ON RELIGION

BENJAMIN CONSTANT

On Religion

Considered in Its Source,
Its Forms, and Its Developments

BENJAMIN CONSTANT

Translated by Peter Paul Seaton Jr.
With an Introduction by Pierre Manent

Liberty Fund

Translation, introduction, editorial matter, and index © 2017 by Liberty Fund, Inc.

This English translation is drawn from the integral French text of
De la religion, by Benjamin Constant, presented by Tzvetan Todorov and
Etienne Hofmann. © 1999 by Actes Sud.

Frontispiece: Portrait of Benjamin Constant by Lina Vallier (fl. 1836–1852),
from the Musée du Château de Versailles. Photo credit: Gianni Dagli Orti / The Art
Archive at Art Resource, NY.

17 18 19 20 21 22 C 5 4 3 2 1
17 18 19 20 21 22 P 5 4 3 2 1

Library of Congress Cataloging-in-Publication Data

Names: Constant, Benjamin, 1767–1830, author. | Seaton, Paul, 1954– translator.
Title: On religion considered in its source, its forms, and its developments / Benjamin Constant ; translated by Peter Paul Seaton, Jr. ; with an introduction by Pierre Manent.
Other titles : De la religion considérée dans sa source, ses formes et ses développements. English.
Description: Carmel : Liberty Fund, Inc., 2017 | Includes index.
Identifiers: LCCN 2017026123| ISBN 9780865978966 (hardcover : alk. paper) | ISBN 9780865978973 (pbk. : alk. paper)
Subjects: LCSH Religions. | Religion—Phliosophy. | Polytheism.
Classification: LCC BL80.3 .C66713 2017 | DDC 200—dc23
LC record available at https://lccn.loc.gov/2017026123

Liberty Fund, Inc.
11301 North Meridian Street,
Carmel, Indiana 46032-4564

Contents

BOOK VI: The Constitutive Elements of Priestly Polytheism

BOOK VII: On the Elements That Constitute Polytheism
Independent of Priestly Direction

BOOK XV: Results of the Work

Translator's Note

The reader has here the first full-length English translation of Benjamin Constant's (1767–1830) massive *De la religion considérée dans sa source, ses formes et ses développements*, published in five volumes between 1824 and 1831 (with the last two appearing posthumously). It is drawn from the integral text presented by Tzvetan Todorov and Etienne Hofmann in *Actes sud* ("Thesaurus," 1999).

Constant's prose is rich, complex, and in places lush—in a word, it breathes the air of nineteenth-century romanticism. It thus presents translation challenges, but none that are insurmountable. My first principle of translation has been fidelity and accuracy; the reader will find no paraphrase here. He will be able to follow Constant's employment of key and even characteristic terms. Insofar as possible, his word order has been respected; and his paragraph divisions have been strictly observed. The reader of a translation of a nineteenth-century French author should feel that he is reading something from another time and place; we don't go to Constant to hear contemporary French, much less the various dialects of America. My aim has been to reproduce a distinctive nineteenth-century French voice and manner of thought speaking in comprehensible twenty-first-century English, albeit with an accent.

Constant worked on this survey and analysis of the human religious experience from fetishism to monotheism throughout his life, in wildly different circumstances. The text bears these marks. Different editions of texts are cited; spellings are not entirely consistent; there is a palpable feel of working *à batons rompus*. Constant himself acknowledged all this. I have made no effort to smooth these features. In an age like ours when individuality is extolled but often fails to be genuine, much less philosophically employed, it is good to encounter a brave mind that took on the most difficult subjects—religion and politics, the soul and its nature—with persistence and gusto. Rather than diminish his achievement because it falls short of contemporary scholarly standards, Constant's warts are pardonable signs of a focus and capaciousness we should admire. What Pascal wrote applies to Benjamin Constant in spades: I went to a book expecting to find an author, and I found a man.

Since Pierre Manent's magisterial introduction to the man and this work is guidance enough for the prospective reader, I can dispense with that task. I only wish to express my thanks to Christine Henderson of Liberty Fund, Inc., who approached me about this project; Colleen Watson, who exercised infinite patience in awaiting its conclusion; and my primary reader and good friend, Dan Mahoney, who introduced me to the adventure of French thought and provided moral as well as translation assistance during the long *durée* of this project. To all, cordial thanks.

Paul Seaton

Introduction to *On Religion*

PIERRE MANENT

In France, Benjamin Constant's fame today is principally due to his literary work, which is largely autobiographical in character.[1] In his own day, he was above all famous for his political activity: across the dizzying succession of regimes that France knew starting in 1789, this man of Swiss origin was constantly at the head of the battle for all the liberties. One could say that when he died shortly after the July Revolution, in which he had fully participated and which had placed the "bourgeois king," Louis-Philippe, on the throne, Constant had embodied the most systematic and combative version of French liberalism. Only recently, however, have people begun to take the measure of the amplitude and complexity of his political and philosophical thought. With Tocqueville, although not quite at the same level, he is the most eminent representative of the "troubled liberalism" that is so characteristic of the French political philosophy of the nineteenth century.

What characterizes the spiritual physiognomy of Constant is that he was a man who was profoundly divided between his mind and his soul, or his heart. On one hand, he adhered without reservation to the doctrine of Enlightenment liberalism, which he defended with as much constancy as trenchancy. According to him, the wellspring of modern history is the struggle between the hereditary principle and the elective principle. The French Revolution marked the definitive victory of the latter over the former, a victory that manifested the perfectibility of the human race, a perfectibility equivalent to a tendency toward equality.[2] On the other hand,

Translated from the French by Peter Paul Seaton Jr.

1. One should primarily mention *Adolphe*, an "anecdote" that appeared in 1816, a first-person account of an unhappy amorous relationship.

2. "*Perfectibilité*" is a key term in eighteenth- and nineteenth-century French thought. Employed by Condorcet before him, Rousseau made it central to the anthropology he developed in the *Second Discourse*. Tocqueville later employed it to understand democratic Americans. Constant, in impor-

his soul suffered from, and therefore was troubled by, certain moral effects of the improved civilization of perfectibility that was in the process of triumphing. The reign of utility and self-interest narrows and weakens souls. They leave idle certain of their highest faculties, and end by putting liberty itself in danger. How to make up for this deficiency in strength and vitality? In order to resolve the problem introduced by the triumph of enlightenment for which he had worked so zealously, Constant's solution was one that would have surprised Voltaire, and even Montesquieu: religion, or a certain version of religion.

Constant's thought on religion is contained in the immense work that the reader of English now has, thanks to this translation. For a long time little appreciated and read in France itself, where it was out of print, this work merits serious study because it is rare that the religious phenomenon is addressed with so much candor and amplitude. The outdated character of Constant's erudition—immense as it was—does not warrant us to treat his enterprise with condescension. It was motivated and borne along by a *sincerity* whose high quality and constancy are always quite rare, but especially so today.

Benjamin Constant was one of the first authors to give voice to a sentiment that has become quite familiar to us, one without which we could not live, so much has it become constitutive of our self-consciousness: the sentiment of living in history, that is to say, in a movement of *irreversible progress*. To be sure, certain disappointments prevent us from formulating this sentiment and conviction with the self-assurance of the first modern generations. It is therefore instructive for us to see how this axiom organized both the form and the content of Constant's thought.

Constant starts with the observation that the reign of religious intolerance is over in Europe. The form of life that gave plausibility, and for a long time its evidence and legitimacy, to the constraint brought to bear on actions, words, and even thoughts in the name of "the true religion," this form of life has been definitively discredited by certain intellectual, political, social, and moral changes—by "progress." The main danger to fear from now on is found less in what remains of barbarism than in the excess of civilization. By giving itself the goal of well-being, and self-interest as its guide, civilization tends to produce a "system of egoism" that confines the individual to himself and makes him the slave of his needs. It is there-

---

tant ways a follower of Rousseau, employs the term and its cognates, such as "*perfectionnement*" and "*perfectionée.*" It is the combination of "perfection" and "ability" in which the exact meaning of both terms is intrinsically indeterminate. "Human perfection" in this optic is rather open-ended and might more precisely (if awkwardly) be translated as "human perfectioning" (translator's note).

fore important to bring another perspective to bear on the human world, by giving man the goal of constant self-perfecting and interior sentiment for his guide.

Now, precisely because intolerance has been irrevocably discredited, and the aggressive unbelief that responded to it has lost its raison d'être, today it is possible to consider the religious phenomenon impartially. What does that mean? With religion no longer having to be regarded as either a truth that has to be defended by all means or as an error and imposture to attack with the same force, one can and should consider it as a *fact*, that is to say, as a reality that is inseparable from the human heart, as it manifests itself at all times and places. Here Constant calls into question what one could call the genealogism of the Enlightenment, which sought to base its arguments on the hypothesis of a natural man who would have lived without religion, as well as without society and language. In this optic, if religion had a beginning—being born from the fear of thunder, for example—then it is reasonable to anticipate that it will have an end—precisely, when men no longer fear thunder. But according to Constant these are untenable conjectures. Religion, like society, like language, belongs to the very constitution of man; and it is as impossible to imagine man without religion as it is to imagine him without society or language.

At this point, one can see a tension between the two aspects of Constant's thought that we just developed. How can religion be the universal and unchanging fact that Constant wishes to place before us while humanity obeys the law of progress; that is, of continuous and irresistible change, an axiom to which he attributes absolute validity? It would seem that, according to Constant, one must say that in human history everything changes and nothing changes.

As it happens, this is the case! With the candor I already mentioned, Constant simultaneously affirms that everything changes and nothing changes in the human phenomenon during the course of history. He escapes from contradiction by having recourse to the distinction between form and substance: the substance is unchanging while the form obeys the law of progressive change, the law of progress. The substance, the substance of man, is therefore the religious sentiment, which is always the same, immutable and eternal. The form is the ensemble of ideas and institutions in which, at each period, the religious sentiment formulates itself and takes form. In the same way as Marx, according to whom the principle of historical change resides in the contradiction between productive forces and the relations of production, according to Constant the wellspring resides principally in the contradiction between the religious sentiment and the forms in which it successively expresses itself. More precisely, change occurs when the sentiment separates itself from the form, and this happens when the latter no longer suits the human spirit. Thus, it is "the human spirit" that ensures the connection between the religious sentiment that does not change and the religious forms that constantly change. One has to acknowledge, however, that Constant hardly explains how this delicate and decisive operation takes place. Historical examples, both numerous and varied, are deemed to furnish the verification of a process, or a mechanism, that is presupposed or postulated rather than described or explained. In fact, the way in which Constant comprehends the religious sentiment makes it difficult to conceive of its relationship with "the human spirit." We should pause on this point.

What is the religious sentiment, according to Constant? It is very much a *sentiment*, which is to say, an involuntary disposition that we do not have the power to govern, much less to suppress at will. In other words, it is a disposition that cannot be translated into strictly rational terms; it necessarily possesses a vague and mysterious character, but one that allows us to glimpse a domain where interest does not reign. Instead of dissimulating this vagueness or obscurity, Constant underscores these characteristics of the religious sentiment: it is in this type of emotion resistant to clear and distinct ideas that, according to him, human life above all experiences its disinterested desire for something better. If one has to give the word "sentiment" its most exact equivalent, it would be "revery." It cannot escape the reader, however, that revery excludes judgment, and first of all, the judgment of real existence. The religious sentiment neither affirms nor denies the existence of the object of its desire or revery. The most that one can say, it seems, is that the religious sentiment does not positively rule out the actual existence of God or a divine object.

One would be wrong to call Constant's sincerity into question. To be sure, he positively affirms nothing apropos to the existence of God, and one can see that even if he invokes certain Christian teachings with respect, his reticence is equal to his respect. His sincerity demands this reserve. To his eyes, the mystery that surrounds human life is so profound and encompassing that one cannot claim to dispel it by any judgment of the mind. The three great parties that claim to judge with certainty—the orthodox, the unbelievers, and the partisans of natural religion—all suppose that man can come into possession of an absolute truth, one that is always the same. On this point, says Constant, they all are equally mistaken. This does not mean that one must renounce every idea of truth. But it does mean, as the Germans were the first to recognize, and it is the sole general truth available to the human mind, that "everything is progressive in man," or as we would say today, "everything in man is historical."

This is not the place to comment on what one could call Constant's "historicism." One can, however, point out a consequence of this "historicism." In his eyes, the period in which one lives determines, or in any case circumscribes, the possible religious attitudes. There are epochs when it is impossible to cast doubt on the established religion; there are others when it is impossible to shore up religious conviction, that is, to escape from doubt. As Constant never tires of underscoring in all his works, the time in which he lives is of the second sort. The moderns cannot escape from doubt, from the fear of being mistaken. Their habit of constant reflection weakens and hampers the movement of the soul necessary to affirm anything of importance with certainty. This being his diagnosis, one can understand why Constant brings the religious quest for the divine object back to the human subject. There is always a truth to grasp and to cherish concerning religion, but it is not a truth concerning God, it is a truth concerning man. At the core of man there is always and everywhere this indestructible but mysterious sentiment by which man experiences, paradoxically, that he is greater than himself, and that his destiny is not measured in terms of his pleasures and his pains but according to a perfection that is found in the way he approaches the joys and challenges of life. According to Constant, it is only in these terms that one can understand the idea of divine Providence. Understood in these terms—the joys and pains are the means of perfecting man—divine Providence equates with human self-perfecting, and vice versa.

Constant's immense investigation, which, we should note, essentially leaves Christianity and Islam to the side, is organized by a determinate polarity—that between priestly religions and the religions free of the priesthood. In his presentation, the difference that one could call "political" between the sacerdotal religions and the others is more determinative than the properly religious differences between fetishism, polytheism, and theism (this last notion approximately covers what we call monotheism). To be sure, Constant shows religion progressing along with society from the fetishism of savages to the polytheism of barbarians, with the latter tending with the progress of civilization to theism. However, this vector of religious progress is subject to a decisive influence, according to whether the religion is priestly or independent of the priesthood. The priesthood, whatever the religion might be, by claiming the monopoly of all the human goods, or at least the most precious (for these are at the root of all priestly powers), installs a system of castes that, even when they are not institutionalized as they are in India, hampers the natural movement of human faculties and gives, as it were, a vicious form to human life. Even if he takes the precaution to concede that all the ills and evils of men do not flow from the priesthood, there is no doubt that for Constant the priesthood as such is simultaneously the great inhibitor of human progress and the great corrupter of human life. After having sequestered and protected what religion has of properly religious in the religious sentiment that the Enlightenment had ignored, Constant takes up again its aggressivity (against which he was otherwise very severe) in a political analysis that absolutely condemns a social and political form: the priesthood.

Constant's argument therefore combines the idea of a continuous progress of civilization and the idea of an alternative between priestly religions and those without priesthoods. The first are essentially enemies of progress; or, as he regularly says, they are "stationary." The second are open to the progress of the human spirit. Now, and this is the decisive juncture of the investigation, in human history there has been only one religion independent of the priesthood, that of the Greeks. At least since heroic times, that is, barbaric times, the Greeks were free from priestly power. He finds the proof of this in the subordinate place in which Homer places them in his poem. Hence, too, the importance that he accords to the dating of the Homeric poems in order to understand human history: the *Iliad* furnishes the authentic portrait of the religion of heroic times. To be sure, the Greeks welcomed many divinities brought by foreign colonies, in particular Egyptian and Thracian ones, but they nationalized these imports, purifying the divinities that had become Greek of what they contained that was originally bizarre, somber, abstract—in short, priestly. In particular, the Greeks never adopted astrolatry, which is the decisive element in priestly religion. Thus Constant celebrates the "national sovereignty" of Greece, without which the human race would have remained in a petrified state and would have everywhere been what it once was in Egypt. It is "a hundred times fortunate," he says, that the Greeks won the victory over the priestly corporations that oppressed the rest of the earth. By keeping themselves free from the priesthood, the Greeks made themselves available to the natural development of religious ideas. Under their independent polytheism, all the aspects of the social state developed in a spontaneous and measured way. Far from crushing men, the qualities attributed to the gods were human qualities on a larger scale. In short, while everything in the priestly religions is obscure, enigmatic, abstract, and contradictory, with the Greeks nothing shocks reason at the time, that is, nothing hampered the progress of human faculties that had already begun.

It is also true that Constant underlines the limits of the religion of the *Iliad*. If the figure of the gods answers to the Greeks' need for ideal beauty, the external and moral beautification toward which the Greeks advanced was disturbed by the intervention of interest. Hence the gods, created by the need to adore, became the objects of fear and hatred, and the Greeks conducted themselves vis-à-vis the gods in as self-interested a manner as the savages do with their fetishes. But the Greek soul is not only divided between the religious sentiment and self-interest. A third element intervenes, which Constant calls "reasoning." We would perhaps say: the logic of the idea. At the same time human society crystalized, the Greeks formed an idea of the divine society, which was going to develop according to its own logic, with the gods turning away or growing distant from men. Henceforth, the gods and men were two different species who lived apart. No less than self-interest—but for a different, even opposed, reason—religious sentiment struggled against this religious form, and while self-interest wanted to make the gods mere human auxiliaries, the religious sentiment wanted to make them judges. Now in the final analysis, sentiment is always stronger than interest. As little moral as was the individual conduct of the Homeric gods, the love of order inherent in man entered the divine world, and sentiment postulated that the gods protect the weak and punish iniquity.

This is the moment to pause over what Constant says about the relations between morality and religion, because it is here that the most significant difference between priestly religions and free ones is found. Considered in themselves, morality and religion are notions or realities that are essentially distinct, with religion defining the relations of men with the invisible world, and morality defining the relations of men among themselves. In fact—as just noted above—the life of the gods of the *Iliad* is essentially lacking in morality. Priestly religions, on the contrary, operate an artificial fusion of religion and morality. The gods (in truth, the priests) are its direct legislators, which leads to the fabrication of unprecedented virtues and vices; hence the imposition of an artificial moral code, one very distant from morality as it develops spontaneously in human life when it is left to its free movement. Priestly moralities are therefore, according to Constant, more corruptive than corrective. Does this mean, however, that the free religions remain, and ought to remain, distant from morality, as was the religion of the *Iliad*? That is not the case at all.

As essentially distinct as they may be, free religion and human morality ought to encounter one another, and their relation assume a certain form. This is the teaching of the *Odyssey*, which according to Constant is not by the *Iliad*'s author and presents the portrait of another society, one more advanced and milder. In the *Odyssey*, morality becomes a constitutive part of religion because the gods intervene, as it were, ex officio in the relations of men among themselves. The progress of civilization from one poem to the other is seen in particular in the progress that marks the condition of women in the *Odyssey*. As soon as civilization develops according to its natural movement, the morality that expresses and sums it up enters more and more into religion, and affects it in every way. It becomes the touchstone of religion, in fact. And by a necessary consequence, the introduction of morality into religion implies a progress in unbelief, since the gods henceforth can be done without as the tribunal of morality.

It is because it is essentially distinct from morality that free polytheism leaves morality free to develop according to its own movement, that is, according to civilization's progress. Numerous and different gods, thus necessarily in disagreement, can hardly be recognized as competent judges, and even less as moral legislators. In contrast, constituting a type of public that, while it is neither infallible nor incorruptible, but is still more impartial and respected than mortals typically are, they naturally will be regarded as the guarantors of morality or justice, such as men spontaneously and gradually come to understand them. On the contrary, by pretending to put the divinity in the position of a moral legislator, the priestly religions are led to construct a moral code that corresponds to a surpassed phase of civilization, and in the final analysis to impose a morality that is both artificial and barbaric.

One does not know quite how to reconcile the progressivism that is so marked in Constant's general conception with the unique value he accords to Greek life and experience. Civilization has made great progress since the *Iliad*, and that ought to be seen in particular in modern religion, that is, in Christianity. Now, not only does Constant halt his inquiry even before the decline of polytheism, not only does he include a good part of historical Christianity in his critique of priestly religions, but without making any explicit reference to this, he points out the features of priestly religions—the notions of a fall, of sacrifice, of a divinity that is triune and mediating—that are so many Christian teachings, confessed by the Catholic as well as the Reformed churches. Everything that makes for the properly religious content of Christianity in its various confessions seems marked with the stamp of priestly construction, as Constant understands and condemns it. This does not mean that the praise directed at the Christian religion is insincere. In order to understand it, however, one must consider what Constant has to say about tolerance. He emphasizes that ancient tolerance was essentially different from modern tolerance. While the latter rests on the respect owed by society, and first of all by government, to the opinions of individuals, the tolerance of Greek or Roman polytheism was "a species of national tolerance." Each people admitted that other peoples had their gods. Under the regime of ancient tolerance, no one had the right to adopt a foreign cult, even though the cult was authorized for the foreigners who practiced it. As Constant points out, the emperor Julian particularly reproached Christians for having abandoned the religion of their fathers. Thus, by appealing to the new possibility that is *conversion*, Christianity freed the individual from the constraining bond that attached him to the community in which he was born. In this way, in Constant's eyes, it was radically liberating, and one can understand that he would say in all sincerity that Christianity constituted the most important and decisive of all the progress that the human race has made to this very day. To be sure, the benefits of this liberation were largely shackled and distorted by the priestly interpretation of Christianity, but the irresistible ending of intolerance warrants the hope that the highest potentialities of the religious sentiment will soon be deployed in a Christian society delivered from the monopoly of priests.

Many things have changed, many sorts of progress have occurred, in the direction Constant desired since the time he wrote. In particular, the abolition of the priestly monopoly has largely taken place in the Western societies marked by Christianity. Have Constant's hopes therefore been fully realized? One would hesitate to say that the depth and vigor of the religious sentiment in our societies effectively correct or counterbalance the concern for material well-being and the reign of self-interest. Despite this observation, however, far from making Constant's perspective anachronistic, it confirms its relevance. The material means of civilization have been perfected to an extent that Constant could not anticipate. The risks to the vigor and refinement of the superior human faculties, however, have grown in tandem. Among other things, if the domain of the exact sciences has infinitely enlarged, the part of things that we do not know, and especially human things, has not diminished at all, and it is always on the borders of this mystery that the religious sentiment takes its flight. Constant's investigation into religion was prompted by an anxious questioning of the ambivalence of civilization and its progress. Progress today has not ceased aggravating the disequilibrium between the external and the internal. To this disequilibrium there are doubtless other remedies than the one Constant recommends. In his eyes, however, the religious sentiment has a very particular advantage by rendering our lives especially precious, because it is our means of improvement, of making us capable of even sacrificing our life because there are things greater and higher than it.

On Religion

Considered in Its Source,
Its Forms, and Its Developments

Μεμνημένον ὡς ὁ λέγων, ὑμεῖς τε οἱ κριταὶ
φύσιν ἀνθρωπίνην ἔχομεν.

Reminding ourselves that the one who speaks and
the one who judges are only human.
—Plato, *Timaeus*, 29d

Preface

The fragmented way we went about publishing this work has been criticized several times. The criticisms are well founded. A work such as this does need to be presented in its entirety if it is to be correctly assessed. Parceling it out necessarily leads to many objections. Although subsequent portions will answer them, the objections can appear to win the day since they are not immediately addressed.

We therefore would never have willingly chosen such a way of proceeding. But an understandable suspicion made us doubt that the public would pay attention to a work on such a subject, given the grave circumstances that surround and trouble all of us. Moreover, these investigations appeal to no particular passion, and they neither threaten nor serve momentary interests.

However, once we were reassured on this point, we would have willingly changed our procedure if commitments we had already made were not absolutely binding. The only thing we thought we could do in this case was to join the two books and publish them together. In this way we hope we have adequately treated each period. And we think that the first volume will give a clear enough idea of the perspective in which we view the important subject with which we are concerned.

The inconvenience, however, is only partly attenuated. There will be impatient judges who will take advantage of the fact that we were not able to talk about each thing immediately, but waited until its proper place.

Thus, for example, when in the first volume we establish that the majority of the notions that constituted the worship of primitive peoples are found again, taken up and consolidated, in the priestly religions of Egypt, India, or Gaul, some will oppose to this claim the profound sorts of learning attributed to the priests of Memphis, the often subtle philosophy of the Brahmins, or the sublime doctrine of the Druids. We will not be able to address this objection until the next volume, when we can treat the learning, philosophy, and doctrine themselves.

In the same way, when we later deepen our understanding of Greek polytheism and we show that the views borrowed from the priestly religions, and presented to the Greeks by travelers, philosophers, and priests themselves, were constantly rejected by the popular genius of this nation, some will counter with the fact of the mystery religions. Our answer will be complete only when we have later proven that the mysteries were the special depositories of foreign doctrines, traditions, and ceremonies precisely because there was an incongruity between them and the public religion.

On these points, and on many others that are no less important for the development of beliefs, and for the history of religious ideas, we have to ask for the fairness of our readers. Since the different volumes will follow one another rapidly enough, the patience we ask for will not be exceedingly demanding as readers wait for the evidence for various claims.

We also ask for such fairness in order to forestall another objection, one of another kind.

We would be deeply pained if we were put in the camp of those writers who, full of a brutal vehemence, or unscrupulousness in the choice of means of succeeding, take aim at all the objects of respect that humanity has created for itself. It was the evidence of established facts, however, that compelled us to express ourselves with a certain severity (that we nonetheless believe justified) concerning the baneful influence of the priesthood among many peoples of antiquity.

To affirm that we are speaking only of ancient nations and the priests of polytheism would only be to remove ourselves from the field of battle rather than defending ourselves from attacks. So it is best to declare our entire thinking; it contains nothing that we fear to avow, and we will thereby gain the advantage of not being thought to have wrapped ourselves in allusions. Allusion is a type of aggression that is rather timorous, and it joins the inconvenience of distorting facts to that of giving animosity an impertinent cast of fear.

Thus I declare that among the accusations against the priesthood of the ancients, especially those concerning its adverse influence on the civilization of that epoch, there are many which are totally inapplicable to the priests of modern religions.

In the first place, the priests of antiquity were condemned to deception by their very functions. They had to have wondrous communications with the gods, they had signs to read, oracles to utter; all this made fraud a necessity. Our beliefs today, which are more purified and refined, have freed the priests of our day from these corrupting obligations. Happily for them, as organs of prayer, as consolers in affliction and confessors, they no longer have any miraculous attributes or functions such as those mentioned above. Such is the progress of our knowledge, and such is the calm that less material doctrines have bestowed upon minds, that fanaticism itself (where it continues to exist) has been forced to respect the limits it was the essence of the ancient priesthood to transgress, because the source of its influence was placed beyond them.

Even if certain individuals attempt to overthrow these barriers, these attempts—partial, interrupted, and resisted—are wrongs, not dangers, objects of blame and not means of dominion.

Secondly, the unlimited power of Druids or magi can never become the lot of our priests. Inclined as we are to understand, and even to find reasonable and well-founded, the apprehensions of those who warn that the priesthood tends to constitute an independent body in the State, we would nevertheless think we were much too sensitive if we supposed that the prerogatives they possess, or those they might momentarily usurp, placed them on the same level as the castes that formerly dominated royalty and deposed kings. Those who monopolized all learning and even literacy, and even created an independent esoteric language, and, presenting themselves as judges, doctors, historians, poets, and philosophers, closed the sanctuary of science to all who did not share their privileges; that is, the vast majority of mankind.

Against the tendencies of some individuals who aspire to resurrect what an interval of twenty centuries has made impossible to revive, we can trust in collective prudence. There is an instinct in social bodies which instructs them about what is unfeasible. And if misguided calculation urges this-or-that effort at restoration, this same calculation instructs them to disavow any such thing at the least sight of danger.

Moreover, if political authority is mistaken about its interests and sometimes seems to lend itself to the undue extension of so-called spiritual authority, still the conditions of the pact between the two are clear and precise. If there are monarchs who desire that Leo XII would denounce certain political doctrines, none of them wants to see in his hands the lightning bolts that Gregory VII launched against thrones. At the moment I write, a once redoubtable religious body was just banished from the States of a prince in whom it had probably invested high hopes. Let us have confidence in the times, and let us not exaggerate the threat of the clouds that two countervailing winds bring together, and which they eventually will disperse.

Therefore nothing that we have to say about the immense power of the theocratic bodies of India, Ethiopia, or even the West should be turned—even with the best intention in the world, joined with the greatest talent for interpretation—into an attack on the priests of the contemporary communions to which we owe respect as citizens, or special regard as Protestant.

As a matter of fact, our judgment against the priesthood of certain polytheisms is less harsh than the verdict brought against them by the Fathers of the Church or the theologians who followed them. We have even sometimes softened the severity of their indictments. We have pointed out the relative good that the ministers of an erroneous worship could do, because, in our judgment, when it comes to the religious sentiment, error is better than absence.

In the previous century, our attitude in this regard would perhaps have drawn much different criticisms. We would have been accused of too much indulgence. This, however, would have been an impolitic and rash act on the part of the priests of a regnant cult, to declare that they make common cause with those of an overturned cult.

As for the various measures of blame which could be applied to the priests of all religions, independently of the beliefs, epochs, and forms of the institutions, it will be obvious to anyone who knows how to read and reflect that today this blame can be merited only by those individuals who misunderstand the character of their own ministry.

The Brahmins wanted to pour burning oil into the mouth of every profane person who opened the Vedas, so much did they fear the instruction of the people and what they called the "indiscipline" of the people resulting from it. By exposing this narrow, albeit cunning policy, we do nothing to wound a clergy which claims the honor of having powerfully encouraged the rebirth of letters. And if there exist today a few individuals who would proscribe the means of extending the various sorts of knowledge to all classes, and thereby improving citizens by enlightening them, the clerical body as a whole would join us in criticizing these reborn Brahmins.

The priests of Meroë deprived their kings of the crown or put them to death. By rising up against these regicide priests, we will only scandalize those who make the throne the footstool of the altar.

The magi declared to Cambyses that his commands were above the laws. Our critique of this alliance of the priesthood and despotism does not touch at all a Church in whose name Fénelon, Massillon, and Fléchier constantly told monarchs that the laws were the foundation and limit of their power.

These explanations seemed necessary to us. As faithful historians, we have not distorted any fact nor sacrificed any truth to secondary considerations. We have attempted to forget the present century and contemporary circumstances and opinions when writing. It is from this scrupulously observed resolution that we have drawn the sort of courage that was most difficult for us: that of separating ourselves, on questions of great importance, from many men whose principles we otherwise share, and whose noble character we greatly respect.

Struck by the dangers of a sentiment that exalts itself and errs, and in whose name countless crimes have been committed, these men set themselves against all religious emotions and want to substitute for them the exact, dispassionate, invariable calculations of self-interest rightly understood. They say that such interest is sufficient to establish social order and to cause the laws of morality to be observed.

We ourselves are far from sharing the pious exaggeration that attributes all the crimes of unbelieving epochs to the absence of religious sentiment. These deplorable results of blind passions, effects that are independent of beliefs, are common to religious and unreligious centuries. Under Alexander VI communion preceded, and confession followed, murder.

We likewise recognize that the necessity of the religious sentiment is not adequately proven by the excesses of the revolutions invoking liberty during which rebellious peoples took pleasure in trampling underfoot venerable ancient customs. Revolutions are stormy times in which men, forced to precipitous judgments and hasty actions in the midst of all sorts of tumult and violence, without any guides to direct them, without observers to chasten them, even with the best of intentions, can easily be mistaken and become criminals with the purest of motives. The revolutions caused by religious convictions in their turn have not been exempt from the criminal, even savage, actions liberty herself has inspired. The violence and chaos of the Protestant wars, their thirty years of massacres, were equal in misdeeds and anarchy to those that darken the pages of the French Revolution. The fierce piety of the Puritans showed itself to be no less bloody than the shameless atheism of our demagogues.

But after having begun with these well-known concessions, we still would have to ask whether, by rejecting the religious sentiment, we fail to distinguish among the forms of religion, and if by solely operating according to the rule of self-interest the human race would not deprive itself of everything that constitutes its superiority, thereby abdicating its most beautiful titles, falling away from its true destination, and confine itself to a sphere that is much less than its true stature? In short, whether we condemn it to a diminishment that is against its nature.

Self-interest rightly understood must destroy everything that is contrary to itself. If man, directed by this motive, triumphs over the passions that would lead him contrary to it, it also must overcome all the emotions that simply distract it from that end. Much then will be lost. If rightly understood interest is powerful enough to defeat the delirium of the senses, the hunger for wealth, and the fury of vengeance, it will overcome even more easily the movements of pity, of tenderness, of devotion, which are constantly under assault by considerations of prudence, egoism, and fear. Without doubt, by listening to the precepts of self-interest we can renounce present pleasures; but this can only be in order to obtain future advantages. We therefore ought to abstain from everything that would harm us in a lasting way. And this very rule—the sole morality acknowledged by interest— ought to apply to our generous passions and our virtues as well as to our selfish passions and our vices.

Thus, there is no noble movement of the heart against which the logic of interest cannot be directed. There is not one that, following this logic, is not a weakness or a blindness. There is not one that interest does not overthrow by its exact calculations and its convincing equations.

In response, do you tell me that interest itself opposes the foregoing depravation of our nature, since it invites us to seek the inner satisfaction that comes from the accomplishment of a courageous duty in the midst of trial and misfortune? However, do you not see that by your own words you return to these involuntary emotions which transport us into another order of ideas? And as they are alien to all calculation, they disconcert and call into question the arid doctrines of self-interest. In order to escape the consequences of the system you adopt, you falsify the system—which in truth is unworthy of you. You reintroduce into it an element it officially rejects. You give the human soul the faculty (for it truly is a faculty, and the most precious of all) to be subjugated and dominated, but also exalted, independently of, and even contrary to, its interest.

If this self-interest triumphed completely, man would not experience any regret except when he was mistaken concerning his interest. He would feel only the satisfaction of having carefully observed its precepts.

But no, nature did not place our guide in self-interest, but in an intimate sentiment. This sentiment tells us what is evil and what is good. Rightly understood, interest only lets us know what is advantageous or harmful.

If you therefore do not want to destroy the work of nature, respect this sentiment in each of its emotions. You cannot bring an axe to bear on any of the branches of the tree without sooner or later cutting the trunk and causing death.

If you treat as chimerical this indefinable emotion which seems to reveal to us an infinite being, the soul, creator, or essence of the world (what do the imperfect names we give it matter?), your criticism will go even further despite your intention, and even against it.

What happens in the depths of our soul is finally inexplicable; and if you always demand mathematical demonstrations, you will end up with only negations and denials.

If the religious sentiment is folly because it cannot be proved, love is also a folly, enthusiasm a delirium, human sympathy a weakness, devotion an irrational act.

If the religious sentiment must be silenced because, you say, it misleads us, one would also have to eradicate pity because it has its perils, and often troubles and torments us. One would have to reprimand the high-heartedness that moves us to fly to the aid of the oppressed, because it certainly is not in our interest to call upon us blows not destined for us. Above all—pay especial attention here—one must renounce the liberty that you so cherish. From one end of the earth to the other, the soil upon which mankind walks is full of the corpses of its defenders. It is not self-interest that erects altars to this deity of proud and noble souls! It waits for others to do so, and to provide a safe haven for it; and if strong winds come up to shake that edifice, you will see it desert liberty's worship or, at most, take a shameful pride in neutrality.

Has not experience proven this? What have we seen the past twenty years in Europe? Self-interest rightly understood reigning without rival. And what has been the fruit of this reign? (I repeat: we are not speaking about crimes. We grant that interest rightly understood condemns them, and that its counsels would have spoken against them.)[1] But this indifference, this servility, this persistence in calcu-

1. Here we grant to our adversaries a point that we could very well have contested. Nothing is less assured than the victory of self-interest rightly understood over the passions that contradict morality. In the man dominated by passion, this interest is, first of all, to silence this passion if it can. But if this victory is above its forces, the interest becomes to satisfy this passion in order to put an end to the trouble that torments him; for this torment can become such that this man succumbs to it. When an accident or an illness that is alien to the temperament of the person puts his life in danger, doctors seek to get rid of the imminent threat without calculating if the remedies they use at the moment of crisis might have consequences for his future health. The interest of the man in the grips of passion is to escape from the violent condition in which his unsatisfied passion has placed him; when the present destroys him, what does the future he will not see matter?

The principal founder of the system of self-interest rightly understood, Helvetius, was much less incoherent than his successors have been. Admirer of the passions, he nowhere exhorted his disciples to conquer them. On the contrary, he told them that if they ceased being passionate, they would be lation, this versatility in endless pretexts—what is that but interest rightly understood?

It served, it is true, to maintain order in times of disaster. Order is necessary to well-being. But interest sacrificed to external order all the sentiments whose appearance and exercise could be hazardous. Order is always, at least in appearance, on the side of force. Self-interest placed itself alongside force, if not to second it at least to remove obstacles to it. It bemoaned its victims, but when they were being taken to the place of execution it made sure that order was not troubled. It allowed heads to roll, and it guaranteed property. It called for the end of pillage while facilitating legal murder.

It served the development of the intellectual faculties, yes, but while developing them it degraded them. It claimed to be "spiritual" because intellectual, but the mind so construed directed itself against every sentiment that was not egoistical. Self-denial became the object of derision. Human nature itself was mocked by irony, even disdained, while interest's advocates claimed to offer a "reasonable" appreciation of things (or at least a witty barb).

By the very fact that it was held to be "truly intellectual," its adherents flattered themselves as a sort of loyal opposition. As long as there was no danger, interest rightly understood allowed itself the luxury of criticizing indifferently good as well as evil. Once danger appeared, though, self-interest counseled the prudent applause of evil along with the good. In this way, under moderate authority one was rebellious, and under violent power one was servile.

The virtues suffered the same degradation as the faculties. They lost the charm that attests to their celestial origin. They were so prudent, so reserved, so anxious that they might do too much, that one could guess that the soul played no part in them, and that the real source of virtue had dried up.

One was charitable because interest said to the wealthy that poverty without hope is to be feared. But charity was thereby denatured. The alms that flow from pity and compassion were forbidden by interest. Moreover, one deprived the poor of his liberty in exchange for his subsistence. The rich thought they were benevolent when they gave the poor bread through prison windows.

Calculation did not stop there. Intruding in advance upon the generations to

---

stupid. He wants the passions, but he allows pleasures. He gives self-interest as the motive, but he does not claim to denature it by a false elevation and invest it with a wisdom or foresight it will never possess. We nonetheless have wanted to make this concession to the partisans of this system because, even after this concession, it seems to us to be as false and harmful as without it.

come, the indigent was reproved for his natural inclinations to procreate, and his children for their very existence. People calculated just how many human arms were needed to do necessary work. The rest of the human race was proscribed as being superfluous. Life was transformed into a carefully tended park, its owners empowered to close its walls to outsiders, entrance to which depended wholly upon their good pleasure.

The domestic virtues were practiced, it is true. It is more in keeping with interest to enjoy life in peace at home than to encounter hostility there, and sexual scandal troubles a quiet life. But the domestic virtues themselves were lowered and abased as a result. Now one considered one's family with an egoistical eye. One's threatened friend was turned away for fear of alarming an anxious spouse. The country's cause was abandoned because interest demanded that a daughter's dowry not be compromised. Unjust authority was obeyed because interest did not want to inhibit a son's career.

It was said that there were no vices in all that; in fact there was prudence, what we could call moral arithmetic. We had the logical and rational part of man, but separated from his noble and elevated part. In a word, this was interest rightly understood.

To be sure, honorable exceptions consoled our gaze. But these exceptions, were they not incompatible with, even deviations from, the system of egoism? Were they not the homage paid to the reality and power of our emotions?

And please note: the picture we just sketched supposes prosperity, calm, a state of things in which nothing disturbs calculation. A situation in which interest calmly and without any effort always knows what it ought to do, and can always make itself heard and understood. It is a beautiful ideal, that of a society governed by rightly understood interest. But what does it possess that goes beyond a group of industrious beavers or the well-regimented activities of bees? And if circumstances change, if serious dangers trouble this methodically arranged society, the system will have other consequences.

Its natural effect is to make each individual his own center. But when each is his own center, isolation results for all. And when all are isolated, the result is dust. When the storm comes the dust is scattered.

O friends of liberty, it is not with such elements that a people obtains, establishes, or preserves liberty. It comes from habits absent from your system, an elevation of soul that your system was not able to destroy, a generous disposition that inspires and transports you yourselves despite your teaching. You are mistaken about the human race and, perhaps, about yourselves. Contemplate the man dominated by his senses, besieged by his needs, softened by civilization, and more enslaved to his pleasures as civilization makes them easier to obtain. See how many opportunities it offers for corruption. Take stock of the flexibility of language that surrounds him with excuses and masks the shamefulness of egoism. Are you going to deprive him of the sole disinterested motive that does battle against so many causes of degradation?

All moral systems reduce to two. One gives us self-interest as our guide and well-being as our goal. The other proposes improvement, betterment, progress in perfecting ourselves as the goal, and interior sentiment as our guide, a certain abnegation of ourselves, and the capacity for sacrifice.

By adopting the first, you will make of man the most able, the most astute, of the animals. But it is in vain that you put him at the top of this material hierarchy. He still will be below the last rung of any moral hierarchy. You in fact put him in a sphere different from the one you think you are assigning him. And when you have circumscribed him within this sphere of degradation, all your institutions, all your efforts, and all your exhortations will be useless. You will triumph over all external enemies, but the interior enemy will be invincible.

Institutions are empty forms when no one will sacrifice for them. When it is egoism that overthrows tyranny, it knows only how to distribute the spoils of tyranny.

Once before, the human race seemed plunged into the abyss. Then too a long period of civilization had enervated it.[2] The intelligence that knows how to analyze everything had cast doubt on truths as well as errors.

Self-interest and calculation united the enlightened classes under their stan-

2. The effects of civilization are of two sorts. On one hand, they add to discoveries, and each discovery is a means of power. In this way civilization adds to the mass of means by which the human species perfects itself. On the other hand, it makes pleasures and enjoyments easier and more varied, and the habit of these pleasures that man contracts makes them a need that distracts him from all elevated and noble thoughts. As a consequence, each time the human race arrives at an exclusive civilization it seems for some time to be degraded. Then it rises from this temporary degradation and, as it were, puts itself back to work, but now with the new discoveries, and arrives at a higher degree of perfection. Thus we ourselves are perhaps as corrupt as the Romans of the time of Diocletian; but our corruption is less revolting, our mores milder, our vices more veiled, because we lack a polytheism that had become licentious and an always horrible slavery. At the same time, we have made immense discoveries. Future generations more fortunate than us will profit from both the destruction of the abuses from which we were delivered and the advantages we have produced. But for these generations

dard. An iron yoke held the laboring classes immobile. In this situation, how many useless efforts, how many victims, were found among the small minority which harkened back to a less abject past and which looked forward to a less miserable future? Everything was fruitless, even success was sterile. After Caligula, after Nero, even much later under the reigns of Galba, Probus, and Tacitus, noble citizens believed for a moment that liberty could be reborn. But liberty struck down saw its defenders fall with it. The times failed to support them. Self-interest abandoned them.[3] The world was populated with slaves, either exploiting servitude or suffering it. Then the Christians appeared. They placed their point of reference outside egoism. They did not dispute the material universe, which material force held enchained. They did not kill, they died, and it was by dying that they conquered.

Friends of liberty, proscribed first by Marius then by Sylla, be the first Christians of a new empire. Liberty is nourished by sacrifices. Return the power of sacrifice to the enervated race that has lost it. Liberty always needs citizens, sometimes heroes. Do not extinguish the convictions that serve as the basis of the civic virtues. Create heroes by giving them the strength to be martyrs.

---

to be able to advance in the path that is open to them, they must have what we lack, and what we lack is conviction, enthusiasm, and the power to sacrifice interest to opinion.

From this it results that it is not civilization that one must proscribe; in fact, one neither should nor can arrest it. This would be to want the child to cease growing because the same cause that makes him grow will also make him grow old. But one must correctly appreciate the period in which one lives, see what is possible in it, and support the partial good that can still be done; above all, one should work to lay the foundations of a good to come, which will encounter fewer obstacles and will be paid for less dearly, to the extent it is better prepared.

3. It is remarkable that at this period every enlightened class, except for the Neoplatonists and the Christians, professed the Epicurean philosophy, which, at bottom, is only the doctrine of self-interest rightly understood.

Notice to the Second Volume (1825)

In order to forestall as much as we can certain objections that will be leveled by that portion of our critics whose critical art consists in pointing out minutiae in order to discredit the essential, we believe we need to forewarn our readers of the following. Having pursued our researches at different times and in different countries, we have been obliged to use different editions of the same works and to draw the facts we have made use of from books written in different languages, sometimes even from French works translated into English or German. We therefore have a diversity of citations and a variety of spellings for the same proper names. For example, while speaking of the Jews we have cited the Books of Samuel sometimes by that title, sometimes by the customary title of Books of Kings. And when, in order to demonstrate the absurdity of certain arguments of theologians, we have extracted certain passages from *The Monarchy of the Hebrews*, a work translated from the Spanish of the Marquis de Saint-Philippe, we were not always able to indicate the exact page. Yet again, while treating the Indians we have written either *Bhaguat Geeta* or *Bhaguat Gita*, Petrees or Pitris.

Our intention was to clear up these disparities, no matter how insignificant they were. But several escaped our attention and we noticed them too late. We also have often preferred designations more generally known to those with a more scientific appearance, and more familiar spelling to what was more exact. We used the word *paria*, for example, instead of using *tschandala*. Most of the time we wrote *Oromaze* instead of *Ormuzd*, and we always wrote *cuttery*, instead of *kchtriya*, and so forth.

These statements were not needed for readers who do not have a *parti pris*, either for or against our views. But we do anticipate some who are ill-willed, from whom we cannot expect good faith. We therefore believed we needed to deprive them of the facile pleasure of trying to be more erudite than we are in matters we know as well as they.

Notice to Volume Four (May 1830)

We now publish the last two volumes of a work that we could not finish sooner. Political duties prevented us from making it less imperfect than it no doubt is. We however do not say this to excuse ourselves: the reader judges the intrinsic merit of the book, not the personal situation of the author.

One observation, however, is necessary, especially concerning the first half of the fourth volume. There we deal only with the externals of the priestly religions, and we bring together indiscriminately the facts that pertain to them and characterize them.

This is because for the peoples dominated by priests, the externals were the entirety of the religion. Because the self-interest of the priests was everywhere the same, everywhere they had the same teachings and the same rites, except for modifications owing to climate and circumstance.

If we had disdained and dismissed this popular aspect and had occupied ourselves only with its mystical sense, we would have given an air of profundity to our work that would have charmed many readers.

There are those who still swoon when they hear about the priests of Egypt, or the Brahmins, or the magi. One would say that by admiring these purported sages they become as wise as them.

We say this of the gullible portion of our readers; there are others, however, of a different stamp.

They extol what was, because what was powerfully suits them. What is, and above all what announces itself, suits them very little.

We have been criticized for having taken as our point of departure the primitive state, because, we are told, it has not been proven that it was the first state of mankind.

But we recognized long before our opponents that the origin of our species is enveloped in shadows impossible to dispel. We made clear, though, that wanting to follow the intellect in its development and progress, we have had to start at the point where this progress began. That the primitive state was the first state matters little to us: man fell into it. All nations indicate a time when this was their state; that is enough for us.

Some have claimed that we ought to have taken as our basis some universal revelation, showing it being gradually lost and then rediscovering its traces in the midst of its corruptions and distortions.

If there was a universal revelation, it was gradual, individual, and entirely interior. Does one want us to be even more orthodox? The revelation restricted to one people remained alien to other peoples. They operated in the midst of the errors of darkest ignorance, barbarism, and the fiercest or most licentious superstitions. May it never happen that we seek the traces of a divine revelation in the human sacrifices of Tyre or the debauchery of Ecbatana!

Third Notice (October 1830)

These two volumes ought to have appeared at the end of last July. The happy events of the time delayed the publication. But since the entirety was printed except for the analytic index, nothing has been changed except for a note of five or six lines (bk. XV, ch. III, n. 2). The readers therefore should not be surprised by a few statements that three months ago perhaps may have taken some courage and which today would only be anachronistic, or of a few rather severe judgments concerning some men who at the time called for our heads. They have been defeated. But forgetting offenses is one thing, esteeming the perpetrators, another. While we impose the former as a duty, we do not feel obliged to feign the latter when we do not feel it.

FIRST BOOK

CHAPTER I

On the Religious Sentiment

Montesquieu, the author of *The Spirit of the Laws*, rightly said that all beings have their laws, the divinity as well as the world, the world as well as men, men as well as the other species of animals.[1]

These laws constitute the nature of each species. They are the general and permanent cause of the mode of existence of each species; and when external causes bring some partial change to this mode of existence, the core resists and always reacts against the modifications.

One therefore should not want to assign causes to these primordial laws; rather it is from them that one should explain particular phenomena.

Why does this class of animals live in groups while in another each individual lives alone? Why is the union of the sexes more or less lasting in this one while in another, once desire is satisfied, the primitive instinct regains its power?

One cannot say anything beyond "these species are this way." It is a fact whose truth is established and for which explanations are arbitrary. For the weakest among these species are not, as one might expect, the most sociable. Even in coming together they do not extend any assistance to each other. What they do is obey their nature, which imposes laws upon them, that is, a disposition that characterizes them and determines their mode of existence.

If, therefore, there is in the heart of man a sentiment not found in the rest of living beings which always occurs, whatever the condition in which he finds himself, is it not plausible that this sentiment is a fundamental law of his nature?

In our judgment, such is the religious sentiment. The primitive hordes, the barbarous tribes, the nations which have attained the social state, those that languish

1. *Spirit of the Laws*, bk. 1, ch. 1.

in the decrepitude of civilization—all experience the power of this indestructible sentiment.

It triumphs over all interests. The primitive for whom fishing or a difficult hunt provides bare subsistence will devote a portion of the catch to a fetish. A bellicose people will lay down their arms to come together in front of an altar. Free nations will interrupt their deliberations to call upon the gods in their temples. Despots will grant their slaves days of respite.

Passions as well as interests yield to it. When suppliants grasp the knees of sacred statues, vengeance is halted, hatred appeased. Man imposes silence upon his most imperious passions. He forbids himself pleasure, swears off love, launches himself into suffering and death.

This sentiment, however, joins itself to all our needs and all our desires. We ask the gods for everything that we do not sacrifice to them. The citizen calls upon them for the sake of his country; the lover separated from what he loves confides his beloved to them. The prayer of the prisoner pierces the walls of the cell that encloses him; and the tyrant is disturbed on his throne by powers invisible, and can hardly be reassured by imagining them to be mercenary.

Would one oppose to these numerous examples a few miserable peoples who are described as wandering on the earth without religious ideas? Their existence, however, is based upon the dubious testimony of a few travelers who are probably inaccurate. One certainly can doubt the accuracy of writers who on the basis of mere report affirm the atheism of a people they have never seen or visited,[2] or those who, failing to see the religion that was actually in place, have concluded from the absence of another form of it that it does not exist.[3] In any event, how

---

2. This is the case of the majority of the travelers Robertson cites in his *Histoire d'Amérique*, and one can say the same of the author of *Description de la Nigritie*, which appeared in Amsterdam in 1789. It was upon the word of his language teacher that he maintained that the Seraires, a tribe of black Africans surrounded by other fetishistic tribes, and who had both priests and sorcerers, nonetheless did not worship any divinity.

3. Collins (*Account of the English Colony in New South Wales*) claims that the inhabitants of New Holland worship no visible or invisible being; but immediately afterward he speaks of the sacrifices that they offer to the souls of the dead, of the fear that the deceased inspire in them, of their trust in sorcerers, and the crude artifices they employ to increase their influence. Now, a people who invoke those who are no longer, who have recourse to the power of magic, who believe in supernatural forces, as well as in the relations between these forces and man, and in means of disposing them in their favor, obviously profess some sort of religion. It is the same with the German author, Berger, in his *Relation de Californie*. The Californians, he says, recognize neither a single god nor several. But they bloody

important an exception can be the tribes who eat human flesh, and whose condition resembles that of brutes?

We therefore can consider this sentiment to be universal, even if it is nothing but a great error.

From time to time, some men affirm that it is just such an error. To hear them speak, the real first causes of religion are fear, ignorance, authority, and cunning.[4] In this view, one would have to say that external and accidental causes have changed the inner, permanent nature of man, and have given him another nature. What is even stranger, he would not be able to undo this nature even when the causes no longer exist!

For it is in vain that his knowledge grows, in vain that having the physical laws of the world explained to him, he is taught to no longer ascribe any causal power to beings to whom he can pray. The teachings of experience cause religion to be relocated to another domain. But they do not banish it from the human heart. As he is progressively enlightened, the sphere from which religion withdraws becomes larger. Again religion retires, but it does not disappear. What mortals believe, and what they hope for, always places itself, as it were, on the circumference of what they know. Cunning and authority can abuse religion, but they cannot create it. If it were not already in our souls, authority would not have been able to use it as an instrument, and ambitious castes make a trade of it.

But if it is found deep within the human soul, where does the opposition to this general conviction, to this universal assent of mankind come from? Should we suspect their motives or their understanding? Should we charge them with a presumptuous ignorance or accuse them of being interested in rejecting a teaching which, while reassuring to virtue, is threatening only to vice?

No. In many eras these men are the most educated, the most knowledgeable, the most respectable of their times. In their ranks we find generous defenders of liberty, irreproachable citizens, philosophers devoted to the search for truth, and ardent enemies of all arbitrary or oppressive power. Most of them, being devoted to sustained and difficult study, are preserved from corrupting temptations by the pleasures of study and the habit of reflection. How, then, can religion, which has

---

their heads by striking them with stones during the funerals of their relatives; they provide them sandals for their voyage to the other world. They have jongleurs who retire into caves in order to confer with superior beings. Is this not a religion?

4. See Democritus, *ap.* Sext. Empir., *Adv. mathem.*; Cic., *De nat. deor.*, II, 5; Hume, *Natur. Hist. of Relig.*; Boulanger, *Antiquité dévoilée*, I, 323–67; II, 133.

nothing frightening for such men, become such a repugnant object? Is its absurdity so clear and evident to them? But they themselves recognize that reasoning leads only to doubt. By what singular reversal of ideas, then, has the natural and innocent recourse by such an imperfect being as man to beings deemed capable of helping him sometimes provoked their fierce hatred instead of exciting in them the sympathy that it appears to call for?

Casting a glance on the entirety of life's trajectory, who would dare to say that this recourse is useless or superfluous? The causes of our misfortune are numerous. Authority can pursue us; lies can publicly injure us. The bonds of a thoroughly artificial society wound us. Fate strikes what we hold most dear. Old age comes toward us, a somber period of life when objects grow dim and seem to withdraw, when something cold and dark casts its shadows upon what surrounds us. We seek everywhere for consolation, and almost all of our consolations are religious. When the world abandons us, we form an alliance beyond the world. When men persecute us, we create an appeal above men. When we see our dearest illusions—for justice, liberty, the homeland—vanish, we console ourselves by believing that there exists somewhere a Being who will be able to reward us for being faithful to them, despite our adverse circumstances. When we regret the loss of a beloved object, we erect a bridge across the abyss and cross it in thought. Finally, when life escapes us, we thrust ourselves toward another life. Thus religion is the faithful companion, the ingenious and indefatigable friend, of the unfortunate. It would seem that it is especially the one who regards all these hopes as erroneous who ought to be most profoundly moved by this universal agreement of all suffering beings, by these requests and pleas of suffering rising from all points on the globe toward a heaven of the coldest, sternest bronze, where they are bound to remain unanswered.

But religion has been perverted. Some have pursued man even to this last haven, into this intimate sanctuary of his existence. Persecution, however, provokes revolt. Deploying itself against this or that particular opinion, authority stirs all worthy minds to demonstrate on that opinion's behalf. There is in us something that grows indignant at any intellectual constraint. To be sure, this principle can go as far as fury; it can be the cause of many crimes, but it belongs to what is noble in our nature.

Hence, in all the centuries when men demanded their moral independence, one saw this resistance to religion. This resistance appeared to be directed against the sweetest of affections, the religious sentiment, but in fact was really directed against the most oppressive of tyrannies. By placing force on the side of faith, one placed courage on the side of doubt. The zeal of believers gave rise to the vanity of unbelievers, and men made a point of pride a teaching whose principal merit lay in the audacity it took to profess it.

I have often been struck with horror and astonishment when reading the famous *System of Nature*. This lengthy diatribe of an old man who wanted to close any possible future ahead of him, this apparently inexplicable hunger for destruction, this enthusiasm against a gentle and consoling idea, seemed to me to be a bizarre sort of madness. But I eventually understood what was going on by recalling that authority had lent violent and artificial support to this idea. Hence, from a sort of repugnance felt toward the writer who triumphantly presented to his reader the great void as the truth of what awaited him and the objects of his affection, I passed to a certain esteem for the intrepid opponent of an arrogant authority.

But now the reign of intolerance has passed. Notwithstanding the efforts a narrow and antiquated policy might still make to reestablish it in a few countries of Europe, we will not see it reappear. The civilization of our day rejects it; it is incompatible with it. To return the human race to these iniquitous laws, it would be necessary for a new invasion of barbarous peoples to bring about the overthrow and destruction of our present societies. This danger is not to be feared. No part of the globe today harbors such primitive conquerors of civilized nations. And if probabilities do not deceive, the excess of civilization is the sole danger we have to fear.

But with the demise of intolerance's dominion, the animosity engendered by oppression must go away as well. Whoever makes such hostility his chief point of pride must cease and desist. Unbelief has lost its greatest charm, that of danger. Where there no longer is peril, there no longer is attraction.

The moment therefore is auspicious for us to take up this vast subject without partiality and without animosity. The moment is favorable to consider religion as a fact whose reality no one can contest, and whose nature and successive developments need to be considered and grasped.

The inquiry is immense. Even those who have seen this have not appreciated its full extent. Even though many have already written on the subject, its principal question remains unrecognized. For a long time a country can be a theater of war and yet still remain in all other respects quite unknown to the troops that crisscross it. They see in plains only fields of battle, in mountains, possible command posts, and valleys as transportation channels. It is only in peacetime that one can examine the country for its own sake.

This has been the fate of religion, a vast country that has been attacked and defended with equal tenacity and violence on both sides, but which has not had a disinterested visitor able to provide a faithful description.

Until now only the exterior of religion has been considered. The history of its inner sentiment remains, in its entirety, to conceptualize and execute. Dogmas, beliefs, practices, and ceremonies are the forms that the interior sentiment takes, and then subsequently breaks and remakes.[5] According to what laws, though, does

5. In order to make sure that no one makes use of the sentence, by giving it a meaning that it does not contain, to accuse us of denying the revelation that serves as the basis of the belief of all the civilized peoples of Europe, we must make clear that, in saying that the interior sentiment takes a form and then subsequently breaks it, we do not contest that this form can be presented to it in a supernatural way when it receives it, and that it cannot be freed from it in a supernatural manner when it breaks it. This in fact is what has happened according to the literal and formal meaning of our sacred books. The Jewish law was a divine law, offered to the Hebrews by the supreme power that enlightened them and accepted by the religious sentiment of this nation. This law, however, was only good for a time; it was replaced by the new law. That is, the ancient form was broken by its author, the religious sentiment was invited and authorized to detach itself from it, and a new form was substituted. To affirm that the seed of religion is found in the heart of man is not the same as assigning a purely human origin to this gift of heaven. The infinite being has deposited this seed in our bosom to prepare us for the truths we must know. We can appeal here to the authority of Saint Paul, who said that God had allowed the nations to search with their own forces, until a certain time. The more one is convinced that religion was revealed to us by supernatural ways, the more one should admit that we have the faculty of receiving these marvelous communications. This faculty is what we call the religious sentiment.

By starting in our inquiries from the crudest state of the human race, and by showing how it left it, we do not weaken the narratives of the sole people that we are obliged to place in a separate class. These narratives, while recounting the celestial manifestations that surrounded the cradle of the world, also inform us that the human race profited but little from this benefit. The truths that the supreme power made known to it were rapidly effaced from its memory, and, with the exception of a specially favored tribe, it was quickly plunged back into ignorance and error. Far from saying that religion is but the creation of fear or the work of cunning, we have proven that neither deceit nor fear suggested to man his first religious notions.

We will go further. In the course of our inquiries a fact has struck us, a fact that was repeated more than once in history. The religions established, reworked, and exploited by men have often done evil. All religious crises, on the other hand, have done good. Behold the Arab: a pitiless brigand, a remorseless assassin, a merciless spouse, an unnatural father, the Arab was nothing but a ferocious animal. On this score one can consult the observations made by Sale at the beginning of his commentary on the Koran. The Arabs before Mohammed considered their wives property. They treated them as slaves. They buried their daughters alive. Then the Prophet appeared, and two centuries of heroism, generosity, and devotion—two centuries equal in many respects to the most splendid periods of Greece and Rome—leave a brilliant record in the annals of the world. We have deliberately cited Islam, of all the modern religions the most immobile and unchanging, and hence the most defective and deleterious.

it take these forms? According to what laws does it change them? These are questions no one has examined. They have described the outside of the labyrinth; no one has penetrated to its center, no one could. Everyone sought religion's origins in circumstances outside man, the devout as well as the philosophers. The former would not believe that man could be religious without some particular and local revelation; the latter, without the action of external objects. Both shared in a fundamental error from which followed a series of errors. Yes, to be sure, there was a revelation, but this revelation was universal, it is constant, it has its source in the human heart. Man needs to listen only to himself. He needs to listen only to that nature that speaks to him in a thousand voices in order to be brought irresistibly to religion.

To be sure, external objects influence beliefs, but they only modify the forms, they do not create the internal sentiment that serves as their basis.

It is this sentiment, though, that they have constantly misunderstood. We have often been shown the primitive filled with fear at the sight of the often harmful phenomena of nature. In his fear he divinizes rocks, tree trunks, the skins of beasts—all the various objects that offer themselves to his sight.

From this some have concluded that terror is the sole source of religion. But in reasoning this way it is precisely the fundamental question that is neglected. Where the terror at the idea of hidden powers comes from is not explained. No one accounts for the need that man experiences to discover and to adore these occult powers.

The more one considers the various systems that are expressly developed against any religious idea, the more this disposition becomes difficult to explain. If man does not differ from the animals except because he possesses a higher degree of the faculties with which they are endowed, if his intelligence is of the same nature as theirs but only more developed and extensive, then it follows that everything that intelligence produces in him it ought to produce in them (to a lesser degree, to be sure, but to some degree). But it does not.

If religion comes from fear, why, then, are animals—many of whom are more timorous than we—not religious? If it comes from gratitude, and the gifts (as well as the rigors) of physical nature are the same for all the living beings, why

---

We would have had too many advantages had we chosen the Christian religion for our example. We therefore believe that the main idea of our work does not undermine any of the bases of that religion, at least as it is conceived by the Protestantism we profess, and which we have the legal right to prefer to all the other Christian communions.

does mankind alone have religion? If ignorance of causes is the cause of religion, we are obliged to apply the same reasoning to animals. Since ignorance of causes exists more for animals than for man, how does it happen that man alone seeks to discover unknown causes? At the other extreme of civilization—that is, at times when ignorance of natural causes no longer exists and man is no longer subject to the terrors of a nature he has subjugated—do we not see the same need for a mysterious correspondence between the world and invisible beings reappear?

When one attributes religion to our more perfect constitution, one fails to see a very essential distinction. Do you understand by "constitution" the ensemble of all our faculties, our organs, our judgment, our power of reflecting and synthesizing, as well as our sentiments? I agree. But what you call our constitution is nothing but our nature, and you should therefore recognize that religion is in our nature. Do you understand by "constitution" only the superiority of *physical* means with which man is endowed? But if that superiority was the root of the religious sentiment, since there are animals that are better organized than others, one ought to see in them some signs and expressions of this sentiment, which would be more or less proportionate to the perfection of their constitution.

If by means of memory and foresight man combines ideas and derives from the facts he sees the consequences that follow from them, then we have to acknowledge that animals too have memory, they too have foresight. The dog corrected by its master avoids repeating the same behavior. How, then, does it happen that being no less exposed than man to physical accidents, the canine does not seek to know their causes, while he does seek to avoid, or at least disarm, the anger of an offended master?

Moreover, whatever foresight you attribute to a primitive human being, of all creatures none is more forgetful and careless of his present interests than he! When his needs are satisfied, the Eskimo sleeps in the crease of rocks, meditates about nothing, observes nothing. The Carib Indian does not extend his reflection beyond today. However, when it comes to religion the Eskimo becomes curious, the Carib farsighted. This is because religion is for them a need more vital and more imperious than all the others, a need that takes precedence over the rest of their nature, over their indifference, their apathy, and their lack of curiosity.

Even supposing that the religious sentiment, and the hopes and enthusiasm it inspires, are empty illusions, they still would be illusions peculiar to man; they would distinguish him from the rest of living things. And from this there would result a second, no less singular, distinction. All beings perfect themselves insofar as they obey their nature. Man would perfect himself the more that he departs from his. The perfection of all other beings is found in truth; that of man would be found in error!

We will go further. If religion was not natural to man, the superiority of his constitution would lead him away from it rather than to it. Why? The result of this superior constitution being that he better satisfies his needs by the forces and powers he has come to understand and has arrived at controlling, he would have fewer motives to suppose or invoke unknown powers. The better he finds himself on the earth, the less he would be inclined to raise his eyes to heaven.

This observation is applicable to all the states of human society. There is no condition in which, if you do not recognize religion as being inherent in man, it would not be a superfluous ornament to his existence. Look at our civilized institutions. Agriculture serves our need for food. Our walls and our roofs protect us from the seasons. Laws protect us from violence. Governments are charged with maintaining these laws, and for better or worse they acquit themselves of this duty. There are punishments for those who break them. In another vein, there are luxury, refinements, and pleasures for the wealthy. There are sciences to explain to us the phenomena that surround us, and to parry those which threaten us. There are doctors for the ill. As for death, it is an inevitable accident, needless to worry about. Is not everything wonderfully arranged? What need does this arrangement not meet? What fear or worry is there without ways of assuaging it? Where, therefore, is the external cause that makes religion necessary? Religion, however, is a necessity that everyone feels, some always, others from time to time. This is because it is not found outside us, it is within us, it is part of us.

People have never really wanted to recognize what man is. They have questioned external objects concerning man's inherent dispositions. It is not surprising that they have not been able to provide an answer. People have sought the origin of religion in the same way they sought the origin of society and the origin of language. The same error was at work in all these investigations. One began by supposing that man had once existed without society, without language, and without religion. But this presupposed that he could do without these things because he had been able to exist without them. From this false presupposition error proceeded. Society, language, and religion are inherent in man; the forms vary. One can ask about the cause of the variety. One can seek to know why man in society has this or that sort of government; why in this religion there is this practice or that dogma; why this language has affinities with that one. But to claim to go back before all of them is a fanciful effort, a sure means of arriving nowhere. To assign religion, sociability, and language to anything other than the nature of man is to be mistaken, and wilfully so. Man is not religious because he is fearful, he is religious because he is human. He is not sociable because he is weak, he is sociable because it belongs to his essence. To ask why he is religious, why he is sociable, is to ask the reason for his physical structure and for what constitutes his very mode of existence.[6]

People have fallen into a second error. They have believed that because we are dealing here with something that has a great deal of influence on men, one must either destroy it or maintain it. And in the various projects of either destruction or preservation they have confused what was transitory and perishable with what was necessarily eternal and indestructible.

As we have said, there is something indestructible in religion. It is not a discovery of the enlightened human being which is foreign to the ignorant, nor an error of the ignorant from which the enlightened can free himself. But one still must distinguish the substance from the forms, and the religious sentiment from religious institutions. Not that we intend here to speak ill of either these forms or these institutions. We will see during the course of this work that the religious sentiment cannot do without them. We will go even further. At each stage, the form that was established naturally was good and useful. It became noxious only when individuals or castes took control of it and perverted it in order to prolong it. But it is no less true that while the substance is always the same, immutable and eternal, the form is variable and transitory.

Therefore, that this or that religious form is attacked does not mean that man is able to do without religion. The philosopher may direct his arguments against it, the irony of his sarcasms, the indignation of his intellectual independence—in Greece Epicurus may dethrone the gods of Olympus, at Rome Lucretius may proclaim the mortality of the soul and the vanity of our hopes, Lucan may insult Homer's teachings, or Voltaire other religious dogmas, an entire generation of men may applaud the contempt directed at a longtime respected belief—this in no way entails that man can do without religion. It indicates only that the current form

6. If one believes that he sees here an analogy with the system of innate ideas, he would be mistaken. Man certainly has in himself no preexisting idea concerning religion. Philosophically speaking, his religious notions come to him from his senses, as is the case with all his notions. The proof is that they are always relative to his external situation. But it is in his natural disposition to always conceive religious notions, in keeping with the external situation in which he finds himself and the impressions he receives.

no longer suits the human spirit, that the religious sentiment has separated itself from it.

But someone will ask, how do you get at the religious sentiment independently of the forms it assumed? We never find it thus separated in reality, to be sure, but by entering into the depths of our soul it is possible, we believe, to grasp it in thought.

When one examines the human species through the prism of the relations that obtain between the place it occupies in the world and the goal it appears destined to attain on earth, one is struck by the harmony and the just proportions that exist between this goal and the means man possesses to attain it. To master the other species; to press a large number of them into its service; to destroy, or keep at bay, those that refuse to obey; to compel the earth it inhabits to abundantly satisfy its needs, and to provide enough variety for its pleasure; to climb the summit of mountains in order to submit them to cultivation; to descend into the abyss; to extract metals and to employ them for its purposes; to master wave and fire, to make them cooperate in marvelous transformations; to brave the weather by clothing, and time by buildings; in a word, to subjugate physical nature; to enslave it and to turn its own forces against it: these are only the first steps of man toward the conquest of the universe. Soon enough, raising himself even higher, he directs his reason enlightened by experience against his own passions. He imposes a uniform yoke upon his internal enemies who are even more rebellious than the external obstacles he defeated. He obtains from himself and others sacrifices that one would have said were impossible. He manages to have property respected by the one who has none, the law by the one it condemns. The few exceptions that are easily put down do not fundamentally disturb the general order.

Thus man—again, considered only in his earthly relationships—seems to have arrived at the peak of his moral and physical perfection. His faculties are admirably combined to guide him toward the goal. His senses are more perfect than those of inferior species (if not in particular at least in their ensemble) by the assistance they lend each other. His memory is so faithful that it allows him to retrace different objects without confusing them, his judgment allows him to classify and judge, his mind each day reveals new relationships. All cooperate to lead him rapidly to successive discoveries and thus to consolidate his dominion.

However, in the midst of these successes and triumphs, neither the universe he subjugates nor the social organizations that he establishes, neither the laws he proclaims nor the needs he has satisfied, not even the pleasures he refines and varies, are sufficient for his soul. A desire constantly rises within him and asks for something else. He has examined, traversed, conquered, even decorated the worldly manse within which he finds himself, and yet his gaze still seeks another sphere. He has become the master of visible, limited nature, and he thirsts for an invisible, unlimited nature. He has provided for a variety of interests that, because more complicated and artificial, seem to be of a higher order. He has known all and calculated all. And still he experiences a weariness, that of only being occupied with interests and calculations. A voice cries from his very depths and says to him that all these things are but mechanisms, more or less ingenious, more or less perfect, but they cannot serve as either the goal or the final boundary of his existence. What he has previously taken as the goal turns out to be a series of means.

This disposition must be inherent in man because there is no one who has not been gripped, more or less strongly, by it, perhaps in the silence of the night or on the shores of the sea or in the solitude of the fields. There is not a human being who has not, at least for an instant, forgotten himself and felt himself carried away, as it were, on the waves of a vague contemplation, plunged into an ocean of new and disinterested thoughts without any strict connection to this life. The man who is the most controlled by active and self-interested passions nevertheless, sometimes despite himself, has felt these movements which take him away from all particular and self-regarding ideas. They arise in him when he least expects it. Everything that in the physical order belongs to nature, to the universe, to immensity; everything that in the moral order stirs tenderness and enthusiasm—the spectacle of a virtuous action, of a generous sacrifice, of a danger bravely confronted, the pain of another attended to or comforted, disdain for vice, devotion to the unfortunate, resistance to tyranny—all these reveal and nourish in the soul this mysterious disposition. And even if the ingrained habits of egoism prompt it to smile at this momentary exultation, it does not do so without a secret shame, one it hides beneath the mask of irony. A silent instinct tells it that in doing so it is disrespecting the noblest portion of our being.

We should add that in studying ourselves at these moments—admittedly so brief and so unlike the rest of our existence—we find that at the very moment when we fall back from this exaltation and find ourselves recaptured by the interests that constantly solicit us, we feel ourselves having descended from an elevation into a denser, less pure atmosphere. We have to do violence to ourselves to reengage with what we typically call reality.

There is therefore a tendency in us that is in contradiction with our apparent goal and with all the faculties that help us to advance toward that goal. These faculties, all adapted to our use, correspond among themselves in order to serve us; they aim toward our greatest utility and they make us our sole center. The tendency we just described, however, impels us outside ourselves and imparts a motion that does not have utility for a goal, but rather seems to bear us toward an unknown, invisible center, one without any analogy to our habitual existence and our mundane interests.

This tendency frequently creates great disorder in us. It nourishes itself with what our logic calls chimeras. It entertains emotions that our intellect cannot account for. It disinterests us in our ordinary interests. It forces us to believe despite our doubts, conversely, to afflict us in the midst of prosperity, to make us sigh in the midst of happiness. It is remarkable that traces of this disposition are found in all of our noble and refined passions. Like it, all these passions have something mysterious and contradictory about them. Ordinary reason cannot explain this in any satisfying way. One finds it in love, in the exclusive preference for an object which we have been able to do without for a long time, and which many others resemble;[7] in the need for glory, that thirst for a fame that will last beyond us; in the pleasure we find in devotion, a joy that is contrary to the habitual instinct of our nature; in melancholy, that sadness without a cause, but in whose midst we find a pleasure that escapes analysis; and in a thousand other indescribable sensations that cannot be explained by reason.

Here we will not seek the origin of this disposition which makes of man an ambiguous and enigmatic being, and sometimes makes him not at home on earth. Believers can see in this the memory of a fall, philosophers the germ of a future perfection. This is a question we will leave undecided.

But we do affirm that if one connects this disposition to the universal sentiment we spoke of above that moves man to address himself to invisible beings, to make his destiny depend upon them, to place more importance on the relations he has with them than on the more immediate advantages of the visible world, one can-

---

7. Brought before the tribunal of a rigorous logic, love could very well lose its case. Would it thereby feel less itself? Would it cease to be the destiny of the most delicate and sensible souls during the best part of their lives? The religious sentiment is not, like love, a transitory inclination. Its influence is not limited to youth. On the contrary, it grows stronger, it grows with age. By destroying it—if one could destroy it—one would not only deprive the time of the passions of some ecstatic pleasures; one would deprive the times of isolation and weakness of a last ray of light and a last breath of warmth.

not deny that these two things appear to go closely together, and that the second is, in a certain manner, but the practical application of the first.

We experience a confused desire for something better than we know: the religious sentiment presents us something better. We are troubled by the boundaries that hem and offend us: the religious sentiment announces to us a time when we will transcend these limits. We are tired of the troubles of this life, which never go away completely and thus render any repose impossible: the religious sentiment gives us an idea of an ineffable rest, one that is exempt from the surfeit of satiety. In a word, the religious sentiment is the response to that cry of the soul that no one can silence, this élan toward the unknown, toward the infinite, that no one can entirely master, no matter what the distractions are with which he surrounds himself or the dexterity with which he deafens or abases himself.

If someone charges this definition with being obscure or vague, we will ask, how can one precisely define something that transforms and modifies itself in every individual, in each country, in every epoch? All our intimate sentiments seem to mock the efforts of language. Words fail what they express by the very fact that they generalize, serving to designate and to distinguish rather than to define. An instrument of the mind, they render well only the notions of the mind. They fail in everything that belongs either to the senses or to the soul. Define the emotion that the consideration of death causes in you, the wind that echoes through ruins or tombs, the harmony of sounds or those of form. Define reverie, the inner stirring of the soul, in which all the pleasures of the senses or of thought come together in a mysterious confusion.

In placing the religious sentiment at the peak, but in the same category as our most profound and pure emotions, we are not thereby denying the reality of what it reveals or divines. In order to deny that this sentiment has a real basis, we would have to suppose that there is an incoherence in our nature, which would be even more strange and implausible because it would be the only one of its kind. Nothing appears to exist in vain. Every symptom indicates a cause; every cause produces its effect. Our bodies are destined to perish, thus they contain the seeds of destruction. These seeds, even when they are combatted by the vital principle that ensures our temporary existence, eventually triumph. Why would the tendency that we have described and which is perhaps determined by a seed of immortality, why wouldn't it also triumph? We feel our bodies led toward the tomb; the tomb opens before them. But we feel another part of ourselves, a more intimate part (although less well known), attracted to another sphere. Who would dare to say that this sphere does not exist? Or that it is closed to us?

If you wander in the night, knowing only the idea of darkness but still experiencing a secret pain at the darkness, when suddenly you see in the distance the horizon gradually lighting up, would you not think that behind the dark horizon is a luminous universe, one that your inexplicable desire had already indicated?

Thus, even though the religious sentiment never exists without some form, it can still be conceived independently of every form by abstracting from everything that varies according to the different situations, circumstances, and relative levels of knowledge in society and history, and bringing together everything that remains unchanging in them.

It is because this sentiment adjusts itself to all conditions, all centuries, and all conceptions that the appearances with which it clothes itself are often crude. But despite this external deterioration one always finds in them the traits that characterize it and cause it to be recognized. Even when it associates itself, as we have already seen, with the most common interests, with the most vulgar calculations, it nonetheless resists this alliance. In this it is like a celestial envoy who, in order to give order to a barbarous tribe, accommodates himself to their highly imperfect mores and language. His voice and his visage nonetheless will always attest that they come from a superior race and originate in a happier kingdom. What is more ignorant and more superstitious than the ignorant savage who daubs with mud and blood his primitive fetish? But follow him to the tomb of his deceased; listen to the lamentations of warriors for their chieftains, of the mother for the child she lost. You will discern something in them that will penetrate to your soul, that will stir your emotions, that will revive your hope. The religious sentiment will seem to you to break free of its present form.

CHAPTER 2

On the Necessity of Distinguishing the Religious Sentiment from Religious Forms in Order to Understand the Development of Religions

The distinction that we attempted to establish in the previous chapter has gone unrecognized, or been misunderstood, up until now. However, it is the key to unlocking a host of problems to which no one has been able to provide a solution. Not only is the origin of religious ideas inexplicable if we do not acknowledge the existence of the religious sentiment; but one also encounters a thousand phenomena during the course of religious development that it is impossible to account for if we do not distinguish the sentiment from its forms. Nothing must be neglected, therefore, to make this truth clear and to support it with ample evidence.

The religious sentiment is born of the need that man experiences to put himself in communication with invisible powers.

The form is born of the need that he equally experiences to render both regular and permanent the means of communication he believes he has discovered.

The consecration of these means, their permanence and regularity, are things he cannot do without. He wants to be able to count on his belief; he must find it today as it was yesterday; it must not seem to disappear like a cloud at each moment. Moreover, it is necessary that he see this path supported by those with whom he has relations of interest, habit, and affection. Since he is destined to live with his fellow human beings and to communicate with them, he does not even enjoy his own sentiment unless it is connected with the universal sentiment. He does not like to commit himself to opinions no one else shares. He desires the approval of others for his thoughts as well as his actions; and external approval is necessary for his internal satisfaction.[1]

---

1. "In the same way that, in the ordinary affairs of life, language gives man the certitude that he is not the plaything of a dream that transported him into an imaginary world, but that the one in which he finds himself is the real world, common to all his fellows (Heraclitus), the public cult is a

From all this it results that at each period a positive form is established that is proportionate to the level of development of the period.

But every positive form, no matter how satisfactory it might be for the present, contains a seed of resistance and opposition to the progress of the future. By the very fact of its permanence, it contracts a dogmatic and unchanging character which refuses to follow intelligence in its discoveries and the soul in its emotions. Each day, however, renders the latter purer and more refined. In order to make more of an impression on its followers, the form is forced to make use of almost material images. Soon, the religious form offers to the human beings who are tired of this world simply another world that resembles it. The ideas that it proposes become more and more narrow, like the earthly ideas of which they merely are a copy. Finally the time arrives when it only presents to the mind assertions it cannot accept, to the soul practices that do not satisfy it. The religious sentiment then separates from this petrified form. It demands another form that does not offend it. It seeks and strives until it finds one.

Behold the history of religion. You can see from it that if the sentiment and its forms are confused, one understands nothing.

Without this distinction, how can you explain a whole series of religious phenomena that strike any reader of the annals of different peoples?

Why, for example, when a religious form is well established and civilization has developed to a certain degree, does unbelief inevitably manifest itself, and with growing boldness and audacity? Greece, Rome, modern Europe: all show this.

To want to explain it by the prominence of a few individuals who all at once (one knows not why) took it upon themselves to undermine respected beliefs is to confuse an effect for the cause, a symptom for the disease.

Writers are but the organs of dominant opinions, and their consonance with these opinions and their fidelity in expressing them are the basis of their success. Place Lucan in Homer's time, or merely in Pindar's, have Voltaire be born under Louis IV or under Louis XI, and neither Lucan nor Voltaire will even attempt to shake the belief of their contemporaries. If they did, it would be in vain. The plau-

---

form of assurance that his is not the fantastic product of his imagination, but the true means of communication with the objects of his religious adoration" (Néander, *Sur le siècle de Julien*). One could see in this disposition one of the causes of intolerance, when it is united to good faith. The intolerant man persecutes the opinions opposed to his as if their existence weakened the truths he cherishes; in this way the intolerance that one attributes to pride would have for its source distrust of oneself and a sort of humility.

dits they obtained in their day, the praise that encouraged them, came less from their own merit than from the conformity of their teachings with those that were beginning to gain credit. They said without restraint what everyone thought. Each reader recognized himself in their writings, he admired himself in his interpreter.

It is not an arbitrary fact that peoples are devout or irreligious. Logic is a need of the mind, as religion is of the soul. No one doubts because he wants to doubt, just as no one believes because he wills to believe.

There are times when it is impossible to sow doubt; there are others when it is impossible to revive conviction.

Where do these contrary impossibilities come from?

When the intellect has progressed but the religious form remains the same, the form is no more than deceptive. The religious sentiment struggles against it. True, despite the intention of those who have it, it sometimes slips into positive religion, but the ministers of the religion detect this and fight the sentiment.

The philosophers of antiquity, up to but not including Epicurus, for the most part expressed only this tendency of the religious sentiment.[2] They did not have irreligious or antireligious intentions. Their efforts to purify belief were so unhostile

2. A modern author seems to insinuate that the religious sentiment did not exist until the establishment of Christianity. "Until then," he writes, "God had only manifested his power. . . . This notion . . . produced a sentiment of respect and of fear . . . God then completed his self-revelation . . . and an immense love took hold of the human heart" (*Essai sur l'indifférence en mat. de relig.*, t. II, pref. 87, 88). To demonstrate the inaccuracy of this assertion, it suffices to cite a passage from Plutarch. One will clearly see the religious sentiment amidst the polytheism that the intellect is trying to purify. "No feast, no ceremony, no spectacle," said the philosopher of Cheronea, "has for man a charm equal to that he finds in the adoration of the gods, in participation in the solemn dances, sacrifices, and mysteries. Then his soul is not beaten down, sad, and discouraged, as if it had to fear malign and tyrannical powers. On the contrary, it is delivered of all fear, all sadness, all restlessness, and is intoxicated with ineffable joys. These joys are alien to the one who does not believe in Providence. Neither the magnificence of ornaments nor the profusion of perfumes, nor the abundance of wine and meats, please the soul in the sacred rites. What pleases, what enchants, is the thought that the gods attend these sacrifices and accept with favor what piety consecrates to them. For the one who does not have this conviction, the temple is a desert; the ceremony, an empty and sad pomp; the prayers, words without meaning; the priest, a vile mercenary who kills an innocent animal" (Plut., *Non posse suaviter vivi secundum Epicuri decreta*, cap. 22). We can also find a thousand passages in Seneca where he gives himself over, in philosophical words, to the exaltation of the religious sentiment. The epoch invited him, he lived under Nero, and, hard-pressed by tyranny, took refuge where tyranny could not come. Traces of the same sentiment can be seen in the Neoplatonists, although they were inhibited in two opposite ways by their tendency to abstractions and their desire to prolong the existence of ancient forms.

to religion that with great conviction they defended the ensemble of beliefs while they wanted to modify (and sometimes discard) a few details. But the positive religions know nothing of this sort of benevolence. For them reformers are enemies. The death of Socrates and the exile of Anaxagoras are well known. Two thousand years later Fénelon's doctrine of pure love, which was nothing but the religious sentiment seeking to find a place among fixed dogmas, was condemned as a heresy.[3]

Persecution, however, has inevitable effects. The desire to break the vexatious yoke of a form that reveals itself to be oppressive becomes the sole purpose toward which thought works.

The imagination's own activity, and reasoning's subtlety, turn against what reason formerly found plausible and what imagination was formerly pleased to revere. In a word, the religious sentiment separates itself from the old form.

Then, however, the persecution intensifies. But it causes a sort of fanaticism of unbelief in the rebellious souls, one that intoxicates the enlightened portions, the superior classes, of society. Soon enough, this unbelief attacks the religious

---

3. As it is probable that the public of our day has forgotten the motives for the brief of Innocent XIII against the archbishop of Cambrai, and the doctrines that were condemned by the Roman Church, we will recall a few of the propositions that were condemned.

1st Proposition. "There is a habitual state of the love of God that is pure charity, without any mixture of the motive of self-interest. . . . Neither the fear of punishment nor the desire for reward has any part in this love."

2nd Proposition. "In this state, one loses every interested motive of fear and hope."

22nd Proposition. "Although the doctrine of pure love was the pure and simple perfection of the Gospel acknowledged by the entire tradition, the ancient pastors ordinarily proposed to the majority of the faithful the practices of interested love."

23rd Proposition. "In pure love consists the interior life in its entirety, becoming the sole principle and unique motive of all disinterested and meritorious acts"

(Brief of Innocent XII, containing the condemnation of the *Maximes des saints*, 12 March 1699).

One sees that all the condemned propositions tend to promote the religious sentiment over interested motives. This preference was necessarily prejudicial to the priestly authority. It placed man in direct communication with the divinity and rendered the intervention of intermediaries superfluous. It impairs the influence of those who are the organs of the requests addressed to heaven to obtain favors or avoid punishment. He who aspires to rewards, or who fears punishments, must turn a more docile ear to the directions that are given him than the one who, finding his happiness in the religious sentiment, has no need of anyone else to find this happiness and enjoy it; and if this pure love, that is, the religious sentiment, all by itself is the interior life, then external worship and rituals—forms, in a word—lose much of their importance.

sentiment itself. Previously merely hampered by the material form of the religion, that sentiment now finds itself subject to the frontal attack that unbelief makes on religion. Just as revolutions against despotism are ordinarily followed by a period of anarchy, so too the shaking of popular beliefs is accompanied by an unchecked hatred and disdain for all religious ideas. And even though the religious sentiment continues to possess its rights even in the face of this assault, the overall appearance is that unbelief is total, that man has abjured forever anything belonging to religion. This is despite the enthusiasm for Nature, for the great Whole, that we note among the most unbelieving authors and which, truth be told, is the religious sentiment in atheism itself, reproducing itself under a different name.

But a new problem presents itself, and again it is only the distinction between sentiment and form that can resolve it.

Why does it happen that whenever positive religions are entirely discredited, men give themselves over to the most frightful superstitions?

Consider the inhabitants of the civilized world during the first three centuries of our era. Look at them as they are described by Plutarch. He was an honorable writer who would have wanted to be a believer, who sometimes imagined himself to be one, but was drawn away, despite himself, by the current of contemporary unbelief and caught the contagion of skepticism.

First of all, at that time there is skepticism, invincible in its arguments, peremptory in its denigrations, and triumphant in its ironic tone. But alongside it one finds a torrent of crude, often wild superstitions sweeping through the civilized world. The old polytheism had fallen, but another replaced it, the latter given to the occult, the somber, and the bizarre. Individuals gave themselves over to it while also being ashamed of it. The official ceremonies of the pontiffs were succeeded by the tumultuous processions of the priests of Isis, the last auxiliaries and (suspect) allies of the dying cult. They were alternatively summoned and rejected by its ministers, who despaired of their own cause. The newcomers included unruly and despised emissaries; indecent dancers; fanatical prophets; intrusive beggars; men with disheveled hair, lacerated bodies, and bloodied chests; and eunuchs deprived of the gender they had foresworn, as well as of the reason they numbed. They paraded images and even relics of divinities throughout the towns and cities. They filled the air with their cries, they astonished the crowd with their grotesque contortions and frightened it with their hideous convulsions. But remarkably, this crowd, no longer moved by the ancient pomp and ceremonies, felt its devotion revived by this troupe of crude charlatans and tricksters. All this occurred among peoples who were believed to be enlightened.[4]

The practices that no longer sufficed were replaced by the hideous bloodbaths of bulls. Despite the best efforts of civic magistrates, revolting rites came streaming into places of worship from the most despised peoples. Human sacrifice was reintroduced into religion and thus dishonored its fall as it had sullied its birth. The gods exchanged their elegant forms for monstrous deformities. In fact, imported from everywhere, these gods were better received the stranger they appeared. It was as a group that they were invoked, it was as a group that the imagination wanted to deal with them. Terrified of finding the heavens empty and silent, it wanted to repopulate the deserted heavens with any sort of being. Sects multiplied, individuals claiming to be inspired wandered everywhere, and political authority no longer knew how to deal with the disbelief that threatened the status quo as well as the mad doctrines that wanted to replace it. Authority contracted unavailing alliances with the priests of the undermined cults. It exhausted itself with exhortations that were more useless than pathetic. It sought to defend the past,[5] but it succeeded only in maintaining deceptive appearances. Reason meanwhile disputed the future with the unexpected errors that also claimed the future as their conquest.

Nor were these errors the sole possession of the ignorant classes. Madness invaded all the ranks of society. Even the most effeminate Roman males and the most delicate females made their way face-down up the steps of the Capitol and congratulated themselves for arriving at the top with bloodied knees.[6] In the palaces of emperors and in the apartments of Roman ladies one found all the monsters of Egypt, images of dogs, wolves, and sparrow hawks. Once upon a time these were symbols of creative power in the mystery religions, but now they were simultane-

---

4. Phed. bk. III, fab. 20; Apul., *Metam.*, VIII; Pliny, XXXV, 12; Dionys. Hal. II, 7; Ovid, *Fast.*, IV, 180–370; Tibull., I, IV, 604; Branch., *De sist. ap. Groev.*, VI; Ovid, *Epist. ex Pont.*, I, 37–40.

5. It was at this period that the Romans who called themselves religious wanted the books of Cicero to be burned as being contrary to the State religion. See Arnob., *Adv. gentes*. Arnobius responds: "*Intercipere scripta et publicatam velle submergere lectionem, non est deos defendere, sed veritatis testificationem timere.*" (To suppress writings and to want to forbid reading is not to defend the gods, but to fear the truth.)

6. Juvenal, *Satyr.*, VI, 523–25; Dion Cass., XLIII, 21; XLVI, 23. This superstition goes back much further, but to a period when religion was already destroyed (Tibull., I, 3, 85). It is said that Caesar and Claudius submitted themselves to it (Senec., *De vita beata*, 27).

ously objects of derision and of public veneration. They indicated the enigmatic character of the current mixture of all the gods.[7]

All this, however, still did not satisfy the human race. It rediscovered religious terror but sought in vain for belief, and it was of belief that it had need. The same Plutarch shows us men of every condition—rich, poor, young, old. Sometimes without any visible cause they are seized by a frantic despair, they tear their clothes and roll in the mire, crying out that they are cursed by the gods.[8] Sometimes they talk about the gods in bantering and ironic tones, then they repair to obscure locations and consult with sorcerers and sellers of amulets and talismans. Sometimes they go at night to cemeteries to disinter the dead or to sacrifice infants or let them expire on tombs, so that they can read their own fate in their entrails. And finally, despite their enervated natures, braving both pain and the law, they sometimes submit their weakened bodies to incredible lacerations in order to compel the unknown power they blindly seek, in this way snatching from hell what they no longer hope to obtain from heaven.

Where did this moral disorder come from, at a time when philosophy had spread its teachings everywhere, and when enlightenment seemed to have dissipated the darkness of ignorance?

At that time, men applauded themselves for having overcome all the prejudices, errors, and fears that had previously bedeviled them—and yet every prejudice, error, and fear seemed to be unleashed. The empire of reason had been proclaimed, and the entire universe was struck by madness. All the systems were based upon calculation and appealed to self-interest, they permitted pleasure and recommended repose—and never were aberrations more shameful, human endeavors more disordered, pain and suffering more poignant. This was because in its attacks against the religious form, skepticism also attacked the sentiment that the human race cannot live without. Having emerged victorious from the battles he waged, man cast a look at the world he had created, one deprived of protective powers, and he was astonished at his victory. No longer did the excitement of battle, the thought of danger that had animated his courage, and the desire to regain contested rights sustain him. His imagination, previously preoccupied with an uncertain victory, was now released and, as it were, deserted; it turned upon itself. Man found himself alone on an earth that eventually must swallow him.

7. The entire sixth satire of Juvenal is a striking portrait of the Roman superstition of this period.
8. Plut., *De superstit.*, ch. 3.

On this earth, the generations pass one by one, transient, isolated, subject to chance. They appear, they suffer, they die: no bond connects them. No voice prolongs the existence of the previous races of men, and the voice of living ones must soon be swallowed up in the eternal silence. What will man do without memory, without hope, poised between the past that abandons him and the future that is wholly closed before him? His petitions are no longer heard; his prayers remain without answer. He has rejected all the supports with which his predecessors had surrounded themselves. He is reduced to his own powers. It is with them alone that he must confront old age, remorse, and the innumerable ills that besiege him. In this violently unnatural state, his actions constantly belied his reasonings, his fears and terrors were a constant atonement for his mockeries. One would say that he was struck with a double vertigo: sometimes insulting what he should revere, sometimes trembling before what he ought to disdain.

An eternal law that one must acknowledge, whatever opinions one might otherwise have on questions that we believe are insoluble, seems to have willed that the earth is uninhabitable when an entire generation no longer believes in a wise and benevolent power watching over men. Separated from heaven, this earth becomes a prison, and the prisoner hits his head on the ceiling and walls that contain him. The religious sentiment beats wildly against the broken forms because a form is lacking that advancing understanding could acknowledge.

Let this form appear and opinion will gather round it, morality attach itself to it, and authority, even if resistant for a time, will end by yielding. Everything returns to order, and restless spirits and troubled souls rediscover repose.

This is what happened when the Christian religion appeared. The religious sentiment took hold of this purified form. Its vague, melancholic, and touching part found asylum in Christianity at the very moment when man had acquired knowledge of the laws of physical things and the existing religion had therefore lost the support that ignorance gave it.

Under the dominion of the ancient form, religion had raised itself from earth to heaven; but its basis had eroded. By giving it a foundation, the new form caused religion to return to earth from heaven. One can consider this period as the moral resurrection of the human race. The political world remained subject to chaos, but the intellectual world was reconstituted for several centuries.

One more thing remains to be observed. At this period the religious sentiment was full of the memory of what it had suffered in the confines of a positive form. It feared in the new form everything that resembled the shackles imposed on it by the previous form. It enjoyed all its freedom. Happy to have rediscovered axioms that it believed were certain and truths that seemed undeniable to it, it savored the delights of believing, but it also rejected creeds for which it had no need, as well as practices that to it were indifferent or superfluous and hierarchies that reminded of the previous yoke that had so much injured it.

It wanted no priesthood. We are all priests, said Tertullian. We are all consecrated as such before the heavenly Father.[9]

It disdained the magnificence of ceremonies. It was concerned only with the infinite, universal, invisible Being, to whom every man should erect a temple in his heart.[10] Wearing the humblest of clothes, and sometimes only half-covered, Christians disdained pagan pomp, the ornate decorations of sacred buildings, and pontifical vestments; they did not erect altars, they did not revere images. Tolerant because it was sincere, the religious sentiment joyfully opened admission to Heaven to all nations, to all prayers, to all times.[11] It delighted in sharing its happi-

---

9. Tert., *De baptismo. Nonne et laici sacerdotes sumus?*; idem, *De castit.*, cap. 7. At the beginning, every Christian claimed the power to cast out demons (Greg. Naz., *Carm.* 61, *ad Nemes*). Every member of the primitive Church, without distinction of rank or sex, enjoyed the right of fulfilling the function of prophet (Mosheim, *Diss. ad. hist. eccl. pertin.*, II, 132).

10. Origen said that the primitive Church proscribed temples and altars. See also Minutius Felix: To this question: *cur nullas aras habent, templa nulla, nulla nota simulacra?* He answered as the Persians or peoples of the North would have. Why build a temple when God inhabits the entire universe? (III, 10, 26, 27).

11. "In every nation, he who fears God and who practices justice is agreeable to Him" (Acts of the Apostles, ch. 10, v. 35). "You know," said Saint Peter (ibid., ch. 28)—and Saint Peter was the least tolerant of the apostles—"you know that it is not permitted to a Jew to have contact with a stranger, nor to go to his home; but God made me see that I ought not to call any man impure." This spirit of tolerance continued to reign for a long time in the primitive Church. "The priests who governed the Church over which you preside," wrote Saint Irenaeus to Pope Victor, "never broke harmony with those who came to them, although they were members of other churches in which other customs were observed. On the contrary, immediately upon their arrival they sent them the eucharist as a sign of peace" (Euseb., *Hist. eccl.*, bk. V, ch. 24; Socrat., bk. V, ch. 22; Sozom., bk. VII, ch. 19; Phot., *Bibliot.*, ch. 120). The word "heresy" was used from time to time among the first writers of Christianity. The Apostles' Creed did not appear for the first time until the fourth century, after the councils of Rimini and Constantinople (Pearson, *Comment. in Symb. Apost.*; Mosheim, *De reb. christ. ant. Const. magn.*, p. 88). "The just does not differ from the just, whether he lived under the law or not; those who before the law lived well are reputed children of the law, and are recognized as just" (Clem. Alex., *Stromat.*, VI). "All men who have lived, or who live, according to reason, are truly Christians and sheltered from all fear" (Saint Justin Martyr, *Apol.*, II). "Glory, honor and peace to all those who did the good, whether Jew or Christian" (Saint Chrysostum, *Homel.*, 36, 37). If one attentively examines all the religious quarrels,

ness with the entire human race because this happiness was purely spiritual. A time will come, though, and under a form that already was being prepared, when temporal goods would again be the objects of desire, and religion would come to be prodigious with exclusions and stingy with benefits, because its ministers became avid for gold and power.

The religious sentiment also claimed this same liberty with regard to rituals and ascetic practices. It proclaimed man freed from every man-made obligation; no one could impose upon him an artificial duty.[12] No external thing could stain him, no fast was prescribed for him, no food was forbidden him.[13] So much did the religious sentiment at this period of its rebirth take care to declare itself independent of forms, and so much did it fear to sully its purity by practices that likened it to the old cults it had come to disdain.

---

persecutions, and massacres that followed the conversion of Constantine, one will see that all these distressing things came from the efforts of some men to give to the new religion a dogmatic form.

12. Confession itself was not considered to be obligatory. Saint John Chrysostom says formally (*Homel.*, II, in *Psalm.* 50) that one must confess to God, who knows all, and who never condemns the faults that are revealed to him. "I do not want," he adds, "to force men to discover their sins to other men."

13. "[H]aving canceled the bond which stood against us with its legal demands; this [Christ] set aside. . . . Therefore let no one pass judgment on you in questions of food and drink or with regard to a festival or a new moon or a Sabbath. These are only a shadow of what is to come. . . . Why do you submit to regulations, 'Do not handle, Do not taste, Do not touch'" [referring to things that all perish as they are used], according to human precepts and doctrines?" (Letter to the Colossians, ch. II, vv. 14, 16, 17, 20–22). We could also cite the authority of Saint Peter, an even greater authority because he was much more attached to Judaism than Saint Paul; he had need of a miraculous vision to abandon the restrictions of the old law (Acts of the Apostles, ch. X, vv. 13–15). "The Christian," said Tertullian, "cannot be stained by anything from the exterior; God has prescribed to him no fast, he has forbidden him no food; what he has forbidden are bad actions; what he has ordained are good actions" (*De jej. adv. psych.*).

CHAPTER 3

That the Moral Effect of Mythologies Proves the Distinction That We Just Established

It is not only in order to understand the general development of religion that one must distinguish the religious sentiment from its forms. One must also recognize the distinction in order to resolve particular questions of detail that have been unanswerable until now.

Powerful and civilized nations have worshipped gods that provided examples of all the vices. Who would not have thought that this scandalous example would corrupt the worshippers? On the contrary, as long as they remained faithful to this worship these nations presented the spectacle of the highest virtues.

That is not all. These same nations abandoned their beliefs, and it was then that they were plunged into the abyss of corruption. The Romans were chaste, austere, and disinterested when they burned incense to the pitiless Mars, to the adulterer Jupiter, to Venus the immodest, and to Mercury the protector of fraud. When they deserted the altars of their cruel or licentious deities, they showed themselves depraved in their mores, insatiable in their greed, and barbarous in their egoism.

How did this strange phenomenon arise? Do men become better by adoring vice? Do they become perverse when they cease to worship it?

No, of course not. But as long as the religious sentiment dominates the form, it exerts a reparative power. The reason for this is simple. The religious sentiment is an emotion of the same sort as all of our natural emotions. Therefore, it is always in harmony with them. It is always in accord with sympathy, pity, justice—in a word, with all the virtues.[1] It follows that as long as it remains united with this religious

1. A writer who lacks neither ability nor talent, Mr. de La Mennais, has attempted to obscure this truth. He has anathematized the religious sentiment. He first of all portrayed it as not existing, then as launching men into the most deplorable excesses. We thought that a lengthy discussion in the body

of the text would interrupt the thread of our ideas. However, not wanting to leave without response assertions that, put forth with a certain art, could produce some effect, we will devote this note to a somewhat detailed examination of his system. As it happens, he has very much aided our work; as the reader will see, his contradictions will provide the majority of what we need to refute him.

The author of the *Essai sur l'indifférence en matière de religion* asks, what is *the religious sentiment*? "No dogma," says he, "is written in our heart; and God did not exist for us before someone named him" (II, 194).

He thought this way in his second volume. Here, however, is his thought at the time of the publication of the first: "Religion," he said, "is so natural to man that there is perhaps no *sentiment* more indestructible. Even when his mind rejects it, there is still something in his heart that recalls it: and this *religious instinct* that is found in all men is the same in all men. *Entirely sheltered from opinion's vicissitudes, nothing denatures it, nothing alters it.* The poor primitive in the New World who adores the great spirit certainly does not have as clear and distinct and extensive an idea of the divinity as Bossuet, but he has the same *sentiment*" (I, 85).

"The sentiment," he continues, "is passive in nature: it denies nothing, it affirms nothing" (II, 183); consequently, it teaches us nothing. But he then cites approvingly these words of Tertullian: "The testimonies of the soul are more true, the simpler they are . . . more common, the more natural they are, the more natural, the more divine. Nature is the master, the soul is the disciple" (*De testim. animae*, bk. *Adv. gentes*, caps. 5 & 6, t. II, p. 266). What is this nature, if it is not that which prompts man to the religious sentiment? What is this soul whose witness is so striking, if not the soul dominated by the religious sentiment?

Mr. de La Mennais claims "that the sentiment of the true and the false is changeable and variable" (II, 200); "[t]hat man sometimes does evil with real approval" (ibid., p. 201); and "that those who admit sentiment as their authority can hardly distinguish virtue from crime" (ibid., pp. 201–2). In order to refute these fallacies, what can we do better than appeal to his own words? He will tell us "that the *sentiment* of divinity, of the just and the unjust, and of good and evil, are found among all peoples" (II, 119); "that everywhere, and at all times, man has recognized the essential distinction between good and evil, justice and injustice; that no nation has ever confused the opposite notions of crime and virtue" (I, 172–173). He also will teach us "that when someone tells us that justice and injustice do not exist, neither crime nor virtue, that nothing is intrinsically good or evil, that feeding one's aged father or eating him are indifferent actions, every man grows indignant at the thought and his conscience utters its protest" (ibid., p. 87). Finally, he will tell us "that man can violate the laws of the just and the unjust only by violating his reason, his conscience, his entire nature, and thus renouncing peace and happiness" (ibid., pp. 366–67), "and if we consider the entire world through all the centuries, we will see a frightful proliferation of crimes and vices, multiplied to infinity, and a continual violation of the most sacred duties; at the same time, we will see the immutable distinction between good and evil constantly recognized and proclaimed by the universal conscience" (III, 487).

"Do you feel," he asks, "that another life will succeed to this one, one that will never end? No, you answer" (II, 202). The author is mistaken. To formulate our affirmative answer, we again will use his own words: "The human race, defended by a powerful faith and by an *invincible sentiment*, sees in death only a change of existence" (ibid., p. 142). "People have worked to destroy the titles of man's greatness. A vain effort. They remain, they will display themselves, they are written *in his nature*. All times have read them there; all, even the most depraved" (ibid., p. 139).

"If religion," he continues, "is a matter of sentiment, all men would then find the true religion written at the bottom of their heart.... But if this is the case, could someone explain to me the variety of religions" (II, 198). Does one really think the difficulty is insurmountable? The author himself is going to overcome it. "Everything of a general nature in paganism," he says, "was true. Everything false in it was local superstitions" (ibid., pref., CIII). "Let no one raise the multiplicity of different cults as an objection" (II, 78). "The diversity of cults only proves that men could neglect the means that God gave them to recognize the true religion" (t. II, p. 179). And further on: "Idolatry, properly speaking, was not a religion" (III, 147).

If in order to reconcile these palpable contradictions Mr. de La Mennais claims that by attributing conscience, the sentiment, to a divine revelation in order to honor God, he deprives them of the force we grant them, we will answer that one of these ideas is not incompatible with the other. We take man as he is, with the sentiment that guides him; and our assertions remain the same whether this sentiment had its first and oldest source in a supernatural manifestation, or is such because of its intrinsic essential nature.

There is, however, an objection in Mr. de La Mennais that he himself did not refute. We will attempt to replace him; we hope it will be with equal success.

"Is it by sentiment," he asks, "that certain peoples offered to horrible deities the blood of their children, or sacrificed the chastity of their daughters to them?" (II, 200). No, it was not by sentiment. Does Mr. de La Mennais ignore a fact attested to by all the ancient historians? Among almost all the peoples of antiquity there were certain corporations that took control of the religious sentiment for their own advantage, who usurped the right to speak in the name of the invisible powers, and who— lying interpreters of these powers—ordered men mad with terror to commit the barbarous acts that the sentiment rejected. No, it was not the religious sentiment that bound the Gauls to sacrifice human victims to Teutates. It was not the religious sentiment that drove the knife of Mexicans into the breasts of their little children before the statue of Vitzliputzli; it was the priests of Vitzliputzli. It was not the religious sentiment that forced female Babylonians to prostitute themselves, or the daughters of India to engage in lascivious dances before the Lingam; it was the priests of this obscene divinity. This is so true that these sorts of crimes and indecencies only episodically tainted the worship of nations lacking the formidable corporations. The demonstration of this truth will form an essential part of our subsequent inquiries.

Mr. de La Mennais ends by pronouncing a formal anathema against the religious sentiment. "If this sentiment must be our guide," he says, "there is no disorder that will not be justified" (II, 202). "The religious sentiment is only fanaticism. It is not slow to reveal to each different teachings. If it encounters an enthusiast with an ardent but somber character, there is no crime that it cannot commit under the pretext of inspiration" (ibid., p. 207). We will not stop to recall to Mr. de La Mennais what he assured us previously, in explicit terms, that "the religious sentiment is entirely sheltered from errors of opinion, nothing can denature it, nothing alters it" (*vid. supr.* and I, 85). We will oppose to him another passage also written by his hand: "What do men not abuse? They abuse foods destined to nourish them, the forces given to them for action and preservation; they abuse language, thought, the sciences, and liberty, even life; they even abuse God. Must one say then that they are pernicious things?" (I, 470). Behold what Mr. de La Mennais said to Christianity's detractors, and what we respond to the detractors of the religious sentiment.

No doubt men have abused this sentiment, some by delivering themselves over to the reveries of an unhinged imagination; others, guiltier still, by employing it to create abominable, intolerant, oppressive, and bloody religious forms. But sentiment remains the surest guide given to us. It is the intimate light that enlightens us at the bottom of our soul. It is the voice that protests at all times, in all places, against all that is cruel, vile, or unjust. It is the judge to whom men make final appeal. This is even true for our author! When he wants to prove the principal points of his system, it is sentiment he invokes, the sentiment that he rejected, excoriated, and portrayed as a blind guide, faithless and deceptive. "On this decisive point"—that of knowing if the human race has always respected the common sentiment and what he calls "universal reason"—"on this decisive point," he says, "I appeal to conscience. I will choose it for judge, I am ready to submit myself to its decisions. Let everyone enter into himself and interrogate himself in the silence of his pride and his prejudices. Let him take care, though, not to confound the sophisms of reason with the responses of the *interior sentiment*. . . . If a single individual found in this condition can truly say in his heart: What is proposed to me as truths of experience are belied by what I experience in myself and by what I observe in my fellows, I will declare myself wrong and will consider myself a foolish dreamer" (II, 47).

Such is the force of the evidence. It brings to their knees the most rebellious minds, and at the very moment when they believe they have obscured it, it extorts from them a confession of their own impotence and errors.

If you reject the sentiment, what will you substitute for this divine monitor placed in our heart? Self-interest? A wretched system founded on an egregious equivocation that leaves passion to be the judge of this interest, and thus puts on a par the narrowest egoism and the most sublime devotion. Authority? If so, you sanction with the word all the corrupting or barbarous commandments found in each country, in Gaul as well as India, in bloody Carthage as in licentious Babylon, whatever is said to emanate from the gods. Those who possess authority always believe they have a pact with fortune. They dream they are the masters of force, while they are but its temporary possessors. Authority is their banner, as if a thousand examples did not teach that they can become its victims rather than its holders.

Let us now examine the second part of Mr. de La Mennais's system. We will not need long developments to do it justice.

He begins by establishing a false principle in order to draw even falser conclusions. The false principle? That one must discover a reason that cannot err, an infallible reason. "Now, this infallible reason," he tells us, "must necessarily be either the reason of each man or the reason of all men, human reason. It is not the reason of each man, because men contradict one another, and nothing is more different and opposed than their opinions; therefore, it is the reason of all" (II, 59). One, however, can hardly understand, with the reason of each only able to lead him to error, how the collection of partial errors would constitute the truth. But the vice is not only in the fallacy, it is in the first principle, the starting point of the entire system. It is not true that one can find an infallible reason; nor is it true that one must find one. To be sure, it can exist in the infinite being. It, however, does not exist in, or for, man. Endowed with a limited intelligence, he applies this intelligence to each object he is called upon to judge, on each occasion he is forced to act, and, if I can be permitted this phrase, as need requires. This intelligence is progressive, and precisely because it is progressive it is not immutable, there is nothing infallible in what it discovers, and there is no necessity that it find anything infallible or immutable. What nature felt needed to be immutable it placed, not in our reason but in connection with the physical world, in our senses; and in connection with the moral world, in our heart. Our sensations are always the same, when the same objects act on us, in the same circumstances. Our sentiments are always the same when the same questions present themselves. Everything due to reasoning, on the contrary, is essentially variable and contestable. Logic furnishes irrefutable syllogisms for and against every proposition.

It is the same with the infallible reason of the human race as it is for the unlimited sovereignty of the people. Some have believed that there has to be an infallible reason somewhere; they placed it in authority. Others have believed that there has to be somewhere an unlimited sovereignty; they placed it in the people. Hence, from one have come intolerance and all the horrors of the persecution of opinions; from the other, tyrannical laws and all the excesses of popular agitation. Religious authority has said: What I believe is true because I believe it; therefore all must believe it; therefore those who deny it are criminals. The people have said: What I will is just, because I will it; therefore all must conform to it; therefore I have the right to punish those who resist. In the name of infallible reason Christians were led to the lions and Jews sent to the flames. In the name of unlimited sovereignty, hiding places were searched for innocents and pyres raised for all the virtues. But there is no infallible reason; there is no unlimited sovereignty. Like private individuals, authority can be mistaken, and when it wants to impose its dogmas by force, it is as guilty as the first individual without a mandate. The people as a mass can err, just as each citizen individually, and when it makes unjust laws, its will is no more legitimate than that of a tyrant surrounded by his satellites, or a brigand in the forest.

The principle is therefore false; but the consequence that one seeks to draw from it is even more absurd. "Authority," we are told, "is the general reason, manifested by testimony or word" (II, pref., XCIII). "Man ought to submit himself to it because his individual reason is fallible, while the general reason cannot err" (ibid., p. 270).

It follows, therefore, that when testimony or word is produced by common consent in support of no matter what rites or opinions or practices, individual reason must admit and profess them. "No," he replies, "these things are local errors, particular superstitions" (ibid., p. CIII). But in order to discover that they are this way, individual reason must examine, that is, separate itself from, the general reason that, at least in appearance, places it under its protection. You say so yourself. "Authority exists in fact, everywhere there are *any sort* of dogmas, *any sort* of worship, *any sort* of law" (I, 179). To be sure, you add: "The difference is always that between legitimate and usurped authority." But who will determine if authority was usurped or legitimate? This certainly will not be the general reason; it is manifested only by testimony or word; it will not be manifested therefore under a persecuting religion or under an oppressive government, except in favor of that religion or government. It must therefore be individual reason. But how can it manifest itself? By separating itself from the general reason; and haven't you expressly forbidden it to do so?

These truths are so palpable that the author we are critiquing finds himself forced to acknowledge them. "Every man whose circumstances make it impossible for him to know the spiritual society would be held to obey only the authority known to him, or the authority of the human race" (II, 283). But how to discover the authority of the human race? You accused Rousseau of demanding that a person study all the religions of the world in order to discern the true religion; thus misrepresenting his thought you arrange an easy triumph for yourself. But the same pilgrimage you reproach him for proposing, you make necessary in order to assure oneself what universal reason or the authority of the human race maintains.

As for the authority recognized by each, in virtue of the authority he recognizes, a Mexican will sacrifice other men, and a Babylonian will hand over his wife or daughters to prostitution. If one or the other refuses to do so, will this not be an exercise of individual reason separating itself from the general reason, and thereby committing the crime you find so odious, that of preferring itself to authority? And are you not obliged to acknowledge that the most licentious, the bloodiest idolatry had its universality? "This universality," you answer, "is similar in all respects to the universality of vices, which never establish a law but rather are the violation of a law, and never acquire authority by multiplying" (III, 165). "There is nothing universal in idolatry but the forgetting of the true God" (ibid.). But if this forgetting were universal, it would have assumed all the characteristics you attribute to your purported general reason. It would manifest itself by witnesses or by word. The priests of Molach had their witnesses, those of Cotytto, their traditions. What would then be the recourse of the human race? Individual reason, or rather the natural sentiments which cried out against the deceptions of authority.

It is in vain that you flail about in the vicious circle you yourself chose as the field of battle. The arguments you add to these fallacies are worse; they are so puerile that one is ashamed to respond, or even to repeat them. When you claim "that man does not use food except in virtue of belief, that one says to the child 'to eat' and he eats, without demanding that one prove to him that he will die if he doesn't eat" (II, 125), do you not sense that you provide the precise example that best shows how absurd your hypothesis is? Certainly the child takes food not because reasoning has convinced him or because tradition has revealed it to him. He eats because he *feels* hunger.

We summarize, and grant Mr. de La Mennais that religion has to have as its basis either reasoning or sentiment or authority. But we add that the reasoning whose sphere is wholly material leads us only to skepticism concerning objects that are not material. Authority will deliver us entirely defenseless to all the calculations of authority, greed, and self-interest. Sentiment alone, no doubt liable to error (as are all of our weak and limited faculties), nonetheless always retains something that will rise up against these errors if they are noxious.

Also notice that most of the time they do not become problematic except when they leave the sphere of pure sentiment and take on the positive forms that grant them legal support. Deprived of this support and left to itself, if it errs, sentiment is contained by human laws.

Take the most horrible crime that the religious sentiment has ever caused humans to commit: insane men have killed innocent creatures in order to send them to heaven or to purify them by means of public penance and torture. But after a single example of this madness, measures are taken against the repetition of such an assault, and the disorder has ceased.

form, the weak ones of this religion can be scandalized, its gods can be corrupt, and this form nonetheless will have a positive effect on morality.

The tales of a religion are the object of an incredulity that neither requires nor provokes reflection. They are lodged in a separate compartment of the human brain and do not interact with the rest of its ideas. Just as arithmetic is the same in India as elsewhere despite the Indian Trimurti, so morality was the same in Rome as elsewhere, despite the traditions that seemed contrary to it. The people that attributed its own origin to the love affair between Mars and a vestal virgin nonetheless inflicted the strictest punishment upon any unfaithful virgin.

Nor does the moral character of the gods have the influence one might suppose. Whatever this character, the relationship established between the gods and men is always the same. The gods' particular misconduct does not affect this relationship, much as the misconduct of kings does not affect their laws established against the misdeeds of individuals. In Alexander the Great's army, the Macedonian soldier convicted of murder was condemned even though his judge had assassinated Clitus. Like the great of this world, the gods have a public character and a private one. In their public character they are the supports of morality; in their private

---

What if, less exaggerated in your accusations and no longer drawing from a small number of facts that in truth are very rare, you limit yourself to saying that the religious sentiment leads men to what are called superstitions? We would agree with you. But are these superstitions so noxious? Truth be told, it is not the superstitions you fear. You welcome them when you can enlist them. You fear them only when they are uncontrolled and independent. But that is when they are not only innocent, but often consoling and beneficent. What is gentler and less offensive than this thought: that the prayers of the living can lighten the pains of the dead? It was only by transforming this hope into a formal obligation that, in the fifteenth century, it became a source of corruption for the believer and of persecution for the unbeliever. Left to individual sentiment, it would only have been a pious connection between beloved souls that fate would have separated. What is more natural than the desire to seek refuge in some harbor in order to escape the tumult of the world, to avoid the temptations of vice, and to prepare oneself for a death without fear? What is more touching than the need to acknowledge one's faults, to confide the secrets of one's weakness to a revered guide, and even to request penance so as to expiate them? But by making it a duty, you detract from its merit; compelling what ought to be voluntary, you open the door to barbarous vexations. Spontaneous confession consoles the living guilty, forced confession becomes the torture of the dying.

Do not distrust so much the nature of man. You yourself said it: it is the work of God. This nature can fail, so many causes work each day to degrade it! But it has never lost all trace of its divine filiation. Sentiment remains to it. Do not stifle it by detailed laws. Do not persecute it with thundering anathemas. Man is not what you claim. It is not true "that evil pleases him." It is not true "that born for heaven, he seeks hell, as a lost traveler seeks his homeland" (IV, 37).

character they obey only their passions. But they do not have a relationship with men except in their public character.[2] It is to this that the religious sentiment exclusively attaches itself, since it is pleased to respect and admire what it worships, even to the point of casting a veil over everything that might detract from it.

But when the sentiment separates from the form that it formerly purified by its powerful action, everything changes, even though this might not be immediately perceived. The corrupting traditions that it left in the shadows, or that it interpreted in a way to avoid their adverse consequences, reappear and add their support to depravation. Thus, in a paradoxical manner, one could say that the less man believes in the gods, the more he imitates them.

2. Failing to grasp this truth, people have been constantly mistaken concerning the effects that the licentious mythology of ancient peoples ought to have. Judging by what they have written concerning this mythology, one would say that the gods approve in mortals all the actions they themselves commit.

CHAPTER 4

That This Distinction Alone Explains Why Several Religious Forms Appear to Be Enemies of Liberty, While the Religious Sentiment Is Always Favorable to It

There is another problem even more difficult to resolve, about which error is even more dangerous.

Take according to the letter the fundamental precepts of all religions, and you will find them always in accord with the most extensive principles of liberty. One could say that they extol a liberty that is so extensive that even to this day applying them has seemed impossible in political life.

But now consider the history of religions, and you will often find that the authorities they established worked in concert with earthly authorities to banish liberty. India, Ethiopia, and Egypt show us the human race subjected, decimated, and, as it were, penned in by priests. Some periods of our modern times present, albeit under somewhat more attractive traits, a hardly different spectacle. And not so long ago the most complete despotism we had known had taken hold of religion as an obliging, even zealous, auxiliary. During fourteen years of servitude religion no longer was the divine presence come down from heaven to astonish, or reform, the earth. Dependent and timid, it had bowed before the throne of power, received its orders, and passively observed its deeds, giving flattery and receiving disdain. It no longer caused ancient walls to resound with the sounds of courage and conscience. And far from instructing the great of this world about a severe God who judges kings, it sought the haughty gaze of its earthly master in the way it should have sought its God. It judged itself happy if it was not constrained to command invasions and wars in the name of a message of peace, or to undermine the sublimity of its teachings with the sophistries of politics, or to ask heaven to bless successful injustice. This would be to slander the divine by accusing it of complicity with evil.

These contradictions between the theory and practice in the majority of religious systems have accredited two opinions that can be extremely harmful and are equally false. The first is that religion is a natural ally of despotism; the second, that the absence of the religious sentiment is favorable to liberty.

Only our distinction between the sentiment of religion and its form can spare us from this double prejudice.

Considering the religious sentiment in itself, and independently of all the forms it can assume, it is obvious that it contains no principle or any element of servitude.

Liberty, equality, and justice (which is but equality) are, to the contrary, its favorite ideas. The creatures who have emerged from the hands of a god whose goodness directs his power, who are subject to the same physical destiny and endowed with the same moral faculties ought to enjoy the same rights.

By studying the epochs when the religious sentiment triumphed, one sees that in every one liberty was its companion.

In the midst of universal servitude under the Roman emperors, whose thirst for absolute power had degraded them even below their slaves (which is saying something), the first Christians resurrected the noble doctrines of equality and fraternity among all men.[1] In another case, nothing was more independent (we would say: more democratic) than the Arabs when Islam was in its first fervor.[2] Protestantism saved Germany from universal monarchy under Charles V. Present-day England owes to it its constitution.

The absence of religious sentiment, on the other hand, favors tyranny's pretensions. If the destinies of the human race are handed over to the vicissitudes of blind material fatalism, is it surprising that they often fall into the hands of the most unfit, the most cruel or despicable of human beings? If the rewards of virtue and the punishment of crime are only the vain illusions of weak and timid imaginations, why, then, should we complain when crime is rewarded or virtue proscribed? If life at bottom is only a strange and transient appearance, without

---

1. The pagans treated them as bad citizens, as rebellious subjects (Korholt, *Pagan. obtrectator*, pp. 112, 525). "*Quibus,*" said Vopiscus in speaking of Christians, "*proesentia semper tempora cum enormi libertate displicent.*" There is one observation to make concerning this sentence of Vopiscus. He adds the word "*semper*" (always) in order to indicate that it was a habitual attitude of the Christians to rise against the crimes and despotism that desolated the known world. Under tyranny, one always presents the demands of free and honorable souls as the effects of a vicious inclination to censure the status quo. It is quite probable that the courtiers of Nero said of those who blamed the burning of Rome: "These are men who are never content."

2. Mohammed, in chapter 9 of the Koran, reproached Christians for submitting themselves to priests and to monks, and thus to have masters other than God.

a future, without a past, and so short that one would believe that it is hardly real, why should we sacrifice ourselves for principles whose realization is in the future? It would be better to profit from each present hour, uncertain as we are that the next will come, and enjoy pleasure as long as it is possible. Thus, closing our eyes before the inevitable abyss of death, we should prostrate ourselves and, rather than resisting, give ourselves over to servitude, perhaps making ourselves masters if we can or slaves if that place is occupied, becoming betrayers rather than betrayed, torturers rather than victims.

The period when the religious sentiment disappears from the souls of men is always close to the time of their subjection. Religious peoples can be slaves, but no irreligious people have remained free. Liberty cannot establish itself, nor can it preserve itself, without disinterestedness, and every morality in which the religious sentiment is lacking can base itself only on calculation. In order to defend liberty, one must know how to sacrifice one's life, and what is more than life for the one who sees in death only his annihilation? Thus, when despotism joins forces with the absence of religious sentiment, humanity is left prostrate in the dust; everywhere force is deployed. In their disdain for everything connected with religious ideas, men who styled themselves enlightened are seeking a miserable recompense for their slavery. One would say that their certainty that another world does not exist is their consolation for their shame in this one.

Nor should one think that what we call enlightenment gains by this. When the inquisitor's whip is raised, this unbelieving host returns to the foot of the altars on its knees, and while leaving the temples, atheism joins itself to hypocrisy. What a deplorable condition for a nation arrived at this state! It asks nothing from authority but wealth, from the law only impunity. It separates action from speech, speech from thought. It believes itself free to betray its own opinion, provided that it can congratulate itself on its indifference to its own duplicity. It considers force as legitimating everything that it pleases. Flattery, calumny, and ignobility pretend to be innocent by claiming to be commanded. By declaring himself compelled to act, everyone regards himself as being thereby absolved. Created by heaven for magnanimous resistance, courage makes itself the executor of unworthy decrees. One risks his life not to overcome oppressors but to kill victims. One fights heroically for causes one disdains. Dishonorable speech goes from mouth to mouth, idle noise, which because it does not come from any real source, nowhere imparts conviction, allowing truth and justice no expression that is not gravely marred. The mind, the basest of instruments when it is separated from conscience, still proud of

its miserable flexibility, elegantly parades itself in the midst of the general degradation. People laugh about their own servitude and their own corruption without
being any less enslaved, any less corrupt. And this sort of joke, lacking both judgment and limits, is itself the truly ridiculous symptom of an incurable degradation.

When a nation has for a long time suffered a religion that in itself is defective,
or is disfigured by its ministers, the friends of liberty can become unbelievers, and
often these unbelievers are the most distinguished men of the country. When a
vexatious government has maintained by force the superstition which supports its
injustices, the friends of liberty can become unbelievers, and these unbelievers can
then become heroes and martyrs. Their virtues, though, are based on the memory
of another teaching. It is a noble incoherence in their system, the heritage of the
religious sentiment. They owe their internal strength to this inheritance.

Is not this sentiment the refuge where, above the action of time and beyond the
reach of vice, the ideas come together which are the true worship of all virtuous
men on earth? Is it not the center where the grand tradition of what is good, great,
and noble is preserved across the baseness and iniquity of the centuries? Does it
not speak to virtue in its own language when the discourse of everyone around
it is that of baseness and servility? When the friends of liberty are deprived of
these consolations and this hope, their souls always try to regrasp the support denied them. Raised on the maxims of Epicurus, like him denying any existence after
this life, in the midst of his great struggles Cassius invoked the shade of the great
Pompey. And in his last conversation with Brutus he said: "Yes, it would be beautiful if there were *genii* who take an interest in human affairs. It would be beautiful if
we were strengthened in such a noble and holy cause not only by our infantrymen
and our fleet, but also by the assistance of immortals."[3]

This is the invariable tendency of the religious sentiment. Between it and liberty,
between the absence of this sentiment and tyranny there is an identical nature, a
principle of homogeneity.

But something of an opposite nature sometimes enters into religious forms. A
spiritual authority, born from the need of establishing regular communications
between heaven and earth, may ally with political power. Religion that had proclaimed the liberty and equality of all too often becomes the auxiliary of someone's
tyranny.

Note the following, though: even then, it is not truly religious men who sign

3. Plut., in *Bruto*.

this pact. The members of the priestly bodies in Egypt that tyrannized the people, or which in other countries, Persia for example, lent their support to political oppression, did not regard the cult they abused as a divine thing, which they then abused. The religious sentiment had nothing to do with this abuse. One does not compromise things one believes to be divine.

Thus, to resolve this question, as well as all others, one has to distinguish the religious sentiment from the forms that make it visible.

Far from being the author of the evil that certain forms of worship can cause men, this sentiment is the victim. Far from sanctioning these oppressive forms, it rejects them and protests against them.

CHAPTER 5

That the Triumph of Emerging Beliefs over Older Ones Is a Proof of the Difference between the Religious Sentiment and Religious Forms

Last of all we ask each reader of good faith, if one does not admit the difference between the religious sentiment and the religious form, how can one explain the immense advantage that new forms have in the struggle with those worn by time?

Let us return to the period that has already provided us numerous examples.

Two religions disputed the universe.

One was supported by authority; it was strong with ten centuries of continuous existence. Better put: its origin was lost in the mists of time. Poets had embellished it, philosophers had purified it, it had cast far from itself everything that might shock reason.[1] It was the religion of all civilized nations; it was the authorized cult of the dominant people.

The other had neither the protection of authority nor the support of ancient traditions. Poetry gave it no ornamentation. It was not accompanied by philosophy's brilliance. It certainly had not contracted an alliance with the imposing profundities of metaphysics. It was born in an obscure country, among a people odious to the rest of humanity (even among them, from the least respectable portion of that people); hence it was an object of universal disdain.

Who would not believe that the first religion must triumph over the second? All enlightened men thought so; all smiled when rumor brought to their attention the existence of a few fanatics who were scattered, unknown, and persecuted.

1. This assertion has nothing that contradicts the portrait we drew of Roman superstition at the time of polytheism's decadence. This superstition was not part of the public religion; on the contrary, it came to replace it. Moreover, polytheism had received all the improvements of philosophy; and in theory it was incomparably better than the belief of previous centuries. But conviction was no longer there; and when this is the case, all the improvements are but branches taken from a living tree, which one foolishly wishes to insert into a dead trunk.

How did it happen that the event overcame these proud predictions? It was because, separated from the former form, the religious sentiment had sought refuge in the new one. And why? Because despite the purifications the ancient form had received, it still recalled the epochs that the sentiment now rejected, especially the vices and imperfections of the former times. The names of these gods were attached to the memories of crudeness and ignorance. Shaken from every direction by human investigations, it had lost its charm and had become, as it were, profane. The new form, on the other hand, was devoid of every noxious memory. The name of its founder and of the God it taught recalled no previous epoch that had harmed the religious sentiment. That sentiment therefore gave itself enthusiastically to the new form. It adopted its banner; it was by the mouth of its followers that it spoke. They owed to it that consciousness of strength and the certainty in their speech that contrasted so strikingly with the timidity and hesitation of their opponents' language. The apostles of the new form went forward surrounded by miracles, which were undeniable by the sole fact that those who affirmed them were full of an unshakeable conviction. The defenders of the old form based themselves upon wonders that they themselves doubted, worn copies of no longer imitable models. The former made fearless use of both faith and reason, of reason against their opponents, of faith for their own teaching. Engaging in philosophical dialectics, they did not fear to compromise a cause that could not be undermined by such reasoning. Their attack-weapon was critical examination, their banner a deep and personal conviction. The others hesitated between a reason that threatened them and an enthusiasm that paled before the one opposed to it. The skepticism they wished to direct against their adversaries turned against them, and because they were not firm in their belief they were timid in their refutations. Their apologies were marked by condescension, by avowals that were first extorted, then retracted, with insinuations that allowed others to see that the religion they recommended was intended only for the weak, and that the strong could do without it. To be sure, they placed themselves in the camp of the strong, but one is a poor missionary when one places oneself above one's own profession of faith.

One could believe that they were zealous for yet another reason. They were moved by their interest, while the martyrs of the other side were far from the time when the victory of their faith would procure personal advantages to those who espoused it. But disinterestedness is the first of powers. In areas when it is necessary to persuade and convince, obvious self-interest weakens rather than strengthens one's case.

So, please note how all these ideas congregated around the religious sentiment and, obedient to its least indication, were modified, even transformed, to serve it. In the older belief that philosophy had subjugated, man had been lowered to the rank of an imperceptible atom in the immensity of the universe. The new form made him the center of a world that had been created for him. He was at once the work and the aim of God. The philosophical notion is, perhaps, truer, but how much more is the other one full of warmth and life! And from another point of view it possesses a yet higher and more sublime truth. If one locates grandeur in what really constitutes it, there is more grandeur in a proud thought, in a profound emotion, in an act of devotion, than in all the mechanisms of the celestial spheres.

Thus see the older form constantly propose exchanges and deals with its rival, and how these offers were met with disdainful refusal. What a remarkable thing! Looking only from the outside it was strength that hesitated and weakness that wanted the battle. This was because true force was entirely on the side of apparent weakness. The ancient form was dead; it aspired only to the peace of the dead. The new form wanted to fight and conquer because, being full of the religious sentiment, it had reanimated the life of the soul and had awoken the skeletons in the tombs.

CHAPTER 6

On the Way in Which Religion Has
Been Envisaged until Now

If we now apply the previous reflections to the way in which religion has been envisaged until now, you will not be surprised that almost all those who have engaged
this vast topic have been misled. In general, three groups have emerged, who fell
into grave errors because they mistook the nature and the progressive development
of the religious sentiment.[1]

The first group considers religion to be inaccessible to man by his own lights
and efforts; it is communicated to him by the Supreme Being in a positive and
unchanging manner. Religion suffers diminishment only when it is modified by
the human spirit. Therefore, when this occurs it must be brought back as much as
possible to its original state, to its primitive purity. Shaken beliefs at all costs must
be shored up. However, this view did not ask if such an endeavor is in the power of
any existing authority. History reveals that all precautions in this vein were useless,
all rigors powerless. Socrates drinking the hemlock, Aristotle fleeing Athens, Diogoras outlawed—none of this halted Athens's unbelief. Greek philosophy came
to Rome. Initially chased from Rome, it soon returned and triumphed. And the
austerity of Louis XIV's old age only prepared France for an even greater, more
open, and bolder irreligion.

The second group was rightly sensitive to the evils produced by fanaticism and
intolerance. However, it saw only falsehood in religion, sometimes quite vulgar,
sometimes sophisticated, sometimes rather material, sometimes more abstract, but
always more or less harmful. This perspective concluded that it was desirable to

---

1. In placing the three positions we are going to speak about on a par, and in saying that it was
error that moved the first group to maintain by force what was falling apart, we perhaps have been
too gentle. Often it was calculation, not error that moved men. The priests of decadent polytheism
knew very well that it was not for the triumph of truth that they sent Christians to their martyrdom.

64

found morality on a wholly mundane basis, and to extirpate the religious sentiment. Had it consulted human experience, however, it would have seen that religion is always being reborn at the very moment when enlightenment proudly thinks it has killed it. Juvenal wrote that only children believe in another life. However, at the same time an unknown sect arose in the empire, its eyes fixed on a world to come, and the present world became its conquest. If religion is necessary to us, if a faculty is found in us that demands to be employed, if our imagination needs to transcend the limits that enclose us, if the suffering and troubled dimensions of our being need a world they can make use of and embellish, in vain would one reproach religion for its drawbacks or its dangers. Necessity will always conquer prudence. The one who can no longer inhabit the land must confront the waves, no matter how littered with reefs the ocean may be.

Finally, the third group takes what it believes to be the golden mean between the two extremes. They acknowledge only what they call natural religion, which they reduce to the purest dogmas and the simplest notions. But this group differs from the other two groups, the orthodox and the unbelievers, not by their path but only by their goal. Like the others, they believe that man can be put in possession of an absolute truth, hence that he can remain always the same, totally stationary. Whoever maintains these dogmas possesses this truth. But whoever falls short of them by his unbelief, or goes beyond them by acknowledging miraculous revelations, is equally mistaken.

With these three perspectives, we can say that until now no one has considered religion under its true aspect. A glance at the religious and the anti-religious writings of France, England, and Germany will provide irrefutable proofs of this claim.

Before the eighteenth century all the works published in France by the defenders of the different religious communities were dedicated to the victory of their own sect. However, they all shared an underlying consensus that ruled out the fundamental questions or dispensed them from raising them.

A fruitful source of disputes, heresy was seen by Catholics as a voluntary fault and was treated as a crime.[2] The adherents of this view agreed with their opponents on the basics and contested only some of their consequences.

2. For a number of years people have been able to flatter themselves that this narrow and hateful way of considering differences in religion had given way to more tolerant principles. During a long period of very unjust vexations, Catholic priests attempted to convince us that all of the reproaches directed at their Church concerning its hostile and persecuting spirit were the calumnies of their adversaries. These ministers of a worship that at the time was proscribed were doubtless speaking

Even more discredited than heresy (although less persecuted), unbelief was rejected by a French public opinion drawing, on one hand, on the lively interest stirred by the wars of religion, and, on the other, on the prestige of a king who had made belief fashionable and a means of advancement.

---

in good faith; and we would love to think that nothing has changed in their new conciliatory and peace-making teachings. But one cannot fail to sigh upon seeing one of the most distinguished members of this Church, with a sort of fury that France, happily, had not seen for some time, reproduce anathemas that are puerile if they are without force and condemnable if they do have force. One hardly believes one's eyes when he reads at the beginning of the nineteenth century that those who do not acknowledge this or that dogma are guilty because "if it does not depend upon reason to understand, it always depends on the will to believe what is attested to by the testimony of a sufficient authority" (*Essai sur l'indifférence en matière de religion*, I, 514); as if it depended on our will to accept as sufficient a testimony that was insufficient for our reason, and if the same difficulty—only removed one step—did not remain. Astonishment doubles when one sees a man who apparently has not left the sanctuary of the Druids or the sub-basements of the Holy Office become indignant at the *abject attitude* the Reformation displayed toward the memory of Socrates, Aristotle, or Cato (ibid., I, 67); who declares tolerance to be an *abyss in which religion is going to be lost* (ibid., I, 225); who would make it a crime for an enlightened defender of Christianity to have considered saved deists in good faith, whose conduct is morally good (ibid., I, 223); and finally, in a country in which many forms of worship simultaneously exist under the protection of the laws, to declare that *no religion can subsist except by rejecting all the others* (ibid., I, 225), thereby risking reigniting the religious wars and bringing back the calamities that caused two kings to be murdered and cost the lives of thousands of men. And let not the one who wrote these inflammatory lines try to excuse himself by saying that as a Catholic he damns no one (ibid., pref., XLIII): his indignation against the Protestant minister who does not damn those who do not think like him (ibid., II, XLIII); his anger at the idea that following the principles of Protestantism one cannot exclude as heretics either Jews or Muslims or pagans from salvation (ibid., I, 231); in a word, this thirst to hand out eternal punishments to those all around him (ibid., II, 262), all seem to us to be the most direct sort of assault on a worship devoted to peace and love. Does one truly serve religion by saying that God condemned to the sword entire nations (ibid., III, 47)? To hurl curses and insults at a portion of one's fellow citizens protected by the law? To say that "[those] such as the gravely guilty ones of which antiquity speaks, a people" of whom a tenth today are French, "have lost their reason; that crime troubled its reason; that to disdain and outrage it opposes a stupid insensibility . . . that it is thus made for punishment; that suffering and ignominy have become their nature" (ibid., III, 57); that "the blood their ancestors shed two hundred years ago still hangs over them"; and, after having thus insulted them as much as one can by words, [declared] "send it to torture" (IV, 202), behold—we will not hesitate to say that these things are not permitted by religion, morality, policy, or decency.

Were he to prescribe to us "silence concerning the ruin of our decayed intellect" (ibid., II, 105); were he to treat us as "rebellious spirits who will find the law and its torments, and who will have [the stigma of] crime eternally accompany us" (ibid., III, 60), we will still congratulate ourselves for professing a belief that allows us to love all men and hope for the salvation of all.

When Bossuet thundered against the pagans in his *History* or prosecuted Protestants in his *Polemics*, he appeared as a judge condemning the guilty rather than as an impartial narrator of events or a calm examiner of various doctrines. And when he directed his blows against unbelievers it was verdicts he issued, verdicts, to be sure, that were accompanied by arguments, but arguments in which authority played a much greater role than reasoning.

Far be it from us, though, to diminish the real merit of a great man. If the perspective in which Bossuet viewed religion necessarily lacked impartiality and scope, it was admirable in its nobility and elevation. In his mouth religion spoke a dignified and proud language, one it, sadly, has abandoned since then. Despite the orator himself, led (perhaps even overcome) by his own genius, the last sparks of liberty found refuge in his eloquence. What he did not say to an absolute monarch in the name of the fundamental laws and the people's true interest, he said in the name of the God before whom all creatures return to their original equality.[3]

Nonetheless, while rendering justice to a writer whose panegyrists praise only what is violent and hateful in his works, we believe that we can say that nothing Bossuet has left us—and a fortiori, nothing left us in the other works of the century—can be usefully applied to the new questions we have raised. This includes anything concerning the distinction between the substance and the forms of religion, the development of religious ideas, the gradual changes in beliefs, as well as those successive and irresistible improvements found in mankind's religious experience. These questions were unknown, and completely foreign, to the earlier religious debates.

After Louis XIV the scene changed. Freed from the authority of an old king and from the etiquette of an old court, France launched itself on the path of license. This was the natural effect of a longtime repression. Madame de Prie succeeded Madame de Maintenon, and ecclesiastical honors went from Bossuet to DuBois. Unbelief emerged from hypocrisy's tomb.

To be clear, I am not simply presenting the unbelievers of the last century as the heirs of the orgies of the Regency. Nobler motives inspired many of them. A slow but sure reaction prepared itself over a long period of time. The Saint Bartholomew Day's Massacre had repulsed everyone. The murders of Henry III and Henry IV

---

3. Nothing better proves the natural alliance of religion and liberty. By his character, Bossuet was the most despotic of men; all his opinions favored absolute power. *La Politique de l'Ecriture sainte* would have merited printing by the imperial press at Constantinople. But when he censored power in the name of religion, one would have called him one of the first Christians, one of the firmest apostles of equality, and one of the most intrepid adversaries of tyranny.

had stirred opinion against religious assassination. Then Louis XIV succeeded in enlisting all the sentiments of mankind against priestly oppression. He did so by means of the cruelties that accompanied the revoking of the Edict of Nantes. He did so by ordering the stationing of troops, by confiscations, by torturing fathers and incarcerating mothers, and by kidnapping children. The philosophers' indignation against him was both just and sincere. But even this anger and the works it inspired, the sorts of associations they formed to wage war against the doctrines they accused of so many crimes and evils—all these things inculcated in them the spirit of a sect. And everywhere this spirit dominates, it employs the same means.

Voltaire had said that it is better to strike hard than to strike justly. And all his imitators, a great and active throng who ran from the literary heights to the most obscure ranks, raged against religion. They did so with a fury that was almost always the inverse of the learning they possessed and the talents at their disposal.

In some circumstances Voltaire's maxim is useful. While violent persecutions had ceased, less obvious ones remained to be overcome. Every means seemed legitimate to inspire horror at any sort of persecution. But disarming fanaticism is not the same as adequately understanding and appreciating the religious sentiment. From these tactics came an insulting and sarcastic way of talking about something dear to the majority of human beings. And while this style is always certain to attain momentary success in an old and corrupt nation, it necessarily inspires disgust in refined and sensitive souls—those who are a powerful if unnoticed minority, who will always end up laying down the law even in the midst of general decadence.

Those philosophers who, even while they attacked the existing religion wanted to preserve the principles serving as the basis of all religion, considered the principles only in their most ignoble and crudest version, as a supplement to criminal laws. Reading their writings, one sees that they wanted religion to serve them immediately, as a sort of police force; they wanted religion to help guarantee their property and their lives, to discipline their children and maintain good order in their marriages. They are so utilitarian that they seem to fear believing for nothing.[4] They want religion to repay them for believing in it.

---

4. One could apply to our moral character what one says of the physical laziness of the Turks. It is said that the secretary of an ambassador of France at Constantinople every day took a walk in his garden; the Turks near to the ambassador besought him to forgive his secretary and not to impose such a harsh punishment on him. They could not conceive that one could walk for no particular reason and without any special purpose.

This narrow and partial way of looking at religion has several drawbacks.

Just as by seeking in the beauties of nature immediate utility, and their direct application to society, one tarnishes all the charms of this magnificent spectacle, so too one degrades religion by seeing only what is useful in it. Secondly, practical utility does not at all imply the truth of the theory, and men are not more religious because they are told that religion is useful; one does not believe in utility. Finally, the social utility of religion serves as a pretext for rulers to violate the consciences of the governed. In arguing this way, authors give unbelieving peoples masters who persecute them.

This need for immediate and, as it were, purely material utility is the characteristic vice of our national spirit.[5] It has some advantages, to be sure. It gives greater regularity and more coherence to the concatenation of ideas. People walk more directly to the goal and do not lose sight of it. But when one examines every question in only one way, one runs the risk of failing to see all of its aspects. In following this path, one rejects all involuntary sentiments, impressions, and emotions. They, however, are sometimes exactly what is needed to cause strict reasoning to take another look; sometimes they possess the key that logic by itself does not.

Three authors, however, sometimes rose above this narrow and degrading view. One we have already spoken of: Fénelon. We saw, however, that he was stopped in his tracks by the authority of the Catholic Church, which indicted him for having maintained that man can love God with a pure and disinterested love. The second author was Jean-Jacques Rousseau. Some of his writings are imbued with a genuine religious sentiment that is pure, disinterested, entirely devoid of ulterior motives. But Rousseau was complicated. He teemed with a thousand contradictory thoughts, and he combined them in confused and discordant ways. This was as true of religion as of politics. He who was the most positive and affirmative of men was also the most impatient with the affirmations of others. He shook everything, not because he wanted to destroy everything, as some have said, but because everything seemed to him out of its proper place. With prodigious force he shook the foundations and toppled the columns upon which human existence had rested, for good and for ill, until then. But he was a poor architect, and he could not con-

5. Mr. de Chateaubriand himself, whose talent is undeniable and who certainly is the premier writer among us, when he depicts the dreamy and melancholic aspect of the religious sentiment succumbs in the most bizarre way to this mania for utility. He extols the utility of Christianity for poetry, as if a people sought in their belief a way of obtaining material for their versifiers.

struct a new edifice from these scattered materials. Only destruction resulted from his efforts, and from the destruction a chaos that still bears his mark.

Lastly, Montesquieu—more by his penetrating mind than by his soul—would have been able to shed new light on religion. There was no subject he approached without detecting many new truths. And since all truths are connected, he advanced truth. Ascending from the facts that he discerned and put forth with admirable sagacity, he rose to the cause common to these numerous effects. Turning to religion, he might have been able to detect the general principle in the midst of its infinitely varied modifications. But besides the fact that even a genius can surpass his century only to a certain extent, in the *Spirit of the Laws* Montesquieu examined religion only tangentially, as it were. He said only what he had to say. Reading this great work of the eighteenth century one gets the impression that the author dismissed a host of ideas that presented themselves to him as being beside his purpose.

The French Revolution occurred because we had too much enlightenment to live any longer under arbitrary authority. It lost its way, however, because we did not have enough enlightenment to profit from freedom. The Revolution unshackled a multitude totally unprepared by any experience or reflection for the sudden emancipation they experienced. It quickly transformed itself into a merely material force, one without rule or brake, directed against all the institutions whose imperfections had provoked it.

Religion became the object of a detestable persecution. Then, what followed had to follow: the reaction was as strong as the original action had been unjust and violent. Among contemporary authors in France, many present themselves as defenders of religion. They, however, are no less ignorant of history than their predecessors, the demagogues. No less obtuse concerning what history teaches about the consequences of all tyrannical measures, they propose the old strictures that failed under François I, Philippe II, Mary of England, and Louis XIV. Pitiful sophists, they betray both governments and peoples!

Thus, religion has always been treated in France in a partial, and often in a superficial, way. It has been defended with virulent pedantry and attacked with indiscriminate hostility.

What about England? There, did religion find less obstinate partisans or more equitable opponents?

Thanks to a fortunate set of circumstances, even though established by force under Henry VIII, because of the cruelties of Mary and the fruitless efforts of the

Stuarts, Protestantism became identified with the constitution that was England's glory for so long. In addition, however, there also resulted from this that religion, more so than in any other enlightened country, became a dogmatic matter[6] immune to all free and impartial discussion.

Warburton, Hurd, and Tillotson possessed the domineering spirit of Bossuet but without his genius. The English Church was for them what the Catholic Church was for the bishop of Meaux, with this difference, that intolerance is even more absurd in their case. By denying others the right to be heretics, they abdicated their own right to be Protestants. Writers in England of a lesser order generally have more classical learning than our theologians, but their perspective is no broader. They understand no better the animating spirit of ancient times or foreign peoples. Nor is their thought more liberal, while their logic runs in the same vicious circle.

To be sure, the English sectarians have shed some light on the first Christian centuries. Every controversy generates some light. But these dissidents (who are as subject as the defenders of orthodoxy to the dogmatic spirit that characterizes the entire nation) do not depart from the narrow circle traced by dogmas. They fight over their interpretation. Even here, though, all the parties share common presuppositions, so no one addresses more fundamental matters and primary truths. Their dispute is over how far to go in developing principles they all agree to be true.

Unbelievers are looked down on more in England than elsewhere because the English recall that one of the means Charles II used to destroy the nation's liberty was to ridicule religion. Among the unbelievers, Collins, Tindall, Woolston, and later Toulmin occupy a lesser rank. We intentionally omitted Hobbes. Religion appeared to Hobbes as a means of tyranny, and he publicly massaged it without believing it. He cannot be considered religion's friend, because he dishonored it, nor as its enemy, because he recommended it. Toland owes whatever is meritorious in his thought to Spinoza. Shaftesbury, Bolingbroke, Cherbury, and Hume are the

---

6. This dogmatic disposition is an obstacle even to investigations that have for their purpose simply to know the opinions, and to deepen our understanding of the past, of other countries. "What can one expect," rightly says one of the most incisive critical spirits of Germany (Mr. Rhode, *Ueber Alter und Werth einiger morgenlaendischer Urkunden*), "what can one expect from the investigations of authors who begin with the following words: Either the first eleven chapters of Genesis are true or our religion is false. Now, our religion is not false, therefore the first eleven chapters of Genesis are true" (Sir W. Jones, *Asiatick Researches*, I, 225 [*Asiat. Res.*]). Of course, there is the unbeliever who draws the opposite conclusion from the alternative. Sophistry belongs to all times and all sects.

only writers in this category who have real value. But they all also have the defects of the French thinkers: an imperious tone, epigrammatic utterances, bitterness, malevolent insinuations, deliberately distorted facts, and artfully mutilated narratives.

In his *Natural History of Religion*, Hume showed a good deal of wit but little profound learning. His irony is effective because of its apparent mildness, and his sallies often hit their mark. But the work is nonetheless quite unworthy of its serious subject.

With a sometimes treacherous adroitness, which he used when he thought he could get away with it, Gibbon spoiled his immense learning, his tireless research, and the often remarkable subtlety of his views. He did so as well by a complete lack of sympathy for enthusiasm. Sympathy for it, however, is the necessary condition for describing a young religion. And, finally, he did so by a revolting indifference toward both misfortune and courage.

Thomas Paine only reproduced in a commonplace and often crude style the shallow metaphysics of Baron Holbach. Embracing a widespread error, he saw in religion only an enemy of the freedom he cherished (without, however, understanding freedom). Because he exaggerated the principles of liberty, he misunderstood the nature of religion.

Even though Godwin is much more profound and ingenious than Paine in developing his sometimes utopian political ideas, when it comes to religion he barely goes beyond Paine. Dominated by the prejudices of a vulgar philosophy, he abdicated his characteristic penetration. In his attacks against an indestructible sentiment, he appeared to be ignorant of the human heart, which in many ways he was able to describe with remarkable fidelity.

Between the two, religious dogmatism and violent (or frivolous) unbelief divide the minds of England. But neither speaks to the human soul. And the essence of religion is found in neither the subtleties of dogma nor the abstractions of unbelief.

Looking closer at the religious attitudes of the two countries we just surveyed, one can detect a certain likeness, although one must look closely. The English sects are limited in their religious aspirations by the letter of the dogmas they wish to retain. The upcoming generation in France, which is beginning to experience a need for religion, is doubly inhibited. On one hand, by a tradition of unbelief that has become a kind of philosophical dogma, one they do not dare abandon, and, on the other, by the unfortunate alliance of religion and politics. These causes inhibit among us and among our neighbors the development of the religious sentiment.

Protestant Germany presents a better scene. Almost all the Germans have the great merit, or great good fortune, of recognizing a fundamental truth without which one discovers nothing true nor establishes anything good. This truth is that everything in man is progressive. None of his ideas remains fixed; they develop even despite resistance, coming to light through various obstacles. At the end of any significant interval of time they are found to have undergone modification, having received essential improvements.

Of all truths, this is the one most rejected in France. We have a certain self-complacency, which at any given time makes us believe that we have arrived at perfection, and therefore the human race should stop and admire us.

Germans are less content, less satisfied with themselves in the present, and less envious of future generations. They know that each generation is placed at some point on a great continuum in order to draw profit from what came before and to prepare what is to be done later. Social, political, and religious forms appear to them as they are: indispensable supports for man, but which must be modified when he changes. This attitude by itself is an excellent criterion for judging religion.

For the past century, a particular circumstance has confirmed them in this attitude and caused them to make progress on this path.

Previously, Protestantism in Germany was what it still is in England: a belief-system as dogmatic as the Catholicism from which the reformers broke. The ministers of the two main dissident communions forgot that their leaders could not justify their reforms except by proclaiming freedom of belief in matters of worship. They rose indignantly against the limits laid down by the Roman Church. But in an absurd and cruel contradiction—one for which their leaders had provided the model—they claimed to be authorized to propose no less arbitrary ones. They demanded liberty for themselves but refused it to their enemies. They railed against the injustice and folly of intolerance, and they made use of both.

Frederick II ascended to the throne. The literature of his country was in its infancy. He granted all his favors to French letters. Excepting Voltaire, who could not live for long in an atmosphere of patronage and dependency, these writers were second-rate, even mediocre. Vain, ambitious, and second-rate, as are all those who condescend to become the entourage of power, they had founded their reputation in France on glib unbelief and were totally lacking a spirit of serious investigation. Depending upon how you look at it, seriousness of purpose either motivates or excuses unbelief. In any event, called to a foreign court, they brought with them this unbelief, the instrument of their success. Therefore Christianity saw itself under constant assault from this philosophical monarch, his sycophants, and their eager imitators. All the sides of the faith which appeared weak were ruthlessly exposed; all legends were mercilessly ridiculed.

A few German writers, much superior to their French models, joined this audacious, impious order. From among them came the Wieland-school in poetry, the school of Nicolai in prose, and Lessing himself. We would be embarrassed to compare him to the Marquis d'Argens and La Metrie in terms of good faith, learning, and genius, but sometimes he resembled them. The vexations by authority in several German principalities furnished the adversaries of religion more than pretexts. Professors denounced for their views and preachers persecuted for heterodoxy indicated the need for more intellectual freedom. And the hatred generated by the persecutions extended to the ideas that the persecutors claimed to vindicate.

But the German spirit finally repudiated both of these sterile dogmatic approaches. It is naturally meditative, too serious to be distracted for long by such superficiality, too sincere to sacrifice what it deems true to applause. The German character itself inclines to enthusiasm, and it finds happiness in religion—as in love—only in exaltation and reverie. It therefore rejected the two quarreling parties, one advancing as proofs only sarcasms that every equitable judge knew were unjust, the other propounding as facts what every learned man knew were not so.

As a result, many defenders of threatened belief presented themselves. Because of the liberty of writing and publishing that Frederick allowed, the new apologists of religion made their case, each in his own way. Thus there was an army, but one without a general and with all-important differences among the troops.

Some attached themselves to the old system and propped it up as much as they could on the old supports of miracles and prophecy. Others renounced these means and restricted themselves to the purely moral aspect of religion, casting into the shadows the historical, traditional, and, especially, the miraculous parts.

This did not occur at once, however. This was an honorable retreat, with each post successively abandoned, the better to preserve all the others. What were later called improvements at the time appeared to be sacrifices.

Then Frederick died. Now authority adopted a policy toward religion contrary to his. It wanted to reunite under a common banner all the different theologians. Those who refused to do so came under attack from those who had remained faithful to the old doctrines. Their previous modifications were termed crimes, their previous sacrifices were called apostasy. You have extreme parties in religion just as you do in politics. Edicts of persecution appeared, apparently dictated from the tomb.

In this way many zealous supporters of Christianity were declared to be enemies. They did not accept this title, though. From their efforts to defend themselves, combined with the impossibility to reprise the doctrines they had disavowed (or simply left behind), emerged a system which contained the germ of an idea we believe is eminently just.

In this system, man, having emerged from the hands of the supreme power, was guided by the divine from his first steps. But the creator proportioned his assistance to the condition and faculties of his creatures. The Jewish religion led the Hebrews to the point where they were capable of a purified faith. Christianity then replaced the Law of Moses. The Reformation made Christianity compatible with the Enlightenment to come in the next century. Other improvements will some day come to reform the Reformation.[7]

7. It was as a consequence of this system that, at the time of which we are speaking, Germany saw multiple treatises on the benign condescension of God toward men, the gradual development of revelations, the education of the human race, and on Christianity finally adapted to the needs of the time. To give an idea of the dominant thinking that presided over these writings, we will recount the arguments of these theologians concerning miracles.

"Miracles," they said, "whether they be supernatural or simply natural phenomena whose cause the ignorant men who observed them did not know, miracles were valuable and even necessary proofs in the times when they took place. The human race was too little enlightened to be convinced by arguments. It needed more striking—and shorter—proofs. Proofs of a different sort are necessary for us today. It is by logic, by morality, by the sentiment of the beautiful and the honorable, that we can be convinced. Miracles ought not to be contested, but left aside." They said the same thing about the mysteries and the prophets.

Quite remarkably, the same idea had presented itself to an Englishman a century earlier. He had proposed that one can calculate the duration of a religion following the gradual lessening of its consonance with contemporary opinions and interests (John Craigs, *Theologiae christianae principia mathematica* [London, 1689, in-4; Leipzig, 1755]). But the dogmatic spirit of the English rejected this hypothesis as being impious; in Germany, though, it took on an eminently religious character. "As an external establishment," said one of its defenders in 1812, "Christianity has been subject to inevitable modifications and changes in time, but the core of the doctrine has nothing to fear from them. On the contrary, it will appear even more sublime and divine. Whatever form it might take on, the fundamental and eternally true ideas of this religion will always be more clearly expressed. At the end of two thousand years, the forms of Judaism have survived its spirit. The spirit of Christianity will survive its forms by taking care to appropriate to itself each intellectual and social situation of the human race" (*Journ. littér.* of Jena, 3 September 1812).

This system bears some resemblance to the Indian doctrine of successive incarnations, which took place every time God wanted to make the truth known to men. It is also rather remarkable that one finds an analogous idea in a Jewish hypothesis. The Jews attributed the same soul to Adam, Abraham, and David, and believed that this would be the soul of the Messiah (Bartholocci, *Biblioth. rabbin.*).

We will leave to the side the supernatural aspects acknowledged by this system, aspects that will fail to satisfy the devout and will displease the philosophers. But, as we said, it contains the germ of a new and important thought, one we will develop in a moment. For now we need to finish our investigation into Germany's religious condition.

The system we just sketched is consoling and noble. There was only one more step to take to rid religion of that narrow and threatening tendency which consists in supposing truth to be a gift of chance or caprice and condemns to eternal damnation those who without any fault of their own are deprived of it.[8]

However, lacking all historical, metaphysical, and moral proofs, and stamped with anthropomorphism, the weak spot of all beliefs, this system could hardly satisfy the mind which demands demonstrations nor a certain sentiment of the heart. This sentiment loves to clothe the Being it adores with infinite benevolence and goodness. Propose faith as a matter of revelation, it can triumph over objections and doubts; and the most bellicose prophet has proclaimed a very similar idea as the source of his divine mission. But as something proposed by man to man, like all other human inventions it had to float in the ocean of conjectures that surrounded it, only to reappear when oblivion had given it an air of novelty.

At the end of a few years, the Germans went beyond this hypothesis and embraced another, broader one. In some respects it was more satisfactory.

They also claimed that one must not distinguish Elias from Phineas, son of the high-priest Eleazar, and that the prophet who lived among men, sometimes under the name of Phineas, sometimes under that of Elias, was not a man but an angel who was incarnate in order to give council to the people of God (Orig., *Tract.*, VII; Aegidius Camart, *De rebus gestis Eliae*).

8. To consider all religions as the manifestations of the divinity proportionate to the enlightenment and customs of peoples is to establish between Providence and men relations that make the virtues and knowledge of men a matter for gratitude and love. The Greeks were free, enlightened, and happy. The Romans, despite their thirst for conquest, which initially was a fruit of necessity and then of habit and the love of power, and despite the too frequent atrocities of their foreign policy, provide us the picture of man perfected in his faculties, his courage, his patriotism, with all the virile and grand virtues carried, perhaps, beyond what we can conceive of today. The religion that had so much influence on these two peoples, and which consequently contributed to their perfection, can it not be considered a benefit of Providence? The Providence to which one owes these successive revelations, always purer and more salutary, does it not thereby display itself in features worthy of its goodness and its justice? Is it not reassuring to see this goodness and this justice watch over the liberty of Athens, the patriotism of Sparta, and the devotion of republican Rome; to see it inspire Socrates; encourage Timoleon; call Cato of Utica to itself; arm Brutus; and support Seneca's courage?

Since we have to explain it in a few words, we beg the French reader's pardon for the vagueness he may experience at first. It will go away, we hope, and we also hope he will see that the fog contains a clear idea.

The advocates of the new system say that religion is the universal language of nature but expressed in different signs, doctrines, symbols, and rites. All peoples, or at least the enlightened class among them, the priests, spoke this language. The differences one observes are only temporary anomalies, unimportant forms, that the one who desires to understand and judge religion must set aside in order to enter into the mysterious vital center in which they all converge.

This newer point of view, the one through which learned Germans view religion today, has been of immense utility. To it we owe admirable discoveries concerning the relations of religions among themselves, concerning peoples' interactions, and the common thread among mythologies. To it we owe the knowledge we have of antiquity, both in its depths and in its charms. Our savants have studied the monuments, records, and traditions of long-ago times much as geologists study the earth or zoologists the skeletons of extinct species. The Germans have rediscovered the nature of man in these traditions and monuments. This nature is always the same, although diversified. Consequently, it must be the living basis for every investigation and for all systems of explanation. In the writings of Fréret, Dupuis, and Sainte-Croix, Greece and the Orient resemble dessicated mummies. Under the pens of Creuzer and Goerres, these same mummies become elegant and admirable statues worthy of Praxiteles and Pheidias.

Everything serves the intellect in its eternal search. Systems are instruments by which man discovers the truth about details while being mistaken about the whole. When the systems are superseded, truths remain.

Moreover, there is a just side to this hypothesis, one that appeals to the religious sentiment chased from its haunts and seeking a refuge. Moreover, this occurs at a time when dogmatic unbelief inspires a sort of fatigue among us. I predict we will soon enough see it arrive in France and replace the narrow and arid system of Dupuis. This will be a triumph of the imagination and in some respects a gain for science.[9]

9. It is with genuine pleasure that we announce that the entirety of this new German system will soon be put before the eyes of the French public by a young writer who combines vast learning with rare sagacity, and with a good faith that is even rarer, along with an impartiality of which our literature offers few examples. Mr. Guigniaut will soon publish a translation of the *Symbolique* of Creuzer, a work that commanded the attention of all of learned Europe, but which in the original had the

However, its adherents seem to have misunderstood a connected truth, without which this system will suffer from the defect characteristic of all systems.

Without doubt, religion is the language in which nature speaks to man. But this language varies; it has not been the same in every epoch, whether coming from the people's mouths or the enlightened classes that governed them. Religion for both classes is subject to a regular progression. Priests obey it, as well as the tribes they dominate. This progression is more mysterious in the priestly doctrines because under the priestly yoke everything is more mysterious. Sometimes, too, it is slower, because the priests do everything to slow it down. But for all that it is no less inevitable and determined by fixed laws, which have their origin in the human heart.

One is therefore mistaken when, instead of seeing a purer teaching as the result of the labors and the progress (in a word, the moral and intellectual amelioration) of the human race, one supposes that this or that doctrine came before all the other ones for no particular reason, or when it is placed at a time when man in fact was incapable of conceiving it, simply in order to protect the honor of the priestly caste. These priests, however, even though more learned (and, above all, craftier) than the mass of people, were very far from being able to rise to the level of certain ideas that could only be the result of constant efforts, accumulated discoveries, and uninterrupted meditation.

To want to make religion something immutable and veiled only to the vulgar, to hope that one will discover this single natural language and that, then, the cults, dogmas, and symbols of all the nations will reveal themselves as parts of this sacred language, is to be captive to an empty hope. It is not in these symbols or in the doctrines that this unity can be found. But if you penetrate into the nature of man, you will gain access to the unique source of all religions and the germ of all the modifications they undergo.

---

defect of lacking that method and clarity that France alone seems to have need of and to appreciate. The translator remedies this grave defect by reworking the book and by putting the important ideas it contains in their natural order. What the plan of our work and its limits forbid us to address will, by Mr. Guigniaut's labor, receive unexpected developments. And even though his opinions and our doubts sometimes are opposed, we think that without aiming to do so he often strengthens, by means of incontestable proofs, the truths we have tried to establish. In any case, the work of Mr. Guigniaut will be of immense utility to the friends of thinking and the admirers of antiquity by opening a new path and enlarging the sphere of ideas concerning ancient religions, a sphere much too limited by the learned of the previous century. In particular, during the past twenty years the great work of Dupuis has made us take a small part for the whole.

CHAPTER 7

The Plan of the Work

The sketch we just provided of the different ways in which religion has been considered up until now seems to us to prove that there is an important lacuna in the treatment of this subject. In this work we have tried to fill it in as much as our powers allowed.

In doing so, we have not declared war on any doctrine; we have not attacked the divinity of any faith. But we have thought that we could respectfully set aside the thornier questions connected with religion and begin with an obvious fact. That fact? That the religious sentiment is an essential attribute, an inherent quality, of our nature.[1]

---

1. We have tried to define the religious sentiment in a previous chapter. But during the printing of this work the premier English poet gave it a definition that is so much in keeping with ours that we could not stop ourselves from including it here.

How often we forget all time, when lone,
Admiring nature's universal throne,
Her woods, her wilds, her waters, the intense
Reply of hers to our intelligence?
Live not the stars and mountains? Are the waves
Without a spirit? Are the drooping caves
Without a feeling in their silent tears?
No, no. They woo and clasp us to their spheres,
Dissolve this clog and clod of clay before
Its hour, and merge our soul in the great shore,
Strip off this fond and false identity?
Who thinks of self, when gazing on the sky?
(Lord Byron, *Island*)

We are told that some men accuse Lord Byron of atheism and impiety. There is more religion in these twelve lines than in the writings past, present, and future of all these naysayers put together.

We studied the forms that this sentiment can assume. We found them necessarily commensurate with the situation of the individuals or peoples who profess a religion. Is it not obvious that the primitive human being who is solely occupied with subsistence cannot have the same religious notions as a civilized one? When society is established, but the physical laws of the world are unknown, is it not understandable that natural forces would be objects of worship? But at a more advanced period when the laws of physical nature are better known, adoration retreats to the plane of morality. Later still, when the causal relations in the moral order are known, religion retreats to metaphysics and spirituality. Later still, when the subtleties of metaphysics are abandoned as powerless to explain anything, it is in the sanctuary of our soul that religion finally finds its impregnable asylum.

This therefore was our first principle. We said: since civilization is progressive, religious forms must be tied to this progression. History confirmed us in this first result of our researches.

We next examined what were the different periods of this progressive development. We noticed that each religious form divides into three distinct periods.

Man first of all runs toward a religion. That is, in accord with his instinct and level of intellectual development, he seeks to discover the relations between him and invisible powers. When he believes he has discovered them, he gives them a determinate and regular form.

Having provided in this way for this first necessity of his nature, he develops and perfects his other faculties. But these very developments render the form he had given to his religious ideas unsuitable to his subsequently developed faculties.

At this point the destruction of the form is inevitable. The polytheism of the *Iliad* is unsuitable to the century of Pericles. In his tragedies Euripides makes himself the spokesman for the naissant irreligion.

Now, if the disappearance of the former belief is inhibited by existing institutions—and this is the natural course of things—this artificial prolongation is only a matter of inertia; the human race then seems deprived of life. Enthusiasm and real faith desert religion. There are only formulas, practices, and priests left.

But this unnatural condition cannot last. A struggle ensues, not only between the established religion and the intellect it offends, but between the religion and the sentiment it no longer satisfies.

This struggle leads to the third period: the destruction of the old form, followed by crises of total unbelief. These are disordered and sometimes terrible moments, but they are unavoidable when man must be liberated from what has become a shackle. These crises are always followed by a form of religious ideas better adapted to the faculties of the human spirit, and religion itself emerges younger, purer, and lovelier from its ashes.

From his most primitive state man follows this path. But he does encounter obstacles of various kinds along the way. Among them there are some that are external and some that are internal.

The internal ones are, first, his ignorance; then the domination of his senses and domination by the objects that surround him; his own egoism; and, finally, his own reason, at least in certain respects.

There is in reason when it is separated from sentiment what I could call a material part, one that opposes all élans of the soul.[2] We saw earlier that it cannot account for any of our intimate emotions. To apply it to religion, with its coolness and inherent limitations, is to apply arithmetic to poetry. One denatures reason and falsifies it when applying it outside its sphere. In our daily lives it shows us very well the obstacles and pitfalls before us. But turned toward heaven it is only an earthbound torch, one that obscures the splendor of the stars.[3]

The external obstacles are, first, the calamities which by troubling the physical

---

2. The Nymphs, said Callimachus, discovered three mysterious stones that could be used to foresee the future. They presented them to Minerva, who refused them, saying that they were better suited to Apollo.

3. There are some ideas that are correct as long as they remain in their proper sphere. Such are the ideas of time, space, and extension; such, too, is the idea of cause and effect. These ideas are suggested to us by the observation of phenomena, i.e., of appearances that strike our senses. They are therefore applicable, even indispensable, to direct our judgment in the sphere of these appearances. But the interior sentiment seems to go beyond this sphere; for the results of strict logic applied to the intimate sentiment are almost always in opposition to it, even though in certain cases it is so strong that all the rigor of reasoning cannot triumph over its resistance. For example, the idea of cause and effect in what relates to external objects and to our relations with these objects is the foundation of all rational logic. But if we transport this idea of cause and effect to the nature of the soul, it leads us directly and irresistibly to deny all free will; that is, it leads us to a result that our interior sentiment cannot admit despite all our efforts. Now, if a way of reasoning that on certain objects leads us to conclusions that are obvious to our intellect, as well as conform to our interior sentiment and are satisfying to our mind, but on other objects results in consequences that revolt our intellect, contradict our intimate sentiment, and, far from satisfying our mind causes it to experience the pain of not being able to refute what it finds repugnant, is it not obvious that this way of reasoning, suitable in the first sphere, is inappropriate in the second? The distinctive character of correct reasoning is to give man the peace of mind that accompanies conviction. When it does not obtain this repose, it is not always the case that the reasoning is false; it can also be applied to objects to which it ought not be applied.

existence of man, retard his moral progress; and, second, the various interests that lead other men to cause him, willingly or not, to take the opposite path.

Man is thus placed among three opposing forces which contend for control. One could say that heaven calls him from on high, earth retains him below, and his fellow human beings attend to him horizontally. Nonetheless, even in the midst of the various obstacles he must overcome, he advances in conformity to the impulse his nature imparts to him. His progress is set; it is necessary. It can be contravened or suspended for a time, but over the long term nothing can give him a different orientation.

This is the series of ideas, or rather facts, that we propose to prove. If we are successful, the result will be salutary in several ways.

Since religion is inherent in human nature and always reemerges under a new form when the previous one is broken, and since religion naturally adjusts itself to the developments and progress of each epoch, it follows that philosophers, while working to purify religious ideas, ought to renounce any effort to fight against the religious sentiment, to try to destroy what is indestructible. On the other hand, authority neither can nor ought to try to shackle, redirect, or even speed up the improvements brought to religion by the labors of the intellect.[4]

We said it ought not even attempt to speed them up. This is because as much as free and gradual improvements appear to be desirable, we find premature and violent reforms to be repugnant. We detest intolerant authority, although we fear philosophical authoritarianism too. Louis XVI's persecutions did much harm, but the purported enlightened learning of Joseph II caused almost as much. The imprudent decrees of the Constituent Assembly caused no less harm, if not by their immediate effects at least by their proximate consequences.

Let authority be neutral. Human intelligence, heaven's gift, will take charge of the rest. It is not religion's enemy except when religion persecutes. It will better accomplish its tasks of impartiality and improvement if it is not hampered by artificial obstacles, troubled by artificial threats, and forced to overreach in order to overcome stubborn resistances.

The neutrality of authority will even serve to preserve a while longer the religious forms to which habit or conviction ought to attach some importance. These

---

4. "A people that perfects its laws and its arts is quite unfortunate and very much to be pitied when it cannot perfect its religion" (de Pauw, *Recherches sur les Egyptiens et les Chinois*, I, 178). See, on the same subject, Herder, *Phil. de l'hist.*, III, 138–150.

forms will last longer when they do not resist imperceptible improvements. It is normally in the midst of conflict that they break down. It was the priests of Athens who first broke the entente that existed between philosophy and polytheism, which philosophy still wished to respect. The inflexibility of Leo X precipitated the full-scale Reformation that Luther himself did not envisage when he began his attacks against the abuses of the Catholic Church.[5]

5. This would not be the only utility of this way of envisaging religion. It has the further advantage of making intelligible many events that seem to us to be the effects of chance, or that we attribute to partial causes, while they are the necessary results of an invariable development. Thus, when we see Cyrus and Bonaparte in the same position, both conquerors of an ancient kingdom whose political as well as religious institutions were hostile to their power, we will be able to understand why the first, by means of a concordat with the magi, established the religion of Zoroaster as the court religion in the midst of the crude belief of these semibarbarous Persians, and why Napoleon did as much vis-à-vis Catholicism in the midst of national unbelief.

We will find many traits characteristic of the revocation of the Edict of Nantes in the sudden persecution of Christians by Diocletian, in the hesitation of this emperor, in the zeal of his courtiers, in the fury of the priests of the ancient cult. We will learn that Julian did not remain without imitators. Modern times are illumined by past times, as those are by modern times.

CHAPTER 8

Concerning Questions That Would Be a Necessary Part of a History of Religion but Are Irrelevant to Our Purpose

Having explained to our readers our aims and our plan, we need to explain why several questions that would naturally enter into a work of history will be omitted here. We also need to indicate the precautions we have had to take in order to attain the goal we set ourselves. We will speak of them in the following chapter.

To discover how man rises from crude beliefs to more sophisticated ones, we had to go back to the least advanced stage of human society, the primitive or savage state.

Here a question presented itself. Was the savage state the original state of our species?

The philosophers of the eighteenth century declared themselves in the affirmative, but with inadequate arguments and reflection. All their religious and political systems are based upon the hypothesis of a human race originally found in the condition of brutes, animals wandering in the forests, competing for the fruits of trees and the flesh of other animals. But if this was the natural condition of mankind, how did men emerge from it?

The reasonings attributed to early human beings for them to adopt the social state contain a clear *petitio principii*. They suppose an already existing social state. One cannot know its benefits unless one has experienced them. But in this view, society itself is the result of the development of human intelligence. In truth, however, the development of intelligence is the result of human social existence.

Some philosophers invoked chance. To do so, however, is to employ a term without definite meaning. Chance does not overcome nature. Nor has chance civilized the lower species. But according to these philosophers, they too were subject to chance, including what we could call fortunate chance.

The civilizing of primitive peoples by foreign ones leaves the problem untouched. Superiors may instruct inferiors, but who instructed the teachers? It is a causal chain suspended in mid air. In addition, primitive peoples reject civilization when it is presented to them.

The closer men are to the savage state, the less given they are to change. Scattered at the ends of the earth, the wandering hordes we have discovered have not taken one step toward civilization. The inhabitants of the shores that Nearchus visited centuries ago are still today as they were two thousand years ago. Today, as then, they gather an uncertain subsistence from the sea. Today, as then, wealth consists in sea-borne bones thrown up by waves upon the shore. Physical need has not instructed them; wretched poverty has not enlightened them. Modern-day travelers have found them just as Alexander's admiral did twenty centuries ago.[1]

The same is true of the savages described in antiquity by Agatharchides,[2] and in our days by Lord Bruce.[3] Even though surrounded by civilized nations, and living next to the kingdom of Meroë with its well-known priesthood (equal in authority and learning to that of Egypt), these hordes have remained in their primitive condition. Some sleep under trees, bending their branches and fixing them in the ground; some capture rhinos and elephants and cure their skins in the sun; some chase ostriches; others collect the locusts the wind wafts to them in the desert or the cadavers of crocodiles or seahorses washed up on the shore. Therefore, the diseases that Diodoras described centuries ago as the result of these filthy foods still afflict the descendants of these unfortunate races.[4] The centuries have passed them over with no improvements, no progress, no discoveries. We acknowledge this truth.

We therefore will not take the savage state as the original condition of mankind. We do not place ourselves at any purported cradle of mankind. Nor do we attempt to determine how religion began, but only in what way, when it is in the crudest state one can conceive, it rose and gradually arrived at purer notions.

We do not positively affirm that this crude state was the first condition of mankind. Nor do we put ourselves in opposition to a point of view that sees this condition as a decline, a fall. But it is the point furthest removed from perfection. That

---

1. See *The Periplus of Nearchus*, by D. Vincent (London, 1798); Niebuhr, *Desc. de l'Arab.*; and Marco Polo.

2. Agatharch., *De rubr. mar.* in *Geogr. min.* Hudson., I, 37ff.

3. Bruce, *Voy. en Abyss.*, II, 539, III, 401.

4. Diodorus, I.

is enough for us to feel compelled to place ourselves there in order to better survey the distance the species has traveled to arrive at the opposite pole.

To be sure, one could make the following objection.

When one returns to the most obscure historical periods, one can see only the outlines of enormous masses that the darkness both covers and renders more imposing. Moreover, the different masses present remarkably similar traits even when separated by chasms.

Surveying Europe, Asia, and what we know of Africa; starting from Gaul, or even Spain, and passing through Germany, Scandinavia, Tartary, India, Persia, Arabia, Ethiopia, and Egypt, we find everywhere similar practices and cosmogonies, and religious bodies, rites, sacrifices, ceremonies, customs, and views all with undeniable similarities. And we find these practices, cosmogonies, corporations, rites, sacrifices, ceremonies, and opinions in America, in Mexico, and in Peru.

It is vain to assign some general dispositions of the human spirit as the cause of these similarities.[5] In many details and particulars there are such minutely exact resemblances[6] that it is impossible to find the reason for them simply in nature,

---

5. Fréret, "Mém. sur les Gaulois," *Acad. des inscript.*, XXIV, 389.

6. On the feast of Bhavani in India, which occurs on the first of May, Indians, and especially shepherds, erected *mais*, which they decorated with flowers. The same ceremony took place the same day by men of the same profession among several nations of the North and the West. April Fool's Day is practiced in India as in Europe, in feasts called Huli (*Rech. Asiat.*, II, 333). The foxes of Samson are also found in a feast of Carseoles, a town of Latium (Ovid, *Fast.*, IV, 681–712). There is a good deal of likeness between the red heifer of the Fordicules and the red heifer of the Jews. There is hardly less between the machinations of Vishnu to obtain the drink called *amrita*, which provided immortality, and those of Odin to obtain the hydromel that enlightens sages and inspires poets.

This resemblance in details extends from ceremonies to traditions. Among the Germans, Mannus, son of Tuiston, had three sons, the founders of the principal German nations. The Scythes spoke of three sons of Targytaus, their founder (Herod. IV, 6 & 10). Polyphemus and Galatea gave birth to Celtus, Illyricus, and Gallus. Saturn had Jupiter, Neptune, and Pluto. Heaven and Earth engendered Cottus, Briarea, and Gyges. Noah's three sons are well known.

But what is even more remarkable is the perfect conformity of the Roman fable of Anna Perenna and the Indian fables concerning the goddess of abundance named Anna Purna Devi, or Annada. Ovid says that Anna Perenna was sometimes considered as the moon, and Annada carries a crescent; sometimes as Themis, and Annada is the spouse of the god of justice, Vrichna Iswara; other times as Io, and Annada is represented under the form of a heifer; or as Amalthea, the nurse of Jupiter, and Annada, seated on a throne, feeds the young Shiva, who offers his hand to receive it. Finally, the tradition concerning Anna Perenna as an old woman, feeding the Romans on the Sacred Mountain, applies to the Indian Anna Purna, who, according to the Puranas, miraculously fed Vyasa Muni and his ten thousand students reduced to starvation by Shiva, who was irritated that their master had preferred much less in chance. However, given what we are daily learning about the antiquities of India, in which English scholars recognize the principal dates of Jewish history and the tales of the Greek, Roman, and Scandinavian religions, a nearly certain hypothesis has emerged. It posits a single people as the common source—the universal stem—of the human race, long since disappeared. Is it not from this people that we ought to seek religion's point of departure, instead of the miserable hordes whose nature barely resembles our own?

To be clear: we are not saying that it is impossible for a diligent scholar or inspired genius to one day come to the great truth, the great, decisive fact that can reconnect in a single chain the scattered links we deal with here. We wish to acknowledge those learned men, indefatigable seekers, who aim at such a discovery. We certainly admire their infinite patience, the courage that nothing daunts and which braves unimaginable difficulties. For this can occur only by studying each people in its smallest particulars and details, by comparing the smallest practices and the most confused traditions; by collecting the debris of many ancient languages. And we are not here speaking of the languages that are ancient for us, but those that were already dead for our predecessors. It is, perhaps, only by traveling through the entire world and, as it were, excavating the accumulated layers of history that they will be able to amass all the materials required for the final success of the work in which a truly noble hope sustains them.

But as precious as it would be, this success would only lead to the point where we are now. The hypothesis of an original people creates an additional difficulty for those who adopt it. On one hand, since this takes them back beyond recorded history, they have to study geological history as well in order to discover the physical revolutions by which this original people was destroyed. (Here is another example of the great truth that whenever you wish to thoroughly pursue a question, you have to attend to everything.) On the other hand, the destruction of an original people being uncontestable, many of its surviving parts were forced to recommence the great work of civilization. One can at most suppose that some countries retained memories of a previous situation, some traditions and practices from it. But these memories would be vague, the traditions confused, the practices unintelligible because their original motives were forgotten. The system one develops, therefore, will have to begin with this condition of crudity and ignorance from which we believed we were obliged to commence.

Vishnu to him. Cf. Ovid, *Fast.*, III, 657–674; and Paterson, "Memoire sur la religion indienne," *Rech. asiat.*, VIII.

CHAPTER 9

The Precautions That the Special Nature
of Our Inquiry Obliged Us to Take

Many precautionary measures have been necessary for us to attain the goal we proposed in this work.

The first has been to distinguish the different epochs of each religion.

A nation does not have at the end of a century the same beliefs it had at the beginning. Even though it worships the same divinities, it does not preserve the same ideas for long.

By entering into civilization, peoples contract an impulse that never ceases, but the changes it prompts are imperceptible. No visible sign indicates them. The exterior of a religion remains unchanging, even when its doctrines are modified. Only the names of the gods do not change, which is a new cause of error in understanding religion.

In the minds of many learned readers, each mythology contains an ensemble of opinions without any particular chronology. Homer's religion and Pindar's seem to them to be exactly similar; and finding on the shores of the Tiber the same celestial agents as those they find on the shores of the Simoeis, they believe that Homer and Virgil described a fairly similar religion.[1]

---

1. An error of this sort, and even greater ones, diminished the merit of a work that contained great beauties. One can hardly regret too much that, in his *Martyrs,* Mr. de Chateaubriand committed an anachronism of about four thousand years. He presented as simultaneous two things of which one no longer existed and the other did not yet exist. The first was the polytheism of Homer, the second was the Catholicism of our days. After Euripides and after Epicurus, and almost in the presence of Lucan, Greek virgins did not ask the first young man they encountered: *Are you an immortal?* On the other hand, the Christians of the time of Eudorus and Cymodocea did not as a matter of course submit themselves to the priesthood or to fixed dogmas, or to many of the other things that characterize the discourse of the virgin and the martyr in more than one place in his work.

This is not true. The gods of the *Iliad*, far from being those of the Roman poets, are not even exactly those of the *Odyssey*. The gods of Greece have nothing in common with those of Ovid and of Virgil except the names and a few stories whose meaning has changed. Their moral character, the relations they have with men at the two different periods, have no connection.

Until now, people have collected rather than critically appreciated the materials. In connection with Greek religion, people cite indifferently Homer and Virgil, Hesiod and Lucan. Modern mythologies have been consulted to understand the

---

The illustrious author of this poem was also led by this error to make use of a genre of marvels that was entirely contrary, and much inferior, to the one that naturally suits his subject. His netherworld has all the defects of Virgil's, because one senses that it is written at a parallel time, when none of the elements of the description was found in any belief. The talent of the stylist could not overcome this defect of conception. The paradise of Mr. de Chateaubriand, copied from Olympus, is equally marred by an imperfection that does not allow it to compete with its original. It has less diversity of colors, and more metaphysics, than the latter. More generally, purity in the midst of corruption, certainty in the presence of universal doubts, independence under tyranny, disdain for riches in the midst of avarice, respect for suffering when everyone there was the example of indifferent cruelty and contemptuous harshness, detachment from the world when all the rest of men had concentrated their desires on it, devotion when all were egotistical, courage when all were cowardly, elevation when all were base—these were the marvels that he could have had come down from heaven. Placed in the souls of the first believers and thereby renovating the face of the world, these would have had at least as much interest as angels, pale imitations of the gods of the *Iliad*, crossing the sky like Venus wounded by Diomedes, or Juno wanting to deceive Jupiter.

If this critique, and an observation placed in a previous note, appear to be attacks on the author they concern, we believe ourselves obliged to further explain our thought. Our work proves well enough that we do not share the religious opinions defended by Mr. de Chateaubriand, and on many other questions we certainly have opposite views. But we do not at all equate him with the men who later embraced the cause that he was the first to take up, the defense of Christianity. When he published the *Génie du christianisme*, the contest was open to his adversaries; the proud power that held all the world at its feet based itself only on its own force and permitted discussion of everything that did not touch politics. Mr. de Chateaubriand therefore engaged the critics in full liberty, which is always the proof of an honorable sentiment convinced of its own value. His successors arrived under other auspices. And even when they would, like him, have the merit of talent, they would not have that of combatting equally armed enemies. What would happen if, by chance, they were immensely inferior to him in this regard? If they had only vehemence for eloquence, unconventionality for originality, and for courage the certainty that no one could return the blows they offer? Between them and Mr. de Chateaubriand there is the same difference as that between a knight in a tournament, who has for himself only his skill and his strength, and the inquisitors of the Holy Office, having for them their henchmen and lackeys.

most remote periods, not to mention referencing ancient philosophers whose clear aim and interest was to purify ancient polytheism.[2]

Running together both dates and doctrines, the authors of most systems have

2. In order to give an idea of the excesses to which this faulty method has led, we would point to the author of the *Essai sur la religion des Grecs*. In the midst of a great display of erudition, when he wishes to speak to us of the netherworld of Homer, he pens a note, and in this note we find verses of Virgil; and another note reports passages of Proclus and of Iamblicus. It is also true that sometimes we find Racine and Boileau listed among his authorities.

What Mr. Leclerc de Septchênes did for the religion of the Greeks, other writers have done for the religion of the Persians. They have invoked as worthy of great confidence not only Plutarch but also Porphyry; his devotion to Neoplatonism is well known; Eubulus, a contemporary of Porphyry, no less inexact than he but much less learned; Eusebius, a learned man but of a puerile credulity; Dion Chrysostomus, a mind imbued with all the subtleties of Alexandria; finally, Eudemus, whose century is unknown to us and who was already suspected of being an impostor by the compiler who preserved for us a few fragments (see *Excerpta ex Damascii libro de principiis*, p. 259). They have not considered that, for the most part, these men wrote close to six centuries after the fall of Darius's empire, when Greek polytheism and philosophy, an eclectic theurgy, Judaism and Christianity, and all the superstitions that political upheavals, as well as the mixing of peoples, servitude, fear, and unhappiness, would have penetrated into the religion of the Persians.

No one, however, has brought the lack of a discerning spirit and the confusion of all authors to a higher degree than Mr. de La Mennais, in the third volume of his *Essai sur l'indifférence en matière de religion*. In order to prove what he calls primitive religion, he cites indiscriminately Pythagoras, Epicharmus, Thales, Aeschylus, Plato, Sanchuniathon, Diodorus, Pausanias, Iamblicus, Clement of Alexandria, Maximus of Tyre, Cicero, Plutarch, Anaxagoras, Lactantius, Archelaus, Porphyry, Seneca, Epictetus, Proclus, etc. He grabs random expressions from each of them in order to conclude that they professed the same doctrine. The skeptic Euripides, who like every tragic author had his characters express the pro- and the contra-, seems to him a witness as respectable as the religious Sophocles. The credulous Herodotus is called upon to be a witness along with the unbelieving Lucan.

The author makes use of a word of Aristotle to present him as having professed theism and the immortality of the soul as we do; while the truth is that the god of Aristotle, a being deprived of all virtue, of all qualities, of any relationship with men, is an abstraction that no religion can make use of; as for the soul, after death it is without memory, without consciousness, without any sentiment of individuality; in other words, it is another abstraction that neither punishment nor reward can affect.

He does the same thing with Xenophanes, the most audacious pantheist who ever existed, who because he recognized only a single, immobile substance (the world) certainly does not merit being called a theist even though he called this substance "god." Pliny the Elder, too, who at the beginning of his work declared that the universe alone is God, is invoked to attest to the permanence of the revelation made to our first fathers. Sanchuniathon, a generic name, one attributed to works that are obviously conjectural—the verses of the purported Pythagoras, the hymns of Orpheus—everything is good for Mr. de La Mennais as long as one finds in them the word *theos*, to whom each philosopher and each poet assigned a different meaning! That includes Horace himself: "*Epicuri de grege porcus, parcus deorum cultor et infrequens*" (A hog from the herd of Epicurus, a sparing and infrequent wor-

brought together the views of different periods; they have failed to distinguish teachings borrowed from abroad from indigenous ones, stories that always belonged to the nation's beliefs from those that were gradually introduced or that entered suddenly by some unexpected event.

It is true of the ancient religions as it is of their geography: everything is progressive. Homer's geography is not Hesiod's, Hesiod's is not that of Aeschylus, Aeschylus's is not Herodotus's. One has to factor progress into everything concerning antiquity.

But what further complicates the difficulty is that almost all the mythologies have suffered chronological distortions. More recent views have been placed in the most remote times, and the most ancient views have been presented as being degenerations of earlier ones. Why this has occurred is easy to understand, however, once it is pointed out.

When the progress of enlightenment has broken the connection between religious ideas and the rest of a people's ideas, a thousand refinements, a thousand subtle explanations, are introduced into the religion. But the inventors of these refinements do not present them as deviations from current worship. The majority of political innovators do not say they want to establish a new order. To hear them, they want only to restore institutions to their original purity. It is the same with religion.

Philosophers and enlightened minds claim the mantle of antiquity for their additions, as well as their more or less ingenious (abstract or learned) interpretations.[3] This is also, even especially, true of priests. As we will show elsewhere, they are subject to two impulses. The first is to preserve current views because it is their immediate interest. The second is to introduce into religion (which they tend to regard as their property) all of their subsequent discoveries because this is the long-

shipper of the gods), which he makes use of to proclaim the immutability, antiquity, and purity of primitive theism.

It really was not worth the trouble to tell us that today we have discovered that Antiquity was little known, in order to instruct us with a compilation that would return science to what it was before the first efforts of historical criticism.

3. This is what caused our learned men to be mistaken. "*Theologia physica prima veteribus innotuit,*" says Villoison, in Sainte-Croix, *Les mystères*, p. 235, "*deinde apud solos remansit doctos et philosophos ac mysteriorum antistites.*" Here we have both a truth and an error. It is true that the physico-mystery theology appeared rather early in the countries where the priesthood exercised a good deal of influence; but it is false that it originally was the popular religion, then became a secret doctrine reserved to philosophers and the initiated. It began by being secret; then, despite the priests, it expanded little by little.

term interest of the priesthood. In order to better control the present generation, they borrow the voice of past generations.[4]

The Bhagavad Gita is a work composed with the obvious intention of substituting a more philosophic teaching for the Vedantic doctrine.[5] Krisha says to his disciple that he earlier revealed to others the sublime truths he is communicating today. The lapse of time had covered them over. Like all reformers he attributes his teaching to antiquity. Similarly, in a dialogue falsely attributed to the Egyptian Mercury and translated by Apuleius,[6] addressing himself to Egypt, this legislator exclaims that a time will come when instead of a pure cult there will be only ridiculous fables. This is the utterance of a philosopher who, while depending upon the forward march of the human spirit moving from ignorance to enlightenment, reverses the movement in order to give his views greater authority.[7]

One can see an analogous procedure among the wise men of Greece. Empedocles, Heraclitus, even Plato[8] tried to identify their hypotheses with what they called the ancient theology. Plato, for example, attributed the worship of stars to

4. Even independently of their intentions, the writers who treat the primitive periods of religion always belong to a later one; this causes them to confuse the opinions of their times with those they wish to describe.

5. It appears, says the English translator of the Bhagavad Gita, that the principal aim of the dialogues that compose this work was to bring together all of the cults existing at the time when these dialogues were written (they are believed to have been written about fifteen hundred years ago), and to overthrow the dogmas prescribed by the Vedas by establishing the doctrine of the unity of God, in opposition to idolatrous sacrifices and the worship of images (Bhag. Gita, pref., p. 20). (This isn't quite right: the Bhagavad Gita establishes pantheism and not theism.) In this passage the English translator clearly recognizes an earlier, cruder religion. However, because of an unexamined prejudice he says elsewhere that in translating the Bhagavad Gita his intention was less to make known present-day superstitions than the primitive religion of the Indians.

6. Dialogue entitled *Asclepius*.

7. Independently of the natural march of ideas, events modify religions; then the priests of these religions, not wanting to acknowledge that their doctrines have ceded to an external force that is purely human, attribute the modifications they have undergone to a fictitious past. Thus, Egyptian religion is divided into several periods. The ancient religion of this country experienced several alterations because of the invasion of the Persians under Cambyses. The religion that resulted from the mixing of the old religion and Persian opinions was modified again under Alexander and his successors, as Greek opinions then entered Egypt. The Egyptian priests, while adding to their cult the fables and doctrines of their conquerors, bent every effort to persuade them that they had come originally from Egypt (Brucker, *Hist. phil.*, I, 281, 283).

8. Plato in the *Cratylus*.

the first Greeks, a practice which was always alien to them.[9] It is only on the basis of his testimony, against the entire historical record, that people believe the Greeks began with star worship.

It is obvious that all the refinements of religious beliefs are subsequent to an initial simple credulity. In the same way it is obvious that civilization follows barbarism.[10] But another quite natural motive caused these innovations to be placed before the original popular stories and fables. Placed there, they contribute to making religion respectable. They are imposing phantoms that add to the somber majesty of an ancient edifice. If they were overtly substituted for traditional belief, they would appear to be impieties.

This observation is verified among almost all the ancient peoples. In Persia, we see the refined and mysterious views of the old Bactrian Empire attributed to Persian barbarians and the vestiges of their early, cruder religion presented as the corruption of a purer worship.

If we accepted the history of Scandinavian mythology as it is recounted today, we would believe that the peoples of the North began with theism and allegory and ended with fetishism. We are told that the first of the Scandinavian deities was called Alfadur, All-Vater, Father of All; then came Odin and his two brothers. The Norns (or Fates) initially numbered three, and presided in a general manner over the past, the present, and the future. It was easy to see its allegorical character, but later it was lost sight of. Then there were as many Norns as there were human beings; they became the fetishes of individuals. This development would be inexplicable, however, if we accepted it as it is recounted. But it becomes easy to understand when we note that it was brought in by the Drottes, or priests, who had acquired great authority among the Scandinavians.

---

9. When we say that the worship of stars was always foreign to the Greeks, we do not at all mean that they did not place stars among the divinities. But we will prove: (1) that the stars divinized by the Greeks occupied only a lower rank; and (2) that the divinities that directed the stars in Greek mythology had an individual character, one that was entirely distinct from the functions that were attributed to them.

10. Let us show by a single example how, as authors are more modern, they attribute a more refined meaning to customs and rites that ancient authors explained in a simpler way. Herodotus and Plutarch both recount that Egyptian priests shaved their bodies. But Herodotus attributes the custom to a natural cause, physical wellness in a very hot climate. Plutarch sees in it a mysterious idea: "The Egyptians acted so," he says, "because hair of the head and the face and wool are impure products that man ought to reject in order to arrive, by way of purity, at perfection."

In the same way in Greek polytheism, cosmogonic deities—Chronos, or Time, Rhea, Sky, Erebus, Night, Ocean, and Earth—apparently preceded real divinities.

It is essential to have these observations in mind as one reads this work. Its nature does not allow us to bring in all the facts, to enter into all the indispensable details, to demonstrate how well-founded the distinctions we establish between the different periods of beliefs in fact are. We do need to ask the readers who may think that a particular fact contradicts our theses, whether it was introduced later than people today believe. Who was the first author to report the fact? When did he live? Did he, perhaps, confuse the opinions of his time, or his own conjectures, with earlier views?

The second precaution we had to take was to set aside the scientific explanations of ancient worship that have been given by several distinguished scholars. To be sure, the works of these learned men were very useful. They have shed a great deal of light on little-known portions of the history of remote times. They have illuminated several essential questions. They have offered often-interesting conjectures, sometimes probable ones. No truth is to be disdained. The solution to a much smaller problem, one whose investigation seemed rather unimportant, has cast an unexpected light on subjects of the greatest importance. Science is always salutary, as ignorance is always harmful.

Nonetheless, these learned men, we dare to affirm, have committed a grave error.

For some, religion was nothing but the symbolic representation of agriculture, for others, of astronomy; for still others, only historical facts distorted by traditions or allegories misconstrued by ignorance. In certain respects, each and all of these explanations contain some truth. In all the countries of the earth a class of more or less powerful men has sought to make religion the depository of human learning. But to conclude from this that religion was invented to contain this hidden treasure, and that popular views were only the disguise, or corruption, of this teaching, is to fall into error. Religious fables only gradually became the hieroglyphs in which the learned class registered its observations and calculations concerning facts, or its hypotheses concerning causes.

The error of these learned men does not consist in the fact that they attributed some scientific meaning to religion, but that they put it before the popular or literal meaning. Instead of considering religion as a sentiment, they envisaged it as a combination of ideas; instead of recognizing in it an affect of the soul, they wanted to transform it into a work of the mind. Instead of seeing nature, they saw only art.

Moreover, as if this fundamental error were not enough, each one chose one particular hypothesis as the sole source of religion. Thus, a system that is defective at its base became fanciful and strained in its details.[11] One system took no account of the most natural inclinations of man; another called into question the most credible testimony of antiquity. Another rejected both what the direct study of ourselves reveals and what history teaches.

Open *The Primitive World*. There you will find neither the sentiment of that profound and virile piety, that intimate and serious conviction that characterized the Romans, nor knowledge of the events that occasioned the introduction of national festivals into worship and made it a source of political patriotism as well as religious veneration. The Regifugium (the King's Flight), obviously intended to commemorate the expulsion of the Tarquins,[12] while also connected with priestly traditions borrowed from abroad, becomes exclusively the departure of the sun at the end of the year. Jupiter Stator is the sun that comes to a halt. The Fortuna of women ceases to recall the mission of Veturia. An author changes it first of all to a festival of Victory, on the pretext that it recalled a victory of filial piety. Then it became the triumph of the sun over winter. Nero founded the Juvenalia[13] to celebrate the great event when he first cut his beard; that is, when he offered the spectacle of the emperor of the world presenting himself as an actor and poet.[14] It became an emblem of the renewal of the seasons.[15]

Thus distorting everything, scholars arrive on the scene, each one carrying his

---

11. What was nothing, said the translator of Warburton, but the origin of a single branch of idolatry Abbé Pluche wanted to make the origin of all idolatry. One can say the same about almost all those who have written on religion, even those who have pointed out this fault in others. In this way error follows error, as it were. All the fables of the religions are susceptible to different interpretations, according to whether one applies them to history, to cosmogony, to physics, or to metaphysics. The victory of the gods over Typhon in the secret teaching of the Egyptian priests, for example, was sometimes the symbol of the expulsion of shepherd kings, sometimes the drying up of Lower Egypt. It is entirely understandable that the priesthood repairs to religious language for its narratives, as for its teachings and its hypotheses: the various explanations can coexist without any problem; each has its own sort of truth; but they are entirely irrelevant when it comes to any real influence on worship.

12. Even when one would cast doubt on the historical truth of the first events of Roman history, it would remain no less obvious that the moral impression produced by belief had to occur in virtue of this belief and not from the mysterious sense or the scientific allusion of which the people would have no inkling. If the Romans attached ideas of devotion to republican government and the hatred of monarchy to the commemoration of the fall of the Tarquins, it matters little that some learned scholars of Rome could have known that this ceremony also had an astronomical meaning and that this meaning was the first, and the only real, meaning in the thought of the founders.

13. Tacit., *Ann.*, XIV, 15; XV, 33.

14. Xiphilin., 61.

15. *Monde primit.*, IV, 292.

favorite banner,[16] behind which he drags captive facts, bizarrely clothed.[17] One of them sees the flood everywhere, another, fire. One sees a succession of months, another a succession of dynasties.[18] None of them, however, has pushed the audacity and ingeniousness of this genre as far as the man who dominates the field in France;[19] for him all the gods and heroes from Osiris to Mohammed were only the

16. What the learned have done for scientific explanations the historians did not fail to do for historical explanations. Levesque, who wrote *Histoire de Russie*, placed the source of all religions in Tartary. Each wishes that what he knows the best be the principle of what all the others know.

17. The mutually exclusive explanations of the learned remind us of the anecdote recounted concerning the author of *Acajou*. Seeing the etchings destined for a book he did not know, he wanted to explain them and composed his novel concerning them. He then discovered that these etchings were prepared for a text of a different genre; the novel, nonetheless, remained.

18. Cudworth perceived in Mithra the sole God. His commentator, Mosheim, saw only a hunter with his deified hounds.

19. It is enough to consider the chain of assertions that make up Dupuis's system to see its falsity. "I examine," he says, "what the men of all times and all countries have thought about the divinity." It therefore is not only of the philosophers and their hypotheses that he speaks, but also the people and their beliefs. "I proved," he continues, "by the historical testimonies of all the peoples of the world, by the inspection of their religious and political monuments, by the divisions and distributions of the sacred order and the social order, and, finally, by the authority of the ancient philosophers, that it was to the universe and its parts that men originally, and most generally, attributed the idea of the divinity." Since among almost all peoples the priests were at the beginning the only historians, it is not surprising that the historical testimonies placed the refined doctrines of the priests above or beside the popular religion; and by the very fact that they were forced to mention this popular religion, we can know that it was the sole religion of the people. And since the religious monuments were constructed under the direction of this caste, the allegories of science had to occupy a greater place in them than in the public worship. As for the authority of philosophers, it is simple enough that, finding in the symbols of the priests cosmogonic doctrines analogous to their own, they would make them prevail at the expense of the popular teachings and opinions. It follows that the priestly metaphysics and physics would become philosophical metaphysics and physics, but not that the multitude would recognize in these religious ideas only personified abstractions. Now, if the people did not recognize them as such, they were not the primitive or general religion.

"The history of the gods," continues Dupuis, "is nothing other than that of nature; and since it has no other adventures than its phenomena, the adventures of the gods will be the phenomena of nature cast in allegories." The history of the gods is not that of nature except for the men who have studied nature. The vulgar do not study it. The history of the gods is for them that of the impressions of various sorts they receive from external objects, combined with their need to adore something that is above them. The motives they attribute to the actions of these external objects, the passions they ascribe to them, gave rise to fables without any relationship with the phenomena of nature, but which were later interpreted in a way to attach them to these phenomena.

"The ancient religion of the world," adds the author, "is still the modern one." Nothing is more false, if this assertion is applied to the moral part, to the real influence of the religion. One can very well prove a thousand times that all the objects of worship from Osiris to Jesus Christ were—in the language of priests—only the sun itself, but the influence religion had over the Egyptians and what Christianity exercised in its primitive purity were nonetheless quite different. The human race changed destiny, and took an immense step forward, by passing from Egyptian polytheism, and even from Greek polytheism (which, as we shall see, was much superior), to the concept of theism, and a theism founded on justice, not force, on goodness and not necessity, on love, not terror.

Dupuis answers: "Light and the darkness that is in eternal contrast with it; the succession of days and night; the periodic order of the seasons, and the movement of the brilliant planet that rules that order; the night and the innumerable fires it lights in the azure of the heavens; the revolution of the stars, more or less extended on our horizon, and the consistency of this length in the fixed stars, its variety in the wandering stars or the planets; their forward or backward march, their momentary stations; the phases of the crescent moon—full, waning, deprived of all light; the progressive movement of the sun from low to high and high to low . . . the successive order of the rising and the falling of the fixed stars that marks the different points of the sun's course, which the varied faces that the earth assumes here below mark the same periods of the annual movement of the sun; the correspondence of the latter in its forms with the celestial forms to which the sun unites itself; the variations that this same correspondence undergoes during a long stretch of centuries; the passive dependence that the sublunary part of the world experiences vis-à-vis the part above the moon; finally, the eternal force that stirs all of nature with an interior movement similar to that which characterizes life . . . all these different scenes, exposed to man's gaze, have formed a great and magnificent spectacle that forms the backdrop to the moment *when the gods are going to be created.* . . . He has not deceived himself concerning omnipotence, concerning the variety of these partial causes that make up the universal cause. In order to prove it, I opened the books in which man from the most remote antiquity has inscribed his reflections on nature; and I have made it clear that none of these scenes has been forgotten. This is what he chanted; this is what he adored."

We have cited this long passage because it puts forward in the most obvious way the profound error of Dupuis. Man in the infancy of the social state, and in the ignorance in which he then was plunged, certainly notes the transition from light to darkness, the succession of days and night, the order of the seasons; but he equally certainly did not comprehend the revolution of the stars, their forward or retrograde march, their momentary stations, nor the correspondence of the earth in all its forms with the celestial forms, and the variations that this correspondence underwent *during a long period of centuries.* This last phrase reveals all the falsity of the system. Dupuis supposes man surrounded by this spectacle, enlightened by these observations, which a long series of centuries had to precede before he is going to create the gods! Thus, he would have remained without religious ideas during all these preceding centuries. This supposition, however, is refuted by the facts we have before our eyes. The Ostyaks and the Iroquois have no need of being learned astronomers to prostrate themselves before a fetish or a manitou.

Dupuis bases himself upon the books in which man, from the most remote antiquity, has consigned his reflections. But religion in its crudest form preceded all books. His discoveries in astronomy, his observations of the course of stars, these triumphs of human intelligence, these were what man celebrated; but these are not what man adored primitively; in fact, they are what man has never adored, because these physical phenomena, even though they have been clothed with religious emblems, have never been the object of adoration. Man could have adored the beings who authored these phenomena, but he has always ascribed an individual character to them, independent of their relations with the phenomena of nature.

"This nature," continues Dupuis, "has always shown itself to men as the principle of all, which has no other cause than itself." Nature has never shown itself to the mass of men under such an abstract form, which is quite unintelligible even for minds that are very developed. This notion never penetrated into human heads except after ages of study and reflection.

"Men have judged what is by what they see and by what they sense." Exactly, and it is because of this that their religion was formed by conjectures concerning external appearances and not by discoveries that they had not yet made; it was composed of sentiments found at the bottom of their soul and not from reasonings that were the product of long meditations. "The nations that we have pleased to call savages have remained there. How many centuries were required for men to return; and how little are they capable of receiving this sublime lesson!" If this lesson is so sublime that so few men are capable of receiving it, how did it happen that the primitive nations made their way to it? They certainly had first to come to it before remaining in it. But one sentence of Dupuis reveals to us the source of his error. "The empire of the senses," he says, "precedes that of reflection. The notions drawn from the physical order have existed during many more centuries and among a much greater number of men than the metaphysical abstractions that were later imagined." The vice is in the use of the word "notion" when one should speak of "sensations." The empire of the senses is as foreign to physical notions as to metaphysical abstractions. The ones belong to science as well as the others; and religion precedes natural science as well as metaphysical hypotheses.

In refuting the fundamental idea of Dupuis's system, we believe we have also refuted Volney's. The foundation of the two systems is the same, and the vices of reasoning upon which they rest are of the same sort. Both believe that the essential is to prove that this or that fable was born from a cosmogonic or astronomical allegory. This may be good to know, but it tells us nothing about the moral effect of the religion in which this fable was, or still is, contained. We ask our readers, even when Volney would have clearly demonstrated that Abraham is only the personified *genius* of Sirius the star, and that in the sacrifice of Isaac he becomes the planet Saturn (*Recherches nouvelles sur l'histoire ancienne*, I, 155–159), if that changes anything to the relations established between Jehovah and his worshippers by the narrative of this sacrifice? In order to judge the real influence of the Jewish religion, is it not these relations that we ought to deal with? When the same author speaks to us of the care that the author of Genesis took to give his narrative a historical and moral character suitable to his aim (ibid., p. 158), he puts us on the right path; but how does it happen that he immediately departs from it? Isn't it the same with the seven *richis*, or Indian patriarchs (ibid., p. 155)? That they should be the *genii* of the seven stars of the (Bear) constellation that guides the sailors and laborers who contemplate it, so be it; but in order to understand the religion of the Indians, would it not be worthwhile to seek how much the example of the *richis*, so astonishing in their practice of penitence, could have encouraged the contemplative spirit of the peoples of these countries, or rather to what point this contemplative sun and the stars. But the truth is that agriculture, astronomy, history, metaphysics, and above all allegory in any of its forms were subsequent to religion. They became parts of religion but are not its basis. Religion took them to its bosom but does not owe its existence to them. Scientific systems have been introduced into every religion, but no one has ever made a scientific system into a religion.[20]

---

spirit, itself the effect of the climate, favored the invention or adoption of such fables? Finally, when he explains what he calls the mythology of Adam and Eve by the signs of the Bear and the Dog; when he attributes to the heliac setting of these two constellations the notion of the fall of man and the fecundity of a virgin (*Ruines*, p. 219), does he not leave to the side the most important part of these traditions, the one that connects them to the ideas of a bad nature or original degradation of the human race, and to the notions of purity and impurity, a doctrine that from time immemorial has divided India into castes; and which later populated the deserts of the Thebaid and the convents of Europe; and which ended by dividing Christianity and ushering in all the revolutions that the world has suffered for several centuries?

In so freely criticizing a famous author, we do not at all fail to acknowledge his merit. More clearly than anyone, and in an eminently ingenious way, he has applied astronomical calculations to the religious systems of antiquity. In the examination of several questions of detail, he deployed an admirable sagacity. For example, he perfectly describes how astrology comes from the observation of celestial phenomena (*Rech. nouvel. sur l'hist. anc.*, I, 172); and from time to time we will make use of his learning, proving in our turn that, by the fact that astronomy produced astrology, religion was something entirely different from astronomy. He has also demonstrated very well that the corrections brought to the initial division of time introduced into the mythologies a complication that gave rise to many uniform fables among different peoples (ibid., p. 177). In this way he dissipated many clouds and sowed along the way a great number of truths. But when he ends his investigations by claiming for a single science the privilege of having served as the basis of the doctrine "that, professed first of all secretly in the mystery religions of Isis, Ceres, and of Mithra, ends by conquering all the earth" (ibid., p. 211), he does not stop to reflect that the doctrine that invaded all the earth was the moral portion of religion. The scientific, allegorical, and cosmogonic traditions could have made their way into earlier cults; but these hidden meanings, misunderstood and received without examination and transmitted without explanation, changed nothing of its influence on the human race. And when he claims that the aim of all religions was to deceive, lead astray, and enslave all peoples (*Ruines*, pp. 324ff.), he slanders religion out of hatred for priests; and when he concludes that *one must draw a line of demarcation between verifiable objects and those that cannot be verified, and separate with an impassable barrier the fantastical world from the real world, and to grant religious opinions no importance* (ibid., p. 224), he proposes what was never done and can never be done, because verifiable objects are always very inferior to the objects that cannot be verified, and because (the world of realities being insufficient for us) our imagination and our soul will always launch themselves toward a world called fantastical.

20. Warburton (*Div. Leg. of Moses*) assigns two origins to the fable. According to the first, it was invented by the most ancient sages in order to express symbolically their mysterious wisdom; but this opinion implies either that these sages fell miraculously from heaven into the midst of primitive

Once admitted into the worship, however, these scientific systems have never had a direct relationship with the moral effects of the beliefs. They were never in popular circulation, if I can put it that way. The most allegorical portion of the Greek religion, that which dealt with the origin of the world, the Titans, and Prometheus, was what the people occupied themselves with the least. The allegorical divinities played almost no role in the national religion. Uranus, Ocean, Saturn were the objects of neither hope nor fear nor petition. Herodotus seems to be ignorant of what Homer meant by Ocean, so little were the cosmogonic personifications connected with popular views.[21] He never spoke of the anger or the protection given by the beings of this class.[22] Their festivals were of another sort than those of the reigning deities. They were ceremonies with no other point than commemoration without practical effect, and they assumed no reciprocal influence of gods on men or men on gods.

Nothing is more likely than that the mutilation of Uranus is an allegory; that a philosopher (probably before the Greeks) in this way wanted to represent the end of creative force, a cessation that dates from the beginning of (natural) order because by subjecting generations to the cycle of procreation, nature seems to forswear the creation of new forms. Or that the philosopher attributed this mutilation to Chronos—that is, Time—because the idea of time is inseparable from that of a fixed and regular succession; or that Hesiod, who had gathered together priestly doctrines from everywhere in order to introduce them into Greek religion, painted this allegory in poetic colors. But what moral or political effect could this allegory have on the people?[23]

It is certain that in the astronomical language of the Roman religion Pan represented the sun. But if in the public worship this god was only a subordinate di-

---

peoples or that religion did not exist before civilization had arrived at the period when it produced philosophers. The second conjecture is that the fable is only the corruption of ancient history: but then one must suppose that during a rather long interval man did not have religious ideas; because if religion was formed only from historical facts, it had to await not only the occurrence of these facts but also their disfigurement by the lapse of time. All these hypotheses are inadmissible.

21. Herod., II, 23.

22. Hermann, *Handbuch der Mythol.*, I, toward the beginning.

23. Heyne, *De Theogon. Hes.*, 140; *Com. Soc. Goet.* The superior divinities of all nations have incontestable relations with astronomy. This truth is adequately proved by the number of these divinities, a number fixed at twelve in Greece and Rome, as well as in Egypt and Chaldea. We will see, however, that nothing is more different than the gods of the Greeks and the Romans from those of Memphis and of Babylon.

vinity, rather malign in his intentions, grotesque in his forms, and the object of the people's high spirits rather than their fear or adoration, who cannot see that the "astronomic Pan" had no real connection with the national religion? What does it matter if Heracles is said to be the sun and his twelve labors the zodiac, or that Jupiter and Juno, or the loves of Mars and Venus, are physical systems, if the nation that worships these divinities sees them as real beings upon whom its destiny depends, and if in the stories told about their actions, it only seeks ways of propitiating them?

What we are saying here in no way is intended to denigrate the usefulness of the works to which we refer. It is worthwhile penetrating to the hidden sense of ancient cults. But even the discovery of this secret meaning does not suffice to help us understand religion in its essential relationships. The mass of men take religion as it presents itself. For them the form is the substance.[24] It is in the letter of mythologies that one can observe the progress of morality and the successive modifications that religions underwent. Allegories and symbols can remain the same in all periods because they express ideas that do not change. Popular fables change because they express ideas that do change.[25]

Thus, to choose an example known to all our readers, Apollo's anger at the Greeks was leveled first against animals; subsequently it was directed against men. It is clear that by this the poet wanted to depict the advance of a plague and its ravages. Just as well as Homer, Ovid (or, for that matter, any modern poet who would employ ancient mythology) can use this allegory to convey a natural phenomenon.[26] But the popular account—that is, the one that refers to Apollo's character

24. I read in a poem that otherwise is very well done and quite learned, but that is based upon Dupuis's system, the following verse addressed to the Jews: "You celebrated the sun and not Jehovah." However, if the Hebrews believed they adored Jehovah and belief constituted their religion, it was really Jehovah they worshipped.

25. Even when one is only trying to discover the scientific meaning of ancient religions, it is still necessary to distinguish the successive periods of the mythologies. For example, those scholars who want to relate everything to astronomy, and who claim that the astronomical meaning was the original meaning, have recognized in the function of conducting the souls of the dead to the netherworld, a function attributed to Mercury, the Anubis Mercury who descends into the hidden lower reaches of the hemisphere (Bayeux, trans. of *Fast.* of Ovid, V, 616). But the function of conducting the souls of the dead to the netherworld was attributed to Mercury only in a mythology posterior to the Homeric mythology. There is no trace of him in Homer; Mercury probably became the conductor of the soul after the teachings and fables of Egypt were introduced into Greece.

26. *Metam.*, VII, 536–552.

and to the motives that moved him—was necessarily subject to the changes that took place in the moral views of the religion. If, as in the polytheism of the *Iliad*, the gods are simply egoists, the anger of the sun-god was motivated by the fact that he was not offered enough sacrifices or because someone offended one of his priests.[27] If, however, a purer morality is an essential part of the religion—which happens as civilization progresses—the poet will recount that the god was angry at the Greek army because of its crimes.[28]

Scholars,[29] however, have unfortunately always had a certain disdain for this part of mythology. One of them says that it is more important to know the real teaching of philosophers and savants about divinity, the universe, the soul, and nature than to collect the stupid fables of the vulgar and the absurd embellishments of the poets.[30] We think the exact opposite. The philosophers' doctrines produced hypotheses and systems; the stories revered by the vulgar constituted the real influence of religion. They decided the morality of peoples. They prepared and introduced all the religious struggles, wars, and revolutions.

Nor is it correct to say that the scientific theology was the sole religion of the learned and the philosophers. We find traces of popular religion in the most learned men and among almost all the sages of antiquity. If one day we treat Greek philosophy, we will show Socrates consulting the Pythia, Xenophon following oracles, Plato according implicit faith to divination.[31]

Even when men depart in many respects from the teachings professed by those before or around them, these doctrines do not lose all their rights. They resemble a defending army that is dispersed and yet which goes to battle in small platoons.

27. *Iliad*, bk. I.

28. *Odyssey*, bk. I.

29. The reproach we level against modern scholars was no less merited by ancient ones. Balbus in Cicero (*De nat. deor.*, II, 24), after having assigned as one of the causes of idolatry the apotheoses of men who civilized their fellows and made discoveries useful to the human race, adds that this was not the only cause of idolatry; but that natural theology having degenerated gradually because of ignorance and the lapse of time, men had forgotten the meaning of things, adhered to the external bark of the tree, and took the shadow for the reality. This was a new reversal in the order of ideas. Ignorance deified physical objects. Natural theology came much later. All the pagan authors who wrote at the time of polytheism's decadence fell into the same error. See Varo and Scaevola in August., *De civit. Dei*, IV, 27; and also Dionys. Hal., II.

30. Villoison, *ap.* Sainte-Croix, pp. 222–223.

31. One sees the same thing in the learned Romans. As proof, see the faith that Tacitus granted to the miracle that prompted Corbulo to destroy Artaxata, the capital of Armenia (*Annal.*, XVI, ch. 41).

At first glance the terrain belongs to the invader. But the defenders have their refuges, their redoubts, their strong places, which they defend and from which they sally forth to counterattack from time to time. Even when philosophy is ascendant over the learned class, fragments of the popular religion continue to be found in the opinions of this class. And even to understand these opinions one has to study this vulgar religion.[32] When they invent, poets themselves still conform to the received religion in order to give their inventions the appearance of truth. As the most judicious of Romans (Varro) said,[33] the ancient religions were for the people what the poets represented at each period. To consider only their hidden meaning is like wanting to analyze the history of drama by describing the pulleys and ropes that help move stage scenery.[34]

Finally, men have neglected to distinguish carefully enough the religions dominated by priests from those that remain independent of sacerdotal direction. It is obvious upon minimal reflection, however, that the path of religion is different depending upon the degree of authority possessed by the priesthood. This is true from the first developments of religious ideas.

It is not necessary for us to seek here how it happened that some peoples were subject to priests from the first moment of their coming together in society, while others enjoyed complete independence for a long time and were never wholly subjugated by them.

We will enter into the examination of the facts when we treat the Greek religion of Homeric times, and when we describe the Egyptian religion as it existed until the mixing and destruction of all the cults of antiquity. Now it is enough to establish the difference between the two species of religion that are often confused.

When a priestly body takes control of a religion from its beginning, the religion follows a different path than when the priesthood, gradually establishing itself,

32. We do not believe that we have to say that one must also avoid the other extreme. Professor Meiners of Göttingen, a man otherwise learned and judicious, wanted to see in religion only its crudest part. He pushed to ridiculous extremes the mania of seeing fetishism everywhere. In order to prove that this or that people was given to this sort of worship, he cited the way in which they groom the manes and hair of their various pack animals. With this logic the mule-drivers of Spain would be fetishists. This basic error greatly diminishes the usefulness and merit of his investigations.

33. Varro, *ap.* August., *De civ. Dei*, VI, 6.

34. In treating religion, the learned have seen neither the priests nor the people, but only science. Unbelievers have seen only impostors in priests. Believers have seen in every other religion but their own the deception of the devil. No one wanted to see in all these beliefs the human heart and the nature of man.

arrives later at constituting itself as a regular and recognized body. The authority of priests has to be unlimited when it exists from the formation of the society. The more intellectually crude the belief, the more authority the ministers of this belief have if they form an independent class.

The little influence that the jongleurs of many savage tribes possess comes from the fact that, since the condition of the tribes is one not organized by fixed rules, everything in them is hazy and uncertain, everything follows momentary impressions and unreflective habit. Nothing has the force of law, the priesthood no more than everything else. But when a people sees a priestly institution arise before there is any political institution capable of fighting against it or restraining it (as was the case with Egypt), it must suffer the yoke of this priestly power. Henceforth religion, which left to itself is composed of all the sentiments, all the notions, and all the conjectures natural to man, in the hands of priests becomes the subject of premeditated calculation and systematic arrangement.

When man occupies himself with religion as something that belongs to him, example and habit lead him to prefer the worship he sees in use around him. Wanting to have the targets of his prayers listen to him, he speaks to them in the words spoken by his ancestors and his contemporaries. Nonetheless, everything in the worship is individual. The individual adds or subtracts or changes without anyone else arrogating the right to be offended. He runs the risk of displeasing the gods, but not of being punished by other men. Prayers and sacrifices, whether offered on domestic altars, in forest retreats, or at the tops of mountains, rise directly to the invisible world without having to seek a privileged channel. Everything is free and open between heaven and earth.

In priestly religions, on the contrary, heaven is closed; a triple rampart encloses the immortals. All access is guarded by jealous intermediaries. Everything is submitted to priests: all the individual's conjectures, his fears, his presentiments of the future, the accidents that happen, the strange things that surprise him, the phantoms he perceives in the darkness, the noises he hears, the shadows he sees in his dreams. From these, the priests compose laws and a special science. Every victim not offered by them is rejected as impious; any incense offered by others is sacrilegious. In order to obtain divine assistance or protection, it is necessary to gain their favor along with that of the gods.

The character of the gods also changes significantly. The person who asks religion only to bring about divine benevolence seeks to discover what the gods want. The priest who expects from religion the means to govern men seeks how he must portray the beings in whose name he wishes to govern. One must not exaggerate, however, the priest's activity. While submitting religion to different changes in accordance with his calculations, he invents nothing, he makes use only of what already exists. His work is not a work of creation but of arrangement, of form and order. Nor does one invent religious opinions; they arise in the minds of men independently of their wills. Some adopt them, others make use of them. The priesthood has found the seed of all religious notions in the heart of man,[35] but it then despotically directed the development of this germ. In this way it imprinted a development on religion that it would not have followed naturally.

It is because of the failure to distinguish these two types of belief that people have committed so many mistakes in the history of religions. By confusing them, they attempted to blaze a path that led at the same time to two opposite extremes, and they exhausted themselves in vain efforts for a chimerical end. The distinction between religions subjected to a priesthood and those that are independent is the first condition for conceiving adequate ideas in this area.

One can see how vast is the range of ideas that we have to deal with. It is so huge that to comprehend it, both in its entirety and in its details, is above the powers of man, and perhaps above the public's capacity to attend to in the present circumstances. In this work, therefore, we restricted ourselves to indicate and to demonstrate, both by reasoning and by facts, the fundamental truth from which all the others flow.

We have begun from the crudest form that religious ideas can assume. We have shown the religious sentiment creating this form then struggling against it, and sometimes arriving, by means of its own marvelous and mysterious energy, at rendering the form noble and heart-touching despite itself. We then said how this form was modified, whether by sacerdotal bodies or by the progress of the human spirit among peoples who were free of sacerdotal authority.

We began with the priestly religions. To be sure, one cannot follow the human spirit in its natural progression except by studying the independent religions. All the changes occur openly in these religions, while under the empire of priests the work goes on behind closed doors, in the mysterious interior of these privileged corporations. But the cults that the priests dominated are historically the oldest; and the very small number of nations among whom the priesthood had little authority were most likely emancipated from the former rather than preserved from it. It follows then that the simplicity of religions left to themselves comes above all

35. "Nothing establishes itself without a principle taken from nature, even if it subsequently becomes against nature," quite reasonably observes a German author (Wagner, *Mythologie*, p. 77).

from the fact that the human spirit successively removed the crude notions that belong to the infancy of belief, ideas that the priesthood, in contrast, had turned into dogmas. Because of this, in order to understand the simplest cults one must have profoundly studied the most complicated ones.

One will see, we hope, that the majority of the reproaches that are addressed to religion really touch only some of its ministers. The religions that have struggled with the greatest success against their power have been the gentlest, the most humane, the purest. If our readers accept this, and derive from it appropriate consequences, we believe that the admiration customarily bestowed on the Persian, Egyptian, or Frankish priestly bodies will be much diminished.

We have limited ourselves to this part of religious history.

With the fundamental truth being recognized, it would be easy to deduce its consequences and to follow it in its innumerable and admirable modifications. After having seen how the two forms that religion takes are constituted, one that the human spirit creates for itself and one that priests most often have imposed upon it, the reader can discern the principle of perfectibility that presides over one and the principle of stasis that weighs on the other. When peoples come together these two forms encounter and are mixed. If it is human intelligence that emerges victorious, its ideas concerning the divine nature are improved and undergo a rapid and positive development. But one can also see the seeds of decline that even these improved ideas contain, as well as the irresistible religious impulse that will lead to even greater refinement.

At that point the most purified and refined religious form becomes the only one that is admissible, it becomes the imperious need of the civilized world. Then, the collapse of the old and discredited beliefs leaves man grief-stricken amidst the rubble he has called down upon himself. He does not regain his courage except by means of a new belief. But this one too undergoes decline. It seems to take a few steps back toward the periods of ignorance and resuscitates barbarous doctrines. But the nature of the human spirit being the same, it reacts as before against these temporary relapses. Each century considers whatever is proportionate to its learning and enlightenment to be the final and unchangeable attainment of the good and the true. But a new century arrives and the limit is pushed back. New ones are then posed, which subsequent generations are destined to replace by pushing them even further back.

Therefore, it is not a detailed history of religion that we have undertaken. To retrace the religious revolutions of all the nations would be to write the history of all nations. Religion is connected with everything. Just as it penetrates into the most intimate regions of man, everything that touches him touches religion. As it modifies everything it touches, it is modified by everything that touches it. The various causes come into contact, clash, and modify one another. In order to explain the development of a religion, one has to examine the climate, the government, the present and past habits of the people who profess it. What exists certainly influences, but what no longer exists does not cease influencing. Memories are like Epicurus's atoms, elements that constantly enter into new combinations. To embark upon these investigations would be to write a universal history. We therefore have tried to avoid a strictly historical form of writing, both because of the length that would be required and because of the infinite repetitions it would entail. One cannot simultaneously develop the history of every religion. Since all peoples have not advanced in the same way because of the changes in their opinions brought in by events and circumstances, we would have had to constantly repeat observations made about one nation when dealing with another.

However, it is impossible to give to these investigations the purely didactic form that Montesquieu gave his reflections on the laws. Laws are written; consequently their revolutions can be precisely connected to definite periods. But religion, existing in large measure in the heart and in the spirit of man, changes insensibly without being perceived;[36] and some of these changes can only be treated historically.

We have tried to present to our readers only results, based, to be sure, upon many facts. We have refuted some objections, but we have passed over others in silence. Perhaps we have failed even to think of others. If we had developed everything, this work would have been too long to read. The history of exceptions would have become longer than that of the general rule. The rule is one and simple, the causes of exceptions innumerable and complicated.

---

36. The idea, or rather the sentiment, of the Divinity has existed at all times. But its conception has been subordinated to everything that also existed at each time. The more crude and simple the state of man the more limited and narrow were the notions of Divinity. Man could not conceive of others. As time progressed, his conceptions were enlarged and ennobled. In its essence religion is not tied to any time, and it does not consist at all in traditions transmitted from age to age. As a consequence, it is not subject to fixed limits imposed upon the generations to come in a literal and unchanging manner. On the contrary, it progresses with the times and human development. Each epoch had its prophets, its inspired men, but each spoke the language of the period. Therefore, as for its substance there is nothing in religion, or in the idea of Divinity, that is historical; but everything in its development is historical.

BOOK II

ON THE CRUDEST FORM THAT RELIGIOUS
IDEAS CAN ASSUME

CHAPTER I

The Method We Will Follow in This Book

We have defined the religious sentiment, the need man experiences to put himself in communication with the nature that surrounds him and the unknown forces that seem to him to animate that nature.

The religious form is the means he employs to establish this communication.

It is obvious that the choice of this means is not arbitrary. Man does not decide from pure caprice for one form over another. He is determined in his choice by the sentiments that are found naturally in his soul, by the ideas that reflection suggests to his intellect, and by the demands that egoism inspires. Some have wrongly considered self-interest as his sole motive. While this is an overstatement, its action is quite powerful inasmuch as it is constant and ineradicable.

In order to detect the results of these different causes, two ways present themselves. One can try to observe and describe the work of each one of the faculties separately, and then the work of them together when a religion is created. Or one can bring together the best-established facts relative to the religious beliefs of the most ignorant peoples, and then seek to find what in these beliefs should be attributed to sentiment, to intelligence, and to self-interest.

The first method seems to us to be too metaphysical and abstract. It is better to start with the historical facts, in order to ascend to the causes of the facts.

CHAPTER 2

On the Form the Religious Sentiment Takes
On among the Primitive Savages

Many of the primitive tribes we know of are in a state little different from that of animals.[1] Some are ignorant of the use of fire; others provide for their subsistence like beasts of the forest, while others, even less industrious, use neither cunning nor force to feed themselves, but simply wait for the death of other animals and eat their wretched and unhealthy flesh. Some only have five or six barely articulate cries as their language.

The hordes just above them are more or less advanced in their means of survival. They have invented some instruments for hunting or fishing. They have developed greater variety in the articulate sounds they make use of to express their passions or their needs. They have built huts. Some have tamed animals. The union of the sexes has acquired a more stable form, or at least it has been extended beyond mere desire and enjoyment.

The first groups resemble wolves and foxes, the second, beavers and bees.

The primitive savage is born into this crude state. When he suffers, he cries; when he is hungry, he hunts or he fishes. The need to reproduce makes itself felt, he satisfies it. He grows old, he dies, or his children kill him.

Nonetheless, what we have called the religious sentiment stirs in him. He sees himself surrounded and dominated, or at least influenced, by forces whose nature and origin he cannot grasp. And an instinct that is peculiar to him[2] among all the beings on earth appears to inform him that the power that animates these un-

---

1. In order to bring together the traits that must enter into a portrait of the ways and customs of primitive savages, we have preferred to consult the most ancient travelers. Each day primitive tribes disappear from the earth. Despite their repugnance toward them, what remains of the half-destroyed hordes undergoes the effects of neighboring Europeans. Their practices grow lax, their traditions grow faint, and modern travelers barely find vestiges of what their predecessors had noted.

2. See Constant, bk. I.

known forces is not without some relationship to him. He experiences the need to establish relations, to determine them in some fixed way. He seeks, haphazardly, this superior power. He speaks to it, he calls upon it, he adores it.

As we have demonstrated, it is not simply fear that causes this instinct to appear within him. The objects of fear are neither the sole nor the principal objects of his worship. To be sure, he sometimes places among them some that caused him harm. But he often adores some that do not inspire any fear in him.

To conclude from the terror he feels when he believes that some objects are full of a divine nature, that it was the terror that caused him to adore them, is to mistake an effect for a cause.

Nor is it any idea of self-interest that creates his first worship. He prostrates himself before objects that cannot be of any use to him. After having deified them, he seeks to make them useful, but that is another movement of his nature. To consider it as the primary is again to confuse effect and cause.

The savage worships different objects because he must adore something. But what objects will he worship? He consults his environment. There is nothing that can enlighten him. He turns to himself. He draws his answer from his own heart. This response, though, is commensurate with the weakness of the reason he barely employs and his profound ignorance. This reason does not have the faintest notion of the idea of Divinity of a later period. This ignorance especially deceives him concerning the causes of natural phenomena.

As we have already said,[3] man always places his religious ideas in the sphere of the unknown. For the savage everything is unknown. His religious sentiment therefore will apply itself to everything he encounters.

Everywhere there is motion he believes there is life. The stone that falls seems to be either fleeing or following him. The torrent that rushes heads toward him; some angry spirit dwells in the steaming waterfall. The wind that moans is the expression of some suffering, or some menace. The eerie echo of some canyon foretells the future or answers a query. And when a civilized European shows the savage a magnetic needle, he sees a being taken from its native land and anxiously desiring to return home.[4]

Everywhere there is movement the savage assumes there is life. And everywhere he supposes there is life, he supposes that there is some action or intention that

3. Ibid.

4. A primitive, seeing a letter for the first time and observing the impression produced by the news it conveyed, regarded it as an indiscreet, even perfidious, being who had revealed some important secret.

has him in view. Man exists for a long time before he recognizes that he is not the center of all things. The infant imagines himself to be this center toward which all tends; the savage reasons like an infant.

Surrounded by powerful, active objects that constantly impact his destiny, he adores those among these objects that strike his imagination most forcefully. Chance decides this.[5] It can be a rock, a mountain, sometimes a stone, often an animal.

This worship of animals seems to us to be strange. Upon reflection, however, it is very natural.

In animals, there is something that is unknown—we could say mysterious—that must dispose the savage to worship them.

So much makes them enigmatic beings: the impossibility of comprehending

---

5. The reader will soon see, and even in this chapter, that there were things other than the adoration of objects in the primitive's worship. But we had to begin here because the homage given to these objects formed, as it were, the exterior, or the matter, of this worship. It is therefore quite certain that American savages chose as their fetishes objects that presented themselves to them in dreams (Charlevoix, *Journal*, p. 243; *Lettr. édif.*, VI, 174). The Malabars make gods according to the chance and caprice of the moment: a tree, the first animal they perceive, becomes their divinity. The Tongouses plant a stake where it seems appropriate, put the skin of a fox or a sable on it, and say: Behold, our god. The savages of Canada prostrate themselves before the carcass of a beaver (de Pauw, *Recherches sur les Américains*, I, 118). Among the African blacks of Guinea-Bissau, each invents or makes his own divinity (*Hist. génér. des voy.*, II, 104). In the deserts of Lapland isolated stones have a crude resemblance to the human form. When the Laplanders pass by these stones they never fail, even today, to sacrifice some reindeer, whose horns can be found around the stones (*Voy. d'Acerbi*).

The reader may perhaps be surprised that we have not assigned a separate place in the worship of savages to the worship of the sun and the stars. This is because when astrolatry is the dominant worship of a tribe, its religion takes a very different path from the one we are now considering. We will treat it in the following book; therefore we will postpone until then what we have to say about star worship. As for the primitives for whom the sun and the stars are simply objects of adoration like all the others that strike them, this worship does not change the character of the religion, of which stars are but a part. Almost all the American savages give worship to the sun (*Allgemeine Geschichte der Voelker und Laender von Amerika*, I, 61–64), but their religion is nonetheless very different from that of the peoples among whom star-worship is in vigor. It is the same with the worship of fire. When this worship is only an isolated thing, like that which savages render to the first animal or tree they encounter, nothing is changed in the religion. Thus the hordes of Siberia and those of South America adore fire, while the peoples of Africa have always remained without this worship (Meiners, *Crit. Gesch.*, I, 237). However, no essential difference distinguishes the religion of Siberia or that found on the banks of the Ohio from that found on the shores of Guinea. When fire worship belongs to the worship of the elements, this is the sign of an entirely different religious form, which we will be able to speak about later.

and judging them (which we share with the savage, although habit inhibits us from seeing it); their instincts, which are surer than our reason; their facial expressions, which so vividly express what is going on within them; the variety and wonderful strangeness of their forms; the often frightening rapidity of their movements; their sympathy with nature, which allows them to sense approaching natural occurrences that man cannot foresee; finally, the eternal barrier between them and man because of the absence of language.

"It would be necessary," said the judicious Heeren,[6] "to have been a primitive oneself, to understand the relationship he believes he has with animals."

As long as he has not stripped them of their aura by domesticating them, he shares both his life and his dominion with them. They are his equals in the forests, while they defy him by taking wing or by plunging into the depths of the seas. They possess to an eminent degree many of his individual faculties. They take turns being his prey or his predators. One can easily see why he sometimes places the hidden seat of the invisible forces in the beings whose existence he finds utterly mysterious, not to mention their purpose.

Primitive veneration for animals even survives into the time when man domesticates them and uses them for his purposes. In fact, the acquisition of domestic

---

6. Heeren, *Ideen ueber die Politik, der Verkehr und den Handel der vornehmsten Voelker der alten Welt*. The Iroquois and the Delaware Indians bring to animals the level of civilization that they have achieved. Each one of their tribes distinguishes itself by the name of an animal, in commemoration of a benefit they still speak of with gratitude. The Munsees recount that at the beginning they lived in the bosom of the earth underneath a lake. One of them discovered an opening by which he made it to the surface. A wolf that was seeking its prey killed a deer, which the Munsee took with him back to his subterranean abode. Taken by this unknown food, the entire tribe left its somber abode in order to take residence in a place where the sunlight delighted the sight and the hunt provided abundant nourishment. Hence the veneration for wolves that was established among them. "It is obvious," adds the author from whom we borrow these details, "that the Indians originally considered themselves as bound in some way to certain animals. All of living nature, to whatever degree it might be, is in their eyes a great Whole from which they had not yet tried to separate themselves. They did not exclude animals from the resting grounds where they hoped to go after their death" (*Histoire, moeurs et coutumes des nations indiennes qui habitaient autrefois la Pensylvanie et les Etats voisins*, by J. Heckewelder, a Moravian missionary [Paris, 1822], pp. 397, 406). The opinion that there exists a sort of lineage between animals and men is found throughout the islands of the West Indies and the South Seas (Hawkesworth, *Account of the Voyages, etc.*, III, 758; Marsden, *Hist. of Sumatra*, p. 257; Valentyn, *Oud en niew ostindien*, II, 139 & 400). Some tribes maintain that women sometimes give birth to crocodiles, which they immediately take to a nearby swamp, but which are always recognized, and which children treat as brothers (Hawkesworth, ibid.).

animals produces such an important revolution in his life that he is even more disposed to attribute an almost divine nature to this new companion of his labors.[7]

The Kamtschatka have domesticated only one species of animal. After their death they have themselves torn apart by the members of that species in the hope of rejoining their ancestors. The faithful dogs that shared life's adventures with them become their guide to the future world.[8]

The preference that a savage accords to one sort of animal over others comes from chance circumstances rather than the complicated reasons that many have tried to come up with.[9] The Troglodytes that Pliny talks about simply worshipped the tortoises that swam to them.[10] Striking colors, the sheen of their scales, the rapidity of their movements were, perhaps, what garnered religious respect for serpents, who then acquired a distinguished place in the majority of mythologies.[11]

7. Herder, *Ideen zur Philosophie der Geschichte*, I.

8. They give their dead to the dogs to devour (Steller, *Beschreibung vom Kamtschatka*, p. 273). The Persians had a similar custom. And did it not also have its origin in the same motive, i.e., the extreme value that the ancestors of the Persians who lived well before Cyrus, mountain dwellers who were almost as wild as the Kamtschadales, placed on the possession of a domestic animal? It often happens that motives are erased but customs continue.

9. When we treat the worship of animals among the civilized nations—the Egyptians, for example—we will demonstrate the futility of the explanations given of this worship by the majority of ancient and modern writers.

10. Pliny, *Hist. nat.*, IX, 12.

11. To indicate all the causes that furnish ignorance with objects to worship would be both superfluous and endless. The least circumstances contribute, and the enumeration of them would be infinite. Those who work the mines in Ireland believe in *genii* who work with them. They call them "knockers." They stop hearing them only when they themselves cease their work (Staeudlin, *Magazin zur Religions Kunde*, I, 518–519). It is clear that these are echoes. And who would doubt that a people among whom there was no established worship would make these knockers its divinities? The same thing happened to Scottish mountain men who even today give a kind of worship to a good *genius* to protect their flocks, as well as to flesh-eating animals so that they will spare them (Pennant, *Scotland*, p. 97). The blacks of Whydah made a large, nonvenomous, easy-to-tame snake their principal fetish because one had slid into their camp before their victory over a neighboring tribe and they attributed the victory to it (Desmarchais, *Voy. en Guinée*, II, 133). According to a tradition of the same sort, the Delaware Indians give a kind of worship to the rooster. In a war they fought against a powerful nation, they were sleeping in their own camp, aware of no danger to them. Then the great sentinel of the human race, the rooster, gave the alarm. All the birds of this species started crying in a voice that seemed to say: "Arise! Arise! Danger! Danger!" Obeying this summons, each man took up his weapon and, to their great surprise, they saw that the enemy was trying to surround them and that they would have been massacred during their sleep if the roosters had not alerted them (Heckewelder, *Moeurs des Indiens de Pennsylvanie*, p. 339).

But in all these cases, the idea of utility has so little place in the motives for worship that often when the idol is alive, the worshipper kills it in order to be able to carry it around with him.[12] And it is even more true that the unknown is the sphere where adoration takes place, that at the time when man adores almost all the animals he never renders worship to his fellows. Man is what he knows best; this is the source of a great exception that has struck many writers without their being able to explain it.

This crude worship is so natural to man in his ignorance that he returns to it as soon as he is freed from the bonds, or cast away from the advantages, of public religion.

The pariahs of India are denied all interaction with the other castes; being neither admitted nor subject to any other worship, they have reprised this belief. We are told by travelers that each of them chooses his own deity, sometimes this or that animal, sometimes a stone or a tree.[13]

In China, where religion is only a form and the mandarins are pantheists or atheists,[14] the people worship serpents and offer them sacrifice.[15]

12. *Lettr. édif.*, VI, 174.

13. Roger; Pyrard, I, 276; Hamilton, *New Account of the East Indies*, 310; Sonnerat, I, 47.

14. We do not mean to claim that among the religious philosophies of the Chinese there is none that approximates to theism. One of the strongest minds and one of the most distinguished savants we have in France, Mr. Abel Rémusat, appears to have discovered a system of Chinese Platonism that is very remarkable for its conformity to that of Greece. Not having a firsthand knowledge of his text because we have not been able to obtain it, we cannot decide the question.

In the impossibility in which the human race finds itself of remaining inactive while unbelief oppresses it and skepticism troubles it, it seems to us rather plausible that for a long time in China, as in the last periods of Greek philosophy, people exhausted themselves in attempts to rise toward belief by means of abstraction. We, however, are speaking about the established and, as it were, the ostensible state of the Chinese religion. The China that Europe more and more resembles each day, the China that is governed by the imperial journal and palace eunuchs, has fewer religious convictions as it has more religious forms, and has to have more superstitions as it has fewer convictions. The sad result of despotism and an excess of civilization, China represents for the European nations what the mummies of Egypt signified: the image of a perhaps inevitable future that one dreads, but toward which one continues to walk.

15. Barrow, *Travels in China*, p. 534. In Tonkin, each small town worships a particular *genius*, which it represents (as in ancient Egypt) in the form of a dog, a serpent, or some other animal (Abbé Richard, *Voy. au Tonkin*). The theocracy of the Hebrews did not always preserve them from every trace of fetishism. It would perhaps be risky to see the worship of stones in the adoration of the rock at Beth-el consecrated by Jacob. But the serpent of bronze that Moses raised in the desert and to which the Hebrews offered incense is an obvious vestige of the worship of animals. The zealous and severe order of Levites does not seem to have become indignant over it. The kings who were most attached

However, the activity of the religious sentiment does not limit itself to the creation of this narrow and crude form. Above the fetishes[16]—material deities, if I can put it that way—that are created, invoked, and then destroyed by the successive needs of the moment, there always hovers a vaguer notion, one that is more mysterious and less applicable to ordinary life, which nonetheless fills the soul of the worshipper with an even more profound respect and a more intimate emotion.

With the savage, as with the civilized human being, the religious impulse directs itself toward the idea of the infinite and the immense. From this comes the idea of the Great Spirit, which resides in the clouds high above the mountains or in the depths of the seas. Always invisible, it is rarely invoked because it takes so little part in the destiny of the inhabitants of the earth. But the soul rises toward it, as if it were trying to mount to nobler thoughts than those that ignorance provides.

This tendency is very imperious; it is found even in the most savage of hordes. The Cucis, the mountain people of Tipra found in northeastern India and Bangladesh, are the most ignorant and wildest of savages. They think that there is a divinity in each tree. They have no positive laws. Murder among them is punished only by the relatives of the deceased, if they have the ability to avenge the death. Society does not intervene at all. They cut off the heads of the females of their enemies if they find them defenseless; and when they kill a pregnant woman, it is an occasion of rejoicing and glory. Nonetheless, they recognize a Great Spirit different from all the other deities they adore;[17] they do not dare to represent it in any image.[18]

An American savage who had a bull for a fetish told a missionary one day that he did not worship the bull itself but the manitou of bulls, who was hidden beneath the earth and animated the animals of that species with his breath. He added that those who adored bears also believed in a manitou of bears. And when he was asked if there was one for men, he replied in the affirmative.[19]

---

to the Law of Moses, David, Josaphat, and Jonathan, tolerated it. It was only under Ezechias that it was forbidden.

16. We have given the name "fetishes" to the divinities of the primitive savages because this is the customary designation, hence the most intelligible. Everyone knows that the word was the invention of European travelers, borrowed from a Portuguese word. The name of the fetishes varies among the different peoples who profess this worship. The Ostyaks call them *starryks*, Iroquois their manitous, etc. This specific nomenclature seems to us to be not worth the trouble to retain, since the idea expressed by different terms was always the same.

17. *Asiatic Researches*, II, 187–93.

18. Ibid., VII, 196.

19. Vogel, *Veruch ueber die Relig. der Aegypt. und Griech.*, p. 101; Lafiteau, *Moeurs des Sauv.*, I, 370; *Lettr. édif.*, VI, 171; *Culte des dieux fét.*, pp. 58–59.

This is obviously an effort on the part of savages to generalize their conceptions. It is the religious sentiment struggling against a crude form that encloses and hampers it.[20] This effort on the part of the religious sentiment to rise to a notion of a god superior to fetishes suggests to the savage an even more abstract conception, one that in the philosophies of civilized periods will undergo immense developments.

At this point we would like to speak of a division into two substances, or of a spiritual nature. While it will occupy a large place in our subsequent investigation, here, when it is but an imperceptible seed, we can say only a few words about it. It is enormously important in religious history, especially to the battle that all philosophical systems wage against positive religions, as well as playing a great role in the hidden or esoteric doctrines of all these religions.

To be sure, we do not claim that the savage himself conceives a division into two substances, or a spiritual nature, in the same way that the ancient or modern philosophers do. The ease with which he attributes life to all objects in fact seems to be an obstacle to being able to divide them into animate and inanimate. However, continuing his observations concerning the nature that surrounds him, he notes two aspects in all the phenomena that present themselves: rest and motion. Since the cause of motion is never visible to him, he is very quickly led to suppose that it belongs to another nature from the being to which motion is communicated. Hence, there arises a distinction between the substance that impresses the movement and the one that receives it.

The element (air) within which we exist, and which simultaneously envelops and enters into us, is by itself capable of suggesting the idea of a spiritual nature. The invisible and, in a certain sense, intangible air acts upon us constantly, but also variously. Sometimes it is an unseen benefactor, refreshing us in the midst of stifling heat; sometimes it is a terrible enemy, freezing us with a chilly blast; sometimes moaning all around us, it shakes the earth, stirs waves, and with unimag-

20. If we were able to give full credence to the reports of Father Labat on the religion of the blacks, we would have a quite striking proof of the distance that they put between their fetishes and their supreme God. He reports that a black whom a missionary asked how his tribe could adore such a noxious reptile as the snake, answered that the deity was not its choice, but came from the order of the supreme God. The Creator, knowing human pride and wanting to humble it, had ordered man to prostrate himself before the vilest of animals. If he had established a human being as the object of adoration, he would have grown proud, and the human race would have believed it was equal to God. To be candid, we find it difficult to attribute to savages such detailed subtleties; and we suspect the missionary who interrogated the black person either poorly understood his answers or embellished them.

inable violence overturns our walls and pursues us into our last shelters, destroying our most impregnable refuges. In these ways the idea of active but invisible and intangible beings naturally comes to mind, which we are easily tempted to conceive of as incorporeal.

Turning to himself, man notes a quite obvious struggle between the active principle that controls his organs and the passive being in which this principle seems to be enclosed. The soul controls the body; the body, though, resists the soul, which in turn sighs, or becomes indignant at being disobeyed, and accuses the body of its own defects. It is the body's organs that are deceived and deceive, its senses that mislead and seduce the soul. The same complaints to this effect are found with the primitive and with the philosopher, in the forests of the New World and in the academy. The old Iroquois gives to his son the same counsel that Socrates gave to the youth of Athens. From this it results that the more that man wants to conceive a perfect being, the more he frees it from matter.

The religious sentiment eagerly grasps this distinction and applies it to the divine nature. In it, the religious sentiment finds liberation from all limits and a grandeur, immensity, and purity that please it.

All the travelers who have reported the religious opinions of the Tahitians report that they distinguish the supreme Deity from the matter it puts in motion.[21] The same opinion is found among several tribes in Florida. And if we give credence to the observations of more than one attentive observer, it is not wholly absent from the beliefs of some tribes of Siberia.

If these primitive conjectures are vague, if their hypotheses are confused, this only better proves that sentiment precedes intelligence when the human race takes its first steps; it glimpses what intellect cannot conceive, what it does not even dare conceive, and what it often combats with the severe strictures of logic.

Up until now we have spoken only of the action of sentiment in the creation of the religious form. But man possesses other powers, other faculties, which also cooperate in this creation and which cannot do so except by following the rules of their nature.

If sentiment nourishes itself with vague emotions, the intellect is more demanding; it wants reasoning whose rigor satisfies it. The inner need that man experiences to adore beings who communicate with him, whose protective cares watch over him, is enough for sentiment to conceive of tutelary deities. Intellect in contrast

21. Cook, Forster, Wilson.

observes before judging. It collects and compares external phenomena and from them draws somewhat different conclusions. If several of these phenomena declare a benevolent force, others indicate hostility and hatred. This opposition shows itself at each moment, and in each particular, of physical and moral nature; at each epoch it is an insoluble enigma for the most developed minds. Who does not know the multiple efforts of the philosophical schools to resolve the problem of the origin of evil?

The much less subtle and less scrupulous intellect of the savage determines the question more simply. In the world there is good and evil. Therefore, there are hostile gods and benevolent ones. Dualism, which plays such a great role in the sophisticated religion of Zoroaster and which almost triumphed in Christian belief, in principle goes back to the religious notions of the savage.

The Araucanians believed in a hostile god,[22] and the Iroquois exhorted one another not to listen to the perverse deity whose pleasure was to destroy them by leading them astray.[23]

But sentiment always rises up against this distressing conception. Not being able to destroy it because it conforms to the rules of logic, the sentiment at least softens it by maintaining the supremacy of the good principle over the evil one.[24] This supremacy, which we will see presented in brilliant poetic colors in the Persian religion, is a fundamental dogma in the worship of primitive tribes.[25]

22. Vidaure, *Hist. du Chile*, p. 119. For other savage hordes, Pyrard, *Voy.*, I, 132; and Forster, *Voy. Round the World*, II, 14.

23. Lafiteau, *Moeurs des Sauvages*. It is probable, moreover, that the missionaries helped to greatly develop this idea among the savages by talking to them constantly about the devil (Mayer, *Myth. Lexic.*, II, 545).

24. Cranz, *Catéchisme des Groenlandais*; Lindemann, *Gesch. der Meyn.*, III, 195. Observed elsewhere, the fact that the primitive savages worship the evil as well as the good principle does not undermine the truth we assert. They continue to hope that the good principle will definitively triumph; and their worship of the bad principles will be explained in a later chapter by the influence that their jongleurs exercise over them.

25. Simply inspecting the epithets that accompany the invocations of the Great Spirit proves the supremacy attributed to him. The Laplanders call him Ibmel, Jabmal, Radien-Atzhie, powerful sovereign, father of all (Leems, *Relig. des Lapons*). The Canary islanders call him the great and good God, preserver of beings. The Quojas, a tribe of blacks, acknowledge his omnipotence, omniscience, and omnipresence; and it should be noted that blacks, who repair to their fetishes when it is a matter of their passions, have the Great Spirit intervene when morality enters in; for example, when they suspect murder or poisoning. We will see very shortly, however, that morality is naturally foreign to fetishism.

If sentiment has its emotions and intelligence its laws, self-interest has its desires and wishes. Religion must accommodate itself to them. The less man is enlightened, the more his self-interest is impetuous, while at the same time enclosed in a narrow and base sphere. His passions are more violent, his ideas of the useful limited to the present moment.

Therefore, as soon as the religious sentiment creates objects of worship, man is pressed by self-interest to employ them for his use. He thus enters into a new path on which self-interest works to falsify the religious sentiment.

Sentiment had led him toward the unknown; self-interest leads him back to known quantities. Sentiment had raised him above himself; interest brings him back to his own level.

We are going to follow him on this new path. We will show religion as self-interest made it. Later we will return to the struggle that the religious sentiment wages against self-interest.

As soon as man believes he has found the hidden power that he sought so persistently, as soon as he has before him the object that he supposes possesses supernatural forces, he works to turn these forces to his advantage. He studies from this point of view the object he adores. It is no longer the religious sentiment that dominates; it is the mind, working for self-interest, that reflects upon the object originally presented to it by the religious sentiment.

To please this object, to obtain its favor, and to interest it in its projects is now the purpose of the primitive. It is no longer a need of the soul that he satisfies by worshipping, but some benefit for which he hopes. He no longer obeys the sentiment; he pursues a calculation.

In order to attain his goal, he tries to judge this mysterious object. Now, he can only do so by analogy, and by analogy with the single thing of which he has some knowledge—himself. Since he grows angry when someone offends him and he is appeased when someone apologizes, or he becomes benevolent when someone serves or pleases him, he concludes that the object he worships will do the same. When some calamity strikes, he seeks the cause in the malevolence of the idol that he has unwittingly offended.[26] He then tries to disarm it with prayers and praise by all the means his own experience suggests to him and which would be successful with him. All this presupposes that his relationship to the unknown is similar to men's among themselves.

---

26. When the primitives of Siberia are ill, they toss a handful of tobacco into the fire, prostrate themselves, and cry out: "Accept this, smoke it, and cease your anger."

Soon he takes another step. Having appeased this being, he seeks to render it favorable. The same means he used to disarm its anger are used to attain its favor.

The idea of sacrifice is inseparable from every religion. One could even say that it is inseparable from every lively and profound emotion. Love is pleased to sacrifice everything it holds dear to the beloved; it even loves consecrating itself to the beloved by the cruelest of sufferings and the most painful of deprivations. Turkish lovers beat their breasts and tear their arms beneath the windows of their beloved. The knights of the Middle Ages inflicted voluntary sufferings upon themselves and imposed difficult trials in order to honor the ladies whose colors they bore.[27] And in the ecstasies of her tender yet passionate devotion, Madame Guyon sought everywhere for antipathies to vanquish, repugnancies to overcome.

Like all the movements of man, this movement is found in the savage. Barely are there gods, when the idea of sacrifice presents itself.

Initially lacking all refinement or sophistication, the idea leads him to share with his idols everything he finds agreeable, depriving himself of some portion of his food, his clothing, or the spoils he has acquired by some victory, which he attributes to supernatural assistance.

But soon the notion of sacrifice becomes more complicated. It is not only material offerings that the gods demand; they require from their worshippers proofs of submission, of devotion, of self-denial. From this come fasts,[28] self-lacerations, and voluntary austerities.[29] The shores of the Orinoco in Spain and the steppes of Tartary have seen penances as austere as those once found in the deserts of the Thebaid; and the celebrated celibacy of our saints has its own martyrs among the savages.

It seems to us that philosophers have not sufficiently reflected upon this ten-

27. See Sainte-Palaye, *Mémoires sur l'ancienne chevalerie*, II, 62, especially for the Gallois, or the penitents of love.

28. The savages of America observe severe and more or less lengthy fasts before going on the hunt or to war. During these fasts, it is forbidden even to drink a drop of water. What savages mean by fast, says Charlevoix (*Journal*, p. 115), is to take nothing at all. When they approach puberty they fast for eight days without eating or drinking anything (ibid., p. 346). In French Guiana the candidates for the dignity of chief refuse all food (Biet, *Voy. dans la France équinox.*, III, ch. 10).

29. The inhabitants of French Guiana, Florida, and the islands of the South Seas mutilate themselves, tear their body, cut off fingers, and remove teeth, precisely as do the devout Indians (*Sammlung der Reisen*, XVI, 504; *Dern. Voy. de Cook*). The women of Florida strike themselves with thorns or whips and toss their blood in the air to do homage to the gods. Chiefs are not recognized by their tribes except after trials, during which each member gives them a certain number of blows that cause deep wounds (Biet, *Voy. dans la France équinox.*, I, ch. 20).

dency of men to constantly refine sacrifice. They have too often attributed to artifice and calculation what in fact is nature's doing. For example, they have seen only the caprice of priestly tyranny in the ideas of impurity connected to the union of the sexes found among almost all peoples. These ideas, they say, are an attempt to afflict human beings with arbitrary denials. To be sure, the priests have profited from this notion of impurity in order to extend their power over that part of human existence that seems to be the most removed from their despotism. But the original notion has deeper roots than priestcraft. If it did not have such roots, it would not be found among savage tribes as well as civilized nations.

Everywhere nature has connected the need for secrecy, the sentiment of shame, to the tenderest of sentiments. It does so with an artfulness that one might initially call bizarre, but which reveals itself to be quite admirable when one follows it through all of its consequences.

Everything delicate, touching, and pure in the relations of love rests upon this marvelous connection; we also owe to it everything that is regular and orderly in our social organization. It is by yielding to one man alone this mysterious reserve whose divine rule is imprinted on her heart, that a woman devotes herself and her modesty to him. For him alone she pulls back the veils, which continue to be her refuge and her glory. From it comes the deep trust of the spouses, the fruit of an exclusive relationship. Each recognizes the sacrifice as well as the exquisite combination of desire and respect it entails. Because of it they share a thousand intimate memories that time only embellishes, kept even more pure and profound by the fact that they finally cannot be expressed in words.

Now, this instinct that attaches a sentiment of shame or modesty to the pleasures of love could easily have suggested to men the idea of a certain degree of wrongdoing attached to these pleasures, while the great intensity of the pleasures that accompany love made forgoing them a sacrifice worthy of being offered to the gods.

Like all the instincts that civilization develops and refines, this instinct is not the work of civilization. It is also found in the savage heart. The Iroquois have their sacred virgins;[30] and among the Hurons there are many who profess a vow

---

30. Lafiteau, *Moeurs des Sauvages*, I, 174. It is curious to read what the same author said on this subject a few pages later; the passage is important enough that we believe we ought to cite it in its entirety.

"They [the savages] have a high opinion of virginity. The term that means virgin in the Abenaki language means 'she whom one respects.' . . . They attribute certain qualities and particular virtues to virginity and chastity; and it is certain that if continence appears to be essential to the success of what of perpetual chastity. Young blacks, both male and female, despite the hot climate in which they live, oblige themselves to practice strict abstinence from the pleasures of the senses.[31] The greater number who cannot wholly resist their attraction atone for this fault by painful penances, or make newly born infants expiate it by such cruel procedures that their lives are put in danger.[32] Man is always shadowed

their superstitions suggest to them, they guard it with great scruple, and would never dare to violate it, for fear that the fasts and everything else they could do would be completely useless because of this violation. They are persuaded that the love of this virtue extends even to plants, some of which are believed to have a sentiment of shame, as though they were alive; they also believe that in order for plants to be effective in medicines, they must be employed by chaste hands; without them they will be useless. Many have often told me in connection with their illnesses, that they know very well the secrets for healing by their means; but being married, they could not use them" (ibid., p. 340).

31. Proiart, *Hist. de Loango*, I, 167–170.

32. Among many peoples, as soon as the signs of pregnancy are detected in a woman, she is plunged into the sea in order to purify her; and on the way, young people of both sexes insult and mistreat her (Bossman, *Voy. en Guinée*, p. 250). This, in a way, is virginity reproaching the senses whatever they may have of impurity. Among the Jagas, a species of tribe or priestly caste (and the fiercest of all the black tribes), the women who give birth in the *chilombo* (the place where the horde is encamped) are punished with death. Elsewhere, it is the fathers who submit to the punishment that they believe is merited. The Caribs fast and tear their members after the birth of their children (Dutertre, II, 371–373; Lafiteau, I, 256). The same thing takes place in Paraguay (Charlevoix, *Journal*, I, 182) and in French Guiana, where the fathers are not only whipped but treated as slaves during a greater or shorter period of time. Others wound the generative organs even before marriage (*Hist. of the Boucan.*, I, 241): this is punishment preceding the fault. The Salivas of Orinoco mark their newly born with incisions that are so grave that some die (Gumilla, I, 183). The mutilations that the Hottentots inflict on theirs are well known (*Beschryv. van de kaap van geode hope*, I, 186; Levaillant, *Deux. Voy. en Afr.*, II, 290). The same motive suggests tortures for the young girls approaching puberty. Their entire bodies are covered in blood (Barrere, *Descr. de la Guyane*, 168; Lafiteau, *Hist. de Loango*, I, 291; Thevet, *Cosmogr. universe.*, II, 913; Leri, *Hist. du Brésil*, ch. 17). Circumcision, which has a great affinity with these customs, does it not come from an analogous idea?

Sometimes the practices were modified in a way to no longer recall the original meaning. Thus the custom among certain peoples that husbands had of going to bed when their wives gave birth, a custom of which one could still see traces in a few southern provinces of France toward the beginning of the eighteenth century (Lafiteau, *Moeurs des Sauvages*, p. 50), probably came from the same source, without those who observed it being able to recall it. It is the same with the use prescribed to the newly married of several tribes not to consummate the marriage except after an interval of a greater or lesser duration:

"Even though the spouses pass the night together, it is without violating this ancient custom. The parents of the wife pay especial attention, and they take care to maintain a large fire in front of their hut which constantly illumines their conduct, and which can serve as a guarantee that nothing goes by the thought that he is not here simply to enjoy himself, and that to be born, to procreate, and to multiply are not his only destiny.

Later we will see the priesthood of more than one ancient people make perverse use of this indefinable but indestructible sentiment; we will see that what nature engraved in the heart of human beings to bring the two sexes together by means of a common modesty, and which means that each for the other is the sole beloved on earth, was interpreted by priests as entailing the rejection of the first law of this nature, the union of the sexes. An absurd celibacy became a slow but terrible torture that ignores the senses, overturns the imagination, and brings acute pain and trouble to the most delicate souls. In the priestly religions it became the best way of honoring the gods. But even as we bring this criminal abuse to light, we also have to recognize that the primitive notion of impurity preceded the abuse.

Self-interest, however, did not wait long to intervene in this powerful notion of sacrifice, which when it seizes hold of men takes turns perfecting, then misleading, them.

Sentiment wanted sacrifice to be disinterested. Interest wants it to be an exchange of services. Religion is thus reduced to commerce. And worship ceases when its profitability does. Man goes from one fetish to another, always seeking a more faithful ally, a more powerful protector, a more zealous accomplice.

Directing religion toward this ignoble aim, self-interest deprives it of every moral aspect. The fetish is a greedy, egotistical being allied to a human being as egotistical as it is, although weaker. The sacrifices it rewards only refer to it. The duties it imposes consist in victims, in offerings, in expressions of submission—agreed-upon currency that will be required in the future. It is payment demanded by the fetish for the protection it accords. Let this payment be given exactly, neither of the contracting parties cares one whit about a third party.

Religion then becomes such a commercial exchange that man establishes, as it were, an account with his god. He looks to see if this god has adequately acquitted itself of the engagements he supposedly contracted. And if the balance does not

___

on contrary to the prescribed order. . . . A husband instructed by missionaries failed in the respect he ought to have for the ancient custom and wanted to emulate the Europeans. His wife was so outraged that even though those who had arranged the marriage had been made aware of his inclination, they were never able to make her again receive this indiscreet spouse. Whatever representations were made to her, she never came around, and finally they were obliged to separate them. . . . Among the Abenakis, a wife who found herself pregnant before the first year of marriage had elapsed became a subject of both astonishment and scandal" (Lafiteau, *Moeurs des Sauvages*).

square, the worshipper abandons or punishes the deity, strikes it or breaks it, consigns it to the flames or the deep.[33]

It would be unreasonable to protest too much at the absurdity of such revenge. Such puerile conduct has its counterpart in more enlightened times,[34] and the most refined religion has not always preserved its more ignorant followers from it.[35]

33. African blacks sold, cast away, burned, or drowned the fetishes with which they were discontent (Bossman, *Reise nach Guinea, aus dem Franzoesischen uebersetzt*, p. 445). After a fruitless hunt, the Ostyaks struck them with rods, then reconciled with them, hoping that the punishment would have corrected them (*Voy. au Nord*, VIII, 415). Struck by the plague, the inhabitants of the Congo burned all the fetishes they had invoked in vain (Proiart, *Hist. de Loango*, etc., p. 310). A traveler saw a Laplander burn his fetishes because his reindeer were infertile (p. 219). The inhabitants of Hudson Bay aimed rifles at their idols when they believed they had cause to regret them (Umfreville, *Present State of Hudson's Bay*). The peoples of Ouechib in the Sandwich Islands canceled their religious festivals because they were angry at their divinities, who had allowed their king to die (Staeudlin, *Relig. Magaz.*).

34. When the idol they invoke does not answer their prayers, the Chinese lash its statues, break its altars, and haul it before tribunals to be judged. If they condemn it, it is demoted and its cult is abolished. Lecomte reports in this connection a rather remarkable anecdote. A Chinese official of a high rank, alarmed because of his dangerously ill daughter, did not limit himself to consulting with all the doctors he could summon; he had recourse to all the bonzes of the environs and put into practice everything they indicated to him in order to obtain from the gods, and above all from the local divinity, the life of his daughter. The priests of this divinity gave him formal assurance. But despite all his sacrifices, all the prayers and gifts he offered, the sick daughter died. Angry at seeing himself thus deceived and disappointed in his hopes, the father wanted to avenge himself on an implacable, or impotent, deity. He brought suit before a judge and requested, as recompense for all the gifts the idol had accepted without helping him, that its temples be destroyed and its priests be banished. The matter seemed so serious to the magistrate of the locality that he believed he had to refer it to the governor of the town, who then referred it to the viceroy. He initially tried to appease the complainant, but the father in his despair refused to withdraw his accusation and declared that he would give himself over to death rather than not see the wicked or lying divinity punished. This stubbornness forced the viceroy to continue the process and to send the parties before the supreme tribunal in Peking. This court had the accuser and the accused appear, i.e., the father and the god, represented by his priests. After having over several days heard lengthy arguments, the court ordained the god to be banished from the empire, his temples to be razed, and that his ministers, the bonzes, suffer severe punishment in his place. The sentence was promptly executed (*Mem. sur les Chin.*, II, 128–129).

Sometimes the tribunals take the initiative. They fix a definite time within which the gods who protect the towns or provinces are supposed to remedy the calamity from which they suffer, under pain of the destitution and destruction of their temples (Du Halde, *Descr. de la Chine*, II, 38).

35. Christians of the Middle Age, discontent with one of their saints, solemnly announced to him that they were renouncing his cult, taking away his ornaments, and casting him into the river. An extra-

When one savage becomes the enemy of another their fetishes do, too.[36] Later, when two nations fight, the gods divide and each nation has its heavenly auxiliaries. This is the same thought adapted to the social state of each period. Among civilized peoples, as with ignorant tribes, divine assistance is given not because of the justice of the cause but because of the liberality of the worshippers.

Here, too, we have to caution our readers against the hasty disdain that civilization lavishes upon savages. Whatever the belief might be, the main thing is to see if sentiment or self-interest predominates. If it is self-interest, the purity of the doctrine does not matter. Religion then is only worship of fetishes. And in civilized souls corrupted by egoism and blinded by fear, this fetishism is as revolting as it is among the Iroquois. Louis XI put himself on the level of these miserable tribes when, prostrate before Our Lady of Cléry, he tried to atone for a fratricide by bribing the saint with magnificent gifts.

In times of great danger the savage does not rest content with his customary fetish, he seeks the assistance of all those of which he has any knowledge; their number can mount into the thousands.[37] In the same way, when their harvest has been poor Russian peasants (whom absolute power believes it has converted) borrow their saints from their more fortunate neighbors, because they have shown themselves more effective.[38] Before the battle of Marathon, the Athenians instituted the cult of Pan, whom they had not worshipped before that time.[39] Louis XI, of whom we just spoke, when he was on his deathbed gathered relics from everywhere on earth.[40]

---

ordinary drought is thought to have cost Saint Peter his dignity as a saint toward the middle of the sixteenth century (Saint-Foix, *Essais sur Paris*, V, 103). Frézier recounts that in a voyage undertaken in 1712, not being able to obtain a favorable wind, the captain of a vessel took an image of the Virgin to the mainmast and told her that it would remain there until the wind changed (Frézier, *Relation du voyage de la mer du Sud dans les années 1712–1714*, p. 248). Even more recently—who would believe it?—in 1793 the Neopolitans on the occasion of the French victories had Saint Janvier condemned by a sort of legal proceeding, and they treated him the same way in November 1804 during an eruption of Vesuvius.

36. Bossman, *Voy. en Guinée*, p. 179.

37. Roemer, *Machrichten on der Küste Guinea*, p. 16.

38. Weber, *Veroendertes Russland*, II, 198. The tribes that inhabit the frontiers of Russia have put Saint Nicholas among their gods (Levesque, *Excurs. sur le schammanisme*, in his translation of Thucydides, III, 292).

39. Herod., VI, 105.

40. The pope, said Philippe de Commines, sent him the corporal on which Saint Peter had said Mass. He had the holy ampule of Rheims sent to him, and many miraculous things were brought to

Once he has entered this path, man is forced to follow it to the end. Having conceived gods who are similar to him by their passions, he has to conceive them similar to him in their needs, their habits, and their destiny. The goddesses of the Kamtschatka carry their newborns on their backs, like human women do. These divine infants suffer and cry like human infants. And every night coming down from the mountains, the pregnant Olympia runs to the river as eager to fish as humans, but more adroit and fortunate than they.[41]

---

him from Constantinople that had remained in the hands of the Grand Turk (Phil. de Comm., *Faits et gestes du roi Louis XI*).

41. Primitives even believe that their fetishes are exposed to the calamity of death. Greenlanders say that the most powerful of theirs, Tornarsuk, can be killed by the impetuosity of the wind, and that the pawing of a dog can cause him to die (Egede, *Nachrichten von Groenland*, pp. 93, 256). Our sacred books show Jehovah bending to the weakness of men and even submitting to their ceremonies. When he swore the alliance he concluded with Abraham, he passed through the immolated victims divided in two because this symbolic formality would make oaths more binding among the Jews.

CHAPTER 3

The Religious Sentiment's Efforts to Rise above This Form

Such is the worship of man in the primitive state.[1] It is religion at the most animal-like period of the human spirit. It is behind all the forms that we will describe in the sequel. The gods are not brought together in a body, as with the polytheism of civilized nations. Its vague notions of the Great Spirit do not rise to the level of theism. It chooses its protectors from a much lower sphere. It does not have the zealous spirit of theocracy, which, by placing its god in perpetual hostility to all other gods, by means of intolerance creates the national spirit and patriotism.

In this narrow and undeveloped conception, however, is contained the seed of all the elevated ideas that will be developed later.

The sacred objects of primitive worship are negligible, useless, monstrous, and ridiculous. But is this not another proof of the need that man has to worship?

He attributes life and intelligence to all objects. He thinks that all concern themselves with him, that they speak to him, threaten him, and warn him. The spiritualist who sees nothing in nature that is not animated by the divine spirit, and the pantheist who conceives divinity to be inherent in every part of the physical world, only follow the path originally blazed by the savage with his confused notions and halting steps. His worship is but the religious sentiment in its original form. It is man asking the nature he neither understands nor can understand where force, power, and goodness are to be found. No matter how crude it may appear, this religious sentiment is nobler, and even more rational, than all the systems that see in life only a matter of chance, and in intelligence a transient accident.

---

1. Here, we could present only the principal and general traits of this worship. As with all beliefs, there are several gradations; we could not detail all of them. Each form and each period of religious ideas could itself be the subject of a history of the sort we are trying to present in broad strokes.

We have already indicated some of the efforts that the religious sentiment makes to purify its form. We saw such efforts in the prototypical Manitou, the Great Spirit of the heavens or the seas.

To clearly see the struggle this effort entails, it will help to contrast the prayers the savage addresses to his fetishes with those he offers to the Great Spirit.

The Koryak says to his idol (while sacrificing dogs and reindeer to it): "Receive our gifts, but in turn send us what we expect from you." In this prayer, everything is base, egoist, greedy.

In contrast, the Delaware Indians' battle hymn, sung in honor of the great Manitou of the earth, seas, and skies, is characterized by an entirely religious, and entirely moral, resignation.

> To arms to fight the enemy!
> Unsheathe your axe and brandish your mace.
> Will I ever see my father's roof, the wife of my marriage bed, or the infants she carries on her back and nourishes at her breasts?
> Supreme Spirit, Great Spirit above, take pity on my spouse and watch over the children she has given me.
> I am a weak and powerless creature, not an instant of my life belongs to me, not one of my limbs.
> I go where duty calls me for the honor and freedom of my nation. Let not the tears of those close to me flow because of me.[2]

The religious sentiment does not limit itself to distinguishing the infinite being toward which it rises from the vulgar idols that self-interest has created. It exerts its influence on the idols themselves, which it constantly seeks to ennoble and embellish.

As we have seen, the savage does not attribute human form to his fetishes. He likens them to it as much as he can, however, because for him this figure is the ideal of beauty. He sculpts them, he decorates them. The Laplanders, the Caribs, the inhabitants of New Zealand, those who live on the banks of the Amazon, the Africans of Loango, the tribes of Central or South America—all fashion idols of mud, stone, wood, and the cloth they acquire from more civilized peoples. They attempt to give them a human form. Pieces of coral or pebbles represent the eyes,

---

2. This avowal of impotence is even more remarkable in the primitive human because it contrasts so strongly with the barbarous savage spirit. See Ajax in Homer.

animal skins serve as clothes, then they decorate them in a thousand ways.[3] The Russians subjugated the Tamertones and the Tartars of Attai but without civilizing them, and forced them to submit to a few Christian practices without eradicating their penchant for fetishes. In their world, they knew no more beautiful apparel than the uniforms of the Russian dragoons. They therefore believed their fetishes were dressed like the officers.[4] It is difficult not to smile at this. But this is the poor savage's attempt to attach to his god everything magnificent that he knows. Thus one sees in this creature the germ of the idea that with Phidias's chisel will produce the Olympian Jupiter.

We have shown that morality remains foreign to the contract established between man and his fetish. In truth, it is very possible for reason to conceive of religion apart from morality. The relations of men with the gods constitute religion. The relations of men with one another constitute morality. These two things have no necessary relationship with each other. The gods can be simply concerned with men's conduct toward them without any interest in men's behavior toward one another. And men can be concerned with the gods simply in connection with the duties of worship. Morality can exist in complete independence.

One cannot conceive of a religion that does not represent the gods as powerful. But it is easy to conceive a religion that grants them no other attribute but power. This in fact would be very natural if terror was the sole source of religion. Natural phenomena only suggest the idea of power. There is no affinity between the lightning that strikes, the flood that carries away, the abyss that swallows, and moral good or evil. Even after having personified the accidents of nature by attributing them to intelligent beings, and after having established the communication with them that serves as the basis for the exchanges between the two parties, man still has many steps to take before imposing upon them disinterested duties or gratuitous actions.

If sentiment, therefore, did not succeed in altering the state of things established by self-interest, religion would inevitably become harmful to morality. The worshipper of a mercenary god, counting on an assistance paid for, would trample on justice with more boldness if he thought he was assured of supernatural assistance.

3. Georgi, *Beschreibung einer Reise durch das Russische Reich im Jahre 1772*, p. 313; Marion, *Voy. à la mer du Sud*, p. 87; Dutertre, *Hist. gén. des Antilles*, II, 369–370; D'Acugna, *Relation de la rivière des Amazones*, I, 216; Pallas, *Reisen*, II, 683; Hogstroem, *Beschreib. des schwed. Lapplands*, 201; *Lettr. édif.*, VII, 8.

4. Muller, *Samml. Russ. Gesch.*, I, 150; *Voy. au Nord*, VII, 337, VIII, 410.

Fortunately, even in this degraded condition sentiment calls upon morality, and in a thousand ways causes it to enter religion.

First of all, we can look at the relationship in its narrowest form; that is, the contract between the two parties. It implies the idea of fidelity to engagements, which is a moral notion.

In the second place, even in the primitive state a kind of human association exists. The individuals of a tribe are united by a common interest. This common interest needs to have its tutelary divinity.[5] Religion takes the association under its protection. It protects the association against its own members, and the members of the association against one another.

The greatest and most difficult problem of society consists in finding some sanction for the engagements that men assume among themselves. The need for this sanction makes itself felt during each human transaction. We never deal with someone whose interests differ from ours without trying to read in his eyes if his real intentions correspond to his words. And sad experience constantly informs us of the inadequacy of our efforts. Voice, gesture, and look can all be the accomplices of deceit.

Religious conviction creates a safeguard: the oath. But with the disappearance of the conviction, the guarantee disappears as well. All too often in the course of history an irreligious people goes from one oath of obedience to another, but not really believing that it is bound by either. It considers them to be mere formulas that authority has the right to demand; therefore the current authority supersedes the previous. For their part, authorities who are as hypocritical as they are irreligious repudiate the promises made the night before, without any concern for the public scandal thus caused. In such a situation, all bonds are severed, justice no longer exists; duty disappears with it, and mere force reigns. Perjury on both sides makes society a permanent state of war and deceit.

But in the primitive state the oath has greater force. One should be grateful to religion that from the very origins of societies it creates this guarantee. The Malabars,[6] blacks,[7] Kalmucks,[8] and Ostyaks[9] all call upon their fetishes as wit-

---

5. Fishing peoples worship in common a god of fishing (*Voy. au Nord*, VIII, 414, 419–20); those of hunters, a god of the hunt (Gmelius, *Reisen*, II, 215).

6. Wolff, *Reise nach Ceylan*, p. 176. For other peoples of India, see *Asiat. Res.*, III, 30.

7. Loyer, *Relation du voy. du roy. d'Issiny*, p. 253; Desmarchais, *Voy. en Guinée*, I, 160.

8. Pallas, *Reisen*, I, 332; idem, *Mongol. Volkersch.*, I, 220.

9. *Voy. au Nord*, VIII, 417. Who would not sigh on reflecting upon the fact that Europeans worked with all their might to undermine the sanctity of oaths in the souls of primitives. Here is what one

nesses on solemn occasions. In this way they submit their momentary passions and changing humors to an invisible yoke.

To be sure, egoism fights this salutary influence of religion; it persuades itself that the gods it invokes will never come forward against it. Several fetish-worshipping tribes believe that they can perjure themselves with impunity when they deal with strangers: they believe their fetishes cannot take up the latter's cause.[10] We will see this contradiction continue among civilized peoples.

Nonetheless, it is an advance to have created a guarantee within a people. The notions at the base of this guarantee will not be slow to expand beyond the narrow confines of a particular territory. Exerting its influence from savage to savage, later religion will exercise it from nation to nation; in fact, it already prepares this move.

The beliefs of American tribes imposed a duty upon them of respecting the envoys of neighboring nations. Placed under the protection of the Great Spirit, these envoys could not be mistreated without committing a crime, and the guilty were delivered over to immediate death. Thus, continues the missionary from whom I borrow this fact,[11] messengers who were charged with declaring a war of devastation and extinction were listened to in silence, then escorted with respect to the borders of the territory.

Thus even in its crudest state religion is beneficial. To be sure, this direct utility is neither the sole nor the most important aspect of it, and we adamantly oppose

---

European recounted, himself the agent in the odious scene he describes. An African black came to find this man, then an agent in a Danish firm, on the coast of Guinea, and told him that he had a young woman, to whose father he had sworn in the presence of a fetish that he would never sell her. The merchant of human beings suggested to him the expedient of making himself compelled by violence to deny the oath he had sworn, which would appease the fetish who had witnessed the oath. The black went to seek the unfortunate female he was going to hand over and returned; then the agent, Roemer, the author of the narrative, had her put in irons. Immediately, the husband who had just sold her uttered pitiful cries, and the agent's slaves took to beating him with their maces. Either because he wanted to obtain from the fetish an even more certain pardon or because conscience had regained its voice in him, he did not agree to the exchange except after having received numerous severe blows. The European reproached him for this prolonged resistance. Fetishes, he said, are not so difficult to satisfy, and this one would have been satisfied at much less cost (Roemer, *Nachrichten von Guinea*; Lindemann, *Geschichte der Meinungen*, etc., VI, 286). These were the lessons given by civilized men to savages, by Christians to the heathen.

10. Cavazzi, *Hist. de l'Ethiopie occidentale*, I, 304. It is sad to think that much later popes reasoned as did these blacks.

11. Heckewelder, p. 283.

the idea that it should go in first place. In a moment we will show that it is even more salutary because of the emotions it causes than the crimes it forbids. But we should spend some time on this first sort of usefulness even though it is subordinate. We wish to prove that it follows even from fetishism.

According to a traveler,[12] on the island of Nuku Hiva all the laws and all social order rest on religion. These laws and this order consist in declaring that such-and-such a thing is sacred; that is to say, that the owner alone has the right to touch it. This consecration takes place by means of the priests. They call *taboo* everything they have consecrated. The persons and the properties of all the inhabitants of the island are *taboo*. No one dares to steal from them or attack their lives. Their wives share the same guarantee, and no one dares to perpetrate violence against them. When a baby is born, one or two fruit trees are declared *taboo* and reserved for his use alone. Since two of these trees are sufficient to nourish a man during the entire year, each has his subsistence assured. The person who violates a *taboo* is universally condemned and cannot escape the punishments the invisible spirits inflict upon such a one.

We must confess: we feel real emotion when we see religion even in its most imperfect form, as found among the most ignorant peoples, associating itself with the ideas of justice and beneficence, and, even as childish as it may be, doing the work that the wisdom of legislators has always recommended: providing for the lives of citizens, the subsistence of the poor, the chastity of women. It is truly moving to see the savage employing his confused ideas and finding in them a safeguard for everything dear to him.

The sentiment that we feel will become even livelier and more profound when we come to see the human spirit making progress, when we see, for instance, the *taboo* of Nuku Hiva at work in the Greek Jupiter, the protector of the weak and suppliants.

If man derived his religious ideas only from the material actions of external objects; if religion was only the work of the mind, a result of self-interest, ignorance, or fear; its alliance with morality would be neither so rapid nor so inevitable. But morality is a sentiment. It associates itself naturally with the religious sentiment because all sentiments cohere. The worship of invisible beings and the ideas of equity encounter and join together from the earliest days of societies. The savage's fetish to us seems to be a vague and ridiculous chimera; it however is a great boon to his moral development and to his future improvement.

12. *Journal für Land und See Reisen*, fifth year, June 1812.

The reader will see in what follows that we have not at all concealed the abuse suffered by the religious sentiment when it was captured by a class that wanted to monopolize it and make it an instrument of power, an object of calculation, the privilege of a few directed against all. But just as much as we believe we have to highlight and condemn the assaults on such a noble sentiment, we also believe we have to show the advantages of religion left to itself.

CHAPTER 4

On the Ideas of Another Life in the Worship of Savages

It is above all by carefully considering the conjectures of primitive tribes on the state of the dead and on the life to come that we can clearly discern the struggle between the religious sentiment and self-interest.

If, as we think we have demonstrated, religion always places itself in the unknown, the center of all religious conjectures must be death, because death is the most imposing of all unknown things.

By his nature man is not at all disposed to believe in another life. Even when his reason adopts the idea it remains foreign to his instinct. In the universe he conceives only himself, and about himself, only life.

The closer he is to the primitive state, the stronger instinct is and the weaker his reason. Therefore his intellect refuses to think that what lived can die.

Blacks,[1] and several peoples of Siberia,[2] attribute death to heaven's anger or to magic; savages of Paraguay,[3] each time one of them dies, seek its soul in bushes and, not finding it there, say that it is lost. The Daures bring food to the dead for several weeks: so extraordinary does the phenomenon of death appear to them, despite so much experience of it.

Finally, however, the terrible conviction settles. The dark abyss opens, but no look can penetrate it. Man immediately fills the abyss with religion. The immense void is peopled; the darkness takes on colors; and terror, even if it does not wholly disappear, is calmed and softened.

It is from the idea of death that the religious sentiment receives its most expan-

---

1. Oldendorp, *Hist. des missions*, I, 299–301; Dobrizhoffer, *Hist. des Abipons*, II, 240.

2. Georgi, *Reise durch das Russisch. Reich*, pp. 278–312, 600.

3. *Lettr. édif.*, VIII, 335.

sive and most beautiful developments. If man were fixed on earth forever, he would end by so identifying with it that religion would flee his soul. Calculation would have too much time, cunning too many advantages, and experience—whether sad or fortunate—would end by extinguishing all emotions that belong neither to egoism nor to success. But by interrupting these calculations, death renders success futile; it dethrones authority, strips it bare, and casts it naked into the pit; it is an eloquent and even necessary ally of all the sentiments that transport us beyond this world, which is to say: all of our generous and noble sentiments. Even in the primitive state, all that religion possesses of the most pure and profound stems from this idea. When the forest-dweller of America displays the bones of his forefathers and refuses to abandon them, when the captive warrior chants while braving the most painful torture and is worried about only one thing: that he bring no shame to the shades of his ancestors, this heroism is entirely religious. It is composed of memories of the past and promises for the future. It triumphs over the present; it presides over his entire life.

However, the degradation we have already noted in the savage's conceptions of his gods also tarnishes those of the next life. Self-interest wants to arrange this imagined world for its own use; the intellect wants to describe it; and because it cannot create from nothing and has to use existing materials, the ideal world becomes a copy of this world.

The inhabitants of Paraguay think that in the next life the individual is exposed to hunger and thirst, to the inclemency of the weather and the attacks of wild beasts, and that the shadows there are divided into rich and poor, masters and subjects.[4] The savages of Louisiana refuse to believe one can do without food there.[5] Tahitians believe they are reunited with their wives and can have new children with them.[6] The people of Guinea, those of Greenland, the tribes of South

4. *Lettr. édif.*, IX, 101; Charlevoix, *Hist. du Paraguay*, II, 277–278; Ulloa, *Voy. dans l'Amér. mérid.*, II, 182.

5. *Voy. au Nord*, V, 331.

6. *Dern. Voy. de Cook*, II, 164–165. The story of Orpheus and Eurydice is found almost word for word among the primitives of Canada. A father, having lost his son and inconsolable at his loss, resolved to go seek him in the land of the souls with a few faithful companions. They confronted many perils and put up with many trials. The adventurous troop, reduced to the most intrepid and the most vigorous, finally arrived at their destination. They first were surrounded by a crowd of animal shades of all sorts, there for the service of their owners. The fir trees and cedars, whose branches were constantly rejuvenated, were decked out in an eternal green; and the sun, which descended twice a day to this place, warmed it and flooded it with light. But a terrible giant, the king of this land of the dead,

America, fear a second death after which all is over for the individual.[7] So strong is the human inclination to envisage what will be from what is.

The conjectures about the next life differ according to climate and local or individual situation. But they do not differ in fundamental nature. The one who has never left the place of his birth points to the mountains in the distance, beyond which one day he will live with his ancestors; there in his canoe he will ride the waves and cast his spear. The Indian taken to Europe awaits the fetish who can take him on the wings of the wind back to his native country.[8] He wishes for a speedy death, so as to escape from the European monsters and return to his former pleasures.[9] The unfortunate soul born into slavery has more humble hopes: one implores his idol that he will no longer be the slave of a white man.[10]

The anthropomorphism that affects the ideas of the savage has a negative consequence. It removes morality from every idea concerning the state of the dead. Even those tribes that distinguish a place of happiness and one of torments do not populate the former with the virtuous and the latter with criminals. The difference of destiny depends upon accidental circumstances. The inhabitants of the Marianne Islands, even while they acknowledge a place of sufferings and one of happiness, do not connect them with the ideas of punishment and reward. Those who die a violent death are the damned of this mythology; those whose death is easy are the elect.[11]

However, it should be noted that every time that travelers or missionaries have made use of the distinction in order to introduce the idea of distributive justice,

---

threatened those who had profaned it by crossing the border of his domain. Prostrate before him, the father asked, with lowered eyes intended to persuade, for his son. The giant relented and returned the soul who had been sought and besought with such insistence. The father brought it in a wineskin to the body it was to reenter. A woman, however, led by a fatal curiosity, undid the skin, and the soul returned to the land of its ancestors (Leclercq, *Relat. de Gaspésie,* p. 312).

7. Meiners, "Geschichte der Meinungen roher Voelker ueber die Natur der Seele," *Goett. Magaz.,* II, 744.

8. Simple nature to his hope has given,

Behind the cloud topt hill, an humbler heaven,

Some safer world, in depth of woods embraced

Some happier Island in the wat'ry waste.

(Pope)

9. Levaillant, *Prem. Voy. en Afrique.*

10. Roemer, *Nachrichten von der Küste Guinea,* pp. 86–87.

11. Gobien, *Hist. des îles Marian.,* pp. 65–68.

and have asked the savages if guilty souls were not separated from innocent ones, the savages eagerly embraced the separation. Even if nothing in their previous stories had said so, this immediately became part of their beliefs. One would say that the religious sentiment was merely awaiting this ray of light, and that it took over this hope as if it were its natural possession.

Nonetheless, from this likening of the next life to this life, a certain abasement of religion results, and for man, constant restlessness. A host of practices emerges aimed to place the deceased beyond the needs that even the tomb does not guarantee. And long in advance, the living take prudent precautions, providing for their stay in the place that, sooner or later, awaits them. The hunter has his arrows placed beside him, the fisherman his nets.

When a Greenland child dies, the most faithful dog is buried with him in order to lead him to the relatives who have gone before him.[12] The same victim, placed at the foot of the bedside of a sick Huron, is to announce their arrival to the shades that await them. In days gone by the Iroquois placed beside each deceased warrior weapons, skins, and colors with which to paint himself.[13] Some even buried their fetishes with them.[14] Even today the Laplanders place flint and tinder in their silver coffins in order to light their way.[15] And the islanders of Car Nicobar in India consider depriving someone who just died of the future service of the animals he owned to be a sacrilegious theft.[16]

Who can fail to see in this a combination of self-interest and sentiment? What the savage does for himself is only egoism; what he does for the deceased that he loved belongs to religion. Religion, from this time on a consolation, trumps sadness. The father who buries with his young warrior son his bow and arrows thus represents the son to himself as running through the forests of another world, full of the vigor that recently caused the heart of the father to swell with pride. Having stopped at a cabin, a traveler found two savages, male and female, in despair over the death of a four-year-old child. The father died a few days later; the mother's tears ceased immediately; she appeared calm and resigned. Queried by the traveler, her sadness had been caused by the idea that her son of four years could not find

12. Cranz, *Hist. du Groenland*, bk. III.

13. Lafiteau, *Moeurs des Sauv.*, II, 413.

14. *Culte des dieux fétiches*, p. 72, German trans.

15. *Voy. d'Acerbi*; Leems, *De la rel. des Lapons*.

16. *Asiat. Res.*, II, 344. The Arabs before Mohammed let the camel destined to be their mount die of hunger on the tomb of their friends (Gibbon, ch. 50).

his own subsistence in the land of the souls; now that her spouse had rejoined him she was not worried about him and looked forward to rejoining them.[17]

Unfortunately, however, as consoling as they initially are, these opinions and the practices they confirm become cruel. In Nigeria,[18] and among the Natches[19] and the Caribs,[20] slaves were buried with their masters, prisoners with their conquerors, even wives with their husbands. The Yakuts only recently gave up this practice. American tribes torment their captives in honor of their ancestors;[21] and while they torture these unfortunates they invoke the shades of the heroes who died in battle.[22]

On the island of Borneo, the inhabitants believe that those whom they kill become their slaves in the next life; this idea has infinitely multiplied assassinations.[23] Among all these peoples time is split between ambushes to capture potential victims and negotiations to redeem them. Such is the danger, too little observed until now, of applying known ideas to the unknown.

In order to inhabit a world similar to ours, the soul must resemble the body. Primitives compare it to the shadow that follows them on earth. Earthly shadows probably suggested this comparison.[24] Many believe it to be of an invisible and intangible material.[25] Sleep and dreams give them the idea that the soul can exist independently of its organs. Greenlanders say that when it abandons its crude envelope, the soul hunts, dances, or travels to far-away places. But it nonetheless

17. Carver, *Travels through North America.*

18. Isert, *Reise nach Guinea*, pp. 179–180; Desmarchais, *Voy. en Guinée*, I, 315.

19. Charlevoix, *Journal*, p. 421.

20. Oldendorp, *Beschreib. der Caraib.*, I, 317; Cavazzi, *Hist. de l'Ethiop. occid.*, I, 396; Bernier, II, 113.

21. Charlevoix, *Journal*, p. 352.

22. Ibid., p. 247.

23. Among the mountain men of the northeast of Bengal, at the funeral of a distinguished man, the head of a buffalo is cut off and is burned with the body. The buffalo becomes the property of the deceased in the next life. At the funeral of a *bonneah*, or chief, it is the head of a slave that is cut off and burned; and for the funeral of a chief of the first rank, his slaves go on expeditions down the mountain and, on the plain, seize a Hindu whom they immolate in the same way (*Asiat. Res.*, III, 28).

24. Among the Patagonians, the soul is the transparent image of the living man; and the echo that resounds in the creases of rocks is nothing but the response of souls when they are called. Even the peoples who believe that they pass into the bodies of animals represent them in a human form; this is a contradiction of anthropomorphism, of which there are many.

25. Meiners, "Gesch. der Mein. roher Voelker uber die Natur der Seele," *Goett. Mag.*, II, 746.

always remains dependent upon its body, whose accidents and sufferings affect it. When the body is mutilated, it is also. It feels this mutilation even beyond the grave and forever bears the marks. Blacks fear much less to be put to death than they do to be deprived of any member.[26] And one of the abilities with which the *angekoks* of Greenland flatter themselves, which especially recommends them in the eyes of believers, consists in healing—or in their own parlance, stitching up— wounded souls.

A strange thing! This same opinion that seems absurd to us, almost beneath the first stage of society, reproduces itself at the other extreme of civilization. When the Mogols conquered China, they ordered the conquered to shave their heads the same way they did. Throngs of Chinese preferred torture, fearing that if they appeared before their ancestors bald, their souls would not be recognized and they would be rejected.[27]

One might be tempted to think that the idea of metempsychosis is incompatible with these ideas. But in the wave that tosses him, man is close to this contradiction.

In and of itself, the idea of metempsychosis is a very natural one. The instinct of animals sometimes resembles reason. And when one recognizes the motives that direct humans' actions, one is tempted to seek in their bodies the souls that have disappeared. We therefore observe some version of metempsychosis among almost all the savage tribes. But this hypothesis does not satisfy any of the subsequent needs of the imagination. Therefore in religious practice it is more or less rapidly abandoned, or at least separated from the consequences that would follow. Even though, as we saw, Greenlanders believe in it, and the poor among them make use of it to obtain benefits from the rich,[28] they nonetheless bury with their children dogs who are destined to serve as guides. As for the Iroquois, they also speak of the next life where the dead reprise the occupations of this life.[29] Among them, as is the

---

26. Roemer, *Nachr. von der Küste Guinea*, p. 42; Snellgrave, *Nouv. Relat. de la Guinée*, p. 218.

27. A passage in the Gospel would give us to believe that among the Jews who did not deny the immortality of the soul, several supposed its resurrection in the state of a body. "It would be better," it is said there, "that you be reborn to eternal life lame, etc., than that you go to the netherworld with all your members" (St. Mark, IX, 43; St. Matthew, XVIII, 3–9).

28. When a rich Greenlander has lost his son or his daughter, the women of the poor class seek to persuade him that the soul has passed into the body of their children, thus seeking to have him care for them.

29. Mayer, *Mythol. Lexicon.*

case with the mystery religions and the Gospel itself, the grain that is cast in the ground is the symbol of immortality, and they bury the remains of their relations on the side of paths so that their souls may be closer to vivify the bodies formed in the bellies of pregnant women.

Nonetheless, the religious sentiment—which improves everything that falls under its influence—in the primitive state appears to prevail over the idea of metempsychosis by making it a mode of gradual purification and an exercise of divine justice. According to the mountain dwellers of Rajahmahal, the body of animals is the abode of degenerate souls,[30] and if vice likens man to beasts, virtue must liken him to divinity. Nothing more resembles the migrations of souls in the priestly philosophy of Egypt and in the Greek mystery cults where this philosophy was transplanted.

After having fashioned his future dwelling place after the image of what he conceives rather than what he desires, the savage wants to decorate it in brilliant colors. He wants it to be richer in pleasures than his earthly dwelling. Tormented in this life by a hostile sky, the Laplander hopes for a milder climate and a better species of reindeer.[31]

However, despite the hope he gives himself, the savage is struck by an invincible terror. Despite himself, he depicts the situation awaiting him as miserable.

The drama of his last moments, the anguish and convulsions of his final agony, shed a somber hue over the unknown abode that defies every effort of the imagination to dispel.

The Patagonians say that souls dwell in the bodies of aquatic birds characterized by their halting flight and their doleful cries. According to the inhabitants of Chile, the food of the deceased is bitter to taste and black in color. In the Homeric netherworld, the stars are dimmed and flowers are darker. This is the conception of the primitive, decked out in the images of poetry.

The dreams and imaginings of self-interest, whatever they are, speak only to the egoistical part of our nature; they do not satisfy the religious sentiment, which alone can achieve victory over the repugnance the image of destruction naturally inspires in every living being. This sentiment takes no part in these fantastic paradises that address themselves only to the eyes and the senses. And from time to time an unexpected idea shines through, like lightning lighting up the night. The

---

30. *Asiat. Res.*, IV, 32.
31. Georgi, *Russ. Voelkerkunde*, p. 383.

idea of an eternal reunion with the Great Spirit appears among the vague conjectures of the savage; it is thus that in the midst of barbarism the noble hypothesis vaguely hovers that one day will console Socrates. It is the core of a sublime system that nourishes man with the sole hope able to satisfy his soul, fill the martyr with exaltation, and the dying with confidence.

Nonetheless, at the period we are now considering the uncertain glimmers that the savage glimpses from time to time do not suffice to reassure him. He yields to visible impressions, and they dishearten and frighten him.

He would like to place the deceased in a place of pleasures, but he sees them wander miserably around their old dwelling places. Hunger, thirst, and cold torment them, and their constant suffering inspires resentment and hatred toward men.[32] According to Caribs, they take on the form of venomous reptiles or of malevolent demons.[33] The inhabitants of Tahiti and of New Holland, the island-dwellers of Ambon, think that they enter into huts and drink the blood of those they surprise while asleep.[34] The Tschermisses encase tombs so that the dead cannot get out and eat those who survive.[35] The women of Matamba dive into the sea in order to drown the souls of their husbands, who otherwise may return and revenge themselves on them.[36] Several tribes do not even dare to pronounce the names of those who no longer exist, and become angry at the rashness of the individual who would utter them and thus trouble their sleep.[37] Others silently ride the waves and fish in silence so that the manes do not get angry at being awakened.[38] Among the Abipones, when a family loses one of its members, it burns his clothes and weapons, leaves its hut, and changes its name.[39]

Let us pause a moment and reflect upon these diverse movements, incompatible and contradictory. When it comes to the dead, where do this respect, this horror, and this calculation, all found together in his spirit, come from? First, whence the respect that he barely satisfies by multiple commemorations, sacrifices, and honors

32. Mariny, *Nouvelles des royaumes de Tunquin et de Lao*, p. 395.

33. Dutertre, *Hist. gén. des Antilles*, II, 372; Rochefort, *Hist. nat. et mor. des Antilles*, II, ch. 4; Delaborde, *Rel. des Caraïbes*, collection of voy. made in Africa and in America, p. 15.

34. Foster, *Observ. dur. a Voy. round the World*, 470; Collins, *Account of New South Wales*, I, 594–596.

35. Rytschow, *Orenburgische Topographie*.

36. Cavazzi, *Relation historique de l'Ethiopie occidentale*, I, 405.

37. Charlevoix, *Journal*; Dutertre, II, 411; Rochefort, II, ch. 24; Laborde, p. 377; Labat., *Voy.*, III, 182.

38. Gobien, *Hist. des îles Marian*.

39. Dobrizhoffer, *Hist. des Abipons*.

of every sort? Then, the horror that he calms only by the distancing, disappearance, or forgetting of the being who no longer exists, and everything connected with his memory? Or calculation, which transports egoism beyond physical destruction and forces him to create a place in an imaginary universe, which he furnishes and provides with everything he finds useful or agreeable?

We find nothing similar among the other animals. The sole instinct that belongs to their nature moves them to seek and find a solitary place where they can expire without witnesses. They seem to be instructed about one thing alone, that they must get rid of the ugly remains and not foul the air with noxious odors. As for anything else, no foresight, no anxiety about their individual destiny after death; no memory, no commemoration of those who have lived by those who survive. There may be some dubious exceptions, perhaps produced by the habits contracted by a few domesticated animals, but which probably are exaggerated observations of those who have a certain prior view. In no way do they change the general rule.

Man, on the contrary, while he is instinctively repulsed by the dead, finds himself again attracted to them by a movement that overcomes this instinct. Everything that strikes his eyes frightens him; everything that comes to his senses wounds him; nonetheless he constantly returns to these beloved (and fearful) objects.[40] When decomposition renders this back-and-forth impossible, and being forced to separate from the body, he attaches himself to their tombs. The warrior reddens them with his blood; the virgin deposits a lock of hair; the mother pours her milk on it or sprinkles flowers.[41] Friendship makes it a duty to descend, living, to the netherworld.[42] Even egoism, sacrificing the present for the future, puts aside the better part of its possessions so as to preserve them intact for another world.

---

40. Nothing is more curious than to read on this subject the description of the feast of the dead among the Hurons and the Iroquois. After having described what was repulsive in the spectacle of these dead being exhumed every twelve years—some, bare skeletons, others, recently deceased bodies—Lafiteau continued as follows: "I don't know what should be more striking, either the horror of such a revolting scene or the tender compassion and affection of these poor people for their deceased relatives; for nothing in the world is more worthy of admiration than the zealous care with which they acquit themselves of this sad duty: gathering the least of the bones, caring for the corpses (even picking out worms), and carrying them on their shoulders during a several days' journey without being repulsed by the disgusting odor thus created, and without allowing any other emotion to appear but that of regret for having lost persons who were, and are, quite dear to them" (*Moeurs des Sauvages*, II, 449).

41. Ibid., II, 433.

42. Among the Natchez Indians, the chiefs have a certain number of people who willingly attach themselves to them, and who are called their *devoted*. At the death of these chiefs, the *devoted* accompany the body to the place of burial; a cord is tied around their necks and they begin a sort of dance

And despite all this, some do not recognize that man is totally different from the rest of animated matter! From the beginning of the social state, when nothing is yet developed in him, death, which for the animals is only the sign of a dissolution that it undergoes without foreseeing and fearing it, without being aware of anything but the present moment, death occupies in the soul of the primitive a place greater than life itself. He does not live except, as it were, to prepare himself to die. He employs his faculties here-below only to arrange—in accordance with his still-childlike desires—the invisible abode where he must live. He is the owner who has taken lodging in a small house in order to oversee the construction of a palace. And some would have us believe that this instinct has no other cause than the vague imaginings of an ignorant, animal-like creature! But what, we must ask, would have suggested to this creature these vague imaginings? Why are they so deeply inherent in him, reserved so exclusively to him?

The obvious crudeness of the hopes and fears of the savage, therefore, do not undermine our arguments. We have already explained how the religious sentiment, the original source of all worship, is not the only faculty of man that contributes to their form. Here, as elsewhere, one sees the traces of the different impulses that share this being who is at once egoistical, rational, and moral. To logic belongs everything that is anthropomorphic, to self-interest everything that is calculated, to sentiment everything that is emotion. Reason, at once guided and deceived by analogy, brings to the abode of the dead the imitation of life. Making its calculations on the basis of this imitation, self-interest suggests to the master the barbarous requirement of sacrificing captives or slaves, to the husband the cruel affection that leads his spouse into the grave or upon the pyre, to the hunter or the warrior the desire to bring with him his bow and his arrows, his spear, or his mace.

Finally, sentiment struggles against a limited intellect and an ignoble self-interest and binds up religion's wounds. The regrets and the respects it devotes to the dead ennoble the narrow religious conceptions. It makes use of the limited images of anthropomorphism, but it purifies them. Sometimes it teaches disinterestedness and controls avarice.[43] Sometimes it wanders into metempsychosis, but

---

during which two men increasingly tighten the cord until the victims expire as they dance until their last breath (ibid., II, 411).

43. "All the labor, all the sweat, all the exchanges of primitives are almost solely aimed at honoring the dead. They have nothing too precious for this purpose. They bestow their beaver skins, their hatchets, their pottery in such quantities that one would believe they hold them in no esteem, even though they are the wealth of the country. They are often seen naked during the rigors of winter, while

there is still something touching and affectionate in the savage's commiseration for the soul that suffers, being separated from the body, and in his efforts to find another for the suffering soul. At other times, it makes use of the crude notions that lower the next life to the level of this one, but inserts self-denial and sacrifice. Finally, by its prayer—which combines regret for the departed and hope in the deity—it purifies cruder notions concerning the nature of this divinity. In this way he elevates the material form, animating it with a spirit in which one can already recognize something divine.

---

in their boxes they have furs and wraps destined for the funeral duties, each one making it a point of honor or religion of being liberal to the point of prodigality" (ibid., II, 414).

CHAPTER 5

On the Errors into Which Several Authors Have Fallen Because They Failed to Note the Struggle of the Religious Sentiment against the Form of Religion at This Period

The struggle of the religious sentiment against its form in the worship of primitive tribes leads to contradictions that have given rise to many errors.

Because the savage, in addition to the fetish that is his customary protector, recognizes a Great Spirit, an invisible god to whom he attributes the creation and even the general direction of this universe, some have concluded that a pure theism existed from the beginning as the religion of primitive tribes.

The theologians of the seventeenth century, and the historians of the eighteenth century who had not overtly enrolled under the banner of philosophy, imposed upon themselves the adoption of this hypothesis as a sacred duty.

In vain did all the monuments, narratives, and annals of antiquity agree in attesting to the polytheism of all peoples during the first reported period of their history. Modern authors dismissed this concert of witnesses with truly remarkable ease.

Since theism was the sole natural religion, when they were asked where polytheism came from they replied, "Worship was corrupted, men grew weary of seeing so simply." But what sudden cause produced the fatigue? "Because it is difficult to conceive that a single mover impressed on the universe of beings so many contradictory motions." But the difficulty could not have been less when men were very primitive; and if they were unable to remain at the heights of theism, they hardly could have attained it with their first steps! To this it was replied "that polytheism was the result of the human tendency to worship the things that fall under his senses."[1] But this tendency has existed at all times, with all men; how could it hap-

---

1. See Mallet, *Introduction à l'histoire du Danemark*, pp. 71–72. We could have cited many other works to this effect. The same faulty and defective arguments are found everywhere, and on this subject the most sober writers have given themselves over to the most romantic assumptions. According to Court de Gébelin, "the men of the primitive world are not at all those stupid and despicable beings

pen that they ceased fighting it precisely when their reason was more developed and provided them with greater means of resistance?

Nonetheless, this conventional opinion was oft repeated and the priority of the-

---

who live only on water and roots . . . and who take stones and the vilest of animals for divinities. . . . If they did not understand metaphysical discussions, if they had neither the time nor the inclination necessary to devote themselves to them, if the exact knowledge of the most important truths made any discussion about them useless, they nonetheless acknowledged a creation and a sole master of the universe. . . . For a long time all the families were united in the bosom of peace, joy, truth, and virtue. But gradually the sages disappeared; the sublime ideas grew confused and weak; the hymns were no longer heard. Less enlightened generations remembered that they used to come together, and they continued to do so; that the sacred places were exalted, and they exalted them; but they believed that they were exalted for their own sake. They believed they saw in them some divine power, and limiting their crude ideas to external objects, idolatry and superstition took the place of resplendent truth. Thus people honored fountains, mountains, high places, or marshes, Mars or the sun, Diana or the moon. One only saw the creature when everything ought to have announced the Creator."

We ask every man possessing common sense: how could the first men, who had neither the time nor the inclination to give themselves to metaphysical discussions, how did they arrive at the metaphysical notion of a single master of the universe? Whence came this exact knowledge of the most important truths, which dispensed them from every other investigation? Please note: the author does not speak of a supernatural revelation of these truths; he shows us families living for a long time together in joy, peace, truth, and virtue. He does not refer to sacred traditions, and he cannot invoke them for his system. He admits nothing miraculous in the way in which these truths came to man. As a result, we have the right to ask him: how did man discover them? Did he receive them from the sages who disappeared? Whence came these sages? Who enlightened them? By what chance were they the only ones above the level of their time? Who gave them this privilege? Finally, why did they disappear?

When man grasps a truth it is his nature to consider it on all sides, to follow it in its consequences, to enlighten himself concerning what he does not know by employing what he does know. How did it happen that *the men of the primitive world* followed the opposite path?

What a strange hypothesis! There were sages before any experience would have helped them to know the world in which they lived, the laws of this world, the connection of causes and effects, when they were lacking every means of acquiring even the simplest notions. And when experiences had accumulated, the sages departed. The radiant truth was eclipsed at the time when light began to come from all quarters. And the worship that is found to be too abject for ignorant man has become the sole religion of civilized nations.

Nonetheless, this is how people argued for a century. They were intoxicated by mere words, and people devoted precious time and rather taxing efforts to built edifices on sand. If we would have a real need to refute such chimeras, we would make use of a comparison that the author himself employs. "The arts," he says, "are founded on principles that escape the one who simply works by hand and by habit; without them, though, one will never arrive at perfecting them." That is all quite true, but simple manual effort preceded the artisan. Practice existed before principles were discovered. Huts were built before palaces. To say that polytheism is only a degeneration from theism is to say that cabins are a degeneration of palaces.

ism acquired the force of received wisdom. Then a small number of minds, more reflective and less disposed to simply parrot sonorous phrases, demonstrated the error of such a system. However, as it often happens in times of philosophical or political parties, going from one error they passed through the truth and ended with new errors.

They say that the admirable regularity of this universe could not have struck intellects still in their infancy, since nothing yet manifested it. Order seems to an ignorant man to be a simple thing. He does not seek its cause. What captures his attention are convulsions and disruptions. The harmony of the spheres says nothing to the savage's imagination. But he lends an ear to the thunder that crackles or the lightning that shakes the forest. In its meditations on invisible forces, science occupies itself with fixed rules. Ignorance is wholly captive to the disorder of exceptions.

Now, these exceptions suggest to the mind notions that are entirely contrary to a single god. Different forces seem to do battle in the heavens and on earth. Human fortunes are exposed to a thousand unforeseen and contradictory influences. One is therefore tempted to attribute these different effects to different causes.[2]

Up to this point, everything is correct in these reasonings. But the philosophers then inferred that in its primitive state the human race had adored only pebbles, animals, and tree branches, and had worshipped them only out of self-interest and fear. To see man prostrate before such base divinities was a triumph for unbelief. Our ears had been worn out by a century of pious embellishments concerning the purity of primitive theism, as well as pious lamentations concerning its deplorable degradation; they were no less pestered the next sixty years by equally monotonous and ill-founded declarations concerning fetishism, presented as an absurd and shameful concept, the source of all religious ideas.

The error was obvious in both directions. If it is certain that ignorant man cannot rise to theism, it is equally certain that even in fetishism there is a movement that goes far beyond the adoration of fetishes. The savage who invokes them certainly considers them to be beings stronger than he; in this they are gods. But when he punishes them, breaks or burns them, they are enemies he mistreats, and no longer gods he adores. The Great Spirit, on the contrary, the prototypical Manitou, is not exposed to these vicissitudes of worship and outrage. It is in this idea that the savage concentrates his ideas of perfection. To be sure, he thinks about it less, he

2. Hume, *Natur. Hist. of Relig.*

only does so at irregular intervals. The interest of the moment calls him away; it constantly distracts him. Perhaps even a mute instinct informs him that he ought not to bring the being he so respects into the vulgar conflict of base passions.[3] But he returns to it each time profound emotions or tender affections stir in him.

One therefore can envisage primitive worship under two points of view, depending upon whether one considers what comes from sentiment or what interest is doing. Sentiment distances the object of worship in order better to adore it; interest brings it closer, the better to use it.

Hence, on one hand, there is a certain tendency toward theism, one, however, that must remain without fruit for a long time, because divinity so conceived is much too subtle for a barely awakened intelligence. On the other hand, this is the source of crude notions that cannot soon fail to be insufficient for developing intelligence because they are too material. As it advances, it is forced to reject them.

Only to see fetishism in the belief of ignorant savage tribes is to fail to see the élan of the human soul and the first efforts of the human spirit. But to see pure theism is to anticipate the later progress of the human race and to honor primitive man with the difficult discoveries that come only later from a more developed reason.

3. This idea will appear to be much too subtle for primitives. It is certain, however, that every time one asks them if they render habitual worship to the Great Spirit, they answer that it is too far above them and has no need for their homage. It is also to be noticed that, when they solicit assistance or indulgence from invisible powers that does not conform to the rules of justice, they do not address the Great Spirit, but their fetishes. Louis XI, in the prayer we reported earlier, invoked Our Lady of Cléry: he hoped to corrupt the saint; he did not dare attempt to corrupt God himself.

CHAPTER 6

On the Influence of Priests in the Primitive State

As soon as man has conceived the idea of beings superior to him with whom he has means of communication, he must acknowledge that the means are not all equally sure. It becomes important to distinguish among their degrees of reliability. If he does not hope to find the best and most sure ways by his own efforts, he naturally turns to those whom he believes are knowledgeable because of more experience, or who declare themselves to possess greater knowledge. He seeks around him privileged, favored, confident organs of the gods; and as soon as he seeks them, he finds them.

Hence, one finds among primitives the class of men whom the Tartars call *schammans*; the Laplanders, *noaïds*; Samoyeds, *tadiles*, and whom travelers typically designate by the generic name of jongleurs.

This still-undeveloped seed of the sacerdotal order is not the effect of fraud, ambition, or imposture, as is often said. It is inseparable from religion itself. It is not established by priests themselves; they are established by the force of things.

But as soon as the savage has created priests, the priests tend to form a corporate body.[1] Here too one should not accuse them; this is also natural.

Give a certain number of men an interest distinct from the common interest: these men, united by a particular bond, by the same token will be separated from

---

1. On the associations of priests in North and South America, see Carver, *Travels through North America*, p. 272; Charlevoix, *Journal*; Dutertre, *Hist. génér. des Antilles*, II, 367–368; Biet, *Voy. dans la France équinoxiale*, IV, 386–387; Lafiteau, *Moeurs des Sauvages*, pp. 336–344. Among many black tribes there is an order of priests or a priestly school designated by the name *belli*. One has to belong to it in order to exercise any priestly functions (*Hist. gén. de l'Asie, de l'Afrique et de l'Amérique*, IV, 651). Mr. Court de Gébelin was struck by the analogy between the initiations required to be admitted to this order and those that were practiced among the Phoenicians (*Monde primitif*, VIII).

everything not belonging to the body. And they will think that bringing everything under the influence of the caste is legitimate and meritorious. Bring men
together around a banner and you will have soldiers; bring them around an altar
and you will have priests.

The jongleurs of the savages therefore work to construct an enclosure the vulgar
cannot penetrate. They are no less jealous about everything that pertains to their
sacred functions than the Druids of Gaul or the Brahmins of India. They become
indignant at anyone who encroaches on their territory without obtaining their
permission. They impose trials and a novitiate upon those who seek admission into
the privileged body.[2] The novitiate lasts several years. The trials are long and painful, even bizarre. At every period, fasts, self-lacerations, flagellations, sufferings,
and vigils are the customary means for approaching the invisible powers.[3] The
primitive jongleurs are already led by the somber, lugubrious spirit of hierophants
and mystagogues.[4]

When profane individuals reject this severe apprenticeship and declare themselves priests on their own authority, their rivals refuse to grant this title. They are
called magicians, and whatever they are able to foretell is attributed to immoral
dealings with *genii* hostile to humans.

Here one discerns, albeit obscurely, a distinction that will become quite important in the development of religion, the distinction between religion and magic.

Properly speaking, magic is nothing but religion separated from the religious
sentiment and reduced entirely to the notions that self-interest suggests. All the
characteristics self-interest gives to religion are reproduced in magic. A more than
human power, the assistance obtained from this venal force by sacrifices detached
from morality (and sometimes in opposition to its precepts)—in a word, the em-

2. The *noaïds* of the Laplanders are methodically instructed in their art or profession (*Voy. d'Acerbi*).

3. *Voy. au Nord*, V, 12. In Guyana the apprenticeship lasts ten years, and fasting—that is, a reduc-
tion of food taken as far as human power could support—lasts a year. In addition this fasting was
accompanied by tortures of all sorts (Lafiteau, *Moeurs des Sauvages*, I, 330; Biet, IV, ch. 12). Among
the Abipones, whoever wanted to become a priest submitted himself to a complete privation of food
for several days (Dobrizhoffer, *Hist. des Abipons*, II, 515–516). In order to be admitted into the order
of the *belli* that we spoke about above, candidates allowed their neck and shoulders to be carved and
patches of flesh removed.

4. This instinct is the same everywhere. Nothing is more similar to the admission of candidates
to the priesthood among the mountain dwellers of India than that of the jongleurs (*Asiat. Res.*, IV,
40–46).

ployment of unknown forces to satisfy the passions and desires of men—this is what devotion motivated by egoism seeks in every land, and what sorcerers promise in every country.

Even though they promise the same things by the same means, the priests of the primitive tribes distinguish themselves from sorcerers. This is because the rivalry that occurs between priests forces them to seek accusations against their rivals, but these accusations cannot undermine the basis of priestly authority.

Accusations that are based on the existence of malevolent gods (whose origins we analyzed earlier) marvelously combine these two objectives. They fortify belief instead of undermining it; they create two supernatural empires, rivals to one another. They employ the same weapons, appeal to the same hopes and fears, and both condemn to similar reprobation. Therefore, to the applause of Iroquois[5] or Indian[6] tribes, pyres are lit to devour sorcerers, or they are cast into the waves to drown. This savage acclaim was echoed in the great satisfaction expressed by the equally ignorant populaces of Paris or Madrid of yesteryear.

It is only when reason's progress has discredited magic that priests come to see only impostors, not rivals, in magicians. They, however, delay such progress as much as they can. For how many centuries did men have to believe in lots, under penalty of impiety?[7]

We will return later to this subject. We will see the ministers of defeated cults

---

5. Lafiteau, *Moeurs des Sauvages*, I, 390–393.

6. Wizards are equally punished with death among the primitives of the mountains of Rajamahal in India. But they can purchase their lives with the consent of the family of the ones they have enchanted (*Asiat. Res.*, IV, 63). In the Congo, it is enough that a priest names someone a wizard; he is immediately killed by the bystanders. In the kingdom of Issini on the Gold Coast they are condemned to be drowned.

7. One can still see a great reluctance in our missionaries to deny the supernatural character of the jongleurs' deeds. "Many of our Frenchmen," says Fr. Leclercq, "have believed a bit too easily that these deeds were nothing but trifles and *jeux d'esprit*.... It is true that I have not been able to discover any explicit or implicit pact between the jongleurs and the devil; but I cannot persuade myself that the devil does not work in their deceptions ... because it is difficult to believe that a jongleur can naturally make burning trees appear, which burn without being consumed, and who can strike a savage dead even if he is forty or fifty miles away, when he buries his knife or his sword in the ground, then withdraws one or the other dripping with blood, saying that such-and-such is now dead, who actually does die and expires at the very moment when he pronounces this death sentence on him ... and with the small bow he uses to wound and kill the infants in the belly of their mothers, when they carve their arrows above the simple figure of these small innocents, which they draw for this express purpose" (Leclercq, *Relat. de la Gaspésie*, pp. 332, 335).

proscribed as magicians, and their gods portrayed as malevolent *genii*. The erstwhile objects of a Saxon's legitimate devotion became demons of the underworld
in Charlemagne's capitularies. And the pagan Roman pontiff's prayers to the most
high Jupiter will become damnable words for Christians, issuing from a dark and
illicit power. Here, however, we will limit ourselves to a brief indication.

The difference between the two notions was not so clear, the boundary line
between the two professions was too fine, for the savage to give it serious attention.[8] More than other factors, success decides the degree of respect and confidence. Jongleurs who fail are treated as sorcerers.[9] The chiefs of African blacks or
Caribs put them to death indifferently as soon as they are suspected of imposture
or found guilty of impotence.[10]

Priests or magicians, sorcerers or jongleurs, have the same functions. Their mysterious operations obtain the protection of a fetish or preserve the savage from the
snares hostile fetishes extend before him. If he is dissatisfied with his god, jongleurs
recommend another or fabricate one.[11] When prayers are inadequate, violence is
allowed, and, like the magi, the shamans pride themselves on being able to compel
the immortals.[12]

The same conviction concerning the supernatural intervention of the devil in the initiatives of the
Caribbean soothsayers shows through in Lafiteau's narrative (*Moeurs des Sauvages*, p. 348), where he
shows himself to be full of indignation against those who would call this intervention into doubt. "It
is an endeavor of atheists," he says (p. 374), "and an effect of that spirit of irreligion that today makes
so much progress in the world, to have somehow destroyed in the thinking of those who still pride
themselves in having religion, that there are men in the world who communicate with demons by
means of enchantments and magic. This belief has been attributed to a certain weakness of mind....
In order however to establish this spirit of unbelief, these purported 'strong minds' had to bend every
effort to blind themselves in the midst of light, they had to overturn the Old and the New Testament,
they had to contradict all of antiquity, and all of history, sacred and profane" (ibid., p. 374). He then
recounts several facts that seem to him to prove the supernatural (or infernal) power of the jongleurs.

8. The distinction between priests and wizards is so little pronounced at this period of religion
that according to some mountain dwellers of India, the souls of their *demaunos*, or priests, become
evil *genii* (*Asiat. Res.*, IV, 71).

9. Cranz, p. 274; Oldendorp, *Hist. des missions chez les Caraïbes*, I, 303. It is remarkable that it is
almost always women and old women who are accused of wizardry (Keysler, *Antiq. Sept.*, p. 456).

10. Sparrman, *Voyage au cap de Bonne-Espérance*, pp. 196–198. A king of the Patagonians had all
the priests he could find killed because none of them could end the smallpox (Falkner, *Description of
Patagonia*, p. 117).

11. Desmarchais, E. c., 296; Charlevoix; and *Lettres édif.*, passim; Georgi, p. 384.

12. Cranz, pp. 265–268; Cauche, *Rel. de l'île de Madagascar*.

They conduct these operations at night in far-away locales, howling and convulsing horribly,[13] accompanied by the beat of drums,[14] their fires emitting only a somber flickering light.[15] They use every means of inspiring fear; their costumes, for example, leave the human form barely recognizable.[16] Sometimes they walk on burning coals, sometimes they pierce bodies with swords.[17] The approach of the god is announced by a noise similar to an oncoming storm, and it is probably by means of an art we Europeans employ for entertainment that they make the voice of an invisible fetish respond to their requests.[18]

Their invocations are cast in a language that is unintelligible to those who attend the ceremony, which makes the priestly monopoly an even more inaccessible secret. Nigeria and Greenland, like Egypt, have their hieroglyphics and, like India, their sacred languages.[19]

The jongleurs deftly draw advantage from everything in nature or life that departs from the norm, because everything that does not follow the common rules strikes the savage with surprise and fear. Imbecility and dementia are revered. The

---

13. For the priestly convulsions of the shamans, one can consult Lévesque, *Excurs. sur le schamanisme*, pp. 298–304. These convulsions are so violent and terrible that Europeans cannot conceive how one can survive them (Gmelin, *Reise durch Sibirien*, II, 353; Charlevoix, *Journal*, pp. 361–362; Leri, *Voy. au Brés.*, pp. 242–98; Carvet., p. 271; Georgi, *Beschr.*, pp. 320–77, 378; Isbrand, *Voy. au Nord*, VIII, 56–57; Roemer, p. 57; Bossman, *Voy. en Guin.*, p. 260). The *demaunos*, or priests, of the mountain dwellers of India suck the blood of victims and fall—or pretend to fall—into delirium (*Asiat. Res.*, IV, 69).

14. Georgi, *Beschr.*, p. 378; Gmelin, *Reise durch Sib.*, I, 289, II, 49.

15. Cranz, p. 268; Biet, p. 387.

16. Here is the portrait of an American jongleur, closely drawn by a missionary not so long ago: "The jongleur was entirely covered with one or several extremely black bear skins; they were so well stitched together that they entirely concealed the man; the head of the bear, as well as the feet with their long nails, had the same appearance as if they had belonged to a living animal. He had placed on the head an immense pair of horns, and an extremely long tail trailed behind; when he moved, the tail looked as if it had springs. When he walked on all fours, one would have taken him for a very large bear, except for the horns and the tail. He had cut openings in the skin in order to be able to use his hands; but one could not see them because they were covered with long naps of the animal, and he looked out from two other holes to which he had attached pieces of glass" (Heckewelder, p. 373).

17. Gmelin, II, 87; III, 72.

18. When *angekoks* announce the arrival of a god, one first of all hears an undifferentiated sound that grows louder as it approaches the place of the ceremony, then two distinct voices, that of the *angekok* and that of the fetish, at some distance from one another (Cranz, p. 268).

19. Roemer, *Nachricht. von der Küste Guinea*, p. 80; Cranz, *Hist. du Groenland*, p. 273; Egede, *Beschr. v. Groenland*, p. 122.

hair of albinos serves as talismans for the blacks of Loango.[20] The islanders of the South Seas worship madmen.[21] Their priests make use of this natural disposition. Epilepsy becomes a gift and a privilege. In fact, it is upon this malady that they found their dynastic pretensions, requiring it to be inherited, or at least required for admission.[22]

Three things especially favor their authority: the fear, or the memory, of nature's disturbances; the astonishment that dreams cause in the ignorant; and his ardent desire, his illusory hope, to know the future.

At different times, all parts of the globe have suffered violent disturbances. Everywhere the earth bears the imprint of these upheavals, which so many times have disrupted the great work of civilization. We live atop volcanoes; we walk over abysses; the sea surrounds and threatens us. While death each day leisurely chooses its victims among us, nature silently prepares even greater devastations. And in its implacable although undetected work, it views with disdain our foolhardy hopes, our fragile accumulations, and foresees the future of our vain efforts. By a single motion, with one turn of the globe, it can blot out the future while erasing the past.

The religious sentiment loves to plunge into the contemplation of these great catastrophes. Either because, being convinced of its immortal nature it flatters itself with being above the wreckage of the world, transcending a destruction that cannot touch it; or because (with a secret pleasure) it discerns the overturning of all the obstacles that separate it from the infinite Being, and which signal its reunion with this Being. Even today, when all our habits turn us away from extensive meditations and propose as life's goal the interest of the day, we become silent and absorbed when our modern natural scientists tell us about the accumulation of strata in the earth, the remains of a thousand destroyed generations that seem to call to us and alert us as to our end. The savage meditates in his hut in his own way, not on what he knows, but on what he fears. Among all tribes one discovers traditions relating the annihilation of the world.[23] Benevolent gods barely forestall the ter-

20. Proiart, p. 172; Ulloa, *Voy. dans l'Amér. mér.*, II, 171.

21. *Dernier Voy. de Cook*, II, 11; III, 131. One sees vestiges of this view among the Turks, the Persians, and the Arabs. The inclination to think that there is something supernatural in the delirium or derangement of the intellect is not as far from philosophy as one would initially believe. "*Aristoteles*," says Cicero (*De divin. l.*, 37), "*eos qui valetudinis vitio furent et melancholici dicerentur, censebat habere aliquid in animis proesagium atque divinum.*"

22. Georgi, *Beschr.*, p. 375. The *angekoks* choose as their pupils epileptic children (Cranz, pp. 268–70).

23. Chappe d'Autroche, *Relation d'un voyage en Sibérie.*

rible moment. To whom can the primitive address himself in order to have his protectors encouraged and his enemies disarmed, if not the jongleur whose prayers are thought to be efficacious and whose terrible voice can compel, after having merely petitioned? When the stars are veiled, when eclipses diminish the pale light of the moon, the tribes, gathered on the summits of mountains or the shores of the sea, accompany the cries of their priests with their own; the lugubrious ceremonies found among all peoples[24] are but the terrors of the savage submitted to a regular order, and reduced to a systematic form, by the priests.

Dreams have no less of an influence on him.

Habit familiarizes us with even the most astonishing phenomena; let the unexplained last awhile and it seems simple to us. But dreams must produce an impression on childish peoples whose depth is impossible for us to measure today. They are bizarre parodies of reality, fantastic images of life, that cross both reality and life and stir up trouble that even our reason, which has become quite rigorous and demanding, can barely contain. Not so for the savages. Those of America and Siberia begin no expedition, they conduct no exchange, they enter into no pact without the encouragement of dreams.[25] These dreams take the place of inspirations, guidance, and prophecy.[26] Whatever they possess that is most precious to them, that which they would defend with their lives, they abandon on the authority of a dream. Kamtschadalian women yield to whomever says he possessed them in his dream.[27] An Iroquois dreams that someone cuts his arm, and he cuts it himself.[28]

---

24. Boulander, *Antiquité dévoilée par ses usages.*

25. Hennepin, *Voy. au Nord*, vol. IX.

26. Ibid., IX, 275.

27. It is the same in America. "A former missionary told me," says Lafiteau (*Moeurs des Sauvages*, I, 365), "that a savage had dreamed that his life's happiness was connected to the possession of the wife of one of the more considerable men of the village where he lived. He proposed to the latter to give her to him. Now, the husband and wife lived in great conjugal unity and loved one another very much; however, they dared not refuse the request. They separated therefore. The woman was engaged to the man; and the abandoned husband, having been beseeched to provide another wife for himself, did so, both out of inclination and to dispel all suspicion that he still thought of his first wife. He, however, remarried her after the death of the one who had separated them, who happened to die shortly afterward."

Having dreamed that he was taken prisoner by his enemies, a savage wanted his friends to fulfill the dream, that is, to surprise him as though they were the enemy and to treat him as a slave. He endured this for a long time so as to escape the prediction of such a terrible dream (ibid., p. 366). Respect for dreams has led several American tribes to celebrate in their honor a feast that resembles in certain respects the Saturnalia of the ancients and the carnival of the moderns (ibid., p. 367).

28. Charlevoix, *Journal*, p. 354.

Another dreams that he kills his friend, and he does so.[29] Entire tribes head out to conquer whatever one of their members dreamed they would.[30] One can easily see the power that this conviction would confer on the interpreters of heavenly signs.

Finally, the need to read the future is a cause of the dominion of these men.

It has been observed more than once that the ignorance of the events that threaten us is the greatest of the benefits that we owe to nature. The past already makes life hard enough to endure. No one has arrived at the one-third milestone of his life without having had to weep over broken bonds, dashed illusions, and disappointed hopes. What would be the case if man was provided with real foresight? Next to the tombs of those who no longer exist, he could see the grave that must welcome those who still remain. Wounded by the ingratitude of a perfidious friend, he would recognize in advance a traitor in the friend who replaced him. The present itself, transitory, barely perceptible, would be placed between two frightening phantoms. The moment that no longer exists and the one that is not yet would come together to poison the time that does exist. But man escapes the past because he forgets it, and he believes he has a future because he does not know what it contains.

However, he constantly seeks to overcome this salutary ignorance. As soon as he believes he can make religion serve his self-interest, he asks religion for the means of penetrating the beneficent obscurity that surrounds him. And the less extensive is his knowledge and the less diversified his experiences, the greater, more explicit, and affirmative are the promises he extorts from religion. Knowledge of future events is therefore placed on the first rung of the attributes that give credence to primitive jongleurs. Superstition asks them for it, ignorance implores them; if they acknowledged their own ignorance, they would abdicate their authority.

In order to preserve it, they obey the demands of superstition and ignorance. And what they reveal comes closer to the goal that is proposed, the more they are connected to the two things that most inspire fear in men: the appearance of malign *genii* and the return to life of those that have departed. It is the Nitos, the hostile powers, that the jongleurs consult on the island of Amboina. It is the dead that they invoke among the Iroquois, against whom the savage defends himself with so much care, these manes that he imagines to be transformed into fierce monsters, into bloodthirsty vampires. The credulous Huron hears the shades of his ancestors respond by moaning. The Carib and the black see their hair moving

29. Ibid.
30. Ibid., p. 355.

at the bottom of the vase in which they are kept, from which prophetic sounds emerge.[31]

Other epochs of religion will recall these dismal notions. In order to pierce the darkness of the future, Ulysses will go down to the netherworld to consult his mother.[32] Men have always concluded that because the dead belong to the past, the future belongs to them. Or rather, it is because, in the depths of his soul, he worries about death that he interrogates those who have already experienced it.

Ministers of these frightful ceremonies, the jongleurs share (or pretend to share) the fear that they cause. They do their best not to trouble the peace of the shades. They fear that the disturbed shades would revenge themselves upon those who troubled their eternal rest. They also fear that these gods who know what destiny holds might punish the temerity of those who want to steal its secrets. It is telling to the observer that in all cults the act of prophesying is painful.[33] This idea probably owes its origin to the fact that when the imagination receives one of these violent commotions that appear to raise it above its customary sphere, this commotion is accompanied by pain and contortions. But in this area, as in others, working with the givens of nature, the jongleurs have adroitly profited from this to raise the price of their activity. Even today those who arrogate to themselves the gift of prediction affect profound terror. It is with great regret, as though confronting immense dangers, that they resign themselves to unveil what the future holds.

---

31. Cavazzi, *Relat. hist. de l'Ethiopie occidentale*, II, 222–234; Dobrizhoffer, *Hist. des Abipons*, II, 84. This credulity of primitive savages ought not to surprise us. The Spanish themselves assure us that they have been spectators at the apparitions of invoked shadows (*Hispani complures persuasissimum sibi habent manes spectabiles fieri*; Dobrizhoffer, ibid.).

32. *Odyss.*, XI.

33. For proof, one need only recall Proteus in the *Odyssey*; Sybil and Silenus in Virgil; Elias and the prophetess in the Old Testament. The contortions of the Pythia were perfectly parallel with those of the jongleurs (*Mém. de l'Acad. des inscript.*, XXXV, 112). Terror at the action of the god in her regard was so strong that she sometimes attempted to escape (*Veritam se credere Phoebo. Pharsale*, bk. V).

CHAPTER 7

Consequences of the Influence of Jongleurs on the Worship of Savages

As one can well imagine, the appearance of a priesthood in the worship of savages is accompanied by very important consequences.

We have depicted man, in matters of religion, besieged by two conflicting movements.

One is disinterested and is nourished by the very sacrifices that it imposes upon itself, while it delights in devotion and in all elevated and sublime conceptions. It spreads a sort of general perfume over these conceptions, and in its rapid, unpremeditated élan sometimes places the beliefs of the most ignorant tribe on a par with the most purified doctrine.

The other movement is egoistical, demanding, and mercenary; it transforms sacrifice into commerce, admits only positive notions, and casts worship into the narrow and turbulent sphere of mundane interests.

It is to the second movement that jongleurs must initially apply themselves in order to become masters. Their authority grows with every support they give to the notions suggested by self-interest. They therefore turn the attention of the savage as exclusively as they can toward this portion of religion. They distract it from the idea of the Great Spirit, who, in its immensity and distance from the human race, is far beyond daily supplications and the needs of the moment. They concentrate the desires of the tribes that listen to them upon their material relationships with fetishes, subordinate powers who are more at man's level, and who belong to the one who offers them the most. They confirm men in the supposition that the gods make their favors a subject of commerce, that one assures oneself of their protection by satisfying their voracious hunger or by flattering their unpredictable vanity. By means of a calculated exaggeration, they dilate on the avidity and wickedness of these idols. The tales of blacks concerning the god

Nanni,[1] and of the Kamtschatka concerning their god Kutko,[2] give an idea of the perversity that goes beyond the fictions of the *Iliad*.

The path along which the jongleurs guide their docile disciples thus seems to prepare the inevitable victory of egoism over sentiment. Resignation to suffering is a more difficult and rarer achievement than is fervor in devotion. The worship that flatters immediate desires accords better with the demands of passion than that adoration which is inapplicable to the details of life.

But after having profited from the cruder side of religious notions, the priesthood soon notices that it can derive even greater profit from their exalted and enthusiastic part.

We have already spoken of the tendency of men to refine things connected with sacrifice. As much as the effects of this tendency are admirable when sentiment is at work, it can become terrible when imposture and calculation make it an instrument.

From the fact that, in order to be agreeable to the gods, sacrifice must be painful to the one who offers it, it follows that new sacrifices will constantly be invented, always more painful and hence more meritorious. From the fact that the gods are pleased with the deprivations of their worshippers, it results that their number will be multiplied and the nature of the deprivations constantly refined. Man launches himself into an endless series of exaggerations, errors, extravagances, and barbarities, whether inflicted merely upon himself or upon himself and others. Disoriented superstition is frightened by its own hopes, and it desires to atone for them by new pains or cruelties.

Human sacrifice no doubt has had several causes.

The dedication of a portion of the booty taken from defeated enemies was extended to captives. The victor felt he had to immolate a percentage of them proportionate to the number the fortunes of battle had given him.[3]

We have already seen that the assumption that the future life resembles this life causes the dead to be buried with their living slaves or concubines, or burned on the same pyres with them.

The leaders of tribes have sometimes thought that by slaughtering other men they would forestall the time fixed by nature for their own demise, or that these

1. Roemer, *Nachricht. von Guinea*, pp. 43ff.
2. Steller, *Description du Kamtschatka*, pp. 253ff.
3. Proiart, *Hist. de Loango*.

victims would serve them as messengers to the invisible powers, that is, as conduits of their homage and their prayers.

Finally, the desire to steal from the future the secrets it contains, which the gods perhaps have hidden in human viscera, has moved primitive curiosity to bloody its hand by digging into their victims' entrails.

These various causes introduced human sacrifice into a great number of primitive tribes.

But the principle of refining sacrifice had to favor the practice of these despicable rites in a special way. The shedding of human blood had to become the most precious offering, because in man's eyes life is the most precious thing. And among these horrible offerings the most meritorious had to be those that struck down the dearest of victims. Nothing is more terrible than logic at work in absurdity.[4]

It is in accordance with this principle that we find that terrible denial of blood ties among the inhabitants of Florida and the coast of Africa:[5] children immolated in the presence of their mothers. These are horrifying customs that we were habituated in our childhood to admire when it was a matter of Abraham's obedience, but which revolt us now in the tribes we are in no way accustomed to respect.

It is so true that these practices are the effects of the calculation and authority of jongleurs that the less a tribe is subject to them, the less one encounters these barbarous rites. Then, however, it is the soothsayers who demand them as an indispensable condition for the revelation of the future.[6] Moreover, we will note when we treat the peoples who have entered into civilization that human sacrifices always fall into disuse among peoples not subjugated by priests, while they are continued among all the nations who are broken to their yoke.

It is the same with the notion of chastity that we saw earlier win out in the heart of the savage over his most imperious passions. As we have already observed, not

4. This theory of refinement in sacrifice sometimes turns against the priests who make use of it. In times of danger, the Burattes sacrifice priests. They think that a victim of this importance ought to be of greater efficacy.

5. In several countries of Africa, and in the South Sea islands, children are immolated while their mothers are compelled to attend (Snellgrave, *Relig. of Guinea*, introd.; Cook, *Dernier Voy.*, I, 351, II, 39–203; asee also Lindemann, *Gesch. der Meyn.*, III, 115). On the island of Sulawesi fathers kill their children with their own hands. In Florida the mother of the victim places herself before the fatal chopping block, covering her face with her hands and deploring her fate (Lafiteau, *Moeurs des Sauvages*, I, 181).

6. *Parallèle des religions*, vol. I.

only does the priesthood make use of this idea to recommend cruel and exaggerated abstinences, but it soon demands an abnegation of a totally different sort, one that is even more bizarre and outrageous.

In the kingdom of Whydah female priests take the daughters of the most distinguished families and, after having subjected them to the most rigorous trials, instruct them in the arts of pleasure, then dedicate them to the profession of courtesan.[7] Among other blacks, a priestly corporation or a religious confraternity[8] composes obscene hymns that are publicly sung at solemn festivals.

In this way, by returning to the savage state, we can detect the hidden motive of the prostitution of female Babylonians and the immodest dances of the women of Memphis, established facts that are denied all too easily by writers who do not know their cause.[9]

7. *Culte des dieux fétiches*; Lindemann, *Gesch. der Meyn.*, etc.

8. The *belli*, about whom we spoke earlier. The hymn that is sung is called the *belli-dong*.

9. Of all our writers, Voltaire fought the most obstinately against the accounts of the ancients relating to licentious feasts and the prostitution of female Babylonians. He found it advantageous to ridicule a man who, no doubt, was much less intellectual than he, and whom his own irascibility caused him to place among the enemies of philosophy because he had the temerity to contradict Voltaire's own sometimes incomplete accounts and hasty assertions. So be it. But one cannot understand how Voltaire, who had studied more than anyone the effects of superstition, and who knew all of its power, stubbornly considered inadmissible the malpractices to which all the historians of antiquity attest, and which were certainly no more unbelievable than many other well-established facts. Even in Christian sects, have we not seen female promiscuity, nudity, immodest touching, and the most obscene practices made into religious duties? Was it harder to impose on a spouse the sacrifice of her shame than to force a father to stab his son or to cast his daughter into the flames?

A time will no doubt come when autos-da-fé will seem to us as impossible as licentious rites. A time will come when no one will believe that the kings of civilized nations ordered the terrible torture of women, children, and old people, and a queen thought she pleased heaven by gouging out the eye of her confessor, who was being led to the pyre. However, unless it be at the cost of not believing a generation who lived shortly before us, we must admit these horrors, which others will have the good fortune of no longer comprehending.

In all his researches into past times and foreign peoples Voltaire seems to have thought that men were the same in every epoch and in every country, and what proper people could not do in Paris, they could not do at Hieropolis or Ecbatana. This principle is able to satisfy a hasty mind, one that is impatient when it comes to dealing with questions, but can only lead to error. To be sure, one has to adopt as the basis of human opinions and actions the inclinations and dispositions that belong to our nature. But the knowledge of these dispositions and these inclinations ought to lead us to the discovery of causes, to the explanation of motives, and not to the denial of facts, especially when they are attested by respectable authorities. It is impossible to assign limits to the extravagances and disgraces to which

From his first steps man has believed that he has never done enough to honor his gods. His nature invites him to seek pleasure, he sacrifices pleasure to please them. Nature prescribes modesty, he offers it as a holocaust to them. But this last refinement comes from the priests. The priesthood discovered in the conflict arising between the religious sentiment and obscene practices the opportunity for a new triumph for religion, one that is the contrary of the one it had earlier attained over sexual attraction. After having forbidden the young virgin the chaste embraces of her spouse, it brought her before hideous divinities in order to profane and demean her.

This truth will become evident when we later show in the religions subjected to priests—and in them only[10]—terribly scandalous feasts that were authorized, even mandated, by the priesthood, the same priesthood that, on one hand, punished the least deviation from the commands of chastity with the most terrible pains, and, on the other, condemned any hesitation before prescribed obscenities and mandated orgies.[11]

Therefore, it is not the religious sentiment that one should accuse when it comes to these deplorable deviations. It is susceptible, to be sure, of being mistaken, as are all the emotions of our soul; but it finds in these very same emotions an assured remedy against its excesses. Purity, pity, sympathy, and that heavenly virtue which in religious language is called charity, and which is nothing but the impossibility of seeing another's pain and misfortune without being moved to attend to it, are its inseparable companions. Soon enough, it is forced by their common nature to abjure the wild or licentious practices that foul its cradle. During the course of our

---

superstition leads peoples. And if retorting with epigrams to unanimous and incontestable testimony is a good way of having success in a time of intellectual levity and ignorance, it is a deplorable way of reasoning, and the most defective of all for arriving at the truth.

10. If someone were tempted to object to us the mysterious feasts of Greece and Rome, we would ask him to suspend his objections until our exposition of the composition of priestly cults, compared to Greek and Roman religion. We put forward nothing without proof, but we cannot say everything at once.

11. In indicating at this point the moral cause of these licentious ceremonies, which were an essential part of the worship of Egypt, India, Phoenicia, and Syria, we are far from excluding scientific and cosmogonic explanations. But these explanations, which belong to the system of priestly philosophy, can only be examined later. It is natural to recognize in the jongleurs the same calculation as can be found in the priestly corporations that take their place, since their corporate self-interest is the same as the jongleurs'. But it would be absurd to attribute to them the same science or the same errors under the façade of science.

work we will furnish a number of incontestable proofs that they are prolonged only by an authority that has nothing in common with the religious sentiment.

This terrible, implacable authority regularizes human folly and transforms delirium into doctrine, the terrible into a system, and barbarism into duty.

Then appear the baneful results that have often been attributed to religion. It is complicated by a thousand cruel and ridiculous practices. Hideous in form, the gods are fierce in character. The religious sentiment seeks to beautify them, the priesthood keeps them horrible, and their very success transmits these repulsive figures to more civilized periods.[12]

Bloody offerings, revolting rites, and terrible holocausts must be offered to such idols.

This disastrous influence of priestly artifice crosses the centuries. If we were to take according to their letter the epithets that most often accompany the mention of divine forces or divine will in more purified belief-systems, we would think that man found a strange pleasure in trembling before the odious and barbarous beings to whom he submitted his destiny. All the evils with which the human race is afflicted, man sees their origin in the malevolence of these frightening opponents. Sometimes they sow disease, unleash storms, raise floods, arm the sun with devastating heat or winter with unbearable cold; sometimes they conspire against the very world they have created and are eager to destroy it. They shake it to its foundations; the moon and the stars are threatened by monsters;[13] the abyss is set to swallow it. Thus the doctrine of the destruction of the universe (about which we spoke earlier) becomes even more terrifying; soon enough, under the imposing forms of a dark cosmogony it will occupy an eminent place in the doctrines of the priests.

The foregoing considerations appear to indicate that we must consider the existence of jongleurs as a scourge of savage tribes. But other reflections must cause us not to pronounce so quickly on the question.

In the first place, the influence of the sacerdotal caste is rather limited in the primitive state, despite the efforts of the caste. The fetish of the black and the manitou of the American Indian are portable, even disposable beings. To be sure, they are the faithful companions of the hunt or war, the allies of his hatreds, the con-

---

12. We will see that while the gods of Greece were raised to an ideal beauty, those of Egypt and India always remained monstrous.

13. Lafiteau, *Moeurs des Sauvages*, I, 101.

fidants of his loves. But as we have seen, he not only can consult his idol in every circumstance, he can leave it for another or punish it when it has disappointed his hopes.

This volatility in his relations with his god inspires little reverence for its ministers; and the ease with which he can interact with his god and treat directly with it often makes the intervention of others either intrusive or superfluous.

In all of South America, jongleurs limit themselves to indicating the sacrifices that will please the gods. It is the fathers of the family, or the most eminent in each hut, who by right preside over the ceremony.[14] It is the same with the Tscheremisses and several neighboring, or dependant, tribes of Russia.[15] Thus, whatever they do, the jongleurs have only what we could call accidental and precarious credit. They are hardly less ignorant than the rest of the tribe that they govern. And while they are associated in a corporate body, they are rivals at each particular moment; they therefore criticize one another more often than they band together.[16] And despite their efforts, others—adventurers without authority—dispute their authority.[17] At bottom their trade is but a dubious means of personal gain, one that is diminished by competition.[18] Their authority is at the mercy of varying and fluctuating opinion. Creatures of this opinion, they rarely become its masters.[19]

Secondly, the quite real and very serious drawbacks connected with the influence of jongleurs are only one aspect of the question.

14. Charlevoix, *Journal*, p. 364.

15. Rytschow, *Journal*, pp. 92–93; Gmelin, II, 359–360. All the Daures (a tribe of blacks) claimed to be soothsayers. In the kingdom of Issini there is only one priest, called *osnon*, who is consulted only by the king. Individuals choose a soothsayer, whom they consult and change as they please.

16. When in some pressing danger or on an important expedition a savage calls together several jongleurs, each bringing his fetish, discord ordinarily arises among them, and the conference ends by quarrels and blows (Dobrizhoffer, *Hist. des Abipons*, II, 84; Dutertre, *Hist. gén. des Antilles*, II, 368).

17. Among the Laplanders, the Americans, the Kamtschadales, whoever sees his *genius* appear to him becomes a priest (Charlevoix, *Journal*, 364). Among the mountain dwellers of Rajamahal, it is the *maungy*, or political head, who officiates at the religious rites (*Asiat. Res.*, IV, 41).

18. The shamans of Siberia are so poorly paid that they are obliged to hunt and fish for themselves.

19. In establishing that the power of priests is ordinarily very limited among primitive tribes, we do not deny that there are exceptions to this rule that merit being explained. Thus in the kingdom of Whydah in Nigeria, the offerings to the national fetish, which is a large serpent, are placed in the hands of the priests, who alone have the right to enter into the temple, and who form a hereditary body equal in power to the king of this tribe (*Culte des dieux fétiches*, p. 31). But it is in the following book [book III] devoted to the causes of the unlimited authority of the priesthood of several countries that we will treat these exceptions.

In order to grasp it in its entirety, one must recognize that the less a people is enlightened, the more the priesthood is inseparable from the religion. Therefore it is not a question of simply deploring an inevitable evil; one must seek to find out if the evil exceeds the good with which it is necessarily connected.

Would it be better if the savage had no religious notions and, at this price, was freed from the jongleurs? There would be many fewer human sacrifices, terrifying rites, painful self-lacerations, and voluntary deprivations. But there also would be neither religious sanction for his emerging morality nor hope for another life (or any of the consolations that lighten the weight of his miserable existence). He would be only a wild animal, but more miserable than the other ones, his equals and his rivals. Consider the picture of American tribes drawn by a traveler known for his talent for observation and his accuracy.[20] Look at these tribes tormented by physical suffering, by constantly recurring needs, by the prospect of being abandoned when they receive incurable wounds, diseases, or old age; often they take their own lives to end their prolonged agony. Cast into such an abyss, can man pay too dear for the hope that revives him? His communications with the gods, his dreams concerning future existence, his preoccupation with the dead he hopes to rejoin, the emotions religion causes in him, the duties it creates—these are all inestimable treasures for him. It shifts the weight of reality, whose burden crushes him. It transports him into the world created by his imagination; and his labors, his pains, the cold that freezes him, the hunger that devours him, and the exhaustion he feels are but the tossing and heaving of the vessel carrying him to the other shore. To be sure, the actions of the jongleurs trouble him, even in his religious consolations. But to take away this noxious influence it would be necessary to do without its consolations. It is better that he possesses them, even in an imperfect, burdensome way.

Moreover, is it certain that the jongleurs do only evil?

Without them, entire peoples would die of torpor and wretched poverty.[21] They rouse them out of their apathy and force them to activity. The tribes without priests are those that are the most animal-like.[22] The jongleurs, whether ignorant

20. Volney, *Voy. aux Etats-Unis.*

21. Roger Curtis, *Nachricht von Labrador,* in Forster and Sprengel, *Beytroege zur Voelkerkunde,* I, 103; Herder, *Ideen,* II, 110.

22. Travelers assure us that the Peschereys at the extreme tip of North America have no priests (Herder, I, 65). Therefore they are the most backward and least intellectually developed of the savages (ibid., p. 237).

or crafty, deceptive or mistaken, nonetheless preserve certain medicinal traditions, some part of which is salutary.[23] For the slothful savage, they make a duty of the hunt or fishing. They make a duty of the pleasures of love, to which certain climates render him almost insensitive.[24] They entertain him with dreams that are not without a certain sweetness. They spread a certain charm over an otherwise deplorable life, grief-stricken by nature. We should not begrudge them that they know how to embellish desolate shores, and place their inhabitants' hopes beyond the mountains or on the other shore of the seas.

Evil is never in what exists naturally, but in what is prolonged or reestablished by craft or force. The true good is proportion. Nature always maintains proportion when it is left free. All disproportion is pernicious. What is overripe and what is premature are equally noxious. Institutions much less crude than the priesthood of jongleurs can cause much more harm when they become unsuited to the ideas inevitably developed by the advancement of the human mind.

When we later compare the actions of jongleurs with those of the priestly bodies so lionized by writers down through the ages, the reader will perhaps be surprised to see the preference remain with the former. Priestly bodies inhibit the human race in all its progress, while jongleurs, despite themselves, push it toward an imperfect civilization. One should see in them a bit of fraud and a good deal of superstition. The others, though, will have at most a bit of superstition and certainly a good deal of fraud.

23. See Heckewelder, *Moeurs des Indiens*, chs. 29 and 31.

24. Herder, *Ideen*. This is not in contradiction with what we said above concerning the deprivations the priesthood imposes. These privations can only be an exception to the rule; otherwise the society would perish, which is not in the jongleurs' interest.

CHAPTER 8

Why We Believed That We Needed to Write in Such Detail about the Worship of Savages

We have entered into detail in treating the religion of primitive tribes. This was necessary because in this religion are contained the seeds of all the notions that make up later beliefs. This truth must have struck our readers, even if they paid only the slightest amount of attention.

We saw not only the worship of material objects, multiplied to the infinite, but unexpected intimations of the purest theism, as well as the division into two substances and the presentment, as it were, of spiritual nature;

Not only the natural idea that the gods are pleased with sacrifices, but the need to refine them; hence human victims and children placed on the paternal pyre, the merit of celibacy and the mysterious price of virginity, and the holiness found in voluntary self-torture, as well as decency offered up on the altars;

Not only the fear of malevolent gods but the classification of divinities into two categories ranged eternally against one another, and the distinction of religious practices into licit ceremonies and perverse rites;

Not only the hope of a new life after death, but abstractions concerning the state of souls and their reunion with the infinite Being;

Not only metempsychosis, but with it the migrations and purifications of souls;

All the things, finally, that we will later see more developed among civilized peoples and cast in clearer terms, clothed with more sublime images and endowed with more attractive colors, the instinct of the savage already divines, grasps, and works with them in every way, trying to arrange them in some order that his intellect either conceives or senses. (Our proud disdain has much too much overstated the limits of this intellect.)

Whether man be a savage or civilized, he has the same nature, the same basic faculties, the same tendency to employ them. The same notions, only less subtle, must therefore offer themselves to him; the same needs and the same desires must direct him in his conjectures. However, distracted by the struggle he must wage against a natural world not yet mastered, and against a moral state devoid of guarantees, he cannot persevere in a straight and regular path. His conjectures arise and evaporate like clouds in the sky or like the phantoms of our dreams when our reason leaves us to our vagabond imagination.

Nothing, however, disappears without leaving its traces; later epochs collect them, elaborate on them, and give them regularity and consistency.

It was therefore important to describe them with some precision; they serve as the baseline of our subsequent inquiries. We will see how the human spirit works on these givens, and how it purifies them when it is left to itself and operates independently of every foreign influence. The crudest aspects are effaced, and more reasonable ones are combined and coordinated. But when it is reduced to servitude, the more reasonable ones are corrupted and perverted while the cruder ones are preserved in all their primitive absurdity.

BOOK III

ON THE CAUSES THAT FAVOR THE GROWTH OF PRIESTLY POWER FROM THE FIRST STEPS OF THE HUMAN RACE TOWARD CIVILIZATION

CHAPTER I

The Object of This Book

In the previous book we described the religious notions of savage tribes. Our readers were able to be convinced of two truths: one, that these notions were commensurate with the ignorance and crudeness of these wretched tribes; the other, that the religious sentiment made itself felt through this inchoate and repulsive envelope.

Now we are going to seek what religion must be at the lowest rung of the social state.

The passage from the savage state to the social state is an enigma, one for which no historical fact provides the key. We therefore will take no position on the way in which the transition occurred. We have already recognized that the savage state could have been a degradation rather than the initial state of mankind, one perhaps caused by some material calamity, or a fall, the sad result of a moral fault.

This question, however, is totally outside our investigations. The only truth we wish to demonstrate is that as soon as a revolution occurs in the state of mankind, religion undergoes an analogous change. We will base our reasonings only on facts we believe are established, and we seek to explain these facts. We have no intention of talking about things on which history sheds no light. We have therefore prescribed to ourselves a law: never to speak about what we do not know. If this rule has the drawback of necessitating more than one regrettable lacuna in our treatment, it has the advantage of keeping us from more than one fanciful hypothesis.

CHAPTER 2

On the Social State That Is the Closest to the Savage State

We will consider as the first rung of the social state the condition of those peoples larger in size than the Tartar, African, or American tribes, who cultivate the earth rather than hunt for their subsistence; who no longer content themselves with the shelter of isolated huts but build permanent buildings in proximity to one another; who know how to work with metals; and, finally, having more or less mastered physical nature, they begin to develop their moral forces, acquiring notions of property, laying down fixed laws, and, according to circumstances, choose or recognize leaders whose authority commands obedience and inspires respect (although it is still contested from time to time).

This state of the human race is generally designated as barbarism; it is in-between the animal-like stage we described in the earlier books and civilization, which will occur only much later. At this stage, peoples are just above the savage state and just below the civilized state. An almost equal distance separates the Samoyed or Iroquois from the Greek contemporary of Theseus, and the latter from the Athenian citizen under Pericles.

To be sure, the general characteristics of the barbarous centuries are modified by secondary differences determined by local factors or accidental occurrences. Nonetheless, looked at in connection with religion, the period is subject to a common rule. The notions suggested to the savage by the narrow horizons of egoism no longer satisfy the human being who has taken his first steps to a better state. Even though he is ignorant of the laws of nature he has discovered some aspects of its workings. Religion must withdraw itself from them. Man has consolidated his empire over inanimate matter and the majority of living species; he no longer can solely worship pieces of wood, animals, and stones. At the same time, the vague élan of the religion sentiment that propelled the savages toward more sublime and mysterious notions now wants them to be clothed in more fixed forms, to give them more constancy and more reality, as it were. In this way, by a double work unnoticed by him, the human being progressing toward civilization tries, simultaneously, to have what is too far above him come down to him and to raise up what is base and beneath him.

Likewise, the isolation in which fetishes live ceases being suitable to the gods of peoples united in societies. Men brought together in social bodies need to be united in their sentiments. To see these sentiments shared is itself a pleasure. They put their gods in common; in fact, this reunion of the gods occurs necessarily as soon as the coming-together of men occurs. Human society being formed, a celestial society forms too. The objects of worship compose an Olympus as soon as worshippers form a people.

By a similar necessity the gods divide power. Being the god of an isolated individual, the fetish had to satisfy all the needs of its devoté. All the fetishes, therefore, had the same functions. Now the gods have distinct functions.

In some way, this revolution is the counterpart of the division of labor among men that occurs with the development of society. In the savage state each individual alone provided all his needs. In civilized society, devoting himself to a particular occupation, each one provides not only for himself but for the similar needs of others. In fetishism, the fetish is responsible for everything that pertains to the individual; when nascent polytheism succeeds it, each deity is charged with one thing, although for everyone.

For this same reason, the gods then take on distinctive names, while fetishes did not have individual names. It was at the moment when, thanks to the arrival of Egyptian colonies, the Greeks passed from fetishism to polytheism that they assigned special names to each of their divinities.[1]

It is not that fetishism disappears entirely with the appearance of this new form. We have already shown that even at much more advanced periods, under different guises it remains an essential part of religious ideas. Even more so, therefore, must it continue in those peoples among whom whatever imperfect knowledge there exists remains the property of a class interested in the perpetuation of ignorance; and among other peoples that are occupied with war and pillage,

---

1. Herodotus.

who concentrate their indomitable passions and developing understanding on the struggles and conflicts of this world. Thus we find traces of fetishism both among the Greeks of the heroic period, when the priesthood had no influence, and among the Egyptians, whose priests subjected them to an iron yoke. Only, these vestiges of a belief the human spirit has risen above combine with the worship that replaces it, and the old fetishes, now disciplined, submit themselves to the greater national deities.[2]

These are the first developments of religious notions that the birth of civilization causes. Whatever the power of priests may be otherwise, the steps are the same. However, if we wish to go further, two paths open before us that grow further apart the further they go. One is the path man follows when he is left to his own powers and his own instinct. The other path is the one that priesthood leads him on when it reduces him to slavery.

Here appears the distinction we established earlier between priestly religions and those in which no priesthood succeeded in subjugating it. Our first concern, therefore, must be to name the causes that favored, and those that limited, priestly authority.[3]

2. Fetishism even survives the establishment of theism, when this sophisticated belief is extended to barely civilized peoples. Blacks in Islam preserve the usage of Mumbo-jumbo, one of their former fetishes terrifying to disobedient women, whom they drag before this idol for it to devour them (*Parallèle des relig.*, I, 175).

3. A distinguished German writer (Rhode, *Ueber Alter und Werth einiger morgenloendischer Urkunden*) has detected the distinction of which we speak here, but it seems to us that he has not adequately sought its cause. "Among the most ancient peoples," he says, "in a time prior to the beginning of the most ancient history as it is presented to us, two systems of religion are found, directly opposed to one another. The first, which certainly preceded the other, consisted in a simple adoration of nature. The physical world was all. Everything flowed from it, everything depended upon it. Active forces and the bodies by which they acted were divinized; and these gods were always imagined as corporeal, and similar to men. Their reciprocal relations were expressed in myths, which soon were mixed with the history of their first worshippers.

The second system is of an entirely different sort. Based upon an ancient and sacred revelation, the supernatural is found here, pure and sublime. It attracts to itself and absorbs, as it were, the worship of nature. In this system everything depends upon a creative being, spiritual, eternal, infinite, immeasurably above creatures. The physical world is but a means spontaneously chosen in view of a moral aim, and has no value or existence except because of its aptitude to realize this aim. As soon as it is achieved—that is, when the disorder that troubles the spiritual world will have ceased—the material creation will be destroyed and the reign of the spirit will begin for all eternity.

This second system dominated from time immemorial in upper Asia beyond the Euphrates and the Tigris, in Persia, in Media, in Bactria, in Tibet, in India, China, and perhaps in Egypt. The other was adopted by the peoples who lived beneath these rivers, with the exception of the Hebrews. It made its way, with its multiform myths, into Greece and Italy; but Greek philosophy modified it; and fragments of the second system were introduced there, making up the mystery cults of Eleusis and of Samothrace."

In all this there are many truths. But the author does not see that he has left two great lacunae: (1) What was the cause that split the religious ideas into two dissimilar categories? (2) The metaphysical system that in our work we regard as sacerdotal, did it descend to the people? We do not believe so. The first system was always placed under the second. The people directed its homage toward visible objects, and priestly abstractions never influenced it.

CHAPTER 3

On Causes That Could Contribute Only in a Secondary Manner to the Increase of Priestly Authority

While they favored the accidental influence of isolated jongleurs, the religion of the savage state and the character of the tribes that professed this religion worked against the regular establishment of priestly power. Despite the superstition of these ignorant tribes, they harbor at the bottom of their hearts a deep aversion to this class of men. The Chiquitos of Paraguay once massacred them all, saying they were more harmful than useful.[1] The Kalmuks and Laplanders often express the same opinion about their soothsayers.[2] How, then, does it happen that emerging from this condition of savagery, men often grant an extensive authority to these purported organs of heaven? To the contrary, given that they are growing in knowledge, should they not liberate themselves from a dominion that rests only on their ignorance?

In order to solve this problem—which contains all of history's problems—one has to discover a cause whose action is uniform. That means one in the absence of which the priesthood would have only precarious, limited authority, while being present confers awesome, immense, unlimited credentials upon priests.

Should we seek the cause of this development in the religious disposition itself, which, when it takes control of the soul, elevates it above all present and visible interests? If so, the priesthood would everywhere have unlimited influence.

Should we attribute it to the factors that in certain countries restrained its influence? To rivalry with political authority or the ascendancy of a warrior caste? But the contest between the interpreters of heaven and the rulers of the earth occurred

---

1. *Lettres édif.*, VIII, 339–345.

2. Pallas, *Voy.*, I, 359; Georgi, *Beschr.*, XIII; Hogstroem, p. 15.

everywhere. All have seen a warrior caste arise among them. From the identity of the cause, the sameness of the effect ought to exist.

Should we attribute it to climate? It is easy to think that in countries where the climate disposes man to contemplation and gives great energy to his imagination at the same time that it dispenses him from material labor because of the fecundity of the soil, that the class that has assigned itself the task of providing for the needs of this imagination greedy for tales and terrors would rapidly acquire unlimited power.

Nonetheless, the climate cannot be considered the primary cause of the subjection of the human race to priestly corporations. The priesthood has been invested with an unlimited authority in all climates. The Druids of the Gauls in their forests; the magi of the Persians on mountaintops; the priests of Egypt in their marshes: they not only have exercised an equal authority, but owe this power to a similar organization. The Brahmins of India and the Drottes of Scandinavia, the former under burning skies, the others in the midst of snow, are brothers wearing different clothing owing to the degree of heat or cold. They nonetheless display an unmistakable family resemblance.

On the other hand, there are very hot climates where we find no powerful priesthood. The jongleurs of several black tribes have little more power than the shamans of Tartary. Among the Greeks, the priesthood always had very little power, while its influence among the Gauls was almost unlimited.

Now, for a cause to be recognized as sufficient, it is not strictly necessary that the effect exist only because of that cause, because it could have occurred for another reason; on the other hand, it is at least indispensable that, everywhere the cause exists, the effect is found. In this light, we have to see climate as a secondary, accessory cause.

It is the same thing with the terrors inspired by the calamities of nature.

There is no doubt that one must place natural catastrophes among the factors of social, and especially religious, institutions whose memory is preserved in the traditions of almost all the peoples of the earth.

In ordinary circumstances, man is threatened only by the dangers resulting from the customary actions of the objects that surround him. Even then, however, he is propelled by the fear these objects inspire to address himself to those who say they are heaven's confidants, the gods' favorites and intermediaries. How much more, therefore, when all the elements are unleashed and he experiences great calamities, must he rush headlong into all the excesses of superstition and fall at the feet of whomever appears to have some credit with the powers that now threaten him? It is not fraud that engenders terror, but terror that solicits fraud. It presents an easy target, which in fact runs under the yoke, crying out for divine assistance and supernatural support in the face of inexplicable calamities.

However, there are peoples among whom great natural disasters have occurred who are not subject to priests. The annals of Greece are full of traditions relative to a flood. Everywhere this country experienced terrible upheavals. But at least since the heroic age, the Greeks are remarkable for their independence from priestly authority.

It is the same with the effects of colonies.

All nations attribute their departure from the primitive state to the arrival of some foreign colony. The Indians speak of the Samaneens come from the North, who removed them from a condition very little different from that of brutes.[3]

According to plausible hypotheses, Egyptian civilization comes from Ethiopian[4] and Indian colonies. Greek civilization was the work of Phoenicians and

---

3. In recalling this Indian tradition, we do not claim to raise here any of the questions that pertain to the origin and existence of the Samaneens, either as a nation or as a sect. It is indifferent to us whether someone considers them to be a Chinese colony that entered a part of India or a sect of indigenous philosophers, religious reformers, disciples of Buddha, and enemies of the division into castes who were chased from their homeland and triumphed in other countries. Each of these opinions contains its plausibility; the last one is based upon great probabilities. The name "Samaneen" can come from a Sanskrit word *sammen*, which means "men who have overcome their passions." In this connection, it is remarkable that Clement of Alexandria and Saint Jerome, who gave to the gymnosophists the names *semnoi* and *samanaioi*, also mention Buddha, while Porphyry attributes to them a monastic regimen similar to that of Buddhist priests. But whatever is true about these conjectures, one fact remains constant. The Indians say they owe their learning to the Samaneens, Brahmins speak of the *nation of Samaneens* they replaced (Lacroze, *Christ. des Indes*), and the oldest and most universal tradition in India maintains that the ancestors of the Brahmins and the *nayrs* or *cutteries* (warriors) came from the south and subjugated the first inhabitants of this country (Legentil, I, 90–91). This proves that despite their claims to antiquity, the Indians themselves follow the common opinion of all peoples, according to which each relates their civilization to colonies. As for the substance of the question, see Klaproth, *Asia polygl.*, pp. 42ff.

4. Since the recent discoveries of Mr. Champollion, discoveries that confirm the investigations of learned Germans, we could have replaced the word "plausible" with "certain," while taking the precaution of observing that the civilizing of Egypt by the Ethiopians does not determine the question of the originality of Ethiopian civilization. It could have been brought to Ethiopia from India, then subsequently transplanted to Egypt.

Egyptians. Etruria was inhabited by primitives when the Lydians, then the Pelasgians arrived. It appears that Phoenicia civilized Gaul, and that Gaul rendered
the same service to portions of Germany. To this we can add that the inhabitants
of Scandinavia did not know the social state when the victorious Dacians made
their way there.

But one must distinguish four sorts of colonies in antiquity. Some were wholly
military, others both military and priestly; others, purely sacerdotal; a few, finally,
neither military nor sacerdotal.

By military, we refer to those colonies that took over the entire country. A few
partial victories do not justify the designation. No colony is established without
battle, but when the result is the mixing of the two peoples, this is not military in
the sense we give the term.

Purely military colonies do not advantage priestly authority. The effect of the
conquest is not theocratic government but military or feudal government (if we
can use a modern term in talking about antiquity). The conquest sometimes even
destroys, or at least limits, priestly authority. This authority was much less in the
new establishments of the barbarians in the Roman Empire than in their former
homelands.

Purely sacerdotal colonies introduce a priesthood that becomes all-powerful
only by degrees. Such was probably the Phoenicians' influence on the Gauls.

Colonies that are neither military nor priestly eventually mix with the indigenous people. Civilization progresses as a result, but priests as a body do not gain in
stature. We will see the Greeks civilized by colonies that came from a country that
was wholly subject to priestly authority but remain free of this authority because
these colonies did not have priests for leaders.

Finally, sacerdotal and military colonies establish a priesthood that, if it is not
the sole power, is always the first of powers. Ethiopians[5] exercised this influence
on Egypt.

5. On the similarities of the Ethiopians and the Egyptians, and the mutual exchanges and invasions of the two peoples, see Heeren, *Idées*, etc., I, 431–434. The first civilization of Egypt evidently
came from priestly colonies, which gave fixed abodes to nomadic tribes and subjugated them (ibid.,
175). The priests of Meroë in Ethiopia, having the custom of sending colonies everywhere their admission seemed possible, planted colonies that, whether by acceptance or force, caused the triumph of
the worship of their gods and of a government similar to that of the metropolis. Ammonium in the
desert was, according to the formal testimony of Herodotus (II, 42), a colony of this sort. Not only
did one find a temple and an oracle based on the Ethiopian model there, but the caste of priests chose

It is certain, therefore, that colonies could extend the dominion of priests over countries in which they would not have naturally arisen. But it also is obvious that their action cannot be regarded as a first cause. To say that one colony has imposed certain institutions on another is to explain why the latter has received them. But one still has to explain why they were established in the home country of the colony.

It therefore is not in man's nature nor in the climate, not in natural catastrophes nor in the migrations of peoples, that the cause we are seeking can be found. It resides in a circumstance that, because it is connected with the ideas that man conceives of the beings he worships, is both necessary and sufficient to solve the problem.

---

a king drawn from themselves and who was, like Meroë, only their instrument, or rather their slave (Diod., 11). Thebes and Elephantine in Upper Egypt were two other similar colonies; but the numerous political revolutions of Egypt prevented them from remaining as faithful to the customs of their original homeland as Ammonium, separated from the rest of the world by the desert that surrounded it (Heeren, *Idées*, etc., II, 441–518, 567).

The memory of several of these colonies had to be lost. Sometimes, though, monuments rise against the silence of history. At the time of the destruction of Persepolis by Muslims, someone discovered in the foundations of one of the principal temples of this city a precious stone called *tutya*, which exists only in India, without anything indicating how it could have been brought there (Goerres, *Mythen Gesch.*, I, 261). Chaldeans, says Abulfarage (*Hist. dyn.*, p. 184), taught the men of the West to raise temples to the stars.

A remarkable thing! The organization of the Indian priesthood is reproduced on some of the islands of the South Seas (Forster, *Voy. round the World*, II, 153–154; Fréville, I, 458). Thus it is probable that these islands were populated by Indian colonies. The Gauls did not know the use of statues except by their commerce with the Phoenicians (*Mém. de l'Acad. des inscript.*, XXIV, 359–360). Justin, as the summarizer of Trogue Pompey (who was born in Gaul), merits a certain confidence in what he tells us about Gaul. He affirms that before being civilized by colonies, the Gauls worshipped stones, trees, weapons: in other words, at this period they professed a worship similar to that of primitive savages. Phoenician colonies arrived. Phoenicia was always subject to priestly corporations, and their colonies brought to Gaul all their doctrines and usages. There is the most perfect conformity between the institutions and even the teachings of the two peoples. (On the interactions of ancient peoples with the Gauls, see Bochart in Chanaan, *Mém. de l'Acad. des inscript.*, VII; on the worship of Isis, which extends even to Thuringer and Silesia, Meiners, *Crit. Gesch.*, I, 124; Laureau, *Hist. de France avant Clovis.*)

CHAPTER 4

On the Cause That, Whenever It Exists, Gives the Priesthood Much Power

There are peoples whose entire existence depends upon the observation of the stars. This may be because their geographical situation invites or requires them to sail and navigate; or because the nature of their soil requires, as a condition of their subsistence or their safety, precise astronomical calculations.

There are other peoples among whom natural phenomena of all sorts abound that are helpful to foresee or at least natural to observe with attentive curiosity.

When man finds himself in such circumstances, because of the nature of the religious sentiment he must infallibly direct his adoration toward either the torches in the sky or the unknown forces he supposes govern the terrestrial phenomena.

Once again, it is not his gratitude toward one or his terror before the other that initially suggests to him the idea and the need of worship. But the idea that possesses him, the need that torments him, leads him to seek objects of worship. He naturally puts in first place those that have the most influence on his existence.

Therefore there are peoples who have been led to substitute the worship of stars for the crude worship we described earlier. There are others that an equal necessity forced to worship the elements.[1]

Often these two kinds of divinities are invoked together: the sun, at once a

1. We do not present the view that star-worship is one of the two primitive forms of religion as exclusively our own. It comes close to the system that makes astronomy the basis of all worship. However, the learned men who have adopted this hypothesis seem to us to have committed two errors. First, they applied it indiscriminately to all the nations of the earth, while several could have followed a very different path. In the second place, they have not sufficiently appreciated that even among the peoples whose religion was based solely on astronomy, underneath the scientific cult there was a purely popular one. Its explanation cannot be sought in science but rather, on one hand, in the passions; on the other, in interests; both of which are always and everywhere the same.

globe of fire and the king of the planets, is the center or common feature of the two religious systems.

Now, these two systems immediately create a priesthood vested with an authority that the jongleurs of savages could not have had. It is impossible to transform the elements or stars into individual fetishes. No one can claim them as his exclusive property. They necessarily become collective deities, and priests are needed to represent the nation to them.

Moreover, to come to know the movements of the stars—to observe natural phenomena in general—a certain amount of attention and study is required.

From the beginning of societies, when the mass of people is still quite ignorant, this necessity establishes corporate bodies whose occupation is the study of

---

We will see later that this popular worship was necessarily more or less disguised fetishism, but, elaborated by the priests, it was associated with the scientific cult and mixed with it. It follows that any explanation that begins with only one idea is necessarily more or less false.

The worship of stars and of the elements once introduced into fetishism, fetishism is placed under them. On one hand, because the peoples who begin with star-worship desire for their daily use gods who are more individual; on the other, because those who begin from fetishism place the stars and the elements among their fetishes (Georgi, *Beschr. Russ. Voelkersch.*, p. 289; Adair, *Hist. of the Amer. Indians*, p. 217). The fetishistic tribes that in Africa (Desmarchais, *Voy. en Guinée*, I, 100), in America (Ulloa, *Voy. en Amér.*), and among the Kamtschatka (Steller, *Descript. du Kamtschatka*, p. 281) render no worship to the stars are the most primitive of all. The less primitive tribes, and at the same time the most numerous, without making them their sole divinities, nonetheless place them among the divinities (Acosta, *Hist. des Indes occidentals*; Laet, *Beschryv. v. Vest-Ind.*, 164; Torti, *Relation de la Louisiane*). But a fundamental distinction always exists. Among the nations who begin with star-worship, the terrestrial gods occupy only a subordinate place. The elements and the stars are on the first rung. According to Diodorus (fragment cited by Eusebius, *Praep. Evangel.*, bk. II), the Egyptians distinguished two classes of gods: the first, eternal and immortal, such as the sun, the moon, the planets. They added the winds and all the beings of that nature. The gods born on the earth formed the second class. On the other hand, the peoples who were initially fetishistic and who later divinized, as visible objects, the constellations or the elements as mysterious forces, did not place them at the head of the celestial hierarchy. Apollo and Diana in Greek mythology, for example, are secondary gods, distinct from the sun and the moon, whom the Greeks called Helios and Selene. It was only at a much later period of Greek polytheism that the poets brought them together. At the time of the tragedies this had not yet occurred. Aeschylus distinguishes the rays of the sun from those of Apollo (*Suppliant.*, 198). Euripides does not consider Diana to be the moon but rather the tutelary *genia* of this planet (*Iphig. en Aulide*, 1570). It follows that despite all these later additions, the two worships retained their original tendencies.

the stars and their goal, the observation of nature. Their discoveries become their property.[2]

Since these corporations make themselves the exclusive depository of the emerging science, they cannot fail to acquire a greater influence than naturally belongs to the priesthood in religions whose gods are not the objects of scientific observations.

There is more. Alongside the study of the regular movements of the stars, soon there is the study of their supposed relations with men. Next to the observation of earthly phenomena is placed the interpretation of these phenomena, which seem to speak a sacred language to mankind.[3] The worship of celestial bodies that leads to astronomy also leads to astrology,[4] the worship of elements leads to divination:[5] two quite extensive, and much more immediate, means of influence for the priesthood.[6]

2. "What is more natural than for the Egyptians, whose well-being is connected to a periodic event, to have a class of calculators, geometers, and astronomers from the first moment they established themselves in the Delta?" (Herder, *Phil. de l'hist.*, III, 117).

3. Pyromancy was a part of the religion of the Persians. Fire, said the Zend Avesta (Izeschne, II, 67), gives knowledge of the future, science, and inspires charming speech.

4. "The Egyptian priests," said Diodorus (I, 2, 23), "had astronomical tables from time immemorial, and the love of this science was hereditary among them. They studied the influence of the planets on sublunary beings and determined the goods and evils that their different aspects announced to men." There was an order of priests especially devoted to astrology. During their feasts they carried the symbols of this science (Clem. Alex., *Strom.*, bk. VI; Schmidt, *De sacerdot. et sacrif. Aegypt.*, pp. 152–156).

5. For the peoples who worship the elements, natural phenomena are so many signs by which nature itself speaks indiscriminately to all men, a language that only the learned can understand (Creuzer, trans. by Mr. Guigniaut, p. 4).

6. "A class of men devoted specifically to the observation of stars," says Volney, "had arrived at the discovery of the cause of eclipses and could predict them. Struck with astonishment at this ability to predict, the people imagined that it was a divine gift that could be extended to everything. On one hand, we see anxious and credulous curiosity, which constantly wants to know the future; on the other hand, crafty greed, which constantly wants to add to its pleasures and possessions; when they act together results a methodical art of deception and charlatanism that is called astrology, i.e., the art of predicting all the events of life by studying the stars and by knowing their aspects and influence. True astronomy being at the basis of this art, its difficulties restrict it to a small number of initiates who, under different names such as seers, diviners, prophets, and magicians, became an all-powerful priestly body among all the peoples of Antiquity" (*Rech. sur l'hist. ancienne*, I, 172–173).

As a consequence, one finds that priests, while they have little authority over fetishistic peoples (or who come to polytheism from fetishism), have an immense authority over the nations given to the worship of the stars and the elements.

The religion natural to the savage neither requires nor allows for priests other than the isolated jongleurs. Worship of the stars calls for astronomers; worship of the elements, natural scientists, or at least men who claim to know and control the hidden forces of the universe. From all this comes an indefinite increase of authority.

Now let us consider the facts. They will support the reasonings just provided.

In this passage the author perhaps attributes too much influence to artifice and subterfuge. Perhaps astrology had a different origin than deception. The stars, and in general the natural phenomena, before civilization could exercise a more marked influence on man and the discoveries that it occasions, would have surrounded him with boulevards that would protect him from external impressions. This influence still weighs upon animals; the sick experience it, and savages are not insensitive to it. In the infancy of the human race, a more intimate correspondence could exist between physical nature and man. This correspondence never had the result of predicting the events belonging to the moral world, i.e., that depend upon the intellect and the will. But it could have allowed man to have a presentiment of physical events such as storms, earthquakes, and other large material catastrophes in a way we no longer can conceive. A poet has said: "In subjugating nature, we have placed barriers between her and us: and to revenge herself for being made a slave she has become mute." This does not mean that the human race was wrong to do so. In triumphing over the material world it has fulfilled its destiny, it follows its path. But it ought not to be the case that, master today of what formerly mastered it, it therefore simply denies the possibility of another condition; a state in which man, without strength against the impressions from without and subject to their then-irresistible action, sought resources proportionate to this unarmed position and interrogated these impressions rather than defeating and dominating them.

CHAPTER 5

Facts That Support the Previous Assertions

Let us return for a moment to the savage tribes. It will convince us of this truth.

In America, the inhabitants of Florida principally worshipped the sun and the moon.[1] All-powerful priests maintained them subject; and the cruelest as well as most lascivious priestly practices characterized their worship.[2] In Africa, the Jagas[3] hold the sun as the highest deity; stars direct them in their wars; and temporal as well as spiritual authority is united in the hands of the *calandola*, or high priest.[4]

We do not deny that accidental circumstances could have subjected some peoples among whom star worship was not present to theocratic authority. Thus, among the blacks of Whydah, whose national deity is a serpent of a particular type, the priesthood forms a powerful body. But this is because formerly, at the time of a decisive battle, this serpent deserted the enemy and became their miraculous ally: adroit jongleurs took advantage and devoted themselves to its service.[5] This small example does not weaken the general rule. The neighboring tribes were not seduced by it; and since no other event caused them to deviate from their natural path, and because they do not render exclusive worship to the sun, their own priesthood has remained without influence or regular authority.

---

1. Lafiteau, *Moeurs des Sauvages*; *Allgem. Gesch. der Laend. und Voelk. von America.*

2. Rochefort, *Hist. nat. et mor. des Antilles*; Coreal, *Voy. aux Ind. occid. Allgem. Hist. der Reis.*, XVII; Lescarbot, in Purchas, *Pilgrim.*; Garcil. de la Vega, *Hist. Flor.*

3. It is doubtful that the Jagas are a tribe; they perhaps are a sect; but if this were the case, our claim would be even better proven, since by bringing together savages of several tribes, the worship of stars would have created a separate horde, one professing a distinct worship and subjugated by the pontiffs of this new cult.

4. *Parallèle des religions*, I, 70.

5. *Culte des dieux fétiches*, p. 31.

If from savage tribes we pass to civilized peoples,[6] the same fact will strike us with the same evidence.

The Egyptian religion was founded on astronomy.[7] The authority of the Egyptian priesthood was unlimited. Near to Egypt, Ethiopia was also inhabited by tribes that worshipped stars; it was also famous for the absolute power of the priests of Meroë. Syrians adored the sun and the moon under the names of Aglibolos and Malachbul.[8] All the world knows of the shameless orgies, the fanatical rites, and obscene mutilations of the Syrian priesthood. Similarly, the veneration the Persian religion had for the elements is too well known to need proof.[9] These

6. We need to tell our readers that even though we are now treating only the social state closest to the primitive state, distinguishing their various periods is impossible in the case of those peoples who were subjugated by a priesthood, while the relevant distinctions strike all eyes in the annals of independent peoples. This comes not only from the shortage of historical records, as Goerres notes (*As. Myth. Gesch.*, II, 445–447) with respect to Egypt, which ran a course of more than two thousand years, but of which we only know the last fifth; of all countries Egypt was the least "national" and the most marked by foreign importations. This difficulty also comes from the fact that, when they hold power, priests immediately bring the human race up to the level of civilization that is necessary to their existence and power. Then, however, they stop without allowing one further step. It is wholly otherwise with nations that enjoy their liberty. Compare the Greeks of Homer and those of Pericles: you will see in the entire nation regular, manifest progress. Compare the Egyptians as they are depicted under Menes or Technatis and those about whom we have more certain ideas from the time of Psammetichus: you will see the same ignorance in the nation; only the priests will have advanced.

It follows that in treating in this chapter the power of priests at the first degree of civilization, we are forced to draw our proofs from the entire span of their history, while for the Greeks we must never go beyond the heroic times.

7. Everything in Egypt, observes Mr. de Pauw, makes reference to astronomy. The cuirass of Pharaoh Amasis, consecrated to Minerva in the island of Rhodes, was remarkable by its weave, in which each thread was woven with 364 others, thus alluding to the length of the year. Herodotus describes this cuirass (*Rech. sur les Egypt. et les Chinois*, II, 319). The largest constructions of Egypt, the Labyrinth, Memnonium, etc., were intended to present to view the symbols of the astronomical cycles and at the same time to preserve knowledge of them. Conjointly, for a reason we indicated earlier, the elements were worshipped with the stars. The names of the eight great Egyptian gods could be read on an obelisk. These gods were Fire, Water, Heaven, Earth, Sun, Moon, Day, and Night (Theo Smyrn., *De mus.*, c. 17; Zenobius, *Cent. Prov.*, c. 78).

8. Selden, *De diis Syr.*; Montfaucon, *Antiq. expl.*, II, 2, 389.

9. Herodotus says "the Persians offered sacrifices to the Sun, the Moon, the Earth, Fire, Water, and to the Winds. These were the only gods they worshiped from time immemorial. . . . They called the vault of the heavens Jupiter" (I, 131). See also Diogenes Laertius (*Prooemium*). Clement of Alexandria says that the elements were for the Persians what statutes were for the Greeks and animals for

peoples put to death anyone who sullied either fire or waves.[10] Among them, this worship was combined with star-worship.[11] Therefore, even though they were often threatened by kings, and sometimes were the victims of cruel persecutions, the magi successfully fought their enemies and always regained authority.

The observation of the stars was an essential part of the Indian religion,[12] and

---

the Egyptians. Descendants of the Persians, the Guebres, still have such respect for fire and water that they do not dare employ one to extinguish the other. To pit two sacred elements against each other would seem to be a crime.

10. Firmicus; Herodotus; Strabo, XV; Zend Avesta, passim.

11. The Chinese historians who speak of the religion of the Persians under the reigns of the Sassanides express themselves in the same terms as Herodotus. The majority of the prayers contained in the Zend Avesta are addressed to the elements and the stars. According to Porphyry (*De antro nymph.*, 6), the cave where Zoroaster lived on the frontier of Persia represented the terrestrial zones and personified elements (Clem. Alex., *Strom.*, V, 5).

We said above that the worship of stars and the worship of the elements always end by being combined. One can see how this combination operated in Persia in the researches of Mr. de Hammer (*Annales de Vienne et de Heidelberg*, and *Mines de l'Orient*). "The Zend books," says Creuzer (French trans., I, 352), "in concert with all the records and testimony of the Greek authors, prove that Mithras is the sun. The Zend Avesta calls this star the Eye of Ormuzd, the resplendent hero pursuing his destiny with confidence, he who gives life to the deserts, the highest of Izeds, who never sleeps, the protector of the country." See ibid., p. 355. The seven prophet-kings of Persia, named in the *Désatir* (V, III, viii, 20), were each distinguished by the special worship of a planet. In the sequel (we will have the opportunity to prove this when we treat the purported theism of the Persians), many foreign notions having entered into their religion, the worship of elements was concentrated in some sects of magi (Cassiodor., *Hist. tripart.*, X, 30). One of the principal ones attributed the origin of things to the three elements, fire, earth, and water (Hammer, extracts of *Burbani-Katii*).

12. In India today there is still a sect (in truth very small) that recognizes no other god than the sun. All the Indian tales have a manifest relationship to astronomy. We pick one at random. The god Agni, having become lustful toward the wives of the seven *rishis*, so celebrated in Indian mythology, fearing the anger of these holy men being directed against him if he seduced their wives, the wife of this god assumed the figure of each of them and in this way satisfied her husband, albeit by deceiving him. Nonetheless, the indignant *rishis* put away their wives, who were placed in the zodiac and became the planets (*Asiat. Res.*, IX, 86–87). In the same way the twelve Adityas, the sons of Aditi, the daughter of Dakcha, the son of Brama, are the sun traversing the twelve signs of the zodiac; close by are the twelve *genii* who preside over the twelve months of the year.

Alongside star-worship one also finds the worship of elements. The Brahmins invoke the Earth, the Air, Fire, Water, Heaven, and especially worship the Earth. In the prayers of Yajurveda, the elements are invoked, sometimes by themselves, sometimes with the gods who preside over the elements being invoked. The worshipper says: "O Fire, grant me prudence in virtue of my offerings"; and a moment after: "let Fire and Prajapati grant me wisdom! Let Air and Indra give me science!" (*Asiat. Res.*, VIII,

India has always recognized the dominion of the Brahmans. Everything leads us to believe that China, while atheistic today, in the midst of the crudest superstitions, in former times professed a religion that subjected the people to priests.[13] And we find astronomy[14] at each stage of its records, and in its rites, vestiges of the worship of the elements.[15] Mexican priests exercised a terrible authority; the sun was the principal divinity of Mexico.[16] The bloody despotism of the Carthaginian priesthood is attested to by all historians.[17] The Carthaginians were devoted to

433–434). In a dialogue that is part of the Samaveda, several sages go to consult a king versed in divine things, Aswapaty, son of Cecaya, over the nature of the divine. He questions each of them concerning the object of his worship. One says he adores the Sky, the other the Sun, a third the Air, the fourth, Ether, a fifth, Water, a sixth, the Earth. The king tells them that this is to worship the Supreme Being, the universal soul, in its separate parts, and that they should adore it as the reunion of all these things (*Asiat. Res.*, VIII, 473–467).

13. See the last chapter of book VI.

14. "China's history speaks of astronomy from its beginnings, and its first kings were astronomers. Everywhere we see immense observatories, towers elevated to the heavens, and vast palaces that are constructed astronomically, and temples, pyramids, and cities of the Seven Portals in honor of the seven planets, as well as empires divided into as many provinces as the sky, bearing the name of the Decan or of the sign that presides over it, the numbers 3, 7, 12, 28, 36, 52, and 360 regulating societies and towns, and entering into the most ordinary things of life. The king of China is dressed in the color devoted to the sun. Several emperors have descended from this luminous body, from the Moon, as well as from the Dog or the Great Bear" (Rabaut, *Lettr. sur l'hist. primit. de la Grèce*, p. 242).

15. Formerly the Chinese addressed their religious homage to the Air and the Earth (Notice of the *Yï-king*, p. 428, *Mém. de l'Acad. des inscript.*, V, 118). Their musical system is still based upon the relations they suppose to exist between these two elements. The barbarous custom of casting children into the river is perhaps a vestige of the worship of rivers (*Mém. sur les Chin.*, II, 40).

16. Like those of the Egyptians, the gods of the Mexicans were divided into three classes. Those of the first were the Sun, the Moon, the planets, Water, Fire, the Earth; that is, the elements and stars. At the birth of their children, the Mexicans mainly invoke Water, the Moon, and the Sun. The oldest and most remarkable monuments of Mexico, the pyramids of Teotihuacan, were devoted to the Sun and the Moon. They served as tombs of kings and as observatories (Clavigero, Humboldt). The kings of Mexico devoted themselves ardently to the study of astrology. Their solar year was more perfect than that of the Greeks and the Romans. The king of Tenochtitlan, Nezahual, who reigned when the Spanish came, was so renowned for his expertise in this science that Montezuma, frightened by negative auspices, appealed to him to explain them. The number of priests, *topitzqui*, was prodigious in Mexico. There were six thousand in a single temple in the capital (Gomar, *Crónica della Nueva España*, cap. 80). The number in the entire empire may have reached four million. Two high priests, probably elected by the priestly corporation, were at their head.

17. Among the Carthaginians, the priesthood does not seem to have formed a corporation similar to that of the Brahmins or the Druids. However, it was a deputation from the order of the clergy that,

star-worship.[18] The nations that neighbored the Jews were for the most part subject to a tyrannical clergy, and they led the people of God into astrolatry. When Ezekiel wanted to depict its guilty defection, he showed the Levites turning their back on the tabernacle and rendering homage to the rising sun. And when Josiah declared a war to the death on idolatry, he confiscated the horses and burned the chariots devoted to this fiery idol.[19]

If we leave the East and South for the West and the North, we will find that the worship of the elements produced the same effects in Germany and Gaul[20] as astronomy did in India and Egypt. We will see the forests of this part of the globe still harboring the hideous monuments of the absolute and bloodthirsty authority of the Druids: at the head of the idolatrous objects proscribed by Canute are the Sun, Fire, Moon, and the Earth.[21] This last deity was invoked under the name

---

together with some chief citizens, was sent to the Roman camp during the final siege of Carthage in order to learn the will of the Senate from the consul Censorinum (Appian., *de Bello punico*). In any case, the priests were very powerful in this republic. Many of them wore the purple, symbol of command. Generals were subject to soothsayers, whom they dared not disobey (Diod., II). Without any hesitation, they gave their children over to the sacred knife; and their colonies were constrained to keep intact and practice the worship of the metropolis (Diod., ibid.), an obligation that, as we shall see later, is an essential characteristic of priestly polytheism in contrast to free polytheism.

18. The proof of star worship and the worship of the elements among the Carthaginians is found in the treaty concluded in their name by Hannibal with Xenophanes, the envoy of Philip of Macedon. In it, the gods of the Carthaginians are distinguished from those of the Macedonians and the rest of Greece; and the principal ones of these gods are the Sun, the Moon, the Earth, the Sea, and the Rivers (Polyb., VII, 2). The sun was worshipped under the names of Baal, Belsamen, Moloch, and Melkarth; the moon under those of Astarte and Urania. In a particular way the elephant was consecrated to these divinities, because a religious sense prompting it to give homage to them was attributed to the beast (Aelian., *Hist. anim.*, VII, 44; Pliny, *Hist. nat.*, VIII, 1). After his defeat in Sicily, Hamilcar sacrificed victims to the Sea, tossing them into the waves (Diod., XII, 86); and Polybius reports (XV, I) that before their conference with Scipio, the Carthaginian ambassadors worshipped the Earth.

19. II Kings, ch. 23.

20. See Pelloutier, *Hist. des Celtes*, and the testimony of Gregory of Tours, who is more worthy of belief because a chronicle is more impartial than a system. "*Haec generatio fanaticis semper cultibus visa est obsequium praebuisse, nec prorsus agnovere Deum, sibique silvarum atque aquarum ... et aliorum quoque elementorum finxisse formas, ipsasque ut Deum colere, eisque sacrificial delibare consueti*" (bk. II, ch. 10, *ap.* Bouquet, *Recueil*, vol. II). It is probable that the fires of Saint John are a vestige of the worship of elements.

21. "What we understand by pagan idolatry," says Canute, "is when they serve idols, such as the Sun, the Moon, Fire, etc." (*L. L., Politic Canuti regis*, cap. 5, *apud* Lindenbr. in *Glossar.*, p. 1473).

of Hertha by the tribes described by Tacitus;[22] the Slavs adored the god of Air; Chen-Yk, with his Tatars, sacrificed to Heaven, whose son he said he was.[23] And when a new Odin, simultaneously a warrior and a priest, wanted to subjugate the Scandinavians, he preached the identity of their supreme god with the sun.

Thus in quite different countries, among peoples with very opposite customs, thanks to the worship of elements and the stars, the priesthood acquired a power that we can barely conceive of today.

22. Tacitus, *German.*, ch. 40.
23. D'Herbelot, *Bibl. Orient.*, VI, 96, 144–148.

CHAPTER 6

On Two Apparent Exceptions

History appears to present two exceptions to the principle we just articulated. These two exceptions, the Arabs and the Germans, are found in two different climates and at almost the two extremes of the world.

Caesar tells us that the Germans recognized only visible gods: the sun, the moon, Vulcan.[1] The worship of stars and the elements is clearly indicated. Caesar, however, adds that the Germans had no Druids presiding over sacred matters. They built no temples and only rarely offered sacrifice. In this way we have peoples who both worshipped heavenly bodies and remained independent of sacerdotal power.

But Tacitus contradicts Caesar.[2] According to Tacitus, the Germans had all-powerful priests, and by the ministry of these priests they sacrificed not only animals but humans. People have tried to reconcile these two impressive authorities by supposing a forced migration of Gallic Druids into Germany. This migration would have taken place under the reigns of Tiberius and Claudius; both persecuted the Druids with implacable hostility.[3] The fugitive priests would have brought with them the institutions of their former homeland. All this would have occurred in the interval between Caesar and Tacitus.[4]

This hypothesis, however, is refuted by several uncontestable facts. The unlimited power of the priests of Germany goes back long before the time when, according to the hypothesis, the priestly authority would have been established. The Germanic divinities have indigenous names that rule out a Gallic origin. The German priests sang hymns and canticles that were peculiar to them, and that were com-

1. *B Gall.*, VI.
2. *German.*, 2, 7, 9.
3. *Sustulit (Tiberius) druidas eorum.*
4. Fénelon, *Acad. des inscrip.*, XXIV.

posed in their own language. They were preserved without change after the arrival of the fugitives from Gaul. The latter were received as brothers, not teachers.[5]

Caesar knew only the frontiers of Germany. Tacitus, writing a century later when the interior of the country was invaded if not conquered by the Romans, had to have more exact information and ideas. His testimony is therefore preferable. The Germans do not make an exception to the rule.

We cannot say the same thing about the Arabs. It is certain that even though the stars figured among their divinities, the authority of the priesthood among them was almost nil. Until Mohammed, each tribe and each family created, and changed at will, the objects and rites of its worship.[6] This is because the Arabs were a tribe of hunters, with man being the prey. They laid in wait for travelers in order to plunder them. As hunters, they were fetishists. They worshiped lions, eagles, gazelles—in a word, all the animals of which their environment abounded.[7] Stars were placed among their fetishes,[8] as we showed must happen. But the worship of rocks, a clear indicator of fetishism, held first place.[9] They washed them in oil and wine, a practice we will find among the Greeks. Such was their attachment to one of these idols that we will see this stone resist the efforts of Islam and reappear in the temple of

---

5. Fréret, *Acad. des inscrip.*, XXIV.

6. Gibbon, ch. 50.

7. Des Broses, *Culte des dieux fétiches*, p. 111, drawn from *Alsharistani*. For the ancient idolatry of the Arabs, see Pococke, *Specim. hist. arab.*; Sale, *Prelimin. Disc. to the Koran*; Assemanni, *Bibliothèq. Oriental.*

8. The Hamyarites worshipped the sun and the Takif tribe the moon. Mohammed destroyed their idols, to which they were so attached that they made several attempts to preserve them (Abulfeda, *Vita Mohammed*; Pococke, *Specim. hist. arab.*, p. 90). It is probable that the Turkish crescent has its origin in the ancient worship of the moon (Selden, *De diis. Syr.*, p. 189).

9. The three most famous idols, Allat, Alazza, and Mana, were, respectively, a stone-idol, a piece of wood, and a nondescript stone (Maximus of Tyr, *Dissert.*, 8; Clem. Alex. in *Protrept.* Arnob., *Adv. gent.*, VI). The idol of Thushara was a square black stone, six feet tall and two feet wide, placed on a gold base. The Arabs worshipped it, said Suidas, by sacrifices, libations, and feasts; and Porphyry adds that the Dumatians in Araby annually immolated to it a young man, whom they buried under the altar. The Arabs also worshipped a tree, probably acacia, and even built a temple for it, which Mohammed had destroyed by his general, Khalid bin Walid. The tribe of the Mudaites rendered worship to a lion, the tribe of Morad to a horse, that of Hamyar to an eagle (Pococke, *Specim. hist. arab.*, p. 93; Hyde, *De rel. pers.*, p. 133; Sale, *Prelim. Disc.*, p. 24). Each head of a family had his own god or fetish, to whom he bid farewell when he left and whom he saluted when he returned (Pococke, ibid., p. 95). Certain idols were subject to the influence of the stars: they were called Therapim.

the Kaaba, where, despite the Prophet, it received the homage of Muslims.[10] The character of the Arabs constantly triumphed over the circumstances that could have subjected them to priestly power.[11] Dispersed after Alexander's conquests, the magi took refuge in the desert and lived with its wild inhabitants.[12] But their influence did not survive into the safe haven, and at most they introduced a few of their rites into Arab fetishism. Even these were isolated and barely recognizable.[13] In fact, these rites, which we will speak about later, will allow us to prove several of our assertions concerning the character that the priesthood gives to religion.

10. The worship of the black stone is of most ancient lineage in Araby, and above all in Mecca, according to what the authors of the country tell us. When Mohammed had the Kaaba rebuilt, he placed this stone—an object of popular worship—in the wall, wanting to remove it from their view and thus end this worship. But still attached to their ancient habit, the new converts forced the ministers of Islam to find pretexts for their indulgence in this regard, and they invented various traditions to explain the worship of the black stone (*Asiat. Res.*, IV, 3, 88). The Muslims named it Hagiar-Alassovad. Abdallah, son of Zobair, had it removed and transported to the sanctuary of the Kaaba. Hadschadsch had it put back in its original place. When, under the caliphate of Moctader, the Carmathians pillaged Mecca, they again removed the stone, rightly suspecting it of being an ancient idol. It was not returned for twenty years. The caliphs had a piece placed in one of the columns of the portal of their palace in Baghdad, and all who entered and left the palace felt obliged to kiss it. No Muslim thinks he has satisfied the pilgrimage to Mecca if he has not kissed this marvelous stone several times. To it is attributed the capacity to float, to fatten the camel that bears it, and to sometimes become so heavy that several oxen or camels cannot move it. The ancient history of the Arabs recounts that this stone was worshipped at all times and, hidden in the Zemzem fountain so that it would not be profaned, was rediscovered by Abdul-Muttalib, Mohammed's grandfather, instructed by a miraculous revelation. This anecdote proves the antiquity of the worship of stones among the Arabs, and the traces it has left.

11. Strabo, bk. XVI, attributes to the Arabs, on the credit of some unknown authors, a sort of division into castes. But with respect to Araby, Strabo collected many obviously false things.

12. Gagnier, *Vie de Mahomet*, III, 114; Pococke, *Specim. hist. arab.*, pp. 146–150.

13. Human sacrifices were probably of this number.

CHAPTER 7

On the Variety in the Organization and Forms of Priestly Authority

The organization of the priesthood was not the same among the nations that star-worship, or the worship of the hidden forces of nature, had subjected to the power of priests. Nonetheless they can be reduced to two categories: hereditary castes or tribes, and corporations in which elections seem to have played a part in their composition.

CHAPTER 8

On the Division into Castes

The division into castes could only have had a religious notion as its primary cause. The other causes that have been put forth—the superior beauty of privileged races, the legislator's will, conquest, or the reasonable submission of peoples—are inadequate and superficial explanations.

The beauty of the races upon which some have wanted to endow this sort of superiority itself requires an explanation. The difficulty is postponed rather than resolved.

With modern scholars,[1] we acknowledge that the two or even three superior castes that dominated in India originally formed only one nation, and that when this nation came down from the mountains and defeated the indigenous people, it was distinguished from them by a whiteness of color and regularity of features.[2] It confirmed its rule by fixed institutions clothed with the authority of religion. We, however, must also recognize that these fixed institutions had already existed in the highlands of the Himalayas and the Caucasus before being established on the plains of Indostan. It is impossible to believe that the second caste, that of warriors, at the very moment when victory would have swelled its pride and stoked its courage, would have agreed to an innovation that was to its detriment. Soldiers guided by priests, however, can preserve in the midst of their military successes a superstitious respect for the mysterious theocracy to whom they attribute their

1. Klaproth, *Asiat. polygl.*, pp. 42ff.

2. "The difference in color and profile between the Spanish Creoles and the Peruvians is not as great," says Heeren, "as what one observes between the Brahmins and the pariahs; I chose this comparison," he adds, "because the establishment of the Spanish in the New World, sword and cross in hand, perhaps offers a faithful image of the armed establishment of the Brahmins in the midst of the natives of India, if we knew the history of these latter" (Heeren, *Idées*, I, 610).

victories. But this theocracy must rest on earlier customs and habits. Altars can be brought into camp, but they cannot be raised there de novo. As long as we have not discovered the cause of the priestly preeminence, of which the division into castes is only the development, we will be no closer to a solution. Thus the beauty of the conquerors and the deformity of the defeated, even granting them their fullest extent (and despite notable exceptions),[3] do not explain the establishment of castes. One has to seek among the conquerors to find the principle.

When Aristotle[4] attributed this to Sesostis, he followed the custom of the Greeks, who attributed all the institutions of whose origin they were ignorant to this conqueror. No legislator, however, assaults natural equality in this way, unless he finds some support in preexisting opinion.

The Indians of today speak of an earlier experience of anarchy and the sentiment that then would have led the people to avoid it at all costs by establishing innumerable barriers against disorder. Like us, however, they are civilized men who when they form conjectures concerning very distant times lend them the refinements of their own civilization. In the abasement of the inferior castes and their acquiescence in it there is something that neither the exhaustion caused by anarchy nor the desire for order explains. Nor can it be the result of a simple political arrangement. It must go back to a social state where the majority of human beings did not yet possess knowledge of their rights or the awareness of their strength.[5]

As we said above, priestly government is not the result of conquest. Nothing resembles these mysterious barriers raised among the inhabitants of the same country. In a military government, the inequality of ranks has a real difference, that of force, as its principle. The principle of the inequality of castes owes to an opinion of an original stain, an indelible mark that no disproportion between forces can efface. The Brahmins of India did not acquire political authority by right. They do not form the caste of warriors from whom most often kings are drawn.[6] We, however, see these kings and these warriors try in vain to enter into the sacred caste, and finally sheathe their swords before the barrier separating them from the

3. See n. 32 below.

4. *Politics,* VIII, 10.

5. "The natural duty of the Brahmin is peace, abstinence, zeal, purity, patience, rectitude, wisdom, science and theology. The natural duty of the *cuttery* is courage, glory, generosity, and nobility. The natural duty of the *vaisya* is work, the cultivation of fields, and the conduct of business. The natural duty of the *soudra* is servitude" (Bhag. Gita, p. 130).

6. Herder, *Phil. de l'hist.,* III, 35.

unarmed Brahmins. Niebuhr[7] notes as a most unusual occurrence that during his time in India a prince had succeeded in entering the order of Brahmins by means of gifts and adroitness.[8]

It is not that we consider the division into castes exactly as a priestly invention. It could have found its source in a natural disposition of man. He is inclined to render his institutions more fixed by a more or less regular distribution of the different occupations of life among different classes. This tendency, which sometimes prevails in the bosom of civilization, already is seen among savage tribes. The Iroquois and the Algonquins joined together a few centuries ago, on the condition that one would be farmers, the other hunters.[9] Among some African tribes, there are hereditary fishermen and hunters.[10] Among the Turks,[11] the administration

7. *Voy. en Arabie*, II, 17.

8. A German author (Meiners, *De orig. castar. Comm. Soc. Goett.*) has proposed an ingenious system concerning the origin of castes, but which is admissible for only one of the countries that history clearly shows us to have been divided into castes, that is, Egypt, India, and Ethiopia. He supposes two migrations, with the people of the first being subjugated by those of the second, and he considers the intermediate class as the product of the mixing of the two original classes. This hypothesis becomes probable when it is confined to Egypt. We already had the occasion to observe that Egypt was peopled by Ethiopian and Indian colonies (Meiners, *Hist. gén. hum.*, p. 29; Kaempfer, *Hist. du Japon*, II, 90; Rooke, p. 23; Heeren, *Idées*, II, 565–68, and especially n. 7); and the division into castes established in India and in Ethiopia could have been transported by the colonies to their new establishments. And it had to be more easily maintained when the differences of races came to its assistance. Herodotus declares the Egyptians are a dark people with frizzy hair (Herod., II, 104). It is certain that there were several races of men in Egypt, who fought violently: on some newly discovered monuments one sees red men striking or killing dark men (Denon, *Voy. en Egypte*, II, 228; Heeren, II, 544–51), while on an even greater number, on the bas-reliefs of the temple of Osiris on the island of Phila, for example, it is dark men who are killing red men, whom the learned have taken rather plausibly for Hyksos, shepherds, or Jews (Goerres, *As. Myth. Gesch.*, pref., xxxii–xxxiii).

But when the author of this hypothesis that would satisfactorily explain the transplanting of the caste system from one country to another wants to apply it to the origin of this institution, his arguments become false. Every colony whose original homeland would not have already known this division into castes would not have been divided into them. One can therefore attribute to Indian or Ethiopian colonies the origin of this division in Egypt; but one has to look elsewhere to explain the division in India or in Ethiopia; and if, following a widely received tradition (*Voy.* of Legentil, I, 90-91), one claims that the ancestors of the Brahmins were themselves foreigners, the objection would have been pushed back only one step.

9. Charlevoix, *Journal*.

10. Iserts, *Voy.*, p. 224.

11. Porter on the Turks.

of justice is the property of certain families who practice it, if I can put it this way, hereditarily. The Laplanders have races of magicians;[12] and among the mountain dwellers of Scotland one finds races of doctors and poets up to the end of the eighteenth century.[13]

Without the self-interested calculations of the class, therefore, men could consider the children of those they believed favored by the gods to be called to inherit this favor. But the priesthood took advantage of this human inclination, as it does with everything in nature; and in order to better profit from it, the priesthood combined it with an equally natural idea, the distinction between purity and impurity.

There are climates that render certain foods harmful and certain illnesses widespread or contagious. Very hot climates oblige their inhabitants to frequent baths and ablutions. From this came the abstinences or precautions that are indicated by necessity, and soon are consecrated by habit. Priests find in these precautions or abstinences the germ of a mysterious notion that they develop and extend. A thousand indifferent circumstances, a thousand fortuitous encounters, in their doctrine become causes of impurity. Nothing will seem so understandable if one reflects on the multitudes of ceremonies, expiations, and purifications that this notion entails, and in which the intervention of priests was always presented as being indispensable.

Thus the ideas of impurity occupy an important place in religions subject to priests. One sees in Strobius's purported extracts from Hermes that the elements complain of being defiled.[14] The respect the peoples of the West and the North had for them is well known; the fear of profaning them by mixing them with unclean objects; and the view that placed in this latter category everything connected with man—his breath, his hair, and his mortal remains.

What proves that these ideas had become the subjects of an interested calculation is that arbitrariness was soon introduced in the interdiction of various foods. Their healthfulness or lack thereof ceased to be the primary concern. The distinction being already established, people wanted to explain prohibitions in that way, but in most cases this was found to be false.[15]

The religious sentiment itself also can have a role in the establishment of castes.

12. *Voyages d'Acerbi.*

13. Pennant, *A Tour in Scotland.*

14. II, 968–76.

15. Meiners, *Crit. Gesch. der Relig.,* I, 229–51.

The idea of purity is one of those ideas that it cherishes the most; and it had to eagerly adopt what was laid down in this regard by the privileged mortals who commanded both respect and fear.

Once the notions of purity and impurity were admitted, it had to happen that among the occupations necessary for life, several had to condemn those who performed them to different sorts of taint. With these professions rather naturally passing from father to son, a sort of gradation was established among the classes. No one could approach a member of another class without a preliminary purification, and soon enough each one took the greatest pride in being approached by the fewest possible number of individuals, because those whose contact he avoided seemed to him to be creatures of an inferior order.[16]

Placed at the summit of the social hierarchy, the priesthood encouraged these ideas, which were most favorable to its views because they established a distinction that was permanent, because hereditary; incontestable, because the will of the gods; applicable at every moment, because it prescribed forms that had to be observed in the most everyday relations. In a similar way the Egyptian priests, not content to keep from them foreigners who ate unclean foods, obliged all those who appeared before them to perform repeated ablutions.[17]

In this way, separations that nature and custom had introduced into the different classes, but which their own will and the progress of civilization could have reversed and would have overturned, became insurmountable barriers because of the priesthood. In this perspective, the establishment of castes could be regarded as their work. The interpreters of the divine law, they supported this institution with their authority. As accidental and precarious as it was, they made it sacred and inviolable. The priesthood, if I can put it this way, penned in the human race and subdivided it into isolated fractions, thus preventing it from uniting against the tyrants who said they were its guides.

The countries where the institution of castes is found most clearly and solidly established are precisely those that combine the worship of stars and the heat of climate; the latter is a secondary cause, as we said, but still very favorable to the

---

16. The ideas of impurity found among the Hebrews, who had no relationship to the caste system, nonetheless introduced some parallels into certain Jewish sects. The Essenes were divided into four classes separated from one another almost as much as the Indian castes. When a member of a superior caste was touched by an individual of one of the other three, he purified himself, as if he were tainted by the physical contact of a stranger.

17. Porphyry; Schmidt, *De sac. et sacr. Aeg.*, p. 57.

power of priests. They therefore always attribute this division of the human race to the gods. Among the Indians, Brahma is its author.[18] Isis established it among the Egyptians. Directed by a hero under the direct inspiration of Oromaze, Diemschid divided the inhabitants of Bactria into four classes.[19] And in ancient Assyria it was Mahabad,[20] the first legislator and king, but also the first prophet and the inventor of the first language, who divided the subject people into castes.[21]

In general, this division is rather uniform. The unimportant variations found

18. Seeing the earth devoid of inhabitants, Brahma created from his mouth a son he named Brahman, who was the root of the caste of Brahmins. He revealed to him the Vedas, which came from his four mouths. Brahman, whose mission was to interpret and to spread the divine word, retired to the depths of the forest. There he was threatened constantly by wild animals. He appealed to his father against these dangers. From the right hand of Brahma came a *cuttery* (warrior) who, marrying the sister whom the creator had drawn from his left arm, was the source of the second caste. But wholly devoted to the defense of his older brother, he could not work the land or provide for his needs. From the right thigh of Brahma was born Vaisya, from whom the caste of farmers and merchants owed their birth. Finally, with the servile works remaining to be done, the right foot of Brahma gave birth to a son, Soudra, who, along with his descendants, was devoted to servitude (Polier, *Myth. des Indiens*).

19. Arrien, VII; Strabo, XVI.

20. *Dabistan*, pp. 35–50; trans. by Dalberg. For a long time the *Dabistan* passed for the Persian translation of a Pahlavi manuscript written by a Muslim of Cashmere, Sheik Mohammed Mohsen, surnamed Fani. But today, after the researches of Mr. Silvestre de Sacy, it appears more probable that this work, as well as the *Désatir*, another purported Pahlavi manuscript to which the *Dabistan* makes frequent reference, is the work of some Indian forger writing after the establishment of Islam and under the influence of this conquering faith. However, since the author of this forgery declares that he will provide the portrait of the religions of Asia dating back to the oldest antiquity, he had to gather the oldest traditions in this regard: and the one that attributes this division into castes to a supernatural origin is certainly of this sort because it is consonant with what all the other myths say on this point.

21. One fact proves how much the priests are attached to the division into castes. The only persecution that took place in India was conducted against the Buddhists, not because of their religious doctrine but because they had attacked the division of castes and wanted to destroy it (Schleger, *Weish. der Indier*, p. 183). This peculiarity explains the contradictions of the Indians with respect to Buddha. According to them, he is the ninth avatar, or ninth incarnation of Vishnu (see Aboul-Fazel, in *Ayin Akbery*). But he receives no worship: his temples are deserted, his idols overturned. Everything that concerns him is surrounded with a sort of horror. The planet over which he presides (Mercury) is accused of exercising a baneful influence. However, as Creuzer observes (French trans., p. 300), there is only one small step from the Vedantic philosophy to Buddhism. By surveying the Brahmic doctrines, A. W. Schlegel demonstrated this identity (*Indisc. Bibl.*, I, 4, 414). But Buddha's reform tended to erase the distinction of castes. Hence the negative connotation attached to his name and the proscription of his followers.

in the accounts of travelers do not disturb the reality, and change nothing of the nature, of the principal fact.

In our day no less than in the remotest past, the first order in India is that of the Brahmins,[22] while the second belongs to warriors.[23] It does not much matter that reports differ concerning the inferior orders.[24] The institutions of a country constantly exposed to invasions and perpetually subjected to foreigners necessarily had to be affected by this series of disturbances. But it still is the case that the individuals of the different castes are separated by a religious barrier, and even in the ordinary encounters of life can approach one another only at the distance prescribed by religion.[25] When this distance is violated, the member of the superior caste is expelled from his rank, and he escapes servitude only by apostasy or flight.[26] The

---

There is more: the division into castes has so much attraction for the priesthood that the Buddhist priests who dominate in the island of Ceylon have reintroduced, against the intention and precepts of their founder, something similar. The *radis* or *radias* are the pariahs of this island. Whoever touches them, even by accident, becomes impure. They are obliged to throw themselves on the ground when they encounter a member of a superior caste. This behavior by the Buddhist priests recalls the first Protestant reformers who, proscribed in Catholic countries for having claimed the right of free examination of doctrine, in their turn, in the States in which they had become powerful, proscribed those who appealed to the same freedom. As compensation for being proscribed, nature granted the *radias* of the island of Ceylon women who were more beautiful than those of other castes. However, the rich then took them, having adopted a rule that women are impure only for other women. This fact overturns the hypothesis that would attribute the degradation of pariahs to their ugliness.

22. They say they are issued from the head of Brahma.

23. Issued from the shoulders of Brahma. This divine genealogy of the castes is contained in the symbol or creed of the Brahmins. Perhaps, add the authors of this symbol, these genealogies are allegorical, but we believe them to be real (Bhag. Gita, pref., xxxvi). We find the caste of warriors, or *cutteries*, in the Cathaei of Arrian (bk. V, 22).

24. Pyrard (I, 265) claims that there are only three orders. Anquetil (p. 145) counts five. Hamilton says there are eight (I, 310). These authors deny that the merchants form a separate order, while Dow, Sonnerat, and Niebuhr affirm that they do. Lacroze (*Christianisme des Indes*, pp. 433–476) takes the number of castes all the way to ninety-eight. But all place the priesthood at the head.

25. Between the Brahmin and the warrior interaction is permitted, but physical contact is illicit; between the farmer and the Brahmin, the distance must be thirty-six steps; between the warrior and the artisan, twelve; between the Brahmin and the artisan, fifty; between the artisan and the warrior, thirty; and the artisan must remain twelve paces from the farmer. See in the *Recherches asiatiques*, volume V, the extract from the book entitled *Kerul-Oodputter*, which is held in great veneration among the inhabitants of the coast of Malabar.

26. When an Indian is expelled from his caste, his father, mother, and wife—everyone—abandon him.

same fate awaits the one whose lips touch food prepared by someone of an inferior caste.[27] The poor Brahmins who are employed as secretaries by wealthy Indians believe they are degraded by eating with their masters.[28]

So great is the authority of these ideas concerning the distinction of castes among these peoples that they even override the interest of religion itself. Indians who have become unclean seek refuge in Islam, even in the face of the threat of being sold as slaves. The Muslim author who reports these details attributes this intolerance to the will of God, who in this way compels his enemies to facilitate the triumph of his faith and the increase of the faithful.[29]

A fortiori, marriages between unequals are forbidden. Formerly, death was the inevitable punishment. The softening of mores has substituted banishment, and Brahmins have arrogated the right to take wives from the warrior caste.[30] But even if time and nature have mitigated the severity of the institutions, the mixed races that result from these impious alliances are still looked upon with disfavor, and the ignoble professions are assigned to them.[31]

At the lowest rung of this tyrannical hierarchy one sees a proscribed race cast outside the social state. The unfortunate pariahs, for the most part fishermen and tanners, are not found among the ranks of men.[32] They are excluded from all society, not allowed on roads, at fountains, or in temples. Their touch, their mere presence, and even their breath are impure. Formerly, one could kill them with impunity. Even today, the other castes would think twice about lending them assistance.[33]

27. *Asiat. Res.*, V, 5–16.

28. Niebuhr, II, 7. It even belongs to the dignity of the first two orders not to know the food that the rest of the nation eats. Mr. Hamilton recounts that having consulted a *zamindar* concerning the use of a tree called *madhora*, he regarded these questions as an outrage and retorted, with a tone of reproach: What can I know about a tree that only serves the people? (*Asiat. Res.*, I, 305).

29. *Description du Malabar*, by Zerreddien-Muikdom, written in Arabic around 1579.

30. *Asiat. Res.*, V, 16.

31. Ibid., V, 53–67.

32. Herder, *Phil. de l'hist.*, III, 42; Roger, *Pagan. indien*, I, 2; Pyrard, I, 276. One can find a detailed and disturbing description of this wretched caste in the *Voyage au pays de Bambou*, p. 76. The Laws of Menu sanction the proscription of the pariahs (Laws of Menu, p. 381). They are the executioners of criminals condemned to death. But this fact proves that their being executioners is not the reason that they are unclean, because their number is so great that they could not be confined to this profession. They are not disgraced because they perform it, but they perform it because they are disgraced. The Indians who take care for snakes and insects will let a pariah die out of fear of touching him.

33. Some have called into doubt the character of the proscription in which religion casts the pariahs. They have objected that it is impossible in commercial cities such as Benares, Patna, Delhi, and Agra to prohibit the pariahs, themselves commercial agents who would constantly encounter *cutteries*

By a singular reversal, in the midst of oppression men seek to console themselves by exercising it themselves rather than resisting it. Pariahs are divided among themselves into orders that transmit the disdain others bear to them. The horror they can display seems to them to be a recompense for the horror they inspire in others.

The institution of castes was consecrated in Egypt in an equally immutable way.[34] The main divisions were the same. The differences in details that owe to incomplete enumerations or misrecognized subdivisions are of little importance.[35] It suffices for us that the priests are always, by heredity, the first of all the classes,[36]

---

or Brahmins, and would have frequent communications with them, to have dealings with them. We willingly grant that time and commerce modify institutions and deprive them of their original rigor. But it is nonetheless true that the religious principle remains; that the sacred books of the Indians establish and recommend it; that it is expressly said in several of these books that the murder of a pariah is a permitted action. The period when these murders took place with impunity is, according to a writer who wanted to defend the Indians against this imputation, further from their current customs than we are from the laws of Saint Louis, who ordered the lips burned and tongues pierced of those who swore or blasphemed (*Des castes de l'Inde, ou Lettres sur les hindous* [Paris, 1822]). But these very words from the mouth of a declared apologist of the ways and customs of India prove that formerly, at least, the accusation he rejects in their name was well founded.

We do not need to examine here what could have been the origin of pariahs, or, to use a term less customary in Europe, the *tchandalas*, whom another writer presents as subject to fixed laws and previously governed by monarchs. It is enough that after having based himself upon hardly demonstrated facts and vague traditions—that, for example, of an alliance between Indian princes and the sovereigns of the *tchandalas*—he recognized that these *tchandalas* were considered vile beings; that in order to explain the degradation into which man falls by his own faults, the Indian tales show him transformed into *tchandala*, that is, descended into the rank of animals; that these *tchandalas*, or pariahs, eat cadavers, that they can never regain favor, and that their name is given to all malefactors indifferently. The ingenious discovery of Mr. Schlegel concerning the identity of the pariahs and the bohemians who emigrated from northern India, whose ways and abominable practices are still those of their ancestors, only better proves the degradation that can result for the human race from priestly proscription.

34. On the Egyptian castes, see Hecataei, fragm. *ap.* Creuzer, fragment; *Hist. antiq. Graec.*, p. 28; Creuzer, *Symb.*, I, 277; Heeren, *Idées*, II, 554. What we are told about Egypt also applies to Ethiopia: "*Plurima utrique genti fuisse communia: reges pro Diis habere: statuarum formas et litterarum caractera, coetum sacerdotum,*" etc. (Diod., I).

35. Herodotus (II, 164) counts seven classes, whose members must remain faithful to their fathers' professions. In one place Diodorus indicates only three (I, 2–8); and Strabo (XVII) confirms this assertion with his own testimony. However, the same Diodorus elsewhere (I, 73–74) brings the number to five; and Plato distinguishes six orders: priests, soldiers, farmers, artisans, hunters, and shepherds (in *Timaeo*).

36. From the time of Joseph, the priests who interpreted the hieroglyphs already formed a separate class (Euseb., *Praep. evang.*, bk. II). The Egyptians counted at Thebes, from Menes until the time of Hecatus of Milet, 385 priests, who succeeded from father to son (Herod., II, 143).

and the warriors form the second.[37] It is also remarkable that the shepherds in Egypt, like the pariahs in India, were the objects of universal disdain.[38] Herodotus tells us that alone among the Egyptians they could not enter the temples. And no one wanted their daughters to marry them, nor to marry theirs. They only inter-married.[39]

One, however, must not fail to note the differences between the Indian and the Egyptian institutions. They perhaps owe to politics as much as religion.[40] The

37. The military caste was composed of two large tribes, the Hermotybians and the Calasirians, to whom were assigned some of the most fertile provinces of Egypt. All mechanical occupations were forbidden them (Herod., II, 164, 368; Diod., I, 73; Letronne on Rollin).

38. Gen., XLVI, 34.

39. Herod., II, 47. The disdain of Egyptians for those who tended pigs came from their hatred of the nomadic tribes that perpetually threatened their peace and property. Similar in lifestyle to shepherds, says Heeren (*Idéen*, II, 635), they were regarded in Egypt like enemies that one had to bear with, because one could not rid oneself totally of them. The vast and mountainous country where they lived was only imperfectly subject to the pharaohs, and placing them under the yoke was always uncertain and precarious. Hence the Egyptians' aversion to them, feelings the priestly caste maintained with great care. The passage from Genesis cited above proves that this disfavor goes back to the most remote times.

40. A German author whose learning I admire as much as profit from, Mr. Heeren, nonetheless seems to me to have exaggerated the part that policy plays in this matter. "The castes," he says (*Idéen*, II, 594), "were not firmly established in Egypt except after the unification of the country into a single kingdom. Even though the origin of this institution cannot be historically proven, one can base it upon the difference of peoples. Having believed that it discovered in the strict separation of profes-sions a way of favoring the improvement of naissant societies, policy hastened to make use of it. The proof of this is that later, new castes were created, that of the interpreters, for example, at the time of Psammeticus." In granting such a large part to policy, Mr. Heeren supposes something that does not exist, that men actually calculate about what they do not know. It is true that people always speak of what the heads of societies have invented in order to make these societies progress. But the leaders do not even know if these developments were desirable. They do not even know if this-or-that mode of organization that has not yet been tried truly is a way of contributing to these developments. The leaders of societies did not fall from heaven. They are barely superior to their subjects, but people at-tribute to them a prescience they could not have had.

As for the new caste of interpreters, the only caste whose origin we actually know, if its creation proves the progress of civilization (at least under a certain aspect), the circumstances that accompa-nied it demonstrate the difference between this caste and those that can truly be regarded as Egyptian. To coin a phrase, Psammeticus wanted *to grecify* his nation, and for this purpose he had many young people raised by Greeks whom he brought to Egypt to teach their language and to impart the cus-toms of Greece. But national hostility showed itself against these teachers and their students. A great number of the members of the superior castes emigrated, and the children raised in Greek customs passage from Herodotus to which we just referred points to an exception made against shepherds. It gives rise to the thought that the hereditariness of professions was reinforced more rigorously than that of races. This would mean that marriages between and among the inferior castes were not as reproved as they were in India. India's castes, in contrast, were treated more with despotic harshness than with religious horror. Calculating everything in view of social utility, Egyptian policy did not cast them from the social state, but made them bear all its burdens and pains.[41] In India, the division into castes was purely a matter of conscience; in Egypt, it was linked with administration.

became an impure race as far as the people were concerned. No one wanted to have them or keep them in any caste. They were forced to form one of their own, which took its name from the profession they practiced, and which was always odious in Egypt as being tainted and alien.

41. The labors that the Jews in the Bible complain of being subject to by the Egyptians is clear evidence of what was imposed on the lower classes in Egypt.

CHAPTER 9

On Priestly Corporations Replacing Castes

The Ethiopians, the Indians, and the inhabitants of Egypt are the peoples of Antiquity among whom one most clearly perceives the division into castes. Among many other peoples, various signs seem to indicate that this division had existed, but then had weakened. For example, it is probable that in the original country of the magi, in Media and especially in Bactria, this order was a veritable caste. But the revolution that transported them to Persia properly speaking, having placed it more or less under the royal power, denatured the institution. Even though formally prescribed by Zoroaster,[1] the division into castes was never scrupulously put into practice. Among the Persians, we see a class of nobles, one of warriors, and one of laborers, but nothing proves that the classes were necessarily hereditary. The hereditary priesthood is the only one attested by the ancients.[2]

---

1. We will deal elsewhere with the reform operated in the religion of the Persians by Zoroaster, the protégé and instrument of a conqueror, who attached a despotic religious and political code to the ancient memories of a civilized people subjugated by barbarians. He based the caste divisions on sacred traditions, thereby separating the nation either into seven classes corresponding to the seven Amschaspands, the servants of Oromaze, or into four, analogous to the four elements. But this theocratic classification, the heritage of a defeated priesthood, was rapidly modified by the effects of the conquest. The political barriers remained, but the religious notion weakened.

2. Hyde, *De rel. persar.*, p. 354. "*Per secula multa ... apud Persas nemo nisi sacerdotis filius in sacerdotio succedebat*" (Schmidt, *De sacerd. et sacrif. Aeg.*, p. 8). For the constitution of the clergy among the Persians, one can consult Ammianus Marcellinus, XXIII; Solin, cap. 55. The magi had a leader named the archimage (Sozomene, II, 73). They were divided into three classes: the *destur-mobeds*, accomplished masters; the *mobeds*, masters; and the *herbeds*, apprentices (Zend-Avesta, II). The observance of religious customs, of religious formulas, prayers, or liturgies, was confided to them (Herod., I, 132).

The same is true among the Mexicans,[3] the Hebrews, and all the southern peoples subject to the power of priests. But going toward the West and the North, hereditary disappears, and we find corporations that appear to be elective.

Caesar reports that members of the nobility could enter into the order of Druids.[4] Porphyry goes even further. According to him, the sacerdotal corporations were composed of all those who, without any distinction of race, obtained the approval of the city or the country.[5]

However, one cannot maintain that priests invested with an immense authority were disposed to share it with first-comers. It seems probable to us that if these corporations were elective by law or custom, they were hereditary in fact.[6] We read in Diodorus that among these same peoples of the North, certain families were charged, descending from father to son, with everything that concerned the worship of the gods.[7] Young nobles were constrained to a novitiate of twenty years under the direction of the Druids.[8] And even the nations that had preserved the right to elect their princes recognized that the priests had the right to choose the head of the priests.[9]

Finally, the difference in forms can be explained by the difference in situations. An active, bellicose, vagabond way of life takes away some of the fixity of institu-

---

A fairly similar hierarchy exists among the Guebres. Five classes of priest share the sacred functions. Their principal college is at Yesd, a city in the north of Isfahan.

3. Certain families had the right to be the hereditary priests of Huitzilopochtli (Acosta, *Hist. nature. et morale des Indes occident*).

4. Caes., *B Gall.*, VI, 14; Pelloutier, VII, 265.

5. Porphyry, *De abstin.*, IV, 17.

6. One must be very wary of the assertions of those who pronounce apodictically concerning facts separated from us by such a distance of time and place. Meiner (*Crit. Gesch.*, II, 527) believes he sees an elective priesthood in Mexico alongside hereditary priests. The character of the Mexican religion argues against this assertion, and the authority of the most accredited writers confirms this moral inference (Acosta, *Hist. nature. et morale*).

7. Diod., II, 47. The priests of the Celts said they were of the race of Bor, or the gods, because Bor was the father of Odin (Edda, 4th fable).

8. Noble Gauls prided themselves on bearing the name Druid and being affiliated with their order (Pelloutier, VII, 282). Christians have similar affiliations with religious orders, Jesuits of the short robe, etc.

9. "*His autem omnibus Druidibus praeest unus, qui summam inter eos habet auctoritatem. Hoc mortuo, si quis, ex reliquis, excellit dignitate, succedit, aut si sunt plures pares, suffragio Druidum eligitur. Nonnumquam etiam armis de principatu contendunt*" (Caes., *B Gall.*, VI, 13, 14; Tacit., *German.*, 7–11).

tions, even if their strength and intensity of action are not diminished. In the next chapter we will see that the power of the Drottes, the Druids, and all the ministers of religion who governed the nations known under the names Getes, Scythians, Celts, Scandinavians, and Gauls were often as despotic as the Brahmins of India or the priests of Egypt.

CHAPTER 10

On the Various Competences of the Priesthood
among the Nations It Dominated

Among the nations subjugated by priestly corporations, as among those that were divided into castes, the power of priests did not limit itself to matters concerning religion.

To be sure, religious functions always occupied the first place. Priests[1] asserted the exclusive right to preside at prayers, sacrifices, and ceremonies, whether the most or the least important rites of the external worship. Among the Persians, the magi were charged with all the offerings: their invocations alone were efficacious,[2] and the consecration of victims consisted in a theogony chanted by a member of this order.[3] These theogonies, the living transmission of the eternal word, had an irresistible power. The magi repeated them regularly, even perpetually, sometimes alone in the temples, sometimes before the assembled faithful. They varied them according to the sun's position, the seasons, the time of day, but they must never be interrupted. Deprived of their salutary resounding, the world would have prematurely returned to chaos. The silence of the magi would have been the universe's last hour.

---

1. Heeren (*Idées*, II, 60) observes with some reason that the word "priest" in our modern languages gives us too narrow an idea of what the great priestly corporations of antiquity were. They contained in their bosom, he says, the enlightened class of every sort. True, but the monopoly they held was founded upon religion. It was as priests that the members of these corporations declared themselves the owners of this monopoly. As a consequence, there was a priestly spirit; that is, a spirit of mystery, exclusion, and intolerance. It is the common sense of language that often disconcerts the calculations of men, and it is this common sense, we maintain, that has always named them priests and not philosophers and savants.

2. Clearch. *ap.* Diog., I, 6.

3. Herod., I, 132.

Whoever in Egypt sacrificed a victim that was not marked by the sacerdotal seal was punished with death.[4] Among the Gauls, only the Druids[5] interpreted signs.[6] They alone observed the flight of birds. No profane hand dared dig into the entrails of humans sacrificed to the gods.[7] Gete,[8] German,[9] and Breton priests accompanied their armies; they alone could implore heaven for them and consign their enemies to death. Despite their theism, the Jews were not an exception. They closed the sanctuary to all but priests.[10] Abiram and Dathan were swallowed up for having usurped clerical functions. Uzzah perished because he involuntarily touched the ark.[11] Fifty thousand Bethsamites were struck dead because they looked upon it.[12] Even though he had destroyed the worship of idols, Uzziah was chased from the temple by the high priest because he had laid hold of the encensoir.[13]

4. Herod., II; Schmidt, *De sacerd. et sacrif. Aegypt.*, p. 82. If our readers wish to instruct themselves concerning the innumerable functions of the Egyptian priests, they can consult Meiners, *De vero Deo*, pp. 40–41. The most minute functions—that, for example, of covering the statues of the gods with their ornaments—were hereditary to a class of priests, the Hierostolists.

5. According to some, the chiefs of the Druids lived on the island; according to others, in Great Britain. The Gauls of the time of Caesar went to Britain to learn their religion. It was there that the Druids learned the secret teaching.

6. The magi alone had the right to predict the future.

7. Diod., V, 213; Strabo, IV; Caes., *B Gall.*, VI, 13.

8. Jornandès, cap. 2.

9. Tacit., *German.*

10. Nombr., I, 51.

11. Spencer, *De legib. ritual. Hebraeor.*, I, 166.

12. Kings, I, 6, 19. The reflections of a Catholic theologian on this subject, it seems to us, merit being reported. One cannot doubt, he says, that these Bethsamites were deeply guilty. They had to know that it was forbidden by an express law, even to the Levites, to touch the Ark and to look upon it uncovered; however, disdaining these prohibitions, the Bethsamites dared to approach it, to rashly look at it, and, according to the Hebrew text, open it and look within. What difficulty can there be to believe that God punished this voluntary and public disobedience, this sacrilegious curiosity! By the law itself, the fault of the Bethsamites merited death. How many human governments sacrifice millions of men in order to maintain the laws and glory of the State, and their wisdom in so acting is extolled, while people cannot conceive that God would have sacrificed fifty thousand guilty in order to avenge his violated laws and his outraged majesty! "Absolute master of our life," says Grotius, "God at any time, without any reason, can take away from each one this gift of his liberality, whenever it seems good to him." We are not surprised, therefore, that he lists some sacrileges that, according to him, merit the loss of life (*Lettres de quelques Juifs*, I, 326–30).

13. Chronicles, II, 26, 18. It is curious to see how much Bossuet admires the energy of the Hebrew priesthood on this occasion. "When Ozias (another name of Azarias)," he says, "wanted to infringe on

In all the feasts of Indians, Brahmins presided.[14] Who could take their place? Brahma existed and lived in them. They are his children. To honor them was to honor him. He received with equal benevolence the homage directed at him and what was directed to his representatives on earth.[15] Endowed with a miraculous force and virtue, their hand sprinkled consecrated water on the animals that nourished man, the furnishings constructed for the different needs of life, and the weapons destined for its defense.[16] They determined days of rejoicing and days of mourning. They alone taught the faithful their appropriate prayers; and if someone revealed them to another person the latter's head rolled, a very ingenious way of controlling indiscretion and discouraging curiosity. Divination was reserved to them.[17] No one could build a pagoda unless some revelation instructed him concerning the spot preferred by the divinity, and the Brahmins were always the necessary intermediaries of these communications.

All teachings were modified in accordance with this principle. The waters of the Ganges possess a miraculous virtue for the expiation of sins. But it was feared that the guilty, desirous of absolution, would escape the priestly power by plunging into the river on their own. As a result, one had to hold in his hand blades of straw blessed by a Brahmin.[18] Even the gods patiently waited while the priests determined their forms and their abodes. The stones worshipped by Indians owe

---

their sacred rights, the priests were obliged by the law of God to oppose themselves to him, as much for the good of the prince as for their preservation of the right which was, as one knows, God's right. They did so vigorously, and putting themselves before the king, their pontiff at their head, they said to him: It is not your office at all. . . . leave the sanctuary . . . Ozias threatened the priests. . . . they expelled him. Leprosy never left him. He had to separate himself according to the law, and his son Joathan took the administration of the kingdom" (*Politique de l'Ecriture sainte*, VII, v. 10).

14. By mistake some have claimed that in India there were tribes of priests who did not descend from the Brahmins, and who are not Brahmins themselves. This could be true for a few heterodox sects, but it is an exception to, or better put: an infraction of, the religious rule. The Laws of Menu are explicit in this regard (Laws of Menu, I, 88, X, 75–78).

15. *Beschreib. der Relig. der Malabar. Pind.*; Roger, *Pagan. ind.*; Polier, *Myth. des hindous.*

16. Sonnerat, *Voy. aux Indes.*

17. "*Eos solos* [the Brahmins], *esse inter Indos divinandi peritos, neque cuiquam divinationem permit, nisi sapienti viro*" (Arrian, in *Indis*).

18. The Brahmins perform the smallest formalities in the ceremonies—for example, that of tossing the wood in the fire, etc. For the number of feasts and religious actions for which the presence of the Brahmins is indispensable, see Herder, *Philosophie de l'histoire*, III, 39. The sacred branches of the *bom* of Persians cannot be used in religious services until a *destour* has placed them in the sacred water, where they are to remain for an entire year (Anquetil, *Voy. aux Indes.*; Kleucker, Zend-Avesta, III, 6).

their sacred nature to the prayers of Brahmins, who call down divinity upon them. Before this mysterious invocation, the stones of Brahma, Vishnu, and Shiva are but profane pebbles.[19] The lingam becomes a sacred object only when a solemn ceremony has confined the god within the newly sculpted idol.[20] Ancient oaks needed to be sprinkled with blood from the hands of Druids to become worthy of the Gauls' veneration.[21]

But the priesthood does not content itself with only, and exclusively, exercising religious functions. It arrogates a considerable part of political[22] and civil authority as well. A king, Plato says, cannot reign in Egypt if he has not been admitted to the knowledge of sacred things. Every man from another class who ascends the throne must have himself received into the priestly order.[23]

The election of kings was reserved to priests and soldiers, but the votes of priests counted one hundred- or two hundred-fold.[24] After his election, the king who had

---

19. Fr. Calmet, S.J., *Oeuvres*, XXIX, 400; Sonnerat, *Voy. aux Indes*. In the *poutché*, the Brahmins are deemed to attract the divinity from one material object to another by means of their invocations. The ceremony concluded, they send it on its way with another prayer (Sonnerat, ibid.). In the same way Egyptian priests maintain that they have the power to communicate something of the divine nature to statues (Lévèque, *Excurs. sur le schammanisme*, trans. of Thucydides, III, 298). This belief made its way into Greece and Rome. The Greeks and Romans were persuaded that, by the power of consecration, the gods incorporated themselves into statues (Van Dale, *De consecr. in libr. de oracul.*, 477). At the time of the decadence of polytheism, its defenders the philosophers claimed that the simulacra were full of the real presence of the gods (Iamblich. *ap.* Phot., *Bibl.*, cod. 225; Arnob., *Adv. gentes*, VI, 17; Julian, passim; Maximus of Tyre). The pagans said to Arnobius (*Adv. gentes*): We do not regard statues and idols as gods, but we believe that the gods inhabit them because these things are consecrated to them. However, they ordinarily restricted the real presence to the idols worshiped by those initiated into the mystery religions (Iambl., Phot., *Bibl.*, cod. 225; Cic., *De nat. deor.*, II, 17; Procl. *ad* Plato, *Tim.*).

20. Laflotte, *Notice histor. sur l'Inde*, p. 206.

21. Pelloutier, *Hist. des Celtes*, VIII, 67; Mézeray, *Hist. de France*, p. 40.

22. Mexican priests were the counselors of kings. No war could be undertaken without their advice. Their decisions were delivered as oracles (Clav., *Hist. du Mex.*, I). There are even some indications of an even greater union between the priesthood and the royalty in Mexico in the person of Montezuma II, who mounted the throne as the heir of the reigning family and at the same time exercised priestly functions.

23. In *Politic.*

24. The vote of a priest of the highest class was counted as one hundred, that of a member of the second class, twenty, and that of an individual of the third class, ten (Plut., *De Isid. et Osir.*). "*Prolato alicujus ex candidatis nomine, milites quidem manum tollunt, comastae vero, et zacori, et prophetae cal-*

acceded to the priesthood[25] remained subject to the ones who had elected him. He was served not by slaves but by the sons of priests who were more than twenty years old. He had as regular associates only the ministers of worship. The hours of his walks, those of his ablutions and his baths, the moments he was permitted to enjoy venereal pleasures, all were fixed by them.[26] In public ceremonies, after having prayed for the prince, the high priest publicly examined and censured his conduct.[27] And just as the priesthood attended him at his installation, the same priesthood calculated each minute of his final agony, and sanctified him with the purifying waters of the Nile.[28]

Even more powerful, the Ethiopian priesthood not only elected kings but dethroned or condemned them to death.[29] It also decided on war and peace.[30]

During their theocracy, the Jews always consulted Jehovah through the inter-

---

culus ferunt, pauci aliqui, sed quorum praecipua in ea re auctoritas. Prophetarum nempe calculus centum manus aequat, comastarum viginti, zacororum decem" (Synes., *De Provid.*, p. 94).

25. Strabo, XVII; Plut., *De Isid.*; Diod., I, 70.

26. Diod., I.

27. In Egypt the statues of priests were placed next to those of kings in temples. The authority of the Egyptian priesthood even survived the conquest of Egypt by the Persians. Darius, father of Xerxes, having wanted to have his statue placed before that of Sesostris, the high-priest of Vulcan opposed the proposal, and the king dared not do violence to him (Herod., II, 110; Diod., I, 55). This moderation of a despot is very remarkable, but it is not astonishing, because even in Persia, despite the loss of power of the magi under their foreign conquerors, they had retained enough authority that the king was compelled to have himself admitted into their order (Cic., *De divin.*) and to treat them as his customary counselors and the inseparable companions of all his expeditions (Meiners, *De vet. pers. relig. Comment. Soc. Goett.*). They had been much more powerful in Media. When Astyages, king of the Medes, consulted them concerning a dream in which he had been ordered to have his nephew Cyrus put to death, they answered him: "We will tell you the truth out of our own self-interest; this interest encourages us to preserve your empire, because now we have a portion of your government." Darius thus became acquainted in his own country with priestly pretentions.

28. Hammer, *Min. de l'Orient.*

29. The kings of Meroë were chosen by the priestly caste and were drawn from their ranks (Diod., I; Heeren, II, 407). These kings, as well as the other inhabitants of Meroë, killed themselves when this was the order of the gods (Diod., III; Strabo, XVII; Larcher, *Not. sur Hérod.*, II, 87). An original if strange thinker, de Pauw, in his *Recherches sur les Égyptiens et les Chinois* (II, 119) hazards a defense of the priests of Meroë, whom he claims constantly opposed despotism. No doubt they opposed it, but in order to exercise it themselves. There are no more irreconcilable enemies of tyranny than those who wish to seize it for themselves.

30. There was a temple of Jupiter at Meroë, says Herodotus (II, 29); and they went to war wherever and whenever he commanded.

mediary of the high priest concerning the choice of their generals. Their sacred books show judges in many respects placed in a subordinate position.

Some have claimed that Brahmins could neither ascend the throne nor lead the armies. But credible travelers cite several contrary examples,[31] and it was not so long ago that the king of the Marathas was subject to twelve Brahmins who governed in his name.[32]

The institutions of the peoples of the North and the West present a singular mixture of political liberty and priestly despotism. Far from diminishing the power of priests, the guarantees that citizens had established against their civil and military leaders redounded to the advantage of their spiritual masters. The peoples exercised the right of dismissal against the former, but not against anyone cloaked in the priesthood.[33] This naturally gave them a great superiority to the removable detainers of temporal authority.[34] Sometimes we see priests unite the two powers.

31. Niebuhr, II, 7. We learn from Arrian that the cities of India that defended themselves against Alexander, or which rose up against him, were for the most part led by Brahmins (Arrian, V, 1; VI, 7). Even in the Indian republics of which the Greek authors speak, the Brahmins were at the head of the government. Thus the Greeks attribute the foundation of these republics to the Indian Bacchus (Heeren, I, 435–438).

32. In Tibet, the *gellongs*, or priests, present themselves before the kings as their equals, without giving them any mark of respect (Pallas, *Samml. Hist. Nachr. ueber die Mongol. Voelkersch.*). The pontiff of Comana, says Cicero (*Ep. fam.*, XV, 4), was in a position to resist the king by arms. In the towns of Comana, of which there were two, one in Pontus, the other in Cappadocia, the inhabitants, governed by a king, were also subject to a pontiff for life (Strabo, XII).

The spirit of Greek and Roman religion made itself felt in opposition to this priestly spirit when the Romans had conquered these two cities. Pompey and Caesar united the pontifical functions with the royal ones, Pompey in the person of Archelaus, Caesar that of Nicomedus (Appian). The same hierarchy as at Comana was established in Pessinus in Phrygia (Strabo).

33. The Burgundians, says Ammianus Marcellinus (XXVIII, 5), could change their king but not their priest. The first dignitary in the State, the priest was invested with this dignity for his entire life.

34. Dion Chrysostomus shows the Druids as in fact performing the functions of government, the kings being nothing but the executors of the wills of these ministers of religion (Dio. Chrys., *Serm.*, 49). See in Kaysler, *Antiq. septentr.*, and in Dreyer, *Vermischte Abhandlungen*, other examples of the power of priests among the Burgundians, Franks, and Slavs. The priests of the Iberians conducted negotiations with foreigners (Strabo, XI). Among the Scandinavians, the Drottes, heads of the assemblies, maintained peace (Mallet, *Introd. à l'hist. du Dan.*, p. 134). Among the Getas, the order of priests was above all other classes. The nobility occupied a lower rank. According to what the historians recount, Decebalus wanted to obtain peace from Trajan and sent him, first of all, mere gentlemen (*comatos*, with long hair), then priests (*pileatos*, mitred), as the most distinguished personages in the nation (Theod., *Excerpt. ex* Dion Cass. bk. 68; Petr. Patritius in *Excerpt. legat.*, p. 24).

Comosicus, the sovereign pontiff of the Goths, governed them not only as priest but as king.[35] Other times, even though it lacked the visible marks of royalty, the priesthood exercised a most formidable authority over it. Kings were not exempt from the human victims that the ministers of the gods had the right to demand. It was even a widespread view that it was a favorable augur when the lot fell on a prince.[36]

Among almost all these nations, the judicial power belonged to the priests, as well as political authority.[37] Among the Germans, they put the accused in irons, they inflicted punishments, they executed criminals, not as administering the justice of men, but as accomplishing the sentences of the gods.[38] The Drottes of the Scandinavians were both priests and judges.[39] The Druids pronounced on all the

35. Jornand., cap. II. The priests of Thrace at the same time commanded the armies. Polyaenus reports a curious anecdote on this subject. One day, he says, the Thracians refused to obey Cosinga, who was both their general and their pontiff; in response he had several ladders connected together. Seeing this, the spectators, believing that he wanted to rise up to heaven to complain of their disobedience, prostrated themselves at his feet and promised to obey his orders (Polyaenus, VII, 22).

36. Caes., *B Gall.*, VI, 13-14; Tacit., *Annal.*, XIV, 30; *Hist.*, IV, 54; Strabo, IV; Pliny, *Hist. nat.*, XXX, 4; "*Gothi reges ipsos mactabant, ut diis pro Victoria ipsorum auxilio reportata, gratiam referent*" (Kaysl., *Antiquit.*, p. 134).

37. Aelianus (*Var. Hist.*, XIV) says explicitly that the Egyptian priests alone exercised the judicial power, and Diodorus (bk. I) excludes from civil functions the military, the farmers, and all those who did not belong to the priestly order. Heeren proves very well (*Idées*, II, 614) that the administration of justice in Egypt could only be in the hands of the priests. "The science of laws," he says, "and the tasks that depend upon it, were the property of the priestly caste. Possessors of all the sciences, the priests alone knew the laws." He then demonstrates that the grand judge of whom Diodorus speaks, who presided over the supreme tribunal of the Thirty, and who wore the image of Truth suspended on a golden chain, was a high priest, and the ornament that distinguished him was a kind of talisman that revealed the future. "In reading this passage from Diodorus," he adds, "one cannot fail to connect this Egyptian ornament to that of the high-priest of the Jews, where it probably had an analogous purpose" (ibid., 615). This tribunal of Thirty sat at Thebes. Ten priests of Heliopolis, ten from Memphis, and ten of Thebes made it up (Diod., I).

38. "*Silentium* [in the assemblies] *per sacerdotes quibus et coercendi jus est, imperator. . . . Neque animadvertere, neque vincire, neque verberare, nisi sacerdotibus est permissum, non quasi in poenam, sed velut Deo imperante, quem adesse bellatoribus credunt*" (Tacit., *German.*, 7). The Druids even pronounced on the faults of soldiers (ibid., 3).

39. Botin, *Hist. de Suède*, sect. I, ch. 5. The same union of religious functions and judicial ones is found in Persia, where the magi had arrogated to themselves almost all judgments (Dio. Chrys., *Or.*, 49). Momentarily deprived of this portion of authority, they recovered it under Xerxes, and claimed that the king himself had to conform to their counsel (Agathias, II, 65).

disagreements between individuals.[40] They gave clemency by offering safe haven in their sanctuaries. This custom has subsisted to our day in Italy and Spain, the countries most dominated by the Catholic priesthood.

It was as the inheritor of these privileges that the Christian clergy obtained from Constantine, Theodosius, and, finally, from Charlemagne that civil tribunals could not take cognizance of cases brought before bishops;[41] it is well known that they presided over trials by fire and water, and the judgments of God.[42]

Independently of the sentences they pronounced in their capacity as judges, priests employed the instrument of excommunication against those who attempted to resist them; and this excommunication involved the loss of all civil and political rights. How so? It banished the guilty from all places destined for worship, but this was where the citizens came together to deliberate about national interests. Likewise, it was in the depths of the forests that tribunals summoned plaintiffs to appear, and where they rendered their verdicts. And last, these forests were the sanctuary of the gods. It was forbidden to the excommunicated to enter these places. In these ways, they could not attend the assemblies of the people or present themselves before tribunals to seek justice. Thus disarmed and without protection, they found themselves subject everywhere to public horror. Everyone fled them, believing they were sullied by their mere presence.[43]

To be sure, among the Persians and the Indians, from time immemorial foreign domination rendered the temporal consequences of excommunication less terrible. But the priests attempted to compensate with the threat of greater pun-

---

40. "*De omnibus controversiis publicis et privatis constituunt*" (Caes., *B Gall.*).

41. *Capitul. Carol.*, bk. VI, leg. 281, p. 1023.

42. Pelloutier, VII, 233. In general, it seems to us that no one has adequately considered the resemblance of the Christian clergy to the hierarchical institutions of the peoples of the North. This resemblance is so striking even in its details that some religious orders have drawn the consequence that they were descended from the Druids. A historian of the community of Carmelites calls the Druids "*sanctos druidas, Eliae filios, fraters nostros et praedecessores*" (*Hist. carmel. ordin.*, I, 1, 4). "*Si vivendi genus et observantias regulares serio discusseris,*" says another writer, "*reperies verso fuisse (druidas) carmelitas*" (a theological thesis defended at Beziers in 1682). People have studied what Christianity borrowed from paganism; but they have not factored in what it borrowed from the barbarians, whose religion, being that of conquerors, and inspiring less hatred than the polytheism of Rome, which for three centuries had fought against Christianity, found few obstacles in handing over to the new faith forms that favored the designs of the priesthood, for whom this new faith was going to become their property for a very long time.

43. Caes., *B Gall.*, VI, 14.

ishments after death. The Sadder is filled with imprecations against the opponents of the magi and frightful descriptions of the eternal torments that await them. "He whom the gods themselves cannot destroy," say the Brahmins, "he who cannot be killed by Indra, or Cali, or Vishnu, will be consumed by fire if a Brahmin curses him."[44] Today, one can see as a vestige of the excommunication formerly in use, the loss of caste these same Brahmins claim to inflict on the members of other castes when they refuse to comply with even multiple requests. This spiritual demotion causes them to descend into an even lower caste.[45]

As one can easily anticipate, so many and so diverse a number of prerogatives were accompanied by vast properties and numerous exemptions. Egyptian priests did not pay any tribute, but were charged with collecting it.[46] They said that Isis had given them a third of Egypt[47] for their maintenance and the upkeep of the

---

44. A passage from the Ramayana. The code of Gentoo commanded whoever caused frequent embarrassment to a Brahmin to be put to death. Their mythology is full of stories proving the effectiveness of the curses of priests. A conqueror, Wiswamitra [Vishvamitra], having attacked a hermit, was about to gain victory. His terrible arrows destroyed by the thousands the defenders of the *rishi*. But an élan of the piety of the latter reduced to ashes the hundred sons of the rajah, who, seeing then how much the power of the priest was above that of the warrior, formed the ambition of elevating himself to the rank of priests by doing penance (extract from the Ramayana). Trishanku the king, cursed by a Brahmin, was turned into a hideous, unclean pariah (ibid.). In the Lamaic religion, the souls of those who incur the anathema of a priest are troubled constantly, not being able to reenter a body, and they become malevolent spirits who torment men (Pallas, *Sammlung. Histor. Nachr. üb. die Mongol. Voelkersch.*, II, 12, 111). At Siam, Thevallut, the brother of Sommonacodom, suffers infinite tortures at the bottom of the netherworld because, having agreed to worship the two mystical words *Putang* (God) and *thamang* (word of God), he refused to adore the third, *sangkhang* (imitator of God, or priest) (Tachard, *Voy. de Siam*, VI, 212–213). But this is not all. Sommonacodom himself, say the Siamese, suffers in hell for fifty generations for having struck a monk with a small stone and wounding him. Behold the supreme god punished for having hurt a priest! No doubt these tales are destined only for the people, but they indicate the priestly mind (Laloubère, II, 14).

45. *Lettr. édif.*, XIII, 144.

46. Diod. Josèph., *Ant. judaic*; Schmidt, *De sac.*, pp. 9 & 82; Clem. Alex.

47. The probabilities that indicate that Egypt was peopled by priestly colonies also lead us to believe that at the time of the establishment of these colonies, the priests at their head became the owners of the entire territory. But this order of things had to undergo, and did undergo, changes. What proves it is that even at the time of Joseph there were properties that did not belong to the caste of priests; and it was they who at the time of the famine yielded their patrimony to the king in order to have grain. The claim of Diodorus that the lands were divided among the king, the priests, and the soldiers is probably not entirely correct. But it still demonstrates that the priests had large properties.

cult. When Pharaoh appropriated the money, flocks, and goods of his subjects, he did not touch the priests' possessions.[48]

In India, in the absence of heirs, the Brahmins inherited.[49] When Gauls died, they transmitted their goods to the gods and to their ministers.[50] Strabo writes of the immense domains belonging to the Druids, and the slaves who cultivated them. There were temples to which more than six thousand serfs were attached.[51] Armenia presents the same spectacle attending the altars of Anaitis.[52] Moses, whose priesthood was in imitation of the Egyptians',[53] gave the Levites a tenth of the harvest and the yield of flocks, as well as everything that fell under interdiction, everything vowed to the Lord, the redemption of firstborn infants, a portion of all the animals that were killed, and, finally, the first fruits of the harvest. Rigorous laws in this world[54] and frightening punishments in the next[55] were the protective hedges of these immense estates. The sword and the anathema, laws and social pressure, gods and demons—all were invoked to guarantee them.

Weighed down with wealth and dispensed from every pecuniary burden, the priests had also emancipated themselves from all other dangerous or painful duties. Even in the most warlike nations, they were not obliged to bear arms,[56] and they could not be put to death for even the most serious crimes.

For a long time, the Christian priesthood claimed a similar privilege. One still sees traces of this exemption in England in what is called the benefit of the clergy.

---

48. Genesis, XLVII, 17–22.

49. Code of Gentoo.

50. Pelloutier, VIII, 111.

51. Strabo, IV, XI, XII. The priests of Cappadocia and Pontus both had large numbers of slaves (Strabo, ibid.).

52. Pliny, *Hist. nat.*, XXX, 24.

53. Outram, *De sacrif.*, I, 4, 43; Michaelis, *Mos. Recht.*, I, 147–57.

54. *Leg. Frisior.*, p. 508.

55. "He who reprises the lands given to the gods or to the priests causes his ancestors to return to the netherworld, even if they were already in heaven" (inscription translated from Sanskrit, *Asiat. Res.*, IX, 411). "Prince, remember Heliodorus and the hand of God that came upon him for having wanted to take the goods placed in the temple. These goods came from kings, I acknowledge; but what they offered, they had first received from God. What an insult to take from God what came from him and which he gave, and to raise one's hand to take what is on the altars!" These words do not come from the Vedas but from the *Politique de l'Ecriture sainte* by Bossuet.

56. "*Druidas a bello abesse consueverunt, neque tributa una cum reliquis pendunt. Militiae vocationis omniumque rerum habent immunitatem*" (Caes., *B Gall.*).

In India, Brahmins formerly enjoyed the same privilege.[57] But now that the time of their unlimited power has passed, this prerogative has become harmful to them, and the punishments that they undergo are even more cruel because of the precautions taken to make sure they do not shed blood when punished.[58]

To justify the accumulation of so much power and so many privileges, the arguments of priests were everywhere the same. The human race is on the earth only to accomplish the will of the gods. All the actions of individuals have a more-or-less direct relation with this will. Priests know this will, and make it known. It belongs to them, therefore, to judge and punish disobedience.

The identity of means is no less noticeable.

An austere, retired life; a difficult, hence rare, admission to it; an affectation of superior purity; care taken to appear before the profane only on solemn occasions when the priest communicates with the gods;[59] ostentatious deprivations and unbelievable austerities: everywhere these make the priesthood appear a separate race. In order to enhance its prestige, no effort is spared. Without any hesitation, it sacrifices its life to its power. Among more than one people, when sovereign pontiffs are struck by dangerous illnesses, they have recourse to suicide or secretly receive death at the hand of an aide in order not to be subject—like the vulgar—to this fatal necessity of our nature.[60]

It is the exclusive possession of the sciences, however, that above all is the foundation of sacerdotal power. This monopoly established the priesthood as the privileged thinker, one might say, of the human race. Therefore this exclusive possession was everywhere the object of its most attentive and scrupulous vigilance. It reserved to itself the teaching of morality, of philosophy, of eloquence, of jurisprudence, of history, of poetry, of physics, of astronomy. In Egypt, the priests were the sole historians.[61] Among the Gauls, poetry was permitted only to the bards, an inferior class of Druids.[62] Still, however, the sacred hymns and canticles that contained the elements of the various disciplines had to be composed by the superior

57. Meiners, *De castar. orig. Comm. Soc. Goett.*

58. Staeudlin, *Relig. Magaz.*

59. Schmidt, *De sac. et sacrif. Aegypt.*, p. 57.

60. This custom is already found among the primitives. Bossman, *Voy. en Guinée*; Desmarchais, *Voy. en Guinée et à Cayenne*; Smith, *Voy. to Guinea*; Oldendorp, *Gesch. der Mission*; Avazzi, *Relation de l'Ethiopie.*

61. Diod., I. Geography is also a science reserved to the priests.

62. Fréret, *Acad. des inscr.*, XXIV, 399.

class.[63] Even as the sole preceptors of the youth—whom they brought into the depths of the forests so as to produce an even greater impression on them—they still refrained from initiating them into their teachings (what they called physiology and magic;[64] that is, their interpretation of nature and the means of obtaining supernatural communications). In the same way, the magi had assumed sole responsibility for education in the vast Persian empire;[65] instruction could come from no other source.[66]

Among all these peoples, medicine, a science with many relations to religion (at least as conceived by priests, as simultaneously positive and conjectural), was associated with the priesthood. We saw this in connection with the savage state in the person of the jongleur.[67] Certain salubrious elements could be touched only by priests performing certain ceremonies;[68] the famous serpent's egg, the virtues attributed to the mistletoe of oaks, the solemnity with which one gathered the

63. Pelloutier, II and VII, 186.

64. Caes., *B Gall.*, VI, 14; Strabo, IV; Pompn. Mela, III, 2; Diog. Laert., *Prooemium*.

65. Notably that of the son of the king (Plato, *First Alcib.*). Mexican priests were also the teachers of kings.

66. Leclerc, *Hist. phil.*, 266; Brucker, II, 165.

67. Plutarch (*Life of Numa*) shows us Fauna and Picus, two ancient deities of barbarous Latium, astonishing Italy by the prodigies they worked with incantations and drugs. Now, the way of life of their priests has often been attributed to the gods. Melampus, whom the priesthood of Egypt (Herod., II, 40) and that of Phoenicia disputed the glory of having educated (Diod., I, 96), and who brought the ceremonies of Bacchus to Greece, was both a priest and a doctor (Apollod., II; Serv. in Virgil, *Georg.*, III, 550; idem in Virgil, *Eclog.*, VI, 48). This double quality is also found in Jinyan Li, whom Chinese annals speak about as living in the remote past (Meiners, *De vero Deo*, p. 145). To this day Brahmins are the doctors in India (Sonnerat, *Voy.*). It was the same in Chaldea (Pliny, Strabo). The Levites were not simply the priests of Jehovah, the guardians, readers, and interpreters of the sacred books. They were also doctors, notary publics, and inspectors of weights and measures. In their sicknesses the Mexicans consult only their priests. The third rank of the priesthood in Egypt was charged with the treatment of all physical maladies; in their treatment they followed the precepts of the last six books of Mercury Trismegistus, who, subordinating medicine to astronomy and astrology, judged the nature of diseases and the effects of remedies according to their purported relationship with the planets (Diod., I, 81; Schmidt, *De sacr. et sacred. Aeg.*, 195). Egyptians gave Isis the surname Salutary (Gruter, p. 83; Fabrett., p. 470) and depicted her in her attributes as goddess of medicine, followed by a good *genia*, in the form of a serpent (Zoega, *Nummi Aegypt. imperat.*, tab. XXI, no. 215). Still in Tibet to this day, the doctors and the astronomers are drawn from the class of the *gellongs*, or priests (Mayer, *Myth. Lexic.*, art. *Gellong*).

68. Pliny, *Hist. nat.*, XVI, 44; XXIV, 11.

samolus and *selago*, were only the combination of a few medicinal secrets with mysterious rites.[69]

All this knowledge, carefully kept in the sanctuary, was shared only with great difficulty with foreigners and the profane.[70] The ancients report the obstacles that Eudoxus, traveling with Plato, had to overcome to obtain from the Egyptians a few fragments of their astronomical views.[71] And the confidences given were always cloaked in darkness. Iamblichus, whose character (and times) inclined to admire everything that was unintelligible, extolled the wisdom of those men who, as he put it, imitated nature by surrounding it with obscurity.[72]

Consider the precautions taken against the vulgar. The people of Egypt could not learn to read without thereby committing a crime.[73] Two or three species of language[74] and of writing,[75] each one a new mystery, served as a double or triple rampart against an indiscreet curiosity.[76] The Druids too rejected writing; and

69. Fénelon, *Acad. inscr.*, XXIV, 19.

70. One of the principal privileges of the kings of Persia was to be initiated into the teaching of the magi (Brisson, *De reg. pers., princip.*, p. 384). This initiation was accorded to others only by a favor whose rarity added to its value. Themistocles received it (Plut. in *Themist.*).

71. Strabo, XVII.

72. Iamblich., *De myst. Aegypt. sect.*, VIII.

73. Diod., I.

74. The priesthood did not even deign to explain to the profane the meaning of the words they commanded them to say. At the inauguration of Apis at Memphis, in the temple of Vulcan, the king and his entire court went forth to greet him, and young people sang verses in his honor that no one understood.

75. Herod., II, 36; Larcher, *Not. sur Hérod.*, p. 125; Diod., I & III; Clem. Alex., *Strom.*; see Porphyry, *De vit. Pyth.* Diodorus says that in Ethiopia the understanding of hieroglyphics was not, as in Egypt, uniquely reserved to priests, and that everyone in principle could learn them. But in Egypt itself, sacred or hieratic writing was not hieroglyphic writing. In enumerating the different species of writing in use, Clement of Alexandria (*Strom.*, V, 4) says that there were three: hieroglyphic, sacred, and alphabetic. This distinction comes close to the one that results from the discoveries of Mr. Champollion Jr. He divides the modes of writing used in Egypt into hieroglyphics; hieratics, which were only abridged hieroglyphics, or, as he puts it, the tachygraphy of hieroglyphics; and demotic, or popular (*Précis du syst. hiérogl.*, p. xiii). The subdivision into which he enters with marvelous sagacity would take us too far afield. But it results from his first and fundamental discovery that the priests had a sacred writing that was independent of hieroglyphics, and that the knowledge of the latter could be permitted to the people without their being able to understand the former. They perhaps, however, took another precaution, that of forbidding to the vulgar the knowledge of hieroglyphics themselves.

76. The books of Hermes were displayed in pomp to the multitude but were never opened for them (Ael., *Var. Hist.*, XIV, 34).

when it was applied to religion, they declared this to be the greatest of crimes.[77] The reading of the Vedas is permitted only to the Brahmins,[78] and boiling oil is poured into the mouth of whoever violates this prohibition.[79]

In this way, since the existence of the priesthood rests on mystery, it gathers together all the developments of force and all the resources of cunning, in order to heighten the darkness surrounding it, and to prolong its existence.

The priests not only put themselves on guard against the peoples they govern: they extend their distrust to themselves. The subdivisions of their hierarchy[80] in India and in Egypt,[81] as well as among the Gauls, had as their natural effect hiding their most important secrets from the lower ranks. Of the forty-two books of Mercury Trismegistus,[82] the first thirty-six were known only by the superior classes.[83]

77. The Druses ordered every infidel, unbeliever, or apostate to be torn to pieces if he was found with a copy of the sacred book, or if he had obtained knowledge of its contents (*Museum Cuficum* [Rome, 1782], L). To examine the religion, in their eyes, was apostasy. As they put it, they delivered such a person, body and soul, hair and navel, to Hakim. The Sabians attach the same importance to the exclusive possession of their teachings (Norberg, *De rel. et ling. Sabaeor.*).

78. Bhag. Gita, by Wilkins, pref., p. 5.

79. *Asiat. Res.*, II, 340–345. We recalled this fact in the preface to our first volume. Some believed that we invented it in order to make a malevolent allusion to the Catholic clergy. To know nothing is a disadvantage in argument, and to attribute to oneself such an importance that everything appears to be an attack, whether direct or indirect, is a bad way to begin criticism.

80. "Not only, the division into castes had as its purpose to separate the races; but there were barriers between priests of the same rank. Those of one deity could not be admitted into the body of priests of another. Those of Vulcan at Memphis would not have been received in the corporation of Heliopolis. These separations could owe originally to the fact that the different priesthoods were founded by different colonies; but the priesthood in general profited. Each corporation was submitted to a high priest. Only these high priests corresponded among themselves" (Heeren, II, 597–598).

81. A passage from Clement of Alexandria (*Strom.*, V, 4), too well known and too long to be quoted here in its entirety, indicates some of the subdivisions of the Egyptian hierarchy (the singers, the sky-watchers, the stolistes, the prophets); because even though the author expresses himself in the singular, it is obvious that he is speaking of classes and not individuals. (See n. 85, below, for the affirmation of Diodorus.) But the enumeration is quite incomplete, as one can see by comparing it with the testimony of other writers of antiquity.

82. The forty-two books Clement of Alexandria characterizes as indispensable formed only a small part of the works attributed to Hermes. The collection that bore his name, in which, as we will see, the priests inserted all their successive productions, rose to 20,000, or according to Iamblichus, to 36,525 volumes.

83. Clem. Alex., *Strom.*, VI; Schmidt, pp. 78 & 195. The division of the books of Mercury Trismegistus into five bodies of works, treating religion and all the sciences, very much resembles the division of the Vedas.

The priesthood showed itself no less farsighted when it came to individuals. Even when he was a member of the sacred corporations, no individual wrote in his own name on religion or philosophy.[84]

Some moderns have noted as worthy of surprise that history, while transmitting the memory of the great sacerdotal bodies that have reigned on the earth, has almost never mentioned a distinguished individual. This is because the priesthood's instinct warned it that in order to attain the common goal, the aspirations of individuals had to be suppressed.[85] What we have taken as the proper names of Chaldean and Phoenician writers probably were the designation of a class. The word "*Sanchuni-athon*" among the Phoenicians signified a savant, a philosopher; that is, a priest.[86] Many Indians assured Lord Jones that Buddha was a generic name.[87] In Egypt, all the works on religion and the sciences bear the name of Thot or Hermes.[88] In all of

84. Pauw, *Recherches sur les Egyptiens et les Chinois*, II, 176.

85. Egyptian priests carried into their ceremonies their precautions against the influence of individuals. "In Egypt as in Greece, it is never," says Diodorus, "just one man or one woman who fulfilled the functions of the priesthood. Several together were always charged with the sacrifices and homage due to the gods."

86. Berger, *Geschichte der Religions-Philosophic.*, pp. 39–40; Theodoret. Bochart, *Acad. des inscr.*, XXIV, 64; Meiners, *De vero Deo*, pp. 66–68; Creuzer, *Symbol.*, II, 8.

87. *Asiat. Res.*, II, 124. "Buddha is a very ancient generic name in Hindu mythology. It signifies savant, sage, excellent or superior intelligence. It is even applied to God, the unique and supreme intelligence" (Creuzer, French trans., p. 286).

88. Iamblich., *De myst. Aegypt.* Hermes, whom the Greeks made a god of the second rank, was in a way the personification of the order of priests, reduced to a single figure. It was in this sense that he was the confidant of the gods, their messenger, the interpreter of their decrees, the presiding *genius* of science, the conductor of souls, elevated above men, but the servant and agent of celestial beings. He was called Thot. According to Jablonsky (*Panth. Aegypt.*, V, 5, 2), *Thot, Theyt, Thayt*, or *Thoyt*, in the Egyptian language signified an assembly, and more specifically an assembly of sages and savants, the priestly college of a city or a temple. Thus, the collective priesthood of Egypt, personified and considered as a unity, was represented by an imaginary being to whom one attributed the invention of language and writing, which he brought from heaven and communicated to men (Plato, *Phileb.*, *Phaedr.*), as well as geometry, arithmetic, astronomy, medicine, music and rhythm, the establishment of religion and sacred ceremonies, not to mention gymnastics and dance, finally, the no-less precious, although less indispensable, arts of architecture, sculpture, and painting. To him were attributed so many works on all the objects of knowledge that no mortal could have composed them (Fabric., *Biblioth. graec.*, I, 12, 85–94). He was even honored for discoveries that occurred much later than when he was supposed to have appeared on earth. All the successive improvements of astronomy, and in general the works of each century, became his property and added to his glory. In this way, the names of individuals were lost in the order of priests, and the merit that each one had acquired by his observations and his efforts—turning to the profit of the priestly association—was attributed to the tutelary *genius*

Egyptian history, says a German author,[89] one never hears of the talents or merit of any priest in particular. No discoverer is known, no individual who had a marked influence on the people.

This supremacy of the corporation, and this absence of any individual preeminence, cannot be the result of chance. The priesthood had decided that the eminent qualities of a few were injurious to the prestige of the rest. They wanted to enjoy in common the veneration of the nation. They wanted to transmit a collective respect to their successors. Everything therefore had to be related to the whole. No one had the right to distinguish himself for his own sake.[90]

In this way, we have an oft-noted phenomenon whose cause has never been sought. The sciences in Egypt rapidly attained a degree of perfection but suddenly were stunted. And the entire enlightened class occupied the same rung, becoming immobile before a barrier that was never overcome.[91]

---

of the association, a *genius* who by his double figure indicated the necessity of a double teaching, with the most important part belonging solely to the priests. The individual found no reward except in the renown he procured for the order of which he was a member.

To this first attribute of Thot was joined another, that of the protector of commerce; and this was also the expression of the influence of the priests on commercial expeditions, an influence that Heeren has clearly demonstrated, and about which we will speak in the next book [book IV]. Here we have to forgo the other ideas—multiplied to infinity—that were combined in the imaginary personage of Hermes: his identity with Sirius, the star that was the precursor of the inundation of the Nile, and whose earthly symbol was the gazelle that flees the approach of a flooding river; his rank in the demonology, as the father of the spirits and the guide of the dead; his quality as an incarnate god, subject to death itself, and as celestial nourishment, vivifying bread, mysterious drink of initiates; his cosmogonic alliance with the generative fire, with light, the source of all science, and water, the principle of all fecundity. We will see later how the Greek spirit modified the Egyptian Hermes to make him Mercury.

89. Vogel, *Relig. der Aegypt.*, p. 88.

90. It is interesting to observe the modifications that the progressive action of centuries caused the priesthood to undergo despite, and contrary to, its wishes. Our modern times have not lacked corporations as ambitious as those of Egypt, who would have wished, like them, to sacrifice all individuality to the whole. One can see among the Jesuits this tendency in its highest degree. However, as the epoch of the domination of castes has given way to that of individual influences, the Jesuit order itself could not succeed in having its members resign themselves to being anonymous in their writings, discoveries, and works. Each Jesuit put his name to his works, certainly wanting the society to profit from his renown, but not wanting to renounce, like the priests of Egypt, his personal renown. It is in vain that one seeks to re-create antiquity, that one exhorts individuals to efface themselves in order to bring back the reign of castes. Those who preach this doctrine exempt themselves from the rule; and even among the admirers of Egyptian *anonymity*, individuality enters and triumphs.

91. At the end of book V we will enter into greater developments to prove this fact, which we would have believed undeniable if an author with whom we disagree with great hesitation when it

Thus everything about these domineering corporations, whether within or externally, was monotonous, immobile, and anonymous. This was a discipline analogous to the military, which renders soldiers more terrifying the more blinkered they are; forcing each member to work together without ever separating from the mass and distinguishing himself. If the priests had encouraged the hope of distinguishing oneself, this would have disturbed their common projects by inconsiderate actions and by imprudent conduct. They wanted their forward progress to be in lockstep, they wanted their look uniform, because they wanted to enslave the earth rather than enlighten it, to dominate by their collective weight, not their individual glory.

---

comes to Egypt had not denied it. This nation, Mr. Champollion says in speaking of Egypt, this nation to which Europe directly owes all the principles of its learning and, consequently, those of its social state, was not delayed in its moral development, as some fine minds claim; they derive this mistaken thought from the entirely false idea that they have formed of the ancient writing system of Egypt (*Précis.*, p. 358). Subsequent researches by this intelligent and indefatigable scholar will lead him, I dare say, to somewhat less affirmative assertions. Already some of his discoveries of detail have compelled some remarkable confessions from him. In speaking of the obscenity of several of the monuments he has studied, he agrees that this obscenity shook his belief concerning Egyptian wisdom (letter inserted in *Le Moniteur* of 6 November 1824). Later we will explain the particular cause of this obscenity. It owes to a general cause, the immobile condition of a people bent under the empire of priests.

Mr. Champollion also agrees concerning the imperfection of the Egyptian language even at the highest point of civilization of this country. The spoken language of Egyptians always retained, he says, numerous traces of the primitive state of the language of savage peoples. The majority of the names of animals are nothing but the more or less exact imitation of the cry proper to each of them (ibid., p. 285).

Mr. Champollion seems to us to be mistaken when he thinks that the doubts expressed by very fine minds (as he himself acknowledges) on the subject of the Egyptian wisdom and knowledge come only from a false idea of the ancient system of writing in Egypt. This system is an effect, not a cause. The cause is the caste system, superstition, and the despotism exercised by kings over the nation, and by the priests over kings; in a word, the priestly power without limit, without counterweight, striking without pity or measure all the faculties of man.

BOOK IV

ON THE INFLUENCE OF
SECONDARY CAUSES ON THE
EXTENT OF PRIESTLY POWER

CHAPTER I

An Enumeration of These Causes

By placing all the nations subject to priests into a single category, we do not claim that priestly power has been exactly the same among these different nations. An infinity of events and circumstances had to modify it in many ways.

Among them there is the climate, which, although it is not a primary cause, nonetheless exercises a good deal of influence because it sometimes renders institutions stationary and sometimes encourages their upheaval or their development; the fertility or sterility of the region; the peaceful or bellicose spirit of peoples; their active or indolent character; national independence or subjection to a foreign yoke; great political revolutions, which, shaking states to their very foundations, extend devastation to palaces as well as huts and, by destroying worldly security, compel the unfortunate to seek repose and place hope in another world; geographical isolation or commerce with others; the more or less imperious necessity of physical labor; accidents caused by the nature of the soil, the density of the air, or exhalations coming from the earth; strange phenomena that constantly strike the inhabitants of certain countries with terror; finally, migrations, whether chosen or compelled. All these things had to produce different effects that it is essential to recognize.

We will attempt to point them out.

CHAPTER 2

On Climate

As we demonstrated earlier, climate does not create the authority of priests, but it does contribute to increasing or prolonging it.

To call its influence into doubt, as Helvetius did, is to close one's eyes to the most manifest evidence. Take a trip to the frost and snow of Iceland, Lapland, and Greenland, then to the smiling, clear skies of India. On one hand, you will see rocks white with snow, arid valleys, and lakes covered with thick fog; on the other, mountains crowned with immense, magnificent forests and fragrant retreats where the air itself appears to be an eager benefactor to man, lavishing upon him its harmonious sounds, sweet freshness, and exquisite scents. In one zone, you will see mournful pines rise above, while moss provides a carpet below; in the other, prodigious amounts of vegetation covering the plains and decorating the hills; in the former, a few animals that seem to reflect the hostility of nature and who in vain ask the companion of their misery, their human master, for a meager nourishment, which he can provide only with great effort; while elsewhere there is an abundance of living beings clothed in resplendent colors, found in sometimes elegant, sometimes gigantesque forms, but always marked with the imprint of a superabundance of life. The mineral kingdom itself, the most imperfect realm because the most material and the most distant from intelligence, is nonetheless subject to the same law dividing the two. In the North it offers only pebbles and rocks, while in the South it displays the splendor of an exuberant wealth, depositing gold in the midst of sands and causing precious stones to lodge in the cavities of the earth. One can easily sense the numerous differences that must result for the inhabitants of these two zones from locations that are so dissimilar. The religious need remains the same, but its expression is not the same, and its appearances vary.

Compare the tales of the Skalds and the songs of the Sacontala. In the former, the cow Audumla has to lick with great effort the frozen snow, and only slowly does a restless, petulant, and suffering race of men appear. A cold sweat that condenses, dark blood that congeals, mutilated members that grow stiff—these are the hideous elements of creation. Depicted in bizarrely poetic colors, the serpent Mitgard, the wolf Fenris, and that prophet of destruction, the raven, all of them witnesses or agents at the birth of the world, offer only dark, repulsive images. One would say that struck by the hostility of everything that surrounds them, the inhabitants of these severe climates find a sad pleasure in noting the rigors of heaven. On the other hand, Brahma rests indolently on the lotus, his cradle; Vishnu emerges from the blossom of a flower; Krishna, when he opens his ruby mouth, displays all the marvels of the universe; and the young Sacontala, in the delightful garden that her presence embellishes, is an emblem of the affection of nature for man. The inhabitants of the woods rejoice around her. At her approach, flowers blossom and spontaneously form lovely garlands. The elements themselves rival one another in serving and pleasing her. She is in the midst of all visible and invisible beings like a favored child in the midst of a family that cherishes and protects her.[1]

1. Had we had the time here to deal with the details of fables, we would have pointed out curious differences introduced into narratives and rites by the diversity of climates. In Santo Domingo, where the heat of the sun is unbearable, the natives depict it as simultaneously a protector and an enemy. The first men, they say, had lived for a long time in the dark caves of a mountain. An enormous giant kept them there. However, desirous of knowing the environs, this sentinel departed the cavern for a moment. The sun cast its rays upon him and changed him into a rock. Delivered from his surveillance, men risked leaving their somber retreat, but only at night for fear of the sun, which was as frightful to them as their guardian. One day, several of them having remained fishing until dawn, the rising sun surprised them and transformed them into fragrant trees. Another time, one of them was changed into a bird. Ever since that time, when the bird perceives the dawn on the horizon, it fills the air with harmonious complaints.

But the Greenlanders, upon whom this orb covered with cold vapors sheds only a weak and somber light, instead of imagining it to be the author of such changes, suppose it to be the victim of a fatal metamorphosis. Separated by invincible barriers, two lovers were transported into the skies in the form of the sun and the moon, and eternally follow one another without being able to join together. They also tell the tale that certain Greenlanders, lost after fishing and unable to find their dwellings, were changed into stars (Cranz, *Hist. du Groenl.*).

Similar oppositions can be seen in the periods of ceremonies and those of feasts. In Italy, the month of November, which seems to deprive the earth of its productive powers, was consecrated to Diana, the virgin, sterile goddess. But in Egypt, the goddess of production (Hathor, in cosmogonic language

Indigenous to some climates thanks to astrolatry, transplanted by migrations to others, the priesthood makes its calculations and modifies these different impressions. The South is its natural domain, the North is its conquest.

Northern climates, when the cold is not pushed to excess (because the extreme of cold, as well as the extreme of heat, almost entirely deprives man of his faculties),[2] northern climates, I say, give an extreme tension to human organs. From this results strenuous activity. Physical needs are satisfied only with difficulty. From this comes a tendency toward theft and violence. When northern peoples fight, they have fierce wars. A life that is always tumultuous leaves them little time for religious ideas. Their risky expeditions make necessary protective gods who are within reach. Priests therefore would have little influence over them unless colonization brought them in contact with an already established priesthood.

Southern climates, on the other hand, when their influence is not counteracted by other circumstances, simultaneously form slothful bodies and active imaginations, and the former encourage the latter. Physical indolence leaves an open field to imagination's reveries. While the body is immobile, the religious sentiment is excited, and the human spirit wanders in its conjectures, exalts in its hopes, and loses itself in its terrors. And those who come in the name of heaven to give order to these terrors, hopes, and conjectures, are listened to with respect and approval.

Thus the roots of priestly authority have always been less profound in northern nations than among the peoples of the South. In India, invasions, conquests, and the devastations wrought by foreigners—calamities that go back to the most

---

the primitive night, the creative principle) presides over the same month, during which nature begins to develop its fecundity.

Sometimes the action of the climate is contradicted by local circumstances, which, without changing the fundamental character of a mythology, introduce singular anomalies. The Kamtschadales' tales, which drew their origin in the midst of wintery weather, are nonetheless stamped with a mixture of pleasure and sensual love that suits only the nations of the South. This strangeness is explained by the subterranean fires and bubbling fountains that are found in the icy regions. Harsh cold and devastating heat are combined there, and hence comes a rapid succession of contrasting impressions, which imparts a direction to the mythology that departs from the ordinary rules (Steller; Krascheninnikov; Herder, II, 153). A similar phenomenon had to influence the Indian fictions. Fonts of warm water have recently been discovered at the head of the Ganges (*Asiat. Res.*, XIV). This explains why Ganga, the goddess of the Ganges, was at once the divine fire and the divine water.

2. Herder, *Phil. de l'hist.*, II, 7 & 133. Immobility and apathy are the first goods for peoples numbed by harsh winter weather, as well as for those burned by an ardent sun. The Eskimos of northern Europe and the peoples of Labrador in America find themselves below the human condition.

remote times, and which have been constantly repeated to today—have barely affected the authority of the Brahmans, while the Romans in less than two centuries destroyed, if not the hidden influence, at least the official rule, of the Druids in Gaul and in Britain.

One does not find in the North the great tenacity of belief that is so astonishing among the peoples of the South (because it seems so difficult to reconcile with their lack of energy). Terribly timid in war, Indians brave the cruelest deaths and the most refined tortures rather than abjure their religion or break its least precept. Much less obstinate, the barbarians of the North have always easily embraced foreign cults.[3] It is also to be noted that while the northern religions have never exceeded their frozen environs, the warm climates have sent their beliefs to the entire world. The men of the North have conquered the South. The opinions of the South have conquered the North.

The need for repose and aversion to every form of struggle deprive southern peoples of every means of shaking off an established yoke. In the same way that Indians cannot repulse the invasions of foreigners, they remain passively subject to the dominion of Brahmins. No one should object to this the religious innovations that under the form of divine incarnations or philosophical systems have taken place in India during different epochs, or the multiple sects that divide it. These innovations appear to us to be so frequent because we see them brought together, while in actuality they were scattered at widely different times; moreover, they have not dispossessed the sacerdotal caste; its power has always been so great that dissidents have always returned to its yoke. Among these dispirited nations, external activity directed toward others is almost impossible. They therefore seek refuge in a sort of interior activity, one that is more compatible with their effeminate disposition, and to which their imagination grants miraculous power.

From this comes the singular teaching of the efficacy of penitence and self-laceration. This doctrine gives their fables a character different from those of all other mythologies. Their penances are not solely directed at the expiation of crimes or to correct mistakes. Their aim is much vaster, and their import much greater. Austerities, fasts, and invocations dominate nature, chance, other men, and the gods themselves.[4] The people of the North present to us nothing resembling

3. Nicephor, *Hist. rom.*, bk. II.

4. The Indian books are full of stories designed to instill this opinion in minds. Rejected by his father, Druwen, son of Utamibaden and Sunady, at the instigation of a new spouse went to do penance in a desert on the banks of the Jamuna. In the first month of his austerities, he remained three

this Indian notion of penitence. The interior vigor that animates them dispenses them from painful lacerations, or from placing their strength in curses. Even in dominating them, the priesthood does not change their nature. Born for battle, it is for battle that they are called upon. Disappointed by certain gods, Scandinavians threaten to scale Valhalla in order to lay hold of these gods. Indians, on the other hand, moved by the sentiment of their impotence, refuse any and all combat, and fall back upon themselves and pray or curse instead of fighting. It is by prayer that they defend themselves; it is by prayer that they revenge themselves. It is by prayer that they shake, or shore up, the world. It is even by prayer that they have children. The five children of Pandu owed their birth to the power of a magic

---

days without taking food, living on fruits the rest of the time. The second month he fasted six days, the third, twelve, drinking only as much water as the palm of his hand could contain. During the fourth month he traversed the eight degrees of contemplation, nourishing himself only on the air he breathed; in the fifth month, fixing his thought solely on the supreme Being, he became a stranger to his own body. In the sixth, he closed all access to external impressions. Finally, even keeping in his breath, he conjured the divinity to appear to him. These austerities and the fervor of his prayer shook the world. All the frightened gods turned toward Vishnu, who revealed to them the cause of this universal disturbance; then, bestowing great favors on the penitent, he avenged him on his stepmother, giving him the kingdom of his father, and had him reign gloriously for twenty-six thousand years (Bhagavatam, bk. IV).

One of the seven *rishis*, wanting to attract the gods to earth, fasted for such a long time that a flame burnt on his head, and the gods obeyed him and appeared (Bhagavatam, ibid.). The five penances of Bagiraden overcame the resistance of Brahma, Vishnu, and Schiva, and caused the Ganges to descend from heaven, distributing its waters in the plains it rendered fecund, and resurrected sixty thousand dead that another penitent had killed with a look (Bhag. Gita, X; Sonnerat, I, 232). Wiswamitra [Vishvamitra], a famous conqueror, aspiring to the sublime rank of Brahmin, gave himself over to such severe penances, says the Ramayana, that he soon surpassed the merit of the gods and the saints; and such was the power that he acquired by his incredible austerities that he could destroy the three worlds by an act of his will. Foreseeing this inevitable annihilation, the gods besought Brahma to grant the terrible penitent what he so vehemently desired; and the creator himself, at the head of the celestial hierarchy, came before Wiswamitra and saluted him with the title he so affected.

By a consequence of the unchanging rule that compels man to depict himself in his gods, this supernatural means of penance was soon transported from earth to heaven and was attributed to the creative divinity of the world. It was by plunging into contemplation and abasing himself in penance that Brahma, the absolute unity, drew from his bosom the golden egg that contained the germ of all things. See the mantras of the Rigveda, and also the third book of the Bhagavatam. In the Bhagavatam, Vishnu declared himself to be so taken by the self-inflicted wounds of his worshipper Ambalischen that he could refuse none of his requests, that he would follow after him like an infant toddles after his mother.

prayer.[5] Anathema, which is a sort of inverted prayer, has no less power. The curse of a single penitent penetrates heaven, chills its inhabitants, and compels them to submit.[6] And this irresistible influence is not reserved, as one might think, solely to believers. Rebellious giants and shades of the dark possess the same advantage.[7]

Indians bring this mysterious weapon into their ordinary relations, the only one that fits with their weakness. They have recourse to it in the business of civil life as well as in their religious interests; they use it against their earthly persecutors as they do against heavenly ones; against the English who oppress them as well as their own inexorable divinities; against their creditors or debtors as well as Brahma or Vishnu.

Any other sort of resistance is beyond their moral faculties. Suicide therefore is very easy for them, and it is by a unique combination of strength and apathy that they often place their resistance in suicide.[8] Disarmed by their own nature, they

5. *Rech. asiat.*, II, 188.

6. Indratuymen, whose celestial chariot crossed the heavens and earth as fast as thunder, was changed into an elephant by the curses of an offended recluse (Bhagavatam, bk. VIII). The head of the demi-gods, Devendren, who had cursed another recluse, saw his wealth cast into the sea by an invisible arm, and was chased from the divine abode with all the gods and *genii* (Bhagavatam, ibid.). There is an even more bizarre notion to note. Reciprocal curses do not lose their efficacy. Schiva and Dackscha cursed each other, and both of their anathemas were realized (Bhagavatam, bk. IX).

7. The giant Erunia-Kasyapa imposed extraordinary austerities upon himself, and by doing so obtained enormous power, which he used to attack gods and men. Vishnu having killed his brother Eruniakschen, he redoubled his penances to be able to avenge him, and he obtained from Brahma the privilege of not being able to be killed or wounded either by gods or by men, by giants or by animals, neither in the day nor at night, in a house or in the open air. Fortified by these advantages, he compelled Vishnu himself to hide; and it was only by means of time, patience, and cunning that he could overcome the prerogatives that the giant had obtained; taking the form of a monster who was neither a man nor an animal but a combination of both, the god came upon his adversary as he was crossing the threshold of a palace and therefore was neither within nor without, at eventide when the day was gone, but night had not yet arrived (Bhagavatam, bk. VI; Sonnerat, I, 137).

8. In a very striking manner, an Indian custom attested to by all accounts reveals the impotence, the inability for active resistance, that characterizes the inhabitants of India. An Indian who wishes to obtain something from another individual places himself at his door or on a path where he is sure to encounter him, bringing with him some poison or a knife or some other instrument of death. At the sight of the one he awaits, he threatens to kill himself in front of him if the individual does not give him what he requires. The latter dares not go further for fear of being the cause of a suicide; but if he is not held back by this fear, it is quite customary to see the first carry out his threat (*Asiat. Res.*, III, 344). Indians make use of this means to win their court cases, to obtain payment for what they claim is their due, to reconcile enemies, etc. (ibid., V, 268). In 1787, force having been used against a Brahmin

are conquered in advance, as it were, by the priesthood, which, peacefully atop a hierarchy, receives their homage without having to take the trouble to demand it.

Their power finds an auxiliary in another effect of the climate.

One would say that nature's creative force in the South is exclusively concentrated in the development of material beings, in the profusion of vegetation, in the enormous number of forms and the wealth of colors in the animal kingdom, and that it neglects the principle of the moral life that is progress. In the majority of the countries of the East and the South man is not occupied, as in Europe, with varying the objects that surround him, nor, if I can put it this way, in varying himself. Time, which destroys individuals, changes nothing with the species. The generations replace one another, without being distinguished from one another. The Arab wears the clothes and sandals he wore at the time of Abraham. The Bedouin of today bakes his cakes and buries his dead like the Bedouin who was Moses's contemporary. The past three centuries, the Indian has seen in the European his master and his scourge. He accepts his yoke, but would be embarrassed by his finery, and rejects his ways. Everything in these burning climates bears the imprint of a necessity that is as invariable as it is irresistible. Custom takes the place of the will. Everything seems to be imposed by chance, but calculated to last eternally. Everything is marked with immobility, and by a natural consequence effects become causes.

The immobility that results from climate's action on the faculties of man further

---

who had refused to fulfill a duty to the government, Brahmins constructed a *khoor*, a sort of circular enclosure, put an old woman in it, sat beside her, and declared that if the officers of justice came near, they would burn the enclosure and all would perish. For her part, the old woman threatened the English, if they wished to do violence to her, that she would throw herself into the first well she could find. We have also seen Brahmins pushed to the limit by sentences pronounced against them, or by creditors' suits, kill themselves or kill others, their children, and their mother, believing that the crime would redound on their persecutors. A Muslim, a creditor of a Brahmin, having taken a purse from the wife of the Brahmin that her husband had confided to her, the mother of the Brahmin came with her son to the banks of the Ganges. There, they demanded from the Muslim the sum he had taken, also demanding reparation for her offended honor. At his refusal, the mother exposed her neck and ordered her son to do his duty, and he cut off her head with a sword. The relatives came together, left the body without burial, and beat a tambourine for forty days and nights to keep the soul awake so that she would become the eternal enemy of the one who had offended her (*Asiat. Res.*, V). Thus, experiencing the moral impossibility to act directly against their enemies, Indians make amends by acting against themselves. Among us, we seek to constrain others by threatening them with evil; in India, it is by threatening to do it to themselves.

enhances this action. The theocratic despotism that it favors keeps its slaves at a distance from one another. The regular communication of individuals and classes among themselves, in Europe the principle of progress and perfecting, is foreign to the East and the South. Religious barriers separate castes, and thanks to polygamy (which is always brought back by the climate whether it be in accordance with religious law or not),[9] the family itself is no longer a united society. Isolated in this way, and without any external distractions, the human species is entirely handed over to the constant, monotonous influence of the priesthood.

On the other hand, while rendering this empire more indestructible, the climates of the South also temper its effects. When man does not stubbornly contradict nature, it almost always adds some sort of remedy to a great evil. The climates that are the most favorable to priestly authority are at the same time those that impart the most gentleness to the character, habits, and customs of peoples. Priests themselves do not remain strangers to this salutary softening. However, when priestly omnipotence is the effect of a transitory accident and thus rests on institutions that have no source in nature (something that has to happen in northern climes), no such compensation can occur. All the periods in the history of the Gauls or of Great Britain attest to the ferocity of the Druids, while Brahmins often show themselves to be benevolent and approachable. The general precepts of their moral teaching are pure and sublime.[10] Their souls are open to pity. All suffering beings stir their sympathy.

This disposition extends itself to their cruelest rituals and somewhat veils the monstrosity of human sacrifice. It is forbidden to sacrifice anyone who has not vol-

9. Polygamy, says Heeren, is an insurmountable obstacle to any other form of government besides religious or political despotism. By investing the head of the family with a necessarily unlimited authority, it renders less revolting the idea of a blind obedience that will be demanded and practiced by others. It places outside the State the sex condemned to servitude, and making the husband a master and women slaves, it establishes, as it were, a microdespotism, establishing despotism in the family, the foundation and model of the society.

10. The forgiveness of injuries is inculcated nowhere with more force and unction than in the poems of the Indians and the Persians. "The duty of the virtuous man," says one of their poets writing three centuries before our era, "consists not only in pardoning but in doing good at the very moment of his destruction to the one who kills him, like the sandalwood tree at the moment it falls spreads its perfume on the ax that strikes it." The same idea is found in Sadi, and the famous distichs of Hafiz develop it with a profusion of images: "He imitates the oyster who yields his pearls to the one who tears him open, the rock yields the diamonds to the pick that opens it, the tree that offers his fruits or his flowers in exchange for the stones one throws at it" (*Asiat. Res.*, IV, 167).

unteered. Even in this barbaric practice, the humanity of Indians has need of the consent of the victim in order to excuse in its own eyes what it is doing. This same desire is even manifest in the very words pronounced by the sacrificing priest.[11]

It is to the mildness of the mores[12] the climate inspires that one should attribute the spirit of tolerance that shines in the religious books of almost all the Indian sects.[13] But watch out: let the priests think their interest is slightly compromised,

11. He begins by addressing himself to the very one he is going to put to death. "All the existing beings," he tells him, "were created for sacrifice, and I commit no crime in depriving you of life." But unsatisfied with this justification, he then goes further in eulogies, homages, and promises. "Oh best of men," he declares, "you, the reunion of all the benevolent divinities, grant me your protection, preserve my children, my parents, and me, who am wholly devoted to you; and since your death is inevitable, renounce life, making it an act of benevolence. Grant me the happiness that one obtains by the most austere devotion, by acts of charity, and by observing the ceremonies, and at the same time, oh most excellent of mortals, also attain for yourself celestial felicity!"

"At these words," continues the chapter of blood, "the gods assemble in the victim; he becomes purified of all his sins. His blood changes into ambrosia, and peace of soul, the banishing of earthly travails, and the supreme good, became his lot for all eternity."

Finally, even when the arm of the executioner had struck the fatal blow, his eyes must avoid contemplating his work. He must turn his gaze while presenting to the gods the head of the one he struck down (*Asiat. Res.*, V, 371–391).

Compare these rites with those of the peoples of the North and the West, who believe they add value to the offering by the prolongation of suffering and the refinements of cruelty. We cannot fail to detect the effect of the climate.

12. Even when they go to war, this gentleness of mores does not leave the Indians. When a private interest or affection calls them to the enemy army, they go and return without encountering any obstacles, and without incurring any danger (La Flotte, *Ess. hist. sur l'Inde*, p. 260).

13. Each one, say the Indians, can go to heaven by his own path (Dow, *Relat. des recherche. de Mahumet-Akbar sur la relig. ind.*). "Whatever is the image that the suppliant worships according to his faith, it is me who inspires in him this firm faith," says Krishna in the Bhagavad Gita, "that faith by which he attempts to make this image propitious and obtain from it the object of his desires, as I have determined. Those who, sighing after the fulfillment of what they wish for, follow the indicated religion, obtain a passing reward; but those who think only of me, I assume the burden of their devotion; that is to say, they have an imperishable reward, and will not return into a mortal body. Those who adore other gods with firm faith, adore me too, although unwittingly. I participate in all worship, and I am their reward. Those who adore the Devatas are incorporated in the Devetas, those who adore the *pétrées*, or patriarchs, are united to the patriarchs, the servants of the *bhoots*, or spirits, are absorbed in the *bhoots*, and those who adore me make one with me." Is it not remarkable that while other religious reformers threaten with eternal punishments those who refuse to profess their doctrine, the sole pain that Krishna inflicts on them is to receive a shorter and less perfect reward than that which is accorded to the faithful? Every enemy of God, also say the Indians, every man who while combating him under

and the priestly spirit awakens. It is then in vain that benevolent nature appears to lead them away from bloody superstition. The priesthood triumphs over nature. Then the religions of the South pass quickly from the most affecting tolerance to the most terrible ferocity, from the deepest compassion (even for animals) to the most pitiless cruelty toward men. If one wants proof, let him reread the following passage from the pen of a fine translator: "'From the bridge of Rama to the Himalayas white with snow, whoever would spare Buddhists, whether young or old, let him be put to death,' cried the pitiless Koumaril-Bhatt to his merciless followers, as he ordered the massacre of Buddhists."[14]

---

any of the forms he has assumed is killed by him or by his incarnation, is saved by the very fact that the incarnation touches him while killing him (*Asiat. Mag.*). So much does the gentleness of the climate of India dispose minds to tolerance!

14. Creuzer, French trans., I, 306–307.

CHAPTER 3

On the Fertility or Sterility of the Soil

The fertility or sterility of the soil also ought to enter into account. The Indians and the black peoples of coastal Africa inhabit an equally hot climate. They equally despise work. But the African finds himself compelled to work because nature has condemned him to wrest from the soil the subsistence she otherwise refuses. He thus acquires and retains a habit of action and movement that follows him into his very pleasures. The Indian, on the other hand, whose needs are furnished by a soil that is both fertile and spontaneous, places his supreme happiness in an almost total repose. And after repose, the Indian rests some more, as if fatigued by repose itself. The African, in contrast, after working seeks boisterous games and dances that giddy and numb him. From this it results (with only a few exceptions owing to chance accidents) that the blacks of Africa are much less preoccupied with religion than the inhabitants of India, and the priesthood has much more power over the latter than the former.

In addition, wherever the vegetal kingdom is rich and diverse, the knowledge of medicinal plants acquires a much greater importance than it can in regions of arid soil. The practice of medicine thus becomes an additional cause of priestly influence.

The fertility of the soil has yet another effect. In countries where work is a necessary condition of subsistence, the number of ceremonies that interrupt or suspend work has serious consequences which do not exist when the earth provides for men's needs. It is then that priests profit from their ascendancy to multiply ceremonies, and the great number of solemnities then increases the ascendancy of those who have instituted them. Everything we know about Egyptian religion is proof of this. But as it happens that these institutions can be transported from countries where they were, if not suitable at least harmless, into those where different circumstances render them harmful, the commands of the religion contradict local necessities. In order to overcome these necessities, the priesthood is obliged to exercise its authority more imperiously, and to arrogate to itself even more authority in areas where, according to nature, it ought to have less.

Sometimes the same cause, or better put: two opposed causes, assist the priesthood in its usurpations by suggesting teachings favorable to it. Thus the fertile Delta suggested the idea of the good principle to Egyptians. But by the same token, the aridity of the deserts of Libya appeared to manifest the activity of a malevolent divinity. Now, there is no doctrine that priests seize hold of more eagerly than the notion of a god of evil.

CHAPTER 4

On the Necessity of Material Works and Products for the Physical Existence of Societies

A remarkable thing: while the love of repose and indolence favors the dominion of priests, so too does the urgent necessity for manual labor and material objects on the part of a society; perhaps even more than the former. "No one," writes Diodorus,[1] "by looking at Lake Moeris, could calculate how many thousands of men, and what huge number of years, had to be employed in constructing such an object." Now, its construction naturally fell on the lower castes. Its direction was confided to the ruling caste. This caste had only to indicate what needed to be done and compel its execution. Why? It knew the secret of flooding, it could calculate its return and its phases; it knew how to distribute its waters, how to stop them from being destructive, how to contain or to expand them, to divide them into canals, to construct dams. Under pain of death, the people were condemned to obedience because it was a matter of defending against the return of the waters in a country that had been seized from water's dominion. From this came the most severe oppression, justified initially by necessity, later prolonged by interest, then transformed into a duty by religion and sanctioned by habit.[2]

---

1. I, 2, 8.

2. By an effect of this habit, rather easy to explain although it seems rather bizarre, a people accustomed to necessary works resigns itself more easily than another to nonuseful works. The Egyptian government, theocratic or royal, continued to impose enormous works upon its subjects, or to put it more accurately: its slaves. The kings followed the example of the priests, even while combating them. Cheops and Chephren, persecutors of the priesthood, had the two largest pyramids built; but the people, angered at the end (or more probably, stirred by the priests), swore to withdraw the bodies of these princes from these monuments and to cut them to pieces, which prevented them from being buried (Diod., I, 2, 16).

This circumstance had to imprint a much more somber character on the worship and priesthood of Egypt than was ever the case with Indian religion and its ministers. Thus, we see among the Egyptians no trace of the mildness, humanity, and spirit of tolerance that honor the people of India.

CHAPTER 5

On the Phenomena That Engender Astonishment or Terror

To this cause peculiar to Egypt is joined another, which also operated in Etruria. The rebirth of Egypt seemed to be an annual miracle. The phenomena that accompanied the arrival of the waters, their stay, and their withdrawal astonished observers. Meteors, fumes, and the fetid fogs[1] that rose from the lime of a country submerged under water, upon which the burning sun cast its harsh rays; the numerous and various events that necessarily resulted from the movement of the people fleeing the flooding, then descending from the mountains as the waters receded—so many causes could not fail to dispose souls to superstition and submission to its ministers.

In the same way, earthquakes, frightening apparitions, and noxious miasmas[2] in

---

1. At the beginning, the sky of Egypt certainly was not the clear and serene sky that today is one of the privileges of this country. As long as it was covered with marshes, and before the waters had been channeled into numerous canals, the atmosphere had to be humid and unhealthy. Insalubrious exhalations escaped from Lower Egypt, especially by Lake Serbonis, and Egyptians called these exhalations the vapors of the breath of Typhon (Plut., *Vit. Anton.*, ch. 3).

2. These are the principal causes that Cicero assigns for the great influence of the Tuscan diviners. "*Propter aeris crassitudinem apud eos, multa fiebant, et quod, ob eamdem causam, multa inusitata, partim ex coelo, partim ex terra, oriebantur, quaedam etiam ex hominum pecudumve conceptu et saltu, perterritorum exercitatissimi interpretes extiterant*" (*De divinat.*). Valerius Maximus (bk. I) calls Etruria "*mater omnis superstitionis.*" The word "ceremonies" is derived from the name of the town of Caeres in Etruria, so much were the Etruscans addicted to the ceremonies of the religion (*Fest. v. Caerimoniarum*). The East, said an ancient, read destiny in the stars; Etruria, in the lightning and chance phenomena that struck one's sight.

Earthquakes seem to have been much more frequent in this part of Italy in the past than today. Historians speak of them happening almost every year. This is perhaps because volcanoes erupted less

Etruria encouraged the triumph of the priesthood which had been transplanted in the country by colonies of Pelasgians who had left Greece before the heroic times.[3]

---

regularly. Orosius says (VIII, 10) that Vesuvius did not erupt until the year 829 of Rome, the eruption that caused the death of Pliny the Elder. Worship of the elements, or of the hidden forces of nature, could have owed a great extension to these causes.

Close to the temple of Venus Aphakitis at Aphaca, between Heliopolis and Byblos, was a lake in the midst of which suddenly rose a round-shaped flame. This phenomenon is reported by Seneca (*Quaest. nat.*, 3, 26) and by Zozimus (I, 58); according to the historians, it wonderfully encouraged the people in their submission to the priests.

3. The country of Congo is subject to earthquakes, to flooding, to droughts, and epidemics. It is during these unfortunate times that the power of the *gangas* grows and is deployed (*Parallèle des religions*, I, 719).

CHAPTER 6

The Influence of the Character and Customary Occupations of Peoples

Priestly authority is no less affected by the pacific or belligerent character of peoples. Egypt lived for a very long time as peaceful. The humor of its inhabitants was never warlike.[1] In this country there were never, as in Greece, leaders of armed peoples who limited, much less destroyed, theocratic domination. Nor were there, as at Rome, political institutions that constrained the priesthood by incorporating it into itself. The efforts of soldiers or princes to become independent were fruitless, or at least what success they achieved was temporary, and Egypt was always delivered over to the priests, at first its kings, and tutors of its kings, after they had descended from the throne. These priests recognized so well the advantages a lasting peace held for them that the conquests of Sesostris and the expeditions of his successors were always considered scandalous. The kings of Egypt were condemned to inaction. Their names serve only to designate a succession of years marked by no memorable enterprise. And 330 of them succeed one another like gray shadows that nothing particularly characterizes or distinguishes.

On the other hand, it is probable that without their passion for war the Scandinavians would not have struggled for so long against the usurpations of the Drottes, and that it would not have been necessary to have three revolutions and two foreign invasions in order to overcome their resistance.[2] If we knew the details of the history of Germany and Gaul, it is probable that we would see the ascendancy of the Druids shaken from time to time by the efforts of military chiefs.

In general, the more that man is occupied with earthly interests, the less he

1. "Neither the Egyptians," says Strabo (bk. XVII), "nor the peoples who neighbor them, have bellicose inclinations."

2. We will develop this historical truth when we deal with the development of the Scandinavian religion.

allows himself to be dominated by other men who speak in the name of heaven. Everything that calls him back to the business of life places limits on a power whose justification is found elsewhere than in this world, whose promises can be fulfilled only beyond the grave.

If, despite the scattered facts that indicate the terrible power of the Carthaginian priesthood, priests are rarely spoken of in what is reported to us about Carthage, this can be explained by the spirit of enterprise and the mercantile activity that, among these rivals of the Romans, doubtless had effects comparable to those of the martial spirit of the followers of Odin.

But such is the complicated action of different causes that combine and modify each other, that the same commerce that limited the power of priests in Carthage enhanced it in Ethiopia.

The colleges of Ammonium and Meroë inhabited the fertile oases scattered throughout the sandy deserts. These oases were the resting places of the caravans that crossed the country. Only there did they find water, vegetation, and shade. But they also sought directions to where they were going, as well as the distance and location of places they would have to cross. The priests gave them such information in their temples, in the form of oracles;[3] while indicating to the travelers their route, they also revealed to them the destiny that hung over them.

3. Such was the temple of Jupiter Ammon, situated in an oasis in the midst of a sea of sand.

CHAPTER 7

On the Effect of Great Political Calamities

Great political calamities also influence the extent of priestly power. In the same countries where the climate establishes the narrowest limits to this authority, these limits cannot resist the extraordinary circumstances that lead men back to superstition. Great defeats as well as great misfortunes—a famine, a plague—give it fierce new life, analogous to the bloody character of warlike peoples. Theocratic despotism reappears in its most terrifying extent, along with the most frightful rites. Prosperity, wealth, perhaps even the beginnings of enlightenment, had diminished the empire of the Carthaginian priests; but then Carthage was threatened by Agathocles. The organs of the gods then suddenly regained the fullness of their authority; the children of the most illustrious families were dragged to the temples, and their blood was offered in expiation and sacrifice.[1]

1. Diod. Sic., XX, 3. The same thing happened at Tyre when Alexander besieged the city (Quint. Curt., IV, 4).

CHAPTER 8

On the Effect of Migrations

At first glance, far-off migrations would seem to be prejudicial rather than helpful to priestly power. Even when it is not their primary aim, war is their inseparable companion. Personal courage and military talent, faculties that need regular exercise to develop and which propel men into the active life, as well as force them to have regular contact with the multitude, are hardly compatible with the prestige with which the priestly order covers itself. It thus gives them formidable rivals.[1] We thus observe several nations free themselves from their priests, at least for a time, during the long voyages they undertake to find a homeland. In the migration from Egypt to Greece, and the blending of Egyptian colonies with Greek tribes,[2] the priesthood almost entirely lost its authority. And much later in the New World it was a migration (instigated and directed by a priest, it is true) that led the Tenochtitlán tribe into Mexico, and to choose as its chief Acamapitzin. Even the colonies that were particularly devoted to the sacerdotal cause, those of Ethiopia,[3] for example, which left their country in order to advance this cause, did not always completely escape from this natural effect of expatriation. While in Meroë the king had to be drawn from the sacred caste, history teaches us that in Egypt Sethos, a priest of Ptah who took over the throne, was considered a usurper.

Nonetheless, special circumstances can cause even these migrations to serve the advantage of the priesthood. The Jews are an example. The exit from Egypt, the sufferings of the Jews, and their sojourn in the desert certainly consolidated the rule of Moses and the Levites. This is because the Jewish people had a fixed goal;

---

1. See the following chapter on the struggle between the priestly power and military and political authority.

2. We will prove this in book V.

3. V, III, iii.

and before departing the land of their slavery, their prophet had fixed their gaze upon a country that God promised them. The entire expedition was religious. It rested entirely upon hopes that had faith for their basis and the promise of Jehovah for guarantee.

Moreover, the weakening of priestly authority by migrations is often only temporary. When a fixed and stable life replaces the wandering life, the priesthood, even if it does not always resume its title, reprises its power. It was thus in Egypt and in Mexico, and it did not happen in Greece only because of the reason we will lay out in the next book.

CHAPTER 9

On the Struggle of Political and Military Power against the Priestly Power

Independently of the accidental or temporary causes that can more or less significantly modify the extent and forms of priestly power, there is one that, without having obtained among ancient peoples the more decisive or durable results we just discussed, nonetheless produced very remarkable effects and cast the human race into an all-too-frequent state of turmoil. We therefore think it is our duty to give this subject some development. We mean to speak about the struggle that took place in all the countries subject to priests between them and the holders of the other powers.

This contest is found in the nature of things and is therefore inevitable.

Even in the countries where the priesthood is originally the sole power, a subordinate authority is not slow to establish itself. Occupied with the care of dominating the peoples by religion, priests are forced to delegate to subordinates the administration of the State and its defense against foreign invasions. As a consequence two new powers are formed: the political power and the military power. At the beginning, they appear to be mere emanations from the priesthood. Its delegates receive a revocable mission, and they fulfill a duty of obedience rather than exercise an authority. But henceforth power seems to be divided. Its different branches appear to be confided to different hands, and this appearance soon enough turns to reality. The temporal heads of government and the generals of the armies are gripped by the sentiment of their strength, and the moment arrives when, whether by a spontaneous impulse or because public opinion invites them, they reject their subordination and claim independence. It is the signal of a struggle that, once commenced, will never end.

This is the spectacle that India, Egypt, Persia, and, above all, Judea, present.

Sometimes the *cutteries*, or warriors, puffed up with pride, shake off the authority of the Brahmins. But some avatar avenges the sacred caste and punishes the rebels with terrible severity.[1] Sometimes an impious monarch, having forbidden the worship of the gods, and having provided the example of a sacrilegious mixing of castes, the priesthood's curses strike him dead, and his more compliant successor submits to the sway of the ministers of the altars.[2] Other times, the periodic destruction of the world is attributed to the diminishment of respect for the priestly order, and once again, Brahmans rise from the chaos to govern the restored world.[3]

1. Children of the sun, the *cutteries* oppressed the Brahmins. Then Parasurama, the sixth avatar of the race of the moon, himself a Brahmin but as courageous as a *cuttery*, attacked the oppressors and defeated them in twenty-one pitched battles, filling entire lakes with their blood. He despoiled their goods and took his implacable severity so far that the Brahmins whose empire he had reestablished were themselves distressed at the vast destruction he had wrought (*Mythol. des hindous*, I, 280–290; Schlegel, *Weisheit der Indier*, p. 184). This struggle of the warriors against the Brahmins forms an episode of the Mahabharata. In the fifth book it is said that at Malva reigned a prince named Herghes. His army was made up only of *cutteries*. A war arose between him and the king of the Brahmins. In each battle the *cutteries* were the larger force; nonetheless they were always defeated. He finally went to find the Brahmins and asked them: How is it that you always win the victory, even though we are more numerous than you? The Mahabharata does not report the priests' response (Heeren, *Idées sur l'Inde*, p. 566).

2. Vena, son of Ruchnan, arrived at the throne because of the flight of his father, forbade all worship of the gods and all justice among men. (The priesthood always sees in the assault on its power the disappearance of all justice.) He imposed silence on the Brahmins and banished them far from him. He next entered into an illicit union with a woman of their caste, allowing others to imitate him, and allowing the children of the gods to mix with the children of men. Forty-two mixed-castes came from these impure marriages. Then the Brahmins cursed him and took his life. As he was without children, they rubbed his hands against each other, and from his blood came a fully armed son, learned in the holy sciences and as beautiful as a god. From his left hand the Brahmins caused a daughter to emerge, whom they gave him as wife. He reigned justly, protecting his subjects, maintaining the peace, punishing disorders, and honoring the Brahmins (*Asiat. Res.*, V, 252).

3. At the time of one of these catastrophes, in the second age, say the Indians, a small number of individuals in the caste of Brahmins, of merchants, and that of artisans were spared; but there were none spared of the caste of warriors or princes, because they had all abused their power and their strength. At the rebirth of the world, a new caste of governors was created; but in order that its members would not be inclined to misbehave, it was drawn from the caste of Brahmins; and Rama, the first of this new caste, was the protector of priests, and acted only according to their counsel. The Laws of Menu mention several races of warriors who became savages; that is to say, they freed themselves from theocratic government and the caste-system; among them were the Pahlavi, whom Schlegel conjectures were a tribe of Medes whose language is still called Pahlavi. This fact supports what we said above, that even in Media, and a fortiori among the Persians since the conquest of Media by Cyrus,

It is plausible that analogous revolutions occurred in Egypt during what is called the reign of the gods.[4] The caste of warriors, the second in the State, appears to have risen against the first.[5] But the latter won the victory. The later establishment of the monarchy did not end the struggle.[6] Refractory monarchs succumbed during their lifetime or after their death.[7] And in the division of Egypt among the twelve kings, he who separated from the others in order to place himself at the mercy of priests[8] soon obtained the sovereignty of the entire empire, which he resigned himself to not ruling except in accordance with their orders.[9]

We will mention Ethiopia, which was the scene of much bloodier revolutions, only in passing. We have already seen that the priests of Meroë condemned their

---

the division into castes did not continue in full vigor (Schlegel, *Weisheit der Indier*, pp. 184–185; Laws of Menu, X, 43–45). Indian books still speak of a Brahmin of Magadha, who had Nandha, king of the country, put to death and placed a new dynasty on the throne (*Asiat. Res.*, II, 139).

4. According to the priestly annals of this country, this "reign of the gods" in Egypt would have lasted eighteen thousand years, and it would have ended in the person of Horus, son of Osiris (Diod., I, 2, 3). "Formerly," says Herodotus, "the gods reigned in Egypt; they lived with men, and there was always one who exercised sovereignty." It is probable that among many peoples there was a theocracy prior to temporal government. The reign of the planets, presented among the Chaldeans as having preceded that of men, is the period of the theocracy named in Egypt the reign of the gods.

5. Herodotus (II, 141) mentions an inscription intended to preserve the memory of this event.

6. "The impiety of the kings of Egypt toward the gods of the country," says Diodorus (I, 2, 3), who wrote drawing from priestly sources, "gave rise to frequent revolts."

7. The first king of Egypt was Menes. His laws on religion limited the empire of the priesthood (Diod., I). He thus attracted the wrath of this order, which, after having regained its influence over his successors, authorized or obliged Technatis to have curses against him inscribed on a column (Plut., *De Is. et Osir.*). Two other kings whom annals written by priests called tyrants and rebels, Cheops and Chephren, had the temples closed for thirty years (Diod., I). Mr. Denon notes that it was during the anti-priesthood period that the only palace belonging to the kings of Egypt was built (*Voy. en Eg.*, II, 115). But the priest Sethos once again seized the throne, and took from the military caste the possession that had been given to it; they therefore refused to serve against Sennacherib, king of Assyria (Herod., II, 141). The story of the Ethiopian Sabacon, who, having become king of Egypt, in a dream received an order to cut in two all the priests of Egypt, but recoiling before such a crime, abdicated power—would that not be a garbled tradition of some conspiracy of Egyptian priests against a foreigner become their master?

8. Herod., II, 147–152.

9. It is remarkable that this Psammetichus, who owed his victory over the dodecharchy to his submission to the priesthood, nonetheless sought to prepare the ruin of priestly power by basing himself on foreign troops, and by opening the ports of Egypt to Greek merchants.

kings to death. In revenge, one of these, Ergamenes, a contemporary of the second Ptolemy, had all the priests massacred in their own temple.

The history of ancient Etruria has remained quite obscure. But the order given to the Etruscans by their king Mezentius to give him the first fruits they were accustomed to devote to the gods, can probably be seen as an attack against the priesthood.[10]

We have already said that we will treat in a later book the religion of the Scandinavians and the revolutions that ended with the triumph of the head of a colony of priests.[11]

The same struggle occurred in Persia. But it was complicated by particular circumstances. To be understood here, we need to lay out these circumstances. The digression will be brief.

Three powerful empires, the Babylonians, the Lydians, and the Medes, divided Asia. The nomadic Persians, who lived in a state of extreme barbarism, obeyed the Medes as much as wandering hordes in the vigor of barbarism can obey masters rendered soft by lengthy civilization. In the midst of Persia, mountain-dwelling clans, sometimes defeated but never subjugated, lived in inaccessible retreats.[12] Cyrus, who originally was named Agradatus,[13] had himself proclaimed head of these divided tribes. His efforts and their success, as recounted by Herodotus, confirm how close these tribes still were to the savage state.[14] Having united them,

10. Macrob., *Saturn.*, III, 5.

11. A learned author given to systems (Wedel Jarlsberg, *Abhandlung ueber die aeltere Scandinavische Geschichte*, pp. 173, 269–72) seems to us to be mistaken concerning the development of Scandinavian religion. According to his hypothesis, one of the Odins, by means of ruse and violence, established a monarchy on the rubble of a theocratic government. But his account is too detailed to be trustworthy. When it is a matter of periods that are so obscure, wanting to connect this or that isolated fact, and purporting to fill in all the lacunae, are sure means of adding several errors to a few truths; and the more coherent an account, the more its different parts are harmonized, the more suspicious is the composition, as ingenious as it may be.

12. Herod., I, 125.

13. Strabo.

14. "Cyrus," says Herodotus, "having deliberated with himself concerning the most cunning way of bringing Persians to revolt, judged that the most effective would be the following, which he put in motion. Having written a letter in which he put in what was necessary, he convoked an assembly of the Persians, and opening the letter, read it to them: it said that Astyagus (the king of the Medes) had named him their leader. "I therefore order you, oh Persians, to present yourselves tomorrow, each with your sickle." This is what Cyrus said to the assembly. . . . The Persians having obeyed and arrived the next day, Cyrus commanded them to remove the thickets and brambles from a place in the country,

Cyrus led them against their effeminate masters, who were weakened by the refinements of luxury, the extent of their possessions, and by the despotism that is as
fatal to masters as to their slaves. Cyrus's victory was easy.

What he did otherwise—his conquests, his ruses, and his oft-vaunted institutions (which ended in bequeathing Asia to a madman and founding a dynasty that
lasted a mere seven years)—all that is beside our point. What is of interest to us
is what his conduct was vis-à-vis the priesthood of the old empire he conquered.

The religion of Bactria was a priestly religion. It sanctified the division of
castes.[15] And the caste of priests, itself hereditary and powerful, took part in government and marched at the head of the pomp and ceremony of the court.

The chief of the barbarians was greatly taken with these solemnities and ceremonies. He hastened to surround himself with them, moved by that naïve vanity
that is not at all unknown to kings born on the throne, and which can mark even
more nonhereditary ones. The Median civilization worked a change in him comparable to the one that Chinese civilization operated more than once on the Tartars. All the Median customs were imitated,[16] and religious institutions were not

---

the space of about eighteen or twenty stadia. This work completed, he ordered them to return the next
day to the same place, but in festive apparel. During the interval, he had goats, sheep, and cattle drawn
from the herds of his father killed and prepared, along with the best available wine and cereal foods,
for the Persian army. Returned the next day, he invited them to recline on the manicured ground and
to enjoy the feast. When they were sated, Cyrus asked them which they preferred, the hard work of
the previous day or the feast. They exclaimed that there was a huge difference: that the day before they
had put up with all sorts of evils, while today they enjoyed all sorts of goods. Seizing upon these words,
Cyrus revealed his ambition to them. Men of Persia, he told them, behold what is before you. If you
follow me, you will have these goods and many others, and you will be exempt from all servile labor.
If you do not follow me, you will have to suffer innumerable hardships similar to those of the day
before. Therefore hearken to my exhortation and be free. I believe I am destined by heavenly decrees to
place in your hands all of life's goods, and I do not believe that you are inferior to the Medes, either in
military valor or in any other thing. Separate yourselves, therefore, as soon as possible from Astyagus"
(Herod. I, 126). What was said was done. Astyagus, after having given the order to have some of his
counselors who were magi impaled, was defeated in the first battle, and taken in the second.

15. See the chapter on the division into castes [Constant. bk. III, ch. 8].

16. The testimonies of all Antiquity agree on this point. Herodotus speaks of the facility with
which the Persians adopted foreign practices (I, 135). When they allude to Persian institutions, Jewish
writers always name together the laws of the Medes and the Persians (Esther, I, 18; Daniel, VI, 8). Plato
reproaches Cyrus for the disorders that began under Cambyses and continued after him, disorders that
he says were produced by the influence of women and eunuchs, i.e., by the imitation of the corrupt
mores of an effeminate court (*De legib.*, III).

exempted from this imitation. Nothing being less in keeping with the rustic and barely developed intelligence of the Persians than the abstractions and mysticism of an old cult, the Zend Avesta (which from then on ruled the Medes)[17] never became the national book.

17. In having to go back to a period prior to the conquest of Media, if not the Zend Avesta itself, which could have been redacted by a contemporary of Cyrus, to whom one gave the fabular or generic name of Zoroaster, then the teaching of the Zend books, we find ourselves in disagreement with several writers of the previous century who denied the authenticity of the records brought to Europe by Antquetil-Duperron (see Meiners, *De vet. pers. rel. Com. Soc. Goett.*). But none of their objections convince us. If no Greek writer before Alexander speaks of the works of Zoroaster, this silence is no more extraordinary than that of all of Antiquity relative to the Jewish books. It therefore does not prove that those of the Persian legislator are not authentic. One can only infer that, carefully preserved by the magi, they were not shared with the profane. With conquest having overthrown the barriers this caste had erected, we find in the ancient authors dating from this period frequent allusions to these writings.

From the fact that one can note the conformity of some parts of the Zend Avesta with the Koran, some have concluded that the redactors of the Zend books borrowed these passages from the prophet of the Muslims. It would have been more simple to recognize borrowings from ambient oriental opinions by Mohammed.

To be sure, the actual content of these books corresponds very poorly to the great wisdom that the Greek philosophers extolled in their author. They are overburdened with formulae, invocations, and superstitious rites. But the wisdom of Zoroaster was a Greek prejudice, who loved all the foreign institutions that distance and mystery made imposing. In addition, these books are very consonant with all the scattered information we find in the historians concerning the doctrine, practices, hymns, and prayers of the magi. The more attentively one examines them, comparing them with the books of all the nations subject to priests, the more apparent their authenticity becomes. At most, it is reasonable to suspect a few interpolations or additions. The Bundahishn is perhaps more recent than the others. But the rest is certainly from the most remote Antiquity.

We would be tempted to believe that their redaction, as it has come to us, was the work of a reformer writing by the order and under the surveillance of the Persian ruler of the Median empire, consulting and reworking even earlier materials. For the Persians speak of yet earlier writings, the Sophs, for example, or priestly books attributed to Abraham, and the Gyavidan-Chrad, the treatise of eternal wisdom by Hushang, ancient Median king. To suppose as some have that it was the Persian religion that Zoroaster reformed under the first Darius encounters an insoluble difficulty. How could a people who at the time of Cyrus were plunged into the deepest ignorance and had seen only thirty-eight or thirty-nine years pass between this conqueror and Darius, son of Hystaspus, where would a reformer have found the elements of a teaching that was so sophisticated and so abstract, completely disproportionate to the level of his fellow citizens and his time? Reformers are never anything but the organs of the opinion about to rise and rule. Zoroaster himself tells us that he was a Mede, and that he lived under a king named Gustasp. People have made him the first Darius without reflecting that Gustasp,

The mass of Persians retained their ancient gods, their "paternal gods" as historians call them.[18] Sometimes the religion even modified its own practices, which the magi wanted to compel them to preserve.[19] It was probably not the intention of the magi that Zoroastrianism became the popular religion. Like that of the Indians, Egyptians, and other eastern or southern peoples, this religion of the Medes was the property of the priests. Its adoption in Persia consisted in the admission and presence of magi at the court, rather than the dissemination of their teachings. The worship of Media thus became that of the Persian palace.[20] Cyrus welcomed it as a portion of the ceremonial that flattered his pride, rather than as a conviction of his soul. The demanding activity of a martial life and the cares of despotism rendered him little susceptible to that. In addition, he wanted his authority to profit from it. The religious and political code of an empire long given to servitude contained a fine model[21] for the government he was establishing or

---

far from being a proper name, was the common title of all the monarchs of the East. But the prince that Zoroaster mentions did not live in Persia. He resided in Bactria; the provinces of his empire are indicated in the Zend Avesta (See Kleucker, Zend Avesta, II, 299). Neither Persia properly speaking, nor any of the cities where the kings of Persia lived, belong to this list. How would Zoroaster have passed over in silence, in a long and detailed description of the empire, precisely the province where the capital was located, and which gave its name to the entire empire? This assumption, too absurd to be admitted, is justified by no author worthy of confidence. Neither Herodotus nor Xenophon, nor even Ctesias, speaks of a Zoroaster contemporary with Darius; and Plato, the first who names Zoroaster, places him at an uncertain period, but much more ancient.

18. See the passages cited in Brisson, *De region persarum principatu*, p. 347.

19. For example, relative to funeral practices. The magi exposed the dead to wild animals. They considered it to be a crime to bury them or even to gather their bones. The nobility, over whom this corporation of courtly priests exercised a direct influence, were obliged to respect this law of the priesthood. A Persian lord risked his life by departing from this custom (Agathias, II; Procop., I, 11). Even the people, less dependent because of their obscurity, and the army, which in all countries despots are forced to manage, did not fail to observe these practices. Ammianus Marcellinus (bk. XIX) speaks of a general who had the body of his son who had been killed in battle burned, and brought his ashes back to Persia.

20. Xenophon gives us a clear enough idea of this conversion of the court of the Persians. For the most part, the Persians, he tells us, imitated the worship of the king because they hoped for greater happiness by serving the gods in the same manner (*Cyroped.*, VIII). However, what Xenophon says about Persians in general actually applies almost exclusively to the nobility (Heeren, *Idées*, I, 522).

21. The invisible world and the demonology of Zoroaster are obviously calculated to give a religious sanction to the new institutions of Cyrus. The court of Ormuzd is similar in everything to that of the king; and the number of Amscaspands is, according to some, equal to the number of castes; according to others, to the number of functionaries who surrounded the throne. This Zoroaster—

reviving, and it offered a means of reconciling the formerly insubordinate tribes to the new government. These tribes were once instruments of the warrior, but now they were objects of distrust on the part of the despot. Cyrus surrounded the royalty with divine honors.[22] He turned to his advantage the ideas of purity and impurity that in other countries were useful only to the priesthood.[23]

Whether because he despaired of destroying the magi or because he believed he had found a support in them, Cyrus preserved their dignities and several of the prerogatives that they had enjoyed in their former country.[24] They continued to be the ministers of worship, the counselors of kings, the judges of the people. But authority sells its benefits at a price. Cyrus kept the magi dependent upon him. Corporations, however, possess a kind of flexibility that comes from the certainty of survival and eventual victory. The priestly spirit was preserved, hidden but intact. The dementia and death of Cambyses opened a path to its hopes.

From this time on, the magi constantly attempted to recapture their former power. In these efforts they invoked not only the respect the Medes had for their native priests but also the hatred they had for their foreign conquerors. The usurpation of the false Smerdis was a revolt both of the magi against the kings and of the Medes against the Persians. The kings defended themselves and opposed the priests

---

believed to be inspired, a god-possessed prophet, a sage given to retreat and absorbed in meditation, a legislator speaking in the name of Ormuzd and in full liberty—could have been nothing but a court prophet, someone following orders, writing at the dictation of a master in order to please him. But at the same time he was a magus, imbued with the spirit and devoted to the interests of his order; hence, there are many personal recollections in his rites, and many contradictions in his precepts. Sometimes he commands work, activity, and everything that despotism loves to have happen for its own convenience, without any of this done to benefit the people. This is when Cyrus's will dominated. Sometimes he launches into a pantheism where his dualism is absorbed, extolling the mystical union of man with the divinity, the abnegation of personal existence, a purely contemplative life. This is when the magus reappears.

22. Athenaeus (VII, 13) transmits to us a story of Theopompus, according to which the courtiers of the Persian king raised an altar to the *genius* of the king during their meal; this was worship that, to the great scandal of the Greeks, was imitated by an Argian named Nicostratus. Mention is made of this sort of worship in the discourse Isocrates wrote to Philip.

23. The figures on the ruins at Persepolis that are not clothed in kaftans take care to cover their mouths when they speak to those who are wearing them, for fear of tainting them with their breath (Heeren, I, 303–305). Now, the kaftan was Median apparel used at the court. The monarch granted the privilege of wearing it to his favorites, and this privilege conferred on them a superior purity.

24. Xenophon (*Cyroped.*, VIII) positively affirms that the magi were introduced by Cyrus himself into the empire he founded.

with not only tyrannical, but sometimes terrible, means. The strange, and certainly garbled, anecdote of satraps compelling Darius to forbid praying to gods during thirty days[25] appears to be an obscure indication of some despotic political violence against the power of the clergy. Better known is the annual feast celebrated in all the empire in memory of the massacre involving the priestly order. Already under Cambyses a magus had undergone a terrible torture.[26] Under Darius, another had been suspended on a cross, and before ascending the throne Smerdis had been shamefully mutilated.

Despite these terrible cruelties, the magi continued the struggle with a perseverance that was rewarded.

Several circumstances that we previously indicated as contributing to the power of priests militated in the magi's favor. If they had against them the climate of Persia, properly speaking, where high mountains covered with snow for several months transform the South into the North, as it were, they had for them the climates of Bactria and Media.[27] In this vast empire there was a struggle of climate against climate.

For the same reason, if the bellicose character of the Persians could show itself resistant to a priestly domination that was contrary to their wild customs—a domination founded upon notions much too abstract for their still undeveloped intelligence—the refinement of the civilized portion of the empire and its long habit of seeing the magi as their guides and instructors, had to have won out over the repugnance of the population, itself the artificial aggregate of formerly scattered tribes.

Finally, the action and influence of the phenomena of nature that we spoke about in connection with Egypt and Etruria were no less powerful in several regions either subject to or close by Persia. As Mr. Creuzer observed,[28] Azerbaijan is famous for its sources of coal tar. Its soil is full of resinous substances; bitumen floats on the surface of lakes. Often in the midst of the darkest nights columns of flame rise which seem to the astonished eye the miraculous appearance of an

---

25. Daniel, VI, 7.

26. Herod., III, 179; VII, 194.

27. This variety of climates is proved by the figures one sees on the ruins of Persepolis. Some are naked, as under the most burning sun, others are clothed with fur, as in the coldest countries (Chardin).

28. Creuzer, French trans., I, 319.

avenging or rewarding deity. The priesthood would have turned to its advantage both the astonishment and the fright that such phenomena elicited.

Thus profiting with great address from the prerogatives the conqueror of their country had granted them, the magi extended them under his successors. From the time of Xerxes they were about as powerful as during the time of Astyagus. And during the course of our inquiry we will see all the characteristics pertaining to cults subject to priests gradually reintroduced, if under more or less mitigated forms, in both the teachings and the rites of the Persians.

CHAPTER 10

Continuation of the Same Subject

The Hebrew books provide the most precious and detailed information concerning the causes that lead to the separation of the two powers, and the way in which this separation occurs. It is also in these books that one finds the most detailed discussion of the dissensions and hostilities that result from it.

Initially, Jehovah governs without division. In his name, Moses exercises the supreme authority. Even though invested with the priesthood, Aaron himself obeys the prophet.[1] The two powers only form one. Nonetheless, succumbing to the weight of multiple burdens, Moses delegates the civil and judicial functions to men whom the people present to him.[2] These men are but his instruments; but already the popular choice contains the seed of an authority different from the theocratic authority.

This seed seems to disappear under Joshua. He concentrates both powers in his hands, speaks to Jehovah, transmits His will to the Hebrews, commands the priests as well as the elders of the tribes, sacrifices victims, presides over ceremonies, pronounces judgment, and leads the army. But after his death, invasions and defeats give the military power new importance separate from the priesthood. Warriors, imprecisely called judges, take their place immediately below the high priests, and an independent spirit is not slow to take hold of them. They demand hereditary rights; a portion of the Jews recognize them;[3] and a first appeal is made to es-

1. While instituting the priesthood and giving Aaron as its head, Moses did not strip himself of sacerdotal authority. Aaron was only his instrument and his subordinate. "He will speak for you to the people," says Jehovah to Moses, "and he will be your mouth. With respect to him, you will hold the place of God" (Exod., IV, 16).

2. Exod., XVIII, 17–24; Deut., I, 13–14.

3. Judg., IX, 1, 2, 16–18.

tablish a monarchy.[4] This effort is repressed, and the judges remain on the second rank. They are not named until after the pontiffs, and their borrowed and restricted authority is nothing compared with the priests'.[5] The priests, however, seem dissatisfied with even this supremacy; the priesthood wants to take back temporal authority. Eli was simultaneously judge and high priest, and Samuel, who replaced him, united the two functions at the battle of Masphat.[6]

But finally the idea of the separation of powers triumphed.

The people demanded a king.[7] In vain, the priesthood resisted, in vain, they told the people of the Divine's indignation,[8] and the punishments this anger prepared.[9] An unheeded threat! The priesthood was compelled to accede.[10] The different powers appeared and henceforth will do battle.

One cannot fail to recognize in the history of Saul and Samuel (even though presented from the perspective and for the sake of the priests) the revenge of theocracy against the monarchy it had grudgingly established.[11]

4. Ibid., 6 & 23.

5. "I will not reign over you," said Gideon to the Jews, "nor my son, but the Lord will rule over you" (Judg., VIII, 22–23).

6. I Kings VII, 6 & 11.

7. "You are old," said the people to Samuel; "your children do not walk in your ways; give us a king" (I Kings, VIII, 5–6).

8. "Today you have rejected your God," said Samuel to the assembled people (I Kings, X, 19). "Hearken to the voice of the people," said Jehovah to the prophet. "It is not you but me that they despise, by not wanting me to rule over them" (I Kings, VIII, 7, 8); Josephus, *Antiq. jud.*, IV, 8; Spencer, *De legib. ritual. Hebraeor.*, I, 227–240).

9. The theocracy was perhaps never more eloquent than in its portrait of the royalty. "The king," said Samuel, "will take your children to drive its chariots, it will make them charioteers, and have them run before its chariot. It will make them officers, some to command a thousand men, others to command fifty thousand. It will take some to work its fields and to harvest its wheat, and others to make its weapons and chariots. It will make perfumers, cooks, and bakers of your daughters. It will also take the best of your fields, vines, and olive plants, and give them to its servants. It will make you pay the tenth of your wheat and the yield of your vines in order to give to its eunuchs and officers. It will take your servants, male and female, and your strongest young men, and make them work for it. It will also take the tenth of your flocks, and you will be its servants. Then you will cry against your king whom you have chosen, and the Lord will not listen to you, because you yourselves have asked to have a king" (I Kings, VIII, 17–18).

10. By attributing to God himself this condescension, a famous theologian in a rather strange way applies to divine omnipotence the counsels of prudence and flexibility that Cicero gave to his friends. "*Non permanendum est in unâ sententiâ, conversis rebus, etc.*" (Cic., *Ep.* 9 *ad* Lentul.). Never has anthropomorphism been so openly declared (Spencer, *De legib. ritual. Hebraeor.*, I, 243).

11. Lilienthal, *Gutachten der Goettlich.* Offenb., VI, 212.

The prince, chosen from an obscure rank by the priesthood that wanted to remain his masters,[12] subject to obligations that were equivalent to servitude, consecrated at the hands of the high-priest,[13] obliged himself to take the priesthood as his guide and counselor on every occasion. In his very first expedition, it was in the name of the high priest that he ordered the people to follow him.

This transaction preserved all the advantages for the priesthood. Soon, however, a sacrifice offered in the absence of the high priest,[14] an act of clemency contrary to its orders,[15] stirred its indignation.[16] The monarch defended himself, but in vain. Sometimes he employed force. He had Achimeleck and eighty-five priests who helped his rival killed.[17] Sometimes he prostrated himself at the feet of his rival and besought him not to take revenge against his family when he ascended the throne. Finally, though, he succumbed and bequeathed to his successors (sprung from another race) the sad duty of submission or the dangerous option of resistance.

It is also true that the overthrow of Saul was not the spontaneous movement of the people, that among the twelve tribes of Israel only one declared itself against him, while all the others remained faithful to his family and his person.[18]

After his fall, the Hebrew annals are full of the attempts of priests against the kings and of kings against the priests. Solomon banished the high-priest Abiathar, who had taken sides with his brother Adonija.[19] Asa cast the prophet Ananias

---

12. Even though Saul appears to be designated by lot, the way in which his election is recounted proves that the priests had intervened, and, above all, that they sought to have it believed that they were involved (I Kings, XV, vv. 20ff.). There are even several details that indicate that the priesthood, sensing its inevitable dethronement, caused the election to fall on a little-regarded individual in order to be able to manipulate him more easily (ibid., I, 9). Thus we see the most eminent personages of the Jewish nation witness to their discontent with the choice (ibid., I, 10, 27).

13. Some have claimed that Samuel could not have been a priest, because he does not appear to be of the tribe of Levi (*Lettres de quelques Juifs*, III, 410). But Samuel, an unknown infant taken in by Eli, high priest and supreme judge, replaced him in this double role after having won the victory over the Philistines at Masphat.

14. I Kings 13, 13.

15. I Kings 15.

16. "Because you have not obeyed, you will not long be king" (ibid., 15–22). It was in vain that Saul humbled himself. God had declared to his prophet that he repented of having chosen him, and ordered him to choose another (ibid., XVI, 1).

17. I Kings 22, 9.

18. Ibid., II, 2, 8, 9.

19. III Kings 2, 26.

into a cell.[20] He punished with death several prominent men of Judah who had declared themselves for the prophet. Jehoiada had Athalia killed in order to place the young Joash on the throne.[21] Joash, who owed his throne to Jehoiada, publicly accused him of dilapidation and later, without any regard for the memory of his benefactor, ordered that his son Zechariah should be stoned.[22] This murder was avenged by the assassination of the king.[23] Even though he reestablished the Mosaic cult in its purity, Azariah[24] wanted to shake off the yoke of the priests. The Levites had transformed the temple of the Lord into a stronghold where they could defend themselves; it was their fortress and arsenal. Azariah having forced the doors of the temple, the high-priest called armed Levites against him, and the monarch was chased from the sanctuary.[25] Jeremiah was arrested by the order of Zedekiah, and Joachim punished Uriah with the ultimate torment.[26]

We draw only these episodes from the part of Jewish history that pertains to the two faithful tribes, because one could attribute the active conspiracies of the priests and the violent persecutions of the kings to the idolatrous portions of Israel who resisted belief itself, rather than to a struggle between powers. One clearly sees in the history of Jehu a priestly rebellion parallel to that of Saul and David. Elisha secretly anointed this usurper.[27] Jehu killed Jehoram, had his mother Jezebel killed, as well as seventy-two sons of Ahab and forty-two brothers of Ochosias, the king of Judah, and he assembled all the priests of Baal in a temple and had them slaughtered.[28] As his reward, Elisha promised the kingdom of Israel for him and his posterity until the fourth generation.

The Hebrew kings sought everywhere for help against the always threatening priestly influence. Hence their eagerness to form alliances with neighboring nations, even though they were appalled by those nations' worship. Barely crowned, David sought the friendship of Hanun, king of the Ammonites. Solomon married

20. II Chronic., 16, 10.

21. IV Kings 11, 16.

22. IV Kings 12, 7; II Chronic. 24, 20–22.

23. "His servants rose against him to avenge the blood of the son of Joiada the high-priest, and they killed him in his bed" (IV Kings 12, 24–25).

24. Named Osias in the Chronicles.

25. We have already recalled this fact, III, x. Earlier we needed it as proof of the monopoly; here we cite it as proof of the struggle.

26. IV Kings 26, 20.

27. IV Kings 9.

28. Ibid., 25–30.

the daughter of Pharaoh[29] and made a treaty with Hiram, king of Tyre.[30] Asa allied with the king of Syria.[31]

In vain the prophets thundered against these alliances. Fearless imitators of Moses, threatening instruments of heavenly decrees who were equally independent of the priesthood and the monarchy, they filled Judea with their denunciations. Their faces dark with ashes, their bodies belted with the skins of animals, they left forests and caves to fill the cities with their cries and the councils of kings with their anathemas. All their writings are full of severe descriptions of the luxury, tyranny, corruption, and infidelity of the Hebrew monarchs. Hosea employs every conceit, all the allegories, all the metaphors of oriental poetry to depict the excesses and degradation of these princes, the hedonism of the court, the lethargy of the government, the abasement of subjects, and the apostasy of masters.[32] Amos left Judah to condemn Jeroboam in the very heart of his empire.[33] Micah depicts the earth shaken, the mountains falling, and valleys opening beneath the feet of a guilty people and an oppressive monarch.[34] But by indicating what their weaknesses were to the holders of temporal authority, these threats also made clear the necessity of shoring up the throne.

This conflict of the two powers, more than anyone has noted up until now, contributed to push the kings of the Jews toward idolatry. The condemned worship, observes Spencer, was above all introduced under the kings. All the judges remained faithful, while there were very few princes who did not turn toward idols.[35] They saw in them a weapon against their rivals and a refuge against their implacable enemies. In this way, it could be true of the Jews—as it was among many other peoples—that the priesthood itself caused damage to the cause it believed itself to serve, and that religion had to bear the consequence of the faults, or the ambition, of its defenders.

29. III Kings 11, 1.

30. Ibid., 5.

31. II Chronicles 16, 3.

32. Hosea, II, 7; IV, 4–8, 12, 18; V, 1, 13; VI, 8; VII, 4, 11–16; VIII, 9–13; IX, 3, 13; X, 3, 6; XI, 5; XII, 2; XIV, 4.

33. Amos, II, 9; III, 12; IV, 1; V, 1, 6; VI, 1, 10.

34. Micah, III, 12.

35. *De legib. ritual. Hebraeor.*, I, 245.

CHAPTER 11

A Necessary Explanation of What
We Just Said about the Jews

While expressing ourselves on the Hebrew priesthood with a candor we have tried neither to hide nor to soften, it was far from our intention to attack the religion of Moses in itself. We are very far from wanting to join with those who have placed the Jews at the lowest rung of ancient peoples and have presented their doctrine as a fierce and fanatical superstition. The writers of the eighteenth century who treated the holy books of the Hebrews with disdain mixed with hostility judged Antiquity itself in a terribly superficial way, and the Jews were of all the nations the one they least understood, whether it be their genius, their character, or their religious institutions. In order to join with Voltaire against Ezekiel or Genesis, one has to combine two things that make his mockery rather sad: deep ignorance and a most deplorable frivolity. Far from sharing this view, which became popular at the end of the previous century, we regard the Hebrews as very much superior to the tribes that surrounded them, and even to the despotic empires that reduced them to slavery. However, we recognize (which no impartial judge can contest) that their annals are filled with revolting facts and cruel actions that we have no intention of justifying. In order to explain this apparent contradiction, here we will lay out our entire thought, making use of the right our own faith grants us. This right is to examine and study the records upon which this belief is founded. And nothing obliges us to hide the results this examination yields.

If one admits revelations—that is, direct and supernatural manifestations of the Divinity to man—one ought to consider these revelations as assistance granted by a powerful and benign being to one who is ignorant and weak, when his forces are not enough for him to improve his lot on earth.[1]

1. We ask our readers to reread on this subject a note found in the first book (ch. 6, n. 8) where we planted the seed of this idea, but which we could not adequately explain at the time without disturbing our presentation.

Then a ray breaks through the darkness covering the uncertain traveler seeking his way. But the goal of man is perfecting himself. He cannot do so except by his own efforts, by the exercise of his own faculties, by the activity of his own free will. If he is protected by a wise and benevolent power, whom his sentiment needs to recognize despite the doubts that logic can raise, this power itself must limit its assistance to instruction, by revealing truths proportionate to man's intelligence. These revelations enlighten him without enchaining him, they leave him free to use this gift at his own risk and peril; he can abuse it, even reject it. The struggle that good and evil wage within him, his halting efforts, his fruitless attempts, his errors, and even his crimes do not disprove the revelation he has received. These things belong to the struggle that is his lot, and this struggle itself is the means of perfecting himself. Led toward this goal by a power that would enslave his will, he would lose his quality as a free agent; and reduced to the status of a machine, his perfection would become mechanical. Amelioration would have nothing moral about it. Therefore the Divinity confides truth to man, which he must defend, preserve, and develop. This is the mission of his intelligence. But in charging him with this mission, it changes nothing in his nature. It leaves this nature as it was—imperfect, subject to error, able to be mistaken about means, often choosing defective, bad, even culpable ones.

Apply this framework to the revelation of Moses. We see him born in a country given over to the crudest superstitions, in the midst of a tribe regarded as impure, and even more ignorant than the rest of the people. Now, theism is not compatible with such a degree of ignorance. How, then, could Moses have been in advance of his century? Some have attributed this theism to Egypt. They have thought that, adopted by an Egyptian priest, he must have known the secret teachings of the priesthood of this country and constructed his religion from them. This opinion seems to us to be completely mistaken.

When we later put forth the different philosophies of barbarous peoples, and the mystery religions of the Greeks into which these philosophies were introduced, we will have the occasion to show just how little the theism (which then combined with pantheism) resembled the idea of the unity of God of the Hebrews, presented in a simple and clear way in their books, and entering into moral relations with men. This last characteristic constitutes the essential difference separating the two species of theism: the supreme God of the priestly philosophies had only cosmogonic features. This God was only the union of the hidden forces of nature, personified in an abstraction (even though the two words seem to contradict each other), or the combination of all the attributes of this sort scattered among the popular divinities. The absence of any particular providence, and the denial of intelligence and individuality, were its distinctive features. It is true that at the decline of polytheism, with all sorts of opinions having been introduced into Greece via the mysteries, a less abstract theism, one more susceptible to becoming a real religion, was admitted, not as the dominant system but as one of the systems among which the priests chose what was most suitable to individual initiates.

But this has no relation to the theism of Moses, which existed twelve centuries earlier. With a marvelous sagacity, Moses spoke to unlettered men the language that was suitable to them, while only rarely adjusting his teaching to the exigencies of their limitations. Moreover, his concessions consisted more in words than in things;[2] they were passing clouds that obscured only for a moment what was sublime in the ideas he taught concerning the Supreme Being. Idle questions and insoluble problems were carefully avoided. The legislator of the Jews did not seek, like the priests of Egypt and India or the philosophers of Greece did, what God's substance was, if He exists with, or without, extension, if He is finite or infinite, if His existence is eternal and necessary, or if it was the result of some arbitrary will. The prophet of Mount Sinai avoided those flights of an uncontrolled imagination of the sort found in popular cults that give them a ridiculous and repulsive cast, and those useless intellectual subtleties that ushered the philosophical theism of India into a labyrinth whose end was necessarily either atheism or pantheism. Atheism because reason, forced to proceed by negation, finally transforms the Divinity into a negation. Pantheism because recognizing only a single substance under a thousand illusory appearances, it absorbs the universe in its author, and substitutes for the religious sentiment a certain enthusiasm that pleases itself with sonorous phrases, but deprives religion of everything consoling, tender, and moral, leaving it at most an imposing form and sterile majesty. In the Genesis account of creation, to which one must accord everything the genius of the East merits, one finds neither an inert rebellious matter nor a mysterious egg, nor a giant cut in pieces, and no alliance between blind forces and atoms devoid of intelligence, neither a necessity that chains reason nor a chance that disturbs it.

This superiority of the religion of Moses is not limited to doctrine; it extends

2. We already cited one of these concessions (bk. II, ch. 2, n. 41): Jehovah passing through victims cut-in-two, in order to enter into a pact with Abraham (Gen., XV, 9–17). This ceremony signified that the one who violated his oath agreed to being cut into pieces like these victims. This was a singular effect of anthropomorphism, which applied this minatory ceremony to God himself. One cannot fail to see here a legislator compelled stoop to the level of the people. One of the premier German theologians, Eichhorn, rightly observes that the people of Moses were constantly below their legislator (*Einleit. zum alt. Testam.*, I, 7).

to its rites. Those that the Jewish books prescribed, no matter how bizarre they appear to our minds formed by a more advanced civilization, are less bloody, less corrupting, less favorable to superstition, than those of the peoples subject to priestly polytheism.[3] When we later consider the ceremonies, the customs, and the modes of worship of these peoples, we will always see in first place human sacrifices and obscene feasts. The Hebrews owed to Moses their being preserved from this double opprobrium.[4]

3. The rites of the majority of priestly nations were calculated to accredit the superstitions on which the power of priests rested: auguries, the explanation of dreams, the invocation of the dead. At several places, the Law of Moses forbids these appeals made by cunning to credulity. "You will use no augurs or any other sort of divination" (Lev., XIX, 26). "And let there be found among you no one who consults soothsayers or reads dreams or auguries, or who uses witchcraft, lots, or enchantments, or who consults those who have the spirit of Python and who attempt to divine, or who interrogate the dead to learn the truth" (Deut., XVIII, 10–11).

4. Voltaire claimed that the Hebrews had immolated human victims. Now, the extremes of terror and superstition had to have led all peoples to these abominable practices; but they never were part of the customary worship of the Hebrews, as was the case in India, Egypt, and Gaul. The Law of Moses expressly forbids them (Lev., XX, 23; Deut., XII, 31).

If it were part of our inquiry to examine in detail all the parts of the legislation of Moses, we could easily show the superiority of the Hebraic laws on matters that have no direct relationship to religion. While we see only in Persia a servitude that no law and no custom tempers, and in Egypt a constant and monotonous oppression exercised alternatively by the priesthood and the royalty; while we seek in vain in these countries—today the objects of childish admiration—some traces of guarantees for those who were neither priests nor soldiers; we see seeds of liberty in the institutions of Moses that cannot be denied, and which like his religious doctrine seem to be put in reserve for later times. Alongside the legislator appears a council composed of the ancients of the nation which deliberates and pronounces on all important affairs. The sole thing that is excepted is the teaching concerning the divine unity; on it Moses tolerates no discussion because it was his main means—in fact, his sole means—of transforming the Hebrews into an independent people; it could not be called into question without imperiling his entire enterprise. But for all the rest, Moses consulted the elders of the people (Exod., IV, 29). At the solemn adoption of the law, he was surrounded by this senate chosen by the people (Deut., I, 13). This senate decided on war and peace; and to justify war the consent of all the Hebrews was required. "Behold all of you here, children of Israel, see what you have to do" (Judg., XX, 7).

It certainly is not a small point in Moses's favor that having come from the land of Egypt where the division into castes was established, he rejected this noxious institution. It would have been better, no doubt, to extend equality even further, and not to have created a privileged priesthood; but the good has its proper time that nothing can hasten; the moment of the enfranchisement of the human race had not yet arrived. This emancipation was pronounced only by the divine author of the Christian law. Even then, his successors hastened to violate its precepts. Moses could not go so far, and yet if we carefully study the Hebrew books, we see in them the seed of the abolition of the priestly privilege at some future date. "There will come a time," says Jeremiah, "when the law will be written on all hearts,

We say all this with so much more conviction because our view was formed slowly and, as it were, despite ourselves. The appearance and duration of Jewish theism, in a time and among a people equally incapable of conceiving the idea and preserving it, are in our eyes facts that cannot be explained by reasoning. That subsequent to this acknowledgment, what we call revelation, the instruction of Providence, a light due to His wisdom and goodness, others call an interior sentiment, the development of a seed deposited in the human soul, does not much matter to us. For the one who believes in God, every illumination comes from Him, as well as everything in us that is good and noble; and revelation is found wherever there is something true, noble, and good.

But in the particular case of Moses, what constituted what we call revelation, if not the knowledge of the unity of God and the religious sanction given by this unique God to the moral duties and obligations of man?

The deliverance of the Hebrews, slaves in Egypt, their being brought together in a body as an independent nation, their wanderings, their conquests, all these things are found within the sphere of human things. They therefore ought to be judged like all human things.

Doubtless, Moses's enterprise was noble and generous, and in a certain sense one can say that liberating his fellow citizens is a mission come down from heaven. But this enterprise did not exceed the forces of our nature. Others have tried it, and others have succeeded as well as Moses.

----

when no one will need to teach their neighbors or their brothers, nor to repeat to them: Know the Lord; for all from the youngest to the most eminent will know him" (Jer., XXXI, 33–34).

A fact that is not irrelevant, and which seems to us to cast considerable light on the subject we are dealing with, is the liberty that Moses granted to prophets, even when they did not belong to the priestly order; it is above all important to notice that he defended this freedom against his most devoted followers. "A young man ran to Moses and said: Behold Eldad and Medad who are prophesizing in the camp. Immediately Joshua, son of Nun, who was one of the young men who served Moses, said to him: Moses, my lord, stop them; but Moses answered: Do you have jealous thoughts on my behalf? But would to G–d that all the people of the Lord had the gift of prophecy! And that the Lord would pour out his spirit upon them!" (Num., I, 27–29). Compare this liberality of sentiment in Moses with the institutions of Egypt, where there was a class of priests named prophets, but drawn from the priestly order, and which was hereditary.

Finally, a passage from Deuteronomy (XVII, 14) proves that Moses foresaw the monarchy, that is to say, the end of the government of priests. He announced it without disapproval; in our eyes this is yet another indication that the power of the priesthood was only a temporary means for him; this puissant order, however, made sport of his predictions; it is not given to those who institute it to limit either its power or its duration.

No doubt also, it was always in the name of Jehovah that he commanded. It was in the name of Jehovah that he inculcated humanity in the Jews, fraternity among themselves, and even hospitality toward strangers. And yet it was also in the name of Jehovah that he drew the sword against the Amorrheans[5] and that he had the Midianite women killed.[6]

It therefore requires readers with an upright spirit and an equitable heart—that is, friends of both the truth and religion—to distinguish what the exigencies of Moses's position forced him to confound. We would go further and say: things that in good conscience he had to combine.

According to his deepest, most intimate conviction (and truth, as it is given to man to experience, is entirely found in his convictions), Moses regarded as an inspiration from God the project that he had formed of delivering his compatriots, of rescuing them from the most humiliating conditions,[7] the most burdensome labors,[8] as well as the recurring cruelties constantly suggested to their oppressors by the suspicions they entertained of the oppressed. The year of his birth had been marked by an execrable act[9]—the slaughter of the newly born—on the part of harsh masters whom they had served in an expedition against Ethiopia.[10] A little while later, the murder, certainly legitimate, of one of the agents of the tyranny[11] connected his self-interest with his patriotism. He therefore raised the banner of independence, and the exodus from Egypt was the first fruit of his courage and his perseverance.[12]

5. Exod., XX, III, 4.

6. Num., XXXI, 17.

7. The Egyptians considered the Hebrews unclean (Gen., XLIII, 32). Their hatred for this people was perpetuated from generation to generation. They sent an embassy to Caligula to denounce them. The grammarian Apion, against whom Josephus wrote, was a member of this embassy.

8. Spencer, *De legib. ritual. Hebraeor.*, II, 20.

9. According to the generally received view, Moses was born the same year as the command to drown the first-born of the Hebrews.

10. Eichhorn, *Einleit. zum alt. Testam.*, II, 236ff.

11. Exod., II, 12.

12. Was the exodus from Egypt voluntary, or was the departure of the Hebrews the execution of a sentence of exile? We do not have to decide this question. Both of these conjectures can appeal to impressive witnesses. According to an ancient tradition reported by Josephus, the Hebrews, whom the king of Egypt had relegated to the town of Avaris, took over the entire country, led by a priest of Osiris named Tisithes, and later Moses; but banished once more, they adopted a new religion and invaded Judea (Josephus, *Contr. Apion.*, bk. I). According to this tradition, attributed to Manethon,

But dangers of every sort threatened the tribe he guided and of which he was the mainstay. Fearful, indecisive, and weakened by 430 years of slavery,[13] it had contracted habits that even its hatred of Egypt could not break. Moses always had to fear that it was going to ask again for its fetters, and that even far from Egypt it would become an Egyptian-like people. It was to prevent this backsliding that he designed all his institutions. This aim is as discernable in his fundamental laws as in the most minute regulations; it dictated what he said about clothing, it presided over food, it directed the work of the poor and oversaw the luxury of the rich; it likewise presided at the funerals of all.[14] This aim, however, was never perfectly attained, and Moses was constantly forced to concessions that both angered and grieved him.[15]

---

to Cheremon, or to Lysimachus, it was Amenophis who assembled the Hebrews at Avaris. They were designated by the name of lepers. Policy commanded the Egyptians to rid their country of the remains of these tribes of shepherds who had multiplied in a frightening manner; some natural calamity perhaps also confirmed them in this resolution, and the interest that the Hebrews had in escaping slavery facilitated its execution. As for the epithet "lepers" given to the fugitives, it probably was the equivalent of "impure," the result of the national hatred for the Jews in their character as shepherds (Goerres, II, 467–469); Herder (*Philosophie de l'histoire*, III, 86) has some useful pages on the installation and sojourn of the Hebrews in Egypt. Diodorus recounts the same fact as Josephus, with other details. "A great plague," he says, "having spread in Egypt, the inhabitants of this country attributed the scourge to some offense committed against the gods by the foreigners who professed other religions, and they sent them outside their country; the greatest number of the banished went to a region now called Judea, which then was desert. Their head was Moses, a man superior by courage and prudence" (fragment preserved by Plotinus, trans. by Abbé Terrasson).

On the other hand, the Bible is explicit. According to chapters III–XII of Exodus, the Hebrews left Egypt against Pharoah's wishes.

13. Exod., XII, 40.

14. Thus it was forbidden to Hebrew priests to shave their heads, an Egyptian custom, or to display disheveled hair, which several nations practiced in their funeral ceremonies (Ezek., XLIV, 20; Schmidt, *De sacred. et sacrif. Aegypt.*, p. 12).

15. All the authors who wrote with knowledge of the Jewish religion—Philo, Eusebius, Origen, Saint Jerome, Saint Chrysostom, Maimonides—acknowledged that there are great resemblances between the customs of the Hebrews and those of Egypt (see Larcher, *Not. sur Herodote*, II, 122). The hereditary institution of the Levites among the Hebrews was perfectly parallel to the priestly caste that dominated in Egypt (Schmidt, *De sacred. et sacrif. Aegypt.*, p. 8). The scapegoat of one was the prototype of the other (Larcher, *Not. sur Herodote*, II, 135). Kircher proves (*Oed. Aeg.*, I, 300) that the worship of the golden calf was a recollection of Apis. The oracle of the Jews known under the name Bat Kol, or daughter of the voice, was founded on the signs that the Egyptians gathered from the voices of children who sang while they played before the stall of their sacred cow (Jablonsky, *Panth. Aegypt.*).

While he prepared victories against the countries that he had to invade, it was necessary for him to achieve an ever more difficult victory over the people, more difficult because it could escape him at any moment. Hence the need to inoculate his people from the memories of the past and the seductions of the present.[16] Hence those severe laws against the vanquished, who were more numerous than their victors.[17] Hence those horrifying punishments of Jews who fell back into idolatry. Greater indulgence toward the first would have led to the alteration, then

---

Josephus reproached the Egyptian Apion with having unwittingly attacked the ancient ceremonies of his own country by insulting those of the Hebrews (*De antiquit. gent. judaic. ap.*; Origen, *Contr. Cels.*). Several Greek and Latin authors have confused the rites of the two nations, so great was their similarity (Schmidt, *De sacred. et sacrif. Aeg.*). So opposed to the intention of Moses, this similarity has often embarrassed the theologians. God wanted, says Saint-Philippe (*Monarchie des Hebreux*), to receive homage from his people at any price. While Spencer says that in the institution of the Mosaic rites, God appears to be compelled by a kind of necessity that moved him almost despite himself, *quasi coactus* (Spencer, *De legib. ritual. Hebraeor.*, I, 196).

16. Israel will live alone and in security (Deut., XXXIII, 28; Gen., XLIII, 32). "I am the Lord your God who separated you from the other peoples, so that you would belong to me alone" (Lev., 9, 20, 24, 25, 26). The majority of the ritual laws of the Hebrews end with these words: "Observe this law, for it is a sign between you and me" (Exod., 31, 13). "You will act neither according to the customs of the country of Egypt where you lived, nor according to the mores of the country of Canaan I will have you enter. You will follow neither their laws nor their rules" (Lev., XVIII, 3ff.). Moses's intention can be seen in the designation of particular places for the sacrifices, and in the punishments pronounced on those who would offer them elsewhere. In the part of the laws that bear upon the causes of impurity, a part manifestly borrowed or imitated from Egypt, the legislator still seeks lines of separation (Spencer, I, 115, 195). This is how to explain the thousand interdictions that seem to be arbitrary, those of sowing among the vines, of boiling the lamb in its mother's milk, of eating uncooked flesh, etc. (Deut., XXII, 9ff.). All these interdictions were motivated by some custom in the neighboring nations; the same is true of forbidding working with a cow and an ass. If one wishes to see in detail how emphasized this purpose is in the Mosaic laws, please read the treatise by Spencer we have cited (I, 277, 585).

17. It needs to be seen that in these rigorous measures, Moses almost always has necessity as his excuse. Condemned to conquer a soil that would support them, the Hebrews were forced to destroy the tribes that, having recovered from the first shock and joining their forces, would have sooner or later destroyed them. Devastation therefore necessarily accompanied the conquest. Any other people would have done the same. It is not Moses's religion, it is his position that one must accuse.

Moses, however, foresaw a time when greater indulgence would be possible. "When you will approach a town to besiege it," he says, "you will offer it peace. If it accepts and opens its gates to you, everyone found within will be saved and will be subject to you and give you tribute" (Deut., XX, 10, 11). However, the Hebrew leaders and pontiffs who replaced Moses were much more merciless than he. Samuel surpassed him in inflexibility and barbarity. One would say that an ever-growing increase in cruelty and intolerance was the pleasure of the priesthood, once constituted.

the destruction, of the nascent Jewish nation. Less rigor against the second would have allowed every trace of the theism that was far from consonant with their intellectual development to disappear. This, however, was their only distinctive characteristic and the sole point of cohesion among them. Nonetheless, it is obvious that revelation, properly speaking, this act of supreme power manifesting itself to man in order to explain the meaning of his existence to him and to clothe his duties with a religious sanction, has nothing in common with these steps of a legislator to govern his people, or of a conqueror to consolidate his success.

Even though he was instructed in the great truth that one day would transform the entire human race into a single family, is there any surprise that in order that his people would not lose this knowledge, Moses adopted the means that seemed best to him? That these means had features of the barbaric customs of a time when human life was little respected?[18] That he did not fully gauge the disproportion between his teaching and the level of intellectual development of his compatriots and contemporaries?[19] That even while recognizing this disproportion, he was prematurely condemned to a violent struggle? That this struggle compelled him to excessive severities? That in order to have faithful guardians of the truth of which his soul was so convinced, he established a priesthood invested with a terrible power? That this priesthood abused its authority? All of the foregoing is in the purely human order and has nothing to do with revelation.

---

18. It is indispensable, says the author of one of the best works we have on the Law of Moses (Mr. Salvador), under pain of committing the most egregious errors, to distinguish what the legislator did and willed from what was done later by others; his principles from the applications that circumstances dictated, and the actions produced by the barbarity of the times (*Loi de Moïse, ou Syst. Polit. et relig. des Hebreux*, foreword).

19. The disproportion that existed between the pure theism of Moses and the level of civilization of the Hebrews was the principal cause of the dissent that troubled this people and the crimes reported in its annals; history nowhere offers as striking an example of the consequences of the complete disaccord between institutions and ideas. This subject merits some developments. We will place them in this note.

First of all, despite the explicit teachings of Moses, the Jews did not conceive the unity of God except as a relative unity. Besides the Jehovah they worshipped, they recognized enemy gods. They abhorred them, but they believed in them. Jehovah was for them only a tutelary divinity who, abiding, fighting, and traveling with his defenders and sharing their animosities, treated foreign gods as competitors who were odious to him and as rivals of whom he was jealous, whose altars he wanted overturned in order to replace them with his own, and by destroying other peoples, replace them with his own (Meiners, *Com. Soc. Goett.*, I, 93). We will cite the passage in the original, in order not to be

These were the things that have been confused. The sectarian spirit has maintained that not only did Moses's doctrine about the Supreme Being come from a divine source, but the Hebrew books themselves were divine—even their material redaction. The facts recounted by Moses and the writers who came after him were not judged as historical facts and in accordance with the rules of morality, which

---

accused of impiety for an opinion uttered and received without any scandal in a country at least as Christian as France: "*Ex in numeris sacrae historiae exemplis et locis facile ostendi posset Israelitarum vulgus Jehovam suum, non tanquam omnium gentium numen, sed tanquam suum, gentisque suae peculiarem deum, veneratum esse, quem inter ipsos habitare, cum ipsis in bello proficisci, easdemque porro inimicitias exercere, omnes denique hostiles populos funditus exscindere velle, persuasum habebant.*"

But even when Moses seems to have abandoned this limited notion, even when pure theism is proclaimed, all the classes abandon it, the kings as well as the people, the people as well as the great. Listen to one of the most religious theologians of England on this subject. "*Si populi mores, in historia sacra memoriae proditos observemus, eos se hodie Deo voventes inveniemus, cras idolis, nec citius Deum superstitionis aegyptiacae hydram decollasse quam monstrosa capita denuo repullulassent*" (Spencer, *De legib. ritual. Hebraeor.*, I, 21).

Moses had a bronze serpent made, and the Jews adored it. Gideon transformed the spoils of defeated enemies into a priestly ornament, and the Jews erected it as an object of worship (Saint-Philippe, *Mon. des Hebreux*, I, 175). The priest who placed himself in the service of Micah to offer incense to foreign gods was a Levite (Judg., XVII, 7). Idolatry reappeared after Joshua, after Othoniel, after Shamgar (Judg., IV, 1), after Baruch, after Jair.

The kings were even more favorable to it. From the third generation, the Hebrew monarchs bowed before idols. Solomon raised numerous altars to them. Under Rehoboam his son, the kingdoms of Israel and Judah separated. The first gave itself over entirely to idolatry. In Judah itself, Rehoboam abandoned himself to it (Chronic., XII, 1), and this worship persisted during the entire life of the prince. It was the same under Abia his son, who vainly reproached his subjects for their mad worship (Chronic., XII, 1). It is true that Asa returned to the Mosaic laws: he destroyed the temples, burned the sacred woods, and raged against his mother (Kings, XV, 13; Chronic., XV, 17); but seventy-one years later, Joram returned to foreign gods. Athaliah strengthened their power, Joash overthrew it, and Joad the high priest exterminated all the ministers of this proscribed cult. The king he had crowned soon became an infidel himself (Chronic., II, 24, 18). Following his example, his successor borrowed idols from everywhere to worship (Chronic., II, 25, 14). Azariah once again expelled them, but Ahaz brought them back to the temple in Jerusalem (Chronic., II, 4, 23–25). In vain his son Hezekiah broke their statues and cut down their sacred woods (Kings, IV, 18, 4). Manasseh reestablished them with all their honors (Kings, IV, XXI, 2, 7). The sanctuary, already once stained, was once again tainted by their presence. Manasseh zealously imitated all the exotic superstitions: he established an oracle, he studied the science of augury; and first among the idolatrous kings, he turned persecution against the Mosaic law, he killed a great number of prophets, and had Isaiah die in a terrible torture. Josias avenged Jehovah, and his severity was boundless. Idols were delivered to the flames, the bones of the dead exhumed, priests were slaughtered on their altars; and not content to lead his people back to are the first and most intimate of revelations. People have seen in these facts acts of the divine will, and they have imposed upon themselves the duty of approving what in other circumstances they would have condemned, and of praising what in the annals of any other people would have been judged to be awful.[20] This blind-

---

the worship of the one God, he brought his destruction to the kingdom of Israel, and with the same severity raged against the living and the dead (Kings, IV, ch. XX, III). But who would believe it? His own son hastened to rehabilitate idolatry. The groves reflourished, the destroyed temples were rebuilt, and the prophets who struggled against these efforts were exiled or massacred (Jer., XXVI, 27).

Such is the history of theism in that fraction of the Jewish people who professed it with less infidelity. If we turn our gaze toward the other faction, we will see idolatry very much in vigor, two golden calves replacing or representing the cow Apis (IV; X, 29) and all of Israel giving it homage, with the exception of a few faithful who go secretly to Jerusalem to adore the God of Moses.

Thus among the Hebrew monarchs, among whom only three extended their rule over all the nation, the first two profess theism while the third is already an idolator. After the division into two kingdoms, twenty kings reigned over Judah, and of these twenty, fourteen gave themselves to idolatry. In Israel, out of twenty also, nineteen worshipped idols; and idolatry always had popular assent: public sadness signaled its fall, cries of joy its return.

A strange but instructive fact: the Hebrews attached themselves to Jehovah only when they were captives and their masters imposed other gods on them. Intolerance revolts man, and misses the mark it proposes. But as soon as the Jews were freed from the idolatrous tyrants, they ran to the feet of the idols; this is the consequence of every disproportion between institutions and enlightenment. Imposed by force on barbarous nations, theism itself, this immense means of perfecting men, will display barbarism in the means it employs to triumph over barbarism. Should we conclude, therefore, that Moses was wrong to prematurely establish the theism that an interior or external revelation had made known to him? Before pronouncing one way or the other, a great question needs to be addressed. In its natural development, the human mind arrives at theistic notions only by destroying, by means of reasoning, the crude notions that preceded this pure but abstract idea. When this destruction occurs, does there remain enough strength for it to embrace theism and to take it as the basis of a new religion? Accustomed to doubt and haunted by this doubt, can the intellect give itself over to a strong and fervent conviction?

History offers a memorable test-case, and this example does not speak for the affirmative. All belief was eroded and gone when the Neoplatonists wanted to return man to the religious faith that he cannot do without. They were sincere, studious, eloquent, and intrepid; they rejected none of the means that can strike the senses and captivate souls; they even appealed to the marvelous. What fruit did all these efforts yield? Superstition and skepticism.

If this is the case, was it not good, was it not necessary, that theism was placed, as it were, in deposit with a special tribe, in order to enlighten the world when the world was able to receive the light and understand it?

20. In his *Law of Peace and War*, Grotius cites the massacres of the nations defeated by the Hebrews as rules to observe and examples to follow. Asa, Hezekiah, Josiah, wrote Bossuet, exterminated

ness in one direction produced blindness in the other direction. Our philosophers are enlightened, learned, and friends of the truth, at least at the outset of their career, until the point when the struggle with religion provokes their vanity and tests their impartiality, then they turn to the Jewish books and make them the object of their mockery and their harangues. These attacks in turn provoke defenders who base themselves on a principle that is equally false. These apologists have often had to produce apologies of crime and cruelty.

The distinction we established above would have spared unbelievers many pointless and puerile critiques, and religious men from having to defend many contradictions. Let the Inquisition rise again and the orthodox of every sect threaten us with their anathemas, we do not recognize revelation in massacres or towns reduced to rubble, or in children torn from their mothers. We see in the bloody records of a barbarous epoch, first, necessity imposing its cruel laws on a conqueror, which perhaps can be excused, but certainly do not merit praise. Later, we see the jealous, implacable priestly spirit. On the other hand, we recognize the revelation made to Moses in the parts of the Hebrew books where all the virtues are recommended, filial love, conjugal love, hospitality toward strangers, chastity, friendship (which no other legislation raised to the ranks of virtues), justice, and even pity, even though the epoch of pity had not yet come, for this epoch is Christianity. Here is the divine voice. Here is the manifestation of heaven on earth. And it is only here that one cannot be mistaken in giving praise, because it appeals to all the sentiments, ennobles and purifies all affections, comes well before enlightenment, and even in the midst of barbarism penetrates the soul with truths that reason would discover only much later.[21] Readers, however, have confused facts and doc-

---

priests and soothsayers. Nor did their zeal spare the most august personages, and even those who were closest to them. Jehu was praised by God for having put to death the false prophets of Baal, without sparing one (*Polit. de l'Ecriture sainte*, bk. VII, art. 3, 9th proposition).

21. Of all the ancient codes of legislation, Moses's is incontestably the one most hospitable to foreigners and most humane toward slaves. However, its theory must be distinguished from practice, because the priesthood controlled the latter. It was the only one that granted foreigners admission to the assemblies of the people "to the third generation" (Deut., XXIII, 7–8). The strictness of the Romans in refusing political rights to foreigners is well known. In Latin, the same word originally meant "foreigner" and "enemy." The Hebraic legislation is also the only one that provided the slave with some guarantees against the cruelty and avarice of the master. Thus theism, even if premature and disproportionate to all contemporary ideas, without the action of the priests who perverted it would have had a beneficent influence, destined as it was one day to make all nations a single nation, and all men a people of brothers.

trine. Because the priesthood was established as the guardian of the divine law, as the redactors of the annals of the nation subject to the law everything these annals contained was said to be the divine law. Because the law of the Jews was holy, some wanted to use it to sanctify every event in Jewish history.

People at least should have recalled from what sources, as well as by whom, this history was assembled. Redacted at different epochs, and always by Levites; several times destroyed, notably at the taking of Jerusalem and the Babylonian captivity;[22] reconstituted by Esdras,[23] who belonged to the priestly line,[24] and, his zeal sharpened by misfortune, who exaggerated the severity of Moses's laws:[25] the Hebrew books had to be thoroughly suffused with the priestly spirit.[26] As a com-

22. The sacred books of the Hebrews were deposited in the sanctuary. It was there that Moses had his laws placed beside the Ark of the Covenant (Deut., 31, 26). Joshua wrote his ordinances in the book that contained the laws of Moses (Josh., 26). At the succession of Saul, Samuel placed in it the new institutions of the new kingdom—i.e., the conditions imposed on the monarch by the priesthood—and placed this deposit before the Lord (I Kings 10, 25). It is probable that one also wrote down the genealogies of the families in it, to which the Orientals attach so much importance (Michael. no. 51, *Mosaisch. Recht*).

Now, it is it explicitly said (Kings, IV, 25, 9) that Nebuzaradan, the general of Nebuchadnezzar, burned the house of the Lord with all that it contained, except for precious objects that he seized; in the same passage one finds a list of what he saved, which does not contain the sacred books. We do not deny that copies of some of these books could be found in the hands of individuals, even though the Levites, like all sacerdotal castes, had carefully kept these sacred writings from the multitude, and that every time the leaders invoked them in support of their policies, they had them brought from the depths of the sanctuary to be read publicly (II Esdras 81; ibid., 13, 1). But in admitting that these copies could have survived the national calamity, they were neither complete nor authentic, and only served as materials for the redaction Esdras undertook at the return of the Jews to Jerusalem.

23. Esdras, *Dei sacerdos, combustam a chaldaeis in archivis temple restituit legem* (August., *De mir.*, bk. II).

24. Esdras I (or Ezra) 7, 1, 15.

25. Esdras forced the Hebrews to send back the foreign wives they had married during the captivity, and with whom they had had children Esdras I (or Ezra) II, ch. 10). This was a cruelty that the Law of Moses did not at all enjoin. This law forbade only the marriage of Jews with the women of the country of Canaan (Eichhorn, *Einleit. zum alt. Testam.*, II, 227). Deuteronomy XXI, 14, explicitly allows one to marry a foreigner, even a captive. "Among the prisoners, if there is one that is beautiful and inspires love in you, you can make her your wife."

26. The priestly spirit that is quite striking in the words and writings of the pontiffs, judges, and prophets of Judea suggested to the Albigensians of the Middle Ages a singular error. Supposing two principles, one good and the other evil, they attributed the New Testament to the first and the Old Testament to the second; and all the severities practiced in His name in the Old Testament, His con-

parison, let us suppose that after several thousand years, when the centuries and the changes that they give rise to have reduced our books to bits and pieces, people recover as the records of Christianity the Gospel and a few historians during our times of barbarism, or degradation, when the massacre of the Albigensians or the horrors of the Inquisition or Saint Bartholomew's Massacre are taken to be acts willed and approved by Providence. Is it not certain that a priestly corporation enriched by these heirlooms, and arrogating to itself a monopoly of them, would bend them to its caste interests, and while exalting what cannot be too exalted, the admirable morality of the Gospel and its no less admirable gentleness, would also extol the zeal of the inquisitors and the obedience of the torturers?[27]

---

stantly repeated character as a jealous, terrible, and implacable God, punishing the sins of the fathers for several generations of their descendants, served to prove this bizarre hypothesis.

27. What we present here only as a supposition is, unfortunately, a reality; those who wish to be convinced of it have only to read the *Relation du strategème de Charles IX contre les Huguenots*, by Camille Capilupi, a courtier of Pope Gregory XIII, published in Rome in October 1572, and recently republished in France. The author says in express terms that *it was the will of God* that, by a memorable act of the very Christian king against the Huguenots, the kingdom was reestablished in its initial healthy condition; that with the Protestants reemerging like the heads of Hydra, Charles IX resolved to obtain by *his dexterity* what he could not procure by force of arms; that moved by a depth of thought and prudent resolution well beyond his years, and *led by the all-powerful will of God*, he concluded peace; and in this improvement of things he pursued his aim, multiplying demonstrations of goodwill and forgiveness of injuries, neglecting nothing to fully gain the trust of Admiral Coligny, giving him the most cordial of welcomes while alerting the Holy See at the same time that he was not unworthy of the name of most Christian king; that he succeeded in deceiving everyone; that he had Admiral Coligny give him the names of his friends, under the pretext of accepting their services; that not being able to gather a second time so many birds in the same net, he pressed the marriage of his sister; that vigorously affirming his good intentions and reassuring everyone about his praiseworthy aims, he fabricated numerous false assurances; he called Coligny his father; but also had a murderer hidden, one who had already been handsomely paid, to assassinate Coligny; but with the admiral only being wounded, the king displayed a lively indignation at the mere attempt. Afterward, he placed the friends of the admiral around him in order to have them more easily under his control, in such a way that none of them could escape; and three thousand Protestants were killed without one drop of Catholic blood being spilled; it was said that this could not happen except by a miraculous display of God's omnipotence; the king also had the women of the court who were given to this abominable heresy (continues Capilupi) brought together, with the order that if they persisted in the heresy they were to be drowned. At Lyon, thanks to the marvelous good order and singular prudence of Mr. de Mandelot, the governor of the city, Huguenots were taken one by one like sheep; nonetheless twenty-five thousand still remained. Later, the king had the ambassador of Spain summoned, and told him that he could now know what had been the aim of these enticing words and soft caresses directed at

This is what has happened, and it is in keeping with this confusion of distinct ideas that the Hebrew books have been judged.[28] For our part, we have already said how we think they should be judged. From the principle we adopt, it follows that the purity of teaching is not compromised by the acts that are foreign to it, and that culpable acts are not excused by the purity of a doctrine that does not command them. The Jewish priesthood certainly could have commandeered the truths that heaven had communicated to Moses in order to monopolize them, to bend them to its interests, just as more than one pope or Christian monarch has taken hold of the Gospel and tried to corrupt it. But in the same way that Christianity contributed nothing to the massacres committed by priests in its author's

---

the Huguenots. From all this, one could only conclude, declares Capilupi, that everything had happened *according to the will of God*, who, *touched with pity* (the very words of Scripture) had *deigned to visit his people*; that the men who did these things were chosen by the Redeemer as ministers of his holy will; that what had been done by their means could only come from his immense power; and, finally, that the very night of the Parisian matins (Saint Bartholomew's Day), when one had begun to chase this execrable plague of Huguenots from the world, a long-dead thorn had sprouted green branches and blossoms.

28. See IV Kings, X, 15, 25, 30: "[Jehu] having left [Samaria], he found Jehonadab, son of Rechab, who came before him; he hailed him and said: Is your heart as well disposed toward me as mine is toward you? Yes, Jehonadab responded. If it is, said Jehu, give me your hand; and Jehu had him enter his chariot.... At the same time Jehu assembled all the people and said to them: Ahab gave honor to Baal, but I wish to give him more. Let all the prophets, all the ministers, and all the priests of Baal come to me; let not one be missing, because I wish to offer a great sacrifice to Baal; whoever is not found here will be punished with death. Now this was a trap that Jehu laid for the worshippers of Baal in order to exterminate them all. Jehu said again: Let us have a solemn feast in honor of Baal; and he sent to all the lands of Israel to call all the ministers of Baal, all of whom came, missing not one. They entered the temple of Baal, and the house of Baal was filled from one end to the other. He then said to those who kept the vestments: Give vestments to all the ministers of Baal, and they gave them to them; and Jehu having entered into the temple of Baal with Jehonadab, son of Rechab, said to the worshippers of Baal: Take care that there are among you no ministers of the Lord, but only worshippers of Baal. They were then assembled in the temple to offer their victims and holocausts. Now Jehu had given orders to twenty-four men to keep themselves close by the temple, and he had told them: If but one escapes of those that I give over to you, your life will answer for his. After the holocaust had been offered, Jehu gave the order to his soldiers and his officers and told them: Enter, and let not one be preserved; and the officers entered with the soldiers, and all were put to the sword, and their dead bodies were cast outside the city.... Next came the promise: Because Jehu had carefully accomplished everything that was just ... his children would be seated upon the throne of Israel until the fourth generation."

name, Judaism did not contribute to the attacks ordered by other priests in Jehovah's name. One therefore need not accept absurd sophisms in order to legitimize
terrible acts. Bossuet, who praised Samuel killing Agag and the Levites deposing
Osias,[29] resembles the Italian Capilupi[30] and the courtier Pibrac,[31] who present
Charles IX as directed in his hypocrisy and his murders by the all-powerful will
of God.

We will end this chapter with a reflection that has always resonated with us, and
which we think will do the same with the reader.

There is no doubt the Jewish religion has its terrible parts, and no one can pe-
ruse its annals without walking in blood and over ruins. Nonetheless the world
owes Moses an enormous debt. When in late Antiquity, devoid of every belief, desolated by doubt, degraded by corruption, the whole earth required new worship,
and given the state of enlightenment this worship could only be theism, the theism
of the Jews served as the standard. And one saw man reborn to all that was noble
and precious in life by being reborn to religion. What a marvelous dispensation of
the power that decides our destinies! Things that seem to have no relation among
themselves, either by their time or by their nature, combine at the right moment
to direct the human race to its end.

Twelve centuries before Plato, Moses gave theism a body that permitted this
sublime idea to be preserved until the moment when intelligence became capable
of conceiving it. Twelve centuries after Moses, Plato prepared minds in such a
way that in adopting theism they were able to receive it purified by the divine
author of the Christian religion, and to resist the violent and obstinate attempts
of a sizable portion of Jewish converts who wanted to take Christianity back to
Judaism. Without Moses, it is probable that all the efforts of philosophy would

---

29. *Polit. de l'Ecrit. sainte*, bk. VII.

30. See above, n. 27.

31. *Lettre sur les affaires de France.* The letter of Pibrac on Saint Barthelemy is more an exonera-
tion than a panegyric; between Capilupi's work and his, public opinion had declared its judgment,
and the French pamphleteer took up the pen to soften what the Italian pamphleteer had praised
with such enthusiasm. Nonetheless, like Capilupi, Pibrac invokes the example of Jewish history. "We
see in the Bible," he says, "the massacres of several thousands of men ordered by Moses, a person resplendent with holiness." One cannot accurately calculate how much the confusion against which we
have written in this chapter ruined the ideas of sincere men, and served as pretexts to perverse men's
machinations.

have only plunged mankind into pantheism or a hidden atheism. As we saw at the beginning of this chapter, this was where the philosophy and the religion of the Indians ended. Without Plato, it is possible, humanly speaking, that overcome by the efforts of Judaizing Christians, Christianity would have become a Jewish sect.[32]

32. After this explanation (which no one can accuse of displaying reticence or second thoughts on our part), we dare believe that no one will see anything in our opinion of Judaism that separates us from the Christian communion to which we belong. To begin with, we recognize the revelation made to Moses; we can explain in no other way the appearance of theism in a barbarous time and among a barbarous people. We also recognize the Christian revelation; the regeneration of the human race, fallen into the deepest degree of political and religious corruption, also seems inexplicable to us without the intervention of the power that wishes the moral amelioration of man. What then does it matter if, basing ourselves on the scriptures themselves and on historical knowledge of the way these scriptures have come down to us, and employing the right that the first reformers had the immense merit of regaining for all Christians, we differ on the understanding of a few particular facts? This dissent overturns none of the bases of the faith we profess, but on the contrary places this belief safely away from grave objections and insoluble difficulties by removing everything that wounds the eternal rules of humanity and justice. This is but one more homage directed at the divine character of the two religions granted to the human race by heaven, each at the necessary time and in keeping with humanity's enlightenment or weakness. In our eyes, Moses and his law are different from the Jewish people and priesthood, and likewise the divine founder of our law has nothing in common with those of his priests who have perverted his heavenly word, nor with the peoples that a fierce fanaticism has often caused to err.

CHAPTER 12

That the Struggle between the Priesthood and the Temporal Authority Must End to the Advantage of the First, as Soon as the Principle of Priestly Authority Is Admitted

The picture we drew of the warfare the priesthood waged against political and military power should have demonstrated to our readers that even if the priests have not always emerged victorious from this struggle, they have always retained vast prerogatives that have aided them in regaining those they lost.

This result of a rivalry that has continued from century to century, and which still continues, should not surprise us.

Once the principle of priestly authority is recognized, those who exercise it have in their favor both the religious sentiment that resides in the depths of souls and the constant and irresistible action of habit, which moves men to respect the object of their forebears' reverence. In addition, there is the influence of their particular superstitions, which are the companions of all their days, the solutions to all their doubts, the explanations of every phenomenon, and the soothing of every fear. And, finally, there is logic itself and rigorous reasoning.

When religion is independent, the religious sentiment can defend itself against the usurpations of the priesthood. It believes it is inwardly invested with a mission, and in its inner forum it is its own authority. But when the struggle is engaged, not between consciences but between powers, the religious sentiment must declare itself for the power that most resembles conscience and that, being without visible arms, least resembles power itself. If it were to enlist on the side of force, it would belie its own nature. There is no common ground between it and force. If it were to render homage to force, it would enter into the domain of human calculations and would die of suicide.

But it is not in this sentiment alone that the attacked priesthood finds a defender. Reason, which the laws of its nature constrain to proceed from initial givens to consequences, and from principles to applications, lends the assistance of incontestable arguments.

As soon as man has need of privileged intermediaries in order to communicate with invisible beings, omnipotence belongs by right to these intermediaries. In order to deflate the pretensions of these exclusive favorites of heaven, one has to suppose that religion is the common property of all. Each one, bearing in his breast the torch designed to enlighten him, compares the light offered to him with the one he possesses. But when the monopoly of this light is granted to a small number, how can the ascendancy of this few have any limits? According to what warrant could the temporal power establish its independence? Such a title would be redundant if it were in accord with celestial decrees, criminal if different from them.

In the priestly system, what is the goal of the world? The accomplishment of the divine will. What are political organizations? Means of ensuring this accomplishment. What are the heads of societies? The detainers of a subordinate authority that has no right to be obeyed, except because it obeys the authority that founded it. What, finally, is the natural organ of this sole legitimate authority? The priesthood.

These Jewish or Egyptian kings, these rajas of India, chosen by the gods from among their equals, possess all their rights from the goodness of the gods, as manifested by their priests. These priests consecrate their ascension, pour sacred oils on their heads, command the peoples to consider them their masters; they also observe their actions, listen to their confessions, absolve them from their faults, wash them of their guilt, reprimand them during their lifetime, and judge them after their death. Prostrate at the knees of these dispensers of supernatural favors, these kings begged permission to ascend the throne; they walked up its steps humble and suppliant. Then suddenly they are to declare themselves the equals—the superiors even—of those who made them? They are to raise their authority to the level of the divine authority, treat it as an equal, and assume there are interests other than those of eternity, and declare themselves the guardians of these material interests even against heaven?

Such patent contradictions cannot be admitted. To try to impose them on the mind is to insult it.

To say to peoples: Profess the religion that pleases and reassures you; if it is your desire or your need, take men as ministers of this religion, as the mediators of your worship and praise; and as long as you consider it just and fitting, subject yourself to the direction and instructions of these men. Nothing is more reasonable. But when you say to them: Behold priests who are infallible when it comes to you and to whom an implicit submission is due, as long as they only attack your rights, only restrict your faculties, only limit your thinking. But when it comes to us, your

earthly masters, these priests lose their infallibility. When it comes to your interests, resistance is a crime, but it becomes a duty when ours are threatened. For us
you will brave the anger of heaven, which we otherwise exhorted you to fear. Then
we will punish obedience, when otherwise we punished disobedience.

These arguments apply to modern times as well as to ancient times, to Gregory
VII as to Samuel or Joad, and the concessions of priests transformed into courtiers
and the arguments of statesmen become sophists equally run aground against them.

Therefore, every time the priesthood has seen itself attacked by authority, religious souls have supported it with all their might. A secret voice told them that
when heaven and earth have become divided, heaven must be obeyed. Religious
prohibition has struck all peoples with terror. Anathema has depopulated courts
and camps. As the Indians say: a single word has always done more in the mouth
of a priest than the sword has in the hands of a warrior.

And if we reflect a moment, we will not be tempted to bemoan this inevitable
result.

To be sure, if one were to place on one side the Egyptian castes, the magi, or the
Brahmins, and on the other, freedom of belief and of worship, the choice would
not be in doubt. But between Chephren or Cambyses and the priests who contest
their power, the preference is due to the priests. Not that they were worthy, but if
tyranny in the name of religion is terrible, tyranny in the name of material force is
both terrible and degrading.

Under the first, at least conviction can be found among the slaves, and only the
tyrants are corrupted. But when the oppression is separated from faith, slaves too
are depraved and become as abject as their masters. We candidly acknowledge that
we have never felt much sympathy for Louis the Pious doing penance at the feet of
a papal legate, or for the emperor Henry IV waiting in bare feet for a pope to absolve him. We have reserved our compassion for other objects. We have extended
it to those obscure populations, outlawed and proscribed because they listened to
the voice of their conscience, and refused to commit what for them were betrayals
and sacrileges. For those Vaudois who asked only to be able to exercise their peaceful worship in their valleys; for those Jews who throughout the centuries were
tormented, dispossessed, and burned; for those Hussites who at least were able
to avenge their leader delivered to the fire in violation of imperial promises; for
those Scots who were put to death by the abominable Duke of York[1] because they

1. Later, James II.

refused the Oath of Test, which he himself did not swear; for those Huguenots suspended on the fence or pressed into galley service. As for the unfortunate members of royal families who declared themselves independent of the power that was the mysterious sanction of their despotism, we have been able to see in this belated resistance (according to their own view) only an incoherent rebellion,[2] and we are not sure if Europe would have been better off because of their success.

A great example is before our eyes, and this example raises certain doubts.

Among the priestly nations of Antiquity, the result of the conflict between the temporal and the spiritual authority was always the triumph of the latter. But in a nation that is ordinarily placed among the moderns, because it still exists and because it occupies no place in ancient history, the priesthood has been defeated.

The reader can surmise that we mean to speak of China.

It is incontestable that the ancient religion of China was a priestly religion based like all in this category on the worship of the elements and the stars.[3] Vestiges of this worship show themselves in all the solemn ceremonies preserved till today by the custom that survived the belief. The Chinese cosmogony bears the imprint of the ingenuity of priests. Here one finds the cosmogonic egg,[4] the Trimurti,[5] the misshapen figures,[6] the incestuous gods,[7] the reunion of virginity and fe-

---

2. Princes themselves think this way when the power of the Roman court is to their advantage. Philip Augustus declared Pope Innocent II to be a usurper when this pope put his kingdom under ban; but when, to his advantage, Innocent II deposed John, the king of England, he recognized the rights he had earlier contested.

3. We have already provided the proofs (bk. III, ch. 5).

4. Chaos, under the figure of a mystical egg, containing the seed of all things, produced Pangu, or Pan-Kou, whose head formed the mountains; eyes, the sun and the moon; veins, the rivers and streams; hair, the plants and forests. This has a complete resemblance to the history of creation and the fable of the giant Ymir in the Scandinavian Edda.

5. Tao, an ineffable triple essence, created the heaven and the earth by dividing into three persons, with one being charged with production, another with arrangement, and the third with the maintenance of a regular succession.

6. All the agents, men or gods, of the Chinese mythical period have monstrous figures. Fo-Hi was a serpent with the head of a man; Chinnong, the inventor of agriculture, had the head of a cow, a human body, and the brow of a dragon. The mysterious objects of ancient worship, the Chin, whose nature and attributes we do not know precisely, like the Egyptian divinities had heads of animals on bodies of men or, like those of India, several heads on a single body.

7. The wife of Fo-Hi was at the same time his sister. These incestuous unions of the gods can be found in all the priestly cosmogonies; later we will say why.

cundity,[8] evil-doing divinities,[9] fanciful animals,[10] mystical conceptions (whose origins we will talk about later,[11] and which independent religions never admit into their native accounts). Among their ancient rites one finds human sacrifice.[12] Finally, the annals of China speak of a high-priest named Tai-chi-ling, whose authority formerly was very great.

But by events that have been transmitted in much too vague a manner to allow for detailed accounts or satisfactory explanations, the priesthood succumbed in China. Chased from the altar, religion descended to the throne. The emperor declared himself the principal minister, or the absolute master, which is the same thing. The entire learned class affected a proud disdain for the priests.[13] It is be-

8. Lao-Tsu, mother of Chao-Hao, became pregnant at the appearance of a star. The appearance of a brilliant cloud made Fu-Pao pregnant: she gave birth to Hoang-Ti. Hu-Su, surnamed the Expected Flower or the Daughter of the Lord, was out walking on the banks of a river; a sudden emotion seized her, a rainbow surrounded her, and Fo-Hi was born at the end of twelve years. The most famous of the virgin-mothers in China was Niu-Oua, or Niu-Va, surnamed the Sovereign of the Virgins. Her prayers earned her miraculous births. She had the body of a serpent, the head of a cow, and disheveled hair, and could assume seventy different forms in a single day. It would be worthwhile to examine the relations of Niu-Va with the Indian Bhadrakali and the Greek Hecate (or rather: who became Greek at the time of the introduction of priestly notions into the Greek religion).

9. Chi-Yeou, says the Chouking, with the body of a tiger and a brow of bronze, and who devoured dry sand, was the head of the nine black, or evil, *genii*. Chinnong, son of Hoang-Ti, attacked and defeated him; but he did not die, and he is the instigator of revolts, fraud, and all similar crimes.

10. Independent of dragons, griffons, and winged serpents, the Chinese have a marvelous animal unique to them. It is the Qilin, who announces both great goods and great evils. Yao ruled when the Qilin appeared on the banks of a lake; a terrible flood destroyed all of the works of men. But the Qilin also appeared to the mother of Confucius and announced to her the glory of the son she bore in her womb (*Mem. sur les Chinois*, XII; Kaempfer, *Hist. du Japon*).

11. Bk. VI.

12. The existence of the awful practice is proved by the very law of the emperor Chan-Hi that was intended to forbid it not more than a century and half ago; despite this law, there were still women strangled during the funeral of the prince Ta-Vang, brother of the emperor Chan-Hi. Voltaire says in explicit terms, however, that the Chinese alone never practiced these absurd horrors (*Philo. de l'hist.*, intro., art. "Theocratie"). This is because he wanted to exonerate China, whose religious tolerance or indifference made it dear to him, as causing shame to fall upon France, which still persecuted. But if these inaccuracies, a bit voluntary on his part, are excused by this intention, he at least should not have blamed Tacitus in the same work for having praised Germany in order to satirize the Romans.

13. The mandarins had the greatest disdain for the monks; they expelled them from their pagodas when they wanted to lodge their retinue there (Barrow, *Travels*, p. 86; Du Halde, II, 37–38). The

cause of this disdain that our philosophers have lavished praise upon the Chinese.[14]

But let us examine what was the real result of this so-celebrated victory.

Religion, reduced to trivial and fastidious ceremonies that recalled only disdained or dead beliefs, mere etiquette substituted for sentiment, dead letters re-

---

members of the tribunal charged with rites are subject to the most shameful punishments and are frequently sent away as base slaves.

14. We have already recalled Voltaire's exaggerations concerning China. They are not dangerous today in terms of our historical knowledge because we have better ideas about this vast and old empire and know the fragility of his constructions. But they are useful to examine because they show how little trust one owes to historians who write with any other aim than that of establishing the truth on each point; in addition, when it is a matter of a Voltaire, the errors of the master are the learning of the majority of the disciples.

"The constitution of China," says Voltaire, "is the best in the world; it is the only one that is entirely founded on paternal power; the sole in which a provincial governor is punished if upon leaving office he is not acclaimed by the people; the sole that has instituted prizes for virtue, while everywhere else the laws are limited to punishing crime. . . . The educated mandarins are regarded as the fathers of cities and provinces, and the king as the father of the empire. Rooted in the hearts of all, this idea forms an immense family. The fundamental law being that the empire is a family, people here more than elsewhere regard the public good as the first duty. . . . It is true that travelers have believed they see despotism everywhere in China: . . . but from the oldest times it has been permitted to write on a long table placed in the palace whatever one found to be objectionable in the government. . . . The religion of China is simple, wise, august, and free of all superstition and all barbarism. . . . That of the educated class is especially admirable: no superstitions, no absurd legends, none of those dogmas that insult nature and reason" (*Dict. phil. Philos. de l'hist. Essai sur les moeurs*).

That a friend of absolute power, the author of the *Esprit de l'histoire* and the *Théorie des révolutions*, for example, would declare that the constitution of China is excellent is understandable. But that the Voltaire who defined the constitution of England very well in the very beautiful verses of his *Henriade* would give this title to a government without checks and balances and without guarantees, this is explicable only by the purpose we already pointed out. What results from the fact that paternal government is the basis of China's government? That the power of fathers over their children, a power limited by affection in some and rendered necessary for a certain period by the ignorance of others, becomes an execrable tyranny when the governors lack the affection that softens authority and the governed are not characterized by the inferiority of intellectual faculties that justifies it. The mandarins, these fathers of cities and provinces, exercise with total impunity the most capricious arbitrariness on those below them, distributing punishments according to whim, except when they receive them themselves—no less unjustly—from the mandarins of a superior order. Nor can one trust in the efficacy of this hierarchy of vexations to make them less wicked or more moderate; on the contrary, it worsens them by making the oppression someone exercises the sole compensation for the oppression he receives.

placing real belief, rites devoid of meaning, practice without theory, irreligious abstractions for the enlightened class, stupefying superstitions for the populace; a worship of ancestors, but no hope for a future life;[15] a worship of spirits and the

---

As for the legislation that rewards virtue, we are not inclined to want to confide the appreciation of moral virtues to authority. Let it limit itself to punishing crimes, and, above all, let it abstain from committing them itself. The virtues will come, and be more pure. The author of the *Essai sur les mœurs* ought to have explained to us how it happens that with these prizes for virtue and its paternal administration the Chinese are the most knavish, cruel, and craven of nations. The most knavish, Voltaire himself agrees; the cruelest, we will prove in a later note; the most craven because, despite the Great Wall, whose utility Voltaire extols (even though it has never sheltered the Chinese from any attack), there has never been a conqueror of China who became the master of the empire without then becoming as pusillanimous and fearful as the defeated Chinese, by adopting their wonderful legislation, and then yielding his place to a new aggressor destined like him to triumph, and then be corrupted.

Can one seriously present as a safeguard for liberty and justice the permission to write remonstrances on the long table of the palace? One should just as well conclude that liberty reigns at Constantinople because an ancient custom obliges the sultan to receive the petitions of whoever places himself on his path with a lighted wick. But the emperor of China can put to death the one who has written on the long table, and the burning wick of a Turkish petitioner does not prevent him from being put in a sack and tossed into the Bosphorus.

The State religion is free of all craft and all barbarism, and we have proved that it permitted or commanded human sacrifices! *The history of China possesses this superiority over all the books that recount the origin of nations, that in theirs there are no marvels*, and the Chinese annals begin with the reign of gods with monstrous forms, virgins who give birth, and giants whose scattered members are the materials of the universe! As for the admirable religion of the learned, we will return to it later. While waiting, we believed we had to rise up against so many false assertions employed as means to an end, which thus could have seemed excusable in their author, even though he bitterly reproaches Christians for their pious frauds. Without making ourselves panegyrists for the imperial government of Rome, we would have preferred to live with Tacitus in this capital of the world than in the forests of Germany, and we would have preferred to live in Paris beside the Bastille than under the bamboo of Peking.

15. According to the most widely adopted doctrine among the Chinese, man is composed of different elements, whose separation takes place at death when each one rejoins the universal mass. In this system there is a denial of individuality, of rebirth, of memory, of all that constitutes the immortality of the soul. Leibniz, who made unflagging efforts to find some traces of a more consoling teaching among them, ends by affirming—with regret—that the hope in a life to come does not enter into their beliefs (*Oeuvr.*, IV, 205). One therefore should not ascribe to the majority of the learned a view that belongs to only a small sect. This sect thinks that with the practice of virtue purifying the soul, it gives it new forces that prevent the destruction of its ability to think and to will; in other words, grant it immortality (*Ac. inscr.*, VI, 633–634). To attribute this opinion to the mass of the Chinese population would be to bestow the refinements of Platonism upon the people of Greece.

crudest, most positive materialism;[16] and for the rest, the weightiest oppression, the most absolute arbitrariness,[17] barbarous tortures,[18] limitless corruption, cunning at the service of fear, a complete absence of all generous sentiments, an apathy that coexisted with the love of gain, and even the human figure taking on the degraded traits of a frightful immobility. Behold what we see in China. Without

16. Of all peoples, the Chinese are the most attached to materialism. They have no notion of spirituality. Spirits, they say, are only solidity and fullness. The creative cause, Li, is a material cause (Fréret, *Acad. des inscript.*, VI, 631–632). The invisible world is a world of physical forces, which excludes all free will, and in which fatality triumphs absolutely (Confucius, in the *Chum-yum*, couplet 51). This materialism leads, like spiritualism, to a pantheistic doctrine. The favorite axiom of the Chinese is that all things are but one and the same thing (see the treatise of Longobardi in the *Oeuvres* of Leibniz, IV). But the Chinese doctrine is much more arid than the spiritualized pantheism of Xenophanes. It assumes a single substance without attributes, without qualities, without will, without intelligence; as engine, a blind fatality; and as the goal of perfection, complete apathy: neither virtues nor vices, pains or pleasures, hope or fear, desire or repugnance, and no personal immortality.

17. The works of Confucius, which have been extolled beyond measure, contain no principle favorable to the liberty or the dignity of the human race. One can consider them under three points of view: morality, politics, and magic (because the word "religion" would be inaccurate). As for morality, that of the philosopher of Chang-Tong is composed of commonplaces that are quite praiseworthy, no doubt, but that can be found among all the moralists ancient and modern, with only a bit of local color and a few peculiarities of expression owning to it; Ecclesiastes, Proverbs, and the Book of Wisdom are certainly superior to all of Confucius's writings. We will say nothing of the incomparable morality of the Gospel. Under the aspect of politics, the works of Confucius are only a code of servitude. He prescribes a blind submission to the caprices of the prince, and far from condemning the most egregious abuses—the excesses of paternal power, slavery, polygamy, selling infants—he approves some and authorizes others by silence. Relative to magic or to superstition, does it not suffice to recall that he is the author of the *Yi-king*, or *Book of Lots*?

18. A rather recent occurrence, reported in all the public sheets of the time, noted the cruelty and minimal generosity of the Chinese emperors. In 1775, having reduced the Miaotse, a mountain people who had never been subjugated, the emperor went out to his general to compliment him on his victory; then he reentered Peking in order to conduct the ceremony called *che-ou-fou*: it consists in receiving the captives taken in war and determining their fate; it took place in the third court of the palace. The prisoners were presented to the emperor, who was seated on a throne. They were put on their knees, each having a sort of white cord around his neck. Then they were taken into another room, then to a third, where the instruments of torture were laid out. Seated now on a small throne, the emperor made a sign, and all the prisoners were tortured. Finally, gags were placed in their mouths, and they were thrown on carts and cut in pieces. The president of the tribunal of rites had declared previously that no one had done this ceremony for several years, but it was very suitable for keeping the people in their duty, and it was found in the code of his tribunal. The president was praised for his zeal; and to reward him, the ceremony was performed in the temple where the spirits that presided

detracting from its truthfulness, we could add features to this portrait that would render it both shameful and ridiculous. To wit: in this country where civil authority affects such a proud independence vis-à-vis everything that pertains to belief, there have been many emperors who have surrounded themselves with monks, and lavished on them the treasure of the State, in order to acquire from them the famous elixir of immortality.[19] This has cost the lives of those who have obtained it, the reward of their prodigality and promises.[20] Thus in China, as elsewhere, magic replaces religion.

In vain, some emperors disturbed by this extreme of degradation have wanted to revive religious belief. As means to do so, however, they only had their authority, and in this sort of endeavor its fate is to fail. They have thought that by rendering religion more reasonable, by subjecting it to a more imposing uniformity, and above all by recommending it as useful, they would make it acceptable to the people. But it is not as reasonable or as clothed with regular forms or as useful to its followers, but as divine, that it can be accepted. When utility is placed in the scales, it interferes with religion's earthy foundation. When religion is declared an instrument of the State, its mystique is destroyed. The classes to whom it is destined are by a secret instinct alerted to disdain what other mortals treat with such an arrogant familiarity. The concordat of the emperor Yung-Lo, which in certain respects recalls the Augsburg Interim of Charles V, could never take root among the Chinese, and Qianlong, who, whether out of cunning or madness, proclaimed

---

over the generations were honored (*Gazette de France*, 27 April 1778; *Journal des savants*, July of the same year).

Is it not deplorable to think that the emperor who amused himself with this refined butchery was the same Qianlong whom our philosophers have extolled because he made a rather dry and pompous compilation entitled *Eloge de la ville de Moukden*?

Iliacos intra muros peccatur et extra.

It is not irrelevant to recall here that it belongs to the positive law and habitual custom in China to involve their entire families in the punishment of the guilty.

19. Despite the protests of his court and tribunals (which proves, *pace* Voltaire, that the decisions of tribunals did not have the force of law in China), Chi-tsong lavished riches on the monks of two warring sects (the Fo and the Lao-Tzu), so that they would give him the elixir of life. (One should not confuse this Chi-tsong of the Ming dynasty, who lived toward the beginning of the sixteenth century, or the end of the fifteenth, with another Chi-tsong who reigned toward 955, and who, far from protecting the monks, cruelly persecuted them.

20. The emperor Livent-Song in the eleventh century died of the elixir of life.

himself the Buddha incarnate at the end of his life, did not at all disturb an indifferent public; he encountered neither support nor contradiction.[21]

By stripping priests of their influence, the temporal sovereigns of China seem to have inherited their spirit. Their despotism was no less stagnant, only the people it degraded lost the excuse of conviction. Instead of being the effect of a sincere error, its slavery is one of ignoble fear and craven servility. In a manner of speaking, China is a theocracy of atheists, or if you wish, of materialistic pantheists, who replace religion with the sword and bamboo. The faculties of man are as compromised under the emperors as they were under the priests. The yoke is as harsh, the opprobrium greater. We have to bemoan, but we can also esteem, a nation subject to superstition and ignorance. Even among its errors, this nation preserves its good faith. It continues to obey the sentiment of duty. It can even have virtues, even though these virtues are badly directed. But a race that has only fear as its psycho-

21. What we say about China can also be applied to Japan, even though the temples there are very numerous and the rites are quite diversified. But the priestly power exercised by the Dairi is nonetheless subordinated to the temporal authority, which the *Koubo* possesses in its entirety, and which he extends even over the priests, arrogating to himself the right to depose them and replace them by laymen whom he pays, and who are revocable at will. The so-called precautions with which he surrounds the spiritual leader, thus keeping him always in sight under the pretext of rendering him homage, are mockeries that wound, and hence destroy, all religious sentiment. This Dairi is reduced to governing the invisible world, to assigning the gods their functions, to keeping up secret communications with them, and to extolling the general whose slave he is in the real world; he is an almost grotesque phantom. The Japanese are in the same religious condition as the Chinese, and the identity of this religious state produces identical effects, with the following difference: the more martial Japanese are less contemptible. But their government is despotic, their legislation cruel, their policy merciless. The lightest faults are punished with death. Torture is constantly employed with damnable refinements. As in China, the relatives of a guilty person are involved in his punishment. The father is punished with the son, the master answers for the slave, the neighbor for his neighbor. The streets are prisons guarded by day, closed at night. The Japanese have made no more progress in the sciences than the Chinese. The printing press that they have possessed for such a long time is in a condition of extreme imperfection. Everything is stationary, and stamped, as it were, with moral death.

Let us therefore convince ourselves that it is not at all the absence of religion but the presence of political and religious liberty that one must invoke as the unique source of all intellectual progress, as well as all the virtues. Where the power of priestly corporations has been destroyed by despotism, the human race has gained nothing. Where this power has been replaced by true independence—and we will see in Greece the proof of this—man has assumed and preserved his rank in the intellectual hierarchy. The absence of priestly power has been a good, because religion outlived it; and religion, even when imperfect, was the first of goods because no sacrilegious hand offended or denatured it.

logical wellspring, and as its motive the salary bestowed from above by the power that oppresses it; a race without any illusions that elevate it, and without errors that excuse it, has fallen from the rank Providence assigned to it. The faculties that remain to it, and the intelligence it continues to display, are for it and for the world only one more misfortune and shame.[22]

22. *De l'esprit de conquête et de l'usurpation.* We have been criticized for having announced in our first volume that Europe was threatened with the fate of China. We expressed fears, but did not allow ourselves predictions. Let us only say here, with all the respect that is due to the progress of the exact sciences and the acceleration of industrial discoveries, that while these discoveries and this progress are precious things, they do not constitute the entire inheritance of our species. We should be less distrusted in professing this opinion as we were the first, almost the only one, who when our country and Europe seemed to have returned to the military period because of the will of one man, proclaimed that the present epoch was one of commerce (*De l'esprit de conquête et de l'usurpation*, p. 7). Yes, the industrial discoveries and the progress of the exact sciences are precious things, because they lift up the laboring class and they give the superior class even more leisure; and because to both classes they open a shorter and easier path to their moral improvement. But becoming perfect is the goal. The discoveries and sciences are only means. Industry ought to be an element of liberty; we need to take care that it does not become only a source of ease. It will lose in that exchange; because if it does not defend public liberties, its own freedoms will soon be compromised. The Romans, said Mr. de Pauw, demanded bread and circuses. The Chinese demanded commerce and theaters.

CHAPTER 13

The Summary of the Foregoing

One can see from the content of this book that we are far from closing our eyes to the exceptions (or to put it better: the variations) that have slipped in under the general rule. We recognize these variations, and what we have said about them can guide the reader in applying the general rule to what needs to be said about each people in particular.

We therefore ask our readers not to become distracted by objections based upon particular details that are always easy to gather, but which when generalized yield only error. We are quite aware that someone might point out that we say that the priesthood dominated both under the beautiful skies of India and in the dark forests of Gaul, in order to accuse us of putting on a par the religion of the Brahmins and that of the Druids. In doing so, though, one would be attributing to our researches a systematic character that would suffice to discredit us with every impartial reader. Proceeding in this way lacks only one thing, however: good faith. To deprive our opponents of this pretext, we forewarn our readers. The priestly power was different in its forms, its extent, and its intensity in each of the nations of which we have spoken.[1] Many things mitigated, combated, and modified it. In

---

1. In order to refute in advance another reproach that some perhaps will believe they can address to us, we will recall what we said in our first volume concerning the action of the priesthood. One must not exaggerate this action. "In submitting religion to different changes according to his calculations and views, it invents nothing, it profits only from what exists. Its work is not the work of creation, but of arrangement, of form and order. . . . The priesthood found the seed of all the religious notions in the heart of man, but it directed . . . the development of this seed" (bk. I, ch. 9). Thus we do not attribute to the priests the invention of the teachings that they subsequently so terribly abused. Their principle is in the human soul or imagination. Their transformation into unchanging positive belief, and the consequences of this transformation: behold the work of the priests.

India, the climate; in the North, war; in Persia, the monarchy; in Carthage, commerce. But these softenings, resistances, and modifications were accidental and temporary inflections. The principle remained the same, and the power itself resisted, survived, and overcame.

If some think that we have painted this power in colors that are too unflattering, that we have misunderstood its relative usefulness, at least in certain periods of an imperfect society, and that instead of showing it subjugating, oppressing, and maintaining in ignorance a race created for perfectibility and enlightenment, we should have recognized that more than once it elevated savage hordes, softened the mores of barbarians, united dispersed tribes against the elements that threatened them, imposed fertility on a harsh soil or wholesomeness on a dour nature; that in a word, by means of its special and precocious knowledge, it was the very first author of the civilization that later would dethrone it, we would grant a certain degree of force to these claims. But we would point out to these readers that we have said nothing contrary to them. At such a stage of the social state, the priesthood could have contributed to the great work of the human race and done its part to realize the views of a benevolent Providence. We will not deny this at all.

We say only that the priestly spirit, the enemy—as is every esprit de corps—of the progress and prosperity of the mass of human beings, because this prosperity and these advancements lead them toward independence, has dearly sold its benefits to mankind. We will also say that it is quite fortunate that a people we will speak about shortly liberated itself from this empire. If thanks to the priesthood, the lot of the Egyptians was better than that of today's Eskimos or Samoyedes, it would be quite deplorable if the fate of the entire human race had not differed from that of Egypt. If men were able to gradually elevate themselves to the point of being able to comprehend and embrace a religion like that which all enlightened peoples profess today, it is because there was one people in history who, because of fortunate circumstances and their own energy, were able to escape from priestly power.

Let each one, then, after having well considered the facts, have his reservations. Pointing out these possible exceptions (which, however, were only few and limited) is the most an impartial reader could ask of us.

More extensive developments would have broken the thread of our inquiry. We will frequently be compelled during the course of this work to trust in the learning of those who read us. Our task is already sufficiently vast and difficult, and wanting to fulfill it without violating the limits we earlier laid down, we have neither the time nor the space to take part in discussions and controversies over details.

BOOK V

ON THE PRIESTHOOD'S SMALL AMOUNT OF AUTHORITY AMONG PEOPLES WHO WORSHIPPED NEITHER THE STARS NOR THE ELEMENTS

A great order of the ages arises anew. . . .
Now a new generation is sent down from high heaven

—Virgil, *Eclogues*, book IV

CHAPTER I

That the Little Authority Priests Have among Nations That Do Not Have the Worship of Stars Is Demonstrated by the History of the First Times of Greece

Among the nations who have worshipped neither stars nor the elements, the priesthood has possessed only a very limited authority, and what we could call an accidental ascendancy. The Greeks are the proof.

While the security of Egypt entirely depended upon the precision of calculations based upon astronomy, the geographic position of Greece made the study of this science not particularly necessary. For a long time it was merely a subject of curiosity. The small number of stars that Homer or Hesiod mention indicate only elementary observations and rather traditional, or perhaps imported, ideas rather than those obtained by methodical personal investigation. Greek progress in astronomy goes back at most to the fortieth Olympiad, or to the origin of the first Ionian school.[1] And their astronomical tales are clearly put forth only in their lyrical poetry. Therefore, whatever Plato may say—who is only expressing an opinion[2]—they never professed the worship of the stars.[3] As a consequence, at least

---

1. Plutarch gives the honor of the first discoveries to Thales and Pythagorus (*De placit. phil.*, II, 13; Diog. Laer., *Vit. Thal.*); Diodorus (I, 62) to Oenopides of Chios; Pliny (*Hist. nat.*, II, 8) and Hyginus (*P. A.*, II, 13) to Anaximander and to Cleostratus.

2. "As much as I can judge, the first inhabitants of Greece followed the same gods as several barbarians recognize even today: the sun, the earth, the stars, the sky" (in *Cratyl.*).

3. A passage of Aristophanes fully confirms the opinion we put forth here. "The Sun and the Moon," says Thygaeus to Mercury (*Paix*, act 2, scene 3), "the most perverse of divinities, have conspired against us for a long time and formed the design to deliver Greece to the barbarians." "What could move them to this crime?" asked Mercury. "It is because," said Thygaeus, "we offer sacrifices to Jupiter and the other gods while the barbarians address their praise to the Sun and to the Moon, which is why these two planets would like us to be lost without recourse, so that empire would pass to the Persians and the Medes."

from the moment when we see them appear on the world stage, we find that alone among all peoples they were free from the power of priests.[4]

Consider the subordinate rank they occupy in the poems of Homer, the oldest records of Greece. The heads of nations and the generals of the armies preside over the rites of religion; and in the interior of families the same functions are exercised, and the same privilege claimed, by the elders and the fathers. Agamemnon constantly bears at his side a sword to fight and a sword with which to offer sacrifice.[5] He immolates victims with his own hand.[6] Nestor[7] and Peleus[8] do the same, and the poet adds that everything is done according to custom. Alcinous presides over the religious ceremonies of the Phaeacians.[9] In all the descriptions of these ceremonies, the name of priests is not even mentioned,[10] but rather that of the head of the

---

The historians of Alexander note that this prince, after having crossed the Euphrates, offered sacrifices to the Sun and to the Moon (Arrian, III, 7); this indicates that they considered these sacrifices to be praise given by the conqueror to the gods of the country; that is, to divinities other than those of Greece.

The learned Creuzer recognizes with us the difference that must be acknowledged between the Greeks and the other peoples of antiquity. "The nations," he says, "who worshipped stars and planets were early on led to idolatry. What must it have been, therefore, among those whose religion consisted from the beginning in a sensible and material pantheism!" The last phrase pertains to the Greeks, although it matters little that Creuzer uses the word "pantheism" while we use the word "fetishism." We ourselves have said that the movement that prompts early man to fetishism, i.e., to attribute life and will to all the parts of nature, would lead him to pantheism, toward the worship of nature as a whole, when he has arrived at the last stage of his religious vicissitudes.

4. Diodorus (bk. I), seeking to find among the Athenians vestiges of their founders come from Egypt, recognized as the class corresponding to the priesthood only those men who had greater education and could be admitted to public responsibilities. The same author expresses himself in another place in no less affirmative terms. "The Chaldeans, priests of Babylon," he says, "led a life that resembles that of the priests of Egypt. They carefully studied astronomy and divination. However, they studied them in a way quite different from the way that those who did so among the Greeks approached them. Among the Chaldeans, this philosophy always remained in the same family. . . . The Greeks, on the contrary, for the most part entered this study rather late or without natural aptitude, and when they had studied it for a while, the necessities of life called them away" (II, 21).

5. *Iliad,* III, 271–272; XIX, 251–252.

6. Ibid., II, 293.

7. *Odyss.,* III, 436–463.

8. *Iliad,* XI, 771–774.

9. *Odyss.,* XII, 24–25.

10. Ibid., III, 454. Virgil shows us a priest accompanying Aeneas before his battle with Turnus, leading the victims to the sacrifice (XII, 169–170). But one can recognize in this passage the inadver-

peoples.[11] Moreover it is heralds who, before the prayers, sprinkle sacred water over the hands of suppliants.[12] No priest intervenes in the purification of the Greek army.[13] Now, if on this solemn occasion, when it was a matter of ending a terrible plague, the Greeks had employed the ministry of some priest, it would doubtless have been mentioned. After the victory, the army deliberated to know if they should offer sacrifice. The opinions of the leaders were divided. Some acquitted themselves of this religious duty; others did not. Each consulted only his own sentiment and will.

Men eminent among the people and in the army often read the future. Covered with glory, the gods appeared to these mortals.[14] Each individual could declare, on his own authority, that he communicated with heaven.

Among the Trojans, whom despite himself the author of the *Iliad* depicts as more civilized than the Greeks,[15] Theano, a priestess of Minerva, lives in the

---

tence of a poet who transported the customs of his time to previous eras. Elsewhere, more faithful to Homeric practices, he has Laocoön designated a priest of Neptune by lot:

Laocoön ductus Neptuni sorte sacerdos.

(*Aen.*, II, 201)

In the funeral ceremonies for Anchises in Sicily, Aeneas alone directs all the solemnities (*Aen.*, V, 94–99), and the kingship and the priesthood are united in the person of Anius:

Rex Anius, rex idem hominum Phoebque sacerdos.

(III, 80)

In Apollonius of Rhodes (*Argonautic.*), it is still Jason who prays, and not a priest; and Mopsus, a soothsayer by profession, is at the same time the most valiant of warriors.

11. Diviners exercise more influence in the Messenian Wars reported by Pausanias than in the Trojan War. On the part of the Spartans, the soothsayer Hecateus, and on the side of the Messenians Theocles, decided the conduct of the Spartan Anaxander and the Messenian Aristomenes (Pausan., *Messen.*). This is because it is in the nature of things that the priesthood progressively acquires more authority. "During the heroic ages," says Gillies (*Hist. of Greece*, bk. I, ch. 3, p. 112), "the famous and religious men believed that they were honored on important occasions by the immediate presence and counsel of their heavenly protectors. The secondary information of the priests and oracles was less generally recognized and respected. But as belief in the appearances of the gods in human form weakened, the office of the priest became more important, and people had more confidence in oracles." Nonetheless—and we cannot too often repeat this—despite this progress, the priesthood in Greece always remained in a subordinate and dependent condition.

12. *Iliad*, IX, 174.

13. Ibid., I, 314–317.

14. Ibid., II, 858–860; XII, 211–229; XVI, 604–605; XVII, 208; XVIII, 249–250.

15. On the luxury of the Trojans, see Herder, *Phil. de l'hist.*, III, 142. The poet, however, committed an error in attributing the same religion as his compatriots to the Trojans. The peoples of Phrygia professed a very different worship: they were subject to priestly authority.

temple of the goddess (or at least opens its doors), offers her gifts, and addresses prayers to her.[16] But this priestess was named by the people,[17] and among the Trojans, no less than among the Greeks, the warriors were augurs. The habitants of Olympus communicate directly with them. Helenus; Polydamas; Laogonus;[18] Eunomia;[19] Cassandra, daughter of Priam; and Oenone, wife of Paris,[20] have the gift of prophecy.

Often this faculty is united to royalty, as with Amphilochus[21] and Theonoe, daughter of Proteus.[22] At other times, the gods bestow it upon men without them desiring or hoping for it. Amphiaraus had never been initiated into the mysteries of the future. One night in the house of Phliunte—behind it, specifies the precise Pausanias[23]—the prophetic spirit took hold of him, and henceforth never left him. We cite Pausanias even though he is a very modern author because he gathered on site, with the scrupulosity that is his mark and merit, the most ancient traditions. After the death of Amphiaraus, Apollo chose Polyphides[24] and his son Theoclymenus[25] to be oracles. Neither, however, appears to have been a priest.

Direct communications were much more respected than those obtained by the intermediary of priests. Priam, receiving from Jupiter the order to go and ask for the remains of Hector from his murderer, did not consult the priests about the will of this god, but he asked for a sign, which he received. He expressed himself on this score in a way that merits attention. If a priest, he says, an interpreter of heavenly signs, had given me this counsel, I would have accused him of lying, and I would have turned from him with contempt.[26] Later, though, these same direct communications will be considered criminal. This is due to a natural progression of ideas.

Those who devote themselves exclusively to the worship of the gods, and pride

16. *Iliad*, II, 300.
17. Eustath., *ad Iliad.*
18. *Iliad*, XVI, 604–605.
19. Ibid., II, 858–862.
20. Clem. Alex., *Strom.*, I, 334; Conon *ap.* Photium.
21. Cic., *De divin.*, I, 11.
22. Euripides, *Helen*, 144.
23. *Corinth*, 13.
24. *Odyss.*, XV, 251–254.
25. Ibid., VI, 528–533.
26. *Iliad*, XXIV, 308–314. Ulysses acts in the same way in the *Odyssey*.

themselves on their special favors, gain nothing from this devotion, neither special prerogatives nor uncontested authority. They lead a wandering life, following in the train of the armies, present in councils and at feasts despite generals and kings who typically hate them.[27] They are not called for, they are not sought, except when someone thinks he needs them. Their interpretations of divine wills are often called into question, and they sometimes are the objects of shabby treatment. Banished and outlawed, Theoclymenus escaped from his fellow citizens only by embarking with Telemachus. This is evidence that at the time the gift of prophecy conferred no privileges. Leiodes claimed it in vain as he sought to disarm the anger of Ulysses.[28] Hippotes, one of the Heracleidae, killed the oracle Carnus.[29] Calchas hesitated to speak before Agamemnon out of fear of arousing his anger. I am only, he said, a common man, without defense before a king.[30] When, reassured by Achilles that he revealed the will of Apollo, Agamemnon showered him with reproaches.

Three verses of the *Odyssey* indicate in a very remarkable way the inferior rank the priests occupied. They are represented as men at the service of the public, and put on a par with doctors, architects, and singers, those to whom one grants hospitality, and who subsist on the charity of those who employ them.[31]

It is true that Homer in general appears to be favorable to the priestly cause. In his poems, heaven almost always backs up the organs of its decrees. But the Homeric poems are after the heroic ages of Greece by at least two centuries, and the attitude of the poet in favor of the priestly estate is the natural effect of a development we will describe later.[32]

One would be wrong to consider the existence of priestly families, which were

27. Aversion toward the priestly yoke is inherent in the Greek spirit, even in the philosophers who most admire the priestly corporations of other countries. Plato, the great panegyrist of Egypt when he called to establish a priesthood (*De legib.*, VI), says that the choice of priests ought to be left to the gods, and that for this purpose they ought to be drawn by lot; but that each office should be exercised by an individual for only one year.

28. *Odyss.*, XXII, 320–329.

29. Apollod., bk. II, ch. 3; Aenomaus *ap.* Euseb., bk. V.

30. *Iliad*, I, 77–83, 106–108.

31. *Odyss.* XVII, 384–386. The poet adds cooks.

32. It follows from this that all the facts that belong to periods after Homeric times, and which would lead us to attribute more or less influence to the priesthood, are not applicable to the period of the Greek religion with which we are dealing here.

numerous in Greece[33] and are mentioned in the *Odyssey* itself,[34] as a proof of the power of priests. The idea of the Greeks concerning the gift of prophecy seems to have some analogy with that of modern peoples concerning nobility. They thought that this divine favor was transmitted from father to son. Calchas came from a family that had enjoyed it for three generations.[35] Mopsus owed his birth to Manto, daughter of Tiresias.[36] Amphilochus was a prophet like his father, Amphiaraus. Herodotus recounts that Evenius had received the gift of divination from heaven because the Apollonians had unjustly deprived him of sight. The historian adds, as a natural consequence of this fact, that Deiphonus, son of this Evenius, fulfilled the functions of an oracle in the army.[37]

The foreign origin of these priestly families is of no importance to this question. We will see later that if some had descended from the colonies by which Greece was civilized, and had retained the direction of certain special rites as their patrimony,[38] they nonetheless never became a legally established institution. The public religion did not belong to them at all. Their true monopoly was in the mystery

33. There were few cities in Greece where one did not encounter some priestly family. The Branchides and the Deucalionides lived at Delphi (Herod., IV; Varro, *Divin. rerum liber*; scholiast of Stace, *Theb.*, VIII, 198). The Evangelides, adopted descendants of the Branchides, lived in Milet; the Telliades at Gela (Herod., VIII, 27; IX, 37). Elsewhere, the Clytiades and the Jamides. The latter trace their origin to Apollo, whose son was Jamus, their founder. This god had granted him the ability to hear the voices of the gods and to read the future in the fire's flames (Pind., *Olymp.*, VI, 69–221). It was at Elis that they established themselves. "*Elis in Peloponneso familias duas certas habet, Jamidarum unam, alteram Clytidarum*" (Cic., *De divin.*, I, 41; Herod., IX, 32; Philostr., *Apollon.*, V, 25; Pausan., IV, 5; V, 44; VI, 2 & 17; Apollod., I, 7; Pind., *Olymp.*, VI, 57 & 120–121). Among the Eleians, two or three families claimed the gift of predicting the future and healing the sick, one that went from father to son (Herod., IX, 33; Pausan., III, 11; IV, 15; VVI, 2; Cic., *De divin.*). Finally, the Eumolpides, the Ceryces, and the Eteobutades had the superintendence of the mysteries in Athens (Andocid., *De myst.*, p. 15; Lysander, ibid., p. 130; Diod., I, 29; Thucyd., VIII, 55; Aeschin., *De falsa legatione*). The Leonidas provided the inferior priests, and the priestesses were subject to a woman drawn from the race of the Phylleides (Sainte-Croix, *Les myst.*, p. 45).

34. Maron, a priest of Apollo, lived with his family in a wood consecrated to this god (*Odyss.*, IX, 197–201).

35. Apollon., *Rhod. Schol.*, I, 139.

36. Strabo, bk. XIV.

37. Herod., IX, 92–94.

38. For example, those of Ceres and Proserpine; the Eumolpides were their ministers in all the cities that worshipped them.

cults, and the mysteries were separate from the public religion.³⁹ This is a yet stronger reason to think that these families exercised no influence in the times described by the epics, since their authors appear to know nothing about the place of mystery cults in the Greek religion.⁴⁰

39. The two cults were so distinct that the priests, subordinate in one, occupied the first rank in the other. Thus the Ceryces, mere immolators of victims in the popular Athenian ceremonies, along with the Eumolpides became the supreme pontiffs in the Eleusian mysteries (Creuzer, German ed., IV, 384).

40. The truth we have tried to demonstrate in this chapter will, perhaps, be the most contested of all those we try to establish. There is no doubt that those who have an interest in denying the cause we give for the superiority of the Greeks over other peoples—that is, the absence of priestly authority in Greece—will try to cast doubt on it by perverting facts and confounding periods. Now, since it is important that a false opinion is not accredited before we can refute it, here we will answer in advance the objections that will be made to us, by means of two very clear assertions, one of which we have already proved, the other that we will demonstrate later. The first: priests had no legal authority in the heroic ages. The *Iliad* gives this ample credibility. The second: they gradually acquired more authority, they obtained prerogatives sanctioned by the laws and habit; but they never enjoyed the unlimited ascendancy, or the exclusive privileges, that the priestly corporations of India, Egypt, or Persia did.

One can fix the peak of the power of Greek priests at the time of Sophocles. In the tragedies of this poet, the priesthood speaks an entirely different language from the one spoken in the *Iliad* or the *Odyssey*. Agamemnon threatens Calchas, but it is Tiresias who threatens Oedipus. He says these remarkable words to him, which were repeated by his successors under different forms, and with various nuances: "I am the servant of the gods, and not yours" (*Oedipus the King*). We give our opponents a great opportunity, therefore, in choosing this moment of Greek history as the touchstone of our claims. But even at this period the priests in Greece possessed no civil, political, or judicial authority. They did not form a distinct or independent body. These are the very expressions of the Scythian author Anacharsis, who in France is the authority for everything pertaining to Greece (*Voy. d'Anarch.*, ch. 21). The monopoly of religion was not the patrimony, whether hereditary or not, of one class. No bond connected the ministers of the different temples (*Voy. d'Anarch.*, ibid.). Many priesthoods always remained elective. The priests and priestesses of individual divinities were in large part named by the people. Even at Delphi, a place especially devoted to worship, the Pythia was taken from the women of the city (Eurip., *Ion*, 1320). In the same temple, the service of the sanctuary was performed by the most respectable citizens, who were chosen by lot: the interior of the temple, says Ion (Eurip., *Ion*, 414), was reserved for the leading citizens of Delphi, designated by lot.

The second archon in Athens had the administration of worship and bore the name of king-archon in memory of the ancient union of the monarchy and the priesthood; but he was not a priest: lot chose him like the other archons (Demosthen., in *Neoer.*). Of the epimeletes who assisted him, two were drawn from the families of the Eumolpides and the Ceryces, and two from the body of the people (*Etym. magn. v. Epimeletès*). The hierophantides, priestesses of the Eleusian mysteries, in truth ought to have always belonged to the family of the Philleides, but the Athenian matrons named whomever they pleased to this family (Worsley, *Inscr. nup. edi.*). Thus, even in the mystery cults, priestly privilege was tempered by popular participation (*Acad. inscr.*, XXXIX, 218; Reiske, *Or. Graec.*, VII, 209).

The priestly functions were often temporary, and those who had performed them returned into the class of simple citizens. They were not dispensed from military and civil duties, even during the time of their religious ones. Callias, daduchus of the Eleusinian mysteries, fought at Marathon clothed in the sacred insignias (Plut., in *Arist.*). The priesthood was subject to the ordinary tribunals. The Areopagus judged everything pertaining to religion (Meurs., in *Areop.*), except in the case of a revision of its judgment by the assembly of the people. The college of the Eumolpides, before whom cases of impiety were argued, while at the same time it had the terrible right to decide according to unwritten laws (Lysias, *Contr. Andoc.*), judged only in the first instance. The definitive judgment was reserved to the Senate and, finally, to the tribunal of the Heliastes, i.e., of all the Athenians, because, starting at the age of thirty, all could sit there (Demosthen., *Cont. Andr.*). The Hieromnemons who were charged with religious ceremonies in the assembly of the Amphictyones had an advantage over all the other members of this assembly, but their dignity was not at all an extension of the priesthood, because they were drawn by lot (Den. of Hal., I, 16).

If someone objects that we have spoken only of Athens here, we would reply that we would find even greater advantage for our position in speaking of Sparta. In his singular institutions, which we would never present as models for anything, Lycurgus subjects religion entirely to the royal authority, and even to the military power. At the battle of Platea, the general of the Lacedaemonians, Pausanias, presided over the sacrifices, and immolated the victims himself, just like the heroes beneath the walls of Troy (Herod., IX, 60–61). The interpretation of heavenly signs belonged to magistrates. The two principal priesthoods, that of Uranian Jupiter and Lacedaemonian Jupiter, were extensions of the monarchy (Herod., VI, 56). The kings chose the deputies they sent to Delphi to question Apollo (Herod., VI, 57); and the knowledge of the god's responses was exclusively reserved to them. This prerogative made the oracle of Apollo an instrument of royal power. The history of Sparta is filled with examples that prove it. The Argiens, having proposed a truce to the Spartans, Agesipolis, in his status as king, based himself on the authority of Olympian Jupiter and the Delphic oracle in order to reject the offer (Xenoph., *Hist. gr.*, IV, 7; Cic., *De divin.*). The ephors were the organs of heaven, invested with the right to contemplate the stars. Once every nine years, during a calm, moon-less night, if they saw a star fall, they could deprive the kings of their position (Plut., in *Aegid.*); they were magistrates, not priests.

One must not confuse the influence of the soothsayers with that of priests, properly speaking. The diviners were not members of an established order. An anecdote transmitted by Xenophon (*Anab.*, VI, 4, n. 2) proves that even at this time the Greeks did not consider divination to be the attribute of a particular profession. A sacrifice offered by the Greek army not having had a favorable result, the soldiers suspected Xenophon of having bribed the diviner in order to oblige them to remain where they were and to found a colony there. Alarmed by their suspicions, Xenophon had it broadcast that the sacrifices would recommence the next day, and that if there was another diviner in the army, he was invited to participate.

Based on facts like these, one can see that at all times the Greeks remained independent of priestly authority. Their priests often exercised great influence, but it was by exciting popular passions, and not by direct and legally prescribed action. It was in this way that they provoked the death of Socrates. They suggested the crime; the people committed it. Raised in the State along with the other Greek institutions, the priesthood was accepted, without being dominant. In this way, our distinction between the Greeks and the other peoples of Antiquity is supported and confirmed.

CHAPTER 2

That It Is Nonetheless Possible That at a Time Prior to the Heroic Age the Greeks Had Been Enslaved by Priestly Corporations

The considerations we just submitted to our readers do not, however, lead us to affirm that the Greeks were never governed by priestly bodies. Several facts that have come down to us through the obscurity of the centuries and the confusion of fables, even though they are more or less scattered, seem to indicate that at a period prior to the one we call mythical Greece was momentarily subject to an order of priests, whether indigenous or foreign.[1] We encounter in Homer some indications of the weakening of this power. The priests of the ages that preceded were invested with a greater authority and occupied a rank higher than those that are shown to us under the walls of Troy. Like the kings, Tiresias carries a scepter of

---

1. By a path different from our own, Mr. Creuzer was led to recognize, as we have, a period during which the priesthood, with the authority of a position more elevated than the rest of the human race, could have given to the Greeks its mysterious teachings. But he places this period between the worship of the Pelasgians and the brilliant fictions of Homer. We place it before the primitive state of the Greeks and the Pelasgian fetishism. One can see our reasons in the chapter itself.

Mr. Creuzer seems to us not to have avoided a mistake we have already pointed out. He supposes that an enormous distance existed between the Greek people and those he calls their founders. If he has in mind foreign founders, in treating the colonies that came to Greece, we will show that this distance did not exist. If it is a matter of native founders, it existed even less. The power of images, the authority of symbols, were not inventions but facts that, renewing themselves each time passion or enthusiasm spoke, constituted the language of which the priesthood made use. But this is not, as Mr. Creuzer says, because the priests knew the fundamental laws of the human mind, and therefore they spoke symbolically; it is because the image and the symbol are the natural expressions of the human mind as long as it neither has abstract notions nor knows the forms of logic. Originally, the priests had the latter no more than the people did. In employing images and symbols they did not stoop to them; they used them because they already used them. As is the case today with primitives, it was the language of all. A proportion between priests and people naturally existed, because the people and the priests were on the same level.

gold; he himself is called a king.[2] The tradition—certainly false—that attributed to Theseus the division of the inhabitants of Attica into classes, similar in some respects to the division into castes, seems to be the confused memory of a far-off time when this classification existed in Greece.[3]

We also find in the traditions that have come down to us concerning the customs of the first Pelasgians, teachings and rites that characterize priestly cults. Herodotus speaks of a phallic Hermes, not Egyptian but Pelasgian.[4] Several authors attest that they saw phalluses on the bas-reliefs of the walls of Mycenae, Tirynthe, and other Greek cities, as at Bubustis in Egypt.[5] The Pelasgians had offered human sacrifices.[6] Vestiges of the worship of the elements and stars appear in some ancient Greek temples. The sacred fire burned perpetually in the Prytaneum of Athens.[7] In the same city, there was an altar formerly dedicated to the earth.[8] Elsewhere, the sea was worshipped as a divinity distinct from Neptune. Cleomenes sacrificed a bull to it by having it cast into the waves.[9] The Argiens cast horses into the lake of Argolide in honor of the Seasons;[10] and Titania, the worshipper of the winds, was celebrated over a long period for her quadruple holocausts and magic invocations that go back to Media.[11] The worship of the Ar-

2. *Odyss.*, X, 195; XI, 95–150; Schlegel, *Hist. de la poésie grecque.*

3. Plut., in *Thes.*

4. Herodotus.

5. Herod., II.

6. Sainte-Croix, *Les myst.*, p. 11, and later: "The Telchines, priests of the island of Rhodes who were formerly Pelasgians, worshipped the earth and offered humans in sacrifice" (p. 76).

7. *Etmol. magn.*, v. Prutaneia, p. 694. This worship of fire, Phoenician in origin, admitted only an everlasting flame as a representation of the divinity.

8. Thucydides, II, 16. Sophocles calls the earth the greatest of the goddesses. In the *Iliad* (XVII, 197, etc.), Agamemnon sacrifices a boar to the sun and the earth. It, however, became a subordinate divinity. It was represented in Athens in a suppliant attitude, asking rain from Jupiter.

9. Herod., VI, 76.

10. Pausan., *Arcadia.*

11. Pausan., *Corinth*, 55. These sacrifices were offered in four caves consecrated to the four cardinal winds. As ancient rites always return in times of misfortune, the worship of the winds was momentarily reintroduced in Athens when Xerxes invaded Greece. The Athenians, frightened by the arrival of the Persian fleet on the coast of Magnesia, offered victims to Borea (Athenaeus, IV) in order to obtain her assistance; and a storm having dispersed the enemy, they built a temple to this goddess on the banks of the Ilissus (Herodotus). In the same way, the Thuriens, delivered from a great danger by a storm that ruined the fleet of Dionysius the tyrant, instituted ceremonies commemorating this event at which the gods were worshipped (Ael., *Var. Hist.*, XII, 6).

cadians was noticeably marked with astronomical ideas.[12] The hideous forms of some of the divinities of a much more remote time[13] differed from the elegance of those that embellished the temples and were celebrated by the poets of Greece.[14]

But even while granting to these scattered facts the authority it is reasonable to accord them, what we proved earlier must still be admitted. Formerly enslaved to priests, the Greeks became independent of them.

How did this revolution occur? How did the priests, triumphant in all the other countries they governed, so completely succumb in Greece?

On this question we can only offer some conjectures.

In this matter, however, we have to decline the help of the two principal guides that moderns employ.

Homer gives no indication of a period when the Greek priests would have enjoyed a less limited power than what he attributes to them. He is silent about the event that would have deprived them of their privileges and cast them into a tenuous and subordinate position. Herodotus says nothing about how the phallic cult was banished from the public religion and took refuge in the mysteries. The assertions of these two authors have the character of vague reminiscences rather than of accurate accounts. Such reminiscences can cross the upheavals of the centuries without being affected and inexplicably appear in the midst of a state of things with which they have no relation.

But does the history of other nations yield light that Greece's denies? In an earlier book, we saw that the military or political authority attempted everywhere to break the yoke of priestly authority.

12. Creuzer, IV, 90–91. The Arcadians, says Hermann, cultivated astronomy long before the other tribes of Greece; what characterizes their tales is that, after the most bizarre metamorphoses, the heroes of these metamorphoses always ended by glittering at the top of the heavens. On this subject he cites the daughters of Atlas, who were changed into doves before becoming the Pleiades; Calisto, a bear on earth before becoming the Great Bear, etc. (*Handbuch der Mythol. astronom. des Grec.*, III, 21).

13. Going back to the most remote antiquity, some Greek divinities had bizarre forms, horns, a tail, a monstrous phallus (Voss, *Mythol. Briefe*). Pausanias (*Attica*) speaks of a statue of Minerva with sphinxes and griffons.

14. We could have added some other details. For example, the Greeks and their imitators the Romans, like the Gauls and the Persians, feared going into battle before the new moon (Pausan., *Attica*; Xenoph., *Hist. grecq.*); this obviously was an astronomico-priestly superstition. We also see the prophetesses whom Ariovistus had in his army declare to him that he would be defeated if he did not await the renewal of the moon before attacking the Romans (Caes., *B Gall.*, I; Dio Cassius, XXXVIII; Clem. Alex., *Strom.*, I, 15).

What was attempted everywhere else could have happened in Greece. The mild and temperate climate of this country disposed its inhabitants to develop their intellectual faculties. They did not have to irrigate their territory with large hydrostatic devices. Natural limits divided their country into small States, which were often attacked by their neighbors. The small boundaries that confined them made absolute despotism on the part of an order or caste almost impossible, and the constantly recurring necessity of defense had to make the military authority prevail. Finally, the worship of stars was foreign to Greece. This circumstance was decisive. Without astrolatry's absence, the Greeks would never have been a fortunate exception to the common rule. Etruria was divided like Greece into small, warring principalities, and India could do without material works; but until the third century of Rome, priests governed Etruria, and they still dominate India.

Favored by their location, the Greeks could have been favored by chance; and what did not succeed in Egypt, Persia, or Ethiopia could have succeeded in a country where circumstances rendered the endeavor easier, and obstacles less insurmountable.

We will not try to determine when in the development of Greek civilization this revolution could have occurred. The endeavors of this sort undertaken by various nations took place at different times. But if the thing did occur in Greece, it is certain that the Greeks were not in a completely primitive state, because their priestly corporations possessed learning in astronomy,[15] and the warrior caste had arrogated to itself the possession of lands. In this way, one finds traces of science and notions of property.[16]

The tradition of Danaus and his fifty daughters killing the fifty sons of Egypt, would not this be the garbled memory of a massacre of the warrior caste by the priests? Supposing the type of anachronism that is rather natural to times when no one observed exact dates, could not one assign a similar motive to the attacks on the oracle at Delphi by Pyrrhus, son of Achilles? Would it not be the same for the religious wars that several historians speak about, and locate in various places in Greece,[17] wars the poets cast as the battle of the gods against the Titans? Modern scholars have believed that here they recognized the struggle of the Pelasgians against eastern or southern colonies. (This opinion, however, will be refuted later.)

15. Dupuis, *Origine des cultes*.

16. The word "Danaoi" signifies "possessor of lands."

17. Diod., III, 36–37; IV, 6; V, 42; Apollon., *Argonaut. Schol.*, II, 219; Solin, caps. 8 & 14; Stephan., *De urb.*, 569–620; Justin, X, 4; Strabo, V; Pomp. Mela, II, 5.

What is beyond dispute is that the Titans professed the worship of the elements and the stars, of the earth and the sky,[18] which is to say: a type of worship that necessarily establishes priestly authority.[19] What is also sure is that the Titans were chased from Greece.[20] Is it not probable that they formed a corporation similar to those we have seen in Egypt, India, Persia, and among the Gauls, and that this corporation was defeated and made to flee by men who no longer wished to wear the shackles their ancestors wore?

Perhaps divisions among the priests contributed to their expulsion. A rather plausible although obscure tradition recounts battles at Argos between the priests of Apollo and Bacchus.[21] These battles recall the internal discord of the Egyptian

18. A tradition reported by Diodorus (V, 71), and repeated by Fulgentius (*Mythol.*, 25), says that, before going to battle with the Titans, Jupiter had sacrificed to heaven, the earth, and the sun. Manilius alludes to this:

Nec prius armavit violento fulmine dextram
Jupiter, ante Deos quam constitit ipse sacerdos.

(*Astron.*, V, 343–344)

This tradition comes from the constant practice of the Greeks to attribute the customs of men to gods. As they worshipped the gods of their enemies in order to disarm them, they wanted Jupiter to take the same precaution before going to battle; but the fiction itself indicates an ancient worship of the stars that was abolished.

19. Sainte-Croix, *Les myst.*, pp. 10, 11, & 26. The opinion of Levesque (trans. of Thucydides), Heyne, and Fréret is that the Pelasgians had come from Scythia. The Scythians were subject to priestly authority.

20. The scholiast of Lycophron reports that Ophion and Eurynome, daughter of Ocean, reigned before Saturn and Rhea; that they were defeated in battle, Ophion by Saturn, Eurynome by Rhea; and that subsequently Saturn and Rhea, having cast them into Tartarus, ruled in their place. Prometheus defeated by Jupiter is, in our opinion, a tradition of the same sort; an ancient Athenian monument, the entrance to a temple of Minerva in the Academy, praised the priority of Prometheus, a Titan, over Vulcan, a Homeric god. Prometheus and Vulcan were represented as working together; and as the elder, Prometheus held a scepter (schol. in Sophocl., *Aed. Col.*, V, 55).

21. Struck, as we were, by the vestiges of a priestly domination in Greece before heroic times, Mr. W. Schlegel has published in a review of Niebuhr's *Histoire romaine* in the *Annales de Heidelberg* a very interesting passage on the subject that occupies us here: "Here is," he says, "how we conceive the event that liberated Greece from the power of priests. In the most ancient times, all Greece was subject to them. The name 'Pelasgians' belonged especially to the caste of priests, and this name was given, following the dominant class, to the entire people. Later, the caste of warriors rose up against the one that ruled in the name of the gods. The *Iliad* bears strong marks of this struggle: the dispute between Agamemnon and Chryses and Calchas is an indication. But the Greeks, or better put: the privileged order of warriors, had increasingly freed itself from the priests' rule, and having introduced

priesthood. It most often is by means of dissension among possessors of power that power falls.

If one reflects on the fact that everywhere the Titans went after their defeat they established mystery cults, priestly corporations, and all the customs that characterize peoples subject to priestly control; if one considers that in Etruria, for example, it has been demonstrated that the teachings and ceremonies of religion were brought by a colony of Pelasgians,[22] with colleges of priests invested with a limitless authority, while no such power appears among the Greeks descended from the Pelasgians who remained there.[23] Given all this, the existence of an earlier priestly religion in this country, and its destruction before Homeric times, acquire great probability.

---

new constitutions and mores, the Pelasgians properly speaking, i.e., the priests, either renounced their hereditary functions and became one with the nation, or they separated from them by emigrating. It is from priestly races that the scattered remains of the Pelasgians at the time of Herodotus and Thucydides descended. Herodotus says that to judge the Pelasgians by those of his century, their ancestors spoke a barbarous tongue. Now, everything that the Greeks did not understand without interpreters appeared to them to be not a dialect different from theirs, but a foreign language, and every foreign language was barbarous to them. The Pelasgians of Thrace, Lemnos, and the Hellespont, driven back on themselves and taking no part in the revolutions that changed the face of Greece and its poetic literature, naturally had preserved their ancient idiom.

"According to this hypothesis," continues Mr. Schlegel, "we would divide Greek history into three epochs: the Pelasgian times, domination of priests, and victory of warriors, some generations before the Trojan War; the heroic times, then the destruction of the warrior caste and the abolition of the monarchy; republican times. We know the third period historically, the second by mythology; we are completely ignorant of the first except for some scattered traditions, which are even more inadequate as guides as the poets have placed in it all the mythological genealogies of the second period, thus falsifying the first" (*Annales de Heidelberg*, vol. 9, pp. 846ff.).

22. Many of the superstitions the Greeks had risen above since the departure of the Pelasgians who emigrated were carried by the latter to Etruria. Divination, augury, extispicy, aruspices, the search for premonitions in the most ordinary events—these were not entirely foreign to Greek habits; but they were much less rooted and held a much smaller place in Greece than among the Etruscans or the Romans, heirs of the Etruscan disciplines. The Etruscans always preserved them in their integrity, with all their original authority, such as they had been observed in Greece in only a few cities such as Delphi, Olympia, etc., that were devoted to religion, and in that character were faithful to the old ceremonies and traditions. Sophocles and Thucydides say that the names "Pelasgians" and "Etruscans" designate the same people. Alexander of Pleuron (schol. *Cod. Ven. ad Iliad*, XVI, 233ff.) claims that the Selles of the oracle of Dodona descended from the Etruscans. We believe the opposite; but his claim proves the resemblance between the two.

23. Heyne, *De Etruscis, Com. Soc. Goett.*

This hypothesis would explain the emancipation from the power of priests of which the Greeks offer the sole example. We will prove later that the liberty enjoyed in this respect by the Scandinavians lasted only for a time.

The same hypothesis would explain the disproportion between Homer's elegant language and the social state presented in the *Iliad*. In this way, it is less astounding to see an idiom that one could regard as the *chef d'oeuvre* of civilization employed to depict still semibarbaric mores. By it, one can go back to the origin of those bizarre portions of mythology that contrast so starkly with the customary mythology of the first Greek poets. There is an obvious analogue with the teachings and fables of all countries where the priesthood reigned. These ill-fitting portions thus show themselves to be the fragments of a destroyed whole, disconnected fragments preserved by men who survived its destruction. Certain oddities that struck us in some of the priestly institutions of Greece, especially the most ancient and the most foreign to the popular Greek religion, become easy to explain.

We therefore do not reject the assumption that at a time that is now covered by a thick night there was a priestly religion in Greece, as well as powerful corporations created by it devoted to its maintenance. But a violent revolution destroyed this religion and its priests, along with all the civilization of which they were the authors. All the historical information going back to the first times of Greece shows its inhabitants reduced to the savage state.[24] Nothing is simpler to understand, and more inevitable. Along with the priests, everything of science, arts, and learning had to disappear, at least for a time. In fact, their overthrow cast Greece beyond barbarism. The tendency of priestly power being to hold the people in ignorance, the destruction of the priesthood in the country where it had reigned without challenge must have led to the destruction of all the earlier civilization. This is what has been noted among all peoples subject to priests, the Hebrews, in Egypt, in Phoenicia. The sciences always follow the fate of the priestly order.[25] The ques-

24. See the beginning of Thucydides. Also see Plato, in *Protag.*; Diod., I; Pausan., VIII, I; Euripid., in *Sisph.* fragm. Mosch. *ap.* Stob., *Ecl. Phys.*, I; *Athenea*, XIV; Sext. Empir., *Adv. math.*, II. Goguet, to whom one must acknowledge the merit of being a compiler who coordinates well the facts that he collects, and draws from them rather accurate conclusions, citing a number of the authorities we ourselves have invoked, depicts the first Greeks "as savages who, wandering in the woods and fields without leaders and order, had no other retreats than caves and caverns, did not use fire and ate no food suitable for man, and were wild to the point of eating one another when the occasion presented itself" (*De l'origine des lois*, etc., I, 1, 59).

25. Meiners, *Hist. de l'origine, des progrès et de la chute des sciences en Grèce.*

tion is to know how, when this order is destroyed, the human race begins its march forward again. If, as in the East, it falls beneath the yoke, along with servitude it reprises the small portion of knowledge that its masters tolerate.[26] If it is emancipated, as were the Greeks, its progress, while slow at first, is subsequently inhibited by nothing. Free but ignorant, the Greeks fell back into fetishism because they professed a priestly polytheism, which, as we will see, is always composed of two parts: on one hand, a secret doctrine; on the other, fetishism. The priestly corporations being destroyed, the secret doctrine was forgotten and fetishism alone remained.

For the rest, we ought not to deplore this retrograde movement. Under the domination of the priests, the sciences (contained in a narrow and mysterious enclave) could only be the property in Greece—as elsewhere—of a small number who made it the basis or the instrument of its despotism. In all things, poverty is better than monopoly.

26. Thus when Cambyses, devastating Egypt, had burned its cities, demolished its temples, destroyed its monuments, and dispersed or killed its priests, both religion and the sciences appeared to disappear. But the sacerdotal order having reorganized anew, Egypt entered into its former way. The learning it formerly possessed came back to the same degree as before the Persian invasion: that is, imperfect, inaccessible, and foreign to any progress.

CHAPTER 3

On the Religion and the Priesthood of the Earliest Times of the Greek, According to the Testimony of Greek Historians

Cast back into the primitive state, the Greeks had to cross its phases by degrees, and practice its form of worship.[1] Like the primitives of all periods, they must have assumed that the different parts of nature were animated by a divine spirit, and they worshipped this divine spirit in animals, stones, trees, and mountains.

These, in fact, are the divinities all the Greek writers indicate as the oldest objects of the religious veneration of their compatriots.

1. Here we will not return to the facts and arguments that demonstrate that theism could not have been the belief of the Greeks before heroic times. Independently of the arguments that have been made against the hypothesis of a theism contemporary with barbarism, the testimony of the ancient authors who are most worthy of trust argues against everything that modern authors have maintained because of their trust in the apocryphal writings attributed to Orpheus, Musaeus, and other mythical personages. Far from considering Orpheus the author of a doctrine more refined than popular belief, the Greek philosophers and orators accused him of having accredited the crudest, most revolting fables. "Orpheus, who more than anyone else," says Isocrates (in *Busirid.*), "attributes indecencies to the immortals, was cut in pieces in punishment of this crime." Diogenes Laertius refused the name of philosopher to this same Orpheus, who attributed to the gods the most shameful excesses, those which men barely let pass their lips (Diog., in *Prooem.*, 3). Musaeus, whom some have wanted to pass as a theist, represents heavenly bliss, Plato tells us (*De rep.*), in a much more sensual manner than even Homer or Hesiod, and he claims that perpetual drunkenness will be the most worthy reward of virtue.

However, having spoken of Herodotus's opinion concerning the first worship of the Pelasgians, Mr. de Sainte-Croix adds: "Such was the idea that the polytheists could form of the theism of the first inhabitants of Greece and the way in which they had to express it. Uranism, or the worship of the material sky, had to naturally follow theism. Soon the worship of the earth was added" (*Myst. du pag.*, ed. of Mr. de Sacy, p. 14). To presuppose theism in this way seems to us to be an unjustifiable obstinacy on his part. Happily, one sees that these chimerical ideas are abandoned by the writers of our day. Mr. Rolle, the author of a very commendable work on the worship of Bacchus, recognizes that the first Greeks were savages, and their worship was very crude (I, 102).

In olden times, says Pausanias, the Greeks rendered honors to entirely inanimate stones which, since then, they offered to the images of the immortals.[2] The Thespians adored a branch;[3] the inhabitants of the isle of Euboea and the Carians, pieces of wood;[4] the mountain dwellers of Cythera, the trunk of a tree; at Samos, a simple plank had altars; and the oldest images of the Pallas and the Ceres of Athens were stakes, similar to the idols of the Tongouse.[5] The Venus of Paphos was a stone. Three stadia from Gytheio there was a featureless rock. It was said that Orestes, having sat upon it, recovered his reason. In commemoration of this event, this mysterious rock bore the surname Jupiter.[6] It is probable that it originally was an object of worship, and that the homage rendered it was preserved after the religion was modified, and a tale was invented to explain it. Often the fables that are presented as the source of ceremonies are really their consequences. The Orchomenians maintained a profound respect for stones that had fallen from the sky and were gathered, they said, by Eteocles.[7] But there are two passages in Pausanias that are even more striking.

"In Phares, a town of Achaia," he writes,[8] "by the statue of Mercury Agorean, thirty squared stones are worshipped by the inhabitants in the name of a divinity; this is conformed to the ancient religion of the Greeks." "The statue of Cupid at Thespiae," he recounts elsewhere, "is, as in the earliest times, a shapeless rock that no one used for any other purpose."[9]

We find at Phlius in the Peloponnese the worship of animals. In the middle of the public square arose the divine image of a goat.[10] At Thebes, weasels had obtained celestial honors.[11] And according to an ancient tradition, the citadel of

---

2. *Achaic.*, 22. On the fetishism of the first Greeks, see also Aeschylus, *Prometheus*, 642ff.

3. Arnobius, VI.

4. *Culte des dieux fétiches*, pp. 151–52.

5. Creuzer, *Symbol.*, I, 184.

6. Pausan., *Lacon.*, 22.

7. Pausan., *Boeot.*, 18.

8. *Achaïc.*

9. *Boeot.*, 25. In the temple of Delphi, where priests carefully preserve the ancient customs and traditions, there was a sacred stone to which they attached great religious importance. The Pheneates, people of Arcadia, had near to the temple of Ceres two stones that they used as witnesses for their oaths (*Arcadia*, 15). The Cadmean Bacchus was the trunk of a tree encased in bronze (*Boeot.*, 12; Aenomaus *ap.* Euseb., *Praep. ev.*, V, 36).

10. Pausan., *Corinth*, 13. Later, this worship will be allegorized by saying that the constellation of the goat, Capricorn, harms the vines (Creuzer, III, 269).

11. Ael., *De natur. anim.*, XII, 5.

Athens had a serpent as its protecting god. This tradition existed at least until the time of the war with Persia, because the purported disappearance of the serpent was one of the means Themistocles employed to cause the Athenians to depart their city and set sail.[12]

It would be easy for us to point out in the practices of the Greeks, even in later eras, the traces of the fetishistic primitives. They washed the feet of statues in blood. And what is even more remarkable, the devotées of Athena poured sacred oil over certain consecrated stones.[13] In the same way, the Ostiacs, the Tongouse, and other peoples smeared their fetishes with blood.[14]

Like the primitives, the Greeks of the earliest times mistreated their divinities. Theocritus reminds the god Pan of this in one of his *Idylls*.[15] And the author of the *Theogony*[16] writes of the destruction of their temples, their altars, and their statues as the punishment of perfidious gods.

To be sure, there is a difference between the fetishes of Greece and those of the modern savages that travelers have helped us to understand. Those of Greece were already national. This is because the information we have concerning this fetishism dates from a period when the Greeks already began to form societies. The fetishes of the association had to replace those of individuals. But the latter were not wholly replaced. The Greeks carried on their persons little pygmy gods that they constantly invoked.[17]

Some writers have regarded these diminutive simulacra as mere images, made to recall invisible divinities. But any distinction between divinities and simulacra

12. Herod., VIII, 41. A law of Rhadymanthus, says Ruhnken, in his *Scholies sur Platon*, allowed Cretans to swear by sacred animals, and not by the higher divinities. Did not this law come from the fact that animals were once adored as fetishes? When the beings of one order are replaced by those of a higher one, men preserve the habit of taking the former idols as witnesses; and an idea of respect for the more imposing mixing with this habit, it was forbidden to lightly invoke the latter.

13. Theophr., *De superst.*

14. See the *Essai sur le schammanisme* of Lévêque, trans. of Thucyd., III, 278; *Culte des dieux fétiches*, p. 151; and Guasco, *De l'usage des statues*, p. 47.

15. Idyll., VII, v. 106. "If you grant me the favor I ask," says the poet to his rustic god, "let the children of Arcadia no longer strike your sides when they have a bad hunt."

16. Hesiod, *Theog.*, 793ff. Some authors have claimed that the tale of the Aegis, or the head of Medusa worn on a breastplate, sometimes by Jupiter, sometimes by Minerva, was a vestige of the habit of savages of scalping their enemies and decorating themselves with their hair.

17. Pausan., II, 11. The Cabiri, divinities of the mystery cults, for a long time retained the figure of these pygmy gods (Creuzer, German ed., II, 350).

is premature when it concerns peoples who are still quite ignorant. Among them the simulacra are gods because they move, they cry, they speak, they predict. Superstition is so inclined to confuse the two things that the confusion persists despite subsequent enlightenment and the different spirit of centuries. In contemporary Madrid, Lisbon,[18] and Naples, Madonnas lower their eyes, cover themselves, and sigh; Saint January sheds tears. Fetishism is always in the wings, as it were, ready to reenter religion. It does not succeed today because the priesthood, while profiting from the popular tendency to enhance its authority, is monitored by the learned class and therefore rejects or disavows whatever in fetishism is too absurd. But among the Greeks fallen back into savagery, and among whom there was neither a regular priesthood nor an educated class, fetishism had to triumph.

The roots it put down were profound. We just spoke of the serpent of Themistocles. But at another period a plague produced the same effect as did the invasion of the barbarians. Struck by the plague, the Athenians recalled that their ancestors had killed the inventor of the vine, Icarus, for having led them to the drunkenness that they believed was fatal. They also raised altars to a faithful dog who had not been able to survive his master.[19]

This Greek fetishism had jongleurs for priests, little different from modern ones.[20] It is in vain that the priests of later times attempted to present them in a favorable, even imposing, light. They attribute to crude customs mysterious motives. But the priests of today's savages provide approximate ideas concerning those of yesterday, and the Greek tragedies all agree in the matter, which confirms us in the conviction that the two priesthoods were identical.[21]

If we turn to the words of Homer, we would not elevate even the priests of Dodona above the category of jongleurs. He shows them sleeping on the hard ground, covered with mire, braving the rigors of the cold with naked feet, improvising their oracles.[22] Leather bowls[23] suspended from old oaks, whose prophetic

18. See the work of Mrs. Baillie entitled *Lisbonne en 1821,* etc.

19. Ael., *De Natur. anim.,* VII, 28.

20. Sainte-Croix, *Les myst.,* I, 29.

21. Aeschylus, *Prometheus,* 829–31; Sophocles, *Trojan Women,* 1164–1168; Euripides, *Andromache,* 885–86.

22. *Iliad,* XVI, 233–36. Strabo makes use of this passage from Homer concerning the priests of Dodona to paint them as primitive and wild men.

23. Etienne de Bysance *ap.* Gronox., *Thes. Antiq. Graec.,* VII; Spanheim *ad* Callimach., "Delos," 285; Sallier and Des Brosses, *Acad. inscr.,* XXXIV; Heyne, *Excurs. ad Iliad,* VII.

sound announces the future, are much like the drums of the Laplanders. And despite the equivocation detected by Herodotus, the inspired doves resemble fetishes,[24] and the bag in which Aeolus gives Ulysses the four winds has an unmistakable likeness to the bags full of wind that the sorcerers of the North sell to sailors. Nonetheless, it could be the case that these priests of Dodona were the relics of a destroyed priestly corporation.[25]

More than one writer affirms that they disposed of their manhood, and we will see that this mutilation was practiced in the majority of religions dominated by priests. They were bound to rigorous abstinences and to follow severe rules. This is yet another agreement with the customs of priestly peoples, and a new difference between the Selles,[26] the priests of Dodona, and the later priesthood of the Greeks. Not forming a corporate body, the Selles in Homeric times were not subject to any fixed rule. Herodotus[27] tells us that they treated the popular anthropo-

24. Herod., VIII, 41; Lévêque, *Excursion sur le schammanisme*, trans. of Thucydides, III, 278.

25. Epirus, where the oracle of Dodona was located, always remained nearly totally foreign to the rest of Greece by its mores, rites, and habits. The fable of Echetus, king of this country, who mutilated foreigners whom evil fate had delivered to him, and who had them devoured by his dogs (*Odyss.*), as well as the Greek proverb, "I will send you to Echetus, king of Epirus," prove how little communication there was between civilized Greece and barbarous Epirus. And does not this hatred of foreigners need to be attributed to the action of a xenophobic priesthood?

Certain ceremonies that were practiced at Dodona long after the triumph of the veritable Greek polytheism appear to have been preserved from the ancient Pelasgian religion. Dione, for example, the mother of Venus, who occupies a rather obscure place in Homeric mythology (*Iliad*, V, 370), was worshipped at Dodona as the wife of Jupiter. The same tradition was maintained in Thessaly (Diod., V, 72); and we learn from a passage of Demosthenes (contra *Mid.*) that at Dodona a bull was sacrificed to Jupiter and a cow to Dione. Note that Dione in the Phoenician cosmogony was a daughter of Uranus (the sky) and the wife of Time (Sanchon., *ap.* Euseb., *Praep. evang.*, I, 10); and in Apollodorus (I, II) that one of the female Titans is called Dionide. Other traditions indicate that the priests of Dodona worshipped a water god, a Jupiter pluvius, explained in the priestly teaching as the first creative or generative principle of the world, which is only a scientific interpretation of the worship of the elements. An oracle of Dodona ordered sacrifices to the river Achelous, and several peoples subject to priests cast victims into rivers. The doves of Dodona could have been sacred animals in the ancient religion which, after the destruction of this religion, became the fetishes of Greece fallen back into the primitive state. This is certainly what would have happened to the sacred animals of Egypt if the priestly regime had been destroyed. The leather bowls whose sound is communicated between them when one is struck can have been the expression of the dogma of metempsychosis in the teaching of the priests (Creuzer, IV, 183).

26. Particular name of the priests of Dodona.

27. II, 243.

morphism with great disdain, and called the genealogies of the gods "fables invented only yesterday." This was because in the midst of their present ignorance, the past bequeathed to them traditions that contradicted the new teachings of Greece. We do not think that to explain this opposition of teachings (if such an expression can be used when it is a question, on one hand, of crude notions, and, on the other, of garbled memories) it is necessary to attribute the origin of the priests of Dodona to Egyptian colonies.[28] They would have acted in the same way if they were the descendants of indigenous priests.

Scattered members of a dispersed caste, they had to affiliate themselves with everything that recalled their former power. Everywhere that a priesthood encounters priestly privileges, teachings, or customs, it recognizes itself in its works. There is a natural confraternity among all priesthoods. Rivalries may suspend it, but they do not break it. Behold in the *Iliad* the Greek diviner embracing the cause of a foreign priest. The priesthood has for its homeland only the priestly order itself.

Whatever may be the case with these different hypotheses, whether the priests of Dodona were simple jongleurs, the products of fetishism, or the disfigured remains of a destroyed priestly corporation, it is certain that they remained throughout the entirety of the heroic age in a state of degradation and obscurity, which made their influence absolutely nil.

It was not to them, therefore, that Greece owed its return to civilization, and even when it had entered onto this path, as much as they could, they persisted in not following it. Greece's return to more civilized mores was the work of Phoenician or Egyptian colonies who landed on their shores around three centuries before the Trojan War. Here, however, we encounter new problems to illumine and new errors to refute.

---

28. While Homer, as we have seen, says that the Selles came from the Pelasgians (Heeren, II, 459–62; and III, 11), the priests of this forest attributed the establishment of their oracle to Egypt; but Mr. Heeren (*Idéen*, II, 462) points out, and develops with a good deal of insight, the interest they had in attributing their origin to Egypt. We have borrowed some of his arguments.

CHAPTER 4

On the Influence of Colonies on the Social State and Religion of the Greeks

People have greatly exaggerated the influence of foreign colonies, especially Egyptian, on Greece.[1] They have thought, and continue to think, that the Greeks, having received from these colonies their doctrines, rites, and belief, along with the initial learning suitable to their social state, that the development of their religion

[1]. The most judicious and prudent of all the authors who have treated the first times of Greek civilization, Mr. Heeren, has to a certain extent earned this criticism. "When," he says, "we would not have any historical proof of Egyptian and Phoenician emigrations to Greece, the thing would still be plausible in itself. But rather than having too few indications of this sort, on the contrary, they are more numerous and detailed than we have the right to expect. . . . A thousand traditions demonstrate the influence of these colonies. The institution of marriage is attributed to Cecrops; the citadel of Athens bore his name, as that of Thebes bore the name of Cadmus; and the name of the Peloponnese proves the memorable consequences of the arrival of Pelops in this country."

As for the multiplicity and apparent exactness of the details transmitted by the Greeks concerning these remote periods of their history, this multiplicity itself and this purported exactitude make these details rather suspect. They bear the imprint of later additions to which writers had recourse when, starting with some general facts, they gave themselves over to their imaginations in order to fill in vast lacunae. We have said this elsewhere: in questions of this sort, positive affirmation is a reason to doubt, and detailed accounts are necessarily invented accounts. As for the inference Mr. Heeren draws from the foreign names imposed on the Peloponnese and Attica, it could just as well be the case that these names were not foreign, and that the heads of the colonies, or even the indigenous peoples, adopted those of the countries where they settled or lived. The hypothesis of Rabaut (*Lettr. sur l'hist. prim. de la Grèce*) is certainly as false as all the hypotheses that rest on a single idea. Greek mythology is no more a system of geometry than of astronomy. But there are partial truths everywhere; and it is more probable that the places consecrated by custom—rivers, for example, or mountains—imposed their names upon the remarkable individuals of a barbarous epoch, than it is that these individuals arbitrarily changed customary designations.

was not the result of the natural development of the human spirit, but a chance event that gave this religion a distinctive direction.

This error goes back to the Greeks themselves. Consumed by an insatiable thirst for learning, their historians and philosophers believed that they had to derive all their knowledge from these countries of the East and the South, which were regarded as the sanctuaries of the sciences and wisdom. They therefore found in these renowned regions everything that could strike their already receptive imaginations, as well as their minds rendered credulous by their curiosity. Priests cloaked in darkness listened to their questions with haughty condescension and responded with proud reserve. They offered symbols, images, enigmatic ceremonies, everything that the most striking pomp and the most august mysteries could do to dazzle eyes and penetrate souls. Their revelations were craftily calculated to accord with the dispositions of the hearer. Varied, and only partial, revelations added the greater value of the unknown, of what was still covered in silence, to the value of what was taught. Even the spectacle of a uniform and peaceful despotism contained something seductive for these sages exhausted by the turbulence of anarchy. The sanctuaries of Memphis and Thebes appeared to them more suitable to meditation than the agora of Athens. And when they returned to the midst of their fellow citizens, who were constantly agitated by hostile passions and ephemeral interests, the profound peace and unshakable stability that they had exchanged for the convulsions of democracy seemed quite regrettable.

To these motives rooted in a natural and understandable bias, add the inclination of men to extol what they took so much time and trouble to discover and convey. By elevating the wisdom of Egypt, Herodotus and Plato vaunted their own learning, their studious investigations, and indefatigable zeal.

From this it has followed that today we generally consider the Greeks to be the docile disciples of Egyptian colonists, and we give little weight to the facts that argue against this opinion, one we have adopted on trust. Therefore, we first must examine what sort were the colonies established in Greece by the Egyptians who were their leaders, what teachings they brought with them, what interest they had in causing them to prevail, and the authority that they naturally obtained over the indigenous peoples.

As we have said, the Egyptians were divided into castes. Their priesthood was a monopoly. Their religion was dual: abstract, on one hand, crude on the other, symbolic or material, depending upon the point of view in which one considered it. The people knew only the exterior of this religion, and this exterior, which consisted in the worship of animals that the multitude took to be gods, barely raised the public belief above the level of fetishism.[2] From this country, which was divided into such different classes carefully separated from one another, came the colonies. If these colonies had been composed of priests, and these priests had been victorious, we would have seen in Greece what was seen in other countries: an enslaved people and an all-powerful priesthood, a fetishistic people and a learned, metaphysical, and astronomical priesthood.

But the Egyptians had a great horror of the sea, for them it was the evil principle.[3] No member of the superior castes participated in sailing. Any maritime voyage was forbidden to priests.[4]

2. We will return to this subject when we treat the priestly religions, among which the Egyptian religion occupies the first rank. It suffices now to recall the facts; they are too well known for it to be necessary to support them with proofs; as for their causes, they will be explained elsewhere.

3. Plutarch (*De Is. et Osir.*) says that in their sacred language the Egyptians called the sea Typhon because the Nile ran into it and appeared to be destroyed. However, the Egyptians gave divine honors to fish as well (Herod., II, 117; Minucius Felix; Juvenal, *Sat.*, XV). Schmidt (*De sacred. et sacrif. Aegypt.*) explains this apparent contradiction by supposing that the worship of fish (like that of onions and crocodiles) was particular to certain provinces. Visitors were also surprised to see these peoples in their public feasts carrying the majority of their gods on vessels. But this practice came from the fact that in Egypt, being cut by the Nile, which divides into a thousand canals, people sailed on them like gondolas in Venice. As a consequence, the gods of Egypt rode on boats like the Greek gods rode on chariots.

4. Plut., *Sympos. quaest.*, VIII, I. It is also the same in India. Traces of this prohibition are found in Diodorus, and we see two Brahmins demoted for having crossed the Indus (*Asiat. Res.*, VI, 535–39). It would seem to us that this would prove that one is wrong to seek the aversion of Egyptians to the sea in some superstition that is particular to it. Some have thought that its inhabitants, attaching a great price to the embalming of bodies, detested the element that by enclosing them in its depths makes it impossible to find them. But a similar opinion in India, where the embalming of bodies is not found, calls this explanation into question. The hatred of the priesthood for foreigners offers a more satisfactory explanation; and what seems decisive to us is that religion rejected maritime expeditions in Persia, just as in Egypt (Hyde, *De rel. pers.*). In order to rule in peace, the priesthood has always wanted to isolate itself. It was only by degrees, when interests overcame opinions, i.e., when civilization had made progress, that the Egyptians, led to traffic on the Red Sea and even to India (see Herodotus and Diodorus; and, in support, the *Description de l'Egypte*, II, 63; and Champollion Jr., *Système hiéroglyph.*, pp. 227ff.), forced priests to deal with new ideas and to replace ancient superstitions with others more suitable to the spirit of a commercial century. Become the theater of lucrative expeditions and the source of immense wealth, the sea could no longer remain subject to the evil principle. Typhon and Nephtys his sister, his wife, his rival in hostility to the human race, yielded the scepter to Isis Pharia. New attributes characterize this national divinity, who, charged with these new functions, advances

Perhaps this circumstance ought to cause us to make a distinction among the colonies come from Egypt. Diodorus, speaking of those that Belus led to Babylon, says that this prince established priests there on the Egyptian model and exempted them from all taxes and public duties. But he says nothing similar about the colonies established in Greece.[5]

The emigrants who made up the latter were probably only men of the people, forced by need to overcome the national repugnance, and at most guided by a few leaders of distinguished birth, but much less occupied with science and religion than with the risks of their endeavor.[6] Such colonies can know only the externals

---

toward the lighthouse, the sistrum in one hand, a swelled veil in the other, in order to disarm the treacherous element and compel it to humbly carry the weight of the sailors protected by her.

5. If, as Mr. Creuzer (I, 262) claims, there were priestly colonies among those that landed among the Greeks and civilized them, they did not subjugate them. The priests were forced to tuck away in the mystery cults they established the teachings that were repugnant to the national *genius*. Thus, the worship of Ceres brought from Thrace or Egypt to Eleusis always remained in the secret religion. The tradition relative to Jupiter Apatenor (Jupiter the deceiver), in which the same author (III, 540–543, German ed.) finds proof of the influence of a priestly colony from Egypt, can be explained without his hypothesis. The relations that he indicates between the Greek god and Jupiter Ammon would equally result from memories preserved by Egyptian emigrants, without these emigrants necessarily being priests. Moreover, nothing confirms that the era of the Apaturi, which was celebrated at Athens, goes back to the landing of the first colonies. Later communications of Egypt with Greece could have introduced this feast, like many others, and this is more probable, given that the main authority Mr. Creuzer offers on this occasion is Pausanias.

6. It is with pleasure that I find myself in agreement with a German philosopher, all of whose opinions I do not adopt, but whose learning I would like to acknowledge. "The Greeks," says Mr. Goerres (II, 782), "received their civilization from Egyptian colonies, probably led not by priests but by warriors who only had a most imperfect knowledge of the sacred books of their country." The word "warriors" must not mislead us. There were surely men of that caste among the Egyptian colonists; but their expeditions did not for that reason have a military character. They sought a haven, not conquest; their small number and the fierceness of the natives rendered it impossible anyway. If, besides the authorities I have already invoked I wanted to cite some less known ones, I would appeal to Mr. Clavier, who in attributing to Phoenicians what we say of Egypt, adds that their colonies did not attempt to establish themselves by force in the countries to which they went, but employed only the means of persuasion and the superiority of an already civilized people over those who were not, which they used, at least apparently, only for the advantage of the latter (*Hist. des premiers temps de la Grèce*, I, 8). Despite his erudition, however, Mr. Clavier is an insufficiently discerning author; without the date of his book, one would believe that it was written at a time when our ignorance of the East reduced scholars who occupied themselves with Greek antiquities to hazard both risky and narrow conjectures.

of a religion whose secret meaning was scrupulously hidden from the vulgar.[7] It has often been noticed among all nations that men devoted to war, sailors, and all those who, braving great dangers and undergoing violent trials, find little leisure in their adventurous lives for reflection, ordinarily fall into a wholly external superstition.

Therefore, there was not the distance between the colonies and the first Greeks that has been supposed. The gap was only of a few degrees, and this circumstance was very favorable to the civilization of Greece.

For a colony to civilize savages, there cannot be between them too great a disproportion of force or learning. When the colonies have too great a superiority of force, they do not civilize the natives, they enslave them or destroy them. When they have too great a superiority in enlightenment, the native savages cannot rise from their crude ideas to the much more refined opinions of the colonists. Intermediaries are lacking. The American tribes have remained savage and fetishist because they were able to remain in barbarism and polytheism before attaining theism and civilization. The Europeans have never civilized the savages they discovered, because they have always proposed mores, ideas, and a religion entirely beyond the savages' grasp. The distance was too great.

It was not thus in Antiquity. The difference between the colonies and the natives was much less, communication had to be easier, instruction more effective. But by the same token, an amalgam had to result, rather than a revolution.

The Egyptian colonies had as their goal neither to convert nor to civilize the peoples they discovered. The sole object was to find a soil that would feed them, a shore that could become their new homeland. It, therefore, was in their interest not to have irreconcilable dissonance between their religious ideas and those of the former owners of the land. What was in their interest was also in keeping with their inclination. Polytheism always believes it finds itself in other religions. It sees allies where monotheism sees adversaries.

To be sure, the priesthood seeks to strip polytheism of this character. When they encounter their neighbors or their enemies, peoples given to priestly polytheism

7. Mr. de Sainte-Croix himself recognizes that it is difficult to believe that the emigrants of Egypt brought to Greece the true sacred doctrine of their country. He admits that one can reasonably doubt that members of the priestly order would have been found among them, or even men sufficiently instructed to propagate the doctrines that formed the deposit confided to the ministers of the cult (*Rech. sur les myst.*, I, 403, ed. of Mr. de Sacy).

destroy temples, overturn statues, and massacre suppliants. But this is because they come as conquerors.

The colonists who landed in Greece, in contrast, came as fugitives and almost as suppliants themselves. They therefore worked at mixing their opinions with those of the indigenous peoples. The difference of languages offered a great means for presuming a similarity of opinions. The necessity of being understood caused ideas that were not the same to be translated into a very imperfect language, and translation became a sort of concordat by which a mixed idea was formed of the two primary ideas without anyone noticing. It was by means of a similar process that our missionaries to China, obliged to express the Christian religion in Chinese, were accused of apostasy by those who remained in Europe.

We should add that a distinctive characteristic of polytheism in all periods is that in this sort of belief man does not remain exclusively attached to these gods, but only when they protect him effectively. Titus Livy tells us that the Albans, having lost to the Romans and been brought to Rome, were thoroughly incensed at their gods and gave up their worship.[8] In a moment, we will see polytheistic nations appropriate the divinities of even their enemies, when they believe they find in them more powerful, or more loyal, auxiliaries.

Now, the colonies that arrived in Greece had to have experienced many misfortunes during their crossing. Leaving their native land, battered by winds, menaced by waves, exposed to hunger and to all sorts of physical difficulties, only with great efforts did they attain the soil that promised them a better future. It was natural that they conceived a kind of anger against the gods that had so poorly protected them, and that their souls were open to finding more propitious gods. If they had debarked among peoples whose cult was already established, they would have adopted it without hesitation. But since the fall of their priesthood, the Pelasgians professed only a primitive fetishism, whose anonymous idols were not combined and regimented in a body like those of Egypt. The colonists borrowed what they could from the indigenous belief. As Herodotus tells us, they gave names to gods who until then did not have any.[9] With their own memories they filled in whatever lacunae appeared. They combined some of their own with the opinions of their new fellow citizens; these they also coordinated, some with their own tradi-

---

8. *"Fortunae, ut fit, obirati, cultum reliquerant deorum"* (Tit.-Liv., I, 31).

9. The names themselves were not always Egyptian; several were drawn from the Pelasgian language. For example, the Charidi, the Nereids. See Heyne, *De Theog. Hes.*

tions. For their part, the Pelasgians had to have easily given themselves to this sort of amalgamation. Ignorant peoples think about their gods as about themselves. They believe that foreigners know and can do many things that they do not know and cannot do. They similarly believe that foreign gods (who have the merit of being unknown and the advantage of never having failed) can do and know more things than their own gods.

If one were to argue against this mutual tolerance on the basis of the counter-example of the special intolerance of Egyptian polytheism, that is, by referring to the wars that occurred from time to time in Egypt over sacred animals, we would reply that these wars were started by the rivalry of priests among themselves, and had as their causes not disputes over opinions, but insults leveled at the objects of worship. The absence of priests and the change of place had to return the polytheism of the colonies to the natural spirit of polytheism. This spirit is not tolerant in the sense that moderns attach to the word, which is to say, the respect governments have for all the religious opinions of individuals; but it is a species of national tolerance, of people to people, tribe to tribe. We see this spirit in the permission granted the Pelasgians to consult their oracle concerning the innovations proposed to them.

What we just said about Egyptian colonies applies with a few modifications to those of Thrace.[10] Among all the countries that the historians of Antiquity help us understand, Thrace is distinguished by its barbarous worship, its fanatical rites, and its fierce enthusiasm. There the priesthood was clothed not only with the regular sacred authority possessed by the priesthood of Egypt,[11] but with an even more redoubtable power because it drew from a sort of religious delirium, one inspired and nourished by ceremonies in part obscene, in part cruel. It seems certain that Thrace sent colonies to Greece, and that these colonies had priests for leaders who attempted to have their bloody customs and wild orgies triumph. Their efforts were not without some partial successes, which stained the Greek religion from time to time. But it always did its best to reject these noxious importations, and in general it succeeded. It is probable that the Thracian priests wanted to initiate the Greeks into Orphic teachings (which we will talk about later),[12] which com-

---

10. See the enumeration of these colonies by Strabo, bk. VII.

11. The kings of Thrace had to be initiated into the mysteries of the priests, like those of Egypt and Persia.

12. Only by rejecting the explicit testimony of Herodotus and characterizing as false all the fragments of the most ancient philosophers can one deny the existence of a religious doctrine called "Or-

bined in an unsurprising mixture (once one understands the cause) the most subtle metaphysics with the most revolting external worship. But neither this metaphysics, which was introduced into the systems of philosophy, nor this external cult, which was transformed in the mysteries into a secret cult, prevailed in the public religion.[13] The Thracian colonies were always odious to the leaders of the Greek tribes; they often fought them openly; and the transactions with them that they proposed or allowed had for their purpose and their result preserving the peoples' beliefs from the contagion of a foreign fanaticism.[14]

Nonetheless, some have supposed that whatever their origin, these colonies ar-

---

phic" that was prior to the time of Homer. The authenticity of the poems attributed to Orpheus has no bearing on this question. Orpheus was probably a generic name in Thrace, like Buddha in India and Odin in Scandinavia. The poems that bear his name belong to a rather recent period, after even the time of Pisistratus, although his contemporary Onomacritus was accused of having falsified them. They seem to belong to the literature of Alexandria, and not to go back before the establishment of Christianity. But it is no less certain that before Homer a priestly teaching from Thrace and called "Orphic" had been introduced to the Greeks.

According to Herodotus, this teaching had many analogies with the cult of Bacchus, and its scientific and metaphysical doctrines were the same as those of the Egyptians and the Pythagorians (Herod., II, 81). Aristotle also alludes to this doctrine, which he believes is Egyptian and which he recognizes has been developed by the Greek philosophers. Modern scholars for the most part have considered it a part of the Greek religion, and as a consequence have studied only its relations with mythology, on which, they believe, it ought to have left many traces. This way of looking at it is only partially true. If, as several facts tend to make us assume, the Thracian colonies brought the Orphic doctrine into Greece, it never mixed with the national belief; it was even completely forgotten at the time of the formation of true Greek polytheism, and contributed nothing to its composition. The first philosophers, on the contrary, especially those of the Ionian school, carefully gathered its least remnants and included them in their systems.

13. Mr. Creuzer reproached the Greeks for this. He says that before the Homerides, by means of their new tales and seductive traditions, had fascinated this childish people, a race of poet-priests had placed Greece under the salutary protection of religion. A priestly order, venerable and powerful—as in Egypt—by music and science kept the profane multitude under its protective instruction; and into this national education had slipped a methodically arranged classification (the author here probably alludes to the division into castes). The metaphysics of the East was taught under symbolic forms, and proclaimed the great axioms of the soul of the world where all goes to lose itself, of the double harmony that penetrates the whole, and the identity of life and death (German ed., I, 210). What a misfortune, therefore, that the Thracian philosophy did not prevail in Greece! We would have had pantheism mixed with atheism as its teaching; and for rites, bacchanalia, mutilations, and orgies.

14. See the work of Clavier, *Hist. des premiers temps de la Grèce*. Also see in our chapter 5 [bk. 5] what we have said about the worship of Bacchus.

rived in Greece animated with fervent zeal and an ardor for war; that they waged religious wars against the Greeks; and that having been victorious, they changed the beliefs of the country they conquered.

This conjecture is destroyed by a single fact, however, which no one can contest. The religion purportedly established by the victorious foreigners was in no way the same as that of the country from which they came. Now, one cannot reasonably see how these foreigners, so attached to their religion that they would wage war to the death against the Pelasgians who refused to accept it, nonetheless would have abandoned it on their own in order to embrace an entirely new one. One cannot understand any better where this new religion would have come from, which was neither that of the former homeland of the foreigners nor that of the people they conquered. One would have to suppose that they would have immediately and spontaneously composed a religion different from the two older ones. This supposition runs against everything that reflection tells us about the development of the human race, as well as all that history confirms.

When a conquering people succeeds in making the conquered people adopt its beliefs, the belief that it imposes is precisely the same as that which it professed in its own country, at least during the first phases of its adoption. It is not altered by the change of place, except later. How, then, to explain that after colonies from Thrace[15] or Egypt arrived in Greece, having waged war against the inhabitants of the country to establish their cult, and having triumphed after several fierce battles, a completely different worship resulted than that of Thrace or Egypt?

Nothing is less congenial to the spirit of primitive peoples than the form of intolerance that causes or fuels wars of religion. Even the advocates of this hypothesis had to have sensed this, because they compare the priests of what they call the ancient cult with the American jongleurs of our day.[16] There is no trace of intolerance in the character of these jongleurs. They and their disciples listen with great curiosity, and no hostility, to the Europeans who speak to them about the Christian religion.

I do not know from what secret chronicles, in what contemporaneous memoirs, certain savants have drawn their information concerning times that we know about

15. Our readers will have already noticed that the difference of religion, mores, and customs has led us to speak of Thrace, despite its proximity, as a country wholly apart from Greece; this proximity has led many writers to equate them.

16. See the previous chapter [bk. V, ch. 3], where we recall the opinion of Mr. de Sainte-Croix in his work on the mysteries.

only by the works of authors who were separated by more than twenty centuries from the times in question.[17] They speak to us of Cyclops, Corybants, and Curetes as if they had lived in intimate familiarity with them. They know all the particulars of the life of Prometheus, who they say was a very enlightened man worthy of living in a less barbaric century, and who wanted to reconcile the two parties. For this purpose going from one party to the other, he became the victim of his own zeal and saw himself attacked by unjust calumnies that have lasted until today.[18] In a word, they write the history of these long-gone epochs like someone recounting the intrigues of the court of Louis XIV or Louis XV.

Herodotus, who conveyed with great clarity everything he had gathered relative to the establishment of Greek religion and the influence colonies had exercised on its formation, does not make the least reference to religious wars occurring at this time. "Formerly," he says, "the Pelasgians offered sacrifices accompanied by prayers, as was told to me at Dodona. But they did not distinguish by particular names the beings they worshipped,[19] because they had not received any instruction on this score. They simply called them gods, in order to designate the rulers of all things. Much later, Egyptians taught them the names they had to give them. They consulted the oracle to know if they ought to obey these instructions come from barbarians. They received permission. From then on they made use of them in their religious ceremonies. . . . But they still were ignorant, almost up to our own time, of where each god came from and if they all had existed as they do at present. . . . Homer and Hesiod composed for the Greeks the genealogies of the gods . . . assigning to them their functions and their dignities, and limning their forms."[20]

17. In his work on the mysteries, Mr. de Sainte-Croix cites Ovid as an authority with respect to the Corybantes (p. 57).

18. Mr. de Sainte-Croix.

19. Mr. Creuzer (Introd., p. 3, trans. of Mr. Guigniaut) draws from this passage of Herodotus a result different from our own. Following his exposition of the meaning of the Greek author, one would say that the Pelasgians worshipped their anonymous gods in a collective manner, as hidden powers, and without being concerned with their nature; this would no longer be fetishism but a contemplative and mystical worship, quite beyond the primitive state. After having reread Herodotus's paragraph, even in Schweighaeuser's edition cited by Mr. Creuzer, which correctly takes to task Larcher's inaccuracy, we have found nothing that would support the reading of the German author; and we are surprised that this writer, who in the following pages recommends Pausanias as a respectable authority, did not find in this compiler a thousand proofs of the unsubstantial basis of his thesis.

20. Herod., II, 52, 53.

Even though more learned and philosophic than Herodotus, no more than Herodotus did Thucydides attribute the revolution brought about in the Greek religion to religious wars.[21]

The influence of colonies on the formation of Greek polytheism was therefore very limited.[22] The Pelasgian fetishism furnished most of the materials. The colo-

21. The existence of religious wars in ancient Greece is admissible only by accepting two assumptions, each of which is equally opposed to the system of French scholars. The first is that these wars would have arisen because of the rivalries of priests when Greece was subject to theocratic authority (see above, II). The example of Egypt teaches us that in priestly peoples the rivalry of priests can give rise to fierce wars, while we find no jongleurs among any primitive people doing so. Like the inhabitants of the nomes of Egypt, the Greek tribes could have fought among themselves for their local divinities. There are some traces of a bloody struggle between the cult of Apollo and that of Bacchus (see Creuzer). It is perhaps to events of this sort that the famous passage of the *Theogony* (629–34) relates, which is the most affirmative of all those that have come to us.

The second assumption is that the traditions relative to these wars allude to the overthrow of priests by warriors (see above, ibid.). But then these wars would have been antireligious, since they had for their result the expulsion of priests and the destruction of a priestly cult.

In both hypotheses, the events preceded Greece's falling back into the savage state. In having them follow the period of the second civilization of Greece by colonies, immediately before the heroic times, an anachronism has been committed; and this anachronism seems to us to have led two learned men, Messrs. Fréret and de Sainte-Croix, into a narrow system, as are all systems that follow from a single idea. Seeing in the Greek divinities only the priests of these divinities, and in their legends only the circumstances of the establishment of the worship, and the opposition it could have encountered, they have gathered many details in favor of their position and discovered partial truths; but they have also rendered other facts and details inexplicable, and they have fallen into no less numerous partial errors. Thus, in order to explain the death of Cadmilla in the Cabiric mysteries, Mr. de Sainte-Croix is content to affirm that this story relates to the murder of some ancient priests (*Les myst.*, ed. of Mr. de Sacy, I, 55). A serious mistake! The death of Cadmilla is an astronomical allusion, like the deaths of Adonis, Osiris, etc. The identity of fables would have struck the French scholar, if he had paid attention to the identity of ceremonies.

22. Our readers would be mistaken if they thought that we completely denied or ignored the influence of Thracian or Egyptian colonies on Greek religion. We limit ourselves to saying that these colonies did not influence this religion in such a way as to turn its peoples from its natural development and substitute a priestly one for it. Their influence was more political than religious. Several social institutions are attributed to them. The royal families, at least on the female side, go back to them. These include the Atrides and the Labdacides. Certain countries bear the name of their leaders, the Peloponnese, for example; or, what is more plausible, the leaders took the name of the country in which they arrived. But all this only proves the fusion of two peoples or two degrees of the social state. Religion enters in this fusion as much as, but no more than, the rest. Everywhere there are symptoms of the transaction, and the symptoms are obvious. For example, a Thracian priest at the

nies added several fables and, above all, many rites.[23] But they did not substitute by force[24] one cult for another. They did not transport the beliefs of the former homeland to their new establishments. In point of fact, they had rather imperfect ideas about this belief in the first place. They did not give the Greeks a religion. They only placed them in a state of civilization that had to modify their own religious ideas.

As for a small number of priestly institutions brought from Thrace, Egypt, or Phoenicia, these took root only in a few cities whose particular location favored them; for the longest time, though, they occupied only a secondary rung. Thus, for example, nature had brought together around Delphi everything that nourished and stimulated superstition and enthusiasm. Vast hollows exhaled vapors that rendered those who inhaled them delirious. Countless springs bubbled everywhere. Hidden grottos made it easy to forget the world, and seemed to promise communication with invisible powers. The deep shadows of ancient forests struck minds with religious terror. Moreover, it is plausible that a colony of priests come from Thrace and Macedonia early on established itself in that marvelous place, applying itself to introducing and maintaining priestly ideas and ceremonies. At Delphi, therefore, are found many customs, traditions, teachings, and rites that are imported from elsewhere.[25] But the relations of the priesthood of Delphi with

---

head of the inhabitants of Eleusis, and Erectheus, the king of Athens, sharing in both the priesthood and the monarchy. The king retains his throne, the priest obtains sacred functions for himself and his family (Sainte-Croix, ed. of Mr. de Sacy, I, 115); but these sacred functions were modified according to Greek ideas. The Eumolpides never enjoyed in Greece an authority comparable to that of Thrace their founder, and the public religion never was affected by what it retained of exoteric doctrines.

23. "If the Egyptian religion expanded to the continents of Asia and Europe, at first it was known there less by its secret doctrines, than by its legends and rites" (Sainte-Croix, *Les myst.*).

24. We do not at all want to say that there was not some resistance in matters of detail. In several writers we see the traces of a kind of struggle between fetishism and the polytheism that replaced it. Caenus, contemporary of Theseus, worshipped his spear and forced passers-by to do so (Apollon., *Argonaut.*, I, 56; Eustath. *ad Iliad*, I; Voss, *De orig. et progress. idol.*, IX, 5). The victory of Apollo over the serpent Python could very well have been a similar recollection, which even could have gone further back. Before the defeat of the Phocaeans by the Dorians, the oracle at Delphi was devoted, it is said, to the Earth, a divinity of the Pelasgian priesthood. The success of the Dorians consolidated the divinity of Apollo, who became the national god of Phocidea. But the distance from these partial facts to general wars between the Pelasgians and foreigners is great.

25. There the wolf, for example, was consecrated to Apollo, precisely as in the great Lycopolitan prefecture of the Thebaid.

the national worship were neither regular nor habitual. They did not exist at all in Homer's time; the name Delphi does not appear once in the Homeric epics.[26]

Thus Greece, having regained its independence from a priesthood whose organization we only imperfectly understand, also maintained it against the colonies that civilized it. It maintained it equally against the repeated efforts of the priests of Thrace, Egypt, and Phoenicia to introduce their institutions and found their empire by hook or by crook. This, however, required a long, sometimes violent, struggle. It also did not occur without admitting some portions of the priestly mythology and, especially, more than one foreign rite. Even the institutions a people rejects influence its own; combatants are changed by combat, even victors by victory. But Greece subjugated everything it admitted. We will demonstrate this truth, the most important of historical truths, because the victory of Greece decided the fate of the human race.

26. Pausanias (*Phoc.*, 32) mentions a chapel of Isis in Phocidea that was manifestly one of these foundations of foreign priests. No one could enter without being invited by a dream. A profane person who had entered without permission saw horrible specters and died of fright. This detail is so obviously Egyptian that the Greek author adds: "The same thing happened in our days in Egypt. The Roman proconsul who governed this province engaged a man to hide in the temple of Isis. This emissary having returned, he recounted what he had seen, but upon ending his report he died." In this way the colonies could transplant to Greece scattered shoots of their ancient superstition; but these shoots, even when they took root, preserved their exotic appearance, and always remained isolated.

CHAPTER 5

On the Modifications the Independent Spirit of Greece Always Caused in What Came from Elsewhere

If the Greek genius was hardly favorable to the introduction of priestly teachings and opinions, the geographic position of the Greeks seemed to invite their barbarian neighbors to try frequently to introduce them.

Greece was everywhere surrounded by islands that foreign sailors had chosen for refuge or as a new homeland, and where they brought their religion.

As much as it is possible to conjecture, a priest whom the historians named Olen, whom they place even before the mythical time of Orpheus; or—and this seems more likely to us—a colony of which Olen was either the leader or the collective name, came to Delos via Asia Minor,[1] singing the story of Diana and Apollo in its hymns, as well as of the offspring of Latona;[2] that is, professing an astronomical religion. As a consequence, we see in the religious practices of Delos

---

1. Asia Minor can be considered, says Creuzer (II, 4–6), as the meeting place of all the religions, because of revolutions, commerce, and the intermixing of peoples. The remark of Strabo (bk. XII, *in init.*) on the multiplicity and mixing of languages in Asia Minor can be equally applied to worship.

2. Pausan., I, 18; IX, 27. This writer sometimes says that Olen had come from the country of the Hyperboreans, sometimes that he originated in Lycia. It is false that the tradition of the arrival of Olen at Delos is, as has been said, an invention of Neoplatonists. It goes back to Herodotus; and Plato, whom in this matter one must not confuse with the first-century sect that bore his name, affirms that among the poets, Hesiod, and Parmenides among the wise, borrowed their notions of the creative, or rather ordering, power that presides over the universe from Olen. It is not irrelevant to observe that none of the poet-priests said to be the organs of priestly opinion in Greece were Greek. Eumolpus, Orpheus, Thamyris, and Linus, whether legendary or historical, generic names or individuals, designate foreigners only in the two hypotheses; Pamphus, of whom it is said that he composed hymns for the Athenians, was not an Athenian himself. The explicit and unanimous affirmation that these poets were barbarians is important when uttered by a proud people, because it proves that the conviction was stronger than their vanity.

many ceremonies that are different from the rites of Greece. There we see sacred virgins[3] and fragments of the hymns sung by the islanders that resemble invocations in the Zend books and the Vedas.

Lemnos and Samothrace, formerly named Leucosi,[4] were another route by which priestly religions came to Greece. Situated between this country and Asia, whose shores were not yet populated by any Greek colony, these islands received the first emigrants from Phrygia, Lydia, and Lycia. By their physical circumstances they were favorable to priestly power; they bore the imprint of nature's revolutions. The destruction of the neighboring islands of Lemnos was an accredited prophecy,[5] and Mr. de Choiseul-Gouffier[6] saw traces of the disappearance of Chryse, swallowed up so long ago after having become famous by the misfortunes of Philoctetes.[7] The most ancient sailing people, the Phoenicians, landed in Samothrace. They brought there their Cabiri, misshaped divinities that we will see reappear in the mystery cults, whose name goes back to Indian mythology.[8] They seem to have lived for a long time on this island. It even seems probable that for some time the Phoenician language was the sole in use.[9] Other colonies composed of Phrygians taught there the art of working in metals,[10] and Diodorus speaks of the astonishment that their metal workers occasioned in the inhabitants by their charms and superior knowledge.[11] These metal workers worshipped the elements; they rendered homage to the heavens and to the earth. Since priests bring into their religion everything that they know, this priesthood combined its metallurgic knowledge with astronomy. The dances they conducted while armed retraced both the dominion of man over the iron he had subjugated and the movement of the celestial spheres.[12]

3. Herod., IV, 31ff.

4. Aristot. *ap.* School; Apollon., I, 97.

5. Herod., VII, 6.

6. See de Choiseul-Gouffier.

7. Pausan., *Arcadia*, 53.

8. The word "*cabire*" in Indian means an accomplished philosopher (Polier, *Mythol. des hindous*, II, 312).

9. Munter, *Erklärung einer griechischen Inschrift, welche auf die samothrazischen Mysterien Beziehung hat.*

10. Clem. Alex., *Strom.*, I.

11. See also the scholiast of Apollonius, *Argon.*, I, 1129.

12. We could say the same things about the island of Crete and the island of Rhodes, about the Curetes of the first and the Telchines of the second, as about Lemnos, Samothrace, and the Dactyles.

Each military expedition of the Greeks established relations between them and peoples subject to priests. From the time of the siege of Troy, they encountered the Phrygians, to whom Homer attributes Greek mores, but who clearly were a priestly nation. The cult of Cybele and her mutilations were of Phrygian origin.[13] The Trojans had purchased their palladium from Abaris the Scythian; in other words, they had the same religion as the Scythians, or one not much different.[14] They cast living horses into rivers,[15] a type of sacrifice that expressed the worship they rendered the elements.[16]

From the most remote times commerce had united Greece to the East. At an even more remote and legendary time (because it precedes the era of Semiramis), we see the opulent and celebrated city of Ephesus arise on the site where the Cayster runs into the Aegean Sea. On one hand, it was the entrepôt of the wealth of Asia, on the other, one of the principal refuges of the Ionian colony. What antiquity tells us about the construction of its temple is a combination of traditions whose details differ but whose meaning is the same.

The son of the Amazon Penthesilia, Caistrus was the father of Semiramis by means of his dalliances with Derceto. He was also the father of Ephesus, who built the temple of Ephesus.[17] Others attribute the construction of this edifice to the Amazons. These enemies of males, proud of their virginity and worshippers of a bloody deity Artemis, the Amazons very much resemble a priestly idea or institution.[18] The priests of Ephesus also submitted themselves to mutilations that we also find in Syria,[19] and the flame that burned perpetually on their altars was a sou-

---

One finds among some the boisterous feasts and frenetic dances; among the others, workers in metal, sorcerers, and the makers of the first idols (Strabo, XIV; Diod., V, 55), the worship of the earth and human sacrifices (Sainte-Croix, 73; Creuzer, II, 378). Diodorus (bk. V, 55) and Strabo (XIV) speak of a family of Heliades, or children of the sun, who established themselves at Rhodes, and Pasiphae in Crete is the daughter of the sun; the Labyrinth recalls Egypt; and by its birth and its monstrous figure, the Minotaur takes us from Greece and brings us to the East.

13. Strabo, X.

14. Scalig., *Not.* in Euseb.

15. This custom is proven by a passage from Homer. "This noble Scamander," says Achilles in speaking to the Trojans, "this Scamander to whom you immolate bulls in such great number, and into which you cast living horses, will not save you from my hands" (*Iliad*, XX, 130).

16. Pausan., VII, 2.

17. Callim., *Hymn. ad Dian.*

18. See below, book VI, the chapter on the privations against nature.

19. They were eunuchs, as it appears to be the case according to Strabo.

venir of the worship of fire. The Greeks also began early with Colchis. The inhabitants of Colchis came from an Egyptian colony. One can see an analogy between the fables of the two countries. In Colchis there was a river that bore the name of Isis.[20] Greek merchants must have carried fables from there, which they garbled.

Finally religion itself, even while distinguishing the Greeks from the barbarians, established bonds between these two races of men that reinforced their mutual superstition. Very early on the Greeks consulted the most faraway oracles. Envoys from Elis crossed the deserts of Libya to query the oracle of Ammonius.[21]

It follows from all this that from the first moments of Greek civilization there were paths traced by which priestly opinions laid siege, as it were, to Greek polytheism, and endeavored to penetrate into it. Under a certain aspect and up to a certain point, they succeeded. The Greeks near to Homeric times must have been disposed to eagerly receive marvelous tales and solemn rites, which they did not understand well enough to see how incompatible they were with their own ideas and their national character. Their ignorance, a quality common to all infant peoples; their poetic imagination, which loved everything offered it to explain natural phenomena by supernatural causes rather than the mechanisms of the world (a sad discovery they had yet to make); a lively and spontaneous constitution; their respect for everything that came from afar, a respect that contrasted starkly with their disdain for barbarians; and finally, the constant struggle of their inner sentiment with the form of their belief—all these things prepared a rather easy entrance to foreign teachings. A tradition that many men repeat, said Hesiod, becomes a divinity. This phrase clearly expresses the profound and credulous curiosity of nascent societies, their need to know everything, whose impatient inexperience receives without examination everything told to it, and confounds together everything it receives.

Hence those countless borrowings from foreign nations by the Greeks of the most remote period. There is almost no Greek divinity whose actions or attributes are not a mixture of fables and priestly teachings. But the Greek spirit always triumphed; it reworked the fables, nationalized the imports, modified the teachings, and stripped them of what in the minds of the priests was their essential character.

20. Pliny, *Hist. nat.*, VI, 4.

21. Pausan., *Eliac.*, 15. He cites several examples of these embassies. For the liaisons of the Delphic oracle with foreigners, see Herodotus, IV, 57. On their side, the barbarians had an equal respect for the Greek oracles. Herodotus says (IV, 22) that the Hyperboreans sent presents to the gods across the country of the Scythians, all the way to the Adriatic gulf, and from there to Dodona, and thence to Delos.

Let us support this with few examples, without trying to put them into a regular order. We do so because it seems useful not to leave this fundamental truth without proofs. We, however, have to confess that in so doing we are anticipating a later section in our work, one that requires a good deal of development. It is only in another book that we will present the complete exposition of the dogmas and rites that enter into the composition of the priestly religions of antiquity. There perhaps is a slight inconvenience in showing how the Greeks rejected them before talking about them as a whole. On the other hand, we think we have already sufficiently indicated what these composite religions were; we have seen that they contained science, cosmogonic hypotheses, personifications of physical forces, symbolic language and rites, a metaphysics that ends in pantheism, while being overlaid and mixed with popular fables, falling back from time to time into fetishism. These general ideas suffice for the moment, and it is important to support with evidence our claims concerning the immense distance that separates the Greeks from the rest of ancient nations.[22]

22. Despite the adoption of the most opposed systems, the evidence has forced writers of all opinions to recognize this interval. Dupuis (whom learned France has too long respected as an authority), Dupuis who traces the development of religious ideas in a way totally contrary to ours, exempts the Greeks from the explanations that he proposes for all fables. He regards theirs as recent; and he adds that ever since Hesiod they had been composed by men who, having lost the thread of ancient ideas, had only preserved the names of chimerical beings who were not connected to the visible order of the world (Dupuis, *Orig. des cultes*). In these few words there are errors of all sorts. As we will see, it was Hesiod who ruined the simplicity of the Greek religion by making doctrines borrowed from priestly cults enter it, without giving them enough Greek coloration. But the distinction of Dupuis between the fantastical beings who are not attached to the visible order of the world and the symbolic beings who are, shows on the part of the writer a confused recognition that the gods of the polytheism subject to priests were personified forces or abstractions, while those of the Greeks were creatures of the human spirit left to itself. Rabaut, who like Dupuis sees only astronomy (with a bit of geography) in the religion, nonetheless agrees "that the Greeks paid no attention to the astronomical truths enveloped in the religious mysteries, whether because their spirit was not yet in a condition to receive them, or because they were already misunderstood by the foreigners who brought them to them."

A German author who is rather obscure but still quite ingenious, Wagner (*Ideen zu einer allgemeinen Mythologie der alten Welt*) divides the religious forms into four classes: (1) the search for the divinity in order to unite with it; (2) the distinction between the divinity and the world that is subject to the divine will's direction; (3) the contemplation of the divinity in the visible objects whose action is the most effective and their exterior, the most striking; (4) the adoration of the divinity in the different parts of nature, each taken separately and individualized in anthropomorphic deities. This classification is not exact enough. The author appears to believe that in all periods man can conceive religion under one or another of these forms. This is not true. The first two, which at bottom are

In order to be better understood by the majority of our readers, we will take examples from among the best known divinities, among those, that is, who appear most frequently in the poems of Homer. This way people will better appreciate the supremacy of the Greek genius that while admitting far-off, mysterious traditions concerning these different deities, transformed them into indigenous tales, and removed from the divinities that had become Greek what was bizarre or somber, abstract or frightful, in a word: sacerdotal.

This method will also have the advantage of putting to the side several difficulties concerning details that we will be forced to consider later when we present the tableau of Homeric polytheism. No one will object that we took too literally this brilliant mythology, since we will have already indicated the elements that composed it; the philosophical, metaphysical, or cosmogonic teachings to which it alludes; and how the genius of Greece reworked and completely nationalized it.

Let us first recall an observation we already made in the first book.

The Greeks admitted tales that hardly differed from priestly cosmogonies into their own hypotheses concerning the creation of the world because these tales, at once confused and foreign, did not really interest them. The physical force and moral character of the gods, the relations of these gods with men, their regular influence on the destiny of their worshippers, these were—these had to be—what interested the religious sentiment in its anxious ignorance; they were objects of a constant attention and active curiosity. The Greeks wanted their gods to resemble them because they wanted the means of dealing with them at all times. But that these supernatural beings and the human race that worshipped them owed their existence to Chaos, to Night, to Earth, to chance, even; that they were intended to give a clear signal to following generations that they were no longer subject to fixed laws; that by uniting the dual creative force in themselves, or the active and passive principles, they could reproduce independently of sexual union by mysterious and often obscene procedures, or by strange mutilations, none of that was of any importance to a young people. And the Greeks put up no resistance to the fact that these foreign traditions brought such symbolic and sacerdotal ideas. According to Hesiod,[23] the virgin Earth gives birth to the Sea, the Mountains, and the Sky without the cooperation of a spouse. The Sky produces Time, or Saturn,

---

pantheism and theism, can only be the result of long meditations, and cannot exist except in a rather advanced civilization; but the last two are those we treat here, of which one, the third, belongs to the priestly nations, and the other, the fourth, to the Greeks.

23. *Theog.*, 126–32.

and Saturn raises a sacrilegious hand against the generative power of his father. In all this, the stamp of the East has to be recognized, and the Greek genius made no effort to change these cosmogonic absurdities. It sensed that in the future it would have nothing to do with them, and in order not to be burdened by them, it put them in a separate sphere. Sky, Earth, Ocean, and their entire race of fabulous monsters—Cyclops, Centimanes and Gorgons, Chimera, Hecate, and Echidna, mother of the sphinx—are the object of no national cult. In their depictions, poets allude to them from time to time, and philosophers in their systems. For the rest, these grand shadows remain immobile, as it were, in the dark precincts where they are confined.[24] They never came forth to join with active divinities, those invoked by the people in their temples, objects of prayers and sacrifices. It was upon the latter that the Greek spirit operated, and while examining these divinities one after another, we will see what its action was.

In Homeric polytheism, Minerva is not exactly, as is often said, the goddess of wisdom and prudence. To define her in this way would be to make her an allegorical divinity; the period of allegory, however, has not yet arrived. Minerva is proud, irritable, driven by a thousand human passions, as are all the inhabitants of Olympus. She however is in general more prudent and wiser than the other gods. This is because she is to be identified with the Phoenician Onga, brought with Cadmus to Thebes in Boetia,[25] and because under obscure forms this divinity

24. This observation, it seems to us, responds to a remark of Mr. Creuzer and resolves a difficulty he raised. "One has difficulty," he says, "in reconciling certain bizarre (and sometimes monstrous) fables with the simplicity, no less clear than pure, of the Homeric period: the character of these fables is precisely what dominates in the majority of oriental myths. The imagination there knows no bounds. It freely abandons itself to the most extraordinary fictions, to the most marvelous combinations." (The author should have used another term than "marvelous." Moreover, it is inexact to present these fictions as the work of the free imagination. On the contrary, they are the result of the subjugation of the imagination condemned to feed itself on the artificial symbols and mystical conceptions of priests.) "Every time that Greek mythology was attached more to some religious or philosophical meaning than to the beauty of forms, it gave birth to similar monsters." (Which is to say: every time that it adopted the priestly spirit instead of rejecting it.) "To the incarnations of the Indian Vishnu one can oppose the Orphic myths, especially those that relate to cosmogony; the philosophical symbols of the ancient, Pherecydes, entirely in keeping with the taste of the Orient; finally in Hesiod himself in the *Theogony*, this great and terrible fiction of the old Uranus, deprived of the power to generate by the hand of Cronus, his son" (French trans., I, p. 49).

25. Pausan., *Boeot.*, 13. One of the doors of Thebes bore his name; but the same city had another door named after that of the Egyptian goddess (Jablonsky, *Panth. Aeg.*, p. 244).

represented the intelligence of the universe. But how did it come about that instead of being produced by the couplings of Jupiter, her birth is a marvel, that she has no mother, that she suddenly emerged, entirely armed, from her father's head? This is because the Onga of Phoenicia, who is a cosmogonic divinity, and under this heading either virginal or hermaphroditic,[26] is not subject to the common laws of generation, but came miraculously from the abyss that contains, engenders, and absorbs everything.

Why does this goddess of wisdom, the intelligence of the world, preside over domestic works, the small cares of women in the interior of their homes? This is because to her attributes have been joined those of the Egyptian Neith,[27] transported to Athens by a colony of Sais. This Neith had received from Ptah the canvas of nature and worked on this mysterious cloth.[28]

How is it that Minerva, who thus did not disdain such peaceful occupations, is also the goddess of war and, bearing resplendent weapons, finds herself at home in the melée, in the midst of carnage and death? This is because the caste of warriors in Egypt was devoted to Neith, and bore her symbol, the beetle, on their rings.[29] What connection is there between this bellicose Minerva and the tale that recounts that she invented the flute, but then cast it far from her because it disfigured the nobility of her features? This is because the flute was invented by the Phoenicians, and music and dance are the typical attributes of priestly divinities, expressing the harmony of the spheres.[30] Finally, why did this goddess, bearing all the ideal beauty that characterized the gods of Greece, carry on her standard the terrifying head of Medusa? This is because the Libyan Pallas had appeared for the first time in Libya on the Triton lake,[31] and the dress of the young girls of this country bore a remote resemblance to the serpents of the Gorgon;[32] or perhaps

---

26. Also, in the 31st Orphic hymn Minerva is called, simultaneously, male and female.

27. Mr. Clavier (*Hist. des premiers temps de la Grèce*) claims, not without apparent reason, that the name Athena in Greek was Egyptian. One cannot find, he says, the origin of this name in the Greek language without violating all the rules of analogy; while one can find it quite easily by reversing the Egyptian name Netha, Athen, to which one adds the ending of "a" or "e," depending upon the dialect (I, 36.d).

28. This is the reason the Greeks called Minerva Ergane or Tisserande.

29. Ael., *Hist. anim.*, X, 15.

30. Kayser, *ad Philitae* fragm., p. 55; Boettinger, *Ueber die Erfind. der Flöte. im attisch. Mus.*, I, 2, 334ff.

31. Heyne, *ad* Apollod., p. 297. Hence the surname Tritogeneia for Minerva.

32. Herod., IV, 189.

(here the traditions lose themselves in one another) it was the urn of the Nile, capped by the head of a man and surrounded by serpents, a mute symbol in Egypt but become for the Greeks the object of a detailed poetic account.[33]

Thus the Greek Minerva was originally a composite of incoherent ideas drawn from the different mythologies of foreign countries and reassembled. From this union, however, resulted a divinity who was perfectly conformed to the spirit of Greece's polytheism, an elegant divinity, passionate and majestic, who descends to the earth and takes part in the actions of men, pursuing or protecting heroes. The intelligence of Onga, which in the priestly version had no relation with the destiny of mortals and signifies only the overcoming of chaos, in Greece is applied to the active interests of men, to their daily struggles. The mystical cloth that in the fingers of the Neith of Egypt represents the world is now the emblem of female industry. The head of Medusa, which recalls the terrifying attributes of priestly divinities, becomes the monument of the victory of a warrior whom Minerva assisted;[34] the goddess mounts a chariot, arms herself with a spear, and puts on a breastplate: all these images are purely Greek. In order to finish the task of making her indigenous, her birth is transported to Arcadia.[35] And last, the olive is her favorite tree. Now she is completely Athenian.[36] All traces of her foreign origin are gone. There is nothing more different from the Egyptian Neith than the Minerva of the *Iliad*, and no one would recognize in the protector of Diomedes and Ulysses one of the dark forces personified by the priests of Tyre.[37]

The Egyptian colonies[38] that had brought the worship of Apollo from Egypt

33. The battle of Perseus against the Gorgon.

34. Homer, *Iliad*, V, 738; Hesiod, *Boucl. d'Her.*, 223.

35. In the city of Aliphera (Herod., I, 77).

36. In Egypt, where the olive is rare, Minerva could not have been thought of as having made the gift of this tree to the country under her protection (Herod., II, 39).

37. Nonetheless, traditions survive: the Greeks sometimes admitted a foreign Minerva. Apollodorus (III, 1, 2, 3, ed. Heyne) says that the Libyan Pallas defended the city of Troy, which the Greek Minerva attacked.

38. In expressing ourselves in this way, we do not claim that the worship of Apollo was born in Egypt, but only that it came to the Greeks from there. Its relations with Indian mythology are incontestable. The identity of Apollo with Krishna is found everywhere. Both are the inventors of the flute (*Asiat. Res.*, VIII, 65). Krishna is deceived by the nymph Tulasi, as Apollo was by Daphne. The two nymphs are changed into trees, and the tulasi is consecrated to Krishna, as the laurel is to Apollo (idem). The victory of Krishna over the serpent Caliya Naga on the banks of the Yumuna recalls that

into Greece also had to introduce the traditional tales and rites practiced in their country. We find therefore the same animal, a wolf, dedicated to the sun at Lycopolis and likewise at Delphos; by his sideways gait he can image the indirect course of the sun.[39] This figure brought into Greek traditions tales relating to the battles of Osiris. Under the figure of a wolf, this god came to help his son Orus;[40] and Latona, leaving the Hyperborean countries to seek refuge at Delos had taken on the same form, it was said.[41] Nor can one fail to recognize in the Daphnephoria[42] that the Thebans celebrated every nine years in honor of the Ismenian Apollo, an astronomical feast. It took its name from the laurel carried by the comeliest adolescents of the town. It was surrounded by flowers and olive branches. From an olive tree, itself decorated by laurel branches and woven flowers, and covered with a purple veil, were suspended balls of different sizes representing the sun and the planets, decorated with garlands whose number was a symbol of the year. On the altar burned a flame whose movement, color, and crackling revealed the future; as we have observed, this was a species of divination peculiar to the priesthood, and

---

of Apollo over the serpent Python, and it is remarkable that the defeated serpents shared the honors given to the victors (Clem. Alex.; Paterson, *Asiat. Res.*, VIII, 64–65).

39. To the side of the statues, and close to the altars of the Sminthian Apollo of Troy (Ael., *H. a.*, XII, 5) or of Crete (schol. *ap. Iliad*, I, 39), one saw a mouse. This is also an imitation of a custom of the Egyptians who placed close to the gods animals who were consecrated to them. In Egypt, the mouse was one of the symbols of the primitive night. At the feet of Apollo it signified the victory of the day over the night, and later one saw in it an allusion to the prophetic faculty of the god, who read the future despite the darkness that surrounded it.

40. Pausan., *Corinth*, 10; Diod., I, 88; Synes., *De Provid.*, I, 115; Euseb., I, 50.

41. Aristot., *Hist. anim.*, VI, 35; Ael., *Hist. anim.*, IV, 4. The island of Delos, on whose shifting soil the lover of Jupiter pursued by Juno had deposited her precious burden (Pind., fragm. *ap.* Strabo, X; schol., *Odyss.*, III), was an imitation of the island of Chemnis, which the Egyptians called "floating" (Herod., II, 156), and which had received Isis when she sought to hide her son from Typhon's pursuit. This tale is subsequent to the *Iliad*, whose author has Apollo born not at Delos but in Lycia (*Iliad*, XV, 514). This (to observe in passing) is a proof of the marginal authenticity of the Homeric hymn to Apollo, a hymn that is composed of two poems written at different periods: the first is addressed to the Delian Apollo, and the second, which begins with the 178th verse, contains the praises of the Apollo who defeated Python. Some also claim that Latona was herself an Egyptian divinity named Leto or Lato. She had at Latopolis a frequently consulted oracle, and at Butis a magnificent temple that is described by Herodotus. But in Egypt she was only the nurse of the children that in Greece she was the mother of. In the astronomical mythology, Latona became the star of the night.

42. On the Daphephoria, see Creuzer, II, 149–50.

was especially in vogue at Olympus, the second city of the sacred land, and under this title the center of many priestly customs.[43] The god of the sun was the god of music by a natural analogy to the course of the stars. And the sparrow hawk, the standard image of the divine essence in Egypt, in Homer was called the favorite bird of Apollo.[44] As soon, however, as this Apollo of Egyptian origin took a distinct place in Greek mythology, the national spirit worked to strip him of these astronomical attributes. All the mysterious or scientific ideas disappeared from the Daphnephoria; they became the commemoration of the love of a god for a girl who resisted his desires.

A new god, Helios, fulfills the functions of the sun. In his quality as the son of Uranus and the Earth,[45] this god was placed among the cosmogonic personifications.[46] He played no role in the tales of the poets. He is mentioned only twice by

43. Philochor. *ap.* schol. Soph., *Oed. Tyr.*, 21; *Antigon.*, 107; Herod., VIII, 134.

44. Homer, *Odyss.*

45. Hesiod, *Theog.*, 370.

46. The lyric poets, who belong to a period when the priestly notions had penetrated not into popular belief, but into Greek poetry and philosophy, sang of Helios and Selene in terms that do not in any way recall Apollo or Diana. The 29th Homeric hymn (these hymns, it is well known, are very much after the time of Homer) celebrates Helios, son of Hyperion and Euryphaessa. (Apollo in turn owes his life to Latona and Jupiter.) He never grows weary, says the poet, illuminating both mortals and the immortals. The sparkling eye of the young god burns under his casque of gold, with rays of fire encompassing his head, and his tressled hair gracefully surrounding his shining face. He is clothed in a diaphanous cloak that the winds have woven from their breath, and beneath him whinny his thunderous charges, who descend from heaven into the Ocean. Helios, says Stesichorus, mounts upon a seashell of gold and crosses the waves until he arrives at the sacred abode of the ancient Night, where, with his mother, his young wife, and the children that surround him, he walks under bosquets of laurel. At night, lazily stretched on a winged bed, the work of Vulcan, who made it of the purest gold, he crosses the liquid plain and arrives among the Ethiopians; for it is there that his chariot and his steeds await him until the next sign of dawn (Mimnermus, fragm. in Stobaeus, bk. VI). One sees that Helios is solely the planet that illumines the world, while Apollo fulfills a thousand different functions; Helios is always either on his chariot or in the Ocean; Apollo is by turns on Olympus, where he takes part in the gods' pleasures, and on earth, where he is passionately involved in the affairs of mortals. There is nothing Greek in the fiction of Helios but the beauty of forms, which is inseparable from poetry among a people who resist the dark cast and bizarre creations of cosmogonic depictions. However, the winged bed seems to us to be a deviation from that purity of taste that characterizes the productions of Greece; and in it we recognize, as with the ambulant tripods that served Vulcan (*Iliad*, 373), the fantastical literary form of the Orient. The seventh Orphic hymn carries this deviation even further: Helios has four feet, alluding to the four seasons of the year. This four-footed Helios plays

Homer.[47] He had no priests, no cult; no solemn feast was celebrated in his honor. Thus stripped of all abstract signification, Apollo appears in Olympus, takes part in celestial feasts, intervenes in the quarrels of the earth, is the tutelary god of the Trojans, the protector of Paris and Aeneas, the slave of Admete, the lover of Hyacinth and Daphne. It is so true that the genius of the Greeks was the author of all these changes in the character of the divinities that we see Apollo retain in the mysteries where the priestly traditions had relegated them the astronomical attributes stripped away by the public cult. Later, the Neoplatonists will seek to give him the same attributes when they attempt to make polytheism an allegorical system of science and religious philosophy.[48] But in the popular religion, instead of being the god who makes humans fruitful, he is a simple shepherd who guides the flock. Instead of dying and rising again, he is always young. Instead of burning mortals with his devouring rays, he shoots terrifying arrows from his quiver of gold. Instead of announcing the future in the mysterious language of the planets, he prophesizes in his own name. He no longer directs the harmony of the spheres by means of his mystical lyre; he has an imperfect lyre invented by Mercury, one

---

the harmony of the spheres on his flute. This hymn is also full of an accumulation of epithets that also characterize the priestly hymns.

For her part, Selene is strictly reduced to the attributes of the moon. In the thirtieth Orphic hymn she has wings. A celestial brightness surrounds the head of Selene, while her wings are extended; she sheds a soft light on the earth. Rays escape from her diadem of gold and dispel the obscurity of the night. After having finished her course, wearing a dress of light, she leaves to bathe in the Ocean, she exhorts on her charges with their manes waving proudly, crossing the heaven in all her splendor, granting prophetic signs to mortals. Jupiter once loved her, and the fruit of their loves was Essa, the dew (fragm. of Alcm. in Plut., *Sympos.*; see also Macrob., *Saturn.*, VII). The seventh Orphic hymn adds to the innumerable epithets given to Diana those of "hermaphrodite" and "evildoing," which bear the recognizable priestly mark.

47. As the father of Circe (*Odyss.*), and as revealing the infidelity of Venus to Vulcan. Does not the affiliation of Helios and Selene, children of the Titan Hyperion, indicate that in their memories the Greeks attached their astronomical divinities to the Titans; that is to say, to an ancient priestly cult? If it was true that the names Hellas and Hellene were the original designations of Greece, and that the priests of Dodona would have been named Selles or Helles because of their ancient worship of the sun, the god Helios, worshipped independently of Apollo and alongside him, would be not a new god but a return of the Greeks after the formation of their Homeric polytheism to notions and appellations that belonged to the earlier cult. On this subject, one can consult Creuzer, 1st German ed., IV, 167–89.

48. We could say as much of the function of presiding over medicine, at first attributed to Apollo, then to Asclepius (Voss, *Mytholog. Briefe*; Creuzer, II, 154).

he perfects. He no longer leads the dance of stars, but walks at the head of the nine muses, each one presiding over one of the beaux-arts.[49]

Diana was subject to a no less remarkable alteration. At Delos, she is obviously a cosmogonic power because she is the mother of Eros, who in the theogonies is always taken as a creative force.[50] Among the Scythians, she is a fierce goddess, thirsty for the blood of men, with a frightful form. This is how she initially appeared to the Spartans, because on seeing her they fell into a state close to delirium. At Colchis, she is so little Greek that she defended the Golden Fleece against the Argonauts. Her guardian dogs and their menacing teeth guarded the seven doors of the sanctuary that contained this precious treasure, and her voice commands monsters whose forms recall the fictions of India.[51] At Ephesus,[52] a mere look at

49. In the Orphic teaching, the muses originally were only the seven strings of Apollo's lyre. In Greece, they became the nine muses, and arrived at this number only gradually (Arnob., *Adv. gent.*, bk. III; Tzetzes, in Hesiod, *Op. et Dies*, V, I). The Orphic school was originally from Thrace, where Mount Pieron and the city of Pimpleia are found. The Greeks made the muses daughters of Pieros and the nymph Pimpleida; and, in order to better naturalize them, assigned the foot of Parnassus by Delphi as their abode, where Apollo Musagete was their director.

They had presided over the stars and the seasons, just as did the Graces and the Horae. The Greeks took away these functions in order to leave them only poetic attributions (Hug., *Rech. sur les fables des peupl. anciens*, pp. 241ff.). One still sees on a graven stone the Graces dancing naked on the head of the celestial bull, and two of them turn toward seven stars that they show with their hands (Borioni, *Collect. antiq. roman.*, fol. 1736, n. 82; Passeri, *Thesaur. Gemm. Astrifer.*, I, tab. CXVIX). This is an allusion to their ancient connection with astronomy.

Later, when morality is introduced into religion, the Graces who presided only over beauty took on moral attributions. One was the manner of granting benefits, another how to receive them, the third how to return them (Aristot., *ad Nicomach.*, V, I; Plut., *Philosop. esse cum princip.*, c. 3; Senec., *De benef.*, I, 3).

50. Cic., *De nat. deor.*, III, 13.

51. See in Orpheus (*Argon.*, 868) and in Apollonius (*Argonautic.*, III, 386ff.) the bulls that belch flames, the dragon teeth that become warriors, a fable similar enough to that of the hairs of Shiva or Badrakali becoming monsters, the giants with six hands, etc. (Orph., ibid., 515; Apollon., I, 993).

52. We do not speak of her oldest simulacrum, which still can be found on some medals. It is an almost uncut trunk, fallen from the sky, with a head and feet, which Pliny tells us had to be ebony wood (*Hist. nat.*, XVI, 79); which would make it a black goddess, perhaps Egyptian. But later a statue of gold was raised to it (Xenoph., *Anab.*, V, 3–5), and this statue merits a somewhat detailed analysis.

It is enchained (Herod., I, 26; Ael., V); we will show in book VI that this practice belongs to priests, who sometimes give it rather crude explanations, sometimes subtle ones. By its vestments covered with hieroglyphs, it resembles a mummy (Gronov., *Thes. Antiq. Graec.*, VII, 360; Mus. Pio Clement., I, 32). Like Cybele and the Dindima of the Indians, it has a crown of turrets. It also has her figure reveals the priestly imprint. How different she is in Greek mythology! Yet a closer examination shows that none of these attributes entirely disappeared. If she is the goddess of the hunt, this is because Isis, accompanied by her faithful dogs and Anubis with a dog's head, had sought the body of her spouse,[53] and the companions of Isis became the pack of Diana. If from the heights of heaven she directed the bronze globe that scatters the darkness of the night, and if the half-moon decorated her head, it is because Isis is the moon, and the half-moon is part of the adornment of the goddess of Ephesus. If she is the cause of the infirmities of women, if she strikes them with madness, sometimes with death;[54] if, in the same way, she sacrifices the children of Niobe; it is because she remembers being the Tithrambo of Egypt, that is, the moon considered in its malevolent aspect.[55] But such is the repugnance of the Greeks to transport into religion what belongs to science that in the same way they separated Apollo and the sun, they separated

---

on certain medals the *modius* of Serapis on its head. The numerous breasts that cover her chest are almost all those of animals. A half-moon or crescent is above. On the lower part of her chest one sees heads of lions, bulls, deer, bees, a crayfish even, heads of panthers with horns and wings, heads of tigers with the belly of a woman, monsters of legend: griffons, dragons, sphinxes. There is almost none of these symbols that does not relate to some allegory or to some scientific hypothesis borrowed from a priestly cult. The astronomical meanings of the lion, the bull, and the crayfish are well enough known. The last animal perhaps also indicates some relationship between the Diana of Ephesus and the Syrian Derceto, a maritime deity. (In this very chapter, see where we recall that Caistrus, father of the founder of the temple of Ephesus, had been the lover of Derceto, and had given life to Semiramis.) The longevity attributed to the deer made it the symbol of eternity (Spanheim, *ad Callim., Dian.*, p. 251). The bee was the emblem of civilization, of the social state and the gentling of mores. It recalls the purer race that had preceded the current generations. Its continuous buzzing represented the secret language that the divinity deigned to use to make itself understood by its favorites. A scholar observes that this mysterious sense was not lost in the revolution of beliefs. After having passed through the mysteries of Eleusis, it was reproduced in the Middle Ages, and one can find bees in the sepulchers of Frankish monarchs (Creuzer, I, 375–377). The griffons take us back to Persia, the sphinx toward Egypt. One cannot fail to see the reunion of all the divinities under these traits, and the priests of Ephesus worshipped it as such. For them it was sometimes Night, the first principle of all, sometimes Isis or Nature, varied, multiform, hermaphroditic, containing all the beings, causing them to leave her womb, and then recalling them. The inscription placed on her statues by sculptors demonstrates it: Φυσις παναιολς παντῶν μητηρ.

53. Plut., *De Isid.*

54. Macrob., *Saturn.*, I, 17.

55. Creuzer, II, 158. For the same reason Diana became Hecate, killed by Hercules and resuscitated by Phorcys (ibid., IV, 121–123).

Diana and the moon,[56] thus rendering her freer, more individual, and more independent. A virgin, she defied the power of Love; she harshly punishes the weaknesses of her nymphs. This understanding of virginity, which we have even seen in the worship of primitives,[57] is an idea natural to man, but which the priesthood adopts and amplifies. For the Greeks whom the priesthood does not dominate, this attribute is only a secondary trait, the effect of the caprice or modesty of a young girl; and the poets call into question sometimes its reality, sometimes its duration. Even as a virgin, Diana presides over births, a combination that echoes that of the power to create and the power to destroy.[58] One sees how incoherent are the remnants of the priestly notions that survived this metamorphosis, and at the same time how much they accompany it. They hardly touch upon the fundamental idea. The Hertha of Scythia, the Bendis of Thrace,[59] the Isis of Egypt, and the Diana of Ephesus are no longer; now they have become the lithe young huntress who as swift as the wind pursues the frightened inhabitants of the woods.

Recall what Hermes was in the Egyptian religion.[60] But the Greek Hermes is a

56. See the section on Selene in note 46.

57. See bk. II, chs. 2 & 7.

58. The association of ideas by which the Greeks sometimes called Venus one of the Parcae, or Fates, comes from this combination of the notions of life and death. The grammarians trace the etymology of the name of Proserpina to this double notion. Someone says to Proserpine (*Hymn., Orph.,* XXI, 15): "You are at once death and life, you produce all and you destroy all."

59. *Palaeph.*, ch. 23.

60. We have to explain an apparent error on the subject of the Greek Hermes that a German translator of the first volume of this work has nicely pointed out. "The author will pardon me," he says in a note (p. 225), "if his claim that Mercury or Hermes was not the conductor of souls at the time of Homer, and that this function was probably assigned to him after the introduction of Egyptian tales, and hence after Homer, this seems to me to be irreconcilable with the twenty-fourth book of the *Odyssey*, where Hermes leads the souls of the suitors to the netherworld." This misconception is due to the fact that we had to publish this work in parts. When the one that treats of Homeric mythology appears, the reader will see that we consider only the mythology of the *Iliad* as truly Homeric, which is very different from that of the *Odyssey*. The latter bears the mark of a much more advanced civilization, with the exception of the eleventh book (which, to note in passing, strikingly contrasts with the twenty-fourth book). The *Odyssey* and the *Iliad* are certainly by two different authors from two different periods. Moreover, in more than one of its parts, the twenty-fourth book of the *Odyssey* is obviously an even later interpolation that does not belong to the body of the poem. It contains details concerning the political constitution of Ithaca, the limited authority of the kings, and the power of the popular assemblies, details that are hardly compatible with the social state that the *Odyssey* recounts, and even more irreconcilable with that of the Greeks of the *Iliad*. Thus, the famous Aristarchus re-

wholly other god. He presides over neither sciences nor writing, nor over medicine or astronomy. He has not composed divine books that contain their elements. The interpreter of the gods in Egypt, in Greece he is only their messenger. This is why he retains the wings that elsewhere were an astronomical symbol.[61] If in memory of the directions given by the priests of Ammonium to the caravans crossing the desert he is the protector of commerce, the Greeks stripped all its somber gravity from this attribution. By a grotesque analogy that belied this function, Mercury became the god of fraud and lies.[62] Is this, perhaps, a reaction of the Greek spirit against the pretentions of the priesthood, by way of a recollection of what the Egyptian Hermes had been? Please note how, even if all the priestly attributes are done away with in popular belief, they reappear in the mystical portion that the hymns, whether Orphic or Homeric, have preserved. The Hermes of these hymns has almost nothing in common with the Hermes of the *Iliad* or even the *Odyssey*. He rather recalls sometimes the qualities of the Egyptian Hermes, sometimes the legends of the avatars of India. Born in the morning of the union of Jupiter with Maia (whose name leads us back to the Indian Maia), Hermes escapes from the arms of his mother four hours after his birth, finds a tortoise on the ground, makes a lyre out of it, and sings of the loves of which he is the fruit, and of the nymphs of the maternal grotto. Behold, he is the inventor of music. He later steals the flocks of Apollo, hides them in a cave, kills fifty cows, and roasts them on a brazier: be-

---

garded it as inauthentic. Hermes, who in it is called the conductor of the shades, is not found in the eleventh book, which is especially aimed at describing the empire of the dead. Probably the story that assigned this function to him was, as Diodorus attests (I, 2, 36), borrowed from the Egyptians and excluded from the first Greek mythology, and this fragment of Egyptian mythology was added to it during the interval that separated the eleventh book of the *Odyssey* from the twenty-fourth: we find it again in all the later poets, from Sophocles (*Ajax*, 831–32) until Virgil (*Aeneid*, IV, 242–44). We will devote several pages to the examination of the authenticity of the Homeric epics. This question is of the highest importance not only as a literary problem, but on it depends the entire system that has to be adopted concerning the development of the human race from its emergence from the primitive state; in some ways, it is the entire history of our species about which we have to speak.

61. The crutch of Saturn explains the wings of Mercury: Saturn has a prop because he needs thirty years to finish his revolution; Mercury has wings because twenty-seven days suffice for his.

62. In a manuscript we have seen, Dupuis assigns a very well-researched origin to this attribute of Mercury. This god was sometimes confused, he says, with the constellation called Prometheus: the apparition of this constellation only took place at evening; his small stature, which often hides him from sight so that one could see him only with difficulty, gave rise to the saying that Mercury was the patron of those who escape thanks to darkness, and who show themselves only at the beginning or the end of the night; that is, times auspicious for thieves.

hold, the inventor of fire. He offers sacrifice to the gods; that is, like Thot-Hermes, he regularizes the religious ceremonies. He eats the flesh of his victims, covers the flame he lit, and returns to the grotto. Malleable as a cloud, he enters by the keyhole and settles in his cradle: nothing more resembles the childhood escapades of Krishna. His mother is wroth; he reproaches her for seeing in him only a child, and declares that no one better distinguishes good from evil than he. Is this not Krishna, who, reprimanded by his nurse, simply opens his mouth, and to her great surprise she sees all the worlds united in all their splendor? Apollo pursues him. The flight of a bird, a witness or indiscreet confidant, directs the pursuit and betrays the hiding place of the fugitive. But come to the grotto, Apollo sees only a cradle in which a newly born infant sleeps. He nonetheless grabs him and wants to throw him into the depths of Tartarus. Hermes invokes the infirmity of his age and swears on Jupiter's head his innocence. Apollo brings him to Olympus, and after a thousand burlesque ruses, totally incompatible with the refined tastes of the Greek poets,[63] Hermes returns his flocks to the god and is admitted by the gods.[64]

We will not speak extensively about the stories relative to Hercules. Their foreign origin is well enough known,[65] and their occult meaning has been the subject of tireless researches. Nonetheless, since it is one of the parts of Greek mythology where the triumph of the Greek genius is most obvious, a few words will not be out of place.

63. Many are of a crude and disgusting levity; that, for example, which retraces the dishonorable action that Dante ascribes to Satan.

64. The difference in the Hermes of the religions subject to priests and the Greek Hermes is noticeable at Rome. The Romans at first received the priestly Hermes, brought into Etruria by the Pelasgians before Homer; and since this first Hermes was represented by a column (Jablonsky, *Panth. Aeg.*, V, 5, 15), it was the god Terminus. But when the Romans at the same time as the laws of Solon learned of the twelve great Athenian gods, they adopted the Greek Hermes under the name Mercury, still preserving the memory of their earlier notions.

Hermes, martia seculi voluptas,

Hermes, omnibus eruditus armis, etc.

Hermes omnia solus et ter unus.

(Martial, V, ep. 25)

65. Independent of the similarities that exist between Hercules and Osiris, Mr. Creuzer has very ingeniously discovered no less striking ones between the same Hercules, Diemschid, and Mithras. Like these two Persian objects of worship who are called the eye of Oromazes, Hercules is called the eye of Jupiter. There is also a good deal of likeness between Hercules and the Indian Rama. One finds Hercules and the Cercopes, in Rama aided in his battles by Hanuman and the army of apes (see the French trans. of Creuzer and the fine note by Mr. Guigniaut, p. 203; *Symbolic. allem.*, II, 252–55, 274–77).

Adored at Thebes in Egypt, Hercules is the sun at the renewal of the year.[66] It is he who, by leaving footprints on the earth, ensures a fruitful year.[67] He holds the phoenix in his hand, the symbol of rebirth.[68] He was killed by Typhon, a new proof of his identity with Osiris. He rises from the dead, like the sun after the winter.[69]

Struck by all these allegories, Herodotus tried to reconcile them with his previous ideas. But soon enlightened about the uselessness of the attempt, he declared (while imploring the indulgence of the gods of his homeland) that it was in Egypt and not in Greece that one must seek the etymology of the name of Hercules, and the meaning of the traditions connected with him.[70]

In fact, the Greek Hercules is only a hero. It is not the signs of the zodiac that he traverses, but monsters from which he delivers the world. Civilized and given to agriculture, Egypt saw in him fecundity. Uncultivated and savage, Greece saw only physical force. Each of his exploits is susceptible to a secret meaning, but it was the literal sense that was adopted. And if the epithets that the poets gave him recall the hidden meanings, the external sense soon enough replaces them in the popular interpretation.[71] What did it matter to the Greeks that the victory over Antaeus of this son of Jupiter was, as a very ingenious French savant explained,[72] the triumph of art and work over the burning sands of Libya? What did it matter that Hercules, disposing of his enemy by removing him from the earth that gave

66. This Hercules was the grandson of Perseus, who had his temple at Chemnis, where games in his honor were celebrated (Herod., II, 91). One also named at Olympus, among the founders of the great Panhellenic games, a Hercules descending from Perseus.

67. Herod., IV, 82.

68. Jablonsky, interpret. *Tab. isiac. opuscul.*, II, 237ff.

69. Eudox. *ap.* Athen., IX.

70. Herod., II, 43.

71. Thus, in the eleventh Orphic hymn Hercules is called *aiolomorphos*, of many figures. But the Greeks, although familiar with the metamorphoses of the gods, i.e., with their temporary disguises for the sake of a particular goal, did not conceive the mystical idea that with all forms belonging to the divinity, it assumed them indifferently, not to veil, but rather to display its supreme majesty. As a consequence, while the Orphic hymn by means of the epithet alludes to a notion of pantheism, the Greeks explained it by a wholly material assumption borrowed from life. Hercules, they said, sometimes showed himself with a mace, sometimes with a bow and arrows, sometimes covered with the skin of a lion, other times with resplendent armor.

72. See the excellent piece by Mr. Jomard on the ruins of the city of Antaeopolis (*Descr. de l'Eg.*, II, ch. 12).

him his strength, is really the Nile divided into a thousand canals, thus preventing the arid sand from returning into desert? For them, Antaeus was only a giant and Hercules, his conqueror. Neither the idea they conceived of him nor the homage they bestowed upon him contrasted with the rest of popular mythology. Only, at the end of his glorious career the Greek Hercules reprised in certain respects traits of the Egyptian Hercules. The latter, after having obtained from Jupiter Ammon the privilege of looking upon him, was plunged into an ineffable, all-absorbing contemplation that incorporated him into the infinite being.[73] Here one recognizes the doctrine of the priests—found in the majority of their philosophical systems—of the reunion of partial beings with divinity. Consumed by a fatal tunic, the Greek Hercules desired to return to the earth all that he had received from an earthly mother. He placed himself upon the fire, the flames consumed him, and the divine breath that animated him was lost in the soul of the universe.[74] Thus Greece offered him a double cult. On one hand, he was adored as a hero, on the other, he was worshipped as a god.[75] From this resulted a singular construction in Homeric mythology, unique in its kind. The deified Hercules enjoyed an unalloyed happiness in Olympus while the shadow of Hercules moaned in the netherworld.[76]

We will be even more concise concerning Bacchus. The worship of this god is certainly of Indian origin. But to arrive at Greece it had to cross other lands: upper Asia, Phoenicia, Egypt, and Thrace, and in this crossing its tales had to change and become embellished. It is impossible to deny his identity with Osiris.[77] It is equally impossible not to recognize in him the Shiva of India and the Lingam, his symbol.[78] The way in which his cult arrived among the Greeks, probably by

---

73. Macrob., *Saturn.*, I, 20.

74. Theocrit., *Idyll.*, XXIV, 81; Lucian, *Hermotim.*, 7, and his commentators. This fable is copied almost word for word from that of Horus, transmitted to us by Plutarch (*De Isid.*).

75. Herod., IV, 44.

76. *Iliad*, VI, 130; *Odyss.*, XI & XXIV.

77. The birth of Bacchus, drawn living from the womb of Semele (struck dead by thunder), and his strange transplantation in the cuisse of Jupiter, bear the fantastical character of the oriental imagination. When he escapes the sides of his mother, ivy emerges from a column to cover him with its shadow (schol. Eurip., *Phénic.*); in Egypt, ivy is the plant of Osiris (Plut., *De Is. et Osir.*), and the coffin of the Egyptian god is shaded by an *érica* (Plut., ibid.), which suddenly emerges from the earth and overshadows it. Both Bacchus and Osiris float in a box on the waves. Both have the head of a bull. Hence the Bacchus Bouguereau of which Plutarch speaks.

78. If we wanted to delve into etymologies, we would point to the similarity of the name of Dyonisos with Dionichi, the surname of Shiva (Langles, *Recherches asiatiques*, French ed., I, p. 278).

several successive migrations across very far-off countries, will always be an insoluble enigma, at least with respect to the dates of these migrations and the particular events that accompanied them.[79] The fables of which he is the hero,[80] the rites these tales animate—rites that are sometimes of a profound sadness, sometimes of a delirious gaiety, alternatively bloody and licentious, lugubrious and frenetic—never became part of the Greek religion.[81] Everywhere they appeared they excited horror and fear. The misfortunes and destruction of several dynasties were attached to their sudden and terrifying appearance. Agave tore to pieces her son Pentheus. Ino dove into the sea with Melicertes. Having gone mad, the daughters of Mina committed horrible murders and underwent a hideous metamorphosis. Later, a similar madness seems to have seized the virgins of Athens and provoked

---

One of the symbols of Bacchus is an equilateral triangle; the same is true of Shiva. Both cults have the same obscenities, the same emblems of the generative power (*Asiat. Res.*, VIII, 50). Shiva is represented as taking the form of a lion in the great battle of the gods. He seizes the monster, whom he fights with his teeth and his nails, while Durga pierces him with his lance. The same exploit is attributed to Bacchus, under the same form, against the giant Rhoecus.

Rhoecum retorsisti leonis
Unguibus terribilique mala.

79. One finds in the *Anti-Symbolique* of Voss a work directed against the *Symbolique* of Creuzer; the author, as we will see, is certainly right on the general question at the end of this volume. Still, in criticizing his opponent for his excessive subtleties he has not always avoided falling into the opposite extreme and seeing only the material side of mythologies. As we have said, however, one finds in his work (pp. 65–67) an excellent history of the introduction and development of the worship of Bacchus in Greece, from the twentieth until the sixtieth Olympiad. This cult began in the mysteries of Samothrace, furnished the Ionian school with Phoenician elements, and enriched itself with Asiatic notions by reason of the expansion of commerce; it took hold of Greek philosophy in its cradle, presented Lydian and Phrygian additions as if they were the original stock, and gave a hidden meaning to the public festivals of Olympia. Then it returned to Egypt under Psammeticus, with the Milesian colonies and immense developments, what Egyptian colonies had brought to Greece. It identified itself with the Orphic teaching, but always remained odious and suspect, disparaged by the sages from the time of Xenophanes and Heraclitus, as it had much earlier been proscribed by kings and rejected by the people.

80. Despite what Creuzer says, it could be the case that the legends of Bacchus were enriched with certain details of the conquests of Alexander. Euripides, who alludes to the Indian Bacchus (*Baccant.*, 14–18), in substance speaks only of Media and Bactria, as Voss observes (Voss, *Anti-Symbol.*, p. 85). But these additions have not at all changed the substance of the original fable, and the identity of Bacchus, Osiris, and Shiva is no less demonstrated.

81. The part of the Bacchic ceremonies that consisted in tears and expressions of sadness later entered into the feasts of Adonis; but at the beginning it was vehemently rejected.

them to commit suicide. No matter how fictitious these accounts, they nonetheless indicate a widespread opinion that better established facts support.[82] The style of the poets who entertain us with these traditions is grave and mysterious, and betrays a priestly origin. The philosopher Euripides and the mocker Ovid, who express themselves with so much levity concerning other legends, in describing the death of Pentheus seem to share the bloody pleasure, fierce irony, and fanaticism of the bacchants. One would say that the priestly genius had mastered the unbelieving poets, and that even after ten centuries the frenzy of ancient orgies dazzled their senses and troubled their reason.

At the time of Homer, these melancholic accounts were unknown or dismissed. Bacchus is spoken of only once, on the occasion of the victory he won over Lycurgus.[83] And the scholiasts were astonished that the poet, having placed Bacchus among the divinities, had him take no part in the affairs that divided them. This is because the Greek genius early on refused even to modify this too heterogeneous idea. But they compensated with the companions and satellites of Bacchus.

Silenus, whom we will later see was one of the chief figures in the priestly demonology, Silenus, intermediary between the gods and mortals, son of the still virgin Earth and born without the assistance of a man,[84] became a drunken, ridiculous old man who only recalled grotesque ideas.

The god Pan, who made the woods resound with the music of his flute and who followed behind Bacchus leading choruses of nymphs and satyrs, in Egypt[85]

82. The war of Perseus, king of Mycenes (Pausan., II, 16, 20, 22), and above all that of Anaxagorus, king of Elisa, against the supporters of Bacchus. A work that we have already cited, and which we cannot recommend in terms of critical acumen (*Histoire des premiers temps de la Grèce* by Clavier), nonetheless contains details on the opposition the cult of Bacchus encountered in Argolis, Boeotia, and in Attica (I, 193–211). It appears that the struggle to which this opposition gave rise suggested to Sainte-Croix the idea of those religious wars we talked about earlier. He generalized partial facts, applying to all of Greece what was true only for Argolis, and ended with the most palpable of errors, that of proclaiming as conquerors foreigners who were often rebuffed, and at most tolerated with resentment and defiance.

83. *Iliad*, VI, 130; *Odyss.*, XXIV, 74.

84. Creuzer, III, 223.

85. Herod., II, 16. Some scholars have claimed that this way of conceiving Pan as the great Whole did not belong to the ancient Egyptian religion, but was a later refinement of the Neopythagorians and Neoplatonists (Tiedemann, *Mem. sur le dieu Pan*, in those of the Mem. of the Society of Antiq. of Cassel, I, 65; and Voss, *Lettres mythol.*). But Herodotus clearly says that the Greeks and the Egyptians had very different ideas about this god, and that while one regarded him as the youngest of all

was one of the eight superior gods, and even the first of the eight. He was the great Whole, the Demiurge, the Firmament. Three cities were dedicated to him: Mendes, found on one of the arms of the Nile; Hermopolis at the center of the country; and Chemnis in the Thebaid. In their secret doctrine, the priests formed an abstract and metaphysical idea of him, while the people's fetishism represented him with horns and cloven hoofs.[86] But the allegory combined apparently opposed ideas. His cleft hoofs were the emblem of prolific force,[87] his horns, the rays of the sun and the moon, his visage with a shining aspect, the lit-up sky; while his furred feet were the image of the earth, the forests, and the animals who lived in them.[88] Taken over by Greek mythology, Pan retained all his external attributes, but each one took on a different significance. His head and his feet, far from expressing a cosmogonic idea, made him the god of shepherds. Once representing the harmony of the spheres, his dances became the dances of the inhabitants of hamlets. His jowls, shining a florid red, witnessed to drunkenness. His flute composed of seven reeds that alluded to the seven planets became a rustic pipe. In a word, he was now a secondary god or a demi-god.[89] It was not that the original ideas were not preserved, but they were preserved in a way to astound those who encountered them with their contradictions.[90]

the gods, the other placed him at the highest rank of their eight great divinities. Pindar, by what he says about metempsychosis and several other teachings, seems to have had some knowledge of foreign doctrines; according to Aristippus, he names Pan the dancer and the most perfect of the gods, as do the Egyptian priests; it is said that the god, in gratitude that Pindar had recalled his former dignity, dictated a poem to him and danced before him to one of his odes (Pind., fragm., p. 50, ed. of Heyne). One could also find an analogy between the Pan of the Greeks and the Indian Hanuman, prince of the apes, skilled like Pan in the art of music.

86. Herod., II, 45.

87. The Arcadians recounted that this god had once assumed the form of a ram, and in this way had attracted the moon into a forest, where he had violated her. This manifestly is generative energy joined to an astronomical idea. But the allusion to astronomy and cosmogony has disappeared; all that remained was the notion of the unfettered desires of a shameless god.

88. Schol. Theocr., I, 3; Serv. *ad* Virgil, *Eclog.*, II, 31; X, 27; Sil. Ital., XIII, 332; Macrob., *Saturn.*, I, 3.

89. In general, several divinities who were eminent in the priestly religions in Greece descended into the ranks of heroes or of very inferior gods. We will find the same metamorphosis in Roman polytheism vis-à-vis Etruscan deities.

90. Even though the Homeric hymns and the Orphic hymns often contain the same doctrines, it must be observed that this conformity disappeared when it came to this field-god. The Homeric hymn depicts him with rustic traits that hardly rise above popular notions. Pan, with the feet of a goat, a forehead with horns, and hair loops, the son of Mercury and a nymph, wanders aimlessly in the thick

"The temple of Pan," says Pausanias, "is in Arcadia. There it is said that this god, the most powerful of all, answers the prayers of men, and severely punishes the wicked. Next to his statue burns a sacred fire that never goes out; and at Olympus his altar rises in the interior of Jupiter's temple."[91] This worship, this opinion of the distributive justice of Pan, his place next to Olympian Jupiter, these are things that hardly go together with the status of a field-god. Some purely Greek traditions seem marked with the same foreign souvenirs. Pan assisted the Athenians at Marathon and Salamis.[92] He helped the Macedonians win a victory over the barbarians. He came to the aid of Antigonus Gonatas, who was attacked by the Gauls. Finally, it was his terrible voice that struck terror in entire armies and put them to rout. How can one reconcile such power with the idea of a subordinate, almost laughable deity, whom his own worshippers treat with a levity very close to disdain?[93]

We will leave Vulcan to the side, whose very name directs our thoughts to Egypt,[94] and in whom we could point to the eternal, uncreated fire, the active principle of the world.[95] This fire that burns in the stars, that circulates through

---

forests of Pisa, walking through the mountains and atop the crowns of all the rocks: sometimes he hides in the bushes, sometimes he plays alongside fountains or shoots the beasts of the forest with his arrows. Returning from the hunt, he confines his sheep in caves and plays melodious airs on his flute. The Oreads assemble as a chorus and sing his praises. Covered with the skin of a lynx, he dances beside a clear fountain on a prairie decked with flowers. At the sight of this god with raised fur, his nurse had taken flight. But his father, charmed by his spritely games, brought him to Olympus, and the sight of him gave pleasure to the immortal gods.

The Orphic hymn gives him even more mysterious attributes. He is the horned Jupiter, the inspired one, terrible in his anger, who sends frightful specters to humans. After having taken repose in hidden grottos, he rests among the stars that burn in the sky. If he sings with the nymphs, it is the harmony of the world. He is the god with a thousand names, the powerful, the universe, the creator and regulator of all things, the dispenser of life. By him the earth has emerged from nothing; by him the ocean surrounds it, and air and fire produce the beings, the reunited elements obey it, and multiform nature gives birth to the generations of men.

91. Pausan., *Arcad.*, 37.

92. Scholiast. of Soph., *Ajax*, 707.

93. For more details, see Creuzer, first German ed., III, 241–82.

94. Hephaistos/Phthas. The Egyptian Ptah was therefore the Greek Vulcan; but what a difference! See Wagner, *Ideen zu einer allgem. Myth. Der alt. Welt*, p. 279.

95. First of all cast into the sea, where Thetis and Eurynome found him and hid him in their damp grotto (*Iliad*, XVIII, 395), Vulcan was then thrown by Jupiter to the island of Lemnos, where the wild Sintiens (*Odyss.*, V, 285–294) granted him hospitality: all this certainly contains allegories indicating the generative force attributed to fire, to heat, to humidity, and to the sun (Hydus, *De mensib.*, p. 85).

all the parts of the universe, that organizes inert matter in a thousand different forms,[96] becomes a god whose halting gait and conjugal calamities give rise to inextinguishable laughter on Olympus. We will end with a last example, that of the Cabiri.

In the language of priests, the Cabiri designate the two great opposing forces.[97] They are the earth and the sky, wet and dry, body and soul, inert matter and vivifying intelligence. Their original figure was unshapely and ugly. They were monstrous dwarf gods.[98] They were brought to Samothrace in this form. There, they were called the grand gods, strong and powerful. They were sometimes hermaphroditic and sometimes each of a different sex.[99] Their cult consisted in orgies rather similar to those of the Phrygian Cybele. Loud music stirred their worshippers to wild dances. Greek mythology in turn took them over, and the poets examined what features could be used in the necessary transformation. The statues of the Cabiri had been placed in the port of Samothrace. They presided over the winds. They were made gods favorable to sailors and terrible to pirates.[100] They appeared at the peak of masts in the form of shining flames, announcing the end of storms.[101] They expressed the opposition between light and darkness. One of the gods had to be hidden under the earth while the other shone in the sky. They had emerged from the cosmogonic egg:[102] the two new divinities emerged from an egg, fruit of the lovemaking of Jupiter and Leda. In order to further nationalize them, they became the protective heroes of Sparta and watched over the Olympic

---

Vulcan, produced by Juno without the cooperation of a spouse, represents the air that engenders and contains fire (Wagner, *Ideen*, etc., pp. 402–3).

96. The Stoics had returned to this idea; or to put it better: this idea served as the foundation of the Stoics' system.

97. The number of the Cabiri was not fixed in the priestly religions or in the mysteries. They varied according to the need of the priests to express cosmogonic forces; but these variations have nothing to do with the point of view under which we envisage them here.

98. According to Herodotus, Cambyses could not contemplate these diminutive and disproportionate divinities without laughing (III, 37), images of infants with an enormous stomach, a large mouth, large eyes, and big ears. At the time of Pausanias, one still saw four bronze pygmy statues, of which three were named Dioscures, another name of the Cabiri (Pausan., *Lacon.*, 14).

99. Varro, *De ling. latin.*

100. Nigid., *ap.* schol. *Germ. in imag. gemin.*

101. Diod., IV, 43.

102. This cosmogonic egg is found in all the priestly religions: a sphere divided into two beings, by a natural analogy, the symbol of the universe in all the religions.

games.[103] They were identified, via Helen, with the family of the Atrides. Warrior adventures[104] were attributed to them, to provide a motive for their apotheosis.[105] The gods gave them winged chargers.[106] They were named Castor and Pollux, and the hideous Cabiri became the handsome Tyndaridae.[107]

The application we just made of this principle to a small number of Greek divinities would yield comparable results if we extended it to all the Greek gods. Juno, who in the Orphic teaching was the air or atmosphere and was the moon among the Phoenicians, retained among the Greeks only very contradictory remnants of her priestly characteristics. In this way, she is both the wife and the sister of Jupiter. And people allude to her original personification of the atmosphere when they recall that, once upon a time, she was suspended among the clouds.[108] In the hymns that contained the foreign teachings entering Greece via the mysteries, Juno was incensed that her spouse had caused Minerva to spring from his head. She addressed the Earth, the Heaven, and the Titans, in order to produce by herself

---

103. Pind., *Olymp.* III, 63–67.

104. Their battle against Idas and Lynceus (Pausan., III, 13).

105. They were deified forty years after the battle recalled in the previous note, and fifty-five years after the apotheosis of Hercules (Clem. Alex., *Strom.*, I; Heyne *ad* Apollod. III, 11, 2).

106. Stesichor. *ap.* Tertull. in *Spectacl.*, pp. 9ff.

107. This is neither the place nor the time to clarify, as much as is possible to do so, or at least to try to do so, this fable of the Cabiri which is particularly obscure. In Egypt they initially were five, because of the five intercalary days necessary to complete the year. In the astronomical point of view, they had three fathers: the Sun, Hermes, and Saturn (Plut., *De Isid. et Osir.*). In the transition from Egypt to Greece they lost this triple origin; three remained occult forces, children of the cosmogonic Jupiter and Proserpina, the passive principle of fecundity as well as destruction, the other two took their Greek names of Castor and Pollux, and had Leda, the mistress of Olympian Jupiter, as their mother (Cic., *De nat. deor.*, III, 21). In Egypt their mother was not Leda but Nemesis, one of the appellations of Athyr, the primitive night. Thus the loves of Jupiter have a fantastical coloring that grows weaker in the Greek tale. Not only does Jupiter change into a swan, but he orders Venus to pursue him in the form of an eagle, and he hides himself in the bosom of Nemesis, whom sleep takes hold of and he finds an easy conquest. Next, Hermes takes the egg to Sparta, and Leda nurtures it. Rejecting completely the cosmogonic personage of Nemesis, the Greeks made Leda a true mother, and the ancient Cabiri were established in the national mythology. But the Ionian school, faithful to the priestly philosophies, continued to call them children of the eternal fire, Vulcan, and of the nymph Cabiria, one of the Oceanides, which led them back to generation by water and fire. When astronomy had taken its place in Greek religion, they were the morning star and the evening star. It would be possible to see an allusion to this idea in Homer (*Iliad*, III, 243; *Odyss.*, XI, 302). Later they became the Gemini.

108. *Iliad.*

Typhoeus, who had a hundred arms and one hundred heads. The Earth responded with a groan that announced the fulfillment of her prayer, and soon the birth of the monster caused terror among both the gods and men.[109] Nothing is less Greek than this fiction. Therefore we find no trace of it in Homer. Juno is a jealous and vindictive divinity with human interests, passions, and desires, but supernatural force. But nothing is allegorical in these desires, or cosmogonic in her forces.

The Mars of Thrace, to whom the poets frequently allude,[110] and the Mars of Phoenicia, who served as the chief text for Dupuis[111] and his astronomical hypothesis, and for the German Canne,[112] whose etymological subtleties were no less ingenious and just as admissible, are probably the archetypes of the Homeric Ares.[113] But as indomitable and fierce as the latter might be, he equals neither in excess nor irrationality the priestly version. His forms are more noble, his worship more humane: the human sacrifices offered at Sparta when he first arrived have fallen into disuse.[114] And if we draw from authorities subsequent to Homer, we would see that the impetuous and cruel Mars, formerly avid for human blood and carnage, was called the avenger of the innocent, the guide of the just, and the protector of mortals.[115]

In the cult of Adonis, composed not only of the traditions of various countries but referring to different divinities[116] imported into Greece at different times from

109. *Hymne à Apollon*, vv. 305–54.

110. *Odyss.*, VII, 361; Sophocl., *Antig.*, 968–70; Eurip., *Alceste*, 502; Callim., *Delos*, 62; Antipat., *Sidon.*, XXXIV; in Brunck, *Analect.*, II, 15; Virg., *Enéid.*, XII, 31; Stat., *Théb.*, VII, 34ff.

111. *Orig. des cultes*, I, 15, 251, 319, etc.

112. Canne, *Parenté des Allemands et des Grecs*.

113. The birth of the Thracian or Phoenician Mars differs essentially from that of the same god in Homer, even though Thrace is his homeland and customary residence. But he is the son of Jupiter and Juno, while the priestly legends, always marked with mystical notions concerning generation, recount that he was born of Juno alone, who had smelled the perfume of a flower (Ovid, *Fast.*, V, 229). By the time of Ovid, the traditions of the two polytheisms had mixed and become confused, and the poets gathered them all, indifferent as they were to belief, and solely concerned with the accumulated conceits.

114. Apollod., fragm., p. 396.

115. Homeric hymn to Mars.

116. *Ogygia me Bacchum vocat,*
Osirin Aegyptus putat,
Mystae Phanacen nominant,
Dionyson Indi existimant,
Romana sacra Liberum,

Syria, Phoenicia,[117] Egypt, Cyprus, and later Alexandria; in the cult of Adonis, as we were saying, which involves a mixture of science, lamentations, and obscenities (the mystical images of death and resurrection),[118] the Greeks at first saw only the poetic side, the unhappy loves of Venus and a handsome adolescent. And when they later admitted some of his foreign rites, they separated the Greek Venus from the Syrian Venus, and the feasts of Adonis were exclusively attached to the latter.[119]

The entire history of Pasiphae is borrowed from an astronomical cult;[120] but only the sordid passion of Pasiphae for a bull remains in the Greek fable. The daughter of Inachus is Isis; she gives birth to Epaphus, who engendered the celestial Bull, like Apis born of a heifer impregnated by a moonbeam. But in Greece she retains from her Egyptian origins only the horns on her head, which embellish rather than disfigure her.

The wild, indecent races of Isis or Cybele for their spouses or their mutilated lovers,[121] in Greece becomes the touching story of a mother who seeks a beloved daughter throughout the entire universe.

Arabica gens Adoneum,
Lucaniacus Pantheum.
(Ausonius, *Epig.*, 30)

117. The Greeks, who sometimes wanted to give themselves the honor of the invention of fables that were most obviously foreign, and most contrary to their spirit, maintained to the Phoenicians that the worship of Adonis had a Greek origin. National vanity deceived it, as theological orthodoxy later deceived the learned bishop of Avranches, who maintained that Adonis was Moses.

118. We have already noticed (bk. II, ch. 4) the remarkable consonance between the mysteries of Adonis and an Iroquois opinion that, like the Phoenicians, takes the grain of wheat that dies and is reborn as a symbol of immortality.

119. Pausanias (VII, 26) says that the two Venuses were adored in different temples and with different ceremonies. The melancholy of the festivals of Adonis, observes Creuzer, was repugnant to the Greeks, whose religious ceremonies with few exceptions were bright and gay. The scholiast of Theocritus (*Idyll.*, V, 21) recalls in connection with this subject a precious tradition. He says that Hercules, having seen in Macedonia a crowd of people who returned from the festivals of Adonis, cried out in anger: I recognize neither such worship nor an Adonis among the gods (Creuzer, German ed., II, 105).

120. Creuzer, German ed., IV, 99.

121. The tales of Ceres and Isis are perfectly the same. The motive for the search, the disguise and silence of the goddess, her mysterious means of nourishing the infant confided to her, everything is identical; and in the Greek fable one notices many vestiges of priestly traditions; for example, the drink of water and flour that Ceres substitutes for wine, as in the mysteries, purification by fire of the child of Metaneira, the indecency of words and deeds by Iambe or Baubo, who makes Ceres laugh, and which is not at all in keeping with the elegance of truly Greek fables. It is the same with the leg-

Jupiter[122] owed to Egypt several of the objects of his love;[123] to Libya his shield, one of his mistresses,[124] and his brother Neptune; to Phoenicia his father, his grandfather, Ceres his wife, and his daughter Proserpina; to Thrace his son Mars; to the ancient indigenous cult of the Pelasgians Juno, his wife and sister; to Phrygia his cup-bearer Ganymede; to Scythia his rival Prometheus; finally to India the divine bird, bearer of his thunder; his eagle is clearly a Greek imitation, and thus embellished and stripped of strange additions, but nonetheless a recognizable imitation of Garudha, the king of the birds in India, with a piercing gaze, rapid flight, golden plumage, a wonderful combination of human, eagle, and sparrow hawk, and the mount of Vishnu.[125] Nonetheless, despite this priestly mosaic (if the expression is allowed) the Jupiter of Homer is exactly what the master of the gods ought to be at this period of polytheism.[126]

If Greece in this way incorporated so many foreign ideas into its beliefs, which it subordinated to its genius; even more so it ought to have received from elsewhere many practices and rites. Rites in fact are introduced more easily than opinions can be shared. From this came many customs in Greece that the Greeks themselves could not explain. For example: the invectives that women hurled at one

---

end of Cybele and Attys. When one reads the fable of Agdistis, which becomes confused with the mysteries of Cybele, one believes he is encountering the most fantastic legends of the East. Agdistis is a hermaphroditic being, born of a dream of Jupiter, dreaming that he possessed Cybele. Angry at the impure birth, the gods mutilated Agdistis, and from the parts they took from him came an almond tree. The nymph Nana, daughter of a river, having gathered some fruit from this tree and having placed them on her lap, gave birth to Attis, a young man whose beauty charms all women. Agdistis, whose mutilation had left him a woman, lusted for Attis, and in her jealous frenzy caused him to undergo the same treatment as she had experienced from the gods (Pausan., VII, 17; Strabo, X, 3; XII, 2). Nothing is less Greek than all this.

122. In the fragments of Orpheus (Clem. Alex., *Strom.*, V), Jupiter is called Metropator, in memory of his quality as a hermaphrodite or as the double creative force; but the Greeks hastened to reject a notion so little in keeping with their ideas. It does not appear, if our memory does not deceive us, in any of the truly Greek poets, no matter how familiar they were with the priestly cosmogonies.

123. Among others, Latona and Semele.

124. Io, daughter of Inachus.

125. Creuzer, French trans., I, 195.

126. If so many different elements sometimes contributed to the composition of a single Greek divinity, it also happened that a single foreign divinity furnished Greece with materials for several divinities. Thus the Egyptian Tithrambo is sometimes Diana, sometimes the Ceres Eyrnnis, violated by Neptune in the form of a horse and mother of a mysterious divinity whose name could not be revealed.

another during the feasts of Damia and Anxesia, which were in imitation of Egyptian women during the feasts of Bubastis. From the same source came the duties of continence or even virginity imposed upon certain priestesses.[127] But more compassionate than priestly polytheism, Greek religion ordinarily was more indulgent to the infirmities of nature or sought to anticipate them. Among these priestesses, some exercised their functions only until the time when they became nubile; others made such rigorous vows only when age rendered them incapable of violating them.[128] Finally, from this cause came the theoxenia found in several cities in Greece—in Athens, Delphi,[129] and Achaia[130]—which were solemn commemorations of the admission of foreign gods. But even while engaging in these rites, the Greek people did not inform themselves about their meaning. They were content with the accumulation of striking ceremonies, of dances and pomp, which they enlivened with their own spirit and gaiety. Their previous views remained intact. The practices borrowed from abroad were for them spectacles in which they were both actors and spectators, occasions for celebration and means of coming together.

127. The priestesses of Hercules, Minerva, or Diana were, for the most part, bound to a more or less long continence (Pausan., *Corinth*; *Coel. Rhodig.*, XXXIX, 22).

128. Plut., in *Numa*.; Pausan., *Boeot.*, XXVI; *Achaïc.*, XIX, 25–26; Spanheim, *ad* Callim., 110.

129. Atheneaus, IX, 13. See the notes of Casaubon and of Schweighaeuser, n. 13.

130. Pausan., *Achaïc.*, 27.

CHAPTER 6

The True Elements of Greek Polytheism

If our readers were to bring together what they just read, they would recognize the truth we have attempted to establish. In its spirit, or its tendency, Greek religion has nothing that likens it to the tendency or spirit of religions subject to priests.

Its initial element was fetishism; but the colonies that brought civilization combined the fetishes and changed them into national gods.[1]

To this first modification of fetishism was added a circumstance that completed the transition of this belief to polytheism: the apotheoses of several leaders of the foreign colonies.[2]

1. This transformation did not happen suddenly, but at different times and following different circumstances. Individuals sometimes retained objects of private worship that were not those of the people to which they belonged. Herodotus gives us an example; and even though he places the scene in Sicily, and the event itself does not enjoy historical certitude, it is precious as a proof of the fact that there were vestiges of an individual religion after the adoption of public worship. "A civil war," he says, "having arisen in Gela, the defeated party took refuge in the neighboring environs. One of the fugitives, *full of confidence in his particular gods*, attempted to lead his companions back to their homeland under their protection."

2. One must not confuse the apotheoses that are proper to the Greek religion with the incarnations that are frequently encountered in the priestly religions. They are two diametrically opposed things.

In apotheosis, one assumes that men can rise to the rank of gods by their exploits and their benefits to others. In incarnations, it is gods who take human form for some particular purpose, whether to create the material universe, or to lead its inhabitants back to the knowledge of the truth they have forgotten, or, finally, to redeem them from the condemnation to which their sins have exposed them. Their mission fulfilled, these gods return to their celestial abodes. They are never mere mortals who become gods; they are gods who become, as they will, humans or animals.

The principle of incarnation is in the interest of the priesthood; that of apotheosis its contrary. It is good for priests that it is maintained that gods become incarnate to descend from heaven. The priests

Nothing is more natural than these apotheoses. Men who arrived among the savages with some knowledge of indispensable arts, and who not being the strongest could only be the benefactors of those they instructed, had to appear to be gods. The unfortunate inhabitants of America display the same tendency to divinize the Spanish whom they see sailing their ships or mounted on their horses;

---

can provoke these marvelous descents at will. It matters little to them that men can mount to heaven. They can ascend by their own merit.

This remark seemed necessary to us because modern writers deceived by some of Diodorus's phrases have attributed to Egyptian colonies the introduction of apotheosis into Greece. As an adherent of Euhemerus's system, Diodorus saw all the gods, no matter what religion they belonged to, as deified humans. However, it is incontestable that the Egyptians never raised any of their kings to the rank of gods. Even Sesostris did not enjoy this privilege. If—and the thing is possible—in the death of Osiris is contained some memory of a historical event pertaining to the wars of pastoral peoples, the priestly spirit would have erased the least traces of this event; while in its apotheoses, the Greek spirit carefully preserved the (admittedly embellished) memory of the earthly course some hero has traversed. The death of Hercules is connected to his loves and to the jealous fury of Dejanira; that of Osiris is but the emblem of the sun's revolutions.

With respect to the Persians, Leibniz committed the same mistake as Diodorus did with respect to the Egyptians. On the basis of an etymology, he saw in the myth of Arimanes the apotheosis of a head of a nomadic tribe. Mosheim (*Annot. ad* Cudworth., p. 238) also claimed that Mithras was only a deified hunter, because he is represented in the monuments and records that have come down to us as killing a bull and being followed by a dog. Nothing authorizes these interpretations. Persians never placed their great men among the gods; but systematic writers have sought out great men in all the gods of antiquity.

The distinction that Julian makes between the fables relative to Hercules and those the priests recount concerning the birth and exploits of Bacchus is helpful in showing the difference that separates the apotheoses of the polytheism that is independent of priests and the incarnations of priestly polytheism. "Hercules," he says, "even though from his birth he displayed a divine and supernatural force, always remained within the limits of mortal nature. But in what mythology tells us of Bacchus, it is no longer a matter of a man who became a god but of a divine essence, emanated from the Supreme Being, and manifesting itself in the world for the perfection of the human race. Semele who is called the mother of this divinity was but one of his priestesses. Having announced his appearance, and having provoked him by her impatience, she was consumed by the flames that surrounded the god." All this has a remarkable analogy with Indian mythology, while everything that relates to Hercules is entirely conformed to Greek mythology. (I would add that, in Spanheim's edition, this passage from Julian is garbled. One would think that he wanted to show that there was no difference between Hercules's birth and that of Bacchus. All the following ideas prove the opposite. A slight correction in the text, and the addition of a question mark, would reestablish the meaning.)

and these pitiless conquerors do not disabuse them of their errors, except by the combined force of their cruelties and crimes.

By these apotheoses, a certain number of divinities took on human form. Gradually, all the others followed this example. Rocks, stones, trees, and mountains ceased to be worshipped under their natural form, and events were assumed to explain their metamorphosis.[3]

In their former countries, the colonists had seen priests deify the great phenomena of nature. The memory of these deifications mixed with the apotheoses. From this resulted gods whose character was dual, whose attributes were mixed. But the part of the character and these attributes that was due to the priests disappeared by degrees, and the time of this disappearance can be determined. It was the substitution of the cult of Jupiter for that of Saturn. Jupiter is the center of the popular mythology.[4] Everything prior to his reign is somber, mysterious, incoherent. The vague conceptions of the savages struggled with the strange traditions of foreigners. Everything that follows the advent of Jupiter is elegant, regular, applicable to the needs of a people advancing toward civilization. New gods succeeded old ones. These new gods have a more individual existence that more conforms to that of men. Jupiter and Neptune replaced Uranus and Ocean. In Venus, a seductive deity, passionate like mortals, the generative force was personified, which formerly was scattered among Night, Discord, and the Sea, obscure figures without any direct action on human life.[5]

The same colonies had brought ceremonies and rites whose meaning they had forgotten. Vestiges of these rites were preserved, but without any explanation of their motives.[6] The imagination of the Greeks invented them. Become enig-

---

3. Dulaure, *Des cultes qui ont précédé et amené l'idolâtrie.*

4. "*Novus fabularum ordo, et, nisi fallor, a caeteris diversus, Hellenicae stirpi propius versatur, circa genus Japeti*" (Heyne, *De Theog. Hes.*).

5. The story of Venus emerging from the surf after Saturn had cast into the sea the parts he had taken from Uranus (*Theog.*, 190) rested on the cosmogonic hypothesis that made water the principle of everything. The Greeks rejected it because they give Jupiter to Venus as her father (*Iliad*, V, 370); but they also retained as both graceful and poetic the image of Venus borne by the waves and showing herself nude to the enchanted universe.

6. The sacrifice of a bull at Athens, the ceremonies that followed, and the court of the sacrificing priest, a court in which all parties traded accusations, including concerning the sword used in a murder (Pausan., I, 28; Porph., *De abst.*, II), are the manifest indications of a previous, or foreign, cult of which the Athenians practiced only a few rites. At the feasts of Ceres among the Pheneates in Arca-

matic, priestly practices gave way to fables. Sometimes when the practice fell into disuse, the fable survived it, but without being able to recall the original practice.[7]

Once entered onto this path, the Greeks never stopped. Everywhere one sees a variety of ingenious traditions flower. Some owed their birth to the meaning of a proper name; others to a distant resemblance between two objects that otherwise have no relation; some to an oddity of nature, or to an effect of chance. The river that flows by Mantinea is called Ophis; this is because a serpent served as guide to the inhabitants of this city who were seeking a homeland.[8] The myrtle of Trezene has pierced leaves; this is because Phaedrus, consumed by a deadly love, pierced them with a golden pin when he was in despair.[9] The rock by Mount Sipylus resembles from afar a woman bent toward the earth; this is Niobe bent under the weight of her sadness.[10] An olive tree makes itself noted in the Argolida by its crooked form: Hercules shaped it that way in order to fix the limits of the country of the Asineans.[11] Sometimes the traditions express the patriotic desire to nationalize discoveries claimed by foreigners. Thus, it is no longer the Egyptian Cecrops but the Athenian Triptolemus who was the inventor of the plow.[12]

Each of these traditions served to make the Greek religion more indigenous. They established new bonds between the gods and those who worshipped them, between the soil and those who lived on it. At the death of a hero, the trees, rivers, heaven, and the earth mourned, like his compatriots.

---

dia, a priest wearing the mask of the goddess struck the attendees with loaves of bread (Pausan., VIII, 5). This rite, says Creuzer, allegorically signifies that the goddess struck the material part, the mortal envelope of man, in order to liberate the soul from the body. We do not reject this explanation. All religious customs had different senses, and this one conforms entirely to the priestly doctrines taught in the mysteries. But the hidden sense was unknown to the vulgar, who saw in the external religious pomp only the inheritance of past times.

7. Thus the history of Ocnus the ropemaker, whose ass constantly gnaws the cord he fabricates, the symbol in the Greek netherworld of the unhappiness attached to useless effort. According to Diodorus (I, 36), it was borrowed from an Egyptian ceremony that had an entirely different meaning.

8. Pausan., *Arcad.*, 8.

9. Pausan., *Attica*, 21.

10. Pausan., *Corinth*, 28.

11. Pausan., *Attica*, 22.

12. Hesych. *in voce* Bouzuges.

These scattered traditions were concentrated and, as it were, circumscribed in a span of time determined by a fictional chronology.[13] This length is manifestly too contracted to contain the many confused events found in it. Recalled only by rare and obscure memories, the infancy of nations becomes rather dense and appears much shorter than it was in reality.

13. The heroic ages of Greece contain five generations, including the heroes who fought at Troy, a period when the heroic times had already begun. The first of these generations is that of Perseus and Pelops; the second, that of Amphitryon, father of Hercules; the third, that of Hercules, the contemporary of Neleus, the father of Oeneus and Nestor; the fourth, that of the Argonauts, of Tydeus son of Oeneus, and the warriors who laid siege to Thebes. For a son of Jason who traded with the Greeks camped beneath the walls of Troy *(Iliad,* VII, 467–69). Finally, the fifth generation is that of Achilles and Agamemnon. Homer places the foundation of Troy five generations before Priam. He thus creates five Trojan generations corresponding to the five Greek ones. But 150 years would not have been enough to bring the Greeks from a semi-savage condition to the one described by Homer. We see in the poems that bear his name great inequalities of fortune or power, princes invested with acknowledged authority and almost always respected, and a population much larger than the primitive state can allow. The purely pastoral life was already so foreign to the author of the *Odyssey* that he attributes it only to the legendary race of the Cyclopes (Fred. Schlegel, *Hist. de la poésie grecque*). While traveling through Greece, Hercules everywhere encounters brigands or monsters. Traveling from Trezene to Athens, Theseus was exposed to a thousand dangers. In his voyage from Pylos to Sparta, on the other hand, Telemachus encountered no danger. Pisistratus and he depart in a chariot pulled by two horses, without any retinue or escort, bringing with them provisions for a day. At night they arrive at Pherae, where Diocles, one of the eminents of the country, provides hospitality; the next day they arrive at Sparta; and their return is as peaceful as their going.

CHAPTER 7

The Results

These are the several heterogeneous elements of Greek polytheism. It is a mixture of some remnants of a crude cult with memories of the past, as well as those of far-off countries, together with tales of travelers. It is the history of the migrations and establishment of each people, the settling into each country, the foundation of cities, the exploits of leaders, and the rivalries and misfortunes of their dynasties. It is the story of science disguised as fables, precepts put into action, metaphysical subtleties personified and unrecognizable. In a living religion, these things are commingled. Imagination and belief do not distinguish among them as do reason and reflection. Classification is a kind of anatomy that is exercised only on corpses.

From all these heterogeneous elements, however, a uniform whole results, animated by the same spirit.

If, as we agree was the case, the Greek religion was more than any other enriched by foreign borrowings, these never altered its constitutive genius. The customs and opinions that the Greeks received at different times from different nations entered only partially, separately, some in one place, others in another, but without reconstituting the whole they had formed when in the hands of priests, and without ever dominating the mass of Greek opinions.[1] The changes the latter underwent were always the effect of the progress of enlightenment and the natural development of

---

1. We can hardly overemphasize that this truth was sensed even by those who had the greatest interest in denying it, because they wanted to attribute a profound symbolic sense to the Greek religion. "Despite all the influences that the Greek spirit received from abroad," says Mr. Creuzer, "it preserved its own character in religion. In the same way that the priests of Dodona could not practice Egyptian religion, the other elements could not erase the national character. . . . Everything the Greeks touched became a new being; and the former creed, impacted by the fables, arts, and poetry of this people, was no longer recognizable" (German ed., I, 370, 280–381).

thought. Privileged by nature and by chance, by their own interior force this people subjected to their national spirit the multiform materials from which they composed their religion. The superb climate, the almost unique good fortune they had of being civilized by foreigners without being subjected by them—a combination of circumstances that was never reproduced in history—allowed them to never depart from the natural development of religious ideas. At each period, the religion had the character that the epoch had to imprint. The traditions, ceremonies, truths, and errors come from abroad always bent to this character. The Greeks never accepted these discordant materials, except on the condition that they could fashion them at their pleasure.[2] Drawing from the fetishism of their ancestors some of the fundamental traits of their gods, they ennobled their inclinations and beautified their forms. They accepted from the East only names and rites. While sacralizing the memories of their ancient (and confused) history, they painted these vestiges of barbarous times with more brilliant, and softer, colors. Placing some of the men who had civilized them on Olympus, they so clothed them with celestial attributes that their earthly origin was covered with a veil.

Later we will notice more than once that when the Greeks adopted fables from other peoples, portions of which did not fit with the ensemble of their ideas, they

Another writer, Mr. Stutzmann, distinguishes between the world and the history of the East and the world and history of classical polytheism. Without being aware of it, this is the distinction between peoples who are dependent upon priests and those who are free of this yoke. We, however, will not draw from this fact, as Hermann does in his *Lettres sur Homère* (pp. 64–68 & 141), the consequence that one can come to an adequate idea of Greek mythology without leaving Greece. On the contrary, we think that because one is constantly being brought short before otherwise inexplicable contradictions and allusions, that one must study the East, but must do so by always having in mind the modifications that Greece gave to what she drew or received from abroad.

2. It is so true that Homer's religion is entirely different from the symbolic religion that Creuzer is obliged to suppose that it was voluntarily that Homer passed over in silence the symbolic meaning of the tales he recounts, and that, even though the rites were preserved, the meaning disappeared. Homeric poetry, he says, has caused people to misunderstand the profundity of the symbolic belief. Homer knew the secrets of the priesthood; but as a poet, in the popular fables he attributes human traits and actions to symbolic beings. He presents heaven and the celestial host in the colors in which the people—the kings, the warriors, and the vulgar—were accustomed to conceive them. As a national poet, and fulfilling his public mission, as it were, Homer had to restrict himself to the circle of knowledge and understanding that the Greeks possessed, since it was to them that his poetry was addressed. Voss (*Anti-Symbol.*, pp. 31, 65ff.) rightly (and vigorously) refutes this view, one that nothing authorizes and which everything we know about the different authors and periods that made up the Homeric epics belies.

rejected these parts. And if much later the progress of thought made them more fitting, they would reprise what they had rejected.[3] So much did the national spirit exercise a despotic sovereignty over all these opinions!

A fortunate and salutary sovereignty, without which the human race—become stationary and petrified—would everywhere today be the same as it was in Egypt!

Instead of developing and purifying itself, the religious sentiment struggling under unnatural fetters would have become disordered because of the lack of progress, delirious because of the lack of liberty. This truth will be manifest in all its evidence when we follow the development of Greek polytheism step by step, embellishing the forms of its gods, improving their character, introducing morality into religion, and separating from belief everything that no longer accorded with the new notions concerning humanity and justice.

Priestly polytheism, in contrast, preserved all the deformities and vices of these idols. Wounded by this oppressive disproportion between them and itself, the religious sentiment experienced only terror where it needed to place confidence. It resembled the legendary giant who was immortal but captive, who because of the crushing weight of an enormous burden moved only by convulsions. Sometimes he cast himself into bitter sadness,[4] sometimes he gave himself over to irrational

3. Thus the god Pan, whom we spoke about above, and who by the time of Herodotus had lost his symbolic meanings, was according to this father of history the adulterous son of Penelope and Mercury; however, with the introduction of the philosophy of the barbarians into the Greek systems, he again becomes a son of the Earth and the Sky, that is, he regains a cosmogonic significance (schol. Theocr., I, 123). In this way too the Greeks removed judges of the dead from their initial view of the netherworld (which was an Egyptian notion), because morality will only later enter the religion (see *Odyss.*, bk. XI, and our investigations into Homeric polytheism); but when morality had entered, judges and judgment were reintroduced into the empire of the dead (see Pindar and the other poets).

4. An equal melancholy reigned among the wild Thracians (Pompon. Mela, II, 2; Solin., XV; Herod., V, 4) and the civilized Egyptians. Both professed the same doctrine concerning the brevity of life and the misfortune of existence (Creuzer, *Symbol.*, German ed., III, 176). The Gauls, the Germans, and almost all the tribes of the North held their religious assemblies in the dark of night (Caes., *B Gall.*, VI, 18; Tacit., *Annal.*, I, 65; *Hist.*, IV, 14; *Antiq. Suevo-Gothic.*, IV, 24). Modern scholars who have sought the reason for this custom say they have found nothing in the religion of these peoples that could motivate it (Pelloutier, *Hist. des Celtes*, VIII, 143). A more precise correlation between their opinions and the rites would have resolved the problem. The inhabitants of Massalia (Marseille), imbued with the doctrine of the Druids, rejoiced at funerals, while births cost them tears (Val. Max., II, 6). The Bhagavad Gita exhorts Indians to consider the earth as a place of misery and affliction (see Schlegel, *Weisheit der Indier*). Only the influence of the priesthood can explain the downcast, somber, and passionless disposition of the inhabitants of Egypt, which had the most pleasant climate under the most serene of skies, living on the most fertile soil.

joys.[5] The latter, however, were a kind of inebriation, even more troubling than the melancholy he tried to escape. One would say that among priestly nations, tired of being prey to constant sadness, man foreswears reason in order to escape the suffering that haunts him. But the result of these efforts is not a happy or even calm condition. The shouts of a disordered and artificial exhilaration degenerated into lamentations; frenetic dances were marked by mutilations, battles,[6] and dark commemorations; and debauchery itself was mixed with deep sadness. It was at the somber ceremony of Adonis at Byblos that Syrian women offered the sacrifice of their chastity.[7] Peoples subjected to priests passed from abasement to license, and from orgies to despair. By a singular effect of the symbolizing spirit, sensual ideas combined with lugubrious ones.[8] The gods who presided over death were honored by obscene rituals; those who presided over life by cruel ones. The phallus was planted on sepulchers,[9] and the same phallus was drenched in blood.

Today, it is only with great difficulty that one can conceive the full extent of the evil done to man by the priesthood of Antiquity. At this period, religious notions felt the effects of the unreflective and petulant impulses of the human race in its infancy. In contrast, the excess of civilization of our days condemns the generations to premature fatigue. The past centuries weigh heavily on us; experience takes hold of us from the cradle, and our youth already bears the imprint of the caducity of time. But at least as a kind of recompense, we possess science and enlightenment. Among nascent peoples, man was intoxicated by the fullness of his forces and the pleasures of his new life. All of nature seemed to speak to him, while it is silent to us. Religion had its childish joys, which it has long since lost. It had not put on the robe of the adult. But the priests, merciless preceptors of the nations they con-

5. The priesthood of the Middle Ages followed in this regard the footsteps of the priesthood of antiquity. Beside autos-da-fé, massacres, abstinences, and austerities, the Feast of Fools and dramas known as mystery plays recalled pagan orgies in the bosom of Christianity. The carnival is still a half-erased vestige of these scandalous ceremonies. Thus, they are especially preserved in countries that did not follow the Reformation.

6. In the temple of Hierapolis, the priests of two divinities that Lucian names Jupiter and Juno fought, and their battles were the symbol of the opposition between the active and the passive principle, day and night, wet and dry, etc.

7. Lucian, *De dea syr.*

8. Ovid notes (*De art. am.*, I, 77) the combination of libertinage and sadness in the feasts of Isis that were brought to Rome (see Juven., *Sat.*, VI; Schmidt, *De sacred. et sacrif. Aegypt.*, p. 64). Propertius calls the Isidian mysteries mournful solemnities (II, 24).

9. Creuzer, German ed., II, 81.

trolled, deprived them of these joys without giving them enlightenment in return. They wanted them to be at once as docile as children and as sad as men.

Greek polytheism was the only one that in its public part—we are not speaking here about the mysteries—protected itself from the dual extremes of sadness and license.[10] In the majority of Greek cities, nocturnal rites were forbidden.[11] The Olympic games, both the Pythian and the Isthmian, occupied in the Greek national worship the place that the festivals of Sais, Hierapolis, Memphis, or Bubastis played in Egypt. In Egypt, one's gaze was offended by revolting objects, one's ears struck with discordant clamors; and in order to worship the gods, man seemed to descend from the level where nature originally placed him. While in Greece, elegant games, harmonious choruses, and a noble contest of talents, as well as the beautiful alliance of all the arts, raised him above the earth, as it were, and encouraged both the beauty of forms and the sublimity of thought.

It is therefore fortunate—a thousand times fortunate—for the human race that the Greeks[12] followed the path that nature laid out for them. They alone preserved that liberty of thought that allows the soul its most sublime flights, the spirit its noblest developments. The victory they won over the priestly corporations who oppressed the rest of the earth was the signal and sign of the high destiny reserved to man by the beneficent being who created him. We owe to the Greeks the life of the mind and moral strength. They have passed on these precious goods to us as our heritage.[13] We must carefully guard this inestimable

10. On the gaiety inherent in Greek feasts, see Hesiod, *Op. et Dies*, 735; Hesychius and Suidas in ουδεν ιερον; Spanheim, *ad* Callim., Del., 3224; Meurs., *Graec. feriat*. A writer born in Africa and raised in Greek ways, who could therefore competently judge, says that Egyptian divinities were worshipped by lamentations and Greek ones by dances (Apuleius).

11. Cic., *De leg.*, II.

12. In putting the Greek people entirely apart, and distinguishing them from all the other peoples of Antiquity, we take no position concerning their origin. On the contrary, we are convinced that its beginning was like all others. And we find evidence of this in a host of its traditions and in a great number of its customs, which contrasting with its daily habits nonetheless had retained a sort of empire over it; sometimes mixing with its institutions despite their obvious incompatibility, sometimes partially reproducing themselves when extraordinary or troubling circumstances brought back the memories of obscure Antiquity. But here we have not at all sought for the origin of the Greeks. That investigation would require volumes, and would only conclude with probabilities. The sole truth important to us is that ever since the period when history lets us know somewhat distinctly the inhabitants of Greece, they were separated from the rest of nations by essential and fundamental differences.

13. Surrounded as we are by critics who do not argue in good faith, but who betray their conscience as well as their pen, who are ready to reproach us with fanaticism if atheism were to reappear

deposit. Ancient Greece knew how to acquire it, may modern Europe know how to defend it.

But we must not flatter ourselves that because of the brilliant period of civilization in which we find ourselves, we have no dangers to fear. It is less impossible than one might think to return generations dominated by egoism and weakened

---

in France, and would be equally ready to accuse us of impiety because a powerful party recognizes religion only in the servile submission and praises given to its ambitious hypocrisy; we therefore feel the need to support ourselves with the most irreproachable authorities, those least suspected of irreligious opinions, in order to show that even before us, in works different from ours, and by very different paths, everyone in Europe who had some knowledge of history, some moral value, some elevation of spirit, and some love for human dignity has declared with unanimous voice the view we express here. Therefore let us let a famous writer speak, one whose intentions cannot be blamed or his merit denied.

"The absence of a priesthood such as found in Egypt and the Orient had important consequences for Greece," says Mr. Heeren, one of the most praised scholars of Germany, who occupies an eminent place in one of the premier literary establishments of that country and in this respect, perhaps, more desirous of pleasing power than attacking it. "No class arrogated to itself the monopoly of the sciences and the direction of intellectual faculties; these precious goods, the most estimable of goods, remained common property in Greece. Religion placed no barrier to the free and unflagging efforts of the inquiring mind. In separating itself from religious dogmas, science took on an independent and progressive character, which was transmitted from the Greeks to the peoples of the West, of whom they became the teachers. Their numerous colonies spread the light everywhere, and in all the countries where these colonies went (they were in the number of four hundred), one encounters a tendency toward progressive development, as well as an elegance and moral elevation that can only be attributed to their influence. Rome owed to it their civilization. The hordes that divided the empire owed theirs to Rome. The superiority of Europe over the other parts of the globe, the superiority of the moderns over the barbarians who are their ancestors, in great part had as their prime cause the absence of priestly power among the Greeks" (Heeren, *Idées*, III, first sect., "The Greeks").

We add that in Mr. Heeren's thought, as in our own, the absence of priestly power does not at all mean the absence of all priesthood. We are far from denying that men more deeply penetrated and habitually occupied with the truths the religious sentiment reveals would assume the office of spreading these truths and rendering them clear and fruitful. It is the monopoly that appears to us to be the scourge. We especially recognize the utility of ministers of love and peace in Christianity, which does not solely consist in external rites, but which has this advantage over the religions of Antiquity that it establishes between God and man moral relations as well as a cult. If we wanted to prove this utility by examples, we would take them indifferently from our own communion and the other Christian communions. If we admire in our own pastors their pure life, their fervent zeal, their calm courage, we also revere the virtues of the Fénelons and Saint Vincent de Pauls of Catholicism. And we would do justice to those of whatever belief who devote themselves to the most beautiful of causes, to that which distinguishes man from the brutes and unites earth to heaven. What we fight against is the exclusive privilege of power, science, enlightenment, preaching, and authority, which for the majority of humanity is a condemnation to ignorance, debasement, and servitude.

by luxury to the situation of those ancient peoples that an all-powerful priestly order kept in subjugation and immaturity. If one constantly attacks instructing the laboring classes; if one forbids the most efficient modes of communicating even elementary education to them; if one goes so far as to forbid them the use of the alphabet;[14] if one lavishes terribly misguided admiration upon the priests of former times, whose teachings, rites, and doctrines reason disdains, thus making sincere piety an object of repugnance, the danger becomes great.

We will not go as far in our alarums as the dean of German scholars, who accuses the ingenious commentators on the philosophies and symbolic cults of Antiquity of presaging by means of their learned systems the return of theocracy, subjection to thrones, and the corruption of nations.[15] His fears, however, do not seem to us to be entirely fanciful. A great question is thereby clearly posed, and upon its

14. Would it be true that a government, which is not that of either Algiers or Timbuktu, forbade learning how to read to those of its subjects who did not possess a certain level of material comfort? The Scythians put out the eyes of their slaves; but the Scythians were barbarians; they did not conspire against civilization, they did not know it.

15. "What do they really think?" says Voss in his *Anti-Symbolique*, in speaking of the adherents and advocates of this new system. "Reasonable men, tolerant men, who do not wish to suspect any evil, they need to consider the end of all these efforts, which is nothing but the revival of absolute theocracy by means of ruse and force; of a theocracy in which only the initiate, received in the innermost sanctuary, was allowed to contemplate the light, while in the Egyptian dusk or darkness the people savored what was called the peace of religion, a peace that they will tell us was never troubled during the night maintained by Gregory VII? To revolt after breaking one's oath, the attack on the rights of kings, anathemas launched from the clerical throne, the replacement of the excommunicated father by the rebellious son, pious frauds, venal indulgences, nocturnal orgies, poison, the dagger, the dungeon, the flames, and a death so gentle that the shedding of blood was avoided: all these things you will learn were but the means of arresting the restlessness of rash reason and the invasive entrance of a childish people into the prohibited regions of science; these were benevolent precautions for maintaining this hapless people in this peace similar to the sleep of Ulysses, which Homer says was deep, irresistible, and little different from death. . . . However, despite these advocates of the *Symbolique*, we on the other hand, peoples and princes, have been enlightened by the light of the Gospel, we protest and will always protest, both for ourselves and our posterity, against this peace of the dark. . . . Let them study but for an instant modern history, rather than misrepresenting ancient traditions. What raised States and communities to a dignity suitable to man? Freedom of the intellect, this gift of God, which leads us from the lowest rung of human knowledge up to the highest and most sublime, to the profound conviction, the pure adoration, the intimate presentment, of the Divinity. Apostles of the doctrine of our divine master who has delivered us from the Pharisees and the scribes, you dare to cause the heads of nations to fear the evangelical light! But answer this: In what countries of the contemporary world does it give credence to demagogs and oligarchs, atheists and theocrats pursuing their bloody aims?" (Voss, *Anti-Symb.*, pp. 111–14).

answer depends our future. How did man emerge from the mire in which he lived with the animals?[16] Did he raise himself to the awareness of his celestial origin by the power of his soul and his intellect, divine gifts of his creator, or does he owe his new being to the partial and parsimonious[17] instructions of those corporations

---

It would be imprudent for us to follow the German author in his eloquent developments. We have cited some passages in order to indicate the perspective in which he envisages the admiration for the priestly corporations of Antiquity professed by a class of scholars. And we must add that we are convinced that he wrongly includes Creuzer and Goerres in this indictment; but with a similar candor we declare that we are less assured concerning the intentions of several writers who follow in their footsteps. When we read in the writings of one of these disciples *that the wisdom of primitive times preserved its core of truth for all ages and all periods, that it is not the artifice of the priests of paganism that created the religious and social forms* (these social forms, I add, were the castes, including the pariahs), *the religious and social forms of late Antiquity; that it is the spirit of truth that animated them, even though they were corrupt and degenerate;* when we see *Brahmins and gymnosophists, magi and Chaldeans, the priestly caste of Egypt, the priests of the Pelasgians and the Thracians, the religious senate of Etruria, the Druids, and the pontiffs of Odin depicted as societies of men with sublime genius and the largest views, still penetrated with the divine spirit;* when we are told that their *very errors were the aberrations (whether innocent or culpable) of a grand truth* (we know that this is the way they explain human sacrifices: as the vague presentment of the sacrifice of a god); finally, when one proclaims that *the priesthood and the ancient social order reflected the heavens*: we cannot stop ourselves from thinking that a conspiracy gathers to render the earth similar to this dark and imaginary heaven, and that it is men who dream of the restoration of castes, and the omnipotence of an implacable order that would once again capture the human race in its immense nets and bring about universal abasement and brutalization. Now we believe this project is as absurd as it is odious; but it exists, and Voss is not wrong to denounce it in Germany, in Europe, in the world over.

16. Voss, *Anti-Symbol.*, pp. 234–35.

17. In order to prove in an evident manner the imperfection and inadequacy of the knowledge communicated to, or hidden from, the peoples by the privileged corporations that oppressed them, we would have to anticipate the developments that will be found in our third volume, devoted as a whole to the exposition of priestly polytheism. While waiting, we will cite an impartial observer, an eyewitness to the effects of the religion of India and the legislation the Brahmins have perpetuated. "The laws of Manu," says Mr. Buchanan (*Asiat. Res.*, VI, 166), "which are rather suitable to an absolute monarchy, in the hands of the Brahmins have become the most abominable and degrading system of oppression that has ever existed. . . . They have perverted morality, and elevated the authority of the priesthood on the ruins of the State and at the expense of the rights of subjects. They have not," he continues, "spread any light over the nation, and have completely destroyed the historical record." And if this witness is not sufficient for our readers, we would send them to the excellent *Histoire de l'Inde* by Mills (I, 139–40; II, 22–204).

As for Egypt, we would choose a very popular authority, a writer whose extensive learning one cannot deny, and whose opinions are not always ours. "Moses," Mr. Malte-Brun tells us, "shows us in Egypt a servile people, without property, without courage, divided into tribes, into hereditary castes, that earlier swaddled him in crude fictions, enervated him with subtleties, and frightened him with wild ceremonies or brutalized him with shameful rites?

That the imitators of the magi or the heirs of the Druids would adopt the latter view, nothing is simpler. The independence enjoyed by the Greeks is a scandal for them. The few facts that can please them, the death of Socrates or the exile of Anaxagoras, cannot satisfy them. They demand the entirety, the whole, which charms them by its vast silence, its enormous weight, and its solemn immobility.[18]

---

with no one being able to leave the métier of his father; and the multitude, content with the basest food, working as slaves to erect monuments to pride and superstition; an ignorant despot, priests given over to magic, inhumane laws; no institution in which the people takes part except for the festivals of the national worship—and what a cult! Not only the awe-inspiring and useful objects of material nature, but animals—the most hideous reptiles—receive an ignorant worship that renders the Egyptians the laughingstock of the other nations; and at the same time grand edifices, populous cities, and flourishing arts. How to reconcile these contradictory facts?" We omit the historical conjectures of the writer and come to his conclusion.

"In the moral sciences, in philosophical ideas, and in religious teachings, while dominating the entire nation, the priestly caste, far from having been their teacher and model, had to remain behind and below the Hebrews, the Greeks, and the Romans. When a caste wants to reserve enlightenment and knowledge to itself, it condemns itself to a stationary condition. This is the penalty attached to the monopoly of civilization. Intelligence does not preserve its vigor except by free emulation. The power and science of the priests of Egypt finally expired in the midst of the darkness against which they thought they had raised a rampart." As for the rest, we will not pretend to demonstrate to our adversaries what they know as well as we do: that they do not admire these ancient corporations for what they knew, but for what they inhibited the people from learning.

18. See Bossuet, *Disc. sur l'histoire univ.*, pt. III, ch. 3. It is impossible to read two pages of the history of the Egyptians by the bishop of Meaux without being struck by the errors and contradictions that are found in each line. Here Bossuet extols the law that assigned to each one his work, which forbade him from exercising two, or from changing his profession. He maintains that by this means all the arts arrived at perfection, and later he says that in Egypt everything always was done the same. But if everything was always done the same, nothing was perfected. He praised the skill of Egyptians in medicine, and we know by the testimonies of all the ancient writers that it was forbidden to them to use remedies that were not found in the books of Mercury Trismegistus (Diod., I, 2). And the doctors dared to treat only a single organ (Herod., I, 84), which was an obstacle to healing any complicated disease or malady. Every discovery was forbidden as sacrilegious (Diod., I, 82). Degraded by this servitude, the doctors of Egypt had descended into the ranks of jongleurs. Their science was composed of evocations, spells, and prayers. Predicting maladies (Diod., I, 81), attributing them to the influence of the planets and the malevolence of demons (Orig., *Contr. Celse*, VIII), they begged for the miraculous cures of Isis, who showed herself to the sick during their sleep. In seven days, the doctors of Darius could not deliver this prince from an illness that the Greek Democedes caused to disappear in one hour (Herod., III, 129). Bossuet certainly was not ignorant of these facts attested to

But in a truly strange incoherence, the philosophy of the eighteenth century, because of its irreligious passion, lent its assistance to these enemies of all enlightenment. It declared itself the admirer of the enslaved peoples who bordered the Indus and the Nile. Their worship differed from Christianity: this was enough to obtain the favor of the unbelievers. Basing their superficial learning and biting harangues on dubious witnesses and apocryphal writings, these philosophers wanted to humiliate Christian priests by the praise they lavished upon Brahmans, and to denigrate the Gospel—which they poorly understood—by exalting the Vedas, which they knew not at all. And in a patent non sequitur, in order to mock the Christian Messiah, born of a virgin, dying on a cross, and redeemer of man, they

---

by all of Antiquity. But it was a matter of a people governed by a priestly corporation, which could not make any movement, allow itself any thought, or satisfy any desire (no matter how innocent) without the permission of priests. Hence, the fraternal affection of the bishop for Ammonium and Heliopolis.

If from Bossuet we move on to more modern authors, we will find that they exaggerated his exaggerations and aggravated his mistakes. They run through the facts like blind horses that overturn everything they encounter. Such is their enthusiasm for Egyptian immobility that it renders them indulgent toward all the follies, obscenities, and cruelties of Egypt. "In order to make its divinities," says one of them (Ferrand), "the Egyptian people consulted not their passions, but their gratitude. They did not offer a cruel or base worship to what had inflamed their hatred or their desire." He forgets the sacrifices noted by all the historical records that remain, as well as the cult of Phallus, who was worshipped under a thousand forms, each more revolting than the other. But it is above all the division into castes that he praises, and he regrets. "This constantly observed rule," he says, "perhaps denied Egypt some great men, or better put: some superior men; but it gave her a series of useful men. It prescribed a uniform path to those restless spirits that would have troubled the State by taking only their imagination as their guide; and this is what gave Egypt the character of constancy and stability that made its happiness. It is never because of the lack of talent that a great State can find itself in danger; on the contrary, it is when too many wish to depart from their place. Read the revolutions of all empires. It was the work of some men who wanted to depart from their place and professions." Egypt, however, perished; this country, which was so well organized, so ably defended against the scourge of genius and talent, fell like the others, and more shamefully than the others. "This is," says the same author, "because they had departed from the ancient principles, from those hereditary principles that ought to be passed down from generation to generation." Not at all. It was because when the majority of a nation is dispossessed of all its rights, inhibited in all its faculties, condemned to languish in ignorance and to suffer a double servitude in religion and in politics, it has no interest in defending its masters against foreigners, because the foreigner is for the majority not a worse master. It is so little true that Egypt perished because it departed from its ancient principles, that its ancient principles survived its fall and rendered it as miserable, and maintained it as base, under the Greek dynasties or the Roman proconsuls, as under the yoke of its native priests and kings.

extolled the disciples of Krishna, himself the son of a virgin, killed too by the wood of arrows, for the salvation of the human race.[19]

A general prejudice resulted from this absurd alliance between two opposed fanaticisms, one that continues to influence even the better minds.[20] This prejudice is not without danger, and it would be wrong to view it as merely a historical error. The theocracies of the Middle Ages justified themselves by means of the example of ancient theocracies. Today, some propose the sanctuaries of Eleusis and Memphis as models, and the philosophical panegyrists of ancient Egypt wonderfully serve the aims of those who would like to impose an Egyptian yoke on modern Europe.

Against this yoke, civilization is insufficient. Civilization enfeebles souls; it disposes them to support everything, because it offers them easy resources to withdraw from everything. By teaching the slave to mock his master, it renders obedience less humiliating for his vanity. Servitude believes it is less vile when it can console itself with irony.[21]

Child of civilization, industry is no less ineffective. It hardly worries about oppression, because for a while it can escape from it. It confines itself to a sphere

19. Paulin, *Syst. brahm.*, 147ff.; Sonnerat, I, 169; Polier, *Myth. des Hindous*, II, 144.

20. This reproach is not addressed solely to those of today's writers who because of their status and interest are obliged to regret the passing of the priesthood of Antiquity. Men who otherwise are advocates of enlightenment, and who like us wish the advance and perfection of the human race, have nonetheless repeated the praises heaped upon these oppressive corporations. We have already declared that we do not agree with the measures taken against the author of the *Symbolique* by a segment of indignant scholars; but we cannot stop ourselves from sighing when we see him define the original constitution of castes as the empire of spirit over matter, of moral powers over physical ones. Rather, it is the empire of fraud over ignorance, which becomes the empire of the sword over the unarmed slave. This combination, which lengthens the infancy of nations, silently prepares, he says, the seeds of the institutions and doctrines that will be the pride of their maturity (French trans., p. 144). But the institutions, discoveries, and sciences that are the pride of the human race developed only in Greece, and without Greece the pressure of the usurping caste would have stifled all the seeds of the good and the beautiful. Out of what bizarre prejudice, from what strange monomania, can someone bemoan the fact that Homer's genius replaced the orgies of Thrace? And when one reflects upon the triumph that Greek fables and poetry won over the ululations of the Bacchantes, does one dare to call the charm of this poetry and these fables "a seduction full of dangers"?

21. When it comes to tyranny, "ridicule attacks everything and destroys nothing. Each believes that by mockery he has regained the honor of independence, and satisfied with having disavowed his actions by his words, finds himself able to belie his words by his actions" (*De l'espr. de conquête et de l'usurpation*, p. 88).

where it believes freedom of thought is superfluous; and when its eyes are opened, the light comes too late.

The sciences obtain protection for their material aspects, which they pay for with adroit concessions. Admitted into the inner circle, they become complicit with the monopoly they share.

Left to itself, philosophy is without force. It leads to doubt, and doubt saps the energy of the soul.

The religious sentiment alone can save us. By enhancing the price of life, by surrounding it with an air of immortality, it ensures that this life itself can be an object of sacrifice. It is even more precious, though, because it is our means of improvement. Nor is this all. Because of it, our thoughts are no longer circumscribed in a narrow sphere. And persecution, injustice, and death are but the steps that lead to the source of all good.

We have already said this: the current crisis is the same that threatened human nature at the time of the establishment of Christianity. But one circumstance today is more favorable. At that time, no rallying point offered itself to the dispirited human being. Everything was vague, confused, and uncertain; he sought some form—and every form fled from him like a cloud.

Today we are in possession of Christianity. And of all the forms the religious sentiment can assume, Christianity is at once the most satisfying and the purest. As it was taught by its divine author, it soothes all the pains of the soul. It respects all the liberties of the intellect while also delivering it from doubt. And with its subtle and varied sympathy, it offers to all—from the palace to the cottage—the consolations they need.

Unalterable yet flexible, it engraves essential truths on hearts, it receives the tributes of the centuries, as well as the improvements they bring. Religious people should not be offended that we speak of the improvements of Christianity. In its moral doctrine, in its precepts, in everything that comes from its author, it is not perfectible because it is perfect. But in its forms, and above all in the partial opinions its followers have adopted, it has room for improvement.

Experience shows this. The most ardent defenders of Catholicism, those whose express mission would seem to be to maintain its doctrines in all their rigor, involuntarily witness to this. They themselves reject those harsh and fanatical maxims against which our more enlightened reason and our gentler mores have long since rebelled.

Do we not read in a recently published book by the head of a university in

France, an author who thus, as it were, legally represents the religion of State, did we not read a vigorous refutation of a doctrine that almost the entirety of Catholics believed, and still believes, is imposed by the Roman Church?[22] To be sure, men versed in the history of dogma know that Catholicism, no matter how severe certain of its ministers have made it out to be, never formally pronounced the condemnation of unbelievers who were so because of the chance of birth, or because of invincible ignorance or other circumstances beyond their will. In a spirit of justice, as well as a desire for fraternal tolerance, we are quite pleased to acknowledge the following: the Catholic religion does not question Providence, it does not level terrible anathemas at those who can only be characterized as subject to an involuntary misfortune. The famous maxim, outside of the Church there is no salvation, has been wrongly interpreted; and the Sorbonne itself has restricted the meaning of the axiom, even in writings that continued to display its easily provoked spirit and its hatred of independent thought.[23]

It cannot be denied, however, that an interpretation that both reason and religion reprove has been constantly proclaimed as an article of faith; that it motivated bloody proscriptions and great cruelties; that the Spaniards invoked it when massacring the unfortunate inhabitants of America; that the Sorbonne—to which we just rendered due justice—adopted this interpretation without noting or call-

---

22. "Why," says Mr. Frayssinous in his *Conférences*, "do some suppose that according to Catholic doctrine there will be men condemned to eternal punishments precisely for not having known a law that was not in their power to know? This supposition is fanciful. . . . No one will be condemned by the tribunal of God for being born in the forests of the New World, or for not having known the Christian virtues. Birth can be a misfortune: it is not a crime, and the involuntary ignorance of revelation is not a punishable fault. . . . If the unbeliever did not have—if he could not have had—the means to enlighten himself, then his ignorance is invincible, he is excusable for not knowing. . . . Christian revelation is a positive law, and it is in the nature of a law not to be obligatory except when it is published and known." This rapid and logical series of ideas, which Mr. Frayssinous establishes as evident principle, seemed to Luther to be an impious view. Zwingli expressed it while speaking of the virtuous men of Antiquity; Luther accused him of becoming a pagan. Is it not curious to see the Catholic bishop being more tolerant than the Reformer? See *Parv. Conf. Luth. Hosp.*, pp. 2, 187.

23. Condemnation of the *Emile* by the Sorbonne. "Every man who is in invincible ignorance of the truths of faith will never be punished by God for not having known these truths. This is the Christian and Catholic doctrine" (art. 26, p. 63). As for the separate communions of the Church: "The children and simple faithful of these communions do not participate in either heresy or schism; they are excused by their invincible ignorance of the state of things. . . . It is not at all impossible that those who live in communions separated from the Catholic Church can arrive, insofar as is necessary for their salvation, at the knowledge of Christian revelation" (art. 32, p. 103).

ing attention to the actions contrary to it that its own zeal had prompted;[24] that fanatical preachers, whether from the pulpit or in works directed against other Christian communions, consign to eternal damnation the child who professes the worship imposed on him by birth, as well as the savage of the New World who is ignorant of the name of Christ.

This is therefore an immense step, an uncontestable improvement, in the practical doctrine of a Church proud of its immutability, when it disavows the maxim that, as we said, was never embraced in theory, but which she permitted or accredited for the longest time.

Thus Christianity is perfected, in the sense that it removes the additions that disfigured it less than a century ago. And even in the midst of the retrograde movement that some want to impart to the human race, men of all opinions are following—whether freely or out of compulsion, by craft or conviction—the new path that time guides them on. Time is always active, always irresistible.

24. The same condemnation of the *Emile* that we just cited contains these words: "Those who have never known the Christian revelation will not be saved, they will be condemned" (art. 32, p. 106). For having hoped for the salvation of pagans excused by invincible error, the author of *Bélisaire* was denounced by the Sorbonne, who kindly recalled on this occasion that the prince had received the material sword from God (art. 4 of the censure of *Bélisaire*, propos. XV, p. 121). It is impossible not to see in these two doctrines the struggle of the priestly spirit against Christianity.

BOOK VI

THE CONSTITUTIVE ELEMENTS
OF PRIESTLY POLYTHEISM

CHAPTER I

On the Combination of the Worship of Elements and the Stars with That of Fetishes

To a certain extent we have prepared our future path. We have indicated the first cause of priestly power, described its extent, and pointed out the path that priests have an interest in pursuing from the very origin of societies; we have shown the different direction, imprinted by nature on the free human spirit, taken among nations independent of priesthoods.

We therefore can proceed without fear of well-founded objections to the examination of free and progressive cults, as well as those that are imposed and immobile, determine their respective forms, and seek what the action of the religious sentiment is under one and the other of these forms, an action that is less perceptible the more dogmatic the collective authority is, and the more individuality is constricted. This sort of action therefore is harder to discern in priestly polytheism than in independent polytheism.

We will first of all treat priestly polytheism, then compare it with the latter. Before that, however, we need to tell the reader that even though we will show the path taken by the priesthood, we do not at all claim that in acting in this way it conceived such a determinate plan from the beginning.

The circumstances that we have described had to create its power.[1] According to the demands of the moment, these circumstances suggested its employment. By the fact that such a power existed, it imposed on its possessors the necessity of maintaining it; they were gripped by the need to extend it. Every class whose authority depends upon an intellectual superiority that it cannot preserve except by a monopoly is in a dangerous position. Every progress that happens outside it is a threat to it. And this danger, the same even in variety, imparts a uniform response

1. See above, bk. III, ch. 4.

to the class. It then seems to have conceived a plan, while it only follows the direction daily dictated by the threat of the day. This plan, however, which could not have been conceived at the beginning, soon results from the very prosecution of it. Experience enlightens; the priesthood sees that immobility, ignorance, and the degradation of everything not belonging to it are the very conditions of its existence. It encloses itself in an impenetrable enclosure, where it keeps everything of knowledge and science that it has harvested; it then declares a war to the death upon all science and all knowledge that show themselves without.

We therefore do not attribute to the priests of semi-savage times the gigantic project of governing the world. We only say that once formed by necessity into priestly bodies in different countries, given the position in which they found themselves, like all corporations they obeyed their interest. This interest led them to acquire and defend an empire that their successors over the centuries rendered even more unlimited.

We do not write out of hatred for the priesthood. We would have wished not to have to speak against any class of men, if only to avoid an appearance of partiality in investigations that, as we said, were intended to remain entirely apart from the debates and agitations of the moment. Is it our fault, however, if in the most remote ages we encountered an enemy we were not seeking? Is it our fault if this enemy, so little to be feared on the banks of the Orinoco or the steppes of Tartary, shows itself much more terrible on the banks of the Nile or the Ganges? Finally, is it our fault if we write at a later time when many memories have been effaced and many resentments have subsided, at a time when, as we love to acknowledge, an even milder and purer divine form has most fortunately distinguished the modern priesthood from the priestly despots of ancient times, tyrants at once of kings and peoples, that an imprudent audacity, confusing such different things, would awaken all the memories and take pleasure in reviving all the resentments?

Our work was written well before today's circumstances. If it appears in a few of its parts to be a book of circumstance, we are not to blame.

CHAPTER 2

On the Popular Part of Priestly Polytheism

In the climates that force men to observe the heavenly bodies, the first form of worship is astrolatry. In the countries where star worship is not natural, but where natural phenomena favor the power of priests, the first cult is the worship of the elements. However, the stars that follow their eternal course in the heavens above, and the elements, abstract divinities, so to speak, because their underlying unity escapes our senses, are not entities susceptible to being employed by the still-childish human being; he therefore cannot be satisfied with them.

The religious sentiment could be content. The more its gods are vague, mysterious, and above him, the more they please him.

It is otherwise with interest. Interest demands that its gods descend to earth to protect the human race at a more immediate level. Thus, while the privileged sacerdotal corporations put elements and stars at the top rung of the divine hierarchy, the multitude, finding itself outside these bodies, seeks or retains gods commensurate with its intelligence. Now, since it is kept away from all science and all study, its intelligence is barely more developed than that of the primitive. The gods of the multitude and those of the primitive are therefore pretty much of the same nature.

Among almost all the peoples subject to priestly polytheism, the worship of animals, of stones and trees, and of crudely fashioned little simulacra, and among tribes of a more martial bent, the worship of spears and swords, come to fill the immense distance separating the inhabitants of heaven from those of earth.

The Germans, whose priests offered worship to invisible or heavenly divinities, the air, water, night, sun, the vault of heaven, also worshipped animals[1] and trees

---

1. *Depromptae sylvis lucisque ferarum imagines;* Tacit., *Hist.*, v. 22. See bk. III, ch. 5, n. 20, with the citation from Gregory of Tours.

as fetishes. They washed the trees in blood;[2] they cast victims into rivers.[3] In other words, this was a combination of the two worships. The superstition still found today that each river in Germany is attended by a seductive, deceiving nymph, called by the people Nix, and who is charged with the death of those who perish in their waves, is probably a memory of this.

The astronomic religion of the Etruscans excluded neither the worship of betyles—that is, animated stones[4]—nor homage rendered to the prophetic woodpecker,[5] to the warrior's spear,[6] or to oaks covered with moss in the forests of ancient Latium.[7]

It is with the gods of this second sort that communication is the most frequent and direct. All the Egyptian festivals, those of Heliopolis excepted, were devoted to animal-gods,[8] and it was in their name that oracles were given.[9]

Individuals divided these secondary deities. Each man or each tribe chose a special protector from among them. This is what happened in Egypt with the animals. This is what still occurs in India with consecrated stones.

But priests have a great interest that man cannot approach his gods without an intermediary and conclude his business directly. As a consequence, the priesthood takes over the fetishes and brings them into a single body. Each is no longer, as among the blacks or the Iroquois, the personal ally of the worshipper who chose it. Grouped under a common banner, they form a regular army, as it were, subject to

2. Agathias, I.

3. The capitularies of Charlemagne prohibited this worship (*Cap. Car. Magn.*, I, tit. 63).

4. Ovid, *Fast.*, IV; *Monde Prim.*, I, 8. On the *Lapis manalis* of the Etruscans, see Spanheim, *De veteris latii domestic. religionibus*; and Festus, v. *aquae licium*.

5. Dionys. Hal., I, 2.

6. Clem. Alex., *Cohort. ad gentes*; Arnob., VI; Spanheim, p. 11; Justin., XLIII, 33; Schwarz, *Bemerkungen ueber die Aeltest. Gegenst. der Verebr. Bey den Roemern nach Varro.*; Tit.-Liv., I, 10; Serv. *ad* Virgil, X, 423; Lucan., *Phars.*, I, 136;. Pliny, *Hist. nat.*, XII, I;. *Aeneid*, XII, 766; Festus, v. *Fagutal*; Tibull., I. *Eleg.*, 11.

7. The worship of trees in Latium gave rise to a custom that one would call into doubt if several undeniable authorities did not testify in its favor. When a fugitive found the means of cutting a branch in the forest of Aricia near Rome, a forest consecrated to Diana, he would present it to the priest of the goddess, who was obliged to fight him, and whose place he took if he killed him (Lucan., III, 86; VI, 74; Ovid, *Fast.*, III, 271; *Met.*, XIV, 331).

8. One must not forget that Isis and Osiris had been animal-gods, Isis a cow, Osiris the sparrow hawk. The reader will see in chapter 4 of this book what mystical senses of more than one kind were grouped around these vestiges of fetishism.

9. Herod., II, 82.

the laws of a mysterious discipline. In the assistance they give to those who ask for it, they are directed not simply by the consideration of the meats offered to them or the honors given, but by a will that comes from even higher and that substitutes calculation for instinct and despotism for anarchy. Each species of fetish is brought together under a head, the archetype of the entire species.

We have found[10] the germ of this idea in the worship of savages. The priests took hold of it and developed it.[11] Apis, Anubis, and Bubastis were gods of this sort.[12]

The priesthood thus diverts toward a single individual deity the worship that previously extended to all his peers, while orienting the latter to their natural objectives: work, death, and everything for which men wish to employ them. It thus reconciles the exigencies of superstition with the needs of society. In addition, it gives a more solemn character to the consecrated object. Each individual no longer has an idol that belongs solely to him, but a generic divinity. To please this divinity, he has to have recourse to its ministers.[13]

In principle, this is the make-up of priestly polytheism. At the beginning, it differs from crude fetishism only by, first, the introduction of celestial or invisible divinities that have little relationship with their worshippers, and, second, the putting in common of once-separated idols who continue to be the gods of the people.

10. Above, bks. II & III.

11. Diod., I, 1; Ael., *V. H.*; Ptol., *De Afric.*, IV; Euseb., *Praep. ev.*, III, 4; Plut., *Sympos.*

12. Jablonsky, *Panth. Aeg.*, II, 60. Apis, the representative of bulls, Anubis of dogs, and Bubastis of cats.

13. If priests act this way with respect to fetishism, whose nature seems to resist such a generalization, for even greater reason will they take similar precautions to stop the superior gods from being exposed to too easy communications. This effort is remarkable vis-à-vis the worship of fire. Once discovered, fire ought to shine in all the huts, serve all the needs of all families, and be at the disposal of every individual. But the priests institute a sacred fire of which they alone are the guardians and authorized agents, without which no ceremony is permitted. Even the fire destined for the most common functions of life, at certain times has to be lit by pontifical hands with a flame brought from the altar (Hyde, *De rel. pers.*, p. 19; Maimonid., *Tract.*, VI, 16). Traces of this practice passed into Greece where they were preserved, especially at Delphi, where all the ceremonies come from abroad and alien to the public religion were brought together, and in the temples of Ceres and Proserpina, mysterious divinities honored by rites different from the ordinary ones (Pausanias).

Nonetheless, the tendency inherent in the human spirit resists this effort, or at least combines submission and resistance. It does not reject the priestly god; but it does not abandon its initial notion. Even though Anubis had his temple at Cynopolis as the celestial representative of dogs, many of his fellows in the same city had their particular worshippers (Strabo, XVII).

It later distances itself even further as these idols are likened to human form. This happens independently of the will of priests, or even in defiance of it. Finally, it is distinguished from the primitive savage cult by the symbolic meanings that establish certain relations between the fetishes and the gods of a higher nature. As we will explain, these relations unite, but without identifying, the science of the priests and the belief of the people.

None of these things, however, addresses the religious sentiment in order to be purified or ennobled by it. Considered from the moral point of view, religion has made no progress. A small number of men have monopolized its influence; they have robbed from the majority of their fellows what until then had been their property. As for the rest, no improvement occurs; the form is different, but without being better. It even has this further vice, that it opposes an obstacle to any improvement that did not exist in the former order of things.

But the intellect has laws it is constrained to follow, despite its calculations and even despite its interests. These laws govern the priesthood, it resists them in vain; they force it to open another path besides the public religion; they oblige it to create a secret doctrine wholly different from the fables believed and the doctrines imposed. Priestly polytheism then becomes a much more complicated system; we will talk about it in the following chapter.

CHAPTER 3

On the Secret Doctrine of the Priestly Bodies of Antiquity

In order to form a clear idea of the secret doctrine of the priestly corporations of Antiquity, we first of all have to note that this doctrine divided into two very different branches. The first was composed of the results suggested to priests by the observation of stars and planets and the phenomena of nature. It constituted a science rather than a religion.[1] This science upon which the power of the sacred caste rested had to be preserved for it, and made inaccessible to the rest of the people. Hence, the oral traditions that never left the sanctuary; hence, the mysterious books that remained eternally closed to the multitude.[2] In them were placed the astronomical calculations, the physical discoveries, the remedies indicated by the barely begun study of disease, and the effects of medicinal plants on the human body; in addition, the means of reading the future with the aid of the stars or

---

1. The notorious barbarism of some peoples whom we know were dominated by priests, such as the Thracians, led several authors to deny that any scientific teaching was the property of these jongleurs of almost savage tribes (Iebb. *ad* schol. Arist., I, 118). On the contrary, however, nothing is more compatible than the exclusive ownership of a mysterious science by a corporation and the highest degree of degradation in everything outside this circle. In response to others who exalt the wisdom of these theocratic institutions, one must also add that the praise they lavish upon them would be a disservice to them if the exaggeration was not obvious; for the more one supposes the priesthood to be enlightened, the more one declares it guilty of having voluntarily kept the human race in a state of inhuman degradation.

2. Among the Etruscans, such were the Acheronitic books and rituals of Tages, containing precepts of agriculture, legislation, medicine, rules for divination, meteorology, and astrology, and a metaphysical doctrine we will talk about later; in Egypt, such were the books of Mercury Trismegistus; among the Indians, such were the Vedas, the Puranas, the Angas, and their innumerable commentaries; and such was the divine wisdom of the Druids among the Gauls.

natural phenomena. In a word, everything that two thousand years later Varro will designate under the name of natural theology or sacred physics.

But the very existence of books or traditions of this sort was an invitation to the priests to add to them whatever suited them, a possibility of which they made ample use. Accounts that attributed to them the invention of all the arts, the establishment of laws, the founding of cities, and, finally, the transition from the savage state to civilization;[3] the marvelous modes of communication that had established such intimate relations between heaven and its favorites; rites destined to eternalize the memory of these revelations; institutions dictated by the gods, the division into castes, and all the privileges of the priestly order were enshrined by these traditions or saved in these books.

History itself entered, although under a legendary guise. Expeditions undertaken by the order of priests or directed against them; the prosperity of the kings they had served; the misfortunes, crimes, and fall of the tyrants who had resisted them; natural calamities, the chastisement of peoples, political upheavals, the punishment of kings: all were combined in a fictional chronology and presented with a gilded mythology. These accounts, these annals, and these ceremonies had only a superficial connection with the priests' secret doctrine. The priests, moreover, had an interest in letting them escape in bits and pieces from the darkness that covered them. The crowd was thus struck by an even greater respect for its teachers and guides.

The second part of their secret doctrine is of a more elevated nature, and consequently truly mysterious. The study of celestial bodies and natural phenomena starts by observing certain facts. These facts have causes. It is in the intellect's nature to seek them. To be sure, at the period we are describing the intellect was confined within a narrow circle; and it was the monopoly of a very small number of men who worked assiduously, often with success, at stifling its impulses. But these dark monopolists, these merciless privileged priests, were after all men themselves, and nature had to make itself felt across the fetters they imposed on the disinherited class, and which they attempted to impose on themselves.[4]

3. In a certain perspective, these narratives were not deceptions; for example, it is incontestable that agriculture in Egypt depended upon the calculations by which the priesthood had determined the regularity of flooding, and the theocratic laws of India were certainly the work of priests; they could even claim to be the first founders of the laws.

4. Since no human effort wins a complete victory over natural laws, progress occurs even in the priestly religions, albeit slowly and by contorted paths. But then it has this that is peculiar: with in-

The priests therefore asked themselves what were the beings that presided at the creation or ordering of the world, why did these beings have the will to do so, how were they invested with creative power? Of what substance were they? To what did they owe their lives? Are they one or many? Dependent or independent of each other? Self-movers or compelled by necessary laws?

These questions inevitably present themselves to the mind; and in whatever situation in which it finds itself, in whatever circle it encloses itself, the mind wants to answer them. Its nature constrains it to want to do so.

Here the priests entered into an entirely new career. Without abandoning the sacerdotal character, they took on that of metaphysicians and philosophers. And if they maintained the public religion unchanging and stationary, they also gave themselves over without scruple to the boldest and most abstract speculations.

Independently of mythical accounts and prescribed rites, the Indian books contain numerous, quite different, metaphysical systems. The magi were divided into several sects; and we can discern the same diversity among the Egyptians.

What is truly remarkable is that the hypothesis that most dominated in the sacerdotal doctrines was subversive of all religious ideas. It was pantheism, an abstract theism that implied the uselessness of all worship and the unavailing character of all prayer. In the final analysis, it was atheism under different forms. In their secret doctrine, the Chaldean priests attribute the origin of the world to a necessity without intellect, a force without will. This same necessity, this same force, they say, governs the world through immutable laws. All the beings that exist—products without purposes, forms without permanence—emerge from chaos and return to it. Thought itself is only the chance result of blind elements. There is no life to come where virtue will be rewarded or crimes punished.[5]

This absence of religion in the secret doctrine of a caste whose power is rooted in religion can be explained by the position of this caste. When in possession of its native liberty the human mind reflects upon the infinite, upon eternity, on

---

telligence being concentrated in a caste, progress occurs only in this caste; and with the interest of the caste being opposed to progress, far from being proud of it, it hides it from all eyes, pretending to have always known what it just learned. In free religions, however, with each change operating via changing opinion, it is perceived even before it is fully realized. New ideas show themselves without concealment; everything occurs in broad daylight. Priestly religions, in contrast, change behind closed doors in the darkness. Forms, expressions, and rites remain the same; everything is immobile until the final destruction of these religions (*Encyclopédie progressive*, art. "Religion").

5. Phil., *De migr. Hebr.*; Sext. Emp., *Adv. math.*, V.

the relations of the invisible world with the material world; sentiment takes its place among the judges and participates in the decision. But the position occupied by the priestly corporations of Antiquity had to suffocate and destroy the religious sentiment within them. Everywhere there is calculation, cunning, and self-interested aims, that is, the project of making religion an instrument and bending it to a goal not its own; the religious sentiment first withers, then it disappears.

From their beginnings, the priestly corporations of ancient peoples saw themselves called to transform religion into a means of power. For the Brahmin, the magus, and the priest of Heliopolis, the cult was a trade, as it was for the jongleur. In this respect, it does not matter whether it was exercised with finesse or not, ignorance or learning. Fraud, deception, and lies were its constitutive elements. In excluding belief, fraud degraded the worship. The priest who invents the purported means of communication with heaven knows even more firmly that his inventions are a fraud when he has artfully arranged them to make an impression on the credulous crowd. Profiting from his knowledge of astronomy when he announces the return of an eclipse as the frightful sign of divine anger, he cannot deceive himself concerning the falsity of the cause he is affirming. While the multitude prostrates itself, he remains a stranger to what is truly religious in the emotions of the multitude. He shares neither its terrors nor its hopes, because it was he alone who stirred them by proclaiming himself the interpreter of a voice he does not hear, the minister of an intervention that does not exist. He wants to deceive, so how can he believe?

Thus, the priestly corporations had to lose the capacity for religious sentiment by the mere fact that they degraded religion by employing it for their own self-interest. The only thing that remained to guide them in the meditations the religious sentiment would have contributed to if the priesthood had not stifled it was dry, severe logic. However, every time one puts the soul and its emotions, the conscience and its interior revelations, outside the pale, disbelief, doubt, and even denial fight with at least equal arms against the hopes that our heart constantly demands.[6]

6. "Every religious belief has a characteristic that ought to strike us: inevidence. ... Certainty is not evidence. This word 'evidence' has been overused, it designates a quality of the object; while the word 'certainty' expresses more specifically a state of the subject. Evidence is in the idea or in the fact; certainty is in the man who pronounces on this fact or this idea. ... Evidence is relative to the general and rather defined organization of the human species; certainty to a certain extent depends upon the different, and changeable, states of individuals. There therefore is a great number of truths about which we can obtain the most adequate certainty, which we cannot deny without lying to our

Atheism opposes to these hopes striking contrary arguments. It shows the universal order—invoked by belief in its favor—being disturbed every day by exceptions whose roots are found in the universe itself; these call into question the intelligence or power or goodness of the supreme cause. They mock final causes, charging their proponents with begging the question, or arguing in vicious circles. In a way that is truly deplorable, they exult at the gradual enfeeblement of the soul, which they say is the result of the body's organs and thus shares their decline, and dies when it does. Great is the disadvantage of the religious person who wants to fight by reasoning alone! It can only end badly if he only calls reasoning to his assistance, and not the certainty imprinted by heaven on the bottom of our soul.

The rival of atheism, pantheism presents itself with arguments no less strong, and even more seductive colors.[7] At the sight of all these partial beings, similar

conscience and our reason, and which nonetheless are lacking in the character of evidence; among these, even at their head, are those that are the object of religious beliefs" (*Mémoire en faveur de la liberté des cultes*, by Alex. Vinet).

7. Pantheism is the natural opponent of polytheism: polytheism divides the forces of nature; pantheism reunites them. Atheism is the natural adversary of theism: theism divides everything into two substances, spirit and matter; atheism denies the former and admits only the latter. Thus the philosophers of Antiquity who left polytheism in great number fell into pantheism, while the moderns who rejected theism declared themselves atheists. Pantheism is evidently more reasonable than atheism. Even though forced to recognize the existence of intelligence, the atheist considers it to be only the result of certain partial and transitory combinations; in his eyes, it is the accidental product of a necessary organization and fermentation. In this system, one can imagine that all intelligent creatures disappear from the world and the world would still subsist. We speak here of the atheists who argue as materialists, like the author of the *System of Nature*. This is because at bottom this atheism is only a reaction against dogmatic spiritualism; even though it seems at first glance to be more positive and susceptible of proof, because it appeals to experience, it is unable to explain many phenomena, and it is based upon an entirely gratuitous presupposition. By regarding the intellect as an essential, indestructible, inseparable part, as a sine qua non condition of the existence of the universe, pantheism avoids this reef.

Speaking generally, one cannot deny that until now pantheism has been only weakly and ineffectively attacked. The famous article of Bayle against Spinoza draws from a metaphysics to which the least schoolboy of our days would not subscribe. Bayle bases himself on the difference between extension and thought, as if we knew extension, and as if we knew what thought is. He draws pitiful objections from the idea that with God being all, he ought to be each individual and each separate thing; here dead, there living; here sad, there happy; here cold, there hot, as if he did not know that Spinoza distinguished between the one substance and its modes, between reality and appearances. His other arguments drawn from the coexistence of truth and error, and from the perfections and the felicity of God, are no stronger. Bayle, however, was a good logician; but logic is worthless when it leaves its sphere.

to fantastic dreams, reentering into the indefinable whole only to reemerge, then return again, who has not been tempted to call these appearances into question, and to see in the universe only one real substance, whose brief modifications are similar to shadows cast by objects or stars reflected on the water?[8]

We would go even further. When the religious sentiment is not halted by the imperious need for moral hopes, it finds some attraction in the prospect of plunging into pantheism. There exists between us and all the parts of nature—animals, plants, the winds, the waves, the heavens—a mysterious and ineffable correspondence that seems to reveal to us that we are all parts of the same being, torn from its bosom by a violent separation, but in so transitory a way that it is all but illusory, and that we must return to in order to overcome the division that torments us, as well as the individuality that weighs so heavily upon us. The disposition of our soul to pantheism is such that the mysticism of all the religions, as well as the extreme abstraction found in all the philosophies, ends with this result. Compare the verses of Xenophanes, the eloquent prose of Pliny, the symbols of the Brahmins, the hymns of the Persian sufis, the allegories of the Neoplatonists, the expressions of certain Muslim sects, and those of Japan and the Chinese educated class, the intoxication of our quietists, and the new metaphysics of a German philosophy, and you will find pantheism differently put forth, sometimes in words that are remarkably similar. Yet pantheism is no less destructive of the distinction between the Creator and the creature, of all retributive justice, and all special providence in the first, and moral merit and efficacious prayer in the second; in a word, of everything that could satisfy the religious sentiment.

To be sure, in recognizing that dry and haughty logic gives these doctrines certain unfortunate advantages, we do not insinuate that the hopes of the religious sentiment are false. The reader has already seen as early as our first book that we contest the jurisdiction of reason in whatever does not relate to physical nature and to the relations established by men among themselves. For everything that is not restricted to these spheres, an élan of the soul seems to carry more conviction than the most rigorous syllogisms of logic. Still, the point we have articulated is nonetheless true. From this it follows that irreligion among the philosophers of independent peoples who follow the natural course of their thoughts has often been combated, even overcome, by the invincible resistance of the religious sentiment. On the other hand, irreligion in the bosom of the priestly corporations of Antiq-

---

8. Comparison drawn from the creed of the Brahmins.

uity encountered nothing that resisted and moderated it. Open what remains of the sacred books of the nations bent beneath the theocratic yoke, remembering that these books were exclusively destined to priests. In them you sometimes will see a pantheism that, by identifying the world and its author, reduces all beings to seeming modifications of a single eternal substance; sometimes the denial of any intelligence presiding over the order of the universe, that is, a blind material necessity, substituted for all the conceptions the religious sentiment suggests or demands.[9]

This has been noted long before us by a great number of learned observers who by different routes have arrived, sometimes surprising themselves, at this unanimous, although strange, conclusion: that the secret doctrine of the ancient priesthoods was subversive not only of the particular religions in whose name they ruled, but of all religion whatsoever. We distinguish ourselves from them on only two points.

First of all, they noted a fact; we have sought and pointed out the cause.

In the second place, they have concluded from this fact that these irreligious systems exclusively made up the secret doctrine, which they considered as a coherent whole, one that was connected to a single thought around which were grouped secondary parts of a regular edifice, with ideas all of the same sort, homogeneous among themselves, exempt from contradictions, and contributing by their combination and harmony to the demonstration of the chief thought. Our view is wholly opposite. We believe that the priestly corporations of antiquity did not

---

9. We would have preferred to preface this part of our investigations with the history of philosophy among the nations independent of priests, especially among the Greeks. What we say here would be more complete. The reader would better see how the human mind arrives successively at the hypotheses among which it is divided. One cannot distinguish the different periods of the priestly philosophies and their gradual progress because the priests, being the only philosophers, covered their philosophy with the same veil as religion. In Greece, on the contrary, despite the efforts of some heads of sects to imitate the obscurity with which the oriental priesthood surrounded it, publicity was the rule and mystery the exception; the development of opinions and the succession of doctrines are easy to follow. An insurmountable obstacle, however, brings us up short. Greek philosophy emerged only after the introduction of several priestly doctrines into Greece, and the principal philosophers of this country, especially the Ionian school, took over these doctrines to make them the basis of their systems. The knowledge of these borrowings is therefore indispensable for every history of Greek philosophy. To want to account for it before having discussed the foreign elements that it appropriated would engage us in a vicious circle.

have a single doctrine, and we see the proof of this in the facts, and their explanation in the manner in which their secret doctrine was formed.

Born with the priesthood at the very moment when necessity imposed upon it the law of acquiring the various sorts of knowledge without which society could not subsist, this doctrine was the receptacle and depository of these various forms of knowledge. As they grew, as others came to swell the mass, or as conjectures, suppositions, and systems, true or false, were associated with them, the gradually observed facts, the successive discoveries, and the hypotheses resulting from these facts and discoveries were all placed there in layers, as it were.

Priests always add, and they never subtract. They always add because these additions were required to maintain their doctrine at the level of their own understanding; they never subtract because each retrenchment is an innovation; moreover, the unity of doctrine does not matter one whit to the corporations taken in their entirety. What do these corporations want to do? Dominate. They have the public cult as means, imposed as a yoke and maintained by inflexible laws. Their inner doctrine had relevance to the vulgar only because it inspired more admiration for the holders of the august and impenetrable secrets. From this point of view, the nature and coherence of these secrets was rather irrelevant: individuals attach themselves to different opinions; but the esprit de corps chooses arms, and views with equal indifference truths and errors. In fact, the variety of hypotheses served the priests even better in the explanations they had to give to initiates and foreigners. Partial responses tailored to the dispositions of hearers were most suitable; and the more numerous and different these systems, the more inexhaustible the arsenal of the priesthood.

Let us take the priests of Egypt as an example. They satisfied the gullible Herodotus when they showed him the similarity between their fables and those of Greece; they flattered Plato's inclination when they showed him the most subtle metaphysical notions as their inner doctrine, while they lowered themselves to purely human interpretations with Diodorus, with the events of history reworked in symbolic form being the basis of the religion that the people revered without understanding. They thus flattered each in his preferred opinion, accordingly as he strongly held it or had the flexibility to modify it.

The most opposed hypotheses thus coexisted under the same veil and were designated by the same name. Side by side, atheistic or pantheistic systems, theism, dualism, perhaps even skepticism had their place, and each of these systems was divided into several branches. Pantheism sometimes allied itself with spiritualism, with matter then being conceived as an illusion of the pure spirit. This is how it is presented in modern India, and probably was presented in ancient Egypt. Other times it identified itself with materialism, and what was only one form became the sole substance, spirit only being a deceptive result of these merely apparent modifications of this substance. In this version, it reigns in Tibet, Ceylon, and China.[10] Elsewhere, the unique substance was infinitely divisible, and countless imperceptible atoms were made the constitutive parts of the great Whole, which nonetheless remained changeless and always the same.

Theism also separated into two distinct categories. Submitting to the yoke of logic, sometimes it lost everything that was mild and consoling and no longer offered man that particular Providence whose immense love receives our prayers, accepts our repentance, absolves us of our faults, and has pity on our sufferings. God, creator of the world, had impressed upon it general unchangeable laws that no supplication, no merit, no appeal to justice or goodness could alter. From the instant that this world had received the divine impulse, all events—we would go further: all sentiments, all thoughts—were subject to a chain of necessity which nothing had been able, nothing could, break. Causes had had to produce, they would produce forever, their inevitable effects. In this way, at bottom theism was only a more vivid form of invincible fatality:[11] a sad and disheartening hypothesis which repels sentiment; for it does not demand, like the self-interested fetishism of the primitive, that the being to whom one offers homage should satisfy earthly passions or lend a mercenary support to even culpable desires; nor, on the other hand, does it implore a voice that could answer it, an approval that would sustain it, a heavenly sympathy that would revive it when injustice or adversity assail it.

10. In Chinese pantheism Thai-Kee is the prime matter, the infinite chaos, inconceivable by the understanding, endowed with capacity, greatness, extent, force, and identity with all things, the heaven in the heaven, the earth in the earth, the elements in the elements, without beginning or end, directing everything but without will; producing all but without intelligence, without real movement, at rest in the core of its nature, having divided itself only apparently into two forces, the active and the passive, the Li and the Ki, or, following another terminology, the Yang and the Yin (*Dialogue de Tchin* in Du Halde; *Chou-King* of Deguignes, p. 311). The author of the Latin catechism for Tonkin says that the Tonkinese suppose a material substance, without intelligence and life, that they call Thaieuc, from which come two other substances, Am and Duam, the heaven and the earth.

11. This category of theism was the one that best accorded with the scientific part of the priests' teaching. It explained the constant regularity of heavenly bodies, their uniform courses, their periodic revolutions. It accounted for all the appearances of necessity that the material universe displayed, and it had to satisfy the priestly intellect, which, as we said, was separated from the religious sentiment.

By thwarting this hope, you cast it back upon itself disconsolate, and it is then tempted to sunder itself from a belief deprived of all warmth and life.

Other times, deviating from its original rigor, theism combines with emanationism. Beings separated from God, and always less pure as they grow farther from their source, nonetheless can return to it by successive purifications. This system, which is obviously contained in the secret doctrine of the Egyptians, soon enough emerged from the sanctuary and was introduced into the public belief. Only (and here we commend the priesthood) it was acts of liberality, obedience to priests, and the exact observance of the rites commanded by them that were the means of purification.

Dualism itself was presented in two forms: one that granted a complete parity, an equal force, and an equal duration to the principle of good and the principle of evil; and one that reduced the latter to the status of an inferior being, reserving a definitive victory for the first.

Some have maintained that skepticism was always foreign to the occult doctrines of the priesthood.[12] We grant that of all the systems skepticism was the one the priests had to most carefully conceal. Affirmation always has something imposing: it announces science or it implies authority. It can present itself as a discovery, gather together those who profess it, and give them a common interest. But skepticism, which does not allow affirmation, brings its adherents together only to disperse them, like light troops who by chance fall upon whomever they encounter. Skepticism, whose tendency is to dissolve and disunite, and which calls into question every authority, its own included, is what is most repugnant to the priestly spirit. However, a writer[13] who has long and carefully observed the Brahmins tells us of a school of Brahmin skeptics, and even though we cannot ascribe extensive learning or solid critical skills to him, when it is a question of a positive fact, his testimony is not without value.

In truth, it is impossible to think that among men protected by the darkness that surrounds them, and taking on from every angle those questions that are eternally insoluble, none would have been led to skepticism, which is the natural term of all these investigations, a conclusion that reason comes to consider as a shelter as

12. Up to the present day, says the author of the *Traité sur la sagesse et la langue des Indiens*, even in the midst of the numerous variations that are found in their books, no one has discovered any book that contains a true system of skepticism (Schlegel, *Weish. der Ind.*, p. 152).

13. Abbé Dubois, *Moeurs, institutions et cérémonies des peuples de l'Inde*. He calls this sect Nastica (II, 98).

soon as it ceases seeing it as a stumbling block. If one has not detected skepticism in the doctrines of the priesthood, it is because this system more than any other had to be hidden from the inferior classes marked out for belief, who must not suspect that their masters were reduced to doubt.

All these doctrines were jammed into the secret philosophy of the priests, more ready to mix and blend than to do battle with one another; two causes combined to make this sort of confusion easy.

The first was the terminology that the priests saw they were obliged to employ to express their metaphysical hypotheses. At the moment when they began to occupy themselves with the arduous questions of the origin of things, ignorance on several points was still quite profound, while the knowledge of other points was mixed with many errors. Language, above all, was very imperfect. To convey the notion of cause and effect, it only had words derived from the simplest and crudest ideas, those for example of to engender and to be born.[14]

These words were applied in a thousand ways. To be born does not only mean to be produced, but to be subsequent to an object, or to be inferior to it, or even simply to have borrowed some quality from it, or having received some modification from it. One said of all the properties, all the forces, all the attributes of a substance, that they were born of it, that they had been engendered by it. Applied without distinction to all the systems, this terminology established among them an apparent likeness that made their real opposition less striking and pronounced. The pantheist showed the great Whole engendering the illusion that deceives us by making us see diversity in the unity; the god of theism equally engendered the creatures who become corrupt by going away from their source; and to express the production of the world by an eternal necessity, the atheist had recourse to the image of generation, or, more fantastically, he said that the necessary being had broken up and the universe was born of its fragments.

In a moment, we will return to another effect of this priestly language. Here we limit ourselves to indicating how it brought together divergent hypotheses under similar expressions.

A second cause favored this confusion.

Even though looked at collectively the priestly corporations of Antiquity could not feel any respect for the religion molded by their hands and bent to their purposes, from time to time the religious sentiment that always returns reasserted its

14. Heyne, *De Theog. Hes.*

rights over certain members of these corporations, or over initiates honored with their confidences. Then suddenly reintroduced into the most unbelieving doctrines was an enthusiasm that denatured and disguised them. The soul struggled against logic, and the native emotions of one imposed a form that appeared to be religious upon the arid conceptions of the other.

Listen to Apuleius depicting the pantheism of Egypt, or the disciple of Krishna giving thanks to his master for the revelation with which the heavenly incarnation had just favored him. "O Nature!" cries the former, "sovereign over all the elements, daughter simultaneous with the origin of the centuries, supreme divinity, queen of manes, first of immortals, unchanging figure of gods and goddesses, who with a nod gives the heavens their luminous shafts, winds their healthful breath, to the netherworlds their terrible silence; the unique being whom the universe venerates in a thousand ways by varied rites, under different names, and whom those who are versed in the ancient doctrine call Isis, it is you whom the Egyptians know how to worship by suitable ceremonies that they have transmitted to the Greeks; it is you who surrounds the globe, inflames the sun, governs the world, treads underfoot Tartarus. The stars answer you, times obey you, gods rejoice because of you, the elements are subject to you; at thy breath the winds breathe, the clouds swell, and seeds germinate and grow. Your majesty strikes with a holy terror the birds that tremble in the air, the wild animals that cross the mountains, the serpents that slide in the grass, the monsters that the Ocean contains in its depths. You are the constant and holy protector of mortals, whom you care for with a maternal affection in their afflictions, and whom you receive in your bosom after their death, where everything returns, because everything has come from you."[15]

"Great god," cried Arjuna when Krishna appeared in his true form to him, wearing brilliant robes and magnificent garlands, with countless eyes and mouths, holding in his millions of arms swords, ready to strike, exuding celestial perfumes, and covered with all the marvelous things that shine separately in the universe; "Great god! I see in your breast all the divinities brought together, and all the classes of different beings. I see Brahma on his lotus throne, and from the saints to the celestial serpents. I see you yourself on all sides, with your infinite forms, your eyes, your mouths, your arms that no one can count; but I cannot discover either your beginning or your end, nor your middle, universal lord, eternal source of the worlds. I see you with your resplendent crown, armed with a bludgeon and a terrible sling,

---

15. Apul., *Métam.*, II.

like a shining globe that no one can look upon. You are resplendent with an ineffable brilliance, like fire in all its force and the stars in all their glory: the sun and the moon are your eyes; your mouth is a volcano that spouts flames. The celestial hosts do not know whether they ought to flee or approach you. Some seek shelter with you; others, frightened, extend suppliant hands and sing your praises. When I contemplate you surrounded with so much light, decorated with so many colors, my courage abandons me. When I regard your menacing teeth, emblems of time, which devours all beings, I remain motionless and confounded. I see the warriors of armies and the sovereigns of the earth fall into your mouth, as into a burning furnace. Some remain suspended between your teeth, their bodies severed. But finally all of them, all these heroes of the human race, are engulfed in this abyss, like the rivers that run rapidly and lose themselves in the Ocean, or like a swarm of insects casts themselves into the flame that draws them in to consume them."[16]

Some of these words are eloquent; several seem to indicate a profound sentiment of immensity, of power, of the supremacy of a God distinct from the world he governs and the generations he creates or destroys. But at bottom these are only the fine and touching irrelevancies of individuals who yield to their emotions, which perhaps deceive them into the intoxication of such sonorous expressions.

The symbolic language of the priesthood always introduces into the formulations of pantheism a contradiction that sometimes gives it the external appearance of theism. The principle of pantheism is to not distinguish the whole from its parts. But since when the whole is personified, relations are established that necessarily imply the existence of the parts, the notion of diversity that pantheism would like to avoid reenters the doctrine; and it protests in vain against the accusation of duplicity leveled against it. It is thus that in the same Bhagavad Gita cited above, Krishna says: "I am the humidity in the water, the light in the sun and moon, the entreaty in the Vedas, the sound in the air, human nature in man, perfume on the earth, and devotion in the pious soul; I am the intelligence of sages, the glory of the proud, the strength of the strong. All things are suspended from me, as precious stones on a ribbon that holds and supports them."[17]

By this even Krishna, who claims to be the sole existent, differs from the partial existences, as the ribbon from the precious stones. This extorted inexactitude in the expressions, however, changes nothing in the core of the system, and disguises

16. Bhag. Gita, English trans., p. 90.
17. Bhag. Gita, pp. 69–70.

rather than changes it. This Nature, which Apuleius appears to make an intelligent and compassionate divinity, in the Egyptian teaching is nothing but an impassible Whole, of which partial beings are only forms produced aimlessly, and which it annihilates without pity. This universal lord of the world before whom Arjuna prostrates himself is only the universe itself; and the Bhagavad Gita from which we have drawn this enthusiastic passage contains the system of pantheism that is at once the most subtle, the most rigorous, and the most foreign (as we will see) to every heartfelt sensibility, as well as the most destructive of morality.

This is the perspective in which one should envisage the metaphysical part of the secret doctrine of the priests of antiquity. This doctrine does not limit itself to one system. The hypotheses generated by each series of meditations were received and registered in it. Since no religious sentiment had a hold over the corporation (considered as a collective body dominated exclusively by its self-interest), irreligion was not rejected, but rather was admitted as equal to any other theory, on the condition of remaining a mystery. The corporation profited, moreover, from this diversity of systems by adapting its confidences to the character of each auditor, all the while constantly attentive to preserve the external appearances of unity. Thus, those who have seen theism, dualism, pantheism, and even atheism in the priestly philosophies are both right and wrong. They were right: all these things were there; they were wrong: none was there by itself.[18]

18. What explains, and to a certain extent excuses, the writers who have fallen into this disdain is that, philosophically speaking, all the doctrines tending to merge into pantheism have a certain similarity, at least in the path they follow. Theism with its general laws, the only one that rigorous logic can admit, is distinguished from pantheism only because it recognizes two substances, one intelligent and active, the other inert and without intelligence; here logic finds no obstacle, and even derives from its arguments more than one encouragement to reunite these two substances.

Dualism, which proclaims two beings, one good, the other evil, is led toward the fusion of these two beings in a single being by the comingling of good and evil and the way in which they give rise to, and return to, one another. We see the proof of this in China. The Yang (the heaven, the sun, the heat, the day, the masculine kind, the primitive fire, health, and happiness) is the good principle: it is represented by the straight line. The Yin (the earth, the moon, the cold, the night, the female kind, the primitive water, disease, unhappiness) is the evil principle: it is figured by the curved line (*Yi-King*, couplet, *Confucius Sinarum philosophus*). But almost immediately the two principles are reunited in the great material Whole, the Tai-Kie.

The doctrine of emanation in a way is only a provisional theism; because even though the beings separated from the Supreme Being are individuals as long as the separation lasts, since individuality is a transitory state, one that is *contra naturam* because the tendency of all partial beings is to reunite in the great Whole, and because once this reunion is effected everything is absorbed in the same sub-

Let us now summarize what we just said about the composition of priestly poly-theism. Its basis is astrolatry, or the worship of elements, under which is placed fetishism. Above this vulgar worship hovers a scientific system that the priesthood works to perfect, and which it always holds beyond the reach of the subject classes. To this system of science, which is but the observation of facts, are joined the efforts to discover their causes, and these endeavors end with philosophical and metaphysical hypotheses. These hypotheses do not at all form an ordered whole; each exists apart, unknown by the people. They therefore can neither scandalize the people by their impiety, nor perplex them by their discordance. Finally, these three elements are clothed in one or several symbolic languages, which result both from the imperfection of language and from the priests' tendency toward mystery.[19] These terminologies in turn express (1) the relations of the superior gods,

---

stance and all individuality disappears, such a theism must end in pantheism and remain there. The system of the atomists, ostensibly opposed to pantheism, nonetheless ends with the same result. The atoms, which are infinite in number and of an extreme subtlety, are one and the same substance in which the appearance of division does not constitute real diversity.

When atheism contents itself with denying a first principle of everything that exists, it only broaches the surface of questions, because it does not go deeper into the fact, one of whose causes it rejects; this was the mistake of the majority of unbelievers in the eighteenth century. The atheist, however, only has to go a little further and he is led to join with those of a pantheistic view who, making matter the real substance, consider spirit an illusion. One must not conceal this truth: once the religious sentiment is put to the side, pantheism is the end of all the doctrines. From the crudest fetishism to the subtlest theism, one sees it open its immense arms to seize hold of them and absorb them in itself. What can save the religious sentiment from this metaphysical aberration is that it has need of an object of worship and love outside itself; but it is not abstraction that can lead it there. In treating the decadence of polytheism we will see the head of the Neoplatonists, Plotinus, begin from abstraction in order to arrive at the knowledge of the Supreme Being; but despite his enthusiastic soul and his quite sincere efforts, he constantly fell back into pantheism.

19. We flatter ourselves that this development will fully respond to the objections of one of the men of France whose extensive learning and good faith we most appreciate. Mr. Guigniaut has re-proached us for *not having taken enough account of that spontaneous observation, that intuitive and necessary study of nature and the world, which results in a science, a primitive philosophy, contemporane-ous with the formation of religious systems.* "All things, more or less," he says, "belong to deep Antiquity, where sentiment and thought, idea and belief, science and religion, were joined. It is the priests who have made—not religion, because it is eternal, inherent in the nature of man, identical with reason, the good, and the beautiful—but the religions that have passed through the world, proportioning themselves to the learning and needs of the time, mixing with the errors and passions of men. The priests, however, having always begun by being the learned of each period, as they were more or less the first legislators of all peoples, did they not have to put in the creeds that they proposed to the implicit

astronomical or elemental, with the fetishes or gods in human form; (2) those of metaphysical beings or abstractions with the divinities of the people[20] and the superior gods; and (3) the relations of cosmogonic personifications with the axioms of science and the objects of public worship. But they have yet another consequence.

From the words "to be born" and "engender" result cosmogonies and theogonies that appear behind the popular mythology at a remote distance, as it were. The infinite, the void, and the creative, preserving, and destroying force become a class of gods heretofore unknown, whose loves, rapes, incests, and mutilations represent the different hypotheses aimed at explaining the creation of this universe.[21] Going beyond religion by metaphysics, the priests return to it by the cosmogonies that

---

faith of their contemporaries the relative understandings that, being revealed to the people with the character of absolute truths, also had to command their own belief, and appear to them to be the most solid basis of the religious and political edifice that they wanted to erect?" (9th note on Cr., pp. 895–97). We are ready to agree (with a few reservations concerning the date of the introduction of science into religion and the religious sentiment of priests) to this judgment of Mr. Guigniaut, provided that for his part he grants us that the priestly understandings changed nothing in the crudeness of public superstitions, and by the very fact that it based its power on science, that the learned caste used its ascendancy only to disturb the necessary proportion between the beliefs that pass through the world and the enlightenment or needs of the time.

20. Thus, for example, to express the variety of apparent forms assumed by elemental matter, the soul of Fo passes successively into the bodies of a host of animals: the ape, a dragon, a white elephant; and the worship of these animals connects fetishism to pantheism.

21. It is not useless to observe that these legends greatly resemble each other among peoples who are the furthest removed from each other. Everywhere one finds the cosmogonic egg. The Phoenicians speak of the breath (πνευμα) that was seized with love for its own principles and engendered matter. Matter rounded into the shape of an egg, and from this egg came the wind Kolpiah and his wife Baau, whose names recall the Kol-pi-jah and the Bohu of Genesis. They engendered time and the firstborn, the human race. Among the Egyptians, Cneph produces the egg, from which comes Ptah, the orderer of the world (Euseb., *Praep. ev.*, II; I. Olympiod., *ad* Plato, fragm. *Orphic.*, p. 510).

In China, Pangu keeps himself in an egg for eighteen hundred years, and the parts of his body— precisely like those of Ymer in Scandinavia and like the Indian egg of Pradjapat (see below, bk. VI, ch. 5), become the sun, the moon, the earth, the forest, and the rivers (*Cosmogonie de Taot-Zée*, in couplet, *Tab. Chron. Monarch. Sin.*, p. 13). Everywhere the cosmogonic gods also come together incestuously; Brahman produces Bhavani, nature, the visible world; she has three children, Brahma, Vishnu, and Shiva, and changes into three daughters to wed her sons. Among the Etruscans, Janus and Cama are brother and sister, and husband and wife (Lydus, *De mens.*, p. 57). Everywhere these gods also mutilate themselves. These coincidences prove that all these conceptions belong to the same period of understanding, and the language in which man at this period was forced to express them.

this metaphysics suggests to them. Personified and endowed with will, life, and action, the cosmogonic beings are all the more imposing as they are vague. These gods hover over the public belief, sometimes entering into it, and above all they imprint on it their somber, mysterious, often obscene and revolting colors. Delayed as much as possible even though they are inevitable, the partial revelations in that way become less unexpected, and have a less dangerous effect because less brusque, and the parts that from time to time escape from the secret doctrine are admitted into the public religion with less trouble, and are harmonized more easily with it.[22]

The theogonies and cosmogonies furnish it with incoherent fables and overload it with enigmatic ceremonies;[23] it is to this cause that one must attribute those wild and licentious orgies that are so strange a part of priestly cults. In order to make more sensible the contrast and the union of the creative and destructive forces, the priests of these cults display with great pomp the bloody signs of their shameful mutilations, or fight fiercely at the foot of their altars in order to express the struggle of the elements.[24] Sure of its power, the sacerdotal esprit de corps spares them no pain, and transforms its instruments into victims. Religion, however, in its relations with the multitude remains unchanging, because it is upon religion that the power of the priestly corporations and the authority of the theocracy rest. The priests who within the sanctuary disdain or denature religion with

22. The priests of Egypt found the means of profiting from indiscretion instead of fearing it. After having transformed their metaphysical notions into symbols, they explained these symbols by fables, then confided these fables to their disciples, not as new, but as not revealed until then. Their goal was not that the fable thus confided would remain secret; they wanted it to be circulated gradually, as having always been a part of the religion. What was important to them was not the secrecy concerning the fable, but secrecy concerning its date; and that could not be betrayed because no one knew it; in that way indiscretion served their purposes. This is demonstrated by facts. The fables relative to Osiris, secrets at the time of Herodotus, were known at the time of Diodorus (Diod., I, 21); but then new fables were the objects of new confidences and new secrets.

23. Often it is impossible to determine if the popular rituals come from the secret teaching, or if the explanation of this or that ritual had not suggested a hypothesis that became part of the doctrine. The priests of Thrace preferred night to day for their religious ceremonies; but did not this preference manifested in their public rites come from the mysterious idea of a primitive night, principal of all, an idea admitted in their secret doctrine; or did this mysterious idea come from previous practices to which they wished to assign the cause? Did the material cult of fire give rise to the system of emanation, or did this system introduce the worship of fire into religion? We pose these questions in order to indicate the influence that each of these things could have had on the other.

24. In the temple of Hierapolis, the priests fought among themselves in order to represent the opposition between the active principle and the passive principle.

their interpretations, without practice all its rites with remarkable ardor—perhaps the awareness of their indifference toward its opinions serves to warm them for its practices. Be that as it may, convinced of the necessity of keeping the multitude always fervent, and of offering an example of this fervor, they compel themselves to the most minute practices, as well as the most painful deprivations. The Brahmin and the bonze impose fasts, austerities, starvations, and even tortures upon themselves, which only the most sincere devotion should undertake. The Brahmin's secret doctrine is a pantheism that cannot admit any worship; the bonze[25] is a veritable atheist because he recognizes only—albeit under a different name—a material world lacking in intelligence.[26] But in exchange, reserving for themselves the inner doctrine that declares only absorption or nothingness for man, in public the bonze and the Brahmin proclaim the immortality of the soul and promise happiness in another life to those who enrich and honor them.

This combination whose fundamental traits we have traced here subsequently differs in details according to climates, local situations, the genius of peoples, their habits, even the accidents that influence their destiny. But the core never varies. We will prove this by successively applying the principles we have developed to the religion of Egypt and that of India.

25. Generic name of the priests of Fo, called in China *seng* or *boschang*, in Tartary lamas or *lama-seng*, in Siam talapoins.

26. Unbelief in priestly philosophies did not abolish either the religious language or the observance of cultic worship. Sugat, an atheistic philosopher who lived at Kikof in the province of Behac about two thousand years before Jesus Christ (a thousand years after the beginning of the Iron Age) believed only in visible things. He wrote many books against the established religion, claiming that actions found their reward or punishment only in this life. But he also threatened his adversaries with future sufferings; and in the fragment of one of his writings that has come down to us, he paints the dead recalling their previous existence and desiring to see the kingdoms of the day again. The Buddhists say that Fo, after having taught during his entire life (which was marked by admirable mortifications) teachings that, despite their excessive abstraction, were colored with a religious tint, gathered his disciples near his deathbed and honored them with a particular confidence. He told them that until then he had taught them only his exoteric teaching. "My secret doctrine," he continued, "the sole truth, the fruit of all the meditations of the intellect, what it discovers by its sublime efforts, is that nothing exists: everything is an illusion; there is nothing real but the void and nothing." His hearers respectfully received this confidence; it became their hidden teaching; but they did not cease putting at the head of their works the same formula as the Brahmins, the word "om," symbol of the attributes of the divinity (*Asiat. Res.*, IV, 175), or to perform the ceremonies, or to devote themselves to works of penance that only a lively faith can make a duty.

CHAPTER 4

Example of the Foregoing Combination in the Egyptians

The combination we just described is clearly seen in Egyptian polytheism.

First of all, we see the worship of animals: the cat receives divine honors at Bubastis; the billy goat at Mendes; the bull at Hieropolis; the eagle and the sparrow hawk at Thebes and Phile; the ape at Arsinoe; the crocodile on the lake of Moeris; the ichneumon in the Heracleotic prefecture; elsewhere the ibis, the shrew, the dog, the cock, the lion; at Elephantine and Syene, the oxyrhynchus, lepidotes, and the eel.[1]

People have wanted to explain this worship in several ways; none of them bears serious scrutiny.

To speak, as does Diodorus, of the metamorphoses of the gods is to account for an absurdity with a fable.

To go back to the banners that different tribes would have raised is to reverse the order of things. A people can choose as a standard some representation of what they worship; but they do not worship this-or-that object because they have chosen it as a standard.

The policy of kings seeking to divide their subjects by giving them different objects of religious veneration is a maladroit application of Euhemerus's system,

---

1. For a fuller listing, one can consult Des Brosses, *Culte des dieux fétiches*, pp. 31–32; Strabo, XVII; Ael., *Hist. an.*, X, 23.

At the time of Maillet (*Descr. de l'Egypte*, p. 175), one still saw vestiges of this worship in the care given to the animals that were fed and maintained in buildings devoted to this practice. Plutarch (*De Is. et Osir.*) claims that the inhabitants of the Thebaid did not worship gods who had been mortals. He says Cneph was their only god; thus, they did not contribute to the maintenance of sacred animals. A partial fact inflated into a general truth probably inspired this assertion, against which many other facts testify.

which, as we know, related the origin of all religions to the machinations of legislators. But fetishism was prior to every positive law. Favored by the self-interest of a class, it was able to prolong itself under civilization by the action of authority; but it had to arise freely in the bosom of barbarism.

Finally, we have already shown that the usefulness of different species counts for precious little in the worship that savages offer them.[2] It was the same in Egypt. Useful and harmful animals were equally adored.

When a belief is shaken, it is difficult to imagine what its former credibility rested on. Then one attributes a thousand kinds of subordinate utility to it, none of which is enough to cause it to be adopted, and which only provide after the fact an apparent explanation of what has become inexplicable.[3] Thus in our days Lent has been justified by saying that it helps fishermen because of the rule of abstinence from meat; but those who first imposed abstinences upon themselves only had in mind pleasing heaven.

If the explanations of Diodorus are superficial, those of Plutarch sin by excessive subtlety.

To hear him, sometimes the worship of animals is owing to metempsychosis.[4] But such as primitives conceive it, metempsychosis can hardly serve as the basis of a cult because, vague and erratic in its conjectures, it prescribes neither pity nor respect for the animals whose bodies are the harbors of wandering souls.[5]

Sometimes, he says, understanding animals as the work of the evil principle, the inhabitants of Egypt would have wanted to disarm the principle by adoring them. But this assertion was dictated to the philosopher of Chaeronea by his tendency to find dualism everywhere; it is belied by the facts. Far from being the creatures

2. Bk. II, ch. 2.

3. This was the error of Mr. de Pauw, a writer nonetheless endowed with a remarkable sagacity: "The utility of certain animals," he says (*Recherches sur les Egyptiens et les Chinois*, II, 119–120), "could have motivated their worship in Egypt. Even though quite removed from this worship, the Turks nonetheless did not permit the killing of the ibis. By adoring the crocodile, certain cities in Egypt ensure the maintenance of the canals necessary for them to have potable water, and by which these animals travel to them. The maintenance of these canals was, in a way, under the protection of religion." In writing these lines, how did Mr. de Pauw not see that he refuted himself? Since the Turks, who are very removed from fetishism, protect the ibis without worshipping it, and because the killing of serpents belongs to them, the Egyptians would not have needed to worship crocodiles in order to spare them, and their religious homage toward these amphibians would have another cause.

4. This hypothesis was reproduced by Aeneas of Gaza in the fifth century.

5. Bk. II, ch. 4.

of the evil principle, in the Egyptian view the animal-gods were its enemies, and to appease it they sacrificed them.

Sometimes, finally, Plutarch exhausts himself in efforts at detecting and bringing to light an imaginary resemblance between the qualities that characterize certain species and those he attributes to the gods; but these gods had to already exist in order to note the resemblances, and it was only later that they could have enriched the symbolic language.

In his conjectures, Porphyry comes closer to the truth. According to him, divinity embraces all beings; it also resides in animals, and man adores it wherever it is found. But Porphyry expresses here only the first élan of the religious sentiment in fetishism. He does not account for the combinations by which the worship of animals takes on a regular form and continues long after man has placed the divinity high above physical nature.

The writers of our days have been even more unfortunate in their attempts. There are those who have imagined that the Egyptians worshipped animals only in order to recall the meaning attached to each of them in the hieroglyphs.[6] But if the Egyptian religion was only a kind of writing, a calendar, or an alphabet, it was not a religion. If its scientific meaning was hidden from the people, what idea could the people have of the forms in which the occult calendar or hidden alphabet was cloaked? How could they conceive gods created to signify periods or letters, but whose meaning was concealed from them?

One cannot repeat this too often: what constitutes a religion is the manner in which its adherents understand it.[7]

6. Dornedden, in a German work entitled *Phaménophis*.

7. As much as it is uncontestable that an application of the names of the Egyptian gods to astronomy took place, and that the mythology of Egypt was employed as a calendar, it would be equally unreasonable to claim that it was employed only in this way. Every system that wants to limit the mythology to one purpose is not exactly false, but partial and incomplete. The mythology of a people contains all the mass of knowledge that it was able to acquire in its childhood, but which, by a natural consequence of the poverty of its language and its writing, it could render only by images. Now, this mass of knowledge is not limited to astronomy. As much as they can, the priests occupy themselves with all the sciences; they bring them into their systems, give them a sacred terminology, and the names of the gods that they had used to indicate their astronomical calculations also serve the same purpose in other sciences. If we grant, therefore, that in the astronomical system of Egypt, Osiris was the year, Menes the week, Thauth the first month, it does not follow that outside this system, by means of another combination, these gods did not indicate entirely different things. To limit them to a single meaning is to act like a man who has read only one book and concludes that the letters he has found

The discovery of a cult in vigor among the primitives that is perfectly similar to the external worship of the Egyptians ought to put an end to these fanciful hypotheses.[8] Place among black tribes corporations of priests who have come to the knowledge of the movement of the stars, and who preserve this knowledge in their sanctuary away from the curiosity of the profane: these corporations will not seek to change the objects of vulgar worship; on the contrary, they will solemnize them;[9] they will give them more pomp and regularity. Above all, they will ensure that the assistance of the priesthood is necessary in every ceremony. Then, by means of a mystical or symbolic meaning, they will attach these material objects to their hidden science; and you will have among the blacks exactly the religion of Egypt. Fetishism at its foundation, astrolatry at its ceiling, and within a science founded on astronomy, thanks to which the fetishes, gods for the people, will be symbols for the priests.[10]

To invert this order is a gross error. What was recognized for a long time as a sign cannot suddenly be transformed into a god; but it is easy to conceive that what passed for a god in the opinion of the masses can become an allegory, a symbol, or a sign for a more enlightened class. In this way Plutarch's idea receives its application, and frivolous or fanciful resemblances motivate the choice of symbols. The ox Apis[11] owed to a few spots, at first accidental, then artfully repeated, the

---

can express only ideas contained in that book. This can be proved with incontestable evidence. This same Thauth was in another sense the symbol of the intellect; this same Menes, the symbol of the world; this same Osiris, that of agriculture (Heeren).

8. We see, says Heeren (*Ideen*, II, 664), the worship of animals from Ethiopia to Senegal, among peoples who are completely savage. Why seek another origin among the Egyptians?

9. The priests say that Isis had ordered the consecration of some animal to Osiris, which was destined one day to enjoy the same honors as the god, either during its life or after death.

10. What we offer here as a supposition is precisely what happened. In speaking of the influence of colonies on the establishment of priestly power, we have pointed out those that came from Meroë to civilize (or rather: to enslave) Egypt. They came in rather large numbers, and were independent of each other, but all were led and governed by priests. Now, notes Heeren (*Ideen*, II, 569–75), it was a rule of the Ethiopian priestly caste, wherever it directed its colonies, to attach the natives to them by adopting a part of their external worship, and by assigning animals they worshipped a place in their temples, which became the common sanctuary and the center of the religion of all.

11. Apis was black in color, but shining, and thus represented the passage from darkness to light; he had on his right shoulder a round white spot, emblem of the moon, and a square one on his forehead, emblem of the year; under the tongue, the image of the beetle, whose horns indicate the

honor of being one of the signs of the zodiac.[12] A studied analogy between the productive force and the Mendes billy goat made it the heaven, father of the stars; the cat owed to his shining fur, as the ibis its equivocal color (which appeared halfway between the night and the day), to be the symbol of the moon; the falcon became the symbol of the year.[13] The beetle, which spends six months under the earth, was the emblem of the sun.[14] And what proves that popular superstition combined with science is that the Egyptian believers wore beetles on their necks as amulets or talismans.[15]

It was the same with trees and plants,[16] fetishes no less revered than the animals.

The leaves of the palm, whose longevity seemed to be a divine privilege,[17] decorated the couches of priests, because this tree, putting forth branches every month, marks the renewal of the lunar cycle.[18] The lotus, which we will also encounter in India, the cradle of Brahma[19] as well as Osiris,[20] the *perséa* brought from Ethiopia by a priestly colony,[21] the *arnoglossum* whose seven sides recall the seven planets, and which for this reason was called the glory of the heavens;[22] all these plants had connections with astronomy.[23]

---

crescent. The hairs of his tail were in double tresses, expressing the double movement of the moon and the sun.

12. Gatterer, *De Theog. Aeg. Com. Soc. Goett.*, VII, 1–16.

13. Creuzer, *Symbol.*, II, 323.

14. Zoega, *De obelisk.*, passim, and above all p. 547. He also was the symbol of Neith and the warrior caste (see above, bk. V, ch. 5). We will see later that each symbol had more than one meaning.

15. Denon, pl. 97; Schlichtegroll, *Dactyl. Stosch.*, II, 38.

16. Egyptians' veneration for trees has continued into our day. Mr. Denon recounts the scandal that French soldiers caused when they cut down an old trunk revered from time immemorial by the natives (*Voy. en Eg.*, I, 229).

17. Ol. Cels., *Hierobotan*, I, 534.

18. Diod., I, 34; Pliny, *Hist. nat.*, XIII, 17.

19. Maurice, *Hist. of Indost.*, I, 60.

20. Plut., *De Isid.*

21. Diod., I, 34; schol. Nicandr., *Therapeut.*, 764.

22. Kircher, *Oed. Aegypt.*, III, ch. 2.

23. Not wanting to prove again already established truths, we will not expand here on the importance of astronomy in the Egyptian religion. We send those of our readers who desire more details to all the works where this subject was treated, and for those who prefer a short and luminous summary, we recommend note 13 of the third book of Mr. Guigniaut, pp. 895–931.

The people saw in them objects of an ancient worship; the priesthood found characteristics that helped recall and perpetuate its discoveries.

To these initial elements of worship were added the influence of localities,[24] which sometimes disturbed the uniformity that the priesthood attempted to establish, and sometimes combined practices that referred to a particular location with rites founded on the general principles of science.

Hence, on one hand came the diversity of animals that were worshipped by the different tribes of Egypt. If they were only symbols, would the priests who seek to make their institutions uniform have introduced such varied, and irreconcilable, symbols? These varieties are explicable only by the condescension of the priesthood to the previous habits of the peoples.[25]

Hence, on the other hand came those jumbled allegories not connected by a common bond, forming many separate strata, as it were. Apis, for example, first of all the prototypical manitou of bulls, then depository of the soul of Osiris[26] (and in this capacity the sun), finds that he has a third meaning that is somewhat intermediate between the two previous ones. He is the representative of the Nile, the river that nourishes the country; and while his color, the arrangement of his ebony black skin, the spots of striking whiteness that must cover his forehead, and finally the length of his days, which cannot exceed twenty-five years, all come from

24. No people in the world were more marked by the reality of localities than the Egyptians. This is because Egypt, almost at the same moment and in the same places, offers the most opposite phenomena, hence the most likely to strike the imagination: the most abundant fertility beside the most sterile sands; the deadest and most arid nature beside a vegetation whose lushness Europeans could hardly conceive. This influence of localities is strengthened by the way Egypt was populated. A narrow valley crossed by the Nile, surrounded on two sides by a chain of mountains, limited at the north by the sea, at the northwest by a sandy desert, it was formed of the lime of the river, and the art of man had to conquer it gradually. Upper Egypt, the Thebaid, had to be habitable sooner than Lower Egypt. The priestly colonies therefore arrived at different times, at different points, independently of each other. They adopted as the bases of popular worship the animals worshipped by each primitive tribe, which were not everywhere the same. In this way, the priests of these colonies reconciled to themselves these nomadic tribes, brought them into their temples, and took control of all the power of habits and memory.

25. Vogel, *Rel. der. Aeg.*, pp. 97–98.

26. Diod., I. The soul of Osiris passed at death into the body of the bull Apis, and successively into all the bulls that replaced him. In this notion there is something analogous to the divinity and immortality of the llama. The needs of the priests being the same in all the priestly religions, fables often have a resemblance that cannot be explained when one fails to recognize the identity of positions and views.

astronomy; the festival of his birth is celebrated on the day the cresting of the river begins. He is led in pomp to Nilopolis and, when the end of his time has come, is cast into a fountain consecrated to the Nile.[27]

Historical facts also appear to have entered into the Egyptian religion. Several of its stories seem to allude to the wars of pastoral peoples. The death of Osiris, emblem of the sun in winter, could have been originally the commemoration of a real event;[28] Osiris, then, would have been, not exactly a deified man, but a hero later associated with a divinity that had never participated in the human condition. This is why the monuments of Egypt show him sometimes looking like a mummy, and history speaks of his tombs, while Isis always remained a stranger to particular places and the different forms of departing from this life.[29]

Metaphysical hypotheses came next.

Pantheism is unmistakable in the famous inscription engraved at Sais on the temple of Isis[30] and Neith: "I am everything that was, all that is, all that will be."[31] The Egyptian priests added that Neith and Ptah, intelligence and force, were not separate beings but different manifestations of a universal being. Hathor, the boundless, elementary night, was that primordial unity that knew all beings and made one with them. It was the great Whole, the sole existing being, the unique god not yet manifest.[32]

---

27. Ael., II, 10. In the same way, Anubis, the prototypical manitou of cats, becomes the horizon in the astronomical religion; for this reason, he is simultaneously a god of the heavens and a subterranean god.

28. Herod., II, 128.

29. Zoega, *De obelisc.*, pp. 302–73.

30. Macrob., *Saturn.*, I, 20. It is for this reason that Isis was depicted, like several Indian divinities, surrounded with the symbols of the four elements: the salamander, eagle, dolphin, and lioness.

31. Plut., *De Isid.* A proof that metaphysical hypotheses, of which pantheism is one of the principal, were not introduced except after the popular religion and the astronomical religion is that the inscription of Sais is subsequent to Herodotus: he does not speak of it.

32. *Deus in statu non manifesto;* Damas., *De princip. cep.*; Wolff., *Anal. graec.*, III, 236; Euseb., *Praep. evang.*, III, 6ff.; Iambl., *De myst. Aeg.*, VIII, 5. From this introduction of pantheism into the Egyptian teaching results another consequence that has discouraged the commentators by the confusion it caused. Each god in its turn is represented as the great Whole, Osiris in Diodorus; Isis in Apuleius; Neith, who says of herself: I am the past, the present and the future (Procl. in *Tim.*); Serapis, whose head is the firmament, his ears the air, his body the sea, his feet the earth, his eyes the torches of the sky. The Nile, finally, a local and hence restrained god, is sometimes called the father of all the divinities (Diod., I) and is represented by the circular serpent, emblem of eternity.

Alongside this pantheism, although probably from a less distant period, appear evident traces of theism.

"Escape all these common limits," says the spurious Hermes Trismegistus,[33] "cast yourself far from your body, escape time, become eternity, recognize yourself as immortal, capable of understanding everything and doing everything. Be higher than any height, more profound than any depth; be at once in all the parts of the world, in heaven, on earth, and in the depths of the waters. Grasp in a single embrace all the cycles, all the measures, all the qualities, all the vast extents, and you will be able to comprehend what is God. He has neither limit nor end; he is without color and without figure, eternal and unchanging goodness, the principle of the universe, reason, nature, act, necessity, number, and renovation,[34] stronger than any strength, more excellent than any excellence, above all praise, and only to be worshipped by silent adoration.[35] He is hidden because he has no need to appear in order to exist. The times manifest him, but eternity veils him. Consider the order of the world, it must have an author—a single author—because in the midst of countless bodies and the most varied movements a single order makes itself seen. If several creators existed, the weakest would be envious of the strongest, and the disorder would lead to chaos. There is but one world, a soul of the world,

33. Herm. Trism. no. 12, *De Communi.*

34. *De regeneratione, hymnus,* no. 1.

35. Poemander, no. 2. Porphyry (*De antro nymphar.*) says that the Egyptians venerated in silence the source of all things, and from that came the mysterious statue of Harpocrates, with the finger on the mouth. But here we have an example of the double meanings attached by the priests to each religious notion or personification. They had connected the idea of silent adoration with astronomy: this was the star that is on the head of the dragon in the southern hemisphere of the Greek sphere. Aratus speaks of it. One does not know, he says, what this figure is; ordinarily it is called a man on his knees: he seems to bow, bending his knees and raising his arms in the air (Arat., *Phén.,* v. 64; Cic. *De nat. deor.,* II, 43).

Nixa genu species, et Graio nomine dicta
Engona sis, ingenicla vides sub origine constat.
Engonasin vocant, genibus quia nixa feratur.
(Manil. V. 644)

This figure is found on obelisks. See Denon, Caylus, *Antiq. égypt. étrusq.,* etc., n. II; pl. VII, n. 4; VII, n. 12. The object of its worship is the lyre, before which it prostrates itself. The Greeks sometimes made it Lycaon asking for his daughter, sometimes Theseus raising the stone under which was hidden the fatal sword, sometimes Atlas or Hercules (Herman, *Myth. Handb.,* III), because the fable recounted that Hercules had once replaced Atlas and held up the world in his stead (Hyg., 2, *Fest. Avien., ad* Arat.).

one sun, one moon, one god.[36] He is the life of all, their father, their source, their power, their light, their intelligence, their spirit, and their breath. All are in him, by him, under him. He preserves them, makes them fruitful, and directs them."[37]

Nonetheless, even this theism falls back into pantheism. After this listing of all the epithets, this accumulation of all the attributes, the fundamental axiom returns: one alone is all, and all is but one.[38] Outside of him there is neither god nor angel nor demon, nor even any substance.

The doctrine of emanation also combines with theism;[39] sometimes the movement comes from the bottom, sometimes from the top. In the first case, the soul emanates from matter, intelligence from the soul, God from the intelligence.[40] In the other case, secondary gods emanate from the supreme god, demons from gods, men from demons, birds from men, quadrupeds from birds, fish from quadrupeds, reptiles from fish. The lower animals then mount back to heaven by the same path when they are sufficiently purified by their different metamorphoses.[41]

But soon a bond is established, on one hand, between these metaphysical hypotheses and the astronomical gods, and, on the other, between these same hypotheses and the idols of the people.

The sparrow hawk that can be found on the door of all temples is not only the sun but also the symbol of the divine nature. The shrew that the inhabitants of Athribis worshipped, and whom the Egyptians believed was blind because its eyes are so tiny that they can hardly be detected, signifies for the metaphysician the incomprehensibility of the first principle.[42] The ibis is not only the symbol of the moon but also of Hermes, because Hermes measured the rise of the Nile, and the ibis at the time of the flooding eats the serpents and insects that infest the banks of the river. The Ethiopian vulture figures the passive principle because, it was said, there was no male in the species; and for an opposite reason the beetle, born without the cooperation of a female, is the emblem of the active principle. Thus in Egypt, as elsewhere, the errors of physics are sanctified by religion. Upon

36. Mens *ad* Mercur., no. 11, Asclepiad., p. 121.
37. Herm. *ap.* Cyrill. *adv.* Julian., 33–34; Cedren, *Chronolog.*, p. 26.
38. Herm. Trism., no. 12.
39. Goerres, II, 425.
40. Ibid., II, 422.
41. Ibid., II, 427.
42. Plutarch.

becoming a victim, the prophetic gazelle[43] bequeathed its horns to Hermes Anubis, who learned from her the division of the day into twelve hours; the lotus, a local symbol in its connections with the Nile, an astronomical one in its relations with the sun, cosmogonic as the nuptial bed of the two first principles, reappears in the metaphysical sphere as the emblem of rebirth or immortality. The onion, the most ridiculed and most famous of the fetishes, thanks to the skins that compose it, and which seem to be so many spheres contained one within the other, is the vegetal image of this vast universe, always different and always the same, where each part represents the whole.[44] In other words, the symbol of pantheism. In this perspective, one can understand the importance the Egyptians attached to it.[45]

Finally, for the reason we indicated in the previous chapter, the cosmogonies and theogonies appear. Those of Egypt, like those of all the priestly nations, are the figurative expressions of metaphysical hypotheses concerning the origin of things. Hador, the elemental night, engenders the first gods, Cneph, Ptah, and Neith, who soon dispute their mother for preeminence. They come into the received religion: Neith becomes Isis, Cneph and Ptah both take the name of Osiris. But in their quality as cosmogonic, they cannot remain in the beaten path, and by a mystical nuptial or a forced incest (because contained in the womb of their mother) they in turn engender other divinities. Aroueris is the fruit of the precocious loves of the sister and brother; the birth of Anubis is due to an incestuous adultery, that of Harpocrates to the monstrous union of death and life.[46] Variable symbols of different doctrines, these gods represent, accordingly as they apply to one or another

43. When the rising of the Nile becomes noticeable, the gazelle flees into the desert (Arat., *Phén.*, v. 330).

44. Goerres, I, 291.

45. If the intellectual divinities of Egypt had been contained in the fetishes or popular divinities from the beginning, how would it have occurred that, besides these popular divinities, one would have worshipped intellectual divinities? If Isis under her form as a heifer was already divine wisdom, where did divine wisdom worshipped under the name of Neith come from? This is inexplicable unless one supposes that the priests sometimes presented their secret doctrine in one way and at other times in another, according to the need of the moment. They said to those whom they saw were greedy for novelties, and were disabused of some parts of the popular religion, that their doctrine was different from it; to others who still respected the Egyptian form of worship, they presented their abstractions as a more sublime part of the religion. Divine wisdom appeared alternately under a name that was foreign to the vulgar religion (that of Neith) and under the same name as Isis. She retained her adherents, and those of new ideas were also satisfied.

46. Plut., *De Is. et Osir.* Isis had Harpocrates by Osiris, after he was killed by Typhon.

of these doctrines, matter and the spirit that coordinates and animates it, the creative forces, both preserving and destructive, that struggle with each other, the two principles of good and evil, or, finally, the apparent divisions of the sole substance, that is, sometimes theism,[47] sometimes dualism,[48] and other times pantheism.

Obscene images and licentious tales enter into the religion simply by the effect of the words borrowed from the union of the sexes. Isis crosses the earth to find the organs of which a cruel enemy has deprived her spouse, and her journeys are marked by indecencies and new incests (we will later see the influence of these symbols on the public ceremonies and rites).

At the same time, these gods are connected to science properly speaking; they are the planets. Isis is the moon; Typhon the sad and baneful Mercury; Osiris the sun whom death strikes twice a year: in the spring, a period of excessive heat brought to Egypt by the winds of the desert; in autumn, when the country hidden beneath the waters wonders if the waters that submerge it will destroy it or make it fertile. But, once more, these gods take the names and forms of animals. The cow is Isis, Osiris the sparrow hawk, Typhon the crocodile; and the sphinx that is found on Egyptian coins of the time of Hadrian, because of his complicated attributes, is at once the bringing together of the animals worshipped by the people and the figure of unity in the pantheistic doctrine of the priests.[49] Thus the theogonies and cosmogonies create a new species of mythology that combines, by means of its mystical sense, with philosophy, and by its literal sense, with superstition.

Another circumstance further complicates this combination. The hieroglyphs have an effect almost parallel to that of the cosmogonies. All the hieroglyphic signs being images, the one who makes use of them cannot render his thought except by clothing it in narrative or fabular form. For example, is he trying to indicate an

47. It is worth observing that even to express theism the Egyptians make use of similar images; only the gods do not engender each other. The eternal and unique Being engenders himself; he is alternately his own father, his own spouse, and his father and his son (Firmicus, *De error. profan. religion.*, p. 115).

48. Dualism is expressed by the violent exit of Typhon, who, engendered by the primitive night (or according to others, the earth), leaps from the maternal womb, tearing it. Nephthys, the wife of Typhon, is also an expression of dualism. Sometimes beautiful and seductive like the Mohanimaya of the Indians, sometimes hideous and sinister like their Moudhevi or Boudevi, she is opposed to Isis, as they are to Lakchmi, wife of Vishnu; she deceives, intoxicates, desolates, and destroys.

49. This sphinx is beardless, a lotus on its head, covered with a veil that falls to its feet; an overturned crocodile emerges from its breast, a serpent crawls nearby, a griffon clings to his back holding a wheel, the emblem of the great Whole among many peoples.

astronomical discovery? He designates the different stars by animal figures or other objects that are thought to act upon each other. Hence a number of narratives that in the eyes of the people take on the authority of a revelation, or at least of history. Thus are born several sacred traditions of the Egyptian priests concerning their gods or their kings.[50]

But no matter how the combination of these religious elements happens, and whatever the significance one gives to the symbols, a uniform rule is invariably observed. The gods that the people implore, those that influence its destiny, are always closer to the fetishes than to the symbolic divinities. The Egyptians explicitly said that Osiris, Isis, Horus, Typhon, and his wife or concubine Nephthys were gods of the third class; and even though later they equated them with the planets, they distinguished them in this classification—a contradiction that only better proves the complexity of their doctrines.

It was in their quality as animal or anthropomorphic gods that these beings were worshipped, that they heard prayers and took part in the affairs of mortals. As metaphysical notions or planetary gods, they had meaning only for the priests;[51] and if the progress of science sometimes led to modifications in the rites and the legends (modifications of which there are traces),[52] the spirit of the public religion never felt these modifications.

This complexity of the Egyptian religion, its symbols, its allegories, its constant stream of significations and meanings, in which the most recent or more subtle did not cause the forgetting of the previous ones—all this explains the contradictions found in the majority of ancient authors.[53]

When Plutarch considered the gods of Egypt as local divinities, and for him Osiris is the Nile and Isis the earth that the river makes fertile; when he later rises to the astronomical meaning, and Osiris is the sun and Isis the moon; when else-

---

50. For example, that which relates to Mars (Herod., II, 64) is of the first kind; that which relates to Rhampsinitus (ibid., p. 122), the second. This observation comes from Mr. Heeren (*Afric.*, 499).

51. One of the three sects that divided Japan, the Shinto, whose Dairi is the pontiff, hence the most priestly, offers no worship to the supreme God, but does to the inferior *genii* (of which they recognize 33,333, whom they call Camis).

52. See the excellent work of Mr. Guigniaut, I, 801–3.

53. According to Cheremon, the Egyptians recognize only the planets as gods. According to Iamblichus, independently of the harmony of the spheres, they worship the superior intelligences and place a kingdom of moral liberty above that of material necessity. Each of these hypotheses had a part of the truth.

where he embraces metaphysical or cosmogonic theories, making Osiris and Isis the active and passive principles, and, following the terminology of the Platonic philosophy, the first is the soul of the world, the second is the matter put in order and animated by this universal soul, and Horus their son is the visible world, the result of the overcoming of Chaos, of Typhon, the evil principle contained in matter, which struggles against the divine spirit that ought to animate it: assuredly Plutarch contradicts himself; but if there is contradiction, there is not error. All these meanings existed in the Egyptian doctrine; and Plutarch did not really begin to be mistaken except when he adopted one over the others.[54]

One also understands that by reversing the order of ideas and the course of events, one could construct brilliant and rather plausible systems in favor of a purported Egyptian theism. This was what Jablonsky did, for a long time the sole guide of scholars, who became commentators on his positions. If we are to believe them, the Egyptians would have believed initially in theism alone; but the division of the attributes and activity of the Supreme Being would have given rise to several conceptually distinct divinities. And alongside these divinities, others would have been placed that were aimed at striking the senses; these would include the moon, the planets, and the heavenly vault. To these eight gods would have been joined the solstices and the equinoxes, and soon enough the five intercalary days. The worship of the Nile would have been one of the results of the devastation and benefits of the river. Finally, priestly symbols employed to enigmatically signify the divine nature would have introduced an inferior cult.[55] We will not point out all the particular errors of this system; we will limit ourselves to saying that one must reverse the series of hypotheses and start from the combined worship of fetishes and stars in order to detect them in the secret doctrine of the priests, transformed sometimes into conceptual deities, sometimes into a single God who creates and

54. It is curious to compare these explanations with those of Synesius and Diodorus. Synesius sees only history reworked in fables by priestly traditions. Queen Isis and Osiris king of Egypt are chased from the throne by Typhon, who himself had been cast out because of his crimes. The scepter falls between the claws of wild animals, and the sacred birds sadly lower their heads. But the gods strike the oppressors with a panic terror: Osiris revives and brings back the golden age. In Diodorus, on the other hand, one recognizes the introduction of Greek ideas. Osiris is the inventor of wine. Behind him walk Apollo and the Muses. The conqueror distributes the Greek provinces to his favorites: to Macedon, Macedonia; to Maron, Thrace; to Triptolemus, Attica; these are the successors of Alexander brought back to an earlier time.

55. Jablonsky, *Panth. Aeg.*

directs the universe, sometimes into a sole substance that absorbs in its bosom this universe, these divinities, and the supreme God.

This combination also explains the nature of the gradual communications made to foreigners by Egyptian priests. Even by promising secrecy, Herodotus learns only the least important things from them. Become less insistent, they instructed Diodorus about everything concerning Osiris, without binding the traveler to silence. At the time of the Ptolemies, the priests were constrained to unveil their secret doctrine because philosophy had come to similar ideas and published them; but then the priests had two goals to achieve and several precautions to take. They did not want to let it be known that from its origins their secret doctrine had been so separate from the public religion, that the latter was only an instrument of control. Nor did they want it known that they admitted new ideas. As a consequence, they represented these new ideas as having always been part of their secret doctrine, and this doctrine as being intimately bound—and always having been bound—to the public religion. Hence, the explanation of all the religious customs, explanations that were overly subtle and contrived.[56]

As the philosophic doctrines multiplied and became contradictory, the priests tailored their divinities and their explanations to each of them, each divinity becoming the symbol of all these discordant doctrines.

When the priests saw their religion wholly discredited, they abandoned philosophy entirely and limited themselves to maintaining the superstition of the people by returning, as it were, to fetishism, by way of sorcery.

56. Vogel., p. 149.

CHAPTER 5

Example of the Same Combination in the Religion of India

The same combination is found in the Indian religion; but it is less easy to recognize.[1] A circumstance that at first glance would appear to be favorable to our investigation turns out to be an obstacle rather than an aid. The Indians are a nation that still exists. One could hope that they would provide explanations of themselves and their ancestors. But if their existence has continued for thousands of years despite both time and invasions, it is because they have always harbored a deep repugnance for foreigners and strangers. This repugnance continues today in all its force,[2] and our discussions with men who see us as impure masters and unclean oppressors are adversely affected by a religious prejudice fortified by political hatred.

Moreover, the records[3] of their belief and worship that we possess, even though

1. This chapter is not an exposition of the teachings or rituals of the Indian religion. That exposition will find its place in following books. Here we are only indicating the elements of which this religion is composed and the way in which they are combined.

2. Everyone who has visited India or who has some ideas of the character of the Brahmins, of the high opinion they have of themselves and the distance they keep from the ordinary human beings, will be able to judge how difficult it is to become familiar with them, or even to approach them. The disdain they maintain in their hearts for all foreigners, Europeans especially, the jealous anxiety with which they attempt to hide the mysteries of their religion from the profane, the archives of their various knowledges, as well as their domestic life, raise a barrier between them and the observer that is almost impossible to cross (Dubois, *Moeurs, institutions et cérémonies des peuples de l'Inde*, preface, p. XXX). In citing Dubois, we do not present him as a profound observer or an enlightened judge; but he confirms an important point: the difficulty the ancient authors complained about three thousand years ago has not been overcome by the moderns.

3. At the head of these records must be placed the Vedas, numbering four; the Rigveda, containing hymns in verse; the Yajurveda, prayers in prose; the Samaveda, in which are religious chants; and

the Atharvan or Ajurveda, full of formulas for expiations and imprecations, and prescribing bloody sacrifices, even those of human victims. The authenticity of this last Veda was contested by Jones and Wilkins and has been defended by Colebrooke (*Asiat. Res.*). In the same collection, Mr. Bentley wanted to prove by astronomical observations and the different names of Muslim princes that none of the Vedas existed before the Muslim invasion; but these names, like other parts of the Vedas, could have been interpolated. No one claims that the Vedas exist today in their original state. In addition, Mr. Bentley's claim would be well founded only if the redaction of the Vedas was modern, but the dominant ideas are no less ancient. In addition to prayers (mantras), the Vedas contain precepts and theological treatises. The collection of the first is called the Sanhita of each Veda; those of the second, Brahmanas and Upanishads (Colebrooke, *Asiat. Res.*, VIII, 387–88). The hymns and prayers are not always addressed to divinities, but also to kings whom the writers praise or thank for their benefits. It is probably by chanting such a hymn that Calanus was so remarkable before Alexander (Arrian). The Brahmanas and the Upanishads are the didactic part of the Vedas. For the most part, the Upanishads consist in a dialogue among the gods, the saints, and the elements; the Oupnekat that Anquetil-Duperron has obtained for us is an extract of the Upanishads, and its title is the same word in Persian. After the Vedas come the Puranas, attributed to Vyasa (see later for the details on him). These Puranas number eighteen; they treat the creation of the universe, its revolutions, its renewal, the genealogy of the gods, the exploits of heroes, distributing their fabular history among the epochs of a fictive chronology; in this respect they fulfill the function in Indian literature that the theogonies occupy in Greece.

Alongside the Puranas are the two great Indian epics, the Ramayana, in which the actions of Rama are celebrated, and the Mahabharata, which recounts the wars between the heroes of the Pandavas and the Kauravas. The Bhagavad Gita is an episode thereof. In connection with these poems, Mr. Heeren has attempted to establish a difference more subtle than solid between the religion and the mythology of the Indians. He seeks the first in the Vedas and the second in the epics; this is as if one sought the Greek religion in Hesiod's compilations or in what has come down to us in the Orphic teachings, and rejected the poems of Homer. The divinities of the Vedas, says Mr. Heeren, are the personifications of physical objects or forces that can be reduced to three: the earth, fire, the sun; and these three must subsequently be considered manifestations of a single being (Heeren, II, 430ff.). Be that as it may, the religion of the Mahabharata and the Ramayana is nonetheless the religion of the people; the traditions reported by these poems gave birth to feasts and rituals without number; in addition, one finds the same invocations of the divinities in the Vedas as in the Ramayana and the Mahabharata. Nor are these two epics the only ones that give us information about the Indian religion. We could have pointed to the *Sisupala-Badha*, where the victory of Krishna over Sisupala is celebrated; the *Cirata-Juniaya*, which sing the mortifications, then the martial exploits, of Arjuna, disciple of Krishna; the *Maga-duta* of Calidasa, the celebrated author of the charming drama of *Sacontala*; the *Rhaguvansa*, containing the major deeds of Rama, and several others; but these poems do not belong to the holy books; and even though in the judgment of English critics they surpass the Ramayana and the Mahabharata in poetic beauty, they do not have the religious authority the others do.

Finally, among the sources of our knowledge of India are the commentaries of the different sects — the theists, pantheists, dualists, atheists, those of the Vedanta school, of the two Nyayan philosophies, the two Mimamsan, and the two Sanchyan, who adhere to the Vedas in terms of form but wholly depart from its content. See below for clarification of these different sects or schools.

they are quite numerous and varied, do not at all form a whole. If from time to time, one part sheds light on another, most often they contradict and contend with one another. The exact time of none of these records is incontestable; the authenticity of several is doubtful; and since those that are apocryphal are always marked by a brilliant but bizarre imagination, and by the excessive abstractness that characterizes the literary and philosophical products of this country, one is in even a poorer position to fix the dates, to sift out original opinions, and to determine the development and progression of these opinions.

The original Vedas, the Akho-Vedas, are lost. Even the Brahmins acknowledge this. The details that they communicated to Holwell[4] concerning the revelation and transmission of these books demonstrate that even since their restoration, according to tradition, they were reworked again, and consequently the doctrine they contained was often modified.

According to these details, 4,900 years before our era, in order to reconcile fallen spirits to himself, the supreme God initially entrusted the divine law to Brahma in a heavenly language. Having translated it into Sanskrit, it formed the four Vedas. A thousand years later, Brahmins wrote six commentaries on these books. These commentaries are the six Angas, which treat the pronunciation of the holy vowels, the liturgy, grammar, sacred rhythm, astronomy, and the meaning of mysterious words. Five hundred years went by, and new commentators published a second interpretation, in which they departed from the original meaning and interpolated several allegories and many fables. From that came the four Upavedas, containing the rules of medicine, music, the profession of arms, and the mechanical arts; and the four Upangas, in the first of which were later put the eighteen Puranas.

Finally, three thousand years after the appearance of the original Vedas, five inspired writers presented a new redaction. One of them, Vyasa, the author of the Puranas, is also the author of the great epic poem of the Indians, the Mahabharata. But this Vyasa could very well have been a generic name designating a series of commentators on the Vedas, just like the name Homer probably indicates the authors of the first Greek epics.[5] The uncertainty that covers the time of Vyasa, and which the efforts of Mr. Bentley have not been able to resolve,[6] incline us toward

---

4. Kleucker, IV, 14; *Asiat. Res.*, I, 466.

5. See our investigation into the authenticity of the Homeric poems at the end of the volume (bk. VIII).

6. *Asiat. Res.*, V, 321.

this view.[7] The contradictions of the Indians themselves in this regard are obvious and striking. On one hand, they separate the Ramayana, a poem they attribute to Valmiki, from the Mahabharata of Vyasa by a distance of 864,000 years; and on the other hand, they affirm that these two poets often encountered and consulted one another concerning the redaction of their poems. When this absurd chronology is brought to their attention, they avoid the objection by recurring to a miracle. Vyasa is, moreover, a mythological person; sometimes he is the regeneration of Brahma, born in the third age four years after his mother's intercourse with a *rishi*, sometimes he is an incarnation of Vishnu in the womb of the young Caly, who remained a virgin after giving birth.[8]

The second redactor of the Vedas was Manu, more known than the first as the legislator of the Indians.[9] The collection of his laws is their oldest code; but this code is probably neither the work of a single man nor the work of a single century.[10] The three other redactors are suspect of heresy, as even the Brahmins acknowledge.

We will not examine the truth of the foregoing narrative; but it clearly indicates the repeated reworkings of the Indian religion. Everyone knows the important statements of Wilford concerning the falsifications of the pandit who had furnished him materials for his comparison between the fables of India and those of Egypt.[11] It seems to us that one can draw from this some important consequences concerning the falsifications of Indian books in general. The Indians themselves do not contest these falsifications, but limit themselves to excusing them by saying that the corruption of the world forces the sages to lend the support of a legendary antiquity to more sublime truths.[12] If it were further argued, as Abbé Dubois does, that the climate rather rapidly destroys all records and forces the Brahmins to recopy them each century, one can imagine how many interpolations and alterations of doctrine must result.

7. It is remarkable that the name Vyasa means "compiler" (*Asiat. Res.*, III, 378, 392, and 488), and that in one of its meanings the name Homer means "things put together" (Eurip., *Alcest.*, p. 780). This question, however, is a matter of indifference to us. If Vyasa was an individual, the tradition says that he had several disciples who themselves had many others. If Vyasa was only a generic name, there were several Vyasas, to the point that eleven hundred different schools were founded over the way of interpreting and teaching the Vedas.

8. See the Mahabharata, a poem attributed to Vyasa himself.

9. *Asiat. Res.*, I, 162.

10. Heeren, *Ind.*, II, 440.

11. *Asiat. Res.*, VIII, 251.

12. Ibid., 203.

If one also considers that during twelve to fourteen hundred years these records thus mutilated, these copies thus reworked, these commentaries—whose
authors sought to have a favorite opinion win out—served as either an occasion
or a pretext for works of philosophy or metaphysics that each sect believed was the
sole original and true system, then one will appreciate the wariness that must be
brought to them and to their examination. In fact, it is enough to read them with
a modicum of attention to recognize that far from containing a received doctrine,
for the most part they are the work of reformers or inspired men who wanted to
interpret and purify—that is, modify and transform—the received doctrine. The
Neardirsen, for example, which the Hindus of Bengal and of all the southern provinces of India regard as a holy Shaster, while those of Deccan, Coromandel, and
Malabar reject it, is a pure system of metaphysics, admitted into the holy books
thanks to the progression of ideas; so too could have been the case for the works
of the eclectics, if the polytheism purified by them had been maintained.[13] It is
the same with the Bhagavad Gita; the effort to replace what is already there with
something new, the mark of a reformer who fights and argues with the extant, is
found on every line;[14] and when Krishna releases the souls of women from the
curse that condemned them to pass into the body of a Brahmin before ascending
to heaven, here one recognizes the reformer battling a prejudice sanctified by the
ancient religion.

Therefore, to seek in these books the primitive popular mythology is to take, as
many have done, Neoplatonism for the religion of the first centuries of Greece or

13. The author of the Neardirsen employs a great number of arguments to distinguish the universal
soul from the vital soul. This necessity of proving what one affirms announces a philosophical hypothesis and not a religion. Religions in their vigor reveal, declare, and command, and do not discuss.

14. "I wish," says Krishna to his disciple Arjuna, "to have you learn a mysterious secret, you who
never seek to blame. The foolish disdain me under this human form. . . . No one, except for you, could
obtain the vision of my supreme form, neither by the Vedas nor by sacrifices, not by profound study
nor by ceremonies, not by actions nor by the most severe mortifications of the body. . . . I cannot be
seen except by means of the worship that is offered to me alone. The object of the Vedas has a triple
nature: be free of this triple nature. Abandon every other religion, prostrate yourself before me, and
you will surely come to me" (Bhag. Gita, French trans., pp. 40, 109, 110, 151). Who can fail to recognize
in these words the desire to have a new doctrine emerge victorious over those that are still in vigor?
In the same book there is a passage that betrays very clearly the intention and position of the master
vis-à-vis his disciple. Arjuna says to Krishna: "I am not satisfied by your words." The latter responds:
"Let celestial favors descend upon you." This is an absurd and superfluous prayer in the mouth of a
god who himself dispenses the favors of heaven; but the reformer is touched, as a man could be, by
the submission of his auditor (Bhag. Gita, p. 96).

Rome. Nothing is more similar to the India Shasters, as far as the content of ideas, than the works of the pagan philosophers who in the second and third centuries of our era worked to dress up Greek polytheism as allegories, and to ascribe to it subtleties that were quite foreign to its genius, and wholly unknown to its first adherents.[15]

To the difficulties that result from the alterations of the sacred books, we must add those that arise from the revolutions that the Indian religion underwent.

One must recognize at least four, and even five, principal ones: Brahmanism; Shivism; Vaishnavism, which Krishna did not invent but perfected; and Buddhism, which was expelled from India properly speaking after fierce wars and terrible massacres,[16] but which is triumphant in Tibet and shares Nepal with the religion of the Brahmins.

Everywhere on the surface of India are striking proofs of these revolutions. Several temples are considered to be the work of evil *genii*, and no one dares to practice the rites of the abolished cult. Now, among all peoples abandoned cults pass for sacrilegious magic: their priests are sorcerers, and their gods blameworthy and malevolent beings.

The Vedas also acknowledge these religious upheavals in India. They order bloody sacrifices, and even human sacrifices.[17] The repugnance of Indians for the shedding of blood, even though it has always been inspired in them by the climate,

---

15. Even though the author of the Bhagavad Gita, says his English translator (pref., p. XXXI), did not dare directly attack the principles established by the people, or the authority of the ancient Vedas, nonetheless by offering eternal happiness to all those who worship the All-Powerful, while he declares that the reward of those who worship other gods is only temporary happiness in an inferior heaven during a span of time proportional to their merits, his aim was manifestly to destroy polytheism, or at least move men to believe in the unique God present in the images before which they prostrate themselves, and to regard him as the sole object of their ceremonies and sacrifices. The most learned Brahmins today are proponents of divine unity, but they submit to vulgar prejudices to the point of externally following all the ordinances of the Vedas such as the ablutions, etc. This resembles the philosophers who allegorized polytheism when theism was being established.

16. Batta of the Brahmanical school of Nyaya killed many Buddhists in a general uprising he provoked against them (see bk. IV, ch. 2), then he burned himself to death in order to expiate the blood he had shed. The Brahmin Vegadeva completes his work: the people saw in him Vishnu arming himself against the impious (*Lettr. édif.*, XXVI, 2218).

17. It is remarkable that the divinities to which one offered bloody sacrifices and even human victims were the tutelary divinities of the towns and villages, which is to say: probably the first, and closest to fetishes.

was therefore not a part of their original worship. But when civilization prevailed (despite the priests) against this barbarous custom, the honor of its abolition was given to Vishnu[18] in his incarnation as Buddha,[19] thus attaching all successive reforms to the ancient divinities, as was the custom.[20]

The incarnations reported in the books of Indian religion are for the most part periods of reform. The Bhagavata Purana (the Bhagavatam) says that Vishnu becomes incarnate each time his presence is necessary to combat error and to have the truth triumph.[21] In his fifteenth incarnation,[22] Vishnu corrects the Vedas; Krishna, the great reformer who following one tradition attempted to banish obscene ceremonies from worship, is the eighth or the seventeenth incarnation of Vishnu. Buddha, who undermined the system of Brahmanism by abolishing castes, is, according to different chronologies, the ninth or the nineteenth.

To be sure, this last revolution is subject to much uncertainty. Scholars are divided over the person and epoch of Buddha. Some[23] regard his cult as a deviation, a reform or heresy that was introduced into that of Brahma, and Buddha therefore was later than him. Others[24] have adopted the opposite view. They identify Buddha with Baouth, an ancient idol; one still finds here-and-there shapeless simulacra and ruined temples dedicated to him. They suppose that his religion, which was before Brahmanism, was proscribed and supplanted by the Brahmins and found refuge in Tibet and Ceylon, in Tartary, Japan, and China, while also preserving itself in a few Indian tribes.[25]

18. *Gita-Govinda*, a poem in honor of the incarnations of Vishnu.

19. Sonnerat, *Voyage aux Indes*, p. 180.

20. In the polytheism independent of priests, this inversion of dates does not take place, because the human mind that advances openly does not disguise its steps. Thus, Saturn demanded human sacrifices; Hercules abolished them.

21. The same theory of incarnations is found on almost every page of the Bhagavad Gita.

22. The great incarnations of Vishnu number ten, and Indians still await the tenth, when a white horse will put its fourth hoof on the earth, and thus will give the signal for the destruction of the world. But if one puts together the different periods when this god became incarnate, his incarnations are much more numerous. At the end of this chapter we will return to the Indian theory of incarnations and point out a consequence of this theory to which no one, even until today, has given sufficient attention.

23. Almost all of the collaborators of the *Recherches asiatiques* published in Calcutta.

24. See Legentil.

25. The adherents of this hypothesis base themselves upon a passage of Clement of Alexandria in which Baouth is named as enjoying divine honors in India (Clem. Alex., I; see also Saint Jerome, *Adv. Jov.*, bk. I).

This question is very difficult to resolve. On one hand, the worship of Baouth does appear to be older than Brahmanism. The traditions attached to it and the crude exteriors of its figures indicate fetishism. On the other hand, the Buddha who meditated the abolition of castes was certainly subsequent to Brahma. As we argued much earlier, the castes had to be established originally without any contradiction, or they would never have been established. Buddha could have attacked them after they were sacralized, as modern philosophers attacked existing institutions; but these institutions preceded the philosophers.

The difficulty would resolve itself if we admitted two Buddhas: the first would be the same as the ancient Baouth, and the second would be the author of the religion that divided India and was introduced into China, substituting the name of Fo for that of Buddha.[26] Then, there would be nothing in common between the second Buddha and the ancient Baouth, if not that the first preceded the division into castes and the second was later than its establishment. In other words, one would have been ignorant of an institution not yet existing; the other, finding it established and sacralized, would have fought it.[27]

We, however, can leave the historical question undecided. Today Buddha is nothing but a legendary figure, like Vishnu, Rama, and all the Indian avatars become incarnate for the regeneration of the human race. His adventures are for the most part those of Rama in the Ramayana.[28] Buddhists have transferred them to their favorite incarnation.

"When he descended from the celestial region in order to enlighten the angels and mortals," recount these heretics, "the beautiful Mahamaya, wife of the rajah Sutah, monarch of Ceylon, received him in her chaste womb, which immediately became as resplendent and transparent as the most diaphanous crystal. The divine child, beautiful as a flower, awaited the hour of his birth, supporting himself on

26. Jones, *Asiat. Res.*, II, 123. The hypothesis of two Buddhas was adopted by Georgi and the Cashemirans in general.

27. The difficulty would also be resolved if, with Georgi (*Alphab. Tib.*), one saw the name Buddha, wrongly assumed to be a proper name, as the customary designation of all superior wisdom, virtue, or holiness. The author of a famous Sanskrit dictionary, known by his name as the *Amaracoscha*, strengthens this view by enumerating eighteen interpretations of the word, all of which express one of these ideas. Captain Mahoney in his *Essai sur les doctrines bouddhistes* says that the word "Buddha" signifies universal knowledge or holiness, a saint superior to all saints, a god superior to all gods, in the Pali language and that of Ceylon.

28. For example, the story of the bow that no one could bend, and which earned Rama the hand of Sita, as well as Buddha the hand of Vasutura (Ramay., bk. I, sect. 53).

his hands. After ten months and ten days of a mysterious pregnancy, Mahamaya obtained permission from her spouse to visit her father. The roads, bordered on either side by trees that spontaneously put forth fruit, refreshed by urns full of limpid water, and lit by the light of a thousand torches in her honor, made themselves smooth and straight before her. Not far from the route she followed, a garden offered itself to her sight. She wished to rest there and gather flowers. The pains of childbirth came upon her. Trees bent their heads toward her so as to shelter her from others' eyes. The air was filled with delicious perfumes, sounds at once melodious and sad resounded from afar, and nature itself felt an indefinable shudder, prophetic of divisions, struggles, and misfortunes. Buddha was born, and Brahma received him in a vase of gold; but already endowed with marvelous strength, the future avatar jumped onto the earth and, taking seven steps, rejoined his mother, who brought him back to her home. A holy man, withdrawn into the forest in order to practice silent worship, was alerted to the birth of Buddha by a secret voice. The virtue of his penances enabled him to fly through the air, and he presented himself before the rajah in order to give homage to the new-born god. Seeing him, he displayed alternately an immense joy and a profound sadness. Asked about these contradictory appearances, he replied: I am in pain, he said, because Buddha, once raised to the rank of avatar, will leave me far from him, perhaps will reject me; but I rejoice at his current presence, which absolves me from my sins.

The god—who was not yet one—was named Sacya, and lived unknown for sixteen years. At that time, a famous rajah offered the hand of his daughter Vasutura to the one who could bend a magic bow. A thousand rajahs tried in vain. Sacya, happier in the endeavor, wed the daughter of Chuhidan. He became a father; but a revelation having enlightened him, and followed by a single servant, he left his palace, his son, and his wife, and having crossed the Ganges, he even sent away his companion, along with his horse and armor.

Five flowers, contemporaries of the creation of the world, were put in the hands of Brahma. Sacya discovered in the calyx of one of these flowers clothing of the sort worn by hermits whose humility is maintained by alms. He put them on. Thus disguised, he continued his pilgrimage. A traveler passing by him, weighed down with eight bundles of sweet-smelling herbs, did reverence to the pilgrim, who laid his sacred body on the herbs. All at once a temple rose from the earth; it was thirty cubits high, and in the sanctuary was a throne of gold. Brahma descended in the midst of clouds, holding a dais over the head of Sacya. Indra came to refresh him with a fan, and Naga, the king of serpents, led to him the four tutelary deities that sat enthroned at each corner of the universe.

But the Assurs[29] came running, full of rage, to attack the avatar. The gods abandoned him; defenseless, Sacya implored the Earth, who, more helpful, opened a vast mouth to its subterranean waters. Defeated, the Assurs were put to flight. The five sacred codes proclaimed the divinity of Sacya, who under the name Buddha, after confirming his new dignity by twenty-one days of rigorous fasting, was seated above the highest of the world,[30] enjoying the ineffable happiness of an absolute impassability. He left behind him the sacred codes. By reading them, the faithful delivers himself from the machinations of unclean spirits, opens the paths of redemption, removes his soul from reincarnation, preserves himself from poverty, arrives at honors, heals himself from illness, and obtains by faith *nieban* or *nivani*, the eternal felicity that consists in the absence of all change, in the loss of all individuality, in the annihilation of all sentiment, all knowledge, all thought."

This is the legend of Buddha. Designated Sommonacodom in Ceylon, Godama in Siam, Fo and sometimes Tamo in China, and represented in Tibet by the Grand Lama,[31] he nonetheless has all the characteristics of an Indian incarnation, even though the sect he founded subsequently substituted apotheoses for incarnations. One recognizes these characteristics in the miracles that established his superiority to Bommaza, a god who disputes his empire, and who imprudently defies his skill. Hidden in the center of the earth like an imperceptible grain of sand, Bommaza was discovered by the penetrating look of Buddha, who in his turn was commanded to hide himself. He placed himself in Bommazo's eyebrow and let his rival seek in vain for him in the four great islands, and in the two thousand islands of lesser extent, in the depths of the Ocean, and on the inaccessible summits of Zetchiavala, and even on the peak of Mienmo,[32] thus frustrating all his efforts and compelling him to acknowledge his defeat. In another legend, Buddha is only

29. The evil *genii*.

30. In the cosmogony of Buddhists, the world is composed of an infinity of worlds similar to one another, which enter each other like the homeomeries of Anaxagoras; it has for a summit a rock at the top of which Buddha is seated (*Asiat. Res.*, VIII, 406).

31. Bringing together all the populations that profess the worship of Buddha—the two Tibets, Tartary, China, Burma, Siam, Laos, Cambodia, Cochin China, Japan, Korea, several countries beyond the Ganges, and the island of Ceylon—this religion counts about 450 million believers.

32. Mythological mountain of Burma.

Vishnu who becomes incarnate to destroy the Tripura, three fierce giants living in enchanted cities with walls of gold, leather, and iron, cities they transported everywhere they wanted to extend their works of destruction with the aid of immense wings and by invoking the Lingam. Vishnu-Buddha defeated them by his preaching and his great works.

He nonetheless is considered to be the author of a detestable heresy, and the malevolence of Brahmins in his regard shines through all of their accounts. After having, almost despite themselves, adored Buddha, the gods of Brahmanism refuse him their assistance, and if he is sometimes confused with the three great objects of Hindu worship, most often his rank as an avatar establishes only accidental and temporary relations between him and them. However, the disfavor cast on the enemy of the caste system does not weaken his divine character. The fundamental difference between Brahmin spirituality and Buddhist materialism becomes perceptible only when one leaves aside public rites and the traditions that animate them, and attends exclusively to the philosophic or secret doctrine. The externals of the religions—their ceremonies, their sacrifices, their priestly establishments, their tendency to the contemplative life—have maintained a resemblance between the two that disguises, albeit unsuccessfully, their mutual hatred.

The Cheritras, or sacred books, of one have an evident analogy with the epic poems of the other. The Ramakien of the Siamese appears to be only a translation of the Ramayana, albeit with less poetry and charm. Throughout their fictions, as well as in the orthodox mythology, one sees sometimes a penitent seized with mystical devotion at the sight of a withered fig tree command the elements by his austerities; sometimes a rajah pierced by a magic spear because he wants to make his own a beautiful woman whom this living spear protects; here an alligator plunges into the Ocean, embracing a young princess who miraculously escapes from this frightful lover; there an elephant aspires to the hand of another princess, who is not preserved from this bizarre match except by the penance of a hermit and the valor of a hero; further on, the tiger and the bull, united in close friendship, obtain human form through the prayers of a *rishi*. Krishna, Bhagavatti, and Rama are found in these tales under slightly modified names.[33]

This uninterrupted succession of reforms, whose dates the priesthood deliberately inverted or confused, this absence of any non-falsified records, this priestly effort to disguise the ancient doctrines by amalgamating them with the new or

33. Bhagavatti is called Pookavadi, and Rama, Pra-Ram.

explaining them by them,[34] all these things render the religious history of India a chaos. Light shines only on certain isolated details, although each day the portions that are illumined grow; but it will take more than a century for the whole to be revealed to our eyes.

Nonetheless, one can discern in this religion the same elements as in the Egyptian: fetishism gradually transformed into anthropomorphism, the worship of elements and stars, initially as a cult, then as a science, metaphysical hypotheses, and cosmogonies.

The worship of trees, of quadrupeds, of birds, of stones is preserved in India even to our day by being associated with the worship of the superior gods by the mystical union that assigns them material objects as abodes.[35] Brahma, Vishnu, and Shiva are deemed to reside in the Kolpo, and sometimes to be born in certain pebbles. Routren[36] is pleased to confine himself in the *outrachou*;[37] the god of the pagoda of Perwuttum is only a shapeless stone;[38] and every time some malady or accident strikes the inhabitant of a village, all his fellows come together to seek a black stone, the mysterious sanctuary of the divinity. When they have found it, they carry it in pomp and raise altars to it.[39]

The Indians worship the elephant, the eagle, the sparrow hawk, the crow, the ape, the beetle (who is among them, as in Egypt, an astronomical symbol, because his antennae and the shine of his wings figure the day star); the swan, whose strik-

34. The current books of the Indians, says Fred. Schlegel (*Weish. der Ind.*, p. 196), are probably attempts at harmonization among the different sects, and perhaps none of them conforms perfectly to the popular religion of any period.

35. The stones of Vishnu are called *shaligramas* by the Indians; one finds them in a river of the kingdom of Nepal. They are black, round, and often pierced in several places. Then one supposes that Vishnu entered them as a reptile. When the Indians believe they discover in them some resemblance to a garland of flowers, or the foot of a cow, they say that Lachmi, the wife of Vishnu, hides in them with him. The stones that Shiva inhabits are called *banling* (*Asiat. Res.*, VII, 240). The rocks that the first Christians called *cunni diabolic,* because they supposed they were the asylum of pagan divinities, are worshipped in India; when they are big enough, the faithful often enter the opening, or at least put in their hand or foot when the entire body cannot fit; this, they say, is a purification (*Asiat. Res.*, VI, 502).

36. Another name of Shiva.

37. The seed of a sour fruit (Sonnerat).

38. *Asiat. Res.*, v. 304.

39. Ibid.

ing white color braves contact with the water that surrounds it, is the emblem of the soul winding its way without blemish through the temptations of the earthly world in order to unite with God. They choose their sacred bulls following the same rules as the Egyptians;[40] and the followers of Shiva regularly observe the day dedicated to this quadruped divinity,[41] who bears Shiva in the air, whose three horns are the Vedas, and who is so redoubtable to injustice that the latter's reign cannot begin, except where the tail of the celestial bull ends.[42]

The cow is invoked as representing Surabhi, the dispenser of felicity; Budrani, the well beloved of Shiva, is represented in the figure of a heifer; Lachmi, the beautiful companion of Vishnu, who sometimes assumes the same form and rests on the bosom of his lover. The history of the cow Nandini, so poetically recounted by Calidasa in the Rhagu-Vansa; that of the cow Bahula, who asks life of a tiger, a charming episode of the Itahasas,[43] are embellishments of these memories of fetishism.[44] The fantastical birds Garuda[45] and Aruna are idealized fetishes who are connected to astrolatry. Aruna, weak and imperfect, is the dawn that precedes the sun and emits only a dubious light; Garuda is the sun in all its pomp, the type of the truth, the mount of Vishnu.

The same reminiscences can be seen in the more modern sects. The Jainists, heretics detested by the Brahmins, and about whom we can speak here only in pass-

40. Colonel Pearse having said to an Indian that Egyptians worshipped a bull, choosing this god according to a mark on its tongue, and that they also worshipped birds and trees, this Indian answered that this religion was that of all his compatriots, that they recognized the divine bull in the same way, and that they offered worship to different trees and birds (*Asiat. Res.*).

41. Dubois, I, 9.

42. *Asiat. Res.*, VIII, 48.

43. The Itahasas are a collection of mythological stories and songs. The images of Bahula and her son are worshipped in several temples, and on the day of their feast the passage of the Itahasas that concerns them is solemnly read and chanted.

44. The worship of the cow is so well preserved in India that in 1808 Englishmen who were looking for the sources of the Ganges discovered a fertile plain of considerable extent. An Indian who had accidentally killed a cow had purchased the land at great cost in order to transform it into an expiatory pasture, where herds of cows grazed in freedom (*Asiat. Res.*, XI, 510).

45. The Garuda is not a fantastical bird in its forms and colors except in mythology. The real *garouda* is an eagle of the smallest species that wages fierce war on serpents. But by a natural development of the association of ideas, this bird profits from the veneration of the Indians for the mythical Garuda. To kill one would be a sacrilege, and Indians come together to render it a sort of worship and toss it food, which it adroitly catches in the air.

ing without digressing from our subject,[46] associate each of their saints or deified penitents with an animal that serves as its emblem.[47] Finally, in the forests and on the mountains of the Carnatic region, as well as on different points of the coast of Malabar, fetishism still exists in its integrity. Several tribes of nomadic savages worship only their individual demons or *genii*, and do not worship the great divinities of the country.[48]

The association of this fetishism with an anthropomorphism that can only be regarded as a change of external forms is manifest in the fables that, in attributing the human figure to gods, add to them characteristics borrowed from the animals that were previously worshipped alone.[49]

Alongside this combined fetishism and anthropomorphism is placed the worship of the elements and the stars. One of the very ancient authors who transmitted to us exact information about India saw close by the coast of Coromandel a

46. The Jainists, who, like all dissidents claim to be the remnant that remains faithful to the original ideas, recognize neither the Vedas nor the Puranas of the orthodox; they have their own Shasters and Puranas. Their fundamental Shaster is the Agama-Shastra, which contains the exposition of their religious duties. Divided into four castes, they, like the other Indians, reject the fifth, the pariahs or *tchandalas*; but they differ from the others on several points: not worshipping the dead, not permitting widows to burn themselves on the corpse of their husband, and simply forbidding remarriage. Their opinions on the gods are rather contradictory. On one hand, they suppose that a divine incarnation presided at the establishment of their religion, and that twenty-four incarnations have followed to our day; on the other, like the Buddhists they seem to admit only apotheoses, and to see in the divine natures only the souls of men deified by the effect of a superior virtue. Adyssuara is the most powerful and the most ancient of all. Brahma and the other Indian divinities are for them only secondary beings, and they represent them in their temples always on their knees before the idols they worship. Despite these differences, the doctrine of the Jainist ends like that of the Indians in pantheism, by the reunion of the soul with God (*Asiat. Res.*, IX, 244–322).

47. The ox is that of Rishaba; the elephant, of Ajita; the horse, of Sambhava; the ape, of Abhimandana; the lotus, of Padmaprabha; the moon, of Chandraprabha; the rhinoceros, of Sreyansa; the buffalo, of Varurujia; the boar, of Vimala; the falcon, of Ananta; the lightning, of Dharma; the antelope, of Santi; the goat, of Cunthau; the pitcher, of Malli; the tortoise, of Munisnorala; the lily, of Nami; the serpent, of Parsva; the lion, of Vardhamana; etc. (*Asiat. Res.*, IX, 304–11). These names are those of the twenty-four incarnations or apotheoses that in the Jainist mythology form the great divine chain descending from the creation of the world to the present day, and which must continue until the destruction of the world.

48. Dubois, I, 92.

49. See later in the chapter on the figure of the gods.

temple dedicated to the five elements.[50] The air, fire, and earth invoked under their true names, with the sun, the moon, and the planets, are designated at the same time under the appellations of Brahma, Vishnu, and Buddha (always honored, although always suspect). The origin of the Vedas is attributed to the elements. The Rig-Veda is born of fire, the Yajur-Veda of air, the Sama-Veda of the sun.[51] Sometimes the tendency of the Indians to deify everything transforms the Vedas themselves into divinities. In the Varaha-Purana, Narada recounts that one day he saw on a lake an astonishingly large flower that was resplendent with the most vivid colors. One the banks of the same lake was a radiantly beautiful girl. She rested indolently on the grass, her eyes half-closed and her bosom exposed. Who are you, I said to her, continued Narada, O unknown beauty, the most perfect of virgins, as slender as the birch that rises to the sky? She closed her eyes and kept silence. Then the memory of divine things left me; I forgot the Shasters and the Vedas themselves, and I approached her who had captivated all my thoughts; three celestial forms were on her bosom. The eyes of the last shone with an indescribable éclat, like the sun. After having displayed themselves, they disappeared. The unknown girl remained alone. Tell me, I cried out, how I lost my Vedas. The first form that you saw on my bosom, she responded, was the Rig-Veda or Vishnu, the second was the Yajur-Veda or Brahma, the third was the Sama-Veda or Shiva. Reprise therefore, O Narada, your Vedas and your Shasters, make your ablutions in this lake, which is the Veda-Sarovara, or the lake of the Vedas, and you will recall the different transmigrations that you have experienced.[52] Thus the Vedas are three gods, but three elemental gods who celebrate themselves in mystical chants; for the Rig–Veda begins with a hymn addressed to fire, the Yajur-Veda by a hymn to air, the Sama-Veda by a hymn to the sun.[53]

Above appears the scientific religion—astronomy, astrology, its companion, the observation of natural phenomena—and its application either to religious uses such as divination or to practical ones like medicine.

The history of Krishna is entirely astronomical. The twelve nymphs that con-

50. Abraham Roger, *Paganisme indien.* The five Indian elements are earth, water, fire, and the air, which they divide into two: the wind and ether. In the Indra-Purana one finds these words: "Indra is nothing but the wind, the wind is nothing else but Indra."

51. *Asiat. Res.*, VIII, 379.

52. *Asiat. Res.*, XI, 120–21.

53. See one of the commentators on Manu, Maditihi, cited by Colebrooke (*Asiat. Res.*).

stitute his retinue are the signs of the zodiac; and the inconstancy that carries him from one to the other is the passage of the sun through these various signs.[54] His victory over the great serpent Caliga-Naga, like that of Apollo over a monster of the same species, recalls the action of the day-star purifying the atmosphere. Before the dawn, the Brahmins ask the sacred Trimurti to give to humans the light of the heavens.[55] They associate with it the immortal torches that warm and enlighten us; and it is also to these scientific gods that the *vanaprastas* who sanctify themselves in solitude offer the most meritorious and efficacious sacrifices.[56]

The Surya-Siddhanta, the most ancient of the astronomical treatises, is considered to be a revelation.[57] Its author, Meya, received it from the sun as a reward for his penances.[58] Shiva has his Tontros, which have made known to men the revolutions of the months and the days. Brahma and Vishnu-Siddhanta indicate by their names alone their divine origin. Other Siddhantas are written by simple mortals, but under a supernatural inspiration; all of them together number eighteen, and like the Puranas they bear the title of Shasters, expressive of their superiority over subsequent commentaries, profane works of the human spirit;[59] and what finally gives these Shasters the priestly stamp is when one notices the attempts of the priests to reconcile the infallibility of their teachings with the successive rectifications that were brought on by the development of knowledge. The movements of the planets can change, it is said in the Surya-Siddhanta, but the principles of the science remain the same; and in order to soften the contradiction that exists between the discoveries that have been made and the absurd tales of the Puranas and the Vedas, whose authority one dare not dispute, the pandits have recourse

54. Paterson (*Asiat. Res.*, VIII, 64): "Is it not the heavens which are the true residence of the majority of the personages who figure in Indian mythology? Is not their function to preside over time and its different divisions, to direct the progress of the year, the months, the seasons, and the days? And for those who inhabit the netherworld, their exact correlation, their constant struggles with the inhabitants of the heavens, even this opposition between the sons of light and the children of darkness . . . does not this prove that astronomy was a great part of brahmanism?" (Guigniaut, pp. 258–260).

55. Before the sun has appeared on the horizon, each Brahmin must intone the following invocation: "Brahma, Vishnu, Shiva, Sun, Moon, and all of you powerful planets, make the dawn appear" (drawn from the *Nittia-Carma, ou Grand Rituel des brames*).

56. The *homam*, sacrifice of rice and liquid butter (Dubois, *Moeurs et coutumes de l'Inde*, II, 341).

57. It is entitled Surya-Siddhanta because it was revealed by Surya, the sun.

58. *Asiat. Res.*, X, 56.

59. Ibid., VI, 279.

to interpretations. Sometimes the fables refuse. Thus, the Vedas positively teach that eclipses are occasioned by the dragon Rahu, a horrible monster whose head was cut off by Vishnu. This monster, who would have stolen from the gods a few drops of their *amrita*, the ambrosia of India, bequeathed his immortal head to the heavens and his tail to the earth, from where, rising up, it furiously pursues (like the Fenrir of the Scandinavians) the sun and the moon in order to devour them. The pandits say that the fact is certain; but obliged to apply human intelligence to astronomy, they write like philosophers, and not like theologians. The physicists of the eighteenth century expressed themselves in the same way. The similarity of circumstances necessarily produced similarity of language.

Astronomy is not the only science that religion takes hold of, that it enlists, that it identifies with its fables, and that it submits to its authority. Legislation is contained in the Dharma-Shastra. Medicine is also the gift of a god who revealed it in the Ajur-Veda, of which only a few fragments exist; and one of the Upanishads of the Vedas contains a treatise on astronomy.

In several Puranas, a special section is reserved to geography, and the Brahmins proscribed geographic treatises in the vulgar language. We have the divine Puranas, they said, what more does the human race need?[60]

The seven musical notes are placed under the protection of seven divinities in the Rama-Veda. This divine art was communicated to our species by Brahma and Sarasvatti, his daughter; and their son Nared is the inventor of the lyre, like Mercury among the Greeks. The further divisions of the different tones are personified as so many nymphs in the Sangita-Ratnakara;[61] or at other times associating one science with another, that is, astronomy to music; the Indians reduce the musical notes to six so that they can correspond to the seasons of the year.[62] They devote a particular harmonic mode to depict the melancholy of the harsh months, the gaiety of the return of spring, the harshness of excessive heat, or the rebirth of nature when the rains refresh the burning air; and constantly reducing fables to science, they suppose six Ragas, beings intermediary between gods and men, playing in the air, bestowing their favors upon five companions with unparalleled beauty, each the mother of eight *genii*, who flutter in their wake on the summit of mountains

60. Ibid., VIII, 268. These treatises appear to have been known to Megasthenes and Pliny the Elder (*Hist. nat.*, VI, 29).

61. Ibid., IX, 458.

62. The seasons in India are two months each.

or even the folds of clouds, a most graceful family, one that rivals the most elegant fictions of Greek mythology.[63]

Grammar, finally, the ingenious organization of the most decisive and most inexplicable discovery, the discovery of language, which the animals approach but never attain, and which, serving as the instrument and bond of the faculties of man, assigns him his rank in creation; grammar has the serpent Patanjali as its author, who fixed its laws in his Morabashya.[64] Another famous grammarian, Panini, is extolled in the Puranas as inspired and a prophet.[65] The history of his commentator Catya-Juna is connected to legends;[66] and Bhartri-Hari, a didactic poet who put in verse the rules established by his predecessors, is the brother of Vicrama-Ditya, whose austerities, wars, and miracles figure on each page of the sacred poems.[67] The Agni-Pourana is a system of prosody; and the invention of this art to which the Indians attach so much importance goes back to Pingala-Naga, a legendary being represented (like Patanjali) under the form of a reptile, or perhaps identical with Patanjali himself.[68]

Thus in India as in Egypt, it is always from religion that science comes, it is by religion that it is preserved; and as in Egypt, its possession is a privilege claimed by the priestly order. Misfortune to the one who would try to pry it from them! When the kings of Magadha permitted the educated of their court to publish writings destined for the instruction of all the classes, indignant Brahmins cursed

63. *Asiat. Res.*, VII, 205.

64. Ibid.

65. Ibid., 203.

66. Ibid., 204.

67. Ibid.

68. Ibid., X, 390. By the sole fact that the Brahmins have treated, whether well or not, all the sciences, one was able to easily find all the sciences in India; and taking poetic effusions literally, some have attributed both the most difficult and the most recent discoveries to the Indians. People have claimed that all of Newtonian philosophy, and especially the system of gravity, was contained in the Vedas, which give the sun an epithet expressive of this idea; and they have also based themselves upon the following passage in a poem entitled *Schirin et Féridad*: "An imperious tendency penetrates each atom, and leads the most imperceptible particles toward some determinate object. Examine the universe from bottom to top, from fire to air, from water to the earth, from the sublunary gods to the celestial spheres, and you will find no corpuscle lacking in this natural attraction. It is this impulsion that compels heavy and hard iron to go toward the magnet, the light and frail straw to unite with the odiferous amber. It is this that imprints on each substance its immutable tendency and irresistible need to attach itself firmly to the object that attracts it."

his kingdom with anathemas and declared it a sacrilegious country where no believer could live.[69]

In a more elevated sphere, we find the metaphysical hypotheses, subtler than in Egypt, and subdivided, diversified, and nuanced in such a way that in this work we renounce any effort to treat them, or even to list them. To be sure, like so many others we could give a show of erudition by leaving their native names to these systems and their infinite subtleties. Two or three extracts from Colebrooke and Schlegel would furnish us with more than sufficient material; and by translating these authors without attribution we would appropriate to ourselves the honor of their erudition. But we will not needlessly tire the reader; we do not need to treat these views in themselves, but rather in the way in which the priests, whether Brahmin or Buddhist, introduce them into their learned doctrine, and the influence that the introduction of this doctrine exercised on the public worship. As a result, instead of taking each Indian system and dealing with it, we will remain faithful to the great divisions we have already established: theism, pantheism, emanationism, dualism, and atheism.

Theism is found in almost all the sacred books of India. The Brahmins' creed teaches that the worshipper of the sole god has no need of idols. The Bedang, which in a very long fable concerning the creation of the world, personifies the attributes of this unique god and relates the origin of all things to him alone. The Laws of Manu[70] combine this teaching with that of absolute fatality; the Dirm-Shaster proclaims it, reducing all the accounts that seem to contradict the unity of God to particular manifestations of Providence;[71] and the Bhagavatam recounts fables without number to inculcate and emphasize this unity.

---

69. *Asiat. Res.*, VIII, 270.

70. Schlegel, *Weish. der Indier*; and the *Cosmogonie* of Manu, translated by the same.

71. "You speak of God as if he were one, says human reason to Brimha Narud. However, it is revealed to us that Ram, whom we are taught to call God, was born in the house of Jessaret, in that of Bischo, and in several others. How ought we to understand this mystery? You must, answered Brimha, regard these births as so many particular manifestations of the providence of God to attain a great end. It was thus with the seventeen hundred women called *gopi* when all the men of Sirendiep (island of Ceyland) were killed in war: the widows prayed to obtain husbands. Their desires were fulfilled in the same night, and they all found themselves pregnant. One must not suppose from this that God, who is introduced as the agent of this miraculous event, is subject to human passions or weaknesses, being incorporeal by nature and purity itself: he can at the same time show himself in a thousand different places under a thousand names and forms, without ceasing to be immutable in his divine essence (first chapter of the Dirm-Shaster).

Sometimes it recounts that one of the fathers of the human race, wanting to know the divine nature, imposed upon himself severe penances, and by the force of his fasts and self-afflictions caused a brilliant flame to shoot out from his forehead. All the gods were frightened and sought shelter near Brahma, Shiva, and Vishnu. These three superior divinities presented themselves to the penitent. Then prostrating himself before them, he said: I recognize only one God; which of you is the true God? Tell me, so that I can adore it. The three gods responded: there is no difference among us. A single being is at once the creator, the preserver, and the destroyer. To adore him under one of these forms is to honor him under all three.[72]

Elsewhere, we learn that Sati, daughter of Daksha, the wife of Shiva, scorned by her father, stirred her spouse to avenge her. A giant with a thousand arms produced from one of the hairs he had plucked in his anger entered into the assembly of the gods and cut off the head of Daksha, who cursed his daughter. The gods complained to Brahma, Shiva pardoned his father-in-law. The head of a billy goat replaced the head cut off and consumed by fire, and Vishna declared again that the three gods, depositories of the forms of nature, comprise one essence and are one and the same God.[73]

Theism is equally manifest in another tale, which is also connected with the historical event of the abolition of the worship of Brahma.

Proud of his power to produce, Brahma one day wanted to rival Shiva the destroyer, and claimed to be superior to Vishnu, who maintained all created things. A terrible battle ensued between Vishnu and Brahma. The celestial spheres were shaken; the stars fell from the sky; the earth trembled. In the midst of this terrible tumult, a column of fire appeared; one could perceive neither its summit nor its base. At this sight, the two antagonists were convinced that supremacy would belong to the one who could discover the foundations of this column or who could attain its summit. Vishnu in the form of a wild boar dug in the earth for a thousand years, digging a distance of three thousand leagues each minute. But the foot of the column remained hidden in the abyss. Vishnu recognized his impotence. Brahma changed into a swan and rose into the air to a height that speech cannot describe. In an hour he crossed thirty-six thousand leagues, and his flight lasted one hundred thousand years. Finally, his exhausted wings refused to carry him further. As he re-descended to earth he encountered a flower. He took it in his hand and

72. Bhagavatam, bk. IV.
73. Ibid.

would not release it except on the condition that it would testify to the success of his endeavor. It had barely uttered this false testimony when the column of fire opened up. Shiva appeared, laughing with a terrible laughter, and as punishment for his lie he condemned Brahma to no longer have temples or images or followers. The repentence of the god disarmed Shiva's anger, but he did not retract his sentence, and Brahma was worshipped only by Brahmins, without any public cult and without external ceremonies. In this way, the superiority of Shiva,[74] supreme god, sole master of all, whom all the beings serve and sacrifice to, was recognized.[75]

It is remarkable that in this tale, as well as in several others, the Indians give preference to the destructive principle. This characteristic of their mythology is explained by their disposition to consider annihilation as the supreme bliss. It is a misfortune for all beings to put on earthly forms; the power that destroys them, the power that delivers man from the individuality that weighs so heavily upon him, ought to have preference over the principle that maintains these forms and this individuality. Moreover, for a contemplative people, the idea of destruction is more unchanging, infallible, and hence more imposing, than that of preservation, which is always varied and occurs in time, while destruction is in eternity; hence preservation is always defeated by destruction. Thus, in the wars of the gods against the giants, Shiva is almost always the principal god. Brahma is the head of his army, and four Vedas are his steeds; Vishnu serves as his arrow.

We will not cite the Ezouvedam, since it is now proven that we owe it to the pious fraud of a zealous missionary.[76] But the ease with which the missionary

74. In another place, the Bhagavatam extracts from Vishnu himself homages to the unity of Shiva, a unity that deprives Vishnu of divine honors. He declares the Brahmins above other men, and the *galigueuls* above the Brahmins; now the *galigueuls* are sectarians who deny the divinity of Vishnu. This oddity is explained by the habit of the Indian priests, who always make the gods the organs of their opinions. Here, this habit has led them to ascribe to Vishnu an acknowledgment by which his very existence is called into question. Alongside this doctrine of theism, the Bhagavatam contains a host of popular fables that are favorable to polytheism, and it inculcates them in its readers as articles of faith, a manifest indication of the double movement of the priesthood, which desires, simultaneously, to allegorize or interpret the traditions and to preserve them intact.

75. Sonnerat, I, 129–31; Baldaeus, *Beschr. der Ostind. Küste*, pp. 144–45.

76. Sonnerat had suspected this fraud for a long time; but it was only completely unmasked by Mr. Ellis in volume XIV of the *Recherches asiatiques*. Anquetil-Duperron, who had devoted several years to the study of the religious records of Indian religion, was completely duped by the imposture. And Voltaire shared his error (see *Siècle de Louis XIV*, ch. 29, note); but his mistake is not surprising: he was far from having the requisite knowledge, and he did not succeed in combining critical judg-

could deceive the most careful readers of authentic books thus demonstrates that theism was one of the philosophic doctrines of the Brahmins.

However, should we therefore conclude—as more than one author preoccupied with a single idea has—that theism is the religion of India, or at least that by itself it constituted the entirety of the Brahmanical teaching?

This conclusion would be false. Who does not see that for the ignorant and credulous crowd, the literal sense of these narratives in which the gods fight, destroy one another, and reconcile, or the vestiges of fetishism that appear in them, and where it is a question of their births and their marriages, can hardly be counterbalanced by a metaphysical axiom that, by offering only an abstraction, most often causes the divinity to descend from the rank of a moral being to merely being a substance? This is the formulation of a philosophy, and not the teaching of a religion.

What these fables inculcate, rituals confirm. In nuptial ceremonies, one invokes Brahma, Vishnu, Shiva, Devendren, the twelve Adityas, the eight Vanuras, the nine Brahmas, the eleven Rudras,[77] the Siddas, the Saddias, the Navadas, the seven great penitents, the nine planets, and finally all the gods whose names come to mind.

Theism therefore was never the public belief of India. Even the sects that profess it deviate from it constantly. The exclusive worshippers of Shiva[78] associate with him Bhavani, his wife. Those of Vishnu[79] render at the same time worship to Radha, one of his favorites. Others who claim to offer homage only to Rama[80] include Sita, his spouse, or venerate the two spouses together.[81] One sees in Indian mythology gods struggling with giants, often oppressed by them, compelled by penances,[82] or subjugated by curses, and despite their power submitting to what is most painful to them. Each temple, each pagoda, witnesses to the plurality of gods, their metamorphoses, their weaknesses, their vices. The temple of Tirumaton recalls the triumph of the giant Eruniaschken over gods and men combined, the

---

ment with his otherwise admirable universality. When a fact served his position, he used it without further examination.

77. In the astronomical religion, the Rudras are only the sun considered under difference faces; but the popular invocations make them so many separate divinities.

78. The *saïvas* had Sanchara-Acharya as their founder, one of the most famous commentators on the Vedas.

79. The *vaischnavas*, whose origin goes back to Madhava-Acharya and Wakhaba-Acharya.

80. The *ramanuj*, a branch of the *vaischnavas*, who worship Vishnu only in his incarnation as Rama.

81. *Asiat. Res.*, VII, 279–82.

82. See above (bk. IV, ch. 2), on the power attributed to penitential deeds by the Indians, where we explain the connections of this view to the climate.

prayers of Brahma, which moved Vishnu to pull the earth out of the abyss where this giant had plunged it, the wiles of this god to defeat this terrible adversary in the form of a boar.[83] The figure of Devendren recalls his illegitimate loves and his punishment, at first indecent, then bizarre.[84]

The proof that theism was never the belief in vigor jumps out of the writings of the philosopher-priests who adhered to it. Some of them, more timid and reserved, opened themselves to followers only after prescribing a profound silence. Thus in the Oupannayana, when the father of the neophyte teaches him the existence of a sole god, sovereign master, principle of all things; he adds that it is a mystery not to be communicated to the unintelligent vulgar, to do so would draw the greatest calamities upon the guilty one. Others who were more candid openly combat polytheism.[85] But one does not fight unless the doctrine already

83. On this fable, see IV, ii, 7.

84. Having conceived a violent love for the beautiful Ahalia, wife of a *mouni* (a Brahmin devoted to the contemplative life), Devendren came to her in the form of her spouse, like Jupiter with Alcmena. Deceived by his appearance, Ahalia yielded without any pang of conscience to his desires. But the Brahmin surprised Devendren in the midst of his illicit pleasures, and by means of his curses covered the body of the god with organs similar to those he had just abused. However, allowing himself to be moved, he replaced these organs with the countless eyes with which Devendren's body is filled. Must not this story produce the same effect in the mass of Indians as the loves of Jupiter, or those of Mars and Venus, on the mass of Greeks? It also can be explained scientifically, like many others. In astronomical language Devendren is the air, or the visible heaven, and the eyes strewn throughout his body express the transmission of light. We will also see him reappear in the priestly demonology as the head of *genii* of the second order.

85. We have spoken of the Ezouvedam as an apocryphal book written by a missionary; but this only better proves the existence of idolatry in India. If theism was dominant there, the missionary would not be obliged to direct his blows against idolatry. One of the men most versed in the history of Indian mythology and philosophy, who at the same time had embraced an opinion wholly opposed to ours because he supposes the primitive religion of India to have been an entirely intellectual and abstract religion, nonetheless recognizes that the systems established in the Shasters and the Puranas were nothing but the attempts to bring together a host of different sects, and that they bear the imprint of the irreconcilable doctrines that they tried in vain to amalgamate (Schlegel, *Weish. der Indier*, p. 186). His testimony is even more important because it wars against his own preferred view. He could not have come to it except by the force of the evidence. This homage rendered to the truth does honor to his virtue as a scholar. It is troubling that this virtue has disappeared in the political writer.

In the dialogue between a missionary and Zaradobura, the high-priest of the religion of the Buddhists of Ava, the latter recounts to the Christian that when the end of the first reign of a thousand years had announced the appearance of a new god, there were six false prophets. One taught that a wild spirit was the cause of good and evil; the second denied metempsychosis; the third affirmed that everything ends with this life; the fourth proclaimed an eternal and blind necessity; the fifth exists. No one today, among either Muslims or Christians, would write against polytheism.[86]

If theism seems to dominate in the Bhagavatam and the Dirm-Shaster, it is impossible not to see pantheism in the other sacred books. In point of fact, the Vedas do not contain a pure pantheism. They teach that there are three worlds; one is the thought of the divinity, the second the realization of this thought by the production of an ideal world, the third the material world of which the ideal world is the type. But the commentators on the Vedas have applied themselves to give

---

limited the happiness of the just to a temporary period; the sixth said that a single being had created the world and merited human praise. Godama (Buddha) defeated these six impostors (Buchanan, *On the Religion of the Burmas*). Notice that theism is put among the impious doctrines and its apostle is treated as a false prophet.

86. At the moment when we deliver these pages to the press, some brochures, already old in India but little known in Europe, have come to us, and they seem destined to corroborate the truth we establish. These brochures, the first of which appeared in 1817, are the work of a Brahmin named Rammohun-Roy who, having declared himself against idolatry and for theism, was persecuted by his caste and would have been the victim of priestly intolerance had he not been under the protection of the English government. According to the procedure of every reformer, he first of all affirms that the doctrine he recommends is the religion practiced by the ancestors of today's Indians; that it is taught in the Puranas and the Tantras, as well as in the Vedas; that many commentaries written by the most famous theologians, with Vyasa and Sanchara-Acharya in the lead, proclaimed the unity of the invisible (*A Defense of the Hindoo Theism*, by Rammohun-Roy [Calcutta, 1817]). But he adds that even though many Brahmins are thoroughly convinced of the absurdity of the worship of idols, these erroneous conceptions have prevailed; that the Europeans who seek to soften the revolting traits of Indian idolatry by claiming that all the objects of this idolatry are considered figurative representatives of the supreme divinity do too much honor to his compatriots; that the Indians of today firmly believe in the real existence of countless gods and goddesses who, in their respective functions, possess a complete and independent power; that in order to appease the idols and not the true god, temples are built and ceremonies performed; to say the contrary is deemed a heresy (*Translation of an Abridgement of the Vedant*, preface [Calcutta, 1818]).

This is a very recent avowal, quite clear and authentic; it is a Brahmin who published it, a Brahmin who is a partisan of theism and ashamed of the errors of his country, braving persecution in order to enlighten it. He ends with these words: "In following the path that my conscience and sincerity lay out, I have encountered complaints, reproaches, and even the threats of my closest relatives; their prejudices are deeply ingrained; their temporal well-being depends on them; but no matter how many are my dangers and my sufferings, I bear them with tranquility; the day will come when my efforts will be considered with justice, perhaps with gratitude, and, in any case, how important are men if I am pleasing to him who sees our actions and who rewards them?" Let no one speak today about the pure theism, both ancient and constant, of the Brahmins who persecute theism in 1818.

a pantheistic interpretation to the texts.[87] The universal power, says one of them, this power that shines in the sun and rules the spirit of man, is the luster in the diamond, the sap in trees and plants, in living things their soul; is also the creator, and Providence, and the force that preserves; it projects and absorbs all; it is the sun and all the gods, everything that moves and everything that is motionless in the three worlds. The Vedantic philosophy goes further; it rejects this trinity of worlds (Trilokya); it admits only one, which is multiplied by an illusion. The recognition of this illusion constitutes the divinity that alone exists, and the universe is but a phantom without reality. The substance of the soul, the sentiment it has of its existence, its various knowledges, its perceptions, all these things are God himself, says the creed of the Brahmins.[88] Everything that was from all time is God, all that is, is God, all that will be, is still God.[89] You, me, all the beings are Vishnu.[90] Reject all notions of diversity, and see the universe in your soul.[91] And the Bhagavatam, suddenly forgetting its favorite theme, teaches that there is nothing in the world that is not Vishnu; that this unique being takes different forms; that it acts in different ways; but that all is only one with him, and that the substance of all bodies, of all souls, is nothing but his own, returning to itself after an apparent separation.[92]

But it is above all in the Bhagavad Gita that this doctrine is developed. It is there that Krishna defines himself, saying that he was at the beginning of all things, all that exists but is not perceived; that since then he is all that was and all that will be, and that outside of him there is only illusion. I am, he continues, the sacrifice and the cult, the perfume and the invocation, the fire and the victim, generation and destruction, the sun and the rain, immortality and death, being and nothing.[93]

87. In the Chandogya-Upanishad, which is associated with the Samaveda, Aswapati criticizes the sages assembled around him because they consider the universal soul an individual being. This soul, he tells them, is everything that exists.

88. Sonnerat, III, ch. 14.

89. Prayer of the Brahmins according to the institutes of Timur.

90. *Mohamudgara*, a poem whose title means "remedy against the troubles of the spirit."

91. *Asiat. Res.*, I, 39–40.

92. Bhagavatam, by Guignes, *Mém. Acad. des inscr.*, XXVI, 793.

93. Bhag. Gita, English trans., p. 80. He adds: "The soul is not a thing about which one can say that it was, that it is, or that it will be; it is without birth, constant, eternal, incorruptible, inexhaustible, indestructible, universal, permanent, immutable, inalterable. I have always been, just as you have, just as everything that exists" (ibid., pp. 35–37). It is rather remarkable that in thus affirming the immortality of the soul in the sense of pantheism, the Bhagavad Gita at the same time raises doubts concerning this view, which it declares it cannot resolve. "Whether you regard the soul," says Krishna, "as of eternal

Pantheism shows itself even in the particular notions concerning each divinity. Brahma is at once each man individually and collectively the human race, which means that he is born and dies every day, because at each instant human beings are born and die; and he also dies every one hundred years, because this is the term of the longest human life.[94]

But in the same way that we have seen the adherents of theism carefully attach their doctrine to popular fables, so too the pantheists, far from disdaining the tales, include them in a system that would seem to exclude them. When, in order to better inculcate this pantheistic hypothesis, Krishna describes himself to his disciple and says: I am the soul contained in the body of all the beings, the beginning, middle, and end of all things: among the Adityas[95] I am Vishnu; among the stars, the sun; I am one of the cardinal points of the heaven in the midst of the winds; and the first book of the Vedas; among the faculties, I am life; and in animated beings, reason; I am the most powerful of the eleven destinies, and among the *genii*, that of wealth, among the elements, fire, and Merou among the mountains;[96] among the sages I am their head Vrischapati;[97] among the warriors, Scandra, the god of war; among the rivers, the Ocean; among words, the mysterious *oum*;[98] I am the head of the celestial choirs,[99] and the first of the *mounis* among the pious penitents; among the cults, silent adoration; among the trees of the forest I am Asvatta;[100] among the horses, Urchisrava, who emerged from the waves with the

---

duration, or you think that it dies with the body, you have no reason to be sorrowful. What good is it to bemoan the inevitable? The earlier state of beings is unknown, the present state alone is manifest; their future state cannot be discovered" (ibid., pp. 37–38). This confirms our claims concerning the contradictions inherent in the priestly philosophies.

94. *Asiat. Res.*, V, 247.

95. Signs of the zodiac.

96. Meru, the holy mountain of Indians, celebrated by all their poets, described in the Mahabharata (I, 16).

97. At the same time the planet Jupiter.

98. The sacred monosyllable that the Indians of every sect, and even the Buddhists, pronounce when beginning their prayers, and that they put at the beginning of their sacred books.

99. By a remarkable effect of the confusion that always reigns in the Indian fables, and which at bottom is only the result of pantheism clothed in mythological forms, Chitrarah, the head of the celestial choirs with whom Krishna here identifies himself, is one of the enemies of Arjuna, and his defeat is a poetic episode in the Mahabharata.

100. The *pipal* tree (*Ficus religiosa*).

so-sought-after *amrita*;[101] among the elephants, Airavat, and the sovereign among men; among the weapons, thunder; among the beasts, the cow Kamaduk,[102] daughter of the sea, I am the fruitful god of love; among the reptiles I am their head, Vasuki, among the serpents the eternal serpent, and among the inhabitants of the tides, the god who governs; among the judges, I am Yama, the judge of the netherworld; among the evil spirits, Prahlad,[103] and in all calculations, I am time; among the animals I am their king, and among the birds, the prodigious Vainateya; among the winds that purify, I am the air; in the midst of heroes, Rama;[104] among the fish, Makar,[105] among the rivers, the Ganges, child of Janhnu;[106] I am the first of the vowels, and among words I am *duandua*;[107] I am death and resurrection, fortune, fame, eloquence, memory, intelligence, valor, patience, Gayatri[108] among the harmonious measures, glory, industry, victory, the essence of all the qualities; among the months, *margasirsha*;[109] among the seasons, spring, Vyasa among the inspired;[110] among the poets, Usana;[111] among governors I am the scepter, and the silence among secrets; of all things, be they living or not, there is none that I am not. When Arjuna answered him: You are Vayu, the god of the winds, Agni, the god of fire, Varun, the god of the seas, Sasanka, the moon, Prajapati, the god of

---

101. The potion of immortality, for the possession of which the gods and the giants wage fierce battles, which are described in the Mahabharata.

102. The cow of abundance.

103. Evil spirit converted by Krishna.

104. The incarnation of Vishnu and the hero of the Ramayana.

105. A mythical fish represented with the trunk of an elephant, and at the same time the sign of Capricorn.

106. When the Ganges emerged from its source for the first time to go to the Ocean, its waves troubled the devotion of Jahnu, who was praying on the banks of the Mahadany. Disturbed, Jahnu swallowed the river; but his anger subsiding, he let it flow again through an incision made in his thigh, and in honor of this the river was given the name "daughter of Jahnu" (Ramayana, bk. I, sect. 35).

107. Way of forming composite words in the Indian language.

108. Mysterious prayer of the Indians and, in addition, the pivot upon which all their beliefs turn; this is because it is simultaneously a prayer and a divinity, a festival and the creative force, a mode of worship and the Trimurti, an irresistible invocation and the reunion of all the gods (see a bit later, toward the end of the chapter, the analysis of this combination).

109. The month of October, when the rains finish and the heat diminishes.

110. See above concerning Vyasa.

111. The converter of the evil *genii*, and at the same time the planet Venus.

nations, and Prapitamaha, the powerful ancestor, is it not obvious that the author of the Bhagavad Gita alters the fables he accredits?

Ourchasrva the steed, Kamaduk the cow, Yama the judge of the netherworld, Jahnu father of the Ganges are so many illusions and, as it were, respects paid to received fictions under which pantheism is introduced, and replaces them; they are like an obligatory set of rubrics; but in the end, all the fables come to pantheism. In his infancy, Krishna stole the milk of their flocks from the nymphs. They complained to Yasoda, his nurse. As his sole response, the god opened his glittering mouth, and Yasoda, totally surprised, saw the entire universe in all its splendor.[112] Who does not see pantheism in this account, concealed under a legend that it confirms, all the while establishing a doctrine destructive of all legends?

Sometimes a pantheistic profession of faith concludes a narrative that seems neither to prepare it nor to support it. Trivicrama reigned on the banks of the Godaveri. Each morning a Brahmin presented him a flower. The king received it respectfully, but when it had withered, he tossed it on the floor of his palace. One day, opening the one he had just received, he saw in it a diamond of great value. Queried, the Brahmin promised to explain this mystery if the prince would accompany him into a forest. They set out and, once arrived at their destination, saw a cadaver propped up by the branches of an oak. The Brahmin asked his illustrious companion to carry the body to his home. Overcoming his repugnance, Trivicrama took the corpse over his shoulders; but the dead man, entertaining him with marvelous stories, succeeded in escaping from him twenty-five times. The angry monarch finally took hold of the fugitive stranger, who revealed to him the plot of the Brahmin, who aspired to his throne and was preparing his death by magical rites, for which a body that had ceased to live was necessary. The conspiring priest was punished, and Shiva, revealing himself to the eyes of the prince, said: Three times you came forth from my own essence; two times I have recalled you to my bosom. When ten days will have come, I will receive you again, and you will no longer be separated from me.[113]

Other times, pantheism reintroduces polytheism in ways whose subtlety is interesting to note. To adore the Supreme Being who contains all the beings is to adore oneself, say the pantheists—and this adoration ought to be prohibited. But it is legitimate to worship the parts of the divinity that are superior to others, and this

---

112. *Asiat. Res.*, II, 267.
113. Ibid., IX, 126.

worship can legitimately be addressed to the idols that the divinity, by the power of incantations, is forced to enter.[114]

Ceremonies, too, have a double tendency. The apotheoses of all the instruments used in the celebrations—the vessels, the tripods, the pavilions, or *pandels*, even the herbs that become so many gods who are adored—are a disguised pantheism; and the following is also rooted in pantheism: the homage offered to the instruments of all the professions during the feast of Gauri, one of the names of Paravati, wife of Shiva. The worker prostrates himself before his plows, his picks, his sickles; the mason before his trowel and rule, the carpenter before his saw and axe; the barber invokes his razors, the writer his iron stylus, the warrior his weapons, the fisherman his nets, the weaver his line; the farmer sacrifices to the manure that fertilizes his lands. But if these mysterious rites recall for the Brahmin imbued with the secret teaching its abstract unity, the transformation of material objects into particular divinities inculcates the plurality of gods in the vulgar.

One can say the same about the holy epics, the Ramayana and the Mahabharata. Pantheism frequently shows up in the Ramayana,[115] and in it one also finds the doctrine of the three worlds taught by the Vedas,[116] as well as the priestly notion that attributes to the gods the invention of all the sciences and arts. This idea serves as the introduction to the work, and the episode of the two birds is recounted with particular charm. (One is killed by a hunter and missed by its companion; this touches Valmiki's compassion and inspires the harmonious rhythm that Brahma blesses.)[117] As for the Mahabharata (of which the Bhagavad Gita is a part), the pantheistic doctrine is even more manifest; but its poetry necessarily led the poets to replace abstractions with images and stories in which individuality returned.[118]

114. Ibid., XI, 126.

115. Ramayana, bk. I, or Adi-Kanda, sect. 2, where it is said: "He who reads this section in the midst of a circle of sages, at the time of his death will be absorbed into the bosom of the divinity."

116. Tell me who is great and powerful, preserving the three worlds (ibid., bk. I, sect. 1). Ravana, celebrated in the three worlds (ibid.). Duscharrata, celebrated in the three worlds (ibid., sect. 6). Ravana, troubling the three worlds (ibid., sect. 14). Two formulas or prayers; Bala and Atibala, powerful in the three worlds (ibid., sect. 20). Bali, son of Virochana, renowned in the three worlds (ibid., sect. 27).

117. The *sloka*, thus named from the Indian word *schoka*, "pain" or "sadness," in commemoration of the sadness of the bird whose companion had died. Mr. Chezy has published a short but learned and insightful treatise on this rhythm.

118. The Ramayana offers us a singular example in section 26 of book I. Vishvamitra gives magical weapons to Rama. These arms are simultaneously all the gods and all the forces of nature. After their long enumeration, the poet adds: "And these invincible weapons, repeating the mantras in the pre-

If the color of these epics is in a sense more solemn and philosophical than those of Homer, the gods of the Ramayana are no less individualized, no less passionate, no less different in their characters, penchants, and wills, than the gods of Homer. This variety—which is harmonized with pantheism only by means of a series of arguments that are quite difficult to follow—necessarily had to have an effect on the people. The multitude from whom a most jealous prohibition keeps these sacred volumes[119] is nonetheless allowed to hear them recited in the ceremonies it attends, and what this teaches them cannot but further confirm them in their polytheistic belief.[120]

It is certain that the Indian who, while pirouetting twelve times, exclaims in his prayers, I am Brahma, the universe is me, nothing but I exist in the universe, does not attach to these words any philosophic sense. At the moment when he repeats them, his multiplied worship of divinities who are infinite in number proves that he does not adhere to the exclusive conception in pantheism that denies all diversity. To stubbornly see in pantheism the definitive doctrine of India is, therefore, to take a part, even a fraction, for the whole, and to generalize a partial truth, which is the infallible means of committing an error.[121]

---

scribed form, presented themselves to Rama, his hands joined, and saying to him: 'Command, O son of Ragha, hero with the powerful arm.'" Having examined them and taken them in his hand, Rama answered them: "Go, and when you hear my voice come running." And these terrible arms, humbly lowering their head, retired from him." The incoherence of the image betrays the struggle between poetry and pantheism.

119. By reading the Ramayana, the *cuttery* becomes a monarch, and the *vaisya* obtains all commercial prosperity; the *soudra*, the artisan, does not have permission to read it himself, but he can hear it being read (Ramayana, bk. I, sect. i, *ad finem*).

120. Since the Ramayana is little known in France and so difficult to obtain, when reporting the fables taken from it we have always referred our readers to the *Recherches asiatiques*, where these fables are found, because it was difficult for us to find a more convenient way of verifying our citations; but in the chapter to follow, in which we deal with several modifications that are particular to the Indian religion, we will have to turn to the details of the poem of Valmiki.

121. Mr. Guigniaut seems to us to have committed this error, at least to a certain point. A single spirit, a single soul, a single life coming from one and the same principle, are spread throughout the entire universe, he says, and the universe is nothing but a grand manifestation of the Most High where a thousand forms of the unique substance circulate. Monotheism in India is really a refined pantheism (pp. 276–77). Supposing the Brahmins to be always correct in their logic, no doubt Mr. Guigniaut's assertion is true; but every mind does not arrive at the final conclusion of their premises, and it has been clearly shown to us that several Brahmanistic schools have stopped midway, persisting in theism even though pantheism seems to call to them. The ingenious writer of whom we are speaking felt it

The system of emanation also presents itself under almost the same forms as in Egypt. The divinity is divided into a multitude of gods who, first of all, take on bodies of human form; these bodies, however, are light, diaphanous, and pure. By degrees, their bodies become darker, heavier, and ever more corrupt; these gods thus descend to the condition of men, in order subsequently to return to their original source. Here there is both theism and pantheism:[122] theism in that everything emanates from a single being, to which all are reunited by purifications; pantheism in the tendency of all the partial beings to reunite with the grand Whole, and once this reunion is effected, everything is absorbed in the same substance, and all individuality disappears.[123]

Dualism also makes itself seen. Having entered into metaphysical doctrine with theism and pantheism, both of which have need of it (the one to absolve itself,[124] the other to explain its double appearance), it moves from the sanctuary into the people's fables. In his countless incarnations, Vishnu appears on earth at each moment in order to combat evil, be it under the form of a hero, a reformer, a penitent, a sage; or of a tortoise, a boar, or a lion with the face of a man. Often the good and evil principles are united in the same god considered in two different aspects. Varuna, the god of the seas, sometimes protects and purifies the mortal race; sometimes, surrounded by crocodiles and serpents, it holds souls captive in its depths.

---

himself; because he says on page 263: The most opposed teachings all have, if not their initial source, at least their common sanction, in the Vedas. Therefore there was opposition in the teachings that coexisted, and there was no exclusive teaching.

122. For the system of emanation, see *Extrait des lois de Menu*, by Sir W. Jones (*Asiat. Res.*, V & VII).

123. Mr. Fr. Schlegel wanted to prove that the system of emanation differed essentially from pantheism in that, he says, in the first system evil always remains separate from God. However, he recognized, on one hand, that the teaching of the Bhagavad Gita is a pure pantheism, and, on the other, that in the same work Krishna declares that the wicked, the foolish, and vile souls will not enter him. This apparent contradiction signifies nothing other than that to occasion the return of the different partial natures, or rather apparent natures, into the universal being, the sole that exists, these partial natures must become homogeneous with the universal being; but when this homogeneity is achieved, there is no more individuality. Pantheism is forced by the evidence to recognize the different modifications of the unique substance; but every system in which these modifications end in the destruction of individuality, and the complete fusion of all being in this substance, is on the way to pantheism (*Weish. der Ind.*, p. 59).

124. We will see this later in book X, chapter 4, which treats of the malevolent deities admitted by all priestly religions, in which sense theism has recourse to the doctrine of a perverse being, either equal or subordinate to the good principle, in order to deal with the existence of evil.

Shiva is beneficent when he rests on Mount Kailash, having a bull for a mount and a gazelle for an emblem, pleased with the happiness he grants when his luminous visage turns to transmit to the corrupted world a refreshing current, source of prosperity and delights; but soon malevolent, he demands blood, is pleased with tears, and his mouth emits devouring flames. Finally, Ganga or Bhavani, this goddess of India, the weaver of nature, the dominatrix of the Himalayas, the primitive water that grants all beings the gift of existence, becomes Cali the terrible, who presides in the other world over the torments of sinners, and here demands human victims.[125]

What we have just said about theism, pantheism, emanation, and dualism applies to atheism. In whatever way one interprets and even tortures the doctrine of Fo, the beginning and end of this doctrine are the void and nothing. The ancestors of the human race came from nothing, and they returned to nothing; we all will return there. All living and non-living beings are different only in appearance, like snow, ice, and hail, which are but different forms of water. Matter alone exists. Birth, death, crime, virtue, moral blemishes, and purification on this earth—all are illusions. If one wants to avoid the word "atheism," one can call this a materialized pantheism; but it is based on the same principles as atheism, and it ends with the same consequences; and the special confidence the reformer made to his disciples on his deathbed,[126] which, even if it is not a historical fact nonetheless expresses the basis of the system, testifies against the subtleties that these disciples now invoke to ward off the accusation of atheism leveled against them by all the other sects. Nonetheless, among the Buddhists, as among the orthodox Brahmins, all the hypotheses coexist; and what is more, by means of precautions we spoke about above,[127] this class of men maintains the people in wholly contradictory opinions. This class conforms itself to the external rites, it imposes and extols them, and tradition shows them going out after their master has expired to astonish the people with the austerity of their penances and the fervor of their religious invocations.

---

125. This portion of Indian mythology has many resemblances to Persian ideas. Vishnu shows himself under the same traits as the heroes Rustan and Feridoun, whose exploits are still celebrated. Frederic Schlegel attributes a Persian origin to Indian dualism (*Weish. der Ind.*, pp. 134, 135). Why, he says, since so many things have come from India, would nothing have returned there with the additions or changes wrought in other countries? Whatever may be the value of this hypothesis, what is beyond doubt is that dualism is one of the dominant doctrines in the Puranas.

126. See above, bk. VI, ch. 3.

127. See bk. VI, ch. 3.

The elements that compose the religions of Egypt and India are therefore identical. Both contain fetishism, science, and philosophy, the latter giving rise to hypotheses that have presented themselves to the human spirit everywhere, hypotheses of which the priests do not exclusively adopt one, but which they deposit in the sanctuary.[128]

Finally, a last circumstance completes the identity. Constrained like the Egyptian priests to express the metaphysical hypotheses in figurative language, the Brahmins have transformed them into cosmologies characterized by monstrous intercourse and births, rapes, and incest. It would take too long to enter into the details of these cosmogonies, which are more complicated and incoherent than those of any other people, because the systems they have to explain were more numerous and subtle.

It is enough to show Brahma,[129] the first of beings, pure above all purity, excellent above all excellence, the light of lights, engendering the sacred Word, son of God, parallel to God, the Word whose first letter, presided over by Brahma, contains the earth, the world, men, spring, and the past; the second, presided over by Vishnu, the atmosphere, the vital heat, the autumn, and the present; the third, the sun, winter or the season of rains, and the future that awaits Shiva Mahadeva, the god of destruction. Maya, however, Maya the deceiver, sister and daughter of the all-powerful, Maya, the desire of Brahma, the eternal love, and in its quality as love, illusion, embraces her father with ineffable incestuous desire. Languidly lying on the brilliant fabric woven by her expert hands, she receives throughout time the fruitful seed of him who was alone. A tricolored (red, black, and white) heifer, by the combination of these three colors the emblem of the three forces that create, conserve, and destroy, she gives birth to the deceptive forces that people the world of appearances. She changes lies into truth, truth into lies, hiding the universal being that truly exists behind the partial ones who do not.

The fundamental ideas of this cosmology are found everywhere. According to a tradition, the original force, Adishakti, gave birth to the three gods, the Trimurti,

---

128. Despite what we pointed out above as a slight error on the part of Mr. Guigniaut, he was not able to completely reject the truth we established. His second chapter on India demonstrates, perhaps more than he knew, not the succession but the simultaneous existence of theism, pantheism, emanationism, and dualism in the Indian systems.

129. This very abbreviated cosmogony is drawn from the Oupnekhat; it can be found at greater length in the book on India in the excellent work of Mr. Guigniaut. We did not need to treat it as extensively, since our aim here was only to note its identity with the other cosmogonies of priestly peoples; later we will be called to return to several details.

brought together in a single body. She fell blindly in love with them, and she espoused her children. Following another tradition, from the seed of Adishakti, the
creative energy, was born Siva, the energy that kills. He who existed alone, says the
Yajur-Veda, was seized with fear; but he reflected: what do I have to fear, I who
am alone? But then he was gripped by love; but what did love do for him in his
solitude? He desired the existence of another, and he became like male and female
in their mutual embraces. The two halves then separated, and the woman, fearing
incest, took on different forms: she changed into a cow, but he changed into a bull;
into a mare, he into a stallion; into a nanny goat, he into a billy goat; into a sheep,
he into a ram; in this way the different species were created, from the colossal elephant to the imperceptible insect.

In one of the Puranas, the gigantic Atri, one of the first fathers of the human
race, was practicing rigorous penance in a withdrawn place. A generative drop fell
into the Ocean. It is my son, he cried out, I commend him to you. Lazy Ocean let
the seed float at the whim of the winds and waves. Finally, recalling the neglected
deposit, he placed it in the heavens. A moon was born, but pale, imperfect, exhausted by the buffetings it had undergone. The gods then cast it into the bosom
of the waves, surrounding it with fortifying plants and trees full of precious sap,
and soon a new moon emerged in the resplendent air.

According to another story, the visions of the three gods who existed only in
idea encountered at a single point. The shock engendered the white goddess, who
is the Trimurti, a virgin under a triple form; but who at the same time is Sarasvati,
daughter of Brahma, and Bhavani, the wife of Shiva; she celebrated her joy at being
created by dancing, and from her bosom escaped the three eggs from which the
three gods emerged. Here appears the cosmogonic egg that is found in the traditions of all peoples. This egg, half gold, half silver, of which one portion forms the
heavens, the other the earth; whose seed is the day star, whose yoke, the mountains,
veins, the rivers, and whose heat, alternately burning and fertilizing, hardens the
unfeeling rocks or gives life to living beings. But by a series of contradictions that
are peculiar to cosmogonies that contain a subtle metaphysics, the creator himself
becomes the creature of the egg he produces; and it is from this broken egg that he
emerges, the first time he shows itself.[130]

However, born from the mixture and confusion of all the seeds, Haranguer-

---

130. The Indians call this egg Brahmanda, and in a grant of lands, translated by Sir W. Jones (*Asiat.
Res.*, III, 45), it is placed among the presents the king Viran-Risinha offered to the gods.

Behah,[131] sometimes the principle of production, sometimes the collection of subtle elements, sometimes chaos, engenders Pradjapat, at once the first generation, the figure of the world, and the representative of the year. And this Pradjapat moves his hands to his mouth, and this movement engenders the fire of sacrifices, and this fire appears as a steed whose head is to the east, rump to the west, and sides to the north and south; from Pradjapat's seed comes the earth, and from the union of this seed with the word comes the sun; and in his consuming hunger Haranguer-Behah, like Saturn, wants to devour the newly born; daughter of the fear that he inspires in them, the word opposes him; and dividing itself among the names of the different creatures and the expression of divine thoughts, it incorporates itself in the sacred Vedas. Here one cannot fail to see a universal symbol found in the most opposed cosmogonies. This insatiable hunger of Haranguer-Behah, who devours everything that he produces, and who produces only in order to have more to devour, is the terrifying image of the destruction reserved for all that exists. Creation, a transitory work, seems to be only the illusory means of filling an abyss that is never filled. The Greek Chronos is the Haranguer-Behah of the Indians. Should one conclude that this idea came from India? Is it not more plausible that a law of nature that experience reveals before all others—we mean to say: this rapid tendency of all beings toward the unknown abyss that awaits and engulfs them—in all countries has suggested this image to man as soon as he began to reflect?

But if Indian cosmogonies thus resemble in general ways those of all peoples ruled by priests, their climate gives them a special set of characteristics. The love of inactivity, the passion for a dreamy immobility, and the charms of an inner contemplation that softens the shocks from without—these pass from the character of the worshippers to the character of the objects worshipped; and creation, before being brought into being, encounters more than one obstacle from this disposition. The first being created by Brahma fled to the desert in order to give himself over to contemplation until the end of time. Nine *rishis*, products of a second act of the will of the Eternal, all refused the work of creation;[132] only then was it that Brahma, combining the two favorite ideas of generation by the union of the sexes and the energy of contemplation, united with Sarasvati, and from this incestuous union were born one hundred sons who, in their turn, each engendered one hun-

131. In Sanskrit, Hirannya-Garbha, the Stomach of Gold.
132. Bhagavatam; and Polier, *Mythologie des hindous.*

dred daughters. At the same time, by the force of his thought he drew from the depths of the waters the earth, the gods, and the Rudras, who asked him how they could in their turn form creatures. Brahma entered into himself, meditated, and gave birth to the sacred fire; and all these secondary beings, practicing austerities and penances with this fire, during the course of a year manufactured a single cow, the type of cows, who gave birth to 999 calves.

One cannot account for so many strange inventions that seem to be the crude and confused work of an imagination gone mad, except by attributing them to the need that the priests experienced, for the satisfaction of their own intellect, to attain the first causes of the phenomena they observed, and to show — accordingly as they were inclined to theism or pantheism — sometimes the grand Whole subdividing, sometimes the creative being causing the type of the celestial world to emanate from it, to which the material world would correspond. With respect to the dominion of the priests over the multitude, these cosmogonies were superfluous. This empire rested adequately on fetishism and anthropomorphism. But wanting to register their hypotheses and their systems, and being able to express them only in images borrowed from an imperfect language, they built up a repertoire of the most bizarre and obscene figures, explaining the strangeness by symbolism, and covering the obscenity by allegory.

The mixture of these different elements shines out in India as in Egypt. The Adityas, of whom Vishnu is the twelfth, represent the twelve months:[133] behold the astronomical part. These Adityas are the sons of Adidi, the productive force, and of Casyapa, infinite space.[134] Here a cosmogonic hypothesis mixes with astronomy. Finally, Vishnu is one of the most active gods of the popular mythology, and as such brings together the belief that offers idols, the science that observes facts, the metaphysics that seeks their causes, and the cosmogony that is forced to personify. Even in their prayers most marked with pantheism, the Brahmins allude to the observation of the planets, and even more frequently to the ancient forms in which the fetishism or the anthropomorphism of its cradle had clothed the gods.[135] Combining, for example, on one hand, fetishism with astronomy,

133. *Sketches to the Hist. Relig., etc., of the Hindoos*, I, 188.

134. Bhagavatam.

135. In accomplishing the *sandia*, the daily purification of the Brahmin when he rises, he must represent to himself the Brahma in striking red, mounted on a goose, and holding in his four arms one hundred marvelous things; Vishnu also in red and having four arms, carried by the legendary bird called Garuda; Shiva, of a sad and somber white, with three eyes on each of his five faces, carried by

and on the other, astronomy with music, they gave Surya the sun the epithet of Hamsa the swan.[136]

The famous invocation or prayer of the Indians by which Krishna identifies himself,[137] the Gayatri, is a mysterious and complicated thing in which all these notions are found: it is a rhythm,[138] a sacred language, the text of the Vedas, a teaching, an all-powerful ceremony that the Brahmins are obliged to practice without ceasing, a revelation, and, at the same time, a separate being, a goddess, the mother of the universe, the spouse of Brahma, the female sun; all of which means: superstition, astronomy, abstractions, and mysticism mixed in such a way that it is impossible to separate them.

In Tibet, all of whose doctrines derive from the teaching of Fo and are therefore Indian despite the modifications they have received, Cenresi, represented in the figure of a wheel, which expresses the transformation by which he successively became the substance of all souls and all bodies, Cenresi, at once nature, the world, and necessity, the motor of the world, in popular legends is also an infant descended from heaven, exposed on a mountain, found by shepherds, risen to the rank of legislator by his wisdom and his miracles, but who, despairing of the crimes of men, breaks his head against a rock into twelve pieces, each one of which becomes a head.[139] Here the popular fable combines with pantheism by bringing in, rather confusedly to be sure, the idea of a divine sacrifice and redemption by it, an idea we will have to talk about later.

Dherma in the form of an ox. (See bk. VI, ch. 7 on the form of the gods in priestly polytheism.) Passing then to astronomy: Divine sun, exclaims the Brahmin, you are Brahma when you appear on the horizon; Shiva when you shed your rays in the middle of your course; and Vishnu when gentler and less resplendent, you approach the end of it (*Nittia-Carma, ou Grand Rituel des brames*).

136. A writer who perverts everything, confuses everything, and, we can add, is ignorant of everything wants to reduce the Indian idea of the sun to a purely abstract notion (journal *Le Catholique*, no. 15, p. 527), because in some passages of the Vedas the sun is Brahma, or pure spirit. No doubt, in the purely metaphysical part; but it is no less the material sun worshipped by the people in its literal sense, and an astronomical god in the teaching of the learned. God save us from men who want to see only one idea where a variety of ideas are placed alongside one another and contradict, without excluding, one another.

137. See above, n. 108.

138. This rhythm, called *gayatriyam*, is composed of a stanza of three lines, each with eight syllables, or rather of a single line of twenty-four, separated by a caesura that puts sixteen at the beginning and eight at the end (*Asiat. Res.*, XIV, 49).

139. Georgi, *Alph. Tibet.*

If one sought a final example of the most extravagant fables combined with science and mystical ideas, one would find it in the history of Trishanku, the most bizarre of the episodes collected in the Ramayana. One of the ancestors of Rama, Trishanku conceived the project of ascending, while alive, to the celestial abode. Rebuffed by the penitents he asked, and whose curses changed him into a pariah, he addressed himself to the powerful Vishvamitra, who prepared a sacrifice to which the gods were invited. On their refusal to attend, Vishvamitra, by the power of his austerities, launched Trishanku into the ethereal sphere. The gods cried to him: "Your place, O *tchandala*, is not among us." Cast down from the height of the air, the king spewed torrents of blood. His protector caught him in his fall, and, by a second effect of the penitential practices he had performed, he created new gods, a new firmament, and new stars. The Indian Olympus capitulated; its inhabitants addressed humble supplications to Vishvamitra. Trishanku remained suspended, head toward the earth but surrounded with a brilliant light; and all the stars created by Vishvamitra are maintained in a lower station, resplendent with the light his words communicated to them. This fantastical story obviously indicates astronomical discoveries communicated by the priests in their fabular language; it also contains the customary ideas of India concerning the merit and power of voluntary suffering, the confirmation of the dominion of the Brahmins (who constrain the gods to obey them), and, finally, allusions to geographical science, because the blood Trishanku coughed up reddened the river Sama, which flows in the part of Tibet called Tsan by the Chinese.[140]

This amalgam of popular fictions with science sometimes introduces contradictions that are difficult to account for when one seeks a chimerical unity;[141] sometimes it produces very singular (and often amusing) tales. Suranah or Suranu, the wife of the sun, not being able to support the glare that surrounded her spouse, secretly fled from him. Made miserable by her absence, the sun asked her back from Twashta, his father-in-law. The latter proposed, as the only way to have a lasting reconciliation, to let his rays be shorn. The sun consented, and placed upon a wheel he was shorn of his hair; this is why when the haze clears, he appears without sunbeams, but as a round and reddish mass. But Twashta had performed the operation

140. Another story attributes the red color of the waters of this river to Rama, who was forced to avoid the paternal curse by cutting off the head of his mother, then washed his bloody scimitar in its waves.

141. Mr. Guigniaut asks how one can reconcile the idea of an original fall and pantheism: there is nothing to reconcile when contradictions are the essence of the thing.

inexpertly, and his son-in-law had several wounds; hence the spots that sometimes appear in the evening on the disc of the sun.[142]

Thus, in the priestly religions there is a perfect similarity, not only as far as content but also in the organization of the material. Science is attached to fetishism by way of personifications, to philosophy by symbols; in order to recount the facts observed by science, and to assign them their causes, philosophy borrows fetishism's images and tales; and fetishism, while associated with science and philosophy without the multitude being aware of it, remains the religion of the people by becoming a part of the priestly idiom.

142. It was with these rays that Twashta formed fire that served all earthly uses: until then there was fire only in the sun, and men could not acquire it. Twashta is therefore something of the Prometheus of India; but Prometheus was severely punished for having used cunning and violence, while Twashta, having shorn the sun with its permission, legitimately profited from his deed (*Asiat. Res.*, XI, 68–69).

CHAPTER 6

On the Causes That Modified This Combination in India, without, However, Winning the Day against the Priesthood

In beginning the chapter one has just read, we announced that it would not contain an exposition of the teachings or the rituals of the Indian religion, and that we simply wanted to indicate the elements of which the religion was composed and the way in which they were combined. As a consequence, many questions had to be postponed. Nothing was said about the character of the gods, their relations with men, the influence of these relations on morality, the notions—whether popular or philosophic—concerning the life to come, and on human destiny. These will be treated elsewhere; one, however, demands some treatment at this point.

Identical with the priestly cults in its materials and their organization, the religion of India is superior to them in many respects, however. Made mysterious by the priests, it seems to experience a need to expand, as it were, that fights against the disposition to mystery. Too often cruel under the empire of a caste, there is an innate sentiment of sympathy and mildness to it that the theocratic spirit cannot stifle. One would say about the Indians that they are a people of children accustomed to respect cruel masters, but contemplating their harsh practices with real astonishment; and who combine with the rites they do not understand a cheerfulness that nothing can destroy, and an innocence that nothing can taint.

One departs from Egypt exhausted, oppressed by an atmosphere where breathing is difficult and existence burdensome. One flees Gaul with horror, haunted by hideous and bloody spectacles over which a somber mysticism near to magic hovers. One finds this oppression, this mysticism, and these bloody spectacles in India as well, yet one comes near it charmed. The oppression weighs less, thanks to the elasticity of an imagination that plays with the yoke that has been imposed. The mysticism is embellished with élans of enthusiasm and songs of love. The hideous spectacles are relegated to a distance that veils them, and, mixing them with fabulous traditions, gives to the reality that still exists an air of fictitiousness that softens its horror.

Whence this difference? From two causes. We have already alluded to one;[1] we need to return to it a second time. We will indicate the other, and perhaps these results will appear to be novel and worth considering.

The climate is the first of these causes. Less harsh and more serene than that of Germany and Gaul, no less pure but less monotonous than Egypt's, India's climate benevolently cradles the inhabitants of that country under its riant variety. The material world displays itself poetically, and this poetry penetrates the soul, which reproduces it no less brilliantly and even more fantastically.

To be sure, the priests have exercised their power in order to poison these gifts of heaven; but at least in part they have failed before nature; and they themselves have sometimes yielded to its ascendancy: their creeds have become less severe, their songs more harmonious; and despite their efforts, surrounded by images that charm him, happy when he is permitted to be, peaceful when he is not made mad by a fanaticism foreign to his character, the Indian has remained benevolent despite the Brahmins who command him to abhor what does not belong to his caste, as well as tolerant, even though the Brahmins have often dragged him into bloody wars and pushed him to horrible massacres.

In order to understand the effect of the climate on the Indians, one must read their sacred poems. They clothe their most abstract doctrines in vivid colors; when they encounter traditions containing a too shocking ferocity, they envelop them in a profusion of images that barely allows them to be seen, and when nothing in their religion contrasts with natural affections, they express them with an energy and tenderness that cannot be found in any of the masterworks of antiquity, and that one would seek in vain in the civilized poetry of our modern times. What is more innocent, for example, and more gracious, than the description of the courtesans sent to attract to the court the pious Dasharatha, the son of a sage who has withdrawn into the forest? His ignorance of the distinction between the sexes, his astonishment at the sight of the various female forms, the harmonious movements of these unknown seducers, their white skin, their diaphanous garments, the sound of the bells that decorate their agile feet, the sensuality and alacrity of their dance, the first stirrings of a desire unknown until then, and which enters sweetly into an innocent soul, the heavens resounding with ineffable melodies,

1. See bk. IV, ch. 2.

the gods pouring torrents of perfume on the boat that bears Rishyashringa and his beautiful companions, everything is lovely in this picture.[2] What the other cults of the same nature present as an ignoble mixture of superstition and debauchery is transformed under the fingers of Valmiki into a magical combination in which desire and sensuality become religious, and religion invites to pleasure.

And if we transport ourselves next to Dasharatha, forced to expose his son to the perils of war; if we lend an ear to the groans of this old man burdened with eleven thousand years, and who is bound by an oath against which his paternal heart protests; if we see him casting himself at the feet of the powerful Vishvamitra, asking grace from him, and repeating a thousand times this touching refrain: "Rama, my beloved, is my life, my support, my supreme treasure. I cannot live without Rama. How will he be able to confront these ten-headed monsters? O sage! Do not deprive me of Rama,"[3] without any hesitation we would place these passages alongside the famous description of Venus's girdle, where desire, sweet words, and flattering prayer triumph over wisdom itself;[4] as well as the goodbyes of Hector and Andromache, or Priam's lamentations.

In general, the comparison of the Ramayana with the *Iliad,* whether in literary, philosophic, or religious terms, would be a singularly worthwhile and instructive endeavor. The hatred of priests, a distinctive characteristic of Greek heroes and kings, and the boundless veneration of the Indians for their Brahmins, the contrast of the simple yet sublime poetry of Homer with the exuberant imagination of Valmiki, the similarity of events and difference of mores, would shed light on the changes circumstances and times imprint on the human race.

The first book of the Ramayana presents us with a narrative similar in its details, although opposed in its results, to that which begins the second song of the *Iliad.* Jupiter sends a deceptive dream to Agamemnon in order to move him to lead the Greeks to battle. Vishnu, wanting to become incarnate in the womb of Kaushalya, brings to Dasharatha, her spouse, the potion that is to prepare the miraculous

---

2. O my divine father, says Rishyashringa to Vibandouka who questions him, young men with enchanting looks have come near to me. They have pressed globes against my bosom, beautiful to see and soft to the touch, which decorate their breast. They have pressed perfumed kisses upon my lips. They have sung airs that intoxicated me, and swaying in harmony they have captivated me with a thousand varied and irresistible poses (Ramayana, bk. I, sect. 9).

3. Ramayana, bk. I, sect. 20. We do not cite the charming episode of the death of Yajnatabada, because it is well known by all learned or studious men by the elegant translation of Mr. Chezy.

4. *Iliad,* XIV, 214.

pregnancy. But the description of the heavenly messenger is laconic in the Greek poet: the master of the gods summons the dream, speaks to it; the dream flies to the son of Atreus, fulfills his mission, and disappears.[5] The author, impatient to get to the action, suppresses all the details that would slow it down.

But the Indian poet, in contrast, delights in drawing a picture of everything that would recall the divine splendor. Certain to please his readers, he leisurely depicts the supernatural being that descends from the heavens. "From the midst of the flame that rose on the altar of sacrifice, in the midst of celestial melodies that filled the air, rose suddenly a supernatural being of incomparable brilliance and incomparable stature, clothed in striking purple, powerful, heroic, irresistible; his face was black, his eyes burned with a fire without parallel; his hair and his beard were of an azure color, they covered his breast and his shoulders with tufts of hair; he was equal in height to the highest mountains, strong like a majestic tiger; similar to the sun, his form shone like a burning flame; in his muscles were found the vigor of the lion. His hands were covered with varied jewelry; twenty-seven pearls surrounded his neck; his teeth resembled the king of the stars; he pressed to his bosom, like a beloved wife, the urn of gold with silver sides filled with the divine *payousa*, the ambrosia of the immortals. Approaching Rishyashringa, he says: 'See in me the emanation of Brahma; take this drink, and let Dasharatha receive it from your hands.'"[6]

The same difference between Homeric and Indian poetry is found in an episode of the Ramayana rather similar to the story of Briseis, except that in the *Iliad* she is a captive, and in the Ramayana, the cow Sabala.

Two verses of Homer are enough to recount the departure of the young prisoner,[7] whose mute sadness is recalled only much later. Valmiki devotes fourteen to depict a Sabala who is at once plaintive and threatening: "Sabala, taken away by the monarch with audacious aims, meditates alone while crying, full of despair. How am I forgotten by the penitent with powerful words, and dragged away, the outraged victim of the servants of a king? What did I do to the prophet whose sight penetrates the secret of things, so that the sage exempt from moral taint would abandon me thus, me, so faithful? And meditating, and meditating again, she races away, knocking over thousands of her profane guards, and runs more rap-

5. Ibid., II, v. 6.
6. Ramayana, bk. I, sect. 14.
7. *Iliad*, I, 345, 346.

idly than the wind to the threshold of the hermitage. She arrives, tormented with anguish and bathed in tears, and sobs at the feet of the holy man of bitter lamentations. You desert me, O blessed one, learned in the Vedas, rich in austerities, son of Brahma, you desert your humble companion"; and the sage responds to her as an adopted daughter, as a beloved sister.[8]

Here we are only indicating some examples, but these examples belong to a whole: they demonstrate the opposite character of the two genres of poetry. Homeric poetry is entirely external, ardent, full of movement, squeezed into those of its descriptions that are not indispensable to the action itself, more narrative than lyrical, adapted more to the retelling of deeds than to the vagaries of reverie; as a result, it is little religious, and devotes religion to earthly purposes instead of elevating it above the human sphere. Essentially meditative, Indian poetry concerns itself with the surrounding objects only to draw them to itself, take them in, and, as it were, identify them with itself; one sees in its often overwrought descriptions, its too frequent repetitions, in the accumulation of confused, incoherent epithets that tend by their subtle harmony to give rise to emotion rather than to describe external objects, that it attributes only a relative reality to such objects, and that for it true reality is in the soul, which always aspires to unite itself with God. This disposition makes the poetry of India eminently religious. Movement bothers it, contemplation enchants it; it is never happy except with this daughter of repose; it always leaves her with regret and therefore with a certain effort; and the less that action is its element, the more it employs striking colors and gigantesque forms in its accounts; when it departs from its nature, it does violence to itself, and this violence imparts something convulsive and disordered to it.

Nonetheless, it constantly returns to its native gentleness; it attempts to soften the fierce traditions that revolt it. Omburischa the king wanted to sacrifice a human victim; Indra saved him from the sacred fire. The king persisted. A poor Brahmin sells him one of his sons for millions of the purest gold, heaps of diamonds, and one hundred thousand cows. The unfortunate son encounters Vishvamitra practicing his holy penances. His heart full of anguish, he casts himself at the feet of the famous penitent. "No longer for me," he says, "is there either a father who protects me or a mother who caresses me, no faithful friend, nor companion on the earth. O you whose voluntary sufferings have endowed with divine energy, save an unfortunate one without hope; let the king's sacrifice take place, but let me live."

8. Ramayana, bk. I, sect. 42.

Touched with compassion, Vishvamitra orders his children to replace the stranger who had implored him; they refuse, and his curses make them unclean pariahs. Turning then to the suppliant: "Recite," he said, "at the instant you are offered as a victim this powerful mantra[9] that I give you, agreeable praise in honor of Indra and the other gods." The ceremony begins, the gods approach with eagerness to participate; but the victim intones the mysterious hymn, and Indra, charmed, delivers him by granting the king the fruit of a vow whose fulfillment he prevented.

Everything in this narrative is significant. The poet allows himself no blame: the immolation of a human victim seems to him to be a virtuous act; the victim himself does not want the sacrifice to be interrupted; the prince is rewarded for his pious intention. The priestly influence is completely manifest here;[10] but the Indian character, which does not dare fight against this influence, eludes and triumphs over it by reconciling the merit of the sacrificer and the salvation of the victim.[11]

What we know of the Mahabharata will provide our claims with new proofs. Several parts of this epic have striking likenesses to the *Odyssey*. The voyages of Bhima are analogous to the long travels of Ulysses; and the episode of the giant Hidimbo, a monstrous cannibal, resembles Polyphemus. But the Indian poet throughout adds to the strange adventures he recounts gentler and more profound sentiments than the Greek poet. The love of the sister of Hidimbo contrasts with the brutal ferocity of her brother, while nothing softens the half-burlesque, half-repulsive portrait of the savage Cyclops; and the filial and fraternal devotion of Bhima is painted in much more touching colors than the somewhat cold respect that Telemachus has for Penelope, as well as the so-long-delayed reunion of this queen with her husband.

An analogous character is manifest in all the ceremonies and rituals. The celebration of marriage recounts the alliance of man with nature, be it living or nonliving. It is in the name of the thirst-quenching water, the purifying fire, the restorative air, and the gods who reside in the elements that the young spouse is given to her husband, with these words: "Let all the assembled divinities chain your hearts to each other; let water, air, and fire unite you, and above all be united by love, that intoxicating potion. Three intoxicating beverages are drawn from the grain, from

---

9. Prayer or hymn in honor of the gods.

10. In a subsequent book we will prove that in all countries the prolonging of human sacrifices was solely the work of the priesthood.

11. Ramayana, bk. I, sect. 48.

milk, and from the flowers of Brahma; the fourth is woman. They intoxicate by
their scent, by their looks. It is love that gives this virgin, it is love that receives her.
Sama who directs the silver moon, once confided her to a Gandharba who shone
in the celestial choirs; this Gandharba passed her to the god of fire; the god of fire
yields her to you, and with her, wealth and a numerous posterity. Sun that presides
over the divine harmonies, darting rays, nymphs of the sun, brilliant stars, nymphs
of the moon, fecund rains, nymphs of the air, and you sacred hymns, nymphs of
the intellect, protect this happy couple. Charming Sarasvati by whom all the elements were created, sanctuary where the seeds of the universe developed, hear this
nuptial song, glory of spouses. Be my companion, says the spouse in his turn, while
pouring over the head of the virgin bride water that cleanses all stains, be my companion, the breath of my breath, bone of my bones, essence of my essence, let no
one break our bonds. I invoked the goddess of happiness, and you are this goddess.
I am the Sama-Veda and you, the Rig-Veda. I am the sun and you are the earth. Remove by this water endowed with a marvelous power the sinister omens that might
be hidden in your eyebrows and your hair, everything that would be sinful in your
words or your smiles, everything that would be impure in your gracious hands, in
your lithe legs, and your most secret charms. Daughter of the sun, mount upon
this chariot similar to the seven-petaled flower,[12] painted in various colors, shining
like gold. Source of ambrosia, increase the prosperity of your husband; let all be
gay, let all be caressing, let all be pleasure and joy." Finally, the priest comes to command the gods in a solemn voice: "Air, fire, moon, sun, expiators of evil, remove
all the marks that would tarnish the beauty of this virgin, everything in her that
would harm her spouse. Woman, I banish far from you the threats, dangers, and
enchantments of the evil *genii*, everything that would threaten your beloved, your
race, your flocks, your goods, and your name. Now let the sacrificial cow—other
times offered in sacrifice—today be put at liberty by the prayer of the young wife;
do not kill the innocent cow, the mother of the Rudras, the daughter of Vasus, the
sister of the Adityas, who generously gives us streams of delicious milk; let go her
reins, let her eat the grass of the prairie, and nourish herself with healthy plants,
and drink long draughts of the pure water of the sacred river."[13]

These ceremonies which are so poetic are combined, it is true, with obscene
practices: the image of the Lingam wounds the sight; the priest offends virginal

12. The cobbler.
13. Extracts from the Yajur-Veda and the Sama-Veda.

modesty by bringing indiscreet hands to the generative organ that is to be touched with a holy oil; and it was probably from India that the revolting practice came to Rome in the last days of a corrupt republic that forced the newly married woman to sacrifice the beginnings of the virginity she was to lose to hideous idols.

But here, too, it was the priestly *genius* abusing the idea of sacrifice,[14] and pursuing with its bizarre laws the human race in its most intimate affections and pleasures.

Philosophy itself, even in its rashest speculations, experiences the beneficent influence of the climate. Contrast the pantheism of India with that of China or Tibet. Chinese pantheism offers only a blind and mute force; mechanism dominates in religious thinking, as in political organization. One would call it the ossified debris of a world that no longer exists, whose gigantic forms, while stirring astonishment, present only the idea of death. In India, on the contrary, something living escapes from the priestly clutches: ingenious images, while attesting to the identity of god and the soul, profit from the momentary difference to encourage man to perfection. "Two birds inhabited the same tree: one ate its fruits; the other, not touching them, contemplates and awaits his companion. One is god, the other is the soul contained in the body; it is the plaything of illusion, and deplores its own impotence. But when she discovers the one who lives with her, union occurs, eternal and intimate, and the soul is delivered from all error and all suffering." There is individuality in the account, despite the doctrine that proscribes individuality; and the marvelous diversity of forms lets them escape from the exclusive unity to which logic and doctrine try to reduce them.

The second circumstance that distinguishes Indian religion from all the beliefs subject to priests is the theory of incarnations; a theory that in truth all these religions endorse, but none of which makes the use of that the Indians do. First inculcated by the priesthood for its benefit, this theory later reacted against it.

As the Indians understand it, it has nothing unreasonable about it.[15] They say

14. In a later book we will treat the licentious rituals brought into the priestly religions by the idea of sacrifice.

15. In directing all the force of their logic against this notion, our missionaries have more than once gone further than they would have wanted. In the Chama-Veda, an apocryphal work probably composed by a Jesuit, founder of the mission of Madourai in 1620 (Robert de Nobilibus, or de Nobilis, close relative to the Pope Marcel II and nephew of Cardinal Bellarmine); in the Chama-Veda, we were saying, the author teaches that the Supreme Being never becomes incarnate; that it never had commerce with women, and that it is impious to say or to think this. But an English writer from

that as soon as one admits a benevolent power that created man in order to perfect him and make him happy, by what right can one refuse this power its choice of means toward this goal? When corruption or ignorance causes the work of his hands to err, given his pity and his indulgence, how can one prohibit him from sending an emanation of himself to reopen the path to heaven? By recognizing the miracle of creation one has ruled out denying any other miracle. The real absurdity is when one limits to a determinate country or time the action of this benevolent Providence; on the contrary, it begins anew each time the world has need of it, and the world, they add, constantly has need of it.[16]

This doctrine is found everywhere in the Puranas. The earth complains that under the weight of iniquity it is ready to fall back into the abyss; the gods groan under the oppression of evil *genii*. Vishnu consoles them by promising a savior who will break this tyranny. This savior, he says, will be born among the shepherds and in the hut of a shepherd; and in a further refinement (which belongs to ideas that we do not need to develop here), this savior becomes incarnate in the womb of a virgin.

In order to parry the specious objections that these strange, sometimes scandalous accounts might suggest to hard-to-please judges, the Indians suppose that once incarnate the divinity does not know himself: subject to all the errors, vices, and infirmities—the unhappy lot of spirit united with matter—the god who becomes incarnates loses awareness of his divine nature. He identifies with the form that he took on. The action of the present effaces the memory of the past.[17] Thus Brahma became an unclean *tchandala* who for a long time lived by theft and mur-

---

whom we borrow these facts asks: if the missionary succeeded in convincing his disciple, would he find himself embarrassed when it came to the mysteries of the Christian faith? (*Asiat. Res.*, XIV).

16. See the phrase of the Bhagavatam cited above (ch. 5). Every time virtue loses its force, and vice or error dominates, I come running, says Krishna too, in order to protect justice, punish the wicked, and give to the good the energy it lacks (Bhag. Gita).

17. This singular notion is one of the principal causes of the obscurity that covers Indian mythology. One never knows if the incarnation acts in its quality as a man or a celestial being; and what is even more inexplicable, the knowledge of his divine nature changes nothing in his relations with the inhabitants of the earth. In the Ramayana (bk. I, sect. 62), when another Rama who is not the hero of the poem comes to attack the latter, his father, Dasharatha, is seized by fear; he begs the aggressor not to kill his son; and when this aggressor recognizes as an emanation of Vishnu the foe he has imprudently challenged, he throws himself on his knees and asks for pardon. Dasharatha nonetheless continues to see in Rama his beloved son, and to tremble for his life each time he confronts a new danger and to rejoice each time he avoids imminent death by his valor and strength.

der; but suddenly recalled to his divine essence by the prayers and merits of two penitents, this vile pariah was raised to the first rank of the inspired and the poets. He explains the Vedas, and the wisest humble themselves before his marvelous interpretations. He takes the lyre, and the echoes of his harmonious songs resound in the Ramayana, and the earth is instructed and corrected by learning the history of Vishnu, already descended seven times among mortals, from Valmiki. Finally taking his own flight for heaven, this poet Valmiki, an unclean being who became regenerate, whose name was once the object of horror but is now the object of veneration and enthusiasm: he is Brama atoning for a rash pride, sentencing himself to celebrate Vishnu. In the same way, Vishnu incarnated as Balaramen or Bala-Rama does not recall that he is a god except when, as the destroyer of the giants, he liberates the human race from the sacrilegious worship these giants had imposed.[18]

This theory of incarnations has continued in India until our day. The Sikhs, a sect of deists who for four centuries have undergone bloody warfare against the orthodox and the Muslims,[19] regard Gobind Singh, who won great victories for their belief, as the tenth avatar; Gobind Singh died at the beginning of the eighteenth century.

If one now reflects upon the direct and necessary consequences of this fundamental principle of the Indian religion, one will find it quite favorable to the progressive development of this religion. It prepares the imagination to contemplate new marvels and the understanding to receive new doctrines. It represents doc-

18. Sonnerat, I, 139–140.

19. The origin and development of this sect, founded by Nanak circa 1490, are recounted in a very credible and interesting way by Colonel Malcolm in the *Recherches asiatiques* (XI, 197, 292). The transition from a peaceful and tolerant spirit to a bellicose and persecutorial one, as the chances of success nourish hope or the cruelties of adversaries inflame hatred, is interesting to observe. This is a proof that whenever opinions take over a corporate body and raise a banner, or in our phrase, take on a form, their dangers are the same whatever their nature. Nothing is purer, nothing gentler, than the theism of Nanak. Like original Christianity, it rests upon a universal benevolence and a perfect equality. But nothing is more revolting than the barbarities exercised in the name of this theism by Hargobind, the fifth successor of Nanak, his son Tegh-Bahadur, his grandson Gobind Singh, and, above all, his companion of arms and faith, the fanatic Banda, who, after having shed torrents of blood, killed his son with his own hand without shedding a tear and died torn to pieces by burning pincers without uttering a cry. The history of this sect would have furnished us a superabundant demonstration of the attachment of Indians to polytheism, because it shows us the same Gobind Singh, who was always ready to have theism prevail by sword and fire, nonetheless forced to make numerous concessions to the mythological traditions and ancient divinities his followers refused to abandon.

trine as never being definitively fixed, and always leaves open a space above the law where a better law can appear. As we already said,[20] each incarnation is a period of improvement and reform. The learned Creuzer and his able translator felt this truth in their bones, as it were;[21] but it seems to us that they obscured or falsified it. To hear them, incarnations would be either systems that were originally different, or the remnants of a single system, the work of time and genius, which came from an ancient and primitive Catholicism that was dissolved and fragmented by time.[22] This is an error. There is no unique system; nor were there simply sects with different doctrines. First of all there were crude beliefs, then successive refinements which, despite the priests, the theory of incarnations would favor. To be sure, the times of some of these incarnations could have, even had to have, been inverted, for a reason we gave in our first volume.[23] Thus, even though in the Indian narratives the religion of Brahma preceded that of Shiva,[24] the latter must have been the older because it is the least advanced; and the religion of Brahma, the most metaphysical of all, had to have succeeded Shaivism.[25]

But whatsoever the confusions that had to have been introduced into the mythological chronology by this voluntary reversal of dates (which are impossible to determine with any precision), the progression of ideas, and the myths that express them, is not unrecognizable.[26] This progression makes itself felt even in the forms

20. See above, chap. 5.

21. "One cannot fail to recognize in the religion of India a high development, at once poetic and moral, that had to be the long gestation of the centuries, and the result of a notable progress in the civilization of peoples" (Guigniaut, p. 218).

22. Ibid., pp. 142, 143.

23. Bk. I, ch. 9.

24. Guigniaut, pp. 139–143.

25. In enumerating in the previous chapter the different religious revolutions of India, following custom we placed Brahmanism before Shaivism, because we did not want to dissent from received ideas before putting forth our reason for adopting another chronology, which, moreover, bears more on doctrines than facts.

26. This progression gave rise to several traditions of the Brahmins concerning the manner in which the Vedas were revealed or transmitted. Among these traditions there is one that obviously indicates a reform clothed in a mythological redaction. Vasampayana, the legendary disciple of the legendary Vyasa, had taught the Yajur-Veda to Yajnyawalcya. But this student refusing to assume his part of guilt for a murder committed involuntarily by his master, the latter ordered him to throw up the Yajur, which he immediately had his other disciples, transformed into partridges, swallow. Hence the black or soiled Yajur. However, Yajnyawalcya in his despair invoked the sun. A revelation was granted him, and a new Yajur descended from heaven; it was the white Yajur, which replaced the impure Yajur.

of the incarnations. Vishnu first of all assumes the form of a fish. Soon an amphibian, he extends his action to the earth and the sea; later raising himself higher in the animal kingdom, he becomes a strong and frightening boar; even later, the king of animals, he adds a human head to the body of a lion. His teaching, which is gentler and purer than Shiva's, attests to the march of civilization. The efforts of Krishna against licentious practices,[27] Buddha's efforts against the inequality of castes, are so many steps taken toward less revolting and less oppressive institutions; and these efforts, evaded or proscribed by the Brahmins, nonetheless have the advantage of at least momentarily imparting a salutary direction to minds; and of preserving them from the Egyptian apathy in which the priesthood always tries to keep them.

Unfortunately, the Brahmins constantly fought the salutary influence of the two circumstances we just discussed; and since in this world the good has its inconveniences, as evil has its advantages, the benevolent influence of a climate that bestows so many favors upon the Indians at the same time consolidated the priestly dominion.

A reading of the Ramayana is extremely interesting from this point of view. Everything our travelers have said in blame and disdain concerning the enslavement of the Indians to the Brahmins is surpassed by what we find in the great epic of Valmiki; and his testimony is so much more impressive as it is with real admiration that he reports the proofs of devotion and submission with which they are surrounded. Here it is an opulent city, Uyodhya,[28] where no one dares offer a Brahmin less than a thousand rupees at a time.[29] There, when the son of a hermit approaches, a king leaves his capital at the head of all his court; he returns, modestly following the holy man at a distance; the entire city is decorated with garlands; it sparkles with burning torches, and hymns of obedience resound in its

---

27. One finds in Goerres (II, 556–58) very interesting observations on the reform intended by Krishna, a reformation that by replacing the bloody rites and obscene practices of Shaivism with a purer and milder worship would have procured for India the benefit that Europe received from the substitution of Christianity for the Jewish law (even though we are very far from comparing this law with the barbarous and scandalous worship of Shiva). Then Krishna needs to be considered under two points of view: as the reformer of a popular cult and as a philosopher, having a hidden doctrine contained in the Bhagavad Gita, by attaching it to the names and adventures of the deities adored by the people.

28. She still exists in Indostan under the name Oude, an obvious corruption of the original name.

29. Bk. I, sect. 6.

ramparts.[30] Later, speaking to the priests he employs in the sacrifices, Dasharatha addresses humble petitions to them; he calls himself their servant, their slave; he has thousands of magnificent tents built to receive their brothers, foreign and native, and fills them with exquisite meats and wines. None of them, says the poet, even had to express a wish; all were anticipated by the prince. They constantly extolled the food prepared for them by his command. They exclaimed: "Son of Rhagava, how well you have fed us![31] Let prosperity accompany you!" Elsewhere, this same prince on his knees before sacrificed birds and fish publicly confesses his sins; the Brahmins absolve him of them, and the king offers them immense lands; but they answer: "The study of the Vedas is our mission; far from us the possessions of this world; small presents—cows, a diamond, a bit of gold—this is what we can accept from you." And the king gave them a million cows, one hundred million pieces of gold; four hundred million of silver; seeing that he had pleased the Brahmins, the son of Ikshvaku, his eyes bathed in the tears of a pious joy, prostrated himself at their feet; and their blessings extend in a thousand different forms over the monarch beloved of the gods.[32]

The history of Vishvamitra is no less remarkable. All-powerful king, conqueror without equal, he has defeated all his enemies. He requires the gift of a cow from a Brahmin; the Brahmin refuses; he takes the miraculous animal, which escapes, and by returning to his master[33] reminds him of the superiority of the Brahmin over the warrior. The Brahmin, however, still fearful, doubts his power. "This king," he says, "has innumerable armies of elephants, infantrymen and horsemen; he has a host of chariots, rolling like thunder; his banners are followed by multitudes: what can I do against him?—O Brahmin, answered the marvelous heifer, the strength of the Brahmin is divine and surpasses that of the *cuttery*. Frightening is the arm of

30. Bk. I, sect. 15.

31. Literally translated.

32. Bk. I, sect. 12. We could have cited a thousand other examples. Dascharatha throws himself at the feet of his confessor (Ramayana, bk. I, sect. 11). The hermits that visit Rama do not attend to him except after having adored Vishvamitra (ibid., sect. 27). After a victory, Rama and his brothers prostrate themselves before him (ibid., sect. 28). The king Pramati does the same (ibid., sect. 37). Janaka only approaches the holy man with clasped hands, congratulating himself on being in his presence (ibid., sect. 40). He calls him his master and asks what he commands (ibid., sect. 53). The Brahmins are always called the teachers of kings (ibid., sect. 61). And the gods exhibit no less respect for the sacred caste. Visited by a Brahmin, Krishna embraces his knees, washes his feet, and assigns him a place above his own (Bhag. Purana).

33. See above, earlier in the chapter.

the latter; but the word of the Brahmin is invincible. Command, and I will destroy his fierce soldiers, and I will break the pride of the impious." The Brahmin allowed it, and the bellowing of Sabala caused phalanxes to appear (whose name appears to be an allusion to some historical event);[34] defeated by Vishvamitra, these phalanxes were replaced by others which themselves were constantly replaced; and Vishvamitra, like a torrent deprived of its channel, like a serpent without its teeth, like the sun blocked by an eclipse, fled like a bird whose wings no longer worked. A century of austerities finally gained him the favor of the gods; he obtained enchanted arms from them and returned to attack the Brahmin, the object of his hatred. But even the gifts of heaven yielded to the priestly power. A baton in hand, a cow at his side, the priest called forth the elements and cast flames that consumed the magical weapons; and he cried out: "Madman, now where is your warrior strength? Do you finally know the word of a Brahmin, you insolent ruler, vile like the dust?" And the defeated prince retired, repeating to himself: "The power of the warrior is but an empty dream. Empire belongs to the Brahmin, and to the Brahmin alone."[35]

This is not all: "I too want to be a Brahmin," says the monarch, and by unheard-of penances he overcame the gods. He forced them to compromise with him, to recognize new gods created by his will; nonetheless, when he asked Brahma for the dignity of a Brahmin, he was refused. Then, beginning anew afflictions that lasted a thousand years, he put the world in danger; the gods ran to the feet of Brahma. "Already," they said, "a terrible disorder shows itself at the far reaches of the universe. The seas are troubled, the mountains are shaken, the earth trembles, the winds cease, the human race is going to embrace impiety, and the sun is deprived of its light by the incomparable splendor of an irresistible penitent. Hear his prayer, father of the gods, save heaven from an imminent ruin." And coming forward with the immortal retinue, Brahma addressed himself to Vishvamitra: "We will grant you days without end, power without limits, divine wisdom, unmixed happiness; your austerities have won you the nature and dignity of a Brahmin; be a Brahmin, O Vishvamitra"; thus, alone of all the children of men since the origin of time, Vishvamitra arrived at this eminent and inaccessible dignity.[36]

Finally, to summarize what India thinks of these priests, let us listen to the advice of the old Dasharatha, ready to separate from his son. "Serve the Brahmins

34. The Ramayana calls them Pahlavas, the name that designated the ancient Persians.
35. Ramayana, bk. I, sect. 43.
36. Ibid., sect. 52.

devoted to the study of the Vedas with the greatest diligence. Try to please them; ask their counsel. Let their instruction be received by you like water that gives immortality. O Bharatha! The Brahmins are grand; they are the source of prosperity and happiness. Instruments of the Vedas, the Brahmins are necessary at every moment. In the form of Brahmins, the gods have fixed their abode among mortals in order to ensure the existence of the world. The Brahmins are the gods of the earth; in them reside the Vedas and the Shasters, and incomparable virtue."[37]

Raised in these ideas, the Indians have never shaken off the yoke of the priesthood; it has profited from the mildness of the climate, from the happiness that accompanies repose, and from the credulity of an imagination that reverie lulls in its cradle and which critical examination would have exhausted, in order to preserve and extend its empire. It disarmed the reforms that in the form of incarnations would have been unwelcome, by honoring them in theory and ignoring them in practice. It recognized the divinity of Krishna but maintained the cult of the Lingam. It did not contest Buddha's title as an avatar, but it persisted in the division into castes. Buddhist priests themselves reintroduced it under certain disguises. In a word, the incarnations of India had the fate of the Reformation in more than one country in Europe. The priests unfurled new banners to better establish ancient abuses.

In the final analysis, their fateful skill in manipulation and their invincible tenacity triumphed over the gifts of nature and the developments of the intellect. Cruel in the midst of a gentle people, immobile despite the seed of perfection it contained, absurd in its popular fables, sanguinary and obscene in its rites, fastidious in the duties it imposed,[38] monstrous in its cosmogonies, given over in its

---

37. Ibid., sect. 63.

38. Colebrooke (*Asiat. Res.*, VII, 277) says that Hindu legislators and the authors of the Puranas accumulated a host of precepts that are ridiculous because of their attention to minutiae and often because of their absurdity: sometimes they relate to diet, completely forbidding several foods, prohibiting the habitual use of others, sometimes they regulate the way in which one takes the food that is presented, the hand that one must offer, the plate upon which it must rest, the hour of the morning and evening meals, the places where these meals are permitted, and those where they become a crime; among these latter are on all the kinds of boats, which perhaps is owing to the hatred of the sea that is characteristic of the Indian priesthood, as well as the Egyptian. They indicate the guests next to whom it is permitted to sit (the son belongs to this number while the wife does not), the attitude one must maintain while seated, the point on the horizon where one must fix one's gaze, and above all the precautions one must take to avoid all unclean contact. Later we will see the effect of these multiple precepts on morality, which they corrupt and pervert more than one might believe.

metaphysical hypotheses to all the aberrations to which our mind is condemned (this despite—and perhaps because of—the forms it created to direct itself): this is the religion that weighs heavily upon India. Its excessive spirituality preserves it from neither the crudest notions nor the most repulsive images. In the polytheism that is independent of the priests, we will see spirituality heighten the divine qualities and perfections. In the priestly religions, it adulterates and disfigures them, sometimes by raising them above the grasp of even the most practiced intellect, sometimes by lowering it beneath the conceptions of even the most vulgar intelligence. There, because of certain sacred words, the pure spirit unites to stones, to pieces of wood, to shapeless idols; the infinite is confined in limited beings; change becomes an attribute of the immutable being; movement occurs within the changeless being; the immaterial gods are at the same time animalgods; impassible substances experience pains, passions, and the vanities of our nature; these things coexist because no one perceives the contradictions in the unintelligible;[39] together they make up the strangest chaos; and the result of this chaos for the slaves of the Brahmins is a sort of permanent delirium, the corruption of every idea of the just and the unjust, and the voluntary abdication of every human faculty.

Would someone accuse us of being too harsh? We can cite authorities. We will choose Lord Jones, known for his partiality toward a people that he, as it were, revealed to Europe, and which he has an interest in extolling beyond measure. "The Code of Manu," he says, "forms a system where despotism and the priesthood, both apparently restrained by the laws, in reality conspire to give each other mutual support. This system is filled with absurd notions in both physics and metaphysics, puerile superstitions, and teachings dangerous because of their obscurity, which favor the most bizarre interpretations. The ceremonies are ridiculous, the punishments capricious, often atrocious, while other times indulgent to a fault; its morality, even though generally strict, is on several points—for example, concerning oaths that are violated and perjury excused by pious motives—unimaginably

---

39. Definition of God in the Oupnekhat: "He is great, he is not great; he surrounds, he does not surround; he is light, he is not light; he has and he does not have vision on all sides; he is and he is not the lion that devours everything; he is and he is not terrible; he is and he is not happiness; he makes death vain and he dies; he is and he is not venerable; he says and he does not say: I am in all" (Oupn. 50, n. 178). "He who says I understand him has not understood him; he who does not understand him, understands him, and he who understands him does not understand him" (Oupn., 36, n. 147).

lax."[40] This sentence, which seems to be already quite severe, is not harsh enough according to an observer who is less favorably disposed than Lord Jones. The Brahmins, says Buchanan,[41] have developed no useful science; they have destroyed history, perverted morality, and erected the power of the altar on the ruins of the throne and liberty. In their hands, the laws attributed to Manu, laws which could suit an absolute monarch, have become the most abominable system of oppression ever invented by artifice and ambition; as well as the most degrading.[42]

One could counter with several facts. Those that we have provided concerning the natural influence of the climate of India, for example, could serve to counter us. But if our opponents argue in good faith, let them answer the following questions:

Was not fetishism found in India? Is it not still found there?

By dividing themselves among different doctrines which are more refined than the beliefs of the people, have not the priests of this country let a public religion rooted in fetishism impose itself on this people?

Are not the principal doctrines among which the priests divide themselves theism, pantheism, and atheism?

Is not theism going to be lost in the subtleties that detract from what it has of religious, leaving only what is abstract?

Even though they are more or less artfully connected to the public religion, do not these doctrines remain in fact foreign to this religion, and change nothing in its teachings or rituals?

Does not the combination of a metaphysics that often ends in unbelief among

40. *Asiat. Res.*, V, Preliminary Discourse, IX, X. If a man out of passion lies for a woman, or to save his life, or to not lose his possession, or to render a service to a Brahmin, the deception is excusable (Code des Gentous, by Halhed.).

41. *Asiat. Res.*, V, 166.

42. We have abstained from invoking the witness of the reverend William Ward, to whom, however, we owe a rather useful book on India (*A View of the History, Literature and Religion of the Hindoos*); but this missionary is so fanatical that one cannot have recourse to his authority. Even though we adopt, at least in part, his conclusions concerning the Indian religion, we do not accuse of paganism those who reject them, and nothing seems more ridiculous to us than the lamentations of the missionary over the translation of some Sanskrit hymns by Lord Jones. "It is a violation of neutrality," he declares, "an offense against the Gospel; what would the prophet Elisha have said about such a use of time and talent?" Mr. Ward missed his vocation; it is not Christianity that he ought to defend but Brahmanism: he believes he is their enemy, but he thinks and speaks like them.

the learned classes with an always crude superstition in the mass of the nation produce the most deplorable consequences?

Is it not in vain that theism offers Indians a system that is sometimes consoling
by its hopes, sometimes sublime in its severity? Is it not in vain that pantheism
invites them to repose, emanationism to perfection, and philosophy in general to
disdain for popular superstitions? The divinities of the multitude, are they not individual beings that the faithful beseech according to their desires of the moment,
Indra for the pleasures of the senses, Lakshmi for the success of their endeavors,
Atri and his ancestors to have children, Agni when they want to seduce with their
beauty, Raudra when they want to win with force? Do not the Brahmins persist so
obstinately in the teaching of the ancient fables, that those of Gangotri[43] still recount that the icicles of the rocks of the Ganges are the hairs of Mahadeva.[44] Did
not Abbé Dubois see the feast of Nagara-Panchami being celebrated in honor of
serpents, who were sought in their dens in order to offer them milk and bananas?
And the Pongol of cows, is it not a solemnity in today's India, where believers
prostrate themselves before animals?

At bottom, this is all that matters to us; and none of the foregoing questions can
be answered in the negative.

One is therefore wrong to aspire to elevate the religion of India above all the ancient religions, and for believers of a new sort in our day[45] to place it almost with

43. Gangotri or Gangautri means "cataract." The Ganges has three; and one of them gave its name
to a rather large city (Wilford, "Geography of India," *Asiat. Res.*, XIV, 46).

44. The voyage of Captain Hodgson to the sources of the Ganges (*Asiat. Res.*, XIV, 118).

45. We mean to speak of a recent school that seeks in the theocracies of the East the model of the
theocracy that it hopes to transplant to Europe, and whose intentions are as perverse as its assertions
are deceptive and its tone dogmatic. This school was introduced into France by way of a German
metaphysics that it poorly understands, and a German erudition that it does not possess. One of
the organs of this school is a man of wit who has the learning common to all the students who have
attended German universities, and who knows how to employ this light baggage with a particular
adeptness. Almost always avoiding citations when he affirms something, and adroitly employing citations — albeit often false ones — on secondary points, he utters opinions that are so emphatic that
one has misgivings about contesting anything from a writer who is so convinced of himself. It is only
upon second reading that one discovers his likeness to a great lord disputing on a subject he barely
knew, who ended by saying: "I give you my word of honor that I am right." The aim of this writer is to
establish a grand intellectual authority that would be *the* monopoly of authority, that is to say, which
would make Europe the parody of Egypt. The Brahmins, the Druids, all the corporations that have
oppressed men are the objects of his admiration. Human sacrifices, as well as orgies or debauchery
combined with murder, seem to him to be mysterious representations of an original order, or religious

Christianity, because they hope to derive from the Vedas (works and instruments of a priesthood) means of bending the Gospel to their despotic views; the Gospel, however, is a heavenly teaching that gave back to man his legitimate liberty and his fundamental dignity.

Like the other priestly religions, this Indian religion has all the imperfections of polytheism sans priests, without any of its advantages, and to these imperfections are joined the enslavement of thought, the perpetuation of the errors of each period, and the impossibility of the human spirit to emancipate itself gradually from these errors, which thanks to heaven is a happy potential found in its nature and its destiny.

In ending this chapter, let us repeat once more that we are far from having claimed to have dispelled all the obscurities that surround the subject we just treated. Our readers were able to see the numerous causes that maintain this obscurity. The confusion of records and the uncertainty of their dates, the simultaneity of conflicting doctrines, the indifference of Brahmins toward the contradictions that do not impair their power, the manner in which in pantheism each god is by itself the great Whole, and when we pass to theism, each god in turn is the supreme god under the name of Shiva, Brahma, Vishnu, Indra, or even Devendren (an otherwise subordinate divinity), the peculiarity of the religion that has it that incarnations are at once celestial beings who do not know themselves and human beings who can die, finally, the necessity in which we find ourselves of having to postpone questions that will be treated later:[46] all that has left many lacunae in

---

élans toward a future order: everything is good, provided that liberty plays no role; everything is sublime, provided that individuality is proscribed. The Greeks who had the misfortune of emancipating themselves from the yoke of priests interest the author only by the vestiges of the happier period when priestly domination weighed over their heads. But he sees in the beliefs of India a much higher degree of moral grandeur, and it is to this degree of moral grandeur that he wants to lead us. His work is little read, which we regret. The disguises that the defenders of a lost cause assume are interesting to look at. Defeated by what is actual in the progress of an always growing civilization, defeated in what is abstract by the developments of the intellect (about which they know only their limits), they call to their assistance the errors and oppressions of all the centuries, bending the knee before the symbolic veils that surround this wreckage. They are impotent architects of a building whose plan is lost in the clouds, and whose materials fall to powder.

46. The main questions are: the moral character of the gods that the priestly religions present for worship, the supremacy of one of these gods over the others, the attributes of this god, demonology, the introduction of gods who are wicked by nature, the original fall, the mediating gods, the destruction of the world, the notion of sacrifice and its results, the immolation of human victims, the denial

our exposition. We think we have said enough to be clear and understood, and complete enough to serve as a guide to those who, free of all *parti pris,* would like to enter into a labyrinth for which, until now, no one has been able to find the thread.

---

of the pleasures of the senses, the licentious rites, the holiness attached to suffering, the abdication of intellectual faculties, etc.

CHAPTER 7

That We Would Be Able to Find Examples of the Same Combination among All the Peoples Subject to Priests

The observations contained in the previous chapters apply to all the religions that the ancient priesthoods controlled. Among the Chaldeans,[1] we simultaneously see the dog, the cock, and the goat adored by the people;[2] anthropomorphism, which modifies their external forms: Saturn with the body of a man and the head of an ape, Jupiter with the head of a vulture;[3] Oannes, first of all a fish-god, then a legislator and prophet with the head and feet of a man, entering each night into the sea and reemerging each morning to give laws to mortals and to reveal to them the course of the stars and planets;[4] at the same time, gods as symbols of the planets, that is, science bestowing upon these crude conceptions a more elevated meaning; astronomical calculations serving as the basis of the mythology and presented to the vulgar as the actions of the immortals; trees planted in the name of the divinities who preside over each star, which are the dwellings of these divinities when they come near to humans;[5] astrology forming a great chain that descends from heaven to the earth, of which one extreme is the science of the priests and the other the beliefs of the people;[6] later, metaphysics seeking the causes after

1. Some have regarded the Chaldeans as a caste of soothsayers or priests; but Cicero says in explicit terms that they were a people. "*Chaldaei, non ex artis, sed ex gentis vocabulo nominati*" (*De divin.*, I, 1).

2. The cock under the name Nargal, the billy goat under the name Aschima, the cat under the name Nibchaz (Kings, XVII, 29, 30; Selden, *De diis Syr. Syntagm.*, II, 8, 9).

3. Kircher, *Oedip. Aegypt.*, II, 177.

4. Apollod., fragm., Heyn., pp. 408ff.; Helladius, in Photius, p. 374.

5. Albufarag., *Hist. dynast.*, p. 2; Maimonid., *More nevoch.*, cap. 29.

6. Goerres (II, 435, 439) has noted that as metaphysical doctrine acquired credit, astronomy, which until then was a teaching hidden from the people, became an external doctrine, relative to metaphysical hypotheses. We will have to develop this idea when we treat the further development of religion.

486

science has noted the facts, theism under the name of the primitive fire, the uncre-ated light, and beside it dualism as a dark spirit, the enemy of the good principle; finally, the cosmogonies clothing metaphysical hypotheses in bloody or obscene images; beings with two heads or hermaphroditic, born of night and water;[7] the hideous Omorca cut in two by Bel, her death causing the death of all that has life, her two halves forming the firmament that covers us and the globe we inhabit; Bel cutting off his own head; the living races born of the earth drenched in his blood; Tauthe and Apason, the active and passive principles, brother and sister, husband and wife, engendering the visible world; Bel reappearing as if he were born for the first time; a mythological, historical, and cosmogonic personage, representing the Demiourgos[8] or the orderer who gave man intelligence, and created the sun, the moon, and the other planets.[9]

The same spectacle strikes our eyes among the Assyrians. Their principal divinity is the sun, who, while his brilliant chariot winds its way above their heads, lives in their midst in a rock with a round shape.[10] Here fetishism mixes with astronomy. But to avoid repetitions, from now on we will speak only about the features that are particular to each people.

An egg fell into the sea, say the inhabitants of the Assyrian Hierapolis; fish took it to the bank,[11] doves hatched it;[12] Venus came forth.[13] Behold cosmogony ani-mating fetishism. Derceto, they continue, charmed by this same Venus and having given herself to the embraces of a young priest, exposed the fruit of her weakness in a cavern, and in the form of a fish cast herself into the waves. The abandoned infant, miraculously kept alive by doves, adopted by a shepherd, was elevated by a singular destiny to the throne of Assyria, and was immortalized in its annals under the name Semiramis. Behold fetishism combining with history.

Among the Etruscans, the worship of birds, oaks, and spears appears alongside

7. Pliny, *Hist. nat.*, II.

8. Syncell., *Chron.*, p. 28.

9. Damascius, *De principiis*.

10. Selden, *De diis Syris*; Mignot, *Acad. inscr.*, XXXI, 137.
Religiosa silex, densis quam pinus obumbrat.
Frondibus.
(Claud., *De rapt. Proserp.*, I, 214)

11. Xenoph., *Anab.*, I, 4 and the note of Larcher; Cic., *De nat deor.*, III, 1, 5; Diod., II, 4; Porph., *De abst.*, II, 61; IV, 15. He cites the ancient comic poet Menander as a witness.

12. Tibull., I, 8, 18, and the note of Brockhuys.

13. Hyg., *Fab.*, 199; Caes. *Germ.*, ch. 20; Theon *ad* Arat., 131.

their Tinia, the supreme god, nature, the first cause and immutable destiny,[14] and alongside Janus, the preserver, the mediator, who presides over time and who is time itself; there is astronomy and astrology in the books of the nymph Begoë, the theism attributed to Tages,[15] dualism under the name of Mantus and Vedius,[16] a demonology alternatively astronomical and metaphysical, and the cosmogonic incest of Janus and Cama[17] (with the hermaphroditic gods presenting the same combination).

Among the Persians, the symbolic cock, Hufraschmodad, this celestial bird, victor over Eschem, the monstrous enemy of men, who pursues them in order to devour them;[18] Hufraschmodad, sentinel of the world, terror of evil *genii*,[19] whose piercing eye scans all the earth,[20] whose beak is a sharpened spear, and who three times a day and three times a night, keeping watch over the dwelling of the just, calls the inhabitants of the air to defend the holy fountain of Arduissur,[21] the virgin water, emanation of Oromaze; the Amschaspand, several of which have animal forms, and who preside over the seven planets or perhaps are the seven planets themselves; Haoma, the tree of life, at once tree and prophet, dwelling place of the soul of Zoroaster, who later moved to the body of a cow; Honover, the powerful word uttered by Ormuzd, which to this day he has not ceased uttering; the ox Abudad, who contains the seeds of all things;[22] the cow Purmaje, sung about in the *Shah-namah*—these are obviously the alliance of the worship of animals, stones, and trees with a doctrine that is sometimes dualistic and some-

14. Senec., *Nat. quaest.*, II, 45. What we know of the philosophy of the Etruscans comes to us almost exclusively from this writer, and we cannot grant him entire confidence. A zealous Stoic, he could have easily attributed Stoic opinions to a priesthood whose doctrine went back to obscure times.

Nonetheless, as the core of these opinions is not in opposition to the hypotheses that it is natural to the priesthood to conceive and to conceal, it would be rash to reject the only witness that has come down to us in these matters. If we admit his testimony, the Etruscan doctrine would have floated between theism and pantheism, like the Egyptian and the Indian.

15. Serv. *ad Aeneid.*, X, 198; Anysius, in Lydus, *De mensib.*, p. 68.

16. Lydus, *De mensib.*

17. *Deus Venus, Venus Almus*, Jupiter the mother of the gods.

18. Izeschné, *Ha*, 10 & 25; Vendidad, frag., 10 & 11; Boundehesch, c. 29.

19. Izeschné, *Ha*, 5657.

20. Jescht Sades, 89.

21. Ibid., 84.

22. Boundehesch, 3, 4, 10, 14.

times pantheistic, depending upon whether Zurvan-Akarana, time without end, is the sole principle, or whether Oromaze and Arimanes are two equal principles.

Oromaze, the Word incarnate; this Word that according to common expressions was the firstborn of the seed of the Eternal; Oromaze, sometimes the infinite because light is infinite, and then, similar to Zurvan-Akarana, is alternately eagle and sparrow hawk. Mithra is the sun in science, in the cosmogony a mediating god with whose assistance creation occurs.[23] Zurvan-Akarana himself is sometimes a generative power, time without end,[24] sometimes an astronomical symbol, the grand period of twelve thousand years.[25] Djemschid is the solar year, the inventor of science, and an invincible conqueror. Fabular animals, chimerical mixtures of the bird, the fish, the goat, and the ape, are figures of the stars. An equally fantastical monster[26] represents the impure races, the work of Arimanes; and the unicorn is the symbol of the pure species created by Ormuzd. Behram, the Yazd of fire emerging from his breast, is sometimes a young warrior, sometimes a steed full of ardor, a laboring cow, a peaceful lamb;[27] the dog Sura, who guards the fixed stars from the top of the heavens, and from there watches over the human race and protects its fecundity.

If the cosmogony of the Persians is less obscene than that of the Hindus, this difference perhaps owes to the period when the Zend books were composed and to the influence of civilization on a belated reform.[28] What the Indians explained

23. It would take too long here to detail the various characteristics of Mithra, whether belonging to metaphysics or to dualism, to cosmogony or to an order of ideas we will develop later, that transformed the gods themselves into beings who suffered and died for man (see below, bk. XI, ch. 6); a singular conception that owes on one hand to astronomy and on the other to mysticism, and makes of these dying gods the image of the sun in winter, or of expiatory victims for the human race. Anquetil wanted to distinguish Mithra from the sun; but the Zend books expressly identify him with this planet (Vendidad, frag. 19). Elsewhere, it is true that Mithra is named an intermediary between the sun and the moon (Jescht-Sades) and between Oromaze and the earth, or between Oromaze and Arimanes. This only better proves the complexity that we have pointed out, which constantly shows up in the doctrine of priests.

24. Vendidad, frag. 19.

25. Izeschné, *Ha*, 19.

26. The Martichoros or Manticore, composed of the lion, the scorpion, and man; one finds this symbol in the ruins of Persepolis.

27. Jescht-Sades, 94.

28. See bk. IV, ch. 9.

by the act of generation, the Persians attributed to the separation of darkness and light, of water and fire: nonetheless, the distinction of sexes exists between these two elements, and the reunion of the sexes in the supreme God.[29] Mithra is at once the male[30] and the female[31] sun. Kaiomorts, the first man, also enjoys this double attribute. The seed of the ox fallen to earth and gathered by Ormuzd, purified by the sun, kept for forty years by two tutelary *genii*,[32] transformed into a tree that presented the image of a man and a woman united to each other, and which engendered Meschia and Meschiane,[33] contains details that are no less indecent than the stories of Brahma and Sarasvati, and of Bhavani and Shiva.

In the midst of this mysticism, of this homage offered to a sole God, of this dualism, this pantheism, and these monstrous cosmogonies, we find a living polytheism among the Persians, practiced by the people[34] and invoked by the kings,[35]

29. "*Jovem in duas dividunt potestates, naturamque ejus ad utriusque sexus transferentes, et viri et feminae simulacra ignis substantiam deputantes*" (Jul. Firmic., *De err. prof. rel.*, I, 5).

30. Hammer, *Wien. Jahrb.*, X, 229ff.

31. Kleucker, *Anb. zum. Zend.*, II, 3.

32. Sapandomad and Neriosingh.

33. Boundehesch.

34. In the second book of his *History*, Agathias says that before Zoroaster or Zarades, the Persians adored Saturn, Jupiter, and the other gods of the Greeks. This assertion of a recent historian is important only because it attests to the universal view, held for eleven centuries, concerning the primitive polytheism of the Persians, because one reads almost the same thing in Herodotus, and one must distrust the Greek tendency to rediscover their gods among other peoples. The Persian polytheism was probably much cruder than that of Greece, and rather resembled the fetishism of primitives than the mythology of Homer. A passage of Porphyry attests that each of the magi, in their mysteries, took the name of some animal (Porph., *De abst.*, IV). Now, it was a general practice in antiquity that the priests took sometimes the name, sometimes the form, of their gods. In the explanation of several singular monuments by D. Martin in *Table isiaque*, and in the *Antiquities* of Count Caylus, we see priests with heads of wolves, cats, sparrow hawks, and lions; the adoption of names analogous to these disguises no doubt has a similar motive. The magi left their ancient fetishes to the Persians, as did the priests of Egypt to the Egyptians, by combining them in different ways with their mysterious rituals.

35. This worship of foreign gods by the kings of Persia has led a famous scholar of Germany into a singular error. He thinks that, flattered by the prophecies of the Jehovah of the Hebrews in his favor, and astonished at seeing them accomplished, Cyrus converted to the Jewish religion; and that obedient to his example and lessons, his subjects and his successors repudiated their idols. From this, says this learned man, came the outrages inflicted by Cambyses on the gods of Egypt; from this, the destruction of the temples of Greece by Darius. But if the conqueror of Asia, convinced by the veracity of the oracles of the god of Israel, had consulted the priests of this jealous god, the intolerant and austere spirit of the Levites would have soon reduced him to the alternative of either complete

with which the priesthood often consents to associate itself. Xerxes sacrificed on the banks of the Scamander a thousand cattle to the Trojan Minerva; and following his orders, the magi offered libations to the heroes of the country.[36] After the storm that destroyed their fleet, the Persians sacrificed to the winds, to Thetis and to the Nereides.[37] Their king become master of Athens commanded the exiled Athenians to enter the citadel, and there to worship their gods in keeping with traditional rites.[38] Sending an envoy to consult the oracles of Greece, Mardonius recommended that he go everywhere he would be permitted, in order to learn the decrees of the gods.[39] Datis, general of Darius, had three hundred talents of incense burned on the altars of Apollo.[40] He believed himself obliged to send back to its temple a statue of this god that had been taken by the Persians.[41] The respect

---

submission or an absolute break. Every shared worship would have seemed to them an insult, every ecumenical gesture a sacrilege. They barely would have admitted proselytes. The imperfect acquiescence of Cyrus would have little satisfied them; even—and this is something that we present only as a conjecture, but one that is conformed to the character of the Hebrew priests—if it did have a basis in history. Perhaps they would not have wanted to let themselves be treated as we have seen Cyrus treated the magi (bk. IV, ch. 9); hence the discontent of this prince, a discontent that interrupted the construction of the temple of Jerusalem. But be that as it may, if one attributes to the Persian monarch a sufficiently profound conviction for the theism of the Jews that he removed all other worship, one will never explain why he did not admit the belief revealed to Moses in all its extent, as well as the rituals prescribed by this legislator. The effect will always appear too small for the cause, and this objection will acquire even more force when one sees the same Cyrus adopt the priesthood of another people without any sign of repugnance. A matter of only some sacrifices, some demonstrations of respect for Jehovah, all the conquerors of antiquity believed they owed homage to the gods of conquered peoples; but this was a principle of polytheism, not theism. Without being a theist, Cyrus could bow his head before the national god of the Jews. And while it is true that Cambyses killed the steer Apis and burned the temple of Jupiter Ammon, on one hand, Cambyses had dementia, and, on the other, these acts of violence could have been caused by the resistance of the Egyptian priesthood to a foreign yoke. The motives of Darius were vengeance and avarice, and his successors hastened to load with offerings the altars of the gods of Greece who had been offended by him.

36. Herod., VII, 43.

37. Ibid., p. 91. Here there is a mixture of the worship of elements, the indigenous worship of Media, and the adoration of foreign gods.

38. Ibid., VIII, 54.

39. In his religious ceremonies, the general made use of a Greek soothsayer whose name has come down to us; it was Hegesistratus of Elea. He was the soothsayer of the Persian army, since the Greek auxiliaries of the Persians had their own soothsayer, Hippomachus of Lampsaque (Herod., IX, 36–37).

40. Ibid., VI, 97.

41. Ibid., p. 118.

of Tissaphernes for the Diana of Ephesus[42] served as a rhetorical trope for Cicero to increase the impiety of Verres.[43] If the Persians marched against the temple of Delphi, it was not because they contested the god's right to celestial honors but, as Herodotus says explicitly,[44] in order to bring its treasures to Darius, who, continues the historian, had full knowledge of the wealth this temple contained.[45]

The facts we have borrowed from Herodotus do not consist in vague rumors or opinions drawn from unsure sources, as the Greeks were wont to do; they are established facts about which this historian could not be mistaken. Xenophon, who by his expedition into Asia had acquired some knowledge of the principal traits of the Persian religion, speaks of sacrifices offered to the sun, to Jupiter, and to several other divinities. He describes the nature and rituals of these sacrifices; and what is even more decisive, he shows us Cyrus the Younger invoking the tutelary gods of the empire he wishes to conquer. Aspasia or Milto, his mistress, believing herself indebted to Venus for her elevation, erected a statue to her.[46] After the death of her lover, she became a priestess of the Assyrian Venus;[47] Artaxerxes had established the cult. And the successors of this monarch raised temples to her in their most prominent cities, enriching them with immense gifts.[48] The Persians, therefore, despite the Zend books and the learned and abstract doctrine of their magi, remained polytheistic until the fall of their empire;[49] under the reign

42. Thucydid., VIII, 109.

43. Cic., in *Verrem*. Some have explained this last fact by supposing that the cult of Ephesus had many relations, or a common origin, with that of the Persians. This hypothesis has been ingeniously established by a modern writer (Mr. Creuzer in his *Symbolique*); but the polytheism of the Persians is thereby only better proved.

44. Herod., VII, 35.

45. Darius accused the Athenians of having burned the temples in Asia Minor (ibid., VIII, 8). Does not this reproach indicate that the burning of the temples of Greece was only in reprisal?

46. Ael., *Var. hist.*, XII, 1.

47. This is the same Assyrian Venus that Greek writers sometimes called the Persian Diana, sometimes Venus-Anaitis, sometimes Juno or Minerva, sometimes Zaretis or Azara (Herod.; Polyb.; Plut., *Vit. Artax.*; Strabo, XII & XIV). The worship of this Venus-Anaitis could very well have been the amalgam of astrolatry and a foreign cult. The Ized, or the *genius* of the planet Venus, is named Anahid in the Zend Avesta.

48. Plut., *Vit. Artax*; Polyb., X, 24; Clem. Alex., *Protrept.*, p. 575.

49. We have entered into some detail concerning Persian polytheism because it was above all among this people that some have claimed to find a pure theism. The religion of the Persians was a priestly religion. Among the systems these religions receive (or better put: jumble together), rather

than combine or harmonize, pure theism can be found, because everything is found in them. But this is never as a sole doctrine or as the popular teaching.

One cannot repeat this too much if one wants to have clear ideas about the development of religion: enlightenment has to have attained a rather elevated state, knowledge of the laws of nature has to have acquired a certain degree of depth and truth, for theism to be possible.

Perhaps someone will object that the people are hardly more enlightened among us than among the ancient nations, and that theism is nonetheless the public religion.

We first will answer that the inferior classes of our modern times, in whatever debased condition they find themselves, cannot be compared with those castes that formerly were condemned to the same professions, denied all varieties of knowledge, were ignorant of reading and writing, learning only the mechanical parts of arts, and were subject to a thousand arbitrary subdivisions that allowed them neither to increase their ideas nor to develop their minds. Moreover, the people of our days receive their notions of theism from the upper classes; their own judgment and reflections do not enter in at all. The ministers of the religion, far from covering them in darkness like the priestly corporations of antiquity, far from hiding from the masses the pure doctrine they possess, communicate it to them, teach it to them, even impose it upon them. If one could reproach them, it would not be that like the priests of ancient Egypt they keep their views inaccessible to the profane; on the contrary, it would be that they sometimes want to force the laity to share all their opinions; nonetheless, the inferior classes constantly depart from the rigor of those strictly unitary ideas of religion, invoke the saints, choose protectors for themselves; in a word, they place a multiplicity of gods under the unique God. If this is the necessary relation of ignorance to a more or less disguised polytheism even among the nations where instruction and enlightenment maintain Reformed belief, even more so must it have been the case when contemptuous and jealous castes were bent only on increasing the distance that separated them from the blind crowd.

If as Hyde supposes, the Persians, or as Jablonsky maintains, the Egyptians, worshipped only one God, what was the difference between these peoples and the Hebrew tribes? Why, then, would God in his eternal decrees have separated the Jews by invincible barriers from nations that were no less faithful and who offered him no less pure worship? This objection applies especially to Hyde's system, who claims that the Persians never deviated from the orthodox worship. Why, then, would they have not been the people of God?

We have already said this, we will demonstrate it later, and this will not be one of the least interesting subjects we will treat: in the human heart there is a tendency toward unity, and consequently toward theism; but at every period this tendency displays itself only partially and under different forms; it does not reveal itself or entirely develop until quite late. It is the result of the disproportion between polytheism and the religious need, modified by enlightenment. Now, for this disproportion to make itself felt, is it not necessary that enlightenment exists?

The author of a distinguished work on the development of philosophical ideas in religion (Berger, *Gesch. der Relig. philos.*) has attempted to establish the priority of theism by arguments that are unique to him. This belief, he says, could have been the first religion among certain peoples, not because these peoples, starting from their early years, raised themselves to the idea of abstract and metaphysical unity, but because of the natural tendency of man to create for himself objects of worship that are conof the last Darius, and therefore before the Greek invasion had denatured their beliefs, they worshipped an image of the sun and idols of gold and silver;[50] and if we believe Tacitus,[51] whose authority we have no reason to doubt, they persisted in polytheism long afterward.[52] Thus in Persia as elsewhere, fetishism, polythe-

---

formed to his personal situation. Among nomadic peoples, heads of family charged with the general direction of their numerous flocks, wives, children, and slaves, and being alone in this task, imagined a single god governing the world like they governed their families. This writer confuses, it seems to us, two dissimilar things: a few nomadic hordes could have worshipped only a single god for the reason given by the author; however, we do not know a single example of this; but even then, they would not consider this god as the only one that existed; they would recognize other gods, protectors of foreign nations which only they worshipped. Now, it is not worship but exclusive belief that constitutes theism, and it is this exclusive belief that cannot triumph except in the bosom of civilization. In reasoning like this author, one could see fetishism as a species of theism, because the majority of times, and in ordinary circumstances, each primitive worships only one fetish.

50. Quint. Curt., III, 3.

51. Tacit., *Annal.*, III, 161–62. Vopiscus recounts that the Persians of the time of Aurelius had devoted to Mithra or the sun, if not temples, at least statues. He tells us (*Vie d'Aurélien*, ch. 5) that the king of Persia made a gift to this prince, before his accession to the throne, of a cup weighing the same as was customarily offered to emperors, and upon which the sun was represented in the apparel worn by the mother of Aurelius, priestess of this god.

52. The history of the Persian religion divides into three periods. Until the time of Alexander, it was a mixture of the doctrine of Zoroaster and the previous religion of Persia; from Alexander, these two elements combined with many notions and practices borrowed from the Greeks. It was only under the dynasty of the Arsacids and the Sassanides (who claimed to come from Zoroaster himself) that the doctrines of this reformer were established in the way the books teach. At this period, the kings of Persia, in concert with the magi, worked to expel from their religion everything that had come from abroad. They reestablished the magi in their former dignity and authority, who had been reduced under the Greeks to nothing but sorcerers and mercenaries. They destroyed the temples of Venus-Anaitis; the name of this goddess is found neither in Ammianus Marcellinus nor in Procopus. Agathias speaks of her as a goddess who was previously worshipped. Thus, after the Arsacids, the Persians only had national gods, Mithra, the moon, the earth, air, fire, and finally Oromaze and Arimanes, whose worship did not become public until the conquest of Alexander. They added outrageous ceremonies against Arimanes, but otherwise remained faithful to their old cult, despite their enslavement to the Arabs and the persecutions they experienced.

These persecutions, which continue today, brought them closer to theism. When one asks contemporary Guebres about the worship they or their ancestors lavished upon fire or the sun or other planets, they respond that they do not worship them as gods, but they offer praise that in reality is directed to the supreme and sole God (Hyde, *De rel. pers.*). This is because the Persians, today oppressed by the Muslims as idolaters, have a vital interest in blunting every imputation of idolatry, and in order to bolster their case they try to exonerate their ancestors as well. Surrounded by theistic nations, they ism, science, history, metaphysics, and cosmogony all encounter, are combined and mixed.[53] If the Zend books, a reform commanded by power and executed by calculation, artificially (and increasingly arbitrarily) rework an already ancient belief, one that also was gradually modified by an ancient civilization, and if they, finally, are a work redone at the order of temporal despotism to fight theocratic authority—if, we say, the Zend books seem to be free of some doctrines and certain revolting practices—the priesthood still regained and preserved its empire, and continued to exercise its ordinary influence; all institutions and precepts were stamped with its spirit; overcharged with practices, the cult left man no moment of relief; the notion of impurity relentlessly pursued and troubled him in all his actions; he was consumed by innumerable prayers, purifications, and expiations. These artificial duties were put in the rank of the primary duties, and the mechanical character of the rites weighed on the religious sentiment and eventually choked it.

Let us move to the West and the North; looking first at the Scandinavians, the

---

are inclined to refine the beliefs of past generations, and to ascribe subtleties to them that they were unaware of and distinctions they did not make.

Of this sort is the "purely civil veneration" that, they say, bound the ancient Persians to prostrate themselves before the sun and the fire as before the great and the kings (Briss., *De reg. pers. princ.*). But what does a "purely civil veneration" mean, offered to beings with whom, once they are personified, men cannot but have religious relations?

53. Goerres (*As. Myth.*, I, 236–38) presents some very interesting observations on the insufficiency of every partial explanation of the religion of the Persians, and these observations tell against the partial explanations of any other religion. It would be easy, says this writer, to present the system of Zoroaster as a series of chronological personifications: Zurvan-Akarana would be eternity; Zurvan, the duration of the world; the Amschaspans, the grand periods; Mithras, the solar year; the Izeds, days; the Gaehs, hours or the division of the hours. One could also find astronomical calculations: Oromaze would be the world; Mithras the sun, the mysterious Bull, the vernal equinox, the four Birds, the zones; the Amschaspans, the planets; the Izeds, the fixed stars; Albordi, the zodiac; Meschia and Meschiana, the Gemini; the introduction of Arimanes in the world, the sign of balance, etc. It would also be easy to fit in a geographic interpretation: Albordi would be the Persian Olympus, or the dwelling of Oromaze; Ixhordad would be the Araxe and the places it waters; Schariver, the mineral kingdom; Sayandomad, the flocks; Amerdad, fertility; the Izeds, the gods of cities, rivers, mountains, and the penates of families. Finally, a metaphysical explanation would not be impossible: Zervan-Akarana would be the infinite; Oromaze, intelligence; Mithras, the soul of the world; the Izeds, ideas; Arimanes, destruction; Honover, the creative force. Each explanation would have its true side; but when each becomes exclusive, there remains something inexplicable, which would pose insoluable objections.

Germans,[54] and all the nations known under the name of Celts, having for idols trees,[55] animals,[56] pebbles,[57] weapons,[58] as well as the sun,[59] the elements,[60] and the stars.

The principal god of the Livonians is simultaneously a bird and the day star.[61] The legends of Regner Lodbrog give the title of goddess to the cow Sibylia, whom this conqueror brought with him to all his battles, and whose terrible bellowings forced the enemies to cut themselves with their own swords.[62] The ancient Russians had tame serpents for fetishes; and each village of Poland recognizes a particular god clothed in some monstrous form.[63] The newly born in Bohemia were presented to the flames, and mothers recommended them to the protection of the sacred fire.[64] This fire was maintained among the Finns by the priests, and if it went out, led to their death. The same people offered cocks to lizards, and humans to the gods, as victims; and these barbarous gifts were given by the Slavs to the Bog,[65] the Don,[66] and the Danube. A king of Norway

54. One can find all the facts that confirm this crude cult in Germany reported by Sulzer, *Allgem. Theor. der schoen. Künste*, VI.

55. Gregory of Tours, op. cit., bk. III, ch. 5, n. 20; and in Borlase (*Antiq. of Cornwall.*, pp. 121–22), the concilar decisions. "*Veneratores lapidum, accensores facularum, et excolentes sacra fontium et arborum admonemus*" (*Concil. Tur.* A.D. 567).

56. Tacit., *German.*, 45.

57. Bartholin, III.

58. Mallet, *Introd. à hist. du Dan.*, 184–85; Procop., *Vandal.*, I, 3; Amm. Marcell., XXXI, 2. On the worship of spears, see Justin, XLIII, 3.

59. The sun under the name of Odin, the moon under that of Mana. Everyone knows the list of the elementary gods of the Scythians given by Herodotus: Tabiti, fire; Papraeus, the world-soul or the sky; Apia, the earth; Oetasirus, the sun; Artimpasa, the moon; Thamimasades, water (Herod., IV, 59).

60. Even though he is too systematic and sees only the external form in religion, Pelloutier was nonetheless forced to recognize that the nations he named the Celts did not see the elements as simple images of an invisible divinity, but as being themselves divine.

61. Adam Brem., ch. 224; *Livones honorem Deo debitum, animalibus brutis, arboribus frondosis, aquis limpidis, virentibus herbis, et spiritibus immundis impendunt*, Bulla Innocent., III A.D. 1199; *Ap.* Gruber *in Orig. livon.*, p. 205.

62. Ragnars-Saga., ch. 8.

63. Dlugosz, *Hist. pol.*, vol. I.

64. Hagec, *Boehm. Chron.*, p. 254.

65. The Hypanis of the ancients.

66. The Tanaïs.

worshipped a cow; an Icelandic hero sacrificed to his horse; others venerated stones.[67]

The country of Wales, the seat of the most ancient Druidism, had its sacred oxen and cows, born of a mysterious ox, son of the ancient world.[68] One of these oxen, by the natural linking of martial ideas and religious notions, was the bull of battle.[69] Goddesses lived in the lakes of Great Britain. A Welsh bard of the fifth century invokes the god of the air, another the god of fire,[70] a third, the sun;[71] and in a panegyric of a prince, the memory of the worship of animals seems to be connected with the glory of an incarnation, as in India. Owen appeared, says the inspired singer, in the form of a ringing shield, which a valorous leader wears on his arm before the tumult to come, in the form of a lion with puissant wings, in the form of a terrible spear with sparkling head, in the form of a brilliant sword which mows down enemies and afterward distributes glory, in the form of a dragon before the sovereign of England, and in the form of a devouring wolf.[72]

The polytheism that was introduced did not replace this first worship; each family of Germany has its particular fetish, which its head carries everywhere with him,[73] while the national gods are contained in boxes that take the place of temples, and which are placed on wagons that accompany the wandering tribes.[74]

Science then borrows images from this dual worship in order to perpetuate its

67. Bartholin, III; Rüh, *Scandinavia*, p. 12.

68. *Archaeol. of Wales*, II, 21, 80.

69. Ibid., pp. 4, 72, 76.

70. "Let him dance, sparkle, burn bright in his unconquerable course, the quick fire, the fire that consumes, he whom we adore, high above the earth" (poem of Taliesin, bard of the sixth century).

71. "The elevated leader, the sun, is ready to mount on the horizon, the most glorious sovereign, the lord of the Britannic isle" (poem entitled "Gododin," by Aneurin the Northumbrian).

72. Poem by Cynddelw in *Mythologie des druids* (London, 1809). For the most part this is one of those foolish products of national vanity in which everything is related to a single country, presented as the cradle of all religion and science; in this light, reading it is instructive only for those who love to see how far an exclusive idea can falsify thinking and make erudition ridiculous.

73. These fetishes were called Allrunes, and this name passed from them to the priests, the sooth-sayers, and to sacerdotal writings. *Magas mulieres quas ipse* (Filimer) *patrui sermone aliorumnas cognominavit* (Jornandes).

74. Tacit., *German.*, 40. The absence of temples has been put forth as proof of sublime ideas of the divinity for both the peoples of the North and the Persians. We have demonstrated the falsity of this claim with respect to the latter; as for the former, we would ask if carts and boxes are more suitable dwellings for the Supreme Being than the temples of other nations?

discoveries and calculations without divulging them. The frequent allusions of Welsh bards to astronomy prove their observation and study of celestial bodies.[75] In the depths of this withdrawn corner of the world, the Druids had written treatises of a fabular geography.[76] The three great festivals of the Scandinavians were celebrated at the winter solstice, the new moon of the second month of the year, and the spring equinox.[77] Asgard, their heavenly city, in one of its meanings is the zodiac; and its inhabitants seated on their twelve thrones are the twelve signs.

The same name designates time, the sun, and the citadel where the gods repair to defend themselves against the giants. The dwarfs who occupy such a large place in this mythology, these children of the gods and three female giants who entered into Asgard to seduce them, are thirty-six in number; the first two, Nyi and Nithi, represent the full and new moons, and four others represent the cardinal points of heaven. But since it is necessary that religion brings together all the sciences, these dwarfs also recall the discovery of metals: they penetrate the bowels of the earth, carve precious stones, and fashion gold and iron, from which they forge weapons, the glory of heroes.[78]

The seven heads and seven swords of the Vandal Rugiavith represent the week. Radegast, sometimes resplendent in white, sometimes ebony black, with the solar symbol of the ox on his breast, and like the god of harmony carrying the swan on his head, recalls the attributes of Apollo.[79] Each evening Perkunas, the wife of Ocean, the Thetis of Poland, receives this god covered with dust, who then is refreshed by the bath she prepares, and reappears each morning surrounded by a new luster.[80] Libussa, famous for her knowledge of metals, and for the worship of a golden idol of which she was the priestess; Libussa, who wanted to marry only a laborer, and who having found him behind her chariot, married and made him king of Bohemia, brings together metallurgy and agriculture, and brings both into the religion.

The Russian traditions have a triple stamp of fetishism, astronomy, and history. Volkov, an ancient prince of the country, is worshipped by the inhabitants of the banks of the Volga in the figure of a crocodile. Vladimir, the first king converted

---

75. *Archaeol. of Wales.*

76. Caes., *B Gall.*

77. Mallet, *Introd. à l'hist. du Dan.*, I, 109.

78. *Voluspa*, Resenii ed.

79. Masius, *Antiq. Mecklemb.*

80. Dlugosz, *Hist. pol.*

to Christianity (who had no more to pride himself about in this than Constantine),[81] is called the shining sun, the friend of man, in all the national legends; Kiev, its capital, is also named the city of the sun. Its enemies are evil *genii*, sons of darkness and the cold. All his adventures,[82] like the exploits of the Greek Apollo, consist in carrying off young women and fighting serpents and dragons; they contain a scientific meaning; while they also have this remarkable feature: that the introduction of a new cult which was destructive of the one that conferred upon them a religious character only modified them, without depriving them of this religious character. Thus, while the historical Vladimir became a Christian monarch, the astronomical Vladimir remained a planetary god, and in general the priestly symbols survived the abandoned belief. It was only after a persecution of several centuries that they shared the fate of the original belief.

After science comes philosophy. In the language of science, the god who sends a beneficent breeze to melt the ice and thus prepare creation,[83] is only the articulation of a law of nature expressing the action of heat on cold. Metaphysics, though, makes him the unknown god, the god not yet manifested,[84] which struck us in Egypt as the symbol of pantheism.[85] The serpent Jörmungandr, who mixes his poisons with the primordial water; and the children of Loki, Vali and Nari, who, changed into wolves by the good principle, eat themselves, and their entrails serve as chains for the god of evil, are dualistic symbols. A rather pure theism characterizes some of the poetry of the Welsh bard Taliesin;[86] and one finds dualism among the Vandals in that singular conception that makes of each god a double being, black and white, evil and good; one finds emanation in a series of beings who come from the great Svantevit, corrupting themselves as they move further away from him; one also finds pantheism in this unchanging, eternal Svantevit, who absorbs all things when the hour marked for them to return arrives.

---

81. While he was still a pagan, this Vladimir slaughtered Christians on his altars. He had nine hundred concubines, and here is what the annalists say of him: "*Uxoris hortatu christianitatis fidem suscepit, sed eam justis operibus non ornavit; erat enim fornicator immensus et crudelis*" (Annalista Saxo, *ad* A., 1013, p. 426, *ap.* Dietmar. Merseburg).

82. See *Prince Vladimir and His Round Table, Heroic Songs of Ancient Russia* (Leipzig, 1819).

83. Edda, *in init.*

84. *Deus in statu abscondito.*

85. See above, bk. VI, ch. 4.

86. "I adore the sovereign, supreme regulator of the world" (poem entitled "Dépouilles de l'abîme").

There is more: the Indian Maya, this goddess of illusion, the deceptive daughter of the Eternal, fantastical creator of beings that exist no more than she does, is found in Scandinavia in the imaginary world that the Skalds call Vanaheim.[87] There error, chimeras, and dreams reign. Lying appearances succeed one another, astonish the sight, fascinate the imagination, cast the intellect into vertigo, and force it to constantly ask—and always without receiving an answer—whether anything exists, and if it can distinguish what exists from what does not. Thus everywhere philosophy has felt its impotence; and priests, the most affirmative of mortals, have, alongside the numerous systems about which they, like us, argue, placed in the most secret place of the sanctuary the acknowledgment of this irremedial impotence, while surrounding it with veils calculated to most effectively disguise it.

Cosmogony also presents itself with its bloody battles and monstrous generations. The most ancient god of Finland engenders himself in the womb of Runnotaris, the void or nature.[88] The Ginnungagap, the infinite space of the Scandinavians, corresponds to the Zurvan-Akarana of the Persians, time without end; the two principles of cold and heat, darkness and light, are not two individuals like Oromaze and Arimanes, but two different kingdoms, Niflheim and Muspelheim. The hermaphroditic sun[89] is equated with Odin in the historical traditions: incest unites him to Freyja, his wife and daughter. Chaos[90] engenders three sons, water, air, and fire;[91] their children hail, the mountains of ice, the fire lit with effort, the calcified ember, and the sterile ash, form a cosmogonic family adapted to the climate. The giant Ymir, endowed like Odin with a dual sex,[92] delivers his immense body to the gods, who kill him; similar to the half-gold, half-silver, egg of the Indians, it becomes the visible world or the terrestrial globe; his blood creates the sea and the rivers, his bones the rocks, his teeth the stones, his hair the plants, his

---

87. Stur, *Abhand. ueber Nord. Alterthüm.* (Berlin, 1817), p. 74. *Wabn* still means in German today "illusion, delirium."

88. Rüh, *Finnland und seine Bewohner.*

89. This hermaphroditic quality is still found among the Vandal divinities Rugarth and Harevith, each of whom has four human heads of males and two of females (Frencel., *De Diis sor.*, p. 124). The moon, Potrimpos, is hermaphroditic among the Lithuanians.

90. Fornierd.

91. Ager, Bare, and Lage.

92. *Voluspa.*

skull the clouds.[93] Night[94] unites with twilight[95] to engender day,[96] and, each mounted atop an enormous steed, day and night cross the heavens. The horse of one, covering his bit with foam, produces the dawn; the mane of the other, flowing in the air, gives off light. Two wolves pursue them; they fill the sky and the air with blood; hence the eclipses; and the rainbow is a bridge that rises from the earth to the heavens.

Among the Welsh, Ceridwen, daughter of necessity,[97] an indefinable blind force, is the object of the love of the primordial ox who came from her womb;[98] together with him she gives birth to the cosmogonic egg, which in turn gives birth to the serpent egg of the Druids,[99] which served in England as the model for the sanctuaries of Stonehenge and Avebury.[100]

Thus among the peoples of the north, under forms less gracious than in India, but more vivacious and poetic than in Egypt, the same elements form the same combinations with the same incoherences. This is because the causes and therefore the effects are similar. The coexistence of beliefs and doctrines that are passed on together by means of mystery, and despite their contradictions, this is the first truth one must recognize if one wants to find the thread of the labyrinth.

But it is time to end this chapter; in a work such as ours, we point out the path without taking it ourselves.

93. *Voluspa.*
94. Nott.
95. Dellingour.
96. Dagour.
97. *Archaeol. of Wales.*
98. *Cambrian Biography.*
99. Pliny, *Hist. nat.*
100. *Camden's Antiq.*

BOOK VII

ON THE ELEMENTS THAT
CONSTITUTE POLYTHEISM
INDEPENDENT OF PRIESTLY
DIRECTION

CHAPTER I

That the Combination Described in the Previous Book Is Alien to the Polytheism That Is Not Subject to Priests

The combination we just described is not found in the polytheism that priests do not dominate. The beliefs of peoples free of this domination are not an amalgam of several elements with contrary natures; one does not see abstract divinities appear beside or above material fetishes. Cosmogonic forces play no role. Allegories are rare, accidental, and found in the expression rather than the thought. Nothing recalls this double or triple sense that in priestly religions disorients and confuses the intellect. There are no privileged learned men, because there is no science; there is no mystery, because there are no priestly corporations with an interest in mystery. Having elevated itself above fetishism, the human mind never falls back to it; at most it preserves a few obscure traces. Nor does it lose itself in the subtleties of a metaphysics that, becoming ever more difficult and arduous, ends in a vague pantheism or in insoluble doubt, or even in an explicit denial of all existence. Preserved from these two extremes—which are more dangerous at this period because human knowledge is quite limited and conjectures can be bolder—man rests unshakeable on the most solid terrain, that is, the most proportionate to his capacities, a terrain he, as it were, has conquered by himself, and upon which he builds the edifice of his religious notions.

In priestly religions, everything is disproportionate to the rest of his ideas, the most sublime and abstract as well as the most abject and crude. Sometimes the intellect, snatched from the sphere that appears to open before it, finds itself cast into a fantastical world surrounded by clouds that no ray of light is allowed to dispel. Sometimes it is condemned to fall back beneath the limits it has already crossed, and is violently led back to notions it had very much left behind.

In free polytheism, everything is proportionate to the social state, which becomes orderly and progressive. All the qualities attributed to the gods are human qualities on a greater scale. Nothing is enigmatic, nothing is contradictory, once the nature and time of his views are acknowledged;[1] nothing shocks his reason just beginning its course and hence imperfect, because it lacks the lessons of experience; but this reason is capable of development when there is no enemy power to impede its progress.

As we always seek facts to support our claims, we are going to demonstrate our assertions by an exposition of the polytheism of the first Greeks, that is, the religion of the only people fortunate enough not to have had these imperious bodies erect themselves over their heads.

---

1. We add these words on purpose because we will have to point out contradictions even in independent polytheism; but these contradictions do not owe, as in the priestly religions, to the desire to maintain ancient ideas while adding new ones. They belong to the development of the intellect, which, placed between its progress and its prejudices, walks uncertainly for a while before granting the victory to the former and freeing itself from the memories that the second bequeathed to it.

CHAPTER 2

On the State of the Greeks in the Barbaric or Heroic Times

At the time with which we are concerned, Greece was divided into numerous tribes, each occupying a very restricted territory.[1] Theocratic authority either had never existed or had been destroyed.[2] The authority of the leaders who governed these societies was poorly defined, sometimes oppressive, and often disputed; it left each individual, if not the legal, the material faculty of counterclaim, of resistance, or at least invective; sometimes the peoples and armies assembled to deliberate, and one would have said that the legitimacy of their deliberations was recognized; sometimes the kings decided alone, and their decisions—objects of blame or subjects of complaint—were nonetheless obeyed. Thersites unleashed himself against Agamemnon; Achilles grew indignant; the army remained a spectator and obedient.

These peoples had only imperfect knowledge of the means of providing the needs and pleasures of life; moreover, they owed them to foreigners rather than to their own efforts. Their progress in the arts of luxury appears to be rapid because they were the effects of imitation; for this reason, at this period the superfluous was ahead of the necessary. They, however, had begun to conquer an empire over physical nature: the earth was torn by the plow; the sea had felt the yoke of ships;

---

1. The Greece of Homer's time was divided into a greater number of different States than it was subsequently. Thessaly alone contained no fewer than ten separate States. Boeotia had five kings: the Minyans whose capital was Orchomenus, the Locrians, the Athenians, and the Phocaeans each had their head: and the Locrians even were divided into two kingdoms. In the Peloponnese, one counted the States of Argos, Mycenae, Sparta, and Pylos, that of the Eleans governed by four princes, and of Arcadia. The majority of islands had a particular king. Ulysses reigned at Ithaca, Idomeneus in Crete, Ajax at Salamis, etc.

2. See bk. V, ch. 2.

and the moral faculties profited from the moments of leisure that these developments made possible; but these moments were short, this leisure precarious. Crudely cultivated, the earth often remained stingy; assaulted by frail boats, the sea resisted; and war was still the easiest, most lucrative resource.

The position of the Greek peoples encouraged them in this direction: living next to one another, their relations were customarily hostile. From this came the invasions and pillaging that made the distribution of property so unequal, its possession so precarious, and the vicissitudes of life so incalculable: throne and slavery, wealth and poverty, succeeded one another with frightening rapidity. Hecuba is queen today, tomorrow her arms are in irons.

From this state of things resulted a mixture of perfidy and loyalty, of cunning and candor, of greed and nobility, and vice and virtue that kept moral ideas in perpetual agitation and vacillation.[3]

During their prosperity, kings—or better put: the leaders—had large herds and vast domains where they exercised generous hospitality; their palaces were decorated with the fruits of their rapine or the presents of their guests; a luxury tainted with barbarism, a demisavage elegance, entered their mores. Their fortunate climate prematurely gave them an exquisite sentiment of the beauty of forms. The arts, especially those that captivate emerging nations, music and poetry, which at that time are never separated, entered their festivals and ennobled even their intemperance. War, devastation, pleasure, danger, songs, festivals, and slaughter filled their active and diversified lives, one after the other.

These are the traits in which the poems of Homer depict for us the Greeks of the heroic times: they occupy the intermediate step that separates the primitive state from the civilized state. In our second volume[4] we have indicated the religious form that this period of society needed, and how it created this form.

Bringing fetishes into a corporate body, the division of supernatural power, and distinctive names—these are the initial conditions that are common to priestly religions and independent polytheism. Now, in order to understand the subsequent modifications that characterize the latter, we have before us the most authentic record: the *Iliad*. Questions, however, present themselves that would arrest our inquiry if we neglected to resolve them.

We are going to try.

---

3. Ulysses is the type of this character, even in the *Iliad*. Brigandage and piracy appear to be occupations so honored that kings practiced them openly; and when someone offered hospitality to strangers, he asked, without any intention of offending them, if they were pirates.

4. Bk. III, ch. 2.

CHAPTER 3

On Some Questions That Must Be Resolved before Proceeding Further in Our Investigations

Two distinct races shared Greece: given the dissimilarity of mores, inclinations, and habits that characterized these two races, do they allow us to ascribe a religion completely the same to them?

Does the *Iliad* give us a faithful portrait of the beliefs of the time that its author or authors wanted to describe?

Finally, if we grant the *Iliad* the merit of being faithful and exact, does it follow that we can do without other records to complete the picture?

Let us examine the first question.

We just said that there were two distinct races in Greece; we could have said that there were four: the Aeolians, the Achaeans, the Dorians, and the Ionians; but the first two disappeared or melted into the other two; the Dorians established themselves in the Peloponnese and expanded into Boeotia, Locride, and Macedonia; the Ionians in Attica, the islands of the Archipelago, and Asia Minor.

These two races were very dissimilar to each other, and this dissimilarity extended from language to political and religious organization.

The Dorians were a grave people, constant in their customs, austere in their mores, full of veneration for the aged who were the repositories of the ancient traditions, aristocratic in their forms of government, disdainful of the fine arts, very attached to their religion, whose ceremonies were simple, and carefully consulting the oracles before attempting any enterprise.

Light and mobile, the Ionians easily changed customs, had little respect for ancient mores, an ardent and restless taste for novelty, a limitless passion for perfection and elegance; and because worship, when it is free, always expresses the moral disposition of a people, they sought in theirs brilliance and gaiety, as in their institutions they sought democracy.

The opposition between these two races can be seen at each period of Greek history, and it presides over all the revolutions the inhabitants of Greece underwent. But did this opposition, starting from heroic times, exercise over the polytheism of this country enough influence that from it resulted fundamental differences in teachings, rituals, and, above all, beliefs?

No doubt several facts attest to the dissimilarities; a few examples will enlighten us concerning the general nature of the facts. Placed far from the coasts and in the midst of the land, the Dorians neglected Neptune and the maritime divinities, while the Ionians who inhabited islands or lived along rivers diligently worshipped them. The orgies of Bacchus were much more repugnant to the Spartans than to the Athenians[1] and the other peoples of Greece. The character of Apollo, less irritable than the immortals who surround the throne of Jupiter with him, less carried away than Jupiter himself, and distinguished by the haughty calm that his statues convey to us; the character of Apollo, as we were saying, manifestly bears a Dorian imprint;[2] and the virile tendencies of Diana, her masculine occupations, her excessive love of independence, perhaps owe to the qualities of the women of Sparta, who enjoyed as much freedom as their spouses, whom they equaled in courage. While the Sappho of Sicyon, Praxilla, celebrates Venus, the lover of Adonis[3] and the seductive mother of the god of intoxication;[4] while the courtesans of Corinth are devoted to the public pleasures under the auspices of this goddess,[5] Sparta has its armed Venus, and its Venus protectrix of the chaste flames of the nuptial hymen. The Lacedaemonian stories about Hercules, the customary center of the Dorian mythology, are of another genre than those that are told elsewhere about the same god. When these legends pass from the Dorian to the Ionian race they are modified; the Ionians join to the worship of the son of Ju-

---

1. One must not entirely equate the Athenians with the Ionian race: they held the middle between the two races, although much closer to the latter. Their poetry indicates this approximately intermediary rank. The epic belongs to Ionia and is distinguished by action, movement, and something adventurous and passionate. The lyric genre is Dorian: grave, measured, sententious, and moral. Tragedy is Athenian, and in Aeschylus and Sophocles combines both the Ionian and Dorian characters, again tending toward the former.

2. See, in the *Doriens* of Ottfried Müller, the observations that are as just as they are ingenious on the serious character of Apollo in Homer, who, however, treated with some levity the gods befriending the Trojans (*Dorier*, I, 293).

3. Hesych., Βακχον Δι, ωνης.

4. Zenob., *Prov.*, 4, 21; Diogen., 5, 21.

5. Sicyon and Corinth were nevertheless Dorian colonies; but the luxury and commerce of foreigners had stripped them of their original character.

piter the memory of Theseus, the Athenian hero par excellence. Finally, the Greek religion is simpler and graver among the Dorians than in Attica, Asia Minor, or the islands; and Plato bitterly reproaches his fellow citizens for the ostentation of their extravagant festivals and the egoism of their prayers, contrasting them with the modest rituals and disinterested worship of Sparta.[6]

But all these differences between the two races are much later than the Homeric ages: even those who have best observed the differences have recognized this truth. The Greeks of Homer, says Mr. Heeren, all resembled one another, whatever their origin. There is no distinction to make among the Boeotians, the Athenians, the Dorians, and the Achaeans we encounter in his poems. The heroes of these different peoples have nothing *local* about them. The differences that separate them come from their individual characters and personal qualities.[7] It is the same with the gods. Even though Juno is the special divinity of the Argolid; Jupiter of Arcadia, Messenia, and Elidus; Neptune of Boeotia and Aegialia; Minerva of Attica, all these specificities disappear in the Homeric mythology. Greek mythology, says the author of the most ingenious and profound work on the ancient history of the Dorian tribes,[8] forms a whole in which different materials become homogeneous by the fusion that is effected, in which all the local colors are blended and unite to make one color.[9]

Therefore the separation of the races can help us when we treat the subsequent progress of Greek polytheism; but at this point it is of no importance.

As for the doubts expressed by more than one critic concerning the identity between the Homeric mythology and the beliefs of the people, a few words will suffice to dispel them.

What has given rise to these doubts is, on one hand, stubbornness in wanting to attribute to the Greeks notions that are more subtle, more metaphysical, less material than the *Iliad* does; and, on the other hand, the disproportion some be-

---

6. In the second *Alcibiades*.

7. Heeren, *Ideen Grecs*, p. 117. The tradition that attributes to Lycurgus the first collection of the poems of Homer proves the importance attached to these poems in the Peloponnese, as in Attica.

8. Mr. Ottfried Müller.

9. Idem, *Doriens*, I, 212. This writer cites an example of this that we believe we should report. In an ancient tradition of Elide, Alpheus and Diana were united; they had a common altar (Pausan., VII, 5; schol. Pind., *Nem.*, I, 3; *Olymp.*, V, 10), and their mutual loves were recounted; but the virginal character of Diana prevailed over the national opinion, and the local tradition yielded: the disdain of Diana replaced her love.

lieve they see between a barbarous people and the sublime poetry and harmonious language of Homer.

We think that we have superabundantly proven that the Greek religion as it was when it dominated the spirit of the peoples, either at the beginning, if Greece never knew a priestly caste, or after the destruction of this caste by warriors who revolted against it, contained none of the refinements we encountered in the religions or philosophies of the priests. We saw the Greek genius modify everything that came to it from abroad: mysterious rituals could have continued, enigmatic ceremonies could have been celebrated, even publicly, but their priestly meaning—scientific or abstract—was unknown by those who celebrated them.[10]

If—passing on to the other objection—we are reproached for considering to be a religious code an entertaining and strange collection of ingenious and brilliant stories that poets have presented as they wished, changed in order to embellish them, and varied according to their fancy, we answer that antiquity did not see these religious epics that way. In its eyes, to attack Homer was to attack religion. This fact is proven by the practices of priests, the arguments of philosophers, and the mockeries of unbelievers. In Greece, the Homeric poems had a sacred authority: Plato refuted the tales they contained as being an integral part of the public teachings;[11] and to overturn these teachings, Lucian[12] directed attacks against these poems that resemble those of our bold minds against the Bible in the last century. If one reflects

10. It is much more necessary to return Homeric polytheism to its simplicity, or, if you wish, to its primitive crudeness, because an effort in the opposite direction was early on made by the Greeks themselves, whose progress in morality naturally led them to suppose that it had always belonged to religion. Seeing the respect that surrounded the poems of Homer, the philosophers sought to give them a more suitable, and purer, meaning. Theagenes of Rhegium, Anaxagoras, Metrodorus, and Stesimbrotus followed this path. The stoic Crates especially gave himself to this sort of interpretation (Eustath., pp. 3, 40, 561, 614; Strabo, I, 31); and much later the Neoplatonists Porphyry, Proclus, and Simplicius took it up again with much more refinement and boldness. All these subtleties ought to be rejected as the product of later ages, and as being in direct opposition to the genius of the period of the Homeric rhapsodies. In favor of our refusal to admit these, in addition to our arguments we have the testimony of Xenophon, Heraclitus (Diog. Laert., VIII, 21; IX, I, 18), and Plato, who far from recognizing a moral sense in Homer expelled him from his republic; Aristarchus who declared these explanations to be dreams; and finally Seneca, who observed very justly that when one finds everything in a writer one finds nothing (*Epist.*, 88).

11. *Euthyphro.* On the complaints of the ancient philosophers against Homer, see Diogenes Laertius; and on the immaturity of the Greek people relative to these fables, the *Timaeus.*

12. In all his dialogues, and especially *The Cock.*

on it, one will find that the religion described by Homer is precisely what ought to be the religion of a barbarous and martial people living in a beautiful climate, under a benevolent nature, when no authority inhibits this people. How can it conceive its gods? As beings similar to man but endowed with more colossal strength, more extensive faculties, superior knowledge and wisdom, which, however, do not exclude either passions or even the vices that passions entail. The fetish is greedy and hungry because these physical needs are the sole that the primitive knows. Jupiter is still voracious and mercenary because neither greed nor intemperance has disappeared among the barbarians; but with other passions having developed in the human heart, these also become an integral part of the character of Jupiter.

The moderns, who hardly admit scruples because they have few, or convictions because they no longer have any, have supposed that the Greek poets—and especially Homer (to employ this generic name)—embellished or disfigured the religion and deities of Greece, because this religion and these deities were what the poetic need and genius of a poet would have created; but this is because the nation and the development of the social state were poetic. The poets only followed the lead of their nation and their time.

The Homeric poems, and principally the *Iliad* (because everything we say here about the Homeric epics applies above all to this epic), are therefore the most authentic and faithful painting of the religion of the heroic times;[13] but alongside this precious monument, are there not other sources that we also ought to consult?

What would be these sources? We leave to the side the Orphic hymns, which are a priestly importation or the scattered fragments of a destroyed system to which Homer sometimes alludes,[14] but which are completely foreign to his own mythology. We have already spoken of them above; we will have the occasion to speak of them later.

13. We are glad to base ourselves on the authority of one of the most learned and ingenious writers of Germany. "The gods of Homer," says Ottfried Müller (*Prolegom. zu ein. wissensch. Mythol.*, p. 72), "are the same gods to whom the Greeks had raised their temples. These gods always act in a way conformable to the character ascribed to them by their worshippers; and the Greek fables are the expression of the belief in the gods of the country, whatever might be the origin of these gods, and the philosophical meaning attached to the fables."

14. When Homer (*Iliad*, XXI, v. 34) has Vulcan fight Scamander, this comes from Orphic teachings, says Creuzer following Philostrates (*Heroic.*, p. 110). It is the battle of wet and dry, perhaps; but did Homer see anything other than a real battle between two divinities of opposite parties? And, above all, is not this the way he presented it to his listeners?

There remains, therefore, the poets and prose writers who made use of Homer's narratives, either to decorate later epics, tragedies, or odes, or to recount the same deeds in a simpler style and more methodical order. Let us begin with Hesiod.[15]

This poet describes a social state that is very different from Homer's. The development of this truth, and of its consequences for religion, would be out of place here. Hesiod is the representative of a very important revolution in the religious ideas of Greece. The examination of this revolution will find its place. Here we will say only a few words.

Three ideas dominate in what remains to us of Hesiod's poetry. The first is the necessity of work. It is found constantly in the *Works and Days*. The poet seeks in a thousand ways to inculcate it. One senses that at this period this conviction had the energy that novelty lends to sentiments that have just emerged: it was a recent discovery, resulting from the change in the situation of the Hellenic tribes.

Returned from their military expeditions, fallen into an exhaustion that inspired them with a great aversion for similar enterprises, the Greeks were further drained by the intestine wars that renewed in their own country the evils that they had experienced in foreign ones. During the absence of the victors at Troy, almost everywhere ambitious subjects or perfidious relatives had usurped their thrones and their wealth. Citizens fought one another; families rose against one another. Chased from their homes, entire clans invaded their neighbors and expelled them.

---

15. It has been proven that Hesiod is later than the author, or authors, of the Homeric epics. The tradition that presents a contest between the two is obviously false. Hesiod must have lived around two hundred years after the time when Homer is commonly placed, probably toward the twentieth Olympiad; this is because he alludes to customs that arose after the fourteenth. He speaks of games and races in which the athletes were entirely nude. This is how he describes the race between Hippomenes and Atalanta; now this custom, as well as the word *gumnasion*, was introduced after the fourteenth Olympiad (schol. Homer, *ad Il.*, XXIII, 683; Dion. of Hal., VII, *ad finem*; Voss, *Géogr. anc.*, pp. 16, 20). Some moderns have wanted to conclude from the fact that Hesiod's poems are more imperfect than those attributed to Homer, that they preceded him. We, on the contrary, think they bear the unmistakable marks of a decline in epic poetry that comes, on one hand, from the state into which Greece had fallen, and, on the other, from the fact that from Hesiod's time poets, despairing of equaling Homer, sought new means of effect, which always produces a deterioration. The degeneration of the epic dates Hesiod, like that of tragedy dates Euripides. It is also remarkable that in Hesiod the heroic century is expressly relegated to the past. Everything indicates a state of mores and political organization, as would be the case during the stormy transition from declining monarchies to republics yet to come. The preference that Homer gives to the government of one (*Iliad*, II, 204) would also serve, if needed, as a proof that Hesiod belongs to a later time.

More than once, all the parts of Greece (with the exception of Attica and Arcadia) changed inhabitants, and torrents of blood attended each of these revolutions. The Greeks, therefore, were gripped by a love of repose. The cultivation of the earth, the agricultural life, and hard work in their eyes were the indispensable conditions for their future well-being; penetrated by a profound sentiment of this truth, Hesiod lets himself return to it constantly.[16]

In the second place, the reiterated complaints against the kings who devoured the peoples, and against the iniquity of their judgments, indicate the fermentation among barbarian tribes that had to precede the abolition of monarchies and the establishment of republics.

When men follow their leaders to pillage, they console themselves for their obedience to them by the oppression they exercise in their turn against the defeated. This savage despotism passes from hand to hand; each tolerates it because each practices it; but when peace has succeeded to war, tyranny, having become the privilege of a few powerful men, presents no recompense to the multitude. The need for a greater liberty and some kind of security is therefore one of the first results of the peaceful life. We will soon show in the *Odyssey* itself the seed of this tendency and a certain growth in the authority of the people.[17] The poem *Works and Days*, written later than the *Odyssey*, was probably composed shortly before the birth of the Greek republics, at a time when the great ones of each country abused their authority.

One sees in Hesiod more than in Homer the pressure of the great on the multitude:[18] not that this pressure did not exist perhaps even more in earlier times, but then it did not appear to be anything surprising. It takes time for man to discover that he has the right to complain.

Finally, the frequent invectives against women are a third proof of a change in

16. By that very fact, Hesiod ought to have a good deal less poetical charm than Homer. Even though, to be sure, in the current order of things, which is a hundred times better than what preceded, work is the basis of all our morality and our liberty. Nonetheless, the transition from the martial life to the laboring life is less poetic. It appears to substitute, and in the early days of work it does substitute, a life of monotony and enslavement to the fits-and-starts, the irregularities and violence of the heroic days, which in themselves are harmful, but which imagination and distance easily embellish. Compare the *Iliad* to *Works and Days*, the *Seasons* to *Paradise Lost*, Delille to Le Tasse, and say which most brilliantly displays the magical and marvelous colors of poetry.

17. See bk. VIII.

18. *Works and Days*, 200–209, especially 208.

social relations. The poets who describe the heroic times speak almost only about the women of the superior class; now, the women of this class, sometimes guilty of atrocious crimes, did not influence the life of their husbands in any sustained way. They have slaves that they direct in some uncomplicated arts or tasks; but in the more complicated state of the laboring life, women became more necessary to the individuals of the subordinate class, which begins to find its place. The work of women, their diligence, and their obedience are more indispensable; hence, the complaints of their husbands, which Hesiod repeats ad nauseam.

In general, it should be noticed that the class of the people, which is spoken of in Homer only as a buzzing mass, unworthy of attention, emerges in Hesiod from its nullity; just as one saw the communes come to the fore in the history of our feudal monarchies after several centuries during which the lords (who are the kings of heroic times) were the only ones mentioned in the chronicles. Homer paints in a way the feudal age; Hesiod, the age that began to be industrious, agricultural, and almost mercantile.

We will see later how religion proportioned itself to the new needs of a changing society. Here we need only conclude that Hesiod will be a great aid when we have to compare the two successive epochs; but he would confuse us if we consulted him concerning the first of them, to which he did not belong.

Another circumstance makes the testimony of Hesiod of little help on this subject. During the interval that separates the *Iliad* from the *Theogony*, the communications of the Greeks with the barbarians had introduced into Greece many fragments of priestly traditions, beliefs, and doctrines that Hesiod brought together in his verses, but without understanding them. In this respect, religion as it is found in Hesiod was the Greek religion of no time. To find something in Greece that is similar, we must go to the mysteries, but we are not at the point of considering them.

The Cyclic poets[19] depart less from the actual mythology of the barbarous times; but these poets teach us nothing that Homer does not provide with more

---

19. We know only a few fragments and the names of the authors of these poems. Stasinus of Chyprus had composed the *Cypria* in eleven books containing the events of the siege of Troy before the quarrel of Achilles and Agamemnon. Arctinus of Miletus wrote the *Aethiopis; or the Death of Memnon* and the *Destruction of Troy*, in two songs. Lesches of Mitylene celebrated the dispute between Ulysses and Ajax and the ruse of the Trojan horse in four books. In the *Telegonia* Eugamon recounted the adventures of Ulysses after his return; and the five books of Augias were written to recall the reverses the conquering Greeks suffered when they returned home.

detail and greater poetic beauty. Rather dry and cold transcribers, their aim was nothing but to link together fable with fable, narrative with narrative: their sole merit is to reestablish a few minute details or forgotten traditions that the singer of the *Iliad* had omitted. But since there is no poetry in their souls, there is no religion in their songs.

The lyric poets are in another category. They wrote at a more advanced period of civilization and development; hence the need to conform traditions to the progress of ideas; see Stesichorus and Pindar. The first repents having gathered untoward comments on Helen and declares that, better informed, he knows that she was never at Troy; the second rejects several stories, declaring that they cannot be correct because they are unworthy of the gods' majesty.[20]

We will return to this work of the lyric poets when we show the Greek religion walking stride-by-stride with morality, and purifying itself as the intelligence of man develops. Here we mean only to demonstrate that the religion that the lyric poets thus improve is not the religion that the Greeks professed under Troy's ramparts.

For even greater reason, we must not hope for greater fidelity or precision from the Greek tragedians. They remove what would wound their audience; they invent what would please them. Aeschylus and Sophocles less than Euripides, because Aeschylus and Sophocles were believers, yielded only to a moral sentiment and the gradual purification of ideas, and consequently suppressed only actions that were degrading to the gods, but did not call their existence into doubt. Toward the time of Euripides, however, the progress of enlightenment had caused unbelief to sprout. The death of Socrates had aggravated it. Ambitious for effect like Voltaire, obeying the spirit of his century like Voltaire, by flattering it he influenced it. He bent his mythology to a specific goal; he recognized only natural forces, or abstractions, in the gods of the vulgar.[21] Sometimes he brought several divinities together in one; his imagination made sport of the religious traditions, and his desire to impart a new charm to his plays caused him to prefer the most recent or the least known.[22] Thus we can find in Aeschylus and Sophocles the Greek religion as their contemporaries understood it, and even in the first of them recollections

---

20. *Pyth.*, III, 27; IX, 45; *Nem.*, VII, 20.

21. In Euripides, Jupiter is rarely an individual god; by turns he is the Ether, necessity, nature (*Troj.*, 891).

22. This is why he follows Pindar in what he says about Pelops; Stesichorus in what he says about Helen.

of earlier traditions. Euripides helps us see the emerging hostility of an already persecuted philosophy; but all these things have nothing in common with the purely
martial peoples ruled by Achilles or Agamemnon.

As for the poets of Alexandria, the mythology that one can call the true mythology—that is, that which commanded belief and respect for a long time—is
entirely denatured by them under the weight of learned ornaments and pedantic
erudition. As a religion, it has no faith; as talent, no more enthusiasm; these are
compilers, sometimes elegant, often fastidious, who prefer forgotten traditions to
popular ones in order to give their compositions the attraction of novelty and
themselves the merit of learning. They are useful in their descriptions of rituals
and ceremonies, in their allusions to doctrines created by philosophy or come from
abroad; but the moral distance that separates them from the first Greek polytheism is even greater than the chronological distance.

The prose writers hardly give us more certain resources. Some, translators, as it
were, of the epic poets, recount in a style devoid of ornaments what the epic poets
had surrounded with all the brilliance of a vivid imagination. Others, seeking to
put the received stories in a certain order, chose from these stories those that lend
themselves most easily to that task, and thus become deceptive guides, since their
choice is arbitrary, or the fruit of a system.[23] Others, flattering their native country, torture the traditions in order to place among their fellow citizens the greatest number of gods and heroes that they can.[24] Still others absurdly introduce
historical criticism in the midst of fictions, and discuss if Aesculapius perished
by thunder or some other manner, and if he was resurrected at Delphi or elsewhere;[25] they calculate the years, months, and days of the battle before Troy;[26]
and in this way, even though what they work on once pertained to religion, it is no
longer religion, but erudition, with which they concern themselves.

Even more imposing by their title and their character are the historians. Their
researches take them back to the origin of ancient peoples and mores, and hence
to legendary times. But they have no special way of judging the fables; those who

23. "I write," says Hecateus of Miletus, "what seems to me to be true, because the narratives of the
Greeks are numerous, and several, it seems to me, are ridiculous" (*ap.* Demetr., *Peri egmen*, no. 12).

24. Acesilaus of Argos makes the Argile Phoroneus the first man.

25. Apollod., III, 10, 3; schol. Pind., *Pyth.*, III, 96.

26. It is said that Hellanicus, according to indications found in the poets, had compiled a sort of
calendar in which the dates of all the events of the siege of Troy were determined (fragm., ed. Sturz.,
p. 77).

were religious, like Herodotus, at most sought to reconcile them when they recounted them, if they dared to recount them at all;[27] those like Thucydides, whom no prejudice controlled, rejected them by means of a disdainful silence and simply drew the conclusion of the barbarism of the first ages.[28]

The triumph of unbelief and skepticism later created a subordinate class of critics[29] who undertook the facile task of separating the marvelous from what they claimed to call history. They transformed the gods into mere mortals, into fortunate warriors and deified legislators. These writers aid us greatly when we describe the decadence and fall of polytheism; at this point, however, we can derive nothing from them.

For the same reason, we must leave to the side the philosophers. They either interpret polytheism, without overtly attacking it, in order to bend it to their own hypotheses, or, bolder, they combat it with reasoning and ridicule. The only way they can be useful to us at this point is that they provide even more proof that the Homeric religion was the true polytheism in Greece, since, as we said above, Homer was always the object of their attacks.

In summary, therefore, Homer remains alone, the representative and organ of the heroic religion of Greece; and among the multitude of writers who followed or commented upon him there are only two whom we can sometimes consult when Homer himself seems obscure or incomplete. One is Apollodorus, an unpretentious compiler who gathered everything without distortion because he did not aim to explain anything. The other is Pausanias, a curious traveler, an indefatigable questioner, who profited from the fragments of poets, local traditions, the stories of priests, and the sight of monuments or ruins, to write down in his journal everything he could understand and collect.

27. Herodotus, passim.
28. See the beginning of Thucydides's *History*.
29. Euhemerus, etc.

CHAPTER 4

The Point of View under Which We Will Envisage the Polytheism of the Heroic Times

We are now going to present to our readers a portrait of the Homeric mythology among the Greek peoples, still barbarous and ignorant; in doing so, we will ignore all the historical, philosophical, or symbolic interpretations. The contribution of these interpretations has been made: they showed the probabilities according to which one could admit the existence of a priestly caste or religion among the Greeks before the siege of Troy. We will have new developments in this regard when we speak of Hesiod, when we treat philosophy, and above all when we come to the decadence of polytheism. But if we entered on that path now, we would equate notions that must remain absolutely separate. Now it is a matter of understanding the popular belief of the period we are describing, and the work of the religious sentiment on that belief. Here nothing is hidden; nothing is scientific; even the various symbols, an agreed-upon language for the priesthood and its initiates, is for the crowd a language whose terms all have a literal and positive sense, wholly conformed to their popular meaning. Let no one therefore come and tell us that we take Homeric mythology too materially; we take it as the Greeks of the heroic times understood it, and we repeat our fundamental maxim: a religion is always for a people such as the people understand it.

This is not just a personal opinion or something lightly put forth. Even though the defect of the majority of German writers who have occupied themselves with so much sagacity, and in more than one respect with great success, to the study of mythologies has been to seek the mysterious sense rather than the popular influence, the more reasonable among them have come to this same conclusion.

The celebrated Hermann has clearly demonstrated that Homer, even while reporting some symbolic fables and alluding to several others, has not understood their meaning at all;[1] and Mr. Creuzer himself, who seeks symbolism everywhere, is forced to conclude as follows: "Ancient Greece could have been during a certain time sacerdotal and oriental, as it were. The founders of the walls, doors, and Cyclopean grottos of Tirynthe, Sicyon, and Mycenae[2] could have been priests; but the climate of Greece, the mountains, forests, the rivers that divide it in every direction, the energy of the peoples who invaded it, early on put numerous obstacles before all purely religious power. Their mores and institutions, reflection and poetry, came together to turn the bellicose tribes from abstract teachings and contemplative beliefs; their mythology necessarily became less adventuresome, less extravagant in appearance, but also less elevated, and less profound in reality. Bards presented themselves, saying they were inspired, without being priests: they disdained the hidden science; they formed a separate class that saw in priests their rivals, and were preferred to them by the monarchs and the warriors. While Calchas trembles[3] and Leiodes perishes,[4] Phemius obtains life, and honors are lavished upon him."[5]

Homer, he continues, had his motives for conforming to the popular beliefs. Poetry wishes above all to please. He bent his genius to the reigning mores and

1. Homer, he says, recounts them as facts, believing them, and without seeking their motives and without venturing any explanation; and he gives a rather ingenious example that it seems to us is worth mentioning. In the twelfth book of the *Odyssey*, in order to attract Ulysses to their trap, the Sirens sing (v. 188) of the happiness of the stranger initiated by them into the science of all things, γαρ τοι παντα. These words announce that they will unveil before his eyes everything that occurs on the diversely inhabited earth, επι χθονι πολ υβοτειρη; and yet what do they offer to teach him? The history of the misfortunes of Troy, which Ulysses ought to know better than anyone. Where does this sudden swerve on the road come from? From the fact that Homer, not knowing the Sirens except by uncertain reports, repeated them without ascribing to them any sense except the literal. In the oriental teachings, the fable of the Sirens came from the fundamental priestly idea that science, when it is revealed in a way other than they prescribe, is an evil, a crime that is soon followed by inevitable and severe punishment. Thus, the Sirens want to cause Ulysses to perish by promising him knowledge of good and evil. Other mythologies have taken this same idea as their foundation. But Homer sees in the Sirens only treacherous monsters who sing harmoniously; and following a tradition he did not understand, after having announced that they would expose the secrets of the world, he has them speak about what he does understand, the war he has recounted and the exploits he has celebrated.

2. Pausan., II, 25, 3; VII, 25, 7.

3. Calchas, *Iliad*, I, 74, 83.

4. *Odyss.*, III, 267.

5. Creuzer to Hermann, fourth letter, pp. 48–49.

opinions. He probably knew Egypt and the East; he could have seen the symbolic sculptures of Thebaid, or Ionian sailors, his compatriots, could have described them to him. But when it was a question of inserting these profound allegories into his poems, as an expert artist he blended them into his narrative, identified them with his characters, took away from them their enigmatic aspects, and, wiser than he might appear, attached himself to the form, passing under silence the teaching;[6] and the entire nation, subject to the genius of this great poet, at the sight of his new and brilliant Olympus soon forgot the sublime but half-veiled lessons that they had earlier received from the priests of the East. Beliefs, poetry, sculpture, everything followed this model, which had become the nation's; all other light paled before his.[7]

This acknowledgment suffices for us.[8] We do not have to seek what Homer thought, but what he said in order to conform to his contemporaries' thinking. It is this thinking that it is essential to know; it is the influence of these thoughts that it is important to examine.

6. Sixth letter, p. 127. This correspondence between two men with vast learning and undeniable sagacity is extremely interesting. Whatever our admiration for Mr. Creuzer, we cannot deny that his opponent has several advantages in this contest. To put our readers in a position to judge, it is enough to state the definition of mythology given by each. Mythology, says Mr. Creuzer, is the science that teaches us how the universal language of nature is expressed in this-or-that symbol (Creuzer to Hermann, p. 97). Mythology, says Mr. Hermann, is the science that allows us to know what the notions and ideas of this-or-that people were, and how they were represented by this-or-that symbol, image, or fable (Hermann to Creuzer, p. 1). One immediately sees that the first is vague and inapplicable, while the second is precise and conformed to reason.

7. *Symboliq.*, French trans., pp. 100–101.

8. There is but one man in the learned world who persists in seeing in the poems of Homer only the development of a vast and universal symbolism (if he still belongs to that world). To hear him, in Homer's view Achilles is not an individual being but a symbolic force like Mithra or Krishna. The loves of Helen are not a historical fact, or a fiction that poetry would have borrowed from legendary traditions: she is the struggle between cold and hot, dry and humid, day and darkness, good and evil. A lot of good that does one! Would a German scholar claim that Balaam's ass was nothing but Orpheus? Each is free to dream as he wishes, as long as he restricts himself to dreams about antiquity. Nothing is more innocent. But when one wants to apply them to modern times, and one falsifies the works of antiquity for the sake of the caste that has oppressed peoples for four thousand years in order to forge new shackles for them, the thing becomes a little less innocent.

CHAPTER 5

The Embellishment of Divine Forms in Homeric Polytheism

The first progress that occurred in the beliefs free of all hindrance and bother is the embellishment of the figures of the gods. This embellishment is a human need; we have already seen it among the primitive savages.[1]

In satisfying this need, mankind momentarily departs from that tendency toward the unknown that is inherent in the religious sentiment.[2] And we will see it depart again, when after having attributed physical beauty to the objects of its worship, it will seek what ought to be their moral qualities. The more it reflects on these questions, the more it will make gods similar to itself. But this is a transition, a preliminary work, to which he gives himself only as long as the gods are inferior to him in their qualities or their forms. As soon as he has made them his equals by ascribing to them what is best in his nature, he makes them his superiors by freeing them from his weaknesses and vices; this new work establishes new differences, incalculable and indefinite, and religion returns to its proper sphere.

This metamorphosis, however, does not occur all at once. For some time, the imagination disfigures the gods by more-or-less bizarre additions. It sometimes gives them several arms or heads as signs of strength or intelligence, sometimes wings as a sign of speed; but these fantastical additions gradually disappear. Taste is purified and brings into polytheism—when this belief can freely follow the direction that is properly its own—the beautiful ideal of human forms.

The most ancient Greek divinities were monstrous simulacra.[3] Pausanias speaks of a god in the form of a fish, seen in his day in the sanctuary of Juno at

---

1. Bk. II, ch. 3.

2. Bk. II, ch. 2.

3. Heyne, *Antiquar. Aufsätze*, I, 162; *Ejusd. Apollodor. et de form. Invent. et de fabul. Homer. Com. Soc. Goett.*; Hermann, *Myth. Handbuch*, II, 168.

Olympia;[4] the Arcadians, near to Phigalia, worshipped Ceres with the head and mane of a horse.[5] In the same way, Proserpina had the head of an animal, four eyes, and four horns.[6] Larissa displayed its Jupiter with three eyes;[7] Amykles its Bacchus,[8] Elide its winged Diana.[9] But every time the historians or travelers mention these sacred representations, they add that they go back to an antiquity so remote that no one can attribute a date to it.[10] This is because these monstrosities had softened, been effaced, and gradually disappeared, without anyone being able to point to the precise moment of the disappearance. Aesculapius, first a jar then a dwarf god, took on at unknown periods (because credit for the development is attributed to several sculptors)[11] a more beautiful form; and the sole vestige that remains of his ancient figure was a pygmy statue placed beside him in some of his temples.[12] Cecrops having come from Egypt with a double body and the tail of a serpent, thus represented a double nature, said the commentators: one, agricultural, expressed by the whip and reins in his hands; the other bellicose, indicated by the sword and shield carried in his other two hands.[13] Little sensible to the allegory,

4. Pausan., *Elide*, 41.

5. Pausan., *Arcad.*, 42.

6. Creuzer, *Symbol.*, IV, 85. In one hand she holds a dove, in the other a dolphin; around her are serpents and other animals.

7. Jupiter Patroous or Triophtalmos. Pausanias has this statue go all the way back to the siege of Troy, that is, to an uncertain and legendary time; and if we credit the tradition that said it was brought to this city, we would be led back to Phrygia, a country where the priesthood dominated (see Creuzer, I, 167). The same writer who conveys these details hazards an explanation of this figure of Jupiter that is suitable to his time, but inadmissible if one applies it to the period he talks about. I believe, he says, that the statue maker gave three eyes to Jupiter to indicate that one and the same god governs the three parts of the world, the heavens, the sea, and the netherworld, which others say were divided among three masters (*Corinth*, 24). It is obvious that this conjecture comes from a time when the general tendency was toward theism. But Jupiter Triophtalmos had three eyes for the same reason that an equal, or greater, number was assigned to several Indian divinities. The three eyes of Shiva express the perspicacity of his sight (*Asiat. Res.*, VIII, 60).

8. Pausan., *Lac.*, 19.

9. Pausan., *Elide*, 19. The same country possessed an ancient and primitive statue of Apollo; as descendants of the Dorians, its inhabitants held tightly to the most ancient images of the gods.

10. Pausan., *Elide*, 19; *Arcad.*, 42; *Corinth*, 24.

11. Pausan., *Corinth*, 27; Heyne, *De auctor. formar.*, p. 25.

12. Pausan., *Mess.*, 22; Ottfried Müller claims that the epithets Βοῶπις for Juno and Γλαυκῶπις for Minerva are a memory of the time when one was worshipped as a cow, the other as an owl (*Proleg. zu einer wissensch. Myth.*, p. 263).

13. Jo. Diacon., *ad* Hesiod, *Scut. Herc.*, p. 219; Plut., *De sera. num. vind.*

the Athenians got rid of these deformities. Cecrops for them was a divine legislator who presided over marriage, otherwise similar to all mortals. The winged Bacchus of Amykles was stripped of his unwelcome and useless symbol to become the ideal of voluptuous and effeminate beauty, as Apollo was of majestic male beauty.[14] Scylla, the monster who was terrible to sailors, first of all a dragon with twelve feet and six mouths always open to devour its prey, was later a woman with the seductive form of the high-drawn belt; and the stories that were told about her hid from view her fish-tail, as well as the menacing dogs whose barking frightened pilots.

If we did not fear to anticipate subsequent epochs, we would show that when circumstances introduced the Greek spirit into priestly religions, this spirit caused the tendency to embellish the divine forms to triumph, despite the resistance of priests. The Serapis of Egypt was originally a head on an urn, surrounded by serpents. At Alexandria, Greek artists protected by the Ptolemies gave it a human figure.[15] At Canopus, on the contrary, where the Greek spirit never penetrated, Serapis continued to be worshipped under his ancient form.[16]

The Phallus, this obscene and hideous idol, which constantly reappears in all the priestly cults; transmitted to the Greeks by the ancient Pelasgian theocracy, or come into Greece from Egypt, the Phallus was initially headed by a human face; soon the indecent organ was removed, and the Phallus did not differ from other statues, except in its mysterious rituals.[17]

14. On the questions of winged divinities in Greece, see the works of Winckelmann and the *Lettres mythologiques* of Voss. With the exception of Mercury (and this exception can be contested), who in his quality as the messenger of the gods retains almost invisible little wings that do not disfigure him at all, all the winged deities—Love, Nemesis, good faith, Diké, justice—belong to an allegorical period and therefore are foreign to real mythology, i.e., that which presupposes belief. When allegory enters into religion, the figure of the gods is modified in a direction inverse to that which we are currently describing. Anthropomorphism changes the symbol into an attribute, while allegory changes the attribute into a symbol.

15. With the *modius* on the head, and by placing at his side a figure with the three heads of a dog, wolf, and lion, with a serpent entwining the body.

16. Creuzer, *Zoeg. numm. Aegypt.*, tab. III, n. 5; XVI, n. 8. It is probable that the spirit of the Persian priesthood exercised a harmful influence with respect to the representation of their gods over the Greeks of Ionia who were subject to Persian domination. Several statues that had no wings in the Peloponnese were winged in Asia Minor. Mr. de Pauw attributes this difference to the climate (*Rech. sur les Grecs*). But the spirit and action of the priesthood had to have contributed.

17. Hecate is the only divinity worshipped in Greece who appears to have retained its monstrous form; she has three faces, three bodies, six hands armed with a sword, a dagger, a whip, cords, and torches, a crown and dragon on her head, and serpents instead of hair (Firm., *De error. prof. rel.*, p. 7). She recalls the Indian Badrakaly, daughter of Shiva, with her eight faces, her boar tusks, the two ele-

Thus the intellect works to embellish what the soul adores. The need to contemplate the ideal of beauty in their gods inspired the Greeks with that passion for beauty in itself, the source of masterworks that we will not be able to imitate.[18] Even when the mysterious sense had penetrated into their religion, it always remained in second place; beauty was the goal. Symbolism was constantly sacrificed to it.

And let no one think that it was art alone that profited from this disposition. The proportion, nobility, and harmony of forms have something that is both religious and moral. A man of real genius said that the sight of the Apollo Belvedere or a painting by Raphael made him better. Indeed, the contemplation of the beautiful of any sort detaches us from ourselves, inspires us to forget our narrow interests, and transports us into a sphere of greater purity and unexpected perfection. Corruption can cause this enthusiasm to veer, as it can pervert everything; but the effect of corruption is limited and momentary. It does not influence the masses; and it is incontestable that a people who have need of ideal beauty in their worship, their festivals, and their buildings—in a word, all that strikes their sight—is morally better off than a people lacking this need. This difference is therefore a first superiority of the Greeks; it was a first advantage the Greeks received from their religious independence.

---

phants suspended from her ears, entwined serpents for clothing, and holding in her sixteen hands keys, tridents, and weapons of all sorts. Thus Hecate was not Greek. Eusebius remarks how much she differed from the other deities (*Praep. evang.*, V). Homer does not speak of her. Her name appears for the first time in Hesiod. The Centimanes, Typhoeus, and Briareus who are mentioned in passing in the *Iliad* have no relation with the customary mythology; no worship is given them; no suppliant calls upon them.

18. The admiration of the Greeks for the beauty of forms was a true passion that won out over ancient customs and traditions in their religion, and over the most ingrained national hatreds in their politics. Herodotus recounts (V, 47) that the inhabitants of Egesto in Sicily raised a chapel and offered sacrifices to Philip of Crotona, son of Butacides, even though he had come with Dorieus to invade their country, and they had killed him. The historian finds this an entirely natural thing, because this Philip was the most beautiful of men. At Aega in Achaia, the most beautiful young man was named priest of Jupiter (Pausan., *Achai.*, c. 24).

It is nonetheless worthwhile to note that the embellishment of the deities did not take place on the coins of Greece. Art did not regard money as pertaining to its province. On several pieces, Bacchus appeared in the form of a bull or a serpent, entwining Proserpina in his tortuous embraces, while painters at Naxos represented him invested with celestial beauty, between the arms of Ariadne (Creuzer, III, 494, 495).

CHAPTER 6

On the Character of the Homeric Gods

The efforts of the religious sentiment left to its free and natural tendency are not limited to the external and, as it were, material embellishment of the gods. The same tendency prompts it to work an interior revolution in them. It wants to attribute to them everything beautiful, noble, and good that it conceives. It works to this end as much as its imperfect notions allow; and in its general propositions it grants the gods beauty, justice, and happiness.

But the same cause of degradation that we have observed in fetishism, the action of the interest of the moment, of that always base interest, both impatient and blind, exerts itself against the new worship that man has just succeeded in establishing.

A double movement therefore makes itself felt, and from this a constant struggle is born. This struggle is further complicated by the credulity and youthfulness of imagination that characterize peoples in their infancy. Fables present themselves in even greater number because they are not the monopoly of priests. Faith receives them, interest takes hold of them, sentiment attempts to modify them; from all this comes an often disparate mythology, full of contradictions that pass unnoticed because no one brings them together to compare them, and because destined one day to do battle, they coexist peaceably at present, not yet having encountered one another.

This is the spectacle that the *Iliad*'s portrait of polytheism is going to offer; our readers will recall that we will present it here as it was understood by the mass of Greeks; we will follow the counsel of an able critic[1] and put aside all the doctrines that distort its simplicity.

---

1. Heyne, *De Theog. Hes.*

On the summit of a mountain,[2] which thick clouds hide from profane eyes, lives the assembly of the gods. Each of these gods presents to the mind the notion of a quality, of a virtue, and of a force superior to those possessed by men. Jupiter is the ideal of majesty; Venus, of beauty, Minerva, of wisdom. We do not mean to say that the Greeks made them allegorical beings,[3] but only that they attempted to combine in them all that they imagined was most majestic, most beautiful, and wisest. Mortals respectfully raised their sights to this venerable assembly of supernatural beings who contemplated and protected them. To this point it is the religious sentiment, profound and pure.

But the Greeks wanted to take advantage of their gods the same way that primitives did their fetishes. Self-interest came to tarnish the new form toward which sentiment aspired.

In order to suppose that the gods facilitate our inconstant desires, our greedy or unbridled passions, one has to imagine that they are sensitive to gifts, sacrifices,

2. We take the Greek mythology of the reign of Jupiter; all the earlier cosmology is foreign to it. In book V, chapter 5, we have shown with what indifference the Greeks received it, and with what eagerness the Greek genius relegated it to a sphere where the public religion did not have anything to do with it. See Vesta (Εστια), the oldest daughter of Saturn and Rhea (Hesiod, *Theog.*, 454). She has no attributes; no fable is attached to her. Out of some faint memory, she is offered a sacrifice before the other deities; then she is abandoned; and she never acts.

3. People are very disposed to see allegory where none exists, when they do not have an exact enough idea of allegory. When a people create their gods and assign them special functions, it is very simple that each of them is assigned everything that has any relation to these functions. Thus Venus will intervene in the passions and weaknesses of love; Mars will start the wars that occur between peoples. Minerva will preside over the works of the sages and the councils of nations. But in addition to these determinate functions, the gods have an individual character that is independent of them: this is not allegory. Now, in the Greek mythology of the period of which we speak, Venus gives her heart over to hatred; Minerva yields to anger; there is no divinity who does not belie by its actions the function it fulfills or the post it occupies. The gods, therefore, are not allegories; they are individuals whose profession, if we can put it that way, does not inhibit them from forming projects or experiencing passions or obeying interests that are private and personal.

Having failed to see this truth, poets since the Renaissance have believed that allegory would replace mythological personages in their works. But when Jupiter appears in the *Iliad*, we do not know what he is going to do; he can change his mind, he can allow himself to be dissuaded. On the contrary, personified fanaticism, discord, or liberty must necessarily act in a way foreseen in advance. There cannot be any uncertainty; nothing therefore that would pique curiosity or captivate interest. Thus ancient mythology is most poetic and most lively; while modern allegories, including those of the *Henriade*, are quite boring and cold.

and offerings. Soon enough: behold, they are mercenary; and such are the gods of the *Iliad*.

It is not morality, it is not equity, that decides their conduct; it is sacrifice. If Minerva protects the Athenians, it is because they present to her cakes of pure wheat, lambs without spot, rams whose decorated horns she delights in contemplating.[4] Jupiter is touched with compassion for Hector, not because this hero defends his father and his homeland, but because he has always loaded the altars of this god with wine, meats, and exquisite perfumes.[5] Neglected by the Aetolians, Diana sends against them a wild boar. Proteus declares to Menelaus that he will not return to his homeland except after having offered sacrifices to the gods of Egypt.[6] Attracted by the vow of a hecatomb, the inhabitants of the ethereal dwellings descend to intervene in the least significant circumstances. In the funeral games of Patrocles, Apollo himself directs the arrow of Merion, whose rival neglected to purchase his assistance.[7] The Greeks address to their gods the same language that the primitives address to their fetishes;[8] and in their own conversations, these gods reproach one another for acts of ingratitude that consist in forgetting the oxen, goats, and choice victims the warriors they abandon had immolated to them on their altars.[9]

Thus the religion was once again perverted. Polytheism is only apparently superior to fetishism.[10] The objects that are devoted to the gods have a greater worth; but the relations established between the divinity and man are the same.

The degradation does not end there. The struggle between self-interest and the purity of the religious sentiment is complicated by the intervention of a third power, which comes as a judge to pronounce sentences that the two adversaries are far from expecting.

This power is reasoning. As the human mind is enlightened, it learns to draw

---

4. *Odyss.*, III, 436.

5. *Iliad*, XXII, 170, 172. Thus Priam says (*Iliad*, XXIV, 425–28) that the gods will remember his son, because while he was living he lavished sacrifices upon them.

6. *Odyss.*, IV, 472–81.

7. *Iliad*, XXIII, 863–73.

8. *Iliad*, VIII, 238; X, 291; XV, 372–75; XXIV, 425–28; *Odyss.*, III, 58–59; IV, 352–53, 761–65; XIX, 363–68.

9. *Iliad*, XXIV, 33, 34; *Odyss.*, I, 60–62.

10. This does not contradict what we were saying about the progressive perfecting of religious ideas. One will see the proof in the last chapter of this very book.

consequences from the principles it acknowledges; this is a law of its nature. From whatever point he starts, man is forced to reason correctly, even when his reasonings go against his aim.

It results from this that when he adopts some hypothesis concerning the gods, the mind draws the necessary conclusions; and by means of these conclusions he arrives at a point he did not foresee, which injures both the sentiment that had created the new religious form and the interest that wanted to make use of it.

By the first modifications that occurred in their character, the gods compose a society of beings who are more powerful than mortals, who sell their protection to them in exchange for presents and victims. According their favors out of self-interest, they grant them to the guilty as well as the innocent. Not only can criminals believe that they can regain the gods' benevolence by offerings and sacrifices—doctrines that are found in more advanced religions—but the same means acquire heavenly assistance for the most blameworthy enterprises. Pandarus promises Phoebus one hundred newborn lambs if he will second his perfidy.[11] Aegisthus hangs gifts in the temples, the price of adultery.[12] In this way, all confidence is destroyed: the vices of the gods[13] multiply by a scale that reasoning makes inevitable, and they arrive at the highest point of perversity and corruption. From venality, they pass to perfidy. Men are not sure of their aid, even when sacrifices please them. They accept them and then prepare new misfortunes for the suppliants.

If one supposed that the authors of the Homeric mythology wanted to portray in the character of their gods the abuses inherent in force exercised on beings incapable of reprisal or resistance, one would be astonished at everything that man glimpsed in this regard from the infancy of society; this is because his instinct precedes his experience. In order to judge the evil occasioned by unlimited caprice and power without check, one only has to go into his own heart. The gods

---

11. *Iliad*, IV, 101–2.

12. *Odyss.*, I, 273–75.

13. The vices of the gods impressed themselves so much upon the popular notions that from them came customary surnames, which expressed the distrust of men vis-à-vis these perfidious divinities. Thus Pausanias tells us that on the island of Spheria, which depended on Trezene, a temple was dedicated to Minerva Apaturia, or the deceiver. An ancient tradition explained this epithet. Aethra, the mother of Theseus, it was said, was instructed by Minerva in a dream to bestow the final rites on Spherus, who was buried on this island; there she had been violated by Neptune; in her animosity she had given Minerva the name Apaturia. It was also applied to Venus, but the story was different (Strabo, p. 495) and alluded to cosmogony.

of Homer are what we would be in our excess of passion and violence if we had the certainty of impunity. They do not respect the holiest laws of the peoples who worship them. In this respect alone they depart from the imitation of human actions: they violate even the hospitality that is so sacred in barbarous times. Hercules kills his host, Iphitus, and is still received in Olympus;[14] Jupiter leisurely savors the spectacle of carnage;[15] he is pleased to see the gods fighting furiously among themselves;[16] he spends nights meditating harmful projects;[17] he sacrifices all the Greek army to Achilles's pride and the entreaties of Thetis;[18] he sends on earth Até, his daughter, the source of all evils.[19] The injustice of this master of thunder is depicted very forcefully by Minerva: he will return, she says, full of wrath; he will seize all of you, innocent as well as guilty.[20] But Minerva herself is no less cruel, no less perfidious, when she wants to slake her hatred: she leads Hector to his end by the most revolting ruse.[21] She permits Ulysses and Diomedes to dedicate the corpse of Dolon to her, killed by them despite a solemn promise.[22] Like Neptune, she applauds the ferocity of the son of Peleus, insulting the corpse of his defeated enemy.[23] To deceive Patrocles, Apollo has recourse to a trick a mortal would be ashamed of.[24] The children of Latona sacrifice an innocent family to their mother.[25] To more fully satisfy her vengeance, Juno delivers to her husband the nations who are most devoted to her worship, the most attentive to her altars.[26] All the gods pursue Bellerophon with their unjust hatred.[27]

14. *Odyss.*, 22–30.
15. *Iliad*, XX, 22.
16. Ibid., XXI, 389–90.
17. Ibid., VII, 478.
18. Ibid., V, 595–602.
19. Ibid., XIX, 91.
20. Ibid., XV, 136, 138.
21. Ibid., XXII, 224–47. Minerva prides herself on being the most cunning of the divinities (*Odyss.*, XII, 287–99). In a quite explicit way, she expresses her admiration for lying (*Odyss.*, XIII, 287ff.). In a social state such as the one Homer depicts, fraud and cunning are naturally held in great esteem. The *point d'honneur* only forms with the progress of civilization. Primitives see no shame in deceiving, or fleeing.
22. *Iliad*, X, 383–570.
23. Ibid., XXIV, 25–26.
24. Ibid., XVI, 785–90.
25. Ibid., XXIV, 602–9.
26. Ibid., IV, 40–63.
27. Ibid., VI, 200–202.

Other times, they are the instigators of the crime. Mercury teaches Autolycus how to steal away with address.[28] Angry at Diomedes, Venus corrupts his wife, Aegiale.[29] To revenge herself against the mother of Myrrha, she moves her daughter to crime.[30] When Helen appears to be shaken by remorse, she forces her to persevere in adultery, and this is not an allegory.[31] Love enters not one whit in the new weakness of Helen. Venus constrains her by crude, almost brutal, threats. Yielding to fear, Helen addresses harsh reproaches at Venus;[32] and her speech is above all remarkable because of the idea it provides of the relations that the religion of heroic times supposes between the gods and humans.

Nonetheless, it is these gods that are invoked for the sake of morality. Priam beseeches Achilles to merit the favor of the immortals by his humanity toward him.[33] Menelaus asks Jupiter to avenge the wounded rights of friendship and hospitality. But one must distinguish what men say from what the gods do. In their prayers, suppliants and the offended speak the language of their interest rather than that of their real belief.

In the examination of religions, sometimes maxims that express more the need that humans have for divine assistance than the gods' true character are taken for a complete system of morality. Their justice, like that of kings, is praised in order to invite them to be just. What men in their passion ask the gods does not prove that they hope for it: they invoke them because suffering without resource and impotent indignation address whatever object presents itself. Even before religion officially intervened in morality, men implored the gods against injustice; and in Sophocles, lacking all human support Philoctetes asks vengeance against Ulysses of the rocks, the mountains, and the forests of Lemnos — mute witnesses, insensible to his despair.[34] This appeal to invisible forces proves misery, not confidence.

This reflection also applies to the punishment of perjury, which the gods are officially interested in punishing. It was Agamemnon, it was Idomeneus, it was the Greek generals who announced to the Trojans guilty of this crime that heavenly

---

28. *Odyss.*, XIX, 395–98.
29. Schol. Homer, *ad Iliad*, V, 412.
30. Schol. Theocr., *Idyll.*, I.
31. See what we said about allegory at the beginning of this chapter.
32. *Iliad*, III, 390–420.
33. Ibid., XXIV, 503.
34. Soph., *Philoct.*, 981, 986.

anger would fall upon them;[35] and it is important to observe that the event did not justify their threatening predictions. It was not because the Trojans broke an oath that the fall of Troy was contained in the decrees of destiny; on the contrary, it was to cause the destruction of Troy, still innocent at least of this crime, that the gods stirred its inhabitants to renew the war by breaking an oath. Condemned to fall the tenth year of the siege,[36] Troy did not perish either sooner or later because the Trojans broke a treaty. Olympus remained divided between the defenders and the enemies of this city.[37] The gods who protected it did not abandon its cause because it had violated the faith of oaths. They tried no less to delay the fatal hour of the city they cherished by all the means in their power.

Therefore men know too well how much their recourse to the justice of the gods is unavailing. The same Agamemnon who implored Jupiter soon accuses him of lying and perfidy;[38] and Menelaus, even while invoking him, blames him for all the evils that overwhelm him.[39]

In this way, the beings the religious sentiment had created in order to place its need for worship in them become the objects of hatred and fear instead of love and hope. In speaking of Pluto, Agamemnon makes use of an expression that merits being noted. Pluto, he says, is inexorable and inflexible; of all the gods, he is the one that mortals hate the most.[40] The peoples therefore put themselves on guard against the powerful but faithless auxiliaries they have placed over them. Some chain them in their temples so they cannot go out and join their enemies, who come swearing oaths and making promises to them;[41] others pronounce their

35. *Iliad*, IV, passim.
36. Ibid., prediction of Calchas.
37. Ibid., IV, 439, 507, 516; XX, 32.
38. Ibid., IX, 18, 25.
39. Ibid., XIII, 629ff.
40. Ibid., IX, 158, 159.
41. The Lacedaemonians had a statue of a chained Mars; the Athenians had removed the wings of the statue of Victory. The first, says Pausanias (*Lacon.*, 15), thought that Mars-in-chains could not desert them; and the second, that Victory deprived of her wings would remain with them forever. When these crude notions had given way to purer ones, the Greeks imagined other reasons to chain their gods; or, to speak more exactly, they explained in another way why certain gods were chained. Art, they said, had given them life and movement; it was necessary to chain them to keep them (Jacobs, *Rede ueber den Reichtum der Griechen an plastischen Kunstwerke*, p. 17). Thus the initial notions were effaced but the practices survived; one found new reasons.

sacred names in a low voice, so that foreigners not knowing how to invoke them would have no way of seducing them.[42] Ready to fight Hector, Ajax exhorts the Greeks to pray in a low voice so that the Trojans would not be able to hear them.[43] All peoples admit that the nations can steal the others' gods by means of adroit gifts.[44] Thus at this period of religion the gods are, as it were, always for hire. Their approval is not a proof of merit; their hatred implies no blame; no shame. Obedience to their orders is a means of pleasing them, but not a virtue; resistance is often a means of glory or even success. It was despite Juno that Hercules conquered Olympus; it was despite Neptune that Ulysses regained Ithaca. If the gods sometimes inspire their favorites with certain qualities—prudence, pity,[45] courage—it is in a particular circumstance, and for a particular aim;[46] it is a miracle, it is enchanting. It has nothing to do with moral improvement, with a fixed and immutable rule of conduct; because other times they teach the contrary of these qualities. The gods have given you, says Ajax to Achilles, a cruel and pitiless heart.[47]

Jealousy is an essential part of their character. They are jealous, says Homer,[48] not only of success but of ability and talent. All mortal prosperity darkens the di-

---

42. Helenus proposes to the Trojans to seduce Minerva (*Iliad*, VI, 89).

43. Ibid., VII, 194–96. He then adds: "Or pray loudly, because we have nothing to fear." This last comment is in keeping with Ajax's character, whose courage is always represented as imperious and rash; but the first request is in keeping with the customs of the time. We will see the same precaution in a more regular form taken by the Romans.

44. The Aeginitans, having revolted against Epidaurus, stole the statues of Damia and Anxesia, tutelary goddesses of Epidaurus, the same as Ceres and Proserpina; they placed them in the middle of their island and attempted to gain their favor by means of the sacrifices they established (Herod., V, 82, 83; Pausan., II, 32; VIII, 53; Festus, *voce Damium sacrif.*; Macrob., *Sat.*, VII, 12). The venality of the gods was such a universal belief that in taking over a country, the first care of the Greeks was to seduce the gods. Aiming at the conquest of Salamis, Solon began by immolating victims to the heroes Periphemus and Cichreus, who had been the leaders of the country (Plut., in *Solon*). Oxylus did the same when invading Elide (Pausan., *Elide*, II). To this view was joined another idea that was no less unfavorable to divine dignity, which was that the gods are constrained to follow their idols, even when they were taken by force. But this idea is not purely Greek; it is a priestly idea that we will explain later, and which probably entered Greece from abroad.

45. The proof that this is not a general rule is that when Agamemnon answers with a speech of unsurpassed ferocity to the supplications of an unarmed Adrastus, and prevents Menelaus from granting him his life (*Iliad*, VI, 55, 62), the gods do not at all disapprove of this cruelty.

46. Ibid., IX, 255, 256; XX, 110.

47. Ibid., IX, 636.

48. Ibid., VII, 455.

vine pride.[49] This implacable pride waits for men and empires to attain happiness, in order to cast them into the abyss.[50]

Thus reduced in the moral qualities which the religious sentiment had been pleased to ascribe to them, the gods also lost a great part of the attributes that it had conferred on them out of respect: infinity, immensity, eternity, even immortality. Their view extends far because they are placed at the summit of the world; but they do not see everything that happens there.[51] When they want to know the events of the earth, they send down messengers who report to them.[52] In order to see the Trojans and the Greeks simultaneously, Jupiter places himself atop Mount Ida.[53] While he has his eyes fixed on Thrace, Neptune, despite his order, gives aid to the Greeks, and Neptune himself would not have known the danger faced by the Greeks he favored if, from the peak of a mountain where he had seated himself by chance, he had not discovered their fleet threatened and the Trojans triumphant.[54] Ascalaphus is killed without the knowledge of his father, Mars,[55] who only learns of it from Juno.[56] Even though perspicuity was her distinctive quality, Minerva bitterly complains about not having foreseen the future.[57] The gods do not enjoy the light of day except when Aurora has brought

49. This notion of the jealousy of the gods crosses all the periods of belief, without ever being completely eliminated. Even while denying Providence, Lucretius recognizes a jealous and malign force that pleases itself with overturning human greatness.

Usque adeo res humanas vis abdita quaedam
Obterit, et pulchros fasces saevasque secures
Proculcare, ac ludibrio sibi habere videtur.
(V. 1232)

50. One finds among the modern Greeks a rather curious vestige of this ancient idea, that the gods are jealous of everything that is distinguished. They consider praise as being able to call down great misfortune upon the person who is its object, or who owns the thing one admires; and they earnestly beseech the indiscreet panegyrist to ward off this effect by some sign of disdain that would disarm the celestial anger (Pouqueville, *Voy. en Morée*).

51. The idea that the gods do not know everything lasted a long time among the Greeks after the period of Homeric polytheism. Xenophon says: "Most men think that the gods know certain things and do not know other things, but Socrates believed that the gods knew all" (*Memor. Socrat.*, I, 1; II, 19).

52. *Iliad*; *Odyss.*, passim.

53. *Iliad*, VIII, 5; XI, 81; XX, 22.

54. Ibid., XIII, 3, 16.

55. Ibid., XIII, 521.

56. Ibid., XV, 110, 112.

57. Ibid., XVIII, 366.

it to them;[58] often they yield to sleep[59] or succumb to fatigue.[60] Juno reproaches Jupiter for making her labors and sweat useless, as well as the exhaustion of her steeds.[61] Mercury complains of having to cross the uninhabitable ocean, a vast and deserted expanse unmarked by human habitations. When they want to put an army to rout, they are apprehensive of their natural strength; they have recourse to magical means that betray the insufficiency of the divine forces.[62] They display before the eyes of the combatants the fearful aegis that sows terror everywhere.[63] To be sure, in general they are stronger than men. Minerva rebuffs Hector's spear with a breath.[64] Juno grows angry at encountering obstacles in an action that even a mortal would be able to accomplish.[65] Sighing, Achilles recognizes that Apollo can defy his vengeance.[66] But their forces are still limited. The beauty of the goddesses is due to the oil of ambrosia,[67] to that immortal oil that gives their charms a new brilliance; the purity of their blood to that same ambrosia, which replaces the wheat broken beneath the stone and the grape crushed by the winemaker;[68] the rapidity of their travel to the velocity of the marvelous steeds that bear them:[69] for the gods cannot act upon men without coming near to them, and their mere will cannot transport them from one place to another. Minerva and Mercury have miraculous sandals[70] that bear them over the immense sea and over the land that spreads so far. They put on the forms that they will;[71] but they are often recognized despite their disguises.[72] The single faculty of the gods that is not limited is that of hearing. They hear everywhere, even though they cannot see everywhere.[73] Men

58. Ibid., II, 48, 59; XI, 1, 2; *Odyss.*, III, 1, 2; V, 1, 2.
59. All the gods were sleeping except Mercury (*Iliad*, XXIV, 677–78).
60. Ibid., II, 1, 2; XIV, 233, 253–254, 259; XV, 4–11; XXIV, 677–78.
61. Ibid., IV, 26–28.
62. Pluto's helmet made the god who wore it invisible (ibid., V, 846).
63. *Odyss.*, XXII, 297–98.
64. Iliad, XX, 437–38.
65. Ibid., XVIII, 362–67.
66. Ibid., XXII, 19–20.
67. Ibid., XV, 320–23.
68. *Odyss.*, V, 211–18.
69. *Iliad*, V, 339.
70. *Odyss.*, I, 96–98; V, 44–46.
71. *Iliad*, IV, 389, 390.
72. Ibid., II, 790–95; III, 121–24 and passim.
73. Ibid., III, 396–97; XVII, 322–23.

have need for them to hear, and do not need for them to see. A deaf people would give its gods greater sight.

The idea of death detached itself rather quickly from the conjectures of men concerning the divine essence: death being what men fear most, they hastened to free the gods from this harsh condition of man's own life. However, the gods of Homer are not immortal in the absolute meaning of the term. The infirmities of old age visit them sometimes. Unforeseen accidents, internecine disorders, the audacity of humans can put an end to their career. Hercules stole the tripod of Delphi; Apollo wanted to fight and kill him; Jupiter hastened to separate his two sons. Cast from heaven by his mother, Vulcan preserved his life only thanks to Thetis.[74] Deceived by Sleep, Jupiter sought it throughout Olympus in order to make it perish in the waves.[75] Enchained by the Aloades, Mars moaned for thirteen months in a dark dungeon; and his strength was depleted when Mercury delivered him.[76] Instructed concerning the fate of his son Ascalaphus, the same god swore to avenge him, even if he had to die at the hand of Jupiter.[77] Finally, following one of the Greek traditions, and probably the most ancient,[78] the oath of the Styx originated in the thought that the waters of this river were lethal for the gods. Subsequently, other traditions replaced this one: swearing by the Styx became an inviolable engagement, Hesiod[79] and Apollodorus[80] tell us, because Styx, the daughter of Ocean, had fought the rebellious Titans; in this way, fables change when ideas do.

Thus reduced back to human nature, the gods borrowed man's mores and habits. Vulcan, whom Venus had betrayed, asked her father for the gifts he had given to obtain the hand of this faithless goddess.[81] Jupiter gives Sicily to his daughter Proserpina.[82] Having killed the son of Neptune, Mars is judged by a tribunal of the gods on the hill where the Areopagus held its meetings. Apollo sings and prophesizes in the celestial feasts, like the rhapsodes and diviners at the banquets

74. Ibid., XVI, 515–16.

75. Ibid., I, 591, 592; XVIII, 395, 398.

76. Ibid., XV, 116, 118.

77. Ibid., V, 385.

78. Ibid., XV, 116, 118.

79. See Hermann, *Abrégé de la mythologie grecque suivant Homère et Hesiode*, I; Larcher, *Not. sur Hérodote*, VI, 101.

80. Hesiod, p. 397.

81. *Odyss.*, VII, 313.

82. On this gift of the Anakalypteria or the nuptials transported from heaven to earth, see Diodorus, V, 1.

of kings. Having killed the serpent Python, Diana and Apollo come to Aegiale to be purified of this murder; and the same god, having killed a brigand who had despoiled Delphi, was absolved of the crime in Crete. As long as the use of chariots was infrequent among mortals, the gods go on foot. The seas, the mountains, and the deserts place obstacles to their travel. In their journeys, they avoid the inhospitable countries that would refuse them the food that belongs to them, food that is often similar to that of men, or that at most differs only because it is made of a purer, more ethereal substance.[83]

The feasts of the gods are a very striking imitation of earthly ones, at a time when physical pleasures exclusively filled the intervals that war left to the leaders of nations. In these feasts, the gods who at other times seemed to satisfy themselves with the odor of sacrifices took their part in the food of men. Jupiter loves to stop among the Ethiopians whose piety erects to him splendid tables covered with delicious meats, suitable to repair his exhausted strength and soothe his fatigue.[84] Sent as a messenger, Iris is impatient to fulfill her commission so as to be able to return to Egypt and take part in a feast.[85] At table, Neptune forgets his hatred of Ulysses, spends seventeen days in Ethiopia, and perceives the king of Ithaca only on the eighteenth.[86]

Man cannot preserve a profound respect for such beings; and their will, ceasing to be respectable, becomes troublesome. He therefore attempts to free himself from it; and among a barbarous people, all of whose habits are bellicose, the idea of resistance is close to that of fighting; thus we see those audacious warriors

83. Sometimes the gods of Homer simply feed on the odor of sacrifices; other times they appear to really take part in the meal offered them. We should pardon the Greeks for these material ideas. Noah, says Genesis, sacrificed upon exiting the ark, and the Lord found the odor agreeable (Gen., VIII, 20–21).

84. *Iliad*, I, 423, 425.

85. Ibid., XXIII, 205, 208.

86. *Odyss.*, I, 26. These feasts of the gods, whose scene, as we see, is almost always among the Ethiopians, could have had some connection to an Egyptian or Ethiopian ceremony: every year the Ethiopians came to Thebes in Egypt to seek the statue of Jupiter Ammon and transported it to their borders, where they celebrated a feast in his honor (Diod., II; Eustath., *ad Iliad*). This feast, which probably lasted twelve days, because the Homeric gods were thought to spend twelve days in Ethiopia (Neptune reproaches himself for having stayed longer), obviously had an astronomical significance: the scholiasts on Homer point it out (see the scholiasts published by Villoison); but Homer, or to speak more precisely, the authors of the *Iliad,* did not doubt its reality. The mysterious origin and meaning of the story had been forgotten in Greece, and the literal sense alone had survived in popular opinion.

attacking the immortals, wounding them, putting them in irons. Otus and Ephialtes cast Mars into a dungeon and let him languish for more than a year;[87] Idas fights Apollo with javelins;[88] Bacchus escapes from Lycurgus by flight;[89] Laomedon threatens to transport Phoebus and Neptune to some faraway island and sell them, after having cut their ears.[90] In Homer, these battles are not allegories, but traditions that are perfectly conformed to the spirit of a religion that only saw in the gods more powerful men. When Venus was wounded by Diomedes, she suffered cruel pains and would not have regained Olympus if Mars had not offered her his chariot and horses.[91] A few minutes later, the god himself escaped the son of Tydeus only with difficulty, and the blow he received almost killed him or at least wounded him.[92] Before his apotheosis, Hercules struck Juno in the breast with his arrows[93] and Pluto in the shoulder:[94] the painful arrow remained embedded;[95] and the master of the netherworld dragged himself painfully to heaven, where Paieon with an expert hand staunched the blood and healed the wound.[96]

Let us stop here in order to consider to what extent, and by what path, the gods have so deviated from their original destination. Man had created them for himself; now behold: they exist only for themselves.[97] Even though each of them has a special function and presides over the government of some part of nature, they nonetheless have individual characters. They live among themselves, absorbed by their passions, their rivalries, their quarrels,[98] conforming themselves to the ways of mortals but making sport of the inhabitants of the earth. Here in a remarkable way is manifest that empire of logic that we spoke about above. The gods having

87. *Iliad*, V, 385.

88. Ibid., IX, 555, 556.

89. Ibid., V, 130.

90. Ibid., XXI, 453, 455.

91. Ibid., V, 290–335, 354–58.

92. Ibid., V, 858–85.

93. Ibid., V, 392.

94. Ibid., V, 395.

95. Ibid., V, 397.

96. Ibid., V, 407; VI, 130.

97. Chateaubriand has nicely observed this characteristic of the Homeric gods. Paradise is much more occupied, he says, with men than Olympus (*Génie du christianisme*, I, 481).

98. Like mortals, they are unequal in strength. Neptune says to Juno that the gods protecting the Greeks do not need to attack the tutelary gods of the Trojans, because they are much weaker (*Iliad*, XX, 132, 135).

to answer the prayers of man and to provide his needs, it would have been to man's advantage not to attribute to them passions that are often contrary to the goods that he hopes to receive from them; but the formation of human society had for its result a divine society. And it is of the essence of society to have separate interests. The society of gods therefore had to take care of its own, and to consider men as mere accessories.[99] Human intelligence is subject to laws independent of its desires. Man had hardly made gods for his use and these laws took over and took them away from him. We, however, should wait a moment: we will see him persevering in his attempts and indefatigable in his hopes; he will take up again these gods of which he has need and renew the indispensable alliance with the beings that have escaped from him.

99. Homer expresses this idea in two verses characterized by their bitterness. "The gods," he says, "have assigned anguish and suffering as the lot of miserable humans: they themselves live happy and carefree" (*Iliad*, XXIV, 525–26).

CHAPTER 7

On the Greek Notions concerning Destiny

When men have established the divine race with ongoing relations of self-interest with the human race, and religion has become a regular exchange of offerings and favors, worshippers have to find excuses for the objects of their worship if they do not keep the faith they have promised and fail in the exchange.

A confused and mysterious notion offers itself to veil the divine impotence and soften the gods' infidelity. It is the idea of destiny. It is necessarily subject to many contradictions. Man needs to believe in it in order not to grow thoroughly bitter against the cruelty of the gods he worships; but he needs to doubt it in order to attribute some effectiveness to his prayers; therefore the Greeks at this period considered the laws of destiny as irresistible and as being able to be eluded.

In some places in the Homeric poems, Jupiter limits himself to weighing in the balance the fate of individuals and empires.[1] When Achilles's scale wins out, Hector's protector Apollo is forced to abandon him.[2] But in a host of other passages, no less clear and affirmative, by their own will the gods suspend the accomplishment of destiny. This destiny willed that Ulysses would see Ithaca again, yet the council of the gods assembled to deliberate over his return, and Minerva his protector spoke with doubt and fear when she implored Jupiter on his behalf;[3] and even after the divine decrees, together with those of fate, calling upon Neptune, Polyphemus begged him to at least delay the return of the hero to his homeland.[4] He thus recognized in Neptune a capacity of resistance similar to that which

---

1. *Iliad*, VIII, 69, 74.
2. Ibid., XXII, 209, 313.
3. *Odyss.*, I, 82–87.
4. Ibid., IX, 532.

Phoebus exercised in Herodotus when he answered Croesus that he would be dethroned three years later than the eternal sentence decreed.

The action of the gods does not always stop with this temporary delaying influence. Despite Destiny, says the poet, Neptune would have caused the hero of Ithaca to perish if Minerva had not helped him.[5] These words, "despite Destiny," are found frequently in the *Iliad* and the *Odyssey*. The Greeks would have lifted the siege of Troy despite Destiny if not for the vigilance of Juno.[6] It was despite Destiny that they would have acquired glory if Apollo had not stirred the son of Anchises to put himself at the head of the Trojans;[7] it was despite Destiny that Aeneas, held back in order to rule in Priam's place one day, would have succumbed to the blows of Achilles except for the miraculous intervention of Neptune.[8] Minerva says that the gods cannot save their favorites from death, not even their own children, when the fatal hour has sounded.[9] However, Jupiter saves his son Sarpedon despite Destiny;[10] and he is ready a second time to grant him the same boon;[11] the danger of the example is the only consideration that holds him back. He often shows himself tempted to save Troy from the ruin that awaits it;[12] and Juno does not deny that he has the power to do so. You can, she tells him, but the other gods will not approve.[13] This disapproval of the other gods is their customary threat when the master of Olympus wants to depart from the decrees of fate;[14] the gods are to Destiny what governments are to opinion: they can brave it, but public censure weighs over them.

Thus, ordinarily they respect it, and they make use of it to accuse it for their own faults. Jupiter attributes to its immutable sentences[15] the defeats that the Greeks have to suffer until the reconciliation of Agamemnon and the son of Peleus, while

5. Ibid., V, 436.
6. *Iliad*, II, 155, 156.
7. Ibid., XVII, 321, 323.
8. Ibid., XV, 300–336; XXI, 515, 517.
9. *Odyss.*, III, 236–38.
10. *Iliad*, XII, 402.
11. Ibid., XVI, 432–38.
12. Ibid., IV, 7–19.
13. Ibid., IV, 29.
14. Ibid., XVI, 441, 443; XXII, 181.
15. Ibid., VIII, 471.

it was he himself who promised Thetis that he would satisfy her desire for revenge by granting the Trojans temporary success.[16]

Men are perpetually sent from one to the other of these views. When they want to find rest in resignation, they justify the gods as being subject to laws that they cannot change; when they want to fortify hope, they grant a sort of independence to these beings, and pride themselves on being able to sway them with their supplications or seduce them with their offerings.[17]

The relations of men to fate are exposed to the same uncertainties. Sometimes neither knowledge of the future[18] nor the precautions of prudence, neither the efforts of courage nor heavenly favor,[19] change anything in what the Fates have woven from the birth of humans;[20] sometimes, however, even as weak and blind as they are, mortals escape the decrees of fate by valor, by address, even by crime;[21] sometimes they have a choice between different destinies. Laius could have had or not had a son; but if he had one, the son would become a parricide.[22] At his birth, Achilles had the choice of living a long time but without glory, or of dying renowned in the flower of youth. Amphiaraus was free not to go to the siege of Troy, but death awaited him under the walls of this city. This is a way of allying the doctrine of destiny with a certain human liberty; it is a transaction between the opposed hypotheses.

By rendering divinity useless to man, an absolute fatality would have been destructive of all worship. If some peoples have believed that they were total fatalists, it is because men are often mistaken about their own opinions. They only consider

16. Ibid., I, 516–26. The Greeks also sometimes mixed together destiny and the will of the gods. "We are not guilty, but [rather] the hatred of Jupiter and destiny" (*Odyss.*, XI, 561).

17. In his dialogue entitled *Zeus Catechized, or Cross-Examined,* Lucian develops very well the contradictions that result from the doctrine of destiny, when one wants to reconcile it with the popular religion.

18. *Iliad*, II, 830, 834, 858, 860.

19. Ibid.., VI, 448, 487; XIV, 464; XV, 610, 614; XVII, 198, 208; XXII, 5, 360, 366; XXIII, 78, 81; XXIV, 540, 542; *Odyss.*, VIII, 196, 198.

20. *Iliad*, XXIV, 209, 210.

21. Jupiter complains of Aegisthus, murderer of Agamemnon, despite the action being destined. "Mortals," he says, "attack and destroy one another despite his decrees, and they subsequently accuse us of the misdeeds they have committed" (*Odyss.*, I, 32–33).

22. Euripid., *Phoen.*, 19, 20. Sophocles offers us several examples of a double destiny: one in *Ajax*, V, 778, 779; another in *Ménécée*, ibid., 918, 921.

them under an aspect that temporarily suits them, and they abandon them (against their will) as soon as they need a contrary opinion. Thus, when they find in this belief the means of pushing back against the fear of danger and death, Muslims affirm that no one can escape his destiny; but in their ordinary life, they make no fewer vows, they offer no fewer prayers, they perform no fewer ceremonies, all of which would be in vain if man were subject in all things, great and small, to an eternal and immutable law.

In these fluctuations one recognizes the efforts of the human spirit to discover a system that simultaneously would represent the gods as good and powerful and man's own misfortunes as not implicating them in either injustice or impotence.

Far from resolving this problem, the unity of God appears at first glance to complicate it further. Since polytheism does not attribute omnipotence to its gods, and often shows them to us as divided, one conceives a destiny above that dominates them, which is in some way their common rule. But in the system of the unity of God, his power being without limit, destiny is placed in his will, and at first one has difficulty in reconciling this belief with belief in the effectiveness of worship and man's free will.

It is only when religion is quite purified, when it has stripped from the idea of God all the remains of anthropomorphism, which in some sense are the inheritance of polytheism (and even of fetishism), that all the difficulties relating to destiny, to fatality, and to free will disappear and vanish. Then, to the notions of necessity or exchange, to these two hypotheses that constantly do battle in a still-imperfect religion, succeeds a notion that combines their advantages and gets rid of what is crude in them. Then we conceive man as endowed with liberty, so that his triumphs over himself have greater merit. We know that in frustrating our desires, fate does better than grant them. We unite ourselves to the unknown cause, not to satisfy our caprices but to attain a higher degree of moral perfection, and we elevate ourselves above everything that is merely ephemeral and personal. Then courage has all its strength and resignation all its consolation.

CHAPTER 8

On the Means Employed by the Greeks to Penetrate the Secrets of Destiny

Whatever the transactions of imagination with reasoning, and of logic with terror, men have to seek some means of foreseeing this destiny that hangs over them.

These means are not the same in the two species of polytheism. That which is independent places in the first rank direct and immediate communications; we have shown in our second volume[1] how much the Homeric poems place them above those that are obtained through the intervention of the priests. In this state of opinion, no one gives his trust except to the communications he himself receives. Enthralled to the god that torments them, Cassandra and Laocoön seek in vain to obtain the confidence of the people; it is deaf to their voices, and it is only when they perish that it abjures its stubborn disbelief. These communications can never have an extensive influence; and with what little authority it possesses, the priesthood always seeks to supplant them because they make its interventions superfluous; their divinations must replace them.

But in the heroic times, divination is a subordinate and rather contemptible science. In the *Iliad*, Polydamas speaks with disdain of the flight of birds.[2] Constantly under arms, risking their lives, and endowed with great physical and moral energy, the heroes believe they carry their destiny in themselves, and they reject submitting it to the capricious movements of animals or the doubtful signs that inanimate nature lets escape. It is only at a second period of Greek religion that divination will come into favor. At Sparta especially, its credit is unlimited; and that has to be: whatever name it bears, authority soon sees the advantages for it of

---

1. Bk. V, ch. 1.
2. See the speech of Polydamas to Hector in the *Iliad*.

a systematic interpretation of the most common circumstances. But we are getting ahead of ourselves.

After divination comes oracles, transmitted from Egypt into Greece, or surviving among the Greeks the destruction of priestly government; initially, they had little influence: the revolution that had pitted the two castes was too recent, and the warriors' hatred too vivid. Homer speaks of no oracle, if not Dodona's, very much in passing, and we have already noted that the name Delphi is not found in his poems. Nonetheless, restless curiosity and credulity win the day. Oracles obtain credit: their origins are attached to the most ancient times, and ordinarily to colonies.[3] They are placed next to springs, in the depths of forests, above all near tombs;[4] and despite the complaints of philosophers[5] and the epigrams of comic authors, they acquire a power that often puts the fate of Greece in the hands of their interpreters.

At the beginning, these oracles did not imply the thought that the gods knew the future; only that since they were imagined sometimes as friendly, sometimes as hostile, they were interrogated not about what had to happen, but what they wished to do; in the way we ask a powerful man, or a judge who has to pronounce sentence, without believing in his general prescience, but because we believe him knowledgeable about his own determinations. As with everything that man tries to do to bend religion to his own views, from this came a new inconvenience, as unforeseen as it was inevitable.

By obliging the gods to predict the future, that is to say, to declare their future intentions, one exposes them to be mistaken or to deceive men; and in order to absolve them of error or perfidy one has to suppose that the suppliants who interrogated them understood them incorrectly.

Hence the ambiguity of oracles; they are always susceptible to a double interpretation, and it is the most unfortunate one that is realized; often the prophecy causes the misfortunes that it seemed destined to prevent: mortals walk into the

3. The foundation of the colony of Delphi was attributed to Pegasus and to the divine Agyieus, sons of the Hyperboreans (Pausan.). As for Dodona, see our second volume [bk. V].

4. That of the fountain of Tilphossa near to the tomb of Tiresias and the monument of Rhadamanthus. This confirms one of our claims. Man has always asked the dead for revelations concerning the future, believing that the future belongs to the races of the past, who no longer have anything to do with the present (see bk. II, ch. 6).

5. See Dicéarque in the *Lettres de Cicéron à Atticus*, VI, 2.

net, and run to the abyss, by the very precautions they take to avoid them. And please note that the fateful ambiguity of these prophecies does not belong solely to the centuries of fables and traditions. On the contrary, it increases as man is more and more loathe to retain notions unfavorable to the gods. When he is still inadequately enlightened to suppose them capable of lying voluntarily, predictions can be unambiguous; then one regards the lie only as a proof of the divine anger. But the more that the character of the gods is improved, the less one can admit this hypothesis, in order to spare their honor. The predictions of Jupiter in the *Iliad* are deceptive and not obscure, while in Herodotus the oracles are obscure in order not to be deceptive. Thus, it is not only Laius who, in exposing his newly born son, prepares the accomplishment of the prophecy that he believes he is eluding. It is not only Croesus who runs to his ruin by going before the king of Persia, because the gods told him that by crossing a river he would overturn a great empire.[6] It is much later that the Pythia will get the Lacedaemonians, by an answer of the same sort, to do battle with the Tegeates, who put them to rout.[7] And it is even later that the priests of Donona, counseling the Athenians to establish themselves in Sicily, will stir them to begin a war against Syracuse that is the first cause of their decline and ruin, while the Sicily indicated by the oracle is rather a small hill near to Athens.[8] Finally, it is at a time when enlightenment was universally widespread that Epaminondas, who had always avoided maritime expeditions because the gods had told him to be wary of the *pélagos*—the sea—died in a wood of this name near Mantinea.[9] These anecdotes, even if not authentic facts, nonetheless prove how long lasting was the general belief in this regard, a belief that even influenced the surnames given to the gods.[10]

6. Herod., I, 46–55.

7. Ibid., I, 66.

8. Pausan., *Arcad.*, ch. 2.

9. See also in Pausanias the oracle given to the Messenians in the second war of Messenia, whose ambiguity rested on a word signifying simultaneously the billy goat and the wild fig. In the same way, the oracle of Ammon had predicted to Hannibal that he would find his tomb in Libya; he therefore thought that he would see his homeland after having defeated the Romans. But it was at the village of Libya, in the States of Prusias, who betrayed him, that he was killed. Everyone knows the oracle that deceived Pyrrhus: *Aio te Aeacida, Romanos vincere posse.*

10. Thus, one invoked Apollo Loxias, called this because of his ever-ambiguous answers. When astronomy had entered into Greek religion, this epithet was explained by the obliqueness of the course of the sun; the scientific explanation changed nothing in the moral sense of the popular fable.

In this way, everything confirms one of our claims; nonetheless, given its importance we do not hesitate to revisit it. When our intellect has adopted an axiom apparently favorable to our hopes and our desires, we are forced to reason from this axiom with a rigorous precision that disconcerts our previous calculations and deceives our expectation. Instituted to guide human weakness across the dark night of the future, oracles soon became by their inevitable ambiguities even more terrible than obscurity itself; and the human beings who invented them to reassure themselves find in them only a new motive of doubt and fear. One would say that our two intellectual powers are irreconcilable enemies, one of which tries to revenge itself upon the other, even though it cannot arrest it. Imagination projects its bold conjectures; reasoning takes hold of them, and even when it adopts them, submits them to such rigid forms that it draws entirely different consequences from those the imagination believed prevailed.

As for the rest, polytheism is not the only form of worship in which man exhausts himself with vain syllogisms in order to reconcile his confidence in the being he interrogates with the events that belie his answers or which stamp his promises with falsity.

"The Gabasites," says a pious author, "having defeated the Israelites, the latter asked God if they should continue the war. He answered that they should, and they gave battle. Eighteen thousand were cut to pieces by the armies of Gabaa. It seemed by the result that God had deceived them; but it was they who deceived themselves. No one promised the victory. God had only declared his will of exposing the people to danger, and to have those he destined to death perish. Whoever would judge this event without due reflection would treat the oracle as false: this would be a rash judgment. The response was neither a counsel nor a prophecy; it was a command. In the same way God sent Saint Bernard to order Saint Louis to go on crusade against the Saracens, not because he destined the king to victory, but because he wanted to employ the war to punish the French army."[11]

When religions have fallen, the zealous friends of the new belief sometimes find themselves in a contrary embarrassment. Among the oracles, there are those that are fulfilled; and not being able to attribute these to the veracity of the gods in whom no one any longer believes, another source has to be found. "God," says

---

11. Saint-Philippe, *Monarchie des Hébreux*, I, 44–45.

Rollin, "in order to punish the blindness of the pagans, sometimes permitted demons to gives answers conformed to the truth."[12]

At the time of the fall of polytheism, the ambiguity of oracles served as a pretext for the bitter pleasantries of unbelieving authors. Logic always revenges itself with interest against the outrages it has received; but its vengeance is slow, and it is exercised like the courage of nations: on enemies already fallen to the ground.

12. Rollin, *Hist. anc.*, I, 387.

CHAPTER 9

On the Greeks' Notions of the Other Life

We showed the primitive savage constantly occupied with the idea of death. As civilization progresses, this preoccupation loses its force. Civilization creates so many relations, expectations, desires, and artificial passions that man has too much to think about as he makes his way through the mêlée, always occupied with attacking, or defending himself. Life is so filled with these struggles that the end is hidden, and one might even say that it is avoidable and should not enter into our projects and calculations. Each, however, knows that an hour awaits when he will be separated from everything he saw, and if he loves something, from all he loves; each knows that this hour will be terrible, accompanied by awful convulsions and unknown pains, which no one can really describe and no living being can truly imagine. And after these pains and convulsions comes the silence that will never end. No cry has escaped from this abyss, where for so many centuries so many creatures have gone—some strong and bold, others sensitive and passionate, but all attached to the earth by so many interests and bonds; no information has come to us from this abyss, so full of swallowed-up lives and experiences. The earth yawns and is silent; it is silent again when it closes; and being smoothed over once more, its smooth surface leaves our questions without answers and our regrets without consolation. And yet we walk lightly over these graves, and the daylight that flickers still captivates us; although already dimmed by the night that approaches, to us it seems that it will never have to give way to the thick night it announces.

Less distracted than us from natural impressions, the barbarous Greeks had death more present; and pursued without any relief by this dark phantom, like the primitives they had recourse to conjectures that made it less terrible, transporting the actual world into the unknown world, substituting displacement for destruction. The netherworld of the Homeric Greeks retained all the traits we saw among the wandering tribes, and was modified only in accordance with the development of society.

The son of Atreus is surrounded by his companions, killed at the same time as he was by Aegisthus.[1] Achilles walks in the midst of the warriors who fought at his side under the walls of Troy.[2] In the portrait of the netherworld by Polygnotus, found on the public square of Delphi, Agamemnon carries a scepter in his hand; a hunting dog is lying at the feet of Actaeon; Orpheus holds a lyre, Palamedes plays dice; Penthesileus is armed with a bow and clothed in a leopard's skin.[3] Feeble imitations of the time that is no longer, the shades still do what they did on earth. The hunter pursues the phantoms of animals fallen beneath his blows; the warrior makes the simulacra of his weapons shine; the poet repeats his songs. But the same repugnance toward death, which in the primitive's soul overcomes the desire to paint with happy colors the dwelling place that opens before him, is also found among the Greeks.

As with fetishism, in their world-to-come all is gloomy, dull, lugubrious; everything is diminished. The stars have less splendor: they twinkle in the darkness rather than enlightening it. The winds are colder; the foliage is darker; the flowers are painted in more somber colors: everything suffers, everything languishes. Virgins bemoan their sterile springtime; heroes look enviously upon the most abject of the living: all are pained at the sufferings that troubled their lives, all also are pained at having lost them; all of them regret past days. The always desolate shad-

---

1. *Odyss.*, XI, 388–89.

2. Ibid., XI, 467–68; XXIV, 15–27. In the netherworld, the same Achilles espouses Helen and Medea. Tzetz., in Lycophr. Libanius.

3. Pausan., *Phoc.*, 30. This imitation of life after passing on is not peculiar to this period of Greek religion, even though it is more manifest then than in subsequent epochs, because the younger imagination describes more vividly what it just invented. We still see in Herodotus, Melissa, wife of Periander, emerge from her tomb to complain of being naked and cold (Herod., V). The daughters of Cecrops in Euripides continue their favorite dances (*Ion*, 495–96). Even at the time of Lucian, the Greeks put in the mouth of the dead a piece of silver so they could pay the passage across the Styx. They burned their clothes on pyres and lodged their slaves near their tombs (Lucan, *Nigrinus* and *Menteur*). In the latter dialogue, Eucrates speaks of the finery of her mother-in-law, which was burned with her. Philostratus shows us the shade of Protesilaus running a race; and even though his netherworld is coldly and pedantically philosophical, Virgil does not neglect these details (see the *Excursus* of Heyne on the sixth book of Virgil). They always have a certain charm, they reposition our habits in our hopes, and they respond to the egoism that attaches us to the earth better than more sublime and refined descriptions.

ows (this epithet is constantly repeated)[4] recount their misfortunes:[5] Hercules[6] and Achilles[7] speak in a plaintive voice; Agamemnon sheds torrents of tears;[8] the king of the Greeks cannot forget the betrayal to which he fell victim;[9] Ajax retains his resentment at the unjust refusal that denied him the arms of Achilles.[10] Sadness is so much the destiny of the shades that while Hercules tastes the delights of the celestial feasts in Olympus and enjoys the charms of the young Hebe,[11] his sad and menacing specter groans in the netherworld.[12]

Death! O death! All of Homeric mythology bears the mark of the terror that this inexplicable mystery must cause in the young human being. The youthful imagination of the Greeks regards this dissolution of our being as a violent event, and as a marvel. The souls torn from a body that was necessary to them bear this separation with constant torment.

This way of conceiving human existence after this life does not allow morality to be closely connected with notions concerning the state of the dead. Among the Greeks, they share a common abode, with the exception of those who have personally offended the gods. All the tales that cause morality to enter the future life—judges, tribunals, sentences brought against the shades for faults that preceded their descent into the somber empire—belong to a period after the Homeric.

The error of several writers in this regard comes from the fact that the shades, imitating as much as they can all the features of the previous life where kings and the aged pronounced judgment concerning the differences submitted to them, exercise the same functions in the netherworld. They quell the passing quarrels that trouble the eternal silence. This jurisdiction, however, applied only to what happens in the other world, although some have thought that it extended to actions committed in this one. Because the *Odyssey* represents Minos judging the dead with a scepter in hand,[13] they have thought that he judged them for their earlier

4. Στυγεραί.
5. *Odyss.*, XI, 540–41.
6. Ibid., XI, 616.
7. Ibid., 471.
8. Ibid., 390.
9. Ibid., 391, 451; XXIV, 21, 95–97.
10. Ibid., XI, 542, 545.
11. Ibid., 601–3.
12. Ibid., 616.
13. Ibid., XI, 567–69.

crimes: nothing is more opposed to the ideas of Homer. Minos judges in the same way as Orion hunts,[14] and as Hercules disperses the shades, holding his fearful bow in hand.[15] He does after his death what he did during his life. It is only later that we will see his magistracy change, in keeping with the development of polytheism.[16] Then also Elysium, which is not yet a part of the netherworld, will be brought there. Now it is a place of happiness, but where the dead do not enter.[17] Menelaus, whom Jupiter miraculously preserved from the common law, lives there with Rhadamanthus, who exercises no judicial function there.[18]

The rivals of the gods are confined to Tartarus,[19] who are gods as well as their conquerors, but expelled from the throne. Jupiter keeps the Titans[20] there and Saturn,[21] who himself cast the race of Uranus into it.[22] When the inhabitants

14. Ibid., 572–74.

15. Ibid., 605–6.

16. See in book XII, chapter 5, the changes in the Greek religion from Homer to Pindar.

17. *Odyss.*, IV, 563–64. Elysium in Homer is not a place of the dead; it is a place of pleasure on one or several of the islands of the western ocean. There, near the doors of night, a path leads to heaven; there, near the bedchamber of Jupiter, flows the spring of ambrosia; there, without having suffered death, are the favorites of the gods among humans; and Juno walks not far from this place of delights in her magnificent gardens full of fruits of brilliant color and exquisite taste (Voss, *Alte Welt Kunde*). Strabo (bk. III) places Elysium near Spain in the Canary Islands (see the *Excursus* of Heyne).

18. Not until the Homeric hymn to Ceres is there a question of rewards after this life; but this hymn, composed toward the thirtieth Olympiad for the new Eleusinian mysteries, and hence designed to convey some mysterious teaching, has no relationship with the mythology we are dealing with now.

19. Pausanias claims that Homer had borrowed from Thesprotia his topography of the netherworld; that Acheron and Cocytus were rivers of this country; that Pluto was its king, that his wife was named Proserpina, and his dog, Cerberus (*Attica*, 17). But this claim, which smacks of the euhemerism whose influence Pausanias (despite his sometimes pious intentions) experienced, in no way modified the public belief that, as such, was foreign to all historical or geographic explanations; we therefore do not need to deal with it. We will speak later of the Egyptian practices that entered into Greece and acted upon the Greek opinions relative to the place of the dead, and we will have occasion to notice again how the Greek spirit reacted upon all these importations to submit them to itself.

20. The Titans are thrown into Tartarus without being dead (*Iliad*, VIII, 477; Hesiod., *Theog.*, 717, 820): a proof that the punishments of Tartarus are not reserved for the other life. Why, asks the Prometheus of Aeschylus, did Jupiter not throw me into Tartarus?

21. *Iliad*, VIII, 479–80.

22. Apollodorus, scholiast of Lycophron.

of Olympus resist him, he threatens them with this terrible punishment.[23] The guilty who are tormented in hell are there only because of the outrages directed against the gods. Tityos, whom two vultures eat, is punished for having violated Latona;[24] Sisyphus, for having defrauded death and returned to life;[25] Tantalus for having deceived Jupiter.[26]

Thus the torments that take place in hell are not acts of justice, but of vengeance on the part of the gods. They strike those who have failed to recognize their power, outraged their dignity, or merely contravened their desires. The dungeons that contain these victims are State prisons where merely human-against-human deeds are not punished.

It is not superfluous to observe that the torments are characteristic of the period that gave birth to the tales. Tantalus tries in vain to slake his thirst in the water that surrounds him, and to take the fruit hanging above his head. In vain, Sisyphus rolls the stone to the top of the mountains; it always falls on him. The water escapes the barrel of the Danaids, and the cord of Ocnus is gnawed by the ass whose proximity he cannot escape. One of the harshest penalties that the men of heroic times could imagine was work and useless effort; and this is a new proof that they applied the habits of this world to the ideas of the next. Unlike us, the Greeks of these times did not lead an inactive life, where pain, as it were, can be said to seek us; but an active life that prompted them to brave pain and difficulty in the hope of success.

---

23. *Iliad*, VIII, 16. The decree of Momus in the dialogue of Lucian entitled the *Assembly of the Gods* declares that those who, expelled by the commission charged with purifying Olympus, obstinately refused to leave heaven would be plunged into Tartarus; this is a burlesque memory of the most ancient Greek mythology.

24. *Odyss.*, XI, 575–76. Ixion was in the same way attached to a wheel for having violated Juno.

25. Homer does not say the cause of Sisyphus's torment. One finds it in Theognis. Under the pretext of having himself buried, he left the netherworld, he said, for one day, and did not want to return (see Sophocl., *Philoct.*, 624–25). Pausanias (*Corinth*, 5) says that Sisyphus was punished for having revealed to Asopus where his daughter Aegina was, whom Jupiter had taken. Apollodorus (III, 12–16) says the same thing. This tradition would serve better than the other in support of our claim.

26. *Odyss.*, 578–91. One finds a tradition concerning the crime of Tantalus in the first Olympian ode of Pindar, another in the *Orestes* of Euripides (410), a third in the *Corinth* of Pausanias, a fourth in Hyginus. The latter says that Tantalus was punished for having divulged what happened at the festivals of the gods. This tradition belongs to a century when mystery seemed to be an essential part of religion: Homer says nothing like it. Ovid, the contemporary of Hyginus, reprises the crudest of these traditions. We will return later to the differences between the traditions as proofs of a progress in ideas, and we will say why Ovid mistook or spurned this progress.

For the peoples softened by civilization, to suffer is the greatest of evils; for the people in the youth of social life, engaged all their days in physical dangers and struggles, the greatest evil was not to succeed.

This absence of all morality in the ideas of the next life is so conformed to the genius of this period of independent polytheism that when moral tales are introduced, they will strip them of their meaning before admitting them. The Egyptians refused passage to Acheron to the dead if they could not justify themselves in the face of accusations against them: this is a moral idea. Borrowing from them the fiction of a river and souls crossing it, the Greeks said that when a dead person was not buried, his soul wandered the banks of the Cocytus for a hundred years: this is a tale without morality.

Thus, the treacherous Eriphyle[27] lived in the same place as Ulysses's mother, the venerable Anticlea.[28] Far from receiving reward, virtue shared the universal sadness.[29]

The fundamental thought of Homer's netherworld is the unhappiness of the soul separated from the body. If life is sometimes called a baneful gift,[30] death is always the greatest of evils, and the soul does not leave the body except by emitting a mournful groan. The idea of this misfortune causes the poet to fall into obvious contradictions. Sometimes the shades recall their past relations and sufferings; sometimes, weak,[31] impalpable,[32] without form or color, comparable to light dreams,[33] borne here and there in the air, and uttering inarticulate cries,[34] they flutter about deprived of intellect,[35] strength,[36] and memory,[37] and thirstily

27. *Odyss.*, XI, 325–26.

28. Ibid., 84–85, 151.

29. *Iliad*, XVII, 445–47.

30. Ibid., XVI, 855; XXII, 363.

31. *Odyss.*, X, 521, 536; XI, 29, 49, 404.

32. Ibid., 206–7.

33. Ibid., 221.

34. Ibid., 43, 632.

35. Proserpina let Tiresias alone preserve his understanding (*Odyss.*, X, 494–95). Callimachus says that it was Minerva (*Hymne à Minerve au bain*); but the exception confirms the rule. Elpenor was not yet without understanding because he was not yet buried. Without having drunk blood, he recognized Ulysses (*Odyss.*, XI, 51ff.).

36. *Odyss.*, XI, 392.

37. Ibid., 338. There are several other contradictions in this eleventh rhapsody of the *Odyssey*: judging the state of shades by what Anticlea says to Ulysses, they know what happens on earth (*Odyss.*, XI, 180–95). But judging by what Achilles and Agamemnon say, they do not know (ibid., 457–59,

drink dark blood[38] in order to experience for an instant a passing warmth they quickly lose.[39]

---

492. They ask Ulysses for news of their children, while he himself has come to the netherworld to learn about his father.

38. Ibid., XI, 94, 146–48, 232–33.

39. In a small work of Latin verse entitled *Le Chant des Mânes*, a modern author has expressed very well the ideas of the ancients on the state of the shades.

Saltemus: socias jungite dexteras;
Jam manes dubius provocat hesperus;
Per nubes tremulum Cynthia candidis
Lumen cornibus ingerit.

Nullus de tumulo sollicitus suo
Aut pompae titulis invidet alteri:
Omnes mors variis casibus obruit,
Nullo nobilis ordine.

Nobis nostra tamen sunt quoque sidera,
Sed formosa minus: sunt zephyri, licet
Veris dissimiles, auraque tenuior,
Cupressisque frequens nemus.

O dulces animae, vita quibus sua
Est exacta, nigris sternite floribus
Quem calcamus humum: spargite lilia.
Fuscis grata coloribus.

Aptos ut choreis inferimus pedes!
Ut nullo quatitur terra negotio!
Demta mole leves, et sine pondere
Umbrae ludimus alites

Ter cantum tacito murmure sistimus.
Ter nos Elysium vertimus ad polum.
Ter noctis tenebras, stringite lumina,
Pallenti face rumpimus.

Nos quicumque vides, plaudere minibus;
Cantabis similes tu quoque naenias:
Quod nunc es, fuimus, quod sumus, hoc eris.
Praemissos sequere et vale.

CHAPTER 10

On the Efforts of the Religious Sentiment to Rise above the Religious Form We Just Described

We have presented the passage from the fetishism of primitives to the polytheism of barbarous tribes as an important improvement; nonetheless, if one judges by the portrait we have drawn of this polytheism, man has gained little. The gods, proud of their strength and misled by their passions, do not offer a surer guarantee for morality or justice than the shapeless idols of the wandering hordes. These gods have even another inconvenience. Fetishes only take care of their worshippers; the Homeric gods often forget the mortal race and think only of themselves; when they do remember them, it is ordinarily because of an exigency. They want sacrifices, but outside of that the gods and men are two different species who live separately. One is stronger, the other weaker; each strives, suffers, and takes its pleasures apart. Between them there is an unequal alliance, an exchange of favors and honors that sometimes brings about a common good; but the exceptions are frequent. Oppression comes from inequality; power has a jealous and malevolent nature. And, finally, no positive system was established, no fixed rule was observed. No link extended from this world to the other. Heavenly protection was acquired independently of vices and virtues; chance, caprice, and momentary interest decided in each situation; and left to himself, man drew from his own heart all the motives of actions that regard only other men.

Nonetheless, observe the religious sentiment as it struggles against this form and takes hold of it on all sides to elevate it above what it was externally, to extend its limits and make it more suitable to its needs and desires. Its efforts go in the opposite direction from almost all the established teachings, and it exploits the least pretext to remove from the gods everything that wounds it.

The gods are not incorporeal; however, the religious sentiment loves to conceive them as invisible. In vain do numerous examples prove that mortals perceive and recognize them despite their best efforts. Their invisibility pleases the sentiment, because it accords with the still vague conceptions of purity and spirituality that it carefully preserved from the previous belief,[1] and that it will later successfully develop in its ideas of the divine nature. The same is true of their immortality: if death is presented in Homer as possible for gods, this possibility is never realized.

Too many facts attest to the battles of mortals against the inhabitants of Olympus for man to be able to entirely reject these traditions; but he compensates by attaching severe punishments to these assaults. The one who raises a sacrilegious arm against the gods is pursued by misfortunes that never fail to strike him.[2] Blinded, a fugitive, rendered mad, alone, deprived of his children, banished from his homeland, he wanders without any support, uttering deplorable cries, and death is right behind him. Here man sacrifices himself to the need he has to respect what he worships, so much is it in human nature that sentiment wins out over self-interest.

Logic forces it to recognize that passionate and vicious beings cannot enjoy unmixed happiness. The same passions that lead Homer's gods to persecute mortals divides them among themselves. They deceive one another;[3] they pass their days in rivalries and quarrels.[4] They moan over their internal discords and bitterly complain about their destiny.[5] Sentiment, however, wants the gods to be happy; it always calls them the blessed immortals.[6] With this epithet man belies the stories he admits, and his soul protests against the conclusions his mind imposes on him. All details are modified in this direction. Olympus is not simply a mountain where the gods live, and which belongs to the earth; it is an ethereal dwelling, a brilliant heaven of supernatural splendor poised on columns of immense height that hide it from sight.[7]

If the gods punish perjury, it is as an outrage against them, not a crime against other men; but it results from this that men begin to call the immortals as wit-

1. See bk. II, ch. 2.

2. *Iliad*, V, 407; VI, 130.

3. Ibid., XIV, 197; XIX, 94, 125.

4. Ibid., I, 518, 521, 542–43, 565, 567; IV, 5–6, 20–22, 31, 36; V, 420, 765, 876, 881, 889; VIII, 360, 400, 407, 455; XV, 17, 30, 162, 167.

5. Ibid., V, 874, 875.

6. Ibid.; *Odyss.*, passim. In one place (among others), the gods are called blessed at the times when they are bent on doing evil to men (*Odyss.*, XVIII, 130–35).

7. Creuzer, fragm. *Hist. graece. antiquiss.*, I, 177.

nesses to their mutual engagements. These engagements become more solemn; men are formed in fidelity because they have interested the gods in this cause; the gods are ennobled as the guarantors of pledged faith.

The State prison that is part of the future world receives only the personal enemies of the gods. As we said, this fiction offers no support to morality. But the sentiment that has need of morality meditates on the place of punishment that the objects of its worship created only for themselves. The human being dominated by his self-interest only wants to see in the gods his auxiliaries, but his internal sentiment forces him to make them his judges. He takes hold of this prison, even before religion grants it to him (which will happen later), and already oppressed weakness casts its oppressors into Tartarus by means of its curses.

Would you like an example of the religious sentiment's resistance to the received tales? Homer recounts that Hercules killed his hosts, and he cries out: The cruel hero does not respect the justice of the gods! This is an exclamation that is even more strange since the murderer, far from being punished, becomes a god himself. But does not this exclamation show us the inclination of man to believe that the gods are just, despite all the proofs to the contrary? And this Jupiter, the father of Hercules, who receives him at his table despite the crime, is he not always called the protector, the patron, the avenger of violated hospitality? The religious sentiment goes even further in its efforts to improve the form. Not only does it turn its eyes from the discouraging spectacle of the vices that this form attributes to the divine natures, but it sometimes transforms these vices into virtues. The venality that offers the conquerors of a country an easy means of seducing the gods this country worshipped, by lavishing gifts and honors upon them, descends from the idols to the worshippers, as a sort of fraternity between the victors and the vanquished, both prostrate before the same altars.

The Greeks employed another artifice to escape from the sad consequences of the anthropomorphism that falsified their religion. They turned from the details and sought refuge in the whole; if the gods taken individually are sometimes depicted with immoral and revolting traits, taken en masse the gods always form an imposing and respectable body; then sentiment gives itself over to all the conceptions of grandeur, power, immensity, and morality that make up its natural atmosphere; there it finds itself at ease, breathing freely. It is for this reason that we will see priestly teachings, if not transported into the public religion, at least received by the public opinion that sees only its external contours. The poets allude to it; the philosophers comment on it. This is sentiment discontent with an imperfect form and seeking elsewhere ideas whose mysterious appearance bewitches it, and which it believes are purer because they are vague.

This tendency of man to form the gods into a corporate body is itself a struggle of the religious sentiment against the polytheism that shocks it, even though contemporary notions did not allow it to free itself from them. The mind, which has need of distinctions, divides and classifies; but it is constrained to do so in keeping with its level of enlightenment; the soul, which has need of bringing together, does not fear to mix or confuse, and it often anticipates the period when greater enlightenment will sanction its efforts. This is what often gives polytheism a deceptive appearance of theism, and it is also what will later—when the intellect has made great strides—replace polytheism with unity.

This is the work of the religious sentiment on Homeric polytheism. There is no part of this belief that it does not try to improve.

The ambiguity of oracles, the ambiguity whose harmful consequences we have pointed out, looked at in a certain light is the result of the effort to improve the form. Dissatisfied with being deceived in the hope that the gods had engendered, interest could conceive of them as voluntarily lying; sentiment, however, revolts against this offensive hypothesis. It does not want to admit voluntary lies, and it accuses itself of having badly understood the oracles when their promises fail to materialize. Having in this way sheltered them from harmful suspicions, it submits them to its influence. Their predictions announce to tyrants their fall, to the unfortunate a better future, or they proclaim salutary maxims unknown until that point; and their verses marked with the harshness of the Attic dialect contribute to the triumph of civilization and the softening of mores.

Polytheism thus becomes a system full of contradictions, but which, improved by man, in turn contributes to his improvement. By attempting to represent the gods clothed in beauty, majesty, and virtue, he reflects upon these things and his morality gains as a result.

Until now, people have emphasized the inconsistencies of Homeric religion and they have drawn two false conclusions: one, that it did not exist in this way, and as a result they have lost themselves in allegories; the other, that man did not have any rule for his religious ideas, and that he simply heaped together without judgment or motive irreconcilable absurdities. But even inconsistency has its laws: man does not poorly reason for the pleasure of poorly reasoning. When he poorly reasons, it is because there is a struggle going on among his faculties and he does not know how to bring them together.

We now can resolve the question with which we began this chapter. Man has gained in passing from fetishism to polytheism, because he gave himself a belief that is more susceptible to being ennobled by sentiment. To ennoble it sentiment falsifies it, but the belief lends itself to that, which is an advantage. A famous Englishman observes that Homer is better than his Jupiter: this is to say, in other words, that sentiment is better than its form.[8] How many crude traditions were rejected even at the period of Homeric poetry, when so many crudities dominated? Jupiter recalled to Juno the harsh treatment she had suffered at his hand; but now it is limited to threats, when previously it meant action. Nonetheless, the heroes of Homer are superior to their gods. Compare the domestic life of Jupiter and Juno with the human domesticity of Ulysses and Penelope; contrast the conjugal quarrels of Venus and Vulcan with the touching affection of Hector and Andromache. Mortals precede their idols in moral perfection; but soon enough, thanks to mortals, the idols take their revenge and, speedily overtaking their worshippers, they will leave them far behind them.

There is also this difference between the influence of fetishism and the influence of the polytheism of this period, that one isolates individuals while the other brings them together, by making it a duty to worship in common the same gods. Thus, what was an effect became a cause; and polytheism, the result of the coming together of primitive bands, consolidated this coming-together. Religion instituted festivals where the different tribes encountered one another and became accustomed to live with one another. It consecrated an entire country to serve as a refuge of peace when enemies or internal divisions troubled it. Elide, at the center of which rose the temple of Jupiter Olympian, which later was decorated by the masterwork of Phidias, could never be the theater of war. Upon entering it, the Greeks again became brothers and fellow citizens. The soldiers who crossed this holy land laid down their arms, which they reprised only when they left.[9]

It was equally conciliating when it came to private quarrels; religion established

8. Wood, *Genius of Homer*. One could prove by comparing the traditions that Homer brings to the stage, and which therefore one should consider to be contemporary traditions, with those to which he alludes as being earlier, that Homer's Jupiter is better than his predecessor (see Aristotle, *Poetics*, 25; and Wolf, *Prolegomena Homeri*, pp. 161–68). You will find in the latter a small but telling example of the way in which the Greeks had recourse to grammatical subtleties to transform or reform Homer's text when, with the introduction of morality into religion, the character of the Homeric gods became too shocking.

9. Strabo, VIII.

expiations that not only appeased hatred and soothed remorse, but formed a bond between the expiated and him whose august ministry caused the forgiveness of heaven to descend;[10] it distinguished involuntary homicide from murder, and by a touching refinement, it declared the former sacred because it was a misfortune; it opened the asylums that disarmed the fury of vengeance. Almost all the altars of Jupiter were asylums;[11] and on this subject note how much it is true that the usefulness of everything owes to the period of the social state. The right of asylum is a dangerous abuse when civilization is advanced, because the laws ensure to men everything beneficial in the right of asylum, but in times of barbarism, when there are no legal guarantees and weakness is without protection, it is fortunate that there are asylums, because even if they protect the guilty they are the sole refuge where innocence can be safe.

It was thanks to polytheism, no matter how imperfect it appears, that amphictyonies arose. Everywhere they are located in the temples.[12] Neptune lends his sanctuary to the amphictyonies of Beoetia, Corinth, and Elide; Diana to those of Euboea; Apollo, of Delos; Juno, of the Argolid.[13] Delphi brings together those of all of Greece. Charged with the celebration of the national festivals, these amphictyonies proclaim truces, during which all resentment is put on hold. They are the arbiters, sometimes impotent, often useful, of the differences that arise among peoples. Supported by oracles,[14] their judgments maintain or reestablish peace.

Everything that is dear to men—their cities, houses, families, treaties, oaths,

10. Medea having been absolved and purified by Circe, even though she recognized her niece fleeing the paternal home with Jason, did not dare to keep her captive or to permit any violence against her because of the previous act. Atonement or expiation was so sacred that the descendants of those who had done so for Orestes came together each year to celebrate the memory of it in a feast that took place on the day and place where it had occurred (Pausan., *Corinth*). The kings forgave the guilty who were of a distinguished rank. Copreus was by Eurystheus, Adrastus by Croesus (see Herodotus and Apollonius). In addition, religion had invented means of saving the criminal from his despair when he could not be absolved at that very moment; he then cut the hands or feet of his victim, licked the blood three times, and believed that heavenly vengeance was suspended until he could purify himself by greater expiations.

11. Eurip., *Hercule furieux*, 48.

12. Sainte-Croix, *Des anciens gouvernements fédératifs*, p. 115.

13. Pausan., IV, no. 1. The Argonian amphictyony still existed in the sixty-sixth Olympiad. It condemned Sicyon and Aegina to a fine of five hundred talents for having loaned King Cleomenes vessels in his war against Argos; but it appears to have had at that time Apollo as its protector.

14. Thucydid., I, 28.

hospitality—is connected to religion; it does not yet give morality a positive sanction; but the support it does give resembles that which would result (in a society where there are no laws) from the general opinion of the strongest. A rapid instinct alerts the nations that the gods are the friends of the good; that they want what is just. In the midst of its barbarity, Greece chose the irreproachable Aeacus to beg Jupiter to end the drought that had struck the scorched countryside with sterility.[15] This is because the love of order inherent in men is also inherent in the gods, although with frequent exceptions: they embrace the cause of the oppressed, as a hero encountering a traveler attacked by brigands saves him from their blows. This is not as a judge, however, and one would be wrong to infer that the society to which he belongs took measures to punish the crime and to put the innocent out of danger. Nonetheless, it is fortunate that men thus invested with superior strength would defend the cause of justice. These men are the gods of Homer, and it is already much to have created a powerful race that ordinarily protects the weak and punishes injustice.

15. Pausan., I, 44; Pind., *Nem.*, III, 17ff.

BOOK VIII

A NECESSARY DIGRESSION ON THE POEMS
ATTRIBUTED TO HOMER

CHAPTER I

That the Religion of the *Odyssey* Belongs to Another Epoch Than That of the *Iliad*

Before moving on from the polytheism of heroic times to the priestly religions, some explanations are necessary.

We believe that we have proved that the Greek religion of those times provided morality no solid support. The religious sentiment sought to bring notions of humanity, generosity, and justice into it; but it was rebuffed, and there was disaccord between this sentiment and the form it wanted to modify.

It is otherwise in the *Odyssey*. There morality becomes a rather intimate part of religion. As early as the seventh verse of the first book, it is said that the companions of Ulysses forfeited by their own misdeeds the return to their homeland. And if the principal one of these misdeeds was to have killed the flocks of Apollo[1] — which pertains to the personal interest of the gods — in many other places their justice is independent of their interest. All crimes stir their indignation.[2] If I forced my mother to leave my house, Telemachus exclaims, she would invoke the Furies.[3] Jupiter prepares a fatal voyage for the Greeks because they were neither prudent nor just. The gods warn Aegisthus not to murder Agamemnon in order to marry his widow;[4] when he does murder him, they are not slow to punish him. Minerva approves and shows the fairness of the punishment; and Jupiter adds that Aegisthus committed the misdeed despite what destiny decreed. This new point of view, which forbids men from accusing fate for their own faults, is an improvement in moral ideas. The same Minerva, reproaching the gods for having abandoned the Ulysses she protects, does not base her intercession on his behalf

1. *Odyss.*, I, 8–9.
2. Ibid., XV, 83–86.
3. Ibid., II, 135.
4. Ibid., I, 29–47.

on the number of his sacrifices, but upon the justice and humanity of the hero.[5] I will not retain you by force, said Alcinous to Ulysses, because this action would displease Jupiter;[6] and if I were to kill you after having received you, what confidence could I have when I address my prayers to the master of the gods?[7] Several times Telemachus threatens the suitors with divine anger.[8] Arriving among the Cyclopes, Ulysses sets about informing himself if the inhabitants of the island are well-disposed to strangers and fear the immortals who protect suppliants.[9] This sort of protection already characterized the Jupiter of the *Iliad*; but it belongs even more fully to the Jupiter of the *Odyssey*.[10] The first interests himself only in those who call on him because they embrace his altars, and because their safety is his glory. The second takes in hand their cause because they are without arms and defenseless.

The gods of the *Odyssey* intervene, as it were, ex officio in the relations of men among themselves. Disguised, they cross the earth in order to observe there crimes and acts of virtue.[11]

In the *Iliad*, their resentment is not stirred except by neglected sacrifices or insults directed at their priests; in the *Odyssey*, the attacks of one man upon another attract their severity. In the *Iliad*, they confer strength, courage, prudence, and cunning on mortals; in the *Odyssey*, they inspire virtue, whose reward is happiness.[12]

If in one place in the poem the suitors deliberate about a murder and appear to believe that the gods approve it—until a sign appears that turns them from it[13]—this is because every period when new ideas are introduced before the former ideas are completely discredited is an epoch of contradictions. Moreover, the gods themselves protest against this injurious hope of the suitors: the suitors still believe they are addressing the gods of the *Iliad*; it is the gods of the *Odyssey* that answer them. One would say that a long interval separated the gods of these two poems, and that during this period their moral education progressed.

5. Ibid., V, 8–12.
6. Ibid., VII, 315–16.
7. Ibid., XIV, 406.
8. Ibid., I, 378; II, 68, 148.
9. Ibid., IX, 174–75.
10. Ibid., VII, 165; XIII, 213–14; XIV, 57–58, 284, 389; XIX, 269–71, 478–79.
11. Ibid., XVII, 485–87.
12. Ibid.
13. Ibid., XVII, 485–87.

One must not confuse the effects of religion with the use of mythology. This use is perhaps less frequent in the *Odyssey* than in the *Iliad*; but the effects of religion, properly speaking, are much more diversified. In it men have better combined the means of rendering the gods not only favorable to their individual interests but also useful to public order.

These gods of the *Odyssey* have a much higher degree of dignity. The description of Olympus is more brilliant, the happiness of its inhabitants more complete.[14] Their dissensions were the results of the observations of a nascent people struck by the disorder and irregularities of nature; and these dissensions calm as man discovers the secret order that presides over the apparent disorder. Thus, the quarrels of the gods, the quarrels that occupy such a great place in the *Iliad*, are barely recalled in the *Odyssey*, and are indicated only in traits that are vaguer and softer. Minerva does not dare to openly protect Ulysses, for fear of offending Neptune.[15]

The distance that separates the gods from men is also greater. In the first of these two poems, the gods act constantly, and they all act. In the second, Minerva is almost the only god who intervenes. In one, the gods act in the way men do; they themselves suffer blows; they utter cries that resound in heaven and on earth; they take from warriors their broken weapons. In the other, Minerva acts only by secret inspirations, or at least in a mysterious and invisible manner.

In place of these battles unworthy of celestial majesty, albeit sung with satisfaction by the singer of Achilles, the poet who celebrates Ulysses shows only once—and this as a tradition, and not as an action in his poem—a rash warrior defying Apollo; but the battle is not even mentioned, and the adversary of the god perishes without offering resistance: he is punished rather than defeated.[16]

In the *Iliad*, when the immortals want to hide from view they are obliged to surround themselves with a cloud: their nature is to be seen; the wonder is not to be seen. Often they are recognized despite their efforts. When she comes down from heaven, Minerva is perceived by the Greeks and the Trojans; and in order not to be seen by Patrocles, Apollo envelops himself in thick clouds. But in the *Odyssey*, Homer says that it is impossible to recognize a god against his will. Thus at this second period the nature of gods is to be invisible. A wonder is needed for them to be seen.

14. Ibid., VI, 42–46.
15. Ibid., 329–31.
16. Ibid., VIII, 222–28.

In the *Iliad*, Thetis is forced by Jupiter to wed Peleus.[17] In the *Odyssey*, the gods disapprove of the marriages of goddesses with mortals.[18] The mixing of the two races seems to them to be an unsuitable misalliance. Jupiter forbids Calypso from wedding Ulysses, and he strikes Jason for having contracted an ambitious match with Ceres.

These differences between the two epochs of Homer could furnish many objections to the portrait we drew of the first polytheism of Greece; but even if they were extended to objects other than religion, instead of complicating this particular problem they would resolve it, because they point to a change in the social state that would explain the change in religious form.

Let us examine the *Odyssey* from this point of view.

In it, it seems to us that one discerns the beginning of a period that is tending to become peaceful, the first developments of legislation, the first attempts at commerce, the birth of amicable or interested relationships among peoples, when they replace brutal force with voluntary transactions, and conquests and violent spoliations with freely consented-to exchanges.

The uprising of the inhabitants of Ithaca against Ulysses after the slaughter of the suitors[19] reveals a germ of republicanism, an appeal to the rights of the people against their chiefs, and everything that we will see more clearly in Hesiod (as we have already indicated).

One of the characteristic features of the *Odyssey* is a curiosity and a thirst for knowledge that are the proof of the repose and leisure that commence. It is as having observed and learned much about the ways of many peoples that Ulysses is first presented to us. He extends his travels, and braves a thousand dangers, in order to instruct himself. Praise of knowledge frequently occurs, and this thought is incorporated even into fables. The father of Calypso, Atlas, bearing on his shoulders the columns that separate the heavens from the earth, knows what the depths of the sea contain. Calypso herself gives lessons in astronomy to Ulysses, and the Sirens are represented as seductive mainly because their songs are instructive. In order to satisfy this thirst to learn the marvels of far-off countries, the author of the *Odyssey* gathers from everywhere the deceptive accounts of travelers and inserts them in his poem. Hence Circe, a more primitive version of Armide and of Alcine; the Cyclo-

17. *Iliad*, XVIII, 432–40.

18. *Odyss.*, V, 118–19.

19. Ibid., XXIV.

pes, connected to mythology by their descent from Neptune; the Lestrigonians, whose traces are found in fragments of the first Greek historians.

These features manifestly belong to the period when man, still young enough to imagine everything and childish enough to believe everything, had already advanced to the point when he wanted to know everything. This is obviously a period after that of the *Iliad*, when the Greeks, preoccupied with the immediate interests of their own lives and employing all their energies in attacking and defending themselves, barely looked beyond themselves.

The condition of women, which always marches in step with that of civilization, is described completely differently in the *Odyssey* than in the *Iliad*. The wife of Alcinous, Arete, exercises the greatest influence over her husband and over the subjects of her husband.[20] The delicate modesty of Nausicaa, her refined sensitivity, imply a rather developed society. The fear she expresses to pronounce the word "marriage" before her father,[21] her description of the gossip, and, if we can use the proper term, the bad-mouthing of the Phaeacians,[22] before whom she did not dare cross the city with a stranger, indicate a very refined and reflective observation of social relations in a State that was both peaceful and well regulated.

Some will perhaps say that having to depict the Phaeacians as a commercial people, Homer ably brought to light the characteristics that distinguished the ways of such a people from the martial customs and manners of the rest of Greece. But having to describe in the *Iliad* a people more civilized and less exclusively warlike than his compatriots, Homer saw only the negative side of this progress in the social state; he still spoke of the Trojans as an effeminate race. On the contrary, it is with approval and pleasure that the civilization of the Phaeacians is described in the *Odyssey*. The admiration, or rather the surprise, that Homer exhibits in the *Iliad* toward the luxury of Troy is that of a man who is still unaccustomed to such luxury; but the singer of Ulysses possesses this habit—he appreciates and admires luxury.

The end of the sixth book of the *Iliad*, the farewells of Andromache and Hector,[23] is the sole place where conjugal love is depicted in touching colors; but it is conjugal love in the grips of despair, surrounded by all the horrors of war, subject to all the agitations of a hopeless situation. It is not domestic happiness, the result

20. Ibid., VII, 65–77.
21. Ibid., VI, 66–67.
22. Ibid., VI, 273–85.
23. *Iliad*, VI, 374–502.

of the order and tranquility that the laws guarantee. In the *Odyssey*, in the midst of her grief, prudent Penelope directs her house and gives herself over to regrets only when, after having divided the work between men and women, and after having devoted herself to her domestic cares, she reenters her chamber alone in order to bathe the nuptial bed in tears. Further note that with the exception of Penelope, all the Greek women of heroic times—Eriphyle, Helen, Clytemnestra, Phaedra—are guilty of murder, betrayal, or adultery. Penelope is the transition from this violent and barbarous state to a more moral, more civilized one, hence subsequent to the former which it replaces. The faithful nurse and attentive observer Euryclea, by the regard with which she is surrounded, herself testifies to the importance attached to the administration of women in the state of society characteristic of the *Odyssey*. Helen who in the *Iliad* limited herself to bemoaning her faults and to committing them, in the other epic appears with a dignity that causes one to forget her errors.

In order to prove that the state of women had not changed between the two poems, some have pointed to the fate of female captives,[24] and to the imperious speech Telemachus delivered to his mother.[25] But they have overstated the meaning of the four verses of that discourse, which were obviously dictated by an extraordinary circumstance. Stirred by Minerva herself, who had allowed him to detect that she was a goddess,[26] over Penelope's objections Telemachus desires to leave; he is troubled by them, of course, and he therefore speaks with the intention of dismissing the one who could be an obstacle to his designs. His conduct, therefore, is an exception dictated by special circumstances. The poet adds that Penelope herself was surprised by it;[27] and in the rest of the poem the son of Ulysses exhibits the greatest deference to his mother. She commands in his palace; he is obliged to take precautions in order to escape from Ithaca without her knowledge or permission.[28] She appears in the midst of the suitors as the mistress of the house they are wasting. There are even two verses that prove that she exercises a direct authority over her son. Euryclea says that Penelope never allowed him to command the female slaves.[29] If, however, as the head of the family he inherited all of his father's rights, he would have had the same power over both sexes as Ulysses, who

24. *Odyss.*, I, 356–60.
25. *Iliad*, VI, 454; *Odyss.*, VIII, 526–30.
26. *Odyss.*, I, 271, 305.
27. Ibid., I, 360.
28. Ibid., II, 248–377.
29. Ibid., XXII, 424–25.

had them punished for their misconduct. All this ought to have enlightened the readers of the *Odyssey* concerning the meaning of the four verses that appear to place Penelope in a subordinate position vis-à-vis her son; however, for the most part, people have seen in the writings of the ancients only what they already believed they would find.

The destiny of female slaves is doubtless the same in the two poems. The laws of war, which are more rigorous than the customs of peace, are also slower to be modified. Even when the relations between citizens change and become more relaxed, it is natural that the former barbarism toward enemies continues. However, the fate of female captives in the *Odyssey* is described in more pathetic terms than in the *Iliad*. Does this difference not indicate an improvement in domestic mores, one that by way of an invidious contrast rendered the fate of prisoners more terrible? The happier their life in the bosom of their families, the more odious became slavery. The more honorable the rank their spouses assigned them, the more repugnant the experience of having to grant their charms to the arrogant men who regarded them as their conquest. Briseis in the *Iliad*, whose father Achilles killed, attaches herself to her conqueror without remorse or scruple, while the *Odyssey* shows us a female prisoner who is forced to proceed by means of blows: this severe treatment presupposes resistance on the part of the unfortunate one, a resistance of which the *Iliad* offers no example.

We will go further. One sees in the *Odyssey* not only the proof of a change in the condition of women, but the effects of this change. One there discovers at once its advantages—more gentleness, more charm, more domestic felicity—and its inconveniences, which, to be precise, belong to a later period than its advantages. This probably needs explanation.

The growth in the influence of women has as a natural consequence making men occupy themselves more regularly with their relations with those with whom they share their lives. From this it results that love is considered in a more detailed, more nuanced way than before, and that the perspectives brought to bear on it multiply. Among these perspectives is one that makes love a light and frivolous, more or less immoral thing, one that lends itself to levity and jest. One, however, does not turn one's attention to it in this way until one has exhausted everything else. The people of thoroughly primitive customs treat love without delicacy, but they do not joke about it. Every time you find witticisms on this subject in an author, be sure that he lives among men already more or less civilized. Now, you can find such features in the *Odyssey*, while in the *Iliad* you will find no such thing. The story of the loves of Mars and Venus—which, I will say in passing, belongs to a tradition posterior to the *Iliad*, because here Vulcan has Charis, not Venus, for his wife[30]—this story casts upon the cuckold husband a tincture of ridicule.

Helen's infidelity is treated much more gravely. Menelaus is betrayed, but no one finds, or seeks, a subject of mockery in it. The Mercury of the *Odyssey*, who jokes with Apollo about Mars's fate (whom he envies), is a dandy in a society that is already corrupt.[31] Barbarous people consider pleasure more seriously. It is with a good deal of seriousness that Agamemnon declares to the assembled Greeks that he claims Chryseis for his bed because he finds her more beautiful than Clytemnestra;[32] and it is without any admixture of joking that Thetis proposes to her son, despairing over the death of Patrocles, the distraction of possessing a beautiful woman.[33]

The characters common to the *Iliad* and the *Odyssey* strike an attentive eye with other differences, and these differences are always progressive.

In both poems hospitality is always a sacred duty; but hospitality in the *Odyssey* has something warmer, more affectionate about it. There is only debt and loyalty in the *Iliad*, while there is refinement and sensitivity in the hospitality of the *Odyssey*.

This is not all. These two poems are not distinguished on the moral plane alone; they are dissimilar on the literary one as well. And these dissimilarities, like the former, indicate two periods connected by a growing civilization.

The unity of action that makes it simpler and clearer; a more lively and coherent narrative that concentrates the reader's attention; these are the perfection of art. These perfections, however, are foreign to the *Iliad*.[34] There the action is not

30. *Iliad*, XVIII, 382. In his fifteenth *Dialogue des dieux*, Lucian gives both Venus and Charis as wives of Vulcan, the latter at Lemmon, the former at Olympus. This is because Lucian takes pleasure in pointing out Homer's contradictions; and because in his day indifference toward religion conflated all the traditions without being overly concerned.

31. Lucian, in the twentieth of his *Dialogues des dieux*, imitated Homer by presenting Venus and Mars surprised by Vulcan, and the gods laughing at the discovered couple; but this portrait was better adapted to Lucian's century than that of the *Iliad*: in fact, it is only found in the *Odyssey*.

32. *Iliad*, I, 31, 112–15.

33. Ibid., XXIV, 130.

34. Following Aristotle, people have much extolled the unity of the *Iliad*. Without being aware of it, this celebrated critic has thus led his modern followers into a serious error. To be sure, he was far from claiming that the *Iliad* contained nothing that was not conformed to this unity, or that the focus did not frequently change. He simply wanted to distinguish the Homeric poems from the Cyclical poems (on these poems, about which we have already spoken, see Fabricii, *Bibl. Graece.*, I;

united; and the reader's interest is divided from the beginning: each hero shines in turn. Diomedes, Ulysses, the two Ajaxes, the old Nestor, and the young Patrocles, share with Achilles our unfocused attention. We often even forget Achilles, idle in his tent, and follow the battles of the companions he abandons. There are entire books when his name is barely mentioned; there are those that can be left out without the reader noticing.[35]

Finally, the object of our habitual sympathy is Hector; and if, on one hand, we are led by the talent of the poet to desire the taking of Troy, we experience, on the other, a constantly painful sentiment, when we consider this defender of the ill-fated city, the only character to whom our refined and generous sentiments can attach themselves without any reservation. This defect—for it would have been one if the poet had had the aim of composing a whole with the sole purpose of celebrating the glory of Achilles—this defect, I say, has so struck critics that they have attributed to Homer the intention of elevating the Trojans above the Greeks; and the pity he sought to excite for the misfortune of the former seemed to them to confirm this view. However, it is undercut by the passages where the poet speaks,

---

and Heyne, *ad* Virg., *Aen.*, II, *Excurs.*, I; and on the complete lack of forming a whole among these poems, Wolf, *Proleg.*, p. 126): these poems had neither a plan nor a purpose, neither a regular course nor a progressive development.

But the case would be different if we took into account a consideration that would oblige us not to simply believe Aristotle at his word. He may have been seeking support for a teaching adopted in advance. Unity was in the first rank of principles that Aristotle wished to have win the day. He found the Homeric poems already brought together in two books. They rightly were the objects of the Greeks' admiration; he therefore took them as examples to demonstrate his own teaching. He had to look for it in, and hence find it in, the two national epics. This necessity made him indulgent in several respects. This is a type of weakness (or, better put: bias) that is rather natural to the human mind, and from which the greatest geniuses escape only with difficulty.

35. Given that we today are agreed to regard the *Iliad* as we have it as complete, we treat the supplement to Homer by a later poet as a rash and ridiculous attempt, and we find everything the latter recounts to be useless and misplaced. We would say the same, though, if the *Iliad* had ended with the return of Achilles to the army, which would complete the subject announced by the poet at the beginning. If in Quintus of Smyrna we read the *Theomachia*, the games by the tomb of Patrocles, or the funeral ceremonies of Hector, we would reject these additions, the first as contrary to the mythology of the rest of the poem, the second as retracing the mores of another period, the third as a leaden style wholly unworthy of the epic. However, if the enumeration of the army was not already a part of our *Iliad* and someone wanted to insert it, people would descry the absurdity of placing this boring catalogue in an epic poem; and it would be easy to demonstrate that it could belong to history, but it ought to remain outside of poetry.

we will not say in his own voice, because that is never the case, but in a descriptive form, which is more appropriate for letting the secret inclination of the author be seen, than a narrative or dramatic form. Thus, for example, in the depiction of the first battle offered by the Greeks, their profound silence, the strict order of their ranks, the regularity of their movements, are put in opposition to the tumult, the disorder, the indiscipline, and the almost savage cries of the Trojans.

But if the *Iliad* lacks unity, it still rises above all the works come from the hands of men by a constant increase of interest, vividness, grandeur, and force from its beginning to its end (with only a few episodes as exceptions). The movement becomes ever more impetuous, passions more violent, the characters more colossal, the action of the gods more marvelous and superlative. As a man of much intelligence[36] and deeply versed in these sorts of investigation observed, this sort of development is much superior to that mechanical regularity that limits itself to subordinating everything to a single goal. However, does not this admirable progression make one suspect a succession of bards, each seeking to surpass his predecessors?

The character of the *Odyssey*, on the other hand, is a constant and perfect unity. Not only does everything relate to the return of Ulysses, but the poet, by attaching us from the very first book to Telemachus and Penelope, whom he shows to be quite weak and defenseless, oppressed by the suitors, forces us from the very beginning to hope for the arrival of the father and spouse they wait for, and who alone can deliver them. We desire this arrival, both by the interest the youth of the son inspires and by the respect the noble character of the mother commands, as well as by the hatred we have for the greedy and violent band of their assailants.

The superior art that shines forth in the *Odyssey* is also remarkable in some less important features, which still merit being discussed. Repetition is avoided much more carefully than in the *Iliad*. Seated with Alcinous, and having arrived at the place in his travels that the poet recounted in the previous book, Ulysses interrupts himself in order not to repeat something already said. In general, the idea of having the poem commence in medias res in order to give the hero the opportunity to recount his adventures, and to vary the tone of the narrative, is a progress in the art: all later writers have followed this method.

Thus, on one hand, the art of the poet is more developed in the *Odyssey*; on the other, the poetry of the *Iliad* is more brilliant, an indicator of a younger, more vigorous era.

---

36. A. W. Schlegel, in his *Cours de littérature*.

CHAPTER 2

A Question That Results from the Previous Observations

Are all these differences sufficiently resolved by the view that Longinus transmitted to us, which supposes that the author of the *Iliad* was young or in the prime of life when he wrote his first poem, but composed the *Odyssey* in his old age? We do not think so. With the present question, it is not a matter of more or less boldness of conception or brilliance of colors; rather it is a matter of a fundamental difference in the entire system of the two epics relative to religion, mores, customs, the condition of women, society, and even politics.

No individual, young or old, can shake off the yoke of his century. When this century has made progress, the past is imitated, but it is no longer animated by the same spirit. The impressions of the atmosphere that surrounds us become a part of us; they become identified with our very existence; each of our words is penetrated by them. The knowledge of ancient monuments and opinions is a matter of erudition; and erudition enlightens us without inspiring us; it provides us with developments that are more and less on point, with rapprochements that are more and less apt, as well as allusions and contrasts. But these things are infused with the present times and mores. Consider Virgil: he instructed himself by studying Homer, he studied Etruscan traditions; nonetheless he is neither Greek nor Etruscan; he is a Roman, a courtier of Augustus. We even dare to say that it would have been no more possible for the Homer of the *Odyssey* to compose the *Iliad* than for a Jew of Alexandria to write the Psalms or the Book of Job.

We therefore are obliged to devote a few pages to another hypothesis. Despite our efforts to shorten this digression, it will probably seem too long; but the poems attributed to Homer are the only ones that can be cited as historical records. All the poets who write at an advanced period of civilization write for effect. They know the taste of their times; they have before them the treasures of the past;

they draw from them at their convenience, according to the goal they propose to themselves, many without discernment, all without exactitude. The most faithful limit themselves to embellishing the mores they describe. But to embellish is to denature. The date of the works therefore is only a literary question. This date provides light on the state of literature at the time the authors write, but none on the veracity of their depictions, if they speak of a century not their own. Place the *Aeneid* one hundred years before or after its true time and your ideas of the literary merit of the century would change. However, you would know that one ought not seek a depiction of the mores of the Trojans in the *Aeneid*. This is not true of the poems of Homer. The *Iliad* exactly represents the mores of a people such as the Greeks contemporaneous with the Trojan War would have to be. But the *Odyssey* transmits details of an entirely different sort; if you suppose that these two works were written at the same time, or were separated by only a few years, the fidelity or accuracy of both becomes suspect. The dating of the Homeric poems therefore is not only important in connection with literary criticism, it is decisive for the history of the human race.

CHAPTER 3

That the Composition of the *Odyssey*, and Hence Its Mythology, Belong to a Period after That of the *Iliad*

If it were proven that the *Iliad* and the *Odyssey* do not come from the same author, but that the *Odyssey* belongs to a subsequent century, and to a period of civilization that is more advanced than that of the *Iliad*, all the difficulties we brought to light in the previous chapter would be easily explained. As a preliminary, let us see if the records and authors of antiquity should make us reject this view.

First of all, note that the view is not new. The authenticity of the two poems attributed to Homer has appeared doubtful to learned men of every century.[1]

However, some have wanted to make the solution of the problem depend upon an even more obscure question: to wit, whether the art of writing was in use in the time of Homer.

On the negative side there are many plausible reasons.[2]

1. The scholiasts of Venice say expressly that several ancient critics assigned these two poems to different authors. These critics formed a large enough group that they were designated by a special name: the Chorizontes (Fred. Schlegel, *Hist. de la poésie grecque*). Seneca (*De brev. vit.*, cap. 13) reproaches the Greeks for having always engaged in frivolous inquiries, and he counts among them those who aimed to determine if the *Iliad* and the *Odyssey* were the work of the same poet.

2. Herodotus, it is true, attributes this invention to Cadmus; but we know that Herodotus, who recounted only what he believed to be true, adopted as true everything that was recounted to him. A learned modern (Wolf, *Proleg. Homer.*) nicely calls him the zealous friend of truth and the enthusiastic narrator of fables; still, Herodotus recounts this only as a rumor that he does not guarantee, ως εμοι δοκειν. Elsewhere, he cites three epigrams that he regards as close to the time of Cadmus, and says that he copied them from the temple of the Ismenian Apollo; but the better critics recognize an imitation of Homer's style in these epigrams.

Aeschylus points to Prometheus as having invented writing; others attributed it to Orpheus, Cecrops, or Linus. The Greeks loved to place the origin of the arts in the most remote times, and did not distinguish their successive developments.

But even if one answers affirmatively, no proof of the poems' authenticity results.

First of all, it still would remain doubtful that their author *wrote* them.[3] Who cannot think of all the difficulties that had to present themselves to the dissemination of writing, or which had to arise from the lack of materials upon which to write? What a large interval had to unfold between a few inscriptions crudely sculpted in stone or bronze and the written redaction of works of an entirely different extent!

As a famous learned man observes,[4] there is one fact that marks the period when the use of writing becomes general among a people: this is the composition of works in prose. As long as none exist, this is a proof that writing is barely in use. In the paucity of materials for writing, verses are easier to remember than prose, and they are also easier to get down. Prose arises naturally from the possibility that men acquire of entrusting themselves, as far as the life of their compositions, to another instrument than their memory. Now, the first prose authors, Pherecydes,

---

However, Euripides in a fragment preserved for us by Stobaeus calls Palamedes the author of the alphabet, which would place this discovery at the time of the Trojan War. It is not likely that Euripides, writing for the stage, would have substituted Palamedes for Cadmus if this hypothesis was contrary to the generally accepted opinion. The Greeks were so little advanced at the time of Cadmus that the fable of Amphion building the walls of Thebes by means of the sound of his lyre is later than it by a century! Now, this fable is obviously the symbol of the first efforts of the social genius to bring together primitive savages.

One finds in Homer several details that seem to indicate that writing did not exist in his time. All treaties are concluded verbally; the memory and conditions of them are preserved only by signs; and if there are two passages from which some have claimed to infer the use of letters, the first can be understood to refer to hieroglyphic characters written on wood, and the second would serve as a proof of the alternative (*Iliad*, VI, 167, 168). On the latter passage, see the notes of Heyne, and the *Prolégomènes* of Wolf, p. 76. Apollodorus, in speaking of the anecdote of Bellerophon, uses the words επιςολη, "mandatum," and επιγωναι, which never means "to read" in Greek. The word επιγραφας that is found in this passage proves absolutely nothing. The word γραφειν in Homer's time meant "to sculpt": nothing is more natural. The meaning of words changes with the progress of the arts. The warriors who placed a token in the helmet of Agamemnon in order that the question of who would fight against Hector could be decided by lot did not recognize the one that the herald presented to them, so it is clear that it was not a written name, because each would have been able to read the name of his rival as well as his own, but an arbitrary sign that only the one who had placed it could recognize.

3. Eustathius explicitly says that at the time of Homer, the discovery of writing was very recent. The first written laws of the Greeks were those of Zaleucus, seventy years before Solon (Strabo, VI; Cic., *Ad Attic.*, v. Scymnus Perieg, 313). The Laws of Solon were themselves engraved on material that was hardly portable, four centuries after Homer.

4. Wolf, *Prolégom.*, p. 69.

Cadmus of Miletus, Hellanicus, who belong to the century of Pisistratus, are very much later than Homer.[5]

For a rather long period of time, therefore, the two Homeric epics could have been transmitted only by memory.[6] Memory is a faculty that is perfected to an astonishing point when it is needed, and is lost with an extreme rapidity when it is less necessary.

The example of bards, skalds, Druids,[7] the Hebrew prophets, the Caledonian poets, and, finally, the improvisers of Italy do not allow us to call this point into question. The sagas, or traditions of Scandinavia, conserved and transmitted from father to son, were so long that one was able to fill libraries with them when they were finally written down. They enable us to see how the Homeric poems could have been orally preserved. The entire history of the North, says Botin,[8] was preserved in unwritten poems. Whereas our social life, observes Mr. de Bonstetten,[9] so disperses our faculties that we have no adequate idea of the capacity of memory of these half-savage men who were not distracted by anything and who made it a point of honor to recite the exploits of their ancestors in verse.[10]

One fact is certain: until the time of Pisistratus, the Homeric rhapsodies were

5. A learned Frenchman (Mr. de Sainte-Croix, *Réfutation d'un paradoxe sur Homère*) has aimed to respond to this argument. Being habituated to poetry, the Greeks, he says, could have consented to use prose only slowly and with great repugnance, and their first prose writers affected a poetic style. If this observation were well founded, it would still not explain why these first prose writers would all be separated from the Homeric epics by an interval of four hundred years.

6. This was the opinion at the time of the historian Josephus. We are assured, he says, that Homer only recited his poems orally, and that they were not reduced to their current form until long afterward (Joseph., *Contr. Apion.*, I, 2, p. 439).

7. *Magnum numerum versuum ediscebant (Druidae) litteris non mandatorum;* Caes., *B Gall.*, VI, 14; Pomp. Mela, III, 2.

8. *Histoire de Suède*, ch. 8. Even in our day there are peasants in Finland whose memory equals that of the Greek rhapsodes. Almost all these peasants compose verses, and some recite very long poems, which they retain in their memory, even correcting them, without committing them to writing (Rüh, *Finland und seine Bewohner*). Bergman (*Steifereyen unter den Calmucken*, II, 213) speaks of a Kalmuk poem of 360 songs that has been preserved for centuries in the memory of this people. The rhapsodes who are called *dschangarti* sometimes know twenty of these songs by heart, which is to say: a poem almost as long as the *Odyssey*; because of a translation of one of these songs provided by Bergman, we see that it is hardly less long than a Homeric rhapsody.

9. *Voy. en Ital.*, p. 12.

10. In addition, one must observe that no one supposes that the same individual knew by heart the fifteen thousand verses of the *Iliad*, or the twelve thousand of the *Odyssey*, but only this-or-that book, or this-or-that particular episode.

sung individually on the public squares by the rhapsodes;[11] this usurper was the first who brought them together and put them in the order he felt was suitable.[12] Charlemagne did the same thing with the ancient Germanic poems orally transmitted to him. And it was in this way that the Arabs in the seventh century formed the collections of the unwritten poetry of the previous ages, called Divans, and

11. The name "rhapsode" appears to postdate Homer, but the thing existed at the time of the composition of these epics. Phemius and Demodocus are rhapsodes in the *Odyssey*. Their profession was very much held in honor. They always recited verses from memory, and they retained this habit even after the invention of writing and when written copies of the Homeric poems were common. These poems being the most frequent subjects of their oral recitations, they were sometimes called Homeridae; this has led some scholars, against all evidence, to believe that those so named were descendants of Homer. The effect of these poems had to be so much greater when they were recited in this way. Everywhere that writing is employed to preserve poems, they become the object of study by the educated class more than of enthusiasm by the vulgar mass. The full effect of poetry requires that it be connected with public declamation and song. It was in this way that the Homeric poems were inscribed in the memory and minds of the Greeks. Recited in the assemblies of the people, recited in the bosom of families, they became an intimate part of everyone's existence, both the nation's and the household's. Even long after writing was in use, the ancients speak of the prodigious effect of these poems as they were declaimed before the Greeks. I see, says a rhapsode to Socrates in one of Plato's dialogues (the *Ion*), I see the listeners sometimes cry, sometimes shake, sometimes, as it were, transported outside themselves. If the rhapsodes could exercise such an empire when everything that was divine in their art had disappeared and they only sang for a salary, what had it to have been when they were the sole means of communication between the poets and the people, and the intermediaries between heaven and earth! Their profession grew ignoble as it became mercenary. This is the fate of all those professions that pertain to the intellectual faculties. However, there were still rhapsodes around the sixty-ninth Olympiad: Cynaethus, a contemporary of Pindar, was a rhapsode.

12. Pisistratus, says Pausanias (*2nd voy. en Elide*, ch. 26), gathered the poems of Homer that were scattered from one end to the other. Another tradition recounts, it is true, that the Homeric poems had been previously carried into the Peloponnese by Lycurgus; nothing, however, is less proven than this claim. The first author in whom we find it is Heraclidus. He speaks vaguely about the poetry of Homer without indicating what works comprised this poetry. Aelian adds that it was all of Homer's poetry; but he enters into no detail (in fragment Πολιτειων). Plutarch gives some, but provides no guarantee of the list; these, moreover, if they were admitted, would be of such a nature as to confirm our doubts rather than dissolve them. "In the time of Lycurgus (in Lycurg.)," he says, "Homer's reputation was not very widespread. A small number of people possessed some fragments of his poems, but they were scattered, and differed from one another." What is more probable is that Lycurgus brought back from his travels in Greece and Asia some rhapsodies, or a vague knowledge of the Homeric poems, a knowledge that quickly was lost. Three centuries after Lycurgus, Pisistratus had them gathered, then copied, by educated men who lived in his intimate circle. The author of the *Dialogue d'Hipparque*, which is falsely attributed to Plato, does not ascribe this collection to Pisistratus, but to his sons. Suidas seems to insinuate that Pisistratus's effort was not the first; and in

Macpherson in modern times brought together scattered songs under the name of the son of Fingal.

But could not these rhapsodes—who for several generations sang the poems of Homer in unconnected pieces[13]—could not they have changed the order, or

___

his *Histoires diverses* (III, 14), Elian attributes the order in which these rhapsodies were put not to Pisistratus but to Solon.

Antiquity, therefore, was divided as much over the poems to be attributed to Homer as to the parts of these poems that truly were his. We said above that Herodatus removed the *Cypria* and the *Epigones* from the list (Herod., II, 117; IV, 32). Eustathius tells us that the ancients maintained that the *Doloneia* formed a separate poem, which Pisistratus had had inserted into the body of the *Iliad*. Others rejected the episode of Glaucus (Heyne, *ad Iliad*, VI, 19; schol. Venet. de Villois., p. 158). This is not all: the collection ordered by Pisistratus is not the one we possess. As was the case before the tyrant, so after him there were frequent alterations, not only to the individual texts but to the ensemble, to the entire order of the Homeric poems. The scholiasts of Homer, and especially the scholiast of Venice, tell us of a class of critics whom they name diaskeuasts, who had worked on these poems. It surely was the same with these diaskeuasts as it was with those who took the tragedies for their subject. Now, we know by the scholiast of Aristophanes (*Nuées*, V, 552, 591) that the latter changed, added, removed, corrected—in a word, reworked—these works. The exemplar that Alexander received from Aristotle had been rectified by several scholars, and even bore corrections from the hand of the victor of Arbelles himself (Plut., *Vit. Alex.*; Strabo, XII). Callisthenes and Anaxarchus had corrected the *Odyssey*. Aratus, who had put in order a copy of this poem, was invited by Antiochus Soter, king of Syria, to give the same care to the *Iliad*, corrupted by the rhapsodes and copyists (Suid., I, 309; *Auctor vetus vitae Arati in Petav. Uran.*, p. 270).

One must note that in this time the corrections made to a copy of a poem had only a very limited influence. The manner in which copies multiplied in Greece, either by the efforts of individuals (αι κατςανδρα) or those of cities (αυ κατα πολεις, αι των πολεων), made it that the corrections of one copy were not public, and changed nothing with respect to other copies.

Therefore, in admitting the existence of a composition ordered by Pisistratus, or by him and his family members, this compilation could not have served as the rule except for a very short time, and soon enough new variants would have been introduced, or new corrections, according to the imagination of the copyists or owners of each version. The Homeric poems do not appear to have assumed their final form except under the Ptolemies, and their current arrangement was given to them by the grammarians of Alexandria (Wolf, *Prolégom.*, p. 151), especially by Aristarchus, who lived under Philometor, toward the 166th Olympiad (in passing let me observe that he, as well as Aristophanes of Byzantium, a no less able critic, doubted the authenticity of the end of the *Odyssey*). Moreover, as Heyne notes (*Homér.*, VIII), the grammarians of Alexandria seemed to have had no other goal in their division of these poems than to ensure that the books contained an approximately equal number of verses and had the same number as the letters of the alphabet. Hence, there are books that end in the middle of an account; hence, too, there are useless or repeated verses at the end and beginning of each book.

13. Ael., *Var. Hist.*, XIII, 14. Pindar calls the rhapsodes: Ραπων Επεων ασιδους, singers of sewn-together verses.

corrupted the texts, or mixed the compositions of various authors during their recitations in the public assembly or on the stage? And the friends of Pisistratus, by making a whole of these scattered pieces, did not they choose, arrange, or correct at their pleasure? Among the friends of the tyrant we find Onomacritus of Athens, who only a little time before was convicted and punished for having inserted in the works of Orpheus and Museus lengthy and frequent interpolations,[14] something that does not give a positive idea of his fidelity or scruples. He then sold himself to the tyrants expelled from his country in order to raise another tyrant against his countrymen. From Pisistratus to the Ptolemies, who can tell us how many times someone would have renewed these reworkings, whether in general or in details?[15]

14. Herod., VII, 6. In order to complete the Homeric poems, Pisistratus promised rewards to all those who knew by heart some pieces and would communicate them to him. One can think that these promises had to give rise to interpolations (Heyne, *Com. Soc. Goett.*, XIII, n. 6).

15. These conjectures authorized by reasoning are confirmed by facts. Several verses cited by the ancients, especially by Hippocratus, Aristotle, and Plato (Wolf, *Prolégom.*, p. 37), are not found in any of our current manuscripts of Homer. Pausanias reports a passage of this poet in order to prove that he recognizes the divinity of Aesculapius, since he calls Machaon his son, the son of a god (*Corinth*, 26): nothing similar is found in the *Iliad* or the *Odyssey*, at least as we have them today; on the other hand, there are other verses found both in Homer and Hesiod, for example the 265th verse of book I of the *Iliad*, which is the 182nd verse of the *Bouclier d'Hercule*. Two famous critics, Aristarchus and Zenodotus, rejected the catalogue of the Nereides (*Iliad*, XVIII, 39–49) and regarded it as belonging to Hesiod rather than Homer. This would lead one to believe that the rhapsodes sometimes transported fragments from one poet to the works of another. The interpolated verse on which Solon based himself in order to establish Athens's rights to Salamina is well known.

These interpolations were both inevitable and easy. Rhapsodes reciting poems before the people naturally brought to these poems the changes that they believed to be pleasing to their listeners.

We will give an example. We have already spoken of a verse that was found in both the *Bouclier d'Hercule* and the first book of the *Iliad*. This verse pertains to Theseus, a hero to whom the Athenians had a special attachment; the rhapsodes therefore had an interest in celebrating his glory. But there is another in the same vein in the eleventh book of the *Odyssey*, around line 630. The way it is constructed, and its little consonance with what preceded and followed it, have caused the best critics to regard it as interpolated. I would have wanted, says Ulysses, to see the heroes Theseus and Pirithous. One cannot understand why Ulysses, who had seen almost all the heroes and heroines of past centuries, and who was choosing among the shades, would have had this desire without satisfying it. But one can understand that a rhapsode, wanting to recall Theseus in order to please an Athenian audience, who had proudly named their city the city of Theseus, and who had sent the son of Miltiadus to seek the ashes of this hero, whose tomb had become a temple and an asylum (Suidas; Hesych.; schol. Arist., in Plut., V, 627; Plut., in Milt. et Cimon); one can understand, we were saying, that a rhapsode had slipped this verse into the text; what is more remarkable is that several centuries later

Polygnotus, in his portrait of the descent of Ulysses into the netherworld, had placed Theseus and Pirithous on golden thrones: this, it seems to us, is a striking development. The author of the eleventh book of the *Odyssey* had not named Theseus; a rhapsode, flatterer of the Athenian people, was pained by this silence and softened it with a verse of regret; a painter profited from this verse; and Theseus, forgotten by the poet, desired by the rhapsode, finally appeared under the brushstrokes of a painter. It is true that the latter distanced himself from the rhapsode's intention; he shows Theseus chained to his throne as a punishment for the outrage he had committed against Pluto. But this circumstance is owing to the fact that the portrait of Polygnotus was destined for Delphi, not Athens. When the same painter employed his palette for Athens, he sacrificed to it not only mythology but also history, and had Theseus take part in the battle of Marathon (Pausan., *Attica*, 15).

We could cite another, less fortunate interpolation, one that all critics and translations, both ancient and modern, have condemned. Homer nowhere speaks of the mysteries; neither the name of Eleusis nor that of the Thracian Eumolpus, founder of the Eleusian rites, is found in the two poems. The adherents of the mysteries nonetheless wanted to support them with his authority. What did they do? They introduced, after the 551st verse of the 18th book, where it is a question of Achilles's shield, a verse in which the epithet "Eleusinian" accompanies the name Ceres. It is probable that when the rhapsodes wanted to insert additions into a poem that already enjoyed public approval, they placed the more important at the end of the poem. A scholiast affirms that the twenty-fourth book of the *Iliad* ends with these two verses:

They thus took care of the funeral rites of Hector:
Then came the Amazon, the daughter of Mars, the great destroyer of men.

It is manifest that this was a transition to a new song. The episode of Mars wounded by Diomedes, and that of Diana fleeing the battle, probably are also additions that imitated the much more elegant description of the wounding and flight of Venus.

We would be able to indicate contradictions in the *Iliad* as well as the *Odyssey* that are so obvious that the same author could not have fallen into them, no matter how inattentive one might suppose him. In the fifth book, verse 576, Pylaemenes, king of the Paphlagonians, is killed by Menelaus; and in the thirteenth, verse 658, this same Pylaemenes accompanies the body of his son, Harpalion. The fall of Vulcan, cast down to the island of Lemnos, is recounted twice with different circumstances (*Iliad*, I, 589–95; XVIII, 395–405). In the fourteenth book of the *Odyssey*, Ulysses, Eumaeus, and the other shepherds split up in order to sleep; and in the middle of the fifteenth book, we see them at the same feast that had ended in the previous book. Finally, is it not probable that the poet who in the nineteenth book of the *Odyssey* and the eleventh of the *Iliad* recognized only one Ilithyia, daughter of Juno, is not the same one who recognizes several in the fifteenth and the sixteenth books?

In the *Iliad* as well as the *Odyssey*, there are maladroit transitions that one cannot but feel came after the fact (see *Iliad*, XVII, 356–68; *Odyss.*, IV, 620). Sometimes the precautions of the rhapsodes betray them: one sees that they wanted to respond in advance to objections that they feared.

Thus, in order to explain why one finds no trace of the wall raised by the Greeks around their ships, they inserted two passages (*Iliad*, VII, 443–64; XII, 4–40) in which they recount in advance the destruction of this wall by Neptune, who, jealous of the pride of men, directs the waves of all the rivers subject to his control against their work. The scholiasts of Venice, and several others, regard these two

To the possibility that the *Odyssey* or the *Iliad* would have been, we will not say formed in their entirety from rhapsodies brought together at random, but considerably lengthened in this way, some oppose the uniformity of style and poetic coloring. But the style of all the epic poems of the Greeks is much the same, as well as their idiom.[16] The language of Hesiod, that of the Batrachomyomachy, and of Quintus of Smyrna differ only slightly from Homer's. The superior rank

---

passages as inauthentic, and the second as being obviously out of place. It interrupts the account of a battle in order to entertain the reader with a far-off event, one without any relationship to the action. In the same way, fearing that some might reproach the author of the *Odyssey* for having spoken of a country (Phaeacia) that did not exist, they, as it were, close any access on the part of sailors to this island by means of a ship turned into a rock.

The authority of certain ancient authors who harbor no doubts relative to the two poems is questionable. Closely examined, the authority is reduced to next to nothing.

The first who speaks of Homer is Pindar (*Pyth.*, IV, 493; *Nem.*, VII, 29; *Isthm.*, IV, 63). But what Pindar says of Homer could have been said even if this poet had written only the *Iliad*. He celebrates Ulysses in the *Iliad* as well as Ajax. One must also note that Pindar attributed the *Cypria* to Homer, which is known to be spurious (Ael., *Var. Hist.*; see on the *Cypria*, Heyne, *Excurs. ad* lib. II *Aeneid*, p. 229). Moreover, what modern poet would scruple to name Ossian without seeking to know if he really existed? Herodotus came seventy years after Pindar, and he presents Homer as having lived four hundred years before him, and as being the author of the epics that bear his name (Herod., II, 23, 53, 115; IV, 29, 32; V, 67; VII, 161). But we have already recalled the excessive credulity of Herodotus. Finally, thirty years later, Thucydides cites Homer in order to verify the facts he puts forth.

The name Thucydides commands our respect. It merits our confidence in all he says, not only all that he saw and concerning what happened in his day, but all that he reports concerning the events, mores, and institutions of civilized Greece; but it is not the same when he goes back to the obscure traditions of antiquity. Our best historians recount fables when they go back to the origin of the Franks, the Gauls, and the Germans. They cite authors whose veracity is dubious; they evoke personages whose existence is apocryphal.

Thucydides displayed such little critical attitude toward Homer that in one place he appears to have attributed to him one of the hymns to Apollo (Thucyd., III, 104). Now, the two hymns in honor of this god are recognized by all scholars as being much later than the *Iliad* or the *Odyssey*.

In general, one must not harbor illusions about the state of criticism among the ancients. The same cause that gave so much charm to their literature renders their criticism very imperfect. As they were very sensitive to impressions, instead of judging traditions, they adopted them without deeper reflection. In all the sciences, doubt is the last quality man acquires.

16. We could add that despite this apparent uniformity, men who are the most versed in Greek have believed they recognized different styles in different parts of the *Iliad*. The style of the first books is distinguished from that where the poet describes the battle near the ships. The *Patroclea* differs from the *Achillea*, properly speaking, and above all, the two last books seem to be from a different hand than the twenty-two preceding ones.

of the latter owes to the vigor of the conceptions, the vivacity of an inexhaustible imagination, much more than what we could call the style.[17]

This conformity in the manner of expression is characteristic of the period of society during which the Homeric poems were composed. One cannot read the songs of Ossian without being struck by their uniformity, yet Ossian certainly was not one and the same bard. The individual character of writers develops only much later. As long as the human spirit battles, as it were, against barbarism, there will be a similar style. Here, as elsewhere, the extremes touch. The absence of civilization gives almost the same color to all individuals. In its progress, civilization develops differences; but with the excess of civilization, these differences disappear again. The only difference is that in the first case this is the natural effect of social circumstances, while in the second case it is the result of a premeditated imitation; and what was uniformity becomes monotony.

To these considerations one can add others derived from our ignorance of Homer's life.[18] What is told to us about his miserable vagabond existence does not fit at all with the epoch in which we place him. The Homeric poems themselves do not depict bards in such straits. This sort of condition could only be produced by the decadence and fall of the Greek monarchies. In the martial and barbarous times, as well as the heroic ages, of Greece, poets always enjoyed the greatest respect of the people and kings. We find the proof of this in every one of the historical records of the Scandinavians, who resemble the Greeks in many ways.[19] But as civilization progresses, the life of men becoming more laborious and ideas

17. Nonnus himself, so different from Homer by his mythology, which is filled with oriental allegories and cosmogonies, differs not at all from the Homeric way of writing.

18. That which is attributed to Herodotus is the work of a sophist who lived much later than the historian. The two treatises on the same subject that are found in the works of Plutarch, of which the second, if we follow Galen, was written by Denys of Halicarnassus, are certainly the products of rather modern rhetoricians. Even the name "Homer" is symbolic, and susceptible to several meanings. It signifies what is put together (Euripid., *Alceste*, 780), a gauge or a guarantee, finally a blind person (Lycophron). Of the three meanings, one accords with our conjectures concerning the assembling of the Homeric rhapsodies; the second indicates the confidence accorded the poets; the third alludes to a circumstance that makes even more doubtful the claim that the name was intended for an individual.

19. Harald with the handsome locks gave Skalds the first place on the bancs reserved for the officers of his court (Torfoeus, *Hist. Norweg.*). Several princes gave them the most important missions during war and peace. One hardly ever sees a Skald sing his verses at the court of kings without receiving a ring of gold, splendid arms, costly clothing. By means of a song, the Skald Egyll redeemed himself from the punishment of a murder (Mallet, *Hist. du Dan.*).

of utility gaining in ascendancy, the existence of poets loses its importance. They themselves sense their decline, and they deplore it.[20] If one adopts the idea that Homer really existed, it would be impossible to explain how when he spoke about the rhapsodes, his predecessors, who were so well received and treated, that he would not have reflected upon himself.

No. Chance could not have brought forth, at the precise line that separated the two different civilizations, a single man capable of describing the civilization that no longer existed and the one that was coming to be. Homer is a generic name,[21] like Hercules or Buddha.[22]

The Homeric poems are the work of several bards, each being the organ and representative of his century.[23] Two or even three primitive poems could have arisen and served as the core;[24] but these poems had to have undergone several important transformations; and around them were successively grouped several episodes; in each of them was inserted foreign material; as a result, the date of these parts and episodes, and of the two poems, cannot be determined except by moral proofs; we will see unimpeachable ones in the essential differences that distinguish the *Iliad* from the *Odyssey*; and because these differences would be inexplicable if one

20. See Pindar.

21. Will there be those who decry the assault on Homer's glory, as was the case twenty years ago? (*Réfutation d'un paradoxe sur Homère*, by Mr. de Sainte-Croix). Homer's glory does not enter into the question. Do scholars do battle for the glory of this or that famous name independently of the truth of the matter? Do soldiers fight for their leaders independently of the country?

22. The barbarous centuries tend to combine in a single person everything that is eminent in a class. The Gallic bard par excellence, Taliesin, about whom we spoke earlier, appeared in the first century; he is born of the first woman, in the furnace of Owen, where genius and science were brewed; he sings in the fourth century, now the son of Edeyrin, a renowned prince; and in the sixth, he is the author of the poems that we have already indicated (bk. VI, ch. 7), and his name, like that of Homer, is emblematic; it signifies divine head, resplendent head (*Archaeol. of Wales*, pp. 17, 71).

23. In things that do not belong to mythology one finds progressive developments that bespeak a rather long interval of time; for example, the invention of the cavalry. In the *Iliad*, this invention is not mentioned; one fights on foot or one makes use of chariots. In the *Odyssey*, Ulysses on a mast is compared to a man mounted on a horse. In truth, in the *Doloneia*, Diomedes is said to be mounted on one of Rhesus's horses. But the *Doloneia* is a later interpolation.

24. A. W. Schlegel thinks that the *Iliad* is composed of three poems: the first ends with the ninth book, the second with the eighteenth, and the third includes the deaths of Patrocles and Hector. He regards as separate compositions the *Doloneia* and the twenty-fourth book. The final songs, he says, except for the thirty verses that end the whole, already approach the pomp and premeditated majesty of tragedy.

attributed these two works to the same author and century; one must recognize them as products of two different centuries and authors.[25]

We therefore do not believe that one can oppose the mythology of the *Odyssey* to the portrait we presented of the original Greek polytheism. The *Odyssey*'s pertains to a period later than the polytheism.

In general, one must distinguish three species of mythology in the Homeric poems.

One notices, on an initial plane, a popular mythology, of the sort that had to belong to a people who emerged freely from fetishism. This mythology is that of the majority of the *Iliad*, and the first eighteen books especially, which embrace and complete the principal action. Then one finds the same mythology, but perfected, with religion having progressed and having united itself to morality; this sort dominates in the *Odyssey*; however, the three books in which Ulysses recounts his adventures depart from this second mythology, and belong to that of the *Iliad*.[26]

25. We have said that this opinion was not new, that it was the opinion of several critics of antiquity; we will add that it has been picked up in modern times. Bentley, one of the most learned men of the last century, calls (with a bit of exaggeration) the Homeric poems scattered songs (*Philelheuter Lips.*, p. VIII). Goguet felt the difference that separates the *Iliad* and the *Odyssey*. "I have suspected for a long time," says M. de Pauw, "that the *Iliad*, as it had to have been at its origin, had been composed for the funeral games celebrated in Thessaly at the death of Achilles" (the author ought to have said: in memory of Achilles's death) "by princes who claimed to belong to the family of Peleus and the race of centaurs. These sorts of games were not always one-off feasts, but often annual occurrences; in this way the *Iliad*, or rather the *Achilleid*, could have been composed at different times; and since, people added so many fragments that if Homer could return, he would not at all recognize his own work. There were even at Athens schools of grammar where one gave children an edition of the *Iliad* filled with verses that no longer exist, such as what Aeschines cited against Timarchus."

Finally, one of our most distinguished travelers noted, without seeking its cause, that the *Iliad* depicts mores that have more connection with those of savages than with those portrayed in the *Odyssey*. I find in the Greeks of Homer, he says, especially in those of his *Iliad*, the customs, modes of discourse, and mores of the Iroquois, the Delaware, and the Miami tribes (Volney, *Tableau de l'Amérique*).

There are certain assertions whose force is found in the unanimity with which one assumes they are adopted. This unanimity is assumed by all those who in each century want to fight these assertions; and such critics believe that despite reiterated denials, the assent still continued to be unanimous. This resembles the cunning of certain governments who pretend to base themselves on the will of the people, and who oppose the general consent of the mass to the resistances of particulars, as if these particulars were not parts of the general will. With this way of reasoning, one sometimes ends by posing the entire nation on one side and all the individuals of this nation on the other.

26. It is remarkable that the love of Ulysses and Calypso is completely physical and resembles Agamemnon's for Chryseis. It therefore is inconsistent with the order of ideas that assumes the modesty

The description of the state of the dead is entirely unfitting to a religion that has morality in its belief and its precepts. On the other hand, the twenty-fourth book of the *Iliad,* which many critics regard as an addition,[27] and whose last thirty verses on Hector's funeral are in truth unworthy of Homeric poetry, appears to belong to the mythology of the *Odyssey.* There are ideas concerning the dignity of the gods that contrast with all of their previous conduct. Mercury leaves Priam at the entrance of Achilles's tent, telling him that it would be unfitting for the gods to intervene too ostentatiously in the affairs of men.[28] This reserve is hardly in keeping with the habits of these same gods who in a thousand other places do not believe they are degrading themselves by intervening, and fighting, protecting, or deceiving humans; and one cannot mistake a progress of religious ideas here, an increase in divine dignity. Priam says to Achilles: "Respect the gods and have pity on me"; this belongs to the *Odyssey* more than the *Iliad.*

We would be tempted to believe that with the march of civilization having softened the notions of the Greeks, that in order to preserve Achilles as their national hero they would feel the need to present him under less fierce and revolting traits than those that characterized many of his previous actions. Hence his belated pity and the restoring of Hector's body to his father.[29]

Finally, there are traces in Homer of a third sort of mythology that is cosmogonic and allegorical, and that consists in the mysterious personification of the forces of nature. This mythology is not homogeneous with the two others, which are the same but at different periods. It appears to be entirely transplanted, with a foreign origin, the result of the communication of Greece with Egypt and Phoe-

---

of Nausicaa, and even with the corruption that informed the witticisms of Mercury, because it implies primitive crudeness rather than corruption. Calypso contents herself with coercing the attention of a lover who passes his days weeping on the river, whom she obliges to devote his nights to her by promising him, as the price of his attention, her permission to leave her.

27. Jonsius, *Observ. de stylo Homeri*; Dawes, *Misc. crit.* See also the doubts of Aristarchus relative to the twenty-fourth book of the *Iliad* (V, v, 60); and Heyne, *Excurs. ad Iliad*, XXIV, p. 670.

28. *Iliad*, XXIV, 463, 464.

29. What confirms us in this conjecture is that the mythology of this last book is different from that of the preceding ones, under various aspects. In the twenty-three earlier ones, it is Iris who is the messenger of the gods; in the twenty-fourth, Mercury replaces her. Now, it is known that this function was not attributed to Mercury until a second period of Greek mythology (see above, bk. V, ch. 5, n. 60). The author of the *Odyssey* and the *Theogony* (v. 68) are poets of this second period; and the oldest of the Greek tragedians characterizes it by calling Mercury the new messenger of the new master of the gods (Aeschylus, *Prom.*, 941).

nicia. It is principally found in the twenty-second book of the *Iliad*, the *Theomachia*,[30] in the fable of Briareus[31] (which is incompatible with what Homer says elsewhere about the power of Jupiter);[32] in the metamorphoses of Proteus,[33] which Diodorus said was a copy of those of an Egyptian god;[34] in the marriage of Jupiter and Juno, which the same Diodorus recognized as a part of the cosmogony of Egypt;[35] and, finally, in the island inhabited by Aeolus and his twelve sons and daughters.[36] This third mythology, however, is found in only a very incomplete and fragmented manner in the Homeric poems.

30. Listen to one of the most learned commentators on Homer concerning this subject, in libro XXI. "*Multa nova et peregrina, nemo non qui ad carmen legendum accessit, observare debuit maxime concursu moxque conflictu Deorum facto, inductis etiam Diis qui, superioribus carminibus rerum Trojanarum et Achivarum nullam curam habuerant. Pugna Achillis, παρα ποταμον, ad Scamandrum fluvium novi omnino generis est carmen, ut nec minus pugna Deorum, quae manifesta habet vestigia alieni ortus et diversi ingenii. Magna sunt phantasmata, sed judicium poetae parum severum, nec cum carmine reliquo Iliaco fabula est conglutinata*" (Heyne, ad *Iliad*, XXIV; Exc., II, p. 785).

31. *Iliad*, I, 396–406.

32. Ibid., VIII, 18.

33. *Odyss.*, IV, 385, 480.

34. Diod., I, 20–24.

35. Ibid.

36. *Odyss.*, X, 1–12. The golden chain of Jupiter and his threats to Juno are manifestly priestly allegories, which have the greatest connection with Indian allegories (Creuzer, I, 116, 120). Thus, the commentators who have written before we had any notion of the traditions and teachings of India have found these images completely foreign to Homer's manner, without being able to account for the difference. One still discerns traces of these importations in what is said relative to Vulcan. We have spoken (bk. V, ch. 5) of the walking tripods, which seemed to us to be borrowed from the oriental imagination. We also could have spoken of the golden virgins that aid him in his work (*Iliad*, XVIII, 376); of the bellows that operate by themselves (ibid., 470). He had forged a golden dog, a living dog, that guarded the sacred woods of Jupiter in Crete (schol., *ad* XIX, 518). Finally, the shield he made for Achilles contains the sky, the earth, the sea, the ocean, men, animals, plants, all of nature. There is nothing more like the representations of Brahma; but the Greek poet only made them the subjects of a poetic description, and Vulcan remains a grotesque deity. What would complete the demonstration, if such were needed, that Homer intended nothing concerning scientific or cosmogonic subtleties is the complete absence of any personification of love. If this notion were known, how could the poet not have made frequent use of it in connection with the quarrels and reconciliations of the gods? How many brilliant or charming portraits of love would have been occasioned? How could love have remained indifferent to the wound of his mother, Venus, or inactive in the troubles of Paris and Helen? But Homer speaks neither of the son of Venus nor of a cosmogonic Eros; these are later inventions that Hesiod gathered together.

We, however, will leave these conjectures to those who are practiced in them, and who delight in reflecting upon such matters. What is important to us, and what we believe we have demonstrated, is that there are essential differences between the religion of the *Iliad* and that of the *Odyssey*, and that the two poems cannot be attributed to the same period or to the same author.

Some perhaps will ask, if the *Odyssey* belongs to a more advanced period of polytheism, why have we sometimes drawn passages from it to support our assertions concerning the original polytheism? This is because when we perceived in a few passages of the *Odyssey* the same views that we found in the *Iliad*, we thought that some fragments of the latter found their way into the former. However, when we found in the *Odyssey* different views, since these were always on the advanced or progressive side of the ledger, we recognized the effect of time and the necessary progress of ideas. When we recognized in a poem two contradictory opinions, this was not because the two coexisted, it was because the poet made use of each as demanded, according to the effect he wished to produce, and which would provide the most beauty. However, when in a long and even vast poem such as the *Iliad*, which embraces almost all aspects of human existence, you encounter only one teaching, compact, uniform, that is contradicted at most in only a few details, it is obvious that this view was the sole dominant one at the time described by the author. What the poet does not say can in this matter be a more telling proof than what he does say. In matters of chronology, positive proof can sometimes be less convincing than negative.

CHAPTER 4

Conclusion

The *Iliad* and the *Odyssey* belong to different periods. During the interval that separated them, the social state had changed: mores were softened; the various sorts of knowledge increased; and by this very fact, religion had to change. The objections that seemed to overthrow our system in fact confirm it. The religious form that their original martial civilization had imposed upon the Greeks did not suffice for their descendants, who were less bellicose and more civilized. The religious sentiment continued its work, grew, and purified the form; and equilibrium was established between it and the social state.

BOOK IX

ON THE PRIESTLY RELIGIONS
COMPARED WITH INDEPENDENT
POLYTHEISM

CHAPTER 1

The Purpose of This Book

In the preceding volume we saw the notions that human intelligence given over to its own forces and enjoying an entire liberty conceives concerning the figure and character of the gods, concerning destiny and the other life. Now we are going to examine how these notions are modified under the empire of priests.

CHAPTER 2

On the Form of the Gods in the Priestly Religions

In these religions, the form of the gods remains stationary. The Egyptians, says Synesius,[1] did not permit either workers or sculptors to represent the gods as they wished, for fear that they would depart from the received form. According to Denis of Halicarnassus, the Gauls never allowed themselves the slightest innovation in their rites or in the images of their gods.[2]

The motive for this prohibition is easy to understand, and the precaution taken was not without its rationale. If the imagination could have exercised itself freely vis-à-vis the divine forms, it soon would have extended its ungovernable activity to their moral qualities or their metaphysical attributes; in this way, the slightest alteration in their appearance would have been the fecund source of other, more important and open-ended changes. For the priesthood, it was better that the imagination, enslaved and controlled, would hit its head against immutable idols. These gods, who suffered no changes while everything changed around them, thus seemed to defy time by their ancient appearance. The immobile monuments of bygone ages, they filled souls with respect, appearing to emerge from the darkness of a deep night.

As a consequence, while anthropomorphism replaces fetishism in independent

---

1. *De Providentia*, p. 73. He adds that priests made their kings swear when they consecrated them, that they would never introduce a foreign custom under any pretext whatsoever. See also Plato (*De legib.*, II). In Egypt, observes a German critic, once the priests had laid out the figure of a divinity with all its attributes, or the narrative of a fable with all its parts, artists would work in accordance with this model for thousands of years without changing the least detail, not even the bearing of the personages; as a result, even to the time of the Ptolemies, no one could distinguish any distinct periods of painting, sculpture, or architecture.

2. Denis of Hal., bk. VIII.

polytheism and erases almost all its traces, it is preserved as something of a baseline in priestly religions, and is prolonged even in the midst of civilization's progress.[3] Everywhere that the priesthood is the supreme authority, the embellishment of the divine forms is rejected as a sacrilege. The spades and the tree trunks adored by the Gauls in no period took on more elegant features.[4] And even when the Gauls familiarized themselves with what we could call a barbarous luxury, the ancient figures always attracted greater veneration than the statues of gold erected next to them.[5]

Priests, moreover, do not like to give gods a human form. They always wish to put between worshippers and idols a greater distance. What we said earlier[6] about the mysteriousness that resides in animals makes them more suitable to inspire religious sentiments, including terror, than would beings like us.

The Egyptians, who raised temples to almost all living creatures, never placed man among their divinities.[7] Greek writers who spoke of men who were deified among the Scythians have fallen into an error that is nowadays well known.[8]

3. Starro, a god the Frisons invoked against floods and storms, was only a piece of wood (Sulzer, p. 291). The god of the air among the Mexicans, Quetzalcoatl, was a serpent covered with green feathers. The Mercury of Phoenicia was a fish with the head of a boar, topped with a crown (Proclus, in *Tim. Firmic.*, l. II, c. 7). Dagon had the same form, and Jupiter that of a sparrow hawk. The Teusar-Poulat, fetishes of pagan Britain, were *genii* in the form of cows, dogs, or other domestic animals (Cambry, I, 72).

4. *Simulachraque moesta Deorum*
Arte carent, coesisque exstant informia truncis
(*Phars.*, III)
Et robora numinis instar
Barbarici
(Claud., *Laud. Stilic.*, I, 128)

5. These gold statues existed before Caesar (Polyb., II, 32). He is accused, not without plausibility, of having stolen several, and having seduced his fellow citizens with the gold of Gaul (Suet., *Caes.*, 54).

6. Bk. II, ch. 2.

7. Two passages, one from Porphyry (*De abstin.*, IV, 9), the other from Eusebius (*Praep. Ev.*, III, 4–12), seem to contradict this claim; but in the first place, these authors restrict the worship of man to a single city named Anabin; and in the second place, they belong to a period that allows us to give little value to their testimony. According to Herodotus (II, 142), the priests of Egypt denied any appearance of the gods under a human form during 340 generations of the Piromis, when the gods governed the universe directly by themselves. The idol of Anabin was probably not a man but an ape of the species of cynocephalae (de Pauw, *Rech. Sur les Egypt. et les Chinois*, I).

8. Immortality among the Scythians was the privilege of those who died a violent death or who perished on the altar. They were considered messengers sent to the gods. The Greeks, imbued with their ideas of apotheoses, saw in these victims deified heroes. It is thus that Lucian says of Zamolxis

Nonetheless, the priesthood sooner or later yields to the natural impulse of the human spirit. What is most perfect in the eyes of men is the human form:[9] priests end by clothing their divinities in it.[10] Still, in their ceremonies they recall vestiges of earlier times.[11] Their gods always retain some remnants of their former deformities;[12] and allegories or fables explain these persistent monstrosities. Shiva having in a fit of rage (as we saw in bk. VII, ch. 5) cut off the head of Daksha, his father-in-law; when peace was concluded he agreed to restore him to life. But the head cut off during the battle had fallen into the fire, and a ram's head had been substituted for the human head.[13] The restored Daksha was thus disfigured. In

---

that he became a god after having been a slave, which simply meant that this slave had been sacrificed. See Herodotus, IV, 94–95.

9. This preference on the part of man for his own form is noted by all the mythologies. God made man in his own image (Genesis). *Os homini sublime dedit* (Ovid). "The divinities that stir in the bosom of the Ocean beseeched the creator to give them a form. He shows them that of a horse, a cow, of all the animals in succession; they were not satisfied by them. Finally, he presented that of man, and all were immediately content" (Rigveda).

10. We have already observed that the human form is the attribute of the last incarnations of Vishnu. The same progression strikes us in Syria. Derceto is first half-fish, half-female; soon she is a woman from head to toe. And we will see her form further complicated when we treat the confusion of the two polytheisms.

11. It was said above that the Egyptian priests employed heads of wolves, dogs, and sparrow hawks in their festivals, and that the magi, decked out in skins of bears, lions, and tigers, in their mysteries took the name of these animals.

12. Erlik-Khan, in the Lamaic mythology (Pallas, *Mongol. Voel-kersch*, II, 54) and Huitzilopochtli among the Mexicans (Clavigero, bk. I) are a composite of human and animal; the Phoenician Astarte had the horns of a bull; Saturn, the head of an ape and the tail of a boar; Prithvi, who in India presides over agriculture, often took the form of a cow. The sun among the Chaldeans was a man with two heads and a tail (Beger *ad* Selden, p. 257). Oannes of the Phoenicians was a fish with two human feet and the voice of a man (Hellad., *ap.* Phot., Selden, *De diis Syris*, III). Of the children of Shiva, one is an elephant, another an ape. The Mithra of the Persians has the head of a lion (Luctatius, in Statii, *Theb.*, I, 715); Anubis, of a dog; Typhon, of a crocodile (on this god, see the investigations of Mr. Champollion). Ganeza, the grandson of the Himalaya, the mountain that is so celebrated in the geography, mythology, and history of India (*Asiat. Res.*, III, 40), has the head of an elephant like Poulear (Dubois, II, 421–22). The Ganges is, like Derceto (see above, note 10), half-female and half-fish. The demigod apes, the allies of Rama, are sometimes purely animal, sometimes a mixture of the beast and the human (Guigniaut, pp. 202, 719–25).

13. *Asiat. Res.*, VI, 476–77. The author of the journal *Le Catholique*, who arranges as he pleases what he compiled on India, sees in the fable a memory of a struggle between the two cults. Daksa, he says, pontiff of Brahma, was eaten by Shiva. Later, there was reconciliation, etc. (XXIV, 294). This

order to explain the form of the goddess Ganga,[14] half-female, half-fish, the Brahmins recount that Shiva had transformed an immense flood that had come from the sweat of his brow and placed it on her head, out of fear that it would flood the entire world.[15]

The priesthood therefore always protests against the attribution of the human form to the gods whose worship they control. In the religions they dominate, this form is only secondary; their mysterious significance is the essential thing. It is the opposite in independent religions.[16]

This constant struggle by the priesthood marks the form of the gods with a quadruple mark.

Ancient fetishism contributes various elements that are sacralized.[17]

More refined, the symbolizing spirit expresses divine qualities by images that suggest them.[18]

---

hypothesis is as false and absurd as that of Sainte-Croix concerning the religious wars between the Greeks and the colonies. No doubt there was an abolition of the worship of Brahma, and a proscription of the Brahmins, at a time and in circumstances we do not know; but to interpret in detail as historical events pure fables that have survived from fetishism, and then were invested with a mystical meaning, is a critical hardiness that nothing authorizes. Daksa, in the form of a billy goat, was a fetish; Daksa, the grandfather of Shiva, was a popular god; Daksa, diving into the great Whole, ends by being a pantheistic symbol.

14. The Ganges.

15. For other Indian fables that owe their origin to the same cause, see Hamilton, *New Account of the East-Ind.*, I, 268–77; Sonnerat, I, 153–54; Kaempfer, *Hist. du Japon*, German trans., II, 310.

16. When the gods cease having animal forms, one sees them in their train or serving as a mount. When the worship of spears fell into disuse among the peoples of the North, the gods were represented with a spear in hand. In India, Shiva is mounted on a bull, Brahma on a swan (Paulin, *Syst. braman.*; Sonnerat, I), Cama, love, on an elephant (Colebrooke, *Asiat. Res.*, IV, 415). In the two cases, the form of the god becomes either a symbol (Montfaucon, *Ant. expl.*, I, 22) or one of its attributes. The Indians of our day are still so imbued with these ideas that, seeing some saints of Christianity accompanied by an animal, they attributed to these saints, like their own gods, miraculous transformations.

17. See bk. VII, ch. 5.

18. Porphyry, according to Bardesanes (*De Styge*, *ap.* Stob., *Phys.*, I, 4; Paulin, *Syst. brahm.*, p. 27), gives us a description of Brahma that indicates the effort of the symbolic spirit to express by the figures of the gods all their functions and forces. This creator of the world is represented not only as hermaphroditic but as surrounded by all the objects over which he exercises his empire. At the right is the sun, at the left is the moon, on his two hands extended as a cross one sees winged *genii*, stars, and different parts of the world: heaven, the earth, the sea, the mountains, the rivers, the animals, the plants, all of nature. The Phoenician Saturn had four eyes in front and four behind, two feathers on the head, four wings of which two were folded and two extended. The number of his eyes signified, said the priests,

Then come the scientific allegories, often a hidden part but inseparable from the priestly cults.[19]

Finally, these different elements are put to work and modified by the always-present inclination of the priesthood to fill the souls of the people with surprise and terror. The figure of Chandika or Cali, nicknamed in India the goddess with terrifying teeth, obviously had this purpose. When someone offers her sacrifices, says the Kalika Puran,[20] he must place beside her two assistants who have three inflamed eyes, yellow bodies, red heads, enormous ears, long and menacing teeth, a necklace of human skulls, and who, armed with tridents and axes, hold in their right hand cut-off heads, and in the left, vases of blood. It was with the same in-

---

his uninterrupted surveillance. One of his feathers indicated his supremacy over the intellectual world, the other his authority over the physical universe. His extended and folded wings designated him as the principle of movement and rest. Priestly explanations of the same sort of subtlety can account for the figure of the gods in the Lamaic mythology. Erlik-Khan, about whom we have already spoken, has the mane of the lion, a symbol of force; the visage of a buffalo or a billy goat; an enormous phallus, the emblem of fecundity; two heads to indicate intelligence; and four arms, the sign of the inevitable fulfillment of the will (Pallas, *Nachr. ueb. die Mongol. Voel-kersch*, II, 54). Dagon, by his fish tail, expresses the quality of fecundity (Selden, *De diis Syris*, pp. 261–63; Guasco, *De l'usage des statues*). The Indian Ganeza, god of wisdom, had an elephant's head (Colebrooke, *Asiat. Res.*, IV, 415). Scanda or Cartikeya had six arms; Eswara seventeen; Dourga ten (Laflotte, p. 209); Bhavani eight, with which she held sabers, swords, spears, and axes. Buddha shows himself to his favorites with four arms; Agni or Agnini, the god of fire, the purifier, has the same number (Sonnerat, I, 157). Brahma is always represented with several arms and several heads, like the Dschoeschik of Tibet (Pallas, *Nachr. ueb. die Mongol. Voel-kersch*, II, 54); and such is the inclination of priests to represent superior intelligences as many-headed that they have invented gods of thirty-six heads, forming three stages or ranks. The Tibetan Chenrezig has eleven in the form of a pyramid. The one that is at the peak is surrounded with rays and has a shining visage around which floats hair of azure. It has nine arms: four carry a flower, a bow, arrows, and a vase full of water; three hold a chapelet, a wheel, and a ring; the last two join hands as in prayer (Pallas, ibid.). This tendency to create many-headed deities is not restricted to the peoples of the South and the East. Svetovid, the god of the sun among the Slavic peoples, had four heads and regarded the four parts of the world; Porevith had two, and Porenetz, independently of his four heads, had a face on his chest, and holding his chin in his right hand, touched the stars with his left (Sax. Gramm., *Hist. Dan.*, XIV, 319–27).

19. Thus in Phoenicia, Mercury recalls the succession of days and nights by the white color of one of his arms and the black color of the other (Procl., in *Tim. Firmic.*). The bull's skin that covered the head of Astarte alluded to the moon (Dupuis, III; Creuzer, II, 106), and the ten monsters of the Cingalese were related to the ten constellations (Knox, pp. 30 & 76). One can see in Goerres the astronomical explanations of these different figures (I, 291–95).

20. *Asiat. Res.*, pp. 371–90.

tention that the Vandal priests represented their Pustrich as a malevolent dwarf emitting waves of burning fire through torrents of smoke.[21]

Sometimes, however, the priesthood betrays a contrary desire. If it desires that the forms of the gods remain stationary, which maintains them in their monstrous state; if it desires that they remain terrible, which renders them objects of terror; it also regrets, when it compares them to mortals, not having clothed them with a superior beauty, and it attempts to hide the deformity under luxury. The Greek divinities are simple and elegant, the idols of barbarians are overcharged with ornaments and decoration; and it is by marvelous traits—by the immobility of their members and look, by the faculty of flying in the air without the wind aiding or their clothing being disturbed, that is, by features that do not come from the perfection of art—that the priests distinguish the celestial race. The Mahabharata shows us gods who compete with Nala for the hand of Damayanti, gods surrounded by a constant splendor, crowned with always fresh flowers because no breeze makes them stir; their gaze fixed, they walk above the ground without their feet touching it, while Nala, covered with sweat and dust, bears only a faded crown; his trembling feet rest on the earth, and his body projects a shadow that confirms his nature's inferiority.[22]

The habit of offering public worship to strange or bizarre forms leads artists who work under the orders of priests to introduce parallels in the inferior ranks of the mythological hierarchy. Hence, that host of imaginary animals[23] found in all the priestly mythologies, while there are none that are indigenous to Greek polytheism.[24]

Sometimes the religious sentiment, by means of an effort wholly disproportion-

21. Frenzel, *De diis Soraborum*, cap. 17; Sagittarii, *Antiq. gent.*, p. 6; Pfeffercorn, *Thüring. Gesch.*, p. 59; Nerreter, *Heiden-tempel*, p. 1084.

22. Mahabharata, the episode of Damayanti.

23. See bk. IV, ch. 12; bk. VI, chs. 5 & 7. The king of the birds, with a piercing look and golden plumage, the bird *garouda* or *garouva*, a fantastical combination of man and eagle (or sparrow hawk) (*Asiat. Res.*, I, 200; XIV, 467–68), is the great blue bee (ibid., I, 200), the horse Ourschivara with two or four heads. It is remarkable that the animals of the Apocalypse are perfectly similar to those of the priestly religions. In the ruins of Persepolis, a city whose rubble attests to a luxury brought to the highest degree of refinement, one finds no pure and regular form: the regarding eye is everywhere exhausted by strange combinations, of animals with the body of a lion, the feet of a horse, wings, the head of a man with a long beard, with a diadem and a tiara (*Voy.* of Chardin). For our purposes, it matters little if these figures were indigenous to Media and Persia, or if they crossed the chain of mountains that separates Bactriana from India in order to enter the countries (Heeren, *Ideen*, etc., I, 295).

24. The Sphinx, the Gorgon, the Chimera are obviously inventions foreign to Greece.

ate to the times, experiences the desire and need of rejecting every likeness.[25] The priests, however, take hold of it in order to direct it according to their will. It can be useful to them, in that it makes them more solidly established as the sole intermediaries between men and the invisible deities. But as this conceit is wholly disproportionate to the state of learning and understanding, it cannot be maintained; the use of simulacra has always triumphed.[26] One cannot provide one example of a people who never had idols, even though one can cite several among whom the hatred of idols was a religious principle.

Those writers who have celebrated this repugnance to giving gods a material form, as proof of an élan toward more purified ideas, have not been simply mistaken; but the error began when they transformed a vague sentiment into a notion of the mind. Examining the question more closely, they would have seen that since the intellect was not strong enough to maintain itself at this height, there was no advantage for the priesthood to reduce this hatred of idols to a maxim. On one hand, this maxim would have been constantly violated in practice; and, on the other, invisible and immaterial gods were much less morally valuable in the hands of priests, as we will prove in the following chapter, than the visible and material gods of the free religions.

25. The inhabitants of Holstein had such an aversion for idols and churches enclosed by walls that Charlemagne, wanting to have one built and the symbols of the faith found in it, was obliged to have a village built and Christians put in it, with the order to defend their church. But this hatred of idols was not, as has been believed, peculiar to the people of the North. The religious sentiment, being everywhere the same, has made everywhere the same attempts, and priests have accommodated themselves to these attempts in order to interpret and profit from them. At Hierapolis, where all the other gods had statues, there were two empty thrones reserved for the sun and the moon. When the author of a treatise on the goddess of Syria (which is attributed to Lucian) was informed of the motive for this difference, he was told that these divinities, always visible in the heavens, did not need to be presented to the gaze of men, while simulacra were needed for the gods that the human eye could not see anywhere.

26. In order to satisfy the religious sentiment that rejects idols, as well as the imagination that needs them, the gods, say the Cingalese, have neither flesh nor bones, nor solid bodies, even though people believe they see hair on their heads, teeth in their mouths, and skin on their bodies that is as brilliant and luminous as the sun. What men see is thus only an illusion: the gods are still invisible and incorporeal (*Asiat. Res.*, VII, 35).

CHAPTER 3

On the Character of the Gods in the Priestly Religions

If, before having put forth for our readers the character of the gods in the religions that are subject to priests, we had proposed to them the following problem: there are two sorts of religion; one is the result of the conjectures, fears, and hopes of an ignorant multitude, one given over to all the errors its ignorance can inflict upon it; the other is the long-meditated work of the elite of the human race organized in corporations, who have gathered all the knowledge they could have acquired by tireless effort, profound reflection, the discoveries of science, the subtleties of metaphysics, and the refinements of contemplation: in which of these religions would the character of the gods be the purest, the most sublime, the most re-moved from all imperfection and vice? The preference would be given to the sec-ond. Nonetheless, when we query history, we see the facts range themselves against this answer.

If pride, venality, and perfidy are the distinctive traits of the Homeric gods, those of the priesthood, no less mercenary and no less proud, are a thousand times more capricious, vindictive, and deceiving. The priests need their cruelty, their ca-priciousness, and their capacity to defraud in order to subjugate in their name the credulous populace. Their esprit de corps instructs them concerning this necessary condition of their existence and power. From all this, wherever they rule, results a religion that is more extravagant and oppressive than in the countries they do not dominate.

Instruments of a corporation whose goal is an unlimited empire, the gods must will what this body wills, which is to subjugate man in small as well as large things, in his thoughts as well as his external actions. Thus, there is nothing that compares to the minutiae they require, to the arbitrariness of their will. Countless practices fill each instant of the day, and precede or follow all of life's actions.

The forms of worship of priestly religion bear an imprint of abasement and humiliation foreign to independent polytheism. One cannot enter into most of the sacred forests of Germany without being bound with irons. It was forbidden to stand erect, or even on bended knee, in these sanctuaries. No one dared to leave, except by rolling on the ground.[1] Such displays of servitude were the only homage deemed worthy of the gods. However, the intercourse between these gods, whom the priesthood thus wishes to elevate, and the mortals who worship them, often degrades the former and corrupts the latter. The former imperiously demand victims and sacrifices;[2] and these offerings are compulsory for the latter.

The gods of the priests, like those of Homer, have the mores of the people who worship them. Those of the Indians find their happiness in repose; those of the Scandinavians are bellicose and greedy for carnage.[3] Idly lounging on brilliantly white waves, or retired on the mountain that serves as their Olympus,[4] the Indian gods draw harmonious sounds from the *vounëi*,[5] the rival of the lyre Apollo plays at the banquets of Jupiter. Odin, on the contrary, seated on the seas, holding a sword in his powerful hand, exudes only storms and devastation. His fiery hair is tossed by the wind. His eyes burn like lightning on his dark face, and his voice is like the sound of the far-off torrent.[6]

---

1. Tacit., *German.*, 39.

2. Whatever you do, whatever you eat, whatever you desire, give me an offering, says Krishna to his disciple (Bhag. Gita, French trans., p. 92). All the Brahmins' ruses, and all the fables they recount to obtain gifts from the faithful, rest on the venality and greediness of the gods (see Dubois, II, 362). At the time of the year when the overflowing Cauvery floods the burning and sterile plains that run along its banks, and there spreads life and fecundity, toward the middle of July, the inhabitants come in droves to its banks in order to congratulate the river and to offer it gifts of all sorts: silver for its expenses, cloth for its vestments, jewels for its decoration, rice, cakes, fruits, brooms and the like, baskets, vases, etc. (Dubois, II, 301). One would liken it to a venal or coquettish woman who granted her favors to the flattery that pleases her or the generosity that enriches her.

3. One of the surnames of Alfadur is Kerian, the destroyer; others are Nicar, the conqueror; Vidar, the devastator; Suidor, the incendiary. Being confused with Alfadur, Odin was called the god of battles (Edda, 28th fable), even though properly speaking it was Thor who presided at war; but the concept of a peaceful god directing the universe could not be admitted among tribes exclusively devoted to expeditions of piracy and pillage. In the Scandinavian language there are thirty epithets for expressing the martial attributes of Odin.

4. Mount Meru.

5. The *vounëi* is a species of small Indian harp used by the superior castes, and especially the Brahmins (Dubois, I, 72–73).

6. Edda. Several traits of this description are found in the poems of Ossian, where Scandinavia is named Lochlin and Odin, Loda.

The peoples of the North and the West assemble under great trees to conduct their civil and judicial affairs. Their gods render justice under an ash tree.[7] In Homer, Minerva and Juno sometimes go on foot, sometimes in a chariot; the gods of India ride in chariots that move themselves.[8] Shiva and Parvati would not have been able to cross the ocean and regain heaven if Daksa had not loaned them his chariot.[9] But Skadi, wife of Niord, grasped her bow, and attaching her skates to her agile feet, jumped from heaven to race over the icy tops, hunting wild beasts.[10] Women in the North practice medicine; therefore in the Edda the doctor of the gods is a woman.[11] In general, among the people of the North, this sex enjoys a greater consideration than among the Greeks,[12] and the goddesses in Valhalla have greater credit than in Olympus.

Among the Greeks, we have seen Apollo do penance for the murder of a serpent felled by his blows; Odin, who killed the giant Ymir in order to create the world, also needed such an expiation, and the death of Balder was explained in this way by the mythologists.[13] In India, Indra, who sullied her guilty hands with the blood of her companions, plunged into the waters in order to atone for her crime.[14]

The foods of the gods are modeled on those of men. In Homer, wine gives them almost as much pleasure as nectar; Odin's companions become drunk on beer, and among the Hebrews, who despite the efforts of Moses had adopted many of the customs and locutions of their neighbors, the altar is called the table of God, and the offering, his bread;[15] and salt is necessary for all the offerings, because without it no aliment is tasty to man.[16] These foods are eaten with an eagerness that betrays a devouring appetite. The gods of the Ramayana run in droves to take their

7. Edda, 8th fable.

8. *Asiat. Res.*, X, 150.

9. Ibid., XI, 56.

10. Edda, 12th fable.

11. Ibid., 28th fable.

12. Mallet, *Introd. à l'hist. du Danem.*, p. 272.

13. Mone, *Symbol.*, 421. Here perhaps there is a cosmogonic idea, but it changes nothing in the effect of the fable. Ymir is chaos or unorganized material. Odin kills him in order to form the universe with its members. The death of Balder (the sun) is one of the physical revolutions that threaten to overturn creation and return it to chaos.

14. Ramayana, p. 270.

15. Mal., I, 12; Num., 28, 2; Ezek., 44, 67.

16. Lev., II, 13.

part in the sacrifice;[17] and the peoples of Bohemia, in their complaints against Charlemagne, said: He forbade us from preparing their evening meals for our hungry gods.[18]

The gods of the priesthood are not endowed with unlimited force. Their efforts to draw the bow of Rama are in vain.[19] Thor needs to put on his magical belt in order to regain his vigor,[20] as does Juno to rest with her horses, after having split the clouds in order to hasten the taking of Troy;[21] and Vidar, like Mercury, owes the rapidity of his flight to his miraculous sandals, which support him in the heavens and on the seas.[22]

Sad infirmities threaten these gods. Hother is deprived of the light of day.[23] They succumb to fatigue. The meadow where Rama and his faithful spouse rest during their travels and bathe their tired feet[24] still shades the mountain of Kimur. Misfortune strikes them. Often struck by an unforeseen calamity, with incredible speed they make seven circuits of the world, uttering piercing cries.[25] Freya, sister and wife of Odin, desolated like Ceres or Isis, crosses all climes seeking her spouse—hence the different names she has among the different peoples. Shiva and Vishnu one day lost the beautiful Parvati, and shed so many tears that a lake was formed, to our day still called the lake of tears. These imperfect divinities are subject to fright. Sarasvati, lost in the desert and pursued by horribly shrieking demons, hid in terror in the depths of the earth, and only reappeared much later in the form of a flower.[26] The greatest of evils, old age, does not spare these gods. An apple rejuvenates them; it is under the guardianship of the goddess Idun. Once it was taken from them, and soon their hair grew white and their hands trembled under the weight of their weapons.[27] Their sight is weak and limited. When the

17. Pp. 42, 179.

18. Ancient Bohemian poems, published in German by Wenzel (Prague, 1819). For a host of other examples of this imitation of human mores and customs, see Dubois, II, 377 & 410.

19. Ramayana, p. 550.

20. Mallet, *Introd.*, p. 79.

21. *Iliad*, IV, 26–28.

22. Edda, 15th fable.

23. Ibid.

24. *Asiat. Res.*, VII, 60–61.

25. Ibid., VII, 477.

26. Ibid.

27. Edda, 14th fable.

Ganges, leaving heaven, came to flow on earth, they abandoned their heavenly abodes in order to reassure themselves firsthand of this prodigious change;[28] and when Jehovah wanted to survey the prophets, he got up in the night and rose in the morning, like a mortal master who checks on his lazy servants.[29]

Immortality, the dubious attribute of the gods of Greece, is not a more assured privilege of the priestly gods. They work constantly to acquire *amrita*, the marvelous potion that confers immortality upon them, which fate has hidden in the depths of the sea.[30] Balder dies pierced by the bramble; the gods deliberate whether they should subject Loki to a painful death;[31] and Freya trembles for the days of Odin.[32]

Thus limited in their physical forces, these gods are even more so in their moral faculties. Gna is their messenger when they wish to know what happens among men,[33] as Iris is the messenger of the gods of the *Iliad*. Odin surveys the earth from the summit of his throne; but it is two crows perched upon his shoulders who recount to him all that they observe.[34] A giant bothers him because of its renown. The god wishes to determine whether the knowledge of his rival surpasses his own. Freya restrains him: she counsels him against this dangerous contest. Imperfect gods, he answers her, often have need of human intelligence.[35] She therefore willingly accompanies him. Can you, she exclaims, have enough knowledge?[36] But the very source where one draws knowledge is not in her power. Mimir guards it; Odin cannot approach it without him allowing it, and he is forced to leave an eye as surety in order to disarm this jealous watcher.[37] Error therefore is often the lot of these gods. In the first age, the aim of the Eternal was missed: its will was circumvented.[38] This idea of a god who is mistaken or whom the ruses of the creature

28. Ramayana, p. 396.

29. Kings, IV, XVII, 10; XXIII, 6, 27.

30. Bhagavatam, bk. 8; Sonnerat, I, 134; supplement to the Bhagavad Gita by Wilkins.

31. Edda, 2nd fable.

32. Mallet, *Introd.*, p. 275.

33. Edda, 8th fable.

34. Ibid., 20th fable. Among the Persians, it is equally a crow that is seated on the shoulder of the father of the gods and inspires him with wisdom (*Shahnameh* of Ferdowsi).

35. Sax. Gramm., III, 65, 66.

36. Mallet, *Introd.*, pp. 270–73.

37. Edda, 8th fable.

38. Preface to the Bhagavad Gita, p. viii.

succeed in deceiving recalls the tale of Prometheus and proves the resemblance of these two polytheisms in one of the most important aspects.[39]

But it is above all by their passions or their vices that these priestly divinities are similar to the gods of the *Iliad*: neither debauchery nor cruelty nor perjury gives them pause. You give yourself to the desires of human beings more than any woman, says Loki to the goddess Idun.[40] Lakshmi, the wife of Vishnu, taken by an unbridled desire for Kamadeva, leaves her spouse and shamelessly pursues the lover, who rejects her ardent caresses with disdain.[41] In the North, Odin dishonors the rank he occupies by his flighty loves; the other gods deprive him of rule and choose another master for themselves; and it is only after ten years that he regains their goodwill and, chasing away his rival, his authority.[42] This tradition probably has a historical basis, and we will have occasion to return to it. But in the mind and heart of the people, it tended to convince them of the irregularities and license of their gods. In the South, Brahma was guilty of theft and suffered the penalty of a shameful theft, the loss of his heritage. These gods do not stop before perjury. Disdaining their own oaths, they kill the architect who built the citadel in which they live;[43] and such is their reputation for perfidy that a warrior they called to their midst did not want to enter among them except fully armed.[44] Bound by solemn engagements to Ravana, Brahma set about breaking them from the very moment he undertook them.[45] This same Brahma, far from being touched by the sacrifices of a pious monarch, sought to discover some negligence or defect that would render the sacrifice useless.[46] By means of his signs, Odin sows discord between a king

---

39. Indian mythology teems with anecdotes in which mortals take the gods for dupes. Soane, desirous of the beautiful Narmada, another name for Bhavani, asks for this goddess in marriage. Bhavani sends her slave Johilla to examine the entourage and pomp that attend her lover. Johilla, struck by the beauty of Soane, disguises herself as Bhavani, who, furious at this infidelity, disfigures the guilty slave and casts her lover in the waves. The tears of Johilla form a small river that bears her name (*Asiat. Res.,* VII, 102–3).

40. "Lokasenna."

41. *Asiat. Res.,* XI, 103–4.

42. Sax. Gramm., III.

43. *Gebrochen wurden Eide, Worte und Verspechungen Voluspa.* On the broken oaths of the Scandinavian gods, see Mone, p. 380.

44. *Eloge* of Haquin.

45. Ramayana, p. 183.

46. Ibid., p. 115.

of Sweden and a king of Denmark,[47] just as the son of Saturn deceived Agamemnon in order to avenge Achilles. While Indra, jealous of the austerities of a hermit, clothed a treacherous *genius* with the features of a courtesan in order to seduce him,[48] the god of the Jews blinded the sons of Heli so that they would not listen to the counsel of their father because he had determined to bring about their ruin.[49] He hardened the heart of Rehoboam in order to produce the division of his kingdom. He moved Pharaoh to disobedience, which caused his ruin.[50] He sent an evil spirit between Abimelech and the Shechimites: this is an expression exactly like those in Homer.[51]

It should be observed that the priesthood regularly makes it a merit of the gods that they possess and practice artifice and ruse.

Mohammed, who, despite the severity of his theism had borrowed his ideas on the divine nature from two religions elaborated by priests, calls God the most admirable of deceivers in more than one place.[52] This is understandable when one reflects that gods suspected of lying make priests who protect men from being deceived by them even more indispensable.

Envy torments them even in the midst of their splendor and power. The greatest

47. Sax. Gramm., VIII.

48. Ramayana, p. 532.

49. I Kings, 2, 24–25.

50. Exodus.

51. This similarity is also found in several passages of the Books of Kings and the Book of Judges. God calls together his angels to deliberate with them against Achab, whom he wishes to destroy by leading him into a war against the Syrians. After a long discussion, a spirit of lies presents itself, which will communicate deceptive words to the priests of Baal, who will influence Achab by promising a victory (Kings, XXII, 19–22). Elsewhere, God, the enemy of the Philistines, who lived at peace, inspires Samson with love for Delilah. His relatives are astonished at this sudden passion; but, says the Bible, it was God who sought a quarrel with the Philistines (Judg., XIV, 4).

52. "*Praestantissimus dolose agentium*" (Koran, cap. 3, v. 53; cap. 4, 156). See above (bk. VII, ch. 6, n. 1), where we indicate the natural cause of the admiration of primitive tribes for cunning and lying. Here we show how the priesthood profited from it. It is said elsewhere in the Koran: "We have cast them into uncertainty, and we have lied to them." In the catechism of the Druses (*Monit.* of 9 May 1808), the instructor asks the student: How is it said in the letter of Rhamar-Ebn-Djaich-el-Selimari that a heretic is the brother of God? Answer: It was a trap that God set for Rhamar to better deceive him and take his life; and later: The custom of God is to deceive some and enlighten others. Cali, in the epic poem by Sri-Harsa, "Naishadha," gains the kingdom of Nala, king of Nishada, by fraud.

crime, says the Ramayana, is pride,[53] which is to say: man's confidence in his own forces. Vishnu in his ninth incarnation mercilessly pursued a king whom he put to death despite his prayers; his sole fault was a too-constant prosperity. The followers of this god still celebrate this easy and cruel victory by a feast.[54] The Brahmins of the seven pagodas recount that the jealous gods flooded the city of King Malecheren, who had lavishly decorated his residence and with its magnificence rivaled the heavenly abode.[55] Do we not hear Neptune complaining to Jupiter of the wall raised by the Greeks around their vessels, and Jupiter reassuring him that he will destroy this proud work of men?[56]

Mexican idols fare no better. At the time of the great flood that submerged it, the country of Anahuac was inhabited by giants, a small number of whom sought refuge in the cavities of a mountain. Having emerged from this asylum, they wanted to celebrate their deliverance by the construction of a pyramid. The gods struck them with lightning. One sees in Serbian poems which are much more recent (although bearing the traces of an earlier mythology) traces of the envy of the gods. Maxim Zernojevitch is engaged to the daughter of the doge of Venice. His father, Ivan, announces in proud terms that he will come to see his daughter-in-law. "One will see me," he says, "under the walls of Venice with a thousand men. Venice will also send a thousand elite men to celebrate the glory of my son. But none will equal, none will appear more magnificent and more handsome than Maxim, the beloved son of his father." Destiny heard him, and suddenly a terrible disease disfigured the handsome Maxim. His father looked upon him, and the memory of his proud words came to his mind.

To envy and imposture is joined betrayal. The Mercury of the Germans allowed himself to be seduced by Marcus Aurelius.[57] When Bomilcar, a Carthagenian traitor, wanted to overturn the government of his fatherland, he multiplied ceremonies to seduce the gods.[58] We have already seen Xerxes, during his invasion of Greece, attempt to corrupt the tutelary divinities of this country by practicing the

---

53. Ramayana, p. 180.

54. Laflotte, pp. 172–80.

55. *Asiat. Res.*, I, 156–57. The Indian custom of never congratulating someone over his health or his success comes from the idea of the jealousy of the gods (Dubois, pp. 463, 464). On the same custom among modern Greeks, see bk. VII, ch. 6, n. 50.

56. *Iliad*, XII, 4, 9.

57. Xiphilin.

58. Diodorus.

rites of their cult. Thus priestly nations take against their gods the same absurd or injurious precautions that struck us among the Greeks.[59]

Besieged by Alexander, the Tyrians chained the statue of Apollo; and after mastering the city, the conqueror had its chains taken off, proclaiming him the friend of Alexander.[60]

To be sure, this custom of enchaining treacherous divinities, a custom whose popular meaning we will explore, also had a mysterious significance. What we have already said about the composition of priestly polytheism should have prepared our readers. The gods of these religions, symbols of the forces of nature, were chained in the periods when these forces seemed to decrease. These bonds were taken away when nature was deemed to take on new vigor. This double sense thus served the priesthood by satisfying learned men and contenting the people.

They said to the former that they by turns enchained and emancipated these symbolic simulacra in order to express the regularity of the seasons and the rebirth of the sun when, having defeated winter, it recommenced its annual course. They said to the others that divinities bound with chains could not desert them in order to aid their enemies.[61] But this last opinion, suited to vulgar understandings, alone dominated the public religion.

Gods so imperfect in their physical nature, so vicious by their moral attributes, could no more than those of the Greeks inspire their worshippers with profound and sincere veneration. Priestly traditions no less than the Homeric mythology are filled with tales that show men ready to revolt against the gods. In Scandinavia, they live huddled in a citadel, and their porter Heimdallr[62] closely watches the bridge[63] that facilitates entrance into their abode. Hothar and Biarcon challenge the entire Nordic Olympus, and even Odin himself, to combat.[64] Gylfus breaks the massive mace Thor holds in his hand. In India, the world is hardly created when a giant chases all the divinities from heaven and earth.[65] A mere mortal pierces

59. Diod., XIII, 28; XVIII, 7.

60. See bk. VII, ch. 6.

61. It is rather curious to compare these priestly explanations with those of Greek artists. See bk. VII, ch. 6.

62. Edda, 5th fable.

63. The rainbow.

64. Mallet, *Introd.*, p. 173.

65. *Asiat. Mag.*, I, 131.

their bodies with arrows.[66] Later, struck with terror at the appearance of a king covered with glory, whose austerities rendered him invincible,[67] they multiplied their eyes, their heads, and their arms—which brandished new weapons—in order to resist him.[68] In Egypt, finally, the gods transformed themselves into animals, hiding from the mortals who surpassed them in audacity and strength.[69] What a strange thing to say, yet true nonetheless! These absurdities, these extravagances, this degradation of the divine nature, prove—who would believe it!—the ascendancy of logic over priests, as well as over the people.[70] Their interest constrained them to make the gods passionate beings and, hence, vicious and unjust. Reasoning then obliged them to conceive of them as unhappy because they are unjust and passionate. The religious sentiment fought in vain against the imperfections the priestly religions attached to these idols; the reason that enlightens essayed in vain to make their attributes less incoherent or their conduct less scandalous. The priests oppose themselves. They prefer to frustrate the religious sentiment rather than modify a tradition, no matter how revolting it may have become; they prefer to stifle reason rather than sacrifice a single dogma.

They believe that they escape the consequences that result by lavishing grandiose epithets upon these perverse beings, which every narrative belies. What truly results is that, despite their systematic arrangement, in these religions there are more contradictions—and more palpable contradictions—than in the simple and crude beliefs of the human spirit. Despite the limits that circumscribe the physical forces of the divine essences, the priests proclaim them to be all-powerful; despite the jealousy that torments these envious divinities, they attribute to them an unlimited goodness; despite the vices that stain their moral character and the errors that darken their intellects, they call them perfectly just and perfectly wise beings; and despite the inevitable misfortunes that follow from disordered passions, they assign them supreme happiness. Thus, in all times, in priestly religions man finds himself painfully assaulted by discordant claims. Far from having gained some benefit from his submission to the priesthood, far from having been led by this

66. Ramayana, sect. 53, p. 549.

67. Viranrisinha.

68. *Asiat. Res.*, III, 46.

69. Diod., I, 2. We have rejected the use that Diodorus wanted to make of this fable to explain the worship of animals in Egypt; but it is precious as a popular teaching because it reveals the opinion adopted on the relations of gods and men.

70. See, on the subject of the power of logic among the Greeks, bk. VII, ch. 6; bk. 10.

privileged guide (the only one invested with the right to instruct him) to a better and purer doctrine, our blind and miserable race bent its head beneath fables that were a thousand times more extravagant than its imagination would have produced. It prostrated itself before beings who were more corrupt than the phantoms of its own dreams; it cast itself into a deeper abyss of superstitions and delirium, and the price of the abdication of its intelligence was, for centuries, slavery, error, and terror.

However, another reflection, one that has already occurred to us, presents itself. If man lavished his worship on gods who were imperfect, corrupt, and evildoing, is this not proof that the worship of some sort of divinity is a need of the soul? The Greeks, free from priests, perfected what they adored; the nations subject to the priesthood worshipped what was presented to them without being able to perfect anything. The absurdity of certain religious forms, far from being an argument against religion, is a demonstration that we cannot do without it. We find ourselves even less miserable under the most defective of these forms than we would if we were completely deprived. The history of the decadence of polytheism will prove it.

CHAPTER 4

On a Singular Notion Whose Traces Are Found in Greek Religion, but Which Is Found Developed and Reduced to a Dogma in Priestly Religions

Of all the opinions that the savage gives birth to in his ignorance, the first that seems to have to be discredited is the one that supposes that the gods can be punished by men when they deceive their hopes and betray the tacit engagement that is the basis of religion at this period.

In fact, this opinion, which is inherent in fetishism, weakens as polytheism progresses. If blacks destroy their fetishes when they think they have something to complain about in their regard, peoples who are becoming civilized renounce this foolish act of illusory vengeance. For a long time they believe (they perhaps always believe) that their gods allow themselves to be swayed, but they no longer imagine that one can punish them.

In a passage of Homer, when the son of Peleus accuses Apollo and says that he would revenge himself on this god if he could, he recognizes his impotence even while manifesting his anger. Pausanias reports[1] that Tyndarus, imputing the adulteries and licentious life of his daughters to Venus, had her statue veiled and chained. Pausanias, however, sees only madness in this act. To be sure, in unforeseen calamities, in the midst of transports of despair, civilized man sometimes returns to this idea, because with passion subverting his entire being, the event causes him to relapse from his progress, as it were, and returns him to the savage state. He then launches himself against his gods, overturns their altars, and destroys their statues. After the death of Germanicus, one saw the people of Rome dragging the sacred idols through the streets, and lavishing upon them the insults and blows they wanted to give to Tiberius.[2] After the murder of Caligula, one

---

1. *Lacon.*, ch. 15.
2. Tacit., *Ann.*, II.

also saw them punishing the gods for having allowed such a monster to reign. But this sacrilegious fury is not motivated by any particular teaching; it is not a calculation based on the character of the gods, or a punishment inflicted upon them in the hope of correcting them; it is a dying and disarmed victim who launches himself upon his tormenters, moved by a thoughtless impulse. The absolute power that overturns minds and reduces tyrants to the level of, or even below, the most ignorant populace led Augustus to the same excesses; at the time of the war with the young Pompey, having lost his fleet in a storm, he forbade that the statues of Neptune should receive the honors accorded the images of the other gods when they were led in pomp during the games of the circus.[3] But what is only an accidental and aberrant movement in independent polytheism becomes a consecrated dogma, regulated by solemn rituals, in priestly beliefs.

Plutarch tells us[4] that when excessive heat brought either a devouring pestilence or other misfortunes to Egypt, in the darkness of night priests would carry in silence some of the sacred animals that they worshipped and take them to remote places. There, they attempted to frighten them by threats; but if these gods were unyielding and the evil remained, the priests would sacrifice them. During storms, the Thracians would fire arrows against heaven in order to punish the god who dispensed the thunder;[5] and the south wind having dried up the wells of the Psylles, a people of Libya, they resolved to declare war against the divinity who controlled the south wind.[6] The Indians of our day, discontent with their gods, cover them with insults, and those among them who hold authority close the door of their temples with fagots of spines so that no one can enter and offer sacrifice.[7]

It seems bizarre that the same authority that labors with such sustained ardor and effort to put an ever greater distance between the gods and men would maintain practices that are so injurious to the divine majesty in the religions it controls. This singularity owes to two causes: on one hand, to persistence in all ancient customs; on the other, to the fact that by establishing itself as the sole intermediary between heaven and earth, the priesthood makes itself in a way responsible for the conduct of the gods. It therefore has a need to arrogate to itself a certain jurisdiction over them; otherwise it will be deemed a useless and powerless auxiliary;

3. Suet., in *Aug.*, cap. 16.
4. *De Isid.*
5. Herod., IV, 90.
6. Ibid., 173.
7. Dubois, I, 427.

and if one supposes stubborn gods, this jurisdiction, no matter how respectful the forms in which it is clothed or the subtlety with which it is disguised, has to end, and in fact does end, in violence done to the supernatural powers, and even with punishments inflicted upon them.

All the peoples subjected to priests have entertained more or less similar ideas. The Sabeans concentrated the influence of the stars in talismans and amulets by which they obliged the stars to hear them. Some Jewish teachers taught ways of constraining Jehovah.[8] In India, the mantrams,[9] and even more the two irresistible formulas *Bala* and *Attibala*, draw the immortals to the earth.[10] In several species of sacrifice, and notably in funeral ceremonies, the priest asks the faithful if the gods should descend; he then commands these gods to be seated on the sacred grass; then he releases them and allows them to return to their customary abodes.[11]

For the priests, however, there is a danger they need to fear in the exercise of this mysterious jurisdiction. The gods can fail to be docile. Then the priesthood needs

---

8. Vitringa, *De synag. veter.*, bk. III; Origen, περι ευχης; Casaubon, *Exercit. anti Baron.*, XIV, 8; correspondence of Creuzer and Hermann; Diod., II; Euseb., *Praep. Evang.*, IV, 1; V, 10.

9. Mantras or mantrams are prayers or sacred formulas that have the virtue of compelling the gods and imposing an obligation upon them from which they cannot escape. The universe, say the Indians, is in the power of the gods; the gods are in the power of mantrams; mantrams are in the power of Brahmins; therefore, the Brahmins are more powerful than the gods (Dubois, I, 168, 186–94). Menandros, a heretic, or rather a magician of the first century, the disciple or rival of Simon the magician, said he compelled the *genii* who created the world (Iren., *Adv. haeret.*, I, cap. 21). One finds this idea, softened and refined, in primitive Christianity. Prayer, says Saint Chrysostom, extinguishes fire, chases demons, opens the doors of heaven, breaks the bonds of death, heals the sick, banishes ills, shores up shaken cities, undermines conspirators, etc. (*De incomprehens. Dei*, I, 489; Stauedlin, *Hist. de la morale*, II, 258). To the extent that Christianity degenerated from its purity and priests obtained more control, this notion became cruder, and the Christians of the Middle Ages held ideas of the effectiveness of prayer that were little different from those of Indians concerning their mantrams (see Meiners, *Crit. Gesch.*, pp. 249–55; and *Vergleichung des Mittelalters*, III). Among the Jews, the way in which Jacob (Gen., 27) obtains the paternal benediction recalls the power of Indian formulas to compel the gods.

10. Ramayana, p. 258. For several other examples of gods constrained by the invocations of priests, see Guigniaut, p. 83. In the *Aitareya Brahmana* of the Rigveda, the power of priests is raised far above that of the gods. Neither the divine arrows nor the arms of mortals, it is said, will strike the one for whom instructed Brahmins celebrate *abischeca*, a ceremony in which a liqueur composed of water and honey is poured on the protected one (*Asiat. Res.*, VIII, 407).

11. *Asiat. Res.*, VII, 255–65.

an excuse. Hence the notion that an omission, a neglect, a stain can remove the effectiveness of the ceremony.[12]

If prayer coming from the mouth of priests is endowed with such a great influence, cursing is no less powerful. We have treated this subject in one of our preceding volumes,[13] in connection with the action of the climate on Indian ideas. Here we will limit ourselves to what concerns the jurisdiction the priesthood obtains over gods by their curses. Buddha, cursed by one of his lovers because he had disdained her fires, was abandoned by all of his worshippers. The daughter of Taruka, a demigod or powerful *genius*, was transformed into a monster by the anathema of a sage.[14] Another, by the same means, deprived Rama of the sublime knowledge that belonged to his heavenly nature;[15] and Parvati saw his cult fall because an outraged penitent pronounced imprecations against it in his anger.[16]

The gods of Egypt are exposed to the same perils. We will stay the vessel of the sun, say their priests; we will expose the mysteries of the abyss to the light of day; our commands will be respected by the gods or we will cause them to perish if they resist.[17]

This jurisdiction that the priesthood arrogates to itself over the beings whose organs or ministers they are supposed to be reveals the cause of a celebrated fact in Greek history that has remained unexplained to our day. It was in the presence of magi, and probably by their counsel, that Xerxes had the Hellespont chained, after having it struck with rods.[18] When they heard of this, the Greeks' astonishment was great. This is because their polytheism, which had progressed along with their reason, had left far behind the polytheism of priests. But what was inexplicable to them can be explained by the doctrine of the magi, who claimed to dictate laws to the gods by their enchantments and to punish them when they disobeyed.[19] Here we recognize fetishism prolonged by the influence of priests, and we also recog-

12. Ramayana, p. 115.

13. Bk. IV, ch. 2.

14. Ramayana, p. 276.

15. Dubois, II, 404.

16. Ibid., p. 396.

17. Iamblichus, or the pseudonymous author who took the name of this philosopher, limits these threats to demons, mixed beings found between the gods and men. The more knowledge progresses, the more this strange notion has to be restricted to powers of a second rank.

18. Herod., VII, 35.

19. Pliny, III, *Hist. nat.*, XXX. Several centuries after Xerxes, one of his successors, Sapor II, the adversary of Julian in the war in which the latter died, suspecting his gods of fighting for the Romans,

nize this fetishism in its fluctuations, when we see the king of Persia, after having insulted the sea, wanting to appease it by magnificent gifts cast into its depths.[20]

All these facts are so many proofs of a truth that is often repeated. The human spirit shows itself to be even more incoherent, more unreasonable, even less religious, when a class of men arrogate to themselves the privilege of guiding it than when it follows its natural course in freedom.

---

in his rage shot arrows against them at the siege of Nisibis (Julian, *Orat.*, I & II; Theodoret, II, 26; Zosime, III).

20. The oddities of the worship of the goddess Durga in Bengal, would they not be vestiges of the idea we are talking about here? Her annual festival lasted three days. During the first two, she was given the greatest signs of respect; the third day, however, insults were lavished upon her and, finally, she was cast into a river (Grandpré, *Voy. dans Inde* [Paris, 1801]; Staeudlin, *Rel. Mag.*, II, 148–53). Perhaps at the foundation of this ceremony there is also something of the scapegoat of the Hebrews.

CHAPTER 5

On Priestly Notions of Destiny

We have seen the problems that man's reason encounters, even in free beliefs, when it broaches the great question of destiny, and its relation with the gods.[1] These problems are no less insoluble in the priestly religions. The priests, however, attempt to escape them with more complicated sophisms and more unintelligible subtleties.

Sometimes an immutable, irresistible destiny weighs over the gods and men.[2] It was by the will of destiny that the rape of Sita occurred, despite the interest the immortals took in Rama.[3] Tibetan fatalism, which created the world by a vortex and a flood, has fixed by invariable laws all the events since the beginning of beings to their end. All the gods of Scandinavia vainly attempt to resist the fatal decree that condemns Balder to death. In vain, Freya obtains from all the living or inanimate beings the oath to spare the days of the god she protects. He dies wounded by the bramble that the goddess had forgotten or disdained to address. This story, however, contains an obvious contradiction: without the negligence of Freya, fate's decree would not have been accomplished.

---

1. Bk. VII, ch. 7.

2. We could descend to Naraka (the netherworld), say the Indians, establish our abode in the dwelling of Brahma or the paradise of Indra, cast ourselves into the depths of the sea, climb to the summit of the highest mountains, inhabit the starkest desert or the most magnificent city, we could seek refuge with Yama (the god of the dead), bury ourselves in the bowels of the earth, brave the dangers of the bloodiest battles, live among the most venomous insects, or rise to the moon, our destiny would still be fulfilled, and what was not in our power to avoid would still happen to us (Dubois, II, 199). No one, say the sages, dies before his hour. Nothing is accidental in this world. An irrevocable destiny rules all (Mahabharata, in the episode of Damayanti).

3. Ramayana.

Other times, the gods in principle have some authority over destiny. But once they have pronounced, they cannot go back over their own decrees. At the birth of each one, Brahma inscribes on his head the fate that awaits him, which nothing can then modify, and he then goes on to judge mortals according to their works—a contradiction that is reproduced everywhere. From the origin of the world, Odin has determined everything by irrevocable laws, nonetheless his warriors consume themselves in constant efforts to avoid a peaceful departure, which would deprive them of Valhalla.

Sometimes the glory of the gods takes the place of destiny. They have numerous duties vis-à-vis this glory, and they fulfill them at the expense of human beings.[4] Despite this learned terminology, however, the meaning is the same. The glory of the gods, like destiny, is nothing but a limit to their power.

The prescience of the gods is yet another difficulty. Homeric polytheism leaves this question vague. It would be better to say that the inhabitants of Olympus are foresighted in our manner, for they are not endowed with an assured knowledge of the future. The prescience of God in the Bhagavad Gita, on the contrary, extends to all things, except, adds an Indian master, for the actions of beings that he created free. But the majority of the events that he is deemed to foresee being the result of free actions that he does not foresee, how can one harmonize his foresight of effects with his ignorance of causes?[5] Thus, up against insurmountable obstacles, priests fail just as the rest of mortals do. Their impotent logic breaks against what is inexplicable, just as does the logic of the vulgar. They have only one privilege, that of forbidding examination, and thus to remain longer in their unseen contradictions: a temporary advantage that finds no support in sentiment and rests only on the torpor of the intellect.

4. God wishes to be prayed to, says Saint-Philippe, even by those he foresees will be condemned, not because he wishes to pardon them, because they will die in their final unrepentance, but because he finds his glory in the confirmation of the decree he brought against them.

5. Do you wish an example of these Indian subtleties among Christian authors? "God," says Saint-Philippe (*Monarch. des Hébreux*, I, 56–57), "allowed the gentiles to test Israel; not that his prescience needed experience to recognize at once all of eternity; but he wanted to give the occasion for repentance to man, in case he recognized his fault, or for new sins, if he persists in evildoing; in a word, he does not at all disturb free will, and he acts, while knowing the future, as if he did not."

CHAPTER 6

On the Priestly Means of Communication
with the Gods in Sacerdotal Religions

The immediate communications of gods with men, even in the religions independent of priests, become less frequent as experience shows their opposition to facts, and more suspect as the priesthood, no matter how limited its power, has a vital interest in discrediting them.

The disfavor cast upon the communications of this nature is even more profound, and proceeds more rapidly, in priestly religions. In our third book[1] we saw the countless imprecations of the bonzes, magi, and priests of Egypt against every effort on the part of the profane to open a direct path to heaven. But since one cannot take this hope away from the multitude without some compensating consolation, astrology and divination take on greater consistency and are more widely applied. Their rules are more fixed, their forms more mysterious, their pomp more imposing, and their rituals are often barbarous. We saw the empire of astrology in the hands of Egyptian priests.[2] Its application extended to medicine, and we still have Greek manuscripts from a not-so-long-ago period that, while composed in Alexandria, contain obvious notions from ancient Egypt explaining the relations of the constellations with the planets.[3] The same superstitions reign over the Indians. It is of the signs of the zodiac, and the star under which they were born, that they ask the secrets of the future.[4] They kill or abandon the infants whose first hours occurred under a threatening planet,[5] and love and marriage arrange them-

---

1. Bk. III, ch. 10.
2. Bk. VI, ch. 3.
3. Manuscript of the library of Leiden, cited by Creuzer, *Symbol.*, I, 286–87.
4. Dubois, II, 53.
5. Ibid., p. 226.

selves according to signs.[6] The Chaldeans placed the different professions under the protection of the stars.[7] To each was dedicated a temple, whose structure symbolically signified the divinity worshiped therein. Invoked in the prescribed manner, honored by suitable sacrifices, this divinity descended into the sanctuary and granted his ministers the gift of prophecy.[8]

Mexican priests equally distinguish themselves by their attachment to astrology. To hear them, each period had a special character and a sign that was proper to it, which revealed to them every future event and the outcome of all enterprises.[9]

But however extended and diversified the application of astrology to human things, divination was subdivided into even more numerous and varied categories.[10] It simultaneously contained both the interpretation of phenomena that, even though they apparently disturbed the order of the universe, were only less-

6. Those who are going to ask a woman to marry choose a day when all the augurs are favorable, and while on the way to do so they pay great attention to the signs they see. If they judge them unfavorable, they return. If a serpent, a cat, or a jackal crosses their path, they renounce the union they intended (Dubois, II, 299, and further, p. 397).

7. Farmers were protected under the star of Saturn; the learned, magistrates, and priests were under Jupiter's; warriors and nobles had Mars as a patron, princes and the great, the sun; sculptors, painters, poets, and all artists (among whom were included courtesans) recognized Venus as their tutelary divinity. Mercury watched over merchants, and, finally, the moon extended its influence over the lower classes.

8. "The Chaldeans named the planets 'the interpreters of the gods.' They especially venerated the planet the Greeks called Chronos (Saturn). They attributed a prophetic faculty to them, because instead of being fixed like the other stars, they have a spontaneous course, which announces what the gods are preparing, either by their rising or their falling, or their color. These planets indicate in advance all the revolutions of the heaven or on earth. The Chaldeans called them Βουλαιους Θεους, *Deos consiliarios*, a denomination that corresponds to the *Dii consentes* of the Romans. Half of these stars observe what happens on our globe, the other half what happens in the heavens. Every ten days, a superior star descends among the inferior ones, and an inferior one rises to the superior stars. Their path is commanded from all eternity" (Diod., II, 21).

9. The Mexican periods were composed of the number thirteen: thirteen days, thirteen months, a cycle of thirteen years, etc.

10. We have seen in book VIII, chapter 8, how much divination was disdained in independent polytheism; but this was true only of the systematic divination of priests. The divination each individual derives from his own observations is, on the contrary, very much held in honor. As religion is the élan of man toward the power that is outside him, every action, every event, that takes place independently of his will is inserted in religion. All fortuitous things seem to him to be the language of heaven.

known combinations, and the arbitrary meaning attached to the most frequent of accidents.

The different modes of divination varied according to climate. The Etruscans, of whom we will speak in detail later, sought the future in meteors, and in the prodigies or monsters that arose among them; the Phrygians and the Cilicians, who lived in mountains, sought it in the songs of birds;[11] the Egyptians and the Babylonians solely in the stars, not wanting to subject their predictions to chance or external events, claiming to have learned directly from the gods everything they revealed to them.[12] But among other peoples, all material phenomena had a prophetic meaning.

When the earth trembled, it was to announce the decrees of the heavens. When the stars were covered with a veil, it was to announce some fate; and not only great calamities such as earthquakes, but phenomena manifest to all, such as eclipses, were the language of the gods; everything that we attribute to the laws of gravity, to the mechanisms of bodies, to the result of chance,[13] or the instinct of animals,[14] their movements, their cries, their encounters or their flight, the least accidents of inanimate nature, the shuffling of leaves, the color of flames, the direction smoke takes while ascending, the murmur of the waves,[15] the strike of lightning, everything mechanical or involuntary in man, the beating of the pulse, sneezes, and above all dreams,[16] which are so powerful with savages,[17] dreams where our nature takes pleasure, as it were, in making us doubt ourselves, and in which reason seems to take part in order to humiliate and confound itself, all these things were so many manifestations of the divine will, because the gods—to hear their minis-

11. See Heyne, *Opusc.*, III, 198, 285, and elsewhere, where he explains the divination of different peoples by the natural history of their country, especially the peoples of Latium.

12. Plut., *Conv. sept. sap.*, 33; Ael., *Var. Hist.*, pp. 11, 31.

13. The Arabs before Mohammed had prophetic arrows named *Acdah*. He forbad this practice (Koran, sura 5; Pocock., *Spec. Hist. arab.*, p. 327; D'Herbel., art. *Acdah*; Sale, *Introd.*). Muslims compensated by applying the verses of the Koran itself to divination (Chardin, III, 205). The Greeks had employed in the same way verses of Homer; the Romans, some of Virgil. See, on these, *Sortes Homericae, Euripideae, Virgilianae,* etc., Van Dale, *De orac.*, p. 299.

14. Pelloutier, V, 33.

15. Mallet, *Introd.*, p. 92.

16. Bk. II, ch. 6.

17. Dreams, observes Meiners (*Crit. Gesch.*, II, 617–18), of all the species of divination are the one to which Antiquity, and even the philosophers, accorded the most confidence. It was for this reason that the ancients slept in temples.

ters—do nothing without a reason, and all beings obey them as the bow and arrow in the arms of the archer. Confucius, whom our philosophers have strangely persisted in placing among themselves, taught his disciples several of these modes of divination.[18] The Persians, as we have said,[19] intermediary between the peoples of the North and the South, connected astrology with divination, in particular with pyromancy.

Scandinavian priests interpreted the cawing of crows;[20] the Germans[21] attached an extreme importance to all the words of women because, they said, being incapable of a constant will, and rarely governed by reason, they more easily received the subtle impressions of invisible powers; unwittingly or unwillingly, they were their organs.[22]

Thus antiquity, according to a remark of an author whose name escapes me, spied on nature in its smallest details, with much more attention than moderns; this was an effect of superstition, and this effect in its turn became a cause. For priests, a science resulted that, when applied to all the events of life and the interests of everyday life, had to immensely increase priestly power. Thus, the study of signs that we have recounted was the principal occupation of Druids;[23] and the young nobility whose education was confided to them spent twenty years perfecting the art of understanding and interpreting these signs.[24]

A single people remained foreign to these superstitions, at least in its laws. This

18. Notice of the *Yi-King*, p. 410.

19. Bk. IV, ch. 9.

20. Rüh, *Scandin. antiq.*, pp. 142–43. The adventurous life of Scandinavians makes them attach extreme interest to every sort of presage. The more that men brave danger and attempt expeditions whose result is uncertain, the more they desire to know the future. The Phansicas, a band of thugs who infest the south of India and the kingdom of Mysore, even though they are almost all Muslims, have recourse to Indian divination in their expeditions. Each of their steps is directed by the indications they receive by chance, or the convulsions of sacrificed victims (*Asiat. Res.*, XIII, 263).

21. Caes., *B Gall.*, I, 50.

22. Tacit., *German.*, cap. 8. The prophetesses of Germany are famous. Norns of the earth, their very name (*weih*) came from a word that signified *braid*, which designates both their domestic works and the thread of the Norns. Wizaga, a prophetess, survived in language the demise of religious belief by becoming the verb "to prophesy," *Weissagen* in German. Who does not know the Veleda of the Bructeri?

23. Pelloutier, V, 23; VIII, 127; Sil. Ital., III, 344; Lamprid., in Alex. Sev., p. 927; Diod. Justin., XXIV, 4; Tit.-Liv., V, 34; Tacit., *German.*, c. 10.

24. Caes., *B Gall.*, VI, 14.

people was the Jewish people.[25] This fact confers additional force to an observation we already made, and which we will later recall for the reflection of our readers.[26]

Divination passed from priestly polytheism to nations free of the priesthood. The Greeks owed it to the Phrygians and the Carians;[27] the Romans to the Etruscans.[28] But as we observed earlier,[29] it occupied a lower rank, especially among the Greeks. The late period of its introduction into the Greek religion explains why one encounters many fewer traces in Homer than in later writers. One also finds many fewer in the poets than in the historians. The poets, who sought only applause, remained as faithful as they could to the more splendid and poetic marvels they found in the *Iliad* and the *Odyssey*; while the latter, aspiring to the trust of their readers, dared not entertain them with fictions that were universally rejected, they did recount what we could call smaller prodigies that had retained favor among them. This is because divination as the ancients conceived it belonged to science rather than the imagination; when credulity lost its force, or imagination its agreeable character, divination could still be respected, and could even acquire new credibility because of the supposed-progress of the science.

The trials found among all the peoples dominated by priests, and which, transmitted from barbarous religions to Christianity took the name of judgments of God,[30] were nothing else than the application of divinatory means to the relations that exist among men. These trials took place among the Scandinavians[31] and the Germans. They gave preference to duels, which was a natural consequence of their love of war; but other sorts of trial were not unknown to them.[32] We

25. One does not see idols in Jacob, says Numbers, XXXIII, 21, 22, 23; and one does not see divination or lots; they are a people who trust in the Lord, their god, whose power is invincible.

26. Bk. IV, ch. 11.

27. Clem. Alex., *Strom.*, I; Pliny, *Hist. nat.*, VIII, 56. One can see the enumeration of the different kinds of divination employed by the Greeks in the *Symbolique* of Creuzer, I, 191–96.

28. Clem. Alex., *Strom.*, I; Lucan., I, 635; Serv., *ad Aen.*, VIII, 398; Cic., *De div.*, II, 50; Ovid, *Metam.*

29. Bk. VII, ch. 8.

30. Judgments of God by fire, water, the cross, blessed bread and cheese, the Eucharist, the *caracteres sanctorum*, or *sortes apostolorum*, imitations of *sortes virgilianae*. Despite all protests, the Christian clergy sanctified trials by dueling (Pelloutier, VIII, 156–218).

31. Schonings, *Rikeshistor.*, II, 320; Dalin, *Hist. de Suède*, I, 162.

32. However, individual combat was so preferred that the laws themselves subjected the other forms of trial to almost impossible conditions. In the case of fire, for example, the accuser had to hold

find many kinds among the Indians, who, transporting to the heavens their own customs, subjected their divinities to them.[33] Accused or suspected by Rama, Sita cast herself into a fiery pyre. A voice descends from the invisible spheres; a rain of flowers inundates the earth, and Rama, convinced by the word of Agni[34] that Sita is pure and without stain, grants her his trust.[35] One can consider as belonging to the same notion the opinion of the Persians, who expose the sick to fierce beasts; if the animals spare them, they are considered to be impure.[36] The Hebrews, while rejecting divination, admitted trials,[37] without noting the identity of principle. The Greeks, on the contrary, display not even the slightest trace of similar practices, with the possible exception of a passage in Sophocles's *Antigone* where the guards accused by Creon of having assisted the princess in her pious disobedience want to justify themselves by placing their hands in a burning fire;[38] however, one should see here only an energetic way of protesting their innocence or, what seems to be even more probable, an allusion to foreign customs that the Greeks knew but did not practice. Sophocles put these words referring to these trials in the mouth of Creon's guards; like all the tyrants of Greek cities, Creon had only

---

the fire in his own hand from the period of accusation to the trial itself, i.e., fourteen nights and days without interruption. The trial by boiling water was imposed only on serfs, settlers or *lites*, commoners freed by the Romans, and penniless freemen.

33. *Asiat. Res.*, I, 389; Porph., *De abst.*, IV, 17; *Mém. de l'Acad. des inscript.*, XXX, 113, where marches of trials are spoken of. Trial of Chyddy-Mandy, Dubois, II, 372–73, 546; *Asiat. Res.*, IV, 60–61. Still today, when some object is stolen from a house and suspicion falls upon someone, the person is led to the temple of Ganeza and his hand is plunged into burning oil. If he is innocent, he will suffer no evil; if guilty, his hand will be reduced to ashes (*Asiat. Res.*, I, 389–404). The Laws of Menu contain a singular application of the idea that serves as the basis of trials. The witness who during the seven days prior to his appearance experiences a misfortune or loses one of his relatives is to be condemned as guilty of false witness (Laws of Menu, c. 8).

34. The god of fire.

35. Ramayana, p. 22.

36. Agathias applies this superstition only to the dead and to the future life. Persians, he says, carefully examined if savage beasts tore the bodies, or if they left them intact. In the first case, they congratulated their souls as having gone to a happy place; in the second, they regarded them as the prey of Arimanes (Agath., II, 60). According to Steller, one finds the same hypothesis among the Kamtschatka, who reject as stained and unworthy of living those who fell into the sea or a river without drowning.

37. See the Bible in several places, notably Numbers V, 11–31, and elsewhere, where waters of jealousy are spoken of.

38. Soph., *Antig.*

barbarians for guards. Now, all these barbarians came from countries submitted to priestly religions.

If on certain important occasions these means of justification were admitted by the Romans, it was as an inheritance of Etruria.[39]

Meditating on what preceded, one is struck by a manifest contradiction in the priestly hypotheses. Astrology and divination should lead to the most absolute fatalism, since the destiny of man is determined by the planets at his birth, the direction or even color of a ray points out the unavoidable events of his entire life. Why did the priests never admit the direct and undeniable consequence of their teaching? It is because the uncertainty of the future is necessary to their influence. They validated divination and astrology in order to give themselves the merit of interpreting the decrees of heaven; then they denied its most obvious consequence in order to preserve hope for devotion, and for their own intervention, its necessity.

39. The vestal virgin Tuccia justified herself in this way against the accusation leveled against her (Den. of Hal., II, 69). Trials by fire took place in the sanctuary of Feronia (Tit.-Liv., XXXII, I; Serv., *ad Aeneid*, VIII, 564).

CHAPTER 7

On the Notions of the Future Life in Religions Dominated by Priests

We have seen the world of the dead and the destiny of those who inhabit it to be the constant objects of the thought of man, until, worn out by fruitless efforts, he determined to turn his gaze away from what can never be known. This is a violent and sad resolution that debases him without giving him peace. Until then, he interrogates both his reason which doubts and his interior sentiment which disturbs and causes him to tremble, as well as external nature that says nothing. He invents a thousand augurs, he has recourse to a thousand ceremonies. He attaches arbitrary meaning to a thousand petty circumstances in order to win the obstinate secret that always escapes him. Nothing satisfies him, and the priesthood profits from his uncertainties and impotence.

The future life is the priesthood's domain, and it is toward it that the priesthood directs all eyes, all hopes, and all fears. The Egyptians place importance only in the existence that follows the passing on. The houses man builds on earth seem to them to be hostels for a day; tombs, in contrast, are man's dwellings par excellence, eternal palaces.[1] The bellicose inclinations of the Scandinavians and the Gauls, combined with priestly domination, depicted death not only as the end but as the goal of life. Impatient to attain it, they launched themselves into battle, less to defeat than to die.[2] They did not attempt to overcome their adversaries except to fall in their turn, covered with even more glory. Each success invited them to seek more danger elsewhere; and the warrior who could not find a glorious demise under an enemy's sword was reduced to give death to him-

---

1. Diod., I.

2. Lucan's verses on the disdain of the Gauls for life and their love of death are well-known.

self.[3] The proof that this repugnance for old age and natural death was owing, at least in part, to the priestly religion of the people of the North, was that the Greeks, no less belligerent, entertained no such opinion. Among them old age was an honor and natural death held no opprobrium.

The Indians accorded the same preference to the future life as the Scandinavians or the Egyptians. The immortality of the soul for them is not a vague desire, an uncertain hope, but an absolute conviction, the determining motive of all actions, the source and aim of all laws, institutions, and practices;[4] but with them this opinion takes another form. Neither the means they employ nor the prize they seek is the same. The means are not a warrior's death, but a contemplative life; the prize is not an immortality of battle, of pleasures and feasts, but an eternal apathy, a complete absence of individuality.[5]

This fatigue before the activity of living when one lives under the most beautiful of skies and in the midst of all sorts of pleasures is a most remarkable thing. To reprise in eternity their this-worldly occupations is the greatest hope of the peoples who struggle here below against a strict destiny, and who acquire only with great effort an always-tenuous subsistence. Never to return to this world is the sole desire of those nations that appear to be most favored, whose fertile soil and mild climate

3. It was a custom among the Germans, the Slavs, and other people of the North, that when they felt their strength diminished by age, heroes had their friends, or priests, run a sword or spear through their heart (Pelloutier, I, 441; Moehsen, *Gesch. der Wissensch.*, I, 44–50). Odin, threatened with death by a sickness, rent his own body in order to see his blood flow during his last hour (Botin, *Hist. de Suède*, I, 6, 24). Niort, his grandson, followed this example, and before expiring gave himself several wounds with a sword. Others cast themselves from the top of rocks, believing they attained Valhalla in this way. "Our ancestors," says the ancient saga from which this tradition is drawn, "all took the path of this rock." The rock was named the Rock of Odin. Pliny attests to this custom. "*Mors, non nisi satietate vitae, epulis delibutis senibus luxu, ex rupe quadam in mare salientibus, hoc genus sepulturae beatissimum*" (*Hist. nat.*, IV, 12). "Among the Icelanders," says Solin, "when a woman gives birth to a son, she asks the gods that he might perish while fighting" (cap. 25). After their conversion to Christianity, which forced them to renounce suicide, the warriors of this part of the world at least armed themselves fully at the approach of the fatal moment.

4. Schlegel, *Weish. der Indier*, p. 113.

5. The reward of the good, says the Bhagavad Gita, is to be absorbed in God and to participate in the divine nature, which experiences no emotion. In connection with this subject, the translator of this work observes that the Indians place the supreme good in an insensibility that is equivalent to annihilation. Every time they speak of the soul reunited with God, they depict it as a perfect impassivity, equally removed from pain and pleasure.

preserve them from all pain and dispense from all labor. This is because work, need, and danger attach us to life by presenting challenges at every moment that must be engaged, goals that must be pursued. Repose, on the other hand, by delivering us to ourselves, makes us feel the emptiness of an easy happiness and the insufficiency of our possessions. In order not to succumb to the burden that crushes him, man has need of being forced by obstacles to forget the sadness of his destiny, and to constantly develop his faculties and his forces.

In Indian literature, the ardent desire to be withdrawn from the human condition modifies even works that are not religious. They are out-of-sorts when someone retraces the infirmities of our nature. They wish to put offstage the representation of everything that would resemble too closely material life; and the doctrine of being absorbed in the Divinity also influences the denouement of their dramas. This resolution must never be unhappy: it would contradict the fundamental teaching, the certainty of a definitive reunion with heavenly quietude.

Greek and Indian notions are the two extremes concerning the state of souls after death. The Homeric netherworld presents these souls as individual beings weakened in soul and body, and the world of the dead as an image of this world but without the full reality. The Indian absorption is the negation of every faculty, of every memory, of all personality of the soul, which is reduced to an abstraction deprived of everything that would connect its existence with existence here-below.

Among the nations subject to priestly corporations, there is one that presents a singular exception when it comes to the future life. The Mosaic law maintains an absolute silence on the immortality of the soul. It encourages Jews with only temporal recompenses, and sometimes the prophets themselves seem to see in the tomb only nothing.[6]

We however believe that some have terribly exaggerated the absence of any

---

6. The tomb will not celebrate you, says Ezekiel to the Eternal. Death will not praise you. Those who descend into the ditch no longer await your truth (Isa., ch. 38). After death, one no longer thinks of God, one no longer praises him, one no longer thanks him (Ps., XXX, vv. 9, 10; CXVIII, v. 18). The dead no longer know the goodness of God; their dwelling is the land of oblivion (ibid., LXXXVIII). I resemble the dead of whom you no longer think, from whom your hand is removed. There is no knowledge, no wisdom, or human endeavor, after death (Eccles.). Job (VII, 8–9; XIV, 8–13) appears to indicate in the most explicit way that he believes in neither the immortality of the soul nor the resurrection; and the sect of the Sadducees explicitly denied all reward and punishment after this life.

teaching on future existence in the Jewish religion.[7] In Deuteronomy,[8] Moses speaks of the evocation of the dead; and sacred writers make frequent allusions to the immortality of the soul.[9]

One can reconcile this apparent contradiction by means of a plausible conjecture. Among almost all peoples subject to theocratic government, the priests, even though clothed with an immense power, had to fight against kings and warriors; and the period of the books or traditions that have come down to us do not go back to the times when the priesthood ruled without rivals. The Hebrew annals, on the contrary, witness to a complete and uncontested despotism of priests until the

7. This exaggeration dates from Warburton, who, as is known, wanted to find a new genre of proofs for the truth of Christianity in the hypothesis that the doctrine of the Hebrews did not exceed the limits of the material world, and that this people rejected (or better put: did not know) the world to come. Seduced by the ingenious reasoning and often imposing erudition of a master who was the more pleasing to them as he was more intolerant and passionate, theologians have freely admitted a system by which Christianity would leave Judaism, its cradle, far behind; and unbelievers have not rejected it, happy to have found—according to an orthodox scholar—the people whose law, although abridged, serves as the basis of our own, and who had no notion of the future life and who placed, as they do, the human race in the rank of animals.

8. Deut., XXIII, 11.

9. The story of the witch of Endor proves that the opinion of a place where the dead lived was a common opinion of the people. Isaiah represents the king of Babylon entering this domain, assailed by the mockeries and sarcasms of those who preceded him (XXVI, 19). Ezekiel compares the restoration of the Jews to their former prosperity to the resurrection. To the passage from Job cited in the previous note, one can oppose another passage with the opposite meaning (XIX, 25–27). While resurrecting the child of the widow, Elijah asks God to cause the soul of the child to return, and the soul reenters the lifeless body (Kings, XVII, 3). Ecclesiastes, alongside its materialism worthy of Epicurus, says that dust returns to the earth whence it came, and the soul to the God who created it (XII, 7). Daniel divides into two categories those who are buried in the dust: some will rise for eternal life, and others to opprobrium and punishment (XXII, 2–3). Tobit (II, 15–28) counts on the life that God will give to those who have a firm faith and who walk in his paths with confidence. Finally, several places in the Bible speak of Belial, the king of the shadows, who governed those who are no longer. From the time of the Maccabees, the Jews prayed for their dead and offered sacrifices for them. The Maccabees themselves died hoping for a better life, and their mother encouraged them in this hope (Macc., II, Josephus, Guénée, p. 86). See ibid., p. 94, on the abode of the dead (Sheol); and, moreover, Goerres I, 499, 506, 519, 522; and Staeudlin, *Relig. Mag.* The latter attributes these ideas of the resurrection and the final judgment found in Ezekiel and Daniel to communications with the Persians. In any case, it is clear that the words of Jesus Christ on this subject, even though they contain a very different spiritual and sublime meaning, are founded upon previous notions.

establishment of the monarchy. Now, when priests are invested with all power and directly employ divine authority, they have no need of delaying its intervention, they even, perhaps, fear weakening, by delay, the effect it should produce. But if they encounter rivals jealous of their authority in the temporal powers, they seek to regain the dominion that is disputed by means of fear for the future. When they reign in this world they are less solicitous of the other; but when the possession of this world is contested, they call the other to their assistance. The terrors of the other life are auxiliaries.

Therefore the priests, the immediate successors of Moses, would initially have neglected these views; but after the substitution of the royalty for the theocracy, they would have invoked them. In fact, it was at this period that the myth of the witch of Endor appeared. The foregoing explanation will not lack plausibility if one reflects that this teaching, which was never taught to the Jews as an article of faith, acquired special force with the prophets and the ministers of religion when they had to fight against tyranny, whether native or foreign, and were called upon either to frighten their oppressors or defend the weak.

But even leaving to one side this conjecture concerning a particular fact, one general fact is incontestable. In all the hypotheses that the priests wish to inculcate, in all the descriptions by which they wish to inspire hope or terror, they are constrained to follow the natural bent of the human spirit. These descriptions, these hypotheses, must have at their base a more or less exact imitation of real life. Its customs, its events, its occupations are the mold in which all the notions concerning the future life must be cast.

Egyptian women eager to please in Amenthes,[10] just as in Memphis or Alexandria, had colors and brushes buried with them in order to refresh their makeup or darken their eyes. The Gauls wrote to friends whom death had taken from them and consigned their letters to the flames, adjourning to their reunion after this life the final tallying of their accounts with creditors and debtors.[11] The Persians

10. Amenthes, a copy of the earth, had its gods, its inhabitants, even its animals. Dionysus and Ceres, who, according to Herodatus's explanation are nothing but Isis and Osiris, ruled in this subterranean world, where Dionysus bore the surname Serapis (Zoega, pp. 302–10). This Serapis had his temple in the middle of Amenthes. Wolves guarded it; therefore one often sees figures of wolves on tombs.

11. Diod., V, 20; Val. Max., II, 6, 10. "*Vetus ille mos Gallorum occurrit, quos memoriae proditum est, pecunias mutuas, quae bis apud inferos redderentur, dare solitos, quod persuasum habuerint animas immortales esse.*" In the tomb of Chilperic the First have been found the arms of this king of the Franks

surrounded the funeral monuments of their kings with everything needed for life on earth.[12] The methodical and even minute ancestral worship of China is well known;[13] it has transmitted priestly rituals to the Chinese of today even through periods of atheism. In a solemn feast that the inhabitants of Tonkin celebrate annually, they prepare their houses to receive those who have ceased to live, and to host them as celebrated guests.[14]

Indians place fruit and milk by caskets,[15] and not only the occupations and needs of souls in the other world, but their travels, are borrowed from this one. According to the Garuda Purana, souls, reduced to the diminutive stature of an inch in height, are transported through the air by Yama's servants to mountains where they live for a month. Then they walk to the banks of the western ocean, where Yama judges them. There are two paths, one beautiful and easy for the good, the

---

and the skeleton of a horse he hoped to ride when he presented himself to the god of war. In an open coffin near Guben, a German had buried with him utensils for eating, as well as flasks and cups of all sizes. The warriors of Hialmar, when rendering him funeral honors, make use of gold, which they bury. See the extract from the Scandinavian poem in the *Introduction* of Mallet, p. 303.

12. See the description of the tomb of Cyrus by Arrian, cap. 29. The courtiers of the king of the Persians had to live near his tomb. One of them, Bagorazus, having left the remains of his master, was disgraced by his successor; and Bagapatis, the inspector of the harem of Darius, son of Hystaspe, remained for seven years, and died, near the place where this prince was buried (Ctes., *Pers.*, 46, 19; Heeren, I, 280). Every month the Persians sacrificed a horse on this tomb. Lucian shows us the satrap Arsace asking to mount his horse in the netherworld, because this horse had been buried with him. Chardin instructs us that the Guebres preserved a custom from their ancestors of burying with their dead everything that had served them in this world.

13. Meiners, *Crit. Gesch.*, I, 306, 307.

14. Marigny, *Nouvelles des royaumes de Tonkin et de Laos*, pp. 249–50. "At midnight on the first day of the year, the doors were held open for the dead to enter. Rugs were put down for them to walk on, beds for them to sleep on; baths were prepared, sandals, and canes for them to use. Dishes of food were put on tables for them to eat, and when they are thought to depart, they are shown out with reverence and on bended knees."

15. The *pranata*, or the breath that animates the dead, comes for ten days to drink and eat (Dubois, II, 209). One provides for them so that they endure neither hunger nor thirst, nor nakedness (ibid., 332–33), nor deafness, blindness, or infirmity (ibid., 213). Hindus are obliged by a precept of the Vedas to offer a cake that they call *pinda* to the manes of their ancestors, to the third generation. The Vedas also command bringing them water each day; this ritual is called *tarpa* (satisfaction, appeasement). When it is neglected, the soul is cast into the netherworld and enters the body of an impure animal (Bhag. Gita, note, p. 154). Astrolatry is joined to these superstitions, and the planets have their part in the homage given to the dead (Dubois, II, 220).

other, quite difficult, for the bad. Souls stop twice en route in order to take food and put on clothing.[16]

Finally, if the riches of Scandinavian warriors are burned on their pyres in honor of the gods, it is so that by means of this sacrifice a field of battle might be opened where new combat awaits them. Their dignity in Valhalla depends upon the treasure they have acquired. Admitted into this place of glory, they stroll among their comrades-in-arms, subject to envious gazes. Soon, though, they take up their glorious arms, mount their steeds, and attack one another. The air resounds with the clash of lances and swords. Their blood burns, and the celestial pavilions are littered with champions fallen a second time. The hour of the feast sounds, the combat ceases, the wounds are healed, the dead revive and come together at the table of their leader. There, served by Valkyrians with blond hair and snow-white skin, they devour the wild boar Skrimner, who is reborn each day, and drink delicious beer. Niflheim encloses the women, children, and old who have finished the course of an obscure life. They, too, relive the past, retaining their names, their rank, and their honors, and continue the renewed dream of life as peacefully as they had led it on earth.[17]

---

16. *Asiat. Res.*, XIV, 441. Several ceremonies aimed to assist the voyage of souls, without which they would remain wandering among demons and the wicked *genii*, are nonetheless copied from earthly customs (ibid., VII, 263).

17. Before Balder's destiny was fulfilled (see above, chapter on destiny [bk. IX, ch. 5]), Odin descended into the palace of Hela (death) in order to ask for an explanation of the dreams that haunted him. He saw a banquet prepared, diamond-decorated rostrums, shining banks of gold, goblets filled with hydromel—in a word, everything that characterizes earthly festivals. Balder appeared with his faithful spouse, they seated themselves on two thrones in order to contemplate the subterranean feast; it was wholly similar to those celebrated by the living (Edda, 44th fable).

CHAPTER 8

On the Abodes of the Dead, and the Description
of Infernal Torments, in Priestly Religions

Homeric polytheism indicates only one abode for the dead, which is not a place of punishments reserved for crime, but a vast and lugubrious space where all the shades without distinction display the melancholy that overwhelms them, which is neither aggravated nor done away with by the moral conduct of their previous life.[1] Priestly religions, however, have more numerous and more detailed netherworlds. The Edda counts two, Niflheim and Nastrond; the Indians sometimes three,[2] sometimes fourteen,[3] and a few sects have as many as twenty-four.[4] Among the Persians there are seven;[5] five among the Burmese, twenty-three among the Japanese, three in Tibet, but subdivided into nineteen regions where the pains are differentiated, because it is in the description of torments that the priesthood above all finds its pleasure.[6]

---

1. See bk. VII, ch. 9.

2. Bhag. Gita, p. 134.

3. Laflotte, p. 226.

4. See Dubois, II, 309–26, 522–30; *Asiat. Res.*, VI, 215–24. These peoples relegate the netherworld to a place beyond the ocean, an opinion founded on an error of physics and geography. They believe that some continent must surround the waters so that they do not fall into the void (*Asiat. Res.*, XI, 105).

5. The bridge that leads to the netherworld is common to the Persians and the Scandinavians. On this bridge, see Wagner, p. 453; and Meiners, *Crit. Gesch.*, pp. 771–72.

6. The netherworlds of the Tibetans are *gnielva*, *jang-scijangso*, and *nasme*. *Gnielva* is divided into two zones, one cold, the other hot; each is subdivided into eight others. In the latter, the damned are lying on the ground covered with red fire; they swallow liquid fire; they are crushed between two rocks, then put into burning pots, and demons stir the liquid iron and lead; they are cut in two or cast upon burning thorns, or cut into four, eight, thirty, or sixty parts (Georg., *Alphab. Tib.*, pp. 183, 265–66).

The hells of the Zend books are placed on the banks of a fetid stream, dark as pitch and cold as ice.[7] The condemned souls are troubled without end. A thick smoke emerges from this dark lair, and the interior is filled with scorpions and serpents.

The Ifurin of the Gauls is a country impenetrable by the sun's rays. Venomous animals are the companions and tormenters of the inhabitants of this horrible abode. Hungry wolves devour them. They call for death, but in vain. After having served as prey for fierce beasts, they are reborn—to provide them new prey. The most guilty are stretched in a somber cavern in the midst of countless reptiles. Burning poison falls upon them drop by drop. Everywhere there is a cold so piercing that these miserable shadows would be turned into ice if they were not destined to eternal pains.[8]

Despite the mildness of their natural disposition, the Indians have no less terrible hells. Yama, judge of the dead, pronounces the sentence. Those who have neglected the precepts of religion are punished for a number of years that is equal to the hairs that cover their head. Atheists are pierced through and through by falling on sharpened weapons. Those who have exhibited contempt to Brahmins are cut into pieces and cast into the fire. The adulterer holds idols reddened by the fire. Crows with bronze beaks tear apart the faithless one who has betrayed his caste. The murderer of a man or an animal is plunged into a vile abyss. The sensual walk with bare feet over brambles. The calumniator is bound with chains and fed unclean food. The greedy is himself devoured by insatiable worms. The one whose sacrilegious hand sacrificed a cow becomes a living anvil struck with a burning hammer. The one who gave false witness slithers from rock to rock, leaving his blood on their sharpened points; and the bodies of these wretched, composed of an impalpable material, join together like quicksilver to suffer new tortures.[9]

7. Hyde, *De rel. pers.*

8. "I will see your soul," says a bard to one of these victims in his sacred verses, "I will see your soul, soon suspended in the bowels of a thick fog, soon cast in the bosom of a humid cloud, the unhappy plaything of winds that will bandy you about in a place where the sun never shines" (*Gall. Altherth.*, I, 62–63). This Druid poetry recalls these verses of Voltaire:

...*et moi predestiné,*

Je rirai bien, quand vous serez damné.

9. Bhagavadam, bk. V. It is so true that these refinements in torments are inherent in the priestly spirit that zealous Catholics support them when they are criticized. An English author named Sumner, who in his attachment to Christianity was desirous of showing the superiority of Christianity to the beliefs of pagan peoples, nonetheless praised the latter because they rejected the horrible portraits of

One sees premeditated calculation in these careful portraits, a will to make an impression, and methodical arrangement. This multiplicity of hells, overlapping one another, as it were, betrays the desire to render the impression produced by fear of the future even more profound. Priests never found this impression sufficiently strong; they diversified their conceptions; they expanded them. They treated the heavens and the netherworld like their own property. They invented new cadres so they could fill them in greater freedom. Often they create a new god to preside at the sentencing.[10] In a word, they constantly rework religion while maintaining its ancient teachings, like a worker improves his tools or a soldier polishes his weapons.

They also mix hope with terror. They multiply paradises as well as hells. Among the Scandinavians, Gimlé comes after Valhalla, as Nastrond after Niflheim.[11] The inhabitants of Ceylon count twenty-six paradises toward which the just are successively raised, returning each time to a human body until arriving at the place of complete felicity.[12] The inferior paradises of the Indians are material. Their inhabitants give themselves over to love, to festivals, to crude pleasures. The superior paradises are devoted to purer pleasures, contemplation, and ecstasy. Finally, in the highest of all, the Chattia Logam,[13] the soul is incorporated into the divine nature.[14]

Independently of these promises and threats, the priesthood employs other

---

the torments of the netherworld. An orthodox Catholic immediately responded: I am surprised by the Protestant innovator, but this straw that the Son of the Eternal will burn with an inextinguishable fire, this pain of fire incurred by the one who harms his brother, this drunkard who is destined to the fire at the end of time, those angels to gather the guilty from the four corners of the world and cast them in the burning furnaces, these tears, this grinding of teeth, these cursed who will be at the left of God, and whom he will cast into the eternal fire prepared for the devil and his angels, all this is in the Gospel (*Gaz. de France*, 18 August 1826). The same journal bitterly reproaches (21 October 1829) Mr. de Chateaubriand for having opened purgatory to pagans.

10. At the period when the Drottes of Scandinavia introduced a second netherworld and a second paradise, it was no longer Odin but an unknown god who was the dispenser of punishments and rewards.

11. In another part of this work, we will indicate the differences that distinguish these two netherworlds and these two paradises. Here, we have dealt only with their number.

12. *Asiat. Res.*, VII, 33.

13. They also call this supreme paradise Zabudeba (*Asiat. Res.*, VI, 224, 233).

14. To see in greater detail the paradises of India, Dubois, II, 424, 505; and the *Recherches asiatiques*, VI, 179; and for their descriptions of the pleasures of the other life, Lanjuinais, on the Oupnekhat, p. 83. Despite all these depictions of happiness, the horror of death prevails. The priests

means to spur the liberality of the faithful; it allows the subterranean abyss to open. Three times a year, Larunda Mania in Etruria leads her pallid subjects amid the living, whom they frighten by their pale aspect or pursue with their sharp cries.[15] Invisible ancestors attended meals and sacrifices. Manes sat around the paternal foyer. Lares were the object of periodic veneration; and during the five epagomenal days, the feast of Apherina-Ghan led back to the bosom of Persian families the deceased held captive in the tomb, which then recalled them after a few hours, unless they were redeemed by gifts and sacrifices. If this was done, they would be separated from the unclean world by Oromaze, who opened the way to heaven for them.

An important observation must be made at this point for our readers. If in Homeric polytheism morality had no influence on the fate of the deceased, the priestly religions attributed a great influence to it.

Everywhere one sees judges of those who descend to the netherworld, and torments for the guilty.[16] It is easy to assign the motive for this difference. The priests who do not tolerate the independence of any of our faculties or conjectures, or our relations, whether with heaven or earth, must hasten to submit the relations of

---

who preside at funerals inspire repugnance. They are called Mahabrahmins (*Digest of Hindoo Laws*, II, 175; *Asiat. Res.*, VII, 241).

15. Varro, *De ling. lat.*, VIII; Festus, v. *Mania*.

16. As we have seen, Yama is the judge of the netherworld in India. At the entrance of each hell of the Burmese are placed judges. Everyone knows the famous decrees pronounced in Egypt on the banks of the river that is the image of the one that the shadows cross. People know that before proceeding to the funeral ceremony, a tribunal of forty judges examined the conduct of the deceased and decided if he merited the honor of burial. In the affirmative case, the gods of the subterranean world, presided over by Serapis, were invoked. This tribunal of gods appears assembled on an Egyptian coffin found in the British Museum; Zoega has provided an explanation of it (*De obelisc.*, 308). A papyrus roll buried with a mummy, which the expedition to Egypt obtained for us, reproduces the same portrait (Denon, *Voy. en Egypt.*, p. 141). This antiquarian is ingenious but a bit shallow; he wrongly sees in it an initiation. Osiris is seated with his ordinary attributes, having before him a lotus flower, symbol of eternal life, and a lioness. A small human figure is weighed in a large set of scales by two *genii* with animal heads, one of a dog, which alludes to material inclinations, the other that of the sparrow-hawk, the emblem of the divine nature. Both these *genii* have a hand on the scales and seem to plead with Osiris. Hermes with the head of an ibis, a scroll in hand, writes the vices and virtues that are to form the basis of Osiris's decree. Heeren (*Afric.*, III, 681) believes that this judgment of the dead comes after earlier primitive notions of Egypt; he accounts for this progression pretty much as we will explain that of Greek polytheism. But we think he was deceived by an apparent likeness. The priests in Egypt hastened the natural introduction of morality into religion, and falsified one by subjecting it to the other.

men among themselves to the yoke of belief. This fusion of religion with morality, a fusion that occurs slowly and by degrees in Greek belief, occurs more rapidly in the sacerdotal cults. But in this the human race loses more than it gains. The priestly morality is entirely artificial, founded not on the value of human actions but on the will of the gods. Submission to priests, gifts without measure, lavishness at the expense of justice or affections become the highest virtue;[17] and since nothing ensures obedience better than the servile practice of ceremonies (which are often revolting and always detailed),[18] the code of priests is overburdened with strange laws that are destructive of natural laws.

This observation was necessary, and for now it is sufficient, because later we will compare the moral influence of the perfected polytheism of Athens and Rome with the action of the cults of Brahma, Isis, Zoroaster, or Odin.

17. The one who deceives a Brahmin is reborn as a demon with a hideous form: he can live neither on the earth nor in the air. Relegated to some dark forest, he moans day and night, and drinks the unhealthy juice of the palm tree, mixed with the spittle of a dog, from a human skull (Dubois, I, 240; II, 266, 379, 464). "Hata! Hata!" cried an ape one day, seeing a fox devouring a cadaver. "You have committed an unspeakable crime, since you are condemned to nourish yourself with such food." "Alas!" responds the fox, "I once was a man; I promised gifts to a Brahmin, I broke my word, you see my punishment." Those who during their life have not given provisions to priests, those who have not clothed them, or who do violence to them, or utter insults, are subject in the other world to hunger, nakedness, fire, and torments of all sorts. The murder of a Brahmin is worse than parricide; better to have killed one's own father than to stir up division in the order of Brahmins. Unbelief, the most unpardonable of misdeeds in the eyes of the priesthood, is punished even more severely. The fire that consumes the impious never goes out (*Asiat. Res.*, VI, 215–220). Homicide, in contrast, merits only a temporary punishment, after which transmigration offers the sinner new chances of salvation (Holwel, German trans., II, 51ff.).

18. Buddhists are not saved by their good works if they have not sanctified them by sprinkling water on the ground (*Asiat. Res.*, VI, 215, 220).

CHAPTER 9

On Metempsychosis

We saw in our first volume[1] that the doctrine of metempsychosis entered into the primitive's conjectures on the state of souls after this life. As the intellect develops, the incompatibility of this notion with that of a world to come that is little different from our own acquires greater evidence, and metempsychosis seems to have to be rejected by the religions that become more regular and better coordinated.

Thus, we do not find it among any of the peoples who freely and progressively created their religious forms. Neither the Greeks nor the Romans admitted it in their public worship, even though it had penetrated into their philosophical systems and their mystery cults; but it was sanctioned in the most affirmative manner among all the priestly nations, and one would be wrong to place it in the scientific explanations of the priests.

To be sure, it formed some part of them, sometimes combining with metaphysical abstractions, sometimes with astronomical calculations. Thus, the Indians[2] attached it to their subtleties on nature and the purification of souls, while

---

1. Bk. II, ch. 4.

2. The Vedas assign this universe as a purgatory to the souls that have misrecognized their celestial origin; sunk into matter, they are incarnate in animated bodies. It is the punishment for their infidelity. On the metempsychosis of the Indians, see Dubois, II, 505. As soon as the soul leaves its body, it appears before the judge of the dead to receive its sentence; then it mounts to heaven or descends to the netherworld, where, according to its faults, it takes the form of a bird, a mineral, or a quadruped (*Asiat. Res.*, I, 239–40). The Cingalese have the same notions; they say the dead are judged by one of the inferior gods, Yammah Raya (their Yama), and in virtue of this judgment they are reborn as men or beasts. These rebirths continue until their arrival and their definitive stay in the Bramah-Loke, or paradise (*Asiat. Res.*, VII, 35).

the Egyptians,[3] without rejecting this system of gradual purifications, united metempsychosis to astronomy by means of the cycle of three thousand years they
assigned to transmigrations.[4]

But independently of these scientific meanings, it is incontestable that metempsychosis was part of the public beliefs of the peoples ruled by the priesthood.

Favored in the southern climates by the sympathy and pity that these climates
inspire for all living and suffering things,[5] probably transplanted in the North by
colonies, it was conserved everywhere, perhaps because offering the faithful the
real spectacle of rewards and punishments, to the priests it appeared to be a more
forceful lesson than the teachings that relegated to an invisible world these same
punishments and rewards. We just saw it in India; it penetrated the religion of the
Gauls,[6] the Persians,[7] the Getes, and it is not sure that it was always foreign to
the mythology of the Hebrews.[8]

The maintenance of this teaching, given other hypotheses that ought to have excluded it, confirms what we established elsewhere concerning the double doctrine
of the priests and its little influence on the public religion. Those of Egypt combined metempsychosis with the existence of a subterranean world by making them
two branches of the same system, at once mysterious and scientific. This subterranean world was nothing but the place of repose where the dead destined to new
purifications (which were attached to astronomy) awaited the signal for the trans-

---

3. On the metempsychosis of the Egyptians, see Herodotus, II, 123; Guigniaut, pp. 882–94; Dubois, II, 309–16; Creuzer, III, 176, who claims that Egyptian notions were common with the Thracians; Goerres, pp. 389–93. The Egyptian and Indian doctrines differ in this, that the first is more
scientific and astronomical, and the second more metaphysical and moral.

4. It was in the name of the blessed souls that the Egyptians pronounced over the tomb of the
dead the prayer that Porphyry reports: "Sun, master of all, and you, gods of the universe, dispensers
of life, receive us, and make us the companions of the eternal gods" (*De abst.*, IV, 10; Goerres, II, 370).

5. Herder, *Phil. de l'hist.*, III, 42, 43; *Zerstr. Blaett.*, I, 218.

6. Diod., V, 20; Caes., *B Gall.*, VI. The people of Wales, the cradle of the Druids and, consequently, of the Gallic religion, also admitted metempsychosis (Davies, pp. 463–77).

7. On metempsychosis among the Persians, see Guigniaut, notes, p. 700; Porph., *De abst.*, IV.

8. A passage from Josephus indicates, on the contrary, that it was the belief of at least one sect. All
souls are immortal, he says, according to the view of the Pharisees. Those of virtuous men pass into
new bodies; those of criminals are condemned to eternal torments. Thus, what among the Indians
served as the punishment of the wicked, among the Jews was the reward of the good.

migrations that would purify them,[9] and it was to this temporary waiting place that the practices that are incompatible with metempsychosis were connected.[10]

The multitude remained indifferent to these refined explanations and according to the scattered and partial teachings that they received, believed alternately in metempsychosis or in Amenthes, without being struck by the opposition of the two beliefs they did not think to bring together.[11]

In this way one of our most important assertions is confirmed. Everything that in independent polytheism strikes the imagination in only a vague and passing manner is recognized and enters into priestly polytheism. The most fleeting conjectures, those that appear to be admissible only by minds that are still plunged in the ignorance of the savage state, are combined with the less crude doctrines that

9. Virgil transported this combination into his *Aeneid*. Anchises says to Aeneas that souls dwell a thousand years in Elysium before passing into new bodies. But given the condition of beliefs in Virgil's day, the poet did not restrict himself to these beliefs. In the *Georgics* (IV, 28), he says that the souls of heroes, sages, and virtuous men pass immediately to the stars. Without admitting metempsychosis, the first Fathers of the Church borrowed from Egyptian teaching the idea of a temporary dwelling of souls before their definitive punishments or rewards. The souls descend, they say, into the subterranean world: the just had presentiment of their happiness, the wicked of their pains, and their destiny would then be realized at the resurrection. Only the martyrs went immediately from earth to heaven. See *Traité de la créance des prêtres touchant l'état des âmes après cette vie*, by Blondel (1661); Baumgarten, *Hist. doct. de statu animar. separat.*, 1754. Saint Augustine perfected this doctrine, making this the place of the souls' purification. Caesarius, bishop of Arles, and Gregory VI endorsed it. Hence, purgatory.

10. This observation also applies to the Indian religion, and serves as a response to the objections of Mr. de Pauw. "One can hardly," he says, "believe that Indians claim to rejoin their spouses, obliging them to burn themselves on their pyres, because they maintain that souls travel from one body to another in such a way that the soul of the husband could find itself in the embryo of a mouse, and the soul of the wife in that of a cat" (*Rech. sur les Amér.*, II, 182). The same objections could be brought against the doctrine of the Burmese. Their belief in transmigration ought to preserve them from the fear of ghosts, and yet some persons belonging to the Chinese embassy having died in Amarapura, this event gave rise to terror in the country because people believed the souls of strangers to be more malevolent than those of natives (*Asiat. Res.*, VI, 180). By pointing out the complicated double composition of religions subject to priests, we believe we have addressed the difficulty.

11. The importance Egyptians attached to the preservation of bodies, and the effort they devoted to their embalming (Heeren, II, 675), owed to the doctrine of Amenthes, in which the state of souls destined to recommence their past lives depended, as on earth, on the perfection of material organs. Metempsychosis served as the basis of other portions of the worship, symbolically expressing more abstract notions.

the progress of the intellect brings; and if one must not attribute the difference that exists between these two species of polytheism to the spontaneous inventions of the priesthood, one must still recognize that they come in large part from the care that it takes to gather everything together and make sure that nothing is forgotten.

BOOK X

ON THE TEACHINGS PECULIAR TO
PRIESTLY POLYTHEISM

CHAPTER I

The Object of This Book

In the preceding book we treated the teachings common to the two species of
religion, and we indicated the differences that the priestly spirit introduced into
these doctrines. But there are others that belong more especially to the religions
controlled by priests. We are going to treat them.

CHAPTER 2

On the Supremacy of One God over the Others in the Priestly Religions

Several passages of Homer prove that the gods of Greece were originally equal:[1] Jupiter had acquired certain prerogatives, but the other inhabitants of Olympus braved his power and disobeyed his will.[2]

It is not the same in the priestly polytheism. Among the Indians Shiva, sometimes Indra,[3] and Brahma in the Vedas;[4] among the Persians, Zurvan-Akarana; among the Scandinavians, Alfadur; among the Egyptians, Cneph, all occupy a place apart and reign over the other gods who are sometimes inclined to rebel, but who are always inferior to their master in force and dignity.

Several causes impress this distinctive character on priestly religions.

First of all, since in the scientific teaching of the religion these gods are only personifications of certain parts of nature or symbols of hidden forces, they neces-

---

1. Notably the discourse of Neptune to Jupiter, *Iliad*, XV, 185–99.

2. The supremacy of Jupiter, it is true, would seem to occur even in the *Iliad*, based upon the symbol of the golden chain (Liv., VIII, v. 17). But this symbol, as we have already observed (bk. VIII, ch. 3, n. 36), is obviously borrowed from a priestly religion. It is found word-for-word in the Bhagavad Gita; all those who have studied Homer have been struck by the strange cast of this fable (see Creuzer, I, 120): this is because it did not belong to Greece; it came from the East.

3. In the 38th chapter of the Rigveda, Indra is chosen by the gods as their supreme head. His throne is built with texts drawn from the Vedas, and the ceremonies of his installation are similar in all things to those of Indian kings. By this, one sees that the supreme god of priestly religions is not always the same. The empire of priests is brought along, however, from one to the other, and this variation is one of the causes of the obscurity that reigns in ancient mythologies. Each god appears successively clothed with the attributes of all the previous ones.

4. Brahma, who is sovereign in the sacred books, at most occupies the second rank in fables. He is supplanted by Shiva or Vishnu, according to the different sect. This is due to the abolition of his worship. We spoke of this above.

sarily lose their individuality. The general system that unites and coordinates them classes them as parts of a whole, and in the mythological language the whole becomes the supreme divinity. But with individuality being as necessary to devotion as metaphysics is to science, this supreme god becomes the link between the two doctrines, sometimes having a variable and active nature, adapted to the needs and desires of the people, sometimes an inactive, immutable nature, as demanded by philosophical meditation.

In the second place, when imagination has become overfamiliar with the objects of its homage, the religious sentiment demands something less-known, something more imposing. It is never entirely satisfied with what is presented to it. Every limit wounds it, and every description, every definition, is a limit. It tends to rise higher in order to find itself at liberty in vagueness. Priests then reveal new secrets to it, unveiling a superior essence that until then was unknown, flattering it by these heights and this mystery while they reawaken the imagination with the novelty.

Thus, the supreme god of the religions fashioned by priests is ordinarily a god different from those surrounded by vulgar adoration. In Scandinavia, it is not Odin but an invisible god who, when the centuries will be fulfilled, will emerge from his unknown retreat to plunge the world back into nothingness.[5]

In Egypt, Cneph came late to dominate not only over the popular divinities, Isis, Osiris, and Horus, but also over Phat, who previously was the first principle.[6] It is from the mouth of Cneph that the mystical egg came, whose shell Phat breaks in order to show himself to the universe; he, however, is only a secondary god because he owes his birth to another god.[7]

Among the Persians, Zurvan-Akarana has nothing in common with Oromaze or Mithra. He is separated from the active divinities; and by a consequence of the complications that always inhere in priestly dogmas, he is at once a cosmogonic power and an astronomical symbol, on one hand, and endless time, creature of the word, on the other, the great period of twelve thousand years.[8]

---

5. What proves that this is a development in the religious notions of the Scandinavians is that in the Edda, Odin, with his brothers, governs the earth and heaven, and he is the most powerful of the gods (Edda, 3rd fable); a teaching contrary to that concerning Alfadur, and which is much older because it is cruder. We know that some have wanted to regard this portion of the fables of the North as an interpolation of Christian monks; but the appearance of the same ideas in all mythologies refutes this suspicion.

6. Cic., *De nat. deor.*, III, 2; Diod., I, 12; Arnob., *Adv. gentes*, I, 4; Iamblich., *De myster.*

7. Porph., in Euseb., *Praep. evang.*, III, 9; Plut., *De Is. et Os.*; Jablonsky, *Panth. Aeg.*, p. 93.

8. Vendidad, Izeschiné, XIX; Goerres, *Asiat. myth. Gesch.*, I, 219–20.

This is not all. By the fact that the active divinities of the mythologies take an interest in the destinies of men and associate themselves with their debates, they inevitably contract their imperfections and their weaknesses. There is a certain versatility in their character; their nature is not immutable, sheltered from every passion, untouchable by change.

In order to compensate for this species of degradation, the priesthood places at the peak of the celestial hierarchy a divinity of a nature that seems more elevated because it is vaguer and less definable. Its immobility has something majestic to it. Its complete apathy distinguishes it from variable beings. The god of the Bhaga-vad Gita, even though like the air it penetrates the diversity of beings, is alien to this diversity: no modification affects it.[9] In Japan, Amida is separated from all the elements, indifferent to the world it moves, and whose movements it does not share. Among the Siamese, Sommonacodom is plunged into a repose that no thought, will, or action troubles; but in order to reconcile this conception with the exigencies of anthropomorphism, the Siamese add that their supreme god obtained this impassability only by unheard-of effort, and the violence it imposed on itself replaced the blood that flowed in its veins with a liquid that is white like milk and cold like snow.

This notion is not as developed in the northern regions. The northern peoples, given over entirely to the storms of life, could not admit a repose founded on the absence of all the emotions that were so dear to them, or a felicity similar to noth-ingness. Nonetheless, their supreme god plays no role in their mythology. It only appears to hover over its ruins.

Even though the Jehovah of the Hebrews was a national divinity, one who marched, fought, and struggled with his people, or against them, the rabbis, in their cabal, declared that any action was unworthy of the divine majesty. They called the supreme god the unknown father, the obscure Aleph.

We do not think that our readers need to be alerted to the intimate connection of these conceptions of the impassability of the supreme god with pantheism, the final term of the metaphysics of priests.

Thus, the priesthood simultaneously courts the religious sentiment that, as we said elsewhere,[10] distances the object of its worship in order better to adore it,

---

9. *Asiat. Res.*, II, 230.
10. See bk. II, ch. 2.

and interest, which brings it closer in order to make use of it. It does the same with the ardent desire for abstraction that takes hold of human minds when they take up the insoluble questions they believe they can resolve by going from subtlety to subtlety, from abstraction to abstraction.

CHAPTER 3

On the Inferior Gods or the Priestly Demonology

Placed outside the world and its interests, the supreme god seems to have entirely escaped from man. The religious sentiment that placed it at this height cannot attain it. The feeble mortal therefore directs sad gazes at heaven, astonished at the solitude in which he finds himself and at his powerlessness to reestablish bonds between him and the immutable being that his thirst for perfection sundered.

When religion is independent, these bonds reconstitute themselves. Free to abandon himself to his successive impressions, man is not chained to a system from which there is no departure; and following the needs of his soul, sometimes he plunges into a vague contemplation that paints the Supreme Being as beyond all proportion with his nature; sometimes he crosses the distance and recalls this being to himself, the better to enjoy its protection.

But in the religions controlled by the priesthood, since it records and saves man's conjectures, it inhibits him in present ones by the sanctions attached to his past suppositions. It then must present to the imagination it holds captive some hypothesis that puts religion back at its disposal. From this comes the immense number of subaltern gods, *genii*, and intermediate beings who populate the beliefs subject to priests.[1]

Celsus says that the Egyptians have thirty-six demons that they call decans, or ethereal gods.[2] Three are attached to each superior god, and each demon commands inferior intelligences, which brings their number to 360.[3] These demons

---

1. The Ramayana (p. 415) speaks of 600 million Asparas, or celestial nymphs.

2. Origen, *Contre Celse*. For the Egyptian demonology, see Creuzer, III, 71; and Guigniaut, pp. 47, 456.

3. Lactant., *De falsa relig.*

are not at all absorbed in contemplation, as is the supreme god;[4] they act cease-lessly, and their activity is tireless.[5] Some are pure and benevolent; they protect mortals, warn them, help them. Their head is Osiris, who, covered with a resplen-dent cloak, holds the mystical Phallus.[6] The nature of the others is impure and malevolent; a serpent's tail betrays their malignity.[7] This is the race of giants defeated by Horus or Hercules, whose blood mixed with the earth produced the vine, a dangerous gift that puts in the veins of humans the blood of a criminal race, causing a deadly delirium.[8] The head of these evil *genii* is Typhon. Because of a reason that we will explain in a moment, the notion of evil divinities, which is foreign to free polytheism, is always a part of priestly polytheism; once malevolent divinities are admitted, a certain tendency of our minds to see or produce symme-try institutes a hierarchy in the netherworld, as in heaven.

However, this demonology, which on one side is connected with the popular religion because of the ability attributed to the demons to protect or harm men, on the other side enters into the scientific doctrine by means of relations established between the demons and the stars and planets. To subject three of them to each of the twelve superior gods was to combine them with the twelve signs of the zodiac, and their number of three hundred and sixty is obviously an astronomical division; then, however, the denominations change. The head of the perverse intelligences is no longer Typhon but Serapis, the winter sun, cold and pale, and exercising only a malign influence.[9]

But this same Serapis returns by another route to attach himself to the popular religion. He is the god of the netherworld, he presides over the subterranean world at Amenthes, the abode of the souls that live an earthly life, but under the earth.[10] Thus, as we have said in a preceding volume, popular superstition and the science of priests constantly touch; they constantly enter into each other, borrowing from one another, exchanging reciprocal developments, and they form two systems that are so united, so interlaced (even though many of their details are irreconcilable) that it is impossible, at any moment, not to run the risk of confusing them.

4. Hermes, *Ad Tatium*; Stobaeus; Iamblich., *De myst.*
5. Iamblich., ibid.
6. Kircher, *Oed. Aeg.*
7. Goerres, II, 385.
8. Plut., *De Is. et Osir.*
9. Porph., *ap.* Eus., *Praep. ev.*, III.
10. Plut., *De Isid.*

It is the same with the demonology of the Persians. It has a hierarchy of good and evil *genii* who, independently of the rank they occupy in the public religion, have astronomical, cosmogonic, and metaphysical meanings. All the measures of time are personified. The Fervers, prototypical ideas[11] conceived in the mind of the first being, become living creatures[12] because the divine thought confers life. Men, stars, and animals all have their particular Fervers; they are the source of all purity, of all abundance, of all beauty. The limpid stream descends down the mountain to water the plain? A Ferver directs it. The trees are covered with fruit or foliage, the prairies with flowers, the fields with grass? It is the work of the Fervers, for which man must pray, and at the same time must constantly invoke. Opposed to the Fervers, the evil *genii* work their mischief.

The Indian demonology[13] is little different from that of Egypt:[14] Indra replaces Osiris, Moisazur, Typhon, and the Devatas or the Daints (numbering several million, with monstrous features),[15] the subordinate demons. At the same time, Indra is the mistress of the firmament; beside her are the elements and the stars, slaves of her will.

The Hebrews, too, have their demonology, especially since the Babylonian captivity.[16] Their angels resemble the Indian Devatas. This demonology was principally founded on the system of emanations. Aeons, immaterial substances parallel to the intermediate beings of the Orphic, Pythagorian, and Platonic schools, had come from God: their number was eleven, Aziloth their name. Three of these Aeons—wisdom, the world, and the spirit—had created the world and communicated the divine decrees to men.[17]

Independently, and above this demonology, half-learned, half-religious, another

11. Heeren, *Ideen*, "Perses," p. 272.

12. Goerres, I, 26ff.

13. Dubois, II, 440, 442.

14. Goerres, II, p. 386, in the note; Polier, *Myth. des hindous*, I, 12, 13. Also see Wagner, p. 180; Oupnekhat, I, 215.

15. Goerres, II, 386.

16. From the time of this captivity, the god of the Jews was depicted surrounded by seven angels, like the seven Amschaspands, and became quite similar to the god of Zoroaster. Daniel is from this period.

17. Glasner, *Dissert. de Trin. Cabbal. et Rabbin. non christ. sed mere platon.*; Helmst, 1741; Brucker, *Hist. phil. judaic. cabbal.* According to Creuzer, Christians borrowed their demonology in part from the Hebrews, in part from the Platonic philosophers. On this subject he cites two remarkable passages from Denis the Areopagite and Saint Basil. The Gnostics, counting 365 classes of *genii* in their demonology, had preserved an astronomical number but had forgotten its meaning (Creuzer, III, 86–88).

inferior order was distinguished by all the priestly nations that has fewer relations with religion and none with science, but nonetheless owed its origin to the belief taught by the priests, and is their imitation, or better put: their parody. It is composed of those spirits of the air, rivers, woods, springs, mountains, and caverns, capricious beings whom Germany still designates under a thousand strange names, and which employ their limited power in playing childish games with human beings, frightening girls, misleading the traveller; they are more playful than evil, but malevolent when they are irritated. In India, they are the *genii* who live near the sources of the Bhagarati, and who, full of an ardent love for youth and beauty, entice adolescents of both sexes into their wild retreats. The victims seduced in this way become similar to their victimizers, whose hope is thus dashed. A child who played close to their abode fell in their trap by hearing the voice of his father, a restless shade separated from its body. Fatherly love, however, overcame the charm and the father obtained the freedom of his son at the price of a promise of total silence on the part of his son. This promise was violated and the indiscreet youth was deprived of speech; as late as a few years ago, this was cited as a powerful proof of the power of *genii*, the frightful guests of the banks and waves of the Bhagarati.[18] Here one clearly sees priestly traditions lowering to the ranks of fairy-tales.

The ancient Gauls had an almost identical demonology.[19]

All these notions are foreign to independent polytheism. We will seek for them in vain in the true belief of the Greeks.[20] It was only during its decadence that they reappeared under the name of magic, in order to serve as nourishment for the credulity that did not know where to put them.

Hesiod, who speaks of subordinate gods and of demons watching over men,[21] had drawn from southern traditions these ideas that he confusedly lumped together without understanding them.[22] Later, the philosophers, admirers of teach-

18. *Asiat. Res.*, XIII, 183. The proof that there is a relation between the religious belief and this subordinate demonology is that the Brahmins who entered into the places inhabited by these spirits predict the future, the death of princes, and the revolutions of empires.

19. Davies, *Myth. Celt.*, 155–56.

20. Creuzer (*Symbol.*, 1st German ed., III, 4) recognizes that the demons or heroes, as intermediary beings, are not at all found in the Homeric mythology. The word "demon" in the *Iliad* applies to the gods. Pallas returns to Olympus, where she rejoins the other demons (*Iliad*, I, 22).

21. *Op. et Dies*, 8–9, 122, 251.

22. Everything systematically arranged in the Persian religion, notes Creuzer with a good deal of insight (*Symbol.*, III, 70, 1st German ed.), is fragmentary and incoherent in Hesiod. The notions imported by this poet were so little similar to the Greek spirit that those who lived after him made no use of the wonders he employed.

ings borrowed from the barbarians, took over their demonology in order to purify and refound polytheism, but they always acknowledged that they owed these purported improvements to foreigners.

Plutarch, who praises the Boeotian compiler for having distinguished the different intelligent natures that unite us to the gods,[23] adds that he does not know if this sublime discovery was due to the magi and Zoroaster, to Thracians and Orpheus, to the Egyptians, or the Phrygians.[24] For a long time the popular belief of the Greeks rejected these exotic additions, and if they were secondary gods at rather advanced periods of their polytheism, these gods, abandoned by the public worship and given over as it were to individual superstition, never formed anything more than an anarchic and incoherent mass, without order or goal, without consistency or hierarchy. They only had accidental relations with humans; they never had any with the inhabitants of Olympus. Their number was never fixed. Their existence was uncertain, and their multiplication was spontaneous and fortuitous, depending on the caprice of individuals.

23. He identifies four classes: the gods, the demons, the heroes, and men (Creuzer, III, 14). Theopompus, in Aelian (*Var. Hist.*, III, 14), says that Selene is a being underneath the gods and above the human race.

24. *De oracul. defectu.*

CHAPTER 4

On Malevolent Divinities

Among the conceptions of the primitive savage is that of malevolent gods.[1] This conception is not the work of the religious sentiment, but of interest. Because man wants his gods to be useful to him, when they refuse he accuses them of wickedness. A fortiori he will consider those he suspects of being harmful to him as perverse beings. But as his knowledge progresses, he will set aside this idea; even anthropomorphism rejects it. The gods of anthropomorphism are a mixture of vices and virtues because they resemble man; they gradually improve. No one does good without some interest, but no one does evil for evil's sake. There are none, therefore, whose special vocation, and constant inclination, is to harm the inferior species by whom they wish to be worshipped.

Moreover, as nature is better observed and the connection of facts is better grasped, good and evil, pleasure and pain, by turns the cause and the effect of one another, seem more closely tied; and to be explained, they do not require that one attribute them to two distinct and separate principles. As a consequence, we find no essentially wicked divinity in Greek polytheism.[2]

Plutarch insinuates that the inhabitants of certain countries of Greece recognized two opposite principles;[3] but he supports this assertion with no fact; and he restricts it to a few provinces where this teaching could have been introduced

---

1. See bk. II, ch. 2.

2. When Arnobius wants to suggest that the marvels about which the pagans glorified themselves were the work of Satan: "*Quisnam iste est unus,*" he says, "*interrogabit aliquis? Ne nobis fidem habere nolitis: Aegyptios, Persas, Indos, Chaldaeos, Armenios interroget.*" This is obvious proof that Arnobius knew that these nations believed in an evil principle, and that the Greeks and the Romans did not.

3. *De Is. et Osir.*

from abroad.[4] Moreover, he writes at a period when the different genres of polytheism were no longer distinct. The teachings, divinities, and practices of all the peoples bent under the yoke of a despotic people mixed, blended together, and composed an indistinct mass. Finally, Plutarch, in the curious but inexact treatise in which this assertion is found, had explicitly proposed to discover the doctrine of the double principle in all religions, as well as in all systems of philosophy; this desire had to lead him to twist and distort the opinions he reported.

At first glance, one could believe that the Titans and the Giants, the hideous monsters who were the enemies of the gods, occupied among the Greeks the place of the Egyptian Typhon or Loki of the Scandinavians. But these monsters play no role in the national mythology; they have no relations with men; they are offered no worship. Nor did anyone establish ceremonies to insult them, as was the case in Egypt. Typhon, in Egyptian belief the god of evil, source of vice and moral stain, exercising his noxious influence both in the universe as a whole and over men, in Greece became a monster who was defeated by the gods.[5]

The infernal divinities of the Greeks no doubt had something sinister and somber. The likeness of ideas naturally attached threatening and lugubrious attributes to the beings who presided over destruction and death. The gods of the netherworld, said Euripides, rejoice at our misfortunes.[6] Pluto was pleased at the sight of funeral objects, and during his feasts Greek and Roman women scratched their cheeks and bruised their bosoms.[7] But these infernal gods did not act on earth at all, unless it was to punish some great crime (and even this was at a much later period), and they did not pursue mortals any more than the other gods did.

Hecate clearly is a foreign divinity;[8] moreover, she ceased being malevolent

---

4. In the Homeric tales, Circe is an evildoing divinity because she seeks to degrade those whom chance has delivered into her power; but this tale takes us back to Colchis, and the inhabitants of Colchis were a colony of Egypt.

5. Homer, *Iliad*, II, 78; Hesiod, *Theog.*, 820. The Egyptian Typhon later entered into Greek mythology. Several fables of this mythology were derivative; that of Adonis, for example, whom Mars pursued and killed in the form of a boar (Lycophr., 580), because Typhon, who sometimes is represented in this form, had killed Osiris. In his *Dionysiaca*, Nonnus describes the battles of Jupiter against Typhon in terms rather similar to those the priests employ to depict the struggle of the two principles; but Nonnus is a very modern scholar of myths, imbued with oriental allegories (Moeser, *Ammerk ad Nonni Dionys.*, VIII).

6. *Suppl.*, 923.

7. Voss *ap.* Serv., *ad Aeneid*, III, 67.

8. Hesiod says that Jupiter, before he usurped rule, respected all the prerogatives enjoyed by Hecate. Mr. de Sainte-Croix, whose mind is always struck by the religious wars that, if one were to believe

when, subject to the action of the Greek *genius*, she took on the traits and the name of Diana.

Priestly polytheism, where all notions, once they are received, are maintained intact, does not allow the intellect that it oppresses to repudiate anything of the inheritance of ignorant times. The worship of wicked divinities is perpetuated, and several causes contribute to its continuation.

First of all, it is very simple that the same god who in the astronomical system is the representative of the evening star, of the harsh season, or, in the cosmogony, of destruction, becomes the evil principle in the popular mythology.[9]

In the second place, the religions submitted to the priests have yet another difficulty to battle than does independent polytheism. The latter does not have to reconcile respect for the justice of the gods with the events that appear to accuse them of injustice. Once these divinities are recognized as vicious and imperfect, everything follows in the rest of the system. Man does not seek to know why the character of these gods is the way it is presented. He conceives it to be similar to his own and takes it as a given. But the priests who control the belief cannot admit any imperfection in the beings of whom they are the sole interpreters and

---

him, had substituted the worship of Jupiter for that of the Titans, sees in this passage of Hesiod the indication of the pains to come, which are reserved for crime in another world by the two religions that succeeded one another. It is much closer to plausibility to admit that Hecate was an evildoing divinity, transported by Hesiod into Greek mythology and placed behind the popular divinities (see bk. VII, ch. 5, n. 17), which was natural because the latter are always the present generation (bk. V, ch. 1, 9). This is what Hesiod was expressing when he said that Jupiter had not diminished the power of Hecate. In point of fact, the sphere in which she had been relegated put her outside all contact with the active divinities. She is not mentioned in either the *Iliad* or the *Odyssey*, and her role in the much more recent poem, the *Argonautica*, is that of Proserpina in Homer (see Creuzer, I, 158; II, 120ff.; Goerres, I, 254–55; Hermann, *Handb. der Myth.*, II, 45, n. 87; Pausan., II, 30). Jablonsky (*Panth. Aeg.*) regards Hecate as the Egyptian Titrambo. Her action on nature, her diversified faculties, her innumerable functions are a mixture of physics, allegory, magic, and philosophical traditions concerning the fusion of elements and the generation of beings. She was sometimes represented with the head of a dog (Hesychius in αγαλμα Εχ). Pausanias had seen a similar statue made by the celebrated sculptor Alcamenes (Pausan., II, 30). Hecate was the night, and, by an extension of this idea, the primitive night, first cause or first mover of all things. She was the moon, and hence drew to herself all the accessory notions of the moon: she was the goddess who troubled the reason of men, the one who presided over nocturnal ceremonies and, consequently, over magic: hence her identity with Diana in Greek mythology and with Isis in the Egyptian; hence, too, all of her cosmogonic qualities, which were also attributed to Isis in Egypt.

9. Cali and Bhavani were at once the moon and the destructive force; their worshippers painted a crescent on their forehead. On the relations of Cali with Artemis, see Creuzer, II, 123, 124.

ministers.[10] They commence by giving their cruel or capricious dispositions honorable names.[11] Their unlimited severity is only an inflexible equity; their merciless jealousy is the care they owe to their own glory—a strange glory, at once insatiable and solicitous over minutiae, that prides itself on the misfortunes it imposes, and is fed by the tears it causes. But even this does not end the various objections.[12] Calamities fall equally on the faithful and the impious. It therefore

---

10. The Druses are the only people who positively affirm that God is the author of evil; and to cut short objections, their catechism adds: "The Lord has said: My creatures very much owe me an account of what they do, but I owe them no account of what I do."

11. See above, bk. IX, ch. 3.

12. As long as one wants to stay with logic, the conundrum of Epicurus is unanswerable. He says: either God can destroy evil and he does not want to do so, or he cannot nor does he want to do so, or he can and he wants to. If he wants to and cannot, he is powerless; if he can and does not want to, he is not good; if he does not want to nor can do so, he is both evil and weak; if he wants to and can do so, where does evil come from? (Lactant., *De ira Dei*, cap. 13). Nothing is more obvious, at least according to the rules of dialectic. Human justice would have happiness as the price of virtue. If you apply the same rule to divine justice, either unhappiness must be proof of a hidden crime, or the existence of evil becomes an insoluble problem. Here again arises the danger of anthropomorphism. It confuses divine justice and human justice. It establishes between the Supreme Being and men the relations of a monarch with his subjects. But if these relations are the same, in the same way that a monarch owes his protection to those of his subjects who obey the laws, God owes happiness to the just. To be sure, the debt is rarely paid. On the contrary, if we do away with anthropomorphism, if we conceive the Supreme Being as having marked out not happiness but improvement as the end of the creature, everything is explainable. A new horizon opens. We are raised to a new height. Happiness and unhappiness are only means: God is not unjust in employing them. Every other solution to the existence of evil is inadequate and rests on sophisms. Dualism, the crudest of these solutions, is still the best. If our readers wanted to convince themselves of the truth of these observations, it would suffice to read the most remarkable book of a school to which we are otherwise opposed, we mean: the *Soirées de Saint-Pétersbourg*, by Mr. de Maistre. The author is endowed with great strength of mind, an irresistible dialectic (when he is right), and at the same time an eloquence that draws from a sensibility that combines disdain with bitterness, as is always the case with genius; he fights furiously against the dilemma we posed earlier; and in order to escape from it, he strikes down both final causes and the immutable laws of nature, which he declares contrary to all religion and worship; but when he has sufficiently thundered against these two adversaries, he is pushed to two conclusions: one, that prayer can suspend the general rules that govern the universe; the other, that misery is always the consequence of crime. With the first of these two principles there is no longer any science; with the second, there is no more pity. The course of the sun is at the mercy of the invocations of a priest or a woman, and the innocent who dies on the rack must perish burdened with the condemnation of even the person who knows his innocence, because he merited this torment by some unknown fault. It is not until Mr. de Maistre, forgetting his own theory, is led by the élan of his soul outside the sphere of dialectics, when he

would be dangerous to always see them as the punishment for some secret fault.[13] What would the pontiff say who was struck with some painful infirmity at the foot of the altar, or struck by one of the accidents that fate, thanks to heaven, reserves to power as well as to weakness? One must therefore attribute another cause to evil than divine justice. The evil principle, or a class of gods who do evil by inclination, by their nature, provides a momentarily satisfactory explanation.

One can observe that the necessity of this hypothesis becomes more pressing as belief represents their gods as more sovereignly just and powerful. According to the necessary conclusions of human reason, the doctrine of the evil principle is the inevitable result of divine perfections carried to the highest point the intellect can conceive. This assertion is so true that when the philosophers of Greece were led by the progress of learning to reject the fables of the common mythology in order to purify the character of the gods they went in the direction of dualism. One cannot fail to recognize this tendency in the works of the Platonists. In his treatise on the origin of evil, Maximus of Tyre says that evils and ills cannot descend from heaven, where there are no perverse natures, but that, as for physical evil, it arises from an intrinsic imperfection of matter, and for moral evil, from a depravation inherent in the soul. This depravation is a species of evil principle.

---

returns to the religious sentiment without trying to harmonize it with the traffic in services that self-interest suggests to man, i.e., when he unwittingly foreswears the anthropomorphism whose defense he elsewhere undertakes, it is only then that he becomes both sublime and reasonable; what he says, for example (I, 443) about prayer, by separating it from the puerile effectiveness that he attributes to it a few pages earlier, and by describing its moral effect on the one who prays, as an act of submission, confidence, and love, is applicable to all religious forms and is admirable in all systems (with the exception of dogmatic atheism, the narrowest and most presumptuous of all teachings). But unfortunately committed to the fixed dogmas he wants to have prevail, Mr. de Maistre does not remain very long in this atmosphere of emotion, disinterestedness, and purity. Soon the sophist devoted to an exclusive form replaces the religious man. His thought loses its expansiveness, sentiment its depth, his style its elevation, clarity, and force. Mr. de Maistre, however, is very much the most distinguished man of this school. Mr. de La Mennais comes after him, the sole disciple worthy of the master, but unstable, the plaything of the winds that waft over his spirit from every direction, not fearing to contradict himself. Messrs. Ferrand, de Bonald, and Eckstein have taken only what is false from the system. This would be gibberish without verve, agitation without warmth; in the first two, there is ignorant presumption and absurdity without talent, in the third, superficial erudition and talent falsified by the desire to be authoritative and the need to be pleasing.

13. The Sadducees, believing that happiness was a reward and unhappiness a punishment, considered not helping the unfortunate to be a religious act; this is the natural consequence of the idea of divine justice applied to the events on earth.

Independently of these causes that have their root in the intellect, local circumstances and particular events had to favor dualism. The priests considered the warriors who fought against them to be agents of the malevolent divinities. The peoples threatened by hordes greedy for pillage rather naturally conceived the same thought. They placed the kingdom of evil on their borders. A mysterious tree separated the two empires; it covered the netherworld with eternal shadows. The children of the day and the children of the night warily observed and attacked one another; and the latter, often defeated, nonetheless constantly renewed their sacrilegious aggressions.

The impurity attached to the union of the sexes[14] probably introduced the doctrine of the evil principle into religion by yet another route. The woman is always its victim or its agent, and often both. Eve seduced our first father; the rape of Sita by Ravana, of Rukmini by Shishupala, in the two Indian epics, and of Kriemhild by a monster in the Nibelungen, display the woman, whether guilty or innocent, as the cause of war and carnage, and the fatal source of all human ills. The story of Pandora, and the subject of the *Iliad* itself, have been related (although by an interpretation that is lacking in solidity) to this teaching common to the priestly mythologies; to be sure, the Greek rhapsodes, like Hesiod, separated this tradition from the religious meaning, of which they were unaware.

These different causes make dualism a fundamental teaching in the religions subject to priests. As Loki is the evil principle among the Scandinavians,[15] and Typhon among the Egyptians,[16] two planets exercise a pernicious influence among the Chaldeans.[17] Finally, the Gauls[18] and the Germans,[19] and at the other extremity of the globe, the Mexicans,[20] revered wicked divinities. If the pantheism of

14. See bk. II, ch. 2.

15. The fable of Loki indicates the difference between the two polytheisms. Like Prometheus, Loki is chained to a rock. Like him, he is given over to constantly recurring torments. In place of the vulture that devours the son of Jupiter, a serpent spits venom on the god of the North, which burns him (Edda, 31st fable). But in Greek mythology, Prometheus is a defeated god, a god who is a friend of man. Among the Scandinavians, Loki is the evil principle.

16. Typhon was the object of a special cult in several cities of Egypt. Temples that were always very small rose beside the magnificent temples of the other divinities. They were called Typhoniums, Τυφωνεια (Strabo, VII).

17. Plut., *De Is. et Osir.*

18. Helmold, *Chron. Slav.*, ch. 15; Voss, *De orig. Idol.*; Hagenberg, *Germ. med. Diss.*, p. 8.

19. *Mém. de l'Acad. des inscript.*, XXIV, 345; Caes., *B Gall.*, VI.

20. Among their evildoing divinities, Tlacatecolotl occupies first place; it is an owl endowed with intelligence that pleases itself by frightening men and doing evil to them.

the Indians led them to confound the destructive force with the Supreme Being in the person of Shiva, they nonetheless made the evil principle a separate being, Moisasour, leader of the rebel angels, who led them into revolt, and who was cast with them into Onderah, the place of darkness;[21] half of nature is subject to his empire.[22]

The idea of an evildoing divinity is not at all foreign to the Jewish religion,[23] and Christianity itself, every time that it was badly understood, could not prevent itself from granting the evil principle an eminent place. Christians named it the prince of this world, the god of this seculum.[24]

The notions of the Persians are in this respect shrouded in obscurity. These obscurities owe to a cause we discussed above.[25] The first polytheism of the Persians was not a priestly religion, and it did not admit divinities who were malevolent by their essence. This teaching came from Media with the magi called by Cyrus; but the magi's teaching was not entirely adopted by the nation. Hence, one finds a striking contradiction among authors who were more and less contemporaries. Some—Plato, Herodotus, Xenophon—do not say a word about Persian dualism. Others, however—Eudoxus, a friend of Plato and companion during his travels,[26] Aristotle, and Theopompus, the disciple of Isocrates—affirm it and discuss it in detail. The silence of Herodotus can be attributed to his excessive fear of indiscreetly discussing the mysteries; Xenophon's by the fact that he knew only the public part of Persian religion; and Plato's because he treated it only in passing. But with no historian of the Macedonian wars saying that the Persians in their defeats had attempted to pacify Arimanes, while Plutarch describes terrible sacrifices celebrated in his honor, this would lead us to believe that the doctrine of the evil principle remained for a long time foreign to the religion of the people and was reserved for the order of magi. Its gradual entrance into the public religion was shown by the growing hatred of certain noxious animals. Initially reserved to

21. Shastabad.

22. Four clouds give rain: Kambarta and Drona the generative rains, Abarta and Puchkara, floods and tempests. Seven elephants carry souls, either to heaven or to the netherworld. Four are gentle and benevolent, three are malevolent and treacherous. Seven serpents reign over all the other serpents. Ahanta and Karkata are the enemies, Maha-Padnia the friend of men (Dubois, II, 50–52).

23. One can see a very intriguing exposition of the development of this teaching among the Hebrews in the commentary of Eichhorn on the New Testament (II, 159–60).

24. Gospel of Saint John, XIV, 30; Cor., IV, 4.

25. Bk. IV, ch. 9.

26. See Hermippus in Diog. Laert., I, 8.

the priestly order, as dualism became the common belief this hatred was communicated to all the classes.

After having proclaimed the existence of malevolent gods, the priesthood has need of reassuring man against this frightful creation of theirs. Hence came fables, promises, and solemn ceremonies.

The fables are always based on the same thought, which is essentially sacerdotal: the first virtue of man is submission. The gods give him over to the evil principle so that he will resign himself to their will. This is the dominant idea of the Book of Job, of the episode of Nala and Damayanti in the Mahabharata, and above all of the story of King Harischandra. Cast from the throne, this prince falls to the condition of a *tchandala*. He buries the dead, sweeps the ways—unclean tasks that only the pariahs undertake; his faithful companion, his beloved son, dies. His despair extracts not a single complaint, his confidence is not at all shaken; and after these trials, the gods steal him from the perverted power, granting him not only his crown but also the beloved objects whose loss had broken his heart.

Promises announce that the god of evil will be defeated, and that while awaiting the moment one can disarm him. Oromaze is to win a definitive victory, and until then Arimanes is contained by the imprecations of the magi.[27] But the priests always let doubt and uncertainty hover over this mystery. No one knows, says the Edda, if Thor killed the great serpent.[28] Typhon, bound in chains and tossed into a marsh where he is hidden, seeks the means of escape,[29] and once already he has succeeded because of the imprudence of Isis.[30] It is therefore necessary to constantly guard man from the malevolent divinity, and the precautions taken for the purpose are so many new supports of priestly power.

Nonetheless, one can see the resistance and efforts of the religious sentiment against a doctrine that afflicts and disorients it. It cannot admit the equality of the good and evil principles. It therefore seeks to give the former a supremacy that

27. This is what persuaded writers who are otherwise quite judicious that Persian doctrine did not admit dualism in an absolute way, but as an accidental form of theism. This doctrine, says Mr. Guigniaut (p. 322), does not stop at dualism. No, doubtless it does not stop there, because no doctrine, whether religious or philosophic, stops there: all obey the eternal law of progress; but by that very fact, one must recognize that progress has its stages, and that of dualism is different from that of the theism that comes to replace it.

28. Edda, 27th fable.

29. Jablonsky, *Panth. Aeg.*, V, 10–22.

30. Plut., *De Is. et Osir.*; Diod., 1–22.

dualism denies. Indra strikes with lightning the magnetic mountain, the work of evil *genii*, and from that come the aerolites that fall from the sky.[31] To the good alone, the magi often say, belongs eternity. Evil is circumscribed in time and has only a transitory existence.[32]

But here appears a new difficulty. The eminently just and good being becomes the author of infernal malice. Since the latter is but its instrument,[33] in good logic the agent, not the instrument, is responsible.

Expelled from this post, the religious sentiment takes over another where its defeat is less evident. The god whose boundless goodness it is pleased to conceive, as well as its power, cannot condemn any of its creatures to an endless misery. Thus, the evil principle must be harmonized with the benevolent principle.[34] At the time

---

31. *Asiat. Res.*, XIV, 429.

32. Hyde, *De rel. pers.*, cap. I. He claims that those of the magi who regarded the two principles as eternal only formed a sect of heretics. It was called Thanavea (duality). This testimony, however, is somewhat suspect. Hyde arranged facts in the way that was most favorable to his theistic system. Creuzer, less partial (*Symbol.*, II, 198–99, 1st German ed.), recognized two doctrines among the Persians: unity, Zurvan-Akarena, creator of Oromaze and Arimanes, and dualism, or Oromaze and Arimanes, equal first principles. But he made one of these teachings the secret of the priests, the other the popular belief, and thus mistook the fluctuations of the religious sentiment.

33. "The Demon," says a very religious writer (St.-Philippe, *Mon. des Hébr.*, I, 137), "can do nothing except by God, who can act by himself, and who in his secret purposes grants him a power that is so limited that it is not in freedom that the Demon acts, but out of pure obedience. He is the invisible instrument of the decrees of the one who cast him into hell." It is remarkable to see Persian dualists operate in this circle without being able to get out. Sensing that if light is eternal and darkness created, darkness is the product and, hence, the responsibility of the light, others, the Zurvanites, said that light had created Zurvan, time, from which Oromaze and Arimanes had emanated, thus placing on the second cause the responsibility from which they claimed to absolve the first. Others made light and darkness come from God, but the latter in the way that a shadow always follows the body (Hyde, cap. I). God did not will them, says Creuzer's translator, interpreting their thought (p. 324), but tolerated them. Still others accuse Arimanes of being perverted by his will, not his nature (Izeschné, XXX, Ha). Vain sophisms, which always leave a reproach hanging over the all-powerful, responsible either for beings to whom it confides its power, or for necessity—an empty word when there is omnipotence.

34. This idea is reproduced in certain Egyptian fables, of which the Greek poets speak. Typhon was the enemy of harmony. He pleased himself with contravening the gods and disturbing the order of the world. Hermes, inventor of music, having defeated him, granted him his life; but he made the strings of his lyre from the nerves that he took from Typhon, thus constraining what was discordant to form harmonies, and what was opposed to unity to contribute to unity (Pind., *Pyth.*, I, 25–31; schol., ibid.; Plut., *De Is. et Osir.*, 55).

of the general resurrection, after burning metals will have purified Arimanes in their liquid fire, he will rise, purified of all his previous corruption; and praising the creative being and Oromaze, the longtime object of his envy, he will intone celestial hymns and pronounce the sacred words.[35]

Sometimes simple ceremonies tend to soften the harsh notion of the evil principle. As god of the subterranean world, of death, and of destruction, Serapis was merged with it. In order to disarm his malevolence, one would bring the sick into his temples and he was implored to spare them. Soon this practice suggested another idea, that he heal them. As a result, he became a benevolent god. It could have been the same with the Nile, a wicked divinity when, before the discovery of agriculture, his flooding was entirely harmful, and a protective god after this discovery, because he fertilized the cultivated earth.

Other times, the religious sentiment not being able to entirely remove perversity from the divine natures, preferred them being capricious rather than thoroughly wicked. See the Varuna of the Indians[36] or the Vila of the Serbians, whose long hair and robes with a thousand folds float in the air, distributing roses but also bringing dark clouds together; she casts blood on the plains, sites of future battles, alternately helpful or harmful to lovers, revealing herself to young virgins in order to lead or mislead them.

The activity of the religious sentiment is thus quite manifest. It introduces modifications into the character of the malevolent gods, and inconsistencies, which mitigate their hostile inclinations; it points toward the time when these regenerated beings will be united to the appeased divinity. It thus wrests from the priesthood more or less limited concessions and places hope alongside discouragement, consolation next to terror.

35. Zend-Avesta, Izeschné, XXX; Boundehesch, p. 104.
36. See bk. VI, ch. 5.

CHAPTER 5

Consequences of This Teaching in the Priestly Religions

The assumption of one or several malevolent divinities entails important consequences. These divinities, who are essentially hostile to man, work to make him not only miserable but also criminal. They surround him with traps, they lay ambushes for him, they trouble him by their seductions, they pervert him by their temptations. The Eternal, says the Shastabad, permits the rebellious debtahs to enter into this world in order to tempt the creatures that must be tested.[1] Among the Egyptians, the souls that, instead of having purified themselves, were corrupted, inclined the new bodies in which they entered to evil.[2]

Greek mythology sometimes shows us gods instigating crimes, but for their personal interest, and in particular circumstances. The hypothesis of spirits who devote themselves to tempting man and leading him to evil out of the sole pleasure of corrupting him belongs exclusively to religions subject to priests. The demonology we have spoken of favors the development and extension of this view. The imagination must occupy itself with the beings it created. As long as man did not exist, says a theologian, the devil had nothing to do.[3]

This assumption influences morality in a harmful way. Man never knows if the movements of his heart, the élans of his soul, the activity of his spirit are not the suggestions of a malignant power. Science can be a criminal curiosity; the testi-

---

1. Bhag. Gita, Wilkins preface, p. XCII.

2. Hermes Trism., pp. 3, 10.

3. *"Donec crearetur homo, non erat pro diabolo opus in mundo agendum"* (Hyde, *De rel. pers.*, cap. 3, p. 81). Thus, after having created the devil to explain man's misfortune and unhappiness, theologians have imagined that God had created man to give work to the devil.

mony of a clear conscience can be condemnable pride,[4] pity, a revolt against the decrees of Providence.

This threat hovers over the most innocent heads, and threatens the most correct of intentions. It is even more inevitable as the corrupting divinities are often clothed in pleasant forms. Mohammaya, perfidious illusion, is decked in the most attractive of features. The figure of Loki is full of grace. Even though Arimanes himself is hideous,[5] Dsye, the evil *genius* who accompanies him, is an adolescent of unblemished beauty; and the brilliant colors of the serpent captivate the eyes, his eloquence charms the ears.[6]

In this doctrine everything is danger; everything is a trap on the part of the divinity itself. The best sentiments, the noblest passions are a source of doubts and of terrors. It belongs to the priesthood to calm the terror and to resolve the doubts.

4. The anecdote of the friend of Saint Bruno is well known; he was condemned for having, at the moment of death, congratulated himself for having lived an irreproachable life.

5. Boundehesch, ch. 3; Kleucker, *Anhang zum Zendavesta*, II, 3, 172. By contrast, the benevolent divinities sometimes take on horrible forms in priestly religions.

6. In a bas-relief that can be seen in the Vatican museum in Rome, the Furies are young and beautiful. Their terrible mission is recognized only in the serpents that are entwined in their hair and the torches they carry in their hands. But in Greek mythology, the Furies are not malevolent deities, they are avenging divinities.

CHAPTER 6

On the Notion of an Original Fall[1]

Let man enter into himself, and he is informed of a double tendency and the constant struggle that goes on in his own heart, the theater of always-arising battles, of which he is both the surprised spectator and the miserable victim. It is in vain that he works to reestablish a harmony he is not destined to enjoy on earth. While he abandons himself to one of these discordant halves, he cannot impose silence on the other. Innocence succumbs to temptation, the guilty to remorse. The opposition of good and evil in the external world gave rise to the doctrine of the evil principle. The opposition of good and evil within man gave rise to the idea of a fall, of a transgression, of an original sin. We find traces of it in all the mythologies. They all speak of a fault whose stain is transmitted from the first individual of the human race to the present generation, or even of a crime that having preceded creation itself, explains our depravity and justifies our present misery.

However, it is only in the priestly religions that this hypothesis acquires importance and lasts.

This notion entered into the philosophical systems of the Greeks. The disciples of Orpheus, says Plato,[2] call the body a prison, because the soul there is in a state

---

1. For the germ of this notion, see bk. II, ch. 2.

2. In the *Cratylus*. It is also said in the *Phaedo* that the souls that abandon themselves to the pleasures of the senses remain on earth and enter into new bodies; those that have worked to disengage themselves from every stain, after death retire to an invisible place. There, he continues in the *Timaeus*, the pure unites with the pure, the good to its likeness, and our immortal essence to the divine essence. Also see the allegory of the reign of Saturn in the *Statesman*. Indians express themselves in almost the exact same terms. They say that the soul united to a body is imprisoned in ignorance and sin, like a frog in a snake's belly, until by the practice of contemplation and penance man once again, and forever, reunites with the divinity (Dubois, II, 85). The difference between the philosophical doctrines and the

of punishment until it has expiated the faults it committed while in heaven; and the same view was received in the mysteries, marked with foreign doctrines. But in the public belief this opinion cannot be seen except in a few rather confused traces. The story of Pandora and that of the four ages of the world (whose idea was transported into Greece from the East)[3] are not connected with the popular cult except by some traditions that in no way modify it. Expiations were not in use except for crimes directly committed by those who had to perform the expiation, and they had no connection with a previous crime, or a natural depravation. From the spectacle of the evils and ills of the human condition, the Greeks were only led to the jealousy and passions of the gods.

However, in all the climates where the theocratic empire was established early on,[4] not being able to reconcile their sufferings with divine justice, men imagined an original offense, whether it was before the creation of our race,[5] or transmitted by our first father to his unfortunate children,[6] or committed by them in a previous life and in another sphere.[7]

Priests have a powerful interest in accrediting this notion. It motivates the purifications, penances, mysterious duties, and supererogatory rigors imposed on man by the god who placed him in this world, not as an innocent being who has a right to justice, but as a guilty party for whom misfortune is only a punishment. And the priesthood is the organ, the representative, of this vengeful divinity.

An hypothesis that seems even more strange, but which is explained by a pen-

---

religious systems is that, ordinarily, the philosophers do not suppose that divine assistance is necessary for the atonement of humankind, other than as protecting and encouraging virtue, and giving man the strength to resist temptation, while the priestly religions imagine a divine assistance of a wholly mysterious nature, in which man has no merit, because divinity takes upon itself the atonement. See bk. XI, ch. 5, on the sanctity of suffering.

3. The Golden, Bronze, Silver, and Iron Ages occur in Tibet (Pallas, *Sammlung*, etc.).

4. For India, see the English preface of the Bhagavad Gita, p. lxxxiv; for the Lamaic religion, Turner and Pallas. Goerres (II, 635–38) traces a very ingenious portrait of the progression taken by the dogma of the original fall in several religions. For Persia, see Guigniaut, pp. 279–80.

5. In the Shastabad, the rebellion of the debtahs is the crime they must atone for, by animating new bodies. In Tibet, the crime of the angels is sexual union.

6. The rabbis speak of an innate inclination to evil, the heritage of Adam which weighs upon all his race.

7. Dayamanti in the Mahabharata, chased by the caravan that elephants have dispersed, cries out, seeking the cause of her misfortune: "I had to have committed some terrible misdeed in another existence before this life."

chant in man that we have already often noted, that of attributing to the gods his own adventures, is the assumption of a fall incurred by the divinity itself because of a crime it would have committed. Seized by love for his own daughter Sarasvati, Brahma could not resist her charms, and subject to the reproaches of the Brahmins, his creatures, he abandoned the body he had defiled; or, according to another legend conveyed by the Puranas, filled with pride at his works, this creator god wanted to be the equal of the supreme god whose will he had worked; but he sank into matter, dragging all of creation with him into Naraka.[8]

The Ramayana and the Mahabharata are the development of this doctrine. Their basis is the incarnation of the divine principle, expiating his fault.

The hypothesis of an original fall is easily combined with metempsychosis. The passage of the soul into different bodies is a punishment, and we have already seen in our chapters on the composition of priestly polytheism in Egypt and India the path that souls punished in this way took in order to atone for their crimes and regain heaven.[9]

8. This doctrine is the teaching of the Manicheans, who placed evil in matter and distinguished the god who created this nature from the supreme god.

9. Creuzer (I, 339) has some very good observations on this.

CHAPTER 7

On a Mediating God

Given over without any defense to the capricious and malevolent action of beings who take pleasure in harming him, the victim of ambushes laid for him by superior intelligences seeking to deceive and corrupt him, or vitiated in his nature by an original fault whose crime was attributed to him, and whose punishment was imposed on him, man would fall into despair if he did not cleave to a teaching by which he could reconnect with the divinity. The priesthood who created the evil because it was in their interest also senses that it is in their interest to provide the remedy. A new combination offers itself to them and they put it to work. A supernatural mediation reconciles heaven and earth. Among all the peoples subject to priests we encounter mediating gods. Fohi fulfills this function in the ancient Chinese religion,[1] Mithra in that of the Persians.[2] Several incarnations occupy the same place in the mythology of the Indians; and even though the North is naturally little inclined to refinements of this nature, Thor is sometimes considered a mediator between the divine and the human race.[3]

Greek polytheism admits subaltern gods, but not mediating gods, properly speaking. A lost tragedy whose main idea is known to us, *Prometheus Unbound* by

1. Couplet and Duhalde.

2. The Persians, says Plutarch (*De Ind.*), named Mithra, Mesites, the intermediary between Oromaze and Arimanes. Fred. Schlegel (*Weish. der Ind.*, p. 129) claims that Mithra was the intermediary between man and the two principles. Kleucker (*Anb. zum Zendavesta*, III, 82) supports Plutarch's assertion with several authorities. The astronomical Mithra, who had a double face like Janus (Caius Bassus, *ap.* Lyd., p. 57), and who was sometimes the sun, sometimes an intermediary between the earth and the sun, expressed the religious notion: he led souls back to God by following the sun's course across the zodiac (Guigniaut, pp. 353 & 732).

3. Mallet, *Myth. Celt.*, p. 127.

Aeschylus, contains in certain respects the notion of a mediating god. Hercules, son of Jupiter and liberator of Prometheus, reconciling the immortals and the terrestrial race, is an intermediary rather similar to those of several priestly religions. But Aeschylus had borrowed his traditions concerning Prometheus from sources foreign to Greek religion, whether by country or date.[4]

4. We will treat Aeschylus and his borrowings when we treat the Greek tragedians.

CHAPTER 8

On Triple or Ternary Divinities

These different notions, encouraged and saved by the priesthood, have probably given rise in almost all the religions they have dominated to those triple or ternary divinities that are placed at the head of the supernatural hierarchy.[1]

Among the Indians, this notion is reproduced under a host of different forms. The three letters of their mystical word correspond to their three gods, Brahma who creates, Vishnu who preserves, and Shiva who destroys.[2] The one whose name is unknown to us, say the Vedas, awakens and contemplates the world enclosed in his bosom. He wishes to project it outside himself; his will is love,[3] and the Trimurti is composed of God, love, and the world. Other times, it is fire, product of the eternal being, who is all light; the water that engenders fire; and the earth that rises above the surface of the waters;[4] or the fire, the terrestrial globe, and the air, in which Prajapati, master of everything that was created,[5] resides, and the trident of Shiva is the emblem of this triple energy.[6] Finally, the secondary divinities themselves are sometimes included in the Trimurti. The Puranas reveal to us the triple nature of Sweta-Devi, the white goddess; and Kumari, the divine virgin, was born on Mount Kailash of the reunion of three gods.[7] Among the Persians, Oromaze

---

1. The idea of the trinity, says Goerres (pp. 638–41, 652–59), has one of its origins in the notion of the good and evil principles, and of a mediating god. He gives examples of trinity in all the priestly mythologies.

2. Wagner, pp. 180–84; *Asiat. Mag.*, I, 852.

3. Cama, love, is the Eros of the Orphics.

4. Oupnekhat.

5. Laws of Menu.

6. The Trilinga.

7. *Asiat. Res.*, XI, 112. For other details on the Indian trinity, see Guigniaut, p. 176.

is Brahma, Mithra is Vishnu, and Arimanes is Shiva, and Mithra, whom we have seen is the mediator, absorbs the other two in his triple essence.[8] In Phoenicia, it is light, fire, and flame; in Tibet, the supreme god, the divine law, and the universe created by this god and coordinated by this law;[9] in Egypt, intelligence, the world, and the image of the world, Amun, Phat, and Osiris.[10] The tripod, transmitted to the Chinese by obscure traditions as the object of their oldest worship, presents a Trinity composed of the principles of good and evil and a mediator who converts one and pacifies the other.[11]

All these almost identical forms, despite the diversity of names, are means, sometimes of eluding the immutability of the first being, who is inaccessible to our desires and for whom mediation is necessary, sometimes to counterbalance the perversity of malignant natures by opposing a power that intervenes and intercedes for us to them, sometimes raising us from our own fall by means of a protector who pays for that fall on our behalf and for our salvation.

The triple gods then combine into a single one,[12] because the religious sentiment is pleased with unity and because meditation leads the spirit toward pantheism.

Taken strictly, as its author intended, the Law of Moses appears to offer no trace of a trinity; however, an analogous idea was introduced to the Hebrews by their demonology.[13]

8. Dionys. Areop., Epist., VIII.

9. Georg., *Alphab. tib.*, pp. 272–73. The Tibetan trinity is sometimes even more metaphysical: the universe ceases being a part of it. It is composed of a god who is one and triple, intelligence, word, and love; but this god is no less material: its substance is the purest, most transparent water.

10. Cneph is intelligence; the image of Cneph is the world; the image of the world is the sun (Mens *ad* Mercur., no. 11). There were also one or several physical trinities among the Egyptians; sometimes the earth, water, and fire; sometimes, as in Phoenicia, fire considered under three aspects: flame, light, and heat.

11. On the trinity among the Scandinavians, see the first chapter of the Edda.

12. He who is visible, and whom the eyes see not, is called Ki; he whom one understands, and whom the ears hear not, is called Hi; he who is sensible, and whom touch cannot touch, is called Ouei. The senses cannot teach you anything about these three; but your reason will tell you that they are only one; the substance of Fo is one, but there are three images (Chin, in Duhalde, III, 66). There are only three gods; but Prajapati is the god where these three combine. It is the unity in triplicity (Laws of Menu, ch. 2, p. 78). The syllable contains the three gods: but in reality only one god exists, Mahan-Atma, the great soul (glossary of the Rigveda).

13. The three Aeons, or Aziloth, who created the world (see above [bk. X, ch. 3] and the note on this subject); also Euseb., *Praep. evang.* (VII, 5; XI, 10); and Maimonides, *Bereschet Nabba.*

The public polytheism of Greece did not know any of these subtleties; its gods sufficed as long as it could improve them. When it arrived at the final limit of their possible improvement, it collapsed with them, without taking in the foreign conceptions that its priests appealed to in order to shore up a ruined belief, and which even its philosophers had sometimes adopted as a solution to insoluble questions.

CHAPTER 9

On the Doctrine of the Destruction of the World

We saw in our second book[1] the effect that the memory of physical calamities and upheavals of nature produces on the religious notions of the savage. This effect is prolonged among civilized peoples. Everywhere, there are festivals—whether public or secret, horrifying rituals or mysterious commemorations—that recall these terrifying catastrophes. But here too appears a difference between the cults independent of priests and those the priesthood has fashioned. The first only preserved confused traces of these convulsions, disguised by ceremonies whose meaning was hidden.[2] Legislators attempted to turn minds from the useless terror of an inevitable danger. On the contrary, nations governed by the priesthood have seemed to take a sad pleasure in augmenting these lugubrious souvenirs; they have often connected them to malevolent divinities whom they taught men to fear. Their rituals were at once commemorative of former misfortunes and prophetic of new ones. Their feasts announced the return of terrible events, whose memory they perpetuated. All their mythologies depict gods resisting destructive force, but only by constant efforts and ruses, destined to fail sooner or later.

The scientific and metaphysical portions of the priestly religions give the priests a great advantage in this regard.[3] The learning and knowledge of which they are

---

1. Bk. II, ch. 2.

2. See Boulanger, *Antiq. dévoil. par ses usages.*

3. In Indian mythology, destruction and creation are one and the same thing. Creation is not, as in Greek polytheism, the effect of the separation of chaos, which enters into ferment and produces the universe, the gods, and men. The supreme god exists alone in ineffable repose: he emerges from this repose, contemplates himself, meditates, divides into two parts, and projects outside himself the material world, a part of himself. Hence, it results that when he returns to his repose, when he ceases to contemplate himself in the universality of his attributes, the immortal world he encloses in his bosom remains plunged in the mysterious unity. The material and temporal disappear: the visible creation is

the sole proprietors, their astronomical calculations and observations of natural phenomena, a study they reserve exclusively to themselves, allow them to connect the revolutions they predict either to the return of these phenomena or the course of the stars; their philosophy then inserts itself, and pantheism (which is its final stage) combines the destruction of the world with the infinite being—motionless, unseen, inactive—that they have placed above all the visible and active gods.[4]

At the end of 12,000 divine years, which are equal to 4,390,000 of our years, and which make but a day of Brahma, this god fell asleep and everything that he created disappeared. On waking, he created all things once again; but at the end of a hundred years he died, and his death was followed by the destruction of all the beings.[5] Thick darkness enveloped the globe. Vishnu alone remained as a resplendent point in space. The seas covered the three worlds. The white horse that carried the tenth incarnation put its fourth hoof on the earth, and the weight cast the dwelling of men into the abyss. The tortoise that held it up withdrew. The serpent with a thousand heads, Adiseshan, belched out flames that reduced everything to ashes. Shiva puts aside his various forms and rages like a living flame over the ruins of the broken world.[6]

---

no longer animated by the celestial breath, and everything that is not God is annihilated. It is from me that this universe emanates, says Krishna in the Bhavishya-Purana; and it is in me that it will be annihilated. In one of the Upanishads, the creator god experiences a devouring hunger and swallows his work as soon as he produces it. Hence, a constant struggle between life and death, a struggle that occasions the destruction of the existing world and its replacement by a new world. Wilson, in his voluminous *Traité de la poésie théâtrale des Indiens* (Calcutta, 1827), speaks of a drama written in sacred meter that presents the destruction of the world, the earth being swallowed by the waters and then reappearing renewed and purified.

4. The Mah-pirly, the annihilation of the universe, according to the Bedang ends with the absorption of all things into God.

5. The Indians name these revolutions *menwanturas*. Their *yogas*, which are ages parallel to those of Greek mythology, end with a flood, their *menwanturas* with a universal fire. Several Indian sects count ten thousand *menwanturas*. It is probable that more than once local calamities gave credence to these traditions. The giant Nirinacheren, say the Brahmins of Mahabalipuram, near the place called the Seven Pagodas, rolled the earth into a shapeless mass and carried it into the abyss. Vishnu pursued him, killed him, and placed the earth back in its original position. According to the description of the ruins of Mahabalipuram by Chambers, one can see obvious traces of an earthquake there. The Brahmins of the place generalized a particular event (*Asiat. Res.*, I, 153–54).

6. Bhagavatam, bk. XII. According to other sacred books, six thousand and one of the revolutions have already taken place. The Shastabad recognizes only four: Three times, it says, the human race has

Among the Burmese, a mysterious being descends to earth; its black apparel floats in the air; its hair is thick; it utters sharp cries in a trembling voice. Torrents of rain swell the seas and the lakes. Then a terrible dryness follows these inundations. Plants wither, the earth opens. Men fight one another, but without motive or end. Two suns dart burning fires on the globe. The last tree perishes, totally withered. A third sun dries up the rivers; a fourth and a fifth the seas and the Ocean; a sixth causes bolts of flame to emerge from the abyss; a seventh consumes the dwellings of gods and men, and finally is itself extinguished, lacking the wherewithal to fuel it.[7]

Mexicans also recognize four ages of the world: the first ended by a flood, the second by an earthquake, the third by a windstorm, and the end of the fourth is not far-off. In this expectation, when each century ended (or each period of fifty-two years), they extinguished all fires in temples and houses, and broke furniture and vessels. Bearing the attributes of their gods, the priests went to a high mountain and declared to the standers-by that all the divinities had left the city, perhaps never to return; but in order to know the divine intentions, they were going to try to reignite the fires they had extinguished. Women and children covered their faces with aloe leaves, and the multitude fixed anxious eyes upon the torch that held their destiny. At the moment when the flame appeared, cries of joy hailed the gods, thanking them for the mercy they had shown to men.[8] According to Tibetans, the duration of the world was divided into ninety-nine periods. Seven fires, followed by a flood, were repeated seven times, and at the last catastrophe poisoned arrows filled space; the wellsprings of the universe were broken, and all beings became the prey of nothingness.[9]

The universal fire of the Egyptians was to take place every three thousand years, at the vernal or autumnal equinox. In place of the fruitful floods came a deluge of fire. The entire world was subject to flame, and the sacred land of Hermes vanished in smoke; but this was less a destruction than a renewal of nature. At the solstice of the following summer, with the sun being in Leo, the moon at its right in Cancer, the planets in their respective places, and Aries in the midst of the firmament,

---

been destroyed: the earth covered with corpses has three times led the soul of the god who gave this harsh command to repent. The fourth age still continues; but the moment approaches when all bodies will be annihilated, when God will recall all souls to his bosom (*Asiat. Res.*, VI, 245).

7. *Asiat. Res.*, VI, 246.
8. Clavig., *Hist. of Mexico*, I, 401–2; Humboldt.
9. *Voy.* of Turner and Pallas.

Sothis reappeared and saluted the new order of things at its dawning and the new times that began. A solemn feast recalled and announced these revolutions. In them, flocks and trees were painted the color of blood; this color expressed the extreme heat that was to devour everything.[10]

The sacred books of the North are filled with no less lamentable descriptions. The twilight of the gods,[11] says the *Voluspa*, will begin with three terrible winters[12] that no spring, no summer, will interrupt. Old and decrepit, nature will oppose only a feeble resistance to the forces that conspire for its ruin. All the elements will transgress their boundaries. A monster raised by a magician who is the enemy of humankind will emerge from the forest in which he lives; impetuous winds will sigh on all sides. Flapping its black wings, the prophetic cock will answer the echoes with his sinister cries. Night will cover the rainbow, the mysterious bridge between heaven and earth. Surtr, the king of fire, will come from the south with his invincible cohorts. He will be mounted on a steed whose nostrils will emit flames. The funeral vessel[13] that ever since Hela[14] assumed her reign is slowly built by the bones of her victims, will head to the east, guided by the giant that serves as its pilot;[15] there it receives the *genii* who are impatient to complete the great work of destruction. Loki and Garmr, the Cerberus of the North, will join the children of Galea. The wolf Fenris has broken his chains. The serpent Mitgard rises like a dark phantom, emerges from the waves, and slithers on the bank. Trembling on their foundations, the mountains hit one another with a terrible cracking. The sun pales, the earth sinks. Surtr approaches, the sky cracks. The companions of Surtr advance to the immense plain dominated by the citadel of the gods. Heimdall[16] blows a horn at the top of the tower. At the entrance of their caves, the Nains weep and shed tears. Men die in large numbers, and the eagle devours them while uttering joyful cries. The gods take up their arms; the heroes that Odin assembled in Valhalla go forth and pass in review. On his head is a helmet of gold; his body

---

10. Epiphan., *Adv. haer.* On the flood and the destruction of the world among the Chaldeans, see Goerres, I, 268–72; and on this teaching borrowed from them by the Jews, ibid., II, 522. Staeudlin (*Hist. de la mor.*, II, 14) claims that they took it from the Persians.

11. Ragnarok.

12. Fimbulwetter.

13. Naglfar.

14. Death.

15. The giant Rymer.

16. The heavenly porter.

is covered with sparkling armor. He brandishes his spear, until then always victorious; but he knows the decrees of fate. His defeat is inevitable. He will fight no less valiantly. Fenris opens his enormous mouth. The serpent spits huge streams of venom. Thor gives him a mortal blow; but he swallows his vanquisher and suffocates him. Frey succumbs to the blows of Surtr. The dog Garmr and the god Tyr destroy one another. Fenris devours Odin and falls beneath the sword of Vidar. Loki and Heimdall kill one another. The end of the ages is fulfilled. The unknown god pronounces his decrees. Separated, the good and the evil will live in different dwellings in the future.[17] A new earth will rise from the midst of the waves; a young couple, children of the sun, will repopulate it. While withdrawing, the eagle will carry to the peaks of mountains fish cast up by the storm. The gods will build a resplendent palace where henceforth their felicity will be unbroken, and Loki will foreswear his revolt and identify with the infinite being.

No doubt our readers will notice that in this picture all the priestly ideas are brought together: the supreme god different from the active gods, the struggle of malevolent powers against the preserving force, the introduction of mortality, the division of the dead into two classes, finally, the defeat and conversion of the evil principle.

Everywhere, the same doctrines and the same descriptions are reproduced. The Persians expected a universal fire.[18] A general flood was announced by the Druids.[19] The prophecy of a similar event contained in the *Yi-King* is probably a remnant of the priestly cult that existed formerly in China. The passages relative to this catastrophe in Christian writings are well known:[20] more than once the Church has renewed these somber predictions, and the power or the wealth of priests has always profited from them. What is more likely to give religious terrors an unlimited ascendancy than the permanent expectation of a terrible upheaval that will cause all earthly interests to disappear? The approach of death ordinarily leads individuals to devotion. The dogma of the destruction of the world maintains the entire species in a long agony.

17. The good, Gimli; the wicked, Nastrond.

18. In the Zend-Avesta, as in the Mahabharata, it is comets that put an end to the current world, when they will have fulfilled the time assigned to them (LXVII, Ha).

19. Strab., *Mém. de l'Acad. des inscript.*, XXIV, 345.

20. See the Letter of Barnabas, the disciple of Saint Paul. He fixes the end of the world at the year 6000. Staeudlin, *Hist. de la morale*, II, 14.

CHAPTER 10

On the Phallus, the Lingam, and Hermaphroditic Deities[1]

Finally, in the priestly religions we encounter a class of gods who seem strange, even bizarre to us, and who by degrees will become revolting and scandalous, but with which the independent religions are only sullied, as it were, in their secret rites, rejecting them in their public rituals. We speak of the Phallus, the Lingam, and the hermaphroditic divinities.

First, recall that from the most remote times we have seen priests place a secret doctrine in the religions they take over, where they deposit their cosmogonies, which are expressed in symbols. Recall too that these symbols were most often borrowed from the notion of engendering, of being born, applied to the productive force and to the world it created. What is more natural than to seek the image of this force in the generative organs?

The union of the sexes has to attract the utmost attention of man as soon as he reflects upon himself. It is by it that, on one hand, he belongs to previous generations, and, on the other hand, that he connects with future ones. He ceases to exist in isolation; he removes a part of his being from the ravages of time and takes possession of eternity. But everything that pertains to the union of the sexes is enigmatic and inexplicable. This complete forgetting of our individuality, which otherwise is so pronounced and dominant, this momentary overturning of all the barriers that always separate us from others, and which makes each one of us his

---

1. It is not without repugnance that we have committed ourselves to speak of these obscene and scandalous deities; but they occupy such a place in the ancient mythologies, and in the religions that still exist in India and Tibet, that we could not have omitted them without leaving a gap that would have had the inevitable effect of casting great obscurity on other parts of our inquiries. We therefore had to treat the subject; we have tried to do so with tact and decency. The reader can find details a thousand times more striking in the work of Mr. de Sainte-Croix on the mysteries, and in the *Mémoires de l'Académie des inscriptions.*

own center and proper aim; this mixture of moral affection and physical ecstasy, this suspension or confusion of all our faculties, this imperious, boundless love for the most vivid yet briefest of our pleasures, everything makes the union of the sexes the great mystery of nature. It required the corruption of society to disenchant and degrade this mystery.

It is not astonishing, therefore, that the priests of ancient peoples who were strangers to this effect of civilization took the union of the sexes as the symbol of what they imagined concerning the origin of this universe. Hence the worship of androgynous gods.[2]

Aphrodite[3] and Adonis[4] of Syria; Adogous, revered by the Phrygians;[5] in Egypt, Phat and Neith;[6] in Persia, Urania Mithra;[7] Freyr, hermaphrodite, in his temple of Upsal;[8] Chenrezi in Tibet;[9] in India, Ishvara, who, passionately in love with the

2. The worship of gods of this sort is a wholly natural consequence of the notion of engendering applied to the world. Before creation, the productive power finds itself alone in the immensity. In creating, in a manner of speaking it divides itself: it fulfills the function of the active being and the passive being, of the male and the female. This is the teaching of the Vedas, explicitly established in the Manara-Dharma-Sastra. Also see the Laws of Menu; *Asiat. Res.*, V, 8.

3. The cult of Aphrodite was transported to the island of Cyprus (Aristophanes). Loevinus says that her sex is uncertain, and Philochorus in his *Histoire d'Attique* confuses her with the moon. Suidas also speaks of the bearded Venus, who had dual generative organs, because she presided over all generation, and was a male from the belt up and female from the belt down.

4. Creuzer, II, 12.

5. Herod., I, 105; Heinrich, *Hermaphroditorum origines et causae*, III; Salmasii, *Plinian. Exercit.*; Jablonsky, *De lingua lycaonia*, Opusc., p. 64; Creuzer, I, 350. Agdestis, an androgynous hero who had entered in some little-known, rather recent, fables of Greek mythology, was the son of the Phyrgian Jupiter and the giant Agdus.

6. The Phat of Egypt, says Orpheus (5th hymn), the Protogone, the first-born, who crosses the air on wings of gold, an ineffable hermaphrodite who enjoyed the powers of both sexes, produced men and the gods (Creuzer, I, 350–58). Minerva and Vulcan, Phat and Neith, according to Horapollo, were the sole hermaphroditic gods in Egypt. They were not hermaphroditic in Greece.

7. Jul. Firmicus, *De errore prof. relig.*, 1–5. It was for this that the Greek writers say that Jupiter was hermaphroditic among the magi (Goerres, I, 254). Kaiomorts, the first man, was male and female (Guigniaut, p. 706). The tree of creation had the form of a man and a woman, united one to the other (ibid., p. 707).

8. Goerres, II, 574–75. In the act of generation, say the bards, the husband becomes a woman, the wife becomes a man (Mone, p. 372). A Scandinavian legend could very well be a recollection of hermaphroditic gods. Thor was sleeping; Thrymer stole his coat during the night of the equinox. Disguised as a woman, Thor wed Thrymer. The marriage was consummated, and the false wife killed her husband with the knife he stole back (Mone, p. 406). This tale also has an astronomical meaning.

9. Wagner, p. 199.

beautiful Parvati, gave her half of his body and from this time on was half male and half female;[10] Brahma, whose statue, male on one side and female on the other, was described by Porphyry;[11] Shiva,[12] who in one incarnation is one with Vishnu, becomes his wife named Ardhanari,[13] or Ardhanarishvara;[14] Rahula, son of Buddha, passing from one sex to the other several times a month because of an imprecation; Ila, daughter of Manu and wife of Buddha, first a young hunter, then transformed into a girl by Shiva, under the name of Savitri[15]; the Gayatri, an ineffable prayer by which a husband becomes a wife, as in the Scandinavian tale recounted above;[16] Krishna, who declares himself to be both the father and the mother of all that exists;[17] Vishnu, to whom a division of his followers[18] attribute this double quality; elements like the fire in the Zend books, the moon in several nations of Asia;[19] all these objects of worship combine the two sexes.[20] As a consequence of this symbolic notion, priests change vestments and put on the clothes of women in the ceremonies established in honor of these gods in order to express their double nature.[21]

But a much more common symbol, because it is simpler and easier to explain to the people, was the separate generative organ.[22] Thus we everywhere encounter

10. Roger, *Pagan. in.*, II, 2.

11. Paulin., *Syst. Brahm.*, p. 195; Porph., in Stob., *Eclog. Phys.*, I, 4.

12. Shiva was represented with the bosom of a woman, which made him be taken for an Amazon by Bardesanes, a contemporary of Heliogabalus (Heeren, *Inde*, p. 315; Wagner, p. 167).

13. Bhagavatam; Wagner, p. 167.

14. Sonnerat, I, 148.

15. Colebrooke, *On the Relig. Cerem. of the Hindoos*, XV, 519.

16. See above, n. 8.

17. Bhag. Gita.

18. The ramanajages (Philostrate, *Vie d'Apollonius de Tyane*, III, 34).

19. Spartian., in *Vita Caracallae*, cap. 7; Casaubon, *Not. ad eundem*. On all the hermaphroditic divinities, see in general, Macrob., *Saturn.*, III, 3; Creuzer, I, 350–63.

20. It is remarkable that this notion entered into the reveries of Christian mystics. Antoinette Bourignon saw Adam, endowed with both sexes, impregnate himself when inflamed with the love of God.

21. The priests of Hercules on the island of Cos; those of the hermaphroditic Cybele on the island of Cyprus. Macrobius (*Saturn.*, III, 8) adds that the statue of this goddess was naked with a large beard; her priests disguised themselves as women for their sacrifices, and the faithful who took part wore clothes of the opposite sex.

22. On the worship of the Lingam, see Guigniaut, pp. 145, 147, 149; and for the Phallus, raised by Isis in memory of the mutilation of Osiris, see the same author, p. 392. Lucian describes a huge Phallus seen in the vestibule of the temple of Saturn at Hierapolis.

the Phallus,[23] or the Lingam,[24] sometimes adored alone under a monstrous form, sometimes combined with the statues of gods, animals, and stones.[25]

At the beginning, this worship contained no indecent idea. In Indian fables there are traits of modesty strangely associated with the homage rendered to the symbols that wound our gaze and run counter to our habits. The Brahmins of the temple at Perwattum recount that a woman having approached the Lingam nude in order to worship it, an arm emerged from it to repel her, and a voice was heard that forbade her from presenting herself to the gods in this immodest condition.[26] But as the simplicity of mores disappeared, the cult of the Lingam and the Phallus had to further shock the more refined ideas of modesty and shame that came with the development of social life; thus, it was rejected by the peoples whose independent institutions were not characterized by stasis. Not only did the Greek philosophers, notably Heraclitus and Xenophon, always reject the cult of Phallus,[27]

23. Statues of this god with huge moving Phalluses were carried during the festivals of Osiris in Egypt (Herod., II, 48). The Myllos, or the Cteis, the counterpart of the Phallus, was also displayed. Arnobius explains by an anecdote the origin of this cult. Egyptian women hung the image of the Phallus from their neck. At Hierapolis there were two Phalluses, three hundred feet tall, that Bacchus had offered to Juno. The Arsaphes Osiris was the Phallus deploying its productive energy (Kirch., *Oed. Aeg.*, I). On this cult, see Jablonsky, *Panth. Aeg.*; Zoega, *De obelisk.*, p. 213; Creuzer, I, 319; Goerres, I, 24–25; II, 369. Sesostris had Phalluses erected everywhere he went. Imbued with the Greek spirit, Herodotus explains this fact by saying that Sesostris thus expresses the virile courage of his warriors and the effeminate softness of the peoples he had conquered (Schlegel, *Weish. der Ind.*, p. 120). Several very religious writers have claimed that the cross of Christians had been borrowed from the simulacrum of the Phallus (Jablonsky, *Panth. aeg.*, V, 74; Lacroze, *Hist. du Christ. des Indes*, p. 431; Carli, *Lettres améric.*, I, 499; II, 504; Larcher, *Not. sur Hérodote*, II, 260–72, last edition). One can find on the progressive modifications of the Phallus, from its addition to the consecrated stones to its combination with the statues of Osiris, very curious details in the work of Dulaure on the *Culte du Phallus*, p. 49. In our day, Denon still saw the Phallus in public baths (*Atlas*, pl. CXXV, n. 15).

24. See Dubois (II, 420) on the Lingam of the Indians. This cult took three different forms among them. One sect personified the productive force and chose as its symbol the virile parts; another, those of the female; and the third combined them in a single representation (Paterson, *Asiat. Res.*, VIII, 54–55). The worship of the Lingam is so rooted in the customs of India that missionaries have been forced to negotiate with this idolatry, and to permit women they convert to keep it by combining it with the cross (Sonnerat, I, 2). Female Indians place it in their hair or paint it on their forehead (Roger, *Pagan. Indien.*, ch. 3).

25. Erlik-Khan, god of the netherworld in the Lamaic religion, indicates the reunion of reproduction and destruction by an enormous Phallus (Pallas, *Samml. Hist. Nachr. ueb. Die Mongol. Voelkersch*).

26. *Asiat. Res.*, V, 313.

27. Voss, *Anti-Symb.*, p. 195.

but the public religion did not admit either this cult or androgynous divinities.[28] Adonis, hermaphrodite among the Syrians, in Greece was only a handsome young man.[29] It was different in the mystery cults. The androgynous Eros;[30] Misé, male and female; Minerva;[31] the moon;[32] Bacchus;[33] the Cabiri,[34] who, as we have seen, were the connecting point of all the priestly teachings, appear in this secret worship with the attributes of both sexes. The Orphic hymns celebrate them, the author of the *Argonautica* sings of them,[35] and Plato, whose fertile imagination took hold of everything in order to purify it, drew from it the subject of an allegory. But the Phallus carried in pomp in orgies rarely profaned the public temples; neither the hymns of Pindar nor the choruses of Sophocles ever celebrated this hideous idol; neither the brush of Apelles nor the chisel of Phidias ever offered it to the gaze of the Greeks. The priesthood, on the contrary, combined this inheritance of ancient times with a principle we will treat shortly and made it an instrument to control, in two ways, the inclinations of man.

28. We showed in our previous volumes all the androgynous divinities brought into Greece by the colonies, and shorn of this feature by the Greek spirit. See bk. V, ch. 5, and bk. VI, ch. 7.

29. Alciphron (III, 37) speaks of a chapel of Athena where Hermes and Venus were represented as united to one another. This chapel was called the Chapel of the Hermaphrodite, and widows left their rings there, as warriors left in other temples weapons that had become useless. These traces of ancient or foreign customs, however, change nothing in the general truth of our claim.

30. Διφυςη, Orph. Hym. Hermann, 23.

31. Wagner, p. 308.

32. Ibid., p. 348. See in Selden, *De diis Syris*, p. 40, or in Henrich, *De hermaphr.*, p. 17, the ancient tradition of *lunus* or *luna*.

33. Orphic hymns 29 and 41.

34. See above, bk. V, chs. 4 and 5.

35. The author of the *Argonautica* makes the androgynous Eros the first mover in his cosmogony.

BOOK XI

ON THE FUNDAMENTAL PRINCIPLE
OF PRIESTLY RELIGIONS

CHAPTER I

Exposition of This Principle

Up to this point, the differences we have noticed between the two species of polytheism are only partial; it is time to go back to the principle that makes these two beliefs two entirely different systems. In order to discover this principle, we have to take up again an idea we have already dealt with, but now we are required to develop all of its consequences.

The notion of sacrifice, we said in our first volume,[1] is inseparable from religion. Initially exempt from any and all refinement, this notion leads man to share with his idols everything that is agreeable or useful to him in this life. If, as civilization progresses, man possesses more precious items and offers his gods a portion of them, it is always on the basis of the assumption that they have need of them, and that they really use the things he consecrates to them, just as he himself uses the part that he retains for himself. But with the advent of a form of civilization that we could call material, a moral civilization is also introduced. The notions concerning the divine nature are modified and purified: man rises to less crude ideas; he no longer supposes that the beings he adores have physical needs similar to his own; he conceives of them as all-powerful, he cannot offer them anything that does not already in fact and in justice belong to them. They are beyond him; they have their felicity, pleasures, and enjoyments totally apart from him.[2] Then, sacrifice shows itself to the human spirit under a new point of view: it is no longer meritorious because of the intrinsic value of the offerings; it can only be meritorious as the witness of his submission, devotion, and respect.[3]

---

1. Bk. II, ch. 2. There are very interesting things about sacrifices in Mr. de Maistre's system that make perfectly well known the theory we develop here.

2. What utility, asks Socrates in the *Euthyphro*, could the gifts we make to the gods have for them?

3. In one of the Indian Shasters, human reason asks divine wisdom where the necessity of sacrifice came from. It asks, does God eat or drink like men? God, responds Brahma, neither eats nor drinks

In the independent religions, this manner of conceiving sacrifice only has advantages. Man concludes from it that the gods attach more value to the interior disposition of those who surround their altars than to the number of victims. Morality profits from this nobler, more elevated appreciation; ceremonies lose their importance; virtue, purity of heart, the triumph over vicious inclinations or imperious passions, become the best means of obtaining celestial favor and protection. It was this teaching that the polytheism of Greece endorsed in the succession of writers following the Homeric period, whether they were historians or philosophers, prose writers or poets.

But the priesthood has its particular logic, which, by supplanting that of the human mind, knows how to profit from the latter's errors and accredit itself by means of its aberrations. From the belief that the gods—endowed with unlimited power, unlimited perfection, and unalterable felicity[4]—have no need of men, their ministers do not conclude that ceremonies are superfluous and that virtues suffice. They conclude that these sacrifices have no merit except in virtue of what they cost those who offer them; therefore, one must refine the pain and suffering they cause in order to increase their merit. This is the dominant principle of priestly cults; and every enlightened mind should easily foresee its consequences. First of all, it imposes on man the renunciation of what he has that is most precious; soon it prescribes the sacrifice of what these affections hold most dear; it then imposes a duty to painfully resist his most imperious and legitimate inclinations; finally, it condemns him to violate what is most sacred in the virtues themselves. Then, by a deplorable necessary development, follow human sacrifices, an exaggerated continence that causes nature itself to suffer, licentious rituals that offend modesty, fastings, penances, mutilations, voluntary tortures, suicide, and injurious homages lavished by delirious men on gods they insult while believing they honor them.

To be sure, there was never a more striking example of wholly contrary consequences of the same principle than when intelligence discovers and develops

---

like men; but these goods of this world being the object of all their desires, God wanted men to freely make the sacrifice of them (extract from the Dirm Shaster).

4. This perfection, this power, and this happiness attributed to the gods of the priestly religions are not, as one might believe, in contradiction to the vices, weaknesses, and misfortunes of these same gods. We have explained above (bk. IX, ch. 3, and bk. X, ch. 4) by what subterfuges the priests, forced to present them as unhappy and imperfect in their fables, in their teachings proclaim them perfect and happy.

it in freedom, and when a caste takes hold of it and makes it an instrument of power. The priesthood of antiquity even turned man's own progress against him. What makes religion purer, more disinterested, more sublime when it remains free, served those who called themselves its ministers to stain it with the most barbarous ferocity, the most revolting debauchery. As crude as it was, Homeric polytheism is a thousand times better than the much-vaunted cults of the eastern and southern nations. Egoistic, proud, passionate gods demanding worship that flatters their vanity and victims that stimulate their senses still leave the moral part of man free. The priestly religions violate this sanctuary, make the religious sentiment their slave and accomplice; and what is purest in this sentiment, the need to sacrifice to what it adores, is transformed in the hands of priests into a cause of delirium, brutalization, and cruelty.

CHAPTER 2

On Human Sacrifices

In our second book,[1] we put forth the principal causes that introduced the horrible practice of human sacrifices among all peoples;[2] we repeat: among all peoples, be they civilized or savage, ancient or modern (if we class among the moderns those among whom Christianity, to whom we owe the abolition of these terrifying ceremonies,[3] made inroads only a long time after its triumph in the civilized West and East). But, just as we said in the same chapter,[4] these sacrifices rapidly fell into disuse in the countries independent of priests, while they were perpetuated where the priesthood exercised its empire.[5] A succinct exposition of incontestable facts will convince us of this important truth.

1. See bk. II, ch. 7.

2. On the subject of human sacrifices among different peoples, one can consult Eusebius (*Praep.*, IV, 155), who reprints an extract from Porphyry listing all the nations among whom these sacrifices were in use; Herodotus (II, 4; IV, 103); Pausanias (*Attica*, 43); Pomponius Mela (II, 1); Solin (cap. 25); Lucan (*Dialogues*); Clement of Alexandria (*Cohort. ad gent.*); Cyril of Alexandria (*Adv. Julian.*, IV); Ammianus Marcellinus (XXV, 8); Ovid (*Epist. ex Ponto.*, III, 2–55); Strabo (bk. VII); Minutius Felix (passim); Meursius (*Graecia Feriata*); Meiners (*De sacrif. hum. Com. Soc. Goett.*, VIII, 68; IX, 63); Goerres (I, 42); for the Huns in particular, see Menander (in *Excerpt. legat.*, p. 64); for the Icelanders, Procopius (*Goth.*, II, 15); for the Goths, Jornandès (cap. 4).

3. In acknowledging this immense merit of Christianity, we do not depart from the fundamental idea whose demonstration is the purpose of this work. Christianity is a progress, the most important, the most decisive, of all the progress the human race has made to this day. As a consequence, the terms we employ here reduce to saying that man in making progress necessarily emancipates himself from the opinions and rituals that tainted the periods of barbarism and ignorance.

4. Bk. II, ch. 7.

5. This connection between the power of the priesthood and human sacrifices makes itself seen from the primitive state. Of all the blacks, those of Whydah, or Ouidah, grant the most authority to priests; therefore they are also the most given to these sacrifices.

The Mexicans immolated prisoners, women, and slaves.[6] The Gauls honored in the same manner Teutates, Taranis, and their Mercury, whom they named Hesus.[7] The Scandinavians dedicated to Odin those whom the fate of battle delivered to them.[8] When they celebrated the memory of heroes, they informed their manes by envoys put to death on their tombs.[9] This was done by lot, and kings themselves were not exempt.[10] At the time of the Romans, the forests of Germany were an object of fear for travelers, whose sight was constantly struck by trees covered in blood and skeletons hanging from branches.[11] The inhabitants of Sicily appeased

6. Robertson, *History of America*. At the dedication of the great temple of Mexico by Ahuizotl, the eighth king of this country, sixty to seventy thousand prisoners were sacrificed (Clavigero, IV, nn. 21–23). On another occasion, five thousand captives were dispatched in a single day. The number of human victims rose annually to more than two thousand. In certain festivals, the Mexicans ate them after the sacrifice. They made a female slave clothed in the garments of the goddess Centeotl dance before her statue, then they killed her. They offered three slaves to Tezcatzoncati, the god of wine; infants to the goddess of flowers and rivers, men and women to the mountains (Clavigero, ibid.). The same rituals were conducted in honor of Vitzliputzli. The idols of several divinities were made of a paste of human blood. They had immense buildings where the heads of victims were kept. The Spanish counted as many as one hundred and thirty-six thousand (Lopez de Gomara, *Hist. des Indes occidentales*, ch. 82). A certain number of captives, decorated like the idol, perished on the altar of the goddess Huitzilopochtli, who presided over the saltworks, and the sacrificer then danced with the victim's head in his hand (Gomara, ibid.).

7. *Mém. de l'Acad. des inscr.*, XXVI; Schlegel, *Weish. der Ind.*, p. 120; Pliny, *Hist. nat.*, VI, 2. There were colossal idols made of wicker, which were filled with victims and then set on fire (Caes., *B Gall.*, VI, 16). In all these ceremonies, they had recourse to the ministry of the Druids (Aug., *De civ. Dei*, VII, 15; Caes., ibid.)

8. Keysler, *Antig. sept.*, p. 134.

9. At Lethra in Sweden, every nine years ninety-nine men were sacrificed, as well as the same number of horses and cocks (Dithm. Merseb., *Chron.*, I, 12; Keysler, pp. 159–326; Mallet, *Introd. à l'hist. du Danem.*, 116).

10. Keysler, p. 133; Loccenius, *Antiq. Suewo-Goth*, 15; Bartholin, pp. 323, 393, 394. People have tried in vain, says Rüh (*Einleit. zur Edda*, pp. 29–30), to deny the human sacrifices of the Scandinavians; unanimous witnesses testify to them. Dithmar of Merseburg observes this custom among the Danes; Adam of Brême among the Swedes; several other authors among the peoples of the North in general. Historians prove it by records and positive facts. In the temple of Thor was a great round bronze vase destined to receive the blood of animals and men. By another temple was a stone, the stone of Thor, Thorstein, where the kidneys of victims were crushed. The Icelanders, fearing being forced to convert to Christianity, tried to rebuff this threat by bringing together a great number of foreigners, captives, and even their own citizens whom they chose for the slaughter at the foot of the altars.

11. *"Lucis propinquis (apud Germanos) barbarae area, apud quas tribunos ac primorum ordinum centurions mactavere"* (in the camp of Varus, Tacit., *Ann.*, I, 61). The Germans, says the same author, above

the Palici, sons of a nymph and Jupiter, by similar offerings.[12] Diodorus tells us that Hamilcar, following a Carthaginian custom, when besieging Agrigentum sacrificed a child to Saturn.[13] To the present day, the Chinese cast their children in rivers in honor of the spirit of the river.[14] At Tonkin, they are poisoned;[15] in Laos, they are buried.[16] The Phoenicians practiced no less barbarous rites.[17] In their invasion of Greece, the Persians buried alive nine young men and nine young women; and the queen Amestris, come to a very old age, put to death in the same way fourteen shoots of the most honored families as a sign and act of thanksgiving to the infernal gods.[18]

In the ruins of Persepolis one sees bound figures ready to receive the mortal blow.[19] The Ethiopians immolated men in honor of the sun and the moon,[20]

---

all worshipped Mercury, by sacrificing humans to him (*German.*, p. 10). He describes the ceremonies conducted in honor of Hertha, the Earth; slaves washed the simulacrum of the goddess and then were drowned in a lake (ibid., p. 40). This lake was probably situated in the island of Rugen, because the inhabitants of this island still recount today that their ancestors consecrated virgins to the pleasures of the devil, and point out the lake in which they cast them when they had ceased pleasing him.

12. Virgil says, in speaking of these sacrifices:

Placabilis ara Palici

(*Aen.*, IX, 685)

because they had been replaced by others that were less terrifying (Serv., *ad eund. loc.*).

13. Diod., XIII, 24. He cast this victim into the sea, which appears to belong to the worship of the elements. The same historian also speaks to us about a statue of Saturn at Carthage, in the hands of which one placed infants destined to the sacrifice, and who let them drop into burning coals. By one of those conformities that would make one believe in the common origin of all peoples, in the palace of the Samorin, king of Calicut, there is an idol that one reddened by the fire in order to put children in its mouth; and our missionaries to China tell us that a prince, whom they name Vou-ye, had a sort of automaton built that played chess against select victims, who were put to death if they lost (Mém. of P. Amyot to Mr. de Guiges, inserted into the *Observations sur le Chou-King*).

14. *Mém. sur les Chinois*, II, 400. This is not in contradiction to what we have said about Chinese atheism. Religious fears being indestructible, fetishism and its practices find their place in the atheism of the mandarins, as in the pantheism of the Brahmins (*Asiat. Res.*, II, 378).

15. Ovington, *Voyage*, II, 52.

16. Sonnerat, II, 39.

17. Eusebius of Caesarea, Philo the Jew.

18. Herodatus, VII, 114. The same author reports (ibid., p. 180) that the Persians, having taken a Greek vessel, chose a young man from among the prisoners and sacrificed him on the deck. Photius in his *Bibliotheca*, p. 1448, and Sozomen, *Hist. eccl.*, III, 2, both attest to sacrifices offered to Mithra.

19. *Voy.* of Chardin.

20. Heliodorus, *Theagenes and Chariclea.*

the Egyptians out of hatred for Typhon; and the bas-reliefs of their temples represented these cruel practices in various symbols.[21]

The pleasure experienced by the divinity at the sacrifice of a turtle lasts only one month, say the Indians; the one who receives the sacrifice of a crocodile, three months; a human sacrifice causes a pleasure that lasts a thousand years; three human victims, a hundred thousand years. The chapter on blood of the Kalika Purana contains quite lengthy precepts concerning the rituals to observe,[22] and the sculptures of Elephanta, near Bombay, trace their images.[23]

In Araby, the tribe of the Koreishities sacrificed young girls to its divinity Alura, and the Dumatians, an adolescent at the beginning of the year.[24] A captive king was slaughtered with religious pomp by the chief of the Sarrasins whom the Romans took as auxiliaries.[25] The father of Mohammed himself had been bound to

21. On the immolation of human victims in Egypt, see Goerres (pref., p. xxxviii) and Diodorus (I, 2, 32), with the notes of Wesseling on this passage. Eratosthenes affirms that the tradition maintained that Busiris sacrificed all the foreigners who came into Egypt, meaning by this that the crime of the entire nation was attributed to one man. Herodotus denies these sacrifices. But Schmidt (*De sacerd. et sacrif. Aegypt.*, pp. 276–79) nicely explains Herodotus's mistake (see also Larcher, *Philos. de l'histoire*). Marsham, *Canon. chronol.*, p. 317, and Jablonsky, *Panth. Aeg.*, III, cap. 3, no. 8, have both proven the disdain of the Greek historian, and their arguments are confirmed by the paintings from the ruins of Dendera and the bas-reliefs of the temple of Osiris in the island of Philae (Denon, *Voy. en Eg.*). At the period when the Turks took over this country, a virgin was still cast into the Nile to obtain a favorable flood from the river (Shaw, II, 148; Pococke, V, 27). Nicephorus Callistus (XIV, 37) and Sozomen (*Hist. eccl.*, VII, 20) extensively recount a fact that occurred under Theodosus, and which proves the attachment of Egyptians to these sacrifices. Plutarch reports another (*Liv. des Fleuves*), but he places it in very remote antiquity. These last testimonies have been contested. However, Sozomen's account and, especially, that of Nicephorus seem plausible to us.

22. "On taking the axe," says the Kalika Purana, "one must twice repeat the following invocation: Hail, goddess of thunder; hail, goddess with scepter of fire, goddess with terrifying teeth; eat, tear apart, destroy, sever with this axe, tie up with these irons, take in hand, take in hand, drink the blood, drink the blood, consume, consume." The goddess of darkness then herself directs the blows struck by the one who implores her and the destruction of his enemies is assured. We have said (bk. IV, ch. 2, p. 239) that the words pronounced by the sacrificers attested to the gentleness of the Indian character and the repugnance it experienced even when it forced itself to practice these bloody rituals. But the priesthood will not let this concession made to the national character extend from man to his gods: if it permits the former to be moved by pity, it maintains the latter in all their fierceness and demands.

23. *Asiat. Res.*, IV, 424–34.

24. Porphyry.

25. Procop., *De bello pers.*, I, 28.

this sort of death, and a hundred camels had purchased his release.[26] Finally, in order to shorten this list of terrible incidents, in a few words: among the Scythians, captives;[27] among the Taures, all foreigners;[28] among the Herules, the aged;[29] among the Thracians, virgins;[30] among the Frissons, infants perished at the foot of the altars;[31] the one who offered sacrifice among the Sarmatians drank the blood of victims;[32] and the same horrors were found among the Bretons[33] and the Spanish.[34]

Now, let us turn our gaze to Greece. In the most ancient times, no doubt, we will see its inhabitants give themselves, like all other peoples, to the abominable practices that we just described. We will not speak here of the sacrifice of Iphigenia, or that of the daughters of Erechteus by their own father. These events, which go back to the mythological period of the Greeks' annals, could be dismissed by being placed in the ranks of fables;[35] but it is certain that the Arcadians and the

26. Evagrius, VI, 21; Pocock, *Spec.*, pp. 72–86; Gibbon, ch. 50. We have established in our second volume (bk. III, ch. 6) that the Arabs were not subject to priests. But at the same time, we have said that images dispersed after the conquests of Alexander had carried several priestly customs into the desert, among which were human sacrifices.

A writer with immense learning (Mr. Creuzer), and who mixed hypotheses that were much too systematic with very new and ingenious insights, wanted to make an exception for the religion of Lycia; it, however, is not well founded. He claimed that this worship, consisting in the pure offering of fruits and cakes, had never been tainted by the sacrifice of living creatures. But in order to support this assertion he was forced to belie the testimony of Plato, who says that in Lycia human beings were sacrificed (*Minos*), and he called into question this testimony only by proposing a grammatical correction; this is the easy (and disappointing) recourse of writers led astray by narrow assumptions.

27. Herod., IV, 72; Euseb., *Praep. ev.*, I; Hieronim., *Adv. Jovin.*, II; Vales. *ex* Nicol. Damasc. and Stobaeus, p. 526; Dio. Chrys., XIII, 219.

28. Herod., IV, 103.

29. Procop., II, 14.

30. Steph., *De urbib.*, p. 512.

31. *Nachtraege zu Sulzers Theorie des Schoen. Künste*, VI, 2, 289.

32. Helmold, *Chron. Slav.*, I, 53; II, 12.

33. Athenaeus, IV.

34. Strabo, III.

35. The legend of Iphigenia resembles that of Jephthah, and one can find parallels among all nations, but always in the legendary times; it therefore has no historical weight. The sacrifice of Iphigenia was the consequence of a vow that Agamemnon had made to Diana, promising her the offering of the best fruit of a year: in this year Clytemnestra had given birth to Iphigenia (Eurip., *Iphig. in Taur.*, 20–24).

tribes of Achaia put men to death on the altars of Jupiter[36] and Diana.[37] During the most remote centuries of Athens, a man and a woman were sacrificed at the time of the city's expiation.[38] In the first times of Sparta, the Lacedaemonians put to death children and prisoners of war.[39] This was the fate of the three hundred Messenians fallen into shackles. The Argiens, masters of Mycenae, offered a tenth of their captives to the gods.[40] These facts are, unfortunately, incontestable. But it is equally demonstrated that the Greeks early-on rejected these barbarous practices, and always held them in horror. To be sure, the stubborn persistence of ancient superstitions constrained them to commit them from time to time in difficult circumstances. Thus, the soothsayer Euphrantides forced Themistocles to shed the blood of three young princes on the altar of the Omestes Bacchus,[41] relatives of the king of Persia who had fallen into Greek hands on the eve of the battle of Salamis.[42] But Themistocles resisted the orders of the bloody prophet for a long while, and it was only so as not to cast his soldiers into dark despair that he, with regret, permitted this horrible execution. Human sacrifices continued in Arcadia longer than in other countries of Greece.[43] Greek civilization surrounded Arcadia and yet did not enter into it. Several traces of the religion of the first Pelasgians were preserved there. In the rest of Greece, the divinities whose worship demanded human sacrifices had foreign origins. The bloody rituals of Saturn had been brought by the Phoenicians.[44] We have seen that Diana had the form of the priestly divinities;[45] she had crossed the earth with the head of a bull.[46] By their own account, the Lacedaemonians had borrowed her from Tauris,[47] and the first result of her appearance

36. Aug., *De civ. Dei*, XVIII, 17; Porph., I.

37. Pausan., *Achaea*, ch. 19.

38. One can consult Theophrastus for remembrances of the Athenians relative to these sacrifices (*ap.* Porph., *De abst.*, II, 5); Eusebius (*Praep. ev.*, I); Plato (*De leg.*); Clement of Alexandria (*Strom.*, VII); Aristophanes (*in Pace*, 1020); Aelian (*Var. Hist.*, VII, 3).

39. Pausan., *Lacon.*, 16.

40. Diod., XI, 22.

41. Bacchus fed on raw flesh.

42. Creuzer, III, 342.

43. Porph., *De non edend. animal.*, bk. I.

44. Sainte-Croix, *Les mystères*.

45. See bk. V, ch. 5.

46. Apollod., fragm., ed. Heyne, p. 402.

47. Suidas, in Lycurg.

had been a frenzy that had stirred fierce combats and countless murders. Everyone who had approached her became furiously enraged, so much did she frighten the imaginations of those not accustomed to these monstrous forms or these revolting ceremonies.[48]

Pausanias recounts in great detail how human sacrifices were established in Arcadia, and how they were abolished there.[49] The tradition that attributes their origin to the loves of Menalippus and Cometho, and the adventure of Eurypyle that brought them to an end by bringing a statue of Bacchus from Troy, are irrelevant to our subject. What does interest us is that they ceased almost entirely at the return of the Greeks from the siege of Troy; which is to say, from the first times of their history. The same Pausanias, speaking of the Lycaon who immolated an infant to Jupiter Lycaeus, adds that in the middle of the ceremony this guilty prince was changed into a wolf.[50] The Greeks therefore believed that their gods were unworthy of such barbarous rites.

It is not entirely implausible that the eighth labor of Hercules, causing Diomedes, king of Thrace, to be eaten by the horses that this prince fed with the flesh of strangers, is a garbled tradition of the abolition of these sacrifices.

In truth, however, it rests on an anachronism because it links this abolition, which for Lacedaemonia only dates to the time of Lycurgus, to a much more remote period. But this anachronism only better demonstrates the desire the Greeks had to cast into a legendary antiquity rituals that they were ashamed their ancestors performed.[51]

All the sacrifices that from time to time are encountered in Greek history are explained by national hatreds, by pressing dangers, in a word, by circumstances that

48. Lucian has Juno say that by living among cannibals, Diana had taken on their ways and their cruelty (*Dial. des dieux*, XXI). I cannot believe, says Iphigenia in Euripides, that a goddess is pleased to see the blood of men shed (*Iphig. in Taur.*, 385–91).

49. Pausan., *Achaea*, 19.

50. Idem, *Arcad.*, 2.

51. Lactantius (*Inst. div.*, I, 21) claims that at Salamis on the island of Cyprus until the reign of Adrian a man was sacrificed in memory of a similar sacrifice instituted by Teucer (Porph., *De abst.*, II; Euseb., *Praep. ev.,* IV, 16). But the date that Lactantius assigns to the abolition of this sacrifice proves that he is wrong. The Romans, who from the time of Caesar opposed human sacrifices everywhere their arms went, would not have tolerated them in Cyprus more than a century later. Tacitus, who speaks of the construction of the Temple of Salamis by Teucer, says nothing of this claim (*Annal.*, III), and Saint Cyril (in Julian., IV) affirms that it ceased under the reign of Diphilus, who substituted a bull for the human victim.

departed from the habitual.[52] Everything demonstrates that it was not a sanctioned institution but rather sometimes a deplorable imitation of foreign practices, sometimes a sudden and momentary flight of fanaticism. The horror of the Greeks for these customs shines in all the narratives of their historians. Menelaus is blamed by Herodotus for having offered two Egyptian children to the contrary winds.[53] Agesilaus is praised by Plutarch for having offered a doe to Diana rather than a virgin, even though the inhabitants maintained that the goddess demanded humans and not animals.[54] The signs having been threatening before the battle of Leuctra, the soothsayers of Thebes proposed to Pelopidas to appease the gods by human victims; he, however, rejected their counsel.[55] Everywhere, the Greeks substituted less bloody rituals for these practices. The children of Achaia went to the banks of a river dressed as victims and laid at the feet of Diana crowns of hair that decorated their heads.[56] At Sparta, young men were struck with rods on the altar of the same goddess, who, they said, being accustomed to bloody homages, wanted to preserve at least a pale image of them.[57]

Other tribes of the Doric race reddened the tomb of Pelops with a small amount of blood.[58] Bacchus had approved that the Thebans would replace the human victim they had previously offered[59] with a goat, and we would not be far wrong to recognize a softening of the same nature in the annual ceremony of Leucadia, where a man was cast from the height of a promontory, but was saved by attaching wings to him and preparing boats for his landing.[60]

We see among the Greeks, as well as the Romans, acts of voluntary devotion that are falsely likened to human sacrifices. When Epimenides purified Athens, Cratinus, the handsomest of the youth, offered himself to redeem by his blood the

---

52. In the tragedy of Hecuba, a national subject, where it is a question of the glory of Achilles, the Greek hero par excellence, all the interest focuses upon Polixenes, and all indignation on the tormentors.

53. Herod., II, 119. See the note of Larcher.

54. Plut., *Vie d'Agéslas*.

55. Plutarch.

56. Pausan., *Ach.*, 20. This writer himself notes this progressive softening. The king of savage Arcadia, Lycaeon, he says, had shed the blood of a child on the altars of his Jupiter. Cecrops ordered that one would place cakes on the altar of the Athenian Jupiter (*Arcad.*, 33).

57. Meursius, *Miscellan. Lacon.*, III, 4.

58. Pauw, *Rech. sur les Grecs*, II, 337–38.

59. Pausan., *Boeot.*, 8.

60. Strabo, X, 311.

faults of his fellow citizens;[61] Pausanias, the general of the Spartans,[62] obliged his warriors to remain motionless until Callicratidas had perished. Thrasybulus ordered the Athenians to wait for one of theirs to perish before attacking the Thirty Tyrants.[63] Codrus had himself killed for the salvation of his people. Two Lacedaemonians offered themselves to be handed over to Xerxes as expiation for the assassination of the envoys of Darius by the Greeks.[64] At Rome, Curtius cast himself into an abyss,[65] and Decius called upon his own head the dangers with which the republic was threatened.[66]

But these acts of devotion are the accidental and spontaneous effects of a patriotism worthy of admiration even in its excesses, the heroic and voluntary act of an enthusiasm carried to an excess by extreme danger to the republic. There are no victims dragged to the altar following a regular custom, or a duty whose fulfillment was part of the legal worship.

On the contrary, among the Gauls, who were subject to priests, these sacrifices were always maintained despite the severity of Roman laws forbidding them.[67] In perpetuating them, the Druids profited from the independence given to the subjugated peoples by the civil wars.[68]

This custom was prolonged among the Franks and the Goths until the eighth century,[69] and what is even more horrible—but undeniably attested to—Christians sold them their slaves to be sacrificed.[70] Even until our days, despite the efforts of the English conquerors, the Indians cast into the Ganges men who are devoured by sharks. Families greedy for posterity commit themselves to give back to the gods in this way a fifth of the children granted them; and European sailors have recently seen pitiless parents push back into the water a young boy who saved

61. Athenaeus, XIII, 2.

62. Plutarch.

63. Xenoph., *Hist. grecq.*, III, 4, no. 11.

64. Herod., VII, 134.

65. Tit.-Liv., VII, 6.

66. Ibid., V, 28.

67. Tertull., *Apolog.*, 9; Euseb., *Praep. ev.*, IV, 15–17; Lactant., *Div. inst.*, I, 21; Tacit., *Annal.*, XIV, 30. Suet., in *Claud.*, c. 30.

68. Lucan., *Phars.*, I, 150. The Franks, says Procopius, still observe a great part of their ancient superstitions. They put men to death in honor of the gods, and practice execrable things (*Goth.*, II, 15).

69. Grotius, *Hist. goth.*, p. 617.

70. Gregor. III, *Papae epist. ad Bonif.*, p. 122.

himself by swimming.[71] It seems to us that one must conclude from these facts that, even though human sacrifices have had causes other than the priesthood's calculations, it was always in the mind and interest of the priests to introduce these sacrifices where they did not exist and to maintain them where they did.

First of all, as we have already proved, the priesthood does not renounce any ancient custom. In the second place, the priests to whom the task of designating the victims was naturally confided found themselves thereby invested with the right over life and death; we have already noted this.[72] They could designate the sovereign on his throne,[73] the victorious general in the midst of his army. One can easily conceive the advantage that results from such a right. What indicates both the priestly calculation in this regard and its influence is that ordinarily it placed itself out of harm's way by a special exception. "Let no Brahmin offer his own blood," says the Kalika Purana. "One must never sacrifice a Brahmin or the son of a Brahmin."[74] To be sure, great calamities sometimes triumphed over this privilege. In times of war, pestilence, or famine, the Indians, following the very principle that we are discussing here, chose to sacrifice Brahmins as the most precious of victims.[75]

The scientific and cosmogonic allegories that appear at first glance to be profound and imposing have contributed (and this has not been noticed enough) to the prolongation of human sacrifices; those that connect to the forces of nature, to the creative or destructive power, have frequently united these two forces in a single divinity.[76] Then, in order to express this combination, homicide has be-

71. *Asiat. Res.*, V, 26–29.

72. Bk. III, ch. 10.

73. Among all the nations subject to priests, says a writer who, while entirely devoted to the cause of this caste, sometimes lets slip very remarkable acknowledgments, they have always taught that the earth is tainted by the temporal power, and in human sacrifices they have gone through the victim to arrive at the king (*Catholique*, n. 11, pp. 218 & 340).

74. *Asiat. Res.*, I, 371–81.

75. Sonnerat, I, 189. The Albanians, according to Strabo's report (IX), also offered their priests, and on the tomb of the king of Mexico his spiritual director was put to death (Acosta, *Hist. nat. et mor. des Ind. occid.*).

76. Paterson (*Asiat. Res.*, VIII, 57–58) describes for us an ancient representation of time, which produces and destroys everything, under the name Mahakal. She had eight arms, of which two were broken; with two of those that remained she placed a veil over the sun in order to extinguish it. Her four other arms were employed in the sacrifice of a human victim. One hand grasped the victim, another brandished a sword, a third held a basin full of blood, a fourth sounded a bell that announced

come a symbol. Thus, despite the simplicity of its origin,[77] the cult of the Lingam has produced everywhere not only obscenity but murder.[78] In the Greek fables, Medea resuscitating Aeson by making him boil in a cauldron, which recalls that of the Breton bards;[79] in the mysteries, the rites that commemorate the slaughter of Bacchus and Camilla;[80] in India, the legend of Shiva, who cuts in pieces his spouse Sati and scatters her torn members, are an offering of life to the mysterious power that alternately gives life and death. This is rebirth by sacrifice.

Another dogma that could motivate these frightful rituals was that of the original fall.[81] What is more simple, when one conceives man as being guilty before his birth, than to offer this guilty party to the vengeful divinity as expiation?[82]

---

the sacrifice. One also slaughtered men before Bhavani or Durga, which is the same symbol of destruction and fecundity. See Creuzer, II, 124–125; and Goerres, on the cult of Shiva, II, 557–559.

77. See bk. X, ch. 10.

78. See bk. X, ch. 7.

79. *Archaeol. of Wales.*

80. See Book XIII, below, where we will treat the mysteries.

81. The Vedas explicitly ordered the sacrifice of man (Purushamedha) in order to redeem the world blackened by sin.

82. On this subject, listen to one of the most eloquent and devout apostles of the orthodox Church. "At all times, man has been persuaded that he was guilty," says Mr. de Maistre (*Eclairciss. sur les sacrifices*, p. 372), "that he was living under the hand of an angry power, and that this power could be appeased only by sacrifices." He then establishes that man has two souls, that the soul of the flesh is in the blood (p. 381), and he concludes from this that man being guilty by the soul that is in his blood, it is blood that must be shed. He cites Leviticus (XIII, 12), which says in explicit terms: I have given you blood so that it may be shed on the altar for the expiation of your sins; and even though the Hebrews had not concluded that this blood ought to be that of men, Mr. de Maistre, even though disapproving the extension of this principle, finds it rather natural that all the nations would have attributed an expiatory virtue to the shedding of blood, that they would have believed that remission could be obtained only by blood, and that *someone* ought to die for the happiness of another (p. 394). This efficacy of shed blood is particularly pleasing to Mr. de Maistre. He returns to it constantly. While calling the Taurobolium, where blood ran like rain, a disgusting ceremony, he describes it with a kind of pleasure (p. 397); he is especially pleased with communion by means of blood, "just and prophetic at its root" (p. 471). He loves this metaphor of Saint Augustine: "The Jew converted to Christianity drinks the blood he shed" (p. 470), and he ends his strange treatise with a solemn proclamation of the applicability of the merits of the innocent paying for the guilty and, in italicized letters, *of salvation for blood* (p. 374).

One of his students, whom we have cited in one of the previous notes, says in defending the death penalty: the guilty one is a necessary victim, whose expiatory sacrifice alone can realize reconciliation with God and reestablish harmony that has been destroyed (*Cathol.*, VIII, 272). Elsewhere pursuing the same thought in his mystical style, he says: the doctrine of atonement is manifest in the most

Sometimes a simple likeness in words, or a deplorable desire to imitate, have equally noxious results: Hercules, representing the year, devoured his children, the months and the days. Carthaginians and Tyrians offered him theirs as a holocaust.

But the principle that we have pointed out as essential to priestly religions had to favor the prolongation of these rituals more than any other cause. Among almost all peoples, this principle led the most fiercely pious parents to bring their children to the altar. The more the paternal heart was broken, the more value the offering possessed. Haquin, king of Norway,[83] and Dag, the eleventh successor of Odin,[84] immolated their sons. Aun the ancient[85] offered nine of his to the sacred knife in order to obtain a longer life.[86]

An evident proof of the importance the priesthood attached to these practices is that it always associated them with knowledge of the future. The Druids judged future things as much by the fall of victims as by the palpitations of their members and the flow of their blood.[87] The Peruvians multiplied their number until the signs were favorable to them.[88] The Cimbri dissected them in order to read

sublime way in this primordial legislation. The priesthood was responsible for it. The pontiff was a representative of the human race, whose sin was expiated by sacrifice by immolating a victim at the foot of the altar. The victim was deemed to come back to life and rise to the place of the gods in the midst of a purifying flame. It was thus assumed that the pontiff himself rose toward the empyrean by means of the victim, and the corporal essence of the sacrificed being became the food of the sovereign master of the gods; this was a figure of the absorption of the soul of the sacrificer in the bosom of the divinity (ibid., III, 460). These writers, Messrs. Ferrand and de Maistre, are so convinced of the excellence and necessity of sacrifice that they are inclined to excuse the cannibalism that accompanies it among certain peoples. They define it as an attempt of man to unite with God.

83. Sax. Grammat., X; Bartholin, p. 228.

84. Botin, *Hist. de Suède*, 2nd ep., cap. 9.

85. Ibid.; and Bartholin, p. 700.

86. This reveals the error of Caesar (*B Gall.*, 81), who claims that the people began by offering criminals, and that it was only when they were defeated that they took innocents for victims. The replacement of the innocent by criminals, on the contrary, was a rather late change, indicating the softening of ideas—a relaxation the priests always fought against. The chapter of the Indians on blood explicitly forbids the sacrifice of any man afflicted with a disease or guilty of a crime. "The blind, the maimed, the decrepit, the sick, the hermaphrodite, the deformed, the fearful, the leprous, the dwarf, and he who committed grave crimes, such as killing a Brahmin, or stealing gold, or staining the bed of his spiritual master, he who is not twelve years old, he who is impure because of the death of his parents, all these cannot be offered in sacrifice, even when they are purified" (Kalika Purana).

87. Diod., V.

88. Zarate, *Hist. de la conquête du Pérou*, I, 52.

their entrails.[89] The Lusitanians trampled them underfoot in order to provoke prophetic convulsions.[90] The Scythians smeared their blood over a sword, and fate was made known by the way in which the blood ran.[91] In this way, agony had mysterious significance, and curiosity become ferocious armed itself against nature.[92]

We will not deny that in all these countries human sacrifices tended to become milder;[93] no power can successfully resist the necessary march of the human spirit. Interest and pity combine against a barbarous custom, and even in priestly religions it gradually fell into disuse. At the time of the conquest of America, the Peruvians had renounced it.[94] They were content to draw a little blood from the forehead of children, which they smeared over the wheat they used to make cakes, which were distributed in a solemn manner to the people. The Syrians had substituted a doe for the virgin they previously sacrificed.[95] The tradition of the Guebres recounts that the Persians presented their sons to the sacred fire; this ceremony recalls the victims burned in honor of the gods.[96] The king of Egypt, Ahmose, ordered that waxen idols be cast into a furnace.[97]

The Egyptians preserved the custom of delivering to the Nile an image of a

89. Strabo, VII; Mallet, notes on the 8th fable of the Edda.

90. Strabo, XIII.

91. Herod., IV. Among the Slavs, it was while drinking the victim's blood that the priests obtained the intoxication that unveiled the future to them.

92. "When you sacrifice a man," says the Kalika Purana, "if his head falls to the east, it promises you riches; to the south, something terrifying; to the southwest, power; to the west, success; to the northwest, a child. If tears escape from his eyes, it is an indication of some political revolution; if the head separated from the body smiles, it is a gauge of happiness and longevity for the sacrificer; if it speaks to you, you can believe all its words" (*Asiat. Res.*, V, 371–91). In the Ramayana, Rama kills the terrible Kabandha and burns him on a pyre; he immediately takes on a divine form and reveals to Rama everything he wants to know.

93. Creuzer, II, 481; III, 28, 341.

94. Garcilaso de la Vega, *Hist. des Ind.*, II, 26.

95. Porph., *De abst.*, II.

96. One finds the same custom among the tribes that neighbored the Jews: the idolatrous princes of Israel and Judah, Ahaz and Manasseh, made their children pass through the fire to dedicate them to their idols (II Kings, ch. 16, v. 3, and ch. 2, v. 6).

97. Porph. in Euseb., *Praep. ev.*, IV, 16; Theodoret, *De sacrific.*, ch. 8. In other places these idols were replaced by cakes, as in America (Athenaeus, IV; Marsham, *Can. Chron.*, sec. XI; Meursius, *De rep. ath.*, I, 9). Plutarch reports that the priests marked the animals that they were preparing to strike with a seal representing a man on his knees, with his hands tied and his head threatened by a sword (*De Isid.*). A modern scholar easily recognized in these features a memory of sacrifices that were earlier in force (Schmidt, *De sacerd. et sacrif. Aeg.*, p. 287).

virgin on the day when the dam was opened to facilitate flooding.[98] The majority of the reformers of the Indian religion disapproved of human sacrifices.[99] In the Ramayana, Ombourischa wants to offer one: Indra saves the victim.[100] The Brahmins made use of straw-figures, and then continued the ceremony as if they were immolating living beings.[101]

Thus, the priestly power, despite itself, bends before the work of nature and time; but not without obstinate resistance to these two adversaries, nor without winning several victories over them. It was in vain that a king of Mexico[102] prohibited human sacrifices; he was constrained to reestablish them, and all that he really achieved was to limit them to prisoners of war. In vain, the people asked Centeotl[103] to deliver them from these cruel rituals. The goddess promised, but the priests delayed the accomplishment of her promises. Despite the laws of Ahmose, Egptians offered humans as victims for a long time. Despite the Indian reformers, and despite the authority of incarnations, the Ganges today still swallows infants and women; and the priesthood profits from all these circumstances to fight against the innovations that hamper it and to reestablish the rituals of antiquity. The relaxation is only momentary. As soon as people, no matter how miserable they are from being subject to the priestly empire, experience some reverse or an extraordinary phenomenon frightens them, this neglect of human sacrifice appears to be a criminal attempt to defraud the gods of their due, and men foreswear what

98. Savary, I, 13; Sicart, *Mém. sur l'Egypte. Lett. éd.*, p. 471. It is rather curious to find the same progression in the immolation of animals among the Chinese. The emperor Kangxi wanted to replace them with small images (de Pauw, *Rech. sur les Egypt. et Chin.*, II, 212). The inhabitants of Siam imitated out of economy what other nations did by humanity. All their offerings are in paper, artistically cut, which follow the outlines of the objects that were sacrificed previously (Laloubère, I, 367).

99. Buddha, the 9th or the 19th incarnation of Vishnu, proscribed them in the most explicit way. See the Gita Govinda, or the hymn of Jayadeva, in honor of the incarnations of Vishnu.

100. Ramayana, pp. 412–513. For the details, see bk. VI, ch. 6. The Ashwamedha, a sacrifice of a horse; the Gomedh, a sacrifice of a cow, are softenings of the Purushamedha, the sacrifice of a man.

101. *Asiat. Res.*, I, 265. To the goddess Bhavani, whom we have spoken about above, one offers cocks and bulls instead of men. One sees in the Yajurveda traces of this softening. It prescribes that one hundred and eighty-five men of different tribes, professions, and castes be attached to stones; but, according to a hymn recited in memory of the sacrifice of Nayarana (Vishnu, *Asiat. Res.*, VII, 251), they are then detached and set free. Animals profit from a similar development. At the celebration of a wedding or the reception of any distinguished foreigner the habit was to sacrifice a cow, and in memory of this custom, a guest is still called *gobbna*, killer of a cow. Today the guest intercedes, and the cow led to the altar is released and set free (*Asiat. Res.*, VII, 290–293). See above, bk. VI, ch. 7.

102. Nezahualcoyotl, king of the Acolhua.

103. The goddess of fecundity.

they believe is an impious respect for human life, and what fathers now consider to be sacrilegious pity for the lives of their infants.[104]

The funeral sacrifices that one can regard as of the same nature as human sacrifices gradually disappeared among the Greeks. It would be ignorant to point to a few scattered facts to infer the existence of a permanent custom. When Achilles slaughtered twelve Trojan prisoners on Patroclus's funeral pyre,[105] this barbarous act was neither motivated nor justified by religion, and the horror the poet exhibits proves that it conformed to neither the opinions nor the mores of the nation.

Virgil, all of whose descriptions of religious rituals are borrowed from Homer, except for the inexactnesses introduced by contemporary philosophy or the desire to produce a special effect, shows the Trojans—to whom he always ascribes Greek mores—burning the clothes, trumpet, and weapons of Misenus on his pyre; the idea of bloody sacrifices is not present at all in Virgil's thought.[106] If in another book of the *Aeneid*[107] he speaks of the captives that his hero wishes to offer to the manes of the son of Evander, it is an imitation of Homer. But the imitator does not add that the sacrifice took place.

The priesthood still opposes itself to this effect of the progress of ideas. Under its empire, the fierceness of the savage and the superstition of the ignorant man continue in the subsequent periods of civilization, which unburden themselves of them without being wholly freed of them. Among the Scandinavians, not only was the wealth of princes consumed with the weapons that had served to acquire them, but their slaves were slaughtered and their wives buried or burned with them.[108] Those of the caciques of Saint-Domingo suffer the same fate, either voluntarily or

104. See the fact relative to the Carthaginians in book VI, chapter 7. It is so true that the priestly principle is at the core of all these notions, that the most zealous apologists of the Catholic Church recognize it in explicit terms. "The equally consoling and incontestable theory of the Catholic witness," says Mr. de Maistre, "shows itself in the midst of the ancient darkness under the form of a bloody superstition; and since every real sacrifice, every meritorious action, every fasting, every voluntary suffering, can be truly applied to the dead, polytheism, brutally misled by some vague and corrupted memories, spilled human blood in order to appease the dead" (*Eclairciss. sur les sacrif.*, p. 411).

105. *Iliad*.

106. *Aen.*, VI, 214–21.

107. Ibid., X, 515–17, and also XI, 81–82.

108. *Hist. Norw.*, passim; Olaus, Tryggues, *Sag.* Kempf, *Antiq. Select.*, p. 147. Sigrid, queen of Sweden, separated from Erik, her spouse, because he had no more than ten years to live and she would have been forced to bury herself in the same tomb (Bartholin, *Ant.*, pp. 506ff.). In the Edda, Brunhilde mounts the pyre of Sigurd and intones a song of triumph while letting herself be burned with him.

by constraint that forces them to obedience.[109] In Persia and Ethiopia, the court-iers invested with certain dignities have to die with the monarch.[110] In Mexico and Peru, the brothers of the king perish with him, and despite the exception ordinarily made by priests on their behalf, the one who presided over the private worship of the prince was enclosed in his tomb.[111] Buried with the king of the Scythians were his concubine, his cook, his food-taster, his minister, his riders, and his horses; and at the end of the year, fifty of his strangled servants were placed on horseback around his sepulcher.[112] The Hephtalites enclosed a certain number of warriors in the tomb of their generals who died in battle.[113] The Japanese, who carefully preserve the forms of a priestly religion whose substance has disappeared, buried soldiers and slaves with the heads of the army and the court.[114] The custom that compelled wives to die with their husbands had been in vigor among the Gauls; Caesar tells us that in his time it had just been abolished;[115] it remained among the Heruli,[116] and we find it in India.[117]

The two wives of the Indian Cetes, officer of the army of Eumenes, after the death of Alexander were the prey of the flames.[118] This practice defies European laws in Benares and Bombay;[119] and it is the Brahmins who lead the unfortunate victims to the pyre, sometimes intoxicating them with perfumes and spirits, and deafening them with overwhelming music, sometimes shaming them with the idea of opprobrium, and even employing violence to effect this frightful sacrifice; for if the widow draws back when the ceremony has begun, force is permitted to compel her to continue.[120]

---

109. See above, bk. II, ch. 4.

110. Xenoph., *Cyrop.*, VII, 3; Diod., III, 4.

111. Acosta, *Hist. nat. et mor. des Ind. occid.*, V, 78. One also sacrificed deformed men, so that they could amuse their masters in the other world: a singular mixture of religion, buffoonery, and cruelty.

112. Herodot., IV, 71–72.

113. Procop., *De pers.*

114. *Rel. des voy. qui ont servi à l'établissement de la Compagnie holland. des Ind. orient.*

115. *B Gall.*, VI, 19; Pomp. Mela, III, 8.

116. Procop., *Goth.*, III, 14; Solin, XIV. See Pomponius Mela, II, 2, on other peoples.

117. Valer. Max., II, 6.

118. Diod., XIX, 10.

119. Herd., *Phil. de l'hist.*, III, 43; *Asiat. Res.*, IV, 224.

120. Historical fragment of *The Mogul Empire, of the Marattoes, and of the English Concerns in Hindostan*, p. 126.

CHAPTER 3

On Privations against Nature

We have already observed that there is something mysterious in the sentiment of modesty or shame inherent in the union of the sexes;[1] we have indicated by what very natural transition this inexplicable sentiment could suggest to man the idea of something criminal in the pleasures he blushes at. Even today, when religion and society have sanctified by solemn forms the reproduction of beings, a notion of stain remains attached to it. When our imagination depicts the embraces she just left, the spouse that quits the arms of her spouse seems to us to have lost her purity, and maternity is necessary to return this purity, albeit under a different form. It is not surprising, therefore, that priestly polytheism, steeped in the idea of sacrifice, based itself on modesty in order to command the renunciation of the pleasures of the senses.

Independent polytheism itself has sometimes sanctioned these rigorous injunctions. The majority of the priestesses of Hercules, Minerva, Diana, and Ceres[2] in Greece were constrained to a more or less lengthy abstinence. But the Greeks ordinarily softened the privations prescribed by religion, either by assigning a term to them or by imposing them at an age when the needs of the senses were weakened. Only the priestesses of Hercules at Thespiae were subject to perpetual virginity.[3]

1. Bk. II, ch. 2.

2. We saw in book V, chapter 5, that these divinities were an amalgam of priestly notions, reworked by the Greek spirit: it perhaps was by a memory of these notions that virgins were consecrated to them.

3. Pausan., *Corinth.* On the sacred virgins among the Greeks, see Meursius, *Lect. Attic.*, IV, 21. The Pythia was constrained to continence. Eustathius says that the celibacy of priestesses was not introduced in Greece until long after Homeric times. In fact, Theano, priestess of Minerva, was the wife of Antenor (*Iliad*, XXIV, 503), and the priestess of Vulcan with the Trojans had two children (ibid.).

Priestly polytheism enforces even more severely these privations.[4] Each pagoda in India has a grand-priest to whom marriage is forbidden.[5] The *yogis* and the sannyasis make a vow of continence,[6] and the monks of Tibet and Siam, arrived at the higher ranks of their hierarchy, make the same commitment; and its infraction is punished with death.[7] Celibacy was ordained for the priests of the goddess Centeotl in Mexico; and in their pilgrimages, the Japanese are obliged to abstain from the pleasures of love even with their legitimate spouses. The same artifice that, in order to reconcile men to human sacrifices, made knowledge of the future depend upon these sacrifices, attached chastity to the same knowledge. From the earliest times, it was an indispensable condition of divination among a class of gynosophists, and the *semnai* who observed the stars and forecast the future were sacred virgins. Peruvian provinces sent to the court a certain number of young girls, some of whom were sacrificed and the others vowed to virginity.[8] The terrible punishments that awaited them if they were moved by temptation are well known. Fire consumed them alive, or the earth opened to swallow them. The same fate threatened the three hundred virgins of Carangua.[9]

The Persian religion appears to be an exception. The Zend Avesta expressly forbids fasts, privations, and, above all, abstaining from the pleasures of love. However, some passages of the Boundehesch present the union of the sexes as the first cause of the fall of man and the depravation of his nature.[10] This contradiction can only be explained by the traces of a religion older than that of Zoroaster, which this reformer was unable to make disappear completely.[11]

Since the principle that leads man to this exaggeration is not susceptible of limitation, the faithful soon persuaded themselves that their privations had not been

---

It would be possible that the Greek priests, even though they did not have legal authority, could have succeeded in slipping partial imitations of priestly customs into some portions of the religious discipline. Book XIII will show this imitation being much more complete in the mysteries.

4. On this subject, see Creuzer, I, 190, and the notes.

5. Sonnerat, I, 185.

6. They could bring their wives into their retreat, but without having intercourse with them.

7. No one in the Buddhist sect attained the state of happiness outside celibacy (*Asiat. Res.*, VI, 48). One of the sects of the Lamiac religion allowed its priests to marry; the other forbade it. As one would expect, the more severe one was dominant.

8. Acosta, V, ch. 5.

9. Ibid.

10. Boundehesch, pp. 83–86; Goerres, pp. 530–31.

11. See what we have said concerning Zoroaster's reform, in book III, chapter 9.

sufficiently painful. They have stimulated their senses so that their resistance would be more meritorious. They have sought out temptations so that their gods would grant them more favor to combat them. The fakirs of India, obscene mystics, grow proud in the midst of the caresses of women who are devoutly shameless, that they were not simply continent but totally unmoved.[12] And who would believe it? A distorted Christianity in the Middle Ages renewed these shameful and ridiculous trials.[13] "In the South of Europe," says Montesquieu,[14] "where by the nature of the climate the law of celibacy is more difficult to observe, it has been retained. In the North, where passions are less lively, it has been proscribed." This is because the renunciation of the pleasures of the senses seemed to be meritorious only where it was painful. And it is so true that the priestly religions recommended continence as a sacrifice, as a victory over nature, rather than because of its intrinsic value, that in the same countries sterility was a curse and a shame.[15] But to refuse what one desired and to trample on one's inclinations was a meritorious act of abnegation and of piety.

12. Anquetil, pp. 365–66.

13. Distorted Christianity, we say, because Saint Paul is much more measured than people subsequently were when it came to the renunciation of the pleasures of the senses. He did not make it intrinsically meritorious. He did not regard celibacy as a higher state, one that was purer than marriage. Marriage, he said, is the rule, celibacy the exception (Eichhorn, Nouv. Test., I, 130, 151, 158, 221, 284, 285). It is quite remarkable that all the exaggerations, abstinences, and excessive fastings were disapproved in the first centuries by Christians who were still obedient to the direction of their divine head; in such a way that one can affirm, in all truth, that far from having added to this delirium of the human race, Christianity always worked to moderate it.

14. *Esp. des lois*, XXV, 4.

15. Meiners, *Crit. Gesch.*, I, 239.

CHAPTER 4

On Licentious Rituals

Our observations on the duty of renouncing the pleasures of the senses, and on the privations contrary to nature that are imposed by the priestly religions of the nations that profess them, are applicable to rites of a totally different sort. We mean licentious rites, practiced in the South, in the East, and sometimes entering into the West and the North. These rituals go back to the savage state; they disappear in the independent polytheism, while they are perpetuated under the empire of priests.

In Egypt, women perform lascivious dances around a bull, a divinity of Lycopolis.[1] The religious prostitution of the Babylonians has been contested in vain;[2] vestiges of this custom can be seen in Lydia,[3] in Phoenicia,[4] and in Carthage.[5]

---

1. To learn the indecencies of the Egyptian religion, one can consult Heeren, *Africa*, p. 668; Herodotus (II, 60) on the cult of Isis in particular (ibid., 51), and on that of Diana at Bubastis (ibid.) with the notes of Larcher (II, 267, 268). Also see the fragments of Pindar in Strabo (bk. XVII). The Egyptians at Chemnis gave themselves to the embraces of the billy goat Mendes (Suidas in *Priapo*; Jablonsky., *Panth. Aeg.*, II, 7; Plut., dialogue entitled "Que les bêtes ont l'usage de la raison"). One still sees today a few remnants of the licentious rituals in Achmin, a city built on the ruins of Chemnis: there a congregation of young girls called knowing virgins was consecrated to pleasure.

2. See our observations on this subject, book II, chapter 7. Meiners, *Crit. Gesch.*, I, 393; and Creuzer, II, 21, 22 and 55, 57, on the erotic activities of the priests of Cybele after their mutilation.

3. Creuzer, II, 249.

4. Selden, *De diis syris*, Synt. II, 7, p. 234; *Ac. inscr.*, XXVIII, 59; August., *De civ. Dei*, IV, 10. There, as in Syria and Assyria, one worshipped the Phallus under the name of Peor or Phegor, and young women sacrificed their virginity to him (Bayer, *ad* Seld., 235ff.; Michael, *Mos. Recht*). According to a tradition of the country, during her travels Isis remained in Phoenicia for ten years and practiced the trade of courtesan (St. Epiph., Petav. ed., vol. II). Would not the legends of Mary of Egypt be a memory of the adventures of Isis?

5. See Dulaure's *Culte du Phallus*, p. 170.

The Jewish prophets frequently complained that the priests of false gods seduced the Israelites by shameful practices.[6] Ezekiel rose up against the fabrication of a Phallus, and reproached the Jews for giving to this idol worship that belonged to Jehovah.[7] In fact, we see it erected in pomp in the temple of Jehovah himself.[8] At the time of the apostasy of Osias, king of Judah, the worship of Priapus was introduced into the kingdom. Josias destroyed the huts of the effeminates who were in the house of the Lord, and these effeminates were idolatrous priests who celebrated obscene rituals.[9] Similar ceremonies stained the religion of Mexico.[10] Among the festivals that the reception of Bourroutta gives rise to according to the Ramayana,[11] in first place were the dances of courtesans. Young female Indians thus dance with their breasts exposed before pagodas.[12] Newly married women offer to these hideous images the first fruits of the virginity that they are going to lose; and—a remarkable thing—this practice is in everything similar to the one that the Romans adopted when all the various polytheisms were mixed together. In the cult of Kali, human sacrifices, illicit pleasures,[13] and obscene chants are simultaneously commanded.

6. Baalphegor, one of the gods of the idolatrous enemies of the Jews, had priapic forms, and licentious rites were celebrated in his honor (Kircher, *Oed. Aeg.*, I, 333). A passage from the Bible would lead us to believe that practices of the same sort took place among the Jews at the time of the worship of the golden calf (Exod., 32).

7. Ezek., XVI, 16–17.

8. II Kings 23, 7.

9. Kings, ibid. and IV.

10. Garcilaso de la Vega, *Hist. des Incas*, II, 6.

11. Ramayana, p. 637.

12. One can consult Meiners, *Crit. Gesch.*, I, 263; Hamilton, *New Account of the East-Indies*. The obscenity of the figures of the temple of Shiva at Elephanta surpasses, says Heeren, everything that the most corrupt imagination could conceive (*Inde*, 322). Nothing is more licentious than the story of the goddess Mariathal, and the cult of Durga is a mixture of debauchery and ferocity (Schlegel, *Weish. der Ind.*, p. 119).

13. Laflotte, *Essais historiques sur l'Inde*, p. 216. Among some Indian tribes (Moore, *Narrative of the Operations of Captain Little's Detachm. of the Mahratta Army*, p. 45; Meiners, *Crit. Gesch.*, II, 264), and in some temples of Mexico (Kircher, *Oed. Aeg.*, I, 5; Laet, *Beschryr. van West. Ind.*, V, 5), solemn festivals offered the dramatic representation of pleasures that ran contrary to nature. Creuzer reports a similar fact in connection with the mysteries of Samothrace. Antoinette Bourignon (*Vie continuée*) makes the sin against nature the incarnation of the devil. Would it be the case that despite herself, and because of the reading of some mystics of the first centuries imbued with traditions borrowed from priestly religions, these traditions had mixed with the extravagance of her own conceptions?

The harshness of the northern climates does not preserve their inhabitants from the shameful excesses of a superstition refining itself. At the festival of Thor, during the longest night of the year, the Scandinavians, say several sagas, give themselves over to debauchery of all sorts, and the young priestesses of Frey serve the pleasure of the god or his ministers.[14]

In this regard, as in what relates to human sacrifices and the privations against nature, the religion of the Persians appears to merit fewer reproaches than the others. However, on the day of the feast of Mithra, the Persian monarch had either the freedom or the duty to become drunk, and to dance in public the national dance,[15] which could be a remnant of crude or licentious rites that the reform of Zoroaster had abolished, while making a rare concession to previous customs.[16]

Like human sacrifices, the shameful feasts had their scientific explanations. The story of Attys, the loves of Cybele, the disappearance of her mutilated lover, the orgies celebrated by the faithful who sought him, and the indecencies that characterized their frenetic joy when they found him; all these things are connected to astronomy.[17]

Also like the bloody rituals, the obscene rites tended to fall into disuse. The Indian sects that paid homage to the generative organs divided into two branches, one of which admitted, while the other rejected, immodest practices.[18] Public opinion scorned the first, but the priesthood resisted; and the purest of reformers, Krishna, is still honored today by the indecent ceremonies he sought to banish.[19]

We see nothing similar in the independent religions as they are publicly pro-

14. Oloff Tryggueson, *Saga*; and Bartholin, *Antiq. Danic.*, II, 5. The Swedish *Saga* that has been transmitted to us by these authors is, in truth, the work of a monk, who always presents Frey as the devil and who seeks to render odious the worship that Christianity replaced. But it is not plausible that he simply made up what was not, rather than exaggerating what was.

15. Athen., X, 10; Kleucker, *Anhang zum Zendavesta*, II, 3, p. 194.

16. We could have extended this list to infinity. Licentious rites are found among the Chaldeans (Goerres, I, 270; Paralip., II, 15–16), the Cappadocians (Creuzer, II, 22), the Armenians (ibid., 22–23), and in all the islands where foreign navigators had brought their rituals, such as Samothrace, Lemnos, Cyprus, and Sicily (Athen., XIV, 647; Sainte-Croix, pp. 217, 400).

17. Creuzer, II, 33–47.

18. Indians represent these two subdivisions by two paths, one of which leads to the right, the other to the left. The one on the right is a decent cult, the one on the left consists of more or less crude obscenities. The path on the left is disapproved of by those who do not follow it, and its tantras, or sacred books, are the object of their disdain and rejection (Colebrooke, *Asiat. Res.*, VII, 279–82).

19. See bk. VI, ch. 6, n. 27.

fessed. There were many festivals in Greece where women appeared nude; but these women were only courtesans,[20] while the licentious rituals of the priestly religions forced women of all conditions into indecency or immodesty.

The girls of Sparta danced without clothes with the young men; however, even though we are far from admiring the half-monastic, half-savage laws of Lycurgus, we cannot find any affinity between these laws and the rituals of Egypt or Syria.

The licentious practices introduced into Greece were always connected with foreign gods.[21] In the mysteries themselves, Greek women, when adoring the Phallus, never prostituted themselves like those of Ecbatana or Heliopolis. Diogondas had prohibited obscene feasts at Thebes, and to banish them more completely he proscribed nocturnal rites.[22] In one of his comedies, Aristophanes proposes expelling the gods who prescribed such practices. We will see that it was the same in Rome during the period of the purity of Roman polytheism.[23] This difference between the two species of polytheism can be explained only by the principle whose applications and consequences we are examining here. The priesthood had ordained chastity, the sacrifice of nature. It also commanded indecency, the sacrifice of shame.[24]

---

20. Strabo (bk. VIII) recounts that at Corinth women dedicated to the cult of Venus trafficked in their charms and deposited the payment in the temple's treasury. But the métier of these women, despite this use of their salary, could only have very indirect relations with the religion. Even in our days, in a Catholic country, in France, a portion of the tax placed upon debauchery serves to pay religious writers and, perhaps, the seminaries of priests, without Catholicism being accused of recommending licentious rites; and Strabo calls these Corinthian women *hetairai*, while the prostitution of female Babylonians extended to all of their sex.

21. Strabo (XIII) puts Priapus among the number of the most recent divinities, unknown to Hesiod. According to several traditions, Priapus was the son of Adonis and Venus, or rather the fruit of a double marriage of this goddess with Adonis and Bacchus (schol. Apollon. Rhod., I, 932). Now, Adonis and Bacchus were both foreign gods. When the poets sought everywhere for allegories, they explained this birth of Priapus by the effect produced on physical desires by wine, which makes them both uncontrollable and cruder.

22. Cic., *De leg.*, II.

23. Cic., *De nat. deor.*, III, 23; Sainte-Croix, *Les myst.*, 437.

24. The same deviation in the notions of sacrifice suggested to several heretics of different times the most revolting practices. Manicheans claimed that with the spirit coming from the good principle and flesh from the evil principle, out of hatred for the latter, and in order to sanctify the flesh, one must sully it in a thousand ways, and under this pretext they gave themselves over to all sorts of impurities (Bayle, "Manichéens"). From the second century, Prodicus, and in the eleventh, Taulerus of Anvers, recommended the most scandalous forgetting of all mystery in pleasure as a victory over

nature's instinct (Theodoret, *Haeret.*, I, 7, v. 27; X, 20). Soon after the death of the apostles, the doctrine of the mystical union among the faithful was symbolically represented by the union of the sexes, called the initiation. The Adamites, the Picards, and the Anabaptists imposed nudity upon themselves as a duty (Bayle, "Turlupins"). Hence the processions of flagellants in which men and women without any clothing walked through the streets and grand avenues. These practices lasted until the fifteenth century.

It appears that independently of this way of considering sacrifice there exists a rather intimate relationship between devotion exalted to excess and the most unbridled thirst for pleasure. (See the Canticle of Canticles and the Gita Govinda of the Indians.) All mystics have allowed themselves to be led to very indecent acts, descriptions, allegories, and images. To be convinced of this, it is enough to read the English or French mystics, Barrow, Madame Guyon, above all, Antoinette Bourignon, whose character, at once harsh and dry, did not preserve her from this pitfall. All the expressions used to describe the pleasures of devotion are borrowed from physical pleasures, and details become more explicit as devotion becomes more ardent.

An author we have often cited in this part of our work, because he is a constant apologist (although more and less direct) of all the priestly rituals and the naïve expression of the priestly spirit of antiquity wanting to insinuate itself into Christianity, has written very curious pages on this subject. He begins by attributing the fact of burlesque and obscene festivals being placed next to sacred feasts to a profound knowledge of the human heart. He says that the men who have established these burlesque and obscene feasts, which in appearance are impious (he thus recognizes this), knew with what adroitness the evil genius works to counterbalance the angelic power. These feasts subsist wherever peoples are still religious, and disappear as indifferentism becomes the dominant attitude. Then these feasts are banished as obscene and crude, as an assault on virtue and an outrage against sacred things; but these sacred things at the same time are effaced from hearts and cease to occupy minds. And is it not in the midst of upheavals and disorder that order reemerges? In this way, the Saturnalia begun with debauchery ended with solemnities. Then passing from theory to application, and even to an image, our author gives us the extract of a poem of Jayadeva, which one can call the Canticle of Canticles of Indians. "Krishna," he says, "the shepherd god, made himself beloved of the young shepherdesses, the Gopi or Gopias, before he himself felt love. His childish games are mixed with mystical depictions in a way that often shocks the modesty of our civilized mores. . . . Finally, the fire of desire is lit in the heart of the young god, and the depiction of this development bears a character of naïve gaiety that the reserve of our mores would reject. . . . Radha, the chosen shepherdess of Krishna, becomes alarmed at his dances with the other shepherdesses. It is, says the French or German author, whichever one would like, the symbol of the spiritual communion of the human race that is concerned for its divine savior, its celestial friend. The most brilliant expressions of oriental poetry serve to depict the jealousy of Radha under the colors of an earthly passion. . . . This is a carnal mysticism, which one would be wrong to regard as simply terrestrial and impure. . . . Everywhere celestial love steals for its use the most vivid expressions of profane love. . . . Let one imagine what the Canticle of Canticles offers that is most vehement, what the expression of desire has that is most delirious, and one will have some idea of the transports of Radha, transports next to which the frenzy of Phaedrus seems to pale. . . . Krishna comes, and the modesty that had found a final refuge in the dark pupils of Radha finally vanishes.

In order to hide their sly smiles, the shepherdesses make the motion of shooing away insects. Then they retire from the grotto and Radha reclines with sensuous abandon on the couch spread with new flowers and petals. . . . Morning comes, and the disorder of her clothes and the fatigue in her eyes betray a night spent without sleep. Contemplating her with delight, however, the god meditates on her charms. I cannot, he says to himself, behold her without being transported, even though her hair is disheveled and the luster of her skin is gone, and she seeks with a graceful modesty to hide the disorder of her necklace and the cincture that poorly defended her most secret places. . . . Beloved of my heart, says Radha to him, place on my eyelid which veils the rays softer than the arrows sent by Cupid this beautifully smelling powder which would cause the bee to envy; hang those diamonds from my ears, chains of love, which emit a lively glow; guided by their light, let your eyes, like two running antelopes, survey my charms, and pursue their sweet prey. . . . O you whose heart is so tender, return my clothes to their place, return my jewels to their accustomed place, and let my golden bells once again sound on my harmonious belt." After this very sweet portrait of the indecencies of the Indian author, our writer concludes once again that this poem has the attraction of the soul for its savior as its subject. This poem of Jayadeva is still after two thousand years the object of a religious festival. During the night, a very exact mime presents the scenes of the shepherd's song, and the spectators recite the odes of Jayadeva. See Paterson on the dance of Rasijatra (*Asiat. Res.*, XVII, 318–619).

CHAPTER 5

On the Sanctity of Pain

In the beginning of the chapter relating to the dominant principle of priestly religions, we said that when man begins with this principle he cannot stop. He is not satisfied with any of the numerous and varied sacrifices that he prescribes for himself; his heart does not seem to be sufficiently rent by the loss of what he holds most dear. His senses seem incompletely tested by the deprivation of his most lively pleasures. He does not believe he has done enough by abandoning purity itself in the temples of the gods, before whom he has imposed silence on the most imperious of his inclinations. He must have positive, visible pains that cannot be misunderstood, that leave no doubt as to his intentions. The tendency to painful physical mortifications is therefore in the heart of man.[1] One can even say that it draws from a true idea. It is by pain and sorrow that man improves. It is like a principle of activity, or a means of perfection, that Providence has given us with such abundance, that any other system would make it a gratuitous and inexcusable cruelty. Pain sometimes awakens what is noblest in our nature, courage; sometimes what is tenderest, sympathy and pity. It teaches us to battle for ourselves and to feel for others. Alerted by the instinct that reveals to it so many truths that logic cannot discern, the religious sentiment sometimes seeks pain in order to draw purity or strength from it. But the priesthood takes hold of this movement and imparts a false and deplorable direction to it.

In all priestly cults, the ministers, and those of the followers of these cults who wish to elevate themselves to the highest degree of perfection, condemn themselves to fasts, mortifications, and torments that inspire in us an astonishment close to doubt. Some cut their arms with knives, other strike themselves

1. See bk. II, ch. 2.

with whips[2] or place a burning wick on their chest. Others mutilate themselves, believing they thereby delight the gods by ceasing to be men; sometimes they walk barefoot across burning coals;[3] sometimes they are suspended on iron hooks; sometimes they carry enormous weights, which they have riveted to their neck to avoid the temptation of discarding them.

Other times, raising their arms in the air, which they do not lower toward the ground, they wait for a pious hand to bring food to their mouth, or they receive the waters of the skies and the snow of winter on their bare heads.[4]

2. Lucret., *De nat. rer.*, II.

3. At Castabala, in Cappadocia (Strabo, XII), among the Samnites and the Sabines (Spangenberg, *De vet. lat. relig.*, p. 48).

4. On these facts, one can consult the philosophers of antiquity, the Fathers of the Church, the modern historians and travelers. On the religious fasts among the ancients, see Morin (*Ac. inscr.*, IV, 29); on voluntary tortures among the Mexicans, Robertson (*Hist. of Amer.*); on their mortifications, mutilations, and abstinences during 162 days, Mayer (*Myth. Lex.*, art. *Cammaxtle*); Clavigero (*Hist. of Mexic.*, I, 363); Meiners (*Crit. Gesch.*, II, 164). During entire months, they drew blood from different parts of the body. The Egyptians struck themselves in their mysterious festivals (Herod., II, 61; Müller, *De myster.*, 192). They publicly flagellated themselves during the festival of Isis (Meiners, *Crit. Gesch.*, II, 165). "*Aegyptii sacerdotes, Saturno dicati,*" says Saint Epiphanius, "*ferreis collaribus se ipsos alligab-ant, circulosque sibi naribus affligebant. Ab isto genere sacrorum non minoris insaniae judicanda sunt publica illa sacra, quorum alia sunt matris Deum, in quibus homines suis ipsi virilibus litant. . . . Alia virtutis quam eandem Bellonam vocant: in quibus ipsi sacerdotes non alieno sed suo cruore sacrificant. Sectis namque humeris et utraque manu destrictos gladios exerentes currunt, efferuntur, insaniunt.*" These Egyptian practices were similar in everything to those of the yogis and *sannyasis* of India (Cheremon., *adv.* Jovinian). The mutilation of the priests of Syria is well known (Lucian, *De Dea Syr.*; Müller, *De myst.*, p. 59; Wagner, pp. 210, 211, 216). The Persians who were initiated into the mysteries of Mithra were sometimes subject to mortal torments (Suidas, *Greg. Nazianz.*, ch. 4; Hyde, *De rel. pers.*, p. 109). In their sacrifices, the priests of Baal cut their own flesh while dancing around the altars, which they washed with their blood (I Kings, ch. 19, v. 28). See especially the sacrifice they offered in opposition to Elijah (II Kings, ch. 18, v. 21). The caregivers of the Hebrews regarded every physical pleasure, and even every indulgence to the needs of the body, as the work of darkness (Phil, *Juifs*). The virgins of Peru tear their breasts and cheeks. The priests of the same country put out their eyes (Acosta, V, 14, 15, 17; Zarate, *Hist. de la conquête du Pérou*, I, 153). The popular religion of the Indians recommends voluntary sufferings, either to expiate the faults they have committed or as a means of obtaining the favors they desire. The penances that give man the most assured rights to divine mercy or assistance are exposing oneself to the sun during the hottest days, in the midst of four burning coals, and to cast oneself into the iciest water during the coldest days. "The blood that a faithful draws from his body to make an offering," says the Kalika Purana, "pleases the divinity in proportion to the greatness of the instrument he employs. He who offers his blood and flesh with zeal and fervor sees his prayers heard within six months; and he who allows himself to be burned by a lit wick is soon filled with wealth and

By a consequence of the same principle, no more than a hundred years ago one still admired Saint Simeon Stylites atop his column, Saint Francis of Assisi holding in his arms statutes of snow, and so many others whose sole merit was having sought out pain and hardship;[5] and the letters of our missionaries in China and Japan manifest the same avid desire for suffering.[6]

From this sanctity attached to pain naturally arises the idea of a mysterious effectiveness in the torments that man inflicts upon himself. Hence the prodigious power of austerities among the Indians. Hence those epithets upon which we have

---

happiness" (*Asiat. Res.*, V, 371, 391). See also the Laws of Menu, ch. 5 (Mills, *Hist. of Ind.*, I, 351–52). Mr. Duncan (*Asiat. Res.*, V, 37–52) gives an account of the austerities of two fakirs he encountered: one, after having crossed all of India and Persia, had arrived at Moscow, in traveling he had always held his arms crossed on his head; the second, having first enclosed himself in a cell where he had made the vow of supporting for twelve years the stings of insects that devoured him. Having left it at the end of one year, he had had a bed of iron nails constructed upon which he had spent thirty-five years in reading and meditating on the sacred books, as well as exposing himself during the four months of the winter to the rain and all the inclemencies of the seasons. Buddhists and the followers of Fo in China are no less barbarous toward themselves. These Indian penances go back to the most remote antiquity. The Oupnekhat speaks (I, 274) of a Brahmin, Raja-Brahdratch, who went into the desert and held himself upright until his death, fixing his gaze on the sun—which is what Pliny reports, word for word, of the ancient Brachmanes (*Hist. nat.*, VII). According to Cicero, they rolled entirely naked in the snows of the Caucasus. For the iron hooks from which they hung themselves, see Roger (*Pag. ind.*); Ovington (*Voy.*, II, 74); Lacroze (*Christ. des Ind.*); Sonnerat (in the chapter on "Pénitents indiens").

5. Saint Godin, who died in England in 1170, used three iron shirts that he wore. He put ash in his bread, salt in his wounds, and broke ice in order to spend entire nights in the water (Pennant, *Tour in Scotland*, p. 30; Saint-Foix, *Essai sur Paris*, V, 88). Saint Catherine of Cordova grazed like the animals, and during days of fasting, even less than normal. Pascal, according to his sister, wore an iron belt studded with nails, and when he took some pleasure in the place in which he found himself, or in a conversation, or any other thing, he attempted to atone for it, redoubling the violence of his efforts. Let no one be mistaken: fidelity to the principle of the sanctity of suffering characterizes the priesthood of every epoch; today still, open the *Bibliothèque chrétienne* of Abbé Boudon, published three years ago in Paris. Sister Angelica of Providence is proposed as a model for young women. "Now, this Sister Angelica had an extraordinary bent for cleanliness . . . she therefore had to overcome this inclination, and what did she do? She spread what had been swept up, as well as other filth, throughout the paternal house." Disgust prevents us from continuing, and all the revolting triumphs over her inclination were for Sister Angelica the infallible path to salvation and are admired by her devout biographer.

6. See the letters of P. Brito, in the collection of *Lettres édifiantes*. Saint Ignatius, in a letter to the faithful (*Epist. ad Rom. ap. Patr. apostol.*, II, 27), beseeches them not to deprive him of the crown of martyrdom by their intercessions. Saint Basil describes the duties of the monk in a style that recalls all the austerities of the Indian *sannyasis* (Staeudlin, *Hist. de la mor.*, p. 225).

already fixed our readers' attention, and that constantly return in the sacred prayers and poems of India: "powerful by suffering, rich with austerities"; and these austerities are in fact wealth, because they are the arsenal from which the mortal draws weapons in his struggle with the immortal gods. It was by his austerities that Dasaratha constrained heaven to grant him children.[7] Ravana, hero, *genius*, or rebellious incarnation, by his austerities forced Brahma to make him invulnerable.[8] The starvations of Gautama put him on a par with the gods, with whom he contested victory.[9] Vashistha, the famous penitent of the Ramayana, places austerities among the means of combating and defeating his enemies.[10] But the least relaxation, the least weakness toward pleasure, deprives mortifications of their merit. Vishwamitra, seduced by a woman that the gods had sent, loses the fruit of a thousand years of austerities.[11] He begins them anew, and the defeated gods cry out: Your austerities have been without limit; your energy will be immeasurable.[12]

Sometimes licentious rites are combined with austerities and penances: the same young Indians who dance half-nude before the temples inflict cruel and refined sufferings on themselves.[13] The priests of Cybele who mutilate themselves also give themselves over to impurities with women, impurities which their impotence renders even more horrible,[14] and this double triumph over suffering and shame makes the crowd respect them even more.

7. Ramayana, pp. 105–10.

8. Ibid., p. 190.

9. Ibid., p. 435.

10. Ibid., pp. 240–58. After many fruitless penances, Vikramaditya was ready to cut off his own head when Kali appeared to him. The gods, she says, forced to yield to you, grant you great power and a long life. You will have a thousand years of prosperity, then you will die at the hand of a child born of a virgin (*Asiat. Res.*, IX, 119, drawn from the *Vikrama Charitra*). In the collection of fables entitled *Sucasaptati, ou Récits du perroquet*, one sees a penitent always cutting off his head and tossing it at Kali's feet, who each time grant him his prayer (ibid., 122).

11. Ramayana, p. 265.

12. Ibid., pp. 546–47.

13. Laflotte, *Essais historiques sur l'Inde*, p. 216. The Qedeshim, the effeminates about whom the Bible speaks (II Kings, 23, 7), were eunuchs who had mutilated themselves out of devotion (Selden, *De diis syr.*, p. 237).

14. On the rituals of the priests of Bellona and Cybele that are simultaneously indecent and bloody, see Lactantius (*Inst. div.*, I, 21), Bayle ("Comana"), Strabo (bk. X), and Creuzer (II, 34). Turkish dervishes and santons, on one hand, submitted themselves to the very painful operation of infibulation, and, on the other, to the search for pleasures that we will not spell out here (Locke, *Entend. humain*, I; *Voyage* of Baumgart., II, 1; Pauw, *Rech. sur les Américains*, II, 121). In a principality of Ger-

This refinement in sufferings often goes to the point of suicide. It was common among the Brachmanes to cast themselves into the flames.[15] As the prologue to his drama attests, Sudraka, prince and poet, author of the drama of Mricchatika, burned himself on a pyre at the age of one hundred; and while profiting from the abolition of this custom, modern Brahmins say that it has fallen into disuse only in the Kali Yuga, the age of corruption and impiety. The devotées of Arakan act the same way. The worshippers of Amida have themselves crushed beneath the wheels of his chariot; and in our day, two English sailors witnessed the religious delirium of thirty-nine Indians who cast themselves into the Ganges together.[16]

The idea we have already seen, the supposition of an original fall, one of the causes of human sacrifice, doubtless contributed mightily to the merit attributed to pain and suffering.[17] All the affections,[18] all earthly bonds, have seemed to be a consequence of the degradation that the human race suffered. The desires for the things of this world, says the Neadirsen, are an offense to God; one must control them by mortifications and penance.

The notion of the division into two substances could equally strengthen the penchant of man for austerities. In this system, matter is the enemy and the tyrant, as it were, of the spirit, which is imprisoned in its thick envelope. One must defeat this enemy, dethrone this tyrant. Everything that makes it suffer or that weakens it—fasts, abstinences, resistance to the needs or attractions of the senses, voluntary tortures—are triumphs that free the spiritual substance from its crude bonds; and the pure spirit, returned to its freedom, rises to God, to merge and lose itself in him.

The refinements of cruelty that one sees in the human sacrifices of certain peoples owe to the teaching of the sanctity of suffering. Among the Mexicans, sometimes the victims were dragged by their hair to the top of the pyramid on

---

many near the Rhine, one sees a château where a princess belonging to a house that still reigns lived. In this château was a chamber devoted to austerities. There one finds the iron bed studded with nails upon which the royal penitent slept, the whip that shed blood on her delicate members, and several instruments of torture. Every year the princess spent forty days harming herself, and when she had thus atoned for her faults, she prepared new subjects of expiation for the following year.

15. Philaret., Oneisir, *ap.* Lucian.

16. In November 1801; *Asiat. Res.*, V, 26–29.

17. This idea appears to have been the basis of Mexican beliefs. The nature of man, degraded before his birth, could not rise to Vitzliputzli and identify with this god except by excessive tortures.

18. One reads in the *Vie de madame Guyon, écrite par elle-même*, these curious words: "In the same week I lost my father and my husband; God gave me the grace not to regret either one."

which they were to die; sometimes they were flayed alive and priests covered themselves with the bloody skins; sometimes they were cast into a burning furnace, then removed with hooks while they were still breathing, in order to slaughter them on the altar.

We need to observe, however, that in order to be profoundly imprinted in the religion, the idea of the sanctity of pain must always be seconded by the climate. One would be wrong to confuse the spontaneous mortifications and torments of southern nations with the frequent suicides in the North. These suicides draw their source from martial habits, according to which only a violent death was honorable; impatient heroes grew indignant at the thought of waiting for the slow and gradual degeneration of old age.[19]

Montesquieu, whose observation concerning the merit of continence we recalled earlier, makes another no less apt observation concerning the contradiction that appears to exist between the soft laziness of the South and the way in which its inhabitants run toward death, brave it, and defy it. But he saw only one of the causes of this contradiction, and a secondary one at that. The principal one is the religion that transforms pleasure into a crime, and suffering into merit. The fear of pleasure becomes a furious passion in the climates that imperiously incline men to physical pleasures. Since the senses are tormented rather than subjugated by austerities, and abstinences constantly reassert their empire, weak consciences are horrified to see everywhere the pleasure that they flee; and in order to better fight this stubborn adversary they pile rigor upon rigor, torture upon torture. It is the people who are the most susceptible to lively affections, the most inclined to sensual pleasure, who give themselves over to the most refined austerities and are in the grip, as it were, of the love of pain. Exhausted by an always unsuccessful struggle, they make the excess of suffering a rampart against their weakness and the seductions of nature.

The Greeks always kept mortifications as well as licentious rites out of their public religion. Until the second century of our era, the philosophers, nourished on Greek literature, had such great difficulty in explaining the austerities of the hermits of the Thebaid, as well as the iron chains they put on themselves, that they believed they were struck with delirium as punishment for abandoning the worship of the gods.[20]

19. See above, bk. IX, ch. 7.

20. See an ancient fragment entitled *Le Philosophe*, in volume 9 of the *Mémoires ecclésiastiques* of Tillement, pp. 661–68.

Nor should anyone object that these same philosophers—the Stoics, the Neopythagorians, and the Platonists of Alexandria—imposed hardship and austerities on their disciples.[21] Some imitation of their practices could be found in Pythagoras, who, we are told, was obliged to subject himself to torments of every sort in order to be admitted to the knowledge of the secret teaching of the priests of Egypt; but his school considered them to be tests of the courage and discretion of those who did them, rather than attaching any religious merit to them. The Stoics wanted in this way to show that pain was not an evil; and, as for Platonists, the half-defeated auxiliaries of a religion into which they introduced foreign extravagances, believing thereby to fortify it against the rivals they parodied, they cannot be usefully consulted about the true spirit of a religion that their efforts tended to denature.

21. These philosophical austerities go back to the time of Socrates. Strepsiades, his so-called disciple in Aristophanes (*Nuées*, 38), declares himself ready to suffer anything the philosophers enjoin: "I will give willingly," he says, "my body to the whip, to hunger, to thirst, to cold; and when I will be flayed alive, I will consent, provided that I escape the hands of my creditors."

CHAPTER 6

On Some Doctrines That Could Have Been Introduced into the Priestly Religions as Consequences of Those We Just Discussed

Before ending this book, we must treat some singular effects of a disposition that we have often noticed in man, whether civilized or savage: we mean his penchant to attribute to the gods his inclinations, sentiments, and even his adventures. This tendency was most clearly manifest in all the religions subject to priests, and it causes the most bizarre doctrines to enter them. Thus, the Egyptians believed Apis was born of a heifer impregnated by the sun.[1] The Scythians identified their origin with a virgin who miraculously gave birth to a child they named Scytha.[2] A virgin was the mother of Tages.[3] The Chinese, whose traditions manifestly owe to ancient priestly doctrines, say that the birth of Fo-Hi was miraculous, in that he did not have a father. Xaca, in one of his apparitions, in Tibet,[4] and Mexitli and Vitzliputzli, in Mexico, emerged from the bosom of a young girl who knew nothing of the mysteries of hymen. The Aslomi, the Indian Dioscuri, who, endowed with beauty as well as eternal youth, cross the globe on horseback healing the ills of body and soul; they are born of a mare that the day star impregnated with his rays. Sita, the spouse of Rama, had a furrow for a cradle;[5] and the most glorious

---

1. Vogel, *Rel. der Aegypt.*, p. 175.

2. Diodorus. This virgin's lower belt had the form of a serpent or a fish. Fetishism thus allied with a mystical idea. Instead of supposing her to be a virgin, Herodotus attributed to her a secret liaison with Hercules. In this one recognizes the Greek spirit, that is, antipriestly, always trying to domesticate the priestly fables.

3. Cic., *De divin.*, II, 23; Arnob., *Adv. gentes*, II, 62.

4. Georgi, *Alph. Tibet.*, pref., p. 16.

5. Ramayana, p. 368.

incarnation of Vishnu is the one in which, under the name Krishna, he saw the light of day without his mother having felt the caresses of a man.[6]

Would not this idea have come from the importance attached by priestly peoples to the sanctity of abstinences and privations running counter to nature? The seed, no doubt, is found in the human heart. We have pointed it out in the savage; but the priests developed this seed; they made a dogma of it that they inserted in their mythological accounts. The union of the sexes, both in heaven as well as on earth, was disapproved; and divinity, even when it became incarnate, did not want to owe its birth to an impure act.[7]

It should be noticed that the desire to spare the gods the stains of a mortal birth sometimes impelled the priests to fictions that were even more indecent than the popular notion they wished to avoid. The beautiful Amogha became pregnant with Brahma by means that we cannot describe; and the virginal ear of the young Anjani enabled her to conceive in a way that was as obscene as it was strange the son of Shiva, Hanuman, the satyr of the Indians, and the active and intelligent auxiliary of the gods in their wars.

What confirms the conjecture we hazard is that no similar notion appeared among the Greeks at the time when their mythology became a regular system. If Hesiod or Nonnus transmit a few fables of the sort that we just considered in India, they are before the reign of Jupiter, or only recount adventures of his youth. This god wishing to do sexual violence to Venus, and his ardor disappointed by the resistance of the goddess, he impregnates a stone that gives birth to a son at the end of ten months.[8] This myth goes back therefore to the cosmogonic period that we have proved many times was foreign to Greece. Minerva emerges fully armed from Jupiter's head, and Vulcan is the fruit of the solitary wrath of Juno against her unfaithful husband. But we have explained how these two fables—the first of which goes back to the Phoenician Onga and the second to the Egyptian Phat[9]—entered into Greek mythology. At most, the pride that prompts Diana to remain a virgin and her severity toward her weaker companions would appear to come

6. Roger, *Pagan. ind.*, II, 3; Creuzer, III, 134. Ancient images of the virgin represent her as a woman having her feet on a crescent and her head crowned with stars; and in the Indian mythology, the mother of Krishna is represented in the same way.

7. Hence, perhaps, the disputes among Christians concerning the immaculate conception.

8. Arnob., V, 162; Nonnus, bk. XIV.

9. Bk. V, ch. 5.

close to the priestly rigors; but this myth, borrowed from Hertha, never had any influence on religion, and even ended by being a subject of mockery by the poets, so little analogy did it have with the received and revered teachings of the people.

It was not only in regard to virginity and divine births without the intervention of sexual union that the priests wanted their gods to conform to the notions of men. It was the same relative to human sacrifices and to the mysterious value attached to suffering. The worshipper, considering the offering to be more effective as the object was more precious, first of all preferred animals to plants, then his fellows to animals, finally, the gods to his fellows. From this it resulted that several nations believed that their gods were immolated on their own altars.

This idea, at least such as it is presented in the cults of Egypt, Phoenicia, and India (because it has no relation to a dogma that we must respect as an object of veneration for several Christian communions), brought back the view that even the gods are not exempt from death,[10] a supposition that independent polytheism hastened to relegate to obscure traditions; and it was supported by the cosmogonic allegories.

In the Indian cosmogonies, which are founded on pantheism, creation is a sacrifice. The god who exists alone sacrifices himself by violently dividing, and drawing the world from his own essence.[11]

Such is one of the meanings of the legend of Bacchus torn to pieces by the Titans; of Osiris, whose members were dispersed throughout the universe; of Mithra, under the name Iresch, eaten by his brothers;[12] Chenrezi in Tibet also breaks his head against a rock in order to create the world.

Other times, imitating the practices of their most scrupulous worshippers, the gods sacrifice what they hold most dear, their children, like them belonging to the divine race.[13]

This notion of a divine sacrifice gave rise among the Mexicans to a strange custom. In one of their most solemn feasts, the priests struck the heart of the god

10. Bk. II, ch. 4.

11. See the Rigveda, last chapter of Aitareya Brahmana.

12. Buddha is sacrificed in the same way, torn in pieces by demons, swallowed by his priest, who, discovering that he serves as a prison for the god he worships, kills himself to put him at liberty; he is reborn, and in his turn resuscitates the priest who had sacrificed himself for him.

13. *Mythologie phénicienne;* Wagner, pp. 285–86.

whom their worship had honored and distributed the broken heart to those in attendance, a mystical food that obtains the protection of heaven.[14]

To this fiction of the death of the gods is joined the merit of voluntary suffering. Sommonacodom descends to the netherworld in order to suffer for five hundred consecutive generations;[15] Eshmun and Attis mutilate themselves;[16] Vishnu, in his fourth incarnation, emaciates himself in the depths of a desert.[17] Diti, his spouse, practices terrible austerities during a thousand years. It is the divine suffering, the penitence of God, the *tapasya* as the Vedas say, that produced the world; this same suffering is necessary to save it. At all times the Indians have believed that the divine nature enters into sacrifices as a suffering part.[18] In immolating themselves, their gods expire in a long and cruel agony. The principle that inspired the worshippers to engage in so many austerities that we shudder at them, led them to imagine the objects of their worship imposing upon themselves, according to their more sublime essence, even more astonishing and painful sufferings. But since the intellect, even when it errs, loves to connect conceptions among themselves and to give them a sort of unity, the hypothesis of the original fall is ordinarily the connecting knot of this sort of drama. By their sufferings the gods bestow a supernatural assistance on the fallen human race. The mediating god reestablishes

14. This festival was called Teoculi, the feast of the god one eats. A man who has applied himself to comment on all the mystical ideas of Indian theology, and who connected all the superstitions to this mysticism, says interesting things on this subject, in that they show the series of subtleties by which one has substituted the sacrifice of God himself for sacrifices offered to God: "It is on the altar that man and the divinity encounter. There, the mystical union of the soul with its creator is accomplished. There, man suffers and is regenerated in the flames of the holocaust. In the primitive family, each sacrifice was a meal. The sacrificer communed with the divinity; it then communed with the human race. Each one in eating the sacrificed victim nourished himself with the substance of the creator-become-creature-and-victim. The man-god was sacrificed, and those who assisted at this sacrifice, either as priests or simple faithful, communed with the mediator and nourished themselves with his divine substance. These ideas had profoundly entered the worship of Bacchus, god of wine, which is the blood of the universe, and into the cult of Ceres, goddess of bread, which is the flesh of this same universe" (*Catholique,* XXII, 247).

15. Laloubere, II, 14.

16. On the story of Eshmun, see Creuzer, II, 148; Wagner, p. 286; Meiners, *Crit. Gesch.*, I, 70; and for the different legends of the mutilations of Attis, Wagner, p. 238.

17. On the sufferings and mutilations of Brahma, see Roger, *Pagan. ind.*, II, 1; Sonnerat, I, 128–29; Anquetil, p. 139; and Wagner, pp. 221–28.

18. See the notes of the translator of Sacoutala, p. 294.

the broken communication. The purification of man is effected by the torments of the god who atones for him.[19] The necessity of such an expiation was transmitted from century to century and entered Christianity, maintaining itself until our day.[20] "The faith teaches us," say very modern authors, "that to efface the sin inherent in the nature of man, it was necessary to have a theandric victim, that is, at once divine and human. Perhaps the inventors of human sacrifices among the idolatrous nations had learned this truth by some vague tradition, and the rituals that revolt us were only an attempt to find the victim destined to deliver the human race by his death."[21]

There is nothing equivalent in the independent religions. If the gods of Homer are vulnerable to suffering, it is a consequence of their imperfect and limited nature. Their pain has nothing mysterious and brings no profit to the mortal race.

19. This expiation is indicated in the ancient Chinese religion (Goerres, I, 146), and in the Lamaic belief (ibid., I, 163–64), by the word "redemption." In their prayers, the Brahmins ask the sun for the sacrifice of Indra, descending from the rank of the creator to the rank of creature, dying and being reborn each day, to once again perform the atoning death.

20. It is by the blood, it is by the suffering of the Logos, say the Indianizing Christians of our day, that the world has to be reconciled with its author.

21. Pelloutier, VIII, 34; Ferrand, *Esprit de l'histoire*, I, 374. By a consequence of the same idea, Mr. de Maistre says that "the human race could not divine the blood of which it had need" (*Eclairciss. sur les sacrif.*, p. 455). We hope that no one will see in this refutation of ideas that seemed to us to be false or ill-considered, an attack directed against the belief for which we have often manifested our gratitude and respect. Brought back to its original simplicity, and combined with freedom of examination, Christianity has nothing to lose by disengaging itself from the vain, and sometimes harsh, subtleties with which the imagination of its commentators has surrounded it; and we think we serve this heavenly doctrine by delivering it from those auxiliaries who give it a deceptive likeness to the religions imposed on the peoples of antiquity by those ambitious bodies to which the Christian priesthood today would certainly be wroth to have itself compared.

CHAPTER 7

A Demonstration of the Previous Assertions, Drawn from the Composition of the Polytheism of Ancient Rome

The composition of the polytheism of ancient Rome presents the most complete demonstration of the assertions contained in the chapters one has just read. One sees among the Romans, during the three centuries during which their religious beliefs were gradually formed, the manifest struggle of the priestly spirit against the Greek spirit, that is, against the spirit free of priestly direction.

At the moment of the foundation of Rome, Etruria,[1] which held under its yoke several peoples of ancient Italy, and which exercised authority over several others, was governed neither by a single monarch, nor by an assembly of the people, nor by a senate. It obeyed an oppressive caste, like the priestly caste of Egypt;[2] and it

---

1. It would be wholly foreign to our subject to seek the origin of the different peoples of Italy. For readers interested in inquiring deeper into these difficult questions, we recommend the works of Plutarch, Varro's treatise on the Latin language, and, on the rural economy, the *Fastes* of Ovid, the commentators on Virgil, Servius, Probus, Festus, etc., the *Historia naturalis* of Pliny, the *Naturales quaestiones* of Seneca, the *Noctes atticae* of Aulus-Gellius; and finally, the fragments of Porcius Cato, Fabius Pictor, and Cincius Alimentus collected in several editions of Sallust; and for the moderns, the *Trésor des antiquités grecques* of Graevius, the *Etruria Regalis* of Dempster, the dissertations of Heyne in the *Commentaires* of Goettingue, the works of Winkelmann, the *Symbolique* of Creuzer, and, above all, the first volume of the *Histoire romaine* of Niebuhr. We would only add that in speaking of the worship of Etruria, we treat that of all of ancient Italy until the founding of Rome; for even though the cult of Latium was different in some details, its spirit was no less Etruscan. The Umbrians, Sabines, and Latins were for a very long time dependencies of Etruria and its federation, which was formed of twelve cities, each with its own head. The diet, or general assembly, of this federation met at Volsinium, in the temple of Vulcan (Dionys. of Hal., II, 15 & 61). The political heads were subject to a pontiff common to all the federated States, who governed the entire priestly order.

2. This caste had for a generic name Lucumon, which originally meant "possessed" or "inspired," and was said to be one of the ancestors of Tarquin the Elder. The enormous constructions of Etruria, those huge masses that seemed as though they could not have been raised by mortal arms, and which

was so similar to the latter that up to the time of Cicero the young nobles of Rome were sent to Etruria to be instructed in the sacred science of divination.[3]

We do not need to examine if this division into castes was indigenous to Etruria, a country whose climate favored priestly power,[4] or if it came from the South, perhaps from Egypt itself, with whom the maritime commerce of the Etruscans had early on entered into contact and communication. An incontestable fact is that the colleges of priests were spread throughout Italy,[5] and their power was unlimited. The study of astronomy[6] and medicine[7] was reserved for them. They were the sole historians of Etruria.[8] The education of the youth was confided exclusively to them.[9] The worship of stars and the elements constituted, we have already proven,

---

antiquity therefore called "cyclopean," then later, a less mythological term, "pelasgian" or "tyrrhenian," prove the tasks and labors with which this class, as in Egypt, oppressed the people (see above, bk. III, ch. 8). Thus, the Etruscan annals speak of frequent revolutions, one of which ended with the expulsion of the oppressors. The family of the Cilicians was violently expelled from Arrentium (Tit.-Liv., X, 3). The insurrection of the slaves of Volsinium is well known. This priestly tyranny contributed much to the success of Rome. Slaves do not always have the foolishness to fight for their masters. One can also detect in Etruscan history (as in Egyptian) some attempts on the part of the kings against the priests. (See what pertains to Mezentius in book IV, chapter 9.)

    3. Cic., *De legib.*, X, 3.

    4. See what we have said about the climate of Etruria in book IV, chapter 5.

    5. There was a corporation of priests in the city of Ardea, called the *saurani*, devoted to the worship of the mother of the gods (*Vulp. vet. Lat.*, v. 209; Serv., *ad Aen.*); and in several other Italian cities, corporations of the same sort presided over the rituals of other divinities.

    6. The priestly corporations of Etruria appear to have had rather extensive knowledge of astronomy. From time immemorial, this people had a regular calendar. Numa, who substituted the solar year for the ancient lunar year (Macrob., *Saturn.*, I, 13), used the help of Tuscan priests for this change, and Mr. Bailly has nicely proven (*Hist. de l'astron.*, VIII, 195) that they could not have had help from the Greeks, who were not very advanced in this science at the time.

    7. The Etruscan priests, like the Egyptian, alone practiced medicine. They had the same renown in the West in this regard as the Egyptians had in the East. If Egypt was nicknamed the country of salutary plants, Etruria was called the homeland of remedies (Mart. Capella, *De nupt. philos.*, cap. 6). Theophrastus (*Hist. plant.*, IX, 15) cites a verse of Aeschylus in honor of the Tuscans, masters of the art of healing.

    8. The *Annales des Etrusques* were a priestly history, like the Indian Purana (Niebuhr, I, 76). This history, redacted by Tuscan priests, like that of the Indians by the Brahmins, was placed in an astronomico-theological cycle. Events were adapted to the system, rather than the system to the events. They had to fit within the eight periods, or eight cosmic days, assigned to the human race. Each people had to last one of these days, which is to say: ten centuries or eleven hundred years (Varro, *ap.* Censorin., ch. 17). See below, the note relative to the ten ages of the Etruscans.

    9. Tit.-Liv., V, 27.

the ancient Latin or Etruscan religion.[10] The inhabitants of all of Italy offered sacrifices to rivers, to lakes, to fountains.[11] In this religion, as among all the priestly peoples, fetishism had been placed under astrolatry.[12]

All the teachings, all the rituals, all the usages characteristic of cults subject to priests were part of Italian worship. There one found gods with monstrous figures, the result of the priestly spirit, which is always immobile. Juno Lanuvina bears a goat-skin and horns;[13] Janus is famous for his double face;[14] Cherilus, son of Feronia, the Proserpina of the Sabines, and simultaneously the tutelary god and king of Preneste, owes to his triple body the honor of being sung by Virgil.[15] Tages, the author of the Acherontic books, is a dwarf god,[16] like the Vulcan of Memphis, whom Herodotus compares to the Cabiri.[17] The Penates of Lavinium are little caducei;[18] and these gods bring together in priestly forms the other qualities characteristic of the divinities that the priests reveal. Tages, born from the still-virgin earth, astonishes peoples with his wisdom, teaches man how to rise from the fall that degraded him, teaches him bloody sacrifices that connect him

10. On the ancient religion of Latium, see bk. VI, ch. 2.

11. Pitiscus, at the word "*Fontes*." The Roman religion had preserved remnants of this ancient cult in the festivals of the Tiber, in the months of June, August, and December (Ovid, *Fast.*, III and VI; Horat., III, 13). These practices survived the introduction of Christianity and were perpetuated until the time of Theodosius (Theod., *Cod. de pagan.*).

12. We have spoken (bk. VI, ch. 2) of animals, stones, trees (Jupiter Fagutal, Jupiter Hetre), spears, and the woodpecker giving oracles. Cybele was a stone (Ovid, *Sat.*, IV); Vesta, a globe (ibid., VI); the good goddess, a stone of mount Aventine. Pliny (*Hist. nat.*, II, 197) mentions a miraculous stone at Egnatia; Horace (*Sat.*, V, 1) had already mocked it. People claim, says Dionysius of Halicarnassus, that at Matiene, an ancient town of the Aborigines, also called Tiore or Matiere, that there was a very old oracle of Mars. It was much like that of Dodona, except that at Dodona a pigeon predicted the future from atop a sacred oak, whereas among the Aborigines, another bird sent by the gods prophesied from atop a column of wood (Tit.-Liv. I, 11). If our readers recall what we have said (bk. V, ch. 3) on the combination of fetishism and priestly authority at Dodona, they will see that our observations apply equally well to the Italian oracle, spoken of here by Dionysius of Halicarnassus.

13. Hirt., *Mythol. Bilderh.*, I, 22; Cic., *De nat. deor.*, I, 29; Creuzer, II, 385.

14. For this reason, Ovid makes him say that he is different from all the other Greek gods:
Quem tamen esse deum te dicam, Jane biformis?
Nam tibi par nullium Graecia numen habet.
(*Fast.*, I)

15. *Aen.*, VIII, 564; and Serv., *ad eund. loc.*

16. Serv. *ad Aen.*, I, 6; Amm. Marcell., XXI, I; XXVII, 10; Isidor., *Orig.*, VIII, 8.

17. Herod., III, 37.

18. *Timeaus*, ap. Den. of Hal., I, 15.

to the divine nature, as well as the progressive purifications that place him on the rank of heroes.[19]

The keys that Janus holds,[20] the vessel in which he stands, the doors of the night and the day that are confided to his care; Vesta, his spouse, who is sometimes the moon and sometimes fire; the privilege in virtue of which he (along with some other divinities of Etruria) enjoys the faculties of both sexes;[21] his incestuous hy-

---

19. Arnob., *Adv. gent.*, II, 62.

20. After what we have said about the multiple meanings of each priestly symbol, no one will be surprised by the host of attributes of Janus. First of all, he was an entirely astronomical god, worshipped at the beginning of the year and at the solstices, in a temple with four faces and twelve altars, invoked as the friend of Saturn—that is, time—and the spouse of the moon (Bailly, *Astron. anc.*, I, 99). He was sometimes taken for time itself (Fronticus, *ap.* Lyd., 57–58). Several of his attributes are common with the divinities of Persia and Egypt. He was represented holding a key in his left hand (*Clavemque sinistrâ*, Ovid, *Fast.*, I). Now, Mithra, or the sun, appears with two keys in Montfaucon's *Antiquité expliquée* (I, 2), and Spanheim observes that among almost all peoples, one or two keys characterize the astronomical divinities (*Observ. ad Callim.*, p. 591; Lyd., *De mens.*, p. 55). One sees Janus on several medals, with the *modius* of Serapis (Vaillant, *Familles romaines*, passim), because he led, as did Serapis, the souls of the dead to the netherworld (Lyd., ibid.). Ancient authors did not at all distinguish him from the Mercury of Egypt, and Justin claims that his cult had passed from the East into Etruria (*Hist.*, LXIII). On pieces of Roman coin, one sees his double head on one side, on the other, a bow:

Navalis in aere

Altera signata est, altera forma biceps.

(Ovid, *Fast.*, I)

Now, the Egyptians, says Porphyry (Euseb., *Praep. ev.*, III, 3), in their images of the sun placed him standing in a boat. Fabius Pictor gives Vesta, or fire, instead of the moon, to Janus as a wife. This was a combination of astrolatry and the worship of elements. Virgil, who wanted everything to relate to his hero, claims that the fire of Vesta had been lit by Aeneas in the foyer of the temple of Ilium, and was carefully preserved during the journey. He designates it "Trojan fire" (*Aen.*, II); but Virgil, writing at a time of religious unbelief, is far from being a faithful interpreter of the ancient beliefs, not even of those that survived. Janus is, moreover, the world (Serv. *ad Aen.*, VI, 610; Varro *ap.* Lyd., IV, 2), the seasons (Luctat. *ap.* Lyd., ibid.), the year, and then his two faces are explained by the rising and lowering of the sun (Serv., *ad Aen.*, VI, 607; August., *De civ. Dei*, VII; Heyne, *Excurs.*, V, *ad Aen.* VII; Cic., *De nat. deor.*, II, 27), the principle of all (Varro *ap.* Cic., *De nat. deor.*, II, 16), chaos, and it is when the elements have separated that he took on a form (Ovid, *Fast.*, Fest., v. *Chaos*). Finally, he is a historical personage, a king of ancient Latium (Arnob., *Adv. gent.*, III, 147), to whom almost all the Latin peoples attributed their origin (Plut., *Numa*, 19), who had taught men the ceremonies of religion (Lyd., *De mens.*, 57), and had two sons, one of whom was killed on the banks of the Tiber and gave his name to that river, a tradition that could have been carried into the legend of Romulus and Remus.

21. Janus in his quality as a hermaphrodite was simultaneously the sun and the moon (Macrob., *Saturn.*, I, 7). Etruscans had their masculine god Venus, and their Jupiter, mother of the gods (Creuzer, II, 430–31).

men,[22] his expiatory death,[23] form a mixture of science, astronomy, and mysticism typical of religions subject to priests.

The host of these diverse and enigmatic gods recognizes a head,[24] whose supremacy often is identified with destiny, and always ends in pantheism.[25] This host grows with demonology;[26] malevolent divinities enter in;[27] they deprive man of his innocence, they darken him with indelible stains, they plunge him into terrifying abysses from which his efforts—all in vain—cannot extricate him, and from which he can be delivered only thanks to the intervention of a mediating

22. See bk. VI, ch. 7.

23. Following a tradition, Janus was killed by peasants to whom he had taught the art of cultivating the vine, and who had become drunk (Plut., *Quaest. Rom.*). This tradition has some connections with a Greek fable we have mentioned earlier; but this fable in Greece produced only a fetishistic custom. In Etruria, the same narrative served to envelop a mysterious teaching found in all priestly religions, the doctrine of the redemption of man by the death of a god. See the preceding chapter.

24. The Etruscan Jupiter, named Tina by the priests, occupied a separate rank from all the other divinities (Creuzer, II, 440).

25. The metaphysical doctrine of Tages, like all priestly teachings, led to the combining of all the divinities, that is, all the forces of nature, into a single divinity or productive, preserving, and destructive power (Placid. Luctat., *ad Stat. Theb.*, IV, 516).

26. The demonology of the Etruscans was no less artfully constructed than that of the Egyptians, Indians, or Persians. Their Jupiter had a council of twelve *genii* (who were subject to birth and death) (Varro, *ap.* Arnob., *Adv. gent.*, III). Their Penates were divided into four classes: those of the last class, males and females, protected males on all occasions and women during their marriage, their pregnancy, and giving birth (Creuzer, II, 441, 449). The feminine *geniae* were first called Junos; but with the Greek mythology having given Juno as the wife of Jupiter, this name applied to secondary beings fell into disuse (Pliny, *Hist. nat.*, II, 7; Heyne, *De vestig. domest. relig. in art. etrusc. oper. novi comment.*, VI). The Etruscans, moreover, believed that each god was attached to a *genius* who was subordinated to it and rendered it domestic services, presiding at its morning toilette, refreshed it with a fan, etc. (Heyne, *Comment.*, II, 45).

27. The Pluto of ancient Italy, named Juvia or the destroyer, Jejovis or the young and wicked Jupiter (Creuzer, II, 485), the Mantus of the Sabines (Serv., *ad Aen.*, X, 198), the Etruscan Februs (Anys., *ap.* Lyd., p. 68), have several features similar to the Typhon of Egypt. In the priestly teaching, Mantus was a personification of death, hence sometimes in place of Janus he led the souls of earth to the netherworld, and from there to heaven. He then became a benevolent god. Divinities who are malevolent in the public religion frequently take on an allegorical meaning in the secret doctrine of the priests that modifies their character. Thus the god of destruction, wicked by nature in the popular opinion, is wicked only out of necessity in the cosmogonic system, and he often becomes a benevolent being, in the sense that he presides over rebirths. But the people do not concern themselves very much with these subtleties, and when priests speak to them of the Devil, they pay attention only to the obvious sense of their words.

god;[28] this god is at once triune and one, because the Etrurian priesthood also had its trinity.[29] These same unremitting powers threatened our globe, and Tuscan prophets constantly announce the destruction of the world.[30] Joined to these doctrines painted in funereal colors, the results of the refined calculations of the priesthood are the cruel or obscene rituals we have already encountered among all the peoples who suffer its yoke. Here the blood of men floods the altars;[31]

28. Janus is by turns the supreme god, replacing Tina, and a mediating god who brings the prayers of men to the superior divinities and brings back their favors.

29. See the verses of Martial already cited in book V, chapter 5, note 64.

30. The ten ages (γενη) of the Etruscans resembled the *yogas* of the Indians, even though they were shorter. The first eight comprised in their entirety only nine centuries. The end of each century was marked by prodigious signs (Varro, *ap.* Cens., *De die nat.*, 17; Plut., in *Sulla*; Creuzer, II, 436). This opinion was perpetuated at Rome, since Servius (*ad* Virg., *Ecl.*, IX, 47) reports a prediction of the soothsayer Volcatius, who in the midst of games celebrated by Caesar declared that the tenth age had just begun. The physical revolutions of Italy, e.g., the separation of Sicily from the continent (Justin, IV, 1), had furnished the priests of Etruria, like the Brahmins of Mahabalipura, the means of basing their lugubrious predictions on historical facts.

31. Before the arrival of Greek colonies, all of Italy offered human sacrifices. Lactantius recounts that Faunus sacrificed men to Saturn (*De fals. relig.*, I, 22), and Plutarch adds that all foreigners were sacrificed to him (*Parallelei*). One reads in Dionysius of Halicarnassus (I, 5) about the gods of the Pelasgians of Etruria, who demanded these victims (see also the scholiast of Pindar, *Pyth.*, II), and they obtained them. Not far from Rome in the forest of Aricia, the pontiff himself sometimes perished (Lucan., III, 86; VI, 74; Ovid, *Met.*, XI, 331; *Fast.*, III, 271–72; Serv., *ad Aen.*, II, 116). One sacrificed children before Larunda, the mother of the Lares (Macrob., *Saturn.*, I, 7). Men were burned in honor of Vulcan (Festus), one sacrificed girls to the Juno of Falerii (Creuzer, II, 471–72); three hundred Roman soldiers were immolated by the inhabitants of Tarquinia in the fourth century of Rome (Tit.-Liv., V, 15). The Etruscans washed the simulacrum of Jupiter Latialis in blood (Lactant., I, 21; Tertull., *Contr. gnostic.*, c. 7). Ennius attests to the practice in the following often-cited verses.

Ille sos (suos) deiveis mos sacrificare puellos.

When they found themselves in some danger, the Sabines devoted the produce of the entire year (*ver sacrum*) to Mars, including the boys and girls who were born (Den. of Hal., I, 16; Strabo, V). When human sacrifices declined, these people limited themselves to sending their children who were selected to colonies outside their country (Serv., *ad Aen.*). Virgins were sacrificed in the wood later consecrated to Anna Perenna.

Et quod virgineo cruore gaudet

Annae pomiferum nemus Perennae.

(Mart., IV, 64)

Dis was honored by the same rituals on Mount Soracte (Dionys. of Hal., I, 4). Also see the note of Servius on this verse of Virgil:

Summe deus, sancti custos Soractis Apollo.

further along, severe laws proscribe pleasure[32] while licentious rituals outrage shame,[33] and terrible torments cause nature to shudder.[34] Finally, divinations, this means of empire that is so carefully cultivated, so minutely developed by priests,[35] and always accompanied by a kind of jurisdiction it arrogates to itself over the

---

During the spring festivals, thirty sexagenarians were cast into the Tiber (Pelloutier, V, 139). The sacrifice of these thirty sexagenarians could very well have been a remnant of the custom of primitives to kill the aged who no longer had the strength to accompany them. Then it would be a striking example of the tendency of the priesthood to perpetuate barbarous practices in civilization (Fest., v. *Sexagen.*; Plut., *Quaest. Rom.*).

32. The institution of the vestal virgins was an Etruscan institution brought from the city of Alba to Rome. The torture of Rhea Silvia, mother of Romulus, whether legendary or not, is the memory of a priestly rigor that existed before Roman worship, but which unfortunately was introduced into it and was continued.

33. Creuzer, III, 337. The cult of the Phallus was established among the Etruscans, Sabines, Umbrians, and other peoples of ancient Latium. At Lavinia, during the festival of Bacchus that lasted a month, each day a fig priapus was promenaded in pomp (Fest., v. *Lucem facere*; Macrob., *Saturn.*, III, 6; Den. of Hal., I, 40). The most irreproachable matrons were chosen to crown it (August., *De civ. Dei*, VII, 21). The orgies of the cult had given Etruria a reputation for corruption that had become proverbial (Niebuhr, I, 96). The *complices* gods, the council of Jupiter (see above, note 26), had phallic forms. Several fables, half-Roman, half-Etruscan, were connected with this cult; among others, see the one that concerned the birth of Servius Tullius (Arnob., *Adv. gent.*; see Ovid, *Fast.*). At the festival of Anna Perenna, young women sang obscene songs. The gods who presided over the marriages of the ancient Latins possessed an indecency that combined the licentious worship of priestly nations and the allegorical spirit of the priesthood. From the goddess Virginesis, who undid the belt of the bride, the god Subigus, the goddess Pruna, the goddess Pertuna (August, *De civit. Dei*, VI, 9), the god Mutunus Tutunus (Tertull., *Ad nat.*, II, 11; Creuzer, II, 487–88), the gods or goddesses Anxia and Cincia (Arnob., *Adv. gent.*, III; Martian, Capella, II), the goddess Persica (Arnob., ibid., IV), until Liber and Libera (August., *De civit. Dei*, VI, 9), everything is described with the strangest and most revolting precision. The god Mutunus had a perfect likeness to the Lingam upon which in India one places young married men on horse. Brahmins and Etruscan priests were led by the same series of ideas to the same practices. These divinities of the ancient Italian cult disappeared at the time of the formation of polytheism at Rome, and only reappeared when priestly rituals flooded the empire.

34. Etruscan priests tore their arms, severely wounded different parts of their bodies, or walked on burning coals (Strabo, V); their dances, which were an integral part of these bloody rituals, resembled the frenetic contortions during which the Corybantes and the Curetes mutilated themselves (Spangenberg, *De veterib. lat. religionib.*, p. 48).

35. The Tuscan auguries had divided the heavens into eighteen parts in order to more exactly observe the course of the stars, the flight of birds, the direction of clouds, thunder's point of departure, and the color of lightning. These last phenomena occupied a large place in the Etruscan discipline. What lightning announced was more assured than what other paths predicted. When the entrails of

gods,[36] was brought into ancient Italy with the highest degree of solemnity and pomp. It was traced back to Picus, the first king of the Latiums.[37] All the elements are prophetic. The air reveals the future by the sound of thunder; the movement, color, and fantastic forms of clouds; birds who fly in all directions.[38] The sound of waves has a divinatory meaning, and prophets and gods emerge from the bottom of the liquid abyss. The bosom of the earth is no less fecund. From a furrow cut by a plow, Tages appears, all at once, to the people. In all directions caves allow supernatural inspirations to rise to man; finally, the fire that burns on the altar, the flames that consume the victim, express the mysteries of destiny by their waves and flickerings. The auguries and aruspices of Tuscany are famous in history. Di-

---

victims or the flight of birds presaged sinister events, a flash of lightning dissipated the fears: but no other sign could weaken the prophetic authority of lightning (Coecinna, *ap.* Senec., *Nat. Quaest.*, II, 34). Lightning was divided into several classes: *fulmina monitoria, pestifera, fallacia, deprecanea, peremptalia, attestata, atteranea, obruta, regalia, hospitalia, auxiliaria* (Senec., ibid., p. 49). Some of these epithets are self-explanatory. The Romans had doubts about the meaning of several others. They also distinguished lightning *in publica* (which related to the State) and *in privata* (which concerned individuals); the influence of *fulmina familiaria* was not limited to an event, but extended to all of life. Jupiter presided especially over lightning (Senec., *Nat. Quaest.*, II, cap. 45). He held three in his right hand (Fest., in v. *Manubia*); the first was destined only to warn men; the second, which Jupiter did not launch until after he consulted the twelve great gods, was already a beginning of punishment; the third was the completion of merited punishment. It struck men dead and overturned empires. The gods veiled themselves, hence the epithet *Dii involuti* (Senec., *Nat. Quaest.*, II, cap. 41). The Roman philosopher draws moral rules from this priestly tradition that he applies to earthly powers. The more absolute the authority, he says, the more it ought to be moderated; and the one who is invested with it ought not to employ severity, except after having surrounded himself with salutary counselors (ibid., cap. 41). Seneca was thinking more of Nero than of Jupiter. The principles of divination by the flight of birds or by augurs among the Etruscans had great similarities with those of the Persians. Their prophetic birds (*alites praepetes et oscines*) recall the four celestial birds named in the Zend books (Izeschné, I, Ha 64; II, 89). Pliny notes that there were figures of birds unknown in his time on Etruscan bas-reliefs, which leads us back to the fantastic birds of Persepolis and Ecbatana (Pliny, *Hist. nat.*, X, 15). All the other modes of divination were employed in Etruria, and pyromancy was practiced at Preneste, with pretty much the same rituals as in the East and among the Hebrews, even though it violated the prohibitions of the Mosaic law (Est., cap. III, 7; IX, 26, 28–29, 31–32).

36. Tuscan priests stripped Jupiter of his thunder, and had it come down from heaven at their will (Pliny, *Hist. nat.*, II, 53). The tradition relative to Tullus Hostilius obviously owes to this mysterious power for which the priests vaunted themselves (Tit. Liv., I, 31).

37. Strabo, VII; Plut., *Quaest. Rom.*; Den. of Hal., I, 11.

38. "*Et aves deus movit*" (Senec., *Quaest. nat.*, II, 32).

onysius of Halicarnassus and Diodorus praise their art;[39] and the superstitious Julian, even in the third century of our era, still consulted the aruspices that he had brought from Etruria.

Such was the religious state of Italy when the Greek colonies arrived. Here we will not enter into discussions concerning these colonies; all the historians recount in detail their arrival and establishment. We will simply observe that one must not reject these accounts with a too proud disdain. The author who has given himself most assiduously to understanding this subject, even though he himself is little favorable to the testimonies of a period when information was rare, the critical method and spirit imperfect, and minds were distorted by the claims of national vanity, nonetheless agrees that before the foundation of Rome there were wealthy and flourishing Greek colonies.[40] The first of these colonies apparently did not bring to the cities they constructed the religion of Greece, such as Homer made it known to us.[41] They had left their country before the revolution wrought in their polytheism by Egyptian or Phoenician

39. Dionys. of Hal., IX, 2. The inhabitants of Tuscany, says Diodorus (V, 27 and 40), applied themselves to the study of literature and philosophy, but they were particularly attached to the knowledge of signs. Tanaquil, wife of Tarquin the Elder, was praised by Titus-Livy for having been instructed according to the rules of the Tyrrhenian discipline. *"Perita, ut vulgo Etrusci, coelestium prodigiorum mulier."* We do not cite Tanaquil here as a historical personage; but particular facts, true or false, always prove received opinion, and the tradition composed of fables nonetheless has a fundamental truth that details invented after the fact cannot invalidate. The arrival of Aeneas and the Trojans to Latium, observes Mr. Niebuhr (*Hist. rom.*, I, 126), is surely a fiction; but it would be absurd to refuse any historical foundation to it. Certainly, the taking of Troy is a fable; however, there is a basis in historical fact.

40. Niebuhr (*Hist. rom.*) rejects the traditions relating to the Cenotrian and Peucetian colonies, but he does not deny that Greek colonies exercised the greatest influence on Etruria and Latium. He recognizes that established as republics, and destroyed around the year 400 of Rome, they had flourished for several centuries; hence, they existed before its founding (ibid., I, 105). As for Niebuhr's division between what is historical and what is legendary in Roman annals, even while we render justice to the seriousness of his research and the novelty of his views, we cannot prohibit ourselves from saying that there is a good deal of arbitrariness in this division. One never adequately distinguishes the motive of the author to grant certain facts the authority of "historical" and to refuse it to others of the same nature and almost of the same time. This is the hegemony of one's good pleasure transported into science.

41. The time of the arrival of the first of these colonies is fixed by ordinary chronology at the year 1719 B.C.

seafarers;[42] and their arrival in Italy had no other effect than to establish more frequent communications between this country and Pelasgian Greece.[43] But later, other Greek colonies having debarked on Latium, they began to reform the cruel rituals of the natives. They had left Greece after the formation of Greek polytheism;[44] they built several cities;[45] along with many other customs they brought all those that had to do with religion.[46] At Falerii, there was a temple of Juno[47] built on the model of that of Argos. There, one performed the same ceremonies for sacrifices. Priestesses officiated following Greek rites;[48] and young women called *canephora*, as in Greece, carried sacred baskets in the religious ceremonies.[49] These colonies preserved such close connections with their former country that every year they sent a tenth of their revenue to Delphi.[50] They inspired the natives with enough respect for the Greek gods that Arimnus, king of Etruria, believed he had to pay the homage of a golden throne to Jupiter Olympian.[51] Finally, they communicated to the Etruscans the knowledge and taste for

42. The arrival of these sailors followed the departure of the first Pelasgians for Italy by more than a century and a half.

43. It would even appear that far from destroying the priestly religion of Italy, these colonies enriched it with some equally priestly notions. For example, they brought the worship of the Cabiri, which we treated above. At least the names of the Cabiri were the same in Greece as in Italy: Θεοι μεγαλοι among the Greeks, and *Dii potes, potentes*, according to the explanation of Varro (*De ling. lat.*, IV, 10), among the Romans, the successors and imitators of the Etruscans. See also (bk. V, ch. 5, n. 64) the priestly Hermes brought into Etruria by the Pelasgians, represented by a column, combining with the god Terminus, then remaining the god Terminus alone, the Greek Mercury replacing Hermes. See, finally, bk. VII, ch. 5, the body, and n. 14.

44. A little less than thirteen hundred years before the Christian era.

45. Caere, Pisē, Saturnia, Alsion, Faleries, Fescennes, and Larissa in Campania, which was thus named after the capital of the Peloponnese (Dionys. of Hal., I, 3).

46. Ibid.

47. Another temple of Juno passed for having been constructed after the Trojan War at Lanuvium by the companions of Diomedes.

48. Cicero says that the worship of Ceres had been adopted from the first centuries of Rome, that it had been borrowed from the Greeks, and that priestesses were brought from Naples or Velia to celebrate it precisely (*Orat. pro Balbo*, no. 24, in *Verrem.*; Valer. Max., I, 1). Mr. de Sainte-Croix thinks that this cult of Ceres was brought from Greece by the Tarquins (*Les myst.*, p. 504).

49. Dionys. of Hal., I, 3.

50. Ibid.

51. Pausan., *Voy. en Elide*, ch. 12.

the arts.[52] Their leaders made incursions in different places that were more and less successful, and everywhere they entered successfully, they introduced some changes in the Italian worship.

It was only at Rome, however, that the influence of the Greek colonies worked a complete and decisive revolution. Until the foundation of this city, the two cults subsisted alongside one another. The reason was simple. The Etruscan priesthood opposed itself, as must always happen, to all innovation. The differences between the monuments of Etruria that have come down to us and the same works of art in Greece have often been noted. These differences perhaps owe to the fact that the Greek colonies had left their country before the arts there had arrived at their perfection; but the static, prohibiting priestly spirit was no doubt the greatest cause. In the towns they dominated, the theocratic corporations successfully battled the action of the Greek colonies. It was not the same in Rome. Its inhabitants brought together by chance, and fugitives from all countries, had no preexisting or established institutions, and the disdain of the opulent and peaceful cities that cast them from their midst in fact protected a collection of warrior brigands, preserving them from the ascendancy of the all-powerful corporations of priests found in the cities.

As a consequence, at the moment when their worship assumed a stable form, the Romans drew equally from the religions of ancient Italy and Greece. For a certain time, the two religions contested for the Roman people, which meant disputing for the empire of the world.

In order to describe this memorable struggle, we will cite facts to which, out of a desire to be brief, we will be forced to attach the names of individuals who perhaps never existed; but we will do so in order to designate periods or epochs, and even if the individuals are legendary beings or generic names,[53] our assertions will not be thereby undermined. That Romulus, Numa, Tatius, even Tullus Hostilius (al-

52. Heyne, *De Etrusc. Com. Soc. Goett.*; and Dempster, *Etruria Regalis*, above all on Bacchus and Hercules. It would be absurd to deny, says Niebuhr (I, 87), that the improvements in Etruscan arts were not due to the Greeks, even though their architecture was proper to them. He adds that Etruscan literature was never improved by Greek literature (ibid., 88), which is an effect and proof of the struggle we are going to talk about.

53. Niebuhr regards Romulus as the generic name of the Roman people, and Latinus, father of Romulus, as the generic name of the people of Latium (*Hist. rom.*, I, 148).

though there is a bit more history in his regard)[54] did not exist; that the colonies called Herculean did not land in Italy in the year or the manner indicated by writers, some who were credulous like Titus-Livy, others, compilers like Dionysius of Halicarnassus; that Tarquin the Elder was neither the grandson of a fugitive from Corinth nor from the family of the Bacchiads, all that matters little to us. We still see that all that is priestly comes from Etruria and everything that belongs to independent polytheism arrives from Greece. We grant as fictional everything that the new critics claim; but this concession does not in any respect weaken truths that cannot be contested. We will begin, therefore, with Romulus, or the moment his name designates.

Already the inclination for the Greek cult manifests itself. Ceremonies in honor of Jupiter are substituted for the worship of the sacred oak.[55] But Tatius, king of the Sabines, associated with empire after the combining of the two peoples, has temples built to the sun, moon, fire, and earth.[56] Numa, Sabine like Tatius, transports his paternal gods to Rome. He places a lance in his palace, an ancient simulacrum of the god of war.[57] He forbids his subjects to attribute human form to the immortals.[58] This is a priestly interdiction. When philosophy came to the Romans, they gave the honor of this prohibition of Numa's to philosophical ideas.

It was perhaps because of the favor this prince gave to the ancient religion of Italy that when the books attributed to him were unearthed by a flood, four hundred years after his death, the Senate wanted them to be cast into the flames. The

54. See Niebuhr on Tullus Hostilius. It is not that there are not many fabular aspects in what concerns this third king of Rome; the historians, for example, Dionysius of Halicarnassus (III, 1), call him the son of Hostus Hostilius, a general killed in the Sabine War; that is, he would be eighty years old at his ascension to the throne, yet martial tendencies and bellicose inclinations are attributed to him.

55. See the place where Titus-Livy recounts that Romulus, having stripped an enemy general of his arms, placed this trophy at the foot of an old oak worshipped by shepherds and consecrated this place to a divinity that he called Jupiter Feretrius.

56. Varro, IV; Dionys. of Hal., I, 32, and II, 12; Ovid (*Fast.*, VI) and Plutarch (*Vie de Numa*) attribute the introduction of the worship of fire to Rome to this prince, under the name Vesta; but Numa being Sabine the same as Tatius, for what concerns us here, the result would be the same. Tatius also introduced a martial god in the form of a spear. Tertullian (*Apologet.*, 24) says that it was a god of the Phalisques.

57. Plut., in *Numa*.

58. Ovid, *Fast.*, VI, 295; Plut., in *Rom.*; Varro, *ap.* August., *De civ. Dei*, IV, 31–36. This interdiction was respected for a long time. In the history of the first two kings, Titus-Livy speaks of no image or statue of gods.

care taken in burning them upon a pyre lit by the very officers who served in the sacrifices proves that the books continued to be respected even as they were destroyed.[59] Whatever may be true of this particular fact, the worship reestablished at Rome after Romulus by Tatius or Numa was manifestly one that was professed by all nations subject to priests.[60]

In the history of Tullus Hostius, the rivalry between the monarchy and the priesthood stands out in unmistakable features. But this was not by favoring the Greek religion at the expense of the Etrurian religion; it was by seeking to take over the mysterious forces of the latter that the third king of Rome appears to have wanted to resist the spiritual power. He declared himself the imitator of the Tuscan priests; he claimed to have penetrated the secrets of their magic; he stole their formulas[61] in order to be able to evoke thunder as they did; and they punished him by attributing his death to a sacrilegious omission during the ceremonies he had presided over with a profane hand.[62] Tarquin the Elder[63] rejected even more

59. Tit.-Liv., XL, 29. It is expressly said that the praetor who, in affirming by oath that these books were dangerous for religion, convinced the Senate to have them burned, did not find them so, except because they were contrary to the established worship. Now, it was only as containing unbelief that they would be contrary to this worship; i.e., by containing priestly teachings or formulas. "Orpheus," says Clavier (I, 85), "following the example of his masters, the Egyptian priests, had a secret doctrine that he shared with his chosen disciples only after long trials. It doubtless was this doctrine, contained in the writings that one found in Numa's tomb, that so scandalized the Roman pontiffs that they ordered them to be burned. It is very probable, in fact, that Numa knew this secret doctrine of Orpheus, etc." The entirety of the hypothesis is quite fanciful; but it has this point that is plausible, that in suppressing the legendary name of Orpheus in order to replace it with that of Orphic doctrine, it implies that Numa's doctrine was a doctrine of priests.

60. Dionysius of Halicarnassus adds that Tatius honored gods whose names were difficult to express in Greek. This observation proves the difference in the two species of divinities.

61. These spells had been revealed to Numa by Picus and Fauna after Egeria had warned him to muzzle them. They possessed the art of forcing the gods to make known their will by lightning and the flight of birds, signs that the vulgar only obtained by a favor that the gods could refuse to bestow (Niebuhr, I, 167).

62. "*Tradunt volventem commentarios Numae, quum ibi quaedam occulta sollemnia sacrificia Jovi Elicio facta invenisset, operatum his sacris se abdidisse: sed non rite initum aut curatum id sacrum esse: nec solum nullam ei oblatam coelestium speciem, sed ira Jovis solicitati prava religione fulmine ictum cum domo conflagrasse*" (Tit. Liv., I, 31).

63. Tradition made Tarquin the Elder the grandson of a fugitive from Corinth. It recounts that his ancestor Demaratus, of the race of the Bacchiades, seeing his family oppressed by the tyranny of the Cypelides, had sought asylum in Etruria at the time of the 30th Olympiad, and had brought with him several Greek artists (Pliny, *Hist. nat.*, XXXV, 3–5; Strabo, V). In fact, some years after the expulsion

directly the Etruscan religion in order to introduce the spirit of the Greek religion. He called to Rome Greek families from all parts of Italy where they had sought asylum.[64] He ordered the construction of a temple of Jupiter on Mount Tarpeian; his son completed it, and as there were several altars devoted to Italian divinities on this hill, they were solemnly expelled.[65] Thus, as we said at the beginning of this chapter, emerging Rome saw the two species of polytheism do battle within its walls. The entirety of the struggle escapes us, but undeniable details reveal it.

This struggle had to have its vicissitudes and its phases. The rivalry of the kings and priests probably more engaged the former, whether because they sought support against the latter in the foreigners they welcomed, especially because they brought the antipriestly spirit of Greece, or simply to negotiate with rivals they always had to fear. Romulus had had pontiffs from Etruria come to Rome in order to learn from them the rituals necessary to gain the gods' protection for the newly founded towns.[66] Despite his anathema against the gods of Italy, Tarquin the Elder borrowed from the Tuscans the sacred games, and some religious ceremonies;[67] and his son, initially disdainful of the Sibylline books, then rendered solemn, if barbarous, homage[68] to these pages gathered by Etruscan soothsayers, repositories of Rome's destinies.[69]

---

of the kings, Greek artists had been established at Rome, and two among them, Damophilus and Gorgasus, worked on the decoration of a temple of Ceres (Pliny, ibid., 12; Dionys. of Hal., VII, 17; Tacit., *Annal.*, II, 9). The 170 years during which the Romans, according to Varro, did not have any idols ends exactly under the reign of Tarquin the Elder; this prince, according to the Varronic chronology, died in the year 175 of Rome; and we learn from Pliny (*Hist. nat.*, XXV, 12 & 45) that he had had a statue of Jupiter placed on the Capitol, and in another temple a statue of Hercules. In Tertullian there is a passage that indicates that the Romans had preserved the memory of this revolution: "*Etsi a Numa concepta est curiositas superstitiosa, nondum tamen aut simulacris aut templis res divina apud Romanos constabat, frugi religio et pauperes ritus, ac nulla Capitolia certantia coelo, sed temeraria de coespite altaria, et vasa adhuc Samia et nidor ex illis, et Deus ipse nusquam. Nondum enim tunc ingenia Graecorum atque Tuscorum fingendis simulacris urbem inundaverunt*" (*Apolog.*, cap. 25).

64. Notably Velitrae, a Greek colony (Suet., in *Augusto*).

65. The passage of Titus-Livy (I, 55) clearly proves the revolution effected in the religion by the Tarquins: "*Tarquinius (superbus) Jovis templum in monte Tarpeio reliquit. Tarquinios ambos, patrem vovisse, filium perfecisse. Et ut libera a caeteris religionibus area esset, et tota Jovis templique ejus ... exaugurare fana sacellaque statuit, quae aliquot ibi a Tatio rege consecrata inaugurataque fuerant.*"

66. Plut., in *Romulo*.

67. Tit.-Liv., I, 35–38.

68. He had a Roman who had given these books to be copied put in a sack and thrown into the sea (Den. of Hal., IV).

69. Dionys. of Hal., IV, 14.

What appears to have put an end to this oscillation between the two cults, and determined the victory in favor of Greek polytheism, was the expulsion of the kings and the establishment of the republic. Quite remarkably, this revolution was probably the work of priests! It turned against them. Without it, the pontiffs would probably have allied with the monarchs. The priests would have made the monarchs receive their teachings and their rituals, while lending a sacred sanction to their temporal power; but political liberty, no matter how different what we call liberty in modern times is from what it was among the ancients, political liberty, I was saying, opposed a powerful barrier to the encroachments of priestly power. Popular governments, or even aristocracies that call many individuals to participate in public affairs, balance spiritual authority by means of the interests of this world. Despotism, though, lavishly pouring all sorts of misfortunes and opprobrium upon its slaves, puts them at the mercy of whoever promises them an asylum elsewhere; unless, being able to degrade everything, it also degrades religion; but this only happens in very corrupt nations, by a combination of circumstances that happily is rather rare.[70]

To be sure, the military expeditions of the Romans also contributed to the diminishment of the authority of priests. A French author rightly notes that if the martial reign of Tullus Hostilius had not immediately followed the peaceful reign of Numa, the crudest superstition would have weighed on fledgling Rome. However, the warrior spirit would not alone have saved Rome. More bellicose than the Romans, the Scandinavians suffered the yoke of priests at a late period. Without liberty, peaceful Rome would have experienced the same destiny as the Egyptians; martial Rome, with the differences that climate introduces, would have had the same destiny as Scandinavia. What proves this is that all the reforms that decided the character and tendency of the Roman religion took place in the century that followed the abolition of the monarchy.

The gods then took on more elegant forms. In adopting the human figure, they did away with the monstrosities with which the symbolic spirit, grafted onto fetishism, had overloaded it.[71] The Penates, for example, instead of being rather shapeless vases surrounded by serpents, were adolescents armed with spears.[72] Human sacrifices were also suppressed.[73] Junius Brutus replaced the children sacri-

---

70. See bk. I, ch. 4.

71. Creuzer, II, 315.

72. Ibid.

73. In all the Italian traditions, the suppression of human sacrifices is attributed to Hercules. He killed Faunus, who sacrificed men (Plut., *Para. Min.*, n. 35). He explained the meaning of an oracle

ficed to Larunda with the heads of poppies, and the thirty sexagenarians who were thrown into the Tiber, with thirty idols made of straw.[74] Solemn games were established in memory of this triumph of humanity.[75] Henceforth, these ceremonies only recurred as sad exceptions in extraordinary circumstances;[76] and even when such circumstances brought back this deplorable superstition, the Romans always turned their gaze away in horror. The death of a man, even though ordered by the gods, did not appear to them, as to other peoples, to be an occasion for feasting, but of lamentation, mourning, and regret.

---

to the Sabines who had offered human victims to gods on the basis of another interpretation of it (Dionys. of Hal., I, 14; Steph. Byz., in Άζοριγ). It is evident that the name Hercules is here a generic name; this hero constantly occupies first place in all the Latin legends. He intervenes in events or fables that are told in Greece without ever mentioning him; his memory mixes with many rituals and institutions of the Roman religion. A sacrifice with purely Greek ceremonies was annually offered at Rome in memory of a tradition relating to Hercules (Dionys. of Hal., I, 9; and VI, 1), and the only priestly families that existed in this city were consecrated to him (Den. of Hal., VIII). Dionysius of Halicarnassus speaks of the traces of temples and altars in his honor that were prior to Rome's founding, even on the spot where it was built (ibid.). We therefore think that the name Hercules was the collective designation of several Greek colonies. This conjecture comports well with the influence of these colonies, and when Dionysius of Halicarnassus (ibid.) tells us that one could hardly find a single place in Italy where Hercules was not given divine honors, it seems to us that he clearly demonstrates the universality of this influence. But at the same time, the abolition of human sacrifices by the Greek colonies proves that these sacrifices owed at least their continuation to the priestly spirit. The Greek colonies were not subject to the priestly power; they weakened or destroyed this power everywhere they went, and human sacrifices disappeared with it. A particular tradition, however, attributes this abolition not to Hercules but to a victor at the Olympic games. One of Ulysses's companions cast up on the coasts of Italy had violated a young woman of Tecmessa; the inhabitants stoned him. He became an evil *genius* who put to death all those he encountered. Having consulted the oracle at Delphi, the inhabitants were commanded to honor the memory of the one they had killed by consecrating a forest to him, building him a temple, and each year sacrificing a virgin. They did so until the time when a Lacedaemonian, Euthymus, who had merited a statue by his victories at the Olympic games, moved by pity and love for the victim, offered to fight the evil *genius* and defeated him. Then the sacrifice was abolished (Ael., *Var. Hist.*, VIII, 18; Pausan., VI, 6). One sees that it is always to a Greek that this abolition is attributed. Saturn and Ops, says another legend, had eaten human flesh; Jupiter had rejected this detestable custom (Macrob., *Saturn.*, I, 7; Arnob., *Adv. gent.*, II; Lactant., I, 20). Ops and Saturn are Italian deities; Jupiter is a Greek god (see bk. I, ch. 9).

74. Ovid, *Fast.*, V; Serv., *ad Georg.*, I, 43; Pomp. Fest; Varro, *De ling. lat.*, VI; Den. of Hal., I.

75. *Ludi compitalitii*; Pitisc.

76. The conspirers who wanted to bring the Tarquins back to Rome had obliged themselves by the sacrifice of a human victim (Plut., in *Vita public.*).

Plutarch, while recounting that in the hope of deflecting the calamities that the incontinence of the vestal virgins, as well as the Sibylline books, made them fear, the Romans buried alive a male and a female Greek and a male and a female Gaul, adds that an expiatory sacrifice was offered annually to the manes of these victims.[77] Ovid denies that such rituals ever existed in Rome. It is natural that a poet writing at the time of Augustus did not want to believe in the barbarous practices of his ancestors. But in the same poet there is a dialogue between Jupiter and Numa[78] that is quite remarkable in this regard; and this dialogue, which under the appearance of a witticism contains an exact history of this revolution in the worship, proves that Ovid's denial was not correct.

From the time of its liberty, Rome's power was always employed to forbid human sacrifices among its allies or conquered peoples. She first of all purified Italy, and then worked to deliver Spain and the Gauls from them.[79] Caesar, praetor in Iberia, abolished this custom, which the Phoenicians had brought to Cadiz.[80]

---

77. Plut., *Quaest. rom.*, n. 83. The same thing took place at the time of Caesar (Pliny, XXVIII, 2); but it is no less true that these rituals had been prohibited at Rome by a formal law in the 655th year of this city.

78. *Caede caput, dixit (Jupiter). Cui rex, parebimus, inquit.*
Caedenda est hortis erecta caepa meis.
Addidit hic, hominis: summos, ait ille, capillos.
Postulat hic animan, cui Numa, piscis, ait.
Risit.
(*Fast.*, III)

"I want a head," says Jupiter.
"You will be obeyed," answers the king. "I will cut the head of an onion that I am growing in my garden."
"I want the head of a man," replies the first.
"I will offer you," says the second, "the tips of his hair."
"I ask for a soul," exclaimed the impatient god.
"You will have the soul of a fish," replies Numa.
The god began to laugh.
Notice that in this dialogue Jupiter seems to be evoked by Fauna and Picus, two divinities of ancient Latium. It is useless to have our readers observe that Ovid wrongly attributes to Numa a reform that will not be complete until more than a century after him. Plutarch (*Vit. Numae*) also makes this error.

79. See in Pliny (XXX, I) the *senatus consultum* promulgated in the year 657 of Rome, which principally regarded the Gauls.

80. Cic., *Pro Balbo*, 43.

And, finally, seeing the obstinate perseverance of the Druids, Tiberius and Claudius pursued and destroyed them.[81]

Some writers have considered the gladiator fights of Rome as a form of human sacrifice; especially in the latter centuries of Rome they had become an essential part of the games and pleasures that were lavished upon a restless, corrupt, and redoubtable people. But these combats were barbarous entertainments, not religious ceremonies. The spirit of conquest, always arrogant and always fierce, in the eyes of the victors stripped the unfortunate victims who had fallen into captivity of all the rights of the human condition. Disdaining their own blood on the field of battle, the Romans were pleased to see the blood of their enemies flow in the amphitheater. It is not their religion, however, but their martial habits that one should accuse. The proof of this is the privilege that the spectators had reserved for themselves to pardon the fighter who distinguished himself by his courage. They would not have deprived the gods of a victim their piety had offered. Finally, it was prisoners that the Romans forced to fight, and Rome would have risen up against the insolent pontiff who attempted to compel a citizen to fight.

Licentious rituals were similarly kept away from the polytheism of Rome. History transmits an attempt by the Tuscan priesthood to introduce some indecent practices into the religion. The Sabine women who had been taken had remained sterile. Their anxious spouses consulted Juno in the sacred forest of Mount Esquiline. The tops of ancient trees suddenly shook, a disturbing oracle made itself heard.[82] Happily, superstition could not defeat the national horror. A soothsayer, the interpreter of the oracle, proposed avoiding the order of the gods by a less ghastly ceremony, which became part of the Lupercalia, in which nude, or almost nude, young men armed with a whip that was made of goat hair struck the women who presented themselves before them. It is impossible not to see in this account the priestly tendency that had dominated Italy until the arrival of the Greek colonies, a tendency that was overcome by the good sense of these colonies. The ordinances that prohibited obscene rituals all came from the Senate after the firm

---

81. Pliny (VIII, 2) makes the abolition of this practice a great subject of praise of his compatriots: "*Non satis aestimari potest quantum Romanis debeatur, qui sustulere monstra in quibus hominem occidere religiosissimum erat, mandi vero etiam saluberrimum.*"

82. "*Italidas matres, inquit, caper hirtus inito*" (*Fast.*, III).

establishment of the republic.[83] We will see them fall into disuse, and licentious practices reappear, with the approach of the empire.[84]

At the same time that the Romans rejected obscene rites, they mitigated, albeit slightly, the privations against nature. At Alba, the vestals were constrained to a perpetual continence; at Rome, they could be freed after thirty years.[85]

Voluntary tortures were introduced quite late into the polytheism of Rome, either as a foreign custom or as a souvenir of ancient practices, a type of souvenir that was easily recalled in calamities and times of danger.[86]

As a result, we see in Rome, in a way more evident than anywhere else, the fundamental opposition between priestly polytheism and independent polytheism. If the inhabitants of nascent Rome were inclined by some earlier habits and traditional memories toward the religion of Italy, which was the cult of their ancestors, and toward the history of Italy, which was their history, the respect that the de-

83. The Senate's decree against the bacchanalia and orgies in which the Phallus was carried dates from the 568th year of Rome, eighty-six years before Christ, one hundred years after the subjection of Etruria by Rome (see Heyne, *Momum. Etrusc. art. nov. Com. Soc. Goett.*, V, p. 49). The Floralia, or Floral Games, famous for their obscenities, from which Cato was obliged to withdraw, date from the Etruscan religion. Varro (*De ling. lat.*, IV) and Dionysius of Halicarnassus (I, 32) make the institution of these games go back to Tatius, king of the Sabines. The tradition that attributes it to a courtesan named Flora is based on the resemblance of the name, but otherwise is highly implausible. The Senate, which could have closed its eyes to an ancient and established custom, would not have permitted a scandalous innovation.

84. The god Mutunus Tutunus, about whom we spoke earlier, and who had been banished from Rome in the times of aristocratic rigor and popular turbulence, which on this one point of religion were in agreement, reappeared in the midst of the madness of tyrants and the abjection of slaves.

85. It was Numa who had the institution of vestal virgins brought to Rome from Alba, and he himself chose the first four (Tit.-Liv., I, 20). In the city of Alba guilty vestals were beaten to death with rods. Numa condemned them to be stoned. Tarquin the Elder ordered that they be buried alive (Dionys. of Hal., VIII, 14; IX, 10). Here one recognizes a concession of this prince to priests. We have spoken of this above.

86. The laws of the Twelve Tablets explicitly forbade women from tearing their cheeks. *Mulieres genas ne radunto.* It was an Etruscan custom borrowed from funeral sacrifices, *ut sanguine ostenso inferis satisfiat* (Varro, *ap.* Rosin; *Antiq. rom.*, ed. Dempster, p. 442). When, toward the end of the fifth century and above all in the sixth century of Rome, the cult of Cybele arrived from priestly countries, the Romans prohibited the frenetic dances of the Corybantes who mutilated themselves (Lactant., *De fals. rel.*, I, 21; Juv., *Sat.*, IV; Propert. Plut., in *Pyrrh.*; Tit.-Liv., XXIX, 10, 11, 14; Appian, *De bello Annibal.*, XLV).

scendants of the colonies had preserved for their original homeland hovered, as it were, over these memories and habits. The Italian religion furnished the Romans with an infinite number of divinities,[87] many legends, usages, and rituals.[88] But the *genius* of the Greek religion took control of these things and modified them,[89] and as the Athenians had nationalized Minerva,[90] the Romans identified Jupiter Stator with their history: a scientific symbol became a protective god of the city. The sun that halted rallied the fleeing legions. The sun that was reborn was Veturia.[91] The Romans retained from the first of these polytheisms everything they could preserve; their policy filled the colleges of pontiffs with the most eminent citizens in the State and army, thus stripping these colleges of the theocratic spirit.[92] The same policy made divination an instrument (which sometimes could run counter to it).[93] It borrowed from the Etruscans something of the division into castes, in order to add a religious sanction to the relation between patrons and clients.[94] As long as Rome was a monarchy, its kings on their elevation to the throne were clothed in Etruscan forms, the signs of their dignity.[95] But the spirit of the priesthood, the teachings that belonged to it apart from the people, human vic-

87. Etruscan names were applied to Greek divinities. Pallas Athena, whom the Etruscans named Menerva or Minerva, preserved this appellation (Micali, II, pp. 48ff.).

88. The music that the Romans used in their religious ceremonies was ancient Etruscan music (Strabo, V; Pliny, *Hist. nat.*, XV, 26; Virgil, *Georg.*, II, 193, *ibiq. interpretes*).

89. Romulus, that is, the personified Roman people (see above), Romulus, says Dionysius of Halicarnassus (II, 7), took what was best from the Greek institutions.

90. See bk. V, ch. 5.

91. See bk. I, ch. 9.

92. The personnel of the pontiffs were changed; the forms of pontifical legislation remained the same (Niebuhr, I, 96).

93. The Senate sent six sons of the most illustrious families to six different peoples of Etruria to learn divination. Labeo translated into Latin the six books of Tages on this science (Tit.-Liv., IX, 36). Roman policy easily attached divination to the most ancient national tradition. Romulus and Remus, it was said, disputing for rule, agreed to leave the decision to the auguries. The one who first perceived favorable ones before his rival would mount the throne. Remus saw six vultures that flew from the north to the south; but at sunrise Romulus saw twelve (Varro, I, 28, *ap.* Censorin., 17; Niebuhr, I, 156). We learn from Cicero that Roman divination was divided into two large branches, each subdivided into several others. The first branch contained what men could regard as direct manifestations of divinity: presentiments, dreams, transports. The second consisted in signs to which one had attached arbitrary meaning. Therefore the first were called natural, the second, artificial (Cic., *De div.*, I, 6).

94. Niebuhr, I, 80.

95. Ibid., p. 96.

tims, licentious rites—all these things were banished from the worship, and only reentered accidentally when terror took hold of souls,[96] or later, when corruption had degraded them.

We will stop here. The truth that we promised to prove seems to us to be beyond doubt; we will not have to return to Roman religion until we treat the later modifications of polytheism.

96. The Etruscan or priestly traditions and teachings left isolated, but still striking, traces in even learned Romans. Cicero, the student, admirer, critic, and judge of the different Greek philosophies, was tempted, in order to revenge himself on the ungrateful and ruthless Octavius, to commit suicide on the altar of an evil *genius*, Alestor or Alastor, who gathered the curses from the mouth of the dying and went to battle armed with these solemn curses against those who had abused their power (see Plut., *Vit. Cicer.*, 34, and *De la décadence des oracles*). This is an idea that is entirely similar to the Indian teaching on the power of curses.

BOOK XII

ON THE DEVELOPMENT OF
INDEPENDENT POLYTHEISM
TO ITS HIGHEST POINT
OF PERFECTION[1]

1. We have tried to move rapidly in this book. With Greece being better known than India, and less enigmatic than Egypt, we believed we could trust in the learning and sagacity of the reader.

CHAPTER I

How the Progress of the Social State
Introduces Morality into Religion

We have established, as the principal truth to demonstrate in our work, that each revolution that takes place in the situation of the human race produces one in religious ideas, and we have already seen polytheism substitute for fetishism by the passage from the primitive to the barbarous state. Polytheism suffers other important changes in the passage from the barbarous state to one that is more civilized; and the notions of a distributive justice, of an equitable and infallible recompense, become fixed and affirmative doctrines instead of being the expression of impotent wishes and confused hopes.

This revolution takes place in a very obvious way among the peoples who are not slowed or shackled by any accidental circumstance, any natural calamity, any religious or political tyranny.

Vigorous with the youthful liveliness of all their impressions, excited by the novelty of what they experience, men do not yet have to defend themselves from inner fatigue or external routine, the sad and inevitable results of lengthy civilization. No second thought weakens them, no skepticism troubles them; they are exposed to many evils, but experience is not there to warn them that there are evils without remedy. They see only obstacles to overcome in what appears to us a necessity to suffer. Where we resign ourselves, they fight; and their activity grows from the difficulties that discourage ours.

In the passage from purely bellicose life to civil life, from a state that is solely martial to the agricultural state, peoples experience needs of a wholly new sort: that of work,[2] which has replaced the use of force by substituting exchange for

---

2. See the passage on Hesiod in book VIII, chapter 3.

conquest; that of property, without which work would be nothing but a series of vain efforts; that of security, without which property would be insecure.

In order to satisfy these until now unknown needs, fixed institutions are indispensable. Soon, they assume the place that necessity assigns to them; a public force is formed that tends to preserve the association from the violence of its members, and its members from their reciprocal attacks. The irregular force of individuals retains for a while its dreadful privileges, but they are increasingly contested. Injustice, which previously encountered obstacles only in those it harmed in an immediate way, now encounters them in the coalition of all those who do not profit from its success. Earlier, there were only offenses that cried out; now, all those who are impartial cry out. The majority bases its calculations on the observation of the laws, that is, on justice and morality. Morality and justice become the center of the majority of interests, the point around which the majority of forces unite.

This revolution in ideas and institutions produces one in religious notions, even when it is only interest that changes them. Interest always wants to employ the authority of the gods for its own purposes. As long as the social state, barely established, influences individuals only in a partial and episodic way, interest principally occupies its gods with the protection of individuals. Now, however, it is a matter of a more general protection; the authority of the gods is devoted to it.

These invisible powers, as we have observed previously, modeling themselves on human beings, and once-isolated fetishes now composing a celestial people, once again follow the example of men. When the latter only occupy themselves with constant war, and their amusements are crude pleasures, with only their vigor or their cunning for means of safety or success and the boldest and most violent men as leaders, the objects of their worship lead an entirely similar way of life atop the heavens. Without distinction, they protect innocent endeavors and culpable designs, unbridled desires and legitimate endeavors. Sacrifices and gifts interest them in any and all causes, and virtue as well as crime are obliged to buy them off. But as soon as men have laws, judges, tribunals, and public morality, then the gods preside over the execution of these laws, monitor the conduct of the judges, themselves compose a supreme tribunal, and give supernatural assistance to morality. All their relations with men are changed in keeping with this tendency. The means of gaining their benevolence are no longer what they were before;[3] homages, vows, and

3. The gods, says Zaleucus in his preamble (see Heyne, *Legum Locris a Zaleuco scriptarum fragmenta*, Opuscul. II, 72ff.), are not pleased with the gifts of wicked men, understood as repulsive human beings, but they want to be honored by generous sentiments and virtuous actions.

offerings lose their effectiveness. While still necessary so that the gods do not become angry at the negligence of mortals, they no longer suffice to assure injustice the assistance of heaven. Faithful to the customs of the first period of polytheism, the people who enter the territory of their enemy seek to gain the favor of the tutelary divinities of this territory, but they believe they cannot better succeed than by making these divinities witnesses of the justice of their cause. Man no longer dares to ask the assistance of the gods for the crimes he wishes to commit; he at most tries to obtain from them forgiveness for the crimes he committed. They no longer are basely envious of all human prosperity, but they are strict enemies of the prosperity of the wicked. Their lightning bolts are no longer directed against the happy, but against the guilty; they no longer persecute, they punish. When some great calamity happens to the powerful of the earth, it is no longer attributed to the jealousy of the gods but to their justice.

The religious sentiment associates itself enthusiastically with this change in religious ideas. These new notions respond to all its desires; they permit it to esteem what it worships; they give a more elevated, nobler character to the gods; they render them more worthy of being honored. Confidence succeeds to fear. Even at the sight of triumphant crime, mortals expect to soon see misfortune fall upon its head. If sometimes an undeniable evidence forces man to recognize that despite the providence of the gods virtue can suffer and iniquity reign, he persuades himself that sooner or later the days of reparation and revenge will come.[4] Thus the idea enters into his heart of an appeal of the present to the future, of earth to heaven, the solemn recourse of the oppressed in all situations, the last hope of the weak who are trampled underfoot, of virtue that is sacrificed; this is a consoling and proud thought that philosophy has never tried to renounce without being immediately punished by its own debasement.

This is therefore the period of the formal introduction of morality into religion. We have proven that even before this, religion favored morality. As a general proposition, the gods must always prefer good to evil, virtue to crime. The love of order is inherent in man as long as he reasons abstractly. The same tendency is therefore inherent in the gods, as soon as instead of being paid individually (if we

4. What deceives mortals, says Theognis (Theog., v. 199ff.), is that the gods do not punish them at the moment they commit a crime. The perjurer cannot hide from the gods, says the orator Lycurgus against Leocrates (see Archer, *Note sur Hérod.*, VI, 119), nor can he escape their vengeance. If he himself is not targeted, at least his children and his entire posterity will experience the greatest misfortunes.

can put it this way), the fetishes are recompensed collectively by society as a whole. The interest of every community is found in morality. Gods who protect the community cannot fulfill their task except by preventing individuals from offending against morality, that is, putting the community in danger.

But as long as they are moved by mercenary motives in the exercise of these functions, as long as they act only out of personal interest, as long as the rewards and punishments that are assured to men in this life and the next have no necessary connection with their conduct vis-à-vis their fellows, morality, properly speaking, is no part of religion. For it to be a part, it is necessary that the injustice of man toward his fellow man attracts the severity of the gods, even though the criminal has not merited their anger by any negligence, or offense, that could have directly injured them.

CHAPTER 2

On the Contradictions That Characterize This Period of Polytheism, and the Way in Which These Contradictions Disappear

The passage from the barbarous to the civilized state is a moment of great fermentation. Justice struggles against violence, the spirit of property against the spirit of theft, the principles of morality against the habit of force. For a long time men seek in vain for a fixed setting. They see themselves simultaneously assailed by the inconveniences of the situation they are leaving and those that are no less great — and are more unforeseen — of the situation they are entering.

Religion experiences this fermentation. The maxims that are introduced run against those that memory consecrates. The opinions that begin to be forgotten, those that begin to be established, encounter one another and clash.[1]

But as civilization progresses, morality identifies more with religion, and the confusion ceases and the contradictions disappear; the venality of the gods is still recognized; egoism cannot renounce this teaching, of which it makes so great use, and in various guises this opinion runs through the epochs. But it has suffered an important change. The gods have not yet become disinterested beings, but they have become honest men, in the ordinary meaning of the phrase. They insist that they be paid for doing good, but they no longer permit anyone to pay them to do evil.

The steps of this improvement are slow; many vestiges of the older notions mix with it and slow it. Even when more honorable opinions concerning the present conduct of the gods are adopted, their previous crimes are still recalled.

---

1. A writer claims that when a people have admitted morality into their religion, they allow virtuous actions only to the gods whom they worship as good, and that if they attribute wicked ones to them, it is because they do not regard them as wicked. Countless examples from every religion prove the contrary. Man has such veneration for force that for a long time he respects actions in the powerful that he believes are forbidden to weakness. However, purification occurs little by little, and the author who was wrong ends by being right.

By stages, however, the traditions that are unfavorable to them are relegated to an obscure past. One is hesitant to recount them, and soon one arrives at calling them into question.

Thus, by a fortunate reaction, morality, which has found a guarantee in religion, purifies and improves the religion that sanctions it.

There is an interesting observation to make concerning the men who at this period stubbornly recall the demeaning traditions. This apparent return to primitive opinions is often a beginning of unbelief. In the polytheism *sans* morality, it was to honor the gods, to exalt their power, that their jealousy and implacable vengeance were spoken of. After the introduction of morality into polytheism, however, it is to insult them and to lower them in men's estimation. What believers once recounted in good faith, as acts worthy of respect, unbelievers later repeated with irony, as scandals. Thus Bossuet and Voltaire meet, and entertain their readers with Samuel hacking to pieces Agag. The first extols this ferocious action, the second denounces it. The faithful of the seventeenth century see in it a model to follow; the philosophes of the eighteenth a misdeed to detest.

Unbelief in fact is always found close to the complete triumph of morality in religion. As soon as men have been thoroughly convinced of the necessity of morality, their logic forces them to compare the facts that religion reports, and the doctrines it teaches, with the new principles it is called upon to sanction. It follows that when these facts or teachings seem to them contrary to these principles, they call the former into doubt; they are even more obliged to do so insofar as the habit of reflection makes progress in all minds, the fables that were previously adopted without any difficulty suddenly serve as a defense of the guilty.[2] Struck by this danger, man no longer accepts the belief except under the express condition that it will protect morality. As the price of not contesting their existence, he demands from the gods that they make themselves useful; and far from recognizing, as previously, that they have absolute rights, he imposes duties upon them. Morality therefore becomes a sort of touchstone, a test, for religious no-

---

2. This is how Ovid justifies incest—for example, that of Jupiter.

Jupiter esse pium statuit quodcunque juvaret,

Et fas omne facit frater marita soror.

(Phaedr. *ad* Hippol.)

And long before this, in Aeschylus, the same abuse of ancient fables can be seen. "Jupiter," says Orestes, "protects paternal dignity; Jupiter who himself struck his father" (*Eumenid.*, 643–44).

tions, which cannot fail to contest a part of them, and to weaken the confidence one has in the rest.

This is a consequence of the intervention of this third faculty about which we have previously spoken: reasoning, constituting itself as the judge of the debates that arise between sentiment and interest, in turn calling into question the desires of the former and the calculations of the latter.

CHAPTER 3

That the Poems of Hesiod Are Contemporaneous with the Revolution We Are Describing

The poems of Hesiod,[1] like those of Homer, have come to us thanks to the rhapsodists who, performing them from city to city on the public squares, transmitted them from one generation to another, until the point when the copyists assembled them, putting them into writing while introducing numerous interpolations that

---

1. The two poems of Hesiod are the *Theogony* and the *Works and Days*. The "Shield of Hercules" is probably a fragment of the *Theogony*, whose last two verses announce that the author is going to speak of the wives of the heroes and their children. Now, it is precisely the son of one of these wives who is the subject of the "Shield of Hercules." By some chance, this portion would have been separated from the poem. However, the grammarian Aristophanes did not regard it as authentic, and declared it very inferior to the *Theogony*, properly speaking.

In this last poem, one recognizes detached portions of one or several priestly systems, dark and mysterious, whose integral version was not understood by the bard who transmitted these scattered details to us. The physical hypotheses of Hesiod on the origin of things, chaos, and unformed matter, on the children of Phorcys and Keto, belong to Phoenicia. In general, his allegories are Phoenician rather than Egyptian. In all the Egyptian cosmogonies one finds as the first principle the mysterious egg, which reappears in the Greek allegories borrowed from the Egyptians; but Hesiod begins with chaos, and the Phoenicians are the people of the South to whom the idea of chaos was most familiar. The Gorgons who live in the West owe their origin to the habit of writers of antiquity to relegate to this part of the world, which was then unknown, all monsters and other extraordinary phenomena. "To hear them," says Voss (*Géogr. ancienne*), "the North and the West were peopled with male and female magicians, who commanded the winds and storms, and killed, or transformed, strangers; man-eating giants with three heads and one eye; dwarfs who were one foot high, who did battle with cranes; griffins guarding treasures; old women having only one tooth; monsters whose looks petrified spectators; men without a head or with the head of a dog, with feet that served them as an umbrella when they reclined, or with ears with which they could cover themselves like a cloak during a storm." The sphinx is an Egyptian import. The traditions relative to Love (Eros, cosmogonic Love, which should not be confused with the one that later poets gave to Venus as a son); the engendering of the have often called their authenticity into question.[2] But the period in which these poems had to be composed is no less indicated by their very nature. These are didactic works, subsequent to the primitive epic; works in which reflection dominates in place of inspiration, in which the desire to produce artistic effects replaces

---

heavens, mountains, and the Ocean, the appearance of the Titans, of which Saturn is the youngest, are, on one hand, fragments of cosmology that Hesiod did not take the trouble to put into any order, but that he accumulated by chance as each notion presented itself to him; and, on the other hand, the beginning of a historical or narrative mythology, because the Cyclopes and the Centimanes are the brothers of the Titans. Now, the Centimanes are, in the language of a people that is becoming civilized, the memory of the savage state.

Uranus mutilated is still a cosmogonic relic; it is nature losing its generative force. We have found this symbol in several priestly religions, with this difference: that it is the basis of all their ceremonies and never ceases to be present in all their fables, while Greek polytheism, after having rendered it hollow praise, discards it like a memory that bothers it. From Uranus's blood, fallen on the earth, come the giants and Erinyes. Venus is the daughter of heaven and the wave (*Theog.*, 187–206). This is the primitive idea under new names. Love had been represented as the daughter of chaos, the principle of all things; Venus, which replaced Love, is called the daughter of the sea, become the first principle in the more recent cosmogonies.

This birth of Venus emerging from the waves, this veneration for the sea, mother of all, probably owed in part to some imperfect knowledge or understanding of the philosophy of the barbarians, and in part to the memories of the colonies and to the memory of their maritime expeditions. The daughters of Ocean bore the names of the different parts of the world, Europe, Asia, etc. Hesiod says that there were three thousand and excuses himself for not naming them all, adding that those who lived near them knew their names. Nereus, this prophetic old man, alludes to the laws of nature, according to which the sea is tossed in winter and calm in summer. This is obviously a symbol of the first observations of sailors concerning the order of the seasons.

In his turn, cast into Tartarus with the Titans, Saturn is the signal of the triumph of the true Greek mythology (see bk. V, ch. 6). The allegories of Hesiod at that time become clearer, more pleasant, more elegant; the Muses are the daughters of Memory, Harmony owes her birth to the embraces of Mars and Venus, but even this part of the *Theogony* experiences priestly borrowings. We have shown elsewhere that Hesiod introduced the oriental demonology into the Greek religion.

Works and Days is an agronomic work that embraces the entirety of the social state, and in which religion is much more applied to human life than in the *Theogony*. It was composed, as was the latter work, of more or less long rhapsodies, with each one forming a whole. It is a precious record of the most ancient civilization. In it one sees the human spirit in its infancy, as it were, developing by means of peaceful and increasing activity, albeit in the narrow boundaries assigned to it by its still recent efforts and its precarious propriety, taking place near newly constructed foyers.

2. The celebrated Heyne, in his dissertation on the *Theogony* (*Com. Soc. Goett.*) points out many passages that are obviously interpolated. With his testimony, Pausanias confirms the claim of the modern scholar. The tradition that Aesculapius was the son of Alcinous, he says, was made-up by

the spontaneous élan and naïve candor of the most ancient poets; finally, in which individuality leads authors to digressions on their personal situation, hopes, and fears. At different times, Hesiod speaks of himself, his position, his private relations, while, whether in the *Iliad* or the *Odyssey*, everything relates to the subject, nothing to the writer.

The different parts that enter into the composition of the poems of Hesiod have no proportion among themselves. Sometimes a dry abbreviator, sometimes an expansive orator, he does not subordinate the extent of particular developments to the measure of the whole; what determines him is the quantity of material that he was able to gather from the most discordant traditions; this is a second symptom that the social state was already more complex and that poetry was a means rather than a goal.

If needed, the style of Hesiod would be a third proof that he wrote at a moment of crisis and social agitation. This style, even though his sweetness has been noted by Quintilian, is somber, serious, often sad; and what demonstrates that this character pertained to his period and not him alone, is that he seized upon all the occasions he encountered or manufactured to give himself over to poetical descriptions and digressions. But in the midst of his efforts to be only a poet, he constantly returned to being a thinker. The earth is full of ills, he says, the sea as well.[3] The description of the different ages of the human race ends with the most ominous prophecies.[4] It is with regret that the Fates allot mortals a few happy days, and Sadness, seated near them, also walks on their spindles, her eyes wet with tears. The complaints of Hesiod against the tyranny of the great and kings are but the expression of the disorders of a social state that is still imperfect, troubled by the

---

Hesiod, or by those who took the liberty of adding their verses to those of this poet (*Corinth*, 26). Pausanias goes even further in his doubts; he declares that after having read the *Theogony* attentively, he holds it to be inauthentic (*Arcad.*, 18), and he bases himself on the opinion of the Boeotians, who claimed, he tells us, that the *Works and Days* was the only poem genuinely by Hesiod; still, he adds, these people drop the exordium, or the invocation to the Muses (*Boeot.*, chs. 27 & 31). This invocation, in fact, is discordant with the rest of the poem. The Muses who dance on Helicon around Jupiter's altar, and who praise this god and his spouse, Juno of Argos; the particular epithets and characteristics attached to each divinity, while priests give only their cosmogonic or metaphysical epithets, are images and conceptions that are entirely Greek. But this is not a reason to reject this invocation of the Muses. Hesiod could have, and had to have, mixed all the genres, as he mixed all the conceptions.

3. *Theog.*, 32ff.

4. Ibid., 163–64.

very ones charged with making it respected.[5] Reflection, the inevitable product of this agitation and malaise, constantly resurfaces, indefatigable and disconsoling. Man has taken the irreversible step, this return to himself and to the misfortune of his condition. He has discovered the pitfalls with which he is surrounded, the dangers of trust, and the deceptions of enthusiasm. After this discovery, no illusion lasts for long. The purity of the soul, the élan of sentiment, sometimes lessen the burden that weighs over the imagination and heart. Some privileged geniuses liberate themselves (we will see an example in Sophocles), but the majority of writers remain bent under the weight: poetry drags after it a second-thought that is against its nature, from which it seeks in vain to be freed. It struggles for several centuries, it varies its forms, it calculates its efforts, it resumes at least the appearances of life, but it carries within itself the seed of death.

The contradictions that the social state under whose influence Hesiod wrote introduces into religious ideas strike the attentive reader at each moment. One first sees, as in Homer, Jupiter consumed by love for a mortal,[6] Minerva encouraging Hercules to wound Mars;[7] Mars, as a consequence, wounded and overturned by Hercules.[8] Olympus is established only by the victory of the gods over the Titans, their rivals, who attack them with equal forces;[9] Typhoeus would have seized the empire of the universe if Jupiter had not prevented him, by striking him with lightning.[10] Hesiod's Tartarus[11] is similar to that of the *Odyssey* in all things. The defeated are confined there;[12] Gyges, Cottus, and Briareus are its wardens,[13] with their one hundred arms and fifty heads.[14] The crimes that men commit against other men are not punished there.

The *Works and Days* contains this fundamental idea of the first period of polytheism, that the gods and the mortals were originally one race, and they were born

5. See bk. VII, ch. 3.

6. "Shield of Hercules," ll. 31–36.

7. Ibid., 331–35.

8. Ibid., 458–62.

9. *Theog.*, 881–85.

10. Ibid., 820–68.

11. Ibid., 724–804.

12. Ibid., 729–31.

13. Ibid., 734–35.

14. Ibid., 148–52.

at the same time;[15] in other words, that the gods do not differ from men except by force and power.[16]

Their perversity is still a received view. Jupiter envies the human race the use of fire because humanity is an object of his hatred.[17] He takes away the warning signs of diseases for fear that the mortals who are thus alerted will avoid them.[18] He condemns them to eternal discords.[19] All the gods agree to make Pandora more attractive in order to cause men to perish.[20] Prometheus knows Jupiter so well that he forbids his brother Epimetheus from receiving any gift from this treacherous god.[21]

But alongside these vestiges of a religion that attributes to its idols all the imperfections and vices, the maxims announced by the poet prove that the gods are already improved. Jupiter, he says, fills just kings and peoples with good things.[22] He punishes the deceitful and deflates the proud.[23] He gave Equity to man as his supreme law.[24] This goddess is seated next to him.[25] Thirty thousand gods constantly cross the earth, strict observers of vices and virtues.[26] The Furies have emerged from the depths of the netherworld to punish perjury.[27] Adultery, incest, the robbing of orphans, and ingratitude toward parents merit severe punishments,[28] and these punishments extend to the posterity of the guilty,[29] because it was sensed early on that for the honor of divine justice, the execution of its decrees

---

15. *Works and Days*, 108.

16. If our inquiries allowed us to enter into all the details of mythologies, we would note that the mythology of Hesiod is closer to the *Odyssey* than the *Iliad*. Mercury, for example, is always the messenger of the gods and replaces Iris, which, as we noted above, was a change in the story made subsequent to the opinion accredited by the singer of the siege of Troy.

17. *Theog.*, 563–68.

18. *Works and Days*, 104.

19. Ibid., 16.

20. Ibid., 81–82.

21. Ibid., 85–88.

22. Ibid., 224–35.

23. Ibid., 7.

24. Ibid., 274–77.

25. Ibid., 254–60.

26. Ibid., 250–53. These gods are demons or intermediary gods. One can see what we have already said in book X on the demonology of Hesiod.

27. *Works and Days*, 800–802.

28. Ibid., 236–45; 325–32.

29. Ibid., 282.

should be placed in another world, or in the future of this one. Finally, the gods reward work, condemn sloth,[30] and take away ill-gotten wealth.[31]

It is not only in these general ideas that Hesiod combines contradictory notions; the same combination is reproduced in his descriptions of particular divinities. Here, Jupiter, subject to error, is the plaything of Prometheus.[32] Elsewhere, he is twice called "he who knows the eternal decrees,"[33] and the poet exhausts himself in theological subtleties to harmonize the omniscience of the god with the success of the artifices of man. The first god, he says, knows ruse, and lets himself be deceived only because he wished ill to mortals.[34] Anthropomorphism has introduced similar sophisms into all mythologies.

In the "Shield of Hercules," the hideous, terrifying Fates are only malevolent and bloody *genii*.[35] They drag the dead through the mêlée; they dispute over the wounded; they even sacrifice those who have not received any wounds. In the *Theogony*, they are the daughters of Justice;[36] they pursue only the guilty, but are unbending in their severity against the crimes of gods and of men.[37] This expression "the crimes of gods" in the same verse where punishment is entrusted to avenging divinities seems to us to clearly indicate the mixing of ideas of different epochs.[38]

We would be able to infinitely extend this list. Hesiod twice calls the Styx an incorruptible divinity,[39] and a few verses later he calls it a horrible, abominable monster.[40] In the *Theogony*, Nemesis is the daughter of Night, the scourge of mortals; she indiscriminately showers evils on them and enjoys the spectacle of their miseries.[41] In *Works and Days*, it is a divinity that lives in the height of the heavens

30. Ibid., 301–8.
31. Ibid., 319–24.
32. *Theog.*, 535.
33. Ibid., 550 and 561.
34. Ibid., 551–52.
35. "Shield of Hercules," 156–62.
36. *Theog.*, 904.
37. Ibid., 218–19.
38. In certain respects, one could compare the persistence of the ancients in preserving the traditions that attributed to the gods morally culpable actions to that of Christians, who, under a religion of gentleness and humanity, no less preserved the Jewish traditions of the jealous and cruel character of Jehovah.
39. *Theog.*, 389–97.
40. Ibid., 775–76.
41. Ibid., 223.

with Shame or Modesty.[42] Venus herself, like Bhavani of the Indians, has two characters. She appears on the Ocean, having in her train love, fecundity, an entourage full of seduction, charm, and joy;[43] but soon she engenders necessity, death, and hatred.[44] Medusa gives birth to Echidna, an admirable, beautiful virgin, whose features the sun loves to display with its rays.[45] Two verses later this beautiful virgin is a frightful serpent.[46]

Here is therefore realized what we said about the characteristics that distinguish the transition from one period to another. Opinions are mixed, men appear guilty of inconsistencies and contradictions that in truth are found in things; but these inconsistencies are going to disappear, these contradictions will be harmonized, as the present triumphs over the past.

42. *Works and Days*, 198. There are also two Erises, one good, the other wicked. The wicked one is older, because she is the daughter of Night. The good Eris is more modern; Jupiter is her father (*Theog.*, 226; *Works and Days*, 17).

43. *Theog.*, 195–202.

44. Ibid., 219–25. It is quite certain that the Aphrodite that Hesiod speaks about in verse 195 and the Night of which verse 219 speaks are one and the same divinity. We have the proof in the third Orphic hymn, where the Night, mother of all, is also called Cypris, an epithet that Hesiod gives her, and in the 55th hymn, where Aphrodite is named the Nocturna, in turn shining and invisible, νυκτεριη, φαινομενη τ'αφανης τε.

45. *Theog.*, 296.

46. Ibid., 298–99. Note that in Hesiod this monster does not have a father: it was much later that Apollodorus assigned him the Earth and Tartarus as parents. Here one recognizes the mixture of two priestly ideas, one relative to the form of the gods, the other connected with miraculous conceptions, independent of sexual union. But Hesiod exiles Echidna far from the sight of the gods and men (v. 384). He seems to have sensed that all these images were rejected by the mythology in vogue.

CHAPTER 4

On Pindar[1]

Pindar writing, at least according to the popular chronology, more than five hundred years after Hesiod, almost never falls into the inconsistencies with which the latter is filled. As much as he can, he rejects everything in the ancient traditions that does not accord with the maxims that have become an essential part of the public belief of his time.

Not only are all his general claims conformed to this tendency. Justice is seated beside Jupiter.[2] All virtues come from the gods.[3] The felicity of the irreproachable man is alone assured, that of the wicked vanishes like a dream.[4] These general assertions would not be sufficient proof of a change in religion, since we see similar ones scattered here and there in the *Iliad* and the *Theogony*, alongside features that belie them; but Pindar makes a positive and explicit principle of the necessity to purify mythology in the direction of morality. It becomes men, he says, only to say

---

1. Our readers ought not to be surprised if we pass so quickly from Hesiod to Pindar. We have scrupulously, and in detail, scrutinized the poets who filled an interval of more than five centuries, but we have hardly found more than a few almost imperceptible signs of the development we are trying to understand. Tyrteus and Sappho offer us nothing; the fragments of Stesichorus are full of Orphic or priestly traditions and images; the dubiously genuine odes of Anacreon barely have any weight; Phocylide and Theognis give us a small number of sentences worthy of attention, and therefore we have sometimes cited them. But the religious revolution that occupies us appears clearly only in the works of Pindar; we still have to set aside his mysterious allusions to foreign or philosophic doctrines, of which he had, and above all wanted to appear to have, knowledge.

2. *Olymp.*, VIII, 28 and 29.

3. *Pyth.*, I, 79–82.

4. *Isthm.*, III, 7–10.

honorable things about the immortals; then, even when they invent something, they will commit no fault.[5]

This passage is remarkable in two respects. It indicates the progress that had caused the tales that are unfavorable to the gods, and even to heroes,[6] to be rejected; and, moreover, it contains the acknowledgment by the poet that he chose among the established traditions, according to certain moral criteria, those that were most in keeping with the new ideas of dignity, order, and justice that had entered the religion.

It should be noted that this moral critique that guides Pindar, even though it ought to end in unbelief, does not yet lead the poet to that conclusion; it is not the reality that he calls into doubt; the marvelous is not what angers him; he does not seek to undermine belief in what really constitutes the mythology—that is, the action of gods vis-à-vis men. He merely thinks that the reality has been disfigured, either by inadvertence or malevolence. Envy and perversity, he says, have secretly accredited this erroneous account.[7] He adds[8] that dazzling lies have often misled men and disguised the truth from them. In this way, the sweet words of Homer and his enchanting verses have clothed deception with an imposing authority, and his genius has captivated the imagination of credulous mortals.[9] Pindar recognizes therefore that the core of the fables is true, that the place occupied by the supernatural ought to remain, but he is distrustful of the later inventions and embellishments; he examines them, not like a mocking or hostile skeptic, but as a serious and orthodox believer; he is attached to the belief even as he purifies it. The tales are not in his eyes materials that one has the right to draw from as he wishes; they are facts from which he has the duty of stripping additions that pervert them.

If he speaks of Tantalus, it is by substituting a more decent fiction for the popular teaching; I cannot regard, he adds, the gods as intemperate and voracious.

---

5. *Olymp.*, I, 55–57; *Pyth.*, III, 27; IX, 45. In the Edda one finds something similar: Do not reveal your destinies to men, says the spouse of Odin to the Scandinavian gods, hide from them what you have done at the birth of time. Even when, says the Edda (23rd fable), Thor would have had the weaker hand in some encounter, he must not speak of it because the world must believe that nothing can resist his power.

6. Stesichorus had already given him this example by making honorable amends concerning what he had said about Helen, because the poets at the time worked to raise the character of the heroes as well as that of the gods.

7. *Olymp.*, I, 47.

8. Ibid., 28.

9. *Nem.*, VII, 20.

Far from us be this wicked thought![10] If he was often moved by the instability of human things,[11] and if he allowed himself to be overcome by that melancholy that is so natural to meditative spirits, he never once uttered a word that would accuse the gods, or tax them with base and cruel jealousy.[12] If we find in one of his odes, as we do in Hesiod, the fundamental axiom of Homeric mythology, the race of gods and that of men declared to be one and the same,[13] elsewhere he speaks of the gods and their superiority over the human race, of their universal knowledge, in a way to indicate the immense distance that, quite recently, had separated the two races.[14] In his ninth *Olympian* ode, following the example of previous poets, he begins by recounting the battles of the gods; but suddenly stopping, he exclaims: Far from me to insult the celestial majesty with my verses; and he brings these profane accounts to a halt.[15] The author of the *Iliad* was very far from experiencing similar scruples. Thus, Pythagoras said that he had seen Homer in the netherworld, tormented like Hesiod for having slandered the immortals.

Finally, in the two places where Pindar speaks of Nemesis, between the two characters[16] that Hesiod gave to this goddess, he chooses the most instructive and moral. It is no longer Nemesis, scourge of mortals, it is Nemesis who punishes the abuse of power, and Pindar invites his hero not to anger her;[17] it is Nemesis who judges the actions of men and whom the Hyperboreans are happy to have never provoked.

We will briefly note here how much the progression of Greek religion lets itself be clearly seen in this conception of Nemesis; in Homer, it is not at all a goddess but an exclamation, a sort of invocation that deflects evil signs and scandal; in Hesiod, she appears doubly, by turns daughter of the abyss or inhabitant of the heavens. Pindar rejects those of her attributes that make her a malevolent force;[18] he

10. *Olymp.*, X, 82–102.

11. *Pyth.*, VIII, 108–11.

12. Phocylides, in the verses reported by Stobaeus, says like Pindar that envy does not exist among the gods.

13. *Nem.*, VI, 1–9.

14. *Pyth.*, 79–87.

15. *Olymp.*, IX, 15, 62.

16. See above, bk. XII, ch. 3.

17. *Olymp.*, VIII, 144.

18. Herder seems to us to have wrongly interpreted the epithet διχοβουλον. It does not at all express a malevolent disposition; it is Nemesis changing disposition, and it is a warning to Alcimedon not to justify this change, by abusing a prosperity of which he would then be unworthy.

does so just in the way that the tragedians will invoke her;[19] and, later, her justice will not be limited to material punishments, by means of a new refinement, by a new delicacy of expression and thought, she will become the companion of moderation; even her statue will recall to the Greeks how dangerous are the errors of a pride without limits and the intoxications of power. The block of marble employed by Phidias will be the one that the Persians, believing themselves assured of victory, destined to immortalize the success of their arms and the enslavement of the Greeks by means of a magnificent monument.[20] Marathon, however, saw them flee, perish in the swamps, or redden with their blood the waves in which they cast themselves, and the marble recouped from them became the goddess who presides over fairness in endeavors and modesty in one's hopes.

This idea is transmitted, refined from century to century, and six hundred years after Pindar,[21] Mesomedes still celebrates it in his verses.

"O Nemesis!" he says, "winged goddess, who decides concerning human life; goddess with stern look, who holds in a strong hand the reins of our destinies, we miserable mortals, prompt to error; you see the pride that destroys us, the envy that devours us; the wheel of fate always turns without leaving a trace, you follow it, invisible, lowering the proud brow that excessive prosperity raises, moderating the abjection of the unfortunate, entering into all hearts to calm them, and always having a finger on the scales in order to reestablish equality; be favorable to us, you who distribute justice, winged Nemesis, with the meditative look, inaccessible to error, never deceiving humans, and only having Fairness as companion, Fairness, which extends its white wings in the air, powerful Fairness, who preserves us from ourselves, and from your severity, and from Tartarus."[22]

19. *Electra*, 793.

20. Pausan., *Attica*, 33.

21. Mesomedes was a contemporary of Hadrian, but, as with all the lyric poets of this period, he had gathered and preserved the moral ideas of the Greek religion.

22. *Anthol. Grecq.*, II, 347. One will easily see in this ode the degeneration of poetry and art. The affectation of Mesomedes in repeating three times the epithet "winged" proves that taste was corrupt and had lost its ancient simplicity. But it was still necessary to recall the substance of ideas.

CHAPTER 5

On the Underworld of Pindar Compared with That of Homer and Hesiod

The comparison between the underworld of Pindar and that of Homer and Hesiod is singularly helpful in casting light on the subject of our investigations; but in order to be truly useful, this comparison demands steady attention and sharp eyes; the differences easily escape superficial inspection.

For the one who looks on the empire of the dead only from afar, nothing seems to be significantly changed. The topography of the future world (if one can use this phrase) remains in many respects the same. The same names are used, the same great divisions continue. Everything, however, has taken on a different destination; everything contributes to promoting the new goal of religion.

We have seen in the primitive netherworld a place of torments where only the personal enemies of the gods groan. By a natural and facile transformation, when the gods declare themselves the defenders of morality, this place of torment is no longer devoted to their particular vengeance but to the punishment of all crimes. The idea of punishment entails that of judgments and sentences. As a consequence, the imagination seeks something from which to form a tribunal among the dead. What is simpler than to extend the jurisdiction of kings and elders exercised over the actions committed during life, a jurisdiction already recognized in Homer's netherworld, but which was exercised only on the particular quarrels of those who live there?[1] Before these judges, therefore, appear, no longer the dead to resolve momentary differences, but each deceased at his arrival at the dark river. He presents himself, burdened with the weight of his faults or accompanied by the memory of his virtues; and this inflexible tribunal, holding the fatal urn in hand,

---

1. See bk. VII, ch. 9.

unmasks ruse and cunning, condemns injustice to atone for its ill-gotten successes, and punishes the arrogant power that the tomb has disarmed.

Rigor exercised against the guilty dead necessarily changes the destiny of the innocent or virtuous dead. They no longer make the place in which they dwell resound with sighs and complaints; they no longer regret life; they no longer give themselves over to crude or sullen pleasures. Their abode becomes one of the purest felicity. Earlier, everything there was sadder, darker, more somber than on earth; now everything takes on more pleasant and beautiful colors; the winds are scented, the grass softer, the sun more resplendent. Commerce with the gods, contemplation of the stars, the revelation of the secrets of nature, all the elevated and refined pleasures are the eternal share of the blessed shades.

Let us see if this is not in fact the underworld of Pindar.

In one of the Fortunate Isles, sweetly refreshed by the ocean winds and decorated with sparkling flowers,[2] live those who, lit by an eternal sun and free of pains and fatigue, three times in this life[3] have rejected the temptation of crime and injustice. They do not laboriously plow the rebellious earth, nor dangerously cross the treacherous sea.[4] Exempt from tears, their days are spent in communion with the favorites of the immortals. Their occupations are songs, hymns, competitions, concerts, games; or in the shadow of the groves scented by the incense offered on earth to the gods, in their conversations they recall the memories of the past. Saturn governs them, assisted by Rhadamanthus, and perhaps Aeacus, who earlier had pronounced on the disputes of the gods themselves. In Erebus, on the contrary, where perpetual darkness reigns, criminals handed over to eternal oblivion are subject to the torments of a restlessness that will never end.

Who cannot recognize the progression of ideas here? The entire kingdom of shadows in Homer is a place of groans and sighs. Pleasures and pains there are entirely physical. There are no judges for the actions of this life. Aeacus is not named there; Rhadamanthus inhabits the Elysium that is not the dwelling of the dead,[5] and the jurisdiction of Minos is only an incidental judgment over passing

---

2. Pind., *Olymp.*, I, 105–45.

3. This is an allusion to the Pythagorian philosophy.

4. Pindar thus banished from Elysium agriculture and navigation, two of the most customary occupations of life; a laudable attempt, but unsuccessful, to make the future life not a copy of this one. If the result did not correspond to the poet's intention, because elsewhere he assigned pleasures that imitated those of this life to his blessed, the attempt is no less a proof of progress.

5. *Odyss.*, IV, 564.

disputes. Pluto punishes the assaults that are denounced to him, but his function is
not to punish crime; he only yields to the demands of those who implore him; he
grants them their request, not as being equitable, but as he would hear any other
prayer. He does not wait for humans in the underworld, he sends the Furies against
those living on earth, like Jupiter and Juno make Iris or Mercury descend to earth
to pursue their enemies.

The netherworld in Pindar, on the contrary, is a place of merited punishments
and rewards; punishments and pleasures there are intellectual and moral. There is
an established tribunal; Saturn presides over it, Saturn, whom Homer presents as
deposed by Jupiter and wearing chains.[6]

Let us further observe how much more clearly and explicitly than Homer the
poet affirms the intellectual and almost divine nature of the soul. The body, he
says, is the prey of all-powerful death; but the soul, which comes from a divinity,
cannot die.[7]

Pindar, however, despite his efforts to escape the law that always influences his
descriptions of the world to come, is despite himself subject to this law. In painting
the occupations of the just, he is forced to return to the pleasures of this life, choosing, however, only the purest and noblest of them. The imagination is so impotent
in its conceptions of happiness that it is reduced to borrow, for the pleasures of
the future world, those of here-below that are insufficient for it. Thus, as perfect
as it is, a certain sadness hovers over Elysium; but this sadness is different from
that of primitive polytheism. The shadows in Homer are sad with the sadness of
barbarism; in Pindar, their sadness is that of civilization. The former are children
who cry and pout; the others are old people who, casting a calm, but serious, gaze
on their past life, still have something melancholic underneath a happy exterior.

Let us end these short observations on Pindar with a reflection pertaining to the
steady changes in the situation of poets, observations that the reading of Hesiod
has already suggested to us and which Pindar confirms. The poets of the time of
Homer, wandering about but welcome in all palaces, seated next to princes, do not
speak of their fate because they could only congratulate themselves on their lot.
At the time of Hesiod, their ideal existence gave way to the common and painful
features of life. The fall of kings deprived them of protectors; the birth of republics

6. Plato in the Apology, in order to better nationalize this tribunal, places alongside the three
judges of the underworld Triptolemus, the favorite of Ceres, who gave agriculture to the Athenians,
and with it, laws and social life.

7. Pind. ap. Clem. Alex., *Strom.*, IV, 640; and Theodoret, *Serm.*, VIII, 599.

is accompanied by storms; they now tell us about their lot because they have something to complain about. From the time of Pindar they forbid themselves from even complaining. It is not that they are happier but that they are more timid. The elegant and superficial author of the *Anacharsis*—we say superficial because profundity is not in the learning that compiles, but in the perceptiveness that appreciates—raised in the literature of the masterworks of Greece, but never entering deeply into their spirit, extols, it is true, the long prosperity of Pindar, his statue that bears a crown,[8] the honors granted him at Delphi,[9] the oracles given in his favor, the sacred banquets he attended; but it suffices to read the poet himself to detect the error of the panegyrist. Pindar is constantly occupied with begging for mercy. Everything frightens him. He exhausts himself in constant efforts to disarm malevolence; he does not succeed. Struck with a fine by his fellow citizens,[10] defeated five times by Corinna,[11] he crawls to the feet of the tyrant of Syracuse, fearing his anger, begging his favors, and in exchange lavishing praise that history belies.[12] A few attempts to repulse the arrows of envy by appearing to disdain it, the sincere, or affected, regret for the days when interest did not sully the language of poetry,[13] the praise of mediocrity,[14] commonplaces of all those who have not been able to acquire power or wealth, do not deprive the songs of Pindar of their striking character of dependency that pains us in the midst of the beauties that dazzle us, and we sigh to see such talent resign itself to occupying a subordinate rank, and hence to become greedy and flattering.

8. Aeschin., Epist. 4, p. 207.

9. Pausan., X, 24.

10. Ibid., IX, 20.

11. Ibid., I, 8.

12. The king of Syracuse whom Pindar celebrates is Hiero I, whom all the historians, and especially Diodorus of Sicily, represent as a bad king.

13. *Isthmiques*, II, 15.

14. *Pythiques*, XI, 76.

CHAPTER 6

That the Same Progression Can Be Seen in the Historians

The progression we just noticed in the poets ought to exist in the historians, albeit with different indicators.

When the poets feel the need to purify religion, they modify the facts, while historians change the causes.

We do not have a Greek historian who is contemporaneous with Homeric polytheism. Greece then only counted poets; but we have a historian who by his religious notions corresponds well enough to the period represented by Hesiod.

This historian is Herodotus. As he is later in date than Pindar, while his polytheism is nonetheless much less refined, one must explain the reasons for this anachronism in his opinions, and therefore we have to look at his character for a few moments, as well as his circumstances, and the influence of these two things on the portrait he transmitted to us.

Herodotus, a man who was simultaneously curious, gullible, and timid, maintained an equal respect for all traditions and beliefs, at whatever time and to whatever people they belonged; his goal, as he himself tells us, was to write down what each had told him.[1] In this endeavor he appears to have abstracted completely from any personal judgment. When he dares to avow that this-or-that anecdote appears doubtful to him, he carefully adds that another may perhaps find it plausible.[2] His superstition is well known; proof is found on every page. Does Hippias announce to the inhabitants of Corinth that they will have much to suffer from the Athenians? No man, adds Herodotus, had a more perfect knowledge of the

1. Herod., II, 122.
2. Ibid., V, 86.

oracles.[3] But Hippias, expelled with all of his family by the citizens of Athens, had an obvious interest in representing them to the Corinthians as dangerous enemies. However, Herodotus preferred to honor a supernatural language rather than recognize the discourse of a fugitive tyrant slandering (as they all do) his fellow citizens. The inhabitants of Potidea besieged by Artabazus, do they attribute an accident that caused many Persians to perish to Neptune's anger, in this way avenging himself on those who had insulted his statue? Herodotus hastens to give his agreement to this explanation.[4] He thinks that if none of the defeated after the battle of Plataea tried to find refuge at the altars of Ceres, it was because this goddess had denied entrance to them because they had delivered her temple at Eleusis to the flames.[5] He does not speak about worship and the various fables except with constant fear; he asks pardon of everything that he writes about the gods, the heroes, and priests;[6] he scrupulously omits nothing, rejects nothing, deepens nothing, explains nothing. Such a historian must confuse all teachings, without distinguishing their dates and without noting their contradictions. He must be the Herodotus of history, and he was.

We first of all find in his histories the character of the Homeric gods. Minerva employs prayers and reasons (these are his own words) with Jupiter, and cannot sway him.[7] On the pyre, Croesus implores Apollo to save him from the danger that threatens him and recalls his many rich offerings.[8] The discourse of this prince is nothing but the translation in prose of Chryses in the first book of the *Iliad*. Jupiter pursues the descendants of Phrixus with implacable anger because Cytissorus, his son, saved an unfortunate man that the Achaeans wanted to sacrifice.[9] The gods legitimate the murder of Candaules by Gyges, and receive with pleasure the gifts of the murderer.[10] They attach the success of endeavors not to justice, but to indifferent things, and to obedience to their arbitrary commands;

---

3. Ibid., V, 96. I do not dare contradict the oracles, and I do not at all approve that others do so (Herod., VIII, 77). Proof of Herodotus's credulity and of the emerging unbelief.

4. Ibid., VIII, 129.

5. Ibid., I, 13–14.

6. Ibid., I, 66–68.

7. Ibid., VII, 142.

8. Ibid., I, 87.

9. Ibid., VII, 197.

10. Ibid., IX, 64; see also VI, 27, and IX, 99.

for example, in the war of the Lacedaemonians against the Tegeans, at the trans-
ferring of the skeleton of Orestes to Sparta.[11] Their oracles are deceptive and
ominous, and even the surnames that are given to several of their divinities allude
to their perfidy. In reporting these surnames, Herodotus does not at all attempt
to explain them, as later authors did. When he speaks of Jupiter Apatenor, it is
Jupiter the Deceiver he indicates.[12] His statements on the jealousy of the gods are
explicit and precise, even though modern scholars had wanted, in this regard, to
be his apologists.[13] Not only does he attribute to Solon an opinion harmful to divine justice, when he has him respond to Croesus that the gods envy the happiness
of men and are pleased to trouble them,[14] but he adds in his own name that the
anger of the gods manifested itself in a terrible manner in connection with this
prince by punishing the one he judged to be the happiest of mortals.[15] He returns
frequently to this idea. God in his jealousy, he says, sends terrors to humans, or
strikes them with blindness;[16] and if life has its pleasures, this is to make their loss
more painful.[17]

　　If we compare this opinion of Herodotus to that of Plato,[18] who says that envy
is not found among the gods, or that of Plutarch,[19] who declares that the divine
nature is incompatible with jealousy, fear, anger, and hatred, or later, that of Am-
mien Marcellin,[20] who regards the fall of the great as an act of heavenly justice,
we cannot mistake the change that progress has brought.

　　At the same time, Herodotus almost always offers a double explanation of the
facts that he reports. This is a new, and striking, similarity of the historian to
Hesiod. Thus, for example, after having said that Croesus was punished by the
gods because of the overconfidence that his prosperity had inspired in him, he

11. Ibid., II, 45.

12. Ibid., I, 147.

13. See the justification of Herodotus by Abbé Geinoz, *Mém. de l'Acad. des inscript.*, XIX, 163.

14. Herod., I, 32.

15. Ibid., I, 34.

16. Ibid., VII, 10.

17. Ibid., VII, 46. See Larcher, *Notes sur Hérod.*, I, 79; and the remarks of Wesseling and Walkenaer
in their edition of the Greek author, on the jealousy of the gods.

18. Plato, in *Phaedo.*

19. Plutarch: "*Non posse suaviter vivere, secundum Epicuri decreta.*" Plutarch rises indignantly
against the malignity of Herodotus in what he says about the jealousy of the gods.

20. XIV, 17.

says elsewhere that he bore the punishment of his ancestor, who had murdered his legitimate master;[21] in this way, in the first view it is jealousy, in the second, divine justice, that accounts for the fall of Croesus. This is a quite singular justice, because the same gods had ordered the subjects of Candaules to submit to the murderer, who in this way rewarded the crime for which they punished his posterity.[22]

In several stories of Herodotus, religion is perfected by the development of human ideas.

Sometimes, the gods receive lessons in morality from humans that they are forced to receive out of shame, as it were; sometimes, they punish their worshippers for having insulted them by questions or prayers that presuppose they are wicked or mercenary.

Pactyas, a Lydian who revolted against Cyrus, having sought refuge in Cyme, a city of Aeolia, its inhabitants consulted the oracle of the Branchides to know if they ought to return the fugitive to the king of Persia, who demanded him. The oracle having counseled the extradition of this unfortunate man, one of their principal citizens who disagreed with this response took away the nests of the birds of the temple. The god indignantly complained that those who had sought refuge near him had been mistreated. Behold! said Aristodicus, you protect suppliants, and you order us to give over ours! Yes, said the god, in order that being guilty of an impiety, you will perish more promptly because of it, and no longer consult the oracles to know if it is permitted to you to commit a crime.[23] Who can fail to recognize here an amalgam of two opposed, and successive, opinions? The first counsel of the oracle had been simple and affirmative; and without the ruse of Aristodicus the inhabitants of Cyme would have followed this barbarous counsel. The second response of the god is but a belated justification which had become necessary and was invented after the fact.

Another anecdote shows us the gods improving by degrees, but in a way to still allow men to count on their venality and perfidy. Cleomenes, marching against Argos at the head of the Spartiates, arrives on the banks of a river in the territory of the Argives. Soon, according to custom he offers sacrifices to the god of this river, that he would protect the Lacedaemonians. But his sacrifices are rejected,

21. Herod., I, 91.
22. See on this subject Cic., *De nat. deor.*, III, 38.
23. Herod., I, 159–60.

and he pays homage to the loyalty of the god who does not want to betray his compatriots.[24] In this narrative, the attempt of the Spartan general to seduce a god by his sacrifices proves the conventional opinion that these means of seduction were effective. The resistance of the god proves that this opinion was beginning to weaken.

The story of Glaucus is of the same kind. Glaucus, consulting the oracle of Delphi in order to know if he ought to return a deposit he received after taking an oath; the oracle in turn declaring the infamy of perjury; Glaucus, terrified, renouncing the iniquity that he was contemplating; but the gods punishing his mere intention, did so to his most remote posterity[25]—all this indicates a phase of religion in which men still thought that the gods could approve crime, but the gods began to be angry at this assumption, taking it to be an insult.

The conduct of the inhabitants of Chios, who had acquired a small province in Mysia by a violation of hospitality, announces yet another step. They did not dare offer in their sacrifices any of the products of this territory. They did not dedicate to any god any of the cakes made of the wheat of that province; they did not sprinkle over the head of any victim the barley they harvested there. In a word, everything that came from an impure source is unclean and is banished from the temples and sacred places.[26]

In this way Herodotus felt the pressure of the atmosphere that began to surround him. He bent every effort to place next to facts, despite traditions, some cause that did honor to the justice of heaven. He was pleased to show us Cleomenes punished by the loss of his reason for having toppled Demaratus from the throne by corrupting the Pythia. He does not want anyone to assign another cause to the madness of Cleomenes.[27] The Spartans attributed it, he said, to the habit he had contracted among the Scythians of getting drunk, but I think rather that he paid this price for Demaratus.[28] Arcesilaus, king of Cyrene, received death

24. Ibid., VI, 76.

25. Ibid., 86. The story of Glaucus, says Herodotus, proves two things: one, that the gods punish not only the guilty but their descendants as well; the other, that the intention is punished as severely as the action itself. This is what Juvenal will say much later.

Has patitur poenas peccandi sola voluntas.

(XIII, 199)

26. Ibid., I, 160.

27. On this anecdote concerning Cleomenes, see Meiners, *Crit. Gesch.*, I, 486.

28. Herod., IV, 205.

as the price of his cruelty against defenseless enemies;[29] Pheretima, his mother, for having avenged her son with too much inhumanity:[30] so certain is he, continues the historian, that the gods hate and punish those who carry their resentment too far.[31]

These assertions of Herodotus more clearly bear the imprint of the revolution operated in the religious notions as they contrast with the preceding legends. In the story of Arcesilaus, for example, it is not for having committed a barbarous action, it is for not having understood an oracle, that this prince is the object of the gods' anger.[32] Herodotus himself recognizes it. He was the victim, he says, of his disobedience, whether voluntary or involuntary.[33] But, after having paid this tribute to previous opinions, the historian returns to the opinions of his time and sees justice there where previous generations only saw power.

Let us move on from Herodotus to the historians who followed him; we will see between him and them the same distance that to us seemed to separate Pindar from Hesiod.

Among these historians we will not place Thucydides; this famous Athenian hardly deals with religion in his work, and when he speaks of it, it is with a good deal of disdain. He seems to have advanced his century in terms of unbelief.

But Xenophon in his *Hellenica*, which he wrote about a hundred years after Herodotus, constantly attributes good and bad fortune to the anger of the gods, based on the virtues and vices of humans. He recognizes that it is in the divine natures to cast down the powerful and raise up the weak,[34] but he does not speak of the envy of the gods, and one must conclude from his words that Xenophon knew more than twenty centuries ago, as we know today, that injustice and power are found together. When Tissaphernes declares war against the Spartans in violation of treaties, Xenophon shows us Agesilaus being happy over this event. Why?

29. Ibid., VI, 24.

30. Ibid., IV, 165.

31. Ibid., 205.

32. The oracle had forbidden Arcesilaus to fire earthen vases that he would find in a furnace; he set on fire a tower where some rebels had taken refuge, and in this way he disobeyed the oracle because he had misunderstood it. This fact supports what we have said about the nature of the oracles among the Greeks.

33. Herod., VII, 197.

34. Ibid., VII, 197.

Tissaphernes, he says, made the gods his enemies and his betrayal indissolubly links the gods to the Greek party.[35] When, in the *Anabasis*, the Persians imprison Clearchus, Xenophon promises victory to his compatriots because justice is on their side.[36] This doctrine is developed still more clearly in the story of the conspiracy that delivered Thebes from the Lacedaemonian tyranny. After having recounted the success of this conspiracy hatched by the Theban exiles, the Spartans, he says, were punished by those against whom they had been unjust. Until then, no mortal force could have defeated them. The gods overthrow their empire without employing any other hands than those of the exiled in order to provide a memorable proof of their power and their fairness. We can, he continues, bring forth many similar examples, among both the Greeks and the barbarians. One would see in them that the gods never neglect to strike those who execute or even plan crimes.[37] If the opinion that the gods were the protectors of morality had not been the conventional opinion, Xenophon would not have professed it, because he of all men was the most subject to the teachings, as well as practices, of the religion of his country. We will demonstrate this truth later, when we consider him as a philosopher.

The introduction of morality into religion places all facts in a new light; this is because now the facts are in the historians' hands, and receive their stamp. The writers subsequent to Herodotus assign moral causes to events to which they previously had assigned no causes. In speaking of the destruction of Sybaris by the Crotonates, he simply says that the latter took this city.[38] Heraclidus of Pontus, disciple of Plato and Aristotle, claims that the Sybarites, having massacred the suppliants, drew the celestial anger upon themselves.[39] Herodotus sees in the tragic death of Polycratus only an effect of the envy of the gods. Amasis, he tells us, learning that the tyrant of Samos had recovered his ring, broke off all communication with him, foreseeing that a felicity that was so complete would infallibly draw the anger of the gods, who are always the enemies of human prosperity.[40] Diodorus, writing at another period of religion, attributes to the king of Egypt a more

35. Xenoph., *Hist. grecque*, bk. V.
36. Xenoph., *Retr. des Dix Mille*, III, 1, no. 14.
37. Xenoph., *Hist. grecque*, V, 4, no. 1.
38. Herod., V, 44.
39. Athen., *Deipnos.*, XII, ch. 4.
40. Herod., III, 40–43, 125.

moral and honorable motive. Amasis, according to him, was not unaware that a prince who governs unjustly cannot avoid the punishment destined for tyranny by heaven.[41] Thus, in this passage of Diodorus (who, however, is not consistent in his religious opinions, because in his time religion was already very much weakened), in this passage of Diodorus, as we were saying, the gods are equitable; in Herodotus, they are only jealous.[42]

41. Diod., I, 95.

42. Philip of Macedonia and Antiochus, king of Syria, Diodorus says somewhere, having undertaken unjust wars and committed several sacrileges and other barbarous acts, the anger of the gods was vented on their States. On the contrary, the Romans having never undertaken but just wars, and having always been faithful to their oaths and their treaties, it was not without cause that the gods always appeared to favor their projects and enterprises (Diod., fragm., XXVI). This is certainly a flattery of the Romans, because no people were more unjust in their wars; but this flattery is based upon received ideas, and that suffices for us.

CHAPTER 7

Of the Same Progression among the Greek Tragedians

One perhaps will be surprised that we seek to discern a progressive development in three authors who lived pretty much at the same time; the Greek tragedians all died within a span of twenty years. But if the first steps of intelligence are slow because of the obstacles it encounters when it begins to walk,[1] the changes it effects in religious ideas soon become much more rapid. When the first occurs, the second becomes a necessity; they follow in this way with an accelerated speed, and writers who are almost contemporary often mark two different epochs.

In a certain respect, it would enter into our subject to go back to the origin of tragedy. The invention of dramatic representations had to precede the pleasure they cause in spectators; nonetheless, the hope of this pleasure is the sole cause independent of religion that one can assign to these representations. It is a vicious circle from which the priesthood helps us escape; its festivals, its ceremonies, opened a career to genius upon which it eagerly entered, but which ended by excluding those who had first given the example. These, in order to revenge themselves, later proscribed what they themselves had invented.

In Greece as in India, tragedy was first a religious form and the act of attending one was an act of worship; this spectacle imported from abroad was then at once terrifying and grotesque, a mixture that eminently belongs to the spirit of priests, some traces of which we perceive in the buffooneries of Aristophanes, which have seemed inexplicable to moderns for a long time. Animals figured in the festivals of Rama, often half-god and half-human; and in the first attempts of the Greeks, in the feasts of Bacchus the Satyrs occupied the place of bears and apes in India.

---

1. See above, bk. XI, ch. 4.

The genius of the Greeks did not wait long to reject this rather chaotic amalgam.

A little after Thespis, the Satyrs no longer appeared on the Greek scene. Mythology continued to furnish the content of dramas; but what was priestly: the monstrosity of the gods, the orgies, the cosmogonic struggles, was increasingly effaced. One still finds them in one of the works of Aeschylus; one does not find them any-more in the works of Sophocles. The mystery cults we will speak about in the following book are for these two poets, as for Euripides (who is in a separate category), the occasion for numerous allusions; but the part of the mystery cults that is especially priestly enters much less than their moral part, and even this part is shown in a different light. The tragedians purify it without doubting it, taking its maxims and its theory, and separating it from the practices and artificial duties that denature and sully it in the mysteries.[2] The great bases of religious morality, submission to the gods, the necessity of a spotless life, the teaching of devotion and sacrifice, were corrupted in the mysteries by the alloy of the priestly spirit. The tragedians, not being dominated by this spirit, emancipated both morality and tragedy from this admixture.

Unfortunately, such investigations would lead us too afar; we cannot forget that we are principally occupied with the popular influence of beliefs, and the way this influence is modified by progress. If we gave ourselves to investigations of the facts that were borrowed, especially by Aeschylus, from foreign mythologies, we would needlessly repeat what has already been said[3] of the triumph of the Greek spirit over the teachings brought by the sailors and colonies, and concerning the elements that constituted the polytheism of Greece.[4] We also ought to reject everything that is only related to the philosophic sects that the tragedians adopted.[5] Elsewhere, we will have to treat this subject extensively when in another work we recount the fall of polytheism, and the part that the philosophers played in this great intellectual event, starting with the Ionian school. Now, however interesting these digressions might appear, whether under a historical or philosophical or literary point of view, we have had to forbid ourselves from pursuing them. We can say nothing that is superfluous when time and space barely suffice for the necessary.

2. See the following book [bk. XIII] on the mystery cults.

3. Bk. V, ch. 5.

4. Bk. VII.

5. According to Cicero, Aeschylus inclined toward the Pythagorian sect. The doctrine of Pythagoras probably influenced the conception of the Furies sparing Orestes in the sanctuary and taking hold of him later, when he wished to leave this religious asylum.

There must be more contradictions concerning the character of the gods in tragedy than in epic poetry. In the latter, character lets itself be known by actions, while in tragedy it is manifested by the axioms that, in the mouths of interested or passionate interlocutors, vary according to their passions or interests; sometimes they want to deceive those who listen to them, sometimes they themselves are deceived; other times they say something other than what they believe, or seek to believe only what they desire. The character of the gods is practical in epic and theoretical in tragedy.

Another feature renders the testimony of the tragedians more or less suspect: their allusions to intrigues, customs, and abuses that are present in the mind of the spectators. Eager to elicit immediate applause, the dramatic poets ascribe opinions to their heroes that are in advance of their time. Thus we see in Aeschylus a constant effort to elevate Athens above Delphi, even in religion, an attempt that was hardly consonant with the respect this holy city inspired in all of Greece as the center of its belief, toward which all its tribes competed in displaying deference and veneration; later, the poet lavished praises on the Areopagus that the subject of the play did not naturally raise but which were the expected defense of this august tribunal, whose authority, already shaky, was soon to succumb under Pericles.[6] Among the traditions relative to Oedipus, Sophocles preferred to choose those that most bring to light the piety of the Athenians, the gentleness of their mores, and their respect for suppliants.[7] One of his tragedies[8] has for its goal nothing but to celebrate Theseus, the favorite hero of Athens, and to better justify his praises the poet puts maxims of moderation and morality in the mouth of the son of Aegeus that the Theseus of ancient fables most assuredly did not profess.[9] This is not to say that the unsuitability did not have its advantages. If these allusions

6. *Oedipus at Colonus.*

7. *Eumenides*, 684–713.

8. *Oedipus at Colonus*, 901, 902, 961, 966, 1155, 1007.

9. The enthusiasm of the Athenians for Theseus caused them to tolerate the most absurd anachronisms. In the portrait of the battle of Marathon by Polygnotus, Theseus takes part in this battle (Pausan., *Attica*, 15). A fact that shows how much the tragedians garbled history to please the crowd is that Menelaus, grave, prudent, valorous in Homer, is both cowardly and cruel in all the Athenian tragedies; this is an effect of the hatred of Athenians for Sparta; and, to complete this case, the plays in which Menelaus is constantly injured are at the same time filled with invectives against Spartan customs (see the *Andromache* of Euripides, 595–601, 444–53). In order to make his allusions more striking, the poet commits an anachronism.

that alter the historical truth reflect badly on the century of the hero, they present the century of the author quite positively.

Aeschylus flourished about the same time as Pindar. Religion, however, appears much less improved in the tragedies of the former than in the odes of the latter. If we grant an implicit faith to his *Prometheus*, we would go back to the *Iliad*. The dominant thought of this drama, which sparkles with severe beauties and is so frightening in its conception, is the hatred of Jupiter for man.[10] This master of thunder is cruel, pitiless, ungrateful, treacherous, and brutal, even in his loves.[11] Olympus is represented as his prey.[12] He governs it by terrible laws that he alone has made, threatening with his spear the gods he has overturned.[13] He is a usurper newly established on a throne he attained by parricide;[14] he is detested by the other gods;[15] antiquity yields to his arbitrary decrees and bends while groaning under his culpable will,[16] because, says Aeschylus, a new master is always harsh.[17] The gods in this play are so similar to mortals that the fall of Jupiter is announced as desirable and possible.[18] The language of Prometheus is that of a defeated faction in a political revolution.[19] He defies the son of Saturn as able to rule only temporarily.[20] The times will change, he cries, they will teach Jupiter himself to know unhappiness.[21] Have I not seen two sovereigns chased from the empire of the heavens?[22] Jupiter, bearing the burden of the paternal curse,[23] will lose in turn this empire at the hand of one of his children,[24] and I prefer to suffer, chained on this rock, than to be his slave.[25]

---

10. Aeschylus, *Prometheus*, 9, 11, 28, 82, 83, 120, 123, 238, 233, 944, 945.
11. Ibid., 304, 306, 734, 737, 893, 905, 1090, 1093.
12. Ibid., 149, 151, 310.
13. Ibid., 403–6.
14. Ibid., 199, 203, 909, 911.
15. Ibid., 1003.
16. Ibid., 149–51.
17. Ibid., 34–35.
18. Ibid., 162–66.
19. Ibid., 199–223.
20. Ibid., 937–39.
21. Ibid., 980.
22. Ibid., 955–58.
23. Ibid., 909–14.
24. Ibid., 759, 967, 906, 926.
25. Ibid., 967–68.

Even in the other tragedies of Aeschylus, the gods are always ready to betray their worshippers.[26] They employ ruse and lying against man.[27] They leave cities when they are taken;[28] and they are retained only by the force of sacrifices.[29] When he puts on his cloak of purple, Agamemnon fears that so much splendor might excite their jealousy.

But to judge Aeschylus properly, one must bring his personal character into the discussion. His impetuous, sometimes wild genius naturally orients him to the most stormy periods of religion and, consequently, the most dramatic. He seems to regret the chaos from which he is sadly compelled to depart. Those cosmogonic forces, teeming in the abyss, impatient to bring forth, as well as to engulf, what they have produced, those terrifying shocks, those struggles of nature, those unbridled passions, transported into the moral world as a legacy of the former disorder of the physical world, please this powerful imagination, which feels strong enough to dominate them; a Titan himself, Aeschylus loves to measure himself vis-à-vis the Titans.

Add republican ideas to these personal traits. Aeschylus composed his tragedies at the time when the king of Persia at the head of a million slaves once again threatened to invade Greece; and the poet whose arm had fought valiantly for his country at Marathon reproduced in his verses that horror for servitude and that love of liberty that had inspired his own exploits.

Hence that proud and restless disposition that influenced his private life as well as his works, and which led him far from that Athens which he had defended when a literary defeat rendered that place hateful to him.[30] This attitude manifests itself not only in his conceptions but in his abrupt, staccato style, often harsh and even bizarre. The aftershock of the storm continued even when the storm began to ebb. The same character marks the splendors with which Aeschylus accompanied his dramatic representations. These colossal splendors bear the mark of a gigantic universe. The terrible effect produced by the appearance of the Furies upon the women who attended the spectacle is well known.[31]

26. *The Seven against Thebes*, 105, 107, 172, 176.

27. *The Persians*, 93–101.

28. *The Seven against Thebes*, 223–24.

29. Ibid., 76, 77, 186, 187, 309, 310.

30. He was defeated by Sophocles, in the judgment of Cimon and the nine generals, his colleagues, named by the head archon to judge between the two rivals (Plut., *Life of Cimon*).

31. Some have denied the presence of women in the theaters of the ancients. However, an anecdote found in a passage of Plato (*De leg.*) where he speaks of the ardent taste of female Athenians for

And yet, one should note, his century obliges our poet to depict a gentler religion and gods who are more just. These Titans, these monsters with one hundred arms and one hundred heads, contemporary opinion forced him to disarm them and to offer to the Greeks who heard him less hideous forms and better idols. Almost despite himself, he made these longtime unconquered powers serve the triumph of eternal justice; and these divinities, once terribly feared, become benevolent toward the men they previously pursued with unbridled hostility.

One must not consider each tragedy of Aeschylus in isolation. The combination of several is necessary to form a complete whole.

Agamemnon, for example, the *Libation Bearers*, and the *Eumenides* composed a trilogy destined to show, first of all, crime triumphant, then this crime punished by another crime; finally, the expiation of this last one putting an end to the calamities and misdeeds of the family of Atreus.

In the same way, the *Prometheus* that we possess is only one-third of the story of Prometheus. Aeschylus had presented him as the benefactor of the human race, then as persecuted by the gods, angry at the favors he had granted mortals, and *Prometheus Unbound* ends this drama by showing this hero set free by Hercules, and with him making peace with Jupiter and with men, those he protected.

These trilogies seem to us the obvious expression of the development of Greek polytheism, since in the same poet traditions succeed one another, always less crude than the previous, because of the mores that grow gentler and the ideas that become more refined. In this way, what was a contradiction in Hesiod is a progress in Aeschylus, and we understand that after having offered to our eyes the acts of violence of the Homeric gods in their frightening starkness, the same author places morality under the aegis of these improved gods. The divinity that mortals call Justice is the daughter of Jupiter.[32] In vain do the guilty flatter themselves that the gods neglect human affairs;[33] on the contrary, their Providence watches over the house of virtuous men;[34] and the prayers of the wicked are powerless to alter them.[35] It is an ancient and sacred law that blood that darkens the earth demands

---

tragedy, and the article of Pollux on *spectatrices*, proves that they were not excluded. They were probably excluded from comedies.

32. *Choeph.*, 949–51; *The Suppliants*, 365.
33. *Agamemnon*, 378–81.
34. *Suppl.*, 28, 29, 386, 389.
35. *Choeph.*, 858–59.

and obtains blood.[36] No one exchanges innocence for crime with impunity.[37] Finally, the song in which the Furies announce the evils that will be spread over the world if someone disheartens them and they no longer punish misdeeds, is a poetic plea in favor of the support that religion gives to morality, because, says the poet, crimes against men are the inevitable consequence of impiety toward the gods.[38]

If it is true, as Quintilian recounts, that the Athenians, still finding some revolting things in Aeschylus, had authorized later poets to correct his plays, when they allowed them, thus corrected, to compete with those of living authors,[39] this would be another explanation of the different maxims that are found in them; but this explanation would lead to the same result.

Study attentively the Minerva of Aeschylus in order to compare it with previous ones and you will see the progression. There are three Minervas in Greek religion: that of the *Iliad*, that of the *Odyssey*, that of Aeschylus in the *Eumenides*. The latter is the ideal-type of the gods, such as the progress of knowledge had constructed it, as Theseus in Sophocles is the ideal-type of the hero.

When one passes from Aeschylus to Sophocles, one believes he has come to a more serene sky and breathes purer air. One experiences a confidence in the immortals not found until then. Sophocles is the most religious poet of antiquity: he has all the grace of India, with the purity of taste of Greece. In reading *Oedipus at Colonus* and *Antigone*, one feels reconciled, as it were, with polytheism, so majestic are his forms, his morality noble and elevated, his teachings useful and, we would say, almost reasonable.[40]

Nature in Sophocles extends her harmony and calm; order and measure reign everywhere. If, despite himself, the poet is sometimes led to traditions that are

36. Ibid., 398–402; *Suppl.*, 418–21.

37. Ibid., 118–19.

38. *Suppl.*, 536–37. We could have multiplied proofs to infinity. The Erynis Fury punishes crime (*Choeph.*, 649–50). Erynis who slowly punishes ravishers (*Agamemn.*, 58–59). The gods do not forget those who commit murders. Finally, the dark Furies pursue him who has become happy by crime (*Agam.*, 469–70). If I deliver you, you who have sought refuge in the temples of the gods, I fear to raise against me a terrible avenger who will never leave me, even after my death, when I am in the netherworld (*Suppl.*, 418–21).

39. On this subject, the Athenians said that Aeschylus had won more prizes after his death than during his life.

40. This impression had to have been very profound, because Mr. de La Harpe, of all critics the one who is the most removed from the moral sense of antiquity, could not prevent himself from feeling it.

injurious to the gods, he hastens either to soften them or to add some words that excuse or apologize for them. Hercules still kills his host, but Jupiter grows angry.[41] We have previously noted[42] that the crime of Hercules had only provoked the indignation of Homer, not of Jupiter, in the *Iliad*.

The chorus, which is always the organ of public opinion, in Sophocles never fails to celebrate the fairness of the gods while exalting their omnipotence.[43] It promises Electra that Jupiter, whose eye nothing escapes, will punish her oppressors;[44] the guilty, it says, are infallibly struck by the vengeance of the celestial Themis;[45] Pluto, Proserpina, Mercury, the Furies with foaming dogs everywhere pursue homicide and adultery.[46] Jupiter is the father of the laws that make the happiness of men.[47] As soon as the immortals, vigilant and just, perceive misdeeds, they prepare their punishment;[48] and if Polynices is unpunished, it is because their gaze has not yet turned toward this rebellious son.[49]

If Sophocles sometimes seems to return to less refined opinions, this step back applies more to rituals than to maxims. The same as in Aeschylus, Clytemnestra mutilates the body of Agamemnon, whom she just murdered, in order to avoid the anger of his manes;[50] in Sophocles she wipes the bloody iron she withdrew from his breast with the hair of her spouse so that his blood would fall upon his head;[51] Oedipus plucks out his eyes so as not to see his father and his mother in the other life.[52] In these details one recognizes the customs of primitive tribes. In the *Alcestis* of Euripides the infernal gods still drink the blood of funeral victims,[53] which is only a slight modification of Homer's description, which makes the shadows drink blood. Finally, an even stranger thing, in Virgil, Deiphobus,

41. *Trachin.*, 38. If, as several critics have thought, the *Trachiniae* was falsely attributed to Sophocles, this circumstance would explain even better the slight difficulty that could embarrass the reader.

42. Bk. VII, ch. 10.

43. *Electra*, 472–515.

44. Ibid., 175–78.

45. Ibid., 1065.

46. Ibid., 110–15.

47. *Oedipus the King*, 865–68.

48. Ibid., 863–910.

49. *Oed. at Col.*, 1370–71.

50. *Choeph.*, 437.

51. *Electra*, 445–46.

52. *Oedipus the King*, 1371–73.

53. *Alcest.*, 844–45.

whose nose, ears, and hands the Greeks had cut off, hides himself, ashamed of appearing thus disfigured in the underworld.[54] In man there is a constant struggle: habits, memories, the entire past attach to him, obstructing his path to the future; but he nonetheless follows this path, and the prolonging of rituals, material forms that are preserved after opinions are modified, only apparently belies the change that has occurred.

At first sight, nothing appears more revolting than the second scene of *Ajax*, where Minerva basely scorns his misfortune, and where Ulysses, whom she protects, shows the most ignoble signs of a laughable cowardice. But with what admirable art the poet effaces this impression, to replace it with a more satisfying and more moral lesson, when Ulysses, the enemy of Ajax, demands from the angered Greeks the burial of the fallen hero, his own victim! This is moderation, the forgetting of injury, pity for the unfortunate, respect for the dead; these are all the generous sentiments personified and sanctioned by religion, under the auspices of Minerva.

This remarkable measure, these subtle improvements, shine forth even more in the depiction of the Furies. Aeschylus presents them to the spectators' eyes as fierce and covered in blood, and it is not until after expiation has disarmed them that the human race breathes safely.[55] Sophocles hides them from the spectators' eyes. He even spares their ears these frightening names. Poetic circumlocutions replace them. In Aeschylus, these divinities emerge from the netherworld, inexorable and pitiless. In Sophocles, they retire to the depths of a sacred wood. The scented breath of the wind appeases them; they rest in silence until new duties rouse their activity against the inhabitants of the earth.[56]

The received notions concerning the justice of the gods, even though admitted and professed by Aeschylus, enter less well into his works and compose much less of a uniform whole than in the tragedies of Sophocles. The poet speaks without any scruple of the crimes of the gods. Morality is a theory that practice still con-

54. *Aeneid*, VI, 495–97.

55. In one place he even depicts them as being held in horror by the gods and men. Here one recognizes the confused and dual mythology of Hesiod.

56. The temple of the Furies was constructed in Athens at the time of Solon, by the order of Epimenides (Dupuis, *Des mystères*, 120–89). Athens was the city in Greece where the Furies were the most revered, perhaps because religion developed there more rapidly and united in a more intimate way with morality than anywhere else. The Furies were the protectors of the Areopagus, and they were invoked immediately after Jupiter the savior and Apollo (Staeudlin, *Rel. Mag.*, pp. 491–92).

tradicts. The formidable tribunal that we have sought in vain in Homer and which we have seen established in Pindar is also sanctioned by the two tragedians; but everything is frightening in Aeschylus. Pluto, the powerful judge of mortals, exercises a belated vengeance in the underworld.[57] It is always only a matter of the torment of the perverse. In Sophocles, Antigone hopes for the felicity of the just: the friendship of the shades, she says to the timorous Ismene, will be more lasting to me than the favor of the living.[58]

In Aeschylus, the gods make themselves feared; in Sophocles, they make themselves loved; this is incontestable progress, this movement from fear to love. Religion identifies itself with the poetry of Sophocles much more than that of Aeschylus. The latter makes it emerge threatening from the dark night; it casts sudden flames in the midst of thunder and lightning. The former by means of harmonious shades associates it with the day-star; the blue of the sky is more brilliant, without being less serene. If we could dare to venture a rather profane comparison, we would say that Aeschylus is the Old Testament of polytheism, while Sophocles is the Gospel.

Even when the goal of the two poets is identical, their means differ. Aeschylus in *Eumenides*, as much as Sophocles in *Oedipus at Colonus*, works to represent Athens as the guardian of the laws, the privileged residence of a superior race, the boulevard before which unjust power halts, the sanctuary where involuntary crime is expiated or crime repents. But in the first, the gods pronounce a decree cast in nearly judicial forms; in the second, the supremacy of the city of Minerva penetrates more slowly, but more profoundly, to the depths of the soul by a series of religious sentiments and emotions, which a miracle completes, without interrupting and troubling them.

Aeschylus appears to be the rebellious slave of his century. Sophocles is its noble interpreter, always faithful and scrupulous; and by a privilege that unfortunately is too rare, the career of this great poet was worthy of his talent. Citizen of the most enlightened country of the ancient world, endowed with the advantages of birth, fortune, and beauty, he attained all honors, he conquered all glories. Chosen in his adolescence to celebrate, at the head of his young companions, the victory of Salamis; in his maturity, he was pontiff and general, colleague of Pericles and Thucydides; he defended, hallowed, and glorified his country. While the irascible

---

57. *Choeph.*, 321, 326, 379, 380.
58. *Antigone*, 80–82.

Aeschylus, like the greedy Pindar, sought the patronage of a tyrant, Sophocles rejected the invitations of barbarous kings.[59] When it reached him, old age itself seemed to respect him. It came alone, without the ugly entourage of infirmities that usually accompanies it. For Sophocles, the ingratitude of his children was only the occasion of a new triumph. One would say that the gods of this polytheism that he rendered so noble and so pure expressed respect and gratitude to him, so much did they lavish their favors upon him. The most striking of these benefits was, doubtless, to spare him the painful spectacle of the decline of his homeland: hardly had his eyes closed when liberty perished in Athens at the hands of foreigners, and the fierce Spartans prevented the body of the poet being buried in the tomb of his ancestors.

To judge polytheism in its childhood, one must turn to the *Iliad*;[60] in order to see its first developments, one must read Hesiod. Aeschylus shows us religion in its successive purifications, although still contested, and if we want to know it in its perfection, it is above all Sophocles who must be consulted.

59. Plutarch (*Life of Pompey*) has preserved for us these two verses from him: "Whoever does not avoid the palaces of kings can enter them free, but will remain there a slave."

60. After having compared Homer with the poets who followed him, we could have compared him with the painters who drew the subjects of their works from his poems. We would have found new proofs of the change of opinions. Even though Pirithous and Theseus are spoken of in the eleventh book of the *Odyssey*, it is not said that they suffer any punishments; but in his painting of the descent of Ulysses (see bk. VIII, ch. 3, n. 15) Polygnotus depicts these heroes chained to thrones expiating their impiety and adulteries (Pausan., *Phocide*, 28–29 and 30). Polygnotus's painting was exposed in the *lesché* of Delphi (the *lesché* was the place in each city where the citizens assembled). The same painter in the same painting represents several guilty being punished under the bark of Charon, while nothing similar is found in the ancient poet; these additions could not have been suggested to the painter except by the ideas of his time.

CHAPTER 8

On Euripides

At first, we had intended not to speak of Euripides: he is such an unfaithful painter of Greek religion, an author so foreign to all precision and scruple, that we believed we should not invoke his testimony on almost any point. As a consequence, far from being pleased with the perfections of religion, he loves to exaggerate its weak sides. Nonetheless, the reader would have reproached us with leaving a lacuna, and we have not wished to merit this criticism. But in order to show with how much distrust one must consider this third Greek tragedian, and what sorts of light he can shed on some details, we first of all have to speak of his individual character, the circumstances of his private life, of the talent that nature had given him, and the application of this talent to tragedy.

The history of dramatic art in Greece, even though confined, as we have observed earlier, to a very short span of time, can be divided into three periods. During the first, genius advanced rapidly and impetuously in its career, but without a determinate direction. During the second, it profited from the experiences and mistakes of its predecessors. During the third, the need for novelty making itself felt, it worked haphazardly, seeking for ways of display. Aeschylus and Sophocles correspond to the first two periods, Euripides to the third.

By itself alone, this circumstance must make his portraits unfaithful, but his particular character adds to the influence of this general cause.

Euripides possessed several brilliant qualities: eloquence, imagination, an extreme mobility, which often resembled sensibility, a remarkable flexibility, a powerful and profound irony: under this last aspect, *Medea* is a chef d'oeuvre. Her scene with Jason,[1] her bitterness with the old man that a confused instinct

---

1. *Medea*, 873–900.

warns to protect her children against her,[2] her return to maternal love when she is ready to seize the iron that is to sacrifice them,[3] even today move the reader to the depths of his soul, even in the absence of dramatic representation. But to these gifts of nature Euripides joined a restless spirit, an unlimited vanity, an excessive appetite for applause, a not-so-sure and not-so-delicate sentiment of appropriateness. The truth of mores, opinions, and customs seemed to him to be subordinate objects. The ancient traditions seemed to him the poet's property; and more than once he treated them as such.[4]

We would be tempted to believe that he at first wanted to devote himself to public affairs, even though antiquity tells us nothing specific in the regard. He was practiced in the art of oratory, and his constant allusions against the orators, demagogues, democracy, the people of Athens — in a word, against all the institutions of his homeland — bespeak a pride that has been crossed. The defects, the pretensions, even the qualities of Euripides opposed themselves to success in the career of political ambition. But he probably renounced it only with difficulty; and, in fact, who in a free State can painlessly renounce the suffrages of his fellow citizens, the pleasures of power, the pleasures of popularity? It is something else entirely when a single man governs. Then it is only the opinion of a single man that one resigns oneself to not winning, and one is consoled by that thought.

Whatever may be the case with these initial desires and first regrets of Euripides, what is sure is that before devoting himself to literature properly speaking, he appears to have wanted to devote himself to philosophy. For some time he was the disciple of Anaxagoras and Archelaus; but he soon enough left abstract (and exhausting) studies, either because he was frightened by the persecutions that Anaxagoras had experienced or because he was seduced by the hope of more immediate and boisterous applause, which dramatic compositions promised to earn him. He retained from his philosophical studies only the habit of formulating axioms, which he placed in the mouths of his characters at every opportunity. For the rest, he brought into his literary works a constantly bitter and discontented disposition; equivocal successes confirmed him in it. Author of at least seventy-five

---

2. Ibid., 901–31.

3. Ibid., 1002–80.

4. The Corinthians, for example, if we believe ancient scholiasts, seduced and for a sum of five talents engaged him to attribute to Medea the murder of her children, whom the inhabitants of this city had stoned (schol. Eurip., in *Medea*, 9; Ael., *Var. Hist.*, V, 21; Pausan., *Corinth*, 3).

plays, he won at most four or five times.[5] Not only was he crushed by the memory of Sophocles's superiority, but he encountered rivals who often defeated him.[6] The biting mockeries of Aristophanes pursued and humiliated him. It is said that domestic embarrassments added to the sufferings of his vanity, and that the infidelity of a wife was the cause of his hatred and invectives against women. Finally, he died far from his country,[7] which rendered only a belated and useless homage to his memory.

The march of the human spirit is always the same; one finds the same three periods of tragedy among us, with Corneille, Racine, and Voltaire. But Corneille is nonetheless quite different from Aeschylus, Racine from Sophocles, and Voltaire is not Euripides.[8]

Euripides and Voltaire always have a goal different from perfection in their works. Both generously sow misplaced generalities.[9] At every opportunity, they allude to contemporary customs, religion, and politics. In a play whose subject precedes by eight centuries the Peloponnesian War, the Greek author alludes to the alliance of the Argives with the Spartiates;[10] later, he insults the orators,[11] demagogues, and democracy, things that did not yet exist when Adrastus reigned over Argos. Elsewhere, he enters into an unexpected digression on popular power and monarchy.[12] Also elsewhere, the same Theseus that Sophocles had already embellished, and who, victor over monsters and brigands, could only have known the barbarous state, retraces in splendid verses the philosophical history of civilization.[13]

Euripides could have made a tragedy like the *Tancrède*; that is, in the same play he could have combined a passionate sensibility with the rage for maxims and declamations that led Voltaire to put in the mouth of a girl when she learns that her lover seeks death in the midst of battle, a dissertation on the rights of women

---

5. Aul. Gell., *Noct. att.*, XVII, 4.

6. Agathon, for example.

7. At the court of Archelaus, king of Macedon.

8. See bk. VII, ch. 3.

9. Ideas on life and old age; Eurip., *Suppl.*, 1064, 1097, 1080, 113; digression on youth, *Herc. Fur.*, 637, 652, 627, 254.

10. *Suppl.*, 1094, 1093, 1181, 1182.

11. Ibid., 734, 738, 744, 749, 864, 865, 879, 880.

12. Ibid., 339, 343–50, 353, 471, 493.

13. *Bacchants*, 249, 252, 270, 271.

and on the injustice that produces, at the end, independence. It is thus that in *Hecuba*,[14] this unfortunate mother asking Ulysses for the life of her daughter, and later crying over the death of Polixena, she stops to examine the influence of education on youth.[15]

If we did not fear to depart too much from our subject, we would notice many other connections between Euripides and Voltaire; both end their tragedies with moral reflections, which indicate the need to declare a result suited to capture applause.[16] In the French author, as in the Greek, the characters do not speak to and between themselves, but for the public. Nature and truth are constantly sacrificed to this aim. Menelaus in Egypt, bringing the false news of his own death to the king of this country, never answers his questions in the way that he reasonably should. His language is full of affected equivocations that run counter to his situation. He only has in mind the spectators who listen to him; and in order to please them he risks his own safety, which is to say, all plausibility.[17] Orestes in *Electra*, arriving disguised (because outlawed) on the stage, meditating the revenge of his father and killing his mother, and in thirty verses covering the different states of life,[18] recalls for us Alzire and the treatise she uttered on suicide when her lover had just murdered her husband.

Sophocles having composed, as had Euripides, an *Electra*, the comparison of the two plays is quite suitable to show the difference between the two poets. In Sophocles, parricide is the effect of an irresistible destiny. In Euripides, this parricide is premeditated; one discusses it on the stage, because Euripides never can turn down a discussion, and this preliminary examination makes the crime a thousand times more revolting.

Voltaire and Euripides have, in general, attacked religion, and both have sought tragic effects in religion itself, the object of their mockeries. Euripides seems to have composed his *Bacchae*[19] to solidify the triumph of the most fanatical superstition, forgetting that elsewhere he touted unbelief. This is how Voltaire made *Alzire* and *Zaïre*; and, for the comparison to be even more complete, the Greek

14. *Hecub.*, 254–57.

15. *Ibid.*, 592–602.

16. *Ion*, 1595–96, 1621, 1622.

17. *Helen.*

18. *Electra*, 263–90.

19. The ancients believed that he had profited very much from a play by Aeschylus on the same subject, a play that has not come down to us.

poet in a play destined to show how terrible the punishments of the gods against impiety are, cannot stop himself from irreligious references;[20] in the same way Voltaire begins his Christian tragedy by these famous verses, so philosophical and so out of place:

> By the Ganges, I was a slave to false gods,
> Christian in Paris, Muslim in these environs.

The plays of Euripides, like those of Voltaire, most of the time are only pretexts for his dominant idea; even his sensibility is subordinated to his systematic intention. The philosopher constantly does battle with the poet, and from it result the implausibilities that destroy all poetic illusion, and, more often, a certain monotony in the characters, as well as constantly returning to the same ideas; in a word, the absence of that dramatic impartiality without which art never arrives at its perfection. All literature that has a goal outside itself is perhaps more useful, more effective, as a means, but it is always less perfect than literature that has itself as its own goal.

The tragedy of *Oedipus the King* in Sophocles, and that of the *Bacchae* in Euripides, have the same tendency. Their outcome is to give an example of the infallibility of oracles and the danger of lacking in respect for the immortals. Destiny attests to the veracity of the gods, says Creon to Oedipus; this is the moral of the play. The same conclusion emerges from the fortune of Pentheus in the *Bacchae*. But these tragedies differ because the character of their authors differs. Sophocles had fulfilled the most important functions, both military and civil, and this practice of life had taught him measure and had imposed gravity. He was thoroughly imbued with respect for religion and love for the constitution of his country. Euripides, whose spirit had not received the education of affairs, grasped only the inconveniences of all institutions. Unbeliever, he could not take up religious language without falling into fanaticism. Sophocles brings to *Oedipus the King* all the seriousness, all the calm, of conviction. Not having conviction, Euripides has no measure. In the *Bacchae* he gives himself to ardor, to inconsistency, to the exaggerations of a man who was never instructed by the sentiment he experiences, of the effect it produces. One can note, albeit to a lesser degree because Voltaire had more taste than Euripides, the same difference between *Athalie* and *Zaïre*.[21] A

20. See the entire scene of Bacchus with Pentheus, *Bacch.*, 910–74.

21. Plutarch reports an anecdote quite suited to convince us of Euripides's indifference concerning the views he ascribed to his characters, and the little connection he established between these views

quite strange thing! The unbelief of Euripides does not preserve him from abusing the miraculous. Of the eighteen tragedies that remain to us, nine end with the appearance of a god on the scene.

The defects of Euripides do not owe, as do those of Aeschylus, to ignorance of the art or the remnants of a barely subdued barbarism. They essentially belong to his ambitious and affected conceptions. They are digressions without connection with the subject, descriptions of a length that destroys all plausibility, allusions that deprive his plays of all historical or local color, epigrams that become absurd in the mouth of his characters. It is against the orators that Hippolyta utters a sally.[22] Orestes loses himself in round-about attacks against the government of Athens.[23] In the midst of her lamentations Andromache interrupts herself and declaims: it is always the obsession of women to have on their lips the pain that torments them, and to fill the air with their woes.[24]

When Aeschylus disappoints us, he has his defense in the memories of mores that once existed. But what shocks us in Euripides belongs to the customs of no nation. Hecuba describing the caresses that Cassandra, her daughter, the slave of Agamemnon, lavishes upon this destroyer of Troy,[25] Admetus with ignoble harshness reproaching his father for not wanting to die in his place,[26] are inexcusable things, whether as depicting nature or depicting manners.

One would believe that the more that authors aim to please the public, the more they ought to perfect the entirety of their works; this, however, is not true. When their sole aim is to cause an effect, they work with only half a pen, as it were, and take care only over the parts that immediately captivate the audience. This, however, is a false move. In order to durably dominate the multitude in literature (as well as in politics), often the surest path is to disdain them.

Like the poems of our day, the plot is sacrificed to episodes and descriptions; like ours, in the tragedies of Euripides the essential is sacrificed to the accidental. The expositions are almost always wretched. I make an exception only for *Andro-*

and their role. He had begun the tragedy of Menalippus with verses that seemed to call into doubt the divinity of Jupiter. The Athenians having displayed their disapproval by murmuring, he immediately substituted verses that expressed a contrary view (Plut., in *Amat.*).

22. *Hippol.*, 486–87.
23. *Orestes*, 885–952.
24. *Andromache*, 92–94.
25. *Hecuba*, 814–32.
26. *Alcestis*, 629–70.

mache, which in other respects is one of the weakest tragedies of this writer. But the exposition is clear and natural, and from the first verses lets it be known what the different characters are to contribute. The choruses, however, hardly have any relationship to the subject. One would say that the poet himself felt this. Euripides displays more defiance toward them than Sophocles. Sometimes the characters threaten them with death if they betray them, sometimes they make them a thousand promises to win them to silence. Sophocles does none of this, because his choruses are an integral part of his plays. Euripides, on the contrary, without even knowing it, constantly puts himself on guard against them because they are intruders, as it were, who appear on the stage only to declaim.[27]

If here were the place to prove how much Euripides departs from the true character of antiquity, we would limit ourselves to citing some aspects of his play *Cyclops*. This play is a collection of impieties, indecencies, intellectual witticisms, and revolting immorality.[28] In a way, it is the *Jeanne d'Arc* of the Greeks, and this is a new similarity of Euripides to Voltaire.

The defects of Euripides do not inspire that curious interest that buoys us in reading the ancient authors, whose very imperfections are instructive because they bear the imprint of their century and their country. The defects of Euripides are shocking, like those of a modern author.

However, it is perhaps for this very reason that we judge Euripides more favorably than he appears to have been judged in his own time. As often happens in the world, this is one more vice that earns him our indulgence. Of all the Greek tragedians he is the least national, and consequently the most like our ideas.

With talent, spirit, alacrity, learning, and verve, one can equal Euripides. But one could put together all the writers who have existed since the rebirth of letters, and probably all those who will exist, and you would not produce a Sophocles. We do not mean to say, as some writers today claim, that the human race deteriorates; but the circumstances of moderns do not produce in them the exquisite sentiment of ideal beauty with which the climate, institutions, and religion of Greece filled all its inhabitants. Our languages are more imperfect, our social order less natural, our calculations narrower, our existence simultaneously more monotonous in its march and more troubled in its egoism: in a word, the entirety of our nature is less

27. Sophocles committed this fault only once, when in *Oedipus the King* the chorus asks in a hymn (which is otherwise quite beautiful) what god gave birth to Oedipus, since he is not the son of Polybius, while everything demonstrates that he is Laius's son.

28. See especially verses 315–45.

poetic. To be sure, this is not an evil: the Greeks owed a part of their poetry to their leisure, their leisure to slavery, which trampled underfoot a proscribed race and denigrated mechanical labor. We prefer to have fewer poets, and not to have more slaves.

The reader will pardon us this digression on Euripides if he reflects that it was necessary to explain the confusion relating to religious opinions that reigns in his works; he covers the entire circle of these opinions, mixes them, and combines them without any regard for the truth of the custom, or for the integrity of characters. If in order to understand Antiquity we possessed only the tragedies of Euripides, it would be impossible for us to see any light in such chaos.

This poet is inexact in small as well as large things. He attributes the usages of his contemporaries and compatriots to all peoples and all times. To take an example at random, he has Medea say that a woman who wants to have a spouse ought to bring him a dowry of considerable riches.[29] This was the Athenian custom at the time of Euripides; but in the heroic ages, hence the time of Medea, men did not obtain their wives except by magnificent gifts. In his tragedy of *Rhesus*, the catastrophe is connected to the presumption of Hector;[30] while in the *Iliad*, Hector is anything but presumptuous.

Sophocles also sometimes changes the character of ancient heroes; but he does so in order to improve and ennoble them. In *Oedipus at Colonus*, Theseus speaks of himself with a reserve and modesty that are in contrast to the self-vaunting of Homer's heroes. Finding in Homer a noble and consistent character, Euripides was unable to remain faithful to this character. What Sophocles did well, Euripides did poorly.

Therefore, as we said at the beginning of this chapter, Euripides is a very unsure witness to the real state of Greek religion at the time when he composed his numerous tragedies. However, in analyzing them carefully one can see in them, through the inconsistencies and inexactnesses of the poet, incontestable proof of the progress of this religion. "I would believe the gods are mad," says Clytemnestra, "if I dared to beseech them for a murderer. What prayer would the murderer of her children dare address to the immortals?"[31] Behold: the efficacy of prayers subor-

---

29. *Medea*, 215–24.

30. Several critics claim that *Rhesus* is not by Euripides. But this tragedy, if it is not by him, is certainly from his school. It has the same defects as his plays, some of his beauties, and is composed according to the same principles.

31. *Iphig. in Aul.*, 1185–90.

dinated to the moral value of actions. When Helen wants to justify her adultery to herself by blaming it on destiny, and on the omnipotence that Venus exercises over the gods themselves, Hecuba accuses her of calumny: "The gods," she says to her, "are not at all the authors of your errant ways; they have not given you a pernicious example. The divinity that seduced you is your own treacherous heart and your mad passion."[32] This is almost Socrates's response to Euthyphro when the latter justified himself for having accused his father, saying that Jupiter punished Saturn.

In this way, reason struggles at each instant against the ancient fables. Hercules rejects all the traditions that are unfavorable to the gods.[33] Euripides recalls them, however; but it is not out of respect, but from hostility: "Phoebus commanded you to murder," says Menelaus to Orestes, "you counted on his assistance. He delays now, following the custom of those that are named the immortals."[34] Apollo, whom Pyrrhus has offended, causes him to die at Delphi; and the messenger who recounts this event observes that the god recalled an old quarrel and, like a wicked man, revenged himself. "Can we," he adds, "after this action, regard him as just or wise?"[35] "O gods!" cries Hecuba, "I invoke, it is true, treacherous allies; but there is a shadow of hope in praying to the immortals when misfortune has struck."[36] Polynices asks Juno, Eteocles, and Minerva to kill his brother.[37] The heart of Jupiter is full of envy against Rhesus,[38] and in the *Oresteia* this same envy is mercilessly unleashed against all the happy.[39]

But these reminiscences are not a step back toward belief; they are a step forward toward irreligion. The works of Euripides are the first in which unbelief took on public and popular forms. And in the same way that Aeschylus shows us the struggle between the ancient fables and morality in original polytheism, Euripides presents us the struggle between a polytheism that has become moral and unbelief. In the *Phoenician Women*, he attributes impious words to the most virtuous character of the play, Antigone.[40] Sophocles never would have committed this mistake.

32. *Troj. Women*, 971–82.
33. *Herc. Fur.*, 1341–46.
34. *Orestes*, 419–20.
35. *Androm.*, 1161–65.
36. *Troj. Women*, 469–71.
37. *Phoenician Women*, 1374–85.
38. *Rhesus*, 456–58.
39. *Orestes*, 340–44.
40. *Phoen. Women*, 1717–18.

The three periods are displayed well enough by the three *Electra*s of the tragedians. In the *Electra* of Aeschylus,[41] fate dominates religion; in Sophocles's, morality allies with it; in Euripides's, this morality becomes a counterargument.

Let us briefly summarize: Euripides, like Hesiod, brings together or confuses doctrines of different times, but for a different reason. Hesiod had found himself between two periods of the religious belief of his country. Euripides wrote when this belief was heading toward its fall. As a consequence, the first drew indiscriminately from opinions that were not yet destroyed and those that were not yet established; the second made use indifferently of all these opinions, because all were equally discredited.

41. Otherwise named the *Choephori*.

CHAPTER 9

A Few Words on Aristophanes

Aristophanes, the sole Greek comic poet who has come down to us, is no less necessary to study than the tragedians. Taken literally, or badly understood, his plays would provide powerful objections to the perfections effected in religion. He represents the gods of Greece as vicious, depraved, ridiculous; and these outrageous portraits, tolerated by the magistrates, received popular applause.

Several causes explain this singularity.

First of all, Greek tragedy had drawn its origin from the serious part of the religion; comedy owed its birth to the grotesque part of the worship, a part transmitted to the Greeks, as we have already said, by the importation of priestly orgies. For we have already noted that buffoonery and license were a characteristic trait of religions subject to priests; they deprive their slaves of all elevated pleasures, and as compensation, brutalize them.

There is something similar in the mystery plays of the Christians of the Middle Ages. Nothing is more audacious, more satirical against the most revered objects; devotion, however, reigned without rival and did not see in these burlesque dramas a profanation of sacred things.

Perhaps a more profound idea presided over these imitations that seem sacrilegious to us. The evil principle, impure matter, struggling against heaven, in these parodies became clownish beings, misshapen in form, vicious in their irony, gay, but of a treacherous or obscene sort.

One must acknowledge this: in gaiety, when it is not the simple development of childish joys, in irony especially, there is something that approaches vice; everything that is good is grave; virtue, affection, courage, the happiness that comes from peace of the soul, are serious things. In the priestly religions, gaiety has often represented the principle of evil. In our civilized societies today, does it not more than ever represent it?

We do not directly apply these observations to the poet with whom we are now occupied. He himself probably did not know what heritage he employed; but we think that these memories of foreign borrowings, even though rejected by the popular worship, could have prepared the Athenians to be somewhat indulgent toward a senseless gaiety that had the authority of a tradition.

Let us add to this preservation of ancient usages the character of the Athenian people, for whom mockery was a need and who believed that the gods, like them, enjoyed wit. No less than the poets, sculptors and painters added features to the mythological accounts that undermined their gravity. On an ancient vase we see Jupiter and Mars in satirical masks, climbing into Alcmene's chamber by means of a ladder.

In second place, the plays of Aristophanes were for the most part parodies of some tragic work, principally the works of Euripides. His comedy *Frogs*, for example, which treats Bacchus with the greatest irreverence, is a burlesque imitation of *Semele*,[1] in which this god descends to the underworld to seek his mother. In *Peace*, sharp mockery is directed against the inhabitants of Olympus, but *Peace* is a parody of *Bellerophon*.[2] *The Clouds*, invoking the Aether, is a parody of *Helen*.[3]

Sometimes Aristophanes mocks Pindar at the same time as Euripides.[4]

The spectators in whose memories the lyrical, and especially tragic, verses were engraved[5] as a result found that Aristophanes was mocking these poets rather than the gods.[6]

1. Tragedy of Aeschylus (see Fabric., *Bibliothèque grecque*), or of Euripides, according to P. Brumoy, VI, 70.

2. See the fragments of Euripides in the edition of Leipzig, II, 481. Bellerophon is seated upon Pegasus, Trigeus on a beetle; Jupiter steals the beetle as well as Pegasus; neither Trigeus nor Bellerophon, however, makes it to the gods, because they have withdrawn to the height of Olympus.

3. Bergler in his commentary on Aristophanes indicates the passages of the tragedians that he parodied. The custom of these parodies lasted long after Aristophanes and the reform of ancient comedy, as we learn from a fragment of *Timocles* in Stobaeus.

4. The voraciousness of Hercules is borrowed from these two poets; see Pindar, *Olymp.*, I, 82, and the passages of *Alcestis*, 747–60, where Admetes's steward computes how much wine Hercules has consumed and how much meat he has eaten.

5. One sees in Plutarch's *Life of Nicias* that the Greeks who were prisoners in Sicily knew Euripides's tragedies by heart.

6. When Aristophanes presents Socrates in *The Clouds* as abandoning the gods of the State and worshipping only Chaos, Air, and the Clouds who invoked Aether, their father (v. 568), the Athenians recognized immediately the allusion to Euripides, giving an epithet to Aether that Aristophanes reinforces in order to render it more ridiculous (*Helen*, v. 872). When he shows Bacchus (*Frogs*, vv. 1469–71) protecting perjury, it is another allusion to a famous verse for which Euripides had been prosecuted.

Finally, the main truth that we have established in our work—that is, the progression of religious ideas—ought to powerfully contribute to the fact that the sarcasms of the comic author were pardoned and applauded.

From what traditions did he draw the tales that seemed to expose the main objects of worship to derision? Was it not in the ancient mythology, which recounted the imperfections and vices of the gods? Why had these vices and imperfections not shocked the Greeks of Homer's time, while they wounded them under Pericles? It is because an immense disproportion separated the earlier notions from the ideas that had replaced them. Far from the success of Aristophanes leading us to deny the various progresses of the Greek religion, his success proves that undeniable improvements had occurred in this religion. The Greeks could no longer tolerate gods without morality, mercenaries, self-interested protectors of crime, bought-off by sacrifices, favoring fraud and injustice; their religious sentiment rose above the initial notions of polytheism, and when they were led back to them, according to the way in which these outdated notions were presented to them, it was either controlled by the need to purify them, and then Sophocles was its guide, or struck by their absurdity; then they applauded Aristophanes.

These explanations seem more natural and satisfying to us than the one some have sought in the purported pleasure the Athenians took in seeing what was above them brought down. This disposition would have protected Aristophanes from the vengeance of powerful men; but the people could not have been pleased at the abasement of their gods. A democratic people loves to see those who dominate them brought low, but no people are pleased when someone denigrates the beings they adore, unless, of course, they have ceased worshipping them; the Athenians, however, were not now at this point. To be sure, the success of Aristophanes indicated a seed of decadence in the religion: the comedy of his play was founded on the disproportion that existed between the unchanging character of the teaching and the capacity for improvement of the idea. A similar disproportion, when the form remains the same, is a principle of death for a belief; each improvement prepares another and, as a consequence, brings closer the moment when the form must be broken.

But one must not conclude that it was broken yet: at the time of Aristophanes, it was not. After having laughed, the people went no less to the temples, respected no less the mysteries. The seed of destruction, which an attentive eye could detect, had not yet developed.

Some will ask, how did the causes that obtained pardon for Aristophanes's attacks against the ancient mythology not preserve from persecution, exile, and death the philosophers who attacked the same beliefs by their reasoning?

It seems to us easy to explain this phenomenon.

Passionate lovers of license and novelties, enthusiasts for the arts that were their delight and that made their glory, the people of Athens had removed the poets from the jurisdiction of the Areopagus and from ordinary judges.[7] A special tribunal exercised jurisdiction over them. The positive laws against impiety were easy to elude, as they always will be in what pertains to thought and the expressions with which it clothes itself. Judgment alone can restrain misdeeds of this sort; and if this is an advantage, it is amply counterbalanced as well; for judgment, while attaining everything, stifles everything, the good as well as the evil, use as well as abuse. And this tribunal, judge of poets, treated them with indulgence. Euripides, guilty of a famous defense of perjury in his *Hippolyta*, was prosecuted but absolved.[8]

Jealous of their liberty, the people of Athens always feared that an authority that they only impatiently tolerated might encroach on their rights; and when they were not led by a political passion, out of instinct and inclination took the part of the accused to whom they owed their amusements; in a certain sense, their own boisterous approbation had made them accomplices.

Aristophanes, moreover, made use of adroit subterfuges against legal strictures. The very traditions he took advantage of served him as a safeguard; they were literally in the ancient Homeric mythology. If in the mouth of his characters they stirred the good humor of the people, no one could accuse the poet of having denied or disgraced them. He took great care to place praises of justice and encomia to the dignity of the gods alongside his harsh witticisms. See in *Plutus* how he rises up against the idea that men can engage them to favor crime by offerings;[9] and how in *The Clouds* he speaks affirmatively of heavenly punishments of the wicked and the impious.[10]

It was not the same with the philosophers. In declaring themselves against ancient polytheism they enjoyed neither the support of the crowd, whose suffrages they did not win, confined as they were in the sanctuary of their schools or the

7. The Athenians had established a legal action against the impious (γραφην ασεβειας, Pollux, VIII, 40) and against atheists (αθεον). This action was brought before the second archon, who was charged with everything pertaining to worship and was called the king-archon, because earlier the administration of the cult was a royal prerogative (Pollux, ibid., 90). The archon submitted the accusation to the tribunal of the heliasts. But the laws against impiety touched only those who denied the gods or who revealed the mysteries. Dramatic works were not submitted to them, and without any danger writers could introduce impieties, provided they were in the mouths of their characters and not in the parts of the poem considered to belong to the poet; for example, in the choruses.

8. Walkenaer and Beck., on Euripides, III, 272; Barthelemy, *Anacharsis*, VI, ch. 71.

9. *Plutus*, 1122.

10. *Clouds*, 1456.

groves of the Academy, nor the resource of praising fables they otherwise attacked; they denied them or interpreted them, neither of which appeased the devout. After the performance of a comedy of Aristophanes, what remained? The memory of a spectacle that had provoked the good humor of those who attended, but to which one could not attribute positive results or formal conclusions. The teachings of Anaxagoras or the lessons of Socrates, on the contrary, led to direct consequences, which were indifferent to the multitude and offensive to the priests.

Despite their limited authority, the priests possessed enough to persecute the philosophers, who as critics of demagogy were odious to the people, as well as wearisome to the enlightened class because they denounced their corruption; and as reformers they were impertinent to all.

Aristophanes wanted to reform nothing: everything was subject to his mockery; he attacked philosophy as well as religion, although in this regard he became religion's useful assistant, and he seemed to have harmed it only out of inadvertence. The priestly spirit treats the enemy of its enemies with a good deal of indulgence; it willingly forgives his license, provided that, along with it, he turns against reason.

Nonetheless, this tolerance always has its limits and its end. Authority suffers impatiently the independence of its instruments. Antagonist of philosophers and orators, raising the suspicions of the multitude and the hatred of power against them, Aristophanes was nonetheless struck by the very power to whom he had denounced philosophy and liberty. This poet who had handed over eloquence to laughter and reasoning to persecution, was gagged by the aristocracy that was triumphant toward the end of the Peloponnesian War. The same tyranny that had punished Socrates's opinions suppressed Aristophanes's wit. He then could judge what masters he had served.[11]

---

11. Some have called into question the influence of the comedy, *The Clouds*, on the trial and death of Socrates. It seems to us that Mr. Cousin (fragm. *Phil.*, pp. 151–59) perfectly clarified the question. The influence was neither sudden nor direct. The death of the philosopher probably did not enter into the poet's intention; but his attacks prepared minds, and we do not think that one can absolve him from the result to which they led. What is clear is that he remained a calm and indifferent spectator of the event to which he had contributed. Socrates perished a long time before he did, and he did not try to save him. This is not surprising. Aristophanes was in his day what the men of today who want time to be reversed are. Now, the best of this opinion observe with indulgence what the worse of the opinion actually do. Inaccessible to ideas, they become worked up against persons, always believing that if this or that man did not exist, the triumph of this or that idea would be impossible. The death of an individual seems to them to be the death of a system. It is for this reason, rather than by natural perversity, that they do not aid or spare any enemy. We should pardon them: nature does against them what they wanted to do against us. One must only wait. They will disappear without being able to gain any more recruits.

CHAPTER 10

Why We Do Not Speak Here of the Greek Philosophers

In this book we do not at all treat the progress of morality in polytheism, such as the Greek philosophers conceived it. Far from working to destroy the popular religion, for a long time these philosophers attempted to reconcile it with morality and to purify it. But since despite their intentions, which were so irenic at the beginning, their efforts led only to the fall of the public belief, it is when we will describe this memorable revolution and the causes that brought it into being, that we will be able to place more suitably some investigations into the march of philosophy and its relations with religion.

CHAPTER 11

On the Relations of Morality with the Two Religious Forms

The improvements of independent polytheism reveal themselves in all its parts. The form of the gods, their character, their adventures, their conduct in heaven, their modes of acting on earth, everything bears the mark of amelioration; but it is above all in what pertains to morality that this improvement is the most obvious and the difference between the two genres of polytheism is most manifest.

Morality introduces itself by degrees into the polytheism independently of the priesthood's direction. It enters and perfects itself as civilization progresses and enlightenment expands. The gods thus do not appear to be the authors, but rather the guarantors of the moral law; they protect it, but they do not change it. They do not create its rules; they sanction them. They reward the good, punish the wicked; but their will does not determine what is good and what is evil; human actions derive their merit from themselves.

To be sure, there are circumstances in which individuals, and sometimes entire nations, place more importance on pleasing the divine power than on the strict rules of morality. Thus the Athenians wanted to banish Oedipus—blind, weak, a fugitive—because this unfortunate old man was the object of celestial wrath.[1] Neptune grows angry against the Phaeacians because they fulfilled the duties of humanity vis-à-vis Ulysses. He changes into a rock the vessel that had transported the hero to the coasts of Ithaca so that this people, he says, would no longer be tempted to lend their ships to strangers who ask for help.[2] Alcinous draws the consequence from this that one must abstain from rendering such service to one's guests.[3] It is by

1. *Oedipus at Colonus*, 233–36, 256–57.
2. *Odyss.*, XIII, 146.
3. Ibid., 151.

obedience to the gods that Orestes plunges the iron into the bosom of his mother; and in exhorting him to this murder, Pylades says to him that it is better to brave the indignation of men than the animosity of the immortals.[4] Finally, much later, the Lacedaemonians violate the rights of hospitality in order to obey the oracle at Delphi; this is what they did, adds Herodotus,[5] because the orders of the gods were more precious to them than any human considerations.

Nonetheless, even then morality does not change its nature; it is sacrificed in the particular occasion, but as a general principle it remains independent.

Hospitality, despite the difficulties that it entails for the Phaeacians, is not considered to be a crime. The Athenians, when they hesitate over whether they will expel Oedipus, feel that even in doing something they believe is agreeable to the gods they will not be doing a virtuous action. It is in vain that Orestes, after having killed Clytemnestra, justifies himself with Menelaus, saying that he only fulfilled the will of Apollo; this god, the king of Sparta answers him, did he not know what is just?[6] And the parricidal son, even though he is the executioner of the decrees of heaven, is no less detested by men and pursued by the Furies.

For morality to cease to be independent in the polytheism that is not subject to priestly direction, two things are required which this belief does not admit: all-powerful gods and unanimous wills among them; but in all the versions of this polytheism, the power of the gods is always more or less limited. One cannot conceive of a great number of beings who are equally invested with an unlimited power; their plurality places an invincible obstacle to their omnipotence; this plurality also suggests the idea of different interests; and to decide between these interests, man has recourse only to his reason. For how can he recognize as competent judges gods who are not in accord? He is therefore never subject to the gods between whom he judges. The protection of one defends him from the hatred of another;[7] and if all the supernatural beings betray him, he retains the right to appeal their decisions to his own conscience. When morality and religion come tightly together in the polytheism left to itself, it is religion that submits to the authority of morality and declares its own dependence. "If there are gods

4. Aeschylus, *Choeph.*, 902.

5. Herod., V, 63.

6. Eurip., *Orest.*, 415–18. It should be noticed in this dialogue of Orestes and Menelaus that it is not said that the order of the gods makes the action they commanded legitimate. One obeys them because of their force, not morality.

7. *Saepè premente Deo, fert Deus alter opem.*

who protect what is equitable, and who interest themselves in noble projects," says the consul Horatius, "we are sure of their protection; if, on the contrary, hostile divinities oppose themselves to our success, nothing will be able to deter us from a glorious and legitimate enterprise."[8] These are the celebrated verses of the author of the *Pharsalia*;[9] but these words are more remarkable in a religious historian, such as Dionysius of Halicarnassus, than in a sententious and philosophical poet.

Thus the gods form a species of public, not infallible, not incorruptible, but more impartial and more respected than the vulgar among human beings. The presumptive opinion and the recognized force of this celestial public are not without advantages. Man suffers before these august witnesses; he disarms them with his virtue; he gains their respect by his courage; and the idea of offering to beings of a superior nature and reason the magnificent spectacle of an irreproachable man, struggling against evil, contains something that exalts the imagination and elevates the soul.

In priestly polytheism, on the contrary, the priests, masters of the people, hasten to give it a code of laws. Morality, instead of spreading through the different fables and fusing itself, as in Greece, with that part of the belief that one can call historical, morality instead composes a body of doctrine. It is produced under this form in the Vendidad of the Persians, the Havamal of the Scandinavians, the Samaveda of the Indians, and in the Laws of Manu.[10] Similar codes do not exist in the Greek religion.

Now, when morality joins in a premature way, and, as it were, violently, with religion, it is inevitably more imperfect than when it is introduced naturally. In the latter case, it enters during an advanced period of society; it enters purified, im-

---

8. Dionys. of Hal., X, 6.

9. *Victrix causa Diis placuit, sed victa Catoni.*

10. See the preface of the Bhagavad Gita. The Athenians had a mysterious, prophetic book: they hid it with such care that no passage has come down to us. Dinarchus is the only author who spoke about it, in his harangue against Demosthenes, whom he accuses of having lacked respect for this book, upon which, according to him, the salvation of the State depended (Reiske and Pauw, *Rech. sur les Grecs*, II, 205). But nothing indicates that this book contained precepts of morality; it probably prescribed rituals, ceremonies, and prayers. Dr. Coray believes that the Athenians regarded it as containing the secret of their destinies, a secret Oedipus confided to Theseus (Chard. de la Roche, *Mélanges*, II, 445–51). The scholiast of Theocritus (*Idylle*, IV) also mentions the books carried by the women in the Thesmophoria; but the observation we just made applies equally to these sacred books. The books of the pontiffs that Flavius, the secretary of this corporation, divulged, and that Ovid put into verse in his *Fasti*, do not contain moral precepts, but indicate the feast days and legends of ancient Rome.

proved, enriched with all the improvements that a people have made while becoming civilized. The priests, in rendering religion changeless, maintain morality as it was in the time of barbarism; hence, with religion having sanctioned it, religion opposes itself to the enlightenment that ought to correct it; in this way, religions that at a particular time could be a relative good, only do evil in later times; their conservative force is exercised in favor of what ought not to be conserved.

This is not all; the gods in the name of whom the code of priestly morality is promulgated are not only judges, they are also legislators; they create the moral law, they can change it, they declare what is evil and what is good. The rule of the just and the unjust is overturned;[11] an incalculable revolution is thus produced in man's conscience. Actions draw all their value from the merit that the gods ascribe to them; they do not please them because they are good; they are good because they please them; hence, two species of crimes and two species of duties: those that are such because of their nature and those that religion declares to be so. A thousand useless things become virtues; a thousand things without any harmful effect are transformed into crimes.[12] What provides no profit to men can be demanded by the gods; what harms no human can offend them. Artificial misdeeds are punished with more rigor than true ones. The first are sins while the second are only faults.

Among the Persians, to bury a dog, to throw water on the fire;[13] among the Egyptians, to involuntarily cause the death of a sacred animal;[14] in India, to violate the prescribed distance when approaching the member of another caste, or to break the branch of a fig tree,[15] or to kill a serpent,[16] are actions that are no less severely forbidden than physical violence, tyranny, and murder. Armenian priests

11. It is so true that in this belief the protection of the gods justified crime that Indian brigands, the Phansigars, about whom we have already spoken once, believed themselves innocent and pious when they followed the rules prescribed in a code entitled *Chaudra-vidya*, science of thieves. In an Indian comedy (the *Mrich-batti*) one finds a slightly travestied formulary of the prayers the brigands addressed to the god who protected them.

12. Several laws of the Jews, says a very pious scholar (Cunaeus, *De rep. hebr.*, II, 24), are dictated neither by reason nor by nature, but by the inexplicable will of God. He even uses the expression *incertâ numinis voluntate*; and by this word, *incertâ*, he indicates that the will of God changing, prohibited things, and consequently bad, would become permitted, and consequently good.

13. Hyde, I; Strabo.

14. Diod., I, 2.

15. Preface of the Bhagavad Gita, p. 62.

16. *Rech. asiat.*, IV, 35–37.

pardon the worst assaults rather than the infraction of required abstinences.[17] A traveler recounts that Illyrian brigands killed the leader who for a very long time led them in battle, and whose fierceness they had admired and imitated, because he had drunk milk during a day of fast.[18] No misdeed, say the Turks, closes the doors of heaven to the one who dies while fasting.[19] According to the code of Gentoo, the man who reads a heterodox Shaster is as guilty as if he had killed his friend. The Bhagavad Gita places the love of work and industry on a par with intemperance and irregular desires.[20]

Greek polytheism in general is a stranger to artificial duties. If we find in Hesiod some innocent or indifferent actions that are forbidden as offending the gods,[21] and if the precepts of this poet in this regard have, both in substance and form, some relation with those that are inculcated in the priestly religions, it is because these precepts were probably borrowed, even without his awareness; but they had no influence on the morality of Greek religion as it was conceived by the people.

In priestly religions, muzzled by a host of commandments and arbitrary prohibitions,[22] man labors blindly in the inadequate space that is left to him; wherever

17. Tournefort, *Voyage au Levant*, II, 167. It is striking, says Spencer, that among his people God attached the death penalty to the least violation of the rituals, while kidnapping, rape, or murder were punished with much less severity. "*Proclivè est observare Deum cuilibet legi rituali, supplicium extremum statuisse, quum tamen peccatis suâ naturâ gravioribus, fornicationi, furto, proximi mutilation, et ejusmodi poenas longè mitiores dedisse*" (ibid., p. 48). As proof, he cites Lev., VI, 2–4; VII, 20, 21, 25, 27; X, 1–2; XI, 44–45; XVIII, 2, 4, 5, 20–23, 30; all of ch. XIX; XX, 7–8; XXII, 3; XXIII, 22, 29–30; XXIV, 19; XXV, 36, 38–39, 43; XXVI, 34; Deut., V, 10; all of ch. VI; X, 12; XI, 26–28; XVII, 12; XXVI, 13, 14, 16, 17, and 18; XXVII, 10; XXVIII, 1, 15; XXX, 8–10; Exod., XXII, 1; XXIII, 22; XXX, 33–38; XXXI, 14–15; Josh., VIII, 24. If a man sins against another man, God could be appeased; but if he sins directly against God, who will pray for him? (Sam., I, 2, 24–25).

18. Taube, *Descript. d'Esclavonie*, I, 76.

19. Chardin, IV, 157.

20. Bhag. Gita, v. 124.

21. *Works and Days*, V, 725–58.

22. Spencer, author of a work of immense erudition and quite orthodox intent, was led by the good faith that struggled in him against his profession as a theologian to recognize this arbitrary character in the imperious style of the Mosaic law. He finds no explication that would explain its cause, either moral or natural. He agrees that the words that precede and follow almost all laws: "I am the Eternal, your God, keep my commandments," cannot be translated except by this despotic paraphrase: "These commandments can appear to you to be futile or contrary to your ideas of good and evil; but it must suffice to you that I am their author, I, your master" (Spencer, *De leg. ritual. Hebr.*, p. 613). Spencer, finally, recognizes that at all times the Jews had regarded the divine laws as emanating from

he turns, he is hampered in his freedom. Soon, he no longer distinguishes good from evil, nor law from nature.

What preserves the majority of men from crime is the feeling of never having crossed the line of innocence; the more that one narrows this line, the more exposed he is to violate it; and however light may be the infraction, by the mere fact that he has overcome his initial scruple, he has lost his most assured safeguard.

Several writers have noted this danger. The laws that make what is indifferent necessary, says Montesquieu, soon make what is necessary indifferent.[23]

Nonetheless, since to arrive at the full truth one must consider questions in all their facets, we will recognize that this demand of religion has its advantage; it accustoms man to sacrifice; it accustoms him not to propose an ignoble goal in anything he does. It is useful that man sometimes prescribes to himself useless duties, if only to learn that everything that is good on earth does not reside in what he calls utility.

But it is with this as with everything that pertains to exaltation, enthusiasm, and the interior sentiment. This sentiment, this enthusiasm, this exaltation, which are sublime when they are spontaneous, become terrible when others abuse them. The power to create virtues and crimes with a word, when it is placed in the hands of a class of men, is but one more terrible means of despotism and corruption.

This class does not limit itself to placing at the first rank of misdeeds any and all resistance to its authority; it does not limit itself to commanding indifferent,

---

a discretionary power (ibid., p. 7). Envisaging their religion under this point of view, the Jews proclaimed the examination of the motives that had moved the Divinity to be sacrilegious (see the book entitled *Coseri,* in Buxtorfio, pt. I, no. 26). In fact, this examination is forbidden by the laws themselves (Num., XV, 39). "You will not seek at all, either in your heart, nor with your eyes." The Jewish commentators add: "Curiosity perverts and denatures faith. Who can, without impiety, want to penetrate into the secrets of his god? If the reason of a precept was known by man, where would be the glory of obedience? [See the book of Gemara and Rabbi Schem-Yobh, in Spencer.] When man discovers the purpose of what is prescribed to him, he is more disposed to discharge it. This knowledge facilitates the fulfillment of the precept; and the mind simultaneously struck by the command and the reason for it, no longer simply is a slave." In this way of conceiving the relations of the Supreme Being with man, there is a striking anthropomorphism. God is then like the despots of the earth, who want to be obeyed without question, as well as without murmuring, and who are flattered when their wills are obeyed without being understood. If they were understood or approved, their authority would suffer; they would lose in authority what they would gain in approval. Bochart (*De Animal. sacris,* pt. 1, bk. II, 491) has so fallen into this anthropomorphism that he calls the authority of Jehovah autocracy.

23. Montesquieu, *Spirit of the Laws,* XXIV, 14.

or useless, actions; it prescribes harmful and criminal ones. Pity for the enemies of heaven is a weakness that is disapproved or proscribed: in contempt of the strongest bonds or the most tender affections, it is forbidden to give assistance to the one who is the object of divine indignation. Cruelty against the impious and infidels is a sacred duty; treachery toward them is a virtue; and, just as the theory of devotion pushed to an extreme makes the most painful sacrifice the most meritorious, when actions have no merit other than because they are in accord with the order of the gods, religious virtues have even more merit when they are the opposite of human virtues.[24] We see in the annals of Egypt a king punished for his gentleness and beneficence. The oracle having indicated to Mycerinus that he only had six years to live: "Whence came it," he asks, "that my predecessors, the scourge of their subjects, came peacefully to an advanced old age and the gods treat me with so much severity, I who have devoted myself to the happiness of my peoples?" "These gods," answered the oracle, "condemned Egypt to one hundred and fifty years of misery and slavery. The monarchs who preceded you fulfilled their decrees; you violated them. Your death is the punishment of your disobedience."

Almost always in priestly polytheism, the interdiction of crimes is accompanied

---

24. An author whom we have sometimes cited, even though he is distinguished neither by erudition nor by talent, but because he brought a candor to his reasonings that becomes precious, because he cannot hide the consequences of the premises he adopts, has a book on this subject that is very curious to read. Every time he recounts some act of clemency or pity on the part of Jewish kings toward their vanquished, "Men," he says, "would have judged this action virtuous, but it was a crime, because it was contrary to the will of God" (Saint-Philippe, *Monarchie des Hébreux*; see the account of Ahab's indulgence toward Benhadad, and a thousand other passages). When he depicts for us the cruel Aza, threatening his mother with the ultimate torture, he continues (ibid., II, 305), "A prince, when it is a question of religion, is bound to other humans by no tie. He is neither a son nor a father, he is simply God's lieutenant, whose power he represents, and who substituted him to exercise his justice." Finally, he recounts the murder of Sisera by Jael (ibid., I, 128): "There is," he declares, "greatness and nobility in respecting the confidence that an enemy displays to us; but religion, is it interested in our conduct? Generosity is no longer appropriate. The love of religion moved the arm of Jael. Religion is the first duty of men. Jael can in conscience employ all sorts of means, invite Sisera with the appearance of a friend, cover him with his cloak, and kill him in his sleep. Thus the angel who announced the incarnation could not find more glorious expressions in honor of Mary than those the Hebrews had employed to celebrate the victory of Jael" (see in the same work the account of the assassination of Aglon by Aod). "If it were true," says Sozomen, in speaking of the death of Julian, of which Christians were accused, "that someone in the service of God and religion had armed himself with a courage similar to that of the ancient liberators of the fatherland, one would have hardly condemned him" (*Hist. ecclés.*, VI, 12).

with an explicit reservation for the case when these crimes are commanded by the gods. Whoever commits a murder on his own, say the Brahmins, will never enjoy heavenly happiness; but if God orders one man to kill another, he does it and lives happily and content.[25]

Religious morality thus conceived can have another inconvenience. Man imagines himself elevated above all duties. The heretics of the fourteenth century, and long before them some Gnostics, thought that, being saved by divine intervention, they were no longer subject to the law, and as a consequence several of them gave themselves over in public to the most revolting libertinage.[26] The bonzes reasoned in the same way. Xaca and Amida, being distressed by the crimes of men, in order to atone for them suffered mysterious pains. Repentence and good works are now so many offenses against these divinities, whose sacrifices have sufficiently erased all our faults.[27]

We have said that in general in polytheism the personal character of the gods had little influence; but this assertion is not completely true, except when morality is independent of religion. The relations of human societies being the same everywhere, the moral law, which is the theory of these relations, is also everywhere the same. When the gods are only charged with the application of this law, their individual character matters little, because in the exercise of this function they abstract from this character. But when the will of the gods decides the moral law, since their character influences their will, every imperfection in this character produces a vice in the law. Man then esteems himself in doing evil. When he obeys religion at the expense of morality, he applauds himself for this, and in violating the holiest of natural laws, not only does he flatter himself that he is making himself agreeable to the gods he worships, but he believes himself morally virtuous, which is yet another grave problem. To subordinate morality to religion in this way is to produce the same revolution in morality that the axiom "if the king wills, so wills the law" does in politics.

The practical consequences of this inversion of ideas are not always equal to its dangers in theory. The priesthood, like every authority established among men, is forced in ordinary circumstances to maintain the great laws of morality so that the

25. *Asiat. Res.*, IV, 36. In a passage of the Bhagavad Gita, the religious principles on the immortality of the soul are employed to get around or justify homicide.

26. Gesen, *ap.* Prateol.

27. Possev., *Bibl. Select.*, X.

society it dominates does not perish; but the door is always open to exceptions, and natural morality is constantly threatened by an artificial one.

This latter morality, at once inexorable and capricious, pursues man in the smallest details and leaves him asylum in neither the sanctuary of his soul nor the secret of his thoughts; it makes ignorance an offense and punishes involuntary actions. From the moment they are born, infants can be criminals. Brahmins present theirs to the moon at the age of eight days in order to obtain absolution for their faults. One's intention is no more than a fragile protection. Remorse announces crime; but peace of soul does not attest to innocence. No longer having the right to consult his conscience, man is never certain that he has not offended the Divinity. Often disfigured by the priestly spirit, Judaism and Christianity furnish several examples. "Lord," says the Hebrew Psalmist, "forgive me those of my sins that are unknown to me."[28] "I reproach myself for nothing," writes an apostle, "but this is not a proof of my innocence."[29]

This uncertainty can be a good thing in a very perfected religion. The man who has very pure ideas concerning the Divinity never knows if his efforts are enough to render him worthy of pleasing him. He works ceaselessly on his own heart, in order to eradicate everything that separates him from the perfect being he adores; his anxiety is, moreover, alleviated by the notion of goodness united to that of wisdom and power. But in a cult whose gods are imperfect and wicked, such anxiety, far from being an encouragement for virtue, is a constantly recurring cause of discouragement and despair.

To escape from it, man adopts a thousand bizarre expedients. Sometimes, exhausted from giving himself to always doubtful actions, over which hover a discouraging obscurity, he condemns himself to a complete inertia; he puts activity, work, and beneficence in the rank of condemnable passions. After the axiom of one of the founders of a priestly religion, when in doubt he abstains; that is, he remains immobile, for fear of rendering himself culpable by a movement, and to

28. Ps., XIX, V, 13.

29. Cor., IV, 4. We have spoken of a companion of Saint Bruno who while dying congratulated himself for not having ever sinned and was condemned to the eternal fires as punishment for his confidence in himself. But see how difficult the theologians are: Prudence, a Christian poet, did not permit himself to hope that his soul would be saved; he only aspired to being plunged into the deepest of abysses; and the same authors who find it just that the companion of Saint Bruno was condemned for having been too certain about paradise, declare the humble request of Prudence to be impious, he who desired only a mitigation of the sufferings of hell (Bayle, art. "Prudence").

escape from crime he forbids virtue to himself; other times, he casts himself at the feet of the priesthood, which arrogates to itself alone the important privilege of expiation. This means of reconciling man with his conscience has its advantages when its effectiveness rests on the interior disposition and future conduct of the one whom religion thus saves from the abyss into which his vices have plunged him. But in priestly religions, expiation changes character. The absolution of the darkest crimes is attached to an implicit credulity,[30] to minute,[31] and even arbitrary[32] practices, to rituals that suppose neither amelioration, reparation, nor repentance:[33] to the sight of a temple,[34] the shadow of a tree,[35] the touch of a stone, washing in the waters of certain rivers,[36] the mechanical repetition of certain words,[37] the reading of certain sacred texts; or what is even more degrading for

30. Catholics have sometimes fallen into this error. I know one who, even today, reproaches Protestants for being zealous about morality and rather cold about faith (*Le Cathol.*, V, 230).

31. Every Indian, whatever his conduct may have been, is saved when he dies in a holy place, or holding in his hand the tail of a cow, or when he is plunged in the Ganges when dying, or is tossed into it after his death, or, finally, when he shakes on himself the branch of a tree dipped into the water of this river (Roger, *Pagan. ind.*).

32. The name Vishnu, pronounced without intention, has the power of effacing all crimes.

33. The prescribed ceremonies and ablutions purify man of the most culpable actions, say the Brahmins, in their expiatory prayers (*Rech. asiat.*, V, 360). It is one of the drawbacks of the ideas of impurity and purification. Man passes easily from the notion of purification to that of purifications that absolve him of his faults.

34. In a Sanskrit inscription found near Gaya, one reads these words: "Amara Deva built the holy temple that purifies from sin. One crime, equal to a hundred, will be expiated by the sight of this temple; a crime equal to a thousand by touching it; a crime equal to a million by adoration" (*Asiat. Res.*, I, 286). The pardon of all of one's sins is attached to the visit to the temple consecrated to Rama on the island of Ceylon (Paulin, *Syst. brahman.*).

35. It suffices to see the *kolpo* or the *toulochi* to be relieved of all one's sins.

36. We have already spoken of the power of the waters of the Ganges; the dying whose lips are moistened with the water of this river are purified of all their sins (Bhag. Gita, pref., pp. LXII, LXX). The opinion of the Christians of the first centuries on the efficacy of baptism is very different from that of Indians. One knows that baptism was often delayed until the moment of death as a sure means of effacing sins during this life. Constantine was in this way baptized a few moments before dying. The Fathers of the Church, in blaming this calculation, did not deny the effects of baptism (Chrysost., in *Epist. ad Hebraeos.*, Homel. 13; Chard., *Hist. des sacrem.*).

37. The syllables *om, am, oum* compose a very effective prayer for the remission of all sins. The Brahmins also attribute an expiatory power to certain words repeated one hundred times or a thousand times in a row, by counting them on their beads (*Asiat. Res.*, V, 356). When the mysterious words have been pronounced over a victim, says the chapter of blood that we cited elsewhere, Brahma and

religion and corrupting for men, expiation is obtained by money,[38] and the indulgence, or rather the connivance of the divine, becomes the object of shameful trafficking. Thus in these religions morality is corrupted both by the dependence in which it finds itself vis-à-vis the will of the gods and by the arbitrariness that is introduced into the number and classification of offenses, and by the means that this arbitrariness provides the guilty to appease heaven and regain innocence. For one must not disguise this: in its relations with morality, religion is always placed between two dangers. If it declares that there are inexpiable crimes, it casts men into despair. If it offers atonement for all crimes, it encourages the guilty with the hope of immunity.

But this danger is much less in the free religions than in the priestly ones. When morality remains itself, it keeps expiations within just limits; when it is subjugated, it has neither rule nor brake. With expiations, it is like the right to pardon under absolute governments and constitutional ones.

One therefore always arrives at this result: with liberty, morality improves religion; with slavery, religion falsifies morality.

---

all the other divinities come together in it, and whatever sin the sacrificer may have committed, he becomes pure and irreproachable (*Asiat. Res.*). The repetition of a sentence of the Vedas absolves from the gravest sins (Laws of Menu, XI, 260). The Chinese who professed the religion of Fo believe that by repeating "*omito-fo*" they obtain a plenary forgiveness.

38. "A donation of lands to pious men, for holy pilgrimages, or for solemn festivals is the means, say the Brahmins, to cross the bottomless Ocean of this world. A donation of lands by sovereigns is the true bridge of justice. . . . He who, by avarice, lays a hand on these donations, makes himself guilty of five great crimes and will dwell longer in the place of punishment. . . . The donor of lands will dwell in heaven sixty thousand years; he who steals them will live in the underworld for the same period" (extract of a donation of lands, trans. from the Sanskrit; *Asiat. Res.*, I, 363–67). The pariahs who do not know, or who cannot themselves perform the prescribed ceremonies pay a priest to perform them in their place; and these ceremonies performed by substitution have the same effectiveness (Anquet., *Voy. aux Indes*; Boundehesch, I). The idea of penance, in priestly religions, suffers in general a singular modification relative to morality. The talapoins, Buddhist monks (see Laloubère, *Relat. de Siam*) and the priests of the Druses (Niebuhr, *Voy. en Arab.*, II, 429) declare that penance is necessary; but that the profane, far from performing it themselves, ought to commit it to the priests, whom they pay. With this precaution they can commit with impunity sins that others will atone for in their place.

CHAPTER 12

On the True Relations of Religion with Morality

In granting this preference to the cults free of all domination, we do not at all mean to say that in antiquity there were any in which the true relations of morality with religion were adequately established.

Those who have written on this subject, whether in the past or today, appear to us to have committed a great mistake.

The ancient legislators did not distinguish between vulgar morality, which limits itself to maintaining order by prohibiting gross misdeeds, and the more refined and elevated morality that prevents crime by inspiring man with a disposition of soul that does not allow him to commit it.

The moderns have followed the ancients on this false path. Let us attempt to depart from it.

To prevent the grossest misdeeds by punishing them, laws and punishments suffice. However, to change the interior of man instead of merely staying his hand, the religious sentiment is indispensable. By restricting religion to a kind of material, and limited, usefulness, one lowers it from its true rank. In this way its dignity, its sanctity, and its noblest influence have always been misunderstood.

The evil did not stop there. Religion has been made into a penal code and as soon as it is a penal code, it is close to becoming an arbitrary code. Hence all the dangers we have described in the preceding chapter. These dangers would be even more terrible in theism because the power of the god of theism is always unlimited.

The most salutary teachings, the purest precepts, cannot repair the evil that every doctrine that thus weakens the eternal rule entails. A worship whose divinities would be cruel and corrupt, but which would leave virtue as the judge of its own heart, would be less pernicious than a religion whose god, invested with the most admirable qualities, could by an act of will change morality.

Religion is not a penal code, it is not an arbitrary code, it is the relation of the Divinity with man, with what makes him a moral and intelligent being, that is, with his soul, his thought, his will. Actions do not belong to its sphere, except as the signs of his interior dispositions. Religion can change nothing in their merit. The work of God like the religious sentiment itself, having come from the same source, morality is uncreated, independent. Its rule is placed in all hearts. It reveals itself to all minds, as they become enlightened. The being that sentiment makes us to know cannot be served or satisfied by any exception to this rule. This would be to want to serve it as we serve the powers of the earth, by flattering their momentary interest, for a given period, in an exigent circumstance.

To be sure, when a religion is excellent, its morality is much gentler, more nuanced, more conformed to all the refinements of sensibility, and thereby more equitable than human justice can be. But it is not the rule, it is only the application that varies because religion distinguishes what the gaze of man cannot perceive. The latter pronounces only on actions; it knows only them; it sees only their exterior, and by that alone its judgments are imperfect and unjust. The same action committed by two individuals in two different circumstances never has the same value. But the social law cannot acknowledge these nuances. Similar to the bed of Procrustes, it reduces unequal sizes to an equal measure. Religion, however, quashes its verdicts for the sake of another world. But this is not because its foundations differ, it is not because religion can innovate in any way; it is only because it is better instructed; and in this respect, it is no less often a recourse against the imperfections of human justice than it is a sanction of the general laws this justice aims to maintain.

Considered under this point of view, the religious sentiment cannot ever harm morality. In the name of the divinity they teach, the ministers of religion can never decide the value of action. Religion leaves to the laws their jurisdiction over effects; it limits itself to improving the cause.

In this way it does the good that human laws have always attempted to bring about, but in vain. The often-repeated axiom that it is better to prevent crimes than to punish them is an inexhaustible source of vexations and arbitrariness when temporal authority wants to determine its interventions accordingly. But the religious sentiment that penetrates to the bottom of souls can attain this goal without arbitrariness or vexation. Laws, in their risky ventures and what they blindly do, are forced to pronounce according to appearances, to govern themselves according to isolated details, to listen to suspicions that prove nothing; and to prevent what could be criminal, they punish what is still innocent. The sentiment in contrast embraces the whole, purifies instead of constrains, and ennobles instead of punishes.

It is only then that one can resolve a problem that has stymied all philosophies. At all times, morality had barely entered into religious belief when all enlightened men, struck by the difficulties we described above, saw themselves forced to go back and try to separate morality from religion. They took to the task in various ways. They disguised their intentions. But the result of their efforts was always the same.

Compare the axioms of the Roman Stoics with the discourses of Homer's heroes. What Hector responds to Polydamas is precisely what Seneca wrote. Thus, at the period when morality was most united with polytheism, the language of the philosophers became similar to that uttered by virtuous men when morality had barely entered this belief.

In the religions founded on theism, the most religious philosophers gave morality the name of religion, leaving to the side and sacrificing everything that constituted religion properly speaking, and everything that gave it a dangerous supremacy to morality. This recently was the endeavor of the most enlightened theologians of Germany. It was another path to the same goal.

But by envisioning religion as we do, placing its jurisdiction at the height that is proper to it, leaving to human justice what is its province, that is, details and effects, in order to subject to religion what is its proper sphere, the ensemble and causes, you will escape all dangers. You will inhibit its ministers, faithless interpreters of its laws, from denaturing it: you will assure morality of divine sanction while confirming its original and inviolable independence.

Here a consideration strikes us. It is so true that the march of the human spirit is progressive; it is so true that despite its apparent steps backward and its deplorable aberrations, it always rises to more refined notions, that religion conceived in this way leads to new perfections in the most admirable teaching man has attained, a teaching that under polytheism was the center that reunited all noble and proud souls, the asylum of all elevated virtues, and which under theism was often envied by the most distinguished thinkers of Modern times,[1] to wit: Stoicism.

Stoicism was a sublime élan of the soul, a Soul tired of seeing morality in the charge of corrupt men and egoistical gods, and, by breaking all its bonds with these gods and these men, attempting to place itself in a sphere above all the injus-

---

1. Montesquieu.

tices of earth and even of heaven. But in Stoicism there was a sort of very labored effort that rendered its influence less salutary and less durable. To arrive at that internal liberty that braved all the blows of fate, it was necessary to stifle in oneself the beginnings of many sweet and profound sentiments. The religious sentiment, however, such as we have attempted to make it understood, ensures the same harbor to man by preserving these emotions that are inseparable from his nature and that make for the charm and consolation of his life. Morality is not at the mercy of either legislators who speak in the name of heaven or those who command on earth. Man is independent of all that can cross or pervert the most noble (or better put: the sole noble) part of himself; but he enjoys this independence under the aegis of a god who understands him, approves him, and esteems him. He is strong, like the Stoic, with the force of his own soul; but he is also strong with the force of a constant and intimate appeal to the Center of all that is good.

This idea brings into Stoicism the life and warmth that were lacking to it. It satisfies that portion of our soul that rejects impassivity, and that Stoicism was forced to try to destroy because it was unable to satisfy it. Resignation becomes the companion of courage. Hope is at once its guide and its reward. With it, resignation is firmer and courage, sweeter.

BOOK XIII

THAT THE GREEK MYSTERY CULTS WERE INSTITUTIONS BORROWED FROM FOREIGN PRIESTHOODS, AND WHICH, WHILE CONTRADICTING THE PUBLIC RELIGION, DID NOT MODIFY IT AT ALL IN ITS POPULAR PORTION

CHAPTER I

How Much the Subject of This Book
Is Beset with Difficulties

More than once in our exposition of priestly doctrines and practices, while demonstrating that they were foreign to independent polytheism, we have recognized that almost all of them were reproduced in the mystery cults that became associated with this polytheism. Here is the place to explain the origin of the Greek mystery cults, and the cause of the identity of what was revealed to initiates with the rituals and doctrines imposed by priests on the peoples they governed. The matter we enter into is beset with difficulties. Men of distinguished knowledge and sagacity have proposed different systems among which it is impossible to choose because all of them had a core of truth mixed with many errors. Here we will only offer some general ideas, which we will support with some facts, but avoiding as much as we can purely historical discussions.[1]

---

1. To know the mysteries thoroughly, it would be necessary to consider them under three distinct points of view: (1) as the place where foreign rituals and doctrines were deposited; (2) as the deal, and dealings, the priesthood had with the opinions that progressively developed, which it adopted to disarm them; (3) as causes of the decline and fall of the public religion. But the two first are the only ones that interest us here. Those of our readers who would like to go further in examining points of detail will find in Meursius (*Graecia Feriata*), in Sainte-Croix (*Les mystères*), in Heyne (*Notes sur Apollodore*), and in Creuzer (*Symbol.*) guides to all the sources that one should consult.

CHAPTER 2

What the Mystery Cults Were among the Nations Subject to Priests

In the human heart there is a tendency to erect barriers around what one knows and what one possesses. The spirit of property shows itself to be egotistical, just as much for what pertains to science as for what belongs to wealth. If this tendency was not combated by others, man would refuse his fellows everything that he could keep from them; but nature has placed the remedy for our defects in our defects themselves. As she forces us by our needs to share what we have, she constrains us by our self-love to make a mutual exchange of what we know; however, the original disposition subsists, and exerts itself with as much force as the interest is important or the science more elevated.

The philosophers of Antiquity had a hidden part in their philosophy, independent of all religious dogma, that was designated in Greek by the same word as the mysteries of the religion.[1] Pythagoras expelled Hipparchus from his school because of some indiscreet revelations and replaced him with a column,[2] and did not leave his books to Damo, his daughter, except with the explicit injunction not to make them known to the profane, a prohibition she respected despite her indigence and the treasure that was offered to tempt her.[3] Zeno, Plato, and—who would believe it?—the Epicureans, superficial and even crude philosophers, had secrets that they did not communicate to their disciples except after trials that were very similar to

---

1. Τελετη. *Etym. Magn.*

2. Iamblich., *De comm. mathem.*; Villois., *Anecd. graeca*, p. 216; Clem. Alex., *Strom.* See Eschenbach, *De poesi orphica.*

3. Gale, *Opusc. mythol.*

initiations.[4] Christianity had barely formed, and Christians divided the public part from the secret part of worship.[5]

It is therefore not surprising that corporations, accustomed to treat with disdain the people they had subjugated, always held the people far from what was most precious and forbade all participation, either in the discoveries that constituted their pride and founded their power or in the theories they had built on these discoveries. Thus we encountered mysteries among all the nations. Diodorus[6] extols those of the Chaldeans, Diogenes Laertius[7] those of Ethiopia. Suidas[8] instructs us that Pherecydes had drawn some of his opinions from the mystery cults of Phoenicia. Herodotus[9] transmits details to us that are more numerous than instructive on those of Egypt. Caesar[10] speaks, although with much less admiration, of those of the Druids. The magi of Persia[11] celebrated theirs in obscure dens; and those of the Hebrews, contained in their kabbalah, served as a pretext for the extravagances of the rabbis and are the despair of modern commentators. Without adopting their reveries, it seems to us proven that from the most remote Antiquity this unfortunate and discontented people deposited in the mysteries their hopes for this life and, perhaps, for the next, by which I mean: expecting a conquering liberator in this world, and some vague notions of a future world.[12]

However, in our opinion it is not under this point of view that the mysteries to which the priestly castes admitted members of others castes by way of initiation rites should be envisaged. Some have erroneously believed that they were made up of the secret doctrine of the priests. To be sure, following a tendency we have already noted,[13] these priests always combined the popular part of worship with their hypotheses and discoveries: fetishes first of all, then less crude gods,

4. Clem. Alex., *Strom.*

5. See Thiers, *Expos. du saint sacrament*, I, 8; and Pellicia, *De eccles. christ. primae, mediae et noviss. aetat. politia*, I, 2ff.

6. Diod., bk. XVII.

7. Diog. Laert., I, 6.

8. Suidas, art. "Pherecydes."

9. Herod., passim.

10. *B Gall.*, VI.

11. Firmicus.

12. Basnage, *Hist. des Juifs*; Buxtorf, *Bibl. rabbin.*, p. 184; Hottinger, *Bibl. orient.*, p. 33; Maimonid., *More Nevoch.*

13. See bk. VI, ch. 3.

became symbols for them; but these symbols were their particular language, their particular property. It in no way entered into their intention, because it was in no way in their interests to communicate their meaning to the profane.

As a consequence, the admission of the initiates to the knowledge of what the priesthood called "the mysteries" did not at all imply the teaching of that doctrine (or better put: these secret doctrines, because as we have seen, there were several).[14] Everything attests that these mysteries revealed by initiation were only dramatic representations, stories put into action, descriptions replaced and rendered more sensible by images; as such they were celebrated on the lake of Sais.[15] The priests had thought that by striking the senses they would produce stronger impressions than by simply addressing the imagination and memory; but the initiates had no other advantage over those who were not initiated but to contemplate a spectacle that the others did not.

Herodotus, admitted into the mysteries of the Egyptians, acquired no knowledge of their hidden theology. He explicitly says that the thing that these people called the mysteries was the nocturnal performance of the gods' adventures; and one can see that the silence to which he had sworn concerned only the names of these gods and a few particulars of their adventures. The priests could recognize allusions to their philosophy in these representations; but the people saw only fables of the popular mythology, offered in a more vivid and animated way to their gaze.

14. Ibid.
15. Herod., II, 171.

CHAPTER 3

How These Mysteries Were Transported into Greece, and What They Became

The period of the establishment of the mystery cults in Greece is irrelevant to our investigation. For us, it suffices that writers who are the most divided on other points take them back to the arrival of the colonies that civilized this country.[1] The Eleusinian mysteries, they say, were brought from Egypt or Thrace by Eumolpus. Those of Samothrace, which served as the model for almost all those of Greece, were founded by an Egyptian Amazon.[2] The daughters of Danaus established the Thesmophoria,[3] and the Dionysian mysteries were taught to the Greeks by the Phoenicians[4] or the Lydians.[5] The truth of these traditions matters little to us; their unanimity demonstrates the principal fact, which is the foreign origin of these first mystery cults. We will add that long after the formation of Greek polytheism institutions of this nature continued to come from abroad. The mysteries of Adonis entered from Assyria by way of the island of Cyprus in the Peloponnese.[6] The dance of the Athenian women at the Thesmophoria is not a Greek dance;[7] and the name of the Sabazian rituals takes us to Phrygia.[8]

1. Sainte-Croix, pp. 77–86; Müller, *De hierarchia*, p. 104.

2. Diod. Sic., III, 55.

3. Herod., II, 171; IV, 172.

4. Herod., II, 49; Apollod., *Bibl.*, I, 9; II, 12. The mysteries of the Cabiric Ceres in Boeotia also had a Phoenician origin. Phoenician sailors had built a temple there dedicated to this goddess.

5. Eurip., *Bacch.*, 460–90. One finds in Wagner (p. 330) proofs that the mysteries of Bacchus were introduced into Thebes from elsewhere.

6. Notably, according to Pausanias, in the *Argolid*.

7. Pollux calls it the Persian dance (*Onomast.*, IV); others, the Mysian dance (Xenoph., *Anab.*, VI, 1–5).

8. Creuzer, III, 360–63. On the foreign origin of the mysteries of Bacchus, even according to the Greeks, see Heeren, *Asie*, pp. 439–40.

We have elsewhere proven that the members of the colonies that landed in Greece for the most part could have only known the external and material part of the religion of the former homeland. But in this material portion there were dramatic representations. The colonists brought these representations into their new establishments; these representations were rejected from the public religion, however, because they did not fit with its spirit, and naturally became mystery rituals, copied on what they had been elsewhere. The mysteries were composed of ceremonies, processions in the interior of temples,[9] and pantomimes. If in the sacred dramas of Egypt Typhon had kidnapped Horus, Pluto in the Thesmophoria kidnapped Proserpina. Plutarch displays the resemblances between the Egyptian stories of Isis and Osiris and the Greek stories of Ceres.[10] The death of this Osiris was based upon that of Cadmillus in the Cabiric mysteries.[11] These dramatic representations probably began by being representations of known fables; then there was nothing mysterious but the performance. Next, new fables were invented that remained secret, and then there was mystery in both the fable and performance. Along with these religious dramas certain names were transported into Greece, exotic formulae, and by that fact unintelligible and unexplainable. That the names of Ceres and Proserpina in the language of the Cabiri are precisely the same as those of the queen of the underworld and her daughter among the Indians can only be the result of chance.[12] The three mysterious words with which, at the end of the great Eleusiniae, the initiates were dismissed,[13] three words which for two centuries have exercised the sagacity of scholars,[14] turn out to be three Sanskrit words

9. In Goerres (II, 379, note) there is an exposition of the processions, the mysteries, and the symbolic meaning of these processions, with very intriguing observations on the conformity of different mythologies.

10. Plut., *De Is. et Osir.*; schol. Apollon., I, 917; Lactant., *De fals. rel.*, pp. 119–20; Diod., I, 2, 36.

11. The founders of the mysteries in Greece sought to add to the fidelity of their imitations by celebrating them in places similar to those of their former homeland. According to a passage of Aristophanes (*Frogs*, 209ff.), it appears that the mysteries of Bacchus at Athens took place on the banks of a lake, because those of Osiris had been celebrated on the lake at Sais. The Lernean mysteries, dedicated to the same god, had as their site the banks of the Halcyon in the Argolid. Creuzer (IV, 50–55) reports that a custom of the Roman matrons was borrowed from a Greek tradition that was itself foreign to Greece. See also the details on the cult of Damia and Anxesia.

12. Ceres, in the mysteries, Axieros: the queen of the netherworld, in India, Asyoruca; Proserpina, Axiocersa; the daughter of the Indian deity, Asyoturscha (*Asiat. Res.*, pp. 299–300).

13. *Conx, om, pax.*

14. Leclerc, *Bibliot. univ.*, VI, 74; Court de Gebelin, *Monde prim.*, IV, 323.

whose meaning applies perfectly to the ceremonies that one brought to a close by pronouncing them.[15]

Thus, the more we enter into the antiquities of India, into that country that seems destined to give us the key to so many unsolved enigmas, the more similarities we perceive between the priestly religions and the mysteries of Greece that were impossible to recognize previously.

Finally, the memory of the dangers of a long and uncertain crossing had to suggest to the sailors who landed in Greece the idea of reunions where they celebrated the memory of the difficulties they had suffered together; and history verifies that these foreigners, founders of the mysteries, added to their local recollections the commemoration of the dangers inherent in long-distance sailing. One of the Cabiri had discovered the art of fighting against the waves;[16] the mysteries of Samothrace had procured a refuge against the storm for the Argonauts.[17] This tradition is a vestige of oriental expeditions combining with Greek expeditions in the stories. In memory of this tradition, the great-priest received on the river those who wanted to be initiated;[18] and many centuries after, the mysteries of the Pelasgian or maritime Isis were celebrated at Corinth.[19]

The mysteries therefore were originally only ceremonies in Greece, as in the countries where they were born, in which initiates were permitted to participate, without obtaining by this admission knowledge of any occult doctrine or philosophy; but gradually they changed nature; here is how.

As civilization progressed, the Greek priesthood, without ever acquiring the authority that this order possessed elsewhere, nonetheless acquired more consistency. Now, in obtaining some power, the priests must have felt even more how limited this power was. Already constituted political authority, the ascendancy of warriors in heroic times, the imagination of the Greeks, active, insolent, and brilliant, the

15. The first, κογε, Sanskrit *cansha*, signifies the object of desire; the second, *om*, is the sacred monosyllable, which the Indians employ at the beginning and conclusion of all their prayers; the third, παξ, Sanskrit *pascha*, signifies Fortune; and it should be noted that the Etruscans placed Fortune among the Cabiri (Serv., *ad Aen.*, I, 325). These were not the only foreign words that were brought into the mysteries. Creuzer (III, 486) cites several others. One could form, he says, a kind of lexicon of the expressions and formulas that were borrowed.

16. Pliny, *Hist. nat.*, IV, 23.
17. Apollon., *Argonaut.*, I, 915–18.
18. Valer. Flacc., II, 435–40.
19. Pausan., *Corinth*, 4; Apul., *Metam.*, XI.

attachment of these peoples to liberty, an attachment that grew from generation to generation—all these circumstances did not permit the priests to take control of the public religion; but outside of this religion they noticed still little-known institutions come from the very countries where the priesthood dominated. We say that these institutions were little known: in truth, it had to be the case that at the period of their introduction they had not made a great impression on the mass of Greeks, since we can find in neither Homer nor Hesiod any allusion to the mysteries, no trace of mysterious customs.[20]

The less general attention that these institutions had attracted, the easier it was for the priesthood to take them over. Their source, their nature, even their separation from everything that existed seemed to invite the priests to take over their ownership, which could not be disputed; or, better put: this ownership had already devolved to them because, by a very simple effect of the establishment of the colonies, several families who descended from these foundations, whom we have spoken about already,[21] already presided over the rituals of the national worship and the celebration of the mysteries.[22]

As a consequence, the priesthood worked[23] diligently to raise the importance of these institutions of which it was the master, while in the national worship it was only a subordinate agent. The mysteries were also multiplied; it was probably in the parts of Greece where foreigners had not brought them that the priests,

20. "Homer and Hesiod," notes Heeren (*Grecs*, 92), "do not speak of the mysteries at all; and even supposing (which is probable) that the mysteries were older than these poets, in their time they did not have the importance they acquired afterward."

21. Bk. V, ch. 1.

22. The foreigners who were founders of the mysteries must have been the first priests, even though they had not exercised priestly functions in their homeland; and the descendants of these foreigners continued to be invested with a dignity that owed to their ancestors. The Eumolpidae at Eleusis represented the superior priests, the Ceryces, the pastophores of Egypt. But the Ceryces, of Athenian origin, were only subordinate sacrificers (*Athenaeus*, VI and XIV), and the first four ministries of the mysteries, the hierophant, etc., all had to be of the family of the Eumolpidae (Heeren, *Grecs*, p. 97). If the national spirit of the Athenians gave the supervision of the mysteries to an archon (Lysias, *Contra Andocides*) and to two administrators chosen by the people (they were called Epimeletes, Pollux, *Onomast.*, VIII, 9, no. 90), all the other priests of the mystery cult had to belong to priestly families (Aristid., *Eleus.*).

23. Creuzer, in his fourth volume (pp. 186–237), analyzes this work of the priesthood with remarkable sagacity, applying himself in particular to Ceres and Proserpina, examining in detail the names and surnames given in the mysteries to these two divinities.

informed of the use they could make of them by the advantage their Egyptian brethren had derived, established some, even before having determined what their content would be. Their mysteries were similar to those sanctuaries where a thick veil hid an empty enclosure from the eyes of the profane. For lack of anything better they closed the entrance of their sacred woods and their temples; certain chapels opened only one time a year and then for a single day.[24] Statues of the gods only appeared veiled;[25] their names could not be revealed without committing a crime.[26] As every type of exclusion shares in mystery, often certain classes were excluded from certain ceremonies; sometimes an entire sex was forbidden. In the same way that the women of the Germans and the Scandinavians had rituals that were reserved to them, the female Greeks had their Thesmophoria where males did not dare enter under penalty of death, the female Romans their festivals of the Bona Dea, the Good Goddess, which became famous by the violation of this rule and the sacrilege of Claudius.

All these mysteries originally consisted in dramatic performances. In the Thesmophoria (to which later people would attribute quite varied, and very profound, significance), Ceres appeared veiled, served and consoled by women. Triptolemus brandished his spear and Celeus measured the earth. At the feet of the goddess were the tripod, a ternary emblem, the boiler, which recalls the cauldron of the Druids, and the mystical mirror (to which we will return), all foreign priestly symbols.[27] But in thus attempting to hide under splendors borrowed from elsewhere the emptiness of the institutions they founded in Greece, the priests applied themselves with filling the void; they worked to have enter these institutions, which depended upon them, everything that was rejected by the independent spirit of the national worship; in other words: priestly customs, rituals, and doctrines.

To describe their efforts in connection with each particular object would be to enter into a path that would exceed all the boundaries of this work; for example, to simply determine the date of the introduction of each opinion or ceremony in the different mystery cults of the Greeks would require discussions with no end

24. Pausan., *Boeot.*, 24.

25. In Greece, there were several statues that only priests had the right to see, the Minerva of Athens, the Diana of Ephesus, etc. They were said to have fallen from heaven.

26. This reticence concerning the names of the gods was a part of the mysteries of Egypt, and it is remarkable that in speaking of the birth of the giant Ymir, the Edda avoids naming the god by whose power this giant was formed (Edda, 2nd fable).

27. See the ancient vase of the collection of Lanzi.

and probably no conclusion. We will limit ourselves, therefore, to proving the fact by showing that in the mysteries all the priestly hypotheses as well as practices are found. But to better grasp this connection, let us observe two things: first, when in proof of the identity of some doctrine or some custom, we cite the meaning it seems to have contained; this is not to say that it did not also have other meanings. Each symbol, each ritual had more than one. Second, several of the facts that we will report occurred, we acknowledge, only toward the last days of the religion. This is because the mysteries, destined by the priesthood of Greece to receive everything that it could borrow from priestly polytheism, only gradually filled up with these borrowings. The composite whole will not be found together except at the fusion of the two polytheisms, that is, toward their fall; but the tendency of the mysteries is shown by this result itself, and the effect, even though late, attests to the cause.[28]

---

28. For the same reason, in violation of our usual rule we sometimes cite authors of a not very remote antiquity. They alone knew the mysteries as they had resulted from this mixture and confusion.

CHAPTER 4

The Conformity of the Teachings of the Greek Mysteries with the Priestly Rituals and Teachings

We have seen that the priestly religions, preserving traces of fetishism in the bosom of civilization, sometimes attributed crude, sometimes monstrous, forms to their gods;[1] the divinities worshipped in the mysteries of Samothrace were, according to Herodotus, shapeless trunks. Bacchus, who in the early times of Greece had borne, as in the East, the head of a bull, but whom the sculptors and poets had separated from this hideous emblem, reprised it in the secret cult that was rendered him under the name Zagreus.[2]

The priests of sacerdotal polytheism adopted the dress of their gods in the dramatic performances, and, going through the entire scale of their accumulated conceptions, sometimes presented themselves as animals, sometimes imitated as best they could the splendor of stars. We find costumes of the same sort in the mysteries of Samothrace and elsewhere.[3] Those who are received at the Leonitica,[4]

---

1. Bk. III, ch. 6.

2. See Nonnus and others. Dionysus Zagreus, with the head of a bull, was the son of Jupiter and Persephone. This misshapen Bacchus is talked about in Pausanias, cited by Eusebius (*Praep. ev.*, V, 36). Bacchus also reprised his wings in the mysteries under the name Bacchus Psitas. One sees him in this way in the monuments of Herculanum. These two attributes that recall the infancy of art express, first, an astronomical notion, and second, the regeneration of the soul and its return to heaven. Ceres in the mysteries was armed with a sword, as in Persia Diemschid was armed with a dagger. The Orphic Saturn or Hercules also had the head of a lion or a bull, wings, and a human body.

3. In the Panathenaea, a priest represented Bacchus. This adoption by priests of the apparel as well as the name of the gods produced great confusion, as much in the fables of the public religion as in the mysteries. It is almost impossible to distinguish the priests from their gods, the history of these gods from that of their priests. In the Idean mysteries, for example, Iasion is a god; in those of Samothrace, a priest. A later tale combined the two traditions by giving Ceres to Iasion as his wife, and for his dowry, apotheosis.

4. Another name for the Mithraic mysteries.

Porphyry tells us,[5] wore the different forms of wild beasts, or traced them on their clothes.[6]

The character of several mysterious divinities is double, like that of Indian divinities. Ceres, the same as Bhavani, is sometimes protective under the name Leucothea,[7] sometimes raging under that of Ceres Erynnis.

The human sacrifices practiced in the mysteries have been denied, and some have suspected the calumny of Christians who imputed these odious rites to their adversaries. But independently of the testimony of historians and the Fathers of the Church,[8] that of Porphyry,[9] whom no one can suspect of any motive of hatred, is explicit and undeniable. In the Dionysia at Chios and Tenedos, he says, a man was immolated in memory of the fable of Bacchus, cut into pieces by the Titans. It was so notorious at the time of Hadrian that the Mithraica were stained by such rites that it was necessary to forbid them expressly. They continued, however, despite this prohibition, and victims served at the extispicies.[10] An ancient tradition to which Euripides refers fixes the sacrifice of a daughter of Erechtheus precisely at the period when the Eleusinian mysteries were established.[11] If we can admit the assertion of Lamprides,[12] who offered only a portrait of these sacrifices without any shedding of blood, this would be no less of a striking conformity with priestly polytheism, where these sorts of performances had always taken place when the softening of mores no longer permitted the reality.

5. Porph., *De abst.*, IV, 16.

6. Sometimes, although rarely, these costumed disguises passed from the mysteries into the public rituals. The scholiast's manuscript of Aristides (*Orat. Panath.*, ed. Iebb., p. 96) notes that in the Bacchanalia a priest fulfilled the role of Bacchus, another priest that of a satyr. In Valerius Flaccus (*Argonaut.*, II, 264ff.), Hypispyle clothed her father in Bacchus's clothes. These customs were brought to Rome in the Cerealia and Isiac festivals. Commodius himself appeared in a festival with the head of Anubis (Lamprid., in *Commodo*, cap. 9), and in the notes of Casaubon one reads verses addressed to a consul who had thus publicly displayed himself in a ceremony.

Teque domo patria pictum cum fascibus ante,

Nunc quoque cum sistro faciem portare caninam.

7. Cic., *De nat. deor.*, III, 19; Ovid, *Fast.*, VI, 545.

8. Socrat., *Hist. ecclés.*, II, 2.

9. De abst., II, 56.

10. Photius, *Bibl.*, 1446.

11. Eurip., *Phoen. Women*, 860–61; Pausan., *Attica*, 38. See also Creuzer for the human sacrifices in the Mithraica.

12. Lamprid., in *Comm.*

Purifications, so customary among the nations subject to priests, were no less so in the mystery rituals transplanted in Greece, and these purifications were of the same sort. Sometimes the profane were made to pass between burning coals or lit pyres;[13] sometimes they were suspended in the air so that the winds could carry away their stains;[14] sometimes they were washed with consecrated water.[15]

The idea of purifications is naturally accompanied by the prohibition of certain foods considered to be unclean.[16] This interdiction is found equally in the priestly religions and in the mysteries.[17]

Among the peoples governed by priests, there were animals it was forbidden to eat, not because they were impure but because of certain teachings that had come to shore up the respect the peoples had already conceived for these animals when they were fetishists. The Syrians abstained from fish because fish had been their fetishes;[18] and their priests giving, as always, an abstract motive for a vulgar superstition, explained this abstinence by their cosmogony, which made the sea a sacred element, and fish, its inhabitants, a sacred race like it.[19] The same privation was commanded at Eleusis.

The renunciation of the pleasures of the senses, homage that priestly polytheism everywhere renders to its jealous gods, was one of the prescribed duties for the initiates, as well as the hierophants who received them: the initiate of Eleusis was obliged to practice continence from the moment he entered the process.[20] The

13. Gori, *Mus. Etrusc.*, I; Pausan., *Boeot.*, 20.

14. Virgil, *Aeneid*, VI. We do not have the habit of citing Roman authors to prove Greek customs; thus, for example, we have kept ourselves from basing our assertions on the authority of Virgil, as certain French scholars do. But it is well known that everything Anchises says to Aeneas in the sixth book of the *Aeneid* is a description of the mysteries established in Greece.

15. All these ceremonies owed to a doctrine inherent in priestly religions, and which we will see shortly become the basis and fundamental principle of the mysteries—that of the return of purified souls to heaven. Ordinarily, Dionysius was the great purifier. This teaching was in fact absolutely necessary for the power of priests. One knows the use the Roman Church made of it until the Reformation. In order to inculcate it even more deeply, one represented the punishment of the soul in hell.

16. Diod., II, 4; Pausan., I, 38; *Attica*, 37.

17. Apul., *Met.*, X; Pausan., *Arcad.*, 15; Porph., *De abst.*, IV, 16. The beans proscribed in Egypt were banished from the Eleusinian mysteries. At Aexone, a small town of Attica, one dared not eat a certain fish because in the mysteries it was considered sacred.

18. See bk. VI, ch. 7.

19. Diod., II, 4; Pausan., 38.

20. Arrian, in *Epictet.*, III, 21. He drank hemlock in order to make this deprivation less harsh. The priests of Diana at Ephesus were constrained to chastity and fasts for one year. The priests and the

priestesses of the Dionysian mysteries at Athens swore between the hands of the wife of the king-archon that they were pure, even from all intercourse with their spouses. Demosthenes has preserved for us the formula of the oath they swore.[21] The female Athenians who prepared themselves for the Thesmophoria absented themselves from the conjugal bed, and this separation from their husbands had to be of some length,[22] since Athenaeus indicates to us what herbs they made use of to support it with less difficulty.[23] Those who had the superintendence of the ceremonies must never have been touched by a man.[24] Celibacy was commanded in the higher levels of the Mithraic mysteries;[25] and, finally, an inviolable chastity was enjoined at Apulia by Isis.[26]

By a natural consequence of this duty imposed on humans, several of the gods honored in the mystery cults were born of a virgin.[27]

The value attached to continence did not exclude the worship of generative organs. Their simulacra had been introduced to Samothrace by the Pelasgians:[28] the representation of Cteis was shown at the Thesmophoria.[29] The canephorae of the Dionysian mysteries carried in the sacred basket the phallus that was brought

---

priestesses of Diana Hymnia in Arcadia submitted themselves to the same obligations during their entire life (Pausan., *Arcad.*, 13).

21. Demosth., contra *Neaeram*. This oath was imposed not only on priestesses but upon all women admitted to the mysteries of Bacchus.

22. Probably of nine days.

23. Hesych., in v. κνεῶροι.; Pliny, *Hist. nat.*, XIV, 9; Dioscor., I, 136; Ael., *De animal.*, IX, 26; schol. Theocr., *Idyll.*, IV, 25; Plut., *De Is. et Osir.*, 69.

24. The very words of Lucan, who, in order to make the fact more salient, opposes them to the hetaerae, trafficking in their charms.

25. Tert., *De praescrip.*, 140. Creuzer establishes a distinction between the Mithraica introduced to Rome and the ancient mysteries of Mithra in Persia (II, 214–217). According to Hyde (*De rel. pers.*), the latter were never celebrated in this country. They were not known by the Romans until after the victory of Pompey over the pirates of Asia Minor (Plut., in *Pomp.*); and even the inscriptions that speak of them do not go back before Constantine (Fréret, *Acad. inscr.*, XVI, 267ff.). The Fathers of the Church saw in the Mithraica only ceremonies borrowed from Christianity to prop up the expiring polytheism. On the contrary, it was a priestly religion transported to Rome under the form of a mystery cult before the triumph of Christianity, and not without a baneful influence on that belief.

26. Apul., *Met.*, XI.

27. Silena, for example.

28. Herod., II, 51.

29. Theodoret, *Serm.*, VII and XII.

near to the lips of the newly received member;[30] and, by a minute conformity, but even more important to notice, this phallus was of fig wood,[31] while dry figs in a similar form were a religious symbol among the Persians.[32] It was by means of the Lernaean mysteries, which were celebrated in the Argolid in honor of Bacchus, that the custom of planting the phallus on tombs was introduced;[33] as in Egypt, it was the emblem of the productive force, which draws life from destruction, and at the same time the symbol of the immortality of the soul, and of metempsychosis.[34]

This secret cult was accompanied in Greece, as the public religion in other nations, with the most licentious ceremonies.[35] Young women, their bosom uncovered, conducted obscene dances at the festivals of Adonis.[36] The debauchery that soiled these feasts is described with pleasure by Ovid,[37] bitterly by Juvenal,[38] and that of the Sabazian mysteries is strongly deplored by the first Fathers of the Church.[39]

30. Theodoret, *Therapeut., disput.*, I.

31. Theodoret, *Serm.*, VII.

32. Plut., *Artaxerxes*. The fig tree was consecrated to Mithras in his mysteries. A hog was also sacrificed, as in Egypt.

33. Pausan., *Corinth*, 37.

34. Creuzer, *Dionys.*, pp. 236ff.

35. Theocr., *Idyll.*, XV.

36. It is because he did not distinguish between the popular worship and the mysteries that a learned man, who otherwise is very much to be recommended, could have written words that are so inaccurate: "In general, Hellenism consisted in absurd and scandalous traditions, in impious or impure rituals, in festivals of pleasure or delight" (Sainte-Croix, *Recherches sur les myst. du pag.*, ed. of Mr. Sylvestre de Sacy, I, 375).

37. *De art. amand.*, I, 75. To explain why we cite Ovid here, we point the reader to note 14 above.

38. Juv., *Sat.*, VI.

39. Clement of Alexandria and others. The *Aulularia* of Plautus revolves around the adventures of a girl who became pregnant during a mystery festival. The elevation of the Phallus, customary in the mysteries, was an Egyptian rite brought into Greece by Melampus (Sainte-Croix, *Les myst.*, p. 17). The indecencies of the cult of Bacchus at Sicyon (Bayle, art. "Bacchus"), the obscenities of the worship of Ceres and Proserpina in Sicily (Diod., V, 4), where the crudeness of words was prescribed because, it was said, in this way one had extracted a smile from the despairing goddess, and the infamy of the Sabazian mysteries (Cic., *De nat. deor.*, III, 13; Sainte-Croix, pp. 437–39), are well-attested facts. The story of Pasiphae, performed in the mysteries of Samothrace, was the importation of pleasures running counter to nature that we have seen to be a part of priestly cults. "What the Eleusinian mysteries have that is holiest," says Tertullian (*Adv. Valent.*), "what is so carefully hidden, what one is not permitted to know until much later, is the idol of Phallus." A passage of Clement of Alexandria in

The hermaphroditic divinities who in the scientific language of priests are the emblems of the creative force, or the reunion of the two active and passive principles, reappear in the mysteries. The Dioscuri at Samothrace,[40] Bacchus in the Dionysian mysteries, are invested with the attributes of the two sexes;[41] and the hare, to whom the ancients attributed the same privilege,[42] as the symbol of Bacchus always figures at the entrance of his grotto on the vases that were used at, or alluded to, the Bacchanalia. Adonis was invoked as being at once a young virgin and an adolescent.[43] The combination of these two principles is also represented in another symbol, that of a marriage between a brother and a sister, and we have seen[44] that the two highest divinities of peoples subject to priests almost always had this relationship. It is plausible that the popular mythology had borrowed the fable of the marriage of Jupiter and Juno from these traditions; but what is sure is that this cosmogonic incest was the basis of the Dionysian mysteries. Jacchus and Proserpina, Coros and Core, Liber and Libera are both brother and sister and husband and wife.

Let us move on from rituals[45] to opinions.

Eusebius proves that these institutions, in which moderns have sought the improvement of morality and the purity of theism, brought together brutality and license. "Do you want," he says, "to see the orgies of the corybants? You will only see killings, tombs, priestly lamentations, the natural parts of a dismembered Bacchus carried in a box and presented for worship. But do not be astonished if the barbarous Tuscans have such shameful worship. What would I say of the Athenians and the other Greeks in their mysteries concerning Demeter?" Note that the author speaks of the cult of the Tuscans in general, hence he is speaking of their public worship, and that in connection with the Greeks he speaks only of their mysteries.

40. Lydus, *De mensib.*, 65.

41. The Sabazian Bacchus; Aristid., *Orat. in Baccho*; Philostratus, *Vit. Apollon.*, III, 34. In Millin (*Peint. des vas. antiq.*, I, 77), one sees Bacchus as a winged hermaphrodite. On the island of Cos he was worshipped as a hermaphrodite with the surname Briseis.

42. Clem. Alex., *Pedag.*, 2. The moderns, more accurate observers, reduced the privilege of the hare to no less desirable faculties, but less miraculous.

43. Lydus (*De mensib.*, 92) says that, in the mysteries of Hercules, the priests put on women's clothing, and referring to Nicomachus, who had written on the Egyptian festivals, he indicates that this custom came from Egypt. By a remarkable extension of this mystical notion, one of the plants that served in the Thesmophoria, asphodelus, passed for hermaphroditic (Dioscor., II, 199).

44. Bk. VI, ch. 3.

45. If we did not fear to go into too many details, we would have pointed out the deviations from the public worship in the mystery cults, which were always aimed at rendering more exact their imitation of priestly rituals. Thus, to cite but one example, the billy goat was ordinarily the victim of

Among priestly nations, all the sciences, all the discoveries, all the decisive improvements in the situation of the human species were attributed to gods. The priests of the mystery cults hastened to assign to all these things an origin that ascribed to religion the merit of everything that was useful in these métiers, as well as beautiful in the arts and wise in the laws. The mysteries of the Corybantes retraced the invention of agriculture,[46] those of the Curetes, the first efforts at navigation,[47] those of the Dactyls, metallurgy.[48] The Bacchants in their frenzy tore the animals they encountered and devoured the scraps of their still-palpitating flesh.[49] This horrible meal became the commemoration of the passage from the savage state to the social state. The initiates at the Dionysian mysteries ate raw flesh at a particular feast in memory of the barbarism to which men had been reduced before priests had civilized them.[50] The establishment of laws gave Ceres the epithet legislatrix,[51] which was given to Themis in other mysteries.[52] The union of medicine and religion was celebrated.[53] The horns of Bacchus were the symbol of bulls yoked to the plow,[54] and his mangled body that of the grape torn from the vine and crushed in the press.[55]

Bacchus; but the mysteries replaced the goat with the pig, because such was the custom of Egypt. The Egyptians, says Herodotus (II, 47–48), regarded these animals as impure and offered them in sacrifice only to Bacchus and the moon.

46. Varro, *ap.* August., *De civ. Dei*, VII, 20–24.

47. Diod., V, 48; Conon, *Narrat.*, XXI; Tzetzes, *ad* Lycophr., 73.

48. Diod., V, 74.

49. Eurip., *Bacch.*, l. 139.

50. Diod., V, 75; Clem. Alex., *Cohort*; Origen, *Contra Celse*, IV; Epiphan., *Adv. haeres*; Macrob., *Somn. Scipion.*, I, 12.

51. Ceres Thesmophora and Thesmothete. Hesych., v. Θεμιστες. Virgil says Ceres Legifera. The name Thesmophoria recalls the establishment of the laws.

52. Euseb., *Praep. ev.*

53. One of the Cabiri was Asclepius. The invention of medicine was attributed to the gods in the mysteries, as to Isis in Egypt.

54. Wagner, p. 333.

55. Ceres was the earth, the Titans the winemakers who crushed the grape and made it ferment; Rhea, who reassembled the members of the divine child cut into pieces, was the wine composed of the juice of different grapes. Diodorus adopts this symbolic meaning, and after him Cornutus (*De nat. deor.*, cap. 10). But never forget that all these symbols had several senses. Even Diodorus, in the place cited, adds that other interpretations of the same fable were hidden from the profane. Of this number was the astronomic meaning. Bacchus torn into seven pieces alluded to the seven planets. What demonstrates this is that according to Orphic teachings, this god presided over each of them under

Astronomy, which occupied in the polytheism subject to priests a place such that it appeared to many scholars to constitute by itself a religion, could not fail to obtain a similar rank in the mysteries. The Sabazian dances were a pantomimic representation of the movements of the sun, the moon, and the planets.[56] The ladder with eight rungs was an astronomical symbol because it revealed that the souls passed from one planet to another in ascending the heavens.[57]

Demonology is also found in them.[58] The entourage of Bacchus which in the popular religion was unbridled, licentious, and boisterous—Silenus, Pan, the satyrs, the nymphs of Nysa, wet-nurses of the god, like the shepherdesses who fed Krishna—became intermediary *genii*; even the initiation was personified under the name Telete; daughter of Bacchus and Nicaea, she was the night dancer, rejoicing in the festivals and pleasing herself with the sound of timpani.[59] The Or-

---

a different name; over the moon, under the name Liknites; Mercury, under that of Silenus; the sun, under that of Trieterica; Mars, that of Bassareus; Jupiter, that of Sabazian; Saturn, that of Omphietes (Girald., *De musis.*). The same fable was also one of the symbols of the original fall. The Titans, it was said, having cut Bacchus in pieces, and having devoured him, were hit with Jupiter's lightning. Their lifeless bodies produced matter, and from this matter men were formed. From this origin comes all that our passions possess that is violent, crude, and fierce. Born of the flesh of the Titans, our bodies have preserved their culpable inclinations. One must punish them for their previous fault, make them suffer, and subjugate them (Plut., *De esu carnium*; Olympiodor., in fragm. *Orph.*, p. 509). Here we can again see, reintroduced by the expiatory power of penance, the notion of the religious merit of suffering.

56. Plut., *De orac. def.*, 10. The priests of Eleusis played the role of astronomical divinities in the mysteries, like the Egyptian priests in the festivals of Egypt. The hierophant represented the Demiourgos; the Dadouchos, the sun; the Epibomus, the moon; etc. Astronomy joined, as always, with astrology. In the sixth Orphic hymn the planets are called the dispensers and declarers of destinies. In general, all the symbols of the Orphic doctrine fix thought on the worship of celestial bodies. The tradition said that Orpheus had declared the sun the first of the gods. The seven strings of the Orphic lyre, which did not differ at all from the Egyptian lyre of Thot or Hermes (Spanheim, 117; Hemsterh. *ad* Lucan, II; Foerkel, *Gesch. der Musik*), represented the seven planets. Their relations with destiny were a natural consequence of the connection of astrology with star-worship.

57. The same combination is found in the mysteries devoted to Hercules among the Athenians. Hercules was at once the god of the sun and he who presided over the purification of souls by fire and light (Lyd., *De mens.*, 93).

58. We will return to the demonology of the mysteries when we treat the demonology of the Neoplatonists, because these philosophers had taken it over and wanted to make it an essential part, and principal support, of the polytheism that they refounded.

59. Nonnus, *Dionys.*, VIII, XI, XIII. It is for this that Pausanias speaks of a statue of Orpheus on the Helicon, alongside of which one saw one of Telete; but he includes no details, and appears not to

phic hymn sung in the Dionysian mysteries, of which we have some fragments in Clement of Alexandria,[60] contains all the oriental traditions concerning the *genii* hovering at the peak of heaven and descending to the bowels of the earth in order to govern the stars, elements, metals, plants, and protecting pure souls, announcing the future to them,[61] and punishing corrupt souls.[62]

Metempsychosis, an opinion, as we have proven, foreign to the popular religion of Greece but inherent in the religions of Egypt and India, was one of the most fully developed teachings, revealed with the greatest solemnity, in the mystery religions. It was designated symbolically in the Mithraic mysteries by the ladder of eight rungs we spoke about earlier, the most secret, and last, of the symbols that the initiates were allowed to see.[63] In the Dionysian mysteries it was combined, as in Egypt, with the notion of the return of souls to the Divinity.

Among the priestly solemnities, the commemoration of the upheavals of nature occupies an important place. In the mysteries, these formidable convulsions are retraced under the symbol of Vulcan, twice cast from heaven into the sea, occupied with subterranean labors for nine years, and reconciled with Olympus by Bacchus, who got him drunk and who, mounted on a mystical ass, saved the central fire, or soul of the world, from destruction.[64] The killing of the same Bacchus symbolized natural revolutions in the Dionysian mysteries.[65]

To the scientific teachings were successively joined fragments of theogonies and cosmogonies.[66] Silenus presents to Bacchus the cosmogonic egg; in the mysteries,

---

have noticed the very natural personification which placed initiation alongside the presumed founder of the mysteries (Pausan., *Boeot.*, 80).

60. *Stromat.*, V, 724.

61. Plut., *De Is. et Osir.*

62. Proclus, in Plato.

63. Cels., *ap.* Orig., VI; Porph., *De abst.*, IV, 16.

64. Aristid., in *Bacch.*, p. 29.

65. See Creuzer for details on the introduction of the six ages of the world in the Orphic cosmogonies. A different god presided over each of these ages: Phanes, Night, Uranus, Saturn, Jupiter, and Dionysius. One recognizes in Jupiter a point where the popular religion and the Orphic cosmogony encountered one another, without mixing. (Creuzer, III, 325–27).

66. The Orphic cosmogony taught in the mysteries was entirely borrowed from priestly cosmogonies. At the beginning was chaos, the incommensurable, the uncreated (Clem., *Recogn.*, XI). With it lived eternal time, the principle of all things (Simplicius, in *Phys.* Arist.). It contained the seed of all the beings, all the qualities, all the elements, but in a shapeless mass. From this was born Aether (Suidas, *voce Orph.*), which until then was enveloped on all sides by night, and which, launching itself

as in Phoenicia, this egg is the great whole which contains all beings; and the son of Night, the organizer of the elements, the prime mover of all existence, Eros, who according to the priests plays such a large role in the engendering of the world, is found in the mystery teachings.

By means of a legend, the mysteries of Samothrace affirm the trinity, always inseparable from priestly cosmogonies. The two Corybantes or Cabiri kill their

---

from the bottomless abyss, shone a ray of ineffable clarity upon nature. This ray, the most ancient and most sublime of the beings, is the god, knowledge of which no one can achieve, which contains everything in its substance and which is called intelligence, light, and life, three words that designate a single essence. Chaos then took the rounded form of a monstrous egg, from which, after several centuries, emerged Phanes, the great Whole, the shining hermaphrodite, with the form of a dragon and two heads, one of a lion, the other of a bull. From two portions of the egg broken by Phanes, one became the heavens and the other, the earth (Athenagor., *pro Christ.*). These two twins united and engendered the three Fates and Destiny. Here are placed the tales of the Centimanes, the Cyclops, the Titans, and the mutilation of Saturn, and one gets to the bottom of the relation of this cosmology with the mythology of Hesiod, since Saturn is expelled by Jupiter. But this mythology, despite the Greek names that enter into it, is far from Greek in its spirit. Jupiter, in the form of a serpent, violates Rhea, his mother: Persephone, with her four eyes, her head of an animal with horns, is born of this incest. A second one unites her to her father, and she gives birth to Dionysus. Behold the many priestly characteristics that are brought together: (1) Chaos; (2) the primitive night, the Athyr of the Egyptians; (3) monstrous figures; (4) time without end, or the Zervan Akarana of the Persians; (5) the trinity; (6) hermaphroditic gods; (7) their incestuous generation, etc.; (8) the cosmogonic egg that we have encountered everywhere. In the Orphic hymns (*Hymne orphique à Proserpine*, XXXI, 15), Proserpina is invoked as at once death and life, producing all and destroying all. This is exactly what the Indians say about Bhavani. In another cosmogony, the Demiourgos confers with Maya, illusion, on the formation of the universe, to which Ophion, the serpent-god, the necklace of Arimanes, is opposed: behold Persian and Indian combined. In a third cosmogony, the periods of the world correspond to the yogas of the Indians, and destruction by fire is still an Indian doctrine.

The Orphic hymns are the expression of the complete emigration of priestly allegories and cosmogonies, not in the popular polytheism, because they never completely and actively entered into it, but into the theological poetry of the Greek mysteries. These hymns were sung in the mystery rites and in an obvious way, resembled the prayers found in the books of Zoroaster that Herodotus called Επωδαι (Pausan., II; and Heeren, *Grecs*, p. 156). Herodotus himself says that the Orphic doctrines came originally from Egypt. These doctrines, consequently, introduced into the mysteries everything found in Egypt, notions on metempsychosis, the sadness of life, and the past and future upheavals of physical nature, as well as orgies, licentious feasts, sometimes bloody ones, the cult of the Phallus, frenzied dances, and mutilations. The Orphic life differed not at all from that of the Egyptian priests. The hymns sung in the mysteries are stamped with the same characteristics, and indicate the same origin, as the Vedas, the Puranas, the Zend books, or the *Voluspa*. There are even traits of similarity with the poetry of the bards, about which we have spoken elsewhere (bk. VI, ch. 7).

brother, place a crown on his head, and cover him with a purple veil, then place him on a bronze shield and bury him at the foot of Olympus; then separating the phallus from the body, which they carry to Tuscany,[67] these two Corybantes form, we would say, a Samothracian trinity with this incarnate God, whom his worshippers, their hands red with blood, invoke in memory of his death.[68]

To have the identity of these doctrines and those of priestly nations stand forth more vividly, let us stop for a moment on the symbol of the cups and the mirror, a symbol that served as a text for the allusions of Aristophanes[69] and the eloquence of Plato.[70] The Demiourgos, Bacchus, the Creator and Redeemer, has two cups. One is the cup of unity; the soul of the world is formed in it. The other is the cup of division, from which partial souls emerge, condemned to birth and rebirth. They cannot escape individuality, either because they have to cooperate in the ordering or preservation of this universe and have not yet taken part in this common task;[71] or because, having already lived in this world, they have committed faults and are reborn in bodies in order to atone for them; or because a fatal curiosity drove them.[72] They cast a glance at the mysterious mirror. The Demiourgos also has contemplated himself it in; he saw his image in it and the desire to create had taken hold of him. Souls look at themselves in it; a mad desire for individuality disturbs and misleads them. They want to know what happens outside the celestial precinct; they want to exist by themselves, another mad desire because individuality is only a wrenching separation. They take their flight toward earth;[73] they drink from the cup of oblivion and become intoxicated; the memory of their noble origin leaves them and they more and more bury themselves in matter.[74] The best resist this temptation for a long time; at the height of heaven they beat their wings,[75] holding them apart from bodies so as not to be cast into them. Finally succumbing, they recommend themselves to their good *genius* who protects them, whom they understand despite the distance. They drink only a measured

---

67. Clem. Alex., *Protrept.*, p. 15.
68. Firmicus, *De error. prof. relig.*, cap. 12.
69. Aristoph., *Frogs*, 154, 321, 390.
70. Plato, *Phaedo.*
71. They were called the new souls, νεοτελεῖς.
72. Celsus in Orig., VIII.
73. Plotinus, *Enneads*, IX, 3, 12; Proclus, in Plato, *Tim.*
74. Macrob., *Somn. Scip.*; Creuzer, *Dionys.*, I, 90.
75. Plato, *Phaed.*; Plot., *Enneads*, IV, 1–8.

amount from the intoxicating cup and preserve a bit of memory of their previous state. The less pure attach themselves to the earth, a place of misery, which appears to them to be full of charms. They no longer listen to the voice of the tutelary daemon.[76] Their bodies become thick and heavy burdens, but which they cherish. They resemble the sea god, Glaucus, who in the depths of the sea attracted to himself shells, stones, and plants, which covered him, but with which he identified, and thus remained crushed under their weight.[77]

However, return is available to these miserable souls. In his pity, the Demiourgos does not want their degradation to be without end.[78] Death, a beneficent god, begins their deliverance and frees them from their ancient evil,[79] and offers them the cup of wisdom.[80] If they drink from it, their misguided desire ceases and the desire to return is awakened; but it is not enough. New appearances in the world, migrations,[81] and purifications are still necessary. The mysteries hasten these migrations, render these purifications more effective, and grant the living before their passing-on, and on this earth, what they would not obtain in the underworld except after death. All these symbols—the cups, the mirror, the misguided distraction of the deceived souls, the repugnance, then the love, then again the exhaustion, of individuality, the terror of rebirth, the efforts to escape from it—the priesthood aids these efforts by revelations, lustrations, penances, and prayers; the definitive deliverance, the supreme good consisting in no longer reentering a mortal body,[82] heaven regained, the Demiourgos receiving the exiles in his bosom, whence they will never depart: all these notions are Egyptian, Persian, and above all, Indian.[83]

76. Hermias, *ad* Plato, *Phaed.*

77. Procl., *De Anima et Daemone.*

78. Plot., *Enneads,* IV, 3–12.

79. *Their ancient evil,* their penchant for individuality, a technical term in the mysteries.

80. Those who drank from this cup, says Mercury Trismegistus (*Monas,* no. 4), although born mortal, become immortal. Their spirit grasps what is on the earth, in the seas, and above in the heavens. They contemplate the good, and because they have chosen the best, they become gods.

81. One can recall that Pindar required three transmigrations for souls to arrive at felicity (*Olymp.,* II, 23).

82. We know from Proclus (in Plato, *Tim.*) the Orphic prayer, tending to close the circle, to breathe freely after distress; i.e., not to return to a mortal body.

83. A connection that is rather unique, and which merits some attention, is that one finds in the mythology of the Welsh the counterpart of the cup of unity in which the Demiourgos mixes the elements of the universe; the cup of Ceridwen combines the substances that compose all the beings. It

The mysterious mirror is the necklace of the Maya of India, and it should be noted that, in her quality as creator or nurse of individual beings, Proserpina is also called Maya.[84]

At the same time, these teachings on the souls are connected to the system in which Bacchus is the sun, hence a double explanation results, at once astronomical and metaphysical, and by means of a chain of subtleties that we will omit, the astronomical system once again is applied to the destiny of souls.

Under a certain aspect, this purifying teaching, both in priestly religions and in the mystery cults, has something beautiful to it; but let us not forget that, on one hand, it does not prohibit the priests, everywhere they dominate, from maintaining their slaves brutalized and ignorant, and, on the other, that it was embellished by the Greek imagination, against which the Greek priesthood, despite its efforts, could not always defend itself.

Finally, all the ancients speak of the austerities, the voluntary torments that the initiates imposed upon themselves or those who aspired to initiation. Fasts preceded the celebration of the Thesmophoria. Those just admitted to the mysteries of Isis had to abstain for ten days from all food that flattered their senses, from the flesh of all animals and from every drink other than water.[85] In the solemnities of Eleusinian Ceres at Phenea in Arcadia, the hierophant struck those who attended with multiple blows,[86] as did the priests of Isis at Busiris in Egypt.[87] Eighty degrees of trials were necessary to participate in the Mithraica.[88] Weakened by hunger, wounded with rods, covered with mud, plunged into foul mire, or thrown into frigid water, for several days or even months the candidates were subject to torments that placed their life in danger.[89] These practices cannot fail to recall the doctrine of the sanctity of pain and suffering that we have seen established in priestly polytheism, and whose source and nature we have attempted to explain; and note well that in the mysteries, as in the priestly religions, the gods, who imi-

---

also is possible that the cup of the Holy Grail, which contained the blood of Jesus Christ, celebrated in our novels of chivalry, was a reminiscence of mystical cups.

84. Porph., *De abst.*, IV, 16.

85. Apul., *Met.*, XI.

86. Pausan., *Arcad.*, 15.

87. Herod., II, 61.

88. Julian, cited by Wagner, p. 239.

89. Justin Martyr, *Apologet.*, I, 86; Nonnus, *ap.* Gregor. Nazianz., pp. 131–45. For other details concerning these austerities, see *Mem. de l'Acad. des. inscrip.*, V, 117–22.

tate mortals, aspire like them to sanctification by torments; like their priests, they mutilate themselves,[90] and while popular belief had attributed these mutilations only to gods who fell outside the national mythology, in its secret conferences the priesthood attributed them to divinities worshipped by the people. Jupiter, they said to the initiates, had mutilated himself in his repentance for having violated Ceres.[91] Eshmun, who in Phoenicia, tired of the love of the goddess Astronoë, had abjured his sex, commits the same assault in the mysteries of Samothrace and becomes the eighth Cabiri, who, under the name Aesculapius or Paean, presides over medicine.

The teaching of a god dead and resuscitated, a doctrine taught by all the priestly religions without exception, contrasts so much with the Greek conceptions that the Cretans who display the tomb of Jupiter on their island[92] were accused of lying by all of Greece;[93] and this tradition of which they made a point of honor, initially a subject of shame, later became the object of the mockeries of unbelievers. Thus the points of view change with the times. In the priestly religions, the death of the gods is a dogma, in the popular religion, an impiety; and from the time of Lucan, only irony recalls it, in order to ridicule it. But in the mysteries the legend continued and was expanded. Attis, Adonis, Bacchus, and Cadmillus are gods who die[94] and are reborn.[95] Juno, jealous of Proserpina, caused Zagreus to die by stirring the Titans[96] against him, in the way that an Egyptian queen, Aso, joins with Typhon and killed Osiris. Turbulent regrets and frenzied lamentations, scru-

---

90. On the god who mutilates himself in the mysteries of Samothrace, see Creuzer, II, 336.

91. Clem. Alex., *Protrept.*

92. Meursius, in *Cretâ.*

93. This claim of the Cretans was the origin of the well-known proverb that Cretans are liars.

94. Staeudlin, *Rel. Mag.*, II, 167–98.

95. If we could compare in an adequate way the deaths of Bacchus Zagreus and Osiris, the reader would be struck by the perfect identity of all the fables and practices. But this comparison would entail so many details that we have been compelled not to enter into it. One can find several of these details in Creuzer, III, 355–60. This writer, without going back to the cause of these tales, was struck by the fact that serves as their foundation. "In all the mysteries," he says, "there were divinities who took part in the human condition and who were suffering and dying beings" (IV, 302–3). Elsewhere he expresses himself in an even more affirmative way. "Bacchus," he says, "born of Jupiter, cut into pieces by the Titans, and ascending to heaven after his members had been reassembled by Apollo, is a god who came down to earth, suffered, died, and was resurrected; and, in this perspective is entirely an Indian incarnation."

96. Clem. Alex., *Protrept.*, 15; Nonnus, *Dionys.*, VI.

pulously based upon foreign rituals, announce the passing-on of these sacrificed gods; but soon overcoming a temporary death, they again see the light of day and bring to the souls of those present a joy as disordered and boisterous as had been their sadness.

To these doctrines perhaps joined some political ideas, as an effect of circumstances peculiar to Greece's location. One sees in Hesiod, we have already noted, the hatred of the oppressed against the oppressors: Hesiod wrote at the time of the destruction of the Greek monarchies. The mysteries, however, had been brought to Greece before this destruction; some of these had perhaps covered with their veils sacred conspiracies in favor of liberty. Obscure insinuations, scattered here and there in the ancients, make it rather probable that men indignant at the yoke of kings, in imitation of the mysteries, or in the mysteries themselves, formed secret societies to overthrow tyranny.[97]

This is not all.

We have shown unbelieving opinions becoming a part of the secret teaching of priests in countries submitted to their empire, but always remaining hidden from the profane. This provides an additional proof that in these countries the priests alone composed the enlightened class.

In independent polytheism, on the contrary, an enlightened class existed alongside the priesthood. Thus the priesthood did not feel strong enough to maintain itself, as its colleagues in Egypt or India, in an isolated position, in a remote camp, as it were; it found itself in a society that not being subject to it, examined its rights and contested its prerogatives. The mystery cults furnished it with a means of calling the profane to its assistance, and to form a body of auxiliaries, by attaching them to itself by means of its revelations; but it was necessary that these revelations be important. It was not a matter of captivating a stupid populace, distracted from all meditations by constant labors, whose faculties were kept within a narrow circle by a priestly caste and who came to attend ceremonies where their eyes were dazzled but their minds did not seek out the meaning; these were men versed in all the sciences, habituated to reflection, men revolted by the crudeness or license of popular fables which in their obvious imperfections needed to be harmonized.

Philosophical doctrines had entered too deeply into the Greek spirit not to have

97. Plutarch is quite interesting to read on this subject. The initiates in the mysteries of Mithras, he says, hoped for a universal republic and the return of the golden age. The entire human race was to be a single family. A fraternal equality was to reign; there was to be a community of goods and unity of language.

attracted the attention of the priesthood. It had to conduct itself in their regard as it had conducted itself vis-à-vis the foreign religions. History shows it persecuting philosophy in public and enriching itself with its victims in secret. The different systems of philosophy had to simultaneously, but separately, become parts of the mysteries.

All these systems were subversive of the public belief. Irreligion was therefore introduced into institutions destined to strike men with religious terror and respect. Not only were the apotheoses of deified heroes called into doubt, but this doubt was carried to the divinity of the higher gods; sometimes one taught, like Euhemerus, that these gods were only mortals; sometimes, like Varro, that they were only personified elements. The ancients, says the latter,[98] in their mysteries have so arranged the idols, the external marks and ornaments of the gods, that at first glance one can recognize the soul of the world and its parts, the true divinities.

Dualism, an essential element of priestly polytheism, was one of the explanations of the Eleusinian mysteries.[99] Julian[100] says that one celebrates these august ceremonies at the autumnal equinox in order to obtain from the gods that the soul does not experience the malign influence of the dark power that is going to prevail in nature; and the fable that says that Venus, having wanted to take the place of Minerva and work like her, feeling the thread break in her fingers, indicates the corruption of matter, resisting the hand of the creator.[101] The same hypothesis is found in the Mithraic mysteries.[102]

Theism[103] depopulated the heaven of its innumerable divinities to replace them

98. *Ap.* August., *Civ. Dei.*, VII, 5.

99. Dio. Chrys., *Orat.*, 12; Themist., *Or.*, 2. All the fables of the mysteries, says Creuzer, among other things, allude to the struggle between good and evil (IV, 37).

100. *Orat.*, V.

101. Nonnus, *Dionys.*, XXIV.

102. *Mém. de l'Acad. des inscrip.*, XXXI, 421–22; *Act. disput. Archel.*; and Manet, *ap.* Zacagni *Monum., Eccles. Gr. et Lat.*, pp. 62–63.

103. Mr. de Sainte-Croix rejects the idea that the unity of God was taught in the mysteries; but all his arguments have force only by supposing them directed against a single and identical teaching. They have no force against a theism that was revealed separately, without entailing the exclusion of entirely different revelations. Theism, says this writer, taught secretly, being in contradiction to the public religion, would have led to the overturning of the altars. Thus the mysteries contributed to this overturning. He thinks that theism was introduced after the birth of Christianity; but at the time of the establishment of Christianity the universal tendency was to theism; how would the mystery cults have escaped from it? (Sainte-Croix, *Les myst.*, 1st ed., pp. 353, 359).

with a single invisible, incorporeal, ineffable, all-powerful being, but who was inaccessible to vows and prayers; or pantheism, depriving the god of theism of his separate existence, made him reenter the substance of which all beings are formed.[104] Atheism itself became part of the mysterious revelation, as a final communication,

104. In the mysteries of Hermione, whose rites, reported by Pausanias (II, 35), indicate an entirely priestly origin, and which were so ancient that the Greeks had forgotten their meaning, there was a fundamental teaching according to which all the divinities that were adored—Ilithyia, Minerva, Bacchus, and Venus (Isis, Demeter, Pluto, Serapis, and Proserpine)—were but one god, with different male and female attributes, and, at bottom, the elemental original night of the Egyptians (ibid., 47). "*In mysteriorum doctrina esoterica*," writes Villoison (*ap.* Sainte-Croix, pp. 227–28), "*quae tota physica innitebatur theologia, ea tradebantur, quibus mythica et civilis ita funditus everteretur theologia, ut velum superstitioni abductum, poetica suavitate ornatum, et potenti eorum qui respublicas administrabant manu sustentatum, penitus removeretur, et sola natura, unica theologiae physicae dea, secum habitans, et orbi, tanquam altari insidens, ac subjecta pedibus falsorum vulgi numinum simulacra proterens, sese oculis offerret*." The slaughter of the young Bacchus that we have often spoken about was also the apparent separation of the parts of the grand Whole, parts that formed the elements, bodies, plants, and animals. It was for this that this god, in Nonnus (*Dionys.*, VI, 174ff.), before falling to the blows of the Titans, transformed himself into fire, air, into all sorts of elements and natures. Plutarch (*De Ei ad. Delph.*) says that all the legends that speak of a dead or disappearing god, resuscitated or rediscovered, always signified the revolutions of the great being that contains the totality of what exists; from this, the complement of this species of drama. Apollo reassembles the scattered members of Bacchus and buries them in his temple at Delphi, i.e., he recomposes the great Whole by bringing together all its parts (Plut., *De Is. et Osir.*). Behold a new explanation of creonomia. It simultaneously signified making wine, the course of stars, the original stain of man, his triumph over his passions and senses, the convulsions of the physical universe, the passage from the savage to the social state, and the absorption of all things by the infinite being. In this pantheistic explanation of the mysteries, Apollo represented unity (Plut., *De Ei ad. Delph.*; Procl., in Plato, *Alcib. Orph.* fragm., Herm. ed., p. 580); Bacchus, the diversity that comes from unity itself. All the ceremonies and representations of the mysteries were interpreted in this sense. Apollo always appears under the same form, that of a young man who is perfectly and eternally handsome because he experiences no change. Bacchus had a thousand different forms; and in human form he was a child, an adolescent, a mature man, an old man. The genre of poems devoted to these two divinities was expressive of these two ideas. The hymn sung in honor of Apollo, which the Greeks called a *paean*, was grave, with a regular rhythm, composing a uniform whole and with a steady beat. Bacchus preferred the dithyramb: fiery, disordered, without succession or rule (Plut., *De Is. et Osir.*). Sometimes it is not Apollo but Vulcan (Hephaistos, the Ptah of Egypt) who is the grand Whole. In the pantheistic symbols of the mysteries, there are images that are entirely Indian. Jupiter, at the death of Semele, confining Bacchus in his thigh, signifies the first cause containing the prototypical idea of all things. In the Dionysiacs it was said that Jupiter, the Demiourgos, had swallowed Phanes, who contained in himself the universe, and that then all the parts of the universe had become visible. In the same way, in the Bhagavad Gita, all things reside in Krishna

a mark of deepest confidence, the result of profound study, a secret, finally, that was transmitted only to a small number of elect, with so many ceremonies, after such preparations, that it was surrounded with an almost sacred obscurity.

What at first glance appears to be inexplicable and contradictory is that these irreligious hypotheses were presented to initiates with all the pomp of religion. The phenomenon of a class that, devoted to the maintenance and celebration of the cult, calls to itself in the midst of festivals, into the very sanctuary of the gods, men in large number in order to reveal to them that the religion that it teaches to the people is only a tissue of puerile fables, this phenomenon will appear less surprising if one reflects that this revolution was not the original goal, nor the sole aim, nor at any time the general goal of the mysteries.

Two motives encouraged the priests to allow opinions into their hidden teaching that daily acquired greater credit: on one hand, the interest of their order; on the other, individual self-love.

In allowing philosophy into the mysteries, they rendered it more indulgent toward external practices that it was important to them to preserve. Fighting publicly against its progress, they secretly connived with it. They disarmed it by adopting it. They congratulated themselves on making an ally of it by granting it the privilege of initiation. Privileges generally corrupt those who receive them. It therefore was not a bad calculation for the priesthood to associate this formidable class with itself, recognizing that in reality nothing was less remote from philosophy than religion rightly understood. It then added that these explanations ought to be carefully hidden from the people; and the human heart contains such an insolent and absurd pride that persuades each individual that he alone possesses a reason strong enough not to abuse what he knows. Each one thinks that the others will be blown away by the light that simply enlightens him. Thus the priests, who because of their estate proscribe irreligion, sought by craft to enroll it under their banner, and as a condition for peace, asked only for silence.

At the same time, individual self-love favored the transaction between unbelief

---

and he reveals them to Jasada, his nurse, by opening his mouth. Phanes was the same as Bacchus, and the latter, by his reunion with Jupiter, was absorbed in the essence of this god. Jupiter, the father of all things, says Proclus (in Plato, *Tim.*), produced them and Bacchus then governs them. Jupiter and Bacchus make but one, says Aristides (Orat., in *Bacch.*). This contradiction, or rather this fluctuation, by which Jupiter and Bacchus were sometimes two separate divinities (even though in intimate relation with one another) and sometimes the same divinity, is identical with what one reads in the sacred books of the Hindus.

and the mystery cults. Like all men, priests are subject to the irresistible impulse imprinted on human intelligence by nature. When doubt enters into minds, it is also seen in the priestly order;[105] now, opinions, and above all vanity, are stronger than interests. Have we not, toward the end of the last century, seen unbelief professed by the ministers of the altars?[106]

In the same way, the priests of polytheism obeyed this tendency and this calculation in their mystery cults; these institutions rendered their role less awkward by dispensing them from fulfilling two contrasting roles on the same stage, before the same spectators.

One would rightly think that morality would enter into the mysteries as soon as it became an integral part of polytheism. Even before, at Samothrace, there was an ancient tribunal that pronounced on crimes, and sometimes condemned the guilty to death; but it appears that this tribunal of purely sacerdotal origin only judged perjury and murder committed at the foot of altars, that is, that were aggravated by sacrilege; now these two assaults were insults against the gods; and we have distinguished between these offenses that every religion from the beginning forbids and the support that religion gives to morality, but only at a later date. For the mysteries, we would place this period at the time of Epimenides. Our readers know that he was charged by Solon with purifying Athens, and Solon, at once a philosopher and a legislator, had to feel the importance of basing the laws and morality on religion.

At that time the exposition of the duties that unite men among themselves was one of the revelations to the initiates;[107] justice was recommended to them,[108] piety toward parents, moderation in desires.[109] A general confession was required from

105. No matter how free each one's opinion seems to be, says a man with a good deal of judgment, Mr. de Bonstetten, in the long run he is always led in the direction of the view of all.

106. On this occasion I recall an article placed in the *Publiciste* many years ago by one of the most spiritual men of our time, and who since then acquired a very great literary reputation. I mean to speak of Mr. de Barante, who in an analysis of the works of Abbé de Boismont made quite clear, by means of an admirable sagacity and striking irony, the way in which the priesthood itself asked for the favor of philosophy when it spoke in the name of religion, attempting to obtain a more welcoming reception for it by veiling it with the name of charity, and insinuating that at bottom it was only another form of philanthropy.

107. Tit.-Liv., XLV, 5.

108. Wise precepts are inculcated in them during the ceremony of initiation (August., *Civ. Dei*, II, 6).

109. Saint Justin, *Adv. Tryph.*, 3, 70.

the newly initiated,[110] and the exclusion leveled against the guilty was the first punishment inflicted on them.[111]

But since the morality of the mystery cults was taught by the priests, it differs
more or less from that of the public polytheism and took on several characteristics that we have noted in the priestly morality. Initiation became an indispensable condition for felicity after this life; at this price, the Corybants promised
their adepts an eternal happiness.[112] It was the mysteries, says Proclus, that liberate
souls from this material and mortal prison, to unite it with the gods.[113] The goal
of initiation, adds Arrian to Epictetus,[114] is to prevent the divine part of man from
being plunged into the dark bog, and to prevent obstacles to its return toward
the Divinity. Aristophanes,[115] Aeschines,[116] and Sophocles (as cited by Plutarch)[117]
represent the initiates as being blessed by this fact alone; they alone could hope
for the rewards of another world. Punishments are the exclusive and inevitable
lot of the profane.[118] The broken jug from which they try to drink was the symbol of their misery. In vain they sought refreshing water, that is, the revelation
that could have saved them.[119] One sees in a painting of Polygnotus at Delphi two
women condemned to eternal torment because they had not been received into
the mysteries of Ceres;[120] this is obviously the introduction into free polytheism
of the dominant idea of priestly polytheism, the idea that crossed the centuries
to enter into a Christian sect, and which proclaims the terrible axiom: outside
the Church there is no salvation, which created a kind of intolerance unknown to

---

110. It was to the *koès*, a priest thus named in order to indicate that his function was to listen, that
one must address oneself. Lysander, required by the *koès* to declare his greatest crime: "Who asks it,"
he said, "the gods or you?" "The gods." "Let them ask me themselves." Antalcidas responded even more
briefly: "They already know" (Pseudo Plat., *Apopht. Lacon.*).

111. Clem. Alex., *Strom.*, V.

112. August., *Civ. Dei*, VII, 24.

113. Comment. in *Pol.* Plato. See also Plot., *Enneads*, I, bk. VI; Iambl., *De myst.*; Julian., *Orat.*, V.

114. III, 21.

115. *Frogs*, 773.

116. *In Axiocho.*

117. *De audiend. poet.*

118. Arist., *Orat. Eleus.*

119. The vases of the Danaides are called νδριαι ατελεις (Aeschin., *Axiochus*), and one recognizes
the Greek word for "initiation."

120. Pausan., *Phocid.*, 36.

previous periods. Athenians considered themselves obliged to be initiated before they died;[121] infants of the tenderest years were initiated,[122] as well as those on their deathbed; one even put the vestments of the initiated,[123] as well as those of hierophants,[124] on the dead. The priestly spirit is the same, whatever the difference in its forms. In the Middle Ages, Christians wanted to be buried in monks' habits.

To engrave this opinion more deeply on souls, one once again had recourse to dramatic performances. Troupes of initiates appeared before the eyes of the newly chosen on meadows dotted with flowers, like the happy inhabitants of Elysium, surrounded with a brilliant and pure light, crowned with laurels, and clothed with robes of shining white.[125]

Expiations acquired a wonderful efficacy, and these expiations were sometimes bought in a way that recalls the selling of indulgences. The Orphic ministers sat at the door of the wealthy, promising to whoever would participate in their ceremonies an immortality during which they would wear crowns and drink delicious wines;[126] while the profane, covered with mud, had to share the punishments of the Danaids. The Orphics added, to be sure, that such treatment would be the reward of justice, or the punishment of iniquity; but in their language, an initiate was always a just man, and no one was unjust except the one who had disdained initiation.[127]

It is not surprising that the philosophers rose up forcefully against this part of the mysteries. Plato, who provided us with what we have reported concerning the Orphics, allows himself the bitterness of a virtuous indignation against it. Diogenes said that it was absurd that brigands and murderers could acquire eternal

---

121. Aristoph., *Frogs*, ll. 362–68.

122. Donat., *ad* Terent., *Phorm.*, act I, 15.

123. Schol. Theoc., *Idyll.*, II, V, 12, 36, 37.

124. Plut., *De Is. et Osir.*, cap. 3.

125. Apul., *Metam.*; Stobaeus, *Or.*, 199; Wyttenbach, *De sera numin. vindicta*; Plut., *De oracul. defect.* According to Jenitsch, a part of the mysteries was the exposition of relics or sacred things and the selling of indulgences (Staeudlin, *Rel. Mag.*, II, 129).

126. Plato, *De rep.*, II. The epithet engraved on the tomb of a young initiate whose inscription has come down to us attests to this notion: "The souls of the dead are divided into two troupes: one wanders anxiously on the earth; the other begins the divine dance with the brilliant stars of the celestial sphere. They belong to this army. The god of the initiation was my guide."

127. Sainte-Croix, p. 582.

felicity by participating in some rites, while Epaminondas and Agesilaus, for not having been initiated, would be cast to the bottom of Tartarus.[128] Demosthenes and Theophrastus similarly castigated them.[129] As the same circumstances suggest the same ideas to men, whatever might be the distance between the periods, Voltaire seems to have put Diogenes's objection into verse when he says in a poem that is famous in so many ways:

> You roast there, wise and learned Cato,
> Divine Socrates, eloquent Cicero.

The testimonies reported here are important in that they prove that this theory concerning the efficacy of initiations was already known before the decadence of polytheism. The religions that are collapsing, unfortunately, sell morality fairly cheaply; and later we will see polytheism call all the vices to its assistance in order to maintain itself. But here, it is the priestly spirit that alone seeks to make morality dependent upon practices and to pervert it for its own interest.

Other features help us to recognize this influence of the priesthood on morality. All priestly religions condemn suicide, and this disapproval is rather remarkable, for these religions inculcate much more expressly than polytheism free of the priests' direction detachment from this world and indifference to all the interests of life. But suicide is a means of independence, and in this regard all authorities hate it. We do not claim to justify it as a general proposition. One must judge it by its motives, as all other human actions. It is often a crime, almost always a weakness, but let us dare to acknowledge: sometimes it is a virtue. It is a crime when, serving as a refuge from the disdain that one wants to merit but without actually incurring, as well as from the punishments that one hopes to brave without actually feeling them, it encourages men to culpable acts by offering them shelter against punishment; it is a weakness when, yielding to one's own pains, one forgets that by doing the good one can mitigate the evils that one experiences; it is a virtue if, hardly reassured about one's physical or moral force, one fears that one will succumb to seductions or fail to resist threats. He who feels that at the sight of torture he will betray friendship, denounce the unfortunate, or violate secrets confided to him fulfills a duty in committing suicide; it is precisely because of this that all tyrannies

128. Diog. Laert., VI, 2–6.
129. Sainte-Croix, p. 417.

proscribe it absolutely.[130] We see it condemned in the mysteries;[131] and Virgil, who had based his depiction of the underworld on what he knew of these institutions, mentions the punishments inflicted on those who have taken their own life; however, suicide was not at all considered a crime by the Greeks, and the Romans saw in it a sign of strength and magnanimity.[132]

130. In the Lamaist religion, those who commit suicide, as well as those who have incurred the curses of priests, constantly shudder in painful anguish, their soul not permitted to reenter a body (Pallas, *Nachrichten*, etc.).

131. Plato, in *Phaedo*.

132. "*Inspectu quodam et instinctu procurrere ad mortem, commune cum multis. Deliberare ultra et causas ejus expendere, prouti suaserit ratio, vitae mortisque consilium suscipere, ingentis est animi*" (Pliny, *Epist.*, I, 22). "*Quidquid horum tractaveris, confirmatis animum, vel ad mortis, vel ad vitae patientiam. In utrumque monendi ac formandi sumus. Etiam cum ratio suadet finire, non tamen temere, nec cum procursu est impetus. Sic fortis et sapiens non fugere debet e vita sed exire*" (Senec.).

CHAPTER 5

On the Spirit That Reigned in the Mysteries

The mysteries being the property of the priesthood, its spirit presides over them, it extends its somber black bunting over them; a profound melancholy rules over them. Plutarch[1] and Proclus[2] speak to us, the former about sad and somber ceremonies, the other of the sacred lamentations prescribed at the Eleusinian mysteries. Almost all the adventures attributed to the gods in the mysteries were tragic. Everywhere one saw funerary rituals. At the Thesmophoria, women seated on the earth as a sign of mourning uttered groans, as in Egypt;[3] even their dance announced discouragement and sadness; but since everything had to be symbolic, the slowness of this dance, and the dejection that it expressed, also indicated the fatigue of the animals employed in work. The misfortune of living, a dogma inherent in Egypt and in India, was inculcated in all the Orphic mysteries; life's brevity and its nothingness were taught in those of Thrace. The expressions of the Bhagavad Gita,[4] that the earth is a sad and limited place, are perfectly parallel to the picture given in the Dionysian mysteries to initiates.[5] Although we have adopted the rule of avoiding as much as possible conjectures that rest only on etymologies and grammatical studies, we find in a modern scholar[6] a very intriguing observation, one that directly applies to the subject that occupies us here, so it merits being reported. Our readers already know that the Greeks had borrowed from the Egyptians the topography of their underworld, the subterranean rivers, the crossing of

1. *De oracul. defect.*
2. Comment. *ad* Plato, *Polit.*
3. Plut., *De Is. et Osir.*; Athenag., *Legat.*, no. 25.
4. French trans., p. 91.
5. Porph., *De antro Nymph.*, 10–12; Plot., *Enneads*, I & IV.
6. Creuzer, I, 341–42.

the shades, and the name of the pilot who received them in his bark; this name, according to Jablonsky, in Egyptian alluded to silence, or, according to others, to the darkness that reigned in the kingdom of the dead. Wanting to naturalize the word in their language, the Greeks made it come from a verb that in Greek means rejoice.[7] This derivation contrasted with all the notions of Homeric polytheism, notions according to which death is always a dreadful event and the shades an inconsolable troupe that envies the living and terribly misses the light of day. It was therefore necessary to find another explanation and Homer's commentators claimed that by a customary euphemism, the ferryman of the underworld had been named Charon because he distresses mortals, and he himself always groans. But in the mysteries, where the priestly teaching of the misery of life prevailed, and the felicity of death as a deliverance, the idea that Charon in fact rejoiced in transporting the unfortunates who suffered in this world to a better one, a melancholic idea that the natural genius of the Greeks had rejected, was welcomed, and the etymology was one of the secrets revealed to the initiates.

Boisterous buffoonery, quite different from the brilliant and lively gaiety of the Greeks, also passed into the mysterious rituals. The Bacchants were subject alternately to a somber and silent melancholy and a frenetic joy.[8] Everywhere, grotesque characters provoked laughter with base and ignoble jokes:[9] the old Silenus drunk on his ass was the amusement of the Dionysian mysteries; a buffoon appeared in Samothrace alongside the Cabiri;[10] and the Eleusinian mysteries show us Ceres distracted from her pain by the immodest poses of two old women.[11] A strange anecdote! One that proves the authority of the traditions even when they depart from the goal proposed by those who respected them. At the festivals of Saturnalia, Julian[12] believed himself obliged to mock the gods. It was by devotion that he did so, nonetheless his mockeries tended to render them ridiculous. It mat-

---

7. Χαιρειν.

8. Hence a proverbial expression to express the rapid succession of these two contradictory states. See Suidas, v. Βακχης τροπων, αδου Βακχος, αδου Βακχη.

9. Gigon in the Cabiric mysteries, Baubus in those of Ceres, Silena in those of Bacchus. Momus, in Lucan, is a buffoon god, prior to those of Olympus and having no place among them. Is this a reminiscence of a priestly cult in Greece? A borrowing made by the Greeks of a foreign priestly custom? A parody of the mysteries?

10. Eustath., *ad Od.*, XX.

11. Apollod., *Bibl.*, I, 4.

12. Julian in his *Caesars*.

ters little to us that these strange customs had signified the satisfaction of the Supreme Being after the arrangement of the universe and the triumph of harmony;[13] it suffices that they were common to priestly polytheism and the mystery cults.

Finally, in them one finds hatred and jealousy vis-à-vis any and all personal distinction. Everything was collective and anonymous in the corporations of Egypt and Phoenicia. Everything had to be the same in the mystery cults where, being unable to expand without, the Greek priesthood had established its empire. Lucan speaks of an Athenian dragged to justice for having named the hierophant and the other priests of Eleusis.[14]

13. Creuzer, II, 298.
14. Lexiphanes.

CHAPTER 6

Summary of the Composition of the Greek Mysteries

The beliefs of the East and the South thus passed entirely into the Greek mysteries, which in this way contained both the public worship and the secret doctrines of these beliefs.[1] But unlike the nations governed by priests, where these two things were in reality two separate cults because the masses of the nation were never admitted to the knowledge of the hidden doctrine, in the Greek mysteries they were brought together, and the crude and material portion became a vestibule where the initiates were retained for a shorter or longer period of time, and then entered more or less deeply into the sanctuary. All the rituals, all the severe or indecent practices, all the doctrines (and in this number the most impious as well as the most religious) composing the secret doctrine of the priests in the East: the supremacy of one god over the others; the mediating or dying god for the salvation of the human race;[2] the trinity;[3] the hypothesis of the degradation of the soul before its inhabiting a mortal body, because of the impurity of matter; the hope of its gradual reascending to the Divinity; theism as principle and result of the system of emanation; or losing oneself in the depths of pantheism; dualism; atheism: all these Persian, Egyptian, and Indian doctrines were consigned to the mystery cults of the Greeks. They were at once the priestly apocalypse and the encyclopedia,

1. Diodorus (bk. V) positively says that the mysteries brought from Crete were the public worship in that island. Several foreign gods, notes Mr. Heeren (*Grecs*, p. 92), obtained from the Greeks a place in the mysteries, even though these gods had no role in the mysteries of these countries.

2. The Logos, as son of God and mediator, is very clearly designated in all the mysteries (Goerres, II, 354 and the citations).

3. Above we have shown the trinity in one of the Orphic cosmogonies. It is while alluding to this trinity that Firmicus says to the Supreme Being: "You are equally the father and the mother of all things, and you, moreover, are your own son."

and their language was often word for word that of the cults that had served as their model.

One would be wrong to object to this the resistance of Greek priests to foreign priests and doctrines. Individuals can very well fight against individuals; that is, the Greek priests could have invoked the severity of the laws against the incursions of the foreign priesthood onto their own ground and even repelled their teachings and rituals from the public religion; but thus rejected, the rituals and doctrines were transported into the mystery cults, and all the priestly doctrines were there received and consecrated.

The priests of the independent polytheism that Greece professed did not differ from those of the East and the South except by success, not by their efforts. Both tended to the same goal; but the first, limited in their power, controlled only the secret part of the religion. The latter, all-powerful, controlled the entire religion without exception. As a consequence, the first transported into the mysteries everything that characterized priestly polytheism and, as much as they could, they created a separate domain for themselves to compensate for the empire that civil society contested with them. The mysteries were the property of the priesthood in the polytheism of the priesthood that had no property.

Of these doctrines and rituals with which the mysteries were successively enriched, none was replaced by another, all coexisted; and not only did they coexist, no matter how contradictory they were, but each of them was itself forged of several heterogeneous and incoherent elements.[4] The most advanced philosophical doctrines were combined with the most abject anthropomorphism. In the pantheistic fable (which therefore is quite refined) of the slaughter of Bacchus by the Titans who burn him in a cauldron, Jupiter is attracted by the smoke of the meal that is being prepared; it is not until he recognizes the victim that he throws lightning at the Titans and has the scattered members of Bacchus interred by Apollo.[5] The slightest ritual was susceptible of several senses; the branches carried in the Thallaphoria sometimes signified the memory of the first foods of

---

4. In the mysteries of Samothrace we find: (1) a system of emanations rather similar to that of India: Axieros, the first of the Cabiri, was the unity from which all the gods and beings emanated; (2) an astronomical system in which the stars were divinized, and which could have come from Egypt; (3) a combination of this system with stones animated by the stars and subject to their action, an Etruscan notion, which established a connection between astrolatry and the worship of stones similar to that which united the stars and animals in Egypt; (4) a hierarchy of intermediary beings, from the supreme unity to man; (5) finally, a doctrine of sufferings and rewards to come.

5. Clem. Alex., in Euseb., *Praep. Evang.*, 9.

man, sometimes the discovery of the olive by Minerva, sometimes the rapid decline of life, figured by a dried branch. In the Cabiric mysteries, the first two Cabiri were popular gods, priestly gods, and symbols, sometimes metaphysical, sometimes cosmogonic.[6] It was for this that it was said that one of the secrets of the mysteries consisted in revealing that Castor and Pollux were not gods. Those of Adonis were astronomical,[7] agricultural,[8] metaphysical,[9] and, moreover, alluded to dualism.[10] At the period when it is unquestionable that the initiates were engaged in the most subtle speculations, the grossest means of acting upon the populace's imagination were still practiced. At the end of the first century A.D., Dion Chrysostom speaks to us of voices that the initiates heard, of light and darkness that passed in succession before them, the dances they witnessed; in a word, he depicts the mysteries as a spectacle.[11]

This is not the place to treat the other sorts of influence they exercised over the philosophical spirit of the Greeks. We will show elsewhere how, even though naturally inclined to a precise and rigorous dialectic, this spirit was imprinted with gigantic conceptions and threw itself into the indefinable subtleties characteristic of the East, and how Greek philosophy lost in logic and clarity what it appeared to sometimes gain in elevation and profundity.[12]

In our opinion, from all that we just laid out, the existence of the Greek mysteries, far from invalidating our assertions concerning the difference between priestly religions and those that remain independent of priests, on the contrary, supports these claims and corroborates them. It is precisely because the Greek priesthood did not have the monopoly of the public religion, as was the case elsewhere, that it created a secret empire in the mystery cults. But as long as the public religion retained some strength, it rejected the opinions and rituals that the priesthood had gathered and, as it were, naturalized in its mystery cults.

6. See what we have said about the Cabiri in book V, chapter 5.

7. Macrob., *Saturn.*, I, 21; Dupuis, *Orig. des cultes*, III, 471.

8. Amm. Marcell., XIX, 1; schol. Theocrit., *ad Idyll.*, III, 48.

9. Gospel of Saint John, XII.

10. Dio. Chrys., *Orat.*, 12; Themist., *Or.*, 2. See in Pausanias (*Archaic.*, 22) the different explanations of the torches of the mysteries.

11. *Orat.*, 12.

12. "The mysteries introduced among the Greeks, and there preserved, all the oriental ideas, which sometimes raised above mere reasoning the philosophy of this people which was naturally addicted to dialectics" (Wagner, *Ideen*, etc., p. 76). I, too, love that the religious sentiment raises itself above dialectics; but I want it to be free, and not that an external authority causes it to deviate from its path and perverts it.

CHAPTER 7

On Gradual Initiations, as the Initiation
into the Priestly Hierarchy

The Greek priesthood, master of the mystery cults, did not content itself with introducing priestly opinions, doctrines, rituals, and customs; it attempted to establish a priestly hierarchy in them. There were different orders of initiates, as in Egypt there were different orders of priests.

The Eleusinian mysteries were divided into great and small mysteries.[1] In the latter, almost the entirety of the Greeks were initiated. They consisted in pantomimes that portrayed several religious fables. Those initiated into the great mysteries were a much smaller group and the teaching was more abstract. In them, the priests combined allegorical or metaphysical explanations with the necessity of hiding these explanations from the people.[2] They were not communicated at a single time.[3] The initiates were more or less instructed according to the level they had attained; no one was sure of being completely initiated. When it comes to trust, it is always useful to be able to say that one has not yet said everything. The

---

1. A scholiast of Aristophanes (*ad* Plut., act IV, scene 2, 23) says that the small mysteries were only a preparation for the greater. There were even three species of Dionysiacs (Ruhnken, *ad* Hesych., v. Διονος; and Wyttenbach, *Bibl. Crit.*, VII, 51; XII, 59). Furthermore, annual mysteries were distinguished from triennial mysteries, or trieterides. Sainte-Croix (p. 428), Apuleius (*Met.*, XI), and Theon of Smyrna (Voss, *De orig. et progr. idolol.*, pp. 828–29) say that there were five gradations. The first consisted in a preparatory purification; the second in the communication of sacred precepts; the third in the contemplation of the spectacle; the fourth in participation in the ceremonies as an actor, the initiate taking in hand the sacred torch; the fifth degree conferred inspiration and complete felicity upon the initiate. The gradual initiations and philosophical doctrines were not shared with the mass of initiates. The initiates in the small mysteries were called μυσται, and the initiates in the grand mysteries εποπται. The first remained in the vestibule of the temple, the latter entered the sanctuary.

2. August., *Civ. Dei*, IV, 27.

3. "*Eleusis servat quod ostendat revisentibus*" (Senec., *Quaest. nat.*, VII, 31).

imagination is struck by the unknown; curiosity is captured by the hope of learning. When a doctrine has weak aspects and one shows only half of it, one can say that the answer to objections is found in the hidden half.

Both sorts of mysteries, the great and the small, were further subdivided and in each subdivision the teaching changed, without these variations destroying respect and trust in the minds of the initiates. The barriers that separated the different classes placed an obstacle to their mutual communication, and the allegorical explanations avoided the contradictions they did not resolve. Each notion that was taught, each practice that had as its purpose rendering the teaching more solemn, had (as in priestly polytheism) a double, often a triple, meaning. What was only a ritual in the first level was a tradition in the second, and in the third, a promise. The present admission was transformed into a commemoration of the past; commemoration became prophecy. The priests had found a pretext for delaying initiations and prolonging trials. It did not depend upon them, they said, to admit candidates; they needed an order, a particular manifestation of the gods; for example, access to the temple of Isis Tithorea was opened only to those summoned by a dream.[4] They compared premature initiation to suicide, and just as mortals did not have the right to leave this life in order to hasten to a better world, but must await the signal of the divine will, in the same way one could not grant the regeneration of the mysteries to the profane, except after having received miraculous authorization from heaven.[5] Apuleius recounts that a year after he had been received into the mysteries of Isis, it was revealed to him that he must present himself to those of Osiris;[6] he sold his clothes to defray the costs of this new initiation, and soon he was initiated a third time. As these initiations were at first free, but then later occurred when one paid the fee,[7] some have considered the mysteries as a means used by the priesthood of enriching themselves. This calculation could have been that of a few individuals, but not the principal aim of the order. We rather see in these pecuniary conditions an effort to keep out the class of the poor without directly rejecting it; in the republican States of Greece, this would have wounded the proud spirit of equality, which was unhappy with even this indirect exclusion.[8]

4. Pausan., *Phoc.*, 31.
5. Apul., *Met.*, XI.
6. Ibid.
7. Apsin., *De art. rhet.*
8. Ibid.

CHAPTER 8

On the Real Object of the Mysteries

In the midst of this accumulation of incoherent teachings and revelations, it has often been asked, what was the purpose of secrecy in the mystery cults? This secret, we do not hesitate to say, did not reside in the traditions or the fables or the allegories or the opinions or the substitution of a purer teaching, replacing a cruder one:[1] all these things were already known. Facts they had heard elsewhere were confided in those who had been initiated, fictions they had read in all the poets, hypotheses that were in the mouth of all philosophers. The travels of Ceres, the misfortunes of the gods, the battles of the Titans, all were represented on the stage, engraved in marble, sung in public hymns. The cosmogonic systems were contained in works open to all the profane. In the initiations, one did not learn philosophic opinions, but when one was philosophic, one recognized them. What was secret, therefore, was not the things that were revealed; it was because these things were thus revealed, that they were revealed as the teaching and practices of an occult religion, and that they were revealed progressively, in a way to always allow future revelations that would at the appropriate time dissipate all objections and remove all doubts. What they had fixed was not at all their doctrines, but the signs and words

---

1. "I am ashamed," says Momus, in the assembly of the gods of Lucan, "to take the inventory of apes, storks, billy goats, and so many other things that are even more absurd, that the Egyptians—I know not why—made rise to heaven. How can you suppose, you other gods, that these ridiculous beings are adored with as much or more respect than you?" "Doubtless," responds Jupiter, "what you say of the Egyptians is shameful; however, several of these things contain puzzles that the profane ought not to mock." "Truly," replies Momus, "I do not need mysteries to know that the gods are the gods, and that those who have the head of dogs are dogs." This passage is important because (1) it attests to the form of several divinities in the mysteries, and (2) one sees the same mockeries directed against the mysteries and against the public religion.

of coming together communicated to the initiates, and the ceremonies that accompanied these communications.[2]

The impious who were persecuted for sacrilegious indiscretions—Diogoras,[3] Aristagoras,[4] Alcibiades,[5] Andocides[6]—were never accused of having divulged a teaching, but of having profaned the ceremonies. The same accusation weighed over Aristotle. No portion of his philosophy was alleged against him by the hierophant, his persecutor, but a sacrifice to the manes of his wife employing rituals reserved to the Eleusinian Ceres.[7]

2. In Epictetus, Arrian blames a man who justified his teaching by maintaining that he only taught what was taught in the mysteries. Yes, he answered him, you teach the same things but in another place, without the ceremonies, without the solemnity, without the purity, without the religious respect that makes them useful. Seneca (*Epist.*, 95), in comparing philosophy to initiation, says that the precepts were known by the profane, but the holiest ceremonies were reserved to the adept. Perhaps there they also learned some different names of the gods.

3. Aristoph., *Birds*, 1073–74; schol., ibid.; Lysias, *Contr. Andocid.*; Athenag., *De legat.*

4. Schol. Aristoph., *Clouds*, 828.

5. Plut., in *Alcib.*

6. Andocid., *De myst.*

7. Diog. Laert., V, 1–5.

CHAPTER 9

On the Explanations That Have Been Given of the Mysteries

It is now easy, it seems to us, to understand the error of the majority of those who have preceded us in these inquiries. This error is of the same nature as that of the scholars we have spoken about in the first volume.[1] Theism, pantheism, the crises of physical nature, the discovery of the arts, the progress of civilization, all these things were found in the mysteries; but none of them was the sole doctrine, none was taught exclusively in them, none was revealed to everyone in them. The priesthood of independent polytheism acted vis-à-vis the profane as we have seen the priests of sacerdotal polytheism act toward foreigners.[2] From the least-instructed faithful to the philosopher most in love with the most abstract speculations, all were found there because of their intellectual instruction and their satisfying revelations.[3] The hierophants of Greece let Plato believe that the mysteries contained precepts of morality;[4] Varro, that truths of nature were contained in them;[5] they let Diodorus recognize historical facts in them;[6] with Plutarch, doctrines, sometimes dualism,[7] sometimes the sufferings and rewards to come;[8]

1. Bk. I, ch. 9.

2. Bk. VI, ch. 4.

3. If the reader would like to find new developments to add to those that we have already presented concerning the variety of explanations that the priests gave at the same time, but to different classes of initiates, he could consult Schmidt, *De sacerdot. et sacrif. Aegypt.*, p. 78.

4. Plato, *Gorgias*.

5. August., *Civ. Dei*, VII, 28.

6. Diod., I, 22.

7. Plut., *De or. def.*, 13–15; *De fac. in orb. lun.*; *De Is. et Osir.*, 45.

8. Plutarch reports the mysteries as teaching the punishments of impure souls and the progressive rewards of souls purified in this life.

to others they revealed the human origin of the gods and the apotheoses of legislators.[9]

Thus the ancients were mistaken like the moderns when they arbitrarily chose what accorded with the system they preferred, and when they rejected explanations that did not comport with this system. When Plutarch rose up against those who, like Euhemerus, attributed historical meanings to the mysteries, or who, like Varro, interpreted them by physics, agriculture, or allegories, he was no more wrong than Warburton, Villoison, or Boulanger.

9. Do we not know, says Cicero (*Tuscul.*, I, 12–13), that all the heavens are occupied by the human race? That the gods of the first rank have risen from earth to the heavens? Remind yourself, because you are an initiate, of what the mysteries teach.

CHAPTER 10

That Our Way of Envisaging the Mystery Cults Alone Explains the Often Contradictory Attitude of the Greeks toward These Institutions

The hypothesis that we have presented, with evidence that it seems to us can hardly be contested, is the only one that places the mysteries in their proper light. It is also the only one that explains the contradictions that astonish us when we consider the Greeks' conduct vis-à-vis these institutions. On one hand, rigorous laws threatened anyone who displayed the least irreverence toward them. These laws could not be repealed, or even relaxed:[1] a redoubtable tribunal composed of priests who were simultaneously judges and parties pronounced capital punishments against the indiscreet and against impiety. Sacrilege was punished with death; one's confiscated goods were put up for auction. A price was put on Diagoras's head[2] and Aristagoras's.[3] The most eminent services rendered to the homeland, the most merited glory in arms and in the sciences, did not serve as a shield. Athens equally failed to recognize what it owed to Alcibiades's arms and Aristotle's meditations; the people grew angry at the slowness of the judges and went ahead of their judgment. In the midst of the applause that his tragedies had obtained, Aeschylus was ready to see himself torn apart by the multitude for having put on the stage objects from the mystery cults, or by some allusion having betrayed a secret of the same.[4] More obscure victims, two young Acarnanians, are murdered as punishment for a fault of the same nature.[5] Despite his hatred for the institutions of his country, and his irreligious intentions, Euripides carefully distinguishes the mysteries of Bacchus from the Dionysian ones so as not to incur an accusation that was inevitably harmful.[6] In

1. Lys., *Contr. Andoc.*
2. Ibid.; schol. Aristoph., *Birds*, 1073; *Frogs*, 323; *Clouds*, 828.
3. Aristoph., *Clouds*, 828.
4. On those of Ceres (Ael., *Var. Hist.*, V).
5. Tit. Liv., XXXI.
6. Sainte-Croix, p. 412.

this regard, the philosophers did not distinguish themselves from the vulgar; they lavished the greatest praise upon the mysteries.[7] Both Socrates, who paid with his life for his public disapproval of the popular mythology; and Plato, all of whose writings tended to flatter this mythology, expressed themselves with a profound respect for the secret cult.

On the other hand, not only is the participation in certain mysteries sometimes a subject of blame,[8] but Aristophanes insulted those that the Greeks revered the most, the Thesmophoria and the Dionysian mysteries.[9] The people of Athens subjected them to the inspection of civil magistrates.[10] It reserved for itself, despite formal declarations disallowing them from any softening of the strict laws of the mysteries, the right to annul the judgment of the Eumolpidae against profaners; and the sages who offered lavish praise of the sublime significance of these institutions nonetheless refused the honor of being initiates.[11] The Romans, who in a previous book offered us the spectacle of the resistance opposed by the Greek genius to the rituals and doctrines of the priesthood, acted toward the mysteries with a more sustained and implacable defiance. This grave and suspicious people promulgated severe edicts against their introduction. The Bacchanalia were forbidden by the Senate;[12] the Eleusinian mysteries were never allowed; even the foreigners who wanted to celebrate the Sabazian Bacchus with occult rituals were prohibited by the praetors, despite Roman tolerance;[13] and when the arms of the republic had subjected Greece, the penalties against profaners were significantly mitigated.[14]

These contradictions will appear to be explained if one reflects that one part of the Greek priesthood employed on behalf of these mysteries all its influence, all

7. Demeter, says Isocrates (*Panegyr.*), enriched our ancestors with two inestimable treasures: wheat, thanks to which we were raised above the animals; and initiation, which fills with sweet hopes concerning the end of life and the existence of man, those who have received its benefit. As the gods are above the heroes, the Eleusinian mysteries are above all institutions established by men (Pausan., X, 31). In general, all the times that the orators, great men, and sages of antiquity speak of the immortality of the soul, taken in its most elevated sense, or of the unity of the first cause, they make allusions to the mysteries of Eleusis.

8. Demosth., *Contr. Ctesiphon.*

9. Bergler, *Not.* in Aristoph., *ad Frogs*, v. 218; *Plutus*, vv. 846–47.

10. The king-archon had the supervision of the mysteries of Bacchus and named their priests. His wife presided over them.

11. Socrates never wanted to be initiated.

12. Tit.-Liv., XXXIX, 15 & 16.

13. Val. Max., III, 3.

14. Hesych., v. Ευνουκος.

the means of acting on the imagination of a restless and credulous nation, and that the general spirit of polytheism, always disposed to receive all gods and celebrate all rites, favored the efforts of the priesthood. The Greeks adopted ceremonies that came from abroad out of the same motive that caused them to raise altars to unknown gods; but the national genius also rose up against all that bore the mark of barbarism and the priesthood.[15] For their part, the philosophers, impatient with the crudeness of the vulgar beliefs, were favorably disposed toward institutions that claimed to purify them. They found their own subtle doctrines in them, the discoveries or conjectures that had cost them so much effort: theism, which alone absolved the Supreme Being of the presence of evil; pantheism, which gives rest to the imagination by realizing that infinity, its promised land, which it perceives through the clouds but without ever being able to enter. But on the other hand, as the philosophers entered into the mysteries' secrets, they saw joined with the opinions that could please them a strange and unnatural mixture of views and practices that gave the national worship an apparently less irrational meaning, but in reality corrupted it with more fantastic hypotheses and scandalous practices.

Hence this mixture of repulsion and attraction, admiration and condemnation, respect and horror. When one said to the Greeks that in the mysteries gods were liberated from their vices, their imperfections, their jealousy toward weak mortals; and always the friends of the human race, always protectors of justice, lending favorable ears to the priests and generous support to the innocent, the religious sentiment of the Greeks believed it saw in these improvements the fulfillment of its hopes, the seal of its stubborn labor concerning the character of these gods; but when in the depths of temples came forth disheveled Bacchants, half-naked, injuring men's sight with the obscene Phallus and filling the air with wild howling, these same Greeks asked where these frenetic hordes could have come from and what terrible prodigy could thus disfigure the cult transmitted by Homer and purified by Sophocles, which such orgies seemed to desecrate.

15. The opposition of the mysteries to the Greek genius has always struck attentive minds. "That the Barbarians," exclaimed Clement of Alexandria, "had such mysteries is no surprise; but the Greeks!"

BOOK XIV

ON THE SCANDINAVIAN RELIGION,
AND ON THE REVOLUTION THAT
SUBSTITUTED A PRIESTLY BELIEF
FOR INDEPENDENT POLYTHEISM
IN SCANDINAVIA

CHAPTER I

Preliminary Observation

Our readers probably expect to encounter among the Scandinavians a very different polytheism from the beliefs of the East and the South, and even from the Greek religion, be it primitive, such as Homer presents it, or purified, as Sophocles allows us to know it. This assumption is natural. The character, habits, mores, and passions of the peoples of the North distinguish them in many aspects from the nations that live in happier climes and more fertile territories. We have already recognized this truth;[1] but we added that if the South was the domain of the priesthood, the North was its conquest. Now the interest of the priesthood being the same, the laws to which its intelligence is subject[2] being identical in all climates, similarities in the religions, whether public or secret, popular or scientific, must occur that would be inexplicable if we did not go back to their cause. In fact, we will see that Scandinavia, which existed only for war and pillage, nonetheless had the same practices, teachings, and cosmogonies, although under harsher forms, as did India, where mildness, softness, and peacefulness reigned. Once the facts prove that all these things were imported, the problem is easily resolved.

Let no one be astonished, therefore, if we do not first see in Scandinavian polytheism a belief that is rather parallel to that of the Homeric Greeks, and later a religion that is not much different in its bases to oriental and southern opinions. We do not maintain that all these peoples were once together; we do not contest that the religion was modified in accordance with climate and circumstances. If instead of limiting ourselves to the history of religious forms, we had undertaken to do a universal history, we would have had the duty and task of entering into

1. See bk. IV, ch. 2.
2. See bk. VI, ch. 2.

the details of all these differences; but obliged as we are to keep to our subject and to follow the path marked out for us, we have only been able to indicate these somewhat summarily, while calling more general and essential agreements to the reader's attention. Thus we have noted that religion, warlike in the North, was peaceful in the East; but this diversity of character did not change much in the action of the priests; it only accidentally, and from time to time, limited the power they exercised, and did not at all prevent them from introducing into the people's belief teachings that were favorable to them and, in the hidden doctrine, notions to which their meditation had led them.

This preliminary explanation being well understood, we will no longer fear being accused of an error that we have often reproached other authors with committing (who otherwise are to be recommended) while taking the greatest care not to commit it ourselves. And we will faithfully paint the authority of the priesthood among the Scandinavians following their second religious revolution as being almost as extensive as it had been among the Egyptians. We will do so without fearing any suspicion of having a blind partiality for an exclusive system.

CHAPTER 2

How the Scandinavians Passed from Fetishism to Polytheism

Before beginning this work, we had proposed to combine in a single book everything that pertains to the religion of Scandinavia. But we have been forced on several occasions to draw facts from this religion aimed at proving our assertions concerning the cults subject to priestly direction.

As a result, many things that ought to find their place here are already spread throughout our four preceding volumes. We have had to leave them aside, and we will not treat the composition and the development of the polytheism of the North except in a general way, and in a considerably abbreviated manner.

Scandinavia includes especially Denmark, Sweden, and Norway.[1]

We have proven by numerous facts that the first religion of the inhabitants of these countries was fetishism.[2] We will therefore leave aside details. We will simply briefly recall that the first gods of the Scandinavians appeared in the form of animals, of bulls, cows, serpents, lizards, for which these people had a particular affection; they carefully nourished these domestic gods, offering them sacrifices. The gods let themselves be seen in dreams in the appearance of inanimate things; they protected their protégés from danger and revealed their future destiny to them. This, certainly, was fetishism.

Scandinavians passed from this belief to polytheism in the same way as the Greeks; that is to say, by the arrival of one or several colonies.

---

1. These countries are designated by Tacitus under the name Germania, and several of the facts that he reports should be applied to the Scandinavians as well as the Germans. However, when he is in contradiction to authors of an uncontested authority, one must prefer their testimony and restrict what he says to the portions of Germany most known to the Romans. This is what a historian who is not without merit said before us.

2. See bk. VI, ch. 7.

It appears certain that the oldest of these colonies had only military leaders as their guide and that no priesthood took part, in the same way that the priesthood of Phoenicia or Egypt had no part in the Egyptian or Phoenician migrations that landed in Greece.

The sole difference one notes is that the colonies to which Greece owed its civilization mixed with the natives without subjugating them, while the people we are dealing with here were subjugated by the bellicose tribes that overran them.

According to tradition, these tribes were under the leadership of the first Odin, king of the Scythians,[3] according to Snorri; king of the Getae,[4] according to Botin; king of the Vandals,[5] according to Eckard.[6]

We say the first Odin; there were several others. Odin, or Wodin, as we know, was only a generic name, like Hercules, Brahma, and Osiris. This generic name appeared in the midst of the obscurity of the northern mythology like a great shadow, around which the various fables were gathered. All the tribes of the North make their origins go back to Odin; their kings said they were his descendants. To him were attributed the discovery of all the arts, the merit of all civil and religious institutions.

This same name, designating at once several stages of the social state and several individuals who succeeded one another over a long interval, has led several writers occupied with the subject we are treating into a serious error.[7] They have not reflected that if it was a matter of different periods, the religion of each one could have been different, and if it were a question of only individuals, each Odin could also have differed from his predecessors in his means, his aim, his doctrines; in all

3. Living between the Black Sea and the Caspian Sea (Mallet, *Introd.*, p. 53).

4. Between the Tanais and the Borysthenes, the Don and the Dnieper.

5. *De orig. Germanor.*

6. We leave to the side the insoluble question of the time or period of Odin's invasion of Scandinavia. Those who fix the date seventy or one hundred years before our era confuse the first Odin with those who succeeded him. It is very plausible that the most ancient of all lived in the time, or before the time, of Darius, son of Hystaspes. We also eschew all inquiry into the homeland of the first Odin. According to Snorri, he reigned over the Ases, people of Asia, and from this came the name Asgard as his capital. In his *Histoire de Suède*, Botin recognizes in him Sigge, who, he says, crossed Estonia and Denmark. Eckard claims that Odin did not come from Asia, and that the error that had him come from there came from the name Ases given to his companions, which means "lord."

7. We speak here neither of those who, wanting to escape from all difficulties, took the easy path of completely rejecting the existence of all Odins, even though they cannot support their denials with any proof, nor of those who ventured the most absurd conjectures, claiming that Odin was Priam, Antenor, or Ulysses, and that Asgard, his capital, was Troy.

of them, they have seen a reunion of the prophet and the warrior; they have made the first Odin like the second or the third, because it perhaps is necessary to count as many as three, an armed Mohammed founding a religion and having made it ascendant by his victories. The first Odin, however, was not someone who was inspired and who established his belief by the sword. He was a conqueror whose success earned him apotheosis. He did not become a warrior, as did Mohammed, because he was a prophet; he later passed for a prophet because he had been a conquering warrior and because later prophets took the same name.

Like the Egyptian colonies that had brought together the fetishes of the Pelasgians, Odin, while civilizing (at least up to a point) the savage tribes of Scandinavia, assembled the idols that these hordes worshipped separately, even individually.[8] A mountain was their Olympus, a huge ash tree provided their shade; and brought into a citadel, like the gods of Greece, they divided the functions that the fetishes previously had exercised indiscriminately. Balder directed the chariot of the sun. Thor presided over the exploits of battle, Freya the pains and pleasures of love.

This revolution did not occur as peacefully as in Greece. The legend of Regnar Lodbrog, to whom the pagan Skald[9] who composed it obviously attributes many of Odin's exploits, alludes to the fierce wars against the worshippers of cows and bulls. Two virgin heifers and the cow Sibylia, whose name recalls the one who in India put the warriors of Vishvamitra to flight,[10] for a long time rebuffed the efforts of Regnar, and his sons were not victorious until after his death.[11]

Because of a circumstance that had not existed in Greece and which was a natural consequence of the victories of the first Odin, the conqueror who had effected a religious revolution had to be placed at the head of the gods.[12]

8. The character of this revolution comports very well with the plausible hypothesis that the first Odin lived five hundred years before the second; because the Cimbri of Scandinavia whom the second Odin subjugated were already in the second period of the social state—i.e., barbarism—and consequently no longer had pure fetishism as their religion.

9. The paganism of the poet is proven by the disdain he displays for the Christian religion. He wrote at a time when this religion worked to establish itself, and he therefore gathered even more faithfully the most ancient legends of the old polytheism.

10. See bk. VI, ch. 6.

11. In other fables, on the contrary, Regnar Lodbrog is the owner of the cow Sibylia, who contributed to his victories (see bk. VI, ch. 7). But this cow is no less a divinity, a fetish.

12. Some students of mythology have noted that it is strange that in a nation of people as bellicose as the Scandinavians, the god of war properly speaking did not occupy the first rank. This is because Odin held it. Thor was regarded as his son (Rüh, *Scandin.*, pp. 32–33).

The glory that surrounded him, the terror inspired by his triumphs, gave him the ability not to impose opinions upon the defeated that were different from those analogous to the ideas of the period: this is beyond all human power, but to bring to these barbarians his cult, which was appropriate to barbarism; he profited from the enthusiasm of his brothers-in-arms to preside over the feasts of the brave after their death, as he presided over their exploits and banquets during this life.

It followed that in Scandinavia the first polytheism was the transplantation in a conquered country of the religion professed by its conquerors but in keeping with the natural development of the belief of the conquered, while the first polytheism of the Greeks had been the peaceful amalgam of the fetishism of primitives with the polytheism of more civilized colonists.

Moreover, the gods of the Edda, like those of Greece, are only powerful and strong beings, protectors or enemies of mortals according to their fancies or interests, and often left to bear the burden of their preferences or their capricious animosities. They come down from heaven, greedy for blood and taking pleasure in carnage. In turn they are victors or vanquished; heroes defy them; mere warriors, above all giants, wound them or force them to flee.[13] Magicians manipulate them with their enchantments.[14]

If one agrees that one must attribute what distinguishes the Greeks from the inhabitants of Scandinavia to accidental differences; if one substitutes a harsh climate[15] for the most beautiful one, sterile and uncultivated land for blessed and

13. Loki, taken by a giant transformed into an eagle, escaped death only by promising to deliver the goddess Iduna, who would rejuvenate the gods (Edda, 51st fable). Odin and two other gods traveled together. They killed the son of a giant. The brothers of the deceased took hold of them and forced them to pay a ransom. It is true that the gods perjured themselves.

14. Thor and Loki had entered into the country of the giants. The king of this country invited them to measure themselves against his subjects. Loki extolled himself by saying that he would eat all the meats presented to him, but the giant that went against him devoured both the flesh and the bones of the animals placed on the royal table. Thor could not finish a cup that he had proposed to empty with a single drink. He tried in vain to move a cat that despite his efforts remained immobile; and Thialfi, the companion of Thor, was beaten in a race by a rival that left him far behind. All these victories were symbolic. Loki's competitor was the fire that consumes. The cup from which Thor drank was connected with the Ocean, whose waves filled it. The runner who was lighter and faster than Thialfi was thought; the cat was the world. After having thus convinced the gods of their weakness and impotence, the giant disappeared in order to escape their wrath.

15. Earlier, the Scandinavian climate must have been even more severe than it is today. Forests had not fallen under the axe, marshes had not become cultivated plains. In the absence of agriculture,

fertile soil, senses tormented by a hostile nature for senses flattered by a gentle and friendly nature, the necessity, then the habit, and, soon, the love of war, the thirst for blood,[16] and the ardor for pillage, for the mixture of repose and action that among the Greeks simultaneously favored the development of the physical faculties, the brilliance of the imagination, and the progress of thought; if one then makes a precise comparison, one will still recognize that the polytheism of the two nations was the same polytheism, establishing between the gods and men precisely the same relations.

The spirit of pillage is more emphasized in the sagas of the peoples of the North than in the Homeric poems, and their Odin, head of the victorious horde, departs Valhalla to participate like a mortal in battles, the prime occupation of the time; Jupiter, on the contrary, limits himself to contemplating from the height of Olympus, deciding but without taking part in the success of the struggle. As for the rest, everything is identical in the two religions.

If the Scandinavian gods, mercenary, cruel, and treacherous like those of the Greeks, are more bellicose, the character of their worshippers is the cause; but these inhabitants of heaven equally have the same direct communication with these warriors. Ingrid and Haquin are soldiers and augurs, like Helenus and Polydamas. The heroes manifest hatred and disdain for the priests, like Agamemnon for Calchas and Chryses; they revolt against the gods and fight against them, like Diomedes. Common morality has nothing to do with the religion. There are no judges of the dead. Niflheim is an imitation of life; Valhalla, a place of pleasure for the companions of Odin. In a word, it is Homeric polytheism but harsher, more somber, and stormier.

---

hunting and fishing were the only means of subsistence; and by a natural transition, with fishing leading the Scandinavians to piracy, fierceness of mores had to result.

16. This difference is striking in the smallest details. The first flood of the Scandinavians, at the death of Ymir, is of blood rather than water (Mone, *Symbol.*, p. 319).

CHAPTER 3

Revolution in the Scandinavian Polytheism

Such was the religious state of Scandinavia when, by an event about whose causes the annalists differ, the priestly power established itself.

Some believe that it was by a domestic revolution. One of the first Odin's successors, they say, having wanted to engage his people in a war against the Romans, was expelled from the throne and a council of priests took over control.

Others attribute this revolution to the arrival of a second Odin, not, like the first, simply a military leader, but a priest at the head of a priestly colony.[1]

They recount in detail the great change that was his work.[2]

At his arrival, they say, Sweden was governed by a king named Gylfi,[3] who at the news of Odin's exploits went in disguise to consult with him. Their conversations bore upon questions of cosmogony and metaphysics, which would indicate the revelation of symbolic and scientific teachings. Gylfi gave his daughter to Skiold, son of the conqueror; but he disappeared suddenly. Would this not be an indication of a revolution wrought against the political power by the foreign priest?[4] In a saga, Gylfi is precisely he who congratulated himself for having

---

1. This second Odin was born, say the chronicles, about a century and a half before Jesus Christ, on the banks of the Tanais. He was named Sigge; he was the son of Friddulf. The motives of his emigration to Scandinavia were defeats in his wars with the Romans or with Mithridates (Rüh, pp. 5–37).

2. See Torfoeus and Saxon the Grammarian.

3. The name Gylfi is the cause of a serious confusion in the traditions. It is given to the head of the temporal government overturned by the second Odin, and to the president of the council of the gods. It is obvious that two individuals of the same name have been assumed, or that the name was transferred from one to the other without the historians distinguishing them.

4. A Danish writer, Mr. de Wedel-Jarlsberg, in his *Essai sur l'ancienne histoire des Cimbres et des Goths scandinaviens* (Copenhagen, 1781), like us claims that the second Odin (which he makes the

broken the mace of a god. Several traditions in fact betray a struggle. Saxon the Grammarian recounts that in the absence of Odin, a competitor who usurped his name and his power overturned the established worship, abolished the festivals where the assembled gods were worshipped, and replaced them with special rituals in honor of each divinity.[5] Do we not recognize in these features an effort of free polytheism (which adores its idols individually) against the priestly tendency to make an assembly of the gods? Odin returned, continues Saxon,[6] killed his rival, degraded the gods whose altars he had erected, and banished the magicians, their accomplices. Now, we have already noted that victorious cults always proscribe the pontiffs of defeated cults as being magicians.

The memory of this struggle seems to have passed from history into the mythology; this is what happens with all peoples. Chased by another god, Odin reenters Valhalla at the end of ten years, puts his rival to flight, and regains the reins of the universe.[7]

Can we not also discern in the giants and dwarfs to whom the legends assign a subordinate, and malevolent, place at the bottom of dens and caverns the adherents of the former religion seeking asylum on mountaintops and in the cavities of rocks?

Whatever might be the case with these two hypotheses, one of which must be admitted, the council of the gods again became a corporation similar to that of Persia and Egypt. The Drottes were at once priests, judges, and legislators;[8] they were called gods, and their words, divine words.[9] They dominated kings, deposed them, took their life,[10] ruled in their place, extended their own authority over in-

---

third) was a high-priest who dethroned Gylfi, the head of the government. He bases his opinion upon a host of authorities drawn from Icelandic chronicles.

5. Sax. Grammat., bk. I.

6. Idem, bk. III.

7. Ibid.

8. After the establishment of the second Odin, the division of the priestly order among the Scandinavians perfectly resembled that of the Druids. The Drottes, properly speaking, like the higher Druids, were exclusively charged with what concerned religion, the teaching of the mysteries, and justice. The Skalds, like the bards, sang the hymns and the glorious deeds of heroes, and the Tyrspakurs, like the Eubages of Strabo, unveiled the future. Freya also had priestesses who kept the sacred fire. Mallet (*Introd.*, p. 67) claims that all of the priestly order was hereditary. The tribunal of the Drottes sat at Sigtuna, a city now destroyed, then the capital of the province where Stockholm is built.

9. Rüh, pp. 123–24.

10. See bk. XV, ch. 2.

dividuals, fixed the belief, maintained it by severe punishments, struck unbelievers with exile or death.[11] Initially paid by a tax levied on the entire people,[12] they soon took over vast domains.

Like the Druids among the Gauls, they established a monopoly over poetry. The Skalds, who from the time of the first Odin freely sang the actions of the gods and the exploits of the brave, henceforth were subject to the order of Drottes by subaltern initiations, and were subdivided into several classes, each of which had a distinct sphere, its determinate revelations, its special rung, without being able to rise higher. The heroic songs became religious chants; but since the subjection of the Skalds did not deprive them of their memory, they often ran together the two worships, hence the mixture of traditions, dogmas, and teachings that confuses us.

However, despite these poetical memories, the Scandinavian religion changed nature. It did not lose its bellicose cast; the first Odin had engraved it too deeply on the soul of his followers, and the harshness of their climate, their greed for wealth, which they could only obtain sword in hand, did not allow them to forget the lessons of their master. Thus the god who orders combats, and whose son was especially charged with war (Thor), Odin continued to maintain the universe under his control. He presided over births, marriages, death. His priestesses with prophetic voices rushed into the mêlée. But the warriors are no less subject to the pontiffs, and the latter decide on enterprises, give the signal for expeditions, and conclude peace treaties, which are but truces.

At the same time they introduced into Scandinavia—that is, they taught and imposed—all the rituals, all the symbols, all the doctrines that we have encountered among the nations subject to priests.[13]

Astrolatry served as the basis of their religion. Odin is the sun, Freya the moon.

11. We have said elsewhere that a Norwegian was condemned to exile for having denied the divinity of the goddess Frigga (Mallet, *Introd.*, 98).

12. This tax was called *nefgioeld, naeskatt* (Snorri Sturleson).

13. The resemblance between the religion of the Scandinavians and that of the Persians has already been often noted. If the second Odin was a Scythian, he could have easily had some knowledge of the teachings of Zoroaster (Wharton, "On the Orig. of Romantic Fiction in Europe," in vol. 1 of his *Hist. of Engl. Poetry*). However, if the teachings and practices present great similarities, the goal and spirit are different. The religion of Zoroaster breathes peace; that of Odin, war. The first announces the return of a lost felicity, the second promises one to come. This opposition probably owes to the fact that the religious revolution of the Scandinavians is, in a certain way, the reversal of the Persian religion. Odin the conqueror gave his religion to the conquered. The defeated Medes gave their religion to the conquerors.

Another goddess, who also presides over this planet, or who is another name of Freya, Ostara, recalls the priestly Astarte. Night and day, which follow each other, while making the circuit of the heavens without burning out; the dawn, which is but the spume with which the courier of the night lathers his frenum; the sparks of the luminous world formed by the stars, the dwarf gods who represent the growth and decrease of the moon; Hati, the morning-star; Sköll, the evening-star; the bridge Bifröst, which is the rainbow; Asgard, the city of the gods, which is the zodiac, the twelve thrones that are its signs;[14] Thor's belt, the reversal of the cuirass of Amasis:[15] all these symbols are astronomical. The festivals are celebrated at periods that also belong to astronomy.[16]

The ancient fables feel this new character. The gods in Valhalla played at dice in order to win the riches each had brought with him while mounting to heaven. Now, these dice, which roll on the celestial table, express the splendor of the stars by their sheen, and by their movement, which is no longer fortuitous, the regular course of the planetary bodies.

One sees hermaphroditic divinities appear.[17] Respect for virginity combines with virgins giving birth,[18] and the North receives with surprise but without resistance the dark and bizarre cosmogonies of the East.[19] The supreme god alone, then with the giants of the Gelae, meditates on creation, like Brahma with the nine *rishis*. The members of these giants formed the world, like the divided body of the

14. Here we reproduce in a few lines some facts that were pointed out in book III, but which seemed essential to recall for the readers. We will do the same thing for the demonology.

15. See bk. III, ch. 5, n. 8.

16. The fable of Iduna, about which we have spoken elsewhere (bk. IX, ch. 3), also has an astronomical meaning. It was under the form of a swallow that Loki went to seek the marvelous apple whose absence condemned the gods to the infirmities of old age. The swallow was the symbol of spring. Spring grants the gods their original strength because it revives the nature that has been beaten down by the rigors of winter.

17. For the hermaphroditic gods of the Scandinavians, see bk. VI, ch. 7; and bk. X, ch. 10. Loki has children both as a man and as a woman; he is the father of Hela, of the serpent Mitgard, and the wolf Fenris, whom he engendered with the female giant Augustabode. He is the mother of Sleipner, whom he procreated with Sua-delfari. Freya, by a striking similarity with Cybele, is androgynous, although the wife of Odin.

18. Virginity has a special protector among the goddesses, Gefion, surnamed the Blessed. Heimdall, the celestial porter, is the son of nine virgins at once (Edda, 25th fable).

19. Rüh, *Scandin.* We have treated elsewhere (bk. VI, ch. 7) the Scandinavian cosmogony, so we will not do so here.

goddess Omorca; this world must be destroyed, and we have already reported the
frightening portrait the Eddas present of this destruction.[20]

But there is more. Independent of this teaching, inherent in all the beliefs
taught by priests, there is a notion that is subtler and no less sacerdotal which
hovers over certain parts of the Edda. Creation is only an illusion, the creator gods
only apparently exist; the time that contains creation no longer has reality, and
only where one and the other vanish do the true, the eternal, the unique begin.[21]
All this is identical with the Bhagavad Gita.

The world being created, a superior god dominates all the other gods;[22] beside
him is found a rival, but inferior, head of the malevolent divinities.[23] A mediator god attempts to reestablish the destroyed harmony.[24] A dying god atones for
the universe, and one must observe that this god, Balder, is the gentlest, the most
irenic, the most virtuous of all; therefore he does not mount to Valhalla. It is in
Niflheim that he is going to continue his peacemaking career. Ideal of the divine
perfection, heavenly lamb without spot, he dies by a mysterious consequence of his
very perfection in order to purify Odin of his first murder, that of the giant Ymir.
Who can fail to see here a priestly doctrine?[25]

A demonology no less regular than that of Egypt or Persia populates the deep
blue of the heavens, the surface of the earth, and the profound caverns where
humans do not enter: the Woles, interpreters of the runic literature, traverse the
fields where the brave fight; the inexorable Fates, breaking the thread they have
spun, or the charming Valkyries, compensating the heroes struck with premature
death with their charms, still other times swans or crows, or invisible, identified
with the murmuring wave and the air they stir. The Elves, children of light and brilliant like the sun, populate a kingdom that bears their name,[26] and they come down
from it to serve men. Others, black like pitch, remain under the earth.[27] Laboring

20. See bk. X, ch. 9.

21. Mone, *Symbol.*, 479.

22. Bk. X, ch. 2.

23. Ibid., ch. 4.

24. Ibid., ch. 7.

25. The gods who, except for Raguarokur, walk to a certain death in order to fight Loki are envisaged by several scholars of mythology as sacrificing themselves in order to destroy evil.

26. Alfsheim, *Grimnismal*, str. 5.

27. Nouvelle Edda, 15th fable.

dwarfs, born of the night and dust,[28] or the union of the gods and giants, because the moment to create man had not yet come, work metals, forge weapons, extract gold from the heart of the depths, thus defending it against mortals who were then growing into formidable giants, or more treacherous, lavishing upon humans this fateful gold, which sows discord, engenders hatreds, and occasions murders.[29]

It should be noted that in the Scandinavian fables, gold holds the place that women occupy in Indian fictions. All the faults of the gods of India, beginning with Brahma taken with Sarasvati, all the weaknesses of the penitents, almost all wars, have as their cause illicit loves or abductions. In the North, without being totally absent, love plays a smaller role. It is treasure that one desires, that one seizes, that one snatches; and sometimes to reestablish peace, this cursed gold, which had misled greedy rivals, is cast into the sea as the source of all evils.

The trinity is found in the three gods full of love, who finally want to manifest themselves (almost an Indian expression); two trees languished sterile and lifeless, the three gods gave them life.[30]

Metempsychosis can be presumed in the virgins who become swans after their death, by heroes changed into wolves, by giants transforming into she-wolves.

Alongside doctrines are cruel rituals, human sacrifices,[31] funeral immolations; Brynhildr, or Brunhild, before burning herself, had eight faithful servants burned on the tomb of Sigurd. Further along there are traces of obscene rituals.[32] Trials by water and fire end judicial proceedings.[33]

28. Nouvelle Edda, 13th fable; *Voluspa*, str. 10.

29. This demonology also has its scientific meaning. The dwarfs that work in metals are the mineral realm; the virgins who emerge from the roots of the tree Yggdrasil are the vegetal realm.

30. Edda, 7th fable.

31. Bk. XI, ch. 2. The priests and priestesses who presided over these sacrifices were called men and women of blood (Mone, *Symbol.*, p. 236); to know if they should offer human victims, they had recourse to a particular mode of divination. They consulted a sacred horse, and according to the hoof that it raised, they decided if the offering was accepted or not. This custom saved the life of a missionary, despite the protest of the priest who accused the god of Christians of invisibly directing the horse upon which he was seated (Mone, ibid., p. 70).

32. Bk. XI, ch. 4.

33. *"Quo evenit ut Dani pleraque causarum judicia eo experimenti genere constatura decernerent, controversiarum examen rectius ad arbitrium divinum quam ad humanam rixam relegandum putantes"* (Sax.. Grammat., X, 294). In the presence of the people, Poppo the Dane put on an iron glove reddened by the flame.

The effectiveness of invocations, imprecations, talismans, and magic letters, so wonderful in Persia and India, is proclaimed by the second Odin.[34] The power of his predecessor was the sword; his was the word, or writing, which is but the written word, and this difference separated the pontiff from the warrior. "Do you know," it is said in the *Havamal*, "how one writes the runes, how one explains them, how one ensures their effects? I know those that queens and the sons of men do not know. They chase away maladies, calm storms, heal wounds. I charm the storms in the atmosphere and they cease. If I pronounce them while pouring holy water on a new-born, he becomes invulnerable. Gods, *genii*, mortals, nothing escapes my sight. I awaken the love of virgins, and my beloved loves me forever." Freyr, recounts the Edda, taken with the beautiful Gerdor, whose marvelous splendor spread throughout the universe, and whose round arms shone with a brightness that dazzled sight, went with a faithful servant to conquer the object of his desires. Gymir, father of Gerdor, held her confined in a palace surrounded by fires that nothing could extinguish. The magical sword of the hero overcame this obstacle. He made his way to the beauty he wanted to possess; he painted in harmonious language the flame that consumed him. It was in vain. He offered her eleven apples of the purest gold, diamonds of inestimable worth, but again in vain. He threatened her with a dazzling sword; a useless threat. His companion, finally, uttered powerful words and the beautiful Gerdor yielded.

Philosophical teachings complete the priestly work. "How will I worship you?" the president of the celestial council asks the supreme god. "Shall I call you Odin, Thor, or This? Alfadur is your name. Under this name our ancestors honored you, before foreign gods had been brought to them." These are sayings characteristic of the work of priests, always attributing to theism, when they insert it into their teaching, a fanciful priority.[35] It is equally impossible to mistake dualism[36] and pantheism.[37]

---

34. "One was convinced that Odin traversed the world in the blink of an eye, controlled the air and storms, took on all sorts of forms, resuscitated the dead, presided over the future, deprived his enemies of their strength and health by his enchantments, discovered treasures hidden under the earth, opened both plains and mountains, and roused shades from the abyss" (Mallet, *Introd.*, p. 43). These exploits of the second Odin will not surprise our readers if they remember that at an earlier, cruder period, the jongleurs already possessed the ability to make use of such means.

35. See bk. I, ch. 9.

36. Bk. VI, ch. 7.

37. Ibid.

Finally, morality takes its place. Gimli and Nastrond, without supplanting Nifl-heim and Valhalla, offer rewards to the virtuous that the first Odin had accorded only to valor, not assigning to vice and crime any punishment because it was only a question of taking up the occupations of this life again.

Several writers have committed the same error with respect to Niflheim that French scholars committed who introduced morality into the underworld of Homer. The texts of the Eddas are clear: the inhabitants of Niflheim preserve their ranks, their dignities, their habits, enjoying terrestrial pleasures, getting drunk with hydromel. They arrive at this dwelling by passing over the bridge, Gjallarbru, on foot or on horse, often in the number of five times five thousand. We have spoken above[38] of the gods who were even confined there because they had not died in fighting. One only sees Hela, who reigns over Niflheim, punish the guilty. All the dead are brought together, the heroes excepted; there they live peacefully, and yet they end even this second career with a battle in which they, like the warriors of Valhalla, perish. It was not until the priests had transformed Gimli, formerly the abode of *genii*, into a place of rewards above Valhalla, and had invented Nas-trond, carefully separated from Niflheim, it was not until then that they assumed a judgment that cast the wicked into a place of torments. It is of Nastrond that the prophetess speaks when she sees the murderers, the perjurers, the seducers who whisper of love when they furtively approach virgins promised to another, struggling in the poisoned waves, and torn apart by wolves and serpents.[39] It is also about Nastrond that these two strophes of the *Havamal* speak, which are not lacking in poetic beauty: "Riches perish, friends perish, you will perish, but the renown that one acquires will not perish at all. Treasure disappears, brothers-in-arms are defeated, you yourself will be; but one thing lasts always: the judgment pronounced on each of the dead."[40]

Nastrond is the underworld of Pindar succeeding Homer's, only with priestly colors. However, because of the unwillingness of priests to remove anything, the original underworld and paradise subsist alongside those that were just created. Among the Greeks, because of the progress of ideas the same underworld is differ-ently employed. Among the Scandinavians, there are two underworlds for different purposes, and in the description of the latter underworld the priestly imprint can-

38. Bk. IX, ch. 7.
39. *Voluspa.*
40. *Havamal*, str. 77–78.

not fail to be seen.[41] The palace of Hela is sadness, her table famine, her sword hunger, her slave slowness, her vestibule the precipice, her bed suffering, her tent curses. The black waters of ten rivers flow through this place of horror; the names of these rivers are anxiety, chagrin, nothingness, despair, the gulf, the tempest, the vortex, moaning, howling, and the abyss.[42]

If from these general features we wish to enter into almost minute details, we would show similarities between the Eddas and the sacred books of other nations subject to priests that would prove the origin and mission of the second Odin. Thus, when Yggdrasil is proclaimed the first of the trees; Skithblathnir, of vessels; Odin, of gods; Sleipner, of horses; Bifrost, of bridges; Bragi, of poets; Habrok, of hawks; Garmr, of dogs, who does not think of Krishna, proclaiming himself the first of each species?[43] The Siegfried of the *Nibelungenlied*, an unmistakable tradition from the Eddas, cannot be wounded except between the shoulders, like the Indian divinity who is vulnerable only on the heel. The cow Oedulma is the fruitful cow created by the reunion of all the gods.[44] The fable of the theft of the poetic potion by Odin and his battles with the giant Suttungr is obviously based on that of *amrita* and the quarrels of the gods and giants for the possession of the treasure that confers immortality. Odin, who at the time of the Ragnarökkr regenerates himself in the midst of flames, differs little from the Brahmins who, from the time of Alexander, were avid for this means of purification, and whose sacrifice was frequently renewed by Buddhists.

The arrival of a second Odin—priest, prophet, and conqueror all at once— explains (and we will add that it alone explains) the contradictions that strike us while reading the Eddas.[45] One then understands how Odin, constantly called

---

41. See what we have said concerning the description of the dwellings of the dead in book IX, chapter 8.

42. Edda, 1st and 6th fables.

43. See bk. VI, ch. 5.

44. Ibid.

45. A German scholar named Graeter, editor of an interesting journal (*Bragur et Hermode*) on Icelandic antiquities, noting many traits of similarity with the doctrines of Greek philosophers, especially Heraclitus and Melissus, in the cosmogonic meanings of the Scandinavian fables, concluded that the second Odin had known the sages of Greece; but other than the fact that this system will always need the hypothesis we present, in order to account for the transplantation of these doctrines into Scandinavia, it rests only on similarities that had to have arisen everywhere from the observation of the most ordinary phenomena, because all of them are connected with the opposition of cold and heat. Another antiquarian, Mr. de Suhm, based himself upon the physical allegories interspersed in

the father of all things, the supreme god, the eternal being, is, however, condemned to perish one day while giving death to the evil principle. This teaching is irreconcilable with the foundation of the previous cult by the first Odin, and does not accord at all with his apotheosis. Would he have announced himself to be a transitory divinity? Would he have predicted the overturning of his own empire? Would he have invented this terrible Ragnarökkr, or twilight of the gods, which must annihilate him along with the universe? But the doctrine of the destruction of the world is a favorite teaching of the priesthood, and we have explained why the religions that it dominates always envelop the active divinities in this destruction.[46]

One also understands why, while the first Odin had so expressly, so emphatically, recommended martial courage and directed all hopes and all fears toward a central point, the love of glory and combat, characterizing every natural death as infamous and peace as hateful, the second Odin, undoing the work of his predecessor, lavished the price of valor upon qualities that until then were secondary. The priesthood had to want to replace teachings that influenced only a portion of human activity with opinions suitable to influence all actions, and thus to ensure it a more extensive and regular power.

We have said that morality did not enter gradually, but all at once, under the form of a code in the religions subject to priests;[47] this is how it appeared among the Scandinavians. It is entirely contained in the *Havamal*, or the sublime song of Odin. "My father sang me this canticle," says a hero in a saga; "this canticle which makes warriors human and just. The one who does not know it offends the weak,

---

the Eddas to conclude that the entire mythology of the North is a system of physics. This is the error of Varro concerning Greek and Roman theology.

46. See above, bk. X, ch. 9. An author whom we have consulted more than once (Rüh, *Scand.*, pp. 268–69), struck by the opposition of this teaching with the fundamental notions of the first polytheism of the Scandinavians, supposed that it was introduced after the establishment of Christianity by Christian monks. This conjecture proves well enough that one cannot study the antiquities of the North without noticing doctrines that come from different periods. But the Ragnarökkr does not need this explanation. It had to be the result of the revolution that gave rise to the triumph of the priestly spirit. The same reasoning leads us with even greater reason to reject the idea that all the Eddas were the work of missionaries. There is no doubt that there were interpolations and pious frauds; but an entire mythology created to ridicule it is itself a ridiculous hypothesis. The resemblances of the mythology of the North with Christianity are no more striking than those of the same mythology with the legends of India. For example, one finds the story of *amrita*, which the Christians could not have inserted, because they did not know it (Rüh, p. 135).

47. Bk. XII, ch. 9.

robs travelers, violates women, devours children. But the one who observes its precepts protects the peasant, the travelers, the senior, the child, as well as the honor of women;[48] and as his reward, after his death he is transported to Gimli, where he lives eternally happy."

Of all the poems that comprise the Eddas, the *Havamal* is the one that the Skalds especially attributed to the first Odin, and in our view this is additional proof that this canticle was the work of the priesthood. What priests must with the greatest care make go back to their legendary founder was precisely what they had added to his doctrine.[49]

Let us now try to determine to which of the two periods of northern religions the traditions and records that remain to us pertain. The Eddas are divided into four parts.[50] We will ignore the subdivisions.[51]

The first is the *Voluspa*, the song of the great female magician: it contains the fables. The second is the *Havamal*, of which we just spoke; to it one must join the *Lokfafnismal*, or the song of wisdom. The third is the *Runatal*, and treats magic. The fourth, which is not found except in the oldest Eddas, that of Soemund, is the *Lokasenna*. Finally, we cannot exclude from this enumeration either the *Nibelungenlied* or the *Book of Heroes*,[52] which were composed by Christian authors a long time afterward and cast in a Christian form; but the features of paganism poke

---

48. Almost all its precepts are opposed to the examples and promises of the first Odin to his companions: pillage is their life, drunkenness their delight, and the *Havamal* forbids pillage and condemns drunkenness (Mallet, *Hist. du Dan.*, II, 280).

49. See Bartholin, *De caus. contempt. mortis*, III, 193; Gebh., *Hist. Dan.*, I, 35.

50. Mallet (*Hist. du Dan.*, II, 33) counts only three; but this is because he rejects the *Lokasenna*. We will see that he does so in error.

51. These subdivisions are numerous and arbitrary. To simplify them, we bring together with the *Voluspa* properly speaking the *Vaftrudnismal*, or the battle of Odin against a giant, as being of the same period; the *Grimnismal*, or the quarrel of Odin and his wife, Freya, for the empire of the world; the song of Alvis the dwarf; the *Thrymskvida*, or the history of Thor, Loki, and the giant Thrymmer; the *Hymiskvida*, or the cosmogonic narrative relating to the giant Ymir; the three legends that recount the struggle of Thor against a dwarf he could not defeat; the loves of the god Freyr, and the puzzles resolved by Svipdagr; the death of Balder; the genealogy of the heroes, the sons of the gods, or the passage of the divine race to the heroic race; the song of the crow, consisting mainly in predictions concerning the destruction of the world.

52. The *Heldenbuch*. This *Book of Heroes*, more recent than the *Nibelungen* and attributed to Henry of Ofterdinger, a poet of the thirteenth century, is nonetheless filled with traditions similar to the ancient legends of the North.

through this form at every moment. The catastrophe of the Germanic poem is obviously borrowed from the twilight of the gods, and the name alone of Sigfried or Sigurd recalls among the Scandinavians the father of one of the Odins.

The *Voluspa* belongs to both periods. In it the priests deposited all the tales that had successively become parts of their legends. Thus the contradictions that attest to the coexistence of several doctrines are piled on top of one another in the work. In certain respects, for the mythology of the North it is what Hesiod is for the Greeks.

The *Havamal* and the *Runatal* (or runic chapter) are from the period of the second Odin. We have shown that the former contained a different doctrine from the original teaching, recommended other virtues, promised other rewards—in a word, established an entirely different religious and moral system. The chapter that treats of magic betrays the precautions of the priesthood against rivals, and by that very fact indicates a moment when the priests were in a position to persecute those who competed with them on their own ground.

The *Lokasenna* is the banquet where Loki, after having caused the death of Balder, came to berate the angered gods. The festival hall is an inviolable haven. Because of the sanctity of the place, Odin himself protects Loki; and the latter, sure of being unpunished, reproaches the inhabitants for their culpable actions and vicious inclinations. This poem must be contemporaneous with the most ancient Scandinavian polytheism and prior to the second Odin.

No doubt, these poems could and must have suffered various transformations. The priestly caste was the sole possessor of them; it transmitted them orally, and partially, to a people lacking entirely in literature and for whom examination was a sacrilege.

As for the *Nibelungenlied* and *Book of Heroes*, what we have said above indicates well enough that one ought to consider them with caution. The memories of two mythologies, reported by writers who professed a third belief, have necessarily been quite disfigured, and the ideas of the two periods find themselves quite mixed together and, moreover, merged and amalgamated with the Christianity that had replaced them, and still attacked them with its hatred and reproaches.

If, despite the moral proofs that we believe have clearly demonstrated our point, one persisted in asking another sort of proof from us, founded on historical witnesses and certain dates, we would respond that because the records of these faraway times were not collected until after their authenticity had become doubtful and their times unknown, the rules of ordinary chronology cannot serve as guides.

The Scandinavians did not have historians until the eleventh century.[53] The use of writing was forbidden in everything that had to do with religion, history, and the laws. Hymns, legends, and mythological narratives were only orally transmitted. If we find in some poems that are still pagan some runic letters attributed to Odin, they were only employed for magical purposes.

Saemund Sigfusson, the first who dared to put the sagas and poems that formed the Eddas into writing, lived in 1057. A century and a half later, his collection was abridged by Snorri Sturluson.

Thus, collected twice at one hundred and fifty years' distance, after the triumph of a new religion, by men who had as their goal inspiring their contemporaries with a high idea of the ancient poetry of the North,[54] rather than retracing the development of religious opinions in this part of the globe, the records of Scandinavian polytheism were simply placed alongside one another rather than classed in their original order. In addition, before being assembled they had suffered many transformations. When for the first time they received a stable form by writing, the opinions they contained were not presently dominant. Those who transcribed them had no interest in seeing if they contained contradictory notions from different periods which had been replaced, or at least succeeded one another, in the spirit of the peoples.

It is therefore impossible to distinguish by precise dates the records that were collected and brought together by compilers, and therefore there is an obvious need to replace an unavailable positive chronology with a moral chronology.

53. According to Torfoeus, eleven centuries passed between Odin and the first Icelandic historian, Isleif, bishop of Scalholt, who died in 1080 (Mallet, *Introd.*, p. 46); and the Odin of whom Torfoeus speaks was not the first but the second Odin.

54. "Edda" signifies poetics, the art of poetry. The Eddas are therefore a collection to form poets, and not a religious book. The Skald apprentices preserved the fictions of the ancient mythology in their poems, even though it was destroyed (Mallet, *Hist.*, II, 25–26). What shows that the compilers of the Eddas were interested only in poetry is the inclusion of a burlesque fable, obviously interpolated, that is a mockery of bad poets. Having swallowed the poetic potion, Odin took flight in the form of an eagle; pursued by one of the giants who were the guardians of this treasure, he let a portion escape, and damaged in this way, this potion became the lot of bad poets.

CHAPTER 4

That the Question Whether There Was a Third Religious Revolution in Scandinavia Is Irrelevant to Our Subject

We could be tempted to resolve another problem. Did Scandinavia experience, subsequent to the second Odin, a new revolution that destroyed or at least greatly diminished the power of priests?

Many scattered facts reported by writers who are extremely careful students of ancient traditions would have us believe so.

A third Odin appears to have destroyed the authority of the council of the gods that the second had established. Initially allied to Gylfi,[1] the president of this despotic council, he soon had him put to death and erected a temporal monarchy on the rubble of the priestly power.

According to this hypothesis, the Scandinavian religion would have changed three times, and each time because of the arrival of a colony. The first would have introduced a polytheism independent of priests, in which the priesthood exercised only a very limited influence; the second would have substituted for this polytheism a religion subject to priests; the third, breaking this yoke, would have put the Scandinavians back into their original independence.

What can give some plausibility to this assumption is that the heads of the government of the island in later times exercised a superintendence over the priests that assigned to them a very secondary rank.[2]

This question, however, is irrelevant to us. What we needed to demonstrate was the existence and succession of the two earlier revolutions. The following chapter will prove how important this demonstration was.

1. In a previous note [bk. XIV, ch. 3, n. 3] we saw the attribution of the name Gylfi to two individuals whose situations were entirely different. It would seem that the same fact has also been placed in the history of both by presenting them as the holders, sometimes of temporal power, sometimes of priestly authority.

2. Wedel-Jarlsberg, pp. 173, 175, 176, 269, 272.

CHAPTER 5

That the Two Revolutions of Scandinavian Polytheism
Confirm Our Assertions Concerning the Nature
and Differences between the Two Polytheisms

One of the truths we have tried to establish is that religion is different according to whether it is freed of priestly domination or subject to this domination.

We have presented this truth under four perspectives, and in each we have found the proof incontestable.

At the time of Homer, in Greece there was no astrolatry, and hence no priests; no priests, consequently in the public religion no bloody or obscene rituals, no theogonies or dark cosmogonies, no subtle teachings such as dualism or pantheism, which would end in a disbelief covered with a mysterious veil, and adversely affecting the solemnity of religion. Later, a priesthood without any influence, and consequently the popular worship remaining without any priestly refinement, gradually improving by the sole effect of the progress and developments of the human spirit; but a secret religion borrowed from abroad and introduced into Greece, almost against the laws, by a priesthood that wanted to compensate itself for the little amount of power it possessed in the State, and this occult religion calling for, invoking, and incorporating all the priestly rituals and teachings.

Throughout the East, in the South, and among the Gauls, there were all-powerful priests, and with them everything whose absence we have noted among the Greeks: a condition of stasis, immobility of intelligence, and servitude.

Among the Romans, the struggle of the priestly spirit against independent polytheism; the preservation of everything that characterizes priestly religions as long as their traces were perpetuated; but the disappearance of all these things as soon as the power of priests was defeated.

Now, we just saw in Scandinavia an opposite movement: first, a polytheism free of the priestly domination, more bellicose than that of Greeks but resting on the same bases, only allowing the same anthropomorphism; then a colony of priests which won a sudden and harmful victory. Simple, natural anthropomorphism, proportionate to the period, was replaced straight away by all the errors, all the barbarisms, and all the subtleties inherent in priestly polytheism.

BOOK XV

RESULTS OF THE WORK

CHAPTER I

Question to Resolve

We have ended our investigations, at least for the first half of the path we intend to traverse. We have described the progressive changes of the first religious form that man created for himself, and we have followed this form to its highest point of perfection. The second half of our researches will embrace its fall. We will indicate the causes of its decadence, the efforts of the religious sentiment when, having improved the form, it finds it resistant to its subsequent needs; its attempts to bend the form to its new needs, and the destruction that follows from them; the fate of philosophy, first of all unthreatening, then soon persecuted, therefore hostile, finally victorious; the apparent immobility of priestly religions, inwardly troubled by an invisible disturbance, their exteriors remaining unchanging, until their foundations crumble. In the midst of the chaos that results from this universal collapse, a new form triumphing over that which had been broken, which the mortal race seemed not to be able to replace or reconstruct, will rally this errant and disheartened race. Around this young and pure form will gather everything that was able to survive the great shipwreck, everything that remained of generous sentiments and consoling hopes; but we will also see arrive all the memories and traditions of the priesthood: corporations, monopolies, tyrannies, impostures, ancient frauds, all eager to reconquer the sanctuary.

However, let us not anticipate the future, let us recollect what the past teaches us.

We will not repeat the facts. For attentive readers this would be superfluous; for the inattentive, useless.

The religious forms are of two species.

Some, subject to corporations that maintain them immobile; others, independent of all corporations, gradually perfect themselves.

Man can find himself under the dominion of one or the other of these forms.

A third hypothesis would be where both forms would be rejected.

Is this hypothesis admissible, though? We do not think so. Historically, we see no example anywhere. Psychologically, the existence of the religious sentiment seems to place an obstacle to it.

The Romans believed they were in this situation toward the first century of our era.[1]

Three hundred years later, religious convictions had once again penetrated all spirits, faith had reconquered all souls.

In France, fifty or sixty years ago, we also thought that we had arrived at a state of disdain for all that was not susceptible of demonstration; many circumstances had conspired to bring us to this point.

A devotion that had had for its object not so much the Divinity as the monarchy expired on the latter's tomb, covered with the people's invectives. These were no longer the times when Madame de Sevigné would have wanted to die for the real presence because she had danced with the Great King.[2] The still established doctrines and the already victorious new ideas clashed, because all proportion was broken. The memories of persecutions (of persecutions mitigated by caprice) angered intellects. Power in contradiction with itself, out of habit raged against principles to which it was attached out of vanity. Liberty of thought was the need of elevated minds; the license of mores tempted corrupt souls; and since one had asserted a positive religion as the basis of morality the fall of this religion favored license.

A clergy that was intolerant in its actions but insouciant in its teachings, and discredited by the conduct of a large number of its members, impressed a complexion that was at once hateful and frivolous on the dominant cult, an incoherent mixture that gave license to ridicule while also giving rise to indignation. Ministers of the altars wrote obscene novels and flattered themselves on their worldly life at the time when Raynal and Rousseau were proscribed, Helvetius was troubled, and the priesthood threatened Voltaire, as well as cast an unhappy look on Montesquieu and a defiant one at Buffon, whom it would have willingly treated like Galileo.

No one should overemphasize the actual mitigations that were made to apparent severities. This inconsistency harmed religion. It was disdained even more

1. Bk. I, ch. 6.
2. Letter 640, Grouvelle ed.

without being hated less. Contempt was united with hostility. All conviction was lost when one saw that nothing was serious for anyone, that professions of faith and practices, even rigors, were only lying forms, with indifference at their core.

The Revolution came. One would have said: the triumph of disbelieving philosophy. In what is related to religious ideas (we will not speak of crimes, of which one must not accuse any teaching, because religion itself would often be accusable), it was a loudly proclaimed unbelief, one received favorably. Forty years have passed: let us examine where we are. What was customary is doubtless gone; what is dead can no longer be reborn; but a mysterious agitation, a desire to believe, a thirst for hope are everywhere manifest. Everywhere you see peaceful sects, because the century is peaceful, but enthusiastic, because the need for enthusiasm belongs to all times. Consider the English Methodists, the Swiss Momiers; in Geneva, those inhabitants of churchyard cemeteries, wanting at all costs to reestablish communication with the invisible world and communion with the dead; in Germany, all the philosophies impregnated with mysticism. Even in France, where the most positive generation, upon taking control of the earth seemed to want to devote itself entirely to the earth; today, in the midst of this grave and studious generation, rise isolated, imperceptible efforts, which protest against the tendency toward materialism, today a tradition rather than a system.

This disposition of mind casts many into strange incoherences. Full of respect for any religious opinion whatsoever, they praise Maecenas for having exhorted Augustus to honor the gods and have them honored, even though these gods were pagan gods and one way of honoring them was to deliver Christians to the wild beasts. They speak with almost the same veneration about holy water and lustral water, of Memphis and the Vatican.

In all this there are elements of extravagance; but the extravagance has a cause. The movement that survives the apparent death proves that the seed is not deprived of life.

And notice how the instinct of this renovation takes hold of our prose-writers and our poets. Where do they look for their effects? To irony, to philosophical apothegms, like Voltaire? No: to vague meditations, to reveries, whose gaze is always turned toward the unbounded future and toward the infinite. Many lose themselves in the clouds; but their élan toward the clouds is an attempt to approach heaven. They sense that it is in this way that a relationship with a new public will be established, a public tired of unbelief and which wants something else, without perhaps knowing what it wants.

The absence of every conjecture, of every sentiment, of every religious hope—
that is, dogmatic unbelief—is therefore impossible for the mass of human beings.

Please observe that we speak here only of dogmatic unbelief. We do not equate
it with doubt. We esteem doubt as much, and more, than anyone;[3] but doubt does
not exclude religious sentiment. Doubt has its recompenses, it has its desires and
its hope; it does not confine man to an iron circle where he struggles with terror
and anguish. From the midst of the obscurity that surrounds him, doubt sees luminous rays break through, it gives itself to presentiments that revive and console
it. Far from rebuffing, it invokes. It does not deny, it simply does not know; and
sometimes warmed by desire, sometimes marked with resignation, its ignorance is
not without its sweetness. But the denial of all power superior to us, of all communication with that power, of all appeal to its goodness and justice against injustice
and perversity, the renouncing of a world better than ours, a world of reparation
and purity, no society will be satisfied with that.

One therefore must return to one of the two estates compatible with our nature:
imposed religion, free religion.

Which of the two is better?

India, Ethiopia, Egypt, and Persia offer the example of the first of these states.
All progress is forbidden to the intellect, all advancement is a crime, all innovation
a sacrilege. Religion does not get rid of the hideous vestiges of fetishism, the form
of the gods remains vague, their character vicious. Morality is falsified, liberty proscribed, crime commanded. At once venal and threatening, religion that is lavish
with terrors is sparing with consolations. Those that it grants, it sells. Crumpled
in the hands of its masters, abased in the soul of its slaves, for the first group it is
an instrument that they degrade, for the second a yoke that weighs upon them.
Object of calculation without any good faith, or obedience without examination,
it corrupts those who profit from it as well as those who are oppressed by it. It condemns fear to hypocrisy, and drags sincerity to the torture chamber, giving a bonus
to whatever is base and reserving punishment for courage.

An oppressive caste successively demands from man the renunciation of his penchants, his affections, his virtues, his intelligence. It applies the same principle to
belief as to all other kinds of offerings. Faith becomes even more meritorious as

3. For me I know nought, nothing I deny,
Affirm, reject, contend, and, what know you?
(Lord Byron)

the teaching that demands it is more difficult to believe or understand. In its exaltation, the religious sentiment favors this demand of the priesthood. It is pleased to immolate its most precious faculties to its gods. The same fanaticism that obtained the holocaust of his son from a father, her modesty from a virgin, obtains from reason the suicide of abjuring itself. Error or truth, it matters not, are equally imposed. Man and his faculties disappear; what remains is the priest and his calculations.

Add the spirit of persecution to all these scourges, the inevitable consequence of such a system. See the massacre of Buddhists among the gentlest people on the earth; among the Egyptians, the oppression of the Hebrews.

In ancient times, this has been the effect of the stationary principle in religion.

We do not wish to exaggerate. We do not claim that the priesthood has been the author of all the evils that have weighed upon the world. Numerous causes of different sorts, external and internal, accidental or permanent, have often, and powerfully, operated. Up to a certain point the aristocracy of warriors has counterbalanced the power of priests, as the despotism of kings later dethroned the warrior aristocracy, and as today industry overturns the despotism of kings. But is it still not true that the priesthood has always hampered that extension of rights and enjoyments that go from one caste to another, and finally from all those who enjoy privileges to the entire species? This is what we affirm; this is what history proves. We grant to all the causes that have determined the lot of man their part in influencing him; but devoting ourselves to describing one of the most active ones, we have had to depict its effects truly.

Distinguished literary men have objected to us that at the period when the priests were the most enlightened portion of societies, it was natural and just that they served as guides. We do not deny this at all. We have recognized that among the savages the priesthood sometimes did good.[4] But the writers to whom we respond, it seems to us, have considered only one side of the question. Doubtless, it is natural and just that superior intelligences march at the head of human associations, even though we would consider the thing to be a fact rather than a right; if one made it a right, the strongest will always call themselves the most intelligent and oppress the others. In order for the intellectual aristocracy not to become as noxious as all other aristocratic systems, its power must be limited to persuasion, to the sharing of its learning without political or coercive means. When the superiority of intelligence calls for the support of authority, it departs from its sphere,

4. See bk. II, ch. 6.

it attributes to itself contestable rights. With this sort of superiority always being disputable, it arrives at various ways of vexation that render it no less odious than material and blind forces. We recognize that when the multitude is plunged into ignorance, the most instructed must direct it; but if, to this faculty that nature has confided in them and which has no need of the law to sanction, they wish to join the right to arrest the progress of future generations, they sacrifice the future to the present; and, in order to prematurely ripen some limited and imperfect knowledge, they strike with sterility improvements that are nobler and more real. Now, this tendency has always been, it will always be, that of a priesthood brought together in a body and invested with temporal power. The priesthood of Antiquity could, sometimes, possess good faith and believe in the legitimacy of its prohibitions as well as the truth of its doctrines. It could be sincere, even in its ruses; to serve God by means of fraud, like one serves a human master, is a rather natural movement in the conceptions of anthropomorphism; but the tendency to which the priesthood obeys has also motived all the tyrannies that have overwhelmed man. It is against this tendency, and not against the legitimate influence of the superiority of knowledge, and consequently the men who in each social period are invested with it, that we have risen.

Now, alongside the priestly immobility, let us consider Greece, free and progressive.

Starting from a crude fetishism, the religious sentiment soon arrives at polytheism, frees it from all the vestiges of barbarism, perfects it and purifies it. Everything is ennobled in its teachings and public rituals. The Greeks borrow from everywhere whatever seduces their active and curious imagination, but they embellish everything they borrow.

They took from the theocratic corporations of the East and the South the elements of the sciences, which these corporations kept captive. From imperfect and languishing as these sciences were in the darkness of the sanctuary, they were revived, expanded, and developed in broad daylight; and the intellect, following its bold march and moving from hypothesis to hypothesis, through a thousand errors, no doubt, nonetheless arrives, if not at the absolute truth, at least to those truths that are the needs of each period, and that are so many rungs to attain other truths, always of a superior order and higher importance. Religion feels this activity of the intellect. Torrents of light inundated it, to enter into and rework it.

Morality, gentler and more refined, because the religious sentiment spreads its refined nuances over it, remains independent of the dryness and harshness of positive dogmas. No capricious will, no arbitrary power, no mystical autocracy[5] transforms good into evil, evil into good. What is virtuous remains virtuous; what is criminal remains criminal. No proud pontiff would dare to order what is culpable, or justify what is atrocious, in the name of heaven. No mercenary priest would make purchased immunity the gage of future impunity (which one would also have to buy). The gods, like humans, submit to eternal laws, and conscience, inviolable and respected, pronounces on the wills of the former as well as the conduct of the latter.

After this comparison, the question is certainly resolved.

And yet the progressive state, the noblest and most worthy of religion, the most salutary for the human species, does not appear to us free of every hindrance even in Greece, and this leads us to demonstrate the disadvantages of a corporation whose interest is that religion be unchanging, even when this corporation does not have the power to maintain it so.

5. See above, bk. XII, ch. 11, n. 22, where we recall that a theologian, while treating the Hebrew laws, says that Jehovah decided the merits of actions in virtue of his *autocratic* right.

CHAPTER 2

On the Disadvantages of the Principle of Stasis, Even in the Religions That Do Not Confer an Unlimited Power on the Priesthood

Even though the Greeks were the sole people of antiquity who had not suffered the yoke of priestly power, there nonetheless was a priesthood in Greece; and this priesthood had some authority. As much as the independence of the national spirit allowed, it had arrived at acquiring a legal place for religion and its teachings in the constitution of the State.

What resulted from this? Enlightenment had spread and rejected absurd fables. Mores that had become gentler opposed themselves to more-or-less barbarous traditions. The character of the gods suffered the changes that this revolution had to entail. It occurred in fact before it was proclaimed in theory. Sages, philosophers, and moralists declared the truth that already existed before their declaration.

Soon, because religious belief was part of the constitution of the State, the priesthood exclaimed that the constitution of the State was being undermined.

Anaxagoras proves that crude and inert matter, which is how the intellect conceived it initially, when it believed it understood what matter and pure spirit are, could not make up the substance of the immortal gods; the Athenian priests accused him of denying their existence, and he was exiled.

Socrates affirms that the divine natures are neither limited nor imperfect nor vicious, that one offends them in wanting to seduce them,[1] that they have neither committed crimes nor protected them. The Athenian priests referred Socrates to the Areopagus, and he was put to death.

It is so true that this attack was due much more to the principle of stasis than to a fervent or passionate fanaticism, that even in this very famous trial, until the mo-

---

1. Those are impious toward the gods, said his disciple (*De leg.*, bk. X), who think that the guilty appease them with their sacrifices.

ment when he drank the poison, the enemies of Socrates allowed him easy means of disarming their attack. But in order to escape, it was either the laws of the homeland that he had to violate or the principle of stasis that had to be recognized by its disavowal. It would have been necessary to reject all the improvements acquired by the noble emotions or by studious meditations; to go back to the times of ignorance and once again adopt their teachings; to renounce all the progress made by reason and morality. Socrates did not want to do this; let us acknowledge his choice. His death was useful to his century and his country. It is still useful today.

Some have strongly protested against one of our cleverest writers because he dared to say that in the given state of the institutions of Athens, the death of Socrates was inevitable and legal. However, the claim is perfectly true. I say it with him: "In an order of things whose basis is a State religion, one cannot think, like Socrates, of this religion, and make public what one thinks about it, without harming this religion, and, therefore, without troubling the State. . . . Socrates did not stand up as a philosopher, except on the condition of becoming *guilty* as a citizen. His death was required, the necessary result of the struggle he had conducted against religious dogmatism."[2]

2. Trans. of Plato by V. Cousin, *Argument de l'apologie*, pp. 56 & 59. This seems to us to answer definitively those of the adversaries of Christianity who, in order to put it below the ancient religions, have attributed the virtue of tolerance to them. Even among the Greeks or the Romans, the tolerance of polytheism did not rest, at all, on the respect owed by society to the opinions of individuals. The peoples who were tolerant toward each other as political aggregates still failed to recognize this eternal principle, that each has the right to adore his god in the way that seems to him best. On the contrary, citizens were held to conform themselves to the cult of the city. The laws of Triptolemus and Draco forbade, under pain of death, all deviation from the public religion (Porph., *De abst.*, IV, where he cites Hermippus, *De legislator.*, I, II; Josephus, *Contra Apion*, II, 37), and the Athenians took an oath to submit themselves to this disposition (Isocrat., *Panath.*; Stobaeus). No one had the freedom to adopt a foreign cult, even though the cult was allowed to the foreigners who practiced it. These foreigners themselves, however, were to remain faithful to the belief of their ancestors. In a letter to the inhabitants of Alexandria, Julian established this principle of polytheism. What he most bitterly reproaches Christians for is having abandoned the religion of their fathers. He calls them rebellious false Hebrews, and judges the Jews more indulgently.

Plato declares accusations of impiety legitimate. One must not, he says, suffer unbelievers. Up to this point, we know more than one modern who would be of this opinion; but Plato adds: One must render worship to the planets, and those who will dare to maintain that the planets are not gods ought to be punished as impious. Here the inquisitors of our day part from Plato. This is what happens to all men who adopt the legitimacy of intolerance. They agree on the persecution of opinions contrary to their own and divide on the one in whose name they ought to persecute.

Nothing is more evident. But from this another thing results: as long as religion serves as a pretext for the existence of a body charged with teaching and maintaining it, depending upon the country and the time, religious dogmatism will have its exiles, its dungeons, its poison, or its pyres.

From this point of view, the reasonings that justify the death of Socrates go much further, if one wishes. The author of the treatise on the laws of Moses has launched himself on this path full of pitfalls; we will not follow him there. But the principle admitted, the religion of the State transformed into law, the consequences he deduces are incontestable. To escape them, one must suppose judges recognizing the divine mission. Then they themselves would have been the enemies of the established order, rebels punishable by law. It would not be on them, but on these laws that reproach would fall. It would be the laws that would have to be abolished.

If we could have treated the entirety of Roman polytheism here, we would have shown even more clearly the harmful consequences of the principle of stasis, which was more solemnly established at Rome than in Greece. To be sure, and we will demonstrate this elsewhere, in its moral part Roman polytheism was superior in more than one respect to Greek religion. But everything that was vicious, oppressive, and cruel[3] in this aristocratic republic must still be attributed to the religious traditions that were perpetuated despite the march of civilization.

The Romans were no more tolerant. "*Separatim nemo habesse Deos neve novos, neve advenas, nisi publice accisos, privatim colunto*" (Law of the Twelve Tables, cited by Cicero). "*Ne qui, nisi romani dii, neuquo alio more quam patrio colerentur*" (Liv., IV, 30). "*Quoties*," says the consul Posthumius, "*hoc partum, avorumque aetate negotium datum est magistratibus, ut sacra externa fieri vetarent, omnem disciplinam sacrificandi, praeterquam more romano, abolerent*" (Liv., XXIX, 16; see also IX, XXVI).

The first philosophers who adopted the principles of true tolerance were the Neoplatonists. This is because positive religion was coming to its end. In ending this note, we cannot refrain from congratulating ourselves on the service one of our most hostile critics performed for us by recognizing that our way of envisaging religion is at bottom identical with that of Mr. Cousin. The author of the *Catholique* (XXXIII, 351–58), in analyzing the course of philosophy of this illustrious professor, expresses himself in these words: "The natural religion is not the instinct of nature traversing the world and soaring to God. The system of Mr. Constant would find itself at the end of this theory. Worship, says Mr. Cousin, is the realization of the religious sentiment. This is exactly what Mr. Constant, in his hatred of the priesthood, previously claimed." However, Mr. Cousin and we began from very different foundations. He admires the great priestly corporations of antiquity, while we detest them. But men of good faith always end by encountering one another.

3. A curious anecdote shows the Roman priesthood, even in a time when enlightenment fought its influence, exercising it at the expense of the dearest affections and most sacred duties. Scylla cele-

The servitude of the plebeians, wandering without any patrimony, deprived of asylum, even on the soil they had conquered, deprived of all real right, and having snatched from their tyrants only a few defensive institutions; who rose up against laws sanctioned by priestly memories—the forbidding of marriage between the two orders, which was the barely softened continuation of the division into castes, and being deprived of an equal part in the ceremonies of the cult—everything that by running counter to interests, and wounding legitimate pride, prepared the endless convulsions that had no remedy: all this was the consequence of the principle of stasis. Thanks to the patriotism of these so mistreated plebeians, Rome had its period of glory; thanks to the Machiavellian energy of a Senate that was despotic without, formidable within, but whose deliberations, even though concentrated in a monopoly still served to maintain the salutary movement of political liberty, Rome had its time of strength and stability.

But the principle of stasis had deposed a seed of destruction in its religious and civil constitution.

Precisely because Roman politics had taken over religion and denied all novelty to it, so that the instrument would more surely remain in its dependency, insofar as it was static religion lost its vital principle, perfectibility, and inasmuch as it was enslaved it lost its real power, conviction.

One no longer believed in anything, because everything had to be believed. Nothing was respected, because calculation was recognized everywhere. It was because the augurs employed a discredited art of divination to govern Rome that they could never encounter each other without a wry smile; and this smile was the infallible precursor of the loss of religion.

We, however, have had to forbid to ourselves these developments and limit ourselves to what we have said earlier concerning the mixture of the Etruscan heritage and the Greek influence. The periods that followed belong to a second work.

---

brated games in honor of Hercules. Metella, his wife, fell dangerously ill. The priests declared that it was not permitted to him, when he was occupied with a religious ceremony, either to see his wife or to allow her to die in his home. He divorced her, she was carried outside while dying, and then she was given magnificent funeral rites.

CHAPTER 3

That the Purity of Doctrine Diminishes Nothing in the Dangers of the Principle of Stasis in Religion

Doctrine, or humanity in its precepts, would extract the poison it contains from the principle we are combating. This would be an error.

The forced preservation of a religious doctrine, rendering it fixed and immutable, entails identical consequences, whatever be the doctrine in itself. Under a form much more purified than polytheism, Catholics have shown themselves implacable against the Reformers, the Reformers against the Socinians, and Socinians, no doubt, would not have been more indulgent toward those who would have denied the human mission of the prophet whose divinity they denied. The cardinal of Lorraine had Coligny killed; Calvin, who would have had the cardinal burned, did have Servetus burned.

To consider a religion as never being able to be improved is to declare it the only good, the only salutary religion. Hence, it becomes an imperious duty to make it adopted by everyone. Not only is it permitted, but it is commanded to employ force in this pious work if the means of persuasion do not suffice.[1]

---

1. All positive religion, all immutable forms, lead by a direct path to intolerance, if one reasons consistently. "Intolerance," says an Italian author, "the intolerance that those who want to tolerate error call a terrible doctrine, and the desire to convert all the nations, are the two finest characteristics of Christianity; and despite the clamors of angered unbelievers, we have no reason to be embarrassed. I would like to know how one dares to deny that since the truth that makes the happiness of this life and the next has finally been discovered, it is a noble, humane, and social enterprise to spread it, to bring it everywhere, and to defend it against the machinations and attacks of its enemies, first by persuasion, then when persuasion is unavailing, by the entire force of the magistrate and the laws. Such is the spirit of conversion and intolerance of Christianity. If it is just to correct, repress, and punish those who advance doctrines contrary to the State, why would it be unjust and cruel to do the same for the good of Christianity, which according to the testimonies of profane writers themselves is the greatest good that men can give or receive, the best of all systems, and even in this life the purest and

If political authority joins with religious zeal to perpetuate the faith, and this principle is once admitted, the political authority must embrace it; it must necessarily invest the priesthood with its means of force. Hence, the introduction of a material power into the domain of conscience; hence, persecutions and tortures.[2]

But this is not the only danger.

As soon as the priesthood has arrived at forming an alliance with political power, it applies itself to fortifying that power, to freeing it from any other resistance than what would come from it; and temporal despotism is the inevitable consequence of the despotism of priests. Consulted by the kings of Persia, the magi applauded their incests and proclaimed them above the laws. Every time the priesthood has had the aristocracy or monarchy as its accomplice, it has pronounced anathema against all the liberties and rights of the peoples.[3] And even in our days, read the works of those who would like to revive theocracy. The mildness to which the century compels them only serves as a thin veil for their regrets, their defenses, and their appeals to the Inquisition.[4] See how much the independence of thought,

---

truest source of earthly and social happiness?" (*Histoire critique des révolutions de la philosophie dans les trois derniers siècles*, by Appiano Buonafede, the general of the Celestines, under the name Agatopisto Oromazziane, V, 55).

2. Even improved, the French Charter is not exempt from this defect. By declaring that the Catholic religion is the religion of the majority of the French, either it declares a fact that is superfluous to declare, or one intends to give, indirectly, this religion supremacy over others, which is a possible danger. Fortunately, later on it establishes the equality of cults, which renders the rights of the majority illusory or inoffensive.

3. In the Middle Ages, says a historian, the clergy declaimed against the communes from the pulpit: it called them "execrable." They were outraged that, "against all justice," slaves escaped from their masters, which proves that if the Christian religion destroyed slavery, its ministers hardly helped in this work of charity. Here is what a writer of the times recounts to Bishop Guilbert: "*Inter missas sermonem habuit de execrabilibus communiis, in quibus contra jus et fas violenter servi a dominorum jure se subtrahunt.*" The word "commune" seemed to him to be a new and detestable word: "novum ac pessimum nomen" (Ducange, Gloss., *verbo Communia*).

4. "Autos-da-fé," says the author of the *Catholique*, "are celebrated with a *pomp that seems horrible to us*. The Inquisition was national in Spain, it did not stifle the Castilian genius, did not inhibit the great poets and historians from flourishing on the Peninsula, did no harm to industry (i.e., since the expulsion of the Moors, and especially since Philip II, the population of Spain diminished by two-thirds), the Spaniards never complained about it; in general, it did not pronounce against atheists and the impious except when they sought to make proselytes; it never tormented consciences, and only struck *the contagion of crime*" (*Cathol.*, XV, 423–24). Not a word of pity for Arnaud de Brescia, or of the satisfaction that Servetus paid for his errors on the pyre, that Savonarola perished in the flames,

liberty of discussion, everything that can spread enlightenment beyond the privileged precinct, wounds and angers them.[5] Listen to Bossuet: Why command men, if it is not that God might be obeyed?[6] Listen to a more modern author: The Church is the true sovereign; it judges the temporal, condemns or absolves it, binds or loosens in heaven as on earth.[7] Today these writers, if they could, would be what priests were six hundred years ago.

So be it. Let them exhaust themselves in emphatic or pathetic lamentations; let them call the servitude from which, after so many centuries, man began to be freed, "the primordial time, the primitive legislation"; let them deplore the cessation of this time when, they say, the world was but a temple; we do not see in this primordial period anything but slavery, in this primitive legislation anything but a revolting inequality, a flagrant usurpation, which no lapse of time can legitimate. These writers consider only the usurping caste; they give them their admiration. We fix our gazes on the oppressed castes; we give them our interest and our pity. They think only of a few hundred men monopolizing the intellectual and material treasures that nature gave to all. We think of the hundreds of thousands groaning in nakedness, ignorance, and irons; and if in this scaffolding of craft and tyranny we see a temple, it is the temple of those maleficent divinities, where the sacrificers are a few, the victims, the immense number. But when these victims no longer bowed down, the sacrificers disappeared.

---

of the approval of the government of Poland for proscribing the entire sect of Socinians (*Cathol.*, VI, 412, 421, 426, 432); and Mr. de Maistre, who, in speaking of the Inquisition and its tortures, calls them the legal execution of a small number of men, ordered by a legitimate tribunal in virtue of an established law, which each victim was perfectly free to avoid, and who carefully calculated the drops of guilty blood shed now and again by law! (*Des sacrifices*, pp. 428–29).

5. "To read ought to be the prerogatives of strong minds, which, after having well understood, would teach what they had thus learned. Minds too weak to give themselves to serious studies deteriorate by reading; it is an act of folly to hand over the treasures of the intellect to the mercy of the greedy crowd, which would waste them, and cannot profit from them. This is one of the greatest crimes that one can commit, initiating the vulgar into the reading of sophistical writings, where they can only draw sinful inspiration" (*Le Catholique*, n. 8).

In reading this, would one not say: here is a magus or a Brahmin wanting to pour burning oil into the mouth of those who speak, or crack the head of those who read?

6. Funeral prayer of the queen of England.

7. *Le Cathol.*, XIX, 86.

CHAPTER 4

How Harmful to Religion Itself Is Every Obstacle to Its Progressive Perfectibility

When one claims to maintain intact a doctrine born at a period when men misunderstood all the laws of physical nature, one sets against this doctrine all the discoveries relative to these laws. The more the material world is unveiled to us, the more the doctrine is undermined. Do we need to recall the advantage that unbelievers have derived from the physics and astronomy of the Bible?

In the same way, when mores have become gentler, when morality has been improved, is it not clear that if one wants to perpetuate in the religion the rituals and practices that existed before this improvement and gentling, a struggle has to arise; and that despite the more or less longer maintained triumphs that an external assistance can lend to the cults whose end has arrived, these cults can only emerge from this struggle discredited and disdained?

It is therefore a grave error to think that religion is rightly interested in remaining stationary; on the contrary, its real interest is that the progressive faculty, which is a law of human nature, should be applied to it.

It ought to be applied to teachings, as well as to rituals and practices. What, in fact, are dogmas? The redaction of the ideas conceived by man concerning the Divinity. When these notions are purified, the dogmas ought to change. What are rituals and practices? Conventions that are supposed to be necessary to the intercourse of mortal beings with the gods they adore. Anthropomorphism serves as the basis of this idea. Men not knowing one another's secret dispositions, their hidden intentions, they remedy this ignorance by attaching a conventional meaning to external manifestations. This artificial language would be useless to them if they could read into others' hearts. Supposing the necessity of this language to address themselves to the infinite Being, however, is to circumscribe his faculties, it is to lower him to the human level, it is to transport into the heavenly abode an imitation of human customs. But with anthropomorphism disappearing, rituals are condemned to follow.

If religious beliefs remain behind the general march of the human sprit, they become adverse and isolated, having transformed their erstwhile allies into adversaries; they then see themselves besieged by enemies they themselves have created. The authority that would like to disperse these enemies cannot defeat them. Each day they grow in number and force; they recruit new members by their very defeats, and they stubbornly renew attacks that cannot fail to end with a victory that will be even more complete, the longer it has been contested.

Henceforth, if one wants to render religion the sole homage that is worthy of it, and to base it on the only foundations that are solid and unshakeable, one must respect its progress.

The human species has no principle that is dearer and more precious to defend. Therefore no other principle has been defended at the price of more sacrifices and more blood. Parallel to the metempsychosis of Brahmins, where souls traverse eighty thousand transmigrations before arriving at God, religion indefinitely regenerates itself; only its forms, subject to death, are in a way like the mummies of Egypt, which serve only to preserve past existences.

This does not at all imply that a people ought to change their religion every time that they have changed. When it comes to politics, it is fortunate that a nation believes it always has the same constitution, even when the constitution improves. For a long time, this made the strength of England, and this persistence in the name is not a lie. A constitution signifies the laws according to which a nation rules itself. That a detail is changed in the law does not mean that the constitution no longer subsists. Religion signifies the ensemble of relations that exist between man and the invisible world. That a dogma is modified does not mean that the religion is destroyed. In general, one must avoid proclaiming these changes unless the necessity is urgent. This would be to stir up resistance. Everything by nature occurs gradually and, as it were, imperceptibly. Men ought to imitate it. Provided that no constraint is exercised on consciences and no obstacle is placed to the practice of different worships, it is useful to preserve the name. It does not harm the substance of things and it reassures spirits susceptible to being scandalized.

Also, let no one fear to injure the divinity of the religion, or better put: the intimate sentiment upon which religious convictions rest. The more one believes in the goodness and justice of a Providence that created man and serves him as a guide, the more it is natural to admit that this beneficent Providence proportions its teachings to the state of the intellects destined to receive them.

This doctrine alone reconciles the ideas that religious men conceive of this Providence with the nature of the human spirit. One cannot deny that the human spirit has an invincible penchant for investigation and examination. If its most imperious duty, its greatest merit, was found in implicit credulity, why would heaven have endowed man with a faculty that he cannot exercise without committing a crime? Why would it have subjected him to a need that he cannot fulfill without making himself culpable? But this sacrifice would reduce him to the rank of a pure machine; this would be, as we have said, a moral suicide; the God who would impose it on man would more resemble the Amida of those idolaters who have themselves crushed under the wheels of a chariot in which their idol is placed, than that pure and benevolent Intelligence offered to our worship and our love.

This implicit credulity, this stasis in doctrines, this static character in beliefs, all these things that are against nature but are recommended in the name of religion, are the things most opposed to the religious sentiment. What in fact is this sentiment? The need to grow close to the beings whose protection one invokes. It is of its essence to try, in order to satisfy itself, each religious form that it creates or that is presented to it; but it is also in its essence, when these religious forms no longer satisfy it, to change them in a way to escape what injures it. To limit it to the present, which never satisfies it, to forbid it that élan toward the future to which the insufficiency of the present invites, is to strike it with death. Everywhere it is thus chained, everywhere it is impossible to successively modify it, there can be superstition, because superstition is the abnegation of the intellect; there can be fanaticism, because fanaticism is superstition become furious; but there cannot be religion, because religion is the result of the needs of the soul and the efforts of intelligence, and because static dogmas put one and the other out of the question.

This system does not at all exclude those supernatural communications about which many minds become indignant, and so many hearts in secret implore. For example, that the idea of theism suddenly appeared as an inexplicable phenomenon in the midst of an ignorant tribe when the religious sentiment, misled by absurd forms, was not able to blaze a better path for itself; that later, an unforeseen assistance came to the human spirit, which, having elevated itself to the idea of divine unity, nonetheless did not have the strength to transform this abstract idea into an animated and living doctrine, each can believe; this does not change anything in what we have affirmed: the tendency existed, and the additional support was exercised only in conformity with this tendency. That man left to himself then recommended his labor following his nature, that he struggled concerning this great discovery, that he gave it crude forms that veiled its sublimity, he nonetheless will have preserved the ineffaceable memory of it, and, by stages, purer forms and more adequate conceptions would have allowed him to enjoy the inestimable benefit without any alloy.

But whatever is the case with divine assistances, let us not mix human hands with these mysterious and impenetrable means. Theologians have said a thousand times that the abuse of religion does not come from it, but from men. To remedy these abuses, it is necessary that men—that is, power, material force—do not mix with religion. Leave it to God and to itself. Always commensurate, it will march with ideas, learn with reason, purify itself with morality, and at each period it will sanction what is best.

At each period, too, let us call for religious liberty, one that is unlimited, infinite, and personal; it will surround religion with an invincible force and guarantee its perfectibility. It will multiply religion forms, each of which will be more refined than the preceding. Each emerging sect aspires to the excellence of morality, and the abandoned sect reforms its own mores. For a time, Protestantism will improve the Catholic clergy; and if we wanted (which we would hardly like to do) to address ourselves to authority, we would prove that religious liberty is in its interest. A single sect is always a formidable rival. Two hostile sects are two camps under arms. Divide the torrent, or better put: allow it to divide into a thousand streams. They will fertilize the ground that a torrent would have devastated.

Index

forgiveness, 241n10; forms of the gods in,
598–604; hermaphroditic gods, 685–86;
Homeric works and, 591n36; human sacrifice, 697, 702–3, 706n86, 707, 709, 720n4;
labor and industry in, 247; licentious rituals
in, 714, 715n18, 717–18n24; Lingam, 50n1,
216, 356, 437, 472, 480, 684–88, 704,
737n33; malevolent dieties and evil principle in, 664–65, 666, 667, 669; mediating
gods, 674; metaphysical hypotheses of, 445;
metempsychosis in, 473–77, 642, 643n3;
minor gods or demons, 656, 657; morality of, 815, 816, 821n31, 821–22nn37–38,
821nn33–34; mystery religions and, 834–35,
850, 851, 862, 865; non-Brahmin priests in,
215n14; original fall of humanity in, 671n2,
673; pain, sanctity of, 720–21n4, 721–23;
pantheism in, 450–56, 462, 463, 473, 664–
65; parallels with other early religions, 86–
87n6, 87; pariah caste, 117, 206–7; political
and military resistance against priestly
power, 255–57; priestly subdivisions and
hierarchies, 226; priests, inability of Indians
to shake off authority of, 477–85; primitive
worship practices in India, 3, 114n5, 118,
133, 140, 141n23, 143, 154n6, 155n8, 156n13;
punishment of the gods in, 617–20; records
and source materials, 427–32; reforms and
revolutions in, 432–38, 476n25; sacrifice in,
691–92n3; sanctity of abstinences and privations, doctrines consequential to, 726–27,
726–29, 730n19; Scandinavians compared,
891, 892; sciences, priestly possession of,
441–45; sea, aversion to, 327n4; soil, fertility of, 244; stars and elements, worship/
study of, 191–92; suicide in, 239; supremacy
of one god over others, 650; sympathy and
mildness characteristic of, 466–67; theism
in, 445–50; trial by ordeal in, 628; triple or
ternary deities, 676; Vedas, limitation of access to, 6. See also Brahmins and Brahmanism; Buddha, Buddhists, and Buddhism

Indianizing Christians, 730n20
Indians, American. See American Indians
Indra (deity), 191n12, 221, 435, 441n50, 470–
71, 483, 484, 607, 611, 650, 656, 667, 707,
730n19
Indra-Purana, 441n50
Ingrid, 885
innate ideas, concept of, 32n6
Innocent I (pope), 290n2
Innocent II (pope), 290n2
Innocent III (pope), 496n61
Innocent XIII (pope), 41n3
Inquisition, 58, 281, 283, 917
interest. See self-interest
intolerance. See tolerance and intolerance
Io, 86n6, 365n124
Ionians, 509–11
Iphigenia, 698, 700n48
Irenaeus of Lyons, 46n11; Adversus haereses,
618n9
Iris (deity), 538, 590n29, 609, 766n16, 775
Irish miners' belief in knockers, 116n11
Iroquois, 97n19, 115n6, 118n16, 120, 124, 140,
142–43, 145n40, 154, 160, 176, 201, 364n118,
392, 589n25
Isaac, 98n19
Isaiah (biblical book): 26:19, 633n9; 38, 632n6
Isaiah (prophet), 279n19
Isbrand, Voy. au Nord, 156n13
Isert: Reise nach Guinea, 141n18; Voy., 201n10
Isidor., Orig., 733n16
Isis (deity): barbarian religions and, 184n5,
204, 224n67; Isis Pharia, 327n4; mystery
religions and, 834, 835, 842, 845n53, 851,
855n104, 869; pre-heroic Greek polytheism
and, 337n26, 347n41, 351, 352, 364, 364n121,
375n8; priestly polytheism and, 392n8,
406, 416n9, 419, 419n30, 419n32, 422–24,
422n46, 423n48, 425n54, 608, 624n10,
651, 661n8, 666, 686n22, 713n1, 713n4,
720n4; religious sentiment and, 42,
99n19

migration of peoples, 253–54

migration of souls. *See* metempsychosis

military resistance against priestly power. *See* political and military resistance against priestly power

Millin, *Peint. des vas. antiq.*, 844n41

Mills, *History of India*, 379n17, 721n4

Milton, John, *Paradise Lost*, 515n16

Mimnermus, 348n46

Minerva/Athena (deity): celibacy required of priestesses of, 710; in civilized state of Greek polytheism, 765, 778, 791, 793, 794, 804; Greek nationalization of, 750; as hermaphroditic god, 685n6, 688; in heroic age Greek polytheism, 511, 524n12, 528, 529, 530n13, 531, 534n42, 535, 536, 541, 542, 555n35; in *Iliad* versus *Odyssey*, 567, 572; Libyan Pallas, 345, 346n37; means of travel, 607; Minerva Apaturia, 530n13; mystery religions and, 837n25, 854, 855n104, 867; origins and development, 344–46; Pallas Athena, 320, 657n22, 750n87, 837n25; Persians and, 491, 492n47; in pre-heroic Greek polytheism, 313n13, 315n20, 321n16, 344–46; virgin birth of, 727

minor gods. *See* demons and demonic gods

Minutius Felix, 46n10, 327n3, 694n2

miracles, German theologians on, 75n7

mirror and cups, in priestly and mystery religions, 837, 849–51

missionaries, Christian, 61, 115n6, 118, 119–20n20, 121n23, 126n32, 134, 139, 154n7, 156n16, 158n27, 330, 447, 449n85, 473–74n15, 482n42, 687n24, 696n13, 721, 891n31, 895n46

Mithra (Persian god), 96n18, 99n19, 489, 490, 494nn51–52, 522n8, 600n12, 651, 674, 677, 685, 696n18, 715, 720n4, 728, 734n20, 842n25; Mithraic cult and, 842n25; Urania Mithra, 685

Mithras and Mithraic mysteries, 191n11, 354n65, 368n2, 495n53, 839n4, 840, 842, 842n25, 843n32, 847, 851, 853n97, 854

Moehsen, *Gesch. der Wissensch.*, 631n3

Moeser, *Ammerk ad Nonni Dionys.*, 660n5

Mogol conquest of China, 142

The Mogul Empire, of the Marattoes, and of the English Concerns in Hindostan, 709n120

Mohammed, 28n5, 57n2, 96, 196, 197n10, 611, 625n13, 697–98, 883

Mohamudgara, 451n90

Molach, priests of, 53n1

Momiers, 907

Momus, 554n23, 863n9, 870n1

Mone, *Symbol.*, 607n13, 685n8, 885n16, 890n21, 891n31

monotheism. *See* theism

monstrous forms, gods/goddesses with, 43, 166n12, 290n6, 293n14, 313n13, 496, 523–26, 598–604, 670n5, 839–40

Montesquieu, 70, 724, 817, 825n1, 906, xvi; *The Spirit of the Laws*, 23, 70, 107, 712, 817n23

Montezuma (Mexican ruler), 192n16

Montfaucon, *Antiquité expliquée*, 190n8, 601n15, 734n20

Moore, *Narrative of the Operations of Captain Little's Detachm. of the Mahratta Army*, 714n13

Mopsus, 308

Morabashya, 444

morality and religion: afterlife, 555; in civilized state, 755–58 (*See also* civilized state, morality of Greek polytheism in); Constant on, xxi–xxii, 7; efforts to found morality on mundane basis, 64–65; evils resulting from priestly impositions, 908–10; heroic age Greek polytheism, character of gods in, 527–40, 558–59; in *Iliad* versus *Odyssey*, 567–68; immoral behavior of Greek and Roman Gods, xxi, 48–55; Jews and Judaism, 815n12, 816–17n22, 816n17, 818n24, 820, 911n5; mystery religions and, 857–61; penal code, religion not to be regarded as, 823–24; primitive peoples and, 132–36; relations of morality with independent versus priestly polytheism, 812–22; in Scandinavia, 893–96; true relations of, 823–26; unbelief and, 760

This book is set in Garamond Premier Pro. The design, by Adobe senior type designer Robert Slimbach, is a new interpretation of book types by sixteenth-century French punchcutter Claude Garamond. Slimbach studied the collection of the Plantin-Moretus Museum in Antwerp Belgium during a visit in 1988. The italics are based on designs cut by Robert Granjon, a contemporary of Garamond.

Printed on paper that is acid-free and meets the requirements of the American National Standard for Permanence of Paper for Printed Library Materials, z39.48-1992. ∞

Book design by Erin Kirk New, Watkinsville, Georgia.
Typography by Graphic Composition, Inc., Bogart, Georgia.
Printed and bound by Edwards Brothers Malloy, Ann Arbor, Michigan